The Study of Religion
under the Impact of Fascism

Numen Book Series

Studies in the History of Religions

VOLUME 117

The Study of Religion
under the Impact of Fascism

Edited by

Horst Junginger

BRILL

LEIDEN · BOSTON
2008

On the cover: Title page of the *Archiv für Religionswissenschaft* 37 (B.G. Teubner Verlag: 1941/42), from the former Library of the Department for the Study of Religion at the University of Tübingen.

This book is printed on acid-free paper.

A Cataloging-in-Publication record for this book is available from the Library of Congress

ISSN 0169-8834
ISBN 978 90 04 16326 3

CONTENTS

Preface ix

Abstracts xi

Introduction (HORST JUNGINGER) 1

PART ONE

THE ARYAN MYTH

From Buddha to Adolf Hitler: Walther Wüst and the Aryan
Tradition (HORST JUNGINGER) 107

Hermann Güntert in the 1930s. Heidelberg, Politics, and the
Study of Germanic/Indogermanic Religion
(BRUCE LINCOLN) 179

"Quand l'Allemagne était leur Mecque..." La science des
religions chez Stig Wikander (1935–1941)
(MIHAELA TIMUŞ) 205

Bernhard Kummer (1897–1962). The Study of Religions
Between Religious Devotion for the Ancient Germans,
Political Agitation, and Academic Habitus
(FRITZ HEINRICH) 229

Irrational Experiences, Heroic Deeds and the Extraction
of Surplus (GUSTAVO BENAVIDES) 263

PART TWO

THE POLITICAL IMPACT IN
SOUTH-EASTERN EUROPE

Leonidas Philippidis and the Beginnings of the History of
    Religions as an Academic Discipline in Greece
    (VASILIOS N. MAKRIDES) 283

War-time Connections: Dumézil and Eliade, Eliade and
    Schmitt, Schmitt and Evola, Drieu La Rochelle and
    Dumézil, (CRISTIANO GROTTANELLI) 303

Entre idéologie de la culture et politique: Mircea Eliade et
    l'étude des religions dans la Roumanie de
    l'entre-deux-guerres (FLORIN ȚURCANU) 315

Raffaele Pettazzoni et Mircea Eliade: historiens des religions
    généralistes devant les fascismes (1933–1945)
    (EUGEN CIURTIN) 333

Raffaele Pettazzoni and the History of Religions in Fascist
    Italy (1928–1938) (MICHAEL STAUSBERG) 365

Politische Myopie, mystische Revolution, glückliche
    (Un)Schuld? Mircea Eliade und die legionäre Bewegung:
    rezentere rumänische Perspektiven (ISTVÁN KEUL) 397

PART THREE

THE CATHOLIC PERSPECTIVE

Maria Laachs "Liturgische Bewegung" im Allgemeinen und
    Odo Casels "Mysterientheologie" im Besonderen. Ein
    doppelter Rückblick auf katholische Religionsgeschichte,
    mit Seitenblicken auf Mircea Eliade und Stefan George
    (RICHARD FABER) 421

Friedrich Andres (1882–1947): ein theologischer
    Religionswissenschaftler an der Universität Bonn
    (ULRICH VOLLMER)   443

Antisemitismus und Antijudaismus in den Werken und
    Arbeiten Pater Wilhelm Schmidts S.V.D. (1868–1954)
    (UDO MISCHEK)   467

PART FOUR

THE PROTESTANT PARADIGM

Religionswissenschaft zwischen Rationalismus und
    Irrationalismus. Ein norwegisches Beispiel: der Fall
    Kristian Schjelderups (SIGURD HJELDE)   491

Haralds Biezais (1909–1995). Ein Religionshistoriker zwischen
    Theologie und Religionswissenschaft (IVETA LEITĀNE)   511

The Essence of Concrete Individuality. Gerardus van der
    Leeuw, Jan de Vries, and National Socialism
    (WILLEM HOFSTEE)   543

Åke Ohlmarks in the Third Reich. A Scientific Career between
    Adaptation, Cooperation and Ignorance
    (ANDREAS ÅKERLUND)   553

PART FIVE

THE QUEST FOR THEORIES

The "Faith of the Enlightened" by Władysław Witwicki. An
    Example of the Conflict between Academic Research and
    Political Correctness (HALINA GRZYMAŁA-MOSZCZYŃSKA)   577

Futures Past: C.G. Jung's Psychoutopia and the 'German
    Revolution' of 1933 (PETTERI PIETIKÄINEN)   591

Strategies in Representing 'Japanese Religion' during the
National Socialist Period: The Cases of Kitayama Junyû
and Wilhelm Gundert (HIROSHI KUBOTA)   613

Joachim Wachs Grundlegung der Religionswissenschaft. Ein
Beitrag zu ihrer Identität und Selbständigkeit
(KURT RUDOLPH)   635

List of Contributors   649

Index   653

PREFACE

Two generations after the end of World War II it is high time to rethink the European study of religion during the 1930s and 1940s. It was in that spirit that the Department for the Study of Religion of the Eberhard-Karls-Universität Tübingen decided to organize an international symposium on "The Study of Religion under the Impact of National Socialist and Fascist Ideologies in Europe" that took place from 16–18 July 2004 at the University of Tübingen. In coordination with the Deutsche Vereinigung für Religionsgeschichte (DVRG, now Deutsche Vereinigung für Religionswissenschaft, DVRW), the European Association for the Study of Religions (EASR), and the International Association for the History of Religions (IAHR), the Tübingen conference offered the opportunity for a thorough debate on that crucial period which affected the study of religion in many ways. There can be no doubt that contemporaneous ideologies had a significant impact on the shaping of its program, on its intrinsic values, and on its academic setting.

Due to the central role National Socialism played within the German study of religion, we felt it meaningful to hold the discussions at the University of Tübingen where, shortly after German troops had begun to spread war over Europe, an 'Aryan Institute' could have been established with the aim to buttress religion and "Weltanschauung" of the Third Reich methodically. The research of the last twenty years has revealed the extent of the ideological correspondence between German scholarship and the Nazi regime. However, political doctrines biased the account not only in Germany. A closer look into the history of our discipline shows that non-scientific orientations could penetrate into the academic field in other countries as well. We must recognize the emergence of similar ideological susceptibilities which ought to be analyzed as part of the complicated relationship between the academic study of religion and those political, religious and other factors determining the course of its development from outside. Which questions were put forth and which kind of answers were given in the era between the First and the Second World War? Was there something approximating a common European approach in the study of religion, and were there comparable distortions?

With these questions in mind we designed the conference as a genuine European undertaking trying to gather at least one half of the participants from non-German countries. It makes no small difference to discuss, for instance, the German occupation policy in Poland either from a German or from a Polish viewpoint. A Polish historian would never arrive at the idea to interpret the German "Reichsuniversität Posen" in terms of a somehow academic normality as it is the case in recent German discussions which, not falsely, stress the point that the German university in Poznan (1941–1945) did not differ very much from other universities in the Reich. But what might appear as relatively normal for one side was gruesome horror for the other. Even 60 years after the Third Reich's overthrow it was anything but normal to organize such a symposium between participants from Germany on the one side and from countries which had suffered from Germany's megalomania on the other. Becoming aware of our different perspectives and exchanging our arguments with the understanding that we belong to an international community of scholars with equal standards, principles and morality turned out to be extraordinarily fruitful.

Besides the organizations already mentioned I particularly thank the German Research Foundation (Deutsche Forschungsgemeinschaft, DFG) for funding the conference. In the time of National Socialism an important part of the ideological stabilization of the regime, the DFG has become the main institution in Germany sponsoring critical research on that period. Processed manuscripts were made possible thanks to a subsidy of the DVRG. I thank Vanessa Cisz for her excellent work in that regard. Stephanie Gleißner provided the book with the index. I would also like to express my gratitude to Brill publishers for comprising this volume in its Numen Book Series. NBS is an eminent place of critical self-reflexivity in the field and has brought forward important volumes on the history of the academic study of religion in the last years. Although the topic we are now dealing with is not very pleasant, it is crucial that we concern ourselves with it.

In remembering the dreadful fate of a prominent French scholar, we dedicated the congress to the memory of Henri Maspero who held the chair "Religions de la Chine" at the École Pratique des Hautes Études until July 1944. Maspero was then deported from Paris to the concentration camp of Buchenwald where he died in March 1945 a few days before he would have been liberated.

ABSTRACTS

Ciurtin, Eugen

RAFFAELE PETTAZZONI AND MIRCEA ELIADE: GENERALIST HISTORIANS OF RELIGIONS AND THE FASCISMS (1933–1945)

Raffaele Pettazzoni (1883–1959) and Mircea Eliade (1907–1986), most likely the greatest scholars in generalist comparative religion, had a notoriously ambiguous relationship with politics, in their home countries as well as in the Europe milieu of the 1930s and 1940s. The article reconstructs different arguments and tries to advance new ones; in the case of Pettazzoni, with the help of his writings (including the minor ones) and of his 2500-page biography offered by Mario Gandini; as for Eliade, with the help of the major contributions, mostly recent, about his political past, especially those coming from historians of religions and including some relevant, yet hitherto unpublished documents. The main argument tries to demonstrate that their scholarly work and cultural and social manifold commitments during 1933–1945, in Italy, Romania or abroad (often intermingled), are a consequence of their generalist project in comparative history of religions. This perspective explains why both Pettazzoni and Eliade took scholarly and personally interest in detecting the most recent challenges in the contemporary European religions during the fascist regimes. The risks were of course great, and the impurities, ambiguities and lamentable consequences for their own work rather numerous. Different aspects of Pettazzoni's and Eliade's images of European politics are rediscussed anew, while some other factual connections are established here for the first time. Thus, the article compares some key themes of their writings such as: religious interpretation of the war, the German and Italian neo-paganism, and the theme of a (European and resurgent) religious substratum. Exhibiting some differences that demand nuance and, the author thinks, with no degree of impartiality, both Pettazzoni and Eliade, when traversing the catastrophes of WW II, admittedly included in their global scholarly legacy that difficult component which still invites us to carefully critique, understand, explain and ultimately abandon their options.

Faber, Richard

THE "LITURGICAL MOVEMENT" OF MARIA LAACH AND ODO CASEL'S "MYSTERY-THEOLOGY." A TWOFOLD RETROSPECTIVE ON CATHOLIC HISTORY OF RELIGION WITH SIDE-GLANCES AT MIRCEA ELIADE AND STEFAN GEORGE

Many religions speak a political language and many political systems articulate themselves religiously. So do poets in joining political and religious features. Then there are scholars of religion who blend arts, politics, religion, and learning. The study of religion provides ample evidence that an unclear distinction between these aspects of life must go to the detriment of its scientific rigor. The article deals with that kind of amalgamation using the liturgical restoration of Catholicism in the 20th century as example. In studying Catholic scholarship on religion, one has to go beyond considering language alone. Rites play an important role as well: gestures, theatricals or, in a theological sense, sacraments. Unlike Protestantism, Catholicism puts much more emphasis on ritualism and sacramental acts. This difference should be reflected on the level of a theoretical occupation with religion as well as in the history of religions itself.

Hjelde, Sigurd

A SCHOLAR OF RELIGION BETWEEN RATIONALISM AND IRRATIONALISM: THE NORWEGIAN EXAMPLE OF KRISTIAN SCHJELDERUP

National Socialist and fascist ideologies found little support in Norway and barely made an impact among the few Norwegian scholars of religion. All the more interesting is the case of Kristian Schjelderup (1894–1980), a liberal theologian who had been searching in many directions for a religion matching the life of the modern world. In so doing he came across the German Faith Movement led by Jakob Wilhelm Hauer. Between 1933 and 1936, Schjelderup presented the ideas of this movement to the Norwegian public in a way that earned him the label of "an involuntary apostle of fascism in Norway." The Norwegian historian Terje Emberland went even further and asked why a liberal humanist like Schjelderup invested so much interest in a nationalistic religious movement (Emberland 2003). With reference to Karl Popper's *Open Society and Its Enemies*, Emberland believed he had found an answer to these questions in the "irrationalism" which Schjelderup shared with Rudolf Otto and other contemporary scholars of religion. Emberland has brought to light a number of interesting similarities between Hauer and Schjelderup regarding their personal development and common idea of religion. Yet, two critical questions are still unanswered: 1) Does Schjelderup, in Popper's terms, really belong to the camp of irrationalism? 2) Is the widespread characterization of the academic study of religion between the wars as "irrationalistic" appropriate or does such a general statement deserve to be refined? The concept of religion in question as well as the corresponding methodology may rightly be labeled as "irrationalism." Interestingly enough, however, these scholars who represented a liberal theological attitude promoted precisely the values which Popper emphasized as essential traits of a rationalistic position.

Keul, István

POLITICAL MYOPIA, MYSTICAL REVOLUTION, 'FELIX CULPA'? MIRCEA ELIADE AND THE LEGIONARY MOVEMENT: RECENT ROMANIAN PERSPECTIVES

The article starts with an outline of some of the more important Romanian reactions to Eliade as a political person between the 1930s and his post-war oeuvre focusing at first on the period up to 1989. The following paragraphs summarize the main arguments as presented in a number of recent publications regarding the interwar period in Romania and Eliade's right-wing political involvement in that time. In trying to explain and interpret Eliade's highly problematic position in those years, authors like Sorin Alexandrescu and George Călinescu emphasize the importance of the contemporary socio-historical context and the impact it had. With no intention of playing down the facts, Eliade's involvement in right-wing politics is presented in these works as the result of a complex constellation of different political, historical, and cultural influences in interwar Romania. At the same time, however, Eliade's political engagement with right-wing movements is seen as an inevitable consequence of his deliberately selective and biased perception of these circumstances.

Leitane, Iveta

HARALDS BIEZAIS (1906–1995).
A HISTORIAN OF RELIGIONS BETWEEN THE STUDY OF RELIGION AND THEOLOGY

Born in Latvia and of Latvian descent, Haralds Biezais was a scholar of religion with a theological provenance. He graduated from the department of theology at the University of Latvia in 1932 where he worked as systematic theologian until 1944. Then Biezais emigrated to Sweden, teaching first at the University of Uppsala and later at the University of Åbo in Finland. In the 1930s, Biezais had undergone additional training at the faculties of theology at the Universities of Zurich and Strasbourg. Throughout his professional activities, Biezais remained invariably rooted in the phenomenological tradition of the study of religion. The key term of his scientific concept was "religious experience" as represented at the University of Latvia by Valdemārs Maldonis, a student of Rudolf Otto, and Gustav Mensching. Biezais described religion in the spirit of liberal theology as a universal phenomenon of human life rejecting any orthodox understanding of Christianity. Emphasizing the importance of religious personality as such, Biezais' early concept of religion was strongly shaped by the values of Latvian national culture. His phenomenological approach – together with his dynamic concept of truth – allowed Biezais to interpret changing religious contents without abandoning his Christian framework. As a result, it was not necessary for him to discard Christianity in reconstructing the Latvian religion. But in opposing the commandment of Christian love, Biezais emphasized natural egoism as an indispensable element of any ethical decision. This basis leads universal duties to reveal themselves as merely *prima facie*. Although he did not give up the idea of a general morality, Biezais defined it in intuitionalist terms. The normative gap inherent in this approach was filled by anthropologically-based and universally postulated religious contents which could be attributed to the Latvian religion.

Mischek, Udo

ANTISEMITISM AND ANTI-JUDAISM IN THE WORK OF PATER WILHELM SCHMIDT S.V.D. (1888–1954)

The article deals with one of the leading figures of ethnology and the history of religions in the first half of the 20th century. Pater Wilhelm Schmidt shaped the scholarly discussion mainly with his idea of a primeval monotheism ("Urmonotheismus") which he declared to be the starting point of religion as such and which ought to verify the biblical book of Genesis. Schmidt was a prolific writer. Not only was his scientific output outstanding, but his theological and political works were extensive as well. Schmidt's political writings in particular conveyed an anti-Jewish undertone although one can also detect anti-Jewish prejudices in his scientific publications. In spite of the racist antisemitism of the Nazis, Schmidt's attitude was strongly influenced by Catholicism. From that perspective, the Jews were above all the murderers of Christ – charged guilty until today. It was the religious structure of Schmidt's dislike of the Jews which distinguished him from other antisemitic traditions in which the "alien" race of the Jews was the main criteria for their otherness and inferiority. Unlike National Socialist racism, Schmidt held that baptism could solve the Jewish problem. Schmidt's political and theological writings are interspersed with anti-Jewish stereotypes which are not so evident in his academic work. However, the "Urmonotheismus" no longer identified or needed the Jews as God's chosen people. Other peoples, for instance the indigenes of Patagonia, lived a life much closer to God's will.

Rudolph, Kurt

LAYING THE FOUNDATIONS OF THE STUDY OF RELIGION. JOACHIM WACH'S CONTRIBUTION TO ITS IDENTITY AND AUTONOMY

Related to the famous Mendelssohn family, Joachim Wach lost his professorship at the University of Leipzig in April 1935 as a result of the racist civil servant law. Wach was the most prominent victim of the study of religion in Nazi Germany. His academic career, which had started a decade earlier, suddenly came to an unexpected halt. After Wach had published his renowned habilitation thesis, he worked as a lecturer ("Privatdozent") until 1929 when he was nominated extraordinary professor of "Religionswissenschaft" at the Leipzig "Institut für Kultur- und Universalgeschichte." With an additional teaching appointment in sociology and focusing on the theory debates in history and philosophy, Wach opened up new vistas for the study of religion. His famous *Religionswissenschaft. Prolegomena zu ihrer wissenschaftstheoretischen Grundlegung* from 1924 remains a classic which is required reading in the academic study of religion until today. Its importance is based on the following points: 1) It provides evidence of the independence of the study of religion specifically regarding theology and philosophy of religion. 2) It underlines the significance of a historical and comparative approach. 3) It opens up new horizons in adjacent disciplines like sociology, psychology, and anthropology which share the same object but have their own, distinct methodological frameworks. It is well-known that Wach did not keep up his concept consistently and only later aimed at the idea of religious experience. The new circumstances he was subjected to in the United States had a strong impact on Wach's scientific work from 1935 on. In Germany, on the other hand, nobody took notice of Wach until 1945. In addition to Wach's scientific development, the article deals with his political conservatism and his reluctance to occupy himself with the political zeitgeist.

Timuş, Mihaela

'WHEN GERMANY WAS THEIR MECQUE'. STIG WIKANDER'S CONCEPT OF RELIGION (1935–1944)

This study is a two-sided analysis of Stig Wikander's position in the history of religions between 1935 and 1944. Most likely in 1935, Wikander encountered Otto Höfler becoming acquainted with a different intellectual *milieu*. Nine years later, he left for Turkey and Greece in 1944 as member of the Swedish Red Cross. The article begins with an overview of Wikander's intellectual interest in the pre-war and war period. This half is based on the unpublished correspondence of Wikander with Höfler which is housed at the University Library of Uppsala and at Austria's National Library in Vienna. It also relies on less-known Swedish articles published by Wikander in Swedish journals. These documents reveal the extent to which Wikander showed interest in the contemporary debates. They illustrate how Wikander tried to contextualize his research as an orientalist in the general German cultural and political framework and enrich our understanding of his controversial *Der arische Männerbund* published in 1938. The second half of the article is dedicated to the structure of *Der arische Männerbund*, analyzing it particularly with regard to Iranian studies to which the work also belongs. While the philological evidence of Wikander's arguing proves scarce, the book is rather well-constructed in epistemological terms. Less based on necessity but on a hypothetical reasoning, Wikander tried to demonstrate the consistence of a social and religious Iranian structure of the *Männerbund*.

Ţurcanu, Florin

BETWEEN CULTURAL IDEOLOGY AND POLITICS: MIRCEA ELIADE AND THE STUDY OF RELIGION IN INTERWAR ROMANIA

Mircea Eliade's early activities in the 1930s can be seen as an intellectual effort to promote the study of religion in his native country which, in his view, ought to become a new and essential part of the national culture of Romania. Eliade stressed in his works of that time the importance of folklore as an important source of the history of religions. Especially with regard to the Balkans, Eliade tried to pave the way for a new intellectual approach in order to redefine the roots of Romania's national identity. Eliade also emphasized the "oriental" character of the pre-modern identity of Romania, trying to de-legitimize modern national historiography as the major source of Romanian collective consciousness. His insistence on the institutionalization of oriental studies in Romania takes the same path. The limited results of this ambitious undertaking, mirrored in Eliade's peripheral and frustrating position in the Romanian intellectual field, partially explains the strong attraction which the fascist Iron Guard – a marginal revolutionary movement – exerted on the young scholar.

Vollmer, Ulrich

FRIEDRICH ANDRES (1882–1947).
A THEOLOGICAL HISTORIAN OF RELIGION AT THE
UNIVERSITY OF BONN

From 1920 until his death in 1947, Friedrich Andres taught history of religions in the department of Catholic theology at the University of Bonn. Andres also held a temporary appointment at the University of Frankfurt from 1926 until 1937 when it was revoked by the ministry. His scholarly work focused on ethnology (following mainly Wilhelm Schmidt's footsteps), the psychology of religion, and introductory topics of general interest. His attitude towards National Socialism can be divided in different phases and aspects. The first stage is characterized by his subordination to the authorities, even using some phrases of national (but not National Socialist) terminology. On one hand, he was judged as an ivory-towered scholar. Yet because he shied away from political opposition, he was promoted to some extent. Unlike Schmidt and some of his disciples, Andres never emphasized terms like race nor demonstrated any contempt for native cultures. Furthermore, he associated with opponents of the NS regime, such as the Dutch theologian Thomas Goossens (imprisoned for a time during the German occupation of the Netherlands) and the Luxembourgian theologian and lawyer Nikolaus Majerus (deported to unoccupied France). In Majerus' case, the authorities forbade Andres from going abroad. In his last publication written in 1944, Andres made his stance clear: contrasting Shintoism as a national religion to Buddhism which he described as an universal religion. Andres classified Shintoism as an outdated epoch of history, his wording comparing it with the Germanic religion and its revitalization by some National Socialist groups.

INTRODUCTION

HORST JUNGINGER

1. *Delay of Interest*

Historical research on the university system of National Socialist Germany has grown considerably during the last decades. During this time, most disciplines in German universities have contributed particular studies, dissecting what happened between 1933 and 1945. However, the study of religion belongs to the latecomers, to those disciplines just embarking on a common effort to investigate their own past. The reasons for this delay are manifold. Of course, dealing with such a disagreeable matter did not meet with great approval for a long time. In the years following the war, critical study of the NS period was anything but popular. Those who had been involved worked hard to obstruct any attempt to examine the preceding era. The scientific mainstream and the so-called "Mitläufer" also had no desire to run afoul of their colleagues in offending against the academic unity which had survived the war. Accordingly, the existing consensus prevented emigrants from re-integrating – emigrants who very likely would have advocated scrutinizing the time of the Third Reich. Instead, the rehabilitation of the former National Socialists and the incorporation of academics streaming in from the eastern parts of the country were given preference. The prevalent cold war ideology in particular impeded any critical inquiry which was seen as playing the game of the political enemy. To act contrary and to lay stress on the Nazi engagement of particular scholars and disciplines would have been hazardous. It would have hindered if not ended one's university career.[1]

---

[1] Not accidentally, the only critical study at that time, Kurt Rudolph's book *Die Religionsgeschichte an der Leipziger Universität und die Entwicklng der Religionswissenschaft. Ein Beitrag zur Wissenschaftsgeschichte und zum Problem der Religionswissenschaft* (Berlin: Akademie-Verlag, 1962), was written at the University of Leipzig. Concerning the situation in the Cold War, see Iva Doležavolá et al., eds., *The academic study of religion during the Cold War: East and west* (New York et al.: Lang, 2001).

It took two generations to arrive at a distance great enough for a less biased and more objective stance on the issue. Mainly as a result of simple biology, a new historical interest cropped up in the 1980s with the passing away of the former academic staff members. Detached from open political pressure and from an intrinsic network of personal and institutional constraints, scholars started investigating the past, even unwilling to exclude their teachers from disapproving judgments. The opening of Germany's archives triggered a qualitative shift in the realm of research. With the death of many persons formerly active in the Third Reich, pleas for the protection of privacy lost their vigor. Under the stewardship of Germany's Federal Archives, state and university archives adopted less restrictive guidelines and allowed historians access to their records. Prior to that, one barely had the chance to work with sensitive material, particularly if one was seen as lacking political discretion. Scholars were frequently threatened with legal proceedings if their examination took a too-critical turn. When those under scrutiny had passed away, their widows often stepped in and defended the memory of their husbands even more rigorously. No wonder, then, that the first historical inquiries relied on data outside of West German archives. I have already mentioned Rudolph's book; its importance for a critical historiography cannot be underestimated. The great achievement of Michael H. Kater's study on the "Ahnenerbe" largely depended on film material in the United States.[2] Fortunately, the Americans had filmed everything before they handed over the documents in their possession to Germany where something resembling a Freedom of Information Act appeared to be a novelty. The duplication "helped" Germany's Federal Archives to disclose its files since nothing could be kept concealed after that. With the end of communism in Europe, many other national archives opened their doors and released a massive amount of new material. Owing to the fact that National Socialist bureaucracy had tended to register everything, the chance to find fitting pieces of the puzzle in complementary records has become rather likely since then. Large parts of the holocaust research and of investigations into the activities of the secret service rely on such documents. The personnel

---

[2] Particularly on the "Captured German Records microfilmed at Alexandria" (T-74, 81, 84, 175, 454) and the "Records of the SS-Ahnenerbe filmed at the Berlin Document Center" (T-580), National Archives, Washington. See Michael H. Kater, *Das 'Ahnenerbe' der SS 1935–1945. Ein Beitrag zur Kulturpolitik des Dritten Reiches* (Stuttgart: Deutsche Verlags-Anstalt, 1974, 3rd ed. 2001), p. 486.

working in these two areas were not only especially interested in hiding or destroying the traces of their behavior, they had the unique power to do so at their fingertips. Nevertheless, what an international community of historians has accomplished to reveal the truth is overwhelming.

Any historical examination of the era of National Socialism solely relying on published texts and oral statements of key players at the time must be deficient if not partial. Any analysis of backstage events and strategies mediating between the political and academic fields remains, at best, insufficient without taking archival sources into consideration. Only more objective data can allow scholars to distinguish facts from claims and apologetic concerns determined by political or personal motives. Under the ideological pressure of National Socialism, academic quarrels for power, influence, and money were often politicized. After 1945, scholars tried to leverage these feuds to minimize their political engagement. Referring to the enmity of this or that prominent National Socialist or emphasizing a strong discomfort one had had with certain points of the National Socialist program, many tried to appear as opponents of the regime. Normal rivalries were twisted to demonstrate a subversive conduct aimed at disguising the degree of one's own consent to the political and ideological agenda of National Socialism. But if, for example, the animadversion against Alfred Rosenberg qualifies as political opposition, Heinrich Himmler would have been the greatest enemy of the Third Reich. The only way to pierce the veil of these kinds of apologetic strategies and to achieve a more differentiated judgment is to enlarge the input of information and adopt a critical stance regarding the authority of one's sources. Unfortunately, historians of religions tend to shy away from applying routine methods well tuned to the science of history, specifically when their own past comes under the microscope. At the same time, secular historians show little interest in things religious and lack a deeper understanding of the problems that the study of religion addresses. This book should be understood as an attempt to unite the strengths of both disciplines.

In addition to the reasons already mentioned, another substantial cause played a role in postponing research on the era of National Socialism. From its beginnings, the problematic nexus between science and religion interfered with the normal development of the academic study of religion. The old tension between a non-religious interpretation of religion and theological priorities reached a new dimension after 1933. Resuming older positions already prevailing in the 19th century, many historians of religions expressed a new-fashioned antipathy to ecclesiastical influences. A great number of scholars took a strong liking to non-Christian features and some even became engaged in Pagan activities. Articulated in terms of a Germanic, Indo-Germanic, or Aryan belief, a fierce hostility against Christianity gained a foothold in the study of religion. In its voelkish parts, the anti-Christian bias dominated everything and ultimately approached criminal conduct in some cases. It was no wonder that the Christian backlash that took place after 1945 affected the study of religion in an exceptional manner. Generally, the political situation in post-war Germany was framed by the return of Christianity in the initial years. Many people resorted to religion hoping to cope with the social and ideological disorder caused by the war. Since the occupying forces believed the churches to be a stabilizing factor, they strengthened their position as much as they could. Christian influence took marked effect at the universities where it fortified the position of theology. Such a development was an unmistakable detriment to a non-theological study of religion. First of all, the former Pagans were barred from returning to their teaching positions. In view of the fact that the adherents of Paganism had been belligerent National Socialists, their exclusion from universities was no great loss. Yet the successful integration of almost all other incriminated scholars shows that less political rather than religious concerns were involved.

What created a much stronger impact than the elimination of Paganism were Karl Barth and dialectical theology. Barth was more than one of the main intellectual adversaries of National Socialism – he was also a fierce opponent of any historical understanding of religion. Considering the Christian revelation and the feeling of religious superiority connected with it a non-historical datum per se, the word "religion" in itself symbolized unbelief for Barth who became one of the most influential intellectuals in the Federal Republic of Germany. Already in the 1920s, Friedrich Heiler had been at odds with Barth.[3] Three decades later, Heiler's position at the University of Marburg still suffered from the influence of dialectical theology. His weak academic stance resembled the plight of the study of religion in the 1950s and 1960s. Heiler reacted with a flight to the international stage and devoted

---

[3] For the antagonism between dialectical theology and a theologically oriented study of religion of Otto's or Heiler's kind, see Horst Junginger, *Von der philologischen zur völkischen Religionswissenschaft* (Stuttgart: Steiner, 1999), p. 78f.

himself to the International Association for the Study of the History of Religions. Being one of the key figures of the IASHR, Heiler held, comparable to Gerardus van der Leeuw, rather unclear and perplexing views on how to cope with the legacy of National Socialism. Exaggerating his own persecution, he did not shy away from supporting former Nazis such as the co-founder of the SS "Ahnenerbe" Herman Wirth whom he helped restore his worldview.[4] Another force which helped disorient the study of religion was the fact that those who opted for a greater distance to Christian theology faced enormous problems in hiding their previous inclination towards National Socialism. Gustav Mensching and Wilhelm Emil Mühlmann were two prominent members of the executive committee of the "Deutsche Vereinigung für Religionsgeschichte" (DVRG) who could have had no interest in opening Pandora's box and embarking on a public debate about the period of the Third Reich.

For these reasons, a general, though outspoken, agreement prevailed in the study of religion not to touch the period of National Socialism. The refusal to take an interest in the history of the German study of religion and to analyze it in the context of the religious developments that occurred in the Third Reich was one reason why the paradigms characteristic of the so-called historiography of the church struggle gained ascendancy. Even secular historians have adopted its shortcomings and embraced the false equation of National Socialism with an anti-Christian counter- or pseudo-religion. This is not the place to discuss the complex and complicated positions of both Christian and non-Christian organizations in Nazi Germany. Suffice it to say that the connection of religious value judgments with political leanings fundamentally opposes the scientific claims and achievements of a non-religious study of religion. Its inadequacies notwithstanding, the paradigm of the church struggle allowed both theologies to establish themselves in the democratic post-war system. In time with the general resurgence of Christianity in the public sphere, the number and influence of church members, mainly clerics and theologians, joining the DVRG significantly increased in the 1950s. Conversely, philologists, historians, ethnologists, and other members of non-theological disciplines stayed away for exactly that reason and concentrated their

---

[4] See my article on Walther Wüst in this volume on pp. 163–165.

activities on their own professional associations.[5] Reactions against the re-Christianization of religious studies did not gain momentum before the 1970s. At that point, a new generation of scholars rose in influence, insisting on the autonomy of the study of religion outside of theology departments and independent of any direct or indirect church influence. The current state of affairs reflects these grounds. But the struggle for emancipation from theology seems to have occupied all resources and left no capacity to deal with the reasons for the disagreeable situation, which undoubtedly have their origins in the period of the Third Reich. Sometimes the historical disinterest was also accompanied by a certain naiveté, as if the academic study of religion had started in 1945 *ab ovo*. The articles in this book try to fill the historiographical gap yawning between 1930 and 1950. Without taking these two decades into account, no real understanding of the post-war development will emerge. From my perspective, many institutional and methodological problems which dominated the study of religion after 1945 are caused by an insufficient understanding of the study of religion under the impact of fascism.

2. *The Weimar Prehistory*

In a speech delivered on July 5, 1941 to mark his appointment as rector of the University of Munich, Walther Wüst expressed his firm conviction that Nazi Germany was about to engender a Nordic master race in which National Socialist scholarship would play a leading role and would, safeguarded by the German army and economy, again become "praeceptor Europae," the teacher of Europe.[6] The academic henchmen of National Socialism can (in extension of Wüst's insolence) be depicted as models of a new type of fascist intellectuals apt to teach the world a lesson about the function of ideology. Talking about the uniqueness of a genuine German understanding of the world, Wüst stressed in this speech the necessity of having a powerful worldview in which the Third Reich's rule over Europe could be grounded. In Wüst's opinion,

---

[5] Cf. Horst Junginger, "Christel Matthias Schröder und seine Bedeutung für die deutsche Religionswissenschaft," *Zeitschrift für Religionswissenschaft* 9 (2001), pp. 235–268, esp. p. 261f.

[6] Walther Wüst, "Indogermanisches Bekenntnis," in idem, *Indogermanisches Bekenntnis. Sechs Reden* (Berlin-Dahlem: Ahnenerbe Stiftungsverlag, 1942, 2nd ed. 1943, a Dutch trans. 1944), pp. 93–118, here p. 118.

a comprehensive ideological substructure was indispensable to winning the war. He saw it as a prerequisite for the success of Germany's second try to become Europe's major power. Yet compared to World War I, many ideologically important things had changed. While in 1914 Christianity had been the only spiritual power capable of uniting the nation and guiding it in the war, the churches lost their predominant position with Germany's defeat four years later. An increasing number of people left the church and workers and intellectuals in particular emphatically rejected traditional Christian tenets. Great parts of the population became critical of the established churches which had supported the hitherto unparalleled killing between Christian nations but still preached brotherly love as the foremost Christian commandment. Their chance to preserve their former hegemony was diminished drastically. Even in the religious realm as such, Christianity faced new groups and movements appearing on the scene and touting attractive spiritual alternatives. Wüst's own life and work is a good example of this development, which led to a rather complicated situation in terms of worldviews and which finally brought an Aryan religion to the foreground.

The German study of religion profited greatly from the decreasing influence of Christianity after World War I and from the general trend towards a more secularized society. Though the separation of church and state was not fully implemented and, for instance, theology departments remained at the universities, extra-theological research on religion augmented considerably. In disciplines such as anthropology, classical, oriental, or Germanic philology, particular religions became an important issue of interest and part of the curriculum. Moreover, independent teaching positions in the history of religions were created. The growth of the study of religion evidently reflected political conditions. From the outset, the scientific impetus of the study of religion aimed at religious pluralism and the equal treatment of all religious traditions. Being perhaps its main principle, religious parity stood in full congruency, and even anteceded, the democratic legislation enacted in the Weimar Republic. But the heightening of the study of religion inevitably meant that the legal status of the Christian churches had been cut down to the position of ordinary religious associations. One cannot avoid the conclusion that the expansion of the academic study of religion depended on the dislocation of Christianity from the public to the private sphere. A state religion and an autonomous study of religion seem mutually exclusive, likely not only in Germany.

However, the social and political reality was not as clear as the Weimar jurisdiction suggested. The aftermath of World War I hampered
a normal development in many regards. Neglecting the reasons of the
war and confusing consequences with causes, the democratic institutions
were held responsible for nearly all calamities at the time. Religion and
religious studies suffered accordingly. Besides the grave economic difficulties touching all spheres of life, the study of religion worked diligently
to escape the ideological vortex prevailing in the post-war period. But
in view of the rampant turmoil that affected all traditional values, it
proved nearly impossible to perform research on religion impartially
and unaccompanied by deep inner emotions. The correspondence
between religious studies scholars and ministry officials, especially when
discussing the establishment of new positions or the appointment of
older ones, indicates that state authorities expected much more than
scientific knowledge. What they wanted was a meaningful contribution to solve the worldview problems of the time and to help ease the
exigency which was seen as a result of the churches' failure to satisfy
the spiritual needs of the masses. With their retrograde orientation
towards monarchy, the churches were obviously unable to give apt and
generally accepted answers to the pressing questions of the day. Losing their cohesive force to unite a nation split into multifarious interest
groups, they actually helped fragment society further. As the influence
of the churches in the educational system shrunk, non-theological
disciplines became increasingly significant. Free of religious favoritism
and doctrinal biases, the study of religion was believed to provide a
better insight into the universals of life than Christian theology, which
many identified with parochialism if not clericalism.

The highly problematic relationship between state and religion
determined how the study of religion played out at the universities.
But it also shaped its theoretical discussions. The widespread ambiguity in things religious was mirrored in the reluctance of the academic
study of religion to theorize the role of religion in a secular state and
the status of religious truth in a secular discipline. The old critique of
the study of religion in which one collected endless quantities of data
unsystematically and concentrated on fact-finding in order to eschew
analytical industry was not unfounded. Very few scholars made efforts
to accomplish a sound methodological framework and clarify the hazy
correlation of science with religion. Joachim Wach's *Prolegomena* was
a good starting point but did not trigger off the broad and intensive
debate which the issues deserved. With no plausible answer to the so-

called truth question, it was easier to ignore its existence or neglect its significance for the study of religion. Although religious truth is the most important thing for the believer and the core of all religions, the study of religion declared it to be scientifically irrelevant and its irrelevance to be a precondition of scholarly research on religion. Instead of theorizing the problem, scholars developed theories on how to abstain from it. The famous *epoché* concept served that purpose. In normal times, perhaps, this blinkered standpoint does no harm. But in times of crisis, it leads to disaster.

Analogous to the laming separation ("hinkende Trennung"), as the religious situation of the Weimar Republic is referred to in today's legal language, theological and non-theological tendencies competed with each other in the study of religion. Research on religion devoid of Christian premises was on the rise, but important currents still endeavored to fuse religious with scientific features. Rudolf Otto's books and activities are exemplary regarding such an intermediate position. I used the notion "theologische Religionswissenschaft" for that approach to describe its two-edged perspective and the wish of its advocates to balance their religious convictions with scholarly maxims valid in the humanities.[7] Considered by the church to be not sufficiently Christian, members of this group were, also correctly, blamed in the academy for not being sufficiently scientific. It is quite understandable that they conceptualized a meta-religion behind religion that was suitable to their persuasions. Such a religion would be located high above the lowly spheres of miraculous feats, objectionable dogmas, and petrified church structures. As an *ecclesia invisibilis* (Heiler's term) or in the form of Otto's "Religiöser Menschheitsbund" it ought to include all true religious people – symbolized by the so-called hominus religiosus – irrespective of their particular faiths. Of course, the abstraction from all doctrinal and tangible concretion has to be understood as reaction to secular criticism. While such a conception perfectly corresponded with the interests of certain intellectuals, it lacked, as a typical "Gelehrtenreligion," real followers and factual religious bodies. The benefit of evading laical critique was offset by the disadvantage of an existence restricted to the realm of creative imagination. Given that the construction of such a meta-religion led to a dead end and attracted very few

---

[7] Cf. Horst Junginger, "Das Überleben der Religionswissenschaft im Nationalsozialismus," *Zeitschrift für Religionswissenschaft* 9 (2001), pp. 149–167, here pp. 155–157.

disciples – outside the academy almost none – the pendulum swung back. Many formerly liberal Protestant religious studies scholars then took up a Germanic or Indo-Germanic religion which they imagined to be deeply rooted in the voelkish soil.

3. *The Time of Fascism in Germany*

After 1933, the situation in Germany was characterized by the return of religion and by a political offensive against all forms of irreligion and unbelief. At first, the Nazi regime took a very pro-Christian course, supporting church interests in every regard. But then National Socialism and the claims of the churches collided, not in all, but in certain fields. The Nazi leaders adopted a position critical of the established churches although they continued to follow the path of a "positive Christianity" (§ 24 of the party program). In contrast with the dualistic assumptions of the historiography of the church struggle, it is important to distinguish a negative assessment of the "reactionary" churches from an affirmative attitude towards religion and "uncorrupted" Christian principles in general.[8] Thus the NS government concomitantly referred to Christian values and attacked the established churches and their prerogatives. Which kind of religion should be given preference was anything but clear and a subject of heated debates. The fate of the German Faith Movement clearly shows that organized Paganism had no chance of becoming the new state religion, at most achieving the status of a third "confession" equally entitled with its Catholic and Protestant counterparts. Pagans in particular failed to realize that the shape of religion as such had changed. They witnessed step by painful step how their religious conception failed to harmonize with the "official" ideology of National Socialism, with Rosenberg's definition, and even less with Hitler's credo of a new faith, which, according to 1 Corinthians 13:2 and Matthew 17:20, would be able to move mountains. The new credence that Hitler unceasingly talked about fitted in much better with the alteration religion as a whole had undergone. In

---

[8] This distinction is one of the main results of Richard Steigman-Gall's notable dissertation *The Holy Reich. Nazi conceptions of Christianity, 1919–1945* (Cambridge: Cambridge University Press, 2004, 1st ed. 2003). Cf. now the special issue of the *Journal of Contemporary History* 42-1 (2007), dedicated to a critical discussion of the book, and Steigmann-Gall's response, ibid., 42-2 (2007), pp. 185–211.

the aftermath of Germany's military defeat in World War I, conventional and long-accustomed forms of religious allegiance had suffered a significant transformation, losing much of their former significance. Opposed to all sorts of religionists, Hitler understood very well that the end of the state church and the disunion of church and religion could not be rescinded by simply pouring new wine in old bottles. The central problem he had to cope with was the integration of millions of unbelieving workers into the community of the folk ("Volksgemeinschaft") which would not be possible on the basis of old-fashioned church structures nor with the help of a rather grotesque voelkish heathendom. But how to overcome the Weimar era of nihilism and secularism? How to unite the nation against all political, social, and class antagonisms? How to subdue unemployment and how to wage the next war already slated as of 1936? In Hitler's eyes, a profitable answer to these questions meant re-establishing a strong belief in the power of superhuman agency. Although he deemed neither Paganism nor traditional Christianity proficient enough to comply with the task sufficiently, history and habit clearly privileged the church which had been such a powerful institution over centuries. The solution of the dilemma lay therefore in a popular and quite conventional credence disentangled from the nomenclature and doctrinal claims of orthodox Christianity. Tapping into the political demands of the churches whenever they were in line with National Socialist goals (and fiercely rejecting them if not), Hitler advocated intensifying of all relations connecting this life with the other world – whether they took the form of normal prayers, sermons, services, or civil rites and feasts. The Almighty and the Providence that he persistently called on had the great benefit of being acceptable for both Christians and non-Christians. Yet most Germans, by reason of culture and education, perceived the Almighty and other features of civil religion in a Christian manner. In particular, the anti-Jewish impetus of National Socialism must be comprehended as part and parcel of the Christian legacy. Whether one prefers to interpret this modernization of religion in terms of a civil or political religion – in my opinion both approaches are useful if they avoid crypto-theological assumptions – one has to emphasize the retention of religion in the face of a fundamentally lessened authority of the established churches.

Filtering out the violent noise which accompanied the religious altercations of the Third Reich, it becomes apparent that the matters in dispute were far from exceptional in the history of religions. Such surging quarrels among religious groups for hegemony and between religion and state belong to the ordinary context of religious change and ought to be analyzed in that regard. With that in mind, the transformation brought about by the National Socialist seizure of power loses its character as a categorical line of demarcation. In spite of the comprehensible wish to keep Hitler's regime at arm's length and to treat it as something alien and incompatible, its political and religious history displays continuity and interrelatedness rather than the total rupture generally attributed to it. My main point is that the modern type of a religious studies scholar was much better equipped than a conventional theologian to fit with the reorganization of the religious field that occurred after the end of World War I and that continued under the reign of National Socialism. Since the political frame of religious reference had basically changed, a more general understanding of religion was required. As representatives of a particular faith, Christian theologians were too petty-minded and not flexible enough to meet the new challenges. While the study of religion flourished in the Weimar years under the aegis of secularism, it positively blossomed in the Third Reich under the rule of fascist irrationalism. The political system of National Socialism yielded even more benefits because it allowed the study of religion to maintain a religious substratum in opposition to its old enemies: illiberal theology and conservative Christianity. In accordance with the alteration that had taken place, the religious commitment of historians of religions could not exceed a certain limit. A blatant involvement in religious activities or an open partisanship for Paganism would have been disadvantageous to one's professional career. Jakob Wilhelm Hauer best exemplifies how an uncompromising agitation in behalf of neo-Germanic heathendom impeded both his academic and political advancement. His involvement with a new anti-Christian religion called "Deutscher Glaube" resulted in severe difficulties with the Reich Ministry of Science and Education. Restricted to an Aryan worldview in his academic teaching, Hauer was not allowed to include "religious education" to his lectureship. His plan to hold special university courses for the instruction of Pagan theologians, clerics and school teachers sputtered to a halt already in the phase of its first planning in 1933–34.

In accord with the reigning religious conditions, the successful scholar of religion in Nazi Germany would be neither overly Christian nor unduly Pagan. Exhibiting political loyalty, he would avoid an inappropriate engagement too far in one direction or the other. The usefulness of religion as such would be his maxim. Conversely, he would oppose any form of irreligion, especially political atheism, the offspring of Jewish bolshevism. Who might fit better to such kind of requirements than a religious studies scholar? With his natural empathy with religion he must appear, at least in his own perception, as the prototype of an intellectual for whom National Socialism was looking. Thus, many scholars of religion became convinced that the Third Reich provided them with the unique opportunity for leaving the peripheral position in which their discipline stayed so long. In their view, time was ripe to step forward and to occupy a place at the foreground of the academy. Comparable to a system of interconnected tubes, the study of religion insisted on making up for the decrease of theology that sharpened dramatically in the second half of the 1930s. Historians of religions considered themselves as the legal successors of Christian theology at more than merely political and institutional levels. In religious regards, too, they believed themselves to be in charge of replacing theological warrants. Whether arguing in favor of voelkish Paganism or in the context of a civil religion, Christian dogmatic theology was blamed for being a counter ideology to National Socialism. For National Socialist historians of religions, the struggle against Christianity therefore materialized as an opportunity to synthesize both their critical and religious bents: appearing critical and remaining religious at the same time; jointly propagating liberation from Christian dogmatism and discarding laicism. What the mainstream of Germany's religious studies scholars did was to shift the scientific antagonism towards theology back to a religious level and adapt it to the reigning worldview conditions.

Though lacking a clear comprehension of the religious transfiguration that had occurred, historians of religions felt intuitively that the non-particular concentration on superhuman agency also entailed a new type of intermediary agent. At the threshold of the spiritual world, a special class of intellectuals was still needed, a class whose members ought to have the hermeneutic expertise to interpret and explain the relevance of the ultimate goals of religion for the political life. Gatekeepers between this world and the other, their function was not only to understand but also to superintend the efficient flow of religious energy. In explicating the usefulness and real meaning of the higher ideas to be found in the history of religions, the study of religion was expected to collaborate in the intricate procedure of energizing politics with religious power. To utilize the potential of the irrational methodically was the responsibility of Christian theology in Christian times. In a more differentiated, secularized, and scientifically oriented society the obligation fell to the study of religion. Rewarded with financial support, new jobs, and a significant extension of influence, this task was received very favorably. Measuring up to it conformed to the intrinsic religious alignment still being extant. Repressed from consciousness or just lying dormant, the religious impetus of the study of religion received a new calling. Yet this wake-up call was, in fact, the kiss of death.

4. *The Problem of Ideology*

In searching for an answer as to why so many German scholars of religion were sympathetic towards National Socialism, one can scarcely avoid taking an intrinsic ideological susceptibility into consideration. Not surprisingly, the percentage of emigrants remained small, with little in the way of opposition or resistance. The eager willingness of Germany's "Religionswissenschaft" to collaborate displayed so few reservations that one would be justified in assuming a natural kinship or a "Wahlverwandtschaft." Immense research into the Nazification of German scholarship has been undertaken in the last three decades. One of its pivotal results is the great degree of consent and free will that characterized the academic professions in Germany. It belongs to the apologetic post-war fictions that scholarly learning and National Socialism had been in opposition to each other due to an innate enmity of science towards ideology. Some years earlier, religious studies scholars had presented their discipline as extraordinarily important for the national awakening. In their view, the strength of the NS state depended on a vigorous worldview and, accordingly, the more a religious dimension was involved, the more important scholars of religion became. Without touching the religious depth of the human soul, any attempt to mobilize the forces of the unconsciousness must be doomed to failure. Since it was equally impossible to return to traditional Christianity and to fall behind a certain limit of rationality, the study of religion was thought to have an advantage over theology in possessing expert knowledge in both areas: science and religion. Most Germans likely consented to the commonplace notion that neglecting the religious nature of man would lead to cynical materialism, overstressing it to an exclusivist dogmatism. What struck the happy medium better than the study of religion? Regarding a well-balanced relationship between the scientific and religious demands of life, the enthusiasm is understandable with which religious studies scholars tried to contribute to the new ideological foundation of the nation. Seizing the opportunity to extend its influence, the study of religion took an active part in the ideological reshaping of the religious field. No wonder, then, that the old cohabitation of science and religion swiftly enlarged to a *ménage à trois* in which ideology became head of the household.

Undoubtedly, the NS regime intensified the pressure on the universities to advance the process of political alignment ("Gleichschaltung") and to achieve a scientific substantiation of its political goals. Notwithstanding disagreements over certain points, one has to admit a far-reaching agreement on the side of the higher education with these aims. Especially the first measures of the new government, that is the exclusion of socialists and Jews, met with anything but disapproval. If criticism surfaced at all, it was sparked off by the impairment of personal interests and private relations and not as a result of political opposition. Though each scholar has to be judged differently, and all circumstances determining one's behavior must be carefully accounted for, it is hardly possible to concur with the lament of Nazi officials over a lack of commitment of Germany's university teachers. Nothing happened in the academy that could be compared to the former resistance against the democratic system of Weimar. Certainly the elite groups in Germany passionately disliked the voelkish crudeness of the NS movement. But things changed in 1933 when National Socialism turned into the official state ideology and shed much of its voelkish bias. From then on, it would have been unwise to express mental reservations openly. Supposing such hidden objections existed, they remained a private matter in most cases and did not take any political effect. On the contrary, what became apparent in public was a mixture of consent and opportunism. The degree of acquiescence and the free choice to cooperate with the administrative apparatus of the Third Reich on every level and in every regard is indisputable evidence that scholars' hearts and minds had been swayed.

However, the essential question is not about personal conduct and the scruples one might have had or not; rather, the issue centers on factual compatibility and the intersection between certain disciplines and certain political requirements. In the case of the study of religion, it is quite obvious that its objects and the way to deal with them bore a close relation to the worldview demands of the day. The occupation with occurrences of a transcendent nature and the reference to the higher ends of National Socialism showed similarities in form and content. If it is true that ideological superstructures and the realm of religious transcendence share a comparable nucleus of irrationality, then religious studies scholars had every right to consider themselves and their work important. One characteristic feature of the NS reign, and of fascist regimes in general, is that the relationship between ideological supply and political demand functioned in a much more direct and explicit manner. Normally, a great number of mediating elements lie between and obscure the unsophisticated nature of political claims. Not so under National Socialism. The habitual function of ideology to blur interests became less important compared to the ideological compression that augmented the performance of the National Socialist propaganda machine. Political theories often overemphasize the instrumental character of ideology which is deemed to serve hidden powers behind the scene. The development of the academic learning in Nazi Germany, particularly that of the study of religion, provides strong arguments to highlight on the autarchic nature of ideological processes. This does not mean that an ideology might be thinkable without material interests. Rather it is a plea to treat ideologies more assiduously as a distinct phenomenon of its own.

Today, the idea of a racial structure of man has rightly fallen into disrepute. But for Nazi scholarship, it served as new leitmotiv that infected almost every discipline in the natural sciences as well as in the humanities. Great efforts were undertaken to prove the relevance of the race principle. In spite of these endeavors, no hard evidence whatsoever could be uncovered to validate the existence of a Semitic or Aryan blood or of characteristics related to it. The race concept remained a mere phantasmagoria. Yet its scientific weakness on one side was its ideological strength on the other. The indeterminate nature of race and the lack of any factual substance made it a perfect ideology, attracting all sorts of prejudices prevailing in the society. It is well known and corroborated by many first-rate studies how Aryans and Semites derived their meaning from different language families. Nothing but language allows one to articulate the notion of an Aryan or Semitic people. What scholarly research treated much less rigorously was the repercussion that religion and, moreover, the study of religion had on the transformation of this philological distinction to a means of political exclusion. Can we really speak of a fortuitous coincidence that the emergence of the study of religion coalesced with the acceleration of racial ideas in the last third of the 19th century?[9]

The two main roots of the modern study of religion in Germany go back to a philological or theological occupation with religion. Both tapped into the grounds of philo-Aryanism or anti-Judaism respectively. A noticeable anti-Jewish undercurrent of liberal Protestantism and the Religionsgeschichtliche Schule has come to light in the last years and is beyond any doubt now.[10] It fueled the ideology of the German Christians in the 1930s and eventually generated a form of scientific antisemitism which aspired to modernize the old religious antagonism towards the Jews with a combination of racial arguments and the methods used in the history of religions. Labeling their undertaking "Religionswissenschaft," its representatives like Gerhard Kittel, Walther Grundmann, and other scholars connected either with the Research Department for the Jewish Question ("Forschungsabteilung Judenfrage") of the Reich Institute for the History of the New Germany ("Reichsinstitut für Geschichte des neuen Deutschland") or with the Institute for the Study and Eradication of Jewish Influence on German Church Life ("Institut zur Erforschung und Beseitigung des jüdischen Einflusses auf das deutsche kirchliche Leben") amalgamated race and religion on a Christian basis.[11] Historians of religions who lost or abandoned their Christian belief preferably turned their interests towards the non-Christian world in which ancient Persia and India obtained a prominent status. Concomitantly to their religious alienation, these scholars

---

[9] Cf. Stefan Arvidsson, *Aryan idols. Indo-European mythology as ideology and science* (Chicago: University of Chicago Press, 2006), esp. the chapter "Language, race, and religion," pp. 37–62.

[10] See especially Uriel Tal, *Christians and Jews in Germany. Religion, politics, and ideology in the Second Reich, 1870–1914* (Ithaca: Cornell University Press, 1975) and Christian Wiese, *Wissenschaft des Judentums und protestantische Theologie im wilhelminischen Deutschland. Ein Schrei ins Leere?* (Tübingen: Mohr Siebeck, 1999), English trans. *Challenging colonial discourse. Jewish Studies and Protestant theology in Wilhelmine Germany* (Leiden: Brill, 2004).

[11] See for Grundmann, Susannah Heschel, "New Testament Scholarship on the 'Aryan Jesus' during the Third Reich," in Benjamin G. Wright, ed., *A Multiform heritage. Studies on early Judaism and Christianity in honor of Robert A. Kraft* (Atlanta: Scholars Press, 1999), pp. 303–321 and for Kittel, Horst Junginger "Das Bild des Juden in der nationalsozialistischen Judenforschung," in Andrea Hoffmann et al., eds., *Die kulturelle Seite des Antisemitismus zwischen Aufklärung und Schoah* (Tübingen: Tübinger Vereinigung für Volkskunde e.V., 2006), pp. 171–220 and in general, Max Weinreich, *Hitler's professors. The part of scholarship in Germany's crimes against the Jewish people* (New York: YIVO, 1946, 2nd ed. New Haven: Yale University Press, 1999).

became magnetized by the Indo-Germanic or Aryan tradition. The dissociation from Christianity and a leaning towards the old Aryans went hand in hand. While scholars of religion sympathizing with the German Christians advocated a solution of the "Jewish question" via a segregation of the Jews, the exponents of a non-theological approach affirmed their expertise for a 'positive' foundation of the ideology of National Socialism. Whether referring to the enmity of Aryan Christianity towards Judaism or proclaiming a version of Pagan Aryanism, both groups heavily stressed racial issues to boost their reputation and influence.

Considering the fact that the study of religion offered nothing that would have been directly applicable to the executive assignments of National Socialist governance, it understandably emphasized its ideological relevance. It made sense to draw on the long tradition and great contributions of Indo-Germanic studies, both politically and scientifically. The development from the language of the Aryans to their culture and then from culture to race mirrored the course of politics from the Second German Reich over the Weimar Republic to the Nazi regime. Substituting the reference point of culture with that of race fully concurred with the change of power that took place in 1933. Aside from their political and religious motives, many scholars now took advantage of race as a hermeneutic tool for a new understanding of religion. Thus armed, they hoped to overcome the old divisions of subject and object, of the rational and the irrational, of science and religion, which had unceasingly harassed the academic study of religion from its inception. The twofold nature of race allowed scholars to use it in both directions. It is a widespread fault to reduce the race concepts of National Socialism to a biological materialism. The idea of a genetically determined religion bears much more resemblance to older religious assumptions of a *prima causa* or a *causa efficiens* engendered by an exterior prime mover. It would be absurd to think that things come to an end in the world with its creation. Likewise, the postulation of a racial origin of religion did not determine its further course unalterably. Nor did it terminate the duty and freedom of men to arrange their lives in accordance with the commandments emanating from one's belonging to a particular race. Scientifically approved by the natural sciences, as it seemed, race functioned as cornerstone of a new theory of religion which permitted reformulating the crucial relationship between the inexplicable "X" of religion and the history of religion as its objective expression, between the inner and the outer side of religious occurrences. Although in a scholarly sense, neither god nor race have any material equivalent, the temptation for scholars of religion was too great not to merge the pseudo materialism of National Socialist race ideology with the deficiencies of their epistemological aspirations. But despite the great expectations aroused by the race concept, it turned out to be anything but a new programmatic modus operandi which would help surmount the theoretical weakness of the study of religion. On the contrary, it inflated its ideological proneness and political corruption in a way and dimension previously unknown.

The main theoretical problem posed to the study of religion is its bilateral disposition – half oriented towards the rational, half towards the irrational – yearning for a *tertium comparationis* to connect both spheres of comprehension. Race served that purpose. With its "materialistic" basis on one hand and its idealistic objective on the other, the race idea functioned as a missing link between the religious and scientific dimensions of the study of religion. Yet it operated in a conventional manner. While the concept of reason developed by voelkish scholars of religion fiercely rejected the Christian notion of revelation, it shared a similar epistemological structure. Feigned corroboration provided by the natural sciences, especially biology and anthropology, cannot hide the fact that only the belief in the revealed truth of racial laws guaranteed their effect. The first article of faith of voelkish scholarship was the postulation that any scientific understanding depended on the nature of one's blood, that is on the belief in the nature of one's blood. In opposition to the Christian type of revelation, voelkish scholars of religion embarked on visionary speculations about the Aryan past which they took for a given, though widely hidden, reality. Synthesizing race and religion, they doubled the tautological assumption inherent in both of its components. The crux of the matter was that the idea of an Aryan race relied to a great extent on the idea of an Aryan culture and religion and that the idea of an Aryan culture and religion relied to a great extent on religious premises and on the negation of what was previously defined as Jewish. The ideological doubling that characterized the amalgamation of race and religion demands the conceptual scrutiny of each of its constituents. Looking upon perverted reality with the *camera obscura* of ideology implies here a binocular focus.[12]

---

[12] I refer here to Stuart Hall et al., eds., *Die Camera obscura der Ideologie* (Berlin: Argument, 1984) and the first volume of Manfred Behrens et al., eds., *Faschismus und Ideologie* (Hamburg: Argument, 1980), particularly to the foreword of Wolfgang Fritz Haug and his article "Annäherung an die faschistische Modalität des Ideologischen," ibid., pp. 7–12 and pp. 44–80.

It is the entanglement of scientific with religious problems that
makes it so difficult to come to grips with the study of religion under
the impact of National Socialist and fascist influences. To deal with the
ideologization of scholarship is an intricate matter in and of itself. Yet
things are even more complicated regarding religious studies and the
unclear epistemological status of its object. Perhaps the occupation with
its inclination towards National Socialist racialism can help to heighten
consciousness of the theoretical questions involved. If it is correct to
attribute the function of ideological criticism to the study of religion,
then it ought to prove its worth by taking its own history into account.
There is no period offering a better opportunity and more material for
critical self-reflexivity than the time of fascism in Europe.

5. *The European Context*

Wüst's arrogant proclamation at the height of Germany's military
success that National Socialist scholarship was about to become the
"teacher of Europe" had some justification in so far as it mirrored the
overwhelming triumph of the German Wehrmacht on all fronts in
the eyes of a leading Nazi intellectual. The kernel of truth of Wüst's
pompous announcement lies in the total ideologization of academic
learning in Germany from which the mission emanated to establish
National Socialism as dominating worldview all over Europe. German science as represented by key figures such as Wüst epitomized an
ideologized and totally politicized scholarship. It displayed the perfect
model of academic learning under the influence of fascism. The more
closely one examines the history of science of the 1930s and 1940s, the
more evidence for the destruction of reason comes to light. However,
setting aside Germany's paramount position in that regard, the question
remains as to whether the situation in other European countries was
substantially different. The extremism of the German example should
not relieve us of the duty to scrutinize the study of religion elsewhere
with the same thoroughness and with comparable critical bearing. In the
light of earlier debates about the nature of fascism in countries others
than Germany and Italy and, more recently, about the autonomy of
racism and antisemitism uninfluenced by the German prototype, we
should focus on the question how to interpret ideological deformations
in other parts of Europe. What accounts for differences in comparison

with National Socialist Germany, and were there similar patterns of distortion? What was the impact of fascist ideas on the study of religion in other European countries, and which segments of its scientific agenda were affected? Was fascism generally advantageous to the development of a non-theological research on religion as it was the case in Germany and Italy, where it set off a forceful institutionalization process? What about scientific or political counter-positions in the study of religion? Many questions of this kind ought to be addressed in order to survey the situation in Europe properly. The most intriguing issue of such a comparative analysis, however, is the possibility of an inner affinity between the study of religion and fascist, voelkish, racist, and similar ideas.

   Owing to the small number of scholars of religion in Europe, most of them knew each other personally or at least from correspondence. Colleagues stayed informed of each other's scientific work despite the absence of today's electronic communication. The correspondence of scholars like Eliade, Hauer, Pettazzoni and others reveals a rather strong cohesion of the European community of historians of religions. Many of them had studied under similar conditions, some even under the same professors, and had received comparable academic training in the time following World War I. The problems they struggled with were not really different, such as living costs, maintenance, academic reputation, seeking a scientific niche, self-assertion against theology, and balancing scholarly and religious persuasions. This makes it rather likely that their worldview orientation embraced common features. It is interesting to see here how they acted on the momentum of their youth and how they dealt with the history of religions when the rise of fascism began to influence, and in some cases to change, the political configuration of their countries. Highly specialized in particular areas of knowledge, European scholars of religion shared very often a similar comprehension of religion. Instead of basically different approaches, one should therefore expect to see the adaptation of a similar scheme of research to particular circumstances. A general trait of likely all religious studies scholars was their profound dislike of Christian dogmatism. Shaped by liberal and enlightened attitudes towards Christianity, they were so far removed from the official church that a position with a theology department appeared unattainable for most of them. The alienation from their personal belief and the lack of prospects to establish themselves in a theological context gave strong stimuli to attend to religious traditions apart from Christianity. It is therefore not astonishing that a scientific or even religious liking of Paganism increased among historians of religions.

Because the established churches had been closely associated with monarchy and the conservative parties virtually all over Europe, the estrangement of religious studies scholars from Christianity brought a forceful political element into play. Religious liberalism automatically took a political shape under such circumstances, and the occupation with non-Christian religions bore the inherent germ of opposition. The percentage of academics with progressive or leftist tendencies seems to have been much higher among religious studies scholars than among other university disciplines, specifically those attached to the state bureaucracy and governmental professions. But their dislike of the reactionary forces, among them, of course, the churches, did not mitigate against a fundamental compassion for religion as such. Accordingly, the drift to religious outsider positions and religious traditions outside of Christianity was a logical consequence. Emphasizing pre- and non-Christian traditions materialized as a general trend in the study of religion throughout Europe although the revitalization of Paganism in the form of a new "church" was restricted to Nazi Germany. Apparently, European scholars of religion reacted not so differently to the problems stirred up in the aftermath of World War I. Progressive intellectuals rejected the parties of the right and their acclaim of Christian traditionalism as well as the worker's organizations with their decided atheism. For that reason, they were easily attracted by the mixture of anti-reactionary and anti-socialist elements characterizing fascist and voelkish ideas. If we define "voelkish" as a term to head an ideological superstructure seeking to equate the flaws of a defective nation-building process, as an ideology that claimed to overcome social, political, economic and other antagonisms on the higher level of the community of the folk, the importance of a renewed access to religion becomes evident. The new order, the new man, a new civilization, a third humanism or Hellenism and whatever terms were used − all these concepts necessitated a new spirituality and the reconciliation of the nation and God. Without reference to the divine, both the future Reich as well as its prophecies lacked inner coherence and a compelling legitimization. Who would be better equipped to rationalize the religious calling for a rebirth of the nation than scholars of religion? Suddenly, their work was catapulted into a new significance which reached far beyond the academic margins they were normally entangled in. It is not surprising that the prospect of becoming part of the nation's intellectual elite held tremendous appeal.

The "positive" program of fascist movements revolved around the hazy theory of a corporative national socialism which greatly relied on the strengthening of the forces of belief for its implementation. Even more important was the other side of the coin, viz a definition of fascism via negation. Those who were declared the enemies of the nation served as negative model displaying inverted attributes and values. Their perversions (*perverso numine et more*) were subject to negation. Outsiders who offended against good taste and an average morality suffered in particular from fascist aggressions. Often attached to a different religious tradition, national minorities were vulnerable to xenophobic chauvinism all over Europe. The boundary shifts caused by World War I had saddled many European countries with serious minority problems. Yet no other group besides the Jews was more appropriate to exemplify the inner enemy and a global threat at the same time. For hundreds of years, they symbolized the forces of evil and darkness allegedly obstructing the better future that everybody yearned for. Primarily a religious problem, hostility against the Jews embraced a large number of modern and secular elements although antisemites had no reason to refuse old and long-established preconceptions of a religious nature. Due to the religious core of the "Jewish question," one might expect a particular inclination of religious studies scholars towards antisemitism and a dedicated role in the anti-Jewish discrimination policy prospering in the 1930s in Europe. But contrary to this presumption, historians of religions appeared to be less antisemitic compared to other groups of intellectuals, for instance Christian theologians who were concerned with the "Jewish problem" for religious reasons. This is only surprising at first glance. Over the course of their alienation from Christianity, historians of religions lost the awareness of the precarious position of the Jews in the Christian salvation plan. Judaism had ceased to be a religious problem for them. For Christians, especially German Christians, the permanent refusal of the Jews of accepting Christian ascendancy meant a suppurating thorn in the flesh. The impossibility to find a solution to this religious aporia finally culminated in the idea that cutting out the cancerous ulcer would be the only option.[13] Whereas

---

[13] Eminent New Testament and religious studies scholar at the University of Tübingen, Gerhard Kittel, developed a rationale for National Socialist antisemitism

anti-Jewish prejudices were not alien to historians of religions as well, they lacked spiritual depth. The principle of religious tolerance, as it seems, continued to have some effect among non-theological scholars of religion even in fascist times.

However, one should not hope for a critical stance on antisemitism and racism within the study of religion in general. Political measures against the Jews and other minority groups met with anything but rejection. Intolerance to the enemies of the in-group became a vital element throughout Europe in forming of a new national identity. To cleanse the country from everything un-national belonged to the foremost claims of all fascist movements in Europe, and not only of these groups. Though failing to arrive at the level of National Socialist racism, the longing for hereditary genuineness and the wish to highlight one's own ancestral heritage cropped up in many parts of Europe. Such a tendency to emphasize ethnic cohesion gained momentum the more a country lacked democratic traditions and the more retarded it was in its economic development. In fact, attempts to establish a sort of ethnocratic order did not hinge on the foreign aid of Nazi Germany. In isolating the German example, one might be tempted to speak of "racism lite" or of a moderate anti-Judaism in these cases. Leaving that comparison aside, the autochthonous character of their racialism cannot be overlooked. The articles in this book provide ample evidence that fascist impulses and a chauvinistic nationalism affected scholars of religion all over Europe. Accordingly, difference in degree – not in principle – ought to be the comparative framework to juxtapose the behavior of religious studies scholars in Europe in the interwar period.

Taking the European context of a fascist reorganization of state and society into account does not devalue the meaning of the German paragon. Though the ideological impairment of the university system in Nazi Germany was outstanding in degree and intensity, there is no danger that an international comparison would belittle the leading role of the German academy in that regard. Particularly after the outbreak of World War II, the expertise of German scholars was utilized on behalf of National Socialist warfare. Approximately 500 university teachers participated in the so-called "Kriegseinsatz der Geisteswissenschaften,"

---

progressing to this extreme degree. I therefore called his approach a "theology of the holocaust." See Horst Junginger, "Das Bild des Juden in der nationalsozialistischen Judenforschung," p. 205.

a project of the Reich Ministry of Science and Education to assemble possible war contributions of the humanities.[14] The "Kriegseinsatz" consisted of various branches which furthered the military aims of the Third Reich ideologically. In Walther Wüst's section "Indogermanische Kultur- und Geistesgeschichte" (History of the Culture and Ideas of the Indo-Germans), Jakob Wilhelm Hauer organized a sub-division titled "Lebensmächte und Wesen des Indogermanentums" (Powers and Nature of the Indo-Germans). Hauer's group consisted of just under 25 collaborators, among them a number of scholars of religion.[15] Another important instrument in the ideological war of Nazi Germany was the establishment of so-called "Reichsuniversitäten" (Reich universities) being instituted as academic outposts of National Socialism in Prague, Strasbourg, Leiden, and Poznán during the war. At the "Reichsuniversität Straßburg," an independent institute of science of religion was erected in 1942 under Otto Huth, a high rank of the SS "Ahnenerbe." One of the ideological tasks of this institute was to produce evidence that Alsace belonged to the German Reich. Together with Hans-Ernst Schneider – who changed his name to Hans Schwerte after the war, becoming rector of the Technical University of Aachen and representative of North Rhine-Westphalia for the academic cooperation with Belgium and the Netherlands in the 1970s – Huth participated in the "Germanischer Wissenschaftseinsatz," a special war project of the SS to strengthen the Germanic worldview of 'Nordic' countries such as the Netherlands and Norway. The situation looked different on the other side of the front. Soon after Germany had declared war, the French University of Strasbourg took flight, expecting a German takeover. It partly re-opened at Clermont-Ferrand in unoccupied France. Among the scholars who managed to escape was the young historian of religions Marcel Simon who became president of the International Association for the History of Religions from 1970 until 1980.

Using the occupation as an opportunity to loot foreign property is a right of conquest that is probably exercised by all invading forces. However, systematically seizing the resources of an occupied nation to

---

[14] Cf. Frank-Rutger Hausmann's standard work 'Deutsche Geisteswissenschaft' im Zweiten Weltkrieg. Die 'Aktion Ritterbusch' (1940–1945) (Dresden: Dresden University Press, 1998, 2nd ed. 2002).

[15] See H. Junginger, Von der philologischen zur völkischen Religionswissenschaft, chapter 17 "Im Kriegseinsatz der Geisteswissenschaften," pp. 233–248, esp. p. 235f. Hauer's co-workers included, for instance, Bernhard Kummer, Hermann Mandel, Otto Huth, Hans Heinrich Schaeder, and Franz Altheim.

augment the taker's fighting capacity seems to have been a German specialty in World War II. A large number of German scholars busily took possession of foreign archives, libraries, scientific institutes, ministries etc. in order to translate, classify, and utilize the appropriated material in these or other ways on behalf of Nazi Germany's ideological warfare. For example, a significant document concerned with the conferences of the International Association for the History of Religions which the "Deutsche Kongress-Zentrale" sent to the Reich Ministry of Science and Education on February 2, 1942, had been stolen from the International Institute for Documentation (Palais Mondial, later Mundaneum), when German troops invaded Brussels. Eventually it wound up in the hands of the Berlin ministry. The first sentence of its cover letter reads: "Enclosed we send you a translation of a report about the International Congresses for the History of Religions that we have taken from the files of the Palais Mondial in Brussels."[16] Recapitulating the history of the first six IAHR-conferences from 1900 until 1935, the communiqué stated that the 7th IAHR-congress had been scheduled to take place in Germany. But due to the many Jews who had been expected as participants, the conference place had been shifted to Italy. Then, as the letter continued, political circumstances forced the entire postponement of the congress although Raffaele Pettazzoni had already been nominated conference president in 1939. Finally, it was announced that Germany would hold the 7th IAHR-conference directly after the war.

It goes without saying that Nazi Germany was eager to organize the renowned international convention of historians of religions in Berlin to demonstrate an objective and unbiased handling of religious matters as well as the country's leading position in the European study of religion. In the preparatory phase of the 6th IAHR-conference from September 16–21, 1935 in Brussels, the German authorities first hesitated to send a delegation to Belgium because they feared international backlash regarding the political situation in Germany. Interested scholars were

---

[16] "In der Anlage übersenden wir Ihnen eine Übersetzung eines Berichtes über die Internationalen Kongresse für Religionsgeschichte, den wir aus den Akten des Palais Mondial in Brüssel entnommen haben." Letter of the "Deutsche Kongress-Zentrale" to the Reich Ministry of Science and Education on February 2, 1942, accompanying a report with the title "Internationale Kongresse für Religionsgeschichte," Federal Archives Berlin, R 4901, 3164, fol. 44, the report itself fol. 45f. The "Kongress-Zentrale" was a department of the Propaganda Ministry responsible for sholarly conferences. Cf. also Michael Stausberg, this volume, p. 379.

barred from participating with the feigned argument of lacking foreign currency. In July 1935, G. v. Langenhove from the organization committee thus wrote a letter to the German ministry in which he complained about the few German scholars who had enrolled for participation.[17] Among 120 foreign scholars from 30 countries less than ten would be Germans. Langenhove explicitly mentioned Friedrich Andres, Alfred Bertholet, Karl Bornhausen, Carl Clemen, Hans Rust (falsely written Ruft), Otto Weinreich, Diedrich Westermann, Hans Alexander Winkler, and, interestingly, Marcel Simon whom Langenhove thought to be located at Berlin.[18] Only six of the Germans, as Langenhove said, would be suited to lecture. Overcoming its hesitancy, the Reich Ministry of Science and Education eventually allowed a small German delegation to attend the Brussels conference. A ministerial note from September 14, 1935 announced that the official delegation would consist of Karl Bornhausen, Franz Dornseiff, Hermann Güntert, and Rudolf Franz Merkel.[19] All others were denied participation. Evidently, the ministry had changed its mind because it put the chance to promote German interests over the risk of international criticism. According to the report of the delegation leader Karl Bornhausen, the group's attempt to advertise the German viewpoint and to explain the real intention of National Socialist policy met with great success. Bornhausen greatly lamented in his account the backward state ("Rückständigkeit") of the International Association for the History of Religions. As concrete evidence of this stagnation he referred to the fact that scholars from the former Entente had been given prominence and that Semitic issues had been a topic of discussion. Opposite to that old-fashioned attitude of liberalism and internationalism, Bornhausen pointed at the favorable result of his endeavors to publicize NS politics. Particularly scholars from Southeast

[17] Letter of G. v. Langenhove to the Berlin Ministry of Science and Education on July 6, 1935, Federal Archives Berlin, R 4901, 2966, fol. 54.
[18] Ibid., fol. 54. In the conference proceedings, Simon appeared as affiliate of the University of Strasbourg. Cf. *Mélanges Franz Cumont. Annuaire de l'Institut de Philologie et d'Histoire Orientales et Slaves*, tome IV-1 (Bruxelles: Université libre, 1936), p. XXXVI. Seen from Germany's perspective, Simon gave a lecture on "La politique anti-juive de S. Jean Chrysostome et le mouvement judaïsant d'Antioche" (ibid., pp. 403–421). For Winkler's failed attempt to come to Brussels, see H. Junginger, "Ein Kapitel Religionswissenschaft während der NS-Zeit: Hans Alexander Winkler (1900–1945)," *Zeitschrift für Religionswissenschaft* 2 (1995), pp. 137–161, here p. 150f.
[19] Note of the Reich Ministry of Science and Education on September 6, 1935, Federal Archives Berlin, R 4901, 2966, fol. 111. The note was based on information provided by the "Deutsche Kongress-Zentrale."

Europe would have been impressed by the German model.[20] Another
illustration of a direct effect of Germany's military aggression on the
study of religion in Europe was the prevention of the first Polish chair
for the history of religions, proposed at the University of Warsaw for
the academic year 1939–1940. Wiktor Niemczyk had already been
nominated, but as a result of the German attack on Poland, he was
never inaugurated.[21] If we consider the situation in Poland and other
European countries, it becomes evident that Germany's imperialistic
attempt to dominate Europe transformed not only the German academy
but also affected scholarly learning throughout Europe.

The Third Reich's military dominance, its ideological hubris, and
its horrible crimes should not tempt us into ignoring the autonomous
nature of fascist tendencies outside of Germany. The contributions
to this book evince an independent liability to fascist ideas in many
countries. They all deal with the question whether the European study
of religion depended upon similar influences, dealt with analogous
problems, and evolved into equal directions. Were there common
features, and what differentiated German, French, British, Italian and
other European scholars of religion, aside from private and individual
factors? However, the current stage of knowledge has not reached the
point to answer these questions properly. Simply speaking, we do not
know enough to generalize about the study of religion under fascism in
Europe. Our only option to advance to a sound comparative approach
is getting seriously involved in specific case studies. Then we may proceed further to more general themes and findings. Usually, history of
science starts with biographies, which subsequently allow the inclusion
of additional topics related to the persons under scrutiny. Due to the
intricate political, cultural and religious context the study of religion
is embedded in, such biographical or other studies of a specific nature
are a demanding task not only for doctoral students. The long-lived
reluctance, not to say unwillingness, of the academic study of religion
to occupy itself with the time of fascism has led to a very unfortunate
scarcity of investigations into the political involvement of individual

---

[20] Report of Karl Bornhausen, October 12, 1935, Federal Archives Berlin, R 4901,
2966, fol. 119–121, 3 pages. Bornhausen, who had taken over the chair of Paul Tillich
at the University of Frankfort in 1934, went on to establish an institute of science of
religion one year later. In Breslau, where he taught previously, Bornhausen gave the
official speech during the book burning on May 11, 1933.
[21] See Halina Grzymała-Moszczyńska and Henryk Hoffmann, "The science of
religion in Poland: Past and present," *Method & Theory in the Study of Religion* 10 (1998),
pp. 352–372, here p. 358.

scholars and into the ideological distortions scholarly research on religion was subject to. Tackling matters of that type often means laying groundwork without applicable secondary literature at hand. Under such circumstances, it is perhaps understandable that emphasizing the contextual relationship outside of one's own narrow subject with due care – that is, to comprehensively focus on the political, religious, and cultural environment in which the study of religion developed – requires more time and capacity than individual researchers normally have at their disposal. Therefore a common effort of today's European study of religion to examine the time of fascism is indispensable to come to terms with its past history and intellectual prerequisites.

6. *The Problem of a Proper Historization*

Scholars had many options of possible conduct in the face of fascism. There was no fixed teleology and university teachers were free to pursue multiple courses of action. Like other intellectuals, historians of religions could freely decide if they wanted to become involved politically and how far this involvement would go. The great variety of potential behavior does not allow for uniform judgments and obliges the historian to assess each scholar differently, striving for differentiation. Deliberating all shades of opinion, one has to avoid black and white representations. Students are well advised to refrain from hasty generalizations and to eschew any attitude of moral arrogance. Each appraisal, positive or negative, has to be based on a profound knowledge of the scientific issues at stake. Attaining this is somewhat difficult as historians of religions usually work in rather specific areas of learning which draw on various language skills and other expertise. Additionally, researchers should be fluent in the political conditions determining the course of events. A close intimacy with the vast corpus of historical and political literature, with both primary and secondary sources, is therefore mandatory. Whereas German publications dominated the earlier debates on fascism and National Socialism, an international community of scholars added great quantities of excellent studies, particularly since the 1990s.[22] It has been rightly criticized that Germans did not take sufficient notice of these books and articles on fascism mainly written

---

[22] See for instance Sven Reichhardt's review article, "Was mit dem Faschismus passiert ist. Ein Literaturbericht zur internationalen Faschismusforschung seit 1990,

in English but also in French, Italian and other European languages. I have already pointed to the fact that archival research is indispensable to grasp the inner side of university affairs. The motives of scholars in the interplay between scientific work, academic duties, and political allegiance become plausible only if one can access the pertinent state and university archives. A membership in fascist associations and other sorts of political engagement would in many cases remain unrevealed without examining the personal files of scholars. Everybody who works with archival material knows that it depicts a different side of things, often deviating significantly from their public appearance. Without such a broad basis of information, thorough and differentiated analyses are inconceivable.

For practical reasons alone it is very difficult for a single researcher to inspect all relevant archives and data pertaining to more than a limited field of research. Maintaining an overview of a constantly growing number of publications germane to the general scientific and political problems drawn in is equally strenuous. Moreover, one ought to be acquainted with mainstream Christianity as well as deviant religious groups in and outside of the Christian realm to understand the religious framework in which scholars of religion developed their theories. Since the European study of religion is strongly contingent upon the relationship between state and church, each change of the status of the established churches must also affect its academic setting. What renders the historiography of the study of religion such an intricate matter is how religious studies are embedded in this context. The dense conglomeration of scholarship, religion and politics symptomatic of the study of religion – especially in the period of fascism – makes it totally impossible to write the history of the history of religions solely on scientific grounds as a history of scholarly ideas. If we take for granted that fascist movements strove to occupy the religious field to leverage the powers of belief for their purposes and, moreover, that a spiritual resuscitation in modern times would not be attainable without a new scientific understanding of religion, the political importance of an extra-theological study of religion appears to be indisputable.

To demonstrate the problem of a proper historization with an eminent example, I would like to focus now on the case of Mircea Eliade,

Teil 1." *Neue Politische Literatur* 49 (2004), pp. 385–406. The announced second part of the review will deal with publications on the issue of political religion.

one of the best-known scholars of religion in our days. Due to his relationship with the Romanian Iron Guard, Eliade is also a highly disputed figure. In the final report of the International Commission on the Holocaust in Romania, presented to the Romanian President Ion Iliescu on November 11, 2004, Eliade is mentioned in a paragraph titled "Background and Precursors to the Holocaust" which ends with the sentence: "The holocaust had deep Romanian roots and must be dealt with as an integral part of Romanian political and cultural history."[23] Although not directly blamed as an intellectual harbinger of the holocaust, Eliade is here unambiguously positioned in the context of an ardent antisemitism and related to the ideology of Romanisation ("românizare") which culminated in the law of August 8, 1940 and which reached a first peak of anti-Jewish violence in November 1940.[24] Radu Ioanid, one of the authors of the report, underscored his harsh critique of Eliade later on, calling him a passionate Iron Guard ideologue.[25] Quite the reverse, Bryan Rennie stated after extensive research that Eliade cannot be held accountable for the vicious antisemitism of the Legionary Movement. In his eyes, on the contrary, Eliade had tried to strengthen the Legion's inherent moral momentum, unluckily in vain. Rennie writes: "It seems that Eliade's agenda was to harness the religious elements of these political movements in a vain attempt to coerce the moral, honorable, virtuous, and dignified behavior of its adherents." Without specifying these noble virtues he continues that in the time when Eliade was sympathetic to the Iron Guard, "antisemitism was not an indispensable part" of its program.[26] Rennie maintained defending Eliade against the accusation of antisemitism being only

---

[23] The report is available on the homepage of the Holocaust Memorial Museum http://www.ushmm.org/research/center/presentations/features/details/2005-03-10/, pp. 37–55, the quotation p. 54f. Cf. also the entry on the Wiesel Commission on http://en.wikipedia.org/wiki/Wiesel_Commission. These and the following websites have been checked at the beginning of August 2007.

[24] See Radu Ioanid, *The holocaust in Romania. The destruction of Jews and Gypsies under the Antonescu regime, 1940–1944* (Chicago: Ivan R. Dee, 2000), pp. 20–25. The law was based on a mixture of religious and biological arguments.

[25] Radu Ioanid, "The sacralised politics of the Romanian Iron Guard," in Roger Griffin, ed., *Fascism, totalitarianism and political religion* (London et al.: Routledge, 2005), pp. 125–159, esp. p. 144. Cf. idem, *The sword of the Archangel. Fascist ideology in Romania* (Boulder: East European Monographs, 1990), esp. p. 82, p. 125f., pp. 143–147, and p. 155f.

[26] Bryan S. Rennie, *Reconstructing Eliade. Making sense of religion* (New York: Albany, 1996), p. 160f. Rennie argues that the Iron Guard became violently antisemitic only after Eliade had left the country.

able if "made out of context."[27] And in sum: There is no evidence for
"egregious wrongdoing."[28] How is it possible to arrive at such contradictory conclusions as exemplified by the quoted statements?

First of all, it should be emphasized that any teleological or retrospective interpretation of history is misleading. Neither an accusatory
nor an apologetic posture would benefit a proper understanding of
the study of religion under fascism. But the call to deal dispassionately
with our history *sine ira et studio* is easier in theory than in practice.
The heated debates about Eliade's political past evince an enormous
inner commitment owing to the great fame Eliade later achieved at the
University of Chicago. These discussions usually address the possibility
of a "tainted greatness," as the title of a book reads which contains
a very critical contribution of Adriana Berger, a former co-worker of
Eliade.[29] It comes as no surprise that her stern criticism met with strong
rejection from the other side.[30] For reasons that are not completely
clear, Berger did not publish the intellectual biography of Eliade she
had repeatedly announced.[31] Albeit not all arguments brought forth
in behalf of defending or indicting a distinguished scholar such as
Eliade should be considered suspicious per se, even if expressed by an
overstretched wording and reasoning, the intention of this book and
its preceding conference leads away from either a positive or a negative predisposition and goes primarily in the direction of a thorough
historical contextualization. It seems that a retrospective interpretation
shaped by the academic post-war discourses in the United States has
encumbered the scrupulous and emotionally uninvolved occupation

---

[27] Bryan S. Rennie, "The meaning and end of Mircea Eliade," in idem, ed., *Changing religious worlds. The meaning and end of Mircea Eliade* (New York: Albany, 2001), pp.
263–281, here p. 267.

[28] Bryan S. Rennie, "Mircea Eliade [Further considerations]," *Encyclopedia of Religion*,
2nd ed., vol. 4 (2005), pp. 2757–2763, here p. 2758.

[29] Adriana Berger, "Mircea Eliade: Romanian fascism and the history of religions in
the United States," in Nancy A. Harrowitz, ed., *Tainted greatness. Antisemitism and cultural
heroes* (Philadelphia: Temple University Press, 1994), pp. 51–74. Cf. also Berger's review
articles "Fascism and religion in Romania," *Annals of Scholarship* 6 (1989), pp. 455–465
and "Mircea Eliade's vision for a new humanism," *Society* 30–5 (1993), pp. 84–87.

[30] See for instance Bryan S. Rennie, "The diplomatic career of Mircea Eliade: A
response to Adriana Berger," *Religion* 22–4 (1992), pp. 375–392 and idem, *Reconstructing
Eliade*, pp. 149–159.

[31] See Berger, "Mircea Eliade's vision for a new Humanism," p. 87 and idem,
"Mircea Eliade: Romanian fascism and the history of religions in the United States,"
p. 72, n. 1. In a letter of March 18, 1994, Berger wrote me that lawyers entrusted by
Eliade's widow had threatened her with legal action specifically to prevent quotation
from unpublished articles and documents.

with Eliade considerably. Yet, if Eliade's subsequent greatness and his position in the academy might be affected by serious research or not should be totally irrelevant to the research itself. The question what to learn from Eliade's early political activities and ideological writings for his later work bears great significance but has nothing to do with a meticulous and uncompromising study of them. A retrospective approach would not only put the cart before the horse. It would – and in fact did – hamper the unbiased examination of Eliade's past as well as that of the study of religion under fascist influences in general.

What is required first and foremost is a comprehensive insight into the Romanian context inclusive of all relevant political, cultural, scientific, and religious aspects.[32] Recently, two excellent studies appeared which contribute immensely to the aim of a proper contextualization of Eliade,[33] though we are still far away from having the full picture. Until today, no critical edition of Eliade's Romanian writings has been published. Attempts have been made to reprint parts of them, but these did not come to fruition.[34] The Romanian texts and documents provided by Mircea Handoca are not generally available; they are not translated; and, even worse, their edition does not follow scholarly rules.[35] The originals Handoca refers to continue to be largely inaccessible and it is unclear to what extent he utilizes or relies on copies (or on copies of copies) of a doubtful provenance. Since Handoca, a private researcher and retired schoolteacher in Bucharest, never made a secret of his candid apologetic intention, a good portion of mistrust is appropriate. Contrary to that, it should be self-evident that historical

---

[32] Regrettably, Armin Heinen's masterful book *Die Legion 'Erzengel Michael' in Rumänien – soziale Bewegung und politische Organisation. Ein Beitrag zum Problem des internationalen Faschismus* (München: R. Oldenbourg, 1986, Romanian trans. Bucharest: Humanitas, 1999), has not been translated into English. Equally important for a thorough understanding of the political background is Hans-Christian Maner, *Parlamentarismus in Rumänien (1930–1940). Demokratie im autoritären Umfeld* (München: R. Oldenbourg, 1997).

[33] Florin Ţurcanu, *Mircea Eliade. Le prisonnier de l'histoire* (Paris: Éditions La Découverte, 2003, Romanian trans. Bucharest: Humanitas, 2003, German trans. Schnellroda: Edition Antaios, 2006) and Hannelore Müller, *Der frühe Mircea Eliade. Sein rumänischer Hintergrund und die Anfänge seiner universalistischen Religionsphilosophie* (Münster: Lit, 2004). The supervisors of Müller's Marburg thesis were Kurt Rudolph and Rainer Flasche.

[34] See for instance the one mentioned by István Keul in his article, this volume, p. 411.

[35] For instance, a letter of Ernst Benz to Eliade from December 21, 1953 is reproduced by Handoca without any reference. Instead, it contains more than 50 (!) spelling mistakes. See Mircea Handoca, *Mircea Eliade şi corrrepsondenţii săi, vol. 1 (A–E)* (Bucharest: Editura Minerva, 1993), p. 84f.

investigations have to be based on primary sources. The hermeticism to
which Eliade's literary remains and political writings have been subjected
in the past is absolutely unacceptable for scholarly research and discussion. Referring to secret data and classified material and retreating to an
unverifiable authentication does not conform to academic scholarship
which should be played with cards face up on the table. To proclaim
on these grounds that Eliade had not written more than a handful of
pro-legionary articles and that his worst article ("Why I believe in the
victory of the Legionary Movement") was not written by himself, are two
examples of a forthright apologetic strategy that historians should not
tolerate. A scientific edition of Eliade's pre-war publications therefore
remains an urgent desideratum. Until this appears, we will never make
fully accurate judgments and be able to reflect about the relationship
of Eliade's life and work adequately. Hannelore Müller summarizes
her dissertation by stating that Eliade's scientific program had been
conceptually fixed when he left Romania in 1940.[36] Discussing that
kind of results brings us to the core of historical analysis.

With the end of communism in Europe, another type of interpretation concerning Eliade and his legacy has emerged. Solely politically
oriented, this pattern of historization tries to link Eliade affirmatively
with the Legionary Movement. Its adherents consider Eliade a Guardist
thinker and venerate him as an intellectual leader of the Romanian
and European right. False friends might be an apposite name for these
admirers of Eliade and their agenda could be entitled with the sentence: Yes, Eliade was a fascist and we are proud of it. The Romanian
"Noua Dreapta" (New Right) and other right wing groups in Europe
pursue that scheme openly.[37] According to Ted Anton's book about the
murder of Ioan Petru Culianu, the extremist right wing Movement for
Romania ("Mișcarea pentru România"), founded by Marian Munteanu
in 1992, made the reading of Eliade's works obligatory for joining.[38]
In the preparatory phase of Eliade's centenary a new upswing of this
interpretative paradigm surfaced. Claudio Mutti, the Italian neofascist,

---

[36] Müller, *Der frühe Mircea Eliade*, p. 169.
[37] See http://www.nouadreapta.org (esp. s.v. "Actiuni 2006"), http://www.miscarea.
com and http://www.romfest.org/rost (both with a great amount of references to
Eliade), or http://www.centrostudilaruna.it.
[38] Ted Anton, *Der Mord an Professor Culianu. Rekonstruktion eines Verbrechens* (Frankfurt
a.M.: Insel, 1999), p. 307. The German edition of Anton's *Eros, magic, and the murder
of Professor Culianu* (Evanston: Northwestern University press, 1996) is based on the
enlarged and revised Romanian translation (Bucharest: Editura Nemira, 1997).

is one of the busiest figures propagating the congeniality of Eliade with rightist ideas. He has gone to great lengths to publicize Eliade's affiliation to the Iron Guard and to conceptualize the pretended ideological kinship of Eliade with the political right.[39] In an interview with the German right wing medium *Junges Forum* Mutti, said to be a grandson of Julius Evola, stressed that it would be essential for the European right to have recourse not only to traditionalist thinkers like René Guenon and Julius Evola but also to established scholars such as Mircea Eliade, Giuseppe Tucci, and Franz Altheim. These authors ought to be taken as reference points to strengthen a new European consciousness and to achieve a "spiritual unity of Eurasia" which should function as bulwark against US-imperialism and Western materialism.[40]

To communicate Eliade's belonging to the right, these self-appointed companions are sedulously in search for evidence that Eliade had personal or intellectual relations to other rightist theorists and, moreover, that he was organizationally attached to the Legion of the Archangel Michael. Already in 1988, Philippe Baillet expounded Eliade's membership of the Iron Guard as a given fact, well known among educated people.[41] Due to their ideological bias, Baillet, Mutti and similar figures do not think it necessary to provide scholarly evidence for their claim. And until today, no exact proof has been found which would manifest Eliade's membership in the Iron Guard prima facie. To the best of my knowledge Hannelore Müller was the first who recently brought to

---

[39] Cf. Claudio Mutti, *Mircea Eliade e la Guardia di Ferro* (Roma: All'insegna del Veltro 1989, Romanian trans. Sibiu: Puncte Cardinale, 1995, German trans. 2007), *Les plumes de l'Archange. Quatres intellectuels roumains à la face de la Garde de Fer: Nae Ionescu, Mircea Eliade, Emil Cioran, Constantin Noica* (Chalon-sur-Saône: Éditions Hérodes, 1993, Romanian trans. Bucharest: Ed. Anastasia, 1997), *Eliade, Vâlsan, Geticus e gli altri. La Fortuna di Guénon tra i Romeni* (Parma: Edizioni all'insegna del Veltro, 1999, French trans. Saint-Genis-Laval: Akribeia, 2002, Romanian trans. Bucharest: Ed. Vremea, 2003), and his internet-articles "Nae Ionescu, maestro di Mircea Eliade e della 'giovane generazione' della Romania interbellica" (posted on July 6, 2003 on http://www.italiasociale.org) as well as "Una tragedia di Mircea Eliade" and "Eliade e l'olocausto" (posted on October 9 and 12, 2005 on Mutti's own homepage http://www.claudiomutti.com, s.v. "Articoli e saggi" and "Polemiche").

[40] *Junges Forum* 3, January 2005. The interview is available in German and in Italian translation at http://www.claudiomutti.com, s.v. "Interviste."

[41] "Nous n'apporterons pas de révélation en disant qu'Eliade fut membre, dans les années trente, de la Garde de Fer, car la chose est établie et connue du public cultivé." Philippe Baillet, "Julius Evola et Mircea Eliade (1927–1974): Une amitié manquée, avec des extraits de deux lettres d'Evola à Eliade," *Les deux étandards* 1 (September/December 1988), pp. 45–55, the quotation p. 46. Baillet later translated the manuscript of Mutti's *Les plumes de l'archange*.

public notice a press announcement indicating that Eliade had been a member of the All for the Country party TPȚ ("Totul pentru Țară"). Müller re-published a reminder of the party appearing in *Buna Vestire* on December 6, 1937 that, together with seven others, Eliade should report if he had already delivered his membership fees to the TPȚ treasury or not. The pronouncement referred not to Eliade's personal contributions but to the fees he had collected for the party.[42] According to this communiqué, Eliade appears not only as a normal TPȚ member but exercised a function on a higher level of the party hierarchy.

Founded in 1930 as a paramilitary subdivision of the Legion, the Iron Guard was banned in December 1933 as a result of its belligerent militancy. Retaliating against the prohibition, members of the Guard assassinated the Romanian Prime Minister Ion Duca. Eliade called the disbanding of the Guard – not the killing of the Prime Minister – an act of practised barbarism ("barbaria exercitată").[43] In March 1935, the Legion constituted the TPȚ to overcome the proscription and to gain access to the state revenues by entering the parliamentary stage. At the beginning, the Iron Guard had a paramilitary function similar to the Storm Troopers (SA) in Germany. But as the Legionary Movement expanded in the mid-1930s, Guard and Legion did not develop further. Conversely, both linked up with each other and membership became identical.[44] Those joining the Legion after spring 1934 were ushered in as ordinary members. To advance to the higher position of

---

[42] "Șefii de judeţe ai partidului 'Totul pentru Ţară' vor achita taxele pentru Cameră şi Senat Luni 6 Decembrie. În aceeaşi zi la ora 6 seara vor răspunde telegrafic pe adresa Neculai Totu, Gutenberg 3, Bucureşti, dacă au achitat sau nu taxele: 1. Sextil Puşcariu, 2. Ion Găvănescul, 3. Niculae Roşu, 4. Col. Piperescu, 5. Col. Christodulo, 6. Mircea Eliade, 7. Ion Cantacuzino, 8. Prof. Pantazi. Neculai Totu. Şeful biroului electoral legionar." ["The county leaders of the party 'All for the Country' shall hand over the fees for the Chamber and the Senate on Monday December 6th. At the same day at 6 p.m. shall report via telegraph to the address of Neculai Totu, Gutenberg 3, Bucharest, if they have paid the fees or not: 1. Sextil Puşcariu, 2. Ion Găvănescul, 3. Niculae Roşu, 4. Col. Piperescu, 5. Col. Christodulo, 6. Mircea Eliade, 7. Ion Cantacuzino, 8. Prof. Pantazi. Neculai Totu, chairman of the legionary electoral office."] "De la Partidul 'Totul pentru Ţară'," *Buna Vestire*, December 6, 1937, quoted from Müller, *Der frühe Mircea Eliade*, p. A94f. (Romanian text and German translation, English translation mine. The text is here reproduced without breaks.). Gutenberg 3 was the home of the TPȚ leader Gheorghe Cântacuzino-Granicerul and served as party treasury as well.

[43] Mircea Eliade, "Câteva opinii despere dizolvarea Gărzii de Fier" [Some opinions about the disbanding of the Iron Guard], *Axa*, December 23, 1933, quoted from Müller, *Der frühe Mircea Eliade*, p. A62f.

[44] Heinen, *Die Legion 'Erzengel Michael' in Rumänien*, p. 278.

a Legionnaire (which itself had different grades), members had to pass through a noviciate of three years or had to distinguish themselves with exceptional accomplishments.[45] Given the fact of his belonging to the TPȚ, it would be justified and absolutely correct to say that Eliade was a legitimate member of the Iron Guard. Another question is if Eliade had formally attached himself to the Guard before the founding of the TPȚ, which seems not very likely in view of his Guardist conversion at the end of 1936.[46] Be that as it may, the All for the Country party had a political program not distinct from that of the Legionary Movement. In the elections held in December 1937, Codreanu's strategy yielded the expected benefit and made the TPȚ, with 15.58 percent, the third largest party in the parliament.[47]

Deeply irritated about his friend's behavior, Mihail Sebastian noted in his diary shortly before the voting that Eliade had "entered the electoral lists" and that he had been electioneering outside of Bucharest "wandering from village to village with Polihroniade," that is with the Iron Guard theorist and editor of the journal *Axa* Mihai Polihroniade.[48] On December 17, three days before the election, Eliade also sought to attract votes for the TPȚ in the legionary journal *Buna Vestire* (Good News). Under the motto "Why I believe in the victory of the Legionary Movement," *Buna Vestire* had carried out a survey and given prominent Guard advocates the chance to promote the legionary cause publicly. Eliade belonged to those who enthusiastically called for a backing of

---

[45] Ibid.

[46] The publication of an extreme right-wing group claimed in March 1936 an earlier membership of Eliade. Leon Volovici quotes that statement but casts doubt on its reliability. See Leon Volovici, *Nationalist ideology and antisemitism. The case of Romanian intellectuals in the 1930s* (Oxford et al.: Pergamon Press, 1991), p. 125, n. 80.

[47] Cf. Maner, *Parlamentarismus in Rumänien*, pp. 239–248 and Heinen, *Die Legion 'Erzengel Michael' in Rumänien*, pp. 352–356. Heinen compares the success of the TPȚ with the triumph of the NSDAP in September 1930 (ibid., p. 356).

[48] Mihail Sebastian, *Journal, 1935–1944* (London: Pimlico, 2003), p. 129 (November 15, 1937) and p. 132 (December 7, 1937). In this context, it is interesting to remember the dispute between Eliade and Polihroniade respecting Eliade's 'first conversion' to a nationalist Romanianism in September 1933 (Mihai Polihroniade, "Convertirea d-lui Mircea Eliade la românism," *Axa* 18, 1933 and Mircea Eliade, "O convertire la românism," *Cuvântul*, September 22, 1933, see Volovici, *Nationalist ideology*, p. 88). Referring to earlier utterances, Eliade claimed he consistently belonged "to a continuum of nationalist political thinking," as Volovici put it. Therefore, Eliade contradicted Polihroniade's opinion that he had now changed his mind. For an improper interpretation of the concept of Romanianism, see Mac Linscott Ricketts, *Mircea Eliade. The Romanian roots, 1907–1945*, 2 vols. (Boulder: East European Monographs, 1988), here vol. 2, pp. 903–909.

the Legion.[49] Interestingly, four contributors to that series had been listed by the *Buna Vestire* announcement on December 6, 1937. These were, besides Eliade, E. Christodulo, I. Găvănescul, and Sextil Puşcariu, the former rector of the University of Cluj and well-known literary critic with early Guardist sympathies.[50] To sum up: There can be little doubt that Eliade had an official affiliation to the Iron Guard and that he bore his part in the overwhelming success of the Greenshirts in this election and in the rise of the Legionary Movement in general. According to an important addendum of a Jewish eyewitness from Czernowitz to the study of Armin Heinen, the Iron Guard's ability to become a mass movement and to achieve such an extraordinary result in December 1937 largely depended on its increased respectability and on "the mild and appeasing attitude of the Rumanian establishment."[51] People who were both willing and capable to function as link between the far right and the center of the Romanian society, for example as representatives of the church, the university or the arts, played a key role in that regard.

The tough and sometimes polemical controversies about Eliade's activities with the Iron Guard reveal how necessary it is to historize the past properly. In a letter written in June 1972, Gershom Scholem demanded a frank reply from Eliade regarding recently emerged accusations about his inclination towards the Legionary Movement.[52] Scholem had come under attack in Israel because of his contribution to a Festschrift for Eliade, a man who was accused of having supported a felonious and rabidly antisemitic movement. Scholem expressed his

---

[49] Eliade's statement with a German translation in Müller, *Der frühe Mircea Eliade*, pp. A96–A103. Müller explicitly rejects the flimsy attempt to dissociate the text from its author. So does Volovici, who also mentions that an eloquent passage of the article was re-published on the front page of *Buna Vestire* with Eliade's signature on January 1, 1938. See Volovici, *Nationalist ideology*, p. 127, n. 85.

[50] Müller, *Der frühe Mircea Eliade*, p. A97.

[51] Zvi Yavetz, "An eyewitness note: Reflections on the Rumanian Iron Guard," *Journal of Contemporary History* 26 (1991), pp. 597–610, here p. 604. The figures of enrolled Guard members increased from 28,000 in December 1933 to 34,000 in May 1935 and to 272,000 in December 1937. See Heinen, *Die Legion 'Erzengel Michael' in Rumänien*, p. 382.

[52] Letter of Gershom Scholem to Mircea Eliade on June 6, 1972, in Itta Shedletzky, ed., *Gershom Sholem: Briefe III, 1971–1982* (München: Beck, 1999), p. 30. A long footnote explains the context of Scholem's request and quotes decisive parts from the introduction to the famous "Dosarul Mircea Eliade" that had been published by the bilingual (Romanian and Hebrew) journal *Toladot* at the beginning of 1972 (ibid., p. 277f., n. 1).

deep concern about the matter and insisted on obtaining from Eliade what he called the "mere truth" to clear up the allegations. Embarrassed, Scholem wanted to remain loyal to his friend but also recognized the vexation of the great many of Romanian Jews living in Israel who understandably had "bitter memories of 'The Iron Guard' and its activities."[53] Eliade's verbose French written answer dated June 25, 1972 and can be understood as a standard model of how people used to respond under the pressure of this kind of accusations.[54] For someone familiar with the denazification of the German university staff, Eliade's arguing seems a very typical and widespread way of acting. Obscuring rather than clarifying the matter, Eliade firmly denied having written a single page of propaganda for the Iron Guard. Since the *Toladot* inculpation included parts of Mihail Sebastian's at that time unpublished diaries, and since Eliade could not simply declare the disclosures of his former Jewish friend untrue, he maneuvered between rejecting their significance and relativizing them by pointing to the fact that Sebastian himself had belonged to the circle of admirers of Nae Ionescu. When touching the critical point of his *Buna Vestire* article, Eliade resorted to gaps in his memory. Nevertheless, he was absolutely sure of not having written one single ideological text in a legionary periodical.

Such a psychological interplay between a good and poor memory, reciprocally connected with pleasant and unpleasant things in the past, was also a very common feature among German university teachers when asked about their involvement before 1945. This is quite a normal reaction and should not be overemphasized. But Eliade's claim that he had never collaborated with *Buna Vestire* ("Je n'ais jamais collaboré à ce journal.")[55] cannot be reduced to a psychological delusion of his memory. It was a barefaced lie. In addition to his political manifesto "Why I believe in the victory of the Legionary Movement," Eliade wrote at least two other articles for that Iron Guard daily.[56] Mac Linscott Ricketts further mentions a eulogizing obituary of Eliade to the TPȚ

[53] Ibid., p. 30.
[54] Letter of Mircea Eliade to Gershom Scholem on June 25, 1972, ibid., pp. 279–281, n. 5.
[55] Ibid., p. 279.
[56] Cf. Mircea Eliade, "O revoluție creştina," *Buna Vestire*, June 27, 1937, re-printed in Müller, *Der frühe Mircea Eliade*, pp. A74–A77. Another article which appeared in *Buna Vestire* on January 14, 1938 is quoted by Radu Ioanid; in it Eliade emphasized once again the Christian nature of the legionary revolution. See Ioanid, *The sword of the Archangel*, p. 146 and idem, "The sacralised politis," p. 144.

leader general Căntacuzino on October 14, 1937.[57] Two months later, *Buna Vestire* introduced Eliade on December 17 as member of the Association of Romanian Writers, thanking him for his "kindness to respond to the survey 'Why I believe in the victory of the Legionary Movement' with the following."[58] What tagged behind was Eliade's article, which undoubtedly has to be regarded as his political credo during that time. Even if this statement were the reported account of a talk, as Eliade later claimed, he would have been responsible. A change in the form of publication would not suspend his liability. But from the viewpoint of independent historical scholarship, it is entirely impossible to lean on the tale started by Eliade himself that someone from the editorial staff (Mihai Polihroniade) ought to be blamed for this undeniably infamous text.

Recent research has shown that Eliade's relationship with the Legionary Movement was closer and more intensive than estimated thus far. There is no avoiding this fact. In his writings, Eliade sometimes spoke like an insider, just referring to the "Captain" when he made mention of the Iron Guard leader Corneliu Zelea Codreanu.[59] Such a formulation indicates that "the" captain was "his" captain as well. Codreanu spoke rather friendly about Eliade, too. During his trial in April 1938, he praised Eliade's eloquence in defending the specific nature of the legionary cause.[60] In light of that closeness, it would not come as a surprise if Eliade indeed had mediated a meeting between Julius Evola and Codreanu that took place the preceding month in March 1938 in Bucharest.[61] Eliade's high esteem of Codreanu endured the times though he avoided publicly speaking about it. His recently published correspondence with Ioan Petru Culianu clearly demonstrates the great respect Eliade still had for the former "Căpitanul" at the end of the

[57] Mircea Eliade, "Mitul Generalului," *Buna Vestire*, October 14, 1937. See Ricketts, *Mircea Eliade. The Romanian roots*, vol. 2, p. 926 and p. 1400, n. 139.

[58] Müller, *Der frühe Mircea Eliade*, p. A96f. The English translation of the introductory note is mine.

[59] See for instance his *Buna Vestire* article on January 14, 1938: "If all the contemporary revolutions have as their goal the conquest of power by a social class or by a man, the Legionary revolution aims, on the contrary, at the supreme redemption of the nation, the reconciliation of the Romanian nation with God, *as the Captain said*." Quoted from Ioanid, *Sacralised politics*, p. 145, emphasis mine. The phrase "cum a spus Căpitanul" is to be found in a similar context in "Why I believe in the victory of the Legionary Movement" as well. See Müller, *Der frühe Mircea Eliade*, p. A98.

[60] Ioanid, *Sacralised politics*, p. 145.

[61] See my article, this volume, p. 137.

1970s. When Culianu asked Eliade about the Iron Guard and his liaison with it, Eliade supplied his student with a legionary publication of Codreanu entitled *Pentru legionary* ("For the Iron Guardists") that ought to provide Culianu with a more accurate outlook on the Iron Guard and its commander. In a letter to Culianu, Eliade not only talked in rather intimate terms about Codreanu, using the confidential abbreviation C.Z.C. He went on to call the former Guard leader "an 'honest' man" who had "managed to awaken a whole generation."[62] Culianu was more than astounded – he was shocked when he realized Eliade's pro-legionary views. Having received Codreanu's text, Culianu wrote in his journal on January 10, 1978: "I'm reading *Pentru legionari* in despair: its delirious antisemitism is appalling... The surprise to learn that M.E. has been the supporter of a totalitarian movement and that he has remained faithful to its mythology fills me with sorrow."[63]

In 1924, Codreanu had executed the police president of Jassy in an ambush because he had taken measures against the violent actions of antisemitic student groups.[64] Today's terminology surely would classify the Iron Guard as a terrorist organization. Calling, in 1978, a brutal murderer and the "Führer" of movement legendary for its atrocities an honest man understandably outraged Culianu. But in defiance of his perturbation, Culianu published some time later an apologetic article in which he strongly denounced all criticism of Eliade's alleged sympathies for the Iron Guard. He particularly rejected the accusations of the Israeli journal *Toladot* using Eliade's own statements as established facts. In obedience to them, Culianu declared that Eliade had never published a single piece in *Buna Vestire*, proving the charge itself untrue.[65] Culianu likewise counted the absence of the *Buna Vestire* articles in Eliade's published bibliographies among the testimonies of a non-involvement in Iron Guard politics.[66] Of course, Culianu felt obliged to defend the reputation of his teacher. But that wish cannot fully explain the discrepancy between his public apologia and his private view that

---

[62] Letter of Eliade to Culianu on January 17, 1978, in "The correspondence between Mircea Eliade and Ioan Petru Culianu" (translated from the Romanian original by Sorana Corneanu), *Archaeus* 8–1/4 (2004), pp. 341–364, here p. 343f.

[63] Ibid., p. 344, n. 3.

[64] Heinen, *Die Legion 'Erzengel Michael' in Rumänien*, pp. 122–126.

[65] Ioan P. Culianu, "Mircea Eliade und die blinde Schildkröte," in Hans Peter Duerr, ed., *Die Mitte der Welt. Aufsätze zu Mircea Eliade* (Frankfurt a.M.: Suhrkamp, 1984), pp. 216–243, esp. p. 234f.

[66] Culianu, "Mircea Eliade und die blinde Schildkröte," p. 242, n. 80.

Eliade had been a supporter of the Legionary Movement. In a review article which appeared several years after Eliade's death, Culianu was much more critical of Eliade's political engagement, relating it to the Romanian "Zeitgeist" of the 1930s, "a period in which Eliade seemed to be more involved than his own recollections would let us suspect."[67] Culianu's dithering statements give the impression that he adopted Eliade's ambivalence in dealing with the past. Other theories try to connect Culianu's own death – he was killed under dubious and still unclear circumstances in a toilet of the Divinity School of the University of Chicago on May 21, 1991 – with his grim critique of the continuity between the Iron Guard ideology and the post-communist regime in Romania.[68]

For obvious reasons, Eliade avoided pro-legionary utterances in public and tried to "minimize" his relationship with the Legionary Movement "throughout his post-war life."[69] His correspondence, his diaries, and other biographical statements are characterized by gaps exactly in those cases when problematic issues were at stake.[70] Eliade seemed to have been well aware that revelations in that regard would have put his academic career at risk. Much of the ambiguity respecting his political past originates from Eliade's own conduct and his efforts to obscure his Romanian years. Understandable as such a behavior is, historical work has to proceed in the opposite direction. Historians are only obliged to go above and beyond acquiescing with Scholem's claim for the "mere truth" – they are charged with striving for nothing less but for the full truth.

The early German history of science occupied with the academic learning under the spell of National Socialism shows in like manner how historians should not deal with the past. Refraining from austere and uncompromising inquiries, they gave nearly full reign of interpretation

---

[67] *The Journal of Religion* 72–1 (1992), pp. 157–161, here p. 157. Culianu reviewed Eliade's *Journal*, his *Autobiography*, and Mac Linscott Rickett's *Romanian roots*.

[68] See Sorin Antohi, "Exploring the legacy of Ioan Petru Culianu" in the *Newsletter* 72 (spring 2001) of the Vienna Institute for Human Sciences (Institut für die Wissenschaften vom Menschen), available on the institute's website: http://www.iwm.at, s.v. "Newsletter." Cf. also the two postfaces to Anton's *Der Mord an Professor Culianu* by Umberto Ecco and Andreij Oişteanu, ibid., pp. 333–347, and pp. 347–357.

[69] Andreij Oişteanu, "Mircea Eliade between political journalism and scholarly work," *Archaeus* 8–1/4 (2004), pp. 323–340, here p. 338.

[70] The apparent incompleteness of Eliade's diaries was criticized by Zwi Werblowsky in his article "'In nostro tempore'," in Duerr, ed., *Die Mitte der Welt*, pp. 128–137, here p. 133f.

to those who had reason to veil rather than to elucidate the connection of science with ideology that was characteristic of the preceding period. It took several decades in Germany until the time was ripe for a more objective and less prejudiced approach. Of course, there were researchers overstepping the mark when they ventured upon repudiating the apologetic scheme of the 1950s and 1960s with its lies and prevarications. But they were few in number and unable to compromise critical historiography as such. Another threat labeled "helpless antifascism" turned out to be even more problematic.[71] Restricted to conspicuous gestures of moral dismay, its interpretative framework relied to a certain degree on the political assumptions and scientific categories already valid in the time of fascism. The rhetoric of an apolitical scholarship whose good intentions had been misused by a bad political system was a widespread way of playing down the political involvement of academics and of saving their former conceptualizations regardless of their ideological bias.

For these reasons, historical research into the study of religion under fascism started with great delay and did not crop up before the majority of formerly active scholars had passed away. That tardiness resulted in new problems before the old ones had been dealt with appropriately. I have already pointed out that this unsatisfactory situation and the lack of interest in coming to terms with a troublesome past carried on much longer in the study of religion than in other disciplines. Basically, one cannot evade the impression that the study of religion is still occupied with the collecting of data and has not yet reached the stage of an in-depth analysis or a systematic explanation of the developments that took place in the 1930s and 1940s. Eliade's case mirrors that state of affairs. Dealing with his past exemplifies many problems characteristic of the German situation on an international level. Confined to the dilemma of defense and accusation, historiography labors until today at rejecting one part of it or another. In my opinion, the study of religion has neither crafted a proper contextualization of its development in the time of fascism, nor has it pinpointed a plausible solution for relating the life and work of distinguished scholars such as Eliade adequately.

---

[71] See Wolfgang Fritz Haug, *Der hilflose Antifaschismus. Zur Kritik der Vorlesungsreihe über Wissenschaft und NS an deutschen Universitäten*, 2nd ed. (Frankfurt a.M.: Suhrkamp, 1968).

7. *The Perspective of this Book*

The first aim of this book and of the conference preceding it is to raise a greater awareness of a highly problematic era of the academic study of religion in Europe. It should be a matter of course to give more prominence to that period in order to comprehend its ideological deformations and, in a second step, to acquire the capability of understanding the way and extent to which scholarship was affected by its legacy after 1945. Though an all-embracing approach lies beyond the scope of a symposium and its proceedings, a representative selection of case studies has been assembled, shedding new light upon this dark and poorly lit part of our history. Divided in five sections, the articles are grouped according to scientific, religious, and geographic features. The first part deals with the "Aryan Myth" and the attempt of scholars to uncover a genealogical lineage along with the attributes of a very old people named Indo-Germans or Aryans. Whether undertaken with a philological, ideological, or religious interest, the resuscitation of the Aryan heritage turned into an attempt not only to describe and determine but literally to create a reality which enveloped the idea of an Aryan or Indo-Germanic race. Research into the Aryans under voelkish premises should be regarded as a *locus classicus* of the invention of a tradition and an imagined community. It is hard to think of gods with a shorter lifespan than those of the Aryan pantheon. By the same token, all things Aryan suddenly disappeared from the academic curricula when the Third Reich ended its short-lived existence after twelve years.

Walther Wüst, with whom I am concerned, is an excellent example to discern how closely the rise of the Aryan Myth and the study of religion had been related. Wüst's work contains much of the 19th-century study of religion and its receptiveness to an increasing import of the Aryan or Indo-Germanic ideology including its sociobiological preconceptions and pseudo-scientific race categories. The probability that the race discourse of the late nineteenth century has been stimulated, perhaps nurtured, by the scholarly work of historians of religions is even more perturbing. Leon Poliakov's accusation that Friedrich Max Müller ought to be seen as main architect of the Aryan Myth should not be taken lightly. What might be discussed for the nineteenth century as a form of creative speculations became laden with inordinate political meaning after World War I. Wüst's adjustment to the race ideology of National Socialism finally embraced a criminal implication in so far as the physical elimination of those considered the enemies of the racially determined nation became a logical consequence. Wüst belonged to the top of Nazi Germany's most influential scholars and can be regarded as model case of an opportunist who profited from the political change. He eagerly delivered the intellectual concepts required of him. But one should keep in mind that Wüst's philo-Aryan penchant was part of a general trend in the history of religions that proceeded from a decreasing influence of Christianity in the academy and in the society as a whole.

In his article, Bruce Lincoln portrays Hermann Güntert as an academic of another scientific caliber. An acknowledged expert in Indo-European mythology long before the emergence of the Third Reich, Güntert taught comparative linguistics as full professor at the University of Rostock starting in 1922 and at the University of Heidelberg in 1926. Following in the footsteps of Albert Dieterich, Güntert quickly and productively incorporated religious and cultural features in his philological approach. "Words and Things" was the title of the linguistic journal *Wörter und Sachen* which Güntert joined as co-editor in 1927 and in which he authored an important article about the causes of Germanic sound shifts – Güntert's special field of research – one year later. In it he argued that non-Indo-European influences must have played a significant role, otherwise the difference between Germanic and other Indo-European languages would remain inexplicable. Lincoln rightly underlines the progressive and anti-essentialist character of Güntert's scholarly work in that time. From a voelkish point of view, Güntert said rather unsympathetic things about the mixed composition of the Aryans and their original homeland, their "Urheimat," located by him in South Russia. The caution with which Güntert drew his conclusions from a well-founded linguistic paleontology to cultural traits is striking. But things changed when the opening of philology towards culture became superimposed by a voelkish chauvinism before and an escalating jingoism after the National Socialist seizure of power.[72]

Referring in particular to Güntert's book *Der Ursprung der Germanen*, appearing in 1934, Lincoln masterfully demonstrates the political shifts his work underwent as it adapted to the ideology of National Social-

---

[72] Clemens Knobloch, *Volkhafte Sprachforschung. Studien zum Umbau der Sprachwissenschaft in Deutschland zwischen 1918 und 1945* (Tübingen: Max Niemeyer Verlag, 2005) has shown that this drift was a general phenomenon in German linguistics and not restricted to Güntert.

ism. Written under the impression of Germany's national awakening, Güntert's publications of the 1930s were gravely vitiated in their scientific value. Nevertheless, one should not read history backwards and should avoid interpreting all of Güntert's former writings from that angle.[73] Lincoln's work makes it clear how necessary it is to concentrate attention on the transitional process in which good and evil, so to speak, have not fully separated. Calling Güntert's development a tragedy is as justified as calling it a "decline of the German mandarins" as Ringer's excellent study reads.[74] When Güntert became the sole editor of *Wörter und Sachen* in 1938, he explained the new course of the journal, stressing the necessity of a rearrangement on behalf of National Socialist interests. A new time, as he said, would require new goals and the new goals would no longer include the false idea of an unvoelkish and transnational humanism.[75] Instead, the task had emerged to widen the conceptual unity of words and objects from its orientation towards culture into racial studies. With exactly the same intent and wording, Friedrich Pfister, another distinguished pupil of Dieterich, delineated in 1936 why the *Archiv für Religionswissenschaft* would highlight now voelkish and racial aspects under his editorship.[76] The statements of Güntert and Pfister were a clear and unmistakable expression of the decline of German scholarship. But things worsened even more and what was a tragedy became a farce. In 1939, Walther Wüst discontinued the interim solution embodied by Güntert and Pfister and personally took over the editorship of the two journals under the auspices of the SS "Ahnenerbe."

The relationship of Stig Wikander with Walther Wüst is unclear. In her article, Mihaela Timuş, who has extensively dealt with Wikander's correspondence, quotes rather disapproving utterances of the doctoral student at the University of Uppsala about the Munich Indo-Iranist. According to them, Wikander considered Wüst a dilettante unworthy

---

[73] This is a mistake in Rudolf Wachter's otherwise well-researched article "Allgemeine und vergleichende Sprachwissenschaft," in Wolfgang U. Eckart et al., eds., *Die Universität Heidelberg im Nationalsozialismus* (Heidelberg: Springer, 2006), pp. 371–389.

[74] Fritz K. Ringer, *The decline of the German mandarins. The German academic community, 1890–1933* (Cambridge: Harvard University Press, 1969, German trans. 1983).

[75] See Hermann Güntert, "Neue Zeit – neues Ziel," *Wörter und Sachen* 19, New Series 1 (1938), pp. 1–11, here p. 7, and the quotation of Lincoln in his article on p. 198.

[76] For the political transformation of the *Archiv für Religionswissenschaft*, see my contribution, this volume, pp. 155–157, for that of *Wörter und Sachen*, Christopher M. Hutton, *Linguistics and the Third Reich. Mother-tongue fascism, race and the science of language* (London et al.: Routledge, 1999), pp. 37–41.

of his academic position.[77] Conversely, Wüst published in the first
ARW issue under his control a heavily critical judgment of a book of
Wikander's teacher and friend Henrik Samuel Nyberg which had been
translated by Hans Heinrich Schaeder into German in 1938.[78] Wüst's
article was preceded by an equally negative contribution by his pupil
Otto Paul.[79] On the other side stood Wikander's friendship with Otto
Höfler, a devoted National Socialist whom Wüst patronized from 1937.
Having heard a public lecture of Hitler in Vienna, Höfler enrolled in
1922 as steward of the National Socialist "Ordner-Truppe" (then the
Austrian SA), whose task was to protect the mass rallies of the Nazis
against their opponents. On May 1, 1937, Höfler joined the NSDAP.[80]
His habilitation thesis submitted to the University of Vienna in 1931,
published as *Kultische Geheimbünde der alten Germanen* in 1934, made a
great impact on Wüst as well as on Himmler. As a result, Wüst tried
to get Höfler appointed to a chair of German studies at the University
of Munich. In October 1937, he informed Himmler about his plans to
incorporate Höfler into the cultural and scientific work of the "Ahnenerbe." Wüst asked Himmler to sign a letter already addressed by him
to the Reich Minister of Science and Education Bernhard Rust to
advance the matter.[81] Using a more academic parlance, Wüst argued

---

[77] See esp. the letter of Wikander to Höfler from November 27, 1937, quoted by Timuş in her article on p. 211.

[78] Walther Wüst, "Bestand die zoroastrische Urgemeinde wirklich aus berufsmäßigen Ekstatikern und schamanisierenden Rinderhirten der Steppe?," *Archiv für Religionswissenschaft* 36 (1939), pp. 234–249. The article referred to Henrik Samuel Nyberg, *Die Religionen des alten Iran* (Leipzig: J.C. Hinrichs Verlag, 1938), 1st ed. *Irans forntida religioner* (Stockholm: Svenska Kirkens Diakonistyrelses förlag, 1937).

[79] Otto Paul "Zur Geschichte der iranischen Religionen," *Archiv für Religionswissenschaft* 36 (1939), pp. 215–234, esp. pp. 228–234. For Paul, who later turned away from Wüst, then working at the Rosenberg Institute for the Study of the Jewish Question, see Gerd Simon's chronology at http://homepages.uni-tuebingen.de/gerd.simon/ChrPaulO.pdf (40 pages, with a biographical introduction).

[80] See Esther Gajek, "Germanenkunde und Nationalsozialismus. Zur Verflechtung von Wissenschaft und Politik am Beispiel Otto Höflers," in Richard Faber, ed., *Politische Religion – religiöse Politik* (Würzburg: Königshausen & Neumann, 1999), pp. 173–203, esp. pp. 178–188 "Otto Höfler und der Nationalsozialismus."

[81] Letter of Wüst to Himmler on October 15, 1937 and letter of Himmler to Rust on October 29, 1937. Rust answered on November 18, 1937 that Höfler would probably be appointed on April 1, 1938. See Magdalena Bonk, *Deutsche Philologie in München* (Berlin: Duncker & Humblot, 1995), p. 325. Cf. also Julia Zernack, "Kontinuität als Problem der Wissenschaftsgeschichte. Otto Höfler und das Münchner Institut für Nordische Philologie und Germanische Altertumskunde," in Klaus Böldl and Miriam Kauko, eds., *Kontinuität in der Kritik. Historische und aktuelle Perspektiven der Skandinavistik* (Freiburg: Rombach, 2005), pp. 47–72, esp. pp. 50–53.

in a petition to the Bavarian Ministry of Education how important it
would be to reorganize German studies and to expand phonology and
text criticism into the realm of the realia through archeology, mythology,
and historical anthropology.[82] Since the chair destined to be reassigned
to Höfler was held by a Rosenberg affiliate (the philosopher Wolfgang
Schultz who died in 1936), some additional problems needed resolving
before Höfler could be appointed in October 1938. The nomination
of Höfler was a key element in Wüst's plan to link the scientific aims
of the "Ahnenerbe" closer with academic learning.

Wikander's employment at the University of Munich as lecturer in
Swedish in 1938 and 1939 should be regarded in this light. Wüst tried
to boost scientifically acknowledged research into the Indo-Germanic
tradition and apparently hoped for a substantial input from both the
Austrian and Swedish scholars.[83] These circumstances provided Wikander with the opportunity to change his mind about Wüst. Most likely, he
also attended Wüst's classes and lectures in Munich. Therefore, it is not
really surprising that Wikander looked forward to publishing his book
Der arische Männerbund with the help of the SS. In November 1938, he
paid a visit to Wolfram Sievers, the general secretary of the "Ahnenerbe"
of the SS, asking him if its publishing house (the "Ahnenerbe Stiftungs-
Verlag") would be willing to adopt his study to its program.[84]

According to the judgment of Klaus von See, Wikander's study on
the Aryan "Männerbund" was an attempt to apply Höflers *Kultische
Geheimbünde der Germanen* to the world of the Indo-Germans. Underlining
that the French Georges Dumézil also helped revive the legendary Indo-
Germanic male societies, von See calls our attention to the fact that this
theory emerged under the auspices of a tripartite joint venture at the
University of Uppsala in the early 1930s.[85] All three scholars were of
a non-German nationality and had been working together in Uppsala
in these years – that is, apart from Nazi Germany geographically and

---

[82] Esther Gajek, "Germanenkunde und Nationalsozialismus," p. 189. The petition
is dated December 28, 1937.

[83] Hopes to enhance Wikander's position did not materialize. Wikander returned
to Sweden and worked as lecturer in Iranian philology at the Universit of Lund from
1941.

[84] Notice of Sievers from November 11, 1938, Federal Archives Berlin, NS 21,
605 E.

[85] Klaus von See, "Der Arier-Mythos," in Nikolaus Buschmann and Dieter Langewiesche, eds., *Der Krieg in den Gründungsmythen europäischer Nationen und die USA* (Frankfurt
a.M.: Campus, 2003), pp. 56–96, here p. 94f.

chronologically. That makes it impossible to interpret the upshots of their cooperation in terms of a National Socialist contamination. The idea of an Aryan or Indo-European line of continuity had a much broader basis and was evidently of a more general nature. A comparative analysis of the writings of Wikander, Höfler, and Dumézil in the 1930s would reveal the common facets of their worldview which appeared, especially in the case of their "Männerbund" speculations, as a chauvinistic and paternalistic ideology notably fitting to the ascendant right wing currents in Europe.[86]

Such an examination would also disclose to which extent older traditions of the study of religion had been entangled. Particularly with regard to Höfler, it is evident that elements of Rudolf Otto's idea of the holy had crept in.[87] It seems that one important gateway for this influence was Lily Weiser's *Altgermanische Jünglingsweihen und Männerbünde* from 1927 which heavily relied on a book of Otto's friend Jakob Wilhelm Hauer that had appeared four years earlier. Hauer's *Die Religionen. Ihr Werden, ihre Wahrheit* adapted Otto's approach of an intuitive religious cognition to the ecstatic experiences he detected in the world of the so-called primitive religions.[88] The adjustment of Otto's conception of a universal spirituality with its various "Momente des Numinosen" to the Indo-Germanic tradition and its simultaneous enrichment with biological arguments perfectly describes Hauer's later program. Without that Pagan bias, Otto's assumption of the holy as a cognitive category developed an even greater standing among educated people and scholars working outside of the study of religion in neighboring areas. The contribution of Mihaela Timuş opens up this

---

[86] Cf. Klaus von See, "Politische Männderbund-Ideologie von der wilhelminischen Zeit bis zum Nationalsozialismus," in Gisela Völger and Karin v. Welck, eds., *Männerbande, Männerbünde. Zur Rolle des Mannes im Kulturvergleich*, 2 vols. (Köln: Rautenstrauch-Jost-Museum, 1990), vol. 1, pp. 93–102 and Stefanie von Schnurbein, "Geheime kultische Männerbünde bei den Germanen. Eine Theorie im Spannungsfeld zwischen Wissenschaft und Ideologie," in ibid., vol. 2, pp. 97–102.

[87] Cf. Harm-Peer Zimmermann, "Männerbund und Totenkult. Methodologische und ideologische Grundlinien der Volks- und Altertumskunde Otto Höflers 1933–1945," *Kieler Blätter zur Volkskunde* 26 (1994), pp. 5–27. Unaware of their origin, Zimmermann relates Otto's ideas to a Jungian influence.

[88] For an interpretation, see H. Junginger, *Von der philologischen zur völkischen Religionswissenschaft*, pp. 57–62 and pp. 90–99: "Hauer, Otto und das Problem der Metaphysik." For Hauer's influene on Weiser, cf. von See, "Kulturkritik und Germanenforschung zwischen den Weltkriegen," *Historische Zeitschrift* 245 (1987), pp. 343–362, here p. 357f. and Christa Niem, "Lily Weiser-Aaall (1898–1987). Ein Beitrag zur Wissenschaftsgeschichte der Volkskunde," *Zeitschrift für Volkskunde* 1 (1998), pp. 25–52, here p. 35f.

non-German, perhaps pan-European, vista of a general utilization
of the Indo-European heritage. Wikander's correspondence with the
Austrian anthropologist and German studies scholar Otto Höfler is of
exceptional value in that regard. The political milieu their scholarship
was embedded in strongly warns against all too hasty generalizations
about people and peoples habitually summarized under the heading
Indo-German or Indo-European.[89]

In his article on Bernhard Kummer, a Nordicist at the University
of Jena, Fritz Heinrich deals with Höfler's greatest enemy in National
Socialist times. Kummer fervently fought Höfler's continuity theory
of an unceasing existence of favorable Germanic traits. Already in his
dissertation entitled *Midgards Untergang. Germanische Kultur in den letzten
beiden heidnischen Jahrhunderten*, printed in 1927 (2nd ed. 1935, 3rd ed.
1937), Kummer expounded the view that the Christianization of the
Germanic peoples had caused their steady decay. Such a reading of
history led to ideological problems; on these grounds, it became difficult to interpret National Socialism as the culminating point of Nordic
and Germanic virtues. Kummer therefore operated with the concept
of hidden powers and a suppressed reawakening of the Germanic
worldview. The quarrel between Höfler and Kummer began in 1935
and ended in 1938 with Himmler's personal interference.[90] It went
along the ideological boundaries of the "Ahnenerbe" and the "Amt
Rosenberg" with proponents named "Höflinge" and "Kümmerlinge."
As an ally of Alfred Rosenberg's voelkish agenda, Kummer was forced
to back down lest he endanger any prospect of a university career. After
Himmler's earnest reprimands and after an intensive talk with Wüst,

---

[89] It is indeed "extremely risky and difficult" to generalize Indo-European features
apart from linguistic lines, as Bruce Lincoln has stated. See idem, "Indo-European
religions: An overview," *Encyclopedia of Religion*, 2nd ed., vol. 7 (2005), pp. 4452–4456,
here p. 4452. The preceding article "Indo-European religions: History of study" of
C. Scott Littleton (reprinted from the 1st edition in 1987, ibid., pp. 4457–4466) speaks
rather uncritically of an "extralinguistic" Indo-Europen heritage with a "common body
of religious beliefs and practices" (ibid., p. 4457).

[90] For the conflict, see Barbara Schier, "Hexenwahn und Hexenverfolgung. Rezeption
und politische Zurichtung eines kulturwissenschaftlichen Themas im Dritten Reich,"
Bayerisches Jahrbuch für Volkskunde (1990), pp. 43–115, esp. pp. 69–78, and Julia Zernack,
"'Wenn es sein muß, mit Härte...' – Die Zwangsversetzung des Nordisten Gustav
Neckel 1935 und die 'Germanenkunde im Kulturkampf'," in idem and Klaus von
See, eds. *Germanistik und Politik in der Zeit des Nationalsozialismus. Zwei Fallstudien: Hermann
Schneider und Gustav Neckel* (Heidelberg: Winter, 2004), pp. 113–208.

Kummer revoked his attacks on Höfler in April 1938.[91] In November 1937, Wüst had provided Himmler with a report on the details of Kummer's "suspecting, outrageously offensive and insidious attacks" on the "Ahnenerbe" and its journal *Germanien* which should not be tolerated.[92] Kummer's formal withdrawal five months later made it possible for him to eventually get a chair of Nordic philology and Germanic religion at the University of Jena in 1942. The feud between Kummer and Höfler had wide repercussions. Many scholars of religion became involved writing evaluations and submitting petitions, for instance Herbert Grabert, Jakob Wilhelm Hauer, Otto Huth, Hermann Mandel, and Walther Wüst.

Heinrich rightly points at the voelkish narrow-mindedness of Kummer as key to understanding his development and thinking. Kummer's nickname "Germanenbernhard" hints at his character as a pettifogging and self-opinionated polemicist who did not shrink from slander and libel to promote his interests. Kummer felt a permanent disregard of his scholarly faculty, which sometimes even approached a type of a persecution mania. He was filled with envy of people like Höfler who garnered an academic reputation without deserving it. Following Bourdieu's sociological interpretation of the academic field, Heinrich analyzes Kummer's behavior in the context of habitual rivalries materializing as scientific conceptualizations with ideological and political undertones. Heinrich's reading reveals the normality of these squabbles whose proponents, nevertheless, believed they were engaged in a momentous battle relevant to the weal and woe of National Socialism as such. Yet, Kummer and Höfler were both ardent Nazi followers who hoped to play a leading role in the university system of the Third Reich.

What is particularly important for our topic is Heinrich's emphasis on the liberal Protestant background of Kummer. Kummer was educated at the University of Leipzig as historian of religions and shared the conventional Protestant aversions to Catholicism. A religion without priests and dogmas, a life oriented piety as well as a sort of voelkish feminism were characteristic features that Kummer detected in the religion of

---

[91] Cf. his internal renunciation on April 1, 1938 to be publicized in *Germanien* as well as in Kummer's own journal *Nordische Stimmen*. Federal Archives Berlin (BDC), personal files Kummer.

[92] Wüst's letter to Himmler on November 3, 1937, concerning "Verdächtigende, unerhört beleidigende und heimtückische Angriffe des Dr. Kummer, Jena, auf 'Germanien' und 'SS'," Federal Archives Berlin, BDC Kummer.

the old Germanic peoples. Obviously, these ingredients originated from his anti-Catholic propensity. Kummer's dislike for exaggerated ceremonies was also a typical Protestant remnant. Re-establishing the old antagonism of a mythological versus a ritualistic interpretation of religion, Kummer's approach went in the direction of an inner worldly piety based on a proper interpretation of the Nordic heritage. But in spite of Kummer's passionate condemnation of the church – the Inquisition, the persecution of the witches and the Christian mission were three important reference points – his way of arguing remained within Christian categories. He simply converted the missiologist narrative of an inner receptiveness of the Germanic peoples for Christianity, transforming it into an idealized apologia of the pastoral life of the old Germans, their religion, and their ethics.[93]

Kummer accused Höfler of having an un-Nordic predilection for strange rites and ecstatic practices. How would it be possible to connect occult mysteries with the Germans, specifically, with a people venerating the light and the sun, he asked. Setting Roman Catholic obscurantism at odds with the clearness and purity of a Nordic Protestant worldview whose roots went back to the Reformation, Kummer redrew the old ecclesiastical conflict lines within his interpretation of the Germanic legacy. This attempt to complete the Reformation with the help of National Socialism must have upset a Catholic scholar like Höfler. Instead, Höfler highlighted the potential for Kummer's voelkish sectarianism to be detrimental to the consolidation of a great German Reich spanning its Catholic territories (especially Austria) and inhabitants. However, neither Kummer's Protestant nor Höfler's Catholic bias warranted their ambitious hopes for an intellectual leadership in Nazi Germany. Kummer remained a theorist on the voelkish margin and Höfler failed to meet the expectations Wüst had for him at the beginning.[94] Though Kummer can be regarded as a talented student of

---

[93] Cf. here Heinrich's dissertation *Die deutsche Religionswissenschaft und der Nationalsozialismus. Eine ideologiekritische und wissenschaftsgeschichtliche Untersuchung* (Petersberg: Michael Imhof Verlag, 2002), pp. 186–200.

[94] See Himmler's letter to the racial hygienist Karl Astel on January 22, 1942, referring to Wüst's disappointment with Höfler. Federal Archives Berlin NS 19, 432, quoted in Gajek, "Germanenkunde und Nationalsozialismus," p. 198. Because he did not want to leave the church, Höfler declined to become a member of the SS. Nevertheless, he collaborated with the SD and the Reich Security Main Office on various occasions, writing, for instance, political memoranda about the situation in Scandinavia in 1942. See the texts (and other primary documents) at http://homepages.uni-tuebingen. de/gerd.simon, s.v. "Nordistik."

religion during his Leipzig years, he entered dangerous territory when turning towards a voelkish revivalism. While his interpretation of the Germanic past and his critique of the misrepresentations of many church historians were worthy of discussion at first, it soon resulted in wishful thinking and led him into a dead end with grotesque misjudgments. Thus "tragic" would be an inappropriate adjective to describe his scientific development. Kummer's reasoning was a mockery rather than a tragedy of scholarship.

In his article, Gustavo Benavides relates the conception of an irrational religious experience, propagated by many scholars of religion in the interwar period, with their attempt to overcome the nihilism resulting from World War I. He shows how sacred texts such as the Bhagavadgita were used by historians of religions to exemplify their own understanding of the world. While written in a scientific tone, these interpretations were anything but innocent. For many of these historians, the idea of an elitist heroic virility emerged as a chance to subdue the pessimistic feeling of death and decay predominating the intellectual debates in the aftermath of the war. With World War II in mind, we often forget to recognize the overwhelming dimension of its predecessor. But first of all World War I epitomized the European catastrophe. As a response to the turmoil it sparked, an increasing irrationality took hold of the academic learning in general and of the study of religion in particular.[95] However, life went on, and a new era necessitated a new intellectual leadership. To come to terms with this transition, historians of religions read the sacred scriptures they were occupied with as a sort of "worldview guideline" which instructed them how to manage the present and move forward.

Benavides gives an idea of how widespread and epidemic this reaction was. The metamorphosis of a pessimistic nihilism into a buoyant self-confidence with the help of religious references was a very common

---

[95] Regarding the German study of religion, see Rainer Flasche's articles "Religionsmodelle und Erkenntnisprinzipien der Religionswissenschaft in der Weimarer Zeit," in Hubert Cancik, ed., *Religions- und Geistesgeschichte der Weimarer Republik* (Düsseldorf: Patmos, 1982), pp. 261–276, "Religiöse Entwürfe und religiöse Wirkungen von Religionswissenschaftlern," in Peter Antes, ed. *Die Religion von Oberschichten. Religion, Profession, Intellektualismus* (Marburg: Diagonal, 1989), pp. 203–217, and "Der Irrationalismus in der Religionswissenschaft und dessen Begründung in der Zeit zwischen den Weltkriegen," in Hans G. Kippenberg and Brigitte Luchesi, eds., *Religionswissenschaft und Kulturkritik* (Marburg: Diagonal, 1991), pp. 243–257.

phenomenon among scholars of religion all over Europe.[96] Alluding
to the supposed a-political bearing of intellectuals, Benavides re-links
their scholarship with the general political circumstances. Placed in
that context, a growing irrationality in the study of religion proved
to be quite destructive. Theories of religion based on purely rational
considerations diminished considerably. In place of them, a theoretical
understanding of religion which relied on introspection and religious
empathy spread in the study of religion, and also in other disciplines
with religion belonging to the scheme of research. Everything depicted
as positivist reductionism was precluded from a genuine and authentic
apprehension of religious phenomena. But the denunciation of reason
delivered the study of religion to arbitrariness and to an uncontrollable
subjectivism. Under the impact of fascist influences, such a development would necessarily become disastrous. As Benavides points out,
the removal of cognitive limitations opened the door for a political
exploitation of the study of religion. Religion then served as a tool
to reproduce and sanctify power relations. Alongside this development, historians of religions mutated into theological experts whose
professionalism in a life oriented explication of religion met with great
political response.

The articles presented in the second part of the book address the
history of religions in South Eastern Europe: Italy, a deeply Catholic
nation; and Greece and Romania, two strongly Orthodox countries.
Vasilios N. Makrides describes the surfacing of religious studies in
Greece centering on the Orthodox theologian and historian of religions
Leonidas Philippidis. Together with Bernhard Kummer, Philippidis
studied in the 1920s at the University of Leipzig under Hans Haas
and Joachim Wach. In 1929, he submitted his doctoral thesis, two
years after Kummer. Having finished his studies at the University of
Leipzig, Philippidis returned to Athens where he worked as lecturer
of the history of religions from 1934 on. In 1939, he was nominated
full professor of history of religions at the Divinity School of the University of Athens, a position he held until 1968. Some years earlier,
the Protestant faculty of the University of Marburg had conferred an
honorary doctorate on Philippidis at the instigation of Friedrich Heiler

---

[96] For an Italian example, see Benavides' article, "Guiseppe Tucci, or buddhology in
the age of fascism," in Donald S. Lopez, ed. *Curators of the Buddha. The study of Buddhism
under colonialism* (Chicago: The University of Chicago Press, 1997), pp. 161–196.

and on the occasion of the 10th international congress of the IAHR that took place in Marburg in 1960.

It was no accident that the establishment of the study of religion in Greece coincided with the dictatorial reign of Ioannis Metaxas that lasted from 1936 until 1941. Not fascist in a strict sense of the word, the Metaxas regime embraced a number of fascist or fascist-like features. Thus historians usually call it an authoritarian dictatorship with fascist leanings. Religion played an important role in the attempt of Metaxas to base his autocracy on solid ideological fundamentals and to embed it in the Greek society. Above all, he needed an ally against the communist party, which had won 15 seats in the 1936 elections. Accordingly, he highlighted the fight against all forms of atheism and irreligion as represented by the archenemy of Orthodox Greece. Though Metaxas had been somewhat of a freethinker during the 1920s, he was a pious man who counted on the church as one of the main pillars of the New State he wanted to create. That he chose the labrys (pelekys) as emblem of his reign had nothing to do with a propensity to Paganism. The double-headed axe of the thundergod Zeus was chosen to symbolize the old age and the strength of the Hellenic civilization on which the new Greece should be based. Combining old Greece with the Byzantine Empire, Metaxas tried to build up a Third Hellenic Civilization, which would amalgamate classical and Christian elements. The Metaxas regime articulated the heroic Greek people in terms of an ethnic and sometimes even racial community. Yet, the idea of an irreconcilable antagonism between the Aryan and the Jewish race remained largely absent, and with it antisemitism and Paganism.

In his paper, Makrides locates the emergence of the study of religion as represented by Leonidas Philippidis in the political context of the so-called Fourth of August regime, named after the suspension of the parliament on that day in 1936. But Metaxas' conduct was motivated by more than the fear of communism. His agenda also included the modernization of the country, which meant removing a sizeable number of the numerous ecclesiastical influences from state agencies. Without the political disengagement of the Orthodox church, it would be nearly impossible to advance Greece to a modern nation. What became necessary under these circumstances was an enlightened understanding of religion based on scientific methods as well as on religious compassion. The contribution of Makrides manifests how well the scholarly approach of Philippidis fitted within that framework. The way Philippidis expounded religion as a vital trait of the Greek nation in history and actuality found a positive response from Metaxas himself. In an enthusiastic letter to Philippidis, the dictator declared in May 1937 that not only his own views but also the tenets of the new Greece would be in full congruency with those of the historian of religions at the University of Athens.[97] Hence, the blending of theology and history of religions advocated by Philippidis turned out to be fruitful for both sides. There can be no doubt that the emerging scholarship of religion supported the Fourth of August regime ideologically. It was also politically promoted, leading to the first chair of history of religions in Greece.

Cristiano Grottanelli's article examines the wartime connections of Georges Dumézil, Mircea Eliade, Carl Schmitt, Julius Evola, and Pierre Drieu la Rochelle. These thinkers shared a common set of political ideas and formed a loose network of like-minded persons who tried to associate more closely during the time of fascism. Their collective worldview orientation embraced fascist elements but focused also on the spiritual dimension of man. Accordingly, they rejected not only parliamentary democracy as such but took a stand against the political concessions of fascism to proletarian concerns as well. As to the non-German members of this web of intellectuals, a predilection towards National Socialism was not very likely. The fallout from World War I meant that anti-German resentments prevailed, especially among the French. Therefore a general fascist design rather than the ideology of National Socialism functioned as reference point of their political aspirations. The common denominator of their intentions was the wish to establish a European counterforce against bolshevism. Another important characteristic was the lack of Protestant values and categories. Instead of the voelkish narrow-mindedness of many scholars of religion with a Protestant background, a broader perspective and the outlook on imperial sovereignty predominated their conceptions.

Grottanelli's portrayal of this international net of theorists with a pro-fascist leaning is corroborated by my research on Walther Wüst and the "Ahnenerbe" of the SS. Wüst's relationship with Julius Evola in particular confirms the theory of a "cultural 'front' of the totalitarian right" in Europe. When Evola traveled to Bucharest in March 1938 to meet Corneliu Zelea Codreanu and Mircea Eliade, he was in search for collaborators to build up a pan-European union of intellectuals against communism. Before and after his journey to Bucharest, Evola

---

[97] See the article of Makrides, this volume, p. 298.

contacted Wüst and Schmitt, hoping to win them as allies as well. Mircea Eliade, the then cultural attaché to the Romanian delegation in Lisbon, visited Schmitt in Berlin five years later when he made a stop during his return trip from the Romanian to the Portuguese capital in July 1942. Although the political objective of Eliade's journey to Bucharest is not fully clear, it was undertaken on the direct instruction of António de Oliveira Salazar. Preceding his departure from Lisbon, Eliade was invited to a private audience with the Portuguese dictator on July 6, 1942. Salazar entrusted Eliade to transmit a message to his Romanian counterpart, Marshal Ion Antonescu.[98] Instead of the Conducător himself, Eliade was received "only" by the Foreign Minister Mihai Antonescu.[99] Eliade's later statements concerning this mission remain rather vague and he obviously tried to minimize its political meaning. However, Eliade encountered various representatives of the Romanian government during his stay in Bucharest. In all likelihood he used his stopovers in Berlin to meet the president of the Romanian Institute ("Rumänien Institut"), Sextil Puşcariu, with whom he had been campaigning in the 1937 elections and who also had contributed to the survey "Why I believe in the victory of the Legionary Movement." According to a German written article of Puşcariu, the main task of the "Rumänien Institut" was to strengthen the relations between Romania and Hitler Germany.[100] A member of the press corps guided Eliade on the second day of his return stop to the home of Carl Schmitt not far away from the Romanian Institute.[101] As one result of their intensive talk, the institute dispatched two issues of *Zalmoxis* to Schmitt on Eliade's demand at the end of August. For that reason Schmitt's expression of thanks, dating September 1, 1942, has been conserved in the files of the Romanian Institute. Two days later the director of the "Institutul Român din Germania" notified Schmitt's appreciation to the "Consilier

---

[98] See Ricketts, *Mircea Eliade. The Romanian roots*, vol. 2, p. 1099f. and pp. 1112–1116 as well as Cristiano Grottanelli, "Mircea Eliade, Carl Schmitt, René Guénon, 1942," *Revue de l'histoire des religions* 219–3 (2002), pp. 325–356, here p. 326f.
[99] Ţurcanu, *Mircea Eliade. Le prisonnier de l'histoire*, p. 326.
[100] Sextil Puşcariu, "Das Rumänische Institut in Deutschland," *Illustrirte Zeitung Leipzig*, no. 4984, p. 190, September 18, 1941 with a picture of the entrance hall of the institute as well as of its president.
[101] The address of the institute was Ahorn-Allee 22–24 in Charlottenburg and Schmitt's was Kaiserswerther Straße 17 in Dahlem. The streets belonged to neighboring districts of Berlin.

Cultural pe lângă Legaţiunea României" in Lisbon, Mircea Eliade.[102]
Two years later, Schmitt visited Eliade in Lisbon during a lecture tour.
On May 23, 1944, he stayed as Eliade's personal guest in his home
in Lisbon. The day before he had given a talk on "Land und Meer"
(Land and Sea) at the German Cultural Institute.[103]

It is noticeable that these encounters took place at the height of
World War II, when ordinary people without a political function had
absolutely no chance to travel throughout Europe. Since these meetings
were essentially political, one cannot reduce them to a private matter
and, for instance, relate Eliade's journey to Bucharest to personal business as Mac Linscott Ricketts does.[104] The set of connections pains-
takingly analyzed by Grottanelli reveals the European character of an
intellectual circle or "Männerbund" with a clear pro-fascist, though not
necessarily pro-Nazi, leaning. His inquiry shows the general disposition
but also the complexity of the relationship between spirit and power
under the spell of fascism. The end of the war did not mean the end
of the network. On the contrary, contacts were reestablished shortly
after 1945 in order to reestablish the network, entrenching it quite
successfully in a different political environment.

In his paper on Eliade's scientific and political development, Florin
Ţurcanu summarizes the findings of his biographical study – *Mircea
Eliade. Le prisonnier de l'histoire* – focusing on the situation at the University
of Bucharest in the interwar period.[105] Ţurcanu's study is one of the best
works about the Romanian historian and philosopher of religions and
was awarded Book of the Year in Romania at the end of 2006. The

---

[102] Federal Archives Berlin, research file 504, Rumänien Institut Deutschland. Cf. also
Alexandra Laignel-Lavastine, *Cioran, Eliade, Ionesco. L'oubli du fascisme* (Paris: Presses Universitaires de France, 2002), p. 313 (with a slight misreading of the letter heading).

[103] See Christian Tilitzki, "Die Vortragsreisen Carl Schmitts während des Zweiten
Weltkrieges," in *Schmittiana* 6 (1998), pp. 191–270, here the "Bericht über die Reise
von Staatsrat Professor Dr. Carl Schmitt nach Spanien und Portugal (Mai-Juni 1944),"
pp. 239–251 and Piet Tommissen, "Briefe an Carl Schmitt: Eine zweite Auswahl," in
ibid. vol. 4 (1994), pp. 249–290, here no. 2 "Mircea Eliade (1907–1986)," pp. 251–256.
Tommissen, the editor of the *Schmittiana*, accentuates, from an affirmative rightist
standpoint, the intellectual countermovement to which Eliade and Schmitt belonged.
For Schmitt's stay in Lisbon, see also Frank-Rutger Hausmann, *'Auch im Krieg schweigen
die Musen nicht'. Die Deutschen Wissenschaftlichen Institute im Zweiten Weltkrieg* (Göttingen:
Vandenhoeck und Ruprecht, 2001), p. 350.

[104] Ricketts, *Mircea Eliade. The Romanian roots*, vol. 2, p. 1112. Ricketts relies here
uncritically on Eliade's own narrative.

[105] An English editon is in preparation. A Romanian translation of the French
original appeared in 2003, a German translation in 2006.

strength of Țurcanu's investigation results from an admirable familiarity with the contemporary background in which Eliade's thinking was embedded. Țurcanu seeks to carefully answer the question of how to relate Eliade's scholarly and political views. He underscores the marginal position of Eliade in the Romanian academy, which characterized the status of his mentor, Nae Ionescu, as well as that of religious and Oriental studies, the objective of Eliade's professional ambitions, more generally. This marginality brought Eliade from an initial opposition to the political and academic establishment and paved the way for an ideological conformity with the rising Legionary Movement. Himself a prolific novelist and a charismatic leader of a group of young intellectuals, Eliade felt predestined to a higher position in the Romanian intellectual life which the political system seemed to withhold from him deliberately. Though Eliade supported the cause of the Iron Guard, his concern was not primarily directed towards politics. What he was interested in was a spiritual revolution, which, in his eyes, would be the precondition of all real political changes.

Eliade's early Indian experience at the end of the 1920s conferred a universalistic touch to his understanding of the world, lifting his religious convictions high above a narrow and parochial conception of religion. Yet Eliade was a child of his time who yearned for a new national identity of Romania, with Orthodox Christianity as its underlying structure. The universalism inherent of his religious views did not prevent him from sharply opposing mass democracy and all expressions of an un-voelkish internationalism. This tension between a universalistic spirituality easily passing over the limits of religions and nations and a very narrow definition of nationhood exclusive of all foreign elements was quite typical of Eliade in that time. Țurcanu convincingly argues in his paper that tensions between universalism and particularism characterized Eliade's thinking much more generally. Striving for a new rapprochement between science and religion, Eliade's reasoning thus oscillated between a spiritual open-mindedness and a jingoistic concept of the nation (românism) with totalitarian tendencies.

In addressing the scientific approaches of Mircea Eliade and his senior colleague Raffaele Pettazzoni, Eugen Ciurtin points to a key intersection in the European study of religion. The intensive cooperation between the two scholars spanned a long period of time and was accompanied by a voluminous correspondence. Though we have a good starting point for examining their relationship in Natale Spineto's excellent edition of their written communication, the information contained there often remains formal.[106] Deeper immersion in their scholarly and political reasoning would require additional sources and data. I have always been astonished by the fact that the life of a giant of the study of religion like Pettazzoni has not found its biographer. Yet Mario Gandini's ample and scrupulous series of articles on Pettazzoni published in *Strada Maestra*, the *Quaderni della biblioteca comunale 'G.C. Croce' di San Giovanni in Persiceto*, demonstrates how this landscape is changing. Gandini, director of this library, acted also as the archivist of Pettazzoni's literary remains, which are preserved there. Exceedingly modest, he calls his accounts – altogether more than 2500 pages – only a collection of materials for a biography ("materiali per una biografia").[107] It is more than astounding that this vast material laying in the public library of San Giovanni in Persiceto has not yet been utilized. Eugen Ciurtin and Michael Stausberg are probably among the first who draw on Gandini's corpus of texts in order to gain better insight in Pettazzoni's life and work. Hopefully others will follow.

In Italy as well as in Romania, the study of religion did not exist when Pettazzoni and Eliade started their university careers. They found themselves at the very fringe of the academy, working from private and professional interests to establish their subject at the university. Their similar outsider experiences gave their relationship a special sense of community typical of the members of minorities. The idea of belonging to a small group of scholars with the task, even the mission, of instituting the study of religion in the face of the ignorance of ministry officials and the powerful influence of the church, characterized the attitude of many historians of religions in the formative era of their discipline. As exemplified by their friendship, the peripheral position to which scholars of religion were restricted forged strong bonds among them, across the borders of different nations and religious backgrounds. Drawing on that spirit of comradeship, Eugen Ciurtin compares Pettazzoni and Eliade in their reactions to the scientific and political challenges raised by fascism in a central phase of their lives.

---

[106] See *Mircea Eliade, Raffaele Pettazzoni: L'histoire des religions a-t-elle un sens? Correspondance 1926–1959. Texte présenté, établi et annoté par Natale Spineto* (Paris: Ed. du Cerf, 1994). The book contains a valuable "Chronologie de la vie et des oeuvres" of both scholars, ibid., pp. 17–30.

[107] For the exact references, see the bibliography of Ciurtin and Stausberg, this volume, p. 361 and p. 393f. Cf. also Mario Gandini, "Il fondo Pettazzoni della biblioteca comunale 'G.C. Croce' di San Giovanni in Persiceto (Bologna)," *Archaeus* 7–3/4 (2003), pp. 291–295.

Although Pettazzoni was twenty-four years older than Eliade, his flirting with Italy's fascist party feels slightly like a youthful folly comparable to the conduct of some of his younger Italian colleagues. Ciurtin, who mentions in this context Eliade's attempt to categorize his political engagement as a "faux de jeunesse," rightly insists on weighing such designations more seriously. Was it only a slip (C.G. Jung on C.G. Jung) or more than a short-term aberration? Under fascist circumstances, the usual *do ut des* between politics and scholarship required a more intensive commitment. Obtaining political support was not without cost; it necessitated various statements and other evidence of loyalty. Additionally, scholars were expected to pay the tribute with their own currency, that is with scientific concepts on the basis of their particular hermeneutic expertise. Referring to Eliade's conceptualization of a creative death, Ciurtin gives a good example of the function of scholarship within an ideological framework. The liberation from death ("on se libère de la mort en mourant"), as expressed in Eliade's *Yoga* book, and the belief that only violent death can have a creative function, as expressed in a contribution to the last issue of *Zalmoxis*, mirrors the Guardist understanding of martyrdom and heroic dying.[108] But the idea of dying a martyr's death loses its emphatic innocence in light of the unbridled brutality and violence of the Iron Guard revealing its innate projective purpose. Perhaps my discussion of a plainspoken lecture of Julius Evola on the Aryan doctrine of the Holy War, given in Berlin some weeks after his return from Bucharest in June 1938, makes it more comprehensible that this sacrificial theory necessarily involved both victims and perpetrators when applied to actual practices.

Michael Stausberg ends his article on Raffaele Pettazzoni and the history of religions in fascist Italy with the conclusion that Pettazzoni had not compromised the veracity of his scholarly writings. The result of Stausberg's detailed examination comes as a surprise insofar as it reveals a number of political concessions of Pettazzoni to the fascist regime. Stausberg mentions, for example, two statements of loyalty Pettazzoni made in 1931 and 1933. Compared to his German colleagues, these acts of proclaiming allegiance were not unusual. In Nazi Germany as well, civil servants had to obey such kind of requirements lest they be regarded as dissidents. When Friedrich Heiler returned to Marburg after

---

[108] See Ciurtin, this volume, p. 350 as well as Cristiano Grottanelli, "Fruitful death: Mircea Eliade and Ernst Jünger on human sacrifice, 1937–1945," *Numen* 52 (2005), pp. 116–145.

his move to the University of Greifswald, he swore an oath not only to
the German Reich but also to Adolf Hitler in person.[109] Yet another
issue was the membership of university teachers in the party. On July
31, 1933, Pettazzoni took that step and joined the "Partito Nazionale
Fascista" PNF.[110] This is hard to digest, considering Pettazzoni's reputation as an anti-fascist, although, to be fair, he never expanded the validity of this claim to the fascist era itself. In 1939, Pettazzoni's assistant
Angelo Brelich, whose early right wing leanings were influenced by
Julius Evola, followed his teacher and became a member of the PNF
as well.[111] Pettazzoni's contribution to the *Enciclopedia Italiana* and his
membership in the Accademia d'Italia were two other focal points displaying his role as public intellectual and representative of fascist Italy.
This political engagement was rewarded with further prestige, influence
and money, allowing Pettazzoni, for instance, to travel abroad and to
publish the journal *Studi e materiali di storia delle religioni*.

Certainly the key to Pettazzoni's behavior has to be located on the
background of his desire to institute the study of religion in the Italian academy. Already the inauguration of his chair at the University
of Rome in 1923 was greatly attributed to the promotion he received
from Giovanni Gentile, the first education minister of the fascist regime
who had been nominated by Mussolini in October 1922. A common
opposition to the Catholic church and traditional Christianity stimulated
Gentile's and Pettazzoni's efforts and led eventually to the establishment
of the new discipline at the University of Rome. In an article written
in 1938 for the official fascist monthly *Civiltà fascista*, Pettazzoni took a
retrospective look at the thriving development of the study of religion
which had gained a footing at ten Italian universities after the advent
of fascism ("dopo l'avvento del Fascismo").[112] Surprisingly, Pettazzoni
related the upswing of the study of religion not to an increasing secular-
ization of the Italian society but, on the contrary, to the victory of the

---

[109] On April 1, 1935, Heiler swore: "I will remain faithful and obedient to the Führer
of the German Reich and people, Adolf Hitler, following the laws and complying with
my official duties consientously." Quoted from Heiler's personal file, State Archives
Marburg, 305a, acc. 1992/55, no. 4283, vol. 1, fol. 35 (trans. mine).

[110] See Stausberg, this volume, p. 373. The fact and date is given by Gandini,
"Raffaele Pettazzoni nelle spire del fascismo (1931–1933)," *Strada maestra* 50 (2001),
pp. 19–183, on p. 132.

[111] See Stausberg on p. 375 with reference to Gandini, "Raffaele Pettazzoni negli
anni 1937–1938," *Strada maestra* 54 (2003), pp. 53–232, here p. 209.

[112] Raffaele Pettazzoni, "Gli studi storico-religiosi in Italia," *Civiltà fascista* 5 (1938),
pp. 194–197. See Stausberg, this volume, p. 369.

totalitarian state over the agnostic spirit of laicism. In a contribution to the newspaper *Il Giornale d'Italia*, Pettazzoni recapitulated on February 28, 1937 the central role of the Italian state in a way that dovetailed well with the fascist myth of Rome.[113]

Being an academic outsider before the onset of fascism, Pettazzoni had the new regime to thank for a great deal of help in advancing his own career and the study of religion in general. Michael Stausberg paves the way for further research on the mélange of political, personal, and scholarly motives of a game whose risk Pettazzoni probably underestimated. These investigations ought to include the delicate question of a political consent and opportunism in Pettazzoni's case as well. Beyond that biographical scope, the general problem has to be addressed regarding the manner and extent to which the post-fascist study of religion was rooted in the preceding era. The 8th IAHR congress that took place in Rome in 1955 should remind us to look more closely at possible lines of continuity and to deliberate on the political context in which the former efforts in the 1930s and 1940s had been undertaken. In 1955, as it seems, everything was done to avoid a discussion of the time of fascism. Otherwise, one would have had to recognize the intriguing fact that study of religion in Italy owed its origin and growth the support of a wicked and inhuman regime – and, as many were all too well aware, not only in Italy.

Political short-sightedness, mystical revolution, and happy guilt are three recognizable elements characterizing the interpretative framework of the reception of Eliade in Romania in the last decades, as István Keul outlines in his review. A number of important books and articles have remained widely unknown outside of Romania because they were written in Romanian. Though these publications often provide new information and insight, they sometimes tend, even wish, to polarize in one direction or the other. The first phase of dealing with Eliade's legacy in Romania was characterized by a harsh rejection. Eliade was called a fascist, a charlatan, and a pornographer, among a host of unpleasant phrases. A number of his books were put on the index and were politically ostracized. However, the situation changed fundamentally when Nicolae Ceauşescu became general secretary of the communist party in Romania. Eliade's writing then found a much more positive response. In particular, those of his works which could

---

[113] See Stausberg, this volume, p. 381f.

be interpreted as a glorification of Romania met with new approval. Evidently, Ceauşescu's national communism tried to press the international reputation of the famous scholar into service of his own political agenda. Due to Romania's political isolation, the discussion about Eliade that cropped up in Israel in 1972 had no impact in the country although many Romanian Jews now living in Israel had participated in it. Quite plausibly, new interest in Eliade arose after the fall of communism. Many of his books were republished and the debate about his relationship with the fascist Iron Guard run high. The publication of Mihail Sebastian's diaries in particular triggered off heated disputes. It separated the two camps further and increased the polarization between those condemning and those lionizing Eliade's political legacy in favor of a new Romanian nationalism. It is to be hoped that these quarrels will calm down and will find more balance. Keul's article makes it clear that an important reason for the inappropriate interpretation of Eliade's life and work is lack of familiarity with Romanian history.

While the Protestant influence on the academic study of religion has persistently been a topic of great interest, its Catholic counterpart has not found a similar, or any, attraction. It remained widely unknown that within the realm of Catholicism a research field cropped up after World War I that aimed at a new scientific engagement with the general history of religions from a Catholic perspective. This Catholic study of religion is the theme of the third section of this book. At a number of Catholic theology departments, lectureships were inaugurated which explicitly contained the terms "Religionswissenschaft" or general or comparative "Religionsgeschichte." In addition, a third theologically oriented type of religious studies arose from within the community of the German Jews when a lectureship of Jewish "Religionswissenschaft" and ethics was established at the University of Frankfort in 1922. Its first holder, Martin Buber, represented the beginning of a third branch of a "theologische Religionswissenschaft" (theological study of religion) as I have called it.[114] The reason why Catholicism is occluded in the historical memory of the study of religion would deserve an investigation of its own. Liberal Protestants probably had a particular interest not to talk about their Catholic counterparts. For them, the Catholic church symbolized the counter-model to the ideas of academic freedom and unbiased research on religion. Their own limitations could

---

[114] Cf. Junginger, *Von der völkischen zur philologischen Religionswissenschaft*, pp. 80–90.

be covered up by pointing to the dependency of Catholic scholars on the directives of their bishops and the pope. And indeed, a scientific study of religion worth its name is hardly thinkable under such circumstances. Until today, the academic study of religion bears a more or less open anti-Catholic stance whose function ought to be addressed more intensively. In the time of National Socialism, the fight against Catholicism received an eminent boost. Historians of religions were given the chance to enlarge their own significance with an intensification of the old anti-Catholic partisanship.

The exclusion of Catholicism from the historical perspective of the study of religion leads sometimes to an inadequate and distorted understanding of certain events and persons. For example, a thinker like Carl Schmitt cannot be understood sufficiently from a narrow Protestant point of view. The Catholic idea of a transnational Reich necessarily remains strange and alien from that angle. Other problems of understanding originate from the strong textual orientation of Protestant scholarship, implying a rationalistic abstraction that is unable to grasp the ritual aspects and the cult mysteries characterizing the Catholic faith. Contrary to this tendency, Richard Faber devotes his article to the liturgical renewal surfacing within Catholicism in the interwar years. One of Germany's foremost experts in Schmitt's political theology, Faber relates the liturgical movement of Maria Laach and of Odo Casel's mystery theology with the general theological and political circumstances. The Benedictine monastery of Maria Laach, situated between Bonn and Koblenz, was a center of the new liturgical movement and Odo Casel, a renowned scholar of liturgical science ("Liturgiewissenschaft"), one of its leading figures. Sometimes called a "Caselism," his ideas included a new vision of the Catholic worship, the Catholic mass, and a renovated meaning of the Christian revelation. As Casel sees it, the liturgical celebration ought to be understood as the concrete reality in which the mystery of man's salvation occurs. This conception of a renewed unification of the religious mystery and the cultic act characterized other Christian traditions as well. Faber rightly mentions on the background of Casel's mystery theology the scientific approach of Eliade in which hierophanies take shape analogous to the Catholic epiphany.[115] The history of religions is the place where hierophanies happen. In the case of Casel and Eliade, the renewed

---

[115] See Faber, this volume, p. 426f. and p. 437.

emphasis on the religious mystery was an explicit attempt to overcome the anthropocentric agenda of a secular study of religion.[116] Whereas the political impact of the deification of the natural order ("ordo universi") – along with the anti-Jewish elements of Casel's work – appears to be plausible at first glance, the fusion of Catholicism and Paganism is a phenomenon of great complexity. Casel's liturgical theory maintained that Catholicism had not only preserved elements of a Pagan spirituality. It moreover enforced its claim to have brought the Pagan mystery to fulfillment. From a Protestant perspective, Pagan religions were to be fought and their cults destroyed. Catholicism instead seeks to absorb them. Thanks to the Pagan input, a spiritual renewal might occur helping to overcome the materialism and skepticism threatening the Church. Evidently, leveraging Paganism involved an in-depth knowledge of the general history of religions apart from missionary interests.

Friedrich Andres, whose development as a Catholic theologian and scholar of religion is described by Ulrich Vollmer, became one of the first Catholic theologians who held a formal teaching position in the study of religion and the first who taught this subject outside of a theology department. In 1920, Andres had completed his habilitation in general science of religion at the department of catholic theology at the University of Bonn, where he received a lectureship in 1922 named "Allgemeine Religionswissenschaft einschließlich der vergleichenden Religionsgeschichte und Religionspsychologie" (general science of religion inclusive of comparative history of religions and psychology of religion). In 1927, Andres was nominated extraordinary professor in the same stream. Parallel to that, he held a similar lectureship at the University of Frankfort. Founded in 1919 as a private "Stiftungsuniversität," Frankfort's university did not include theology departments. After a successful lobby work, the Catholic and Protestant churches – and following them the Jewish community – were allowed to teach worldview matters and the history of religions from a Catholic, Protestant, and Jewish perspective. These lectureships were labeled "Religionswissenschaft." I have already mentioned the position of Martin Buber. What Andres did for the Catholic church, Martin Buber did for the Jewish community. But Buber's teaching position developed more into the direction of an independent study of religion without, nonethe-

---

[116] Ibid.

less, losing its attachment to the Jewish religion. In 1936, Andres was prevented from participating in the 6th IAHR conference in Brussels and in 1937, his lectureship was withdrawn by the Berlin Ministry of Science and Education. Although political implications and a general anti-Catholic penchant played a role in these measures, they were not directed against Andres personally. Otherwise, it would have been impossible for him to become a civil servant in 1939. At the same time, his teaching position was upgraded to an extraordinary professorship. On October 26, 1939, he swore his oath to Adolf Hitler and the Third Reich.[117] The example of Andres illustrates that university teachers were still able to abstain from an open partisanship for National Socialism without being bereaved of their academic position. Of course, such an attitude of restraint was not permitted to go beyond a certain limit of political commitment.

Unlike Andres, Wilhelm Schmidt was an unmitigated enemy of National Socialism. Udo Mischek shows in his article that for Schmidt, National Socialism and international socialism belonged to the same category of godless materialism. Both ideologies threatened the all-embracing claims of the "catholic" Church fundamentally. Schmidt clearly understood the anti-Catholic bias of the voelkish, Protestant-based, parts of the Nazi ideology. He argued not only in his worldview scriptures but also in his scientific works from an unmistakable Catholic standpoint, never denying his missionary background. In 1927, Schmidt became the first director of the newly-founded "Museo Missionario Etnologico" of the Vatican in the Lateran Palace originating from a previously held missionary exhibition. Rudolf Otto's founding of the "Religionskundliche Sammlung" at the University of Marburg (still the only museum of its kind in Germany) must be understood as a reaction to the missionary and ethnographic museum in Rome. Another important facet of Schmidt's scientific endeavors was the foundation of the *Anthropos* journal in 1906 followed by the establishment of the Anthropos Institute 25 years later near Vienna in 1931. After the "Anschluss" of Austria in 1938, the institute was dissolved and Schmidt had to flee to Switzerland. Already at the end of 1937 or at the beginning of 1938, the German anthropologist Wilhelm Emil Mühlmann demanded in a fierce memorandum, possibly written for the Rosenberg office, the

---

[117] Personal files of Andres, Archive of the University of Bonn, no. 116. For the wording of the oath, see here p. 62, n. 109.

abolition of the Anthropos Institute. Mühlmann made his case as a devoted National Socialist, stipulating political measures against the clericalism of Schmidt and the Anthropos circle. One of Mühlmann's allegations called the Catholic worldview of Schmidt a danger to the racial unity of the Nordic peoples.[118] After the war, Mühlmann played an important role in the executive committee of the German Association for the Study of Religion (DVRG).

Despite Schmidt's ardent opposition to National Socialism, he held decidedly fascist views, among them an open antisemitism. Mischek lays bare how Schmidt's reasoning in his scientific and non-scientific writings revealed his antisemitic fervor. An enthusiastic propagator of traditional anti-Judaism, Schmidt regarded the Jews as the killers of Christ and as the source of many if not most evils in the world. He even included racial arguments in that scheme. This did not mean that he adopted the biological arguments and the racial materialism of the Nazis as he saw it. In his mind, race belonged to the constituent parts of the natural order instituted by God himself. The anti-evolutionist stance of Schmidt can be depicted as the driving force behind his scholarly activities. It also shaped his famous theory of primitive monotheism. Schmidt's catholic theological a priori drew heavy criticism from the fields of anthropology and the study of religion. The theoretical rejection of Schmidt's speculative agenda was an important factor in the self-characterization of the study of religion. Interestingly enough, Schmidt was honored as an icon of the study of religion in a series published in Germany in 1996, while Raffaele Pettazzoni, perhaps his most prominent opponent, was denied entry into that gallery of ancestral portraits.[119] From a political point of view, one should emphasize with Mischek the fact that a decided anti-Nazi like Schmidt could, nevertheless, act in favor of an ideology that might be described best as a sort of clerical fascism.

A theological study of religion shaped by liberal Protestantism – the subject of section four – gained considerable influence outside of Germany as well. Particularly in Northern Europe, Rudolf Otto held

---

[118] See Ute Michel, "Wilhelm Emil Mühlmann (1904–1988) – ein deutscher Professor. Amnesie und Amnestie: Zum Verhältnis von Ethnologie und Politik im Nationalsozialismus," in Carsten Klingemann et al., eds., *Jahrbuch für Soziologie-Geschichte* (Opladen: Leske und Budrich, 1991), pp. 69–117, esp. pp. 81–84.

[119] See Axel Michaels, ed., *Klassiker der Religionswissenschaft. Von Friedrich Schleiermacher bis Mircea Eliade* (München: Beck, 1996). The very sympathetic article on Schmidt was written by Hans Waldenfels (ibid., pp. 185–197).

substantial sway over many scholars of religion. Haralds Biezais was a typical representative of the Ottonian paradigm. He studied Protestant theology at the University of Latvia in Riga from 1929 but his interests turned increasingly towards the history of religions. Most of his early writings (which steered Biezais in forming his scientific views) remain untranslated. Iveta Leitane's article on Biezais as an historian of religions between theology and religious studies addresses – probably for the first time – the beginning of the academic career of Biezais, who became a very influential scholar of religion in Northern Europe after 1945. Biezais' early studies fell in a time of an intensive search for Latvia's national identity in which the church played a decisive role. The country had acquired national independence only in 1918, and foreign influence, particular that of the Baltic Germans, was very strong. Gustav Mensching, a prominent pupil of Rudolf Otto, taught as professor of history of religions at the department of Protestant theology at the Latvian State University from 1927 until 1935. He influenced Biezais deeply. In his theological master's thesis from 1932, Bieazais dealt with the work of Mensching who belonged to the group of nationalistic Germans in Latvia and who joined the NSDAP in Riga in 1934. Having completed his theological dissertation in 1939, Biezais embarked on a habilitation thesis on the Protestant theologian Emil Brunner.[120] In June 1941, he assumed the position of a lecturer at the theological department of the University of Riga.

After the German troops invaded in June 1941, Latvia became a province of the so-called "Reichskommissariat Ostland." The occupation was accompanied by the immediate persecution and extermination of the Jews. Chief responsibility for the killing of almost all Latvian Jews was borne by Franz Walter Stahlecker, the son of a Protestant pastor in Southern Germany. Stahlecker had studied at the University of Tübingen where he obtained a doctoral degree in jurisprudence in 1927. With Stahlecker's subordinates Martin Sandberger and Erich Ehrlinger, the leaders of the special task units ("Einsatzkommandos") 1a and 1b, two other former Tübingen students were to be blamed for the Latvian holocaust.[121] After the church of Gramzda, where Biezais

---

[120] Neither study was translated. Cf. Leitane's bibliography at the end of her article.

[121] See Michael Wildt, *Generation des Unbedingten. Das Führungskorps des Reichssicherheitshauptamtes* (Hamburg: Hamburger Edition, 2002), pp. 89–104 and Horst Junginger, "Tübinger Exekutoren der Endlösung. Effiziente Massenmörder an vorderster Front

worked as a Protestant pastor, had been burned during the invasion, Biezais had the structure rebuilt not only with the help of the Germans but, as Leitane found out, by drafting Jewish workers as well.[122] As of September 1941, Biezais had been working at the church archives of Riga, nominated its director in 1942, where his task had been to prepare proofs of Aryan descent ("Abstammungsnachweise") for those Baltic Germans who belonged to the "Wehrmacht."[123] When the first group of Latvian legionaries joined the German army, Biezais preached at the Dome of Riga.[124] Yet according to Leitane, Biezais had no liking for National Socialism. Once the Red Army invaded, Biezais fled to Sweden in October 1944.

What becomes clear from Biezais' early writings and activities is a special appreciation of non-Christian traditions, indicating a certain estrangement from orthodox theology with undertones that might be designated voelkish. The Latvian folk religion in particular became a central area of his in interest and research. At the end of his life, Biezais also published historical and biographical works involving the 1930s and 1940s. Drawing on these studies, Leitane casts new light on the early career of Biezais' life and work. In the highly controversial debates about the Latvian past – but also with regard to the history of the study of religion – a critical biography of Biezais would be very helpful.

Norwegian academics, particularly theologians, held traditionally positive views about Germany. During World War I, many of them supported the German cause. The Old Testament scholar and historian of religions Sigmund Mowinckel, for instance, asserted to his teacher, Hermann Gunkel, his firm solidarity with the German war efforts.[125] In World War II, things changed, especially with the German invasion of Norway in April 1940. Mowinckel himself was interrogated several times by the Gestapo, and in November 1943 he was threatened with imprisonment and deportation.[126] Immediately after German troops had

---

der SS-Einsatzgruppen und des Sicherheitsdienstes," *Schwäbisches Tagblatt*, June 18, 2003, p. 29, available on the internet: http://homegapes.uni-tuebingen.de/gerd.simon/exekutoren.pdf.

[122] See Leitane, this volume, p. 514.

[123] Ibid.

[124] Ibid.

[125] Cf. Sigurd Hjelde, *Sigmund Mowinckel und seine Zeit. Leben und Werk eines norwegischen Alttestamentlers* (Tübingen: Mohr Siebeck, 2006), pp. 86–91.

[126] Ibid., p. 100.

invaded Norway, Walter Stahlecker was ordered to organize the work of the secret police. Nominated "Befehlshaber der Sicherheitspolizei und des SD" (commander of the security police and the SD), he built up various outposts of the SD and the Reich Security Main Office in Oslo, Bergen, Trondheim, and other Norwegian cities. Stahlecker personally resided at the former Foreign Ministry in Oslo. By orders of Heinrich Himmler, Erich Ehrlinger came to Norway in August 1940, trying to drum up Norwegian volunteers for the German Waffen-SS.[127] After the University of Oslo was closed in 1943, about 65 professors and 1500 students were arrested for resisting the occupying forces. Some 650 students were immediately deported to the German Reich.[128] Half of them were taken to the Buchenwald concentration camp, the other to an educational camp near Strasbourg where members of the "Ahnenerbe" of the SS tried to convince them that they belonged to the community of the Nordic race. In the course of this attempt, Walther Wüst and Otto Huth were scheduled to give speeches to the Norwegian students in order to persuade them of their racial origin and of their duty to join to the anti-bolshevist efforts of National Socialism.[129] The objective was to win national collaborators in the occupied territories in order to spread the European agenda of the Third Reich. In the case of these Norwegian students, the plan ended unsuccessfully.

An independent study of religion in Norway emerged after great delay. The only chair of the history of religions, held by Wilhelm Schencke from 1914 until 1939, remained vacant until 1947 as a result of World War II.[130] Sigurd Hjelde states in his article on Kristian Schjeldrup that there were a number of theologians whose interest and teaching included the general history of religions. Schjeldrup belonged

---

[127] Cf. Wildt, *Generation des Unbedingten*, pp. 508–516.

[128] See the moving eyewitness account of Kurt D. Singer, "Norwegian students fight the war," *Journal of Educational Sociology* 18–1 (September 1944), pp. 22–28.

[129] See Kater, *Das 'Ahnenerbe' der SS*, p. 185f. and Junginger, *Von der philologischen zur völkischen Religionswissenschaft*, p. 264.

[130] Hjelde, *Sigmund Mowinckel und seine Zeit*, p. 266. For Wilhelm Schwencke, see Hjelde, "The science of religion and theology. The question of their interrelationship," in Arie L. Molendijk and Peter Pels, eds., *Religion in the making. The emergence of the sciences of religion* (Leiden: Brill, 1998), pp. 99–128, here p. 113f. and Einar Thomassen, "Wilhelm Schencke – Norway's first professor in history of religions," in Sigurd Hjelde, ed., *Man, meaning, and mystery. 100 years of history of religions in Norway. The heritage of W. Brede Kristensen* (Leiden: Brill, 2000), pp. 223–236. Cf. also the account of Ragnhild Bjerre Finnestad, "The study of religions in Norway," *Method and Theory in the Study of Religion* 13 (2001), pp. 243–253.

to them and to those who fought against the German aggression. The later bishop of the Lutheran diocese of Hamar (1947–1964), Schjeldrup had studied under Friedrich Heiler and Rudolf Otto at the University of Marburg at the beginning of the 1920s. In 1927, he founded a union of liberal Christianity ("Verein für freisinniges Christentum") and in 1931 a journal named *Fritt Ord* (free word). As these activities were closely related to the pursuits of Jakob Wilhelm Hauer, Schjeldrup came to meet the Tübingen indologist and historian of religions. He maintained these contacts even after Hauer had become the founder of the German Faith Movement in July 1933. Above and beyond that, Schjeldrup disseminated Hauer's Pagan and now decidedly anti-Christian ideas in Norway. These actions led him to be judged an involuntary apostle of fascism. In one regard, such a harsh criticism of a leading figure of liberal Protestantism in Norway is unjustified. But in another sense, it correctly reflects the elective affinity between Hauer and Schjelderup. In fact, Hauer himself had belonged to the realm of free Christianity and liberal Protestantism in Germany before 1933. In that time, Hauer was a liberal-minded scholar who struggled against the dogmatism and moral hypocrisy of the church. At first, Hauer tried to realize his endeavors for a spiritual renewal within Protestantism.[131] As a result of the open enmity against these efforts he left the church. It is an interesting but thus far unanswered question at what point and for what reasons the relationship, partly friendship, between Hauer and Otto, Buber, or Schjeldrup came to an end. Schjeldrup gave up publicizing information about the German Faith Movement with its end in 1936. In discussing a well-researched book of Terje Emberland on the spreading of Paganism and Nazism in Norway,[132] Hjelde emphasizes that the distinction between rationality and irrationality, Emberland's marker for linking Schjeldrup and Hauer, is not suitable for adequately classifying the different currents in the study of religion.

The designation used for the Dutch German studies scholar Jan de Vries in his post-war trial in May 1948 was that of an "intellectual collaborator."[133] This judgment encapsulated the truth quite well. Less

---

[131] For the liberal Protestant background of Hauer's endeavors, see Hiroshi Kubota, *Religionswissenschaftliche Religiosität und Religionsgründung Jakob Wilhelm Hauer im Kontext des Freien Protestantismus* (Frankfurt a.M.: Lang, 2005).

[132] Terje Emberland, *Religion og rase. Nyhedenskap og nazisme i Norge 1933–1945* (Oslo: Humanist forlag, 2003).

[133] See Willem Hofstee's article on Gerardus van der Leeuw and Jan de Vries, this volume, p. 548.

than four years earlier, the executive director of the SS "Ahnenerbe" Wolfram Sievers had stated that De Vries would be one of "our best and most energetic co-workers in a long time" and that he would stay in permanent connection "with us."[134] Even more explicit was Hanns Albin Rauter, the highest ranking SS leader in the Netherlands responsible for the deportation of the Dutch Jews as well as for the oppression of the Dutch resistance, in a letter to Heinrich Himmler in November 1944. The "Obergruppenführer" and higher SS and police leader in the occupied Netherlands called Himmler's attention to the extraordinary merits of De Vries for the Germanic idea. Among Dutch university teachers, De Vries would have become the most active propagator of "our cause."[135] Rauter continued that De Vries could no longer be employed in the Netherlands as a result of the military situation. With that in mind, he should be given a professorship in Germany to reward him for his advocacy of German interests.

Though De Vries had previously placed his predilection for a greater Netherlands above his pro-German sentiments, he threw himself into the political course of the SS in 1942. Allying himself with the SS "Ahnenerbe," De Vries became a FM, a "Förderndes Mitglied" (supporting member) of the SS in July 1943.[136] On the occasion of the so-called "Dolle Dinsdag" and on orders of the secret police and the SD, De Vries left the Netherlands in September 1944 to relocate to Nazi Germany immediately after his flight.[137] With the help of the SS, he found not only a new domicile at Leipzig but received an extremely

---

[134] Letter of Sievers to Bruno Schweizer, head of the "Ahnenerbe" department of Germanic linguistics (with copies for Walther Wüst and Hans Ernst Schneider), on October 2, 1944, quoted in Andries Dirk Kylstra, *De Leidse oudgermanist Jan de Vries in de ogen van de bezetter* (Roden: Kylstra, 2001), p. 139. Of particular interest in Kylstra's book is the section "Bijlagen," with many reproductions of primary documents.

[135] "Hat sich in den letzten 2 Jahren außerordentliche Verdienste um den germanischen Gedanken erworben und ist unter den Hochschul-Lehrern im letzten Jahr der aktivste Anhänger unserer Sache geworden, sein Sohn ist Staatsanwalt Hans de Vries, dient als Kriegsfreiwilliger beim Landstorm." Rauter's letter to the Reichsführer SS on November 7, 1944, quoted by Kylstra, *De Leidse oudgermanist*, p. 155.

[136] See Barbara Henkes and Björn Rzoska, "Volkskunde und 'Volkstumspolitik' der SS in den Niederlanden. Hans Ernst Schneider und seine 'großgermanischen' Ambitionen für den niederländischen Raum," in Burkhard Dietz et al., eds., *Griff nach dem Westen. Die 'Westforschung' der völkisch-nationalen Wissenschaften zum nordwesteuropäischen Raum (1919–1960)*, 2 vols. (Münster et al.: Waxmann, 2003), vol. 1, pp. 291–323, here p. 315.

[137] See Kylstra ibid., p. 179, and the attestation of the "SS-Ersatzkommando Niederlande" on September 4, 1944, ibid., p. 131. On September 5, 1944, about 30,000 members of the "National-Socialistische Beweging" (NSB) fled from the Netherlands after a false BBC report announcing the invasion of the allied forces. See Jan Zim-

generous grant from the German Research Foundation ("Deutsche Forschungsgemeinschaft", DFG). In February 1945, the DFG extended its grant of 750 Reichsmark per month until September 1945. De Vries, then, had every reason to write a letter of appreciation to Walther Wüst on March 1, 1945. Since he realized that a return to the Netherlands had become rather unlikely for him, De Vries asked the "Ahnenerbe" curator if it would be possible for him to obtain a professorship of Nordic studies or old-Germanic culture in Germany.[138]

Willem Hofstee's paper appropriately underscores the exceptional collaboration of De Vries with the Germans and the SS. This is important the more so because an attempt has recently been made to whitewash the Dutch scholar from his pro-Nazi engagement during World War II. On the basis of a very simplistic and faulty understanding of the German policy in the Netherlands in general and of the tasks of the "Ahnenerbe" in particular, it has been claimed that De Vries would have been in unconcealed contradiction ("unverhohlenem Widerspruch") to the ideology of National Socialism.[139] The example of De Vries is striking in so far as the Dutch scholar fraternized with the Nazis only after the Wehrmacht had overrun the Netherlands and in a phase when the Germans consolidated their vicious occupation policy. Claiming to act in favor of Dutch nationalism, De Vries took the defeat of his country and the humiliation of his fatherland as chance to defect to the enemy. Seen from the German side of the frontline, De Vries appeared as a model of successful proselytization. Especially the "Ahnenerbe" strove to win sympathizing intellectuals among the 'Nordic' countries as collaborators to help disseminate the great Germanic idea ("großgermanischer Gedanke") and the pan-European ideology of National Socialism. To better organize these plans, the

---

mermann, "Alfred Toepfers 'Westschau'," in Burkhard Dietz et al., eds., *Griff nach dem Westen*, vol. 2, pp. 1061–1090, here p. 1084.

[138] Letter of Jan de Vries to Walther Wüst on March 1, 1945, quoted in Kylstra, *De Leidse oudgermanist*, p. 148f. and pp. 185–187. De Vries wrote "Inzwischen ist es mir doch deutlich geworden, daß für mich auch nach dem Kriege eine Rückkehr nach Leiden ausgeschlossen sein wird und ich muß mich deshalb darauf einrichten, außerhalb meines Vaterlandes mein weiteres Leben zu verbringen." Ibid., p. 186.

[139] See the foreword of Stefanie Würth to the third edition of Jan de Vries, *Altnordische Literaturgeschichte* (Berlin et al.: De Gruyter, 1999), pp. XIII–XLV, here p. XIIIf. The poor historical knowledge of the author, a professor of Scandinavian studies at the University of Tübingen, becomes particularly evident from her assertion that Heinrich Harmjanz, a scholarly opponent of De Vries, would have been the chairperson ("Vorsitzender") of the SS "Ahnenerbe."

SS leadership established a special department in the "Ahnenerbe" in 1943 which named "Germanischer Wissenschaftseinsatz" (GWE). It was headed by Hans Ernst Schneider, who became Hans Schwerte after the war. In close co-operation with the SS "Hauptamt" of Gottlob Berger, Schneider established GWE branches in the Netherlands (Friedrich Wilhelm Mai), the Flanders (Alarich Augustin), Wallonia (Léon Degrelle), France (Ludwig Mühlhausen), and Norway (Hans Schwalm).[140] Besides intending to recruit volunteers for the German "Waffen-SS," the GWE tried to join forces with politicians and intellectuals sympathetic to German interests and to make common cause. With that aim in mind, scholars like De Vries were much more useful to the SS than were the genuine National Socialists of the NSB. Anton Mussert's "National-Socialistische Beweging" remained isolated in Dutch society, unable to implement the new order ("nieuwe orde") that the invaders wanted to impose on the Netherlands. In all countries occupied by the German forces, the same sort of conflicts arose. The attempt to set up forms of an indirect rule regularly collided with the wish of the native collaborators to rescue what they considered to be an autonomous position. In fact, the Germans needed and used these quislings. But they never accepted any kind of national sovereignty – if this notion makes sense at all under the conditions of a brutal and oppressive occupation regime.

While De Vries pursued his own projects at the beginning of the German occupation, he sacrificed his plans completely to the great Germanic ideology, specifically to SS interests. Instead of founding a national institute of anthropology and folklore, De Vries joined the pro-Nazi "Nederlandsche Kultuurraad" led by Geerto Snijder. In fact, shortly before he left the Netherlands in a rush in 1944, De Vries earned the German Rembrandt Prize and the Dutch Rembrandt Medal.[141] On June 7, 1944, Schneider praised De Vries in a letter to Hans Rössner, a Germanist and high SD official, as one of the few Dutch scholars who would collaborate "with us" unreservedly and with total commitment to German interests.[142] With "us" Schneider meant the "Ahnenerbe" but,

---

[140] See Joachim Lerchenmüller, "Hans Ernst Schneiders/Hans Schwertes Niederlande-Arbeit in den 1930er bis 1950er Jahren," in Burkhard Dietz et al., eds., *Griff nach dem Westen*, vol. 2, pp. 1111–1140, esp. pp. 1128–1131.
[141] See Zimmermann, "Alfred Toepfers 'Westschau'," pp. 1083–1085.
[142] "Prof. de Vries ist einer der wenigen Wissenschaftler aus dem gesamtgermanischen Raum, der rückhaltlos mit uns mitarbeitet." Kylstra, *De Leidse oudgermanist*, p. 126f.

as it seems, also the SD. In this letter, Schneider additionally reported
an encounter between De Vries and Otto Höfler some days previously
in Oslo where Höfler was very positively impressed with his Dutch colleague. Though the objective of that Oslo meeting was not expressed
openly, it appears less related to cultural politics than to intelligence
purposes. One of Schneider's co-workers in the GWE, partly acting as
his deputy, was Otto Huth, the assistant of Jakob Wilhelm Hauer at
the University of Tübingen and professor of science of religion at the
Reich University of Strasbourg as of 1942.[143] Huth also worked for the
SD. When I met him twice in 1994, I asked him, among other things,
about his engagement in the Netherlands. Huth's answers remained
vague and nebulous, although it became clear that he knew much
more. It may be of interest in that context to add that the leader of
the GWE in the Flanders Alarich Augustin – whose cousin Günther
Augustin wrote a dissertation on Friedrich Nietzsche under Hauer at
the University of Tübingen in 1936 – joined the religious community
of the "Deutsche Unitarier Religionsgemeinschaft" (DUR) after the
war. Alarich Augustin belonged to a group named "Bund deutscher
Unitarier. Religionsgemeinschaft europäischen Geistes" which broke off
from the DUR in 1988 under the leadership of Sigrid Hunke, another
co-worker of the SS "Ahnenerbe" and of the "Germanistischer Wissenschaftseinsatz."[144] In addition, Huth's wife as well as Hunke's sister
Waltraud, Otto Höfler's assistant, worked for the GWE.

Gerardus van der Leeuw, who had been thrown into prison and
interrogated by the SD in 1943, stands in contrast to Jan de Vries,
who was the prototype of an intellectual collaborator. The reason for
Leeuw's arrest was the resistance of his two sons who refused to sign the
declaration of loyalty demanded by the Germans from all students.[145]
Like their Norwegian colleagues, many Dutch students courageously
resisted the German oppressor, facing the same consequences, including confinement, deportation, and, in some cases, death. However,
as Hofstee's paper shows, things were not so clear with Gerardus van
der Leeuw himself. Before the German invasion, Van der Leeuw held

---

[143] For Huth, see Junginger, *Von der philologischen zur völkischen Religionswissenschaft*, pp.
248–268, esp. p. 262f.

[144] Cf. Horst Junginger "Sigrid Hunke: Europe's new religion and its old stereotypes,"
in Hubert Cancik and Uwe Puschner, eds., *Antisemitismus, Paganismus, Völkische Religion.
Anti-Semitism, Paganism voelkish religion* (München: Saur, 2004), pp. 151–162.

[145] See Hofstee, this volume, p. 547 and in general idem, *Goden en Mensen. De godsdienst
wetenschap van Gerardus van der Leeuw* (Kampen: Kok Agora, 1997).

views not so far removed from those of Jan de Vries. And even after the conquest of the Netherlands, Leeuw's pro-German penchant was not vitiated in principal.[146] Besides their philo-German proclivity, the accordance between Van der Leeuw and De Vries included an ardent anti-communism, the mistrust towards parliamentary democracy, the dislike of positivism, materialism and of the dissolution of traditional values connected with authority, family and religion. Both sought for means to strengthen the national identity of the Netherlands, which ought to take a third way between materialist capitalism and atheist bolshevism. Therefore, many political and social measures implemented by National Socialism in Germany met their consent, offering a model for the Netherlands that could frame the voelkish community of all Dutch beyond their class and other barriers as well. So it should not come of any surprise that De Vries wrote an article for a book on the religions of the world that Van der Leeuw edited in 1940 and 1941.[147]

But, to be clear, Van der Leeuw never sympathized with the Nazis or with National Socialism. And he never sided with the German invaders. In his eyes, the German church policy in particular cast the National Socialist government in a very bad light. A pro-Franco utterance quoted by Hofstee has to be regarded in that context of repugnance towards the anti-clericalism and biological racism that reigned in the Third Reich. The ambivalence of Leeuw's views resulted in the futile attempt to maintain what was called a "critical collaboration."[148] Though one should not underestimate the extraordinary difficulties of living under a vicious occupation regime, the idea of a "critical collaboration" failed to harmonize with the reality from the outset. That such a concept proved to be a contradiction in itself becomes more evident in the case of some other Dutch intellectuals who used it as euphemism to hide their collaboration and the benefits that it yielded. Jan van Dam, the Dutch minister of education employed by the Germans, belonged to that group, claiming that he had done his best to defend the national interests of the Netherlands when he joined in the policy of the Nazis. His nickname "Jan Pudding" indicates his opportunism but is less harmless than it may appear. Another pithy aphorism describes better

---

[146] Hofstee, *Goden en Mensen*, p. 87.

[147] Jan de Vries, "De godsdienst der germanen," in Gerardus van der Leeuw et al., eds., *De godsdiensten der Wereld*, 2 vols. (Amsterdam: Meulenhoff, 1940/41), vol. 1, pp. 126–171 (non vidi), 3rd ed. vol. 1, 1955, pp. 475–520.

[148] See Hofstee, this volume on p. 547.

how he behaved and how the roles were allocated in reality: "Van Dam
wikt, Seyß beslist, van Dam slikt."[149]

The comparison between Jan de Vries, whom Van Dam personally
requested (by order of the Nazis) to write a schoolbook on the Germanic
ancestors of the Dutch,[150] and Gerardus van der Leeuw, the successor
of Van Dam as minister of education in 1945 and 1946, raises more
questions than it answers. Perhaps Leeuw's "active cultural policy"
adopted in 1945 was not totally different from the reform plans that
Van Dam had in mind a few years earlier. For Leeuw, the national re-
education of the Dutch society ought to embrace a spiritual renewal
and a moral rearmament based on a modernized Christian agenda.
Shying away from a reflection upon the voelkish nature of the concept
of "Dutchness," he apparently "was blind to the previous ideological
misuse of folk culture."[151] Partly for these reasons, Van der Leeuw failed
as minister and was replaced by the Roman Catholic Jos Gielen in 1946.
Discussions on the re-shaping of the national identity of the Netherlands
after the war boomed. At certain points they also focused on the role
of Van der Leeuw. But in the context of our topic, Van der Leeuw's
miscarriage as minister is less important than the question of whether
he succeeded in bringing his ideas to fruition with the International
Association for the Study of the History of Religions. The IASHR
was founded during the 7th International Congress for the History of
Religions held at Amsterdam from September 4–9, 1950. Nominated
its first president, Van der Leeuw died a few weeks later on November
18, 1950. However, together with Friedrich Heiler, he took an active
part in shaping both the IASHR agenda and the arrangement of the
first International Congress for the History of Religions after the war.

---

[149] Van Dam considers, Arthur Seyß-Inquart – the Reich commissioner for the
occupied Netherlands – decides, Van Dam swallows. Both quotations from Gerhard
Hirschfeld, "Die Universität Leiden im Nationalsozialismus," *Geschichte und Gesellschaft*
23 (1997), pp. 560–591, here p. 571. See also Peter Jan Knegtmans, "Jan van Dam
und die Reform des Unterrichtswesens in den besetzten Niederlanden," in Burkhard
Dietz et al., eds., *Griff nach dem Westen*, vol. 2, pp. 1091–1109.

[150] Jan de Vries, *Onze voorouders* ('s-Gravenhage: De Schouw, 1942). The National
Socialist publisher De Schouw was ordered to print 100,000 copies of the booklet
for school use. See B. Henkes and B. Rzoska, "Volkskunde und 'Volkstumspolitik' der
SS in den Niederlanden," in Burkhard Dietz et al., eds., *Griff nach dem Westen*, vol. 1,
p. 314 and P. J. Knegtmans, "Jan van Dam und die Reform des Unterrichtswesens in
den besetzten Niederlanden," in ibid., vol. 2, p. 1104.

[151] Rob van Ginkel, "Re-creating 'Dutchness': Cultural colonisation in post-war
Holland," *Nations and Nationalism* 10–4 (2004), pp. 421–438, here p. 425.

Immediately before that event, Van der Leeuw had gotten involved in the constitutive sessions of the German historians of religions taking place at Marburg castle from August 28 until September 1, 1950.[152] A newly elected board, the nucleus of the German Association for the Study of Religions, consisted of Heinrich Frick, Friedrich Heiler, Johannes Baptist Aufhauser, Gustav Mensching, and Erich Fascher of whom the first three formed the German delegation to attend the Amsterdam congress.

Considering the religious, scholarly, and political convictions of Van der Leeuw and Heiler, it is not surprising that the IASHR managed to evade all discussion of the past. As if nothing had happened since the 1935 Brussels conference, the IASHR tried to start from scratch, drawing a definite line at its inception. The firm will to avoid touching the preceding era was paramount among the 200 participants. Even those who had not been politically engaged previously associated themselves with the proscription of everything that might have been reminiscent of the time of fascism. If scholars of religions detect such practices among the indigenous peoples of Polynesia, they normally describe them as a forceful taboo to aid in barring bad demons. But how could it be possible to escape from reality to the ivory tower of an alleged non-political scholarship after World War II? What were the reasons for that rampant wish to close the eyes and to press the resume button, so to speak? Some 55 or 60 million people had lost their lives on the various battlefields of the war and as civilians indirectly affected by its consequences. About six million Jews were killed by the Germans. If there was no interest in deliberating on their fate as human beings, the violent and destructive assault on their religion ought to have at least posed a scholarly problem to the international community of historians of religions. Not to mention the great many other crimes and the total destruction of the economic and social infrastructure in many parts of Europe and Asia. A critical debate of the fascist era and of the active role religion and the study of religion had played in it should have been a primary task of the IASHR, if not its raison

---

[152] See the report of Heinrich Frick in the *Theologische Literaturzeitung* 10 (1950), col. 633–637. This "Marburger Schloßkongreß" originated from a previous convention of Protestant university theologians at Marburg in March 1950. On March 29, 1950, the "religionswissenschaftliche Sektion des Theologentages" decided to promote the study of religion in the future. See again Frick's report in the *Theologische Literaturzeitung* 4/5 (1950), col. 306, indicating the close liaison between the study of religion and Protestant theology.

d'être. Yet, everything that could have had the slightest connection with the past was ousted. The IASHR conference in 1950 chose to address "The mythical-ritual pattern in civilization" without any relation to the actual destruction of civilization that had occurred a short time before. The title of Mircea Eliade's lecture expressed the intention of the Amsterdam congress in a nutshell: "Mythes cosmogoniques et guérisons magiques."[153] What the newly established IASHR had in mind was magic healing and an occupation with "eternal" cosmological structures. The founding of the IASHR itself constituted in that regard an imaginative and myth-laden cosmogony.[154]

In May 1945, Ian de Vries, the Dutch scapegoat in Eliade's narrative, was sentenced to twelve months imprisonment and lost any prospect of his reinstatement in an academic teaching post. Consequently, he concentrated on his publications. A.D. Kylstra has counted 16 books and 75 articles De Vries wrote between 1951 and 1964 when he died.[155] Among them were highly problematic texts. In the group of nine articles for the renowned encyclopedia *Die Religion in Geschichte und Gegenwart*, one dealt with the history and development of German studies.[156] Of course, a critical account of that discipline, which had compromised its reputation like no other university subject in Germany, was not to be expected. As it appears now, he was chosen as author exactly for that reason. In his text on the swastika, De Vries managed to omit every mention of the National Socialist period with a single word.[157] And his article on the Indo-Germans was a great setback compared to the excellent contribution of Herman Güntert to the second RGG edition

[153] See the summary of Eliade's paper in the *Proceedings of the 7th congress for the history of religions*, ed. by Claas J. Bleeker et al. (Amsterdam: North-Holland Publ. Comp., 1951), p. 180f.

[154] It is tempting to cross-check Eliade's cosmogonical mythology and to reconnect it with the constitution of the IASHR: "Sur le niveau cosmologique, ces cérémonies [des sociétés archaïques, H.J.] représentaient la destruction de l'Univers et la réactualisation du Chaos, suivies par une nouvelle Création. Le scénario rituel comprenait l'extinction des feux, la confession des péchés, l'expulsion d'un bouc émissaire, la visite des âmes des morts – suivies par des luttes rituelles entre deux groupes adverses, l'allumage d'un feu nouveau, la récitation du mythe cosmogoniques, etc." Ibid., p. 180. However, as it seems, the item *confessione dei peccati* evoked little response compared to the others.

[155] Andries Dirk Kylstra, "Vries, Jan de (1890–1964)," in *Biographisch-Bibliographisches Kirchenlexikon* 13 (1998), col. 108–117, here col. 108. The article is available on the Internet on www.bautz.de/bbkl, s.v. Vries, Jan de.

[156] Jan de Vries, "Germanistik," in *Die Religion in Geschichte und Gegenwart*, 3rd ed., vol. 2 (1958), col. 1242–1245. The other topics were: Fremde I, Freundschaft I, Gastfreundschaft, Glück, Haine, Hakenkreuz, Indogermanen, Mannhardt.

[157] Jan de Vries, "Hakenkreuz," in ibid., 3rd ed., vol. 3 (1959), col. 31f.

in 1929.[158] 30 years later, and 15 years after the downfall of the Third Reich, De Vries returned to racial arguments – though avoiding becoming too explicit.[159] With both his writings and his political past, De Vries conformed very well to the general pattern of the third edition of *Die Religion in Geschichte und Gegenwart*. This eminent Protestant encyclopedia offered a sanctuary for former adherents of National Socialism who faced similar difficulties in their attempt to return to the university and who were in need of publication opportunities. The list of authors in the third edition of the RGG, which appeared from 1957 until 1962, includes high ranking members of the Reich Minister of Science and Education, members of the NSDAP, of the SS, of the Reich Security Main Office, of the "Ahnenerbe" of the SS, of the SD as well as zealous antisemites.[160] A native collaborator from the Netherlands meant another iridescent spot of color in that well-arranged bouquet.

Nordic philologist and historian of religions Åke Ohlmarks, discussed by Andreas Åkerlund, differs from the general scheme of intellectuals addressed in this book in some regards. Quite an average scholar, Ohlmarks does not fit into the usual classification scheme within the study of religion. Yet in 1944, he was lucky enough to be nominated director of a newly founded institute of science of religion at the University of Greifswald. Having studied philosophy, Nordic philology and history of religions at the University of Lund, Ohlmarks had worked as lecturer in Swedish. In 1937, he published his dissertation on old Norse mythology followed by a book on the problem of shamanism in 1939. Both works were influenced by Wilhelm Schmidt's theory of cultural circles and both were poorly received by historians of religions. Most notably, his distinction between a "true-arctic" and a "sub-arctic" shamanism and his connection of the first with a Nordic patriarchal and the second with a matriarchal culture were heavily criticized.

Since establishing himself at a Swedish university proved hopeless, Ohlmarks joined the "Riksföreningen Sverige-Tyskland," the Swedish-German Society founded in 1937 for the promotion of political and

---

[158] Hermann Güntert, "Indogermanen," in ibid., 2nd ed., vol. 3 (1929), col. 249–252.

[159] Jan de Vries, "Indogermanen," in ibid., 3rd ed., vol. 3 (1959), col. 723–726.

[160] To name but a few: Gustav Bebermeyer, Georg Bertram, Heinrich Bornkamm, Ernst Ludwig Dietrich, Karl August Eckhardt, Wilhelm Engel, Karl Epting, Günther Franz, Karl Friedrich Euler, Gerhard Heberer, Johannes Heckel, Johannes Hempel, Otto Höfler, Herbert Jankuhn, Karl Georg Kuhn, Martin Redeker, Franz Taeschner, Reinhard Wittram, Max Wundt.

cultural relations with the new Germany. Particularly the chairman of the society, the antisemitic New Testament scholar of the University of Lund, Hugo Odeberg, gave Ohlmarks the impression that a membership in that organization would be useful for his further advancement. Because Odeberg was also a member of the Institute for the Study and Eradication of Jewish Influence on German Church Life ("Institut zur Erforschung und Beseitigung des jüdischen Einflusses auf das deutsche kirchliche Leben"), inaugurated in 1939 at Eisenach with the intention of cleansing the Christian church from all Jewish remnants, Ohlmarks met a number of academics in Germany. Ohlmarks joined this "Institutum Antijudaicum" which counted several dozen university teachers among its collaborators. The institute was interested in Ohlmarks' expert knowledge of old Norse mythology. But Ohlmarks was neither an ardent antisemite nor did he adopt racial arguments. Nor was he a devoted Christian. He simply wanted to embark on a professional career. His wish turned out successful; the contact with Wilhelm Koepp, who also worked for the Eisenach institute, resulted in a partnership with the theological department at the University of Greifswald. Koepp tried to defend Protestant theology under difficult political circumstances by emphasizing both the objective nature of religious studies and the political usefulness of Nordic studies undertaken by Ohlmarks. Together with a grant from an influential member of the Swedish delegation in Berlin, who was a personal friend of Ohlmarks, a new institute of science of religions at the University of Greifswald was formed in November 1944. Of course, the impact of the institute was limited – it lasted only a few months. But its establishment is significant since it shows that religious studies could be embedded in a general Protestant milieu, even at the end of 1944.

The book's fifth section, on "the quest for a new understanding of religion," starts with the Polish psychologist of religion Władysław Witwicki. His book on "The faith of the enlightened" – a French translation appeared five years after the Polish original under the title *La foi des éclairés* in 1939 – had made a very interesting and valuable contribution to a sound methodology for the psychology of religion. Halina Grzymała-Moszczyńska portrays Witwicki's scientific development in Poland as one which had been hampered by grave difficulties emanating from the far-reaching impact of Catholicism in Poland. Educated and raised in a devout Catholic family, Witwicki emancipated himself from the doctrinal belief of his youth during his studies. Nominated professor of psychology at the University of Warsaw in 1919, his subsequent problems as an empirically oriented scholar exemplify the predicament of an independent occupation with religion in a country where the influence of a state church dominated. An autonomous psychology of religion turned out to be impossible in Poland during those times. Witwicki faced the additional problem that the psychology of religion was not a distinct part of general psychology and that its emergence stood under the influence of church interests regarding possible effects on pastoral theology and speculative cogitation on the religious experience of men.

In a significant innovation, Witwicki turned to experimental methods and well-elaborated oral interviews to scrutinize the religious convictions of educated young people. His findings pointed to a marked discrepancy between the religious dogmas of the church and the religious conduct of his interviewees, which might be interpreted as an early example of a cognitive dissonance between personal faith and ethical judgments. Obviously habit, education, and the cultural background had a much greater impact than church dogmas and religious teachings. This kind of academic scholarship could hardly meet a friendly response in the Polish society of the interwar period. Some years before his book came out in 1935, Witwicki presented his findings at the meetings of the psychological section of the Philosophical Society in Warsaw. His lectures triggered severe calamities. Fearing a backlash from the bishop of Warsaw, the psychological quarterly *Kwartalnik Psychologiczny* refused to publish the work. Wiwicki's public appearance as a scholar with secular views sparked massive opposition. Nationalistic youth groups disturbed his university teaching and threatened Witwicki personally. In their mind, Polishness and Catholicism constituted a uniform entity and every attempt at a secular interpretation of religion jeopardized not only the rights of the church but the fundamentals of the Polish society as such. Witwicki left Warsaw in 1943, after the German attack on Poland. Five years later, he died in Konstancin, a few kilometers south of the Polish capital.

Petteri Pietikäinen's article on "C.G. Jung's psycho-utopia and the 'German revolution'" also addresses the psychology of religion, though Jung's contribution to that discipline remains in dispute. Nevertheless, Jung is typically included in the already mentioned collection of classics of the academic study of religion.[161] Less pertinent to the academic psychology of religion in a narrow sense, Jung's views on religion

---

[161] Christoph Morgenthaler, "Carl Gustav Jung (1875–1961)," in Axel Michaels, ed., *Klassiker der Religionswissenschaft*, pp. 234–246.

were part of a broader spiritually motivated search for a psychological authenticity reaching the religious depth of the human soul. His quest for generic archetypes greatly resembled the occupation of Jakob Wilhelm Hauer with the history of religions in pursuit of so-called religious "Urphänomene" involving a meta-empirical recognition and transhistorical laws. After World War I, both Jung and Hauer looked for new ways and means to regain the lost emotional immediacy between this and the transcendent world, a characteristic of previous times. In Hauer, Jung met a religious studies scholar congenial to his own views who also sought a new scientific understanding of the religious nature of men. When Jung met Hauer for the first time in 1930 at a conference in Baden-Baden, Hauer was anything but inclined towards National Socialism. As Petteri Pietikäinen has shown in an earlier article, the common link between the two was a voelkish utopianism that approached the realm of religion as well as that of the unconsciousness.[162] Hauer repeatedly participated in conferences organized by C.G. Jung. In 1932, Hauer attained the famous Zurich Kundalini seminar, in 1934 the second Eranos conference, and in 1938 the seminar at the Psychological Club in Zurich, where he gave a lecture series on constitutional laws in the history of religions.[163] In fact, the worldview orientations of Jung and Hauer bore significant resemblances, deserving of further research.[164]

The problem with Jung and Hauer is that, as Pietikäinen rightly emphasizes, they both exceeded the limits of their scholarship. What they wanted was not merely a scientific answer to scientific questions but a solution to prodigious worldview problems. Both were on a quest for a spiritual revitalization *extra ecclesiam*, and both shared the prophetic and declamatory style when talking about religious myths

---

[162] Petteri Pietikäinen, "The 'Volk' and its unconsciousness: Jung, Hauer and the 'German revolution'," *Journal of Contemporary History* 35–4 (2000), pp. 523–539. Jung's voelkish background is also emphasized by Richard Noll, *The Jung cult. Originis of a charismatic movement* (Princeton: Princeton University Press, 1994) and idem, *The Aryan Christ. The secret life of Carl Jung* (New York: Random House, 1997).

[163] Regarding all three events, interesting materials have been handed down in Hauer's literary remains. Of particular relevance are the manuscripts of Hauer's two lecture series in 1932 and 1938 (including the subsequent discussions) as well as some unpublished letters not included in Jung's correpondence.

[164] Margarate Dierks has dedicated a special chapter to the relationship between Jung and Hauer in her biography of Hauer. See idem, *Jakob Wilhelm Hauer, 1881–1962* (Heidelberg: Lambert Schneider, 1986), pp. 283–299. Yet the interpretation of Dierks, a former member of the Ludendorff movement, is highly problematic.

and symbols. During the period when Jung and Hauer were close, Jung hoped that the Third Reich might provide the political background for an awakening of the forces of the unconsciousness. Pietikäinen rightly advocates that it would be appropriate to consider Jung's estimation of the political development in Nazi Germany within the context of and as an element of his psychological agenda. He points out that Jung interpreted National Socialism in terms of a positive individuation writ large on the level of German nationalism. After an initial phase of regression, as Jung thought, the positive effects would gain the upper hand and the German Volk would pass through a phase of religious and psychological regeneration. Comparable to Hauer, who wanted to explain the awakening of National Socialist Germany with a racially based theory of religion, Jung intended a depth psychology that would enlighten on the psychological fundamentals of the German revolution. One reason why the relationship between Jung and Hauer came to an end in 1938 was Hauer's embrace of National Socialist racism in a way that Jung could not accept.

Hiroshi Kubota's paper on the two Japanese studies scholars, Wilhelm Gundert and Junyu Kitayama, deals with their efforts to reinterpret the religious history of Japan in accordance with the new political developments in their countries. The rapprochement between Germany and Japan resulted in the Anti-Comintern Pact in 1936 (joined by fascist Italy the year later) and the Triple Axis-Pact in 1941, and it entailed a sort of Japan boom in Germany, leading to a growing number of students of japanology and of scholarly activities concerned with Japan.[165] In this context, Gundert and Kitayama tried to redefine the scientific parameters of Japanese studies, particularly with the history of Japanese religions as their specific area of interest. Their endeavor had a two-pronged intent. First, it sought to reveal religion as the basic principle of Germany and Japan. In their mind, enhancing the power of a nation required its inhabitants to strengthen their religious commitment. Second, it sought to augment the significance of Japanese studies, a marginal discipline at the fringe of the academy, which ought

---

[165] Cf. Herbert Worm, "Japanologie im Nationalsozialismus. Ein Zwischenbericht," in Gerhard Krebs and Bernd Martin, eds., *Formierung und Fall der Achse Berlin – Tokyo* (München: Iudicum Verlag, 1994), pp. 153–186. For Japanese (and Chinese) studies in the Third Reich, see the overview of the German Reich Ministry of Science and Education from 1942, re-printed in the *Newsletter Frauen und China* (now *Berliner China-Hefte*) 7 (1994), pp. 1–17.

to adapt itself to the new political constellation that had emerged in the 1930s. On the basis of an old-fashioned, philologically oriented scholarship, and with the nineteenth-century idea of Humboldtian "Bildung," such an alignment of Japanese studies seemed impossible. Kitayama and Gundert's new conceptualization intended to tap into the general voelkish trend prevailing in the German academy. Its main characteristic was the subordination of scientific learning to the demands of the German people as defined by National Socialism. The Viennese japanologist Ingrid Getreuer-Kargl has correctly stated, during a workshop on Japanese studies under National Socialism, that the principal aim in these days was not scholarly research based on objectivity and disinterest but, rather, the wish to provide politically relevant evidence for parallel developments and corresponding interests between Japan and National Socialist Germany.[166]

The rapid increase of this kind of political parallelism finds abundant corroboration in Kubota's analysis. Gundert's and Kitayama's comparisons of Japan and Germany provoked the detection of "striking" similarities and analogous developments, particularly when religion and national mentalities came under scrutiny. The impressive arbitrariness of their juxtaposition circled around the voelkish paradigm that they applied to the religious history of Japan. Shinto, especially in the form of a "State Shinto," appeared to them as a model of successful Volk formation, as Kubota put it. With the Japanese model in mind, Gundert had hoped that a solution to the confused religious situation in Germany might come forward.[167] Learning from Japan meant, above all, fortifying Germany's own national identity. Grounded on an equally stable voelkish community, National Socialist Germany would be able to fulfill its tasks just as well as Japan. But, of course, the Japanese mirror worked in reverse. It reflected the German state of affairs and expressed Gundert's homemade conceptualization in a roundabout manner. Evidently, he had molded the uniform voelkish entity of the

---

[166] Ingrid Getreuer-Kargl, "Von den langen Schatten der Vergangenheit. Bericht vom Workshop Japanologie und Nationalsozialismus am Institut für Japanologie der Universität Wien, 30. Mai – 1. Juni 1999," *Minikomi. Informationen des Akademischen Arbeitskreises* 2 (1999), pp. 32–36, here p. 34. The report is accesible at http://www.aaj.at/minikomi99.html.

[167] Cf. here also Christoph Kleine, "Religion im Dienste einer ethnisch-nationalen Identitätskonstruktion: Erörtert am Beispiel der 'Deutschen Christen' und des japanischen Shinto," *Marburg Journal of Religion* 7-1 (2002), pp. 1–17. This e-journal includes an English summary at the beginning of Kleine's article.

Japanese people according to the amalgamation of nationalism and Protestantism in Germany.

Minor dissimilarities in the interpretative scheme of Gundert and Kitayama originated from their different personal development. Kitayama was the son of a samurai and Buddhist priest and had been sent to Germany for further studies after his own ordination by order of the Pure-Land-School. At the University of Heidelberg, he completed a doctoral thesis on the metaphysics of Mahayana Buddhism under Karl Jaspers in 1931. Recommended by Heinrich Frick, the book appeared in a series co-edited by Jakob Wilhelm Hauer at the University of Tübingen. Kitayama worked for several years as assistant at the "Religionskundliche Sammlung" in Marburg where he became acquainted with Otto and Frick. On Frick's initiative, Kitayama was nominated honorary professor of cultural and religious studies of East Asia ("Kultur- und Religionskunde Ostasiens") in 1940. In his application, Frick announced that Kitayama would act as the head of the Japanese department of the "Religionskundliche Sammlung."[168] From 1936 on, Kitayama functioned as deputy of the director of the Berlin "Japan-Institut," and in 1944 he was entrusted with the task of founding a new institute for the study of East Asia ("Institut zur Erforschung und Vermittlung der Kultur- und Geistesgeschichte Ostasiens") at the "Deutsche Karls-Universität" in Prague. This plan originated from an earlier attempt by Reinhard Heydrich to establish a chair of Japanese or East Asian studies there.[169] Wilhelm Gundert, a cousin of Hermann Hesse and grandson of Hermann Gundert, the well-known missionary to India, was himself a Protestant missionary to Japan. After his return to Germany, Gundert was appointed professor of Japanese studies at the University of Hamburg. A staunch National Socialist and party member since 1934, he was nominated, in 1937, dean of the philosophy department by the Berlin authorities. From 1941 until his dismissal in 1945, Gundert acted as rector of the University of Hamburg.

---

[168] Federal Archives Berlin, BDC Kitayama, fol. 1052f. The expert opinion of Frick dated June 6, 1940.

[169] Letter of the philosophy department of the "Deutsche Karls-Universität Prag" to the Reich Ministry of Science and Education on June 23, 1943. Ibid., fol. 1076. At the "Reinhard-Heydrich Stiftung," a Japanese department had already been instituted. For the involvment of Japanese studies in foreign affairs politics of the German secret service, see Gideon Botsch, 'Politische Wissenschaft' im Zweiten Weltkrieg. Die 'Deutschen Auslandswissenschaften' im Einsatz 1940–1945 (Paderborn: Schöningh, 2006), esp. pp. 291–294.

Though racial arguments were not absent in Gundert's and Kitayama's attempt to reshape Japanese studies in Germany, their approach
was more inclined towards Karl Haushofer's "Geopolitik," which had
been adapted in a "georeligious" version by Heinrich Frick to the history
of religions. The crux of Gundert and Kitayama's voelkish paradigm
was the mutual dependence of Volk and religion. On one hand, the voelkish pre-structure of religion ought to determine the national renewal
of Japan and Germany. On the other, what shaped the voelkish setting
of a nation most was religion. Nothing determined the voelkish identity
of Japan and Germany more than their religions. Based on that tautology, Gundert and Kitayama intended to reveal two truths: first, that
the new political circumstances in Japan and Germany necessitated a
new connection of the Volk, the nation and its leaders with the divine
powers; second, that a voelkish oriented japanology would be able to
explicate the historical background of that development. However,
and this is the decisive point in Kubota's paper, the voelkish agenda of
Gundert and Kitayama relied on a conventional religious essentialism
that made it possible to assign universal features to the history of religions which then, understandably, generated that astounding parallelism.
As a result, Gundert and Kitayama's voelkish paradigm appeared as an
epiphenomenon of their phenomenological interpretation of religion.
In contrast to their presumption, only the idea of religious universalism
enabled both Japanese religions and the study of Japanese religions to
change over and adjust to the new political demands.

As it is well known, Joachim Wach was the most eminent among
scholars of religion who fell victim to the racial laws of National Socialist
Germany. In addition to him, Hans Alexander Winkler, a lecturer of
general history of religions ("Allgemeine Religionsgeschichte") at the
University of Tübingen, lost his academic position in 1933, due to his
former membership in Germany's communist party in the 1920s.[170]
Outside of the study of religion proper, for instance in oriental studies, indology, anthropology, and sociology, a considerable number of
university teachers with a research focus on religion were dismissed

---

[170] For Winkler, see my two articles "Ein Kapitel Religionswissenschaft während der
NS-Zeit: Hans Alexander Winkler (1900–1945)," *Zeitschrift für Religionswissenschaft* (1995),
pp. 137–161 and "Das tragische Leben von Hans Alexander Winkler (1900–1945) und
seiner armenischen Frau Hayastan (1901–1937)," *Bausteine zur Tübinger Universitätsgeschichte* 7 (1995), pp. 83–110. Later, Winkler joined the Foreign Office and worked at
the legations in Teheran and Cádiz. Not long before his own death in Poland, his son
was killed as a deserter by the Gestapo at the end of the war.

either for political or racial reasons. But within the study of religion, Wach was the only professor of "Religionswissenschaft" expelled from the German academy. His crime consisted in his "racial" affiliation to the Mendelssohn Bartholdy family; his mother and grandmother had been related to the German-Jewish composer Felix Mendelssohn Bartholdy, who himself was the grandson of the famous enlightenment philosopher Moses Mendelssohn. Wach's categorization as a Jew originated from the National Socialist definition of race. Particularly in the study of religion, we should remember that race was no more than an invented tradition. The classification of the Nuremberg Laws depended entirely on the religious beliefs of one's ancestors. This interconnection between race and religion has not been sufficiently recognized to date. Kurt Rudolph properly reminds us of the fact that Wach never considered himself a Jew. In fact, his political position should be characterized as that of a moderate German nationalist having volunteered for the military service during World War I. In 1935, Wach seized the chance to remain in the United States. His emigration and the further development of the Third Reich strongly impacted Wach's views. Like the members of the Frankfort School, Wach significantly modified his scientific program after 1945. This transformation of Wach's scholarship ought to be scrutinized more intensely. In Nazi Germany, Wach fell not only into oblivion but was, analogous to his physical expulsion, actively barred from the academic discourses. In 1943, the German authorities stripped him of his doctoral degree.

Wach's emigration meant an inestimable loss to the German study of religion. In the years prior to his ousting, Wach had published many books and articles promoting an independent study of religion in Germany. In particular, his Leipzig habilitation thesis from 1924 on the epistemological fundamentals of the study of religion furthered the identification process of religious studies outside of Christian theology.[171] Wach's interdisciplinary endeavors were based on an excellent knowledge of the theoretical discussions, specifically in philosophy, history, and sociology. Stressing the empirical fundamentals on which every scholarly occupation with religion has to be grounded, Wach formulated guiding principles for the methodological improvement of the study of religion. Kurt Rudolph's article is an appeal to return

---

[171] Joachim Wach, *Religionswissenschaft. Prolegomena zu ihrer wissenschaftstheoretischen Grundlegung* (Leipzig: Hinrichs, 1924).

to that eminent starting point of the academic study of religion. Its later development should be scrutinized in the perspective of Wach's habilitation thesis, which, in that light, should be considered a classic rather than a prolegomenon.

8. *De Te Fabula Narratur*

The history of the academic study of religion in the 1930s and 1940s cannot be considered apart from the history of fascism.[172] These proceedings document the substantial impact of fascist ideas on scholars of religion in many parts of Europe. Its articles clearly show that the connection between non-theological research on religion and fascist and right-wing developments did not happen accidentally and was based on factual premises. Although elements of political opportunism cannot be ignored, the particular reasons for the susceptibility of religious studies to fascist ideas must be uncovered in its own body of work. In my opinion, this intersection of interests reflected a composite set of religious, political, and scientific traits inherent to the study of religion in general.

Regarding religious and worldview matters, it is quite obvious that criticism of the established churches was an important point of common reference. Going back to older layers of nineteenth-century critiques of religion, traditional Christianity was considered behind the times and opposed to a modern understanding of life. A naïve credence in Church doctrines and Christian revelation was held to be incompatible with a scholarly perception of the world. Notwithstanding this stance, religion was still believed to be essential to humanity. Without religious commitment, the fundamentals of personal life and the strength of the nation would be jeopardized. Thus, impiousness and unbelief were held to undermine the stability of the society. Since "official" Christianity was considered unable to cope with worldview problems and spiritual disarray after 1918, alternative explanations surfaced. Given its proficiency in things religious, the relevance of the academic study

---

[172] While it is justified to differentiate fascism and National Socialism for conceptual reasons, the contrast should not be overstated. Similar to the confrontation of an intentionalist and functionalist approach in the study of antisemitism, the distinction becomes counterproductive at a certain point. Therefore "fascism" is used here in a broad sense as generic heading inclusive of the study of religion under National Socialism.

of religion necessarily increased in such circumstances. As experts in non-Christian traditions, scholars of religion had some bearing on the shaping of oppositional worldviews. Especially in the case of Aryan or Indo-Germanic Paganism, historians of religions had long been considered experts, with access to knowledge reaching far into the past.

In terms of politics, the interwar years were characterized by rising tensions and escalating conflicts approaching, in some cases, the level of civil wars. The old orders had broken down and new ones were not yet established successfully. Fascist movements originated from that turmoil and profited from its progression. Since the war and its outcome had seriously affected the nation-building processes in Europe, fascist and voelkish ideologies articulated a unity of the nation above and beyond the prevailing antagonisms based on ethnic cohesion. The ideological superstructure of the imagined folk community involved a religious point of reference in opposition to Judaism and outside of customary church structures. With that backdrop, the importance of non-theological scholars of religions intensified. For them, political parties connected with conservative clericalism were just as repellent as the parties of the left with their public atheism. Together with a long accustomed anti-establishment attitude, it was the combination of anti-reactionary and anti-bolshevist elements that could make fascism so attractive to liberal-minded intellectuals. Evidently, not the already established and politically conservative scholars of religion developed an interest in fascist ideas. It was the future-oriented, judgmental and progressive "young generation" who became magnetized by fascist reasoning. The German and Italian example clearly illustrates that fascism in power supported this intellectual avant-guard with additional money, influence and teaching positions. In return, religious studies scholars were expected to substantiate central points of the fascist agenda with their hermeneutic expertise. Becoming aware of their new significance, and recognizing the chance to join the intellectual elite of the nation, most of them did not hesitate to respond favorably to that scheme.

From the very beginning of the study of religion, a crucial problem was the question of how to adequately objectify religious phenomena. The unclear distinction between science and religion fuelled hybrid epistemologies, which consisted of elements from both sides and which oscillated between the one and the other. A purely rationalistic and anthropocentric approach was regarded as inappropriate while, conversely, open appeals to religious inspection and to theological teachings appeared to be unscientific. Constricted by the dilemma of

unbelief and dogmatic belief, historians of religions searched for ways
to reconcile the rational and irrational elements of their scientific
undertaking. Unable (and also unwilling) to think through both the
prerequisites and the consequences of that dichotomy, they left the
epistemological status of their objects in suspense. As I have tried to
make plain earlier, voelkish scholars of religion in Nazi Germany sought
to overcome this intellectual quandary with the help of a double-sided
race concept which was intended to function as *tertium comparationis*
between the religious and the rational parts of the study of religion.
But far from providing a solution to that intellectual predicament, this
approach resulted in ordinary belief structures even more dogmatic
than the doctrinaire Christian religion that constituted its point of
departure. Thus, the conventional search for a proper rationalization
of the irrational ended in an argumentative *metabasis* to the worldview
level, where logical reasoning and epistemological precision have no
footing. Pulling down the cognitive boundaries in the study of religion
opened the door for an ideologization since unequaled. If there is a
concrete lesson to learn from the study of religion under fascism, it is
a greater awareness of this destructive potential that renders the study
of religion not only prone to religious subjectivism but to uncontrollable
political exploitation as well.

Yet it seems that, in this respect, the study of religion continues to
maneuver without clear course or reliable compass. It still hopes to
sail safely past the Scylla of irreligion and the Charybdis of dogmatic
religion. With bound eyes and stopped ears, it seeks to hold a middle
course, neither prey to the monster of atheism nor drawn into the
maelstrom of a profound religiosity. To repeat, in stormy seas, such
strategies necessarily lead to unfavorable results. The analysis of the
study of religion under the spell of fascism convincingly illustrates
the importance of coming to terms with the problem of rationality in
the study of religion.

In confronting this intricate and theoretically exposed problem, one
has to take more serious account of ideological distortion in the study of
religion. It is an easy exercise to point out the black sheep, denouncing
them as fascist or fascist-like. Though historical research, especially into
fascism, requires a certain moral momentum, this should not interfere
with meticulous and disinterested scholarship. A more differentiated
approach does much greater justice to the complexity of the situation,
with a considerable range of gradations. What can we conclude from
the fact that most historians of religions shared quite similar scientific,

political, and religious views in the 1920s? Even a Joachim Wach and a Walther Wüst did not differ fundamentally. Only a few years later, Wach, the alleged Jew, left Germany as a victim of National Socialist politics while Wüst, the ideologue of the Aryan race, became one of the closest associates of Heinrich Himmler. At the same time that German authorities revoked Wach's doctoral degree, Wüst accompanied Himmler to the concentration camp of Auschwitz for an inspection tour. That the names of Wüst and Wach appear next to each other on the front page of the *Zeitschrift für Missionskunde und Religionswissenschaft* as joint members of its scientific board at the end of the 1920s is a striking symbol of the intellectual community to which scholars of religion belonged prior to the rise of fascism.

Finding apposite answers to the questions raised by the study of fascism requires further studies. They ought to include examinations of persons, institutions, journals, conferences, relevant patterns of thought, and paradigms – not only in the study of religion proper but in adjacent disciplines as well. Special emphasis should be put on the worrying fact that the study of religion denied the responsibility for its past so fervently and for such a long time. In my opinion, the time is still not ripe for reliable generalizations about the study of religion in Europe. I would be happy if this book were to give rise to further research, but also if it were to trigger intensive, controversial and heated debates. Scholars of religion should not underestimate the danger that elements of a suppressed history will return *mutato nomine*, one way or another. Even a revisionist backlash and the desire to again take up concepts developed in the 1930s appear possible. In particular, the European unification process necessitates a critical study of religion – critical of its objects and critical of itself. If they have a chance to do so, some politicians and parties in the accession countries will certainly try to utilize religion and scholarship of religion in favor of nationalist interests. In that context, scholars and scholarly concepts might be re-interpreted towards an old-fashioned criticism of Western democracy. As I have already pointed out during the jubilee congress of the International Association for the History of Religions at Durban in September 2000, I find it imperative to learn from the past in order to cope with the present. In the case of the study of religion, such a simple statement raises more difficulties than may appear at first glance.

Bibliography

Anton, Ted. *Eros, magic, and the murder of Professor Culianu.* Evanston: Northwestern University Press, 1996, Romanian trans. Bucharest: Editura Nemira, 1997, German trans. Frankfurt a.M.: Insel, 1999.

Arvidsson, Stefan. *Aryan idols. Indo-European mythology as ideology and science.* Chicago: University of Chicago Press, 2006.

Baillet, Philippe. "Julius Evola et Mircea Eliade (1927–1974): Une amitié manquée, avec des extraits de deux lettres d'Evola à Eliade." *Les deux étandards* 1 (September/ December 1988), pp. 45–55.

Behringer, Wolfgang. "Das 'Ahnenerbe' der Buchgesellschaft. Zum Neudruck einer Germanen-Edition des NS-Ideologen Otto Höfler." *Sowi* 27 (1998), pp. 283–289.

Benavides, Gustavo. "Guiseppe Tucci, or buddhology in the age of fascism." In Donald S. Lopez, ed. *Curators of the Buddha. The study of Buddhism under colonialism.* Chicago: University of Chicago Press, 1997, pp. 161–196.

Berger, Adriana. "Fascism and religion in Romania." *Annals of Scholarship* 6 (1989), pp. 455–465.

———. "Mircea Eliade's vision for a new humanism." *Society* 30–5 (1993), pp. 84–87.

———. "Mircea Eliade: Romanian fascism and the history of religions in the United States." In Nancy A. Harrowitz, ed. *Tainted greatness. Antisemitism and cultural heroes.* Philadelphia: Temple University Press, 1994, pp. 51–74.

Berggren, Lena. "Swedish fascism – why bother?" *Journal of Contemporary History* 37–3 (2002), pp. 395–417.

Bleeker, Claas J., et al., eds. *Proceedings of the 7th congress for the history of religions.* Amsterdam: North-Holland Publishing Company, 1951.

Bonk, Magdalena. *Deutsche Philologie in München.* Berlin: Duncker & Humblot, 1995.

Botsch, Gideon. *'Politische Wissenschaft' im Zweiten Weltkrieg. Die 'Deutschen Auslandswissenschaften' im Einsatz 1940–1945.* Paderborn: Schöningh, 2006.

Brunotte, Ulrike. *Zwischen Eros und Krieg. Männerbund und Ritual in der Moderne.* Berlin: Klaus Wagenbach, 2004.

Comité Directeur et Collaborateurs de l'Institut de Philologie et d'Histoire, ed. *Mélanges Franz Cumont. Annuaire de l'Institut de Philologie et d'Histoire Orientales et Slaves.* 2 vols. Bruxelles: Université libre, 1936.

Culianu, Ioan P. "Mircea Eliade und die blinde Schildkröte." In Hans Peter Duerr, ed. *Die Mitte der Welt. Aufsätze zu Mircea Eliade.* Frankfurt a.M.: Suhrkamp, 1984, pp. 216–243.

———. "The correspondence between Mircea Eliade and Ioan Petru Culianu." Trans. from the Romanian original by Sorana Corneanu. *Archaeus* 8–1/4 (2004), pp. 341–364.

Davies, Peter and Derek Lynch, eds. *The Routledge companion to fascism and the far right.* London et al.: Routledge, 2002.

Dierks, Margarate. *Jakob Wilhelm Hauer, 1881–1962.* Heidelberg: Lambert Schneider, 1986.

Dietz, Burkhard et al., eds. *Griff nach dem Westen. Die 'Westforschung' der völkisch-nationalen Wissenschaften zum nordwesteuropäischen Raum (1919–1960).* 2 vols. Münster: Waxmann, 2003.

Dipper, Christof et al., eds. *Faschismus und Faschismen im Vergleich. Wolfgang Schieder zum 60. Geburtstag.* Köln: SH Verlag, 1998.

Doležavolá, Iva et al., eds. *The academic study of religion during the Cold War: East and west.* New York et al.: Lang, 2001.

Dow, James R. and Hannjost Lixfeld, eds. *The nazification of an academic discipline: Folklore in the Third Reich.* Bloomington: Indiana University Press, 1994.

Dubuisson, Daniel. *Mythologies du XXᵉ siècle.* Lille: Presses universitaires de Lille, 1993.

Eatwell, Roger. "Towards a new model of generic fascism." *Journal of Theoretical Politics* (1992), pp. 161–194.

———. "Reflections on fascism and religion." In Leonard Weinberg and Ami Pedahzur, eds. *Religious fundamentalism and political extremism*. London: Frank Cass, 2004, pp. 145–166.

Ellinger, Ekkehard. *Deutsche Orientalistik zur Zeit des Nationalsozialismus 1933–1945*. Edingen-Neckarhausen: deux mondes, 2006.

Emberland, Terje. *Religion og rase. Nyhedenskap og nazisme i Norge 1933–1945*. Oslo: Humanist forlag, 2003.

Faber, Richard. *Roma aeterna. Zur Kritik der 'konservativen Revolution'*. Würzburg: Koenigshausen & Neumann, 1981.

———. *Lateinischer Faschismus. Über Carl Schmitt – den Römer und Katholiken*. Berlin et al.: Philo, 2001.

——— ed. *Der Protestantismus – Ideologie, Konfession oder Kultur?* Würzburg: Königshausen & Neumann, 2003.

——— ed. *Katholizismus in Geschichte und Gegenwart*. Königshausen & Neumann, 2005.

Finnestad, Ragnhild Bjerre. "The study of religions in Norway." *Method & Theory in the Study of Religion* 13 (2001), pp. 243–253.

Flasche, Rainer. "Religionsmodelle und Erkenntnisprinzipien der Religionswissenschaft in der Weimarer Zeit." In Hubert Cancik, ed. *Religions- und Geistesgeschichte der Weimarer Republik*. Düsseldorf: Patmos, 1982, pp. 261–276.

———. "Religiöse Entwürfe und religiöse Wirkungen von Religionswissenschaftlern." In Peter Antes, ed. *Die Religion von Oberschichten. Religion, Profession, Intellektualismus*. Marburg: Diagonal, 1989, pp. 203–217.

———. "Der Irrationalismus in der Religionswissenschaft und dessen Begründung in der Zeit zwischen den Weltkriegen." In Hans G. Kippenberg and Brigitte Luchesi, eds. *Religionswissenschaft und Kulturkritik*. Marburg: Diagonal, 1991, pp. 243–257.

Gajek, Esther. "Germanenkunde und Nationalsozialismus. Zur Verflechtung von Wissenschaft und Politik am Beispiel Otto Höflers." In Richard Faber, ed. *Politische Religion – religiöse Politik*. Würzburg: Königshausen & Neumann, 1999, pp. 173–203.

Gandini, Mario. "Raffaele Pettazzoni nelle spire del fascismo (1931–1933)." *Strada maestra* 50 (2001), pp. 19–183.

———. "Raffaele Pettazzoni negli anni 1937–1938." *Strada maestra* 54 (2003), pp. 53–232.

———. "Il fondo Pettazzoni della biblioteca communale 'G.C. Croce' di San Giovanni in Persiceto (Bologna)." *Archaeus* 7–3/4 (2003), pp. 291–295.

Gentile, Emilio. "Fascism as political religion." *Journal of Contemporary History* 25 (1990), pp. 229–251.

———. "Fascism, totalitarianism and political religion: Definitions and critical reflections on criticism and interpretation. In Roger Griffin, ed. *Fascism, totalitarianism and political religion*. London et al.: Routledge, 2005, pp. 32–81.

Geoffrey, G. Field. "Nordic Racism." *Journal of the History of Ideas* 38–3 (1977), pp. 523–540.

Getreuer-Kargl, Ingrid. "Von den langen Schatten der Vergangenheit. Bericht vom Workshop Japanologie und Nationalsozialismus am Institut für Japanologie der Universität Wien, 30. Mai – 1. Juni 1999." *Minikomi* 2 (1999), pp. 32–36.

Ginkel, Rob van and Barbara Henkes. "On peasants and 'primitive peoples': Moments of rapprochement and distance between folklore studies and anthropology in the Netherlands." *Ethnos* 68–1 (2003), pp. 112–134.

Ginkel, Rob van. "Re-creating 'Dutchness': Cultural colonisation in post-war Holland." *Nations and Nationalism* 10–4 (2004), pp. 421–438.

Griffin, Roger, ed. *Fascism*. Oxford: Oxford University Press, 1995.

——— ed. *International fascism. Theories, causes and the new consensus*. London: Arnold, 1998.

——. "The primacy of culture: The current growth (or manufacture) of consenus within fascist studies." *Journal of Contemporary History* 37–1 (2002), pp. 121–143.

—— ed. *Fascism, totalitarianism and political religion.* London et al.: Routledge, 2005.

Grottanelli, Cristiano. "Mircea Eliade, Carl Schmitt, René Guénon, 1942." *Revue de l'histoire des religions* 219–3 (2002), pp. 325–356.

——. "Fruitful death: Mircea Eliade and Ernst Jünger on human sacrifice, 1937–1945." *Numen* 52 (2005), pp. 116–145.

Grüttner, Michael. *Biographisches Lexikon zur nationalsozialistischen Wissenschaftspolitik.* Heidelberg: Synchron, 2004.

Grzymała-Moszczyńska, Halina and Henryk Hoffmann. "The science of religion in Poland: Past and present." *Method & Theory in the Study of Religion* 10 (1998), pp. 352–372.

Güntert, Hermann. "Indogermanen." *Die Religion in Geschichte und Gegenwart.* 2nd ed., vol. 3 (1929), col. 249–252.

——. "Neue Zeit – neues Ziel." *Wörter und Sachen* 19, New Series 1 (1938), pp. 1–11.

Hall, Stuart et al. eds. *Die Camera obscura der Ideologie.* Berlin: Argument, 1984.

Handoca, Mircea, ed. *Mircea Eliade şi corrrepsondenţii săi, vol. 1 (A–E).* Bucharest: Editura Minerva, 1993.

——. *Mircea Eliade, Europa, Asia, America.... Corresponenţa vol. 1, A–H.* Bucharest: Humanitas, 1999.

——. *'Dosarul' Mircea Eliade.* Vols. 1–9. Bucharest: Curtea Veche, 1998–2004.

Hanisch, Ludmila. "Akzentverschiebung – Zur Geschichte der Semitistik und Islamwissenschaft während des 'Dritten Reichs'. *Berichte zur Wissenschaftsgeschichte* 18 (1995), pp. 217–226.

——. *Die Nachfolger der Exegeten. Deutschsprachige Erforschung des Vorderen Orients in der ersten Hälfte des 20. Jahrhunderts.* Wiesbaden: Harrassowitz, 2003.

Haug, Wolfgang Fritz. *Der hilflose Antifaschismus. Zur Kritik der Vorlesungsreihe über Wissenschaft und NS an deutschen Universitäten.* 2nd ed. Frankfurt a.M.: Suhrkamp, 1968.

——. "Annäherung an die faschistische Modalität des Ideologischen." In Manfred Behrens et al., eds. *Faschismus und Ideologie.* Hamburg: Argument, 1980, pp. 44–80.

Hausmann, Frank-Rutger. *'Deutsche Geisteswissenschaft' im Zweiten Weltkrieg. Die 'Aktion Ritterbusch' (1940–1945).* Dresden: Dresden University Press, 1998, 2nd ed. 2002.

——. *'Auch im Krieg schweigen die Musen nicht'. Die Deutschen Wissenschaftlichen Institute im Zweiten Weltkrieg.* Göttingen: Vandenhoeck & Ruprecht, 2001.

Heinen, Armin. *Die Legion 'Erzengel Michael' in Rumänien – soziale Bewegung und politische Organisation. Ein Beitrag zum Problem des internationalen Faschismus.* München: R. Oldenbourg, 1986, Romanian trans. Bucharest: Humanitas, 1999.

——. "Erscheinungsformen des europäischen Faschismus." In Christof Dipper et al., eds. *Europäische Sozialgeschichte. Festschrift für Wolfgang Schieder.* Berlin: Duncker und Humblot, 2000, pp. 3–20.

Heinrich, Fritz. *Die deutsche Religionswissenschaft und der Nationalsozialismus. Eine ideologiekritische und wissenschaftsgeschichtliche Untersuchung.* Petersberg: Michael Imhof Verlag, 2002.

Heizmann, Wilhelm. "Germanische Männerbünde." In Rahul Peter Das and Gerhard Meiser, eds. *Geregeltes Ungestüm. Bruderschaften und Jugendbünde bei indogermanischen Völkern.* Bremen: Hempen Verlag, 2002, pp. 117–138.

Henkes, Barbara and Björn Rzoska. "Volkskunde und 'Volkstumspolitik' der SS in den Niederlanden. Hans Ernst Schneider und seine 'großgermanischen' Ambitionen für den niederländischen Raum." In Burkhard Dietz et al., eds. *Griff nach dem Westen. Die 'Westforschung' der völkisch-nationalen Wissenschaften zum nordwesteuropäischen Raum (1919–1960).* 2 vols. Münster et al.: Waxmann, 2003, vol. 1, pp. 291–323.

Heschel, Susannah. "New Testament Scholarship on the 'Aryan Jesus' during the Third Reich." In Benjamin G. Wright, ed. *A Multiform heritage. Studies on early Judaism and Christianity in honor of Robert A. Kraft.* Atlanta: Scholars Press, 1999, pp. 303–321.

Hirschfeld, Gerhard. "Die Universität Leiden im Nationalsozialismus." *Geschichte und Gesellschaft* 23 (1997), pp. 560–591.

Hjelde, Sigurd. "The science of religion and theology. The question of their interrelationship." In Arie L. Molendijk and Peter Pels, eds. *Religion in the making. The emergence of the sciences of religion.* Leiden et al.: Brill, 1998, pp. 99–128.

—— ed. *Man, meaning, and mystery. 100 years of history of religions in Norway. The heritage of W. Brede Kristensen.* Leiden et al.: Brill, 2000.

——. *Sigmund Mowinckel und seine Zeit. Leben und Werk eines norwegischen Alttestamentlers.* Tübingen: Mohr Siebeck, 2006.

Hock, Hans Henrich. "Did Indo-European linguistics prepare the ground for Nazism? Lessons from the past for the present and the future." In Brigitte L.M. Bauer and Georges-Jean Pinault, eds. *Language in time and space. A Festschrift for Werner Winter on the occasion of his 80th birthday.* Berlin et al.: Mouton de Gruyter, 2003, pp. 167–187.

Höfler, Otto. *Kultische Geheimbünde der Germanen.* Frankfurt: Moritz Diesterweg, 1934.

Hofstee, Willem. *Goden en Mensen. De godsdienst wetenschap van Gerardus van der Leeuw.* Kampen: Kok Agora, 1997.

Hutton, Christopher M. *Linguistics and the Third Reich. Mother-tongue fascism, race and the science of language.* London et al.: Routledge, 1999.

Ioanid, Radu. *The sword of the Archangel. Fascist ideology in Romania.* Boulder: East European Monographs, 1990.

——. *The Holocaust in Romania. The destruction of Jews and Gypsies under the Antonescu regime, 1940–1944.* Chicago: Ivan R. Dee, 2000.

——. "The sacralised politics of the Romanian Iron Guard." In Roger Griffin, ed. *Fascism, totalitarianism and political religion.* London et al.: Routledge, 2005, pp. 125–159.

Jacobeit, Wolfgang et al. eds. *Völkische Wissenschaft. Gestalten und Tendenzen der deutschen und österreichischen Volkskunde in der ersten Hälfte des 20. Jahrhunderts.* Wien et al.: Böhlau, 1994.

Junginger, Horst. "Ein Kapitel Religionswissenschaft während der NS-Zeit: Hans Alexander Winkler (1900–1945)." *Zeitschrift für Religionswissenschaft* 2 (1995), pp. 137–161.

——. "Das tragische Leben von Hans Alexander Winkler (1900–1945) und seiner armenischen Frau Hayastan (1901–1937)." *Bausteine zur Tübinger Universitätsgeschichte* 7 (1995), pp. 83–110.

——. *Von der philologischen zur völkischen Religionswissenschaft. Das Fach Religionswissenschaft an der Universität Tübingen von der Mitte des 19. Jahrhunderts bis zum Ende des Dritten Reiches.* Stuttgart: Steiner, 1999.

——. "Völkerkunde und Religionswissenschaft, zwei nationalsozialistische Geisteswissenschaften?" In Bernhard Streck, ed. *Ethnologie und Nationalsozialismus.* Gehren: Escher, 2000, pp. 51–66.

——. "Das Überleben der Religionswissenschaft im Nationalsozialismus." *Zeitschrift für Religionswissenschaft* 9 (2001), pp. 149–167.

——. "Christel Matthias Schröder und seine Bedeutung für die deutsche Religionswissenschaft." *Zeitschrift für Religionswissenschaft* 9 (2001), pp. 235–268.

——. "Das 'Arische Seminar' der Universität Tübingen 1940–1945." In Heidrun Brückner et al., eds. *Indienforschung im Zeitenwandel. Analysen und Dokumente zur Indologie und Religionswissenschaft in Tübingen.* Tübingen: Attempto, 2003, pp. 176–207.

——. "Tübinger Exekutoren der Endlösung. Effiziente Massenmörder an vorderster Front der SS-Einsatzgruppen und des Sicherheitsdienstes." *Schwäbisches Tagblatt,* June 18, 2003, p. 29.

—— and Martin Finkenberger, eds. *Im Dienste der Lügen. Herbert Grabert (1901–1978) und seine Verlage.* Aschaffenburg: Alibri, 2004.

——. "Die Tübinger Schule der 'völkischen Religionswissenschaft' in den dreißiger und vierziger Jahren." Ibid., pp. 10–35.

——. "Herbert Grabert als völkischer Religionswissenschaftler: Der Glaube des deutschen Bauerntums." Ibid., pp. 36–68.

——. "Sigrid Hunke: Europe's new religion and its old stereotypes." In Hubert Can-
cik and Uwe Puschner, eds. *Antisemitismus, Paganismus, Völkische Religion. Anti-Semitism,
Paganism voelkish religion.* München: Saur, 2004, pp. 151–162.
——. "Politische Wissenschaft. Reichspogromnacht: Ein bisher unbekanntes Gutachten
des antisemitischen Theologen Gerhard Kittel über Herschel Grynszpan." *Süddeutsche
Zeitung,* September 11, 2005, p. 13.
——. "'Judenforschung' in Tübingen – Von der jüdischen zur antijüdischen Religions-
wissenschaft." *Simon Dubnow Institute Yearbook* 5 (2006), pp. 375–398.
——. "Das Bild des Juden in der nationalsozialistischen Judenforschung." In Andrea
Hoffmann et al., eds. *Die kulturelle Seite des Antisemitismus zwischen Aufklärung und Schoah.*
Tübingen: Tübinger Vereinigung für Volkskunde e.V., 2006, pp. 171–220.
——. "Religionswissenschaft im Nationalsozialismus. Die Geschichte einer gescheiter-
ten Emanzipation." In Jürgen Elvert and Jürgen Sikora, eds. *Kulturwissenschaften und
Nationalsozialismus.* Köln 2007 (in print).
——. "Archiv für Religionswissenschaft," "Brachmann, Wilhelm (1900–1994),"
"Grabert, Herbert (1901–1978)," "Hauer Jakob Wilhelm (1881–1962)," "Huth, Otto
(1906–1998)," "Wüst, Walther (1901–1993)," "Völkische Religionswissenschaft,"
"Zeitschrift für Geistes- und Glaubensgeschichte." In Michael Fahlbusch and Ingo
Haar, eds. *Handbuch völkischer Wissenschaften.* München: Saur, 2007 (in print).
Kallis, A. Aristotle, ed. *The fascism reader.* London et al.: Routledge, 2003.
Kater, Michael. *Das 'Ahnenerbe der SS' 1935–1945: Ein Beitrag zur Kulturpolitik des Dritten
Reiches.* Stuttgart: Deutsche Verlags Anstalt, 1974, 3rd ed. München: Oldenbourg,
2003.
Kippenberg, Hans G. *Die Entdeckung der Religionsgeschichte. Religionswissenschaft und Moderne.*
München: Beck, 1997.
Klee, Ernst. *Das Personenlexikon zum Dritten Reich. Wer war was vor und nach 1945?* Frankfurt
am Main: S. Fischer, 2003.
Kleine, Christoph. "Religion im Dienste einer ethnisch-nationalen Identitätskonstruk-
tion: Erörtert am Beispiel der 'Deutschen Christen' und des japanischen Shinto."
Marburg Journal of Religion 7-1 (2002), pp. 1–17.
Knegtmans, Peter. "Jan van Dam und die Reform des Unterrichtswesens in den besetzten Niederlanden." In Burkhard Dietz et al., eds. *Griff nach dem Westen. Die 'Westforschung' der völkisch-nationalen Wissenschaften zum nordwesteuropäischen Raum (1919–1960).*
2 vols. Münster et al.: Waxmann, 2003, vol. 2, pp. 1091–1109.
Knobloch, Clemens. "Die deutsche Sprachwissenschaft im Nationalsozialismus. Ein
forschungsorientierter Überblick." *Kritische Ausgabe* 2 (2004), pp. 42–47.
——. *Volkhafte Sprachforschung. Studien zum Umbau der Sprachwissenschaft in Deutschland
zwischen 1918 und 1945.* Tübingen: Max Niemeyer Verlag, 2005.
Koerner, E.F. Konrad. "Ideology in 19th and 20th century study of language: A
neglected aspect of linguistic historiography." *Indogermanische Forschungen* 105 (2000),
pp. 1–26.
Krech, Volkhard. *Wissenschaft und Religion. Studien zur Geschichte der Religionsforschung in
Deutschland 1871 bis 1933.* Tübingen: Mohr Siebeck, 2002.
Kubota, Hiroshi. *Religionswissenschaftliche Religiosität und Religionsgründung. Jakob Wilhelm
Hauer im Kontext des Freien Protestantismus.* Frankfurt a.M.: Lang, 2005.
Kummer, Bernhard. *Midgards Untergang. Germanischer Kult und Glaube in den letzten heidnischen
Jahrhunderten.* Leipzig: Pfeiffer, 1927, 4th ed. Leipzig: Klein, 1938, 5th ed. Zeven:
Verlag der Forschungfragen unserer Zeit, 1972.
Kylstra, Andries Dirk. *De Leidse oudgermanist Jan de Vries in de ogen van de bezetter.* Roden:
Kylstra, 2001.
——. "Vries, Jan de (1890–1964)." *Biographisch-Bibliographisches Kirchenlexikon* 13 (1998),
col. 108–117.
Laignel-Lavastine, Alexandra. *Cioran, Eliade, Ionesco. L'oubli du fascisme.* Paris: Presses
Universitaires de France, 2002.

Lerchenmüller, Joachim and Gerd Simon. *Im Vorfeld des Massenmords. Germanistik und Nachbarfächer im 2. Weltkrieg.* 3rd ed. Tübingen: Gesellschaft für Interdisziplinäre Forschung Tübingen, 1997.

———. *Maskenwechsel. Wie der SS-Hauptsturmführer Schneider zum BRD-Hochschulrektor Schwerte wurde und andere Geschichten über die Wendigkeit deutscher Wissenschaft im 20. Jahrhundert.* Tübingen: Gesellschaft für Interdisziplinäre Forschung, 1999.

Lerchenmüller, Joachim. "Hans Ernst Schneiders/Hans Schwertes Niederlande-Arbeit in den 1930er bis 1950er Jahren." In Burkhard Dietz et al., eds. *Griff nach dem Westen. Die 'Westforschung' der völkisch-nationalen Wissenschften zum nordwesteuropäischen Raum (1919–1960).* 2 vols. Münster et al.: Waxmann, 2003, vol. 2, pp. 1111–1140.

Lincoln Bruce. *Death, war, and sacrifice. Studies in ideology and practice.* Chicago: University of Chicago Press, 1991.

———. *Theorizing myth. Narrative, ideology, and scholarship.* Chicago: University of Chicago Press, 1999.

———. "Indo-European religions: An overview." *Encyclopedia of Religion.* 2nd ed., vol. 7 (2005), pp. 4451–4456.

Littleton, C. Scott. "Indo-European religions: History of study." *Encyclopedia of Religion.* 2nd. ed., vol. 7 (2005), pp. 4457–4467, reprint of the 1st ed. 1987.

Maner, Hans-Christian. *Parlamentarismus in Rumänien (1930–1940). Demokratie im autoritären Umfeld.* München: R. Oldenbourg, 1997.

Mees, Bernard. "Völkische Altnordistik: The politics of Nordic studies in the German-speaking countries 1926–1945." In Geraldine Barnes and Margaret Clunies Ross, eds. *Old Norse myths, literature and society.* Sydney: Center for Medieval Studies, 2000, pp. 316–326.

———. "Hitler and 'Germanentum'." *Journal of Contemporary History* 39–2 (2004), pp. 255–270.

———. "'Germanisch Sturmflut': From the old Norse twilight to the fascist new dawn." *Studia Neophilologica* 78 (2006), pp. 184–198.

Meier, Mischa. "Zum Problem der Existenz kultischer Geheimbünde bei den frühen Germanen." *Zeitschrift für Religions- und Geistesgeschichte* 51 (1999), pp. 322–341.

Michaels, Axel, ed. *Klassiker der Religionswissenschaft. Von Friedrich Schleiermacher bis Mircea Eliade.* München: Beck, 1996.

Michel, Ute. "Wilhelm Emil Mühlmann (1904–1988) – ein deutsche Professor. Amnesie und Amnestie: Zum Verhältnis von Ethnologie und Politik im Nationalsozialismus." In Carsten Klingemann et al., eds. *Jahrbuch für Soziologie-Geschichte.* Opladen: Leske und Budrich, 1991, pp. 69–117.

Morgan, Philip. *Fascism in Europe, 1919–1945.* London et al.: Routledge, 2003.

Morgenthaler, Christoph. "Carl Gustav Jung (1875–1961)." In Axel Michaels, ed. *Klassiker der Religionswissenschaft.* München: Beck, 1997, pp. 234–246.

Mosse, George L. *The fascist revolution. Toward a general theory of fascism.* New York: Howard Fertig, 1999.

Müller, Hannelore. *Der frühe Mircea Eliade. Sein rumänischer Hintergrund und die Anfänge seiner universalistischen Religionsphilosophie.* Münster: Lit, 2004.

———. "Mircea Eliade und Nae Ionescu. Der Schüler und sein Meister." *Zeitschrift für Religionswissenschaft* 12 (2004), pp. 79–98.

Mutti, Claudio. *Mircea Eliade e la Guardia di Ferro.* Roma: All'insegna del Veltro, 1989, Romanian trans. Sibiu: Puncte Cardinale, 1995, German trans. 2007.

———. *Les plumes de l'Archange. Quatres intellectuels roumains à la face de la Garde de Fer: Nae Ionescu, Mircea Eliade, Emil Cioran, Constantin Noica.* Chalon-sur-Saône: Éditions Hérodes, 1993, Romanian trans. Bucharest: Ed. Anastasia, 1997.

———. *Eliade, Vâlsan, Geticus e gli altri. La Fortuna di Guénon tra i Romeni.* Parma: Edizioni all'insegna del Veltro, 1999, French trans. Saint-Genis-Laval: Akribeia, 2002, Romanian trans. Bucharest: Ed. Vremea, 2003.

Niem, Christina. "Lily Weiser-Aaall (1898–1987). Ein Beitrag zur Wissenschaftsge-
schichte der Volkskunde." *Zeitschrift für Volkskunde* 1 (1998), pp. 25–52.
Noll, Richard. *The Jung cult. Originis of a charismatic movement.* Princeton: Princeton
University Press, 1994.
———. *The Aryan Christ. The secret life of Carl Jung.* New York: Random House, 1997.
Nyberg, Henrik Samuel. *Die Religionen des alten Iran.* Leipzig: J. C. Hinrichs Verlag 1938,
2nd ed. 1968, 1st Swedish ed. *Irans forntida religioner.* Stockholm: Svenska Kirkans
Diakonistyrelses förlag, 1937.
Oişteanu, Andreij. "Mircea Eliade between political journalism and scholarly work."
Archaeus 8–1/4 (2004), pp. 323–340.
Oldmeadow, Harry. *Journeys East. Twentieth century Western encounters with Eastern religious
traditions.* New York: World Wisdom Inc., 2004.
Paul, Otto. "Zur Geschichte der iranischen Religionen." *Archiv für Religionswissenschaft*
36 (1939), pp. 215–234.
Paxton, Robert O. *The anatomy of fascism.* New York: Knopf, 2004, German trans.
München: Deutsche Verlagsanstalt, 2006.
Payne, Stanley G. *A history of fascism, 1914–1945.* Madison: University of Wisconsin
Press, 1995, German trans. Berlin: Propyläen, 2001.
Pettazzoni, Raffaele. "Gli studi storico-religiosi in Italia." *Civiltà fascista* 5 (1938), pp.
194–197.
Pietikäinen, Petteri. *C.G. Jung and the psychology of symbolic forms.* Helsinki: Academia
Scientiarum Fennica, 1999.
———. "The 'Volk' and its unconsciousness: Jung, Hauer and the 'German revolution'."
Journal of Contemporary History 35–4 (2000), pp. 523–539.
Poliakov, Léon. *The Aryan myth. A history of racist and nationalist ideas in Europe.* New York:
Basic Books, 1974.
Puşcariu, Sextil. "Das Rumänische Institut in Deutschland." *Illustrirte Zeitung Leipzig*,
no. 4984, September 18, 1941, p. 190.
Pringle, Heather Anne. *The master plan. Himmler's scholars and the holocaust.* New York:
Hyperion, 2006.
Reichhardt, Sven. "Was mit dem Faschismus passiert ist. Ein Literaturbericht zur
internationalen Faschismusforschung seit 1990, Teil 1." *Neue Politische Literatur* 49
(2004), pp. 385–406.
Rennie, Bryan S. "The diplomatic career of Mircea Eliade: A response to Adriana
Berger." *Religion* 22–4 (1992), pp. 375–392.
———. *Reconstructing Eliade. Making Sense of Religion.* New York: Albany, 1996.
———. "The meaning and end of Mircea Eliade." In idem, ed. *Changing religious worlds.
The Meaning and end of Mircea Eliade.* New York: Albany, 2001, pp. 263–281.
———. "Mircea Eliade [Further considerations]." *Encyclopedia of Religion.* 2nd ed., vol. 4
(2005), pp. 2757–2763.
Ricketts, Mac Linscott. *Mircea Eliade. The Romanian roots, 1907–1945.* 2 vols. Boulder:
East European Monographs, 1988.
Ringer, Fritz K. *The decline of the German mandarines. The German academic community,
1890–1933.* Cambridge: Harvard University Press, 1969, German trans. Stuttgart:
Klett-Cotta, 1983.
Römer, Ruth. *Sprachwissenschaft und Rassenideologie in Deutschland.* München: Wilhelm
Fink, 1985.
Ros, Martin. *Schakale des Dritten Reiches. Untergang der Kollaborateure 1944–1945.* Stuttgart:
Neske, 1997, 1st ed. Amsterdam et al.: De Arbeiderspers, 1995.
Ruck, Michael. *Bibliographie zum Nationalsozialismus.* Köln: Bund-Verlag, 1995.
Rudolph, Kurt. *Die Religionsgeschichte an der Leipziger Universität und die Entwicklng der Religions-
wissenschaft. Ein Beitrag zur Wissenschaftsgeschichte und zum Problem der Religionswissenschaft.*
Berlin: Akademie-Verlag, 1962.
———. *Geschichte und Probleme der Religionswissenschaft.* Leiden et al.: Brill, 1992.

Schetelich, Maria. "Bild, Abbild, Mythos – die Arier in den Arbeiten deutscher Indologen." In Michael Bergunder und Rahul Peter Das, eds. *'Arier' und 'Draviden'. Konstruktionen der Vergangenheit als Grundlage für Selbst- und Fremdwahrnehmungen Südasiens.* Halle: Franckesche Stiftungen, 2002, pp. 40–56.

Schier, Barbara. "Hexenwahn und Hexenverfolgung. Rezeption und politische Zurichtung eines kulturwissenschaftlichen Themas im Dritten Reich." *Bayerisches Jahrbuch für Volkskunde* (1990), pp. 43–115.

Schlerath, Bernfried. "Georges Dumézil und die Rekonstruktion der indogermanischen Kultur." *Kratylos* 40 (1995), pp. 1–48 and 41 (1996), pp. 1–67.

———. "Religion der Indogermanen." In Wolfgang Meid, ed. *Sprache und Kultur der Indogermanen. Akten der X. Fachtagung der Indogermanischen Gesellschaft Innsbruck, 22.–28. September 1996.* Innsbruck: Institut für Sprachwissenschaft, 1998, pp. 87–99.

Schnurbein, Stefanie von. "Geheime kultische Männerbünde bei den Germanen – Eine Theorie im Spannungsfeld zwischen Wissenschaft und Ideologie." In Gisela Völger et al., eds. *Männerbande, Männerbünde. Zur Rolle des Mannes im Kulturvergleich.* 2 vols. Köln: Rautenstrauch-Jost-Museum, 1990, vol. 2, pp. 97–102.

———. "Shamanism in the Old Norse tradition: A theory between ideological camps." *History of Religions* 43 (2003), pp. 116–138.

Sebastian, Mihail. *Journal, 1935–1944.* London: Pimlico, 2003, 1st ed. Bucharest: Humanitas, 1996, German trans. Berlin: Claassen, 2005.

Sedwick, Mark. *Against the modern world. Traditionalism and the secret intellectual history of the twentieth century.* Oxford: Oxford University Press, 2004.

See, Klaus von. "Kulturkritik und Germanenforschung zwischen den Weltkriegen." *Historische Zeitschrift* 245 (1987), pp. 343–362.

———. "Politische Männerbund-Ideologie von der wilhelminischen Zeit bis zum Nationalsozialismus." In Gisela Völger and Karin v. Welck, eds. *Männerbande, Männerbünde. Zur Rolle des Mannes im Kulturvergleich.* 2 vols. Köln: Rautenstrauch-Jost-Museum, 1990, vol. 1, pp. 93–102.

———. *Barbar, Germane, Arier. Die Suche nach der Identität der Deutschen.* Heidelberg: Winter, 1994.

———. "Der Arier-Mythos." In Nikolaus Buschmann and Dieter Langewiesche, eds. *Der Krieg in den Gründungsmythen europäischer Nationen und der USA.* Frankfurt a.M.: Campus Verlag 2003, pp. 56–96.

Shafir, Michael. "The man they love to hate: Norman Manea's 'snail's house' between holocaust and 'gulag'." *East European Jewish Affairs* 30–1 (2000), pp. 60–81.

Shedletzky, Itta ed. *Gershom Sholem: Briefe III, 1971–1982.* München: Beck, 1999.

Simon, Gerd. *Wissenschaftspolitik im Nationalsozialismus und die Universität Prag.* Tübingen: Gesellschaft für Interdisziplinäre Forschung Tübingen, 2000.

Simon, Marcel. "La politique anti-juive de S. Jean Chrysostome et le mouvement judaïsant d'Antioche." In Comité Directeur et Collaborateurs de l'Institut de Philologie et d'Histoire, ed. *Mélanges Franz Cumont.* Vol. 1. Bruxelles: Université libre, 1936, pp. 403–421.

Singer, Kurt D. "Norwegian students fight the war." *Journal of Educational Sociology* 18–1 (September 1944), pp. 22–28.

[Spineto, Natale] *Mircea Eliade, Raffaele Pettazoni: L'histoire des religions a-t-elle un sens? Correspondance 1926–1959. Texte présenté, établi et annoté par Natale Spineto.* Paris: Ed. du Cerf, 1994.

———. *Mircea Eliade storico delle religioni. Con la corrispondenza inedita Mircea Eliade - Károly Kerényi.* Brescia: Morcelliana, 2006.

Steigman-Gall, Richard. *The Holy Reich. Nazi conceptions of Christianity, 1919–1945.* Cambridge: Cambridge University Press, 2004, 1st ed. 2003.

Strenski, Ivan. *Four theories of myth in twentieth-century history. Cassirer, Eliade, Levi-Strauss and Malinowski.* Basingstoke: Macmillan, 1987.

Stroumsa, Guy G. "Buber as an Historian of Religion. Presence, not Gnosis." *Archives de Sciences Sociales des Religions* (1998), pp. 87–105.

Tal, Uriel. *Christians and Jews in Germany. Religion, politics, and ideology in the Second Reich, 1870–1914*. Ithaca: Cornell University Press, 1975.

Thomassen, Einar. "Wilhelm Schencke – Norway's first professor in history of religions." In Sigurd Hjelde, ed. *Man, meaning, and mystery. 100 years of history of religions in Norway. The heritage of W. Brede Kristense*. Leiden et al.: Brill, 2000, pp. 223–236.

Thompson, Lawrence. "Recent investigations in early Germanic religion." *The German Quarterly* 13–3 (1940), pp. 137–141.

Tilitzki, Christian. "Die Vortragsreisen Carl Schmitts während des Zweiten Weltkrieges." *Schmittiana* 6 (1998), pp. 191–270.

Tommissen, Piet. "Briefe an Carl Schmitt: Eine zweite Auswahl." *Schmittiana* 4 (1994), pp. 249–290.

Totok, William. "Die Generation von Mircea Eliade im Bann des rumänischen Faschismus." *Halbjahresschrift für südosteuropäische Geschichte, Literatur und Politik* 1 (1995), pp. 42–55.

Trimondi, Victor and Victoria. *Hitler, Buddha, Krishna. Eine unheilige Allianz vom Dritten Reich bis heute*. Wien: Ueberreuter, 2002.

Țurcanu, Florin. *Mircea Eliade. Le prisonnier de l'histoire*. Paris: Éditions La Découverte, 2003, Romanian trans. Bucharest, Humanitas, 2003, German trans. Schnellroda: Edition Antaios, 2006.

Volovici, Leon. *Nationalist ideology and antisemitism. The case of Romanian intellectuals in the 1930s*. Oxford et al.: Pergamon Press, 1991.

Vries, Jan de. "De godsdienst der germanen." In Gerardus van der Leeuw et al., eds. *De godsdiensten der Wereld*. 2 vols. Amsterdam: Meulenhoff, 1940/41, vol. 1, pp. 126–171, 3rd ed., vol. 1, 1955, pp. 475–520.

——. *Onze voorouders*. 's-Gravenhage: De Schouw, 1942.

——. "Germanistik." *Die Religion in Geschichte und Gegenwart*. 3rd ed., vol. 2 (1958), col. 1242–1245.

——. "Hakenkreuz." Ibid., 3rd ed., vol. 3 (1959), col. 31f.

——. "Indogermanen." Ibid., 3rd ed., vol. 3 (1959), col. 723–726.

Wach, Joachim. *Religionswissenschaft. Prolegomena zu ihrer wissenschaftstheoretischen Grundlegung*. Leipzig: Hinrichs, 1924.

Wachter, Rudolf. "Allgemeine und vergleichende Sprachwissenschaft." In Wolfgang U. Eckart et al., eds. *Die Universität Heidelberg im Nationalsozialismus*. Heidelberg: Springer, 2006, pp. 371–389.

Waldenfels, Hans. "Wilhelm Schmidt (1868–1954)." In Axel Michaels, ed. *Klassiker der Religionswissenschaft. Von Friedrich Schleiermacher bis Mircea Eliade*. München: Beck, 1996, pp. 185–197.

Weinreich, Max. *Hitler's professors. The part of scholarship in Germany's crimes against the Jewish people*. New York: YIVO, 1946, 2nd ed. New Haven: Yale University Press, 1999.

Weiser, Lily. *Altgermanische Jünglingsweihe und Männerbünde*. Bühl: Konkordia, 1927.

Werblowsky, Zwi. "'In nostro tempore'." In Hans Peter Duerr, ed. *Die Mitte der Welt. Aufsätze zu Mircea Eliade*. Frankfurt a.M.: Suhrkamp, 1984, pp. 128–137.

Wiese, Christian. *Wissenschaft des Judentums und protestantische Theologie im wilhelminischen Deutschland. Ein Schrei ins Leere?* Tübingen: Mohr Siebeck, 1999, English trans. Leiden et al.: Brill, 2004.

Wikander, Stig. *Der arische Männerbund*. Lund: C.W.K. Gleerup, 1938.

Wildt, Michael. *Generation des Unbedingten. Das Führungskorps des Reichssicherheitshauptamtes*. Hamburg: Hamburger Edition, 2002.

Worm, Herbert. "Japanologie im Nationalsozialismus. Ein Zwischenbericht." In Gerhard Krebs and Bernd Martin, eds. *Formierung und Fall der Achse Berlin – Tokyo*. München: Iudicum Verlag, 1994.

Würth, Stefanie. "Vorwort zum Nachdruck" of Jan de Vries. *Altnordische Literaturgeschichte.* 3rd ed. Berlin et al.: De Gruyter, 1999, pp. XIII–XLV.

Wüst, Walther. "Bestand die zoroastrische Urgemeinde wirklich aus berufsmäßigen Ekstatikern und schamanisierenden Rinderhirten der Steppe?" *Archiv für Religionswissenschaft* 36 (1939), pp. 234–249.

———. "Indogermanisches Bekenntnis." In idem. *Indogermanisches Bekenntnis. Sechs Reden.* Berlin-Dahlem: Ahnenerbe Stiftungsverlag, 1942 (2nd ed. 1943, Dutch trans. 1944), pp. 93–118.

Yavetz, Zvi. "An eyewitness note: Reflections on the Rumanian Iron Guard." *Journal of Contemporary History* 26 (1991), pp. 597–610.

Zernack, Julia. "'Wenn es sein muß, mit Härte...' – Die Zwangsversetzung des Nordisten Gustav Neckel 1935 und die 'Germanenkunde im Kulturkampf'." In idem and Klaus von See, eds. *Germanistik und Politik in der Zeit des Nationalsozialismus. Zwei Fallstudien: Hermann Schneider und Gustav Neckel.* Heidelberg: Winter, 2004, pp. 113–208.

———. "Kontinuität als Problem der Wissenschaftsgeschichte. Otto Höfler und das Münchner Institut für Nordische Philologie und Germanische Altertumskunde." In Klaus Böldl and Miriam Kauko, eds. *Kontinuität in der Krise. Historische und aktuelle Perspektiven der Skandinavistik.* Freiburg: Rombach Verlag, 2005, pp. 47–72.

Zimmermann, Harm-Peer. "Männerbund und Totenkult. Methodologische und ideologische Grundlinien der Volks- und Altertumskunde Otto Höflers 1933–1945." *Kieler Blätter zur Volkskunde* 26 (1994), pp. 5–27.

Zimmermann, Jan. "Alfred Toepfers 'Westschau'." In Burkhard Dietz et al., eds. *Griff nach dem Westen. Die 'Westforschung' der völkisch-nationalen Wissenschften zum nordwesteuropäischen Raum (1919–1960).* 2 vols. Münster et al.: Waxmann, 2003, vol. 2, pp. 1061–1090.

PART ONE

THE ARYAN MYTH

FROM BUDDHA TO ADOLF HITLER:
WALTHER WÜST AND THE ARYAN TRADITION

Horst Junginger

1. *Introduction*

Walther Wüst is rightly known as one of Germany's leading academics during the Nazi period. He was a scholar of a new voelkish type. Being on very intimate terms with Heinrich Himmler, he quickly advanced in the SS and was appointed SS-"Oberführer" in 1942, the highest rank he would achieve. His academic career prospered similarly. Full professor since 1935, Wüst was nominated rector of the University of Munich in 1941. At that time, he had already headed Himmler's brain trust named "Ahnenerbe" (ancestral heritage) for four years. Indeed, Wüst represented the archetype of a politically engaged Nazi scholar. It is misleading to raise doubts about his extraordinary position only because Alfred Rosenberg tried to thwart some of his projects. Michael Kater goes too far in his still authoritative book about the "Ahnenerbe" relating Wüst to a somewhat old school of scholarly learning in Germany.[1] Writing his dissertation in the early 1970s, Kater did not see through the widely played game of many post-war university professors who made a virtue of necessity in transforming their former rivalries into opposition and even resistance after the war. But it has to be acknowledged that Kater stood under great pressure from his interviewees, mostly university professors and high ranks of the former "Ahnenerbe" and the Reich Ministry of Science and Education, during his research.[2] They went to great lengths to impose their view on the young doctoral student, even threatening him with legal proceedings if he would go a little bit too far in his interpretation. Their intention was clear: to neglect or, at least, to diminish their involvement in National Socialism

---

[1] Michael H. Kater, *Das 'Ahnenerbe' der SS 1935–1945. Ein Beitrag zur Kulturpolitik des Dritten Reiches* (Stuttgart: Deutsche Verlags-Anstalt, 1974, 3rd ed. 2001), p. 275.

[2] Kater's correspondence with them is to be found in the Institut für Zeitgeschichte München (Institute of Contemporary History, Munich), ZS/A-25 "Zeugenschrifttum Kater."

as far as possible. Some even construed a contradiction between the alleged scientific aim of the SS-"Ahnenerbe" and the ideological claims of the Third Reich. Otto Huth (1906–1998), head of the "Ahnenerbe"-section "Indogermanische Geistes- und Glaubensgeschichte" (History of Indo-Germanic Ideas and Belief) called Himmler's think tank an institution concerned with the development of a Germanic humanism and its journal *Germanien* a place of spiritual resistance against the Nazi regime.[3] Only privately did Kater express his opinion that a scholar such as Wüst should be summoned to appear in court. Why should the "Ahnenerbe"-president remain free when its secretary Wolfram Sievers was hanged for his deeds, he asked in a letter to Germany's chief public prosecutor Fritz Bauer.[4]

Unlike anyone, Wüst epitomized the university system of the Third Reich, its arrogant claims as well as its intellectual and moral decay. A biography of him is an urgent desideratum of Germany's history of science.[5] It should not only center on Wüst's vigor in the field of politics but should also take his influence in indology and the history of religions into account. This article, putting emphasis on Wüst's views pertaining to religion and the study of religion, can in no way replace such an effort.[6]

---

[3] Letters of O. Huth to M.H. Kater from August 21 and September 9, 1963, ibid., MA ZS/A-25; cf. also Horst Junginger, *Von der philologischen zur völkischen Religionswissenschaft* (Stuttgart: Steiner, 1999), p. 295.

[4] Letter of M.H. Kater to F. Bauer from February 26, 1968, MA ZS/A-25, s.v. Bruno Beger, fol. 16f.

[5] Gerd Simon is preparing a book on Wüst with the title *Mit Akribie und Bluff ins Zentrum der Macht. Walther Wüst und das 'Etymologische und vergleichende Wörterbuch des Altindoarischen'*. Helmut Heiber's *Universität unterm Hakenkreuz*, vol. 2.2 (München: Saur, 1994), pp. 216–233 describes the life of Wüst a little bit different compared with Kater's study (op. cit., pp. 43–46). A dissertation of Max Schreiber, Munich, concentrating on Wüst's academic career, ought to appear in 2007.

[6] My main archival sources are Wüst's personal files at the Munich University Archive and at the Federal Archives Berlin (the former Berlin Document Center, BDC), the "Ahnenerbe"-files NS 21 there (consisting of nearly 1000 large volumes), the literal remains of Jakob Wilhelm Hauer laying in the Koblenz branch of Germany's Federal Archives, and the holdings of the Institute of Contemporary History in Munich. I have to thank Gerd Simon especially for information about the "Ahnenerbe"-career of Wüst and his relationship with Julius Evola. The "Gesellschaft für interdisziplinäre Forschung Tübingen" (GIFT), of which we both are members, is providing access to some important files concerning the humanities under National Socialism, see http://homepages.uni-tuebingen.de/gerd.simon/gift.htm.

2. *Religious Background and the World View of Herman Wirth*

Born in May 1901 in Kaiserslautern, Wüst was raised in a traditional Protestant environment. His father was a teacher and a staunch Bavarian civil servant. Brought up by a very pious mother in common Protestant values and virtues, Wüst participated already as a schoolboy in activities against the Versailles treatise which had cut off the left side of the Rhine from the German Reich. At that time, Palatine in the west of Germany belonged to Bavaria. In 1920 Wüst began to study German, English, and Indian philology as well as comparative religion at the University of Munich. Similar to many others, Wüst became aware of new ideas in the course of his academic education. The university widened his horizons and led to a certain estrangement from his parental home and familiar attachments. Becoming acquainted with the religious world apart from Christianity, the belief of his childhood lost much of its cohesive force. Particularly the religions of the East impressed the young student who immersed himself in the cultures of India and Persia during his training in Aryan philology.

Though the notion "Aryan philology" had no negative or racial connotation at the beginning of comparative Indo-European linguistics and was merely synonymous with philological expertise in Sanskrit and Awesta, non-scientific influences were superimposed on it in the second half of the 19th century. To deal with the culture of the Aryans now meant much more than scrutinizing language structures and etymological relations.[7] Something like an Aryan Myth emerged. Léon Poliakov closely related the appearance of the Aryan Myth in Germany with the scientific work of Friedrich Max Müller.[8] Although Poliakov exaggerated his influence in that regard, one should be attentive to the fact that Müller developed a firm interest in the racial theories of Count Arthur de Gobineau at the end of his life. In a letter to Ludwig Schemann, the propagator of Gobineau's racism in Germany, Müller expressed his

---

[7] See Ruth Römer, *Sprachwissenschaft und Rassenideologie* (München: Fink, 1985) and Maurice Olender, *Les langues du Paradis. Aryens et Sémites, un couple providentiel* (Paris: Gallimard, 1989, German ed. *Die Sprachen des Paradieses. Religion, Philologie und Rassentheorie im 19. Jahrhundert*, Frankfurt a.M.: Campus, 1995).

[8] Léon Poliakov, *Der arische Mythos. Zu den Quellen von Rassismus und Nationalismus* (Wien: Europa-Verlag, 1977, English ed. *The Aryan Myth*, London: Heinemann, 1974), esp. pp. 241ff. See also Laurens van den Bosch, *Friedrich Max Müller. A Life Devoted to the Humanities* (Leiden: Brill, 2002), pp. 370ff.

"sincere admiration" of the French count on January 1, 1894.[9] Müller did not even hesitate to support the Gobineau-society Schemann had founded to spread the racial ideas of Gobineau.[10]

The attractiveness of the Aryans in the 19th century had scientific and religious origins. Translating and analyzing a vast corpus of hitherto unknown holy scriptures was an imperative and indispensable, but also a Herculean task. The series *The Sacred Books of the East* Müller inaugurated and edited between 1878 and 1894 provides proof of the enormous progress in this new field of research called history of religions. But in addition to inner scientific motives and developments, historians of religions also turned their interest to the religious world outside Europe because they were dissatisfied with their own religion at home. Liberal-minded scholars were deeply disappointed by orthodox Christianity, its affinity with monarchy and its outdated dogmas opposing scientific progress in many areas of academic learning. If they, nevertheless, wanted to remain religious or, at least, if they esteemed religious values important to one's personal and social life, where should they head? Leaving the church and becoming overt agnostics or atheists was an option for very few. It would have been against their convictions and, perhaps more important, it would have hampered their academic career considerably. To embark on the path of religious reformation was no alternative for them either since they were already on the fringe of their church. My point is A) that many religious studies scholars were attracted by non-Christian traditions as a result of and parallel to their alienation from Christianity. And B), the more they occupied themselves with religions they equally found true, authentic, and respectable, the more their intrinsic critique of Christianity raised. Under such circumstances the wonderland of India functioned as a magnet drawing scientific interests, spiritual needs, and political hopes out of their traditional Christian setting. It is no surprise that a lot of traits then attributed in a positive form to the Aryan people originally stemmed from the catalogue of Christian

---

[9] "Ich habe seit Jahren eine aufrichtige Verehrung für Gobineau gefühlt und mich oft gewundert, daß sein Name so wenig genannt wird." quoted together with two other affirmative letters of Müller by Ludwig Schemann, *Gobineaus Rassenwerk* (Stuttgart: Fr. Fromms Verlag, 1910), p. 188f.

[10] See Günther Deschner, '*Gobineau und Deutschland*'. *Der Einfluß von J.A. de Gobineaus 'Essai sur inégalité des races humaines' auf die deutsche Geistesgeschichte 1853–1917* (Diss. Erlangen 1967), p. 64 and the appendix as well as Junginger, *Von der philologischen zur völkischen Religionswissenschaft*, pp. 145ff.

deficiencies. Because linguistic evidence was not sufficient to verify a close kinship between the old Aryans in India and contemporary Germans in Europe, the importance of non-scientific features increased. Race became such a determining factor amalgamating the people of India and Germany to "Indo-Germans" who were supposed to share a specific Aryan worldview.

Scholars such as Walther Wüst and Jakob Wilhelm Hauer were deeply rooted in the 19th century's study of religion. They projected their own longings onto the Aryan heritage to a much greater extent than their forerunners. As a legacy of the old Protestant text-orientation, Wüst and Hauer aspired to reveal the essence of Indo-Aryanism via interpretative hermeneutics. When the Nazis attained power, both perceived a clear inner calling to come forth with their particular expertise in Aryan philology and religion in order to authenticate and even substantiate the ideology of National Socialism. But in the decade before, in a situation of ideological confusion and political disorder after the lost war, Wüst, Hauer and many others began to think about the Aryan tradition in rather unspecific and ill-defined terms of a cultural and spiritual alternative.

In the course of Wüst's habilitation procedure, the dean of the philosophy department of the University of Munich Lucian Scherman wrote an expert opinion in May 1926 in which he specifically praised the candidate's philological diligence. Scherman, in summarizing the votes of his colleagues Hanns Oertel and Hermann Güntert, however added the warning that Wüst should not leave the path of methodological thoroughness when turning his attention to cultural history in the time to come.[11] Scherman's assessment must be understood in the context of a severe crisis indology faced due to the old age of most of its professors and the great number of solely language-oriented Sanskrit chairs. Wüst was one of the few promising young scholars of Indian and Iranian philology who nurtured hope in a positive development in the future. In those days of little money and great problems, politicians and ministry officials wanted the universities to place more stress on practical relevance. Studying Sanskrit philology or religious

---

[11] L. Scherman's "Gesamtgutachten" from May 10, 1926 as well as the votes of H. Oertel (January 14, 1926) and H. Güntert (n.d.) are to be found in Wüst's personal files, University Archive Munich, ON 7 and ON 14. Perhaps Schermann's admonition was also a reaction to the overtly positive statement of Güntert which Bruce Lincoln quotes in his article on p. 199, n. 70.

traditions far away in time and distance for purely scientific reasons was esteemed superfluous and potentially dispensable. University disciplines like indology and comparative religion reacted to this challenge with a closer orientation towards cultural themes and arguments. In so doing they hoped to gain further legitimacy and to cope with the new demands of a new time. It was probably not astonishing that a young and talented scholar like Wüst saw this as a chance to connect his personal advancement with the overdue modernizing of indology. Consequently, Wüst went one step further and included the interpretation of the Aryan race to the interpretation of the Aryan culture when it soon became necessary. The vagueness and uncertainty of the race-concept did not speak against its utilization. Instead, it was a notion of great hope and expectations.

A growing interest in Indo-European mythology notwithstanding, Wüst entirely remained in the realm of Protestant Christianity in the 1920s. He maintained close contacts with missionary circles long after he had finished his dissertation in 1923 and his habilitation in 1926. Yet in 1931 he participated in the annual meeting of the East Asia Mission in Basle where he gave a lecture on Buddhism and Christianity.[12] Founded in Weimar in 1884, the "Allgemeine Evangelisch-Protestantische Missionsverein," better known as "Ostasien-Mission," had Japan and China as its main missionary fields. Because the East Asia Mission gave less prominence to traditional missionary work and admitted a more scholarly approach based on critical historical methods, it was refused membership in the umbrella organization of the "Deutscher Evangelischer Missionsbund" in 1928 for being not Christian enough. The inclination towards the history of religions found expression in the journal of the East Asia Mission *Zeitschrift für Missionskunde und Religionswissenschaft* edited by Johannes Witte and Hans Haas. Whereas Witte focused on the missionary aspects, Haas accentuated the history of religions as far as he could, resulting in severe difficulties with his co-editor. Together with some 20 liberal theologians and historians of religions – among them Karl Beth, Karl Bornhausen, Wilhelm Brachmann, Carl Clemen, Otto Eißfeldt, and Joachim Wach – Wüst joined the scientific board of the *Zeitschrift für Missionskunde und Religionswis-*

---

[12] Walther Wüst, "Buddhismus und Christentum auf vorderasiatisch-antikem Boden. Vortrag, gehalten während der 47. Jahresversammlung der Ostasien-Mission in Basel, 6.10.1931," *Zeitschrift für Missionskunde und Religionswissenschaft* (1932), pp. 33–63.

senschaft in 1929. In some issues he appears right after Joachim Wach in the list of board members. Wüst wrote several articles and reviews in which he emphatically appraised books of Jakob Wilhelm Hauer, Rudolf Otto, Gustav Mensching, and Hilko Wiardo Schomerus. Wüst even assessed publications of the Jewish indologists Isidor Scheftelowitz and Otto Strauß in quite a positive manner, scholars who were later denounced as racially alien and as a threat to the German university system.

The relationship between Protestant mission and the study of religion is of exceptional importance and has undeservedly been excluded from historical investigation until today. A great bulk of material in church and missionary archives is still waiting to be examined. Its analysis would enable a much better insight in the history of our discipline in particular with regard to the era of National Socialism.[13] Quarrels among the various German missionary societies preceded and pre-structured some of the later conflicts within the study of religion after 1933. Wüst's reservations against Hauer were most likely based in the rivalry between the East Asia Mission and the pietistic Basle Mission Societey, the "Basler Missionsgesellschaft," for which Hauer had worked as missionary in India. Hauer instead fought a fierce battle with Johannes Witte who got the first chair of history of religions (in combination with missiology) newly established in the Third Reich at the University of Berlin in 1935. In a letter to Alfred Rosenberg Hauer attacked Witte as an unqualified Christian apologetic who should be seen as a danger to the German youth.[14] The "Missionsinspektor" of the East Asia Mission Wilhelm Brachmann had been strongly promoted by Witte before he changed sides and became the leading religious studies scholar of the "Amt Rosenberg." Witte himself was nominated head of the German delegation to attend the 6th IAHR conference

---

[13] Cf. Werner Ustorf, *Sailing on the Next Tide. Missions, Missiology, and the Third Reich* (Frankfurt a.M.: Peter Lang, 2000) who puts little emphasis on the study of religion itself. The excellent investigation of Bertelsmann publishers carried out under the directorship of Saul Friedländer contains a valuable description of the missionary scene in Germany written by Helen Müller and Trutz Rendtorff, see S. Friedländer et al., eds., *Bertelsmann im Dritten Reich* (München: C. Bertelsmann Verlag, 2002), pp. 91–101. Cf. also Karla Poewe's article "Liberalism, German Missionaries, and National Socialism," in Ulrich van der Heyden and Holger Stoecker, eds., *Mission und Macht im Wandel politischer Orientierungen. Europäische Missionsgesellschaften in politischen Spannungsfeldern in Afrika und Asien zwischen 1800 und 1945* (Stuttgart: Steiner, 2005), pp. 633–662.

[14] Letter of J.W. Hauer to Alfred Rosenberg on May 23, 1935, quoted in Junginger, *Von der philologischen zur völkischen Religionswissenschaft*, p. 180.

that took place in Brussels in September 1935. Shortly before the event his former membership in a Freemason society became known and he therefore was replaced by Karl Bornhausen. Less than one year before Bornhausen had taken over the chair of Paul Tillich in November 1934, teaching philosophy of religion in a newly created institute of science of religion at the University of Frankfort. Similar examples abound, showing a remarkable expansion of research in religion on Protestant premises that took place in the first years of the Third Reich. It was evident that the Reich Minister of Science and Education Bernhard Rust supported the German Christians and had no interest in fostering a Pagan influence at the universities. Eugen Mattiat, one of his main collaborators in the ministry and a firm German Christian, did his best to prevent 'Pagans' from entering the field – and things did not change before the end of the 1930s.[15]

What is significant of many German religious studies scholars is that they became acquainted with the religions of the East through engaging in missionary activities or through discussions within mission societies which the *Zeitschrift für Missionskunde und Religionswissenschaft* mediated in a Protestant and the *Zeitschrift für Missionswissenschaft und Religionswissenschaft* in a Catholic context. Wüst was far away from being a Pagan at the end of the 1920s. Lacking a deep-seated personal religiosity, he fully stood on the ground of Protestant Christianity. But parallel to his reading of the publications of Herman Wirth (1885–1981), Wüst's religious views appear to have gradually altered. Wirth, a private researcher borne in the Netherlands (demonstrated by his first name Herman and not Hermann), developed a fanciful and imaginative theory of Nordic symbolism. In his book *Der Aufgang der Menschheit. Untersuchungen zur Geschichte der Religion, Symbolik und Schrift der atlantisch-nordischen Rasse* (Man's rise. Studies in the religion, symbolism and scripture of the North-Atlantic race, Jena: Diederichs, 1928) he promulgated the existence of an extraordinarily old Nordic-Aryan culture around the Atlantic Ocean which originally came from the North Pole. Wandering southwards in early times, this eminent white race inhabited Atlantis before it sank, subse-

---

[15] I cannot go into particulars here but I scrutinized Mattiat's enormous impact in another article on "Religionswissenschaft im Nationalsozialismus. Die Geschichte einer gescheiterten Emanzipation," in Jürgen Elvert and Jürgen Sikora, eds., *Nationalsozialismus und Kulturwissenschaften* (forthcoming) in detail. For the Christian views of Bernhard Rust, see Richard Steigmann-Gall, *The Holy Reich. Nazi Conceptions of Christianity, 1919–1945* (Cambridge: Cambridge University Press, 2003), p. 45f., p. 73, and p. 122f.

quently leaving its trace wherever it went. Wirth claimed that Nordic symbols, signs and artifacts could be found everywhere their creators had spread. Yet one ought to have a trained eye for them since later layers of a Christian time covered and obscured the original remains. Lacking scientific talent and grounding, Wirth collected his material in a typical amateurish and eclectic manner. Without any regard for historical contexts and alternative possibilities of interpretation, he pressed heterogeneous things together if they seemed to fit into his system by their outward appearance.

Wirth's theory remained banished from the universities though it achieved considerable success in voelkish circles. His editor Eugen Diederichs praised Wirth as an unappreciated genius and intervened in behalf of his case at the Prussian Ministry of Culture and Education in Berlin. In 1929 Wirth tried to obtain his habilitation at the University of Marburg where he had been living since 1923. The ministry supported his effort and moreover wanted to award him with the title of an honorary professor paying homage to his national merits. But the requested evaluation turned out to be a disaster for Wirth. The dean of Marburg's philosophy department Hermann Jacobsohn (as a German Jew: Hermann), a distinguished linguist who was said to have mastered about 30 languages and dialects, called Wirth in harsh words a total dilettante and his work below the level of scientific scholarship. Wirth's attempt to link his superficial understanding of linguistics with a rather confused Nordic world view upset Jacobsohn.[16] His Marburg colleague, the archaeologist Gero von Merhart, seconded Jacobsohn's opinion that it would be a shame to the university allowing someone like Wirth to teach.[17] But what followed is characteristic of the way things went in Germany. Jacobsohn, who had been full professor and director of the Department of Oriental and Indo-Germanic Studies since 1919, was

---

[16] "Ein Mann der behauptet, dass der Konsonantenwechsel eine 'Jahreslautver-schiebung', der Vokalwechsel ein 'Jahresablaut' sei, dass der Ablaut eine Folge kult-sprachlichen Empfindens sei, dass dem Winter der Vokal *u*, der Übergangszeit des Frühlings der Vokal *e*, dem frohen sieghaften Sommer das *i* usw. zuzusprechen sei, wer Äusserungen tut wie 'das ist das grosse Mysterium der Muttermacht, dass das *u*, der dunkle Vokal, der sich tief in der Höhle des Mundes befindet, zum *a* wird', steht ausserhalb jeder Wissenschaft, jedes vernunftgemässen Denkens. Und dabei handelt es sich nicht um zufällig herausgegriffene Sätze, Höhepunkte des Unsinns. Sondern das ganze Buch steht auf diesem Niveau, auf jedem Wissenschaftsgebiet das Vf. her-anzieht." Jacobsohn to the ministry on November 22, 1929, State Archive Marburg, 307d, acc. 1966/10, no. 221, fol. 14f.

[17] Ibid., fol. 16 (n.d.).

dismissed on April 25, 1933 as soon as the Nazis came to power. His 'crime' consisted not only of his Jewish origin, Jacobsohn was also a staunch democrat and member of the "Deutsche Demokratische Partei" (DDP), then the "Deutsche Staatspartei." Befriended with Rudolf Otto and Martin Rade, Jacobsohn dreamt his whole life of a German nation in which Jews and Germans could live together as equals. In utter despair and unsuccessfully seeking help from Rudolf Otto – who was in Berlin that day to intervene in the case of Heinrich Hermlink – he committed suicide on April 27, one day after he received the telegram announcing his removal.[18] Wirth, on the other hand, profited from the new political system and eventually received the title of an extraordinary professor from the University of Berlin in 1933 which brought him 700 Reichsmark a month without any teaching duties.[19]

In 1929, the year Jacobsohn so heavily criticized Wirth and his book *Der Aufgang der Menschheit*, Wüst published a long review article in the *Zeitschrift für Missionskunde und Religionswissenschaft*.[20] He aligned his examination with Wirth's theory of decay and the view that modern man has fallen victim to materialism. This kind of cultural criticism was widespread in Germany, for the most part a reaction to the lost war. Though Wüst avoided taking sides with Wirth and his Weltanschauung explicitly, it becomes clear that he shared Wirth's basic assumption that the German soul had lost its connection with its religious roots and that Germany's re-ascent to a strong and powerful nation depended on its spiritual rebirth, however it may have been imagined. But interestingly, Wüst completely avoided dealing with the role of religion in Wirth's narrative in which Jewish-Oriental Christianity formed the main opponent of the Nordic civilization. His religious convictions were rather ambivalent at that time and he apparently did not think Christianity

---

[18] See Ruth Verroen et al., eds., *Leben Sie? Die Geschichte der deutsch-jüdischen Familie Jacobsohn* (Marburg: Universitätsbibliothek, 2000), pp. 57–81. Because his Protestant wife helped Jewish friends, Margarete Jacobsohn was imprisoned in 1944. Only thanks to the intervention of Heinrich Frick and the prison doctor, she escaped admission to a concentration camp (ibid., p. 81).

[19] Due to internal quarrels Wirth's certificate was not issued although Hermann Göring had already signed it. See Ingo Wiwjorra, "Herman Wirth. Ein gescheiterter Ideologe zwischen 'Ahnenerbe' und Atlantis," in Barbara Danckwortt et al., eds., *Historische Rassismusforschung: Ideologen, Täter, Opfer* (Hamburg-Berlin: Argument, 1995), pp. 91–112, here p. 105. Nevertheless Wirth bore the title of an extraordinary ("außerordentlicher") professor at the University of Berlin and used it in his letterhead.

[20] Walther Wüst, "Gedanken über Wirths 'Aufgang der Menschheit'," *Zeitschrift für Missionskunde und Religionswissenschaft* (1929), pp. 257–274 and pp. 289–307.

and Wirth's approach were mutually exclusive. Therefore he centered his examination on the book's scientific claims which he criticized from the standpoint of academic scholarship particularly for their linguistic and paleographic failings.[21] In distinguishing between theoretical insufficiencies and, in his eyes, a brilliantly formulated critique of culture, Wüst articulated his commentary in the form of an appeal to push ahead and to improve on it in the future: "Praesens Imperfectum – Perfectum Futurum" was the phrase with which he ended his review.[22]

In the following years Wüst's sympathy for the worldview of Herman Wirth matured. In 1932 he joined a committee that supported Wirth's project to establish a special museum for the material he had collected.[23] When the Nazis obtained the majority in the elections for Mecklenburg-Schwerin's state parliament in May 1932, these plans turned out well and Wirth succeeded at the end of the year in initiating a research institute and an open-air museum named "Forschungsanstalt und Freiluftmuseum für Geistesurgeschichte" in Bad Doberan in Mecklenburg near Rostock. At the same time, a research society "Studiengesellschaft für Geistesurgeschichte Deutsches Ahnenerbe," the precursor organization of the later "Ahnenerbe," was founded in Bad Doberan. It is impossible to adequately translate the terms "Geistesurgeschichte" or "Geistesurreligion," the headings of Wirth's whole endeavor. They meant something like a history of religious ideas extended and inflated by the prefix "ur." Wirth abundantly used the additive "ur" to designate the existence of a very old and very venerable pre-historic Nordic religion becoming visible through Pagan *hierophanies* in later historic times. To learn more about this religion required the study of its symbols and emblems in an approach he called "Urgeistes-" or "Urreligionsgeschichte." Scientifically spoken, Wirth's device involved a typical *circulus vitiosus*. His phenomenology of Nordic symbolism wanted to prove on what it relied: the assumption of a Nordic "Urreligion."

Private money and a subsidy from the Berlin Ministry of Culture and Education enabled Wirth to carry out his first "urreligionsgeschichtliche" exhibition titled "Der Heilbringer" (the 'Savior') in Berlin from

---

[21] Ibid., pp. 272–274.

[22] Ibid., p. 307.

[23] Other members of this supporting committee (consisting of 25 persons) were Karl Bornhausen, Hugo Bruckmann, Niels Diederichs, Eugen Fehrle, Jakob Wilhelm Hauer, Mathilde Merck, Gustav Neckel, Konrad Theodor Preuss, Max Wieser.

May 1–14, 1933. It focused on the Thule culture and displayed Nordic artifacts of a primeval megalith religion dating back to the Stone Age and having a Pagan "Heilbringer," the son of heaven and mother earth, as its main figure.[24] The exhibition aimed not only to memorize the Nordic legacy but to utilize it for the present. Wirth needed the success of such an exhibition and a continuing support from relevant people in order to recieve official acknowledgment and public funds.[25]

At the end of 1933 Wirth published his famous *Ura-Linda-Chronik* which he announced as a historic Friesian chronicle going back to the 3rd century BC.[26] The *Ura-Linda-Chronik* encompassed a wild mixture of sagas, memories and wise sayings of an extraordinarily old and respectable mythology. Wirth, without furnishing any kind of proof, asserted that the chronicle was a reliable document of a solemn Aryan cosmogony ("eine erhabene Kosmogonie des arischen Urglaubens") even older than, and of course superior to, the Old Testament of Jews and Christians.[27] Full of antisemitic prejudices, the *Ura-Linda-Chronik* entered the public stage as a Pagan counter narrative to the Jewish-Christian tradition. Unfortunately, the Holy book of the Nordic race was nothing but a fake written in the 19th century and reflecting the romanticism of that period. Whereas some university professors such as Gustav Neckel, Alfred Baeumler, and Arthur Hübner had estimated Wirth's previous publications with some sympathy, they now turned away, irritated by the apparent misinterpretation. Very view academics kept on supporting Wirth's ideas. Among them were Walther Wüst and Otto Huth. On May 4, 1934 a public debate was held at the auditorium maximum of the University of Berlin in which the authenticity of the *Ura-Linda-Chronik* came under fierce fire.[28] Huth, who spoke in the name of the

---

[24] See Theodor Devaranne, "'Der Heilbringer'," *Zeitschrift für Missionskunde und Religionswissenschaft* (1933), p. 242f.

[25] On April 5, 1933 Wirth requested additional funds for himself and his assistant Otto Huth who had helped him to organize the "Heilbringer"-exhibition. Wirth added a leaflet containing the aforementioned list of supporters with Wüst as last name. Federal Archives Berlin, R 73, 11853.

[26] *Die Ura-Linda-Chronik* (Leipzig: Koehler & Amelang, 1933), translated, edited and explained by Herman Wirth. The chronicle, in fact a compilation, consisted of not more than 128 pages followed by 200 pages explanation and 40 pages of pictures Wirth added.

[27] Ibid., p. 15.

[28] I refer here to an article by Gerd Simon, "Himmlers Bibel und die öffentlichwirksamste Podiumsdiskussion in der Geschichte der Germanistik," published at http://homepages.uni-tuebingen.de/gerd.simon/himmler-bibel.pdf. See also I. Wiwjorra, "Herman Wirth," p. 103f. and Sönje Storm, "Die öffentliche Aussprache über Herr-

"Reichsbund für Volkstum und Heimat," referred to his studies on the Indo-Germanic Vesta cult with its virgin priestesses who light the holy fire and keep it under their surveillance. He experienced laughter from the audience when people shouted "mehr Feuer" (more fire) and "Hut(h) ab" (down the hat).[29] Wüst as second defender maintained the existence of an authentic and trustworthy core of the *Ura-Linda-Chronik* and, once again, suggested further research for a critical text edition that would allow the real essence of the chronicle to be separated from later modifications and external influences.[30]

Wirth's theories raised severe criticism not only from the academy but also from National Socialists and organizations affiliated with National Socialism. For instance, Wirth's postulation of an old-Germanic matriarchy met, not surprisingly, a strong rejection as totally alien to the Aryan race and German mind. His assumption of a Nordic "Urchristentum," that is the idea of a Christian dependence on non-Semitic roots, incurred the displeasure of decided anti-Christian Pagans such as Bernhard Kummer and Mathilde Ludendorff.[31] Even within the NSDAP a great number of people estimated Wirth's speculations to be incompatible with National Socialism, some even considered them as a threat to its respectability. Especially scholars connected with Alfred Rosenberg denied any scientific and political relevance of Wirth's "Ur"-symbolism. Yet Wirth had fortune on his side. In Heinrich Himmler he found a prominent supporter who himself held such exaggerated views of an idealized life of the old Germans. Wirth first met Himmler during a party Johannes von Leers – who was married to Wirth's former secretary – organized in October 1934.

---

man Wirths 'Ura-Linda-Chronik' in Berlin (1934)," in Birgitta Almgren, ed., *Bilder des Nordens in der Germanistik 1929–1945. Wissenschaftliche Identität oder politische Anpassung?* (Huddinge: Södertörns Högskola, 2002), pp. 79–97.

[29] G. Simon, "Himmlers Bibel," loc. cit., p. 7.

[30] "Als zweiter Verteidiger sprach als ein sehr wendiger Advokat für die Echtheit der Chronik der Münchner Indologe Professor Walt[h]er Wüst. Statt sich nüchterner sauberer Sachlichkeit verpflichtet zu fühlen, war ihm vor allem daran gelegen, Erfolg und Gunst beim Publikum zu erhaschen. Die Rolle des Verführers lag ihm näher als diejenige eines ehrlichen Führers des Volkes. Er stellte es als das Ziel der weiteren Forschung über die Ura-Linda-Chronik hin, eine kritische Ausgabe der Chronik zu schaffen, um mit ihrer Hilfe den alten Kern herauszuschälen." Ibid., p. 7, quoting the report of a Max Wegner.

[31] See Wiwjorra, "Herman Wirth," p. 102f.

3. *Walther Wüst and the "Ahnenerbe" of the SS*

On July 1, 1935, Herman Wirth, Heinrich Himmler, Richard Walther Darré, and a handful other voelkish Nazis founded the "Ahnenerbe. Studienurgesellschaft für Geistesurgeschichte." Herman Wirth was the central intellectual figure at its inception. The way he referred to the assumed ancestral heritage of the Nordic race accepted the others as paradigmatic model. Consequently, Wirth became head of the first "Ahnenerbe"-department named "Pflegstätte für Schrift- und Sinnbildkunde," where the occupation with Nordic scriptures and symbols stood in the fore. Already in August 1935 Wirth started his first expedition to Scandinavia to examine ancient rock drawings and to reproduce plaster cards of them. A second research journey followed one year later.

Some months before the constitution of the "Ahnenerbe," Walther Wüst wrote a very submissive letter to Heinrich Himmler on January 27, 1935 "most humbly" reporting his readiness to become engaged in the activities of the new organization. At Himmler's request Wüst added his curriculum vitae rightly speculating that the backing he aspired at could be useful for his academic advancement.[32] From 1926–1932 Wüst had worked as lecturer of Indian philology at the University of Munich, then holding the non-established position of an extraordinary professor before he was assigned to administer the chair of Hanns Oertel in April 1935 whom he eventually succeeded in October, nine months after his letter to Himmler. Concomitant with his appointment as a professor of "Arische Kultur- und Sprachwissenschaft" (the study of Aryan culture and language), he was nominated director of an institute with the same designation. Himmler derived much pleasure from the young scholar who was not only eager to make career but, as Himmler immediately realized, would do everything for it. Wüst's apparent opportunism and his keenness to subordinate himself under the authority of the SS-leader made him a perfect collaborator of the "Ahnenerbe."

Wüst seemed indeed the right man to transform the "Ahnenerbe" from a voelkish association of people with crude ideas into a scientific

---

[32] Letter of W. Wüst to H. Himmler on January 27, 1935, Federal Archives Berlin, DH ZM, 1582, A. 4, fol. 11. It was Herman Wirth who asked Wüst to approach Himmler. Wüst ended with the obedient phrase "mit dem Ausdruck gehorsamsten Danks für die Ehre, durch Ihre Aufforderung ausgezeichnet worden zu sein." Though the 33-year-old scholar thought it better to remain in Munich and to take over the chair of his teacher Hanns Oertel, he generously declared his willingness to succeed Heinrich Lüders at the University of Berlin if necessary.

think tank. Lacking academic reputation and representing the lunatic or, even more, the lunar fringe of the society, it was far away from being the effective brain trust Himmler needed to compete with his rivalries. Vis-à-vis that aim Wirth had become a problem. According to Kater, Himmler decided at the beginning of 1936 to get rid of him. In March 1936 Himmler prohibited Wirth from autonomously corresponding in the name of the "Ahnenerbe" and in October of the same year Wirth got a sharp directive not to surpass his position and capacity.[33] Certainly Himmler had not abandoned his views concerning Germany's ancestral heritage. But he ought to be more careful lest face derision either from the established sciences or from Rosenberg's associates. Therefore he interdicted public discussions on the *Ura-Linda-Chronik* and engaged an Otto Mausser, a germanist, in 1936 to scrutinize internally what could be said about it without leaving safe ground. Himmler also disallowed publications on the "Externsteine," a massive stone monument near Detmold held to be a center of pre-Christian Paganism. Instead, he triggered intensive excavations to sustain a voelkish Pagan interpretation of the "Externseine," however without any success.[34] Not at least under the influence of Wüst, Himmler reached the conclusion that it would be impossible to receive the acknowledgment of the Ministry of Science and Education and public funding from the German Research Foundation if the "Ahnenerbe" would remain on the level of heathenish sectarianism. Himmler had no qualms about removing Wirth and to substitute him with Wüst when he became aware of that relationship. Appointed corresponding member of the board of the "Ahnenerbe"-curators on May 11, 1936, Wüst was officially nominated head of a newly established department called "Wortkunde" (a Germanizing translation of linguistics) in October. Shortly before that, he had the honor of being invited to a working conference at Himmler's home in Tegernsee on August 31, 1936. On February 1, 1937, Wüst became president of the "Ahnenerbe."

Counter to the assumption of Kater, a protocol of that notable August meeting between Himmler, his special representative Bruno

---

[33] Kater, *Das 'Ahnenerbe' der SS*, p. 43.

[34] See Uta Halle, *'Die Externsteine sind bis auf weiteres germanisch!' Prähistorische Archäologie im Dritten Reich* (Bielefeld: Verlag für Regionalgeschichte, 2002). The best contemporary account of the "Externsteine" as a possible Pagan sanctuary originated from Carl Clemen, "Waren die Externsteine ein germanisches Heiligtum?" *Zeitschrift für Missionskunde und Religionswissenschaft* (1935), pp. 210–233.

Galke, the "Ahnenerbe"-secretary Wolfram Sievers and Wüst exists.[35] The consultation had great significance since Himmler articulated his further plans and projects he pursued with the "Ahnenerbe." Wüst himself was given in Tegernsee the unique opportunity to present a detailed statement about his scientific views in general and the way he would exploit the Indo-Germanic tradition for the purposes of the "Ahnenerbe" in particular. Himmler was so impressed that he instantly appointed Wüst director of a new department "Wortkunde" which his authority allowed him to establish on the spot.[36] Point 6 of the protocol notified a lengthy report of the Munich professor about the meaning of the notion "Odal." Himmler had a special interest in that concept which he thought to be an old Nordic law of hereditary nobility. He ordered Wüst to complete his research on this ideologically important issue as soon as possible. Additionally he commanded Sievers to instruct Wirth to wait with his own "Odal" book until Wüst would have finished his linguistic investigations (point 7). Himmler asked Wüst to survey and correct Wirth's 320 page "Odal" manuscript which he already had in hand and which, even in Himmler's eyes, needed to be rethought and revised (point 8). Another order of Himmler forced Wirth to restrict himself on his symbol studies ("Schrift- und Zeichenkunde") and to seek the help of Wüst before going to publish any of it (point 9). One half of the protocol's 16 paragraphs was worded as an "order" or "command." The other 8 mostly contained strong recommendations of Himmler accounting his fancies the "Ahnenerbe" should execute. While Wüst proposed bestowing the venia legendi on Wirth at the beginning (point 4), he recognized in the course of the meeting that the wind blowing Wirth's sail was about to veer. He did not fail to seize on the opportunity and wholeheartedly assured Himmler of his firm will to comply with his every wish. A new self-confidence led Wüst at the end to submit the suggestion that the translation of the Rig Veda should be included to the working schedule of the "Ahnenerbe," a proposal that Himmler immediately moved into an official order (point 14).

The item with the most practical relevance for Wüst was point 13 instructing him with Himmler's directive to deliver speeches in front

---

[35] Galke's "Erinnerungsprotokoll" dated September 1, 1936, Federal Archives Berlin, NS 21, vol. 669 (n.p.).
[36] Ibid., paragraph 5 of the protocol.

of SS-personnel throughout the country.[37] In June 1936 Wüst had given for the first time a talk about "Des Führers Buch 'Mein Kampf' als Spiegel arischer Weltanschauung" (Hitler's book 'Mein Kampf' as mirror of the Aryan worldview) at the University of Munich. It met with such a positive response that Himmler now directed its perpetual repetition in order to edify the ordinary SS-man in all parts of the country with the racial legacy of the Indo-Germans and the political duties arising from it. Several adaptations of the speech exist. In the following I quote from the version published in the journal of SS-sponsors *FM-Zeitschrift* based on the lecture Wüst gave at the Munich beer hall Hackerbräukeller on March 10, 1937.[38]

The talk was structured like a Protestant sermon. Starting with an anecdote about Hegel, Wüst then turned to the explanation of the word "Weltanschauung" before he elaborated on the benefits of the Aryan tradition and finally advanced to a comparison of Buddha and Adolf Hitler. His expounding of the German notion "Weltanschauung" went along with a strong critique of its Jewish counterpart. Though Wüst did nothing else than repeat common Christian prejudices, he declared "with utmost scientific thoroughness" that the Aryan worldview surpasses the Semitic one by far. Grounded on the very ancient scriptures of the old Indians and Iranians, only the Aryan race was able to develop a worldview characterized by 1) a meaningful cosmic order, 2) a solar mythology, 3) an expansive growth shaped by the laws of life and nature ("lebensgesetzliches Wachstum") and 4) by a forward-moving Indo-Germanic vigor.[39] None of these characteristics are to be found among Jews. Compared to a three-dimensional frame of mind the Aryans were provided with, the Jews possessed only two

---

[37] "RFSS [Reichsführer SS, H.J.] ordnete an, dass Professor Wüst im Winterhalbjahr vor sämtlichen Oberabschnitten der SS sprechen solle." Galke and Sievers were ordered to promote ("aufziehen") a lecture series in great style as a sort of advertising campaign in favor of the "Ahnenerbe." Ibid., NS 21, 669, point 13.

[38] *FM-Zeitschrift* 4.3, 1.3.1937. "FM" means "Fördernde Mitglieder." The journal is very rarely to be found in libraries (for instance in the Berlin State Library). See for a copy, Federal Archives Berlin, NSD 41/259, and for other non-published, slightly modified and partly commented versions: ibid., NS 21, vols. 292, 681 and 811 as well as Wüst's BDC-file (BDC AE, fol. 254–270). Karla Poewe, *New Religions and the Nazis* (New York-London: Routledge, 2006) shows a picture of Wüst on p. 27 lecturing in Munich, most likely in the Hackerbräukeller.

[39] "Des Führers Buch 'Mein Kampf' als Spiegel arischer Weltanschauung," *FM-Zeitschrift*, 1.3.1937, p. 3f.

dimensions.[40] No wonder that only the Indo-Germanic race was so successfully taking possession of the world in space and time. Particularly in their painting Wüst detected that the mind of the Jews was restricted to two dimensions: surface and abstraction. Utilitarianism and a superficial materialistic orientation on the Jewish side correlated to an Indo-Germanic attachment to the fate, Nietzsche's amor fati, on the other. Contrary to the cosmic order of the Aryans, the Jewish world was created by chaos and emptiness. It was – as the Old Testament reads in Genesis 1:2 – waste and void ("wüst und leer") from the outset. Wüst, nomen est omen, pointed to the Jewish understanding of the world as a pure vale of tears ("Jammertal") in which a healthy relation to life and nature was replaced by the frail concept of the original sin ("Erbsünde").

Wüst's critique of the Jewish perception of the world partly derived from the old Christian-Jewish antagonism and partly relied on a shallow anti-religious criticism of Christianity now concentrating on its Jewish fundamentals. Such a voelkish reference to post-Enlightenment currents gained momentum among many Nazi leaders particularly during the so-called church struggle and the vexations it caused. In Wüst's case the growing disapproval of the churches was fuelled by his professional inclination towards the language and culture of the Indo-European peoples. Due to his affirmative comprehension of things religious in general, he nevertheless emphasized traditional Protestant values even in such a speech on Adolf Hitler's Aryan roots as to be found in *Mein Kampf.* Above all Wüst attributed the secularized version of a "Tatchristentum" (Christianity of deeds) and a religiosity that becomes effective within the world and as part of its progress ("Weltfrömmigkeit") to the "Führer." Taken this way Hitler displayed the paradigmatic model of a self-sacrificing personality who dedicated his whole life to the service of his people. Having overcome the egocentric nature of man, Hitler perfectly epitomized the heroic fulfillment of one's duties ("Pflichterfüllung"). In the way he described the uniqueness of Hitler's conduct Wüst noticeably relied on a long-established canon of Protestant virtues which themselves originated from characteristics customarily attributed to Jesus Christ. What Wüst did was to expand this Protestant type of inner-worldly religiosity to the East and the Aryan culture. Only at first

---

[40] "Der Jude hat niemals eine dreidimensionale Weltvorstellung gehabt." Ibid., p. 3.

glance does it seem curious that Wüst switched immediately to Buddha after his description of Adolf Hitler as another example of moral leadership. This has to be understood as further extension of the credence of a Protestant intellectual to the East. Shaped by idiosyncrasies such as anti-dogmatism, anti-clericalism, anti-Catholicism, anti-Judaism, a strong historical orientation and scientific leaning, it aimed to revive withered or semi-secularized religious values with new life and faith.

Buddha entered Wüst's tale in the conventional form of a Christian miracle: After a long period of meditation and spiritual seclusion Buddha felt the necessity to return to his people and to normal life. In a wrestle that shattered the foundations of the world Buddha had gained a new understanding of the world.[41] On his way back to ordinary society he met a couple of unbelievers sitting near a grove. Despite the strong inner resistance of the five infidels, Buddha's supernatural power and the transcendent clearness on his face immediately forced them to discard their defiance. Then they easily found their way out of the incarceration amid the desire of selfish materialism and an eccentric self-abnegation inimical to the obligations of life. Exactly the same happened 2500 years later in Austria. The "Führer," at that time an unskilled worker who lived in Vienna under the spell of suffering, became acquainted with the hardship of the poor when walking through the pitiful flats of the workers ("wo er als Hilfsarbeiter im Bannkreis des Leidens stand, durch die Elendswohnungen schritt und die Not der Arbeiter sah").[42] His Viennese experience prevented Hitler either from getting lost in abstract theories or to become subject to a shallow realism. Instead, he arrived at an inspired vision ("geniale Zusammenschau") of reality similar to the one Buddha once had. Realizing the stunning parallelism between Buddha's and Hitler's enlightenment, Wüst felt overwhelmed. The only reason he found to explain the astounding correspondence was the racial kinship between the two.[43] Since Buddha and Adolf Hitler belonged to the same hereditary community, they reacted the same way to the problems of their time. Moreover, their common genetic constitution endowed them with the capacity to guide their people from subjugation to freedom.

---

[41] "Der Buddha hat in einem welterschütterten Ringen sich seine tiefsten weltanschaulichen Erkenntnisse errungen." Ibid., p. 4.

[42] Ibid., p. 4.

[43] Ibid., p. 4.

If we put the question aside what the "Führer" himself would have thought about such a foolish nonsense, we should not ignore the fact that for Himmler and other leading SS-figures, Wüst's fantastic journey into the history of Indo-Germanic religiosity made some sense. Wüst had been careful enough to evade the impression of an unpleasant Aryan proclivity towards self-castigation and long Lentens without eating and drinking. It is somehow bizarre to imagine SS-members sitting in the Munich Hackerbräukeller behind their second or third beer mug considering Buddha's holy life in linen and teetotalism so far away from everything worth living in Catholic Bavaria. Wüst did well to declare swiftly that the Buddhist negation of life was not directed against life itself. What Buddha meant was only the rotten life and the decayed morality of the big cities in India.[44] Since the statement obviously alluded to Berlin and other dens of iniquity in Weimar Germany under the influence of Jewish wickedness, a good beer and a respectable roast pork was not in danger from Wüst's encounter of East and West.

On the other hand, Himmler's notorious asceticism was well-known not to say dreaded in the SS. Its members often had the opportunity to experience that the expression "Himmler-Sekt" was not only a mere saying but another word for mineral water. The SS-records of the Federal Archives contain many admonitions of Himmler concerning alcohol abuses or other improper behavior of SS-members. The great number of internal reprimands clearly indicate the disproportion between moral claims (in terms of SS regularities) and reality. But observed or not, the frequent assertions of puritanical self-discipline strengthened the apprehension of the SS as an honest order with veracious principles. It must have been a great feeling for Wüst, as son of a school teacher, to ascend to the top of such a highly regarded and undoubtedly powerful organization. Having joined the SS on January 26, 1937, he was nominated "Hauptsturmführer" only four days later. From then on he quickly advanced to a "Sturmbannführer" on September 12, 1937, an "Obersturmbannführer" on September 11, 1938, a "Standartenführer" on November 9, 1940, and a SS-"Oberführer" on November 9, 1942.[45]

---

[44] "Der Buddha hat nicht das Leben verneint, sondern er hat das angefaulte Leben der indischen Großstädte, das Leben einer verrotteten Sittlichkeit gemeint." Ibid., p. 4.

[45] The military equivalent of a "Oberführer," Wüst's highest rank, corresponded to a rank between an "Oberst" (colonel) and a "Generalmajor" (brigadier general) in the Wehrmacht. It was nearly impossible for civilians to get such a high rank outside the army.

The enormous success of his ideological output led Wüst to believe that his permanent references to the Indo-Germanic tradition constituted a crucial part of the SS doctrine. In his opinion the SS formed the spearhead of the German master race, and the "Ahnenerbe" was the driving force behind it with the task of elaborating a reasonable and authoritative Weltanschauung.

In the formative phase of the "Ahnenerbe," when the SS-elitism gained intellectual contour, Wüst became acquainted with the prominent Italian fascist Julius Evola (1898–1974). Wüst met Evola on July 13, 1937 when the Italian baron traveled to Germany to promote the cultural exchange between the two axis powers. Seeking to build up an anti-bolshevist frontline in Europe, Evola tried to find possible allies among leading National Socialists. Wüst exhorted him to contact Himmler as well, and Evola swiftly promised. Directly after their meeting Wüst wrote a letter to Wolfram Sievers, the secretary general of the "Ahnenerbe," reporting his very interesting encounter and asking to purchase Evola's book *Erhebung wider die moderne Welt* as soon as possible.[46] Wüst was extremely excited about the German edition of Evola's *Rivolta contra il mondo moderno* which he considered as aristocratic version of popular German cultural criticism. Similar to the verbose and long-winded style of authors such as Oswald Spengler, Houston Stewart Chamberlain, and Herman Wirth, Evola employed the same unscientific and eclectic method of reasoning. However, Evola endeavored at demonstrating a noble discretion in politics and abstained from clumsy agitation in this publication. Besides his aristocratic reticence Wüst appreciated Evola's accentuation of the Eastern world being one of his main reference points. Evola's book, rightly esteemed as his 'masterpiece', was akin to Wirth's *Aufgang der Menschheit* – only better.[47]

---

[46] "Ich teile mit, dass ich heute die sehr interessante Bekanntschaft des Baron J. Evola – Rom gemacht habe. Baron Evola ist führend tätig auf dem Gebiete der faschistischen Kulturpolitik und plant die Errichtung einer über ganz Europa ausgedehnten antibolschewistischen Front des Geistes...Ich habe ihn darauf aufmerksam gemacht, dass unbedingt auch der Reichsführer SS angegangen werden müsse, was Baron Evola gern zu tun versprach." Letter of W. Wüst to W. Sievers on July 13, 1937, Federal Archives Berlin, NS 21, vol. 343, n.p. Two days later Sievers answered that the book was ordered and on July 23 that the book had arrived. Ibid., NS 21, vol. 730 and vol. 596.

[47] Though criticizing Wirth's errors, Evola beneficently conceded that also noteworthy things are to be found in his works. See for instance J. Evola, *Erhebung wider die moderne Welt* (Berlin: Deutsche Verlagsanstalt, 1935), p. 406f., n. 6; p. 432, n. 6; p. 442, n. 7; p. 443, n. 9; p. 446, n. 7; and p. 451, n. 29.

The more Evola's apparent anti-positivism linked positivism, materialism, and rationalism not only with the "Hebrew factor" in general but
with the study of religion and its Jewish representatives in particular,
the more Wüst became attracted by it.[48]

Invited by the "Studienkreis der Deutsch-Italienischen Stiftung," a
study group of the German-Italian Society, Evola gave a lecture on
December 10, 1937 in Berlin about "Abendländischer Aufbau aus urarischem Geist."[49] Here he emphasized in much clearer words the need
for a traditionalist counter revolution that should be based on the old
Aryan spirit and that would lead to a reconstruction of the Occident.
The enemies to be defeated before were the Jews, the bolsheviks, and
the Freemasons. A successful fight first had to overcome the solely negative attitude typical of many political and spiritual counter movements
leading up to the fight. Instead, a positive worldview was required, a
worldview rooted in a higher idea. Evola promised to deliver precisely
that. Two months later the distinguished fascist lectured a second time
in Berlin, now on the topic of "Gralsmysterium und Reichsgedanke."[50]
Since the German Foreign Ministry had taken notice of Evola's public
activities, it asked the "Ahnenerbe" for an expert to step in to provide a
proper understanding of Evola's ideas and intentions. For that reason
Joseph Otto Plaßmann, the editor in chief of the "Ahnenerbe"-journal
Germanien, wrote a short expert opinion in which he argued in two direc-
tions: a qualified approach, but, regarding politics, possibly problematic.
To avoid confusion and heated discussions about the status of Italy in
the medieval German Reich, it should not be published in *Germanien*. In
March 1938 Sievers sent the official "Ahnerbe"-statement to the Foreign
Ministry. Using Plaßmann's words he pleaded for political reservation,

---

[48] See ibid., p. 482, n. 13 where Evola heavily draws on the Protocols of the Elders of
Zion. The statement that Jewish scholars such as Durkheim paved the way for a "befle-
ckende 'Religionswissenschaft' auf 'soziologischer' und 'ahnenmäßiger' Grundlage"
refers to Evola's article "Sulle ragioni dell'antisemitismo" in *Vita Nova* 5–8, 1933.

[49] J. Evola, "Abendländischer Aufbau aus urarischem Geist. Vortragsabend im Studienkreis Berlin, 10.12.1937," Federal Archives Berlin, NS 21, vol. 343, 11 pages.

[50] The lecture took place between February 13 and 23, 1938. Drawn from the
version in the monthly *Geist der Zeit* (March 1939, pp. 145–154) it was translated and
republished as "Il mistero del graal e l'idea imperiale," in *Julius Evola nei documenti segreti
dell'ahnenerbe*, a curo di Bruno Zarotti (Quaderni di testi Evoliani 30) (Roma: Europa
Liberia Editrice, 1997), pp. 17–25.

however he also underscored that Evola stood in high esteem by the "Ahnenerbe"-president Wüst.[51]

Additionally a series of three lectures followed close in June 1938. Evola gave talks titled "Arische Lehre des heiligen Kampfes" (Aryan doctrine of the Holy War, June 13), "Gral als nordisches Mysterium" (Grail as Nordic mystery, June 20), and "Die Waffen des geheimen Krieges" (The weapons of the secret war, June 27).[52] The "Ahnenerbe" sent five envoys to Berlin, among them Sievers and Plaßmann. Wüst refrained from joining the group lest give the false impression of an official SS acknowledging Evola. In his lectures Evola once again stressed the necessity to form an anti-communist and anti-Jewish alliance in Europe. As he said in the foreword, occult forces intended the downfall of the world ("Weltumsturz"). Therefore it was of vital importance to have a valid and operative counter ideology in order to resist the agents of the darkness. In describing the secret aims and malicious practices of the enemies, Evola again referred to the Protocols of the Elders of Zion which unmistakably revealed that the Jews were the main perpetrators of the world revolution ("Haupttäter des Weltumsturzes").[53] What was at stake was the fight between the forces of tradition and anti-tradition, of spiritual hierarchy and revolutionary chaos, generally between light and darkness. While he defined traditionalism as connection with the metaphysical world, Evola denied Christianity any positive role in the resistance block he aimed to establish. Moreover, he saw it as a part of the problem and not of the solution although he eschewed tackling Christianity, obviously for opportunistic reasons. He did not hesitate to criticize groups and movements with a theosophical, occult or 'orientalizing' background which he subsumed under the category of new spiritualism ("Neuspirtiualismus"). Their general claims were not bad in his opinion, sometimes even good, but they painted more often than not a distorted picture of the metaphysical world. This was no wonder because these groups were usually headed by dreamers and half-educated experts in spiritual knowledge leading their good intentions to a bad end.

---

[51] Siever's to SS Obersturmführer Professor Langsdorff on March 16, 1938 answering a request from January 1. Federal Archives Berlin, BDC, personal file Evola, fol. 121, Plaßmann's statement, fol. 122.

[52] The manuscripts of all three lectures are to be found in the Federal Archives Berlin, NS 21, vol. 776 (20, 17, and 15 pages, together with a foreword of two pages).

[53] J. Evola, "Die Waffen des geheimen Krieges," p. 2. Himself he called a pioneer of antisemitism in Italy ("Vorkämpfer des Antisemitismus in Italien"), ibid., p. 10.

Evola believed that only a small elitist minority would be able to act as vanguard of the new order to come. With his idea of spiritual superiority and heroic virility he became rather interesting for a league of ascetic warriors such as the SS. In the first of his three speeches Evola expounded the Iranian doctrine of Mithra, "the warrior without sleep," who leads the "fravashi," the transcendental elements among his followers, into war against the satanic enemies of the Aryans.[54] Together with other examples taken from the religious history of the Indo-Germans, Evola developed an Aryan doctrine of the Holy War, a war that was not primarily undertaken in behalf of material interests but for metaphysical purposes. Culminating in bloody frenzies, the Aryan wars and conquests appear in Evola's explanation as a way of spiritual elevation. Even the "aristocratic idea of immortality" resulted from the Indo-Germanic understanding of heroic fighting.[55] According to Evola's interpretation of the Aryan tradition the victory of the victorious was an observable sign, more than that, an ordeal of a successful initiation and mystical renovatio.[56] What a powerful tautology! In contrast to the half-witted apostles of "Neuspiritualismus," Evola had to submit a skilled proficiency in hermetic traditions. He astutely intimated that there existed certain rites and "objective spiritual techniques" to gain influence over the divine potency either to tame or to unchain it, or, at least, to guide it in specific directions.[57] Evola concluded his lecture in summarizing the destructive elements on the side of the enemies (rationalism, individualism, collectivism, altogether culminating in bolshevism) whose agents were about to prepare their final attack. It was against them in particular he wanted to uphold tradition and the symbolism of the Holy War: "Eine neue Front soll sich bilden und alle die zusammenfassen, die noch standhalten und Träger der Tradition sind."[58]

---

[54] Ibid., p. 7. "Die frawashi heissen 'die schrecklichen, die allmächtigen', diejenigen, die im Sturm angreifen und den Sieg dem geben, der sie anruft." Ibid., p. 16. Cf. Karl Friedrich Geldner, "Fravashi," in *Die Religionen in Geschichte und Gegenwart*, vol. 2, 2nd ed. (1928), col. 747, for the personification of what was only a credo at the beginning.

[55] Ibid., p. 14.

[56] "Krieg: sagen wir es mit lauter Stimme: der Krieg soll für uns weder ein grausames Gemetzel, noch eine traurige Notwendigkeit sein, sondern der Weg zu einer höheren Lebensform und die Prüfung der göttlichen Sendung eines Volkes." Ibid., p. 18.

[57] Ibid., p. 4.

[58] "A new front shall be established to unite all those who keep on resisting, those who are still the bearers of the tradition." Ibid., p. 19.

Such a metaphysical justification of imperialistic warfare ought to be a perfect ideology for an organization such as the SS. With the set up of the four year plan in autumn 1936, the leaders of the Third Reich had began actively preparing the next military conflict which they commenced exactly three years later. It is not surprising that Wüst revealed a very assertive opinion about the way Evola utilized the Aryan tradition, a tradition that the "Ahnenerbe"-president thought to provide an excellent substantiation of the aristocratic warrior caste the "Männerbund" of the SS was. However, Wüst's persuasion did not represent the mainstream in the SS. This becomes quite evident from an evaluation that originated from the Secret Service of the SS, strictly speaking from the SD department II 2112, which openly repudiated Evola's theories and projects.[59] Its author, an SD collaborator named Hancke, probably Kurt Hancke, took great pains to explain over 12 pages why the views of the Italian fascist were not compatible with National Socialism. Hancke criticized Evola's individualism, his overaccentuation of spiritual agency, the lack of a deeper understanding of politics as well as his speculative arguing and high-flown utopia without grounding. After all, Hancke saw in Evola a typical representative of the old nobility, a reactionary Roman ("reaktionärer Römer") entirely shaped by the feudalism of a bygone time. He ended his assessment with four recommendations: 1) no concrete support for Evola's plans and projects, 2) no continuation of his public lectures, 3) to prohibit Evola from taking up high level contacts with party or state agencies, 4) to keep an eye on his propaganda activities in the neighboring countries.[60]

A second evaluation came from the "Ahnenerbe" itself. It was again written by the germanist Joseph Otto Plaßmann, head of the "Ahnenerbe"-department of Germanic cultural sciences ("germanische Kulturwissenschaft"). Plaßmann articulated the official position of the "Ahnenerbe" also taking Evola's Berlin lecture series as starting point. Tone and content were quite different to Hancke and the SD. Already in the first sentence Plaßmann affirmed that the Italian fascist was

---

[59] "Bericht Vortragsreihe Evola," 12 pages, June 30, 1938, Federal Archives Berlin, Dahlwitz Hoppegarten ZB 1, 1224, fol. 645–656 as well as Federal Archives Berlin, BDC, personal file Evola, fol. 83–94.

[60] Ibid., p. 12.

principally regarded as a positive figure.[61] Then he continued with a
moderate critique of Evola's insufficient familiarity with real politics
and with the nature of National Socialist statesmanship. Evola's comprehension of Italy as an outpost of Nordic solar mythology in the
Mediterranean world was, from his point of view, neither false nor
dishonorable, nor his highlighting of a fascist alliance between Italy
and Germany. But in a typical Italian manner of thinking Evola's
Aryan forces of the light ("arische Lichtkräfte") had an existence too
airy and too far away from the concrete social and political life. As
a result of his poor understanding of political reality, Evola did not
shy away from seeking contact with reactionary intellectuals such as
the Catholic universalist Othmar Spann, hereby totally ignoring their
anti-voelkish bias. Plaßmann's arguments were included by Sievers in
the official statement of the "Ahnenerbe" forwarded to Himmler on
July 13, 1938.[62] The most relevant part of it was the final paragraph.
In following Plaßmann and in recapitulating the former assessment for
the Foreign Ministry, Sievers pleaded again for an attitude of reserve.
It would not be advisable to sustain Evola's propaganda campaign, not
at least because it had remained unclear whether Evola really represented the official standpoint of fascist Italy. Nevertheless – and here
Sievers relied on the judgment of Wüst – lines of communication with
Evola should remain open. Basically seen as a valuable thinker and as
a companion in the ideological warfare at stake, either stimulation or
constraint might be applied to guide him in the right direction. How
close the relation and a possible cooperation might become in the
future should depend on a further maturation of Evola's ideas. Sievers
ended with the words:

> Dagegen wird es auch nach Ansicht von SS-Obersturmbannführer Wüst,
> der mit Evola früher bereits gesprochen hat, für notwendig gehalten, dass
> man mit Evola, der an sich eine wertvolle geistige Erscheinung darstellt,
> in ständiger Fühlung bleibt, ihm Anregungen gibt und ihn im Notfalle
> zügelt, wobei man auch von ihm wertvolle Anregungen gewinnen könnte.
> Wie sich eine solche Kraft auf die Dauer auswirkt und wie man sie einmal
> in ein politisches Gesamtziel einordnen kann, das kann erst eine längere
> Zeit der Beobachtung und der Reife seiner Gedanken erweisen.[63]

---

[61] "Die Grundeinstellung von Evola ist von unserem Standpunkt aus im allgemeinen
positiv zu werten." "Aktenvermerk betr. Baron Evola," July 2, 1938, Federal Archives
Berlin, NS 21, vol. 815, 2 pages, here p. 1.
[62] Sievers to the Reichsführer SS on July, 13, 1938, "Stellungnahme zu den Vorträgen
des Baron Evola," Federal Archives Berlin, NS 21, vol. 815, 2 pages.
[63] Ibid. p. 2, emphasis in the original.

One and a half week after the "Ahnenerbe"-statement was sent to Himmler, Wüst received a handwritten message from Sievers indicating him that the matter of Evola had some delicacy.[64] Yet a telegram dated August 11 from Himmler's personal adjutant Rudolf Brandt made clear to Sievers that the Reichsführer SS fully agreed with the assessment of the "Ahnenerbe," especially with its final passage.[65] Evola was to be accepted as a collaborator without endorsing his metaphysical agenda. In the internal quarrels concerning an appropriate estimation of the Evolian sort of Italian fascism, the ambivalent, though generally positive, "Ahnenerbe"-position prevailed. The further relationship of the SS with Evola followed this direction, and Wüst was clever enough not to insist on Evola's spiritual doctrines.

Ironically, the SD delegated "Obersturmführer" Hancke to resume contact with Evola. After a first meeting on April 27, 1939, Hancke wrote a very interesting three page report about it.[66] Referring to the former SD rejection from June 1938, he pointed to its success insofar Evola's plans to found a new transnational and bilingual fascist journal had been thwarted.[67] Because Evola had managed to contact other influential state agencies, for instance the Ministry of Propaganda, and because his official support from the Italian government had become manifest, the Secret Service should reconsider and modify its position. To his great surprise Hancke learned from the conversation with Evola that the Italian fascist was not only very well informed about the earlier SD repudiation but constantly maintained close contacts with high-level SS leaders, namely Alexander Langsdorff, Werner Best, and, of course, Walther Wüst. Yet Hancke met also an Evola who had considerably cut down his expectations and wishes and who no longer wanted material

---

[64] Sievers to Wüst on July 22, 1938, Federal Archives Berlin, NS 21, vol. 776.

[65] Brandt to Sievers on August 11, 1938, ibid.

[66] Hancke's statement dated from May 2, 1938, Federal Archives Berlin, Dahlwitz Hoppegarten, ZB 1, 1224, fol. 657–659.

[67] The name of the journal should have been *Sangue e Spirito* (Blood and Spirit). It aimed to balance the German and Italian version of racism. Evola acted here in compliance with Mussolini himself who later withdrew his approval. See H.T. Hansen in his foreword to Julius Evola, *Menschen inmitten von Ruinen* (Tübingen: Hohenrain, 1991), p. 100. See also the 22 "Posizioni italiane sulla questione razziale per la rivista italo-tedesca 'Sangue e Spirito'," in Nicola Cospito and Hans Werner Neulen, eds., *Julius Evola nei documenti segreti del Terzo Reich* (Rome: Europa, 1986), pp. 93–100 and the list of 15 Italian collaborators, ibid., p. 92. However, this new attempt was undertaken in 1942, that is four years later. Cf. also the report of a Dr. Vollmer from the Foreign Ministry, February 19, 1942 "Colloquio con il Barone J. Evola a riguardo della fondazione di una rivista sulla razza," ibid., pp. 85–91.

support from the SS. What Evola now hoped for was Himmler simply to consent to his publication plans. Evola even agreed to send in the proofs of his new book on the Grail mystery in order to get an official SS imprimatur for the German translation. Moreover, he obediently admitted to rearranging the circle of authors for the intended journal in full accordance with SS interests.[68] Then the proud Italian aristocrat and anti-Catholic dissenter used the occasion to submissively request a personal audience with Himmler. Finally Evola asked for an admission to German archives because he wanted to investigate the secret aspects of Freemasonry. This time Hancke concluded his report with two suggestions: 1) to confer the requested *internal* imprimatur, 2) to await Evola's further research activities if a cooperation might be in the interest of the SD.[69] As a result of their encounter, Evola was allowed to make the personal acquaintance with Hancke's superior Professor Alfred Six, then head of the department VII of the Reich Security Main Office.[70] The "Reichssicherheitshauptamt," established in September 1939, had a special section dedicated to Freemasonry (VII B 1) as well as a division "Archive, museum, special research assignments" (VII C).[71] An undated and unsigned statement to be found in the same file after the aforementioned letters – evidently originating from the Secret Service – informs us that Evola's research work on the Freemasons required not only normal sources but also the use of confidential material confiscated by the German Reich.[72] His aim to write an anti-Freemason book noticeably coincided with the new readiness of Six and the SD to accept Evola as informant and co-worker.

---

[68] ". . . die negativ beurteilten Vorschläge zum Mitarbeiterkreis [seien] nur vorläufiger Natur und jederzeit im Sinne der SS zu ändern." Federal Archives Berlin, Dahlwitz Hoppegarten, ZB 1, 1224, fol. 658 (p. 2).

[69] Ibid., fol. 659 (p. 3).

[70] See the letter of Evola to an unnamed addressee from June 15 and to Six from August 20, 1939, Federal Archives Berlin, Dahlwitz Hoppegarten, ZB 1, 1224, fol. 680 and fol. 662f. In his letter to Six Evola referred to a meeting they had in Rome before.

[71] See Reinhard Rürup, ed., *Topography of Terror. Gestapo, SS and Reichssicherheitshauptamt on the 'Prinz-Albrecht-Terrain'. A documentation*, 4th ed. (trans. from the 7th rev. and enl. German ed. from 1989 by Werner T. Angress) (Berlin: Willmuth Arenhövel, 1995), pp. 78–82. The amount of objects seized by Gestapo and SS grew into enormous dimensions. The SD even entertained a special (non-public) "Freimaurermuseum" in Berlin since 1936. See Helmut Neuberger, *Winkelmaß und Hakenkreuz. Die Freimaurer und das Dritte Reich* (München: Herbig, 2001), p. 199.

[72] Federal Archives Berlin, Dahlwitz Hoppegarten, ZB 1, 1224, fol. 681 (recte et verso). Thus the author argued for a financial and practical support of Evola.

Instead of becoming an organic intellectual of the SS warrior caste, Evola ended as one of the great many subaltern collaborators. In the course of these activities Evola was seriously wounded during an air raid in Vienna on March 12, 1945.[73]

The relationship between Wüst and Evola is of outstanding significance in several regards. First it shows a remarkable change in Wüst's development whose perspective turned from the voelkish narrow-mindedness of a Herman Wirth to Evola's aristocratic idea of an imperial Reich. Though not principally different, Evola's cultural pessimism stood in Wüst's view high above the doctrinaire and pedantic casuistry of Wirth. In the 1920s Evola played a comparable role as Pagan Zealot and anti-Catholic rabble rouser in Italy especially with his book *Imperialismo pagano* appearing in the same year (1928) as Wirth's *Aufgang der Menschheit*. However, Evola became more moderate through defending himself against the counterattacks launched by prominent Catholic fascists such as Egilberto Martire and better comprehending Mussolini's flexible "dual" policy regarding the church.[74] This kind of reflective and controlled animadversion towards the Catholic church became more attractive to Wüst the more so Evola emphasized the Jewish traits of Christianity and resorted to the world of the Aryans in seeking an alternative. Evola's more spiritual and less biological racism came across to Wüst as useful in supporting his endeavor of anchoring the doctrines of the SS in the history of the Aryan tradition. It must not be forgotten that Wüst, who came from a lower middle-class background, was fascinated by Evola's noble appearance and his aristocratic reasoning on large scale and in dimensions previously unknown to him.

Second, Wüst's assessment of Evola clearly demonstrates that within the SS different and even contradictory positions were not only possible but quite normal. If such a rigorous corporation lacked a uniform not to say consistent theoretical basis, one should not expect National Socialism as a whole to have had or to have been a coherent ideology. Wüst's relations with Evola, generally Germany's relations with Italy, offer compelling examples for the wide range of attitudes to be designated by the rubric "fascism." Besides many other issues of minor importance religion was such a highly problematic field of controversial debates

---

[73] The date is given by H.T. Hansen in Evola, *Menschen inmitten von Ruinen*, p. 111.

[74] See Richard Drake, "Julius Evola, radical fascism, and the Lateran accords," *The Catholic historical review* 74 (1988), pp. 403–419.

concerning the ideological substance of a fascist worldview. Fascism
and National Socialism should more appropriately be understood as
flexible aggregations of fitting components prone to modification under
the influence of political, social, economical, and other factors rather
than monolithic blocks. Similar to the concept "religion," the concept
"fascism" implies plurality and variegation, its 'universal' meaning and
semantic function as general notion notwithstanding.

Fascist ideologies embrace a deep-seated animosity towards Jews as
one of their main features. Both Wüst and Evola shared the opinion
that almost all problems exhibited by modern societies resulted from a
Jewish influence. The omnipresence and omnipotence of the secret Jewish threat approached in Evola's thinking sometimes even a pathological
dimension. In his infamous foreword to the second Italian edition of
the Protocols of the Elders of Zion, published by the Catholic fascist
Giovanni Preziosi in 1938, Evola's main point was that their truth and
reliability could in no way be injured by a perhaps lacking authenticity.
He unwaveringly believed that the Protocols "contain the plan for an
occult war, whose objective is the utter destruction, in the non-Jewish
peoples, of all tradition, class, aristocracy, and hierarchy, and of all
moral, religious, or supra-material values." Wherever he looked, Evola
discovered that the Protocols veraciously describe how the Jews corrupt
Western civilization from within: "Liberalism, individualism, egalitarian-
ism, free thought, anti-religious Enlightenment, and various additions
which, following from these, bring about the revolt of the masses and
communism itself."[75] What is astounding here is that a devout Pagan
and a firm Catholic joined arms in their fight against the Jews. Under
the patronage of the fascist state, antisemitism functioned as a powerful
agent to overcome different, even conflicting religious persuasions for
acting in court against a common adversary. Next to anti-bolshevism,
antisemitism was the chief propulsive power to reconcile or, at least, to

[75] "Introduzione a L'Internationale ebraica." *I 'Protocolli' Dei 'Savi Anzani' Di
Sion* (Roma: La Vita Italiana, 1938), pp. 9–33, quoted from the English translation
which is to be found on the right wing website http://thompkins_cariou.tripod.
com/id68.html. In Preziosi's journal *Vita Italiana* two antisemitic articles of Evola
appeared shortly before: "Il processo di Berna e l'autenticità dei 'Protocolli'" and
"La volontà di potenza ebraica e l'autenticità dei 'Protocolli'," ibid., October and
December 1937. Evola did not hesitate to repeat his heinous propaganda in *Menschen
inmitten von Ruinen*, pp. 323ff., the German translation of *Gli uomine e le rovine* (1st ed.,
Roma: Ed. dell'Ascia, 1953).

set back otherwise dominating societal conflicts. The greater the enemy, the greater the need to join forces.

Evola's attempt to extend the front of his anti-bolshevist campaign to Southeastern Europe is another confirmation of the ideological interplay between fascism in general and fascism in particular. Some days after his second and some weeks before his third lecture in Berlin, Evola traveled to Romania where he met with the Iron Guard leader Corneliu Zelea Codreanu in March 1938. Evola continued in Bucharest what he had started in Berlin: to both incite and unite traditionalist impulses to prevent the victory of the forces of the darkness. Their meeting at the "Green House," the guardist center in the suburbs of Bucharest, was made possible "grazie alla mediazione dello scrittore moldavo Lovinescu e di Mircea Eliade," as Francesco Cassata writes.[76] Evola and Eliade had corresponded with each other for an extended period of time. Their fellowship can be described as congenial, perhaps even cordial. It is more than likely that Evola not only wanted to discuss the possibility of an anti-communist alliance with Codreanu in Bucharest but sought to win Eliade as collaborator for his new journal *Sangue e Spirito* as well. If one compares Eliade's articles of that period with the arguments Evola brought forth in his own publications or, more openly, in his lectures given in Berlin, the resemblance is not to be overlooked.

Although an English edition of Eliade's contributions to legionary or pro-legionary periodicals is still missing, the evidence provided by Leon Volovici in his book on *Romanian Intellectuals in the 1930s* clearly validates the correspondence.[77] Most of the catchwords used by Eliade are also part of Evola's reasoning: a national awakening based on the reconciliation of metaphysics (god) and politics (Romania), the political need of a spiritual rebirth, the regeneration of humiliated hierarchic and cosmic structures, national messianism, ethnic unity and so forth. The most striking example for that parallelism is probably Eliade's eulogy of "legionary aristocracy" that appeared shortly before Evola arrived in Bucharest. In a typical Evolian manner Eliade propagated

---

[76] Francesco Cassata, *A destra del fascismo. Profilo politico di Julius Evola* (Torino: Bollati Boringhieri, 2003), p. 222, see also F. Țurcanu, *Mircea Eliade*, p. 283f. and p. 386f.

[77] Leon Volovici, *Nationalist Ideology and Antisemitism. The Case of Romanian Intellectuals in the 1930s* (Oxford et al.: Pergamon Press, 1991), pp. 77–149. The pro-legionary articles published by Hannelore Müller, *Der frühe Mircea Eliade. Sein rumänischer Hintergrund und die Anfänge seiner universalistischen Religionsphilosophie* (Münster: Lit, 2004), here pp. A63–A107 point at the same direction.

the strengthening of aristocratic European values, a new "awareness of the historic mission, worthiness, manliness, contempt and indifference toward the powerless, scoundrels and clever fellows."[78] The laudation of the Iron Guard's unique achievements and spiritual primacy – "Replacing aristocracy of the blood, the Legion creates a new aristocracy: that of the spirit."[79] – concurred to a large degree with the intention of Evola's new journal *Sangue e Spirito*. Two decades later Evola contributed five articles to the "Journal for the Free World" *Antaios* that Eliade edited together with Ernst Jünger from 1959–1971.

Despite the fact that the Iron Guard was a purely Chistian movement with no affiliation with the old Aryans of India and Iran whatsoever, Evola instantly detected an Aryan type when he met Codreanu.[80] The chief characteristic that qualified Codreanu to become a representative of the Aryan tradition was his fervent antisemitism. As it was the case with the Catholic fascist Giovanni Preziosi, we have to notice here the same phenomenon that religious contradictions were annulled in attacking the common Jewish enemy. In fighting against the antagonists of every metaphysical and hierarchic order, the legionaries displayed typical Aryan values. Their success was more than a proof an ordeal for the righteousness of their behavior. What impressed Evola the most considering the Iron Guard's war against the "Yids" was that it totally emerged from a spiritual grounding. The legionaries perfectly accomplished the "Aryan doctrine of the Holy War" which Evola highlighted soon after in Berlin on June 13, 1938. The subject of this lecture was a rationale of heroic fighting and dying not in favor of personal or materialistic interests but for metaphysical reasons. Could Evola have found a better example than the dauntless death of the two Guardist martyrs Ion Moţa and Vasile Marin who lost their life in combat on

---

[78] M. Eliade, "Noua aristocraţie legionară," *Vremea* 522, January 23, 1938, quoted from L. Volovici, *Nationalist Ideology and Antisemitism*, p. 91.

[79] Ibid., *Nationalist Ideology and Antisemitism*, p. 134.

[80] "...azure grey eyes, open forehead, genuine Roman-Aryan type: and, mixed with virile traits, something contemplative, mystical in the expression. This is Corneliu Codreanu, the leader and founder of the Romanian 'Iron Guard', the one who is called 'assassin', 'Hitler's henchman', 'anarchist conspirator', by the world press, because since 1919, he has been challenging Israel, and the forces which are more or less in cahoots with it, at work in the Romanian national life." Julius Evola, "La tragedia de la Garda di Ferro," *La Vita Italiana* 309, December 1938, quoted from the English translation provided by the already mentioned Thompkins-website. Alexandra Laignel-Lavastine, *Cioran, Eliade, Ionesco: L'oubli du fascisme* (Paris: Presses Universitaires de France, 2002) p. 194 quotes this passage from a French translation of Evola's article.

Spanish soil having fought "with all and every means against the powers of the darkness" voluntarily sacrificing themselves "for the victory
of the Savior," as Eliade put it?[81] Evola's entire speech about the holy
war of the Aryans was an adoration of the heroic death of the initiated for whom dying was a medium to achieve a higher spiritual level.
Even the wild frenzies attributed by Evola to the Iranian Mithra and
his enraged followers found expression in Guardist behavior. When ten
legionaries murdered the traitor Mihael Stelescu in July 1936, their
fervor was so great that they not only shot him dead but chopped his
body in pieces. "Then they danced around the corpse, made the sign
of the cross, kissed each other and wept for joy."[82]

It is essential in a historical perspective to disclose the underlying
truth, viz. the underlying lies, of an ideological preaching such as
Evola's. Neither were Jews exempted from material spoliation for the
sake of metaphysical reasons nor led the holy war of the Aryans to any
spiritual enhancement on the side of the enemies and the defeated.[83]
Long before the outbreak of World War II, the Iron Guard as well
as the SS revealed on plenty of occasions their real nature as terrorist
organizations. Evola's justification of Aryan warfare has an exceptional
character in so far he argued straightforwardly without any religious
or other deviation. As an ideologue *sans phrases* he offers the opportunity to better differentiate the positions of less extreme thinkers. Wüst
reached Evola's level of direct and unambiguous ideological arguing
in the second half of the 1930s. As we will see in the next chapter, he
then used the Aryan tradition to corroborate the ideology of National
Socialism without any intermediating factors. Significant differences
notwithstanding, the common denominator between Wüst, Evola, and
Eliade was the collective goal of setting up a spiritual countermovement
against bolshevism, a "antibolschewistische Front des Geistes," as Wüst
had correctly described Evola's endeavors in Germany. Evola's 'opus

---

[81] M. Eliade, "Ion Moţa şi Vasile Marin," *Vremea* 472, January 24, 1937, Volovici,
Nationalist Ideology and Antisemitism, p. 83.

[82] "Sie feuerten jeweils mehrere Schüsse auf den Wehrlosen und zerstückelten die
Leiche mit Äxten. Danach tanzten sie um die Kadaverteile, bekreuzigten sich, küßten
einander und weinten vor Freude." Armin Heinen, *Die Legion 'Erzengel Michael' in Rumä-
nien. Soziale Bewegung und politische Organisation. Ein Beitrag zum Problem des internationalen
Faschismus* (München: R. Oldenbourg, 1986), p. 280f. Cf. H. Müller, *Der frühe Mircea
Eliade*, p. 79f.

[83] Cf. here Cristiano Grottanelli, "Fruitful Death: Mircea Eliade and Ernst Jünger
on Human Sacrifice, 1937–1945," *Numen* 52–1 (2005), pp. 116–145 and the articles of
Gustavo Benavides and Eugen Ciurtin in this book on p. 263f., p. 272, pp. 350–352
and on pp. 355–357.

magnum' *Rivolto contra il mondo moderno* functioned for both Wüst and
Eliade as a key text allowing them to conceptualize their own theoretical agendas. Eliade was even more enthusiastic than Wüst about
the way Evola described modern man's decadence, the reasons for his
decay and the possibilities to regenerate the metaphysical fundaments
of a fallen world. In the review that Eliade published in March 1935
in the Romanian journal *Vremea*, he pronounced an extraordinary positive assessment of Evola's thinking.[84] Eliade was particularly delighted
at the rigor of Evola's analysis, his critical stance, and his courage to
oppose mainstream positivism. Appropriately, Eliade put Evola in one
line with Gobineau, Chamberlain, Spengler, and Rosenberg.[85] Evola's
prodigious erudition ("érudition vraiment prodigieuse") made him
inaccessible "aux dilettanti" but also prevented a greater diffusion of
his ideas. It was for that reason why Eliade proclaimed it as his task to
spread the views of Evola in Romania to an even further extent than
he had already been doing starting in 1927.[86] This was much more
than the "Ahnenerbe"-president accomplished in promoting Evola's
fascist theories in Germany.

One and a half year after Wüst had taken over the presidency
of the "Ahnenerbe" he delivered a speech in July 1938 in which he
resumed the "Ahnenerbe"-development of the foregoing period.[87] Wüst
declared that now 20 departments and 72 collaborators were part of
Himmler's brain trust, a number that increased until the end of the
war to about 40 departments. Most of the "Ahnenerbe"-collaborators
were funded by the German Research Foundation if they did not have

---

[84] Mircea Eliade, "Recension de 'Rivolta contro il mondo moderno' de Julius Evola,"
Vremea 382, March 31, 1935. I am quoting from the French translation that appeared
in the right wing paper *Les deux étendards* 1, September/December 1988, pp. 42–44.

[85] "On peut dire qu l'oeuvre d'Evola se situe dans la ligne de Gobineau, Chamberlain, Spengler, Rosenberg." Ibid., p. 43.

[86] "...il est intéressant de rappeler que j'ai écrit une longue étude sur son œuvre,
qui a paru en plusieurs parties à partir der 1927, tandis qu'en 1928 j'ai entamé toute
une étude sur sa philosophie magique, étude restée à l'état de manuscrit. Depuis, le
seul qui ait mentionné son nom, dans notre pays, a été, en 1933, notre camarade de la
rédaction, V. Lovinescu." Ibid., p. 43. The editors added the note that Vasile Lovinescu
had published an essay under the pseudonym "Geticus" on "La Dacie hyperboréene" in
the journal *Études Traditionelles* in 1936/37, republished as Geticus, *La Dacie hyperboréene*
(Pardès: Puiseaux, 1987).

[87] "Die Forschungsgemeinschaft 'Das Ahnenerbe'," protocoll of Wüst's speech given
at "Schloß Niedernfels" during a "Gaudozentenlager" (July 16, 1938), Federal Archives Berlin, NS 21, vol. 792. This sort of both physical and ideological training camps
("Dozentenlager") had become obligatory for lecturers to raise their qualification from
the habilitation to an official "Dozentur" (lecturership) in December 1934.

an established position at one of Germany's universities. For financial reasons alone it was vital for the "Ahnenerbe" to keep in frequent contact with the Reich Ministry of Science and Education and to win university professors for co-operation. In fact, the "Ahnenerbe" had a clear (and successful) strategy to infiltrate the Berlin ministry with SS members. In pursuing the aim of a greater scientific seriousness, Herman Wirth had been pushed back to the position of an honorary president in March 1937 before he was urged to depart completely in December 1938. Parallel to the first measure Wüst arranged for the name "Deutsches Ahnenerbe. Studiengesellschaft für Geistesurge-schichte" to be freed from the Wirth-additive and changed into "Das Ahnenerbe" in March 1937. With similar intentions, Wüst replaced the designation of his own department "Wortkunde" with the more scientific heading "Abteilung für Indogermanisch-arische Sprach- und Kulturwissenschaft" on March 8, 1938. Another example for someone who released himself from an earlier impact of Herman Wirth was Otto Huth who joined the "Ahnenerbe" in March 1937. He likewise distanced himself from Wirth to proceed with his career. In April 1938 Huth was nominated provisional head of the "Ahnenerbe"-department "Indogermanische Geistes- und Glaubensgeschichte," but became its official director after he attained his venia legendi at the University of Tübingen under Jakob Wilhelm Hauer. With the support of the SS and the "Ahnenerbe," Huth was nominated professor of science of religion ("Allgemeine Religionswissenschaft") at the "Reichsuniversität Straßburg" in occupied France on April 1, 1942.[88]

To open up better fundraising possibilities, Wüst changed his posi-tion with Himmler on January 1, 1939, becoming the new curator and Himmler president of the "Ahnenerbe." The diagram on p. 142 shows that many "Ahnenerbe"-sections had a traditional philological-historical leaning. This resembled Wüst's own scientific background and resulted from his efforts to organize the work along normal academic structures. Space does not allow more than a superficial view of the "Ahnenerbe"-departments. Of course, disciplines dealing with such matters as the old Germans and the Indo-Germanic heritage were strongly emphasized. In both the natural sciences and humanities, excursions like the one Herman Wirth had undertaken in Sweden

---

[88] To Huth's career, see H. Junginger, *Von der philologischen zur völkischen Religionswis-senschaft*, chapter 18, pp. 248–268.

Diagram of the SS-„Ahnenerbe" (1943/44)
Bold frame designates research fields with a philological-historical orientation.

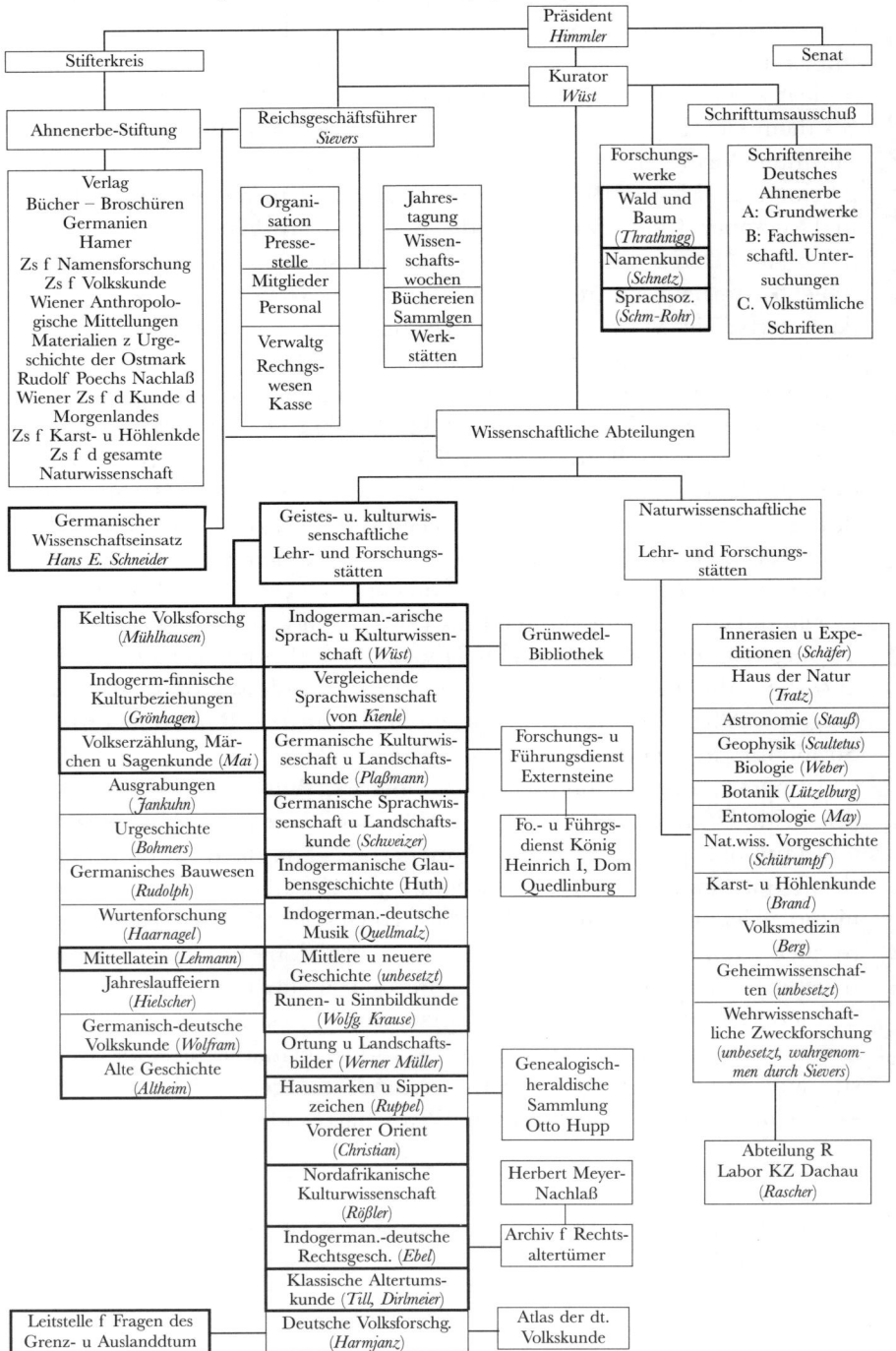

Präsident *Himmler*

Stifterkreis

Senat

Kurator *Wüst*

Ahnenerbe-Stiftung

Reichsgeschäftsführer *Sievers*

Schrifttumsausschuß

Forschungs-werke

Schriftenreihe Deutsches Ahnenerbe
A: Grundwerke
B: Fachwissen-schaftl. Unter-suchungen
C. Volkstümliche Schriften

Verlag
Bücher – Broschüren
Germanien
Hamer
Zs f Namensforschung
Zs f Volkskunde
Wiener Anthropolo-gische Mittellungen
Materialien z Urge-schichte der Ostmark
Rudolf Poechs Nachlaß
Wiener Zs f d Kunde d Morgenlandes
Zs f Karst- u Höhlenkde
Zs f d gesamte Naturwissenschaft

Organi-sation
Presse-stelle
Mitglieder
Personal
Verwaltg
Rechngs-wesen
Kasse

Jahres-tagung
Wissen-schafts-wochen
Büchereien
Sammlgen
Werk-stätten

Wald und Baum (*Thrathnigg*)
Namenkunde (*Schnetz*)
Sprachsoz. (*Schm-Rohr*)

Wissenschaftliche Abteilungen

Germanischer Wissenschaftseinsatz *Hans E. Schneider*

Geistes- u. kulturwis-senschaftliche Lehr- und Forschungs-stätten

Naturwissenschaftliche Lehr- und Forschungs-stätten

Keltische Volksforschg (*Mühlhausen*)

Indogerman.-arische Sprach- u Kulturwissen-schaft (*Wüst*)

Grünwedel-Bibliothek

Innerasien u Expe-ditionen (*Schäfer*)

Indogerm-finnische Kulturbeziehungen (*Grönhagen*)

Vergleichende Sprachwissenschaft (von *Kienle*)

Haus der Natur (*Tratz*)

Astronomie (*Stauß*)

Volkserzählung, Mär-chen u Sagenkunde (*Mai*)

Germanische Kulturwis-seschaft u Landschafts-kunde (*Plaßmann*)

Forschungs- u Führungsdienst Externsteine

Geophysik (*Scultetus*)

Biologie (*Weber*)

Ausgrabungen (*Jankuhn*)

Germanische Sprachwis-senschaft u Landschafts-kunde (*Schweizer*)

Botanik (*Lützelburg*)

Entomologie (*May*)

Urgeschichte (*Bohmers*)

Indogermanische Glau-bensgeschichte (Huth)

Fo.- u Führgs-dienst König Heinrich I, Dom Quedlinburg

Nat.wiss. Vorgeschichte (*Schütrumpf*)

Germanisches Bauwesen (*Rudolph*)

Indogerman.-deutsche Musik (*Quellmalz*)

Karst- u Höhlenkunde (*Brand*)

Wurtenforschung (*Haarnagel*)

Mittlere u neuere Geschichte (*unbesetzt*)

Volksmedizin (*Berg*)

Mittellatein (*Lehmann*)

Runen- u Sinnbildkunde (*Wolfg. Krause*)

Geheimwissenschaf-ten (*unbesetzt*)

Jahreslauffeiern (*Hielscher*)

Ortung u Landschafts-bilder (*Werner Müller*)

Wehrwissenschaft-liche Zweckforschung (*unbesetzt, wahrgenom-men durch Sievers*)

Germanisch-deutsche Volkskunde (*Wolfram*)

Hausmarken u Sippen-zeichen (*Ruppel*)

Genealogisch-heraldische Sammlung Otto Hupp

Alte Geschichte (*Altheim*)

Vorderer Orient (*Christian*)

Nordafrikanische Kulturwissenschaft (*Rößler*)

Herbert Meyer-Nachlaß

Abteilung R Labor KZ Dachau (*Rascher*)

Indogerman.-deutsche Rechtsgesch. (*Ebel*)

Archiv f Rechts-altertümer

Klassische Altertums-kunde (*Till, Dirlmeier*)

Leitstelle f Fragen des Grenz- u Auslanddtum

Deutsche Volksforschg. (*Harmjanz*)

Atlas der dt. Volkskunde

Source: Joachim Lerchenmüller and Gerd Simon, eds., *Im Vorfeld des Massenmords. Germanistik im 2. Weltkrieg* (Tübingen: Gift, 1997), p. 88.

had been an issue of considerable interest. The greatest project in that regard was Ernst Schäfer's Tibet expedition between April 1938 and August 1939.[89] In addition to normal botanical, geographical and anthropological studies, the expedition intended an ethnological survey of the Tibetan populace according to racial criteria. Speculations about secret or even occult aims of the research journey, concerning for instance the World Ice Theory of Hans Hörbiger or Helena Blavatsky's theosophical guesswork about a lost Aryan knowledge that might have survived in Tibet, gained some popularity in the last years. However, while such things might have played a role in Himmler's thinking, no hard evidence for an occult background of the expedition has been revealed. Its scientific and political success led to the establishment of a new "Ahnenerbe"-department called "Innerasienforschung und Expeditionen" (Research on Inner Asia and Expeditions) in January 1940 with the zoologist Ernst Schäfer as its director. Two years later it was reorganized and transformed into the "Sven Hedin-Reichsinstitut für Innerasienforschung," named after the famous Swedish researcher. On June 17, 1942 Wüst applied to the Reich Ministry of Science and Education for funding the institute framing its intention in the context of a new "Großraumpolitik" (policy in large areas).[90] At the beginning of the next year a pompous inauguration was held in the auditorium maximum of the University of Munich on January 16, 1943.[91] Starting with the expedition film "Geheimnis Tibet" in the afternoon, an honorary degree was bestowed on Sven Hedin in the evening. Wüst, who had taken an active part in the erection of the institute and in the exploration of "Inner Asia" as such, held the main speech of the ceremony in front of a great number of invited guests. According to Mircea Eliade's Portuguese diary, the Romanian press, then cultural attaché to Lisbon was personally invited by Wüst to join the Munich opening ceremony in January 1943.[92] Although the context of Eliade's

---

[89] See Isrun Engelhardt, "Tibetan Triangle: German, Tibetan and British Relations in the Context of Ernst Schäfer's Expedition, 1938–1939," *Asiatische Studien/Études Asiatiques* 58–1 (2004), pp. 57–113.

[90] One half of the requested 300,000 Reichsmark was scheduled for labor costs, alone 13,000 for its directer and ca. 7,500 for its assistant Bruno Beger. Federal Archives Berlin, R 21, 10.996, Sven Hedin Institut, fol. 1–20.

[91] A program of the event is to be found in Hartmut Walravens, ed., *W. A. Unkrieg (1883–1956). Korrespondenz mit Hans Findeisen, der Britischen Bibelgesellschaft und anderen über Sibirien und den Lamaismus* (Wiesbaden: Harrassowitz, 2004), p. 162f.

[92] I thank this information Mihaela Timuş and her both extensive and thorough foreword of eadem, éd., *Întotdeauna Orientul. Corespondenţa Mircea Eliade – Stig Wikander*

invitation, delivered by the German ambassador to Romania, remains unclear, it is certain that earlier contacts must have existed – and not only on a superficial level. Otherwise such an invitation in the middle of the war which certainly included the absorption of traveling and lodging costs makes no sense. But of course, Eliade could not journey to Germany in the middle of the war.

The beginning of World War II brought new problems and new centers of interests. The ideological substantiation of the Third Reich's 'Germanization' policy in Nordic countries such as Norway and the Netherlands now became an important focus of the "Ahnenerbe"-work. The more countries Germany's troops occupied, the better possibilities emerged to carry out examinations, excursions, and excavations to justify the various claims of National Socialist ideology. As a consequence of the change from a more theoretical, worldview oriented, to a more practical, application-oriented approach, it was decided to modify the organizational structure of the "Ahnenerbe." On April 1, 1942 it was incorporated as "Amt A" in the SS "Hauptamt" and Himmler's "Persönlicher Stab." Wüst's title changed from "Kurator" to "Amtschef." The establishment of the notorious "Institut für wehr-wissenschaftliche Zweckforschung" (Institute of Scientific Research for Military Purposes) with Wolfram Sievers as provisional director has to be seen as a further step towards a closer military orientation. Under its umbrella top secret experiments were undertaken which included medical experimentations with different sorts of poisons and bacteria as well as lethal tests to find out, for instance, how long humans take to die in cold water or under a progressively decreasing atmospheric pressure. August Hirt, professor at the "Reichsuniversität Straßburg," 'ordered' more than 100 persons from the concentration camp in Auschwitz to use them as 'testing animals'. Then they were killed and functioned as 'stockpile' for a skull and skeleton collection he wanted to establish.[93] Shortly before Allied troops reached Strasbourg in the fall of 1944, Hirt and many other scholars (among them Otto Huth)

(1948–1977) [C'est toujours l'Orient. Correspondance Eliade-Wikander] (Iasi-Bucarest: Polirom, 2005), pp. 15–91, here p. 73 with reference to the entry of January 13, 1942 in Eliade's *Diario português* (Barcelona: Editorial Kairós, 2001). See also E. Ciurtin in his article on p. 354.

[93] Cf. H. Junginger, *Von der philologischen zur völkischen Religionswissenschaft*, pp. 264–268. See also Hans-Joachim Lang, *Die Namen der Nummern. Wie es gelang die 86 Opfer eines NS-Verbrechens zu identifizieren* (Hamburg: Hoffmann und Campe, 2004). Lang succeeded to identify the names of 86 victims of this horrible crime.

fled to Tübingen whose university provided them with shelter and with the opportunity to continue their work as far as possible. After the war, Wolfram Sievers was hanged due to his responsibility for these crimes. His superior Wüst, however, declared to have known nothing about it – undoubtedly a lie. As chief of the "Amt A," Wüst was not only informed but was certainly involved in one way or another.

Between 1991 and 1992, new archival material came to light in a special repository ("Sonderarchiv") in Moscow. Among other things it contained Himmler's official diaries the SS leader had used between 1941 and 1942.[94] Since Wüst's relations with Himmler were mostly informal in character, he does not appear very often in the record. The entry of July 9, 1942, for example, discloses that Wüst acted as Himmlers's translator in a meeting of the "Reichsführer-SS" with the Indian nationalist Subhas Chandra Bose.[95] Soon after we can read the July 14 entry regarding an encounter between Himmler, Wüst, and Dr. Sigmund Rascher who reported on his freezing and high altitude experiments in the concentration camp of Dachau. To stimulate discussion, a film feature of the deadly testing in a low pressure chamber was shown after dinner.[96] Moreover, the entry of July 17 reveals that Wüst accompanied Himmler to an inspection tour to Auschwitz. On July 7 Himmler had ordered the establishment of the "Institut für wehrwissenschaftliche Zweckforschung" and on August 12 Hirt officially affiliated with the "Ahnenerbe." Three days later Rascher started with his freezing experiments in Dachau on August 15. This was the direct context of the journey Himmler and his team carried out from July 17–20 (Friday to Monday), 1942. It aimed to check the orderly functioning of the whole extermination process and, as the contextual relationship indicates, had also to do with the kind of SS-research named "wehrwissenschaftliche Zweckforschung." The group inspected all sorts of installations, the prisoner camps, agricultural laboratories, the IG-Farben factories, building projects and discussed organizational problems with various administrative agencies. A freshly arrived transport of Jews deported from the Netherlands offered an excellent opportunity

---

[94] Published as *Der Dienstkalender Heinrich Himmlers, 1941/42*, ed. by Peter Witte et al. (Hamburg: Christians, 1999).

[95] Ibid., p. 482. With Wüst's assistance Himmler discussed on July 15 with Bose the possibility of including Indian units to the "Waffen-SS." Ibid., p. 490.

[96] Ibid., p. 489. The military aim of the experiment was to discern in which maximum altitude pilots and parachute jumpers could leave an aircraft and, in a second step, how long they would be able to survive in cold sea water.

to examine the separation measures to which these Jews were subjected from the beginning. The high point of the program was the survey of the gassing of several hundred Jews in Birkenau.[97]

Another example of Wüst's connection with Auschwitz is to be found in a thrilling correspondence between Franz Altheim, head of the "Ahnenerbe"-department "Alte Geschichte," and his friend Karl Kerényi. After Kerényi's daughter Grazia was imprisoned on April 3, 1944, she was subsequently committed to Auschwitz because her mother (Kerényi's first wife) was a Jew. Kerényi sent coded messages to Altheim whom he rightly expected to be able to approach higher SS leaders in behalf of her.[98] His letters caused irritations and serious frictions on the side of his friend.[99] But finally Altheim complied with the increasingly urgent requests of the desperate father. He contacted Wüst who used his relations to Heinrich Himmler to have Grazia Kerényi delivered from Auschwitz to the concentration camp Ravensbrück. Ultimately, she survived. What this dramatic story makes clear is that Wüst had entered a level in the political hierarchy of Nazi Germany giving him enough power to arrange for someone's release from Auschwitz. In stressing Grazia Kerényi's rescue, Losemann completely disregards the political and ethical implications of Altheim's and Wüst's behavior. Why Wüst had such power and which role the "Ahnenerbe" played in the interchange between ideology and politics, between ideology and crime, were questions which Losemann does not ask. The moral bankruptcy and intellectual corruption characteristic of the "Ahnenerbe"

---

[97] Ibid., pp. 491–497. As a result of the inspection, Rudolf Höß, the commander of Auschwitz, received an order of Himmler to open all mass graves and to burn the corpses.

[98] See Volker Losemann, "Die 'Krise der Alten Welt' und der Gegenwart. Franz Altheim und Karl Kerényi im Dialog," in Peter Kneissl and V. Losemann, eds., *Imperium Romanum Studien zur Geschichte und Rezeption. Festschrift für Karl Christ zum 75. Geburtstag* (Stuttgart: Steiner, 1998), pp. 492–518. On June 15, 1944 Kerényi wrote: "Meine kleinen Töchter sind gesund, die kleinere von den größeren, Grazia, wurde vor 5 oder 6 Wochen in ein Sanatorium [sc. to Auschwitz, H.J.] gebracht. Es ist eine furchtbar verzweifelte Sache, ich kann es Dir nicht erklären, aber es kann sich sehr wohl um einen ärztlichen Irrtum handeln. Ich wollte Dich bitten, vielleicht kennt jemand von Deinen wissenschaftlichen Mitarbeitern einen von den dortigen Professoren, der die Sache anders ansieht als einen gewöhnlichen Patienten. Du musst Dich aber sofort umsehen, denn gerade in diesen Tagen entscheidet sich viel." Ibid., p. 499.

[99] Now you are seeking help from the same people you have insulted before, wrote Altheim in July 1944 to Kerényi. Not saying on which source he relied, Altheim continued that his friend ought to recognize that his daughter already received a preferential treatment compared to others: "Andere müssen ganz anderes mitmachen." Ibid., p. 501.

as a whole culminated in its scientific director Wüst. It goes without saying that Wüst understood the case of Kerényi's daughter and his own involvement in it as an exception to the rule. Wüst undoubtedly knew the "rule" and he agreed with it, to say the least.

4. *Religion and the Study of Religion in Wüst's Perspective*

As we have seen in the previous chapter, Herman Wirth had to leave the "Ahnenerbe" as a result of his fantasy-laden conjectures about Nordic "Ur"-symbolism which hampered Himmler's and Wüst's attempt to tranform the "Ahnenerbe" into a scientific brain trust. But the lacking academic respectability of Wirth was only one half of the truth. The other one pertained to Wirth's religious affiliation with the German Faith Movement. It was a combination of both that led to his estrangement from the "Ahnenerbe" and his supporters in the SS. Before the church struggle voelkish religious groups such as the ones constituting the "Deutsche Glaubensbewegung" could evolve to a certain degree in the NS state. But their margin drastically diminished in the course of only two or three years. Already in spring 1936 the German Faith Movement – the main of the small number of Pagan organizations – fell apart due to internal dissent and external pressure.

When the working community of the German Faith Movement ("Arbeitsgemeinschaft Deutsche Glaubensbewegung") constituted at the end of July 1933, Wirth became a member of its leaders' council ("Führerrat"), but functioned as a co-editor of and contributor to Hauer's journal *Deutscher Glaube* as well.[100] In March 1934 Wirth wrote a letter to the "Führer" of the German Faith Movement in which he declared that he would be pleased to participate in the work for a textbook of Indo-Germanic religious sources Hauer was about to prepare.[101] Besides that the letter addressed some other, for Wirth more urgent issues. One referred to the impending Berlin discussion about the *Ura-Linda-Chronik*. Wirth expressed his confidence that Walther Wüst and Hermann Güntert (Güntert with a question mark) would partake and defend his cause. Starting on May 1 Wirth and Wüst would edit a new *Zeitschrift*

---

[100] See Ulrich Nanko, *Die Deutsche Glaubensbewegung. Eine historische und soziologische Untersuchung* (Marburg: Diagonal Verlag, 1993), esp. p. 147.

[101] H. Wirth to J.W. Hauer on March 24, 1934, Federal Archives Koblenz, literal remains of Hauer, vol. 61, fol. 430.

für Geistesurgeschichte and, together with Wüst's pupil Dr. Otto Paul, he would publish a new text edition of the *Ura-Linda-Chronik* until the end of the year. Both projects did not materialize. The main problem for Wirth was the harsh critique of other National Socialists who accused him of having taken money from Jews to conduct his research. Rather than deny it, Wirth said that he had thought it a good idea to fight against the Jews with the money of the Jews. His new book should be understood as the final destruction of all Jewish claims and the liberation of the North from them.[102]

Wüst was repeatedly confronted with Hauer's wish to become engaged in the activities of the German Faith Movement. Because such an attachment did not conform to Wüst's own religious views he steadily rejected and refrained from any collaboration. Hauer's and Wirth's heathenish sectarianism disgusted Wüst even more when he realized that A) the German Faith Movement would never play a leading role in Nazi Germany and B) that an involvement of that sort would harm his academic advancement. In 1935 Wüst and Hauer, nevertheless, embarked on a close liaison. But this resulted from the broader frame of an Indo-Germanic or Aryan worldview and not from a commonly shared Pagan religion. And again, antisemitism constituted the pivotal mechanism to render their Aryanism coherence. Even in the Weimar years, when the Aryan Myth was stirring up, anti-Jewish preconceptions were involved as the following example shows: Induced by his friend Rudolf Otto, Hauer had taught indology at the University of Marburg from 1925–1927. When leaving Marburg Hauer received the proposals of two prominent colleagues, Hanns Oertel and Wilhelm Geiger, who supported Wüst to become his successor. Hauer reacted very positively to their suggestion and started reading the publications of the young "Privatdozent" (lecturer) Wüst.[103] Although he finally recommended Helmuth von Glasenapp, Hauer's first goal was to prevent

---

[102] "Und die *Heilige Urschrift* ist die endgültige Zertrümmerung aller geschichtlichen Ansprüche des Judentums und die Befreiung des Nordens davon." Letter of H. Wirth to Werner Haverbeck on August 6 (ibid., fol. 431–433, the quotation fol. 432) given as confidential addendum to the aforementioned letter to inform Hauer. Wirth's book appeared as *Die heilige Urschrift der Menschheit. Symbolgeschichtliche Untersuchungen diesseits und jenseits des Nordatlantik* (Leipzig: Koehler & Amelang, 1936).

[103] See Hauer to Hanns Oertel on October 11, 1927 (answering a letter from October 5) and Hauer to Wilhelm Geiger on October 12, 1927 (answering a letter from October 5), Federal Archives Koblenz, literal remains of Hauer, vol. 123, fol. 14f. and fol. 17f.

the appointment of the Jewish candidate Otto Strauß. This becomes clear from his statement sent to the Berlin ministry in October 1927 in which Hauer argued that Marburg's philosophy department already had enough Semitic blood ("hat schon ein reichliches Element semitischen Bluts").[104] The denunciation, introduced by Hauer's affirmation to be a strong opponent of ordinary antisemitism ("Ich selbst bin ein scharfer Gegner des landläufigen Antisemitismus."), aimed of course at Hermann Jacobsohn, a Jew, a democrat, and a gifted linguist, to wit a threat against Sanskrit studies at the University of Marburg. This nasty, though not uncommon, episode makes evident that antisemitism and Aryanism were inextricably intertwined with each other not only ideologically but also on a structural academic level.

Eight years later Hauer was well-situated to do more for Wüst. When the chair of Hanns Oertel was to be re-occupied in 1935, he was in the position to write the decisive expert opinion for the Munich philosophy department. In addition to that he also utilized his relations with Karl August Eckhardt, an important collaborator of the Reich Ministry of Science and Education and an early member of the German Faith Movement as well. Already in January Hauer had informed Wüst that he was trying to attain a reorganization of the *Orientalische Literaturzeitung*, the main journal of Oriental studies in Germany. There were too many Jews who, by their nature, were incapable of understanding the Indo-Aryan spirit. Hauer said that he would use his contacts to place Wüst on the board of the journal.[105] Wüst fully agreed with Hauer's opinion and was gratified about the offer to become a "Schriftleiter" (co-editor) of the *Orientalische Literaturzeitung*. Wüst promised to bring his own political contacts into play in order to achieve the necessary reform of German indology: "Ich bin gern bereit, mit Ihren und meinen ganzen Verbindungen für dieses wichtige Ziel zu kämpfen."[106] Party member since May 1, 1933, Wüst worked on various levels and occasions for the NSDAP. His relations with the "Gauleitung" of Upper Bavaria were excellent. One of his many assignments and monstrous

---

[104] Letter of Hauer to the Ministry of Culture and Education in Berlin (Prof. Windelband) on October 28, 1927, ibid. vol. 123, fol. 391–394. See also H. Junginger, *Von der philologischen zur völkischen Religionswissenschaft*, p. 183.

[105] Hauer to Wüst on January 18, 1935, Federal Archives Koblenz, literal remains of Hauer, vol. 141, fol. 619.

[106] "I am willingly prepared to fight with your and my own relations for that important goal." Wüst to Hauer on January 26, 1935, ibid. vol. 141, fol. 616–618, here fol. 617 verso.

titles read "Referent für arische Geistesgeschichte, Wortkunde und arisch-indogermanische Weltanschauung bei der Gauleitung München-Oberbayern des NSLB."[107]

On March 4, 1935 Hauer wrote a letter to K.A. Eckhardt advocating Wüst in every regard as a promising young scholar capable to take over a chair in indology even at the University of Berlin.[108] The recommendation was followed by a villainous diatribe against Jewish indologists, especially against Otto Strauß, the editor responsible for indology at the *Orientalische Literaturzeitung*, who, as a Jew, would always try to engage other Jews such as Betty Heymann and Walter Ruben. Thirdly Hauer agitated against the theological orientation of Germany's study of religion, particularly in the case of Johannes Witte at the University of Berlin. However, this was only the covering letter to an official petition he submitted the same day to the Reich Ministry of Science and Education, addressed to Bernhard Rust personally. In it Hauer pleaded for a total rebuilding ("Neuaufbau") of the German university system in general and indological and religious studies in particular, of course on the basis of National Socialism. Hauer therefore wanted to strengthen the Aryan legacy in opposition to the alien worldview of Judaism and Christianity. Every German university should get at least one lectureship or professorship concerned with Germanic or Indo-Germanic traditions. It should be high time to remove general history of religions ("Allgemeine Religionsgeschichte") from all theology departments.[109]

For that bundle of reasons Hauer tried to corroborate research into the Aryan past and to bring Wüst into the position of a full professor at the University of Munich. It comes as no surprise that Wüst entirely shared Hauer's opinion. Also from Wüst's point of view a complete reorganization of Indian studies was an urgent task. It meant in 1935, two years after the shameful Law for the Reestablishment of the Civil Service from April 7, 1933, to free the academe from Jewish, but also from liberal, democratic, and reactionary remnants. "We National

---

[107] Wüst's curriculum vitae – to be found in his personal files at the Munich University Archive, in the BDC-files of the Federal Archives Berlin, and in Hauer's literal remains, Federal Archives Koblenz – includes other designations of that sort. The NSLB ("Nationalsozialistischer Lehrerbund") then became the National Socialist Instructors' Union, NSDDB ("Nationalsozialistischer Deutscher Dozentenbund").

[108] Hauer to Eckhardt on March 4, 1935, Federal Archives Koblenz, literal remains of Hauer, vol. 141, fol. 607f.

[109] Hauer to Bernhard Rust on March 4, 1935, ibid., vol. 141, fol. 609–611.

Socialists," Wüst wrote to Hauer, must be aware and careful to accomplish our mission.[110] Asked by the Munich philosophy department for an expertise, Hauer answered on May 14, 1935 in a very affirmative manner. Wüst would be not only a talented and scrupulous young scholar but also someone who would be able to show Aryan philology new paths in the future. While Oriental studies had concentrated too much on philological and historical work in the past, just collecting masses of material, it totally ignored concerning itself with the spiritual grounds from which all these findings emanate. What was in need instead was a new life oriented synopsis ("lebendige Wesensschau") of the Indo-Germanic traditions. Wüst would be a university teacher from whom a significant contribution to this new kind of scholarship could be expected.[111]

An important if not the main trait of Hauer's and Wüst's inclination towards an Aryan worldview was their more or less openly expressed anti-Jewish resentment. In trying to consolidate the projected working community of National Socialist indologists, Hauer put on November 6, 1935 a second petition for the reorganization of indology in writing.[112] In addition to Wüst Hauer asked other like minded scholars such as Richard Schmidt (Münster), Herman Lommel (Frankfurt), and Bernhard Breloer (Berlin) to join the undertaking.[113] Hauer repeated in his paper the topics of the first petition but argued more plainly: All remainders of a Jewish influence should be eliminated. A situation in which Jews were still allowed to be active in Germany's indology has to be ended. Even under the presupposition of an excellent philological talent Jews

---

[110] "Insbesondere müssen wir beide vor der Lüders-Garde auf der Hut sein." Wüst to Hauer on May 5, 1935, ibid., vol. 141, fol. 603. The menace Wüst connected with the "Lüders-Garde" referred to the influential Berlin indologist and Geheimrat Heinrich Lüders (1869–1943) who, "owing to his anti-Nazi attitude," was not permitted to continue lecturing after his retirement in 1935. Cf. Valentina Stache-Rosen, *German Indologists. Biographies of Scholars in Indian Studies writing in German. With a Summary of Indology in German Speaking Countries*, 2nd rev. ed. (New Delhi: Max Mueller Bhavan, 1990), p. 167. The book includes articles on Geiger, Hauer, Heymann, Oertel, Strauß and many others. Wüst, however, is missing.

[111] Hauer to the vice-dean of the Munich philosophy department Robert Spindler on May 14, 1935, ibid., vol. 141, fol. 462, answering Spindler's request from May 9 (ibid., fol. 463) and getting Spindler's thanks on May 17 (ibid. vol. 461).

[112] Ibid. vol. 141, fol. 21. It seems that the request was not submitted.

[113] For the National Socialist leaning of Breloer, Lommel, and Schmidt, see Sheldon Pollock, "Deep Orientalism? Notes on Sanskrit and Power Beyond the Raj," in Carol A. Breckenridge and Peter van der Veer, eds., *Orientalism and the Postcolonial Predicament. Perspectives on South Asia* (Philadelphia: University of Pennsylvania Press, 1993), pp. 76–133, here pp. 91–94.

were not able to understand the Indo-Aryan spirit. Hauer closed with the voelkish racial credo that only the cognate would have the capacity to interpret the Indo-Aryan or Iranian worldview adequately.[114]

Though Wüst and Hauer were both distinguished ideologues of the Aryan Myth, they expected different things from their occupation with the Indo-Germanic world and from their relationship with each other. Hauer saw in Wüst a probable ally in his quest of a new Pagan religion called "Deutscher Glaube." Even after he had been forced to abandon his hope for a Pagan organization in April 1936, he remained the prophet of a new religion. Wüst instead had absolutely no liking for Hauer's Pagan dogmatism and missionary zest. His doctrinaire model of a "Deutscher Glaube" bore a certain resemblance to Hauer's pietistic past and his former career as Christian missionary to India having shifted now to an Indo-Germanic religiosity. Wüst's own understanding of the Aryan heritage lacked any passionate religious affection. It was much more instrumental than content dependent. The designation of his Munich institute and professorship "Arische Kultur- und Sprachwissenschaft" indicates that Wüst's interest in the legacy of the Aryan tradition had not primarily religious motives. Thus Wüst was also a gifted opportunist who cheerfully accepted the help of the "Führer" of the German Faith Movement to become a full professor in Munich. As soon as he had achieved this goal, Hauer's attractiveness lessened and went to zero after Wüst had been nominated president of the "Ahnenerbe." The role of his former benefactor changed to that of a rival. Although Hauer repeatedly tried to affiliate with the "Ahnenerbe," Wüst prevented any closer collaboration. Only in the so called "Wald und Baum Projekt," a huge project (funded by Hermann Göring) to examine the Indo-Germanic understanding of the German forest, Hauer was able to obtain a little grant. Wüst even wrote a negative assessment when Hauer tried to include "Arische Weltanschaung" in his lectureship at the University of Tübingen in 1939. He declared that

---

[114] "Es muss aufhören, dass in Deutschland, wie das bisher der Fall war, Juden die Indologie betreuen. Ich bin der Meinung, dass auch bei guter philologischer und selbst abstrakt philologischer Begabung nur der Artverwandte die indo-arische oder iranische Weltanschauung zu deuten vermag." Federal Archives Koblenz, literal remains of Hauer, vol. 141, fol. 21.

Hauer held outdated views and had insufficient knowledge of Iranian philology, accidentally his own area of specialization.[115]

The relations of Wüst and Hauer with Heinrich Himmler also illustrate their deviating development and different stance within the SS. Hauer had joined the SS and the SD in 1934 and was honored with one or two personal meetings with Himmler and Heydrich.[116] This was nothing compared to Wüst. Wüst stood in a much closer, even confidential relationship with the "Reichsführer SS," and in June 1942 Wüst and not Hauer held the funeral oration at Heydrich's burial. In his correspondence with Hauer Wüst liked to impress his senior colleague with incidental hints on important encounters he recently had with Himmler. Hauer, vice versa, asked Wüst several times if he could not arrange an appointment for him with Himmler, without success. Hauer did not realize that neither Wüst nor Himmler, nor the SS in general, were interested in his religious agenda. His aspiration to provide the SS with a Pagan substructure or, at least, to advance to its ideological advisor totally failed. In September 1942 Bruno Beger – participant of the Tibet expedition and the one who selected the human 'material' in Auschwitz for August Hirt – wrote a memo for his superior Ernst Schäfer about a meeting he had with Hans Endres, Hauer's assistant at the Aryan Institute at the University of Tübingen. Beger had discussed with Endres his participation in a new SS-expedition which aimed to survey the whole Caucasus region. Moreover, Endres ought to have accompanied Beger to Auschwitz if private problems would not have crossed plans.[117] After the encounter Beger recorded that Endres had cunningly avoided to mention the name of his teacher Hauer because, as the memo reads: The Reichsführer SS as well as Standartenführer Wüst stay in opposition to him. "Den Namen Hauer hat Endres klu-

---

[115] See H. Junginger, *Von der philologischen zur völkischen Religionswissenschaft*, p. 158f. and Wüst's negative letter to the Reich Ministry of Science and Education (Heinrich Harmjanz) on June 21, 1939, Federal Archives Munich, personal files Wüst, O-N-14.

[116] Cf. the reprint of two letters between Hauer and Himmler I added to my article "Das 'Arische Seminar' an der Universität Tübingen 1940–1945," in Heidrun Brückner et al., eds., *Indienforschung im Zeitenwandel. Analysen und Dokumente zur Indologie und Religionswissenschaft in Tübingen* (Tübingen: Attempto, 2003), pp. 177–207, here pp. 183–185.

[117] See H. Junginger, *Von der philologischen zur völkischen Religionswissenschaft*, pp. 280–284. In September 1944 Endres became a lecturer of science of religion with special reference to religion and race at the University of Tübingen (ibid., p. 287f.).

gerweise nicht erwähnt, denn der Reichsführer-SS sowohl als auch Standartenführer Wüst stehen gegen denselben."[118]

Ensuing from the experience with the church struggle, Pagans in and outside the German Faith Movement had become the object of state surveillance by Gestapo and SD. Their religious sectarianism was seen as a potential threat to the ideological unanimity of the Third Reich. In the official NS historiography, and especially in the eyes of Adolf Hitler, World War I had been lost as a result of Germany's disunity. Therefore everything that could impair the unification of the German people in the preparatory phase of the next war had to be nipped in the bud. One of the lessons the Nazi leaders learned from the church struggle was that religious quarrels would lead to a disaster given free play. Considering the fact that the 'official' planning of World War II started in 1936, the policy of National Socialism towards Paganism appears in another light. Hitler was fully convinced that the war was not to be won without the support of the Christian churches. Yet how many members of the "Wehrmacht" did not belong to either the Protestant or the Catholic church? Who of them had read one sentence of the Vedas, had ever heard about Krishna and Arjuna, the famous Aryan warriors? A German army merely consisting of soldiers with an Aryan or Pagan preference would have been a rather negligible seize. Certainly the god appearing in the long-established slogan "Gott mit uns!" that escorted Germany's soldiers as engraving in their belt clasps to Poland, France, and the Soviet Union did not belong to the Aryan pantheon.

In view of that political context the role of Paganism, but also the position and function of the SS-"Ahnenerbe," have to be re-examined. Any interpretation of the "Ahnenerbe" as core of a Pagan counter religion is misleading.[119] Particularly under Walther Wüst the "Ahnenerbe" never planned to establish something like an Aryan church, to develop Pagan rites or to educate Pagan clerics. Only very few "Ahnenerbe"-members deliberately rejected a traditional scientific approach in favor of occult hermetic traditions.[120] Their influence remained mar-

---

[118] Memo of Bruno Beger on September 23, 1942, Federal Archives Berlin, R 135, vol. 48, fol. 164012.

[119] Victor and Victoria Trimondi, *Hitler, Buddha, Krishna. Eine unheilige Allianz vom Dritten Reich bis heute* (Wien: Ueberreuter, 2002) is relying on this misinterpretation.

[120] The most important figure in that regard was Karl Maria Wiligut (1866–1946), named "Weisthor" or "Himmler's Rasputin." But Wiligut was a psychopath who stayed seven years in a mental hospital in Salzburg before he advanced to a spiritual advisor

ginal. It was Wüst who watched over the scholarly appearance of the "Ahnenerbe," who coordinated all projects and who maintained close relations with the Reich Ministry of Science and Education. Under the political circumstances described above, Wüst's religious and scientific development is not astonishing for someone familiar with the history of the academic study of religion: Confronted with rather unattractive religious alternatives, Wüst opted for a closer orientation towards the scientific occupation with religion. This decision was engendered by his personal religious penchant but was also influenced by the ideological function of the "Ahnenerbe." Wüst's famous Indo-Germanic credo is compelling in that regard. Consisting of six speeches delivered between 1936 and 1941, Wüst published in 1942 his *Indogermanisches Bekenntnis*, a profession of his personal worldview but also a manifesto of the "Ahnenerbe"-work in general.[121]

The largest and most important contribution to that book was Wüst's article "Von indogermanischer Religiosität. Sinn und Sendung" (On Indo-Germanic religiosity. Its meaning and mission) which originally appeared in 1939 in the restructured *Archiv für Religionswissenschaft (ARW)* where it served as a key text to denote the journal's new course. Already in 1933 the *Archiv für Religionswissenschaft* had faced pressure from its publisher Teubner, especially from the Teubner manager Hermann Gieselbusch, to align with the ideology of National Socialism.[122] This led to a first reorganization in 1936 and to the inclusion of the classical

---

of Himmler. Wiligut believed in an Indo-Germanic "Krist" who, in the year 12,500 BC, had proclaimed an "Irminglauben." Later Christianity adopted this "Krist" but distorted his teachings. Wiligut's occult capacities allowed him to hold contact with the ancestors and gods of the old belief. In 1939 he fell back in a state of mental derangement and left the SS. See http://www.relinfo.ch, s.v. Wiligut.

[121] W. Wüst, *Indogermanisches Bekenntnis. Sechs Reden* (Berlin-Dahlem: Ahnenerbe Stiftungsverlag, 1942, 2nd ed. 1943): "Germanenkunde. Frage und Verpflichtung" (Detmold, October 5, 1936), "Das Reich. Gedanke und Wirklichkeit bei den alten Ariern" (Munich, February 2, 1937), "Deutsche Frühzeit und arische Geistesgeschichte" (Munich, May 12, 1939), "Von indogermanischer Religiosität. Sinn und Sendung" (Salzburg, August 24, 1939), "Indogermanisches Bekenntnis" (Munich, July 5, 1941), "Überlieferung als völkische Kraftquelle" (Strasbourg, November 24, 1941). Wüst dedicated the book in gratitude and loyalty ("in Dankbarkeit und Treue") to Heinrich Himmler.

[122] I refer here to my article "Archiv für Religionswissenschaft" in Michael Fahlbusch and Ingo Haar, eds., *Handbuch völkischer Wissenschaften* (forthcoming). See also Martina Dürkop, "'...er wird sehen, daß das Archiv wirklich ein Geschäft ist, wenn es richtig behandelt wird...'. Wissenschaftlicher und wirtschaftlicher Existenzkampf des ARW 1919–1939," *Archiv für Religionsgeschichte* 1 (1999), pp. 107–128. A listing of all *ARW*-articles is to be found under http://pomoerium.com, s.v. Archiv für Religionswissenschaft.

philologist Friedrich Pfister as third editor next to Otto Weinreich and
Martin P. Nilsson. In the preface and in two articles Pfister articulated
the political change emphasizing the need to incorporate voelkish and
racial features which in his view had been underestimated thus far.[123]
Hauer's former pupil Herbert Grabert highlighted in the same volume
in plain language National Socialist racialism and the total dependence
of any scholarship on voelkish prerequisites.[124] Hauer himself contributed to the 1937 edition an exposition of the 'natural' relationship
between race and religion.[125] Not all articles appearing in the volumes
33–35 (1936–1938) had that open ideological proclivity. Other authors
refrained from carrying favor with National Socialist ideas and followed
academic rules and standards valid before. But the scientific level of
the *ARW* came to grief alone from the fact that Jewish and politically
undesired authors were excluded from publishing. Even the participation of foreigners not stemming from related nations had become a
problem to the new voelkish scheme.

Nevertheless, the concessions set off were insufficient. Much more
had to be done and a further political tightening was necessary. It is not
surprising that an interference of the SS resulted from that situation.
The "Ahnenerbe" was greatly interested in increasing its respectability
with renowned scientific periodicals and Wüst was keen to take over the
Archiv für Religionswissenschaft. Accordingly Otto Weinreich and Friedrich
Pfister, but in particular the Swede Martin P. Nilsson, had to retire.
With volume 36 (1939) the former flagship of the international study
of religion had come under the patronage of the SS to appear now
as a belligerent organ of National Socialist ideology. Besides Wüst, the
SS-partisan and head of an "Ahnenerbe"-department Heinrich Harmjanz, a professor of German folklore ("Deutsche Volkskunde") and high
rank of the Reich Ministry of Science and Education, acted as second
editor. Hauer wrote a bitter letter to Wüst lamenting over his omission
and pointing to his political and scientific merits.[126] Wüst remained
unimpressed yet allowed Hauer to write a long review article about the

---

[123] Cf. F. Pfister, "Die Religion und der Glaube der germanischen Völker und ihrer
religiösen Führer" and idem, "Die religiöse Sendung des deutschen Volkes," *ARW* 36
(1939), pp. 1–14 and pp. 373–380.
[124] H. Grabert, "Allgemeine Religionsgeschichte und völkische Glaubensgeschichte,"
ARW 33 (1936), pp. 191–220.
[125] J.W. Hauer, "Religion und Rasse," *ARW* 34 (1937), pp. 81–97.
[126] Hauer to Wüst on March 4, 1939, Federal Archives Koblenz, literal remains of
Hauer, vol. 140, fol. 310.

actual situation of Indo-Germanic studies in Germany.[127] However, the programmatic article in the new issue derived from Wüst's own pen. On more than 40 pages and nearly 200 footnotes Wüst made clear that he himself asserted the right to expound the new course of the *ARW*.[128] To exhibit his ideological hegemony Wüst gave an extensive and well informed overview of the state of affairs in contemporary religious studies. But it is interesting that Wüst's conceptual framework grounded on the same racial phenomenology characteristic of Hauer's approach. Wüst, like Hauer, sought to furnish evidence for the old paradigm of an intrinsic correspondence between religion and the study (student) of religion by using racial arguments. Only the racially kindred is able to understand things racially kindred, declared Wüst.[129] Yet Wüst preferred the notion religiosity ("Religiosität") as terminus technicus to describe the inner side of the history of religions rather than Hauer's "Glaube" which was too close to the traditional concept of a Protestant belief. But Wüst's study of religiosity ("Religiositätsforschung") had an identical intention compared with Hauer's "Glaubensgeschichte": to re-conceptualize a direct access to the religious essence of historically discernable religious phenomena. According to two newspaper articles Wüst had put in his public lecture even more emphasis on the racial aspects of the study of religion. A new racial theory would lead to the comprehension that belief and knowledge are not in opposition to each other. Wüst's critique of the failings of contemporary study of religion, and of Hauer's Paganism, must have been much more apparent in his speech given in Salzburg.[130]

Contrary to Hauer, Wüst saw the main tasks of the academic study of religion in the political and not in the religious sphere. Lacking a

---

[127] J.W. Hauer, "Zum gegenwärtigen Stand der Indogermanenfrage," *ARW* 36 (1939), pp. 1–63.

[128] W. Wüst, "Von indogermanischer Religiosität. Sinn und Sendung", *ARW* 36 (1939), pp. 64–108 (= *Indogermanisches Bekenntnis*, pp. 51–91 and pp. 141–150). The article went back to a talk of Wüst during the so called "Salzburger Wissenschaftswochen," a conference with a strong anti-Catholic leaning jointly organized by the "Ahnenerbe" and the Reich Ministry of Science and Education on the eve of World War II. See Kater, *Das 'Ahnenerbe' der SS*, p. 116f. and p. 143f.

[129] "verstehen kann nur der rassisch Verwandte den oder das rassisch Verwandte." W. Wüst, "Von indogermanischer Religiosität. Sinn und Sendung," in idem, *Indogermanisches Bekenntnis*, p. 76 (*ARW* 36, 1939, p. 90).

[130] See the reports in *Die Zeit* (Reichenberg) from August 27, 1939 and in the *Kölnische Zeitung* from August 26, 1939, as copies in the Institute of Contemporary History, Munich, MA 609, fol. 56997 and fol. 56999.

deep-rooted and impassioned personal religiosity, it was much easier for Wüst to recognize the political needs the study of religion was confronted with and, moreover, its possibilities to comply with them. Any relevance of religion and the study of religion depended on their political function and possible utilization. In Wüst's understanding, the academic study of religion had the task to exploit religion as a vein of gold.[131] Emphasizing its instrumental function and practical applicability, Wüst recommended the study of religion as a perfect tool for governance that should be made available to the state rulers' disposal. Though he paid some lip service regarding the necessity of scientific methods and standards, Wüst's voelkish conception completely discarded objectivity and general validity of knowledge. Principles of that sort had lost their value and meaning. They belonged to an antiquated period and had to be abandoned. Since voelkish subjectivity had seized power in Germany's academe, any scholarship devoid of the racial paradigm and not in conformity with the needs of the German people had to be eliminated. A scholar or a discipline unwilling to meet the voelkish demands as defined by National Socialism should and would have no future in Germany. In another article dealing with the "German task of indology" Wüst insisted in an analogous way that the rules of the voelkish order had to be obeyed.[132]

At the height of Germany's military success, Wüst was nominated rector of the University of Munich. On July 5, 1941 he held his inauguration speech commencing it by praising Adolf Hitler and recounting the splendid victories the German army had achieved in the time before.[133] On April 27 the "Wehrmacht" had taken Athens occupying Crete at the end of May. The attack on the Soviet Union on June 22 was followed by the rapid capture of Riga and Lvov only a few days later. Under the fresh impression of these breathtaking victories Wüst wanted to relate the triumph of the German troops with the history of

---

[131] "Daß ein Vortrupp deutscher Religionsforschung der Gegenwart nach verschiedenen beachtlichen Ansätzen in den letzten Jahrzehnten, im Drang nach Innen den entscheidenden Inhalt und die unerhörte Reichweite des Sinnwortes 'Religiosität' erkannt und diese Goldader der Erkenntnis auszubeuten entschlossen ist, wird – davon bin ich fest überzeugt – das Wesensmerkmal unserer gelehrten, aber volksverbundenen Arbeit im kommenden Vierteljahrhundert sein." Ibid., p. 67 (*ARW* 36, 1939, p. 79f.).

[132] W. Wüst, "Die deutsche Aufgabe der Indologie," *Deutsche Kultur im Leben der Völker. Mitteilungen der Akademie zur wissenschaftlichen Erforschung und zur Pflege des Deutschtums, Deutsche Akademie* 3 (1939), pp. 339–348.

[133] W. Wüst, "Indogermanisches Bekenntnis," in idem, *Indogermanisches Bekenntnis*, pp. 93–118, here p. 95.

the Indo-Germanic tradition in his lecture. It was the superiority of the Aryan worldview that caused the military success. The swastika hoisted on the Acropolis just bore testimony of the Aryan legacy symbolized by the vases with swastika ornaments in the national museum of Greece beneath the hill.[134] The same historical process of a powerful worldview coming to fruition could be recognized in Cracow, Warsaw, and Bergen in 1939 and 1940 and occurred likewise in the Netherlands, Belgium, France and Yugoslavia. In an Evolian manner of arguing Wüst declared that the German conquest of these countries did not follow material interests but fulfilled the eternal laws recorded in the holy scriptures of the Aryans for thousands of years. Wüst underlined the expert knowledge provided by indology and religious studies to interpret these venerable texts for the benefit of the political presence. His own proficiency authorized him to declare that the German victories were an Indo-Germanic "Bekenntnis der Tat," a confession by deeds similar to the former "Tatchristentum" being extended to political Aryanism. The military success of the German troops confirmed the righteousness of the Indo-Germanic mission like an ordeal. In accordance with the program of the so-called "Kriegseinsatz der Geisteswissenschaften" – a project of the Reich Ministry of Science and Education to involve the humanities in the ideological warfare[135] – Wüst spoke about the task of the universities to practically and theoretically substantiate the reign of the Third Reich over Europe. Wüst was so exalted about the overrunning power of the German "Wehrmacht" that he started reflecting about the post-war era and the duties of German scholarship in it.[136] He had no doubt that NS scholarship would again become *Praeceptor Europae* (Europe's teacher) making a significant contribution to secure Germany's supremacy in Europe in the next millennium ("während des kommenden Jahrtausends").[137]

---

[134] Ibid., p. 93f.

[135] Wüst played a leading role in the "Kriegseinsatz" organizing the part of Oriental studies in it. Cf. his "Schlusswort" in Hans Heinrich Schaeder, ed., *Der Orient in deutscher Forschung. Vorträge der Berliner Orientalistentagung, Herbst 1942* (Leipzig: O. Harrassowitz, 1944), p. 260f. See in general Frank-Rutger Hausmann, *'Deutsche Geisteswissenschaft' im Zweiten Weltkrieg. Die 'Aktion Ritterbusch' (1940–1945)* (Dresden: Dresden University Press, 1998, 2nd ed. 2002) and for the involvement of Hauer and other historians of religions, H. Junginger, *Von der philologischen zur völkischen Religionswissenschaft*, p. 235f.

[136] W. Wüst, "Indogermanisches Bekenntnis," p. 96.

[137] Ibid., p. 117f.

Wüst's public lecture at the beginning of his rectorship at the second university of the German Reich marked one of the lowest points in the history of academic learning in Germany. Science as prostitution instead of Weber's science as vocation would be a correct description of the role Oriental and religious studies adopted in Wüst's Machiavellian understanding of scholarship. It contained a criminal implication insofar as Wüst deduced from the Aryan tradition that Indo-Germans always had, and still have, the duty to eliminate everything ill and alien to the voelkish community with deadly hatred ("tödlicher Haß gegen den Andersartigen").[138] To eradicate the inner enemy appeared in his speech as implementation of a divine order. With regard to such a teaching of the Indo-Germanic laws of life, Wüst's behavior in the case of the resistance movement "Weiße Rose" appears in another light. At the beginning of 1943 some students distributed leaflets at the University of Munich criticizing the banning of free speech and free learning in the academe. In particular they attacked intellectually corrupted professors who betrayed the academic autonomy. Out of the university with groveling opportunists and SS-ranks, Wüst had to read, and he could not be unclear who was meant. When the caretaker of the university caught Sophie and Hans Scholl while laying out their flyers, they were handed over to Wüst as rector of the university on February 18, 1943. Delivered to the Gestapo and immediately sentenced to death, both were killed by a criminal state apparatus four days later. It is hardly possible to overlook Wüst's role in that issue and to neglect the manifest interrelationship between his theoretical views and their practical consequences.

A comparison between Wüst's position and the religious agenda of Hauer and Wirth makes evident that Wüst lacked any passion for the foundation of a new Pagan church or religion. Especially his commitment to the SS-"Ahnenerbe" demonstrates the difference between their religious claims and his political worldview. To evade an involvement in religious squabbles – either between Pagans and Christians or between the various Pagan groups and individuals among each other – Wüst was keen on pushing Wirth out of the "Ahnenerbe" and on preventing Hauer from entering. Wüst took care not to jeopardize the scientific position of the "Ahnenerbe." Any funding from the Reich Ministry of Science and Education would have ceased if Pagan ambitions would

---

[138] Ibid., p. 101 and p. 108.

have come too much to the foreground. On the other side, a noticeable religious undercurrent gained some influence in Wüst's thinking that ought to be analyzed in terms of a Pagan counter identity to (Jewish) Christianity. But it is rather unlikely that this vague religious leaning would have shifted once to the level of a Pagan church, dogmas or rituals. The fate of the German Faith Movement exemplifies that a Pagan organization, even under National Socialism, had no chance to become the focal point of more than a few thousand outsiders. The failure of Hauer's and Wirth's religious hopes and fantasies should prevent us from taking their utterances for reality itself. For Wüst and the "Ahnenerbe" did the aim to revive the ancestral heritage of the Aryan tradition not mean that they intended to create a new religion. It is therefore necessary to differentiate Wüst's political worldview orientation from a genuine religious approach. The juxtaposition of a Pagan prophet such as Hauer and an unmitigated ideologue such as Wüst serves that purpose to differentiate between a religion and a worldview. Of course an intersection existed that could be labeled as a religious worldview though its religious substance was anything but clear. Neither were Wüst's convictions definitely pro Pagan nor the ideology of National Socialism decidedly anti-Christian. One can only speculate in which direction the religious situation in Third Reich might have developed in the future. The case of Wüst seems to indicate that a religious commitment would have been less traditional and more in the form of a modern civil religion whatever religious ingredients it might have had. Due to its dichotomy of a good and bad (true and false) religious behavior, the so called historiography of the church struggle totally failed to appropriately analyze the non-Christian history of religions under National Socialism until today.[139]

Putting the content of Wüst's Aryan mythology aside, it becomes transparent that his views concerning the study of religion were anything but exceptional. They ranged among the mainstream concepts being in vogue in the interwar period. Seeking for a third way between atheism and dogmatic Christianity, many scholars of that time embarked on the academic study of religion as a possibility to reconcile the antagonism of their religious and scientific persuasions. This could lead to a generalization structured as religion per se (normally Christianity deprived of

---

[139] A recent example for that type of interpretation is Karla Poewe, *New Religions and the Nazis* (New York-London: Routledge, 2006). See my review in *The Journal of Religion* 83-2 (2007), pp. 319–321.

its dogmatic features) or to a new religion outside the Christian realm (Germanic, Indo-Germanic, Aryan) usually followed by a theological agenda even more dogmatic than before. What distinguished Wüst from other scholars was his instrumental understanding of both religion and the study of religion. Compared to the possible utilization of a religion its religious truth claims lost much of their meaning and influence becoming an issue of minor importance. Such a perspective would be inconceivable for a homo religious. True or not, what mattered for Wüst was the political function of religion. The task of the academic study of religion, as he saw it, was to strengthen the sovereignty of National Socialism. Consequently, historians of religions mutated into technocrats of power.

5. *The Aryan Myth and Beyond? Some Final Remarks*

In light of his political opportunism and the total lack of moral scruples it was no wonder that Wüst advanced to one of the most prestigious and powerful academicians in Nazi Germany. The *ordinarius monachensis*, to use a designation of Stig Wikander for the "Munich professor," kept a close watch on university affaires as far as his power reached.[140] And his influence went far. Against his vote an appointment in Oriental studies had become almost impossible in the 1940s. In 1944 Hans Heinrich Schaeder expressed his opinion that without Wüst's consent nobody in Germany could become a professor or only a lecturer in indology.[141] But as Wüst's might was inseparably attached to the NS regime it passed into nothing with its end. Dismissed in October 1945, Wüst was sentenced to three years internment in a labor camp. In 1950 the judgment was reduced to "minderbelastet" (less incriminated) although hardly a German university professor could be found more incriminated than Wüst. In any case, a further continuation of his university career was simply not feasible. His state pension allowed Wüst to live the life of a private researcher and in 1955 he founded a new

---

[140] Letter of Stig Wikander to Otto Höfler on November 27, 1937. Although Wikander called Wüst an ignorant dilettante he asked the "Ahnenerbe" to publish his book *Der arische Männerbund*. See the article of Mihaela Timuş, this volume, p. 211 and p. 213.

[141] "...ohne dessen maßgebende Mitwirkung heute keine indologische Dozentur verliehen und keine indologische Professur besetzt wird." Letter of Hans Heinrich Schaeder to Christel Matthias Schröder on November 16, 1944, literal remains of Schröder, Department for the Study of Religion, Tübingen, s.v. Schaeder.

journal named *PHMA* (Rhema, word) in which he published linguistic studies. Since nearly no one wanted to contribute, Wüst had to write most articles by himself. Having become a persona non grata in the academe, everybody distanced themselves from him. This was not surprising in view of his former political involvement. But the exclusion of Wüst from the scientific community had, on the other hand, also resulted in avoiding any critical discussion about the past. Wüst was a perfect scapegoat whose undeniable guilt ought to bar the incriminations of many others from consideration. The historiography of NS scholarship of the last years has revealed how strong the group spirit among university teachers had been in the first decades after the war. It was unthinkable that a critique of particular disciplines and university teachers would have been articulated from within. Even Wüst was not openly blamed for his commitment to National Socialism. While Wüst's political engagement had been outstanding, his scientific views represented mainstream thoughts to be found among many others in the field of religious and Oriental studies. Therefore the question remains if parts of Wüst's thinking persisted although his person was subjected to a collective *damnatio memoriae*. The following two examples provide evidence of an affirmative answer to that question. They apply to the two main ideological reference points of Wüst I have discussed in this article: Herman Wirth and Julius Evola.

It is quite astonishing that the organizers of the 8th International Congress for the History of Religions allowed a distinguished Nazi ideologue such as Wirth to participate in the Rome convention in 1955. But not only Wirth, also a Bernhard Kummer and Otto Höfler, and in addition to them others like Franz Altheim, Herman Lommel, Gustav Mensching, and Wilhelm Emil Mühlmann who also had had a strong leaning towards National Socialism came to Rome presenting their lectures as if nothing had happened. No protest, not even a slight critical comment raised against the presence of former Nazi academics. Wirth, whose participation was promoted by Friedrich Heiler, resumed the old subject matter and talked about "Die Entstehung der Heerkönigsreligionen der indo-europäischen Völkerwanderungszeit und das Ende des kultischen Matriarchates" (The formation of military leaders' religions during the Indo-European migration time and the end of cult-matriarchy).[142] Directly after the war Heiler had begun

---

[142] See the *Atti dell'VIII Congresso Internazionale di Storia delle Religioni. Roma 17–23 Aprile 1955* (Firenze: G.C. Sansoni [1956]), pp. 373–375. The title of Höfler's lecture was

to intervene verbally and in writing for Wirth's release from internment.[143] His support enabled Wirth to restart spreading his views in
the 1950s. Of course Wirth had to alter the former Indo-Germanic
to a European vocabulary and to omit the previous goal of justifying
the racial superiority of the Nordic people. The Rome conference
acted as a stage for Wirth to carry on with a modified version of his
theories and particularly to seek for assistance for his plans to establish
a museum which now held the title of a "Ureuropamuseum." In Germany Wirth founded a new organization "Europäische Sammlung für
Urgemeinschaftskunde" (ESU, European Collection for the Knowledge
of Primal Community). Heiler sustained Wirth's endeavors as far as
he could. He even became a member of the executive committee of
the ESU. In a very positive assessment Heiler called Wirth an eminent
researcher whom the study of primordial history owes valuable momentum. Heiler's expert opinion dated from 1954 and was of great help
for Wirth in his advertising campaign.

It appears rather strange that the decided Christian Heiler bolstered
the activities of the co-founder of the SS-"Ahnenerbe" and devoted
Pagan Herman Wirth. Two reasons lie behind Heiler's behavior.
First, Heiler naively believed that Wirth had been expelled from the
"Ahnenerbe" due to a political opposition.[144] Relying on the widespread idea of a rightful beginning of National Socialism that had
been distorted by radicals, Wirth was in Heiler's view a credulous but
honest spokesperson of the worthy part of the Third Reich's aspirations. Wirth's maltreatment seemed him to prove that theory. On a
similar misinterpretation depended Heiler's frequent reference to his
own persecution in order to increase the authority of his arguing, not
only in the case of Wirth.[145] But more important, Heiler wanted to
include Wirth's collection of Scandinavian plaster cards to the "Religionskundliche Sammlung." Therefore he repeatedly appealed to the

---

"Der Sakralcharakter des germanischen Königtums" and that of Kummer "Sverre und
Magnus. Ein Lebensbeispiel zur Frage nach Ursprung und Fortwirkung demokratischen
und sakralen Königtums in Skandinavien" (ibid., pp. 359–361 and pp. 368–371).

[143] This and the following after the archive of the Religionskundliche Sammlung,
Marburg, D II 8.

[144] Heinrich Frick argued similarly in a letter to Tor Andrae on December 7, 1953.
Asking for support for Wirth, Frick said that Wirth had suffered political oppression
in the Third Reich. Ibid.

[145] For a critique of Heiler's claim, see H. Junginger, "Christel Matthias Schröder
(1915–1996) und seine Bedeutung für die deutsche Religionswissenschaft," *Zeitschrift
für Religionswissenschaft* 9 (2001), pp. 235–268, esp. pp. 242–244.

Hessian Ministry of Culture and Education for financial and technical support to transfer Wirth's material to Marburg. And indeed parts of it were stored in the Marburg castle. Only in the preparatory phase of the 10th International Congress for the History of Religions that took place in Marburg in September 1960, Heiler distanced himself from Wirth. Wirth had demanded to use the conference as a platform to publicize his museum plans and to guide official congress excursions to his collection. Offended by Heiler's rejection Wirth abstained from participating. In his place other previous Nazi ideologues took part in the Marburg IAHR-conference, for instance Jakob Wilhelm Hauer and a whole 'delegation' of the former Amt Rosenberg.[146] In 1998 Wirth's plaster card collection finally found a new home in Spital am Pyhrn in Austria in the rock art museum of the former "Ahnenerbe"-collaborator Ernst Burgstaller.[147]

In the context of Heiler and Otto one should remember that Wüst's first and Heiler's last semester at the University of Munich (Heiler taught from 1918 to 1920 in Munich) overlapped. Afterwards Wüst studied history of religions with Rudolf Franz Merkel, a pupil of Rudolf Otto, at the University of Munich. In the 1920s Wüst was quite receptive of Otto's phenomenological approach. When in February 1939 Heinrich Frick tried to assemble collaborators for a new Festschrift at the occasion of Otto's 70th birthday, he asked Wüst to join as well. Wüst, as Frick wrote, had already made a contribution to Otto's 60th birthday. Frick now hoped that Wüst might again share the idea that the holy had still a mission to fulfill.[148] Since Wüst does not appear among the contributors, it seems at first that he had donated money. Of course, in 1939 Wüst had no interest to become engaged in a Festschrift honoring

---

[146] Former Rosenberg affiliates were Eberhard Achterberg, Friedrich Cornelius, Matthes Ziegler, and, again, Bernhard Kummer. See the proceedings *X. Internationaler Kongress für Religionsgeschichte, 11.–17. September 1960 in Marburg/Lahn*, ed. by the Organisationsausschuß (Marburg: Elvert, 1961). The record of participants includes the names of Biezais, Eliade, Gundert, Kummer, Philippidis, and Wikander – appearing in this book as subject matter – as well.

[147] See Franz Mandl, "Das Erbe der Ahnen. Ernst Burgstaller/Herman Wirth und die österreichische Felsbildforschung" (with an English summary), in *Mitteilungen der Anisa* 1/2 (1999), pp. 41–67. Luitgard Löw, Bamberg, is currently finishing her habilitation on *Die skandinavischen Felsbilder in der Deutung völkischer Laienforschung. Das Beispiel Herman Wirth und sein Umfeld*; cf. her article "Der 'Fall Herman Wirth'," in *Archäologisches Nachrichtenblatt* 10–3 (2005), pp. 315–320.

[148] Letter of Frick to Wüst on February 13, 1939, personal files Walther Wüst, University Archive Munich, O-N-14.

Rudolf Otto. The political development of Wüst was probably also the reason why his assistant Hans Hartog – the later son-in-law of Friedrich Heiler – changed from the University of Munich to Marburg.[149]

Julius Evola, the eminent Italian fascist and antisemite, replaced Wirth as Wüst's ideological reference point in the second half of the 1930s. Evola's less voelkish and more imperial critique covering (but not limited to) culture, materialism, liberalism, and Judaism attracted Wüst's interest when he had assumed a leading position in the "Ahnenerbe." Wüst was one of Evola's main supporters in the SS. Others rejected Evola's aristocratic thinking as inadequate to National Socialism and its claim to act in conformity with the interests of Germany's proletarians. Wüst met Evola several times in the 1930s and 1940s.[150] He shared with him the intention of establishing a spiritual countermovement against bolshevism and Judaism in Europe. The ideology of the Waffen-SS followed a similar approach to include as much nations and movements as possible into the war against the dark forces of evil, however under the auspices of a German dominion and not on the basis of Evola's ideas. Nazi Germany was, in Franco Ferraresi's words, not Evola's "natural habitat."[151]

After World War II Evola advanced to one of the leading intellectuals of the European far right. His ideological influence even increased with the end of communism in Europe. He is rightly called "a key reference-point for all modern far-right thinkers."[152] To make Evola acceptable outside the radical right it was necessary to purify him from the accusation of being a mere fascist and antisemite. Over the last several years a strategy in bringing Evola in opposition to National Socialism has emerged. The Hancke-assessment of the Secret Service of the SS contributes greatly to that aim. Comparable in that regard is

---

[149] In a letter to his teacher Heiler Christel Matthias Schröder wrote on September 12, 1937 that Hartog had wanted to write a dissertation under Wüst. But his opinion that a conception of sin was to be found in the Vedas caused problems with Wüst. Literal remains of Ch. M. Schröder, Department for the Study of Religion, Tübingen, s.v. Heiler.

[150] See Evola's letter to Wüst on September 16, 1940 announcing his visit a few days later. Evola said that their first encounter took place during the second Nordic Thing in Bremen on October 22, 1934. Personal files of Walther Wüst, University Archive Munich, O-N-14.

[151] Franco Ferraresi, "Julius Evola: Tradition, Reaction, and the Radical Right," *Archives Européennes de Sociologie* 28 (1987), pp. 107–151, here p. 107.

[152] Peter Davies and Derek Lynch, eds., *The Routledge Companion to Fascism and the Far Right* (London-New York: Routledge, 2002), p. 207.

another negative evaluation originating from Karl Maria Wiligut. It is obvious that these texts were translated and published to serve ideological and not scientific purposes.[153] A clear mention of the references is avoided in order to rely on an exclusive interpretation of a hermetic source – the opposite of an open scholarly debate. The "Ahnenerbe"-statement of Joseph Otto Plaßmann and other material from German archives pertaining to Evola is unknown or excluded. From a serious point of view it could be hardly possible to use the vote of a maniac such as Wiligut to 'prove' an antagonism between Evola and the SS or National Socialism. Wiligut's bewildered fantasies and his quest of occult magical forces becomes visible when he asked Bruno Beger before the start of the Tibet expedition, as Christopher Hale writes, to find evidence for his assumption that Tibetan women "carry magical stones lodged inside their vaginas."[154]

Parallel to this strategy of distraction rightist theoreticians try to link Evola with more reputable thinkers many of whom are attached to the so-called conservative revolution.[155] In that scheme of raising Evola's respectability Mircea Eliade has become a corner stone. Particularly Philippe Baillet, Claudio Mutti, and H.T. Hansen emphasize a strong impact of Evola on Eliade.[156] The Austrian esotericist H.T. Hansen, who is esteemed as one of the main and best informed propagators of Evolian thoughts, contributed a foreword of more than 100 pages to the German edition of Evola's *Gli uomine e le rovine* that has become highly influential and is considered a definitive introduction to Evola's thinking.[157] The Hohenrain publishing house that printed the book

---

[153] See B. Zoratto, ed., *Julius Evola nei documenti segreti dell'Ahnenerbe*, pp. 33–43 and Gianfranco de Turris and idem, eds., *Julius Evola nei rapporti delle SS* (Quaderni di testi Evoliani 33) (Rome: Europa Liberia Editrice, 2000), pp. 11–13.

[154] Christopher Hale, *Himmler's Crusade. The True Story of the 1938 Nazi Expedition into Tibet* (London et al.: Bantam Press, 2003), p. 155.

[155] See H.T. Hansen, "Julius Evola und die deutsche konservative Revolution," *Criticón* 158, April-June (1998) pp. 16–32, separately printed as *Julius Evola et la Révolution conservatrice* (Montreuil: Les Deux Étendards, 2002).

[156] Philippe Baillet, "Julius Evola et Mircea Eliade (1927–1974): Une amitié manquée, avec des extraits de deux lettres d'Evola à Eliade," *Les deux étendards* 1, septembre/décembre (1988), pp. 45–55, Claudio Mutti, *Mircea Eliade e la guardia di ferro* (Parma: Edizioni all'insegna del Veltro, n.d. [1989]), esp. pp. 38–55, and H.T. Hansen, "Mircea Eliade, Julius Evola und die Integrale Tradition," in *Über das Initiatische von Julius Evola. Aufsatzsammlung* (Sinzheim: H. Frietsch Verlag, 1998), pp. 9–50.

[157] H.T. Hansen, "Evola's politisches Wirken," introduction of J. Evola, *Menschen inmitten von Ruinen* (Tübingen: Hohenrain, 1991), pp. 7–132, English trans. *Men among ruins. Postwar reflections of a radical traditionalist* (Rochester: Inner traditions, 2002), with an English translation of Hansen's German introduction (pp. 1–104 and pp. 300–310)

belongs to the Tübingen Grabert-Verlag, a leading right wing publisher in Germany particularly proficient in Holocaust denial. Its founder Herbert Grabert was a member of the German Faith Movement and pupil of Jakob Wilhelm Hauer. After the death of his father, Grabert's son Wigbert continued publishing books pointing to a spiritual alternative to the Judeo-Christian model.[158] The second key text of Hansen trying to increase Evola's reputation is the long preface "Mircea Eliade, Julius Evola und die integrale Tradition" introducing a collection of Evola's *Antaios* articles published by Hansen under the title *Über das Initiatische*. Discussing an article of Paola Pisi Hansen accentuates the influence of Evola on Eliade.[159] Because Eliade embarked on an academic career and became a member of the establishment himself, he 'forgot' his former friend and hid the connection with him. Mutti, Baillet, and Hansen stress Eliade's political opportunism although admitting that traditionalist and hermetic ideas could not have been spread in this way without Eliade's belonging to the academe which remained closed for Evola. The metaphor used for Eliade's behavior is that of a Trojan Horse.[160]

Whether (or how far) this is the case with Eliade, the analogy of a Trojan Horse certainly applies to Hansen himself. H.T. Hansen's real name is Hans Thomas Hakl, known as author of a well written and cautiously arguing study on the Eranos movement.[161] To conceal his role as an advocate and propagator of the Italian fascist, Hakl uses Hansen as *nom de guerre* at the Evolian front. His non-fictitious identity is reserved for another kind of audience. Without such a camouflage, as Hakl rightly assumes, his influence in the academic world would be limited. The actual climax of Hakl's plan of action is the successful placing of an article about Evola in the second edition of the renown *Encyclopedia of*

---

and an additional preface by Hansen to the American edition (pp. xi–xvi and pp. 298–300).

[158] See Martin Finkenberger and H. Junginger, eds., *Im Dienste der Lügen. Herbert Grabert (1901–1978) und seine Verlage* (Aschaffenburg: Alibri, 2004).

[159] Cf. Paola Pisi, "I 'tradizionalisti' e la formazione del pensiero di Eliade," in Luciano Arcella et al., eds., *Confronto con Mircea Eliade. Archetipi mitici e identità storica* (Milano: Jaca Book, 1998), pp. 43–133, cf. in this context also Natale Spineto, "Mircea Eliade and traditionalism," *Aries* 1 (2001), pp. 63–87.

[160] Hansen, "Evola's politisches Wirken," pp. 21–26.

[161] Hans Thomas Hakl, *Der verborgene Geist von Eranos. Unbekannte Begegnungen von Wissenschaft und Esoterik. Eine alternative Geistesgeschichte des 20. Jahrhunderts* (Bretten: Scientia Nova, 2001).

Religion.[162] To venerate a notorious antisemite and irreconcilable enemy of the Western democratic system seems to have become quite normal if accompanied by the expression of a few mental reservations which Hakl added to quiet possible criticism. Hakl went so far to quote his own pseudonym in the article. How stupid does the author think about the *ER*-readers? But what calls more attention are the reasons compelling the editors to include such an article. It remains unclear on the basis of which sort of accomplishments (religious, scientific, or political) they decided to reserve six columns for today's most important right wing intellectual in Europe. From Hakl's point of view it is a combination of all three elements that makes Evola an outstanding thinker. Since Evola had nothing produced in terms of ordinary scholarship, Hakl's aim must be to connect him with prominent historians of religions such as Raffaele Pettazzoni, Karl Kerényi, Angelo Brelich, Giuseppe Tucci, Franz Altheim, and, above all, Mircea Eliade. Even if the editors had no knowledge of the real identity of the author it is scandalous to honor one of Europe's most influential postwar fascists, someone who has written the preface of the heinous Protocols of the Elders of Zion, with an entry in the *Encyclopedia of Religion*. Having achieved such an excellent opportunity of advertising Evolian thoughts, Hakl correctly refers to this sort of self-fulfilling prophecy in writing: "Academic circles have become increasingly interested in Evola."[163]

The desire to revive the myths and ideological mystifications prevailing in fascist Italy, National Socialist Germany, and other countries or movements with a fascist leaning after 1945 normally presumed a modification of the former ideas. At least the main fascist catch-phrases ought to be deleted. Evola never undertook the slightest attempt to do so with the result that his influence was restricted to right wing circles. But also Herman Wirth had no chance to be taken serious in Germany although he tried to impart his former Nordic symbol theory with a new European appearance and although he could come, with the help of Heiler, into a loose contact with the academic study of religion. More public success had the former head of the "Ahnenerbe"-department "Ortung und Landschaftsbilder" (Location and Landscape Scenes)

---

[162] H.T. Hakl, "Evola, Julius," *Encyclopedia of Religion* 5 (2005), pp. 2904–2907. A similar article of him with a more plain language appeared ten years earlier in the German right wing dictionary *Lexikon des Konservatismus*, ed. by Caspar von Schrenck Norzing (Graz: Stocker, 1996), pp. 165–167.

[163] Hakl, "Evola, Julius," *Encyclopedia of Religion* 5 (2005), p. 2906.

Werner Müller (1907–1990).[164] Müller transmuted his previous occupation with the Indo-Germans into the study of the North American Indians, becoming a well-known specialist in that field in the 1970s and 1980s.[165] But similar to the situation of his "Ahnenerbe"-colleague Otto Huth, it was impossible for Müller to establish himself as a university teacher in Germany after the war. The career of both Müller and Huth unfolded in parallel and ended in Tübingen's university library.[166]

Their connection with the Aryan Myth in the years of fascism impeded Grabert, Hauer, Huth, Müller, Wirth, Wüst and others from returning to a university position. If their theories still attained a marginal influence, it was restricted to groups at the fringe of the society. The political change after 1945 was connected with a Christian backlash that took effect specifically in the study of religion and barred the former agitators of an Aryan or Indo-Germanic mythology from reentering the academic stage. Under such circumstances a revival of any kind of Aryanism was rather unlikely. But with the end of communism in Europe a new situation emerged, a situation comparable to the ideological confusion at the end of the 1920s. The rising susceptibility to old myths, traditional knowledge, and hermetic texts met a new response from the side of Indo-European mythologies.[167] It brought Evola from an outsider position to the center of the political discourse. Yet a further success would require a more general understanding of what might become the ideological substructure of a new imperial Europe. It is probable that the future quarrels for religious hegemony will occur along the same lines for and against the significance of Christianity.

---

[164] See the diagram on p. 142. The task of this department was to detect places of Indo-Germanic relevance.

[165] See the very positive article of Mircea Eliade, "Werner Müller und die 'allgemeine Religionswissenschaft'," in *Unter dem Pflaster liegt der Strand* (1982), pp. 13–17.

[166] The parallels between Huth and Müller include a dissertation at the University of Bonn under Carl Clemen, the directorship of an "Ahnenerbe"-department, a teaching position at the "Reichsuniversität Straßburg," a common escape from Strasbourg to Tübingen at the end of 1944, and a new beginning at Tübingen's university library. Party member since 1933 and SS member since 1940, Müller was first involved in the "Ahnenerbe"-research on the *Ura-Linda-Chronik*. With the help of the SS he could achieve the habilitation and a lectureship at the German "Reichsuniversität Straßburg" in 1942 and 1944. See http://homepages.uni-tuebingen.de/gerd.simon/ChrMueller-Werner.pdf for further information.

[167] See H. Junginger, "Sigrid Hunke (1913–1999): Europe's New Religion and its Old Stereotypes." In Hubert Cancik and Uwe Puschner, eds., *Antisemitismus, Paganismus, Völkische Religion – Anti-Semitism, Paganism, Voelkish Religion* (München: Saur, 2004), pp. 151–162, for a German approach to re-model the former Pagan tradition.

Which role the academic study of religion will adopt in this game is an open question. Its development in the 1930s and 1940s reveals a greater interest in creating myths instead of analyzing them. The enticement of leaving the academic margin and becoming influential not only at the university but in the society as a whole had an overwhelming charm which only very few historians of religions resisted.[168]

Walther Wüst was a scholar who totally surrendered himself and his scholarship to the ideology of National Socialism. Although compensated with extraordinary might and influence, he served as an intellectual lackey of the NS regime. Wüst internalized his role to such a degree that he believed in the function of the academic study of religion as a mere tool for the exploitation of religious capital in order to secure and fortify the power relations on which his position relied. Though the state he supported lasted only twelve instead of thousand years, his comprehension of the study of religion has perhaps more general and modern features as we would appreciate. To abstract how well both religion and the study of religion functions from its content in behalf of a politically accepted order points far beyond the NS period. Surely opportunism and the lack of self-reflexivity was not confined to Wüst and characteristic of many other scholars attached to National Socialism. But the willingness to identify himself with a criminal regime, becoming all the more involved in criminal activities, distinguishes him from the majority of his colleagues. Since it is hardly possible to learn something positive from such an example, it may serve as a *memento mori* to remind later generations of the destruction of scholarship from within.

---

[168] A special issue of the *Zeitschrift für Religionswissenschaft* with the title "Das Überleben der Religionswissenschaft im Nationalsozialismus" (*ZfR* 9, 2001) is concerned with this group of scholars.

Bibliography

Atti dell'VIII Congresso Internazionale di Storia delle Religioni. Roma 17–23 Aprile 1955. Firenze: G.C. Sansoni [1956].

Baillet, Philippe. "Julius Evola et Mircea Eliade (1927–1974): Une amitié manquée, avec des extraits de deux lettres d'Evola à Eliade." *Les deux étendards* 1, septembre/ décembre (1988), pp. 45–55.

Baumann, Schaul. *Die Deutsche Glaubensbewegung und ihr Gründer Jakob Wilhelm Hauer (1881–1962)*. Marburg: Diagonal, 2005.

Bosch, Laurens van den. *Friedrich Max Müller. A Life Devoted to the Humanities*. Leiden: Brill, 2002.

Boutin, Christoph. *Politique et tradition. Julius Evola dans le siècle (1898–1974)*. Paris: Éditions Kimé, 1992.

Cancik, Hubert. "'Neuheiden' und totaler Staat. Völkische Religion am Ende der Weimarer Republik." In idem, ed., *Religions- und Geistesgeschichte der Weimarer Republik*. Düsseldorf: Patmos, 1982, pp. 176–212 (reprinted in Richard Faber et al., eds., *Antik – Modern. Beiträge zur römischen und deutschen Kulturgeschichte*. Stuttgart: Metzler, 1998, pp. 187–227).

Cassata, Francesco. *A destra del fascismo. Profilo politico di Julius Evola*. Torino: Bollati Boringhieri, 2003.

Clemen, Carl. "Waren die Externsteine ein germanisches Heiligtum?" *Zeitschrift für Missionskunde und Religionswissenschaft* (1935), pp. 210–233.

Cospito, Nicola and Hans Werner Neulen, eds. *Julius Evola nei documenti segreti del Terzo Reich*. Roma: Europa, 1986.

Davies, Peter and Derek Lynch, eds. *The Routledge Companion to Fascism and the Far Right*. London-New York: Routledge, 2002.

Deschner, Günther. *'Gobineau und Deutschland'. Der Einfluß von J. A. de Gobineaus 'Essai sur inégalité des races humaines' auf die deutsche Geistesgeschichte 1853–1917*. Diss. Erlangen 1967.

Drake, Richard. "Julius Evola and the Ideological Origins of the Radical Right." In Peter H. Merkl, ed., *Political Violence and Terror. Motifs and Motivations*. Berkeley: University of California Press, 1986, pp. 61–89.

——. "Julius Evola, radical fascism, and the Lateran accords." *The Catholic historical review* 74 (1988), pp. 403–419.

Dürkop, Martina. "'...er wird sehen, daß das Archiv wirklich ein Geschäft ist, wenn es richtig behandelt wird...'. Wissenschaftlicher und wirtschaftlicher Existenzkampf des ARW 1919–1939." *Archiv für Religionsgeschichte* 1 (1999), pp. 107–128.

Eliade, Mircea. "Recension de 'Rivolta contro il mondo moderno' de Julius Evola." *Vremea* 382, March 31, 1935.

——. "Ion Moța și Vasile Marin." *Vremea* 472, January 24, 1937.

——. "Noua aristocrație legionară." *Vremea* 522, January 23, 1938.

——. *Diario portugués*. Barcelona: Editorial Kairós, 2001.

Engelhardt, Isrun. "Tibetan Triangle: German, Tibetan and British Relations in the Context of Ernst Schäfer's Expedition, 1938–1939." *Asiatische Studien/Études Asiatiques* 58-1 (2004), pp. 57–113.

Evola, Julius. *Erhebung wider die moderne Welt*. Stuttgart: Deutsche Verlagsanstalt, 1935 (1st ed. *Rivolta contro il mondo moderno*. Milano: Heopli, 1934).

——. "Introduzione a L'Internationale ebraica." *I 'Protocolli' Dei 'Savi Anzani' Di Sion*. Roma: La Vita Italiana, 1938, pp. 9–33.

——. "La tragedia de la Garda di Ferro." *La Vita Italiana* 309, December 1938.

——. *Menschen inmitten von Ruinen*. Tübingen: Hohenrain, 1991 (1st ed. *Gli uomine e le rovine*. Roma: Ed. dell'Ascia, 1953).

Ferraresi, Franco. "Julius Evola: Tradition, Reaction, and the Radical Right." *Archives Européennes de Sociologie* 28 (1987), pp. 107–151.

Flasche, Rainer. "Religionsmodelle und Erkenntnisprinzipien der Religionswissenschaft in der Weimarer Zeit." In Hubert Cancik, ed., *Religions- und Geistesgeschichte der Weimarer Republik*. Düsseldorf: Patmos, 1982, pp. 261–276.

——. "Der Irrationalismus in der Religionswissenschaft und dessen Begründung." In Hans G. Kippenberg and Brigitte Luchesi, eds., *Religionswissenschaft und Kulturkritik*. Marburg: Diagonal, 1991, pp. 243–257.

——. "Vom deutschen Kaiserreich zum Dritten Reich. National-religiöse Bewegungen in der ersten Hälfte des 20. Jahrhunderts in Deutschland." *Zeitschrift für Religionswissenschaft* 2 (1993), pp. 28–49.

Friedländer, Saul et al., eds. *Bertelsmann im Dritten Reich*. München: C. Bertelsmann Verlag, 2002.

Grabert, Herbert. "Allgemeine Religionsgeschichte und völkische Glaubensgeschichte." *Archiv für Religionswissenschaft* 33 (1936), pp. 191–220.

Grottanelli, Cristiano. "Mircea Eliade, Carl Schmitt, René Guenon, 1942." *Revue d'histoire des religions* 219–3 (2002), pp. 325–356.

——. "Fruitful Death: Mircea Eliade and Ernst Jünger on Human Sacrifice, 1937–1945." *Numen* 52–1 (2005), pp. 116–145.

Hakl, Hans Thomas [Hansen, H.T.]. "Evolas politisches Wirken." In Julius Evola, *Menschen inmitten von Ruinen*. Tübingen: Hohenrain, 1991, pp. 7–132 (English trans. "Julius Evola's political endeavors." In Julius Evola, *Men among the ruins. Post-war reflections of a radical traditionalist*. Rochester: Inner Traditions, 2002, pp. 1–104 and pp. 300–310).

—— [Hansen, H.T.]. "Julius Evola. Denker gegen die Moderne." *Deutschland in Geschichte und Gegenwart* 4 (1991), pp. 25–27.

——. "Evola, Julius." In Caspar von Schrenck Norzing, ed., *Lexikon des Konservatismus*. Graz: Stocker, 1996, pp. 165–167.

—— [Hansen, H.T.]. "Julius Evola und die deutsche konservative Revolution." *Criticón* 158, April-June (1998), pp. 16–32 (Italian trans. "Julius Evola e la 'Rivoluzione Conservatrice' e Tedesca." In *Studi Evoliani*, 1998, pp. 144–180, French trans. *Julius Evola et la 'Révolution conservatrice' allemande*. Montreuil: Les Deux Étendards, 2002, with a preface by Philippe Baillet and a bibliography of Evola's German writings by Alain de Benoist).

—— [Hansen, H.T.]. "Mircea Eliade, Julius Evola und die Integrale Tradition." In *Über das Initiatische von Julius Evola. Aufsatzsammlung*. Sinzheim: H. Frietsch Verlag, 1998, pp. 9–50.

——. *Der verborgene Geist von Eranos. Unbekannte Begegnungen von Wissenschaft und Esoterik. Eine alternative Geistesgeschichte des 20. Jahrhunderts*. Bretten: Scientia nova, 2001.

——. "Eranos im Spiegel der Geistesgeschichte des 20. Jahrhunderts." *Archaeus* 6–1/2 (2002), pp. 183–200.

——. "Evola, Julius." In *Encyclopedia of Religion* 5 (2005), pp. 2904–2907.

——. "Die Integrale Tradition." *Sezession* 11 (2005), pp. 20–26.

Hale, Christopher. *Himmler's Crusade. The True Story of the 1938 Nazi Expedition into Tibet*. London et al.: Bantam Press, 2003.

Halle, Uta. *'Die Externsteine sind bis auf weiteres germanisch!' Prähistorische Archäologie im Dritten Reich*. Bielefeld: Verlag für Regionalgeschichte, 2002.

Hansen, H.T., see Hakl, Hans Thomas.

Hauer, Jakob Wilhelm. "Religion und Rasse." *Archiv für Religionswissenschaft* 34 (1937), pp. 81–97.

——. "Zum gegenwärtigen Stand der Indogermanenfrage." *Archiv für Religionswissenschaft* 36 (1939), pp. 1–63.

Hausmann, Frank-Rutger. *'Deutsche Geisteswissenschaft' im Zweiten Weltkrieg. Die 'Aktion Ritterbusch' (1940–1945)*. Dresden: Dresden University Press, 1998 (2nd ed. 2002).

Heiber, Helmut. *Universität unterm Hakenkreuz*, 3 vols. München: Saur, 1991–1994.

Heinen, Armin. *Die Legion 'Erzengel Michael' in Rumänien. Soziale Bewegung und politische Organisation. Ein Beitrag zum Problem des internationalen Faschismus.* München: R. Oldenbourg, 1986, Romanian trans. Bucharest: Humanitas, 1999.

Heinrich, Fritz. *Die deutsche Religionswissenschaft und der Nationalsozialismus. Eine ideologiekritische und wissenschaftsgeschichtliche Untersuchung.* Petersberg: Imhof, 2002.

Jacobeit, Wolfgang et al., eds. *Völkische Wissenschaft. Gestalten und Tendenzen der deutschen und österreichischen Volkskunde in der ersten Hälfte des 20. Jahrhunderts.* Wien et al.: Böhlau, 1994.

Junginger, Horst. "Ein Kapitel Religionswissenschaft während der NS-Zeit: Hans Alexander Winkler (1900–1945)." *Zeitschrift für Religionswissenschaft* 2 (1995), pp. 137–161.

——. *Von der philologischen zur völkischen Religionswissenschaft. Das Fach Religionswissenschaft an der Universität Tübingen von der Mitte des 19. Jahrhunderts bis zum Ende des Dritten Reiches.* Stuttgart: Steiner, 1999.

——. "Völkerkunde und Religionswissenschaft, zwei nationalsozialistische Geisteswissenschaften?" In Bernhard Streck, ed., *Ethnologie und Nationalsozialismus.* Gehren: Escher Verlag, 2000, pp. 51–66.

——. "Das Überleben der Religionswissenschaft im Nationalsozialismus." Special issue of the *Zeitschrift für Religionswissenschaft* 9 (2001), pp. 149–167.

——. "Christel Matthias Schröder (1915–1996) und seine Bedeutung für die deutsche Religionswissenschaft." Ibid., pp. 235–268.

——. "Das 'Arische Seminar' an der Universität Tübingen 1940–1945." In Heidrun Brückner et al., eds., *Indienforschung im Zeitenwandel. Analysen und Dokumente zur Indologie und Religionswissenschaft in Tübingen.* Tübingen: Attempto, 2003, pp. 177–207.

—— and Martin Finkenberger, eds. *Im Dienste der Lügen. Herbert Grabert (1901–1978) und seine Verlage.* Aschaffenburg: Alibri, 2004.

——. "Die Tübinger Schule der 'völkischen Religionswissenschaft' in den dreißiger und vierziger Jahren." Ibid., pp. 10–35.

——. "Herbert Grabert als völkischer Religionswissenschaftler: Der Glaube des deutschen Bauerntums." Ibid., pp. 36–68.

——. "Sigrid Hunke (1913–1999): Europe's New Religion and its Old Stereotypes." In Hubert Cancik and Uwe Puschner, eds., *Antisemitismus, Paganismus, Völkische Religion – Anti-Semitism, Paganism, Voelkish Religion.* München: Saur, 2004, pp. 151–162.

——. "Religionswissenschaft im Nationalsozialismus. Die Geschichte einer gescheiterten Emanzipation." In Jürgen Elvert and Jürgen Sikora, eds., *Nationalsozialismus und Kulturwissenschaften* (forthcoming).

Kater, Michael H. *Das 'Ahnenerbe' der SS 1935–1945. Ein Beitrag zur Kulturpolitik des Dritten Reiches.* Stuttgart: Deutsche Verlags-Anstalt, 1974, 3rd ed. München: Oldenbourg, 2001.

Kippenberg, Hans G. *Die Entdeckung der Religionsgeschichte. Religionswissenschaft und Moderne.* München: Beck, 1997.

Krech, Volkhard. *Wissenschaft und Religion. Studien zur Geschichte der Religionsforschung in Deutschland 1871 bis 1933.* Tübingen: Mohr Siebeck, 2002.

Kubota, Hiroshi. *Religionswissenschaftliche Religiosität und Religionsgründung. Jakob Wilhelm Hauer im Kontext des freien Protestantismus.* Frankfurt am Main et al.: Lang, 2005.

Laignel-Lavastine, Alexandra. *Cioran, Eliade, Ionesco: L'oubli du fascisme.* Paris: Presses Universitaires de France, 2002.

Lang, Hans-Joachim. *Die Namen der Nummern. Wie es gelang die 86 Opfer eines NS-Verbrechens zu identifizieren.* Hamburg: Hoffmann und Campe, 2004.

Lerchenmüller, Joachim and Gerd Simon, eds. *Im Vorfeld des Massenmords. Germanistik und Nachbarfächer im 2. Weltkrieg.* 3rd ed. Tübingen: Gesellschaft für Interdisziplinäre Forschung Tübingen, 1997.

Lincoln, Bruce. *Theorizing myth. Narrative, ideology, and scholarship.* Chicago: University of Chicago Press, 1999.

Löw, Luitgard. "Der 'Fall Herman Wirth'." *Archäologisches Nachrichtenblatt* 10–3 (2005), pp. 315–320.

Losemann, Volker. "Die 'Krise der Alten Welt' und der Gegenwart. Franz Altheim und Karl Kerényi im Dialog." In Peter Kneissl and V. Losemann, eds., *Imperium Romanum Studien zur Geschichte und Rezeption. Festschrift für Karl Christ zum 75. Geburtstag.* Stuttgart: Steiner, 1998, pp. 492–518.

Mandl, Franz. "Das Erbe der Ahnen. Ernst Burgstaller/Herman Wirth und die österreichische Felsbildforschung" (with an English summary). *Mitteilungen der Anisa* 1/2 (1999), pp. 41–67.

Müller, Hannelore. *Der frühe Mircea Eliade. Sein rumänischer Hintergrund und die Anfänge seiner universalistischen Religionsphilosophie.* Münster: Lit, 2004.

———. "Mircea Eliade und Nae Ionescu. Der Schüler und sein Meister." *Zeitschrift für Religionswissenschaft* 1 (2004), pp. 3–21.

Mutti, Claudio. *Mircea Eliade e la guardia di ferro.* Parma: Edizioni all'insegna del Veltro, 1989, Romanian trans. Sibiu: Puncte Cardinale, 1995, German trans. 2007.

Nanko, Ulrich. *Die Deutsche Glaubensbewegung. Eine historische und soziologische Untersuchung.* Marburg: Diagonal, 1993.

Neuberger, Helmut. *Winkelmaß und Hakenkreuz. Die Freimaurer und das Dritte Reich.* München: Herbig, 2001.

Olender, Maurice. *Les langues du Paradis. Aryens et Sémites, un couple providentiel.* Paris: Gallimard, 1989 (German ed. *Die Sprachen des Paradieses. Religion, Philologie und Rassentheorie im 19. Jahrhundert.* Frankfurt a.M.: Campus, 1995).

Organisationsausschuß, ed. *X. Internationaler Kongress für Religionsgeschichte, 11.–17. September 1960 in Marburg/Lahn.* Marburg: Elvert, 1961.

Pfister, Friedrich. "Die Religion und der Glaube der germanischen Völker und ihrer religiösen Führer." *Archiv für Religionswissenschaft* 36 (1939), pp. 1–14.

———. "Die religiöse Sendung des deutschen Volkes." Ibid., pp. 373–380.

Pisi, Paola. "I 'tradizionalisti' e la formazione del pensiero di Eliade." In Luciano Arcella et al., eds., *Confronto con Mircea Eliade: Archetipi mitici e identità storica.* Milano: Jaca Book, 1998, pp. 43–133.

Poewe, Karla. "Liberalism, German Missionaries, and National Socialism." In Ulrich van der Heyden and Holger Stoecker, eds., *Mission und Macht im Wandel politischer Orientierungen. Europäische Missionsgesellschaften in politischen Spannungsfeldern in Afrika und Asien zwischen 1800 und 1945.* Stuttgart: Steiner, 2005, pp. 633–662.

———. *New Religions and the Nazis.* New York/London: Routledge, 2006.

Poliakov, Léon. *Der arische Mythos. Zu den Quellen von Rassismus und Nationalismus.* Wien: Europa-Verlag, 1977 (English ed. *The Aryan Myth*, London: Heinemann, 1974).

Pollock, Sheldon. "Deep Orientalism? Notes on Sanskrit and Power Beyond the Raj." In Carol A. Breckenridge and Peter van der Veer, eds., *Orientalism and the Postcolonial Predicament. Perspectives on South Asia.* Philadelphia: University of Pennsylvania Press, 1993, pp. 76–133 (German trans. "'Ex Oriente Nox'. Indologie im nationalsozialistischen Staat." In Sebastian Conrad and Shalini Randeira, eds., *Jenseits des Eurozentrismus. Postkoloniale Perspektiven in den Geschichts- und Kulturwissenschaften.* Frankfurt/New York: Campus, 2002, pp. 335–371).

Römer, Ruth. *Sprachwissenschaft und Rassenideologie.* München: Fink, 1985.

Rudolph, Kurt. *Die Religionsgeschichte an der Leipziger Universität und die Entwicklung der Religionswissenschaft. Ein Beitrag zur Wissenschaftsgeschichte und zum Problem der Religionswissenschaft.* Berlin: Akademie-Verlag, 1962.

———. *Geschichte und Probleme der Religionswissenschaft.* Leiden: Brill, 1992.

Rürup, Reinhard, ed. *Topography of Terror. Gestapo, SS and Reichssicherheitshauptamt on the 'Prinz-Albrecht-Terrain'. A documentation.* 4th ed. Berlin: Willmuth Arenhövel, 1995.

Schaeder, Hans Heinrich, ed. *Der Orient in deutscher Forschung. Vorträge der Berliner Orientalistentagung, Herbst 1942.* Leipzig: O. Harrassowitz, 1944.

Schemann, Ludwig. *Gobineaus Rassenwerk.* Stuttgart: Fr. Fromms Verlag, 1910.

Spineto, Natale. "Mircea Eliade and traditionalism." *Aries* 1 (2001), pp. 63–87.
Stache-Rosen, Valentina. *German Indologists. Biographies of Scholars in Indian Studies writing in German. With a Summary of Indology in German Speaking Countries*, 2nd rev. ed. New Delhi: Max Mueller Bhavan, 1990.
Steigmann-Gall, Richard. *The Holy Reich. Nazi Conceptions of Christianity, 1919–1945.* Cambridge: Cambridge University Press, 2003.
Storm, Sönje. "Die öffentliche Aussprache über Herrman Wirths 'Ura-Linda-Chronik' in Berlin (1934)." In Birgitta Almgren, ed., *Bilder des Nordens in der Germanistik 1929–1945. Wissenschaftliche Identität oder politische Anpassung?* Huddinge: Södertörns Högskola, 2002, pp. 79–97.
Strenski, Ivan. *Four theories of myth in twentieth-century history. Cassirer, Eliade, Levi-Strauss and Malinowski.* Basingstoke: Macmillan, 1987.
Timuş, Mihaela, éd. *Întotdeauna Orientul. Corespondenţa Mircea Eliade – Stig Wikander (1948–1977)* [C'est toujours l'Orient. Correspondance Eliade-Wikander]. Iasi-Bucarest: Polirom, 2005.
Trimondi, Victor and Victoria. *Hitler, Buddha, Krishna. Eine unheilige Allianz vom Dritten Reich bis heute.* Wien: Ueberreuter, 2002.
Ţurcanu, Florin. *Mircea Eliade. Le prisonnier de l'histoire.* Paris: Éd. La Découverte, 2003.
Turris, Gianfranco de and Bruno Zoratto, eds. *Julius Evola nei rapporti delle SS* (Quaderni di testi Evoliani 33). Rome: Europa Liberia Editrice, 2000.
Ustorf, Werner. *Sailing on the Next Tide. Missions, Missiology, and the Third Reich.* Frankfurt a.M.: Peter Lang, 2000.
Verroen, Ruth et al., eds. *Leben Sie? Die Geschichte der deutsch-jüdischen Familie Jacobsohn.* Marburg: Universitätsbibliothek, 2000.
Volovici, Leon. *Nationalist Ideology and Antisemitism. The Case of Romanian Intellectuals in the 1930s.* Oxford et al.: Pergamon Press, 1991, Romanian trans. Bucharest: Humanitas, 1995.
Walravens, Hartmut, ed. *W. A. Unkrieg (1883–1956). Korrespondenz mit Hans Findeisen, der Britischen Bibelgesellschaft und anderen über Sibirien und den Lamaismus.* Wiesbaden: Harrassowitz, 2004.
Wasserstrom, Steven M. "The lives of Baron Evola." *Alphabet City* 4/5 (1995), pp. 84–89.
——. *Religion after religion. Gershom Scholem, Mircea Eliade, and Henry Corbin at Eranos.* Princeton: Princeton University Press, 1999.
Wirth, Herman. *Der Aufgang der Menschheit. Untersuchungen der Geschichte der Religion, Symbolik und Schrift der atlantisch-nordischen Rasse.* Jena: Diederichs, 1928.
——. *Die Ura-Linda-Chronik.* Leipzig: Koehler & Amelang, 1933.
——. "Die Zeit Gottes." *Deutscher Glaube* 2 (1934), pp. 71–74.
——. *Die heilige Urschrift der Menschheit. Symbolgeschichtliche Untersuchungen diesseits und jenseits des Nordatlantik.* Leipzig: Koehler & Amelang, 1936.
——. [Roeper Bosch] *Führer durch das Ur-Europa-Museum. Mit einer Einführung in die Ursymbolik und Urreligion.* Marburg: Eccestan-Verlag, 1975.
Witte, Peter et al., eds. *Der Dienstkalender Heinrich Himmlers, 1941/42.* Hamburg: Christians, 1999.
Wiwjorra, Ingo. "Herman Wirth. Ein gescheiterter Ideologe zwischen 'Ahnenerbe' und Atlantis." In Barbara Danckwortt et al., eds., *Historische Rassismusforschung: Ideologen, Täter, Opfer.* Hamburg-Berlin: Argument, 1995, pp. 91–112.
Wüst, Walther. "Über das Alter des Rigveda und die Hauptfragen der indoarischen Frühgeschichte." *Wiener Zeitschrift für die Kunde des Morgenlandes* 34 (1927), pp. 165–215.
——. *Stilgeschichte und Chronologie des Rgveda.* Leipzig: Brockhaus, 1928.
——. "Gedanken über Wirths 'Aufgang der Menschheit'." *Zeitschrift für Missionskunde und Religionswissenschaft* (1929), pp. 257–274 and pp. 289–307.

——. "Rabindranath Tagores Geschichtswerk. Grundlagen und Zusammenhänge." *Zeitschrift für Missionskunde und Religionswissenschaft* (1931), pp. 33–50.

——. "Wilhelm Geiger." *Yoga. Internationale Zeitschrift für wissenschaftliche Yoga-Forschung*, ed. by Helmut Palmié (co-editors among others H. v. Glasenapp, J.W. Hauer, O. Strauß, W. Wüst, H. Zimmer), no. 1 (1931), pp. 15–21.

——. "Buddhismus und Christentum auf vorderasiatisch-antikem Boden. Vortrag, gehalten während der 47. Jahresversammlung der Ostasien-Mission in Basel, 6.10.1931." *Zeitschrift für Missionskunde und Religionswissenschaft* (1932), pp. 33–63.

——. *Vergleichendes und etymologisches Wörterbuch des Altindoarischen (Altindischen)*. Heidelberg: Winter, 1935.

——. "Des Führers Buch 'Mein Kampf' als Spiegel arischer Weltanschauung." *FM-Zeitschrift* 4.3, 1.3.1937, pp. 1–4.

—— with Kurt Schrötter. *Tod und Unsterblichkeit im Weltbild indogermanischer Denker*. Berlin: Nordland-Verlag, 1938 (2nd ed. 1939, 3rd ed. 1942).

——. "Von indogermanischer Religiosität. Sinn und Sendung." *Archiv für Religionswissenschaft* 36 (1939), pp. 64–108 (= *Indogermanisches Bekenntnis*, pp. 51–91 and pp. 141–150).

——. "Bestand die zoroastrische Urgemeinde wirklich aus berufsmäßigen Ekstatikern und schamanisierenden Rinderhirten der Steppe?" *Archiv für Religionswissenschaft* 36 (1939), pp. 234–249.

——. "Yasna XLII 4, 2/3." Ibid., pp. 250–256.

——. "Die deutsche Aufgabe der Indologie." *Deutsche Kultur im Leben der Völker. Mitteilungen der Akademie zur wissenschaftlichen Erforschung und zur Pflege des Deutschtums, Deutsche Akademie* 3 (1939), pp. 339–348.

——. *Indogermanisches Bekenntnis. Sechs Reden*. Berlin-Dahlem: Ahnenerbe Stiftungsverlag, 1942 (2nd ed. 1943).

——. "Indogermanisches Bekenntnis." Ibid., pp. 93–118.

Zarotti, Bruno, ed. *Julius Evola nei documenti segreti dell'ahnenerbe* (Quaderni di testi Evoliani 30). Roma: Europa Liberia Editrice, 1997.

HERMANN GÜNTERT IN THE 1930s.
HEIDELBERG, POLITICS, AND THE STUDY OF GERMANIC/INDOGERMANIC RELIGION

Bruce Lincoln

I

Hermann Güntert (1886–1948) is less well known than he ought to be, for his reputation was largely eclipsed when Georges Dumézil (1898–1986) and his admirers promoted the legend that the French scholar had single-handedly rescued the study of "Comparative Mythology" after its 19th century collapse.[1] Between the disgrace of Friedrich Max Müller (1823–1900) and the labors of Dumézil, however, there was Güntert, who was one of the foremost linguists of his era and equally accomplished in Religionswissenschaft.[2] Between 1912 and 1923, he devoted five extraordinary volumes to aspects of Indo-European religion, each more brilliant than its predecessor. First came a pioneering monograph, *Über altisländische Berserkergeschichten* (1912), which anticipated the later, less prudent work of numerous authors who came to see warrior rage as a religiously valorized phenomenon.[3] Next, *Über die ahurischen und daevischen*

---

[1] See, for instance, the hagiographic treatment of C. Scott Littleton, *The New Comparative Mythology* (Berkeley: University of California Press, 1966, 3rd ed. 1982) or Daniel Dubuisson, *Mythologies du XXᵉ siècle* (Lille: Presses universitaires de Lille, 1993).

[2] Güntert studied Religionswissenschaft under Albrecht Dieterich and Franz Boll. In many ways, his work has been more influential on students of religion (Dumézil, Herman Lommel, Mircea Eliade, e.g.) than on those of linguistics, although there also he continues to be read and appreciated. For short summaries of his life and work, see Wolf H. Goegginger, "Hermann Güntert als Religionsforscher," *Numen* 14 (1967), pp. 150–158 and Wolfgang Meid, "Hermann Güntert: Leben und Werk," in Manfred Mayrhofer et al., eds., *Antiquitates Indogermanicae. Studien zur indogermanischen Altertumskunde und zur Sprach- und Kulturgeschichte der indogermanischen Völker. Gedenkschrift für Hermann Güntert zur 25. Wiederkehr seines Todestages am 23. April 1973* (Innsbruck: Innsbrucker Beiträge zur Sprachwissenschaft, 1974), pp. 517–520. Also useful is the summary discussion of Rudolf Wachter and Amina Kropp, „Allgemeine und vergleichende Sprachwissenschaft," in Wolfgang U. Eckart, et al., eds., *Die Universität Heidelberg im Nationalsozialismus* (Heidelberg: Springer Medizin Verlag, 2006), pp. 371–389.

[3] Hermann Güntert, *Über altisländische Berserkergeschichten* (Heidelberg: J. Hörning, 1912). Cf. Lily Weiser, *Altgermanische Jünglingsweihe und Männerbünde* (Bühl-Baden: Konkordia A.G., 1927), Otto Höfler, *Kultische Geheimbünde der Germanen* (Frankfurt: Moritz Diesterweg, 1934), Richard Wolfram, *Schwerttanz und Männerbund* (Kassel: Bärenreiter-

Ausdrücke im Awesta (1914) advanced Güntert's understanding of language as rooted in culture and culture as rooted in religion, demonstrating how Zoroastrian dualism structures language itself, such that Avestan (the language of the older Zoroastrian scriptures) employs two parallel sets of nouns and verbs to mark righteous beings and actions as antithetical to those that are evil or demonic.[4] The same sort of argument animates *Von der Sprache der Götter und Geister* (1921), which identified a metalinguistic trope through which many Indo-European languages contrasted a "language of gods" to the "language of men." The latter was normal, unmarked speech, but the former constituted a lofty, highly marked diction, suitable for poetry and other divinely inspired, quasi-esoteric, and self-consciously elegant acts of discourse.[5] Calvert Watkins was still drawing on this work respectfully and productively a half century after its publication.[6] Then there was *Kalypso* (1919), an anguished wartime meditation on the mythology of death, especially the Indo-European goddesses and *femmes fatales* who personify the grave and whose superficial charms mask the horrors of decay, dissolution, and non-being buried in their bodies, the soil, and life itself.[7] Finally, there is *Der arische Weltkönig und Heiland* (1923), Güntert's masterpiece, which treats the imagery of bonds and bondage (social, religious, legal, cosmic and existential), also the promise of liberation from them.[8] Vast in its scope, exquisite in its philological detail, and awesome for its nuanced readings of sources, it is widely – and rightly – regarded as the finest book ever devoted to the religion of the Indo-European-speaking peoples. Inter alia, it inspired Dumézil's *Mitra-Varuna* (1940),

---

Verlag, 1936), Stig Wikander, *Der arische Männerbund* (Lund: C.W.K. Gleerup, 1938), Georges Dumézil, *Horace et les Curiaces* (Paris: Gallimard, 1942), and Mircea Eliade, "Dacians and Wolves," in *From Zalmoxis to Genghis Khan* (Chicago: University of Chicago Press, 1972), pp. 1–20.

[4] Hermann Güntert, *Über die ahurischen und daevischen Ausdrücke im Awesta. Eine semasiologische Studie* (Sitzungsberichte der Heidelberger Akademie der Wissenschaften, 1914–13) (Heidelberg: Carl Winter, 1914).

[5] Idem, *Von der Sprache der Götter und Geister. Bedeutungsgeschichtliche Untersuchungen zur homerischen und eddischen Göttersprache* (Halle: Max Niemeyer, 1921).

[6] Calvert Watkins, "Language of Gods and Language of Men: Remarks on Some Indo-European Metalinguistic Traditions," in Jaan Puhvel, ed., *Myth and Law among the Indo-Europeans* (Berkeley: University of California Press, 1970), pp. 1–18.

[7] Hermann Güntert, *Kalypso. Bedeutungsgeschichtliche Untersuchungen auf dem Gebiet der indogermanischen Sprachen* (Halle: Max Niemeyer, 1919).

[8] Idem, *Der arische Weltkönig und Heiland. Bedeutungsgeschichtliche Untersuchungen zur indoiranischen Religionsgeschichte und Altertumskunde* (Halle: Max Niemeyer, 1923).

Mircea Eliade's article on "the Binder God," and studies of cosmogony by Jaan Puhvel and myself.[9]

Largely as a result of these contributions, Güntert was called to the chair in comparative linguistics at Rostock in 1921, then to Heidelberg in 1926, where he had earlier studied under Albrecht Dieterich (1866–1908), Wilhelm Braune (1850–1926), Franz Boll (1867–1924), and Christian Bartholomae (1855–1925), whose chair he assumed. There, he was warmly received and highly regarded, as is clear from his selection as dean of the Philosophical Faculty (1928–29) and his election to the Heidelberg Academy of Sciences (1931). Initially, he continued his work in Religionswissenschaft, producing a short volume entitled *Kundry* (1928) as an extension of the research begun in *Kalypso* (1919).[10] A programmatic outline dated "Weihnacht 1930" shows that he understood these two books and *Der arische Weltkönig* as parts of an ambitious research program on the theme "Tod und Erlösung," for which he planned to write seven further volumes.[11]

Pieces for several of these projects survive in Güntert's Nachlass, which fills two meters in the Heidelberg library, but none was ever completed.[12] Rather, in the late 1920s he turned his attention to other, more pressing matters and shifted his primary focus from Indogermanistik and Religionswissenschaft to Vorgeschichte and Germanenkunde, assuming responsibility for teaching the latter subject in 1933.[13] In the present

---

[9] Georges Dumézil, *Mitra-Varuna. Essai sur deux representations indo-européennes de la souveraineté* (Paris: Presses universitaires de France, 1940), Mircea Eliade, "Le 'dieu lieur' et le symbolisme des noeuds," *Revue de l'histoire des religions* 134 (1948), pp. 5–36, Jaan Puhvel, "Remus et Frater," *History of Religions* 15 (1975), pp. 146–157, Bruce Lincoln, *Priests, Warriors, and Cattle. A Study in the Ecology of Religions* (Berkeley: University of California Press, 1981), pp. 121–165.

[10] Hermann Güntert, *Kundry* (Heidelberg: Carl Winter, 1928).

[11] This document is reproduced in Meid, pp. 519–20. Under the title, "Tod und Erlösung," four major volumes (Hauptteile) were listed, each to be accompanied by an accompanying monograph (Zwischenstück). The whole ensemble was then to be framed by an opening and closing volume (Vorklang and Ausklang).

[12] The Nachlass is in Heidelberg's archives, but I have not had the opportunity to consult it. According to Meid, it includes several chapters for a volume intended as a Hauptteil of the research project ("Balder, der Heiland der Germanen") and its accompanying Zwischenstück ("Das Geisterschiff," alternately titled "Götterschiff und Totenbarke"). The two volumes meant to open and close the series seem to have been reconceived and published as works for the theater: *Wieland, der Schmied. Ein germanisches Sagenspiel in drei Aufzügen* (Heidelberg: Carl Winter, 1936) and *Prometheus, der arische Heiland. Mythenspiel in drei Teilen* (Heidelberg: Carl Winter, 1938).

[13] Meid, "Hermann Güntert," p. 517.

paper, I will discuss certain problems in Güntert's later publications and the turbulent circumstances in which they were written.

II

The relevant publications begin with Güntert's lead article for *Wörter und Sachen* in 1927. This was a Heidelberg journal founded in 1908 to oppose the neo-grammarian orthodoxy then dominant in linguistics and to foster research that reconnected language to the material realities of culture.[14] Since its inception, the journal's editorial board had remained intact, but in 1926, upon Güntert's return to Heidelberg, he was named to that body.[15] With his first major contribution, he sought to make a mark, arguing – with characteristic rigor, acumen, and panache – that the sound-shifts differentiating Germanic languages from other members of the Indo-European family are so deep and pervasive that they must reflect the profound influence of a non-Indo-European substratum. If this is so, then German should be understood as having originated in the fusion of two different languages spoken by two originally separate populations, one – as he saw it – a "Fäliscan" (*fälisch* or *dalisch*) substratum indigenous to German soil and the other a group of Indo-European intruders from the east.[16]

In three publications of 1930–32, Güntert dilated this argument, adding comparative evidence that, he argued, showed the connection of Indo-European phonology and vocabulary to Chinese, Korean, and other Asian languages, thereby supporting his case for setting the Indo-European *Urheimat* in the east. In taking this position, he implicitly aligned himself with the great Jewish linguist, Sigmund Feist (1865–1943) against most German scholars of that era, who were determined to locate the racial homeland on the shores of the Baltic.[17]

---

[14] See the programmatic "Vorwort" which the founding editors Rudolf Meringer (1859–1931), Wilhelm Meyer-Lübke (1861–1936), Joosepi Julius Mikkola (1866–1946), Rudolf Much (1862–1936), and Matthias Murko (1861–1952) contributed to the first issue, *Wörter und Sachen* 1 (1909), p. 1f.

[15] See the editors' announcement "Zur Begrüßung H. Günterts als Mitherausgeber," *Wörter und Sachen* 9 (1926), I and Güntert's response, "Zu meinem Eintritt in die Redaktion der 'Wörter und Sachen'," ibid., pp. IV–VI.

[16] Hermann Güntert, "Über die Ursache der germanischen Lautverschiebung," *Wörter und Sachen* 10 (1927): pp. 1–22.

[17] For a relatively apolitical history of the debates surrounding the *Urheimat* question, see James Mallory, A Short History of the Indo-European Problem," *Journal of*

Citing select archaeological research, he drew a schematic contrast between the intrusive Indo-European "Streitaxtleute" with the Fäliscan "Megalithgräberkultur" on the grounds of language, economy (pastoral vs. agricultural), religion (celestial gods vs. ancestral spirits), and burial practices (individual vs. collective tombs). That others regarded this argument as important is reflected in the fact that his two articles were given lead position in the volumes where they were published.[18] His third publication was a monograph, *Deutscher Geist* (1932), intended to make some of his Heidelberg lectures available to the general public. The preface to that volume, dated Spring 1931, sheds light on his purposes, saying he wished to engage contemporary issues on a strictly scientific basis and "to warn even the educated public against fearful errors." His goals were not partisan, he insisted, perhaps with some disingenuity. Rather, he hoped only "to help the German nation (*dem Deutschtum*) to what is properly its own."[19] The monograph was intended, moreover,

Indo-European Studies 1 (1973), pp. 21–65; more attentive to the ideological dimensions of such discussions are the classic work of Léon Poliakov, *The Aryan Myth: A History of Racist and Nationalist Ideas in Europe*, trans. Edmund Howard (New York: Basic Books, 1974) and Ruth Römer, *Sprachwissenschaft und Rassenideologie in Deutschland* (Munich: Wilhelm Fink, 1985), pp. 49–102. Feist's contributions to these debates included *Europa im Lichte der Vorgeschichte und die Ergebnisse der vergleichenden indogermanischen Sprachwissenschaft* (Berlin: Jerome Weidmann, 1910), *Kultur, Ausbreitung, und Herkunft der Indogermanen* (Berlin: Jerome Weidmann, 1913) and *Indogermanen und Germanen, ein Beitrag zur europäischen Urgeschichtsforschung* (Halle: Max Niemeyer, 1924), works that were consistently attacked and derided in the writings of German scholars favoring the Baltic homeland. A well-orchestrated – and fairly strident – attempt to show unanimous support for the latter thesis was staged in Helmuth Arntz, ed., *Germanen und Indogermanen: Volkstum, Sprache, Heimat, Kultur. Festschrift für Herman Hirt* (Heidelberg, Carl Winter, 1936). Güntert was careful to maintain a certain distance from Feist, whom he cited critically ("Die Frage der indogermanischen Urheimat," p. 3, n. 1) or in lists along with other, more orthodox authors (*Ursprung der Germanen*, p. 177). That others made the association, however, is clear from the remark of Hans Stahlmann, who found it understandable when Jews argued for an Asian Urheimat, but surprising from an "utterly serious and German-minded scholar like Hermann Güntert" (Hans Stahlmann, *Vom Werden und Wandel der Muttersprache: Ein Hilfsbuch für Studierende, Lehrer und Freunde unserer Muttersprache* [Leipzig: 1940], p. 3, cited in Römer, p. 71).
[18] Hermann Güntert, "Zur Frage nach der Urheimat der Indogermanen," in Hans Teske, ed., *Deutschkundliches: Friedrich Panzer zum 60. Geburtstage überreicht von Heidelberger Fachgenossen* (Heidelberg: Carl Winter, 1930), pp. 1–33 and "Die Frage der indogermanischen Urheimat in neuer Beleuchtung," *Zeitschrift für deutsche Bildung* 8 (1932), pp. 1–8.
[19] Idem, *Deutscher Geist. Drei Vorträge* (Bühl-Baden: Konkordia A.G., 1932), p. 6. The preface, dated "Spring 1931," is worth citing in full.
     Diese Vorträge gehen im Kern auf verschiedene Reden und Ansprachen zurück, die ich bei mancherlei Gelegenheit in Heidelberg gehalten habe. Da ich hoffe, daß sie in unserer heillos verwirrten Zeit zur Anregung, Vertiefung des Denkens und

to set the stage for "my fuller work, *Der Ursprung der Germanen*, which will trace the deepest roots of our ethnicity (*den letzten Wurzeln unseres Volkstums*)."[20]

III

Güntert understood *Der Ursprung der Germanen* as the culminating synthesis of the researches he began in 1927. The volume was initially scheduled to appear in 1932, but its publication was delayed when its original publisher, J.F. Lehmann of Munich, withdrew support for the project.[21] The reason is not hard to divine. Lehmann was a völkisch publisher, and this part of Güntert's work no doubt appealed to them. They were also a racist publisher, however,[22] and his interest in refuting Nazi ideology held ever less interest as electoral support for the National Socialist party rose from 2.6% in 1928 to 37.4% in mid-1932, when the book was scheduled to appear.[23] To this end, Güntert amplified and expanded his case that the Indo-European homeland could not

---

Selbstbesinnung, zur Klärung mancher Streitfragen in Wissenschaft und Leben, zu tieferem Verständnis der gegenwärtigen Lage, zur Warnung und Mahnung vor gefährlichen Irrpfaden vielleicht auch in weiteren Kreisen der Gebildeten ein kleines Scherflein beitragen könnten, entschloß ich mich, wenn auch zögernd, zu einer erweiterten, allgemein verständlichen Um- und Ausarbeitung. Die Aufsätze ruhen durchaus auf wissenschaftlichem, und zwar sprach- und kulturgeschichtlichem Grunde und enthalten sich eines jeden Eingehens auf engere politische Parteifragen; ihr einziges Ziel ist Klarheit und Wahrheit, ihr einziger Sinn: dem Deutschtum zu seinem Recht zu verhelfen! (p. 6).

[20] Ibid. "Zugleich sind aber diese Vorträge als dreisätziges Vorspiel gedacht zu meiner größeren Arbeit 'Der Ursprung der Germanen', die den letzten Wurzeln unseres Volkstums nachspürt."

[21] Güntert cited the book as forthcoming in 1932, "Der Frage der indogermanischen Urheimat in neuer Beleuchtung," p. 8, n. 2. The story of Lehmann's withdrawal is noted by Goegginger, "Hermann Güntert als Religionsforscher," p. 156, on the authority of Friedrich Panzer. Panzer thought he saw the hand of future Reichsminister Richard Walther Darré behind Lehmann's decision, but it is not clear on the strength of what evidence.

[22] Among the titles Lehmann brought out in the relevant period are Eugen Fehrle's commentary on Tacitus's *Germania* (1929), Richard Walther Darré, *Das Bauerntum als Lebensquell der nordischen Rasse* (1929), Hans F.K. Günther, *Rassenkunde des deutschen Volkes* (1930), Ewald Banse, *Deutsche Landeskunde* (1932), and the *Zeitschrift für Rassenphysiologie* (from 1929 on). In earlier years, this house published works by Alfred Rosenberg (*Das Verbrechen der Freimaurerei, Judentum, Jesuitismus, Deutsches Christentum*, 1922) and Houston Stewart Chamberlain (*Das Lebenswerk H. St. Chamberlains in Umrissen*, 1927).

[23] The electoral figures are taken from Claudia Koonz, *The Nazi Conscience* (Cambridge, MA: Harvard University Press, 2003), p. 10.

have been in the Germanic north, which is to say the Indo-Europeans were not a Nordic people, nor were the Germans a pure race, the last preservers of Aryan greatness or the people most continuously in touch with their primordial native soil. Rather, Germanic ethnicity originated with the union of two different populations and the Indo-European ("Aryan") component came from outside. In his view, it was the synthesis of these originally separate peoples and the unresolved tension between their cultures that produced a distinctive genius, which he referred to as the "Faustian spirit."[24]

Güntert claimed that the best and most recent research in three different disciplines supported this picture. To that end, he cited his own work in linguistics against that of Hermann Hirt (1865–1936), while also favoring the archaeology of his Heidelberg colleague Ernst Wahle (1889–1981) over that of Gustaf Kossinna (1858–1931), and the physical anthropology of Egon von Eickstedt (1892–1965) over the Rassenkunde of Hans F.K. Günther (1891–1968).[25] In each case, arguments for an Asian "Urheimat" trumped the Nordic thesis and more tolerant views prevailed over aggressive racism.

The chapter Güntert devoted to the topic "Rasse und Sprache" is, in truth, the most daring piece of a very bold book.[26] Among numerous deliberately provocative points are his decoupling of racial and linguistic categories (p. 73); his rejection of the term "Aryan" (properly reserved for the peoples of India and Iran, p. 73); his ridicule of beliefs in the purity of German blood as "romantisch naiv und unhaltbar" (p. 76);

---

[24] Hermann Güntert, *Der Ursprung der Germanen* (Heidelberg: Carl Winter, 1934), vol. 9 in the series "Kultur und Sprache."

[25] In two sections placed at the end of *Der Ursprung der Germanen* ("Schriftennachweise," p. 177 and "Schlußbemerkung," p. 183) Güntert indicated the structure of the debates in which he sought to intervene. With regard to linguistics, he contrasted his own work, also that of Sigmund Feist, *Kultur, Ausbreitung und Herkunft der Indogermanen* (Berlin: Weidmann, 1913) and Otto Schrader, *Die Indogermanen* (Leipzig, Quelle & Meyer, 1911), with that of Hermann Hirt, *Die Indogermanen*, 2 vols. (Strassburg: K.J. Trübner, 1905–7). The archaeological and prehistorical debate pitted Ernst Wahle, *Deutsche Vorzeit* (Leipzig: Curt Kabitzsch, 1932) against Gustaf Kossinna, *Ursprung und Verbreitung der Germanen*, 2 vols. (Leipzig: Curt Kabitzsch, 1926–27). In anthropology and *Rassenkunde*, the central figures were Egon Freiherr von Eickstedt, *Rassenkunde und Rassengeschichte der Menschheit* (Stuttgart: Ferdinand Enke Verlag, 1934) and Hans F.K. Günther, *Rassenkunde des deutschen Volkes*, then in its 16th edition (Munich: J.F. Lehmann, 1933). Günther responded to Güntert's challenge dismissively in the opening pages of his *Herkunft und Rassengeschichte der Germanen* (Munich: J.F. Lehmann, 1937), p. 11f. A similar position was adopted by Otto Reche, Professor of Rassen- und Völkerkunde at Leipzig, *Rasse und Heimat der Indogermanen* (Munich: J.F. Lehmann, 1936), pp. 202–204.

[26] Güntert, *Ursprung der Germanen*, pp. 73–97.

his decomposition of the German Volk into six different ethnic stocks (p. 76f.); his dismissal of stereotypes about height, skull shape, color of hair and eyes (p. 77f.); and his insistence that not even the Indo-Europeans were racially pure (since they wandered and intermixed with countless other peoples, p. 73). Most striking of all is his treatment of "racial purity" (*Reinrassigkeit*) as either a misguided fantasy or an incestuous practice yielding decadence and monstrosities. In open defiance of current trends, he voiced warm appreciation for racial mixture, constituting the German Volk as a case in point: *Mischlinge ab origine*.

> Another prejudice we can correct is the common view that racial mixture (*Rassenmischung*) must always be unhealthy and produces the decadence of mongrels (*den Niedergang der Mischlinge*). This is undoubtedly incorrect. There are surely races that stick to themselves and are not permitted to form alloys. But on the other side, it is often through favorable mixture of blood that a Volk, like an individual, can particularly advance its own interests. As regards the "Indo-Europeans," it seems to me that their world historical position of power is the direct result of such favorable mixtures and other blood transfusions.... 'Racial purity' (*Rassereinheit*) in the sense of incest is not only historically untenable, but scientifically far from ideal; were it factually accomplished, it would quickly weaken a Volk and render it defenseless in life's struggles (*im Lebenskampf widerstandslos machen*).[27]

Less independent or daring than Franz Boas, Güntert did not reject race outright as a category of analysis. Indeed, he accepted that connections exist between racial characteristics and linguistic structure, but he consistently stressed the importance of language and minimized that of biology, following Albrecht Dieterich (1866–1908), who had been his mentor in Volkskunde and Religionswissenschaft at Heidelberg.

---

[27] Ibid., p. 74f.
Auch ein andres Vorurteil mag gleich berichtigt werden: man meint öfter, Rassenmischung müsse stets unheilvoll sein und den Niedergang der Mischlinge bewirken. Das ist so ohne weiteres sicher nicht richtig. Es gibt freilich Rassen, die sich abstoßen und nicht legieren lassen. Aber andrerseits ist schon oft durch günstige Blutmischung ein Volk wie eine Einzelpersönlichkeit sogar besonders gefördert worden. Was die 'Indogermanen' anlangt, so scheint mir ihre weltgeschichtliche Machtstellung gerade auf solchen günstigen Mischungen und anderer Blutzufuhr zu beruhen.... Die 'Rassereinheit' im Sinne von Inzucht ist also nicht nur historisch unhaltbar, sondern auch naturwissenschaftlich keineswegs ein Ideal; sie würde, wenn sie tatsächlich vorkäme, ein Volk sehr schnell schwächen und im Lebenskampf widerstandslos machen.

IV

As Dieterich explained in his programmatic lecture "Über Wesen und Ziele der Volkskunde" (1902), he differed with those who wished to make Volkskunde a wide-ranging, amorphous discipline and felt that such topics as a people's typical physiology or historic relation to the landscape they inhabited were better treated by ancillary sciences (physical anthropology, geography, e.g.).[28] Like J.G. Herder (1744–1803), Jacob Grimm (1785–1863), and Erwin Rohde (1845–98), he felt that the discipline ought primarily concern itself with the traditional beliefs, stories, poetry, and sagas of the Volk, all of which are transmitted through language. Language he took to be the precipitate of a people's historic experience and the prime instrument for reproduction of their culture and accordingly, he considered philology the most important research tool of the Volkskundler.[29] Ultimately, however, folkloric research proceeds from language to religion, since "Folk customs and practices, sagas, folktales, and folksongs are closely tied up with folk religion, which is the most important item of all in understanding the life of a folk."[30]

Of all Dieterich's students, none embraced these principles more fervently than did Hermann Güntert. Having adopted this model of how Volk, language, and religion were related, he acquired competence in more than thirty languages, as well as in the methods of comparative (Indo-European) philology and comparative Religionswissenschaft. It was this combination of expertise that let him make his early landmark contributions, and it also informed his later work on the relation between Germanic and Indo-European Völker.

---

[28] Albrecht Dieterich, "Über Wesen und Ziele der Volkskunde," *Hessische Blätter für Volkskunde* 1 (1902), pp. 169–194. This text was originally presented at the Generalversammlung of the Hessische Vereinigung für Volkskunde (May 24, 1902), as journals and chairs of Volkskunde were being created throughout Germany. According to contemporary reports, it sparked tremendous enthusiasm at Heidelberg and elsewhere. See pp. 184–187 for the assignment of biological considerations (including race) to other disciplines (anthropology, ethnology, anatomy, physiology).

[29] Ibid., pp. 174–178, p. 185, p. 191, et passim on the importance of language. "Die Kunde von einem Volke im umfassenden Sinne ist wissenschaftlich genommen Philologie" (p. 174).

[30] Ibid., p. 175f., p. 189f., for the importance of religion. "Volkssitte und Volksbrauch, Volkssage und Volksmärchen und Volkslied sind eng verbunden mit der Volksreligion. Sie ist darum das wichtigste in der Erkenntnis dieses Volkslebens überhaupt" (p. 176).

Other students were less assiduous in their devotion to Dieterich's principles, however, if only because few were able to match Güntert's philological industry or genius. Beyond this, some came to feel that other kinds of knowledge should be incorporated within Volkskunde. As a case in point, it is useful to consider the example of Eugen Fehrle (1880–1957).

Initially, Fehrle's studies followed Dieterich's model, focusing on religious sensibility in a Mediterranean context as it can be reconstructed from close reading of textual sources. After completing a dissertation on the practice of chastity in classical antiquity, however, he enlisted in the army and served through the war of 1914–18.[31] After returning from service, he became influenced by the racial theories of Hans F.K. Günther (1891–1968), which construed the Germans as a particularly pure and precious, but embattled and vulnerable part of the Aryan race.[32] Thereafter, Fehrle refashioned Dieterich's *Volkskunde* to take account of race, understanding that part of the discipline's mission was to rally the German Volk against its (racial) enemies.[33] In 1931, Fehrle became one of the first academics to join the Nazi party (after earlier participation

---

[31] Eugen Fehrle, *Die kultische Keuschheit im Altertum* (Giessen: A. Töpelmann, 1910). The work is strongly reminiscent of Dieterich's opus magnum, *Mutter Erde* (Leipzig: B.G. Teubner, 1905).

[32] Hans F.K. Günther, *Rassenkunde des deutschen Volkes* (Munich: J.F. Lehmann, 1920), idem, *Rassenkunde Europas, mit besonderer Berücksichtigung der Rassengeschichte der Hauptvölker indogermanischer Sprache* (Munich: J.F. Lehmann, 1926).

[33] For critical studies on Fehrle, see Martin Scharfe, "Einschwörung auf den völkisch-germanischen Kulturbegriff," in Jörg Tröger, ed., *Hochschule und Wissenschaft im Dritten Reich* (Frankfurt: Campus, 1984), pp. 105–115, esp. 107ff., Peter Assion, "Eugen Fehrle and 'The Mythos of Our Folk'," in James R. Dow and Hannjost Lixfeld, ed., *The Nazification of an Academic Discipline: Folklore in the Third Reich* (Bloomington: Indiana University Press, 1994), pp. 112–134, and Steven P. Remy, *The Heidelberg Myth: The Nazification and Denazification of a German University* (Cambridge, MA: Harvard University Press, 2002), p. 13, p. 39, p. 60, p. 98, and p. 132f. Accounts that reflect the esteem in which he was held during the NS period include Wolfgang Treutlein, "Eugen Fehrle als Forscher und Kämpfer," in Ferdinand Herrmann and Wolfgang Treutlein, eds., *Brauch und Sinnbild. Eugen Fehrle zum 60, Geburtstag gewidmet von seinen Schülern und Freunden* (Karlsruhe, Südwestdeutsche Druck- und Verlagsgesellschaft, 1940), pp. 1–12, Richard Hünnerkopf, "Eugen Fehrle (1880–1957)," *Zeitschrift für Volkskunde* 54 (1958), p. 142f., and Lily Weiser-Aall, "Eugen Fehrle, 1880–1957," *Hessische Blätter für Volkskunde* 49/50 (1959), p. 9f. Assion, pp. 113–116 and Remy, p. 60f. contain good discussions of Güntert's and Fehrle's common debt to Dieterich and the nuanced differences in the way they developed his theories. The postwar change in Fehrle is apparent when one compares the relative unimportance of racial categories in his *Deutsche Feste und Volksbräuche* (Leipzig: B.G. Teubner, 1916) with the prominent position they occupy in the first chapter of *Badische Volkskunde* (Leipzig: Quelle & Meyer, 1924), "Sprache und Art des Volkes," pp. 1–21 or in his theoretical essay "Bemerkungen über Ziele und Grenzen der Volkskunde," *Oberdeutsche Zeitschrift für Volkskunde* 6 (1932), pp. 85–92.

in the Deutsche Volkspartei) and on March 3, 1933, he was one of the three Heidelberg faculty members who signed a petition in the *Völkischer Beobachter* urging support for Hitler.[34] In subsequent years, he joined the SA (1933), then the SS (1939), serving in the ideological service of the latter (the *Ahnenerbe*). After the war, a tribunal charged him with having been a leading figure ("Hauptschuldiger") in the Nazification of Heidelberg. After numerous hearings and appeals, he was convicted on lesser charges, but was banished from academia forever.[35]

Although Güntert shared some of Fehrle's nationalist and völkisch views, a racial component did not figure in his outlook, except as an argument to be refuted (Figure One). Nor did he join the Nazi party until relatively late (1939).[36] Still, the men maintained a friendship, and Güntert's *Deutscher Geist* was published in a popular series edited by Fehrle.[37]

V

Returning to *Der Ursprung der Germanen*, we have noted that the book's scheduled publication in 1932 was delayed when the original publisher withdrew support. Güntert took it to Carl Winter of Heidelberg, who brought the book out in 1934, which is to say, after Hitler had become chancellor (January 30, 1933). In the intervening period, Güntert made several revisions at the beginning and end of the book in a torturous

---

[34] Peter Assion, "Eugen Fehrle," p. 117.

[35] On the trial, see Assion, "Eugen Fehrle," p. 129f. and Remy, *The Heidelberg Myth*, pp. 181–185.

[36] I am grateful to Michael Stausberg for having consulted the personnel files at Heidelberg regarding the question of Güntert's party membership. The most important item in his file (Personalakte PA 421) is his response – in the negative – to a circular sent to all employees of the University on 16 September 1935 asking whether they were members of the Nazi party. This is confirmed by a letter of October 11, 1945 that Gisela Güntert submitted to the administration as part of her attempt to secure retirement and pension for her seriously ill husband, in which she stated that he became a candidate for party membership ("Parteianwärter") in 1938 and a member ("Parteigenosse") in 1939. He did, of course, take the oath of loyalty to Hitler that was required of all professors in November 1934. Wachter and Kropp confirm this information (p. 384), but also note that he became a supporting member ("Förderndes Mitglied") of the SS in May 1934 and played an unpleasant role in controversies at Heidelberg surrounding Emil Julius Gumbel (1891–1966) as early as 1930 (p. 372f.).

[37] Heft 4 in the series *Bausteine zur Volkskunde und Religionswissenschaft*, ed. by Eugen Fehrle (Bühl-Baden: Konkordia A.G., 1932). The series was inaugurated with Weiser, *Altgermanische Jünglingsweihe und Männerbünde*. Eighteen volumes had been published when it ceased publication in 1939.

Figure One: Genealogical relations, Hermann Güntert and Eugen Fehrle.

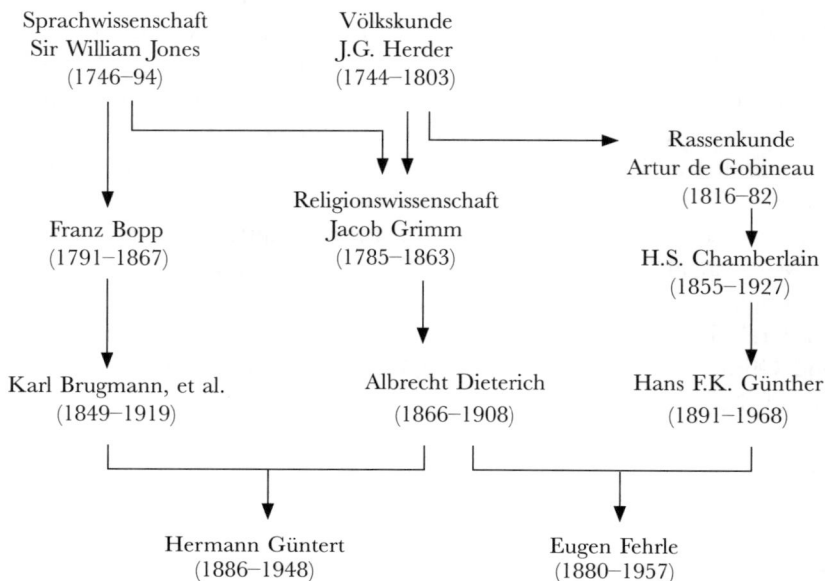

Sprachwissenschaft
Sir William Jones
(1746–94)

Völkskunde
J.G. Herder
(1744–1803)

Rassenkunde
Artur de Gobineau
(1816–82)

Franz Bopp
(1791–1867)

Religionswissenschaft
Jacob Grimm
(1785–1863)

H.S. Chamberlain
(1855–1927)

Karl Brugmann, et al.
(1849–1919)

Albrecht Dieterich
(1866–1908)

Hans F.K. Günther
(1891–1968)

Hermann Güntert
(1886–1948)

Eugen Fehrle
(1880–1957)

attempt to take account of changing circumstances. To that end he added a preface, dated March 21, 1933 ("in the springtime of a new, national Germany"), redefining the volume's goals and effacing its critical project. Although his text was designed to show that German "Blut" and primordial "Boden" were not what National Socialist ideology maintained, here Güntert foregrounded his desire to serve and celebrate the Volk, awkwardly cramming as much NS jargon as possible into the concluding paragraph.

> Only if the German Volk is conscious of its essence and its racial character (*seines Wesens und seiner Eigenart*) and learns to regard and evaluate foreign culture and foreign Geist from that perspective, proud in its own racial nature (*artstolz*), will it be able to hold its own in the ruthless, inexorable struggle for existence among rival Völker (*unerbittlichen und rücksichtslosen Daseinskampf der Völker*). In this sense my book might also assist in defining the goal of German culture in the present: it might clarify and awake, and be perceived as a contribution to a spiritual reconstruction, to laying the foundation of a völkisch-German culture, as an affirmative acknowledgment of our powerful Germanentum and our strongly rooted Deutschheit. For I firmly believe that it is from an understanding of one's historically conditioned essence (*seines geschichtsbedingten Wesen*) and one's völkisch racial

character (*seiner völkischen Eigenart*) that the German Volk must draw the
necessary conclusions for its further development.[38]

A second accommodation falls in the book's closing pages, which are
separated from the preceding text by a large space and a horizontal
line, conventions that appear nowhere else in the volume.[39] Here,
after reasserting his claim to have identified the heroic, Faustian Germanic spirit as the product of a dual ancestral heritage, Güntert went
on – in a much different tone – to discuss the threats this admirable
Volk experienced from its enemies, beginning with the Romans and
continuing through the last war. In the present, two foreign entities
are identified and the first is fairly predictable: "Ungerman groups of
an 'international,' world-bourgeois, or Bolshevik-nihilist sort."[40] The
second is more surprising, for where one expects an antisemitic tirade,
Güntert mentions the Jews not at all, an omission that can only be
intended. Rather, he fulminates against "the South," which is to say
Greece, Rome, and the classic ideals of beauty adopted by Humanism,
which threaten properly Germanic culture (the medieval, Gothic, and
northern) with a "geistige Überfremdung."[41]

The book's final footnote refers to these same pages and apparently
represents Güntert's last revision. It states that after the book had
gone to press, the speech Hitler gave at the Nuremberg party rally of

---

[38] Güntert, *Ursprung der Germanen*, p. 7.
  Nur wenn sich das deutsche Volk seines Wesens und seiner Eigenart bewußt ist
  und daher fremde Kultur und fremden Geist selbstsicher und artstolz betrachten
  und einzuschätzen lernt, wird es sich im unerbittlichen und rücksichtslosen
  Daseinskampf der Völker behaupten können. In diesem Sinne möchte mein
  Buch auch mithelfen an der Zielsetzung deutscher Kultur in der Gegenwart; es
  möchte klären und wecken und als ein Beitrag zu einem geistigen Neuaufbau, zur
  Grundlegung völkisch-deutscher Bildung, als bejahendes Bekenntnis zu kraftvol-
  lem Germanentum und wurzelstarker Deutschheit aufgefaßt sein. Denn aus der
  Erkenntnis seines geschichtsbedingten Wesens und seiner völkischen Eigenart
  muß das deutsche Volk für seine weitere Entwicklung, an die ich fest glaube, die
  nötigen Folgerungen ziehen.
    Heidelberg, am 21. März 1933, dem Frühlings-Werdetag eines neuen, natio-
  nalen Deutschlands.
                                                              Hermann Güntert
[39] Ibid., pp. 172–175. The break appears in the middle of p. 172 and one suspects
that these pages were added between January and March of 1933.
[40] Ibid., p. 173.
  Daher sind alle Lockungen undeutscher Gruppen mit 'internationaler', welt-
  bürgerlicher oder bolschewistisch-nihilistischer Gesinnung die natürlichen Feinde
  des Deutschtums, die am Mark seines Lebens nagen und es vernichten.
[41] Ibid., pp. 173–175. The phrase quoted appears at p. 174.

September 1933 perfectly captured its goals. Two carefully chosen citations from that speech are then presented as the volume's ideal conclusion. However offensive it may be, this gesture should not be dismissed lightly, but is best understood as a complex maneuver executed in a risky situation. Simultaneously profession of loyalty, token of submission, selective appropriation, strategic redeployment, and a desperate exercise in camouflage, its goal was to create the impression that the views of the Professor and the Führer were in perfect alignment, when in fact there was considerable tension and difference between them.[42]

And then there is the book's last gesture of accommodation, its dedication:

> Herrn Ministerialrat Professor Dr. Eugen Fehrle, dem Vorkämpfer der wissenschaftlichen Volkskunde, in alter Freundschaft.[43]

When the Nazis came to power, Fehrle was the best connected of the Heidelberg faculty. Although only a lecturer at the time, in March 1933 he was made advisor for university affairs in the Ministry of Education in Baden as a result of his party membership. In that capacity, he helped secure the appointment of his friend and former classmate, Hermann Güntert to a second term as dean of the Philosophical Faculty (1933–37). Seemingly, the two men negotiated a symbiotic relation in this period, whereby each one supplied the other with what he lacked. For his part, Güntert extended scholarly legitimacy to his less intelligent, accomplished, and original friend, while Fehrle provided political cover. Once in office, Güntert immediately took steps to establish a chair of Volkskunde at Heidelberg, to which Fehrle was appointed in 1934 and which became his base of power.[44] In subsequent years, Güntert would make other appointments in this discipline, repeatedly turning to foreigners who had proved themselves friends and admirers of the German Volk.[45]

---

[42] Ibid., p. 182f.

[43] Ibid., p. 5.

[44] A chair of Volkskunde had briefly existed from 1917–1918, but was not renewed after the war. In 1926, the same year as Güntert's arrival, the Philosophical Faculty obtained approval from the Educational Ministry to have Fehrle (then a lecturer in Classical Philology [since 1924, having previously served as research assistant 1919–1924]) give a two-hour lecture course on Volkskunde. Assion, "Eugen Fehrle," p. 117f. See also Remy, *The Heidelberg Myth*, p. 13 and p. 38.

[45] Remy, *The Heidelberg Myth*, 63, citing the examples of Wilhelm Klumberg (1886–1942), G.A.S. Snijder (1896–?), Sigurd Erixson (1888–1968), and Heinrich Ritter von Srbik (1878–1951).

VII

If Güntert felt these steps would protect him from controversy, he was less than fully successful. *Der Ursprung der Germanen* was widely reviewed and much discussed. Whereas his prior work had been quite favorably received, his views now received sharp criticism.[46] To date, I have been able to collect seventeen reviews, although I am aware of several others that appeared in publications hard to obtain in North America.[47] Of those I have seen, six are favorable, and eleven hostile, with a clear pattern to the distribution. Of the favorable reviews, only two were written by German scholars.[48] The other four were by foreigners and were published in foreign journals.[49] Several were quite attentive to the book's political subtext and purpose, above all Félix Piquet, writing in *Révue Germanique*, who repeatedly praised Güntert's critique of racism.

> M. Güntert est formellement hostile au racisme. Affirmer qu'il y a une race germanique pure c'est, selon lui, émettre une évidente contre-vérité.... Armé d'un savoir étendu, M. Güntert fait appel à l'archéologie, don't il utilise les documents au profit de ses conceptions, à l'histoire qu'il interprète autrement que les racistes, aux faits ressortissant à l'évolution de la culture et des moeurs, qui justifient ses constations chronologiques, enfin et surtout à la linguistique.... En dépit de quelques assertions hasardées, le livre de M. Güntert tend à une louable impartialité. Son patriotisme

---

[46] Thus, the two reviews that were published of the *Friedrich Panzer Festschrift* (1930) both spoke warmly of Güntert's contribution to it ("Zur Frage nach der Urheimat der Indogermanen"): Karl Biëtor, writing in *Zeitschrift für deutsche Bildung* 7 (1931), p. 227 and the unsigned review that appeared in the *Oberdeutsche Zeitschrift für Volkskunde* (a publication edited by Eugen Fehrle) 6 (1932), p. 57. Reactions to *Deutscher Geist* (1932) were also favorable. These include the unsigned review in *Oberdeutsche Zeitschrift für Volkskunde* 6 (1932), pp. 180–182 and Gerhart Streitberg, *Mitteldeutsche Blätter für Volkskunde* 7 (1932), p. 211. More reserved and ambivalent is Otto Eicke, *Volk und Rasse* 2 (1933), p. 107.

[47] These include *Nachrichten aus Niedersachsens Urgeschichte* 8 (1934), p. 116, idem 9 (1935), p. 116, *Die Sonne* 11 (1934), p. 597, *Singgemeinde* 9: pp. 653–656, *Mitteilungen des schlesischen Bunds für Heimatschutz* (1935), p. 307, *Mitteilungen der Handelskammern Breslau* 22: pp. 198–200.

[48] Franz Rolf Schröder, *Germanisch-Romanisch Monatsschrift* 22 (1934), p. 321f. and Hermann Dreyhaus, *Monatsschrift für höhere Schule* 33 (1934), p. 219, the latter of whom minimized the book's critical content.

[49] Félix Piquet, *Revue germanique* 25 (1934), pp. 368–370, Wilhelm Koppers, *Anthropos* 29 (1934): pp. 570–572, Hugo Suolahti, *Neuphilologische Mitteilungen* 37 (1936), pp. 15–19, and the unsigned review in *Neophilologus* 19 (1934), p. 315. C.C. Uhlenbeck also signaled his appreciation, "Oer-Indogermaansch en Oer-Indogermanen," *Mededeelingen der Koninklijke Akademie van Wetenschappen*, Afdeeling Letterkunde, Serie A 77 (1934/35), pp. 125–148, esp. p. 140f. and p. 144f.

194 BRUCE LINCOLN

n'est ni aveugle, ni agressif. La valeur scientifique de cet ardu et considerable travail est patente.[50]

By contrast, the negative reviews were all by Germans writing in German publications, with two exceptions: Fernand Mossé in *Les langues
modernes* and the pro-Nazi Jan de Vries in *Museum*.[51] Among the German
critics, some were respectful,[52] some condescending,[53] and others dismis-
sive, even contemptuous.[54] Several charged him with disloyalty of one
sort or another, as when Rudolf Much said his credulity toward foreign
opinions could neither be disguised, nor forgiven,[55] or when Hans Maier,
writing in the official party organ, *Nationalsozialistische Monatshefte*, accused
him of ignoring the principle that studies of prehistory ought serve
the Reich.[56] Going further still, Lutz Mackensen argued that studies
of Germanenkunde had major political import in the era of "national
revolution," and Güntert's views constituted a problem. "The opinions
expressed in this book have shown themselves mistaken, and the uproar
has taken care of itself. Fine. But was it necessary?" he asked, then
went on to make some ominous suggestions: "I doubt that Güntert

---

[50] Piquet, p. 369f.

[51] F. Mossé, *Les langues modernes* 32 (1934), p. 539f. responded with indignance and
sarcasm at Güntert's hostility toward the Greco-Roman tradition. while Jan de Vries,
who would later be the chief Nazi collaborator among Dutch academics, offered a
nuanced reaction in *Museum* 42 (1934), pp. 77–79. While praising the book as timely,
passionate, original and perceptive, he faulted it for insufficient scholarly prudence in
presenting speculations as if they were fact. "Where does scholarship end and where
does fantasy begin?" he wondered (p. 78), then suggested that while experts might benefit
from Güntert's critical intervention, the book posed dangers for the general public.

[52] Siegfried Gutenbrunner, *Teuthonista* 11 (1935), p. 251f., Willy Krogman, *Zeitschrift
für deutsche Philologie* 60 (1935), pp. 279–283.

[53] Unsigned review in *Archiv für das Studium der neueren Sprache* 165 (1934), p. 288f.

[54] "R.K.," writing in *Zeitschrift für Deutschkunde* 48 (1935), p. 273f., "H.," in *Die deutsche
höhere Schule* 2 (1935): p. 269, Otto Huth, *Germanien* 8 (1936), p. 186f., Franz Specht,
Geistige Arbeit 3/10 (20 May 1936), p. 6.

[55] Rudolf Much, *Literaturblatt für germanische und romanische Philologie* 57/7–8 (1936), pp.
228–231: "Zusammenfassend lässt sich sagen, dass der Aufwand an gelehrtem Wissen
und an Beredsamkeit den Mangel des Blicks für das kulturgeschichtlich Mögliche und
die grosse Leichtgläubigkeit gegen fremde und eigene Gedankengänge nicht verdecken
und aufwiegen kann."

[56] Hans Maier *Nationalsozialistische Monatshefte*, vol. 5, no. 50 (May 1934), p. 92f.:
"Die von ihm versuchte Stützung seiner Theorie durch die Vorgeschichte und Rassenkunde beruht aber auf einer ganz einseitigen Auswertung des Schrifttums.... Die
hier gebotene beschränkte Auswahl aus dem vorgeschichtlichen Schrifttum von 1934
läßt die Hauptrichtung erkennen, in der die Vorgeschichtswissenschaft arbeiten muß,
um ihrer großen Aufgabe gerecht zu werden, aus dem Reichtum unserer arteigenen
Vorzeit Grundpfeiler für den Neubau des Reichs und für die Gestaltung eines neuen
deutschen Kulturwillens zu gewinnen."

would have published his book in this form if he had had to explain his thesis to an expert commission.... The ideal of scholarly freedom must be replaced by the ethos of political accountability. Schooling the scholars is the duty of the State."[57]

VIII

After publishing *Ursprung der Germanen*, Güntert fell relatively silent for several years[58] and his next book, *Altgermanischer Glaube* (1937) was both more guarded and more conflicted than its predecessor. Here, he seems determined to show himself an aggressive enthusiast of the German Volk, while restating his case for its mixed origins on the basis of Religionswissenschaft, rather than linguistics. Thus, chapter one presents the haunting funerary images from the Kivik grave in southern Sweden (c. 1400 B.C.E.) as evidence for the religious ideals and practices of the non-Indo-European megalithic population autochthonous to northern Europe.[59] Similarly, chapter two treats the Old Norse pantheon's distinction of Æsir and Vanir deities as reflecting the two racially and culturally different groups whose synthesis created the German people. Thus, the Æsir (Óðinn, Thorr, and Tyr) were powerful, but ugly warriors, whose names all have Indo-European etymologies. The Vanir (Njörð, Freyr, and Freyja), in contrast, were beautiful and pacific, whose wealth came from the soil and the sea: None of their names is of Indo-European origin. For Güntert, the case was clear, but he used

---

[57] Lutz Mackensen, "Zwischen Skepsis und Legende: Kleine grundsätzliche Bücherschau zur Germanenkunde," *Die Neue Literatur* 10 (1935), pp. 577–593, esp. p. 582f.: "Die Ansicht dieses Werkes hat sich als irrig erwiesen, die Beunruhigung hat sich gelegt. Gut. Aber war sie nötig? Ich bezweifle, daß Güntert sein Werk in der vorliegenden Form veröffentlicht hätte, wenn er seine Hauptbeweise vorher den Fachkreisen zur Erörterung vorgelegt hätte.... Das Ideal der freien Forschung muß durch das Ethos der politischen Verantwortlichkeit ersetzt werden; die Gelehrten hierfür zu schulen, ist Aufgabe des Staates."

[58] The bibliography published in *Antiquitates Indogermanicae*, pp. 523–528. shows that between 1926, when he returned to Heidelberg, and 1934, Güntert published six books, eighteen articles, fifteen encyclopedia articles, nineteen book reviews, and three necrologies. In the years 1935 and 1936, his scholarly publications dropped almost to zero, although he did bring out a play in three acts ("Wieland der Schmied") and a collection of folksongs, *König Laurin. Eine deutsche Sage in Liedern* (Heidelberg: Carl Winter, 1936).

[59] Hermann Güntert, *Altgermanische Glaube nach Wesen und Grundlage* (Heidelberg: Carl Winter, 1937), "Das Grab von Kivik in Südschweden als Denkmal altgermanischen Totenglaubens," pp. 1–35.

a different vocabulary to contrast the two populations than he did in his earlier writings.

> Racially expressed, [this is a contrast, B.L.] between Faliscan and Nordic racial disposition (Sinnesart). Voiced culturally, it is between settled large scale peasants and conquering warrior bands of young men. From the intimate mixture of Fäliscan-Nordic megalith-ceramic tribes of large scale peasants and purely Nordic warrior groups of cordware ceramic and straight-axe people, the historic Germans grew into a novel unity.[60]

Among the changes that should be noted in the argument and diction are a greater willingness to employ a racial discourse; designation of the Indo-Europeans as "purely Nordic" (*reinnordisch*); and a narrative that identifies this ethnic group with martial bands of young males (*jungmannschaftliche, erobernde Kriegerbünde*). Throughout the book, Güntert drew heavily on recent work by Otto Höfler (1901–1987), Rudolf Much's prize student, whose dissertation, *Kultische Geheimbünde der Germanen* (1934), had created a sensation.[61] In the spirit of Höfler, Güntert's discussions of violence, struggle and conquest, the dissolution of individual identities within the male group, the importance of military training for the young, and the joy of submission to the will of the Führer all had obvious contemporary resonance, as descriptions of the "ancient" *Männerbünde* were transparent projections of the SA, SS, Wehrmacht, and Freikorps.[62]

Read as a whole, *Altgermanischer Glaube* presents a sad and terrifying spectacle, and Güntert's last book, *Geschichte der germanischen Völkerschaften*

---

[60] Ibid., pp. 47–54. The passage cited appears at p. 48.
   ...rassisch ausgedrückt: zwischen fälischer und nordischer Sinnesart, kulturell gesagt: zwischen seßhaften Erbgroßbauern und jungmannschaftlichen, erobernden Kriegerbünden. Aus enger Vermischung fälisch-nordischer megalithkeramischer Großbauernstämme und reinnordischer Kriegergruppen der Schnurkeramiker und Streitaxtleute sind die historischen Germanen zu neuer Einheit erwachsen.

[61] Otto Höfler, *Kultische Geheimbünde der Germanen* and Lilly Weiser, *Altgermanische Jünglingsweihe und Männerbünde*, op. cit., note 3. The obsession with *Männerbünde* as a key institution of Germanic culture originated in Vienna with Rudolf Much and his students (Weiser, Höfler, and Wolfram). Höfler's volume was the chief instrument of its popularization, but Höfler and Wolfram both worked assiduously to propagate the idea through their service in the SS Ahnenerbe. On Much and his students, see Olaf Bockhorn, "The Battle for the 'Ostmark': Nazi Folklore in Austria," in James R. Dow and Hannjost Lixfeld, eds., *The Nazification of an Academic Discipline*, pp. 135–155, and Sebastian Meissl, "Germanistik in Österreich: Zu ihrer Geschichte und Politik 1918–1938," in Franz Kadrnoska, ed., *Aufbruch und Untergang: Österreichische Kultur zwischen 1918 und 1938* (Vienna: Europaverlag, 1981), pp. 475–496, esp. p. 478, p. 484f., and p. 488f.

[62] Güntert, *Altgermanischer Glaube*, p. 43, pp. 48–51, p. 58f., and pp. 67–70.

(1943, but written in 1938) is even worse, culminating in a chapter arguing that the etymologically proper meaning of "deutsch" is nothing other than "völkisch."[63] At points, one can still perceive the same philological acumen, religio-historical sensitivity, and penetrating intelligence that characterized Güntert's great work of the 'tens and twenties, but in these two books, ever more passages are burdened – no, animated – by fascist subtexts of one sort or another. Militarism, völkisch nationalism, Nordic triumphalism, anti-humanism, irrationalism, vitalism, totalitarianism, the "Führerprinzip," wounded German pride, and a Wagnerian fascination with the coming *Götterdämmerung* all are present. Occasionally, Güntert maintained his struggle against racism, but ever more frequently he capitulated, creating utter incoherence in the process, as in his statement "The primary components that mix together in the Germans, Faliscan and Nordic, 'stand very close to each other', therefore the Germans can be designated as 'an Indo-European Volk of particular racial purity'."[64] The sentence, like the book, represents an unstable attempt to encompass contradictory positions and interests, without really being able to satisfy either the political demands of the era or the moral demands of posterity.

Güntert's works of 1937 and 1938 were still relatively free of anti-semitism,[65] but an anti-"Southern," anti-humanist, and anti-Catholic polemic reminiscent of the Kulturkampf still mars them badly.[66] Other

---

[63] Hermann Güntert, *Geschichte der germanischen Völkerschaften* (Leipzig: Bibliographisches Institut, 1943), pp. 153–160. Whatever its ideological motivations, the argument is formally elegant and continues to be accepted in standard dictionaries, e.g. Thomas V. Gamkrelidze and Vjaceslav V. Ivanov, *Indo-European and the Indo-Europeans* (Berlin: Mouton de Gruyter, 1995), p. 652f. The root is *theu-th-, "a term for a large social grouping uniting individual tribes and clans," of which Old High German *diutisc* (= German "deutsch") is an extension in -isk-. Cf. Gothic þiuda, Old Saxon thiod[a], Anglosaxon þéod, Old Frisian thiode, and Old Norse þjóð, all of which mean "the people; the folk; the social totality," Oscan *touto* ("community"), Umbrian *totam* ("society"), Old Prussian *tauto* ("country"), etc.

[64] Güntert, *Altgermanischer Glaube*, p. 50 (emphasis in the original): "Bei den Germanen aber stehen die sich mischenden Hauptkomponenten, fälisch-nordisch, sich selbst sehr nahe, und daher können die Germanen als ein besonders rassereines indogermanisches Volk bezeichnet werden."

[65] Antisemitic remarks are rare, but not entirely absent from Güntert's writings. See, for instance, "Das germanische Erbe in der deutschen Seele," *Zeitschrift für Deutschkunde* 48 (1934), p. 459f. or *Geschichte der germanischen Völkerschaften*, p. 6 and p. 8.

[66] Thus, *Altgermanischer Glaube*, pp. 36–40, pp. 72–74, pp. 122–137, *Geschichte der germanischen Völkerschaften*, pp. 124–126 and the penultimate chapter, entitled "Das Kreuz von Rom," pp. 138–152. On the nature of this polemic, see Römer, *Sprachwissenschaft und Rassenideologie*, pp. 8–10.

compromises and surrenders were also evident. Thus, when the last of its founding editors died in 1938, Güntert assumed control of *Wörter und Sachen*. Proclaiming a new era for the publication, he focused it much more tightly on Indo-European linguistics, and gave it a more aggressively völkisch orientation. Under the influence of the new editors he appointed – two of whom (Richard von Kienle [1908–1985] and Walther Wüst [1901–1993]) were active members of the SS[67] – he accepted the terms "Aryan" and Ahnenerbe,[68] while also endorsing the primacy of race and biology over language such that use of a common speech cannot mitigate the ineradicable alterity of those who are "Volks- und Rassefremde."[69] Wüst, whom Himmler had made president and scientific director of the SS Ahnenerbe in 1937, assumed a position

---

[67] According to *Der Ursprung der Germanen*, p. 183, von Kienle served as Güntert's assistant in the Heidelberg linguistics seminar. On his role as the Nazi party's "trusted man" at Heidelberg, see Steven Remy, *The Heidelberg Myth*, p. 69; regarding his later service in the SS Ahnenerbe, see p. 76. With regard to Wüst, see Horst Junginger's contribution to this volume, Anka Oesterle, "The Office of Ancestral Inheritance and Folklore Scholarship," in Dow and Lixfeld, eds., *Nazification of an Academic Discipline*, pp. 201–212, and Michael Kater, *Das 'Ahnenerbe der SS' 1935–1945: Ein Beitrag zur Kulturpolitik des Dritten Reiches* (Stuttgart: Deutsche Verlags Anstalt, 1974), pp. 43–46 et passim. The others named to the board at this time were Heinrich Kuen (1899–1989), Walter Porzig (1895–1961), Kurt Stegmann von Pritzwald (1901–1962), and Leo Weisgerber (1899–1985). Weisgerber had previously served as an editor, but apparently was demoted. On the völkisch – but non-racist – neo-Humboldtian linguistics he advocated, see Römer, *Sprachwissenschaft und Rassenideologie*, pp. 162–165 and Christopher Hutton, *Linguistics and the Third Reich: Mother-tongue, Fascism, Race, and the Study of Language* (London: Routledge, 1999).

[68] Hermann Güntert, "Neue Zeit – neues Ziel," *Wörter und Sachen* (Neue Folge) 1 (1938), pp. 1–11. The term "Aryan" appears at p. 7, "Ahnenerbe" at p. 6.

[69] Ibid., p. 6f.:

Mag eine Sprache auch mit ihrer Art, die Welt begrifflich zu fassen, weitgehenden Einfluß auf den einzelnen Sprachgenossen ausüben – Sprache allein macht niemals zum wahren Volksgenossen. Denn jede Sprache ist Ausdruck der Eigenart eines Volkes, und die ist abhängig von den viel tiefer wirkenden, aus der Tiefe des Unbe- wußten quellenden, biologischen Mächten, von der Rasse, von der Erbmasse, von Veranlagung, von Gemütsart, vom Wohnraum, von der gemeinsamen Geschichte, alles Kräfte, die eine Sprache ebenso wie Sitte, Brauchtum, Rechtsempfinden, Weltanschauung usw. bestimmen. Ein Volks- und Rassefremder wird dadurch, daß er eine ihm ursprünglich fremde Sprache spricht, also nun mit deren Aufbau 'die Welt betrachtet', nicht zum Volksgenossen werden...

This passage anticipates the chilling moment in *Geschichte der germanischen Völkerschaften*, when the author opines "Juden haben überall leicht die Sprache des Volks gelernt und gesprochen, in dessen Reihen sie sich parasitisch festsetzten, ihre Rasse und Ras- seeigentümlichkeiten in ihrer weitervererbten Volkssubstanz haben sie deshalb nicht aufgegeben und aufgeben können" (p. 8).

of special favor and took over the journal in 1939,[70] when Güntert, at the age of fifty-two, was incapacitated by a series of strokes. Whether or not one considers these attacks the somatic expression of other pressures Güntert was experiencing, they effectively ended his career. Although he did not formally retire until after the war, the stroke of 1939 left him paralyzed on one side. Save for some teaching, he was largely inactive thereafter.

IX

Since his death, those who have written about Hermann Güntert have adopted one of two positions. On the one hand, Wolf H. Goegginger, Wolfgang Meid, and contributors to the Gedenkschrift marking the 25th anniversary of his death stressed Güntert's work on the Indo-European homeland, portraying him as an early opponent of Nazi orthodoxy who was made to suffer for his views.[71] Rejecting this as sanitized post-war mythology, Steven Remy and Ruth Römer have been more critical, emphasizing Güntert's role in the Nazification ("Gleichschaltung") of

---

[70] The journal's title page for the first volume of its "Neue Folge" (1938) lists Güntert as editor, "in Verbindung mit Walther Wüst." Volume 3 (1940) lists Wüst as editor, "in Vertretung von Hermann Güntert." The journal ceased publication in 1944. Together with Heinrich Harmjanz (1904–1994), Wüst also took control of the *Zeitschrift für Volkskunde* in 1938 and the *Archiv für Religionswissenschaft* in 1939 on behalf of the Ahnenerbe. Regarding the fate of the latter journal under his direction, see Fritz Heinrich, *Die deutsche Religionswissenschaft und der Nationalsozialismus: Eine ideologie-kritische und wissenschaftsgeschichtliche Untersuchung* (Petersburg: Michael Imhof, 2002), pp. 245–256. Güntert apparently had some respect for Wüst's scholarship, as attested by a favorable review of the latter's *Stilgeschichte und Chronologie des Rgveda* (Leipzig: Deutsche Morgenländische Gesellschaft, 1928), that he published in *Orientalische Literaturzeitung* 32 (1929), p. 381f., well before the expression of such views had any political importance. Less innocent is the opinion he voiced on Wüst's suitability to succeed Hanns Oertel as Professor of Arische Kultur- und Sprachwissenschaft at the University of Munich in October 1935. I am grateful to Horst Junginger for having transmitted the follow-ing text to me, which he found in Wüst's personnel file (Personalakte Walther Wüst O-N-14). Wüst sei "einer der originellsten und anregendsten jüngeren Forscher auf dem Gebiet der altindischen und indo-iranischen Philologie… Somit halte ich Herrn Wüst für den fähigsten und anregendsten unter den jüngeren Indologen; es ist von ihm noch viel zu erhoffen, insbesondere nach der Seite geistes- und kulturgeschichtlicher Durchdringung des indo-arischen Altertums. Solche Forscher sind heute besonders nötig, wenn die indogermanisch-arische Altertumskunde neuen Auftrieb im Geiste der Zeit gewinnen will."

[71] Goegginger, "Hermann Güntert als Religionsforscher," p. 155f., Meid, "Hermann Güntert, p. 520.

Heidelberg and his professional success in the NS era.[72] Both positions strike me as right, but also as partial. Güntert's work published between 1927–1934 did indeed pose a bold and principled challenge to Nazi racism, but in 1933 its author began a process of intellectual retreat and practical collaboration. Neither side of the story can be denied or ignored.

We are thus left with two questions: 1) What prompted his initial commitment? 2) What led him to back away? Together, the two can be used to voice a more general concern: What are the sources – and limits – of scholarly courage and integrity?

Before I could attempt to answer such questions, I would want to have read Güntert's private papers and to have spoken with those who knew him, if any are still living. Not having taken these steps, I can only speculate. There is, however, one possible answer to the first query that can surely be ruled out. This is the view that "the data" – more precisely, the sound shifts in Germanic that Güntert studied so closely – forced him to reach his conclusions, after which his integrity as a scholar forced him to speak out. However appealing such a narrative may be, it commits the fallacy of imputing agency to something inert (here "the data"), while agency is always a human quality and product.

Güntert's training as a linguist – which is to say, the linguists with whom he studied, those who became his colleagues, and those whose publications he read – told him the sound shifts were significant. The same people gave him the tools with which to ponder the implications of connecting phonology to (pre)history. Perhaps most important, they also provided him with an ethos that stressed certain practices and dispositions, which they constituted as cardinal virtues. And as he manifested these virtues – which included rigorous attention to detail, logical consistency, dispassionate evaluation, scrupulous reporting, and so forth – they encouraged and rewarded him, thereby securing the reproduction of those values in him and in the discipline as a whole. Being called to the chair of a Heidelberg Ordinarius in 1926 was the culminating moment in this process, and it is no accident that Güntert undertook his most independent, challenging, and consequential research in the immediate aftermath of that occasion. Collegial acclamation – and the desire for same – strikes me as having been the stimulus for his work,

---

[72] Remy, *The Heidelberg Myth*, pp. 209–10, Römer, *Sprachwissenschaft und Rassenideologie*, p. 179.

the basis for his pride, and the secret of his courage. A sense that he enjoyed the support of colleagues outside his discipline also played a part, as is seen from his regular invocation of ranking scholars (usually from Heidelberg) in Vorgeschichte, Religionswissenschaft, Volkskunde, and even Rassenkunde to buttress his conclusions.

At the first signs that *Der Ursprung der Germanen* was courting a hostile reception, Güntert seems to have felt shaken. Times had changed and he was in an exposed position, in danger of abandonment by his colleagues and condemnation as a traitor to his Volk. Support from abroad provided no solace, and might even make matters worse. One senses his fear and sees him reach out for support from other kinds of colleagues than those whom he previously courted: men who had reason to feel increased confidence with the opening of the Nazi era. First came Fehrle, then Höfler, then von Kienle, Wüst, and others. As he cultivated his relations with such people, the content and quality of his work deteriorated. Striving to please the new powers that be, he opened his own discourse to admit and accommodate theirs, thereby adopting a narrower, more strident völkisch discourse that incorporated racism, militarism, and demagoguery, but became confused and contradictory on countless points. His later work is as sorry as his pre-Heidelberg writings were grand, and the story of his descent from the one to the other is – I submit – nothing less than a tragedy, horror story, and object lesson.

Bibliography

Arntz, Helmuth, ed. *Germanen und Indogermanen: Volkstum, Sprache, Heimat, Kultur. Festschrift für Herman Hirt.* Heidelberg, Carl Winter, 1936.

Assion, Peter. "Eugen Fehrle and 'The Mythos of Our Folk'." In James R. Dow and Hannjost Lixfeld, ed., *The Nazification of an Academic Discipline: Folklore in the Third Reich.* Bloomington: Indiana University Press, 1994, pp. 112–134.

Bockhorn, Olaf. "The Battle for the 'Ostmark': Nazi Folklore in Austria." In ibid., pp. 135–155.

Darré, Richard Walther. *Das Bauerntum als Lebensquell der nordischen Rasse.* München: J.F. Lehmanns Verlag, 1929.

Dieterich, Albrecht. "Über Wesen und Ziele der Volkskunde." *Hessische Blätter für Volkskunde* 1 (1902), pp. 169–194.

——. *Mutter Erde.* Leipzig: B.G. Teubner, 1905.

Dubuisson, Daniel. *Mythologies du XXᵉ siècle.* Lille: Presses universitaires de Lille, 1993.

Dumézil, Georges. *Horace et les Curiaces.* Paris: Gallimard, 1942.

——. *Mitra-Varuna. Essai sur deux representations indo-européennes de la souveraineté.* Paris: Presses universitaires de France, 1940.

Eickstedt, Egon Freiherr von. *Rassenkunde und Rassengeschichte der Menschheit.* Stuttgart: Ferdinand Enke Verlag, 1934.

Eliade, Mircea. "Le 'dieu lieur' et le symbolisme des nœuds." *Revue de l'histoire des religions* 134 (1948): pp. 5–36.

——. "Dacians and Wolves." In idem, *From Zalmoxis to Genghis Khan.* Chicago: University of Chicago Press, 1972, pp. 1–20.

Fehrle, Eugen. *Die kultische Keuschheit im Altertum.* Giessen: A. Töpelmann, 1910.

——. *Deutsche Feste und Volksbräuche.* Leipzig: B.G. Teubner, 1916.

——. *Badische Volkskunde.* Leipzig: Quelle & Meyer, 1924.

——. "Bemerkungen über Ziele und Grenzen der Volkskunde." *Oberdeutsche Zeitschrift für Volkskunde* 6 (1932), pp. 85–92.

Feist, Sigmund. *Europa im Lichte der Vorgeschichte und die Ergebnisse der vergleichenden indogermanischen Sprachwissenschaft.* Berlin: Jerome Weidmann, 1910.

——. *Kultur, Ausbreitung und Herkunft der Indogermanen.* Berlin: Weidmann, 1913.

——. *Indogermanen und Germanen, ein Beitrag zur europäischen Urgeschichtsforschung.* Halle: Max Niemeyer, 1924.

Gamkrelidze, Thomas V. and Vjaceslav V. Ivanov. *Indo-European and the Indo-Europeans.* Berlin: Mouton de Gruyter, 1995.

Goegginger, Wolf H. "Hermann Güntert als Religionsforscher." *Numen* 14 (1967), pp. 150–158.

Güntert, Hermann. *Über altisländische Berserkergeschichten.* Heidelberg: J. Hörning, 1912.

——. *Über die ahurischen und daevischen Ausdrücke im Awesta. Eine semasiologische Studie* (Sitzungsberichte der Heidelberger Akademie der Wissenschaften, Philosophisch-historische Klasse 1914–13). Heidelberg: Carl Winter, 1914.

——. *Kalypso. Bedeutungsgeschichtliche Untersuchungen auf dem Gebiet der indogermanischen Sprachen.* Halle: Max Niemeyer, 1919.

——. *Von der Sprache der Götter und Geister. Bedeutungsgeschichtliche Untersuchungen zur homerischen und eddischen Göttersprache.* Halle: Max Niemeyer, 1921.

——. *Der arische Weltkönig und Heiland. Bedeutungsgeschichtliche Untersuchungen zur indo-iranischen Religionsgeschichte und Altertumskunde.* Halle: Max Niemeyer, 1923.

——. "Über die Ursache der germanischen Lautverschiebung." *Wörter und Sachen* 10 (1927), pp. 1–22.

——. *Kundry.* Heidelberg: Carl Winter, 1928.

———. "Zur Frage nach der Urheimat der Indogermanen." In Hans Teske, ed., *Deutschkundliches: Friedrich Panzer zum 60. Geburtstage überreicht von Heidelberger Fachgenossen.* Heidelberg: Carl Winter, 1930), pp. 1–33.

———. *Deutscher Geist. Drei Vorträge.* Bühl-Baden: Konkordia A.G., 1932.

———. "Die Frage der indogermanischen Urheimat in neuer Beleuchtung." *Zeitschrift für deutsche Bildung* 8 (1932), pp. 1–8.

———. *Der Ursprung der Germanen.* Heidelberg: Carl Winter, 1934.

———. *Wieland, der Schmied. Ein germanisches Sagenspiel in drei Aufzügen.* Heidelberg: Carl Winter, 1936.

———. *König Laurin. Eine deutsche Sage in Liedern.* Heidelberg: Carl Winter, 1936.

———. *Altgermanische Glaube nach Wesen und Grundlage.* Heidelberg: Carl Winter, 1937

———. *Prometheus, der arische Heiland. Mythenspiel in drei Teilen.* Heidelberg: Carl Winter, 1938.

———. *Geschichte der germanischen Völkerschaften* (Leipzig: Bibliographisches Institut, 1943), pp. 153–160.

Günther, Hans F.K. *Rassenkunde Europas, mit besonderer Berücksichtigung der Rassengeschichte der Hauptvölker indogermanischer Sprache.* Munich: J.F. Lehmann, 1926.

———. *Rassenkunde des deutschen Volkes.* Munich: J.F. Lehmann, 1930, 16th ed., 1933.

———. *Herkunft und Rassengeschichte der Germanen.* Munich: J.F. Lehmann, 1937.

Hirt, Hermann. *Die Indogermanen,* 2 vols. Strassburg: K.J. Trübner, 1905–1907.

Höfler, Otto. *Kultische Geheimbünde der Germanen.* Frankfurt: Moritz Diesterweg, 1934.

Hünnerkopf, Richard. "Eugen Fehrle (1880–1957)." *Zeitschrift für Volkskunde* 54 (1958), p. 142f.

Hutton, Christopher. *Linguistics and the Third Reich: Mother-tongue, Fascism, Race, and the Study of Language.* London: Routledge, 1999.

Kater, Michael. *Das 'Ahnenerbe der SS' 1935–1945: Ein Beitrag zur Kulturpolitik des Dritten Reiches.* Stuttgart: Deutsche Verlags Anstalt, 1974, 3rd ed. Munich: Oldenbourg, 2003.

Koonz, Claudia. *The Nazi Conscience.* Cambridge, MA: Harvard University Press, 2003.

Kossinna, Gustaf. *Ursprung und Verbreitung der Germanen,* 2 vols. Leipzig: Curt Kabitzsch, 1926–1927.

Littleton, C. Scott. *The New Comparative Mythology.* Berkeley: University of California Press, 1966, 3rd ed. 1982.

Lincoln, Bruce. *Priests, Warriors, and Cattle. A Study in the Ecology of Religions.* Berkeley: University of California Press, 1981, pp. 121–165.

Mackensen, Lutz. "Zwischen Skepsis und Legende: Kleine grundsätzliche Bücherschau zur Germanenkunde." *Die Neue Literatur* 10 (1935), pp. 577–93.

Mallory, James. "A Short History of the Indo-European Problem." *Journal of Indo-European Studies* 1 (1973), pp. 21–65.

Meid, Wolfgang. "Hermann Güntert: Leben und Werk." In Manfred Mayrhofer et al., eds., *Antiquitates Indogermanicae. Studien zur indogermanischen Altertumskunde und zur Sprach- und Kulturgeschichte der indogermanischen Völker. Gedenkschrift für Hermann Güntert zur 25. Wiederkehr seines Todestages am 23. April 1973* . Innsbruck: Innsbrucker Beiträge zur Sprachwissenschaft, 1974, pp. 517–520.

Meissl, Sebastian. "Germanistik in Österreich: Zu ihrer Geschichte und Politik 1918–1938". In Franz Kadrnoska, ed., *Aufbruch und Untergang: Österreichische Kultur zwischen 1918 und 1938.* Vienna: Europaverlag, 1981.

Oesterle, Anka. "The Office of Ancestral Inheritance and Folklore Scholarship." In James R. Dow and Hannjost Lixfeld, eds., *The Nazification of an Academic Discipline: Folklore in the Third Reich.* Bloomington: Indiana University Press, 1994, p. 201f.

Poliakov, Léon. *The Aryan Myth: A History of Racist and Nationalist Ideas in Europe,* trans. Edmund Howard. New York: Basic Books, 1974.

Puhvel, Jaan. "Remus et Frater." *History of Religions* 15 (1975), pp. 146–157.

Reche, Otto. *Rasse und Heimat der Indogermanen*. Munich: J.F. Lehmann, 1936.

Remy, Steven P. *The Heidelberg Myth: The Nazification and Denazification of a German University*. Cambridge, MA: Harvard University Press, 2002.

Römer, Ruth. *Sprachwissenschaft und Rassenideologie in Deutschland*. Munich: Wilhelm Fink, 1985.

Rosenberg, Alfred. *Das Verbrechen der Freimaurerei, Judentum, Jesuitismus, Deutsches Christentum*, Munich: J.F. Lehmann, 1922.

Schott, Georg. *Das Lebenswerk H. St. Chamberlains in Umrissen*, München: J.F. Lehmann Verlag, 1927.

Scharfe, Martin. "Einschwörung auf den völkisch-germanischen Kulturbegriff." In Jörg Tröger, ed., *Hochschule und Wissenschaft im Dritten Reich*. Frankfurt: Campus, 1984, pp. 105–115.

Schrader, Otto. *Die Indogermanen*. Leipzig: Quelle & Meyer, 1911.

Stahlmann, Hans. *Vom Werden und Wandel der Muttersprache: Ein Hilfsbuch für Studierende, Lehrer und Freunde unserer Muttersprache* [Leipzig: 1940].

Treutlein, Wolfgang. "Eugen Fehrle als Forscher und Kämpfer." In Ferdinand Herrmann und Wolfgang Treutlein, eds., *Brauch und Sinnbild. Eugen Fehrle zum 60, Geburtstag gewidmet von seinen Schülern und Freunden*. Karlsruhe: Südwestdeutsche Druck- und Verlagsgesellschaft, 1940, pp. 1–12.

Wachter, Rudolf and Amina Kropp, „Allgemeine und vergleichende Sprachwissenschaft." In Wolfgang U. Eckart, et al., eds., *Die Universität Heidelberg im Nationalsozialismus*. Heidelberg: Springer Medizin Verlag, 2006, pp. 371–89.

Wahle, Ernst. *Deutsche Vorzeit*. Leipzig: Curt Kabitzsch, 1932.

Watkins, Calvert. "Language of Gods and Language of Men: Remarks on Some Indo-European Metalinguistic Traditions." Jn Jaan Puhvel, ed., *Myth and Law among the Indo-Europeans*. Berkeley: University of California Press, 1970, pp. 1–18.

Weiser, Lily. *Altgermanische Jünglingsweihe und Männerbünde*. Bühl-Baden: Konkordia A.G., 1927.

——. "Eugen Fehrle, 1880–1957." *Hessische Blätter für Volkskunde* 49/50 (1959), p. 9f.

Wikander, Stig. *Der arische Männerbund*. Lund: C.W.K. Gleerup, 1938.

Wolfram, Richard. *Schwerttanz und Männerbund*. Kassel, Bärenreiter-Verlag 1936.

Wüst, Walther. *Stilgeschichte und Chronologie des Rgveda*. Leipzig: Deutsche Morgenländische Gesellschaft, 1928.

QUAND L'ALLEMAGNE ÉTAIT LEUR MECQUE
LA SCIENCE DES RELIGIONS CHEZ STIG WIKANDER
(1935–1941)*

Mihaela Timuş

L'Allemagne – la Mecque

« Si vous avez un examen français ou si vous avez publié un livre qui a attiré l'attention du public français, ce n'est pas du tout méritoire aux yeux de nos professeurs – autrefois, l'Allemagne était leur Mecque, maintenant ils sont bien sans Mecque, mais la France est vraiment trop éloignée... ».[1]

1. *Perspective générale*

Derrière cette expression inspirée, qui risquerait de devenir fameuse, se trouve l'écho de plusieurs itinéraires, parmi lesquels la biographie scientifique de Wikander avant la deuxième guerre. Pour rester dans

---

* Sous le titre "Quand l'Allemagne était leur Mecque..." nous avons par ailleurs publié un sous-chapitre dans l'introduction plus ample de l'édition roumaine de la correspondance Eliade-Wikander, voir *C'est toujours l'Orient. La correspondance Mircea Eliade – Stig Wikander (1948–1977)*, Iasi, Polirom, 2005 (préface par Giovanni Casadio, postface par Frantz Grenet, édition, traduction, introduction et annotations par M. Timuş). Là nous avons suivi plutôt les relations de chacun des correspondants avec l'Allemagne, dans les années 1936–1944, pour mieux mettre en lumière l'emplacement distinct de chacun d'eux. Parfois, il y a également des rapprochements. Pour la présente contribution je m'appuie, davantage que dans le précédent travail, sur d'autres matériaux inédits, notamment les réponses de Wikander aux lettres adressées à lui par Otto Höfler. Je tiens à remercier vivement MM. Frantz Grenet (Paris) et Horst Junginger (Tübingen) pour leurs observations très profitables faites en marge de cette contribution. Un riche et substantiel échange de correspondance avec M. Bruce Lincoln (Chicago) a précédé la rédaction finale de cet article. Qu'il y trouve l'expression de ma vive reconnaissance. Enfin, mais pas dernièrement, je remercie Johan Härnsten (lecteur de suédois, École Normale Supérieure, Paris) pour son assistance nécessaire autour des traductions que j'ai faites après la correspondance suédoise de Wikander.

[1] Lettre de Stig Wikander à Mircea Eliade, Lund, le 18 janvier 1952, voir Mihaela Timuş et Eugen Ciurtin, « The Unpublished Correspondence between Mircea Eliade and Stig Wikander (1948–1977) – 2nd Part », *Archaeus* 4 (2000), fasc. 4, p. 180.

les cadres d'une problématique religieuse, celle que suscite les origines
d'une telle expression, on peut dire qu'elle conviendrait profondément
à un des plus importants historiens des religions suédois, d'ailleurs fondateur de la première chaire d'histoire des religions en Suède, à savoir
le pasteur luthérien devenu archevêque d'Uppsala, Nathan Söderblom.
Dans ses actions œcuméniques, démarches grâce auxquelles il allait
recevoir le prix Nobel pour la paix, Söderblom est resté dévoué à la
cause protestante, parfois jusqu'aux dernières conséquences de cet engagement.[2] La Mecque d'une Suède luthérienne ne pouvait ne venir, au
moins jusqu'à une certaine date, du pays où l'initiateur de la reforme
était né. Cette gravitation confessionnelle se fit, sans doute, au fur et à
mesure, responsable aussi de la configuration culturelle suédoise.

D'une autre part, la veille de l'orientalisme suédois ou, au moins, de
ce qui y est devenu recherche 'aryenne', remonterait à la traduction
en suédois de certains écrits de Friedrich Schlegel.[3] Les historiens des
religions suédois de la génération de Martin P. Nilsson se formèrent
et travaillèrent en étroits contacts avec l'Allemagne.[4] La génération

---

[2] Nous avons pu identifier comment dans son ouvrage iranisant *La vie future d'après
le mazdéisme* (Paris, Leroux, 1901), qui est aussi un exercice d'eschatologie comparée,
l'interprétation d'une notion pehlevie telle *tan ī pasēn* remonte finalement à la lecture
que Luther donna à la *resurrectio carnis*, voir M. Timuş, « Le corps eschatologique (*tan
ī pasēn*) d'après la théologie zoroastrienne », in Eugen Ciurtin, éd., *Du corps humain, au
carrefour de plusieurs savoirs en Inde. Mélanges offerts à Arion Roşu pas ses collègues et ses amis
à l'occasion de son 80ᵉ anniversaire* (= *Studia Asiatica* 4.2003–5.2004), sous la direction de
O. Botto, C. Caillat, P. Delaveau, P.-S. Filliozat, S. Lienhard, G.J. Meulenbeld et P.V.
Sharma (Bucarest, Centre d'histoire des religions – Paris, De Boccard, 2004), p. 779–808,
surtout p. 780–782.
[3] Voir M. Timuş, éd., *Întotdeauna Orientul. Corespondenţa Mircea Eliade – Stig Wikander
(1948–1977)* [C'est toujours l'Orient. Correspondance Eliade-Wikander] (Iasi-Bucarest,
Polirom, 2005), p. 280–281, où les références s'appuient sur le manuscrit inachevé et
inédit de Wikander, *Den ariska romantiken*.
[4] Voir aujourd'hui l'étude très pertinente de Martina Dürkop, «'...er wird sehen,
dass das Archiv wirklich ein Geschäft ist, wenn es richtig behandelt wird...'. Wissenschaftlicher und wirtschaftlicher Existenzkampf des ARW 1919–1939», *Archiv für
Religionsgeschichte* 1–1 (1999), p. 107–128, article qui suit les rapports entre la Suède
et l'Allemagne autour du périodique *Archiv für Religionswissenschaft* qui allait finir par
devenir, à partir de 1938, une revue 'nazifiée', pour reprendre l'expression de Henrik
S. Nyberg dans l'introduction à la deuxième édition de son *Die Religionen des alten Iran*
(Osnabrück, Zeller, 1966). Une telle image de la Suède tournée vers l'Allemagne
devrait être partiellement ajustée par l'étude de Walter H. Capps, « Geo Widengren
on syncretism: On parsing Uppsala methodological tendencies », *Numen* 20–3 (1973),
p. 163–185, très bonne enquête sur les tendances de la culture suédoise, manifestes
déjà à la veille du 19ᵉ siècle, d'éloignement de la philosophie idéaliste allemande et de
réorientation vers le pragmatisme britannique (d'ailleurs, aujourd'hui, le philosophe le
plus souvent trouvable chez les bouquinistes d'Uppsala est Bertrand Russell).

juste après Söderblom s'oriente vers l'Allemagne bien au-delà de cette dimension confessionnelle précise.[5]

2. *Les débuts de la carrière de Wikander*

Oscar Stig est né le 27 août 1908 à Norrtälje, près de Stockholm, comme le deuxième enfant dans la famille. Son père, Åke Magnus Wikander, apothicaire érudit, lui-même auteur d'un guide pour le lexique latin médical et pharmacologique et d'un essai sur les fondements théologiques de la morale, l'avait éduqué dans un esprit de respect pour les langues classiques. En tant qu'élève Stig avait même gagné un concours de composition en hexamètres. A partir de l'automne 1925, il suit les cours de langues classiques et aussi de langues sémitiques (sous la direction du professeur K.V. Zeterstéen) à l'Université d'Uppsala. Ensuite il élargit ses études avec des cours de langues et religions iraniennes, directions qui décident son profile de savant, en obtenant deux licences : une sous la direction de Henrik Samuel Nyberg (cycle d'enseignement conclu le 24 février 1933), puis une autre sous celle d'Arthur Christensen (cycle d'enseignement conclu le 23 septembre 1936) en soutenant une dissertation avec le titre *Karnamak-i-Artaxer och den iranska historietradition*. L'année 1931, il se trouve à Paris, chef des étudiants de la Maison suédoise de Paris (récemment ouverte à l'époque), et c'est la même année qu'il devient, sous le patronage de Sylvain Lévi, membre de la Société Asiatique, fondée en 1822. C'est aussi là qu'il ressent l'attraction pour la pensée de Charles Maurras.[6]

---

[5] À cela il faut ajouter que la carte des orientations reste encore plus nuancée, les modèles de l'école ethnographique britannique (*Myth and Ritual School*) empruntés énergiquement par Geo Widengren, jouèrent eux aussi leur rôle. Pour une esquisse de ce que l'école d'histoire des religions d'Uppsala signifia 50 ans après la guerre et il est à retenir que Wikander n'y figure pas, voir Carl-Martin Edsman, «Ein halbes Jahrhundert Uppsala-Schule», dans Michael Stausberg, éd., *Kontinuität und Brüche in der Religionsgeschichte. Festschrift für Anders Hultgård zu seinem 65. Geburtstag am 23.12.2001* (Berlin, Walter de Gruyter, 2001), p. 194–209.

[6] Auquel il dédiera un article entier dans la presse suédoise à l'occasion de son élection au sein de l'*Académie Française*, voir Stig Wikander, «Ett revolutionärt val i Franska akademien. Dreyfusmotståndaren Maurras bland Frankrikes odödliga» [Une élection révolutionnaire. Maurras, opposant de Dreyfus, parmi les immortels de la France], 18 juin 1938, voir M. Timuş, «La bibliographie annotée de Stig Wikander (1908–1983)», *Studia Asiatica* 1 (2000), surtout p. 215. En faisant une courte présentation des écrits politiques de Maurras, pour le public suédois, Wikander applaudit non

La constellation sous laquelle il va soutenir la thèse de doctorat sur le «Männerbund aryen» se compose de deux savants scandinaves, augmentée par l'ouverture, plus ou moins bénéfique, vers les travaux d'Otto Höfler et ceux ethnographiques issus à l'époque et portant sur la question des sociétés guerrières. Le projet pourrait être daté des environs de 1935, quand Wikander confesse à Nyberg l'intention de «plagier» le livre *Kultische Geheimbünde der Germanen* (Frankfurt am Main, Diesterweg, 1934) d'Otto Höfler dans le domaine iranien ancien.[7] Otto Höfler avait été conférencier à Uppsala (1929) et c'est peut-être là que le jeune étudiant Wikander était entré en contact, pour la première fois, avec les idées du professeur germaniste. Néanmoins, le contact direct entre les deux, concrétisé dans leur correspondance, semble débuter la même année que celle de la 'confession du plagiat'.

A part son amitié et son admiration pour Höfler, qu'il visite à Kiel en 1936, Wikander garde une position, à l'intérieur même de sa propre discipline, qui lui permet de se trouver attaché à l'Allemagne, aux grandes disputes que cette culture porte. Cependant il refuse de se confondre dans l'enthousiasme grégaire des jeunes nazis, amis de Höfler, qu'il rencontre sur place. Bien au contraire, il se retourne en Suède dégoûté, en dénonçant déçu, dans une lettre adressée à son maître, le caractère corrompu et unilatéral de ces organisations:

> Permettez-moi de vous remercier pour votre lettre et d'essayer d'éloigner tout malentendu possible concernant ce que j'avais dit sur Bonn[8] (…). Je n'ai pas l'intention de critiquer la science allemande. Mais on ne peut pas rester indifférent face aux opinions politiques culturelles qui jugent chaque chose comme ayant une valeur plus ou moins politique (…). [J'ai participé] à une rencontre allemande-suédoise des étudiants de Kiel, mais le caractère unilatéral et corrompu de ces organisations est tellement évident que c'est avec le cœur brisé que j'ai dit 'non' aux invitations pressantes des amis de Höfler.[9]

---

sans étonnement que le maître à penser d'un mouvement royaliste soit élu au sein de l'Académie de la république française.

[7] Voir la lettre de Wikander à Nyberg, le 14 septembre 1935, voir Stefan Arvidsson, «Stig Wikander och forskningen om ariska mannaförbund», *Chaos* 38 (2002), p. 55–68, ici p. 58–59.

[8] Il s'agit de l'*Orientalisttåg* (journée des orientalistes) 1936, que Wikander avait décrit, dans une lettre antérieure, comme pure propagande nazie.

[9] Voir la lettre de Wikander à Nyberg, le 27 août 1936, voir Stefan Arvidsson, «Stig Wikander och forskningen om ariska mannaförbund», p. 60.

Cela ne l'empêche pas d'écrire à son tour des lignes exaltées devant lesquelles on peut se rappeler au moins les propos de Dumézil: «le rapport du nazisme et de l'antiquité germanique nous [tous, sociologues et mythologues, en 1938–1939, M.T.] apparaissait, en toute évidence».[10] Encore plus que cela, et c'est la chose la plus substantielle, on le retrouve convaincu que l'importance des études iraniennes est une chose qui peut se traduire en termes de rapport entre la religion et la politique et que c'est surtout cette chose qui serait d'être communiquée aux jeunes nazis de Kiel:

> D'ailleurs, il serait bien de raconter aux gens de Kiel combien la discipline d'études iraniennes est importante – c'est le premier peuple indo-européen dont la conception de l'empire (*rikstanke*) est devenue consciente en tant que nécessité politique et cela dans un ensemble compliqué avec le *Männerbund* et l'église d'état: les trois facteurs y sont issus d'un même fondement national, ce qui donne à la dialectique des problèmes une certaine clarté et simplicité. (…) on peut directement opérer avec des concepts fondamentaux sociologiques sans présupposer des influences étrangères.[11]

Le même intérêt se renouvelle encore trois ans plus tard (quand Wikander est déjà de retour de Munich), lors de la lecture des *Mythes et dieux des Germains*:

> [En ce qui concerne] le dernier ouvrage de Dumézil *Mythes et dieux des Germains* (qui est) paru il y a quelques mois à Paris, je suis encore entièrement stupéfait après la lecture. Décidément, c'est son meilleur ouvrage, qui contient bien partiellement des résultats du séminaire d'hiver. Un petit volume (150 pages) mais avec beaucoup de choses nouvelles et intéressantes, en partie un parallèle frappant ou un prolongement de tes écrits, qu'il cite avec grande approbation. Le chapitre central parle des initiations et des mythes de l'émigration, parce que les émigrations ont été à toute époque un trait dominant, conditionné religieusement dans la vision du monde germanique (…). Dynamiques, instables, indociles

---

[10] Il s'agit des lettres autour de la soutenance de sa thèse: avant la soutenance «Es heulet der Werwolf am baltischen Meer/Es brauset im kavischen Banner der Wind/Wir fordern zum wilden Gelage dich her/LYCANTHROPE PRINCEPS, komm eilends, geschwind», Lund, 16 mai 1938, ou après la soutenance, quand il s'adresse à son ami avec 'Värderade Varulv!' [loup-garou], Uppsala, le 23 juin 1938. Pour les dits de Dumézil, voir Georges Dumézil, «Science et politique. Réponse à Carlo Ginzburg», *Annales. Économies. Sociétés. Civilisations*, 40–5 (1985), p. 985–989, ici p. 986. Belle confession mais qui efface le fond du problème.

[11] Lettre de Wikander à Höfler, Copenhague, le 7 mai 1936 (traduction du suédois). Les lettres adressées par Wikander à Höfler proviennent du fonds *Nachlass Otto Höfler*, *Österreichische Nationalbibliothek* Wien.

aux administrations durables et passionnément dévoués aux chefs éphé-
mères, les anciens peuples germaniques avaient des mythologies à leur
image – c'est la conception fondamentale du livre formulée à plusieurs
reprises. (...) Le plus important est qu'il voit avec clarté trois faits dans le
monde germanique : sa continuité, les fortes liaisons religieuses de la vie
politique (même dans le troisième Reich comme depuis 2000 ans déjà)
et son homogénéité – il dit explicitement que ce qui de nos jours paraît
séparer radicalement les allemands et les scandinaves ne sont que des
divergences temporelles et superficielles, conditionnées par les dernières
évènements politiques. Est-ce que tu peux comprendre comment un
français, qui a vécu à Uppsala au commencement des années 30 et qui
était obligé de fréquenter doc. Lombard,[12] est-il arrivé à une conception
telle ? Cela fait partie d'une série mythologique populaire et on peut lui
reprocher une certaine superficialité nonchalante dans l'émission de ses
idées, pourtant la connexion qu'il établit entre l'histoire politique et la
religion, on ne le retrouve chez personne aujourd'hui, sauf toi. Si le livre
était plus travaillé on aurait eu le complément politique de Grönbech.
Maintenant tu as encore le temps de faire ceci, mais dans ce cas-là il
faudrait que tu le fasses vite.[13]

On voit bien que Wikander est encore assez loin d'entrer 'cadet génial
et original' à l'école du trifonctionnalisme dumézilien. Il l'adoptera avec
une discrétion très grande dans son deuxième livre sur le dieu Vâyu,
mais sans pouvoir aboutir à une vision systématique et cohérente. La
pression du modèle imposé par son maître Nyberg était encore très
forte.[14] Ce qu'il apprécie chez Dumézil, en 1939, est très, même trop
cohérent avec ce qu'il concevait quelques ans avant (1936, Kiel) sur la
religion des iraniens anciens, en termes de résonance pour le monde
contemporain, à savoir toute une série de catégories (e.g. la continuité)
qui ont abouti à jeter les recherches historiques dans le bestiaire des
proto-chronismes, si chers d'ailleurs aux totalitarismes, fussent-ils de
type nazi ou communiste.

---

[12] La référence à Alf Lombard concerne peut-être les sympathies marxistes, fait
qui expliquerait les bonnes relations que celui-ci gardera, après la guerre, avec un
pays communiste comme la Roumanie. Et cela d'autant plus qu'il dirigeait à Lund la
chaire de langue roumaine.

[13] Lettre de Wikander à Höfler, Stockholm, le 22 septembre 1939 (traduction du
suédois). Pour la lecture de *Mythes et dieux des Germains* dans le décor de l'époque, voir
Bruce Lincoln, «Rewriting the German War God: Georges Dumézil, Politics and
Scholarship in the Late 1930s», *History of Religions* 37–3 (1998), p. 187–208.

[14] Je remercie Bruce Lincoln de m'avoir confié certains témoignages de Geo
Widengren qui confirment la résistance que Nyberg avait toujours éprouvé face aux
propositions faites par ses deux jeunes disciples, Widengren et Wikander, celles d'une
ouverture vers le système dumézilien.

Wikander est un personnage parfois difficile à localiser et la pauvreté de témoignages contribue elle-aussi à cette difficulté. Il ne s'exprime pas en tant que fanatique du national-socialisme, ni comme sympathisant des vagues anti-judaïques envahissants de plus en plus les milieux universitaires allemandes. Là où, d'une manière plus ou moins sérieuse, Höfler voudrais voir évacuée toute trace possible d'éléments judaïques dans la mythologie allemande :

> Neulich erzählte mir übrigens Wüst, München, dass im Tibetischen allerlei in uralter Zeit aus dem Indischen dahin gedrungene Überlieferungen erhalten seien, die sich nahe zu meinen germanischen stellen sollen. Hast Du diese Dinge auch untersucht? Es wäre doch tröstlich, wenn Wodan aus dem Tibet das Zeugnis erhielte, dass er kein Vierteljude ist![15]

La réponse de Wikander vient par un filon plus raisonnablement scientifique et se résume à celui-ci :

> Tout discours concernant les sources tibétaines est ici [i.e. Suède ; M.T.] d'un dilettantisme dépourvu de sens. Les littératures tibétaines contiennent seulement des documents bouddhiques tardifs. Peut-être du point de vue ethnologique on pourrait trouver des ordres lamaïstes avec des exercices extatiques et des choses semblables, mais dans ce cas-là ce sont des parallèles folkloriques avec le *Männerbund* tel qu'on le retrouve surtout en Afrique de l'ouest et en Mexique. Ou veux-tu accepter pour le Tibet les 'théories de l'influence' que tu rejettes si énergiquement pour les vieux germains ? Je joins ma réserve contre l'*ordinarius monachensis* W[üst] que tu viens de citer, un des plus ignorants dilettantes qui n'est pas digne de la chaire qu'il détient.[16]

---

[15] Lettre de Höfler à Wikander, Kiel, le 22 novembre 1937. Les lettres de Höfler adressées à Wikander proviennent toutes du fonds *Stig Wikander, Uppsala University Library*. Des rêves tibétanisants, penchés vers le côté mystique, étaient nourris surtout par H. Himmler, le président de l'Ahnenerbe, fonction qui ne l'excusa du mépris que Hitler éprouva pour ce type d'exotisme : « What nonsense ! Here we have at least reached an age that has all mysticism behind it, and now he wants to start all over again. We might just as well have stayed with the church. At least it had tradition », voir Isrun Engelhardt, « Tibetan Triangle. German, Tibetan and British Relations in the Context of Ernst Schäfer's Expedition, 1938–1939 », *Asiatische Studien. Zeitschrift der Schweizerischen Asiengesellschaft/Études Asiatiques. Revue de la Société Suisse-Asie* 58-1 (2004), p. 57–113, ici p. 65–66, n. 38.

[16] Lettre de Wikander à Höfler, Uppsala, le 27 novembre 1937. Ce n'est pas le seul endroit où Wikander s'exprime d'une manière si nettement négative contre Walther Wüst (voir aussi : «Je ne pense pas polémiquer avec W[üst] : sa production jusqu'à maintenant = 0», lettre de Wikander à Höfler, Uppsala, le 31 janvier 1938) ce qui ne l'empêchera cependant de collaborer d'une manière ou d'une autre avec l'officier nazi de la discipline indo-iranienne. Sur l'engagement de Wüst, voir la contribution de Horst Junginger dans ce volume et S. Arvidsson, *Ariska*

En revanche, il est très probable qu'il partage avec Höfler ce que ce dernier expose comme les idées générales autour desquelles les sciences humaines devraient se concentrer et qui relèvent un assez fort ancrage idéologique, lié au verbiage de l'identité du Reich: le pouvoir «créateur d'État» indo-germanique, la «continuité des instincts créateurs d'État»...

> Jedenfalls ist es mir eine besondere Freude, zu hören, dass deine Arbeit schon fertig ist. Ich hatte gemeint, dies würde noch längere Zeit dauern. Sollte nun nicht bald der Augenblick kommen, wo man durch eine 'Kollaboration der Künste' zu einer Geschichte der indogermanischen Gemeinschaftsformen kommen kann? Wie kommt es, dass idg. Sprachen die verbreitesten der Erde sind? Doch letztlich von der einzigartigen staatenbildenden Kraft der Indogermanen. Ich vermute, man wird ausser der Konstanz und Kontinuität der staatenbildenden I n s t i n k t e auch eine solche der staatenbildenden I n s t i t u t i o n e n der Idg. Feststellen können (ich spreche übrigens über derlei beim Erfurter Historikertag, 6 Juli; kommst du hin?).[17]

aussi bien que les projets qui sont en train d'être mis en route, notamment la constitution effective de SS-Ahnenerbe.

> Das *Ahnenerbe*, mit dem ich in den letzten anderthalb Jahren immer mehr zusammengearbeitet habe, hat sich in der erfreulichsten Weise entwickelt, indem es Dilettanten an die Luft setzte und systematisch mit einer Reihe der besten Geisteswissenschaftler Fühlung suchte und aufnahm, so etwa mit Herbert Meyer, Altheim, Jahnkuhn und einer ganzen Reihe von anderen Forschern, besonders solchen, denen es um die Probleme der indogermanischen Kontinuität zu tun ist.[18]

Les rapports de Wikander avec l'Allemagne se concrétisent le plus par un stage prolongé, en 1939 (le plus probablement entre novembre/décembre 1938 et août 1939), dans le poste de lecteur de suédois à Munich, en partie suite à l'échec de sa candidature au poste de 'docent' à Lund, après la soutenance de thèse qui ne se passa pas sous les meilleurs auspices (sur l'échelle de cinq qualificatifs, Wikander n'a obtenu que le moyen: 'med beröm godkänd', i.e. *cum laudatur approbatur*).

idoler. Den indoeuropeiska mytologin som ideologi och vetenskap (Stockholm-Stehag, Brutus Östling Bokförlag Symposion, 2000) qui remarque très soigneusement que le livre de Wüst, *Indogermanisches Bekenntnis*, 1942, avait été dédié à Himmler: «Dem Präsidenten des 'Ahnenerbe' Reichsführer SS Heinrich Himmler in Dankbarkeit und Treue».
[17] Lettre de Höfler à Wikander, Kiel, le 27 mai 1937.
[18] Lettre de Höfler à Wikander, Kiel, le 20 juin 1938.

«J'ai été refusé comme 'docent' à Lund. *Maxima cum ignominia.* (...) Mais heureusement j'ai cet engagement à Munich, ainsi je peux parasiter un peu. (...) je compte beaucoup sur les possibilités d'émigrer en Amérique, où les philologues sont bien payés maintenant.»[19]

La précarité financière semble être une des motivations les plus fortes, et elle pourrait aussi avoir influencé le projet d'une éventuelle collaboration avec l'Ahnenerbe.[20] Des alternatives plus théoriques penchent entre l'émigration en Amérique et un coup d'état : «Après l'échec de Lund j'ai hésité entre émigrer en Amérique et un coup d'état armé.»[21] Le coup d'état est un refrain qui reviendra presque une demi année plus tard, dans sa correspondance avec Ragnar Liljedahl, ami et collègue de rédaction à la revue suédoise *Fri opposition* : il s'agissait d'abord d'une tentative de lutte contre la menace du communisme, d'autant plus grandissante lors de la guerre entre Finlande et la Russie (à laquelle participe, en tant qu'officier son collègue et encore bon ami Geo Widengren).[22] Une raison plus subtile pour ce type d'activisme pourrait être décelée dans un article où Wikander dénonce le 'flirte avec la neutralité' affiché par le gouvernement suédois.

Le séjour en Allemagne apporta sans doute une nouvelle dimension dans la vision générale de Wikander. Il est clair que ses recherches indo-iraniennes, poursuivies là aussi, aux cours de Walther Wüst, se développent dans une stricte contemporanéité avec l'évolution de

---

[19] Lettre de Wikander à Höfler, Lund, le 18 octobre 1938 (traduction du suédois).

[20] Bruce Lincoln avait déjà très précisément remarqué que les passages soulignés par Wikander dans les lettres reçues de la part de Höfler, celles contenant des propositions de collaboration avec l'Ahnenerbe en vue d'une deuxième édition corrigée et peut-être augmentée de *Der arische Männerbund*, concernent les détails financiers, voir Bruce Lincoln, *Theorizing Myth. Narrative, Ideology, and Scholarship* (Chicago-London, Chicago University Press), 1999, p. 122–123. Cela n'exclut bien sûr qu'une deuxième édition aurait pu être 'augmentée' dans le sens des conclusions encore plus éclairantes pour le rapport entre la religion et l'état. Horst Junginger vient de me signaler qu'en novembre 1938 (probablement le 11) Wikander est allé voir Wolfram Sievers, le secrétaire général de l'Ahnenerbe, en lui demandant si 'Ahnenerbe Stiftungsverlag' serait intéressée de publier son *Der arische Männerbund*, voir la notice de Wolfram Sievers (11.11.1938), Archives fédérales allemandes, Berlin, NS 21, vol. 605.

[21] Lettre de Wikander à Höfler, Södertälje 29.10.1938 (traduction du suédois). Le rapport final de Nyberg n'avait pas été entièrement positif, en accusant plusieurs défauts d'ordre philologique : une langue allemande pleine de néologismes suédois (*svedicismer*), les citations pehlevies et avestiques superficiellement transposées et la présentation très insatisfaisante de beaucoup de textes, ainsi que celle des références bibliographiques, voir «Utdrag av Humanistika sektionens i Uppsala protokoll den 28 maj 1938», acte dans l'archive de Stig Wikander, Uppsala.

[22] Lettre de Wikander à Ragnar Liljedahl, le 12 juin 1939, voir, S. Arvidsson, op. cit., donc pendant la période quand le premier se trouvait encore à Munich.

l'idéologie du troisième Reich.[23] Peu après son arrivée en Allemagne, il écrit dans la presse suédoise une longue présentation d'un livre récemment paru (Cristoph Steding, *Das Reich und die Krankheit der europäischen Völker*) et qui devient vite une source pour les discours officiels d'un Walter Frank, directeur du « Reichsinstitut für Geschichte des neuen Deutschland ».[24]

On pourrait essentiellement dégager trois points dignes d'intérêt dans la lecture que Wikander fait au livre de Steding: 1. Le Reich signifie une nation avec une conscience politique forte et vivante, opposé au peuple qui se trouve dans un état d'existence végétative et inconsciente, opposé à l'État, qui est en effet un appareil bureaucratique dépourvu de pouvoir dynamique, c'est un idéal qui apparaît chez différents peuples, mais qui ne se réalise pas vraiment que par une forte volonté et seulement à certaines époques. Pour cela, la politique actuelle d'Hitler est la meilleure. 2. La maladie de la culture européenne, celle qui va conduire à sa morte, s'appelle « Das Prinzip der Abweichung », autrement dit la séparation de la vie spirituelle de l'ordre vital de l'engagement politique, la division des sciences en autant plusieurs disciplines que possible, en vue de l'idéal nommé l'objectivité scientifique (« il y a un pathos assez faible pour faire représenter les sciences et les cultures dans le monde du pouvoir politique »).[25] 3. A cette maladie correspond l'isolement neutre des états germaniques, la Suisse, les Pays Bas et les pays scandinaves. Pour Wikander la pensée de Steding, comme celle de Maurras, est le produit d'une dispute avec les idéologies du 19ᵉ siècle et une confron-

---

[23] Voir d'une part les remerciements inclus par Wikander dans la préface de son livre sur le dieu Vâyu: « Prof. Helmer Smith (Uppsala) und Prof. Dr. Walther Wüst (München) haben mich in liebenswürdigster Weise zu ihren Seminarübungen zugelassen. Ihnen verdanke ich viele wertvolle Hinweise und so manche Aufklärung in exegetischen und wortkundlichen Fragen », Stig Wikander, *Vâyu. Texte und Untersuchungen zur indo-iranischen Religionsgeschichte* (Lund, Lundequistska bokh., 1941), p. XIII–XIV. La chose est certifiée par la source secondaire qui est l'autobiographie de Bernfried Schlerath, où l'auteur cite parfois ce qu'auraient été les paroles de vive voix de Wikander: « Wir haben beide [Davoud Monchi-Zadeh et Wikander, M.T.] zusammen mit Karl Hoffmann in München bei Walther Wüst studiert. Und Sie haben bei Lommel promoviert: Der arische Kriegsgott! », Bernfried Schlerath, *Das geschenkte Leben. Erinnerungen und Briefe* (Dettelbach, J.H. Röll, 2000), p. 198.
[24] Voir Stig Wikander, « En tysk kulturkritiker » [Un critique allemande de la culture], *Sverige-Tyskland* 3 (1939), p. 14–17.
[25] Ibid., p. 15.

tation, voulue pleine de lucidité, avec les problèmes les plus hauts, les plus ardents, de la culture européenne actuelle.[26]

Pourrait-on en conclure que Wikander penche avec cela pour dépasser fermement l'état d'incubation que la vie scientifique semblait lui infliger ?

Une année plus tard, quoique avec des nuances pas trop confiantes quant à l'Allemagne, il milite pour l'engagement politique de la Suède dans la guerre : tenant compte des épisodes de l'histoire suédoise, pas tant la perte de Poltava (1709, les Suédois face aux Russes), que la politique déplorable de Gustav IV Adolf qui aboutit à la perte de la Finlande en faveur des Russes, les Suédois devraient abandonner tout 'flirt avec la neutralité' et se préparer pour être capables de se défendre à tout moment, sans attendre l'aide, d'ailleurs douteuse, de l'Allemagne (d'autant plus que les qualités 'lucifériennes' de Hitler faisaient déjà l'objet des commentaires dans la presse générale suédoise ; ni l'admiration pour Hitler, ni la peur devant lui, dit Wikander, ne pourraient être le fondement d'un jugement, d'une position mature et propre).[27] Un plaidoyer, donc, pas tant pour l'abandon de la neutralité politique par rapport à celle allemande, mais pour la maturité politique suédoise. Avec un tel article, Wikander monte sur la scène publique avec un problème qui deviendra le refrain de ses écrits dans la presse suédoise après la guerre, la défense contre le danger du marxisme :

J'ai dû renoncer déjà à mon lectorat parce que je suis mobilisé et le serai pour longtemps. Peut-être tu sais déjà que nous sommes prêts un peu de tout. Même si je n'étais pas appelé pour le service militaire j'hésiterais à voyager lorsque la situation est assez grave. Ici, dans le pays, le dernier temps, les communistes se sont renforcés en grande mesure sur leurs positions. Tu te rappelles peut-être ce que j'ai dit lors de notre dernière rencontre : la seule constante de la politique suédoise, derrière toutes les fluctuations idéologiques, est l'opposition à la Russie (...) maintenant quand la bolchevisation de l'Europe de l'est est en plein processus et on peut se figurer les conséquences. Au matin, Estonie et Finlande seront des républiques rouges et ensuite (...) cette menace est une réalité ! J'ai écrit même à Wüst, il y a quelques jours, en lui expliquant pourquoi je ne pouvais plus rester pour le lectorat. Je suppose que ce serait aussi impossible déjà pour l'Ahnenerbe d'imprimer quelque chose, d'autant moins

---

[26] Parmi celles-ci, glose Wikander après Steding, le fait qu'après la première guerre mondiale, l'Allemagne a fait appel aux méthodes scientifiques des pays germaniques marginaux et toujours par l'intermédiaire de l'intelligence juive.
[27] Voir Stig Wikander, « 1809 och 1940 », *Folkets Dagblad*, 1 mars 1940.

de faire paraître une nouvelle édition. Peut-être l'Ahnenerbe pourrait collaborer avec une maison d'éditions suédoise.[28]

Il va sans dire que les démarches de Wikander n'ont abouti à rien. En février 1944 il partait vers le front de l'est (Turquie et Grèce) comme membre de la Croix Rouge suédoise, par le chemin de fer, en passant quelques jours à Bucarest où il rencontra d'anciens collaborateurs d'Eliade à la revue d'histoire des religions *Zalmoxis* (1938–1942).[29] Il aurait aimé rencontrer l'auteur du *Yoga. Essai sur les origines de la mystique indienne* (Paris, Paul Geuthner – Bucarest, Imprimeriile Nationale 1936), livre qu'il connaissait assez bien, mais Eliade était encore à Lisbonne, dans le tourbillon des événements qui liaient la Roumanie à la politique allemande.[30] Ils se rencontreront pour la première fois en 1948, à Paris.

Wikander ne connaîtra une position académique stable qu'à partir de 1953 quand il réussit à la candidature pour la chaire de «Langues indo-iraniennes», qu'il occupera jusqu'en 1974, après une longue période (1938–1953) de candidatures, tant à l'Université de Lund (1948/1949, pour le professorat d'histoire des religions et de psychologie de la religion) qu'à celle d'Uppsala (1949/1950, toujours pour la chaire d'histoire des religions et de psychologie de la religion; 1951/1952), échouées successivement.[31]

---

[28] Lettre de Wikander à Höfler, Järnagatan, le 26 septembre 1939 (traduction du suédois). Pour le refrain anti-marxiste chanté par Wikander dans la presse suédoise d'après la guerre, voir M. Timuş, «La bibliographie annotée de Stig Wikander (1908–1983)», *Studia Asiatica* 1 (2000), surtout p. 209–234.

[29] Il s'agit de MM. Ioan Coman (collaborateur à *Zalmoxis*), Alexandru Rosetti (ami d'Eliade, mais surtout d'Alf Lombard; à ce dernier Rosetti écrit juste la même année sur le plaisir d'avoir rencontré Wikander à Bucarest, lettre du 15 mars 1944 (R38), publiée dans N. Mocanu, I. Anghel, H. Hoffmann, éds., *Alexandru Rosetti & Alf Lombard. Corespondenţă (1934–1990)*, vol. I, 1934–1964 (Cluj, Clusium, 2000), p. 76., et l'historien d'origine arménienne H. Dj. Siruni, voir M. Timuş, éd., *C'est toujours l'Orient*, p. 230, n. 4.

[30] Voir Florin Ţurcanu, *Mircea Eliade, le prisonnier de l'histoire* (Paris, La Découverte, 2003) et l'article de Eugen Ciurtin [sur Raffaele Pettazzoni et Mircea Eliade] dans ce volume.

[31] Des renseignements sur les débats qui ont eu lieu autour de ses échecs voir Stig Wikander, *Erinringar med anledning av sakunnigutlåtandena angående lediga professorsämbetet i religionshistoria med religionspsykologi vid Lunds universitet* [Mémoire concernant l'examen de compétence pour le poste vacant de professeur en histoire des religions et psychologie des religions à l'Université de Lund] (Lund, Gleerupska univ.-bokh., 1949), et Carl-Martin Edsman, *Res aut verba? Erinringar med anledning av sakkunnigutlåtandena rörande preceptorsbefattningen i religionshistoria vid Uppsala universitet* (Lund, Lindstedts univ.-bokh., 1949). L'écho d'un échec en 1952, à Uppsala, se trouve dans une lettre que Dumézil adressa

3. Amoindrir ou effacer l'abîme ?

Par rapport à l'histoire des études iraniennes, *Der arische Männerbund* s'inscrit dans la descendance directe de la synthèse plus ample de son maître, *Die Religionen des alten Iran* : Wikander le dit lui-même, de son côté Nyberg le reconnaît d'abord dans le rapport de soutenance de thèse.[32] C'est à Nyberg qu'on doit le paradigme de différentiation entre *Mithra-gemeinde* et *Zarathustragemeinde*, modèles par lesquels il poussait la recherche toujours vers un arrière-plan indo-iranien commun. Le schéma est cohérent avec l'idée de l'orthodoxie réformatrice de la religion de Zarathoustra, dont les textes fondateurs, les *Gâthâs*, contiendraient des allusions, bien plus – des diatribes contre les communautés sauvages, non-pastorales. Si Nyberg est celui qui avait dressait le plan général, il est à noter également que le mot 'Männerbund' n'est jamais présent chez lui : sans le traduire, *mairya* est « ein technischer Ausdruck für die 'soziale Organisation' der Feinde ».[33] Mais, avec ce postulat d'une forme sociale plutôt devinable que démontrable au-delà des textes (d'ailleurs la plupart, sinon tous, à caractère religieux), Nyberg aussi bien que Wikander affrontent le même piège que Dumézil, à la même époque et dans le sillage de l'école sociologique française, Durkheim et Mauss.[34]

à Eliade (le 2 mars 1952, voir Mircea Handoca, *Mircea Eliade şi corespondenţii săi*, vol. I, Bucarest, Minerva, 1993, p. 265–266), en l'avertissant ainsi sur la forme la plus récente du sacrifice dans le monde nordique : le sacrifice académique. Voir également Åke Holmbäck, *Inbjudningskrift till åhörande av de offentliga föreläsningar med vilka Professorn i sanskrit med jämförande indoeuropeisk språkforskning Stig Wikander, Professorn i exegetik Harald Riesenfeld och Professorn i nordiska språk Ivar Modéer tillträda sina ämbeten av Åke Holmbäck Uppsala universitets rektor* (Uppsala, 1953).

[32] Lettre de Wikander à Höfler, Uppsala, le 31 janvier 1938 : « mon livre est un complément à Nyberg ». Pour une vision globale sur la trajectoire scientifique de Stig Wikander, voir M. Timuş, « Stig Wikander », Lindsay Jones (ed.), *Encyclopedia of Religion, Second Edition*, Detroit etc., Thomson Gale, 2005, vol. 14, p. 9734a–9736b.

[33] H.S. Nyberg, *Die Religionen des alten Iran*, 2e éd. (Osnabrück, Otto Zeller, 1966), p. 257. Également : « im Avesta *mairya* das aufgrund von politischen und religiösen Gegensätzen einen üblen Sinn erhalten hat », ibid., p. 332.

[34] Sur le tournant épistémologique chez Dumézil entre 1938 et 1945, voir Daniel Dubuisson, « Contribution a une épistémologie dumézilienne : l'idéologie », *Revue de l'Histoire des Religions* 208-2 (1991), p. 123–140. Si étrange qu'il puisse paraître, le diagnostique qu'Eliade donnait de la popularité de Durkheim, théoricien de l'origine sociale de la religion, est assez éclairant, bien que très discrètement exposé dans une note infrapaginale : « Quant au succès de popularité connu par le chef d'œuvre de Durkheim, il s'explique avant tout par le fait qu'il ait assimilé l'expérience religieuse à un enthousiasme collectif. C'est à dire, en fin de compte, que *Les formes élémentaires* nous aident mieux à comprendre la mentalité occidentale qu'à nous faire une idée

Que toutes les recherches ethnographiques concernant différents types de 'Bund' (Männerbund, Geheimbund) et qui servirent pour matériel d'appui (L. Bittremieux, L. Frobenius, L. Hildebrand, H. Schurtz ou H. Webster) auraient pu être plaquées à l'origine sur une réalité historique, issue au sein de la vie religieuse allemande vers la fin du 19ᵉ siècle et manifestée par la fondation des communautés, déclarées comme «christianisme germanique» opposé au «christianisme judaïque» – telles Deutschbund (1894), Bund für Deutsche Kirche (1921), Deutscher Christenbund (1925), Germanische Glaubensgemeinschaft (1908)[35] – cela échappait peut-être à Wikander. Sur une carte des paradigmes historico-religieux au 19ᵉ siècle, Eliade plaça souvent et généreusement *Der arische Männerbund* au chapitre des «initiations».[36] À vrai dire on ne sait pas encore grande chose sur les rites d'investiture royale iranienne (achéménide ou sassanide), encore moins sur l'initiation au sein de très hypothétiques sociétés guerrières...

La construction de cet ouvrage est en effet très simple, voir même facile : collecter une grande partie des passages avestiques et pehlevis où *mairya*, respectivement *mêrâg*, sont employés et par cette voie, en dépit d'une évidence étymologique, les accorder à un concept dont la structure est déjà donnée, étant en partie fournie par les recherches

---

de la religion primitive. Le succès de Durkheim annonçait ce qui allait se manifester dans la plupart des sociétés occidentales, dix ou quinze ans plus tard. En fait, *Les formes élémentaires* préparaient le lecteur occidental à comprendre les événements de la Première Guerre mondiale, la montée du nationalisme et l'apparition du fascisme et du communisme. Dans une France anticléricale, individualiste et agnostique, Durkheim insista sur la nature religieuse des intérêts et enthousiasmes collectifs. Il préparait ainsi ses lecteurs à comprendre comment l'État, la Classe et la nation peuvent devenir au plus haut point hiérophaniques.» Voir Mircea Eliade, *Les religions australiennes*, trad. de l'anglais par L. Jospin (Paris, Payot, 1972), p. 33, n. 1. Sur les rapports mutuellement féconds entre l'école d'Uppsala (Nyberg, Wikander, Widengren) et l'école française, représentée par Antoine Meillet, voir Jean Kellens, «Sur quelques grandes tendances des études avestiques et mazdéennes au XXᵉ siècle», in Carlo G. Cereti, Mauro Maggi, Elio Provasi, éd., *Religious themes and texts of Pre-islamic and Central Asia. Studies in honour of Professor Gherardo Gnoli on the occasion of his 65th birthday on 6th December 2002* (Wiesbaden, Ludwig Reichert Verlag, 2003), p. 213–222.

[35] Voir Raffaele Pettazzoni, «Il neo-paganismo germanico», in idem, *Italia religiosa* (Bari, Laterza, 1952), p. 115–131. À cela ajouter les données concernant le «christianisme germanique» indiquées par Andreas Åkerlund, «Åke Ohlmarks in the Third Reich. A Scientific Career between Adaption, Cooperation and Ignorance», dans ce volume.

[36] Voir Mircea Eliade, «Les Daces et les loups», *Numen* 6 (1959), repris dans idem, *De Zalmoxis à Gengis-khan. Études comparatives sur les religions et le folklore de la Dacie et de l'Europe orientale* (Paris, Payot, 1970), aussi bien que *Naissances mystiques. Essai sur quelques types d'initiation* (Paris, Gallimard, 1959).

ethnographiques : 'Männerbund' voudrait dire initiation par des rites orgiastiques, comportant des métamorphoses zoomorphes et liés au culte des morts. Mais dès lors, l'avestique *mairya*, le pehlevi *mêrâg*, est déconnecté de son véritable sens contextuel : un jeune homme célibataire,[37] ayant parfois un comportement érotique assez bien marqué, dont l'éventuel caractère négatif se décrirait en termes religieux, comme sont aussi les textes zoroastriens qui en parlent, à savoir que le célibat trop prolongé risque de menacer la continuité de la lignée zoroastrienne et du culte domestique.[38]

La prudence du philologue qu'il est d'abord, avait senti la difficulté : les caractères du 'Männerbund' ne sont pas confirmés d'une manière positive par les textes iraniens.[39]

> Diese Ansichten [Initiationszeremonien der mit Totenkultus und orgiastischen Riten verbundenen Männerbünde, M.T.] skizzenhaft ausgeführt, und wohl darum von Seiten der Philologen nicht positiv verwertet, lassen sich ohne Zweifel mit vergleichenden ethnologischen Material weiter ausführen.[40]

Ce qui n'empêche Wikander de tenter une sorte d'apophatisme, qui ne veut dire autre que cela : l'étymologie devient génératrice des *realia*, faits d'ordre sociologique, et le comparatisme s'y trouve hors de sa tâche, i.e. il devient un rapport censé produire le deuxième terme de la comparaison. Le moindre sens de la comparaison y remonte à une contrainte qui anime une construction purement hypothétique par le vecteur d'une position normative :

> Wenn hinter diesen sprachlichen Tatsachen irgend eine Realität steht, so m u s s es sich um einen Kultus handeln, dessen Hauptcharakteristika die Totenverehrung, die orgiastischen Opferfeste, die Anknüpfung an

---

[37] « young man, husband », David N. MacKenzie, *A Concise Pahlavi Dictionary* (London, Oxford University Press, 1971), p. 55 ; « a (young) man standing in personal association (through family or partnership) with another », H.S. Nyberg, *A Manual of Pahlavi* (Wiesbaden, Harrassowitz, 1974), p. 132 (on remarquera que Nyberg n'a jamais retenu le sens de 'Männerbund').

[38] Voir le commentaire le plus récent chez Jean Kellens, « Langues et religions indo-iraniennes », *Annuaire du Collège de France* 103 (2002–2003), p. 815–845, ici p. 833.

[39] Et il le ressentira encore plus tard, en marge d'un ouvrage tout aussi problématique, *Vâyu* : « Inwieweit man von rein philologischen Materialien zu der Geschichte der ältesten Wanderungen vordringen kann, ist mir noch ganz unklar », lettre de Wikander à Höfler, Lund, le 28 mars 1941 (original en allemand).

[40] Wikander, *Der arische Männerbund*, p. 67.

kriegerische Organisationen, eine positive Einstellung zu den dunklen und dämonischen Mächten des Lebens sind.[41]

C'est dans ce « so m u s s es sich handeln » que se concentre l'enjeu de l'ouvrage de Wikander. Dans cette position normative et, plus encore, dans une passerelle plus ingénieuse, qui elle ne tient non plus : un seul passage de l'*Avesta* (Y. 9. 18) où l'occurrence d'un « *mairyâ* a deux pieds » et du « loup à quatre pieds », collée à la titulature des peuples nomades attestés chez les classiques comme *saka haumavarka*, lui fait interpréter à tort *varka* comme 'loup', lui faisant du même coup conjecturer que le texte sacré iranien témoigne de la pratique de la lycanthropie, donc du 'Männerbund'.[42]

Par cela, toute recherche qui construirait son argument, tenant l'existence du 'Männerbund' iranien pour une certitude acquise par *Der arische Männerbund*, une fois pour toujours par la science nous semble futile. Au-delà de la masse de détails, qui pour la plupart rendent le charme d'une époque ancienne, le livre est altéré dans le principe de l'argumentation.[43] Pour cela, c'est à très juste titre que, assez vite après la fin de la deuxième guerre, Jean de Menasce avait diagnostiqué cette méthode comme purement 'divinatoire'.[44] Mais que le livre sur le 'Männerbund' aryen provoquait le vertige à un savant qui pendant la

---

[41] Ibid., p. 64.

[42] « However we cannot accept Wikander's interpretation of Saka haumavargâ », G. Gnoli, *Zoroaster's Time and Homeland. A Study on the Origins of Mazdeism and Related Problem* (Naples, Istituto Universitario Orientale, 1980), p. 40–41, n. 149.

[43] D'ailleurs c'est ce défaut de méthode qu'Ernst Arbman critiqua (en tant que membre de la commission qui incluait également Harris Birkeland, Uno Harva et Martin P. Nilsson) dans son rapport de la candidature de Wikander pour la chaire d'histoire des religions d'Uppsala, 1947/1948, quand il concoura Carl-Martin Edsman. Ni l'un ni l'autre ne furent élus. Plus tard, s'appuyant surtout sur l'évidence archéologique, Mary Boyce attira l'attention sur le raisonnement déficitaire pratiqué par Wikander : « In general, W[ikander]'s theory of the existence of the p[roto]-I[ndo]-I[ranian] 'Männerbund' remains wholly unsubstantiated, since it rests not on acceptable evidence but on 'analogical and ill-based assumptions' », voir idem, « Priests, cattle and men », *Bulletin of the School of Oriental and African Studies* 50–3 (1987), p. 508–526, ici p. 515.

[44] « M. Wikander était parfaitement armé pour reprendre cette enquête et il faut dire que, dans l'ensemble, son argumentation est convaincante. Même lorsque l'on ne partage pas son avis, *on n'éprouve plus le vertige* que procurait naguère la lecture de son ouvrage sur le 'Männerbund' iranien. C'est que nous sommes ici dans un domaine où les témoignages et les textes sont assez nombreux pour autoriser de raisonnables conjectures et limiter des séductions de la méthode divinatoire », Jean De Menasce, compte-rendu à 'Feuerpriester im Kleinasien und Iran', *Revue de l'Histoire des Religions* 132, juillet-décembre (1946), p. 170–175.

guerre fut contraint à se réfugier en Suisse, cela dit encore plus qu'un défaut de méthode.[45]

Ce qui a suit à *Der arische* Männerbund est également remarquable. Il s'agit du *Vâyu. Texte und Untersuchungen zur indo-iranischen Religionsge-schichte*, conçu comme premier volume d'une série (Questiones Indo-Iranicae) coordonnée avec son ami et collègue Kasten Anders Rönnow (1897–1943). Ce livre, était-il voué à couronner la proposition exposée dans *Der arische Männerbund*, à savoir donner la description de la religion des anciens guerriers indo-iraniens, dévots d'un dieu protéiforme, *Vâyu* (Krieger, Bundesgott, Seelenführer, Todesgott, Hochgott als Schicksalsgott)? Même si le livre débute avec plusieurs paragraphes de type thèse, l'ensemble donne une image différente. Conçu au premier chef comme une suite de commentaires en marge du *Yasht* 15 de l'*Avesta*, structure qui rappelle les travaux d'Eugène Burnouf ou, de nos jours, ceux de Jean Kellens, ce livre est un vrai chantier de tâtonnements.[46] Se situant toujours dans la matrice paradigmatique offerte par Nyberg, Wikander s'efforce d'assimiler d'autres positions théoriques, comme celle de Widengren sur les grandes dieux ('Hochgötter') qui n'a eu part d'une postérité considérable pour l'histoire des religions, ou celle du trifonctionnalisme dumézilien. Si le trifonctionnalisme serait appliquable au système religieux des zoroastriens («Im orthodoxen Zoroastrismus ist Vayu der Gott des zweiten Standes, der Krieger, Ahura Mazda der des ersten, der Priester»),[47] pour la couche antérieure il ne l'est plus («Wenn aber in einem nichtmazdaistischen Kult Vayu der höchste Gott war, so ist zu erwarten dass die Rangordnung der Stände eine andere, als die in zoroastrischer Tradition überall geltende war. Gibt es nun überhaupt Spuren einer solchen sozialen Organisation?»),[48] ce qui finalement donne une assez belle incohérence, car les indo-iraniens aussi bien que les zoroastriens censés avoir été issus postérieurement,

---

[45] Voir Raoul Curiel, «En souvenir de Jean de Menasce (1902–1973)», *Studia Iranica* 7-2 (1978), p. 289–291.

[46] Et par cela ce deuxième livre a des meilleures chances à résister à travers l'histoire des études. Encore plus, l'hypothèse d'un culte dédié à Vâyu assez bien répandu en Asie Centrale (espace indo-iranien) semble être bien confirmée par des travaux récents, voir Frantz Grenet, «The Second of Three Encounters between Zoroastriansim and Hinduism: Plastic Influences in Bactria and Sogdiana», in Gilbert Lazard and D.R. SarDesai, *James Darmesteter Memorial Lectures* (Bombay, Asiatic Soc., 1994), p. 41–57. Mais les données archéologiques centrasiatiques proposent une datation beaucoup plus tardive que l'époque des guerriers de Wikander.

[47] Wikander, *Vâyu*, p. 73.

[48] Ibid., p. 74.

d'après le modèle d'interprétation offert par H.S. Nyberg, sont tous des «indo-européens» dans le système dumézilien, donc tous redevables au trifonctionnalisme. Ce n'est qu'un exemple pour dire qu'à travers ce deuxième livre Wikander se voit de plus en plus découragé à soutenir des positions si fortes comme celles de *Der arische Männerbund*. Encore plus, et c'est la chose remarquable, le mot 'Männerbund' y est très rarement présent.

Autrement dit, c'est le début d'une réorientation. La guerre avait commencé et l'Allemagne se montrait de moins en moins une promesse. Du point de vue académique, du point de vue politique, du point de vue économique.

4. *En guise de conclusion*

Au niveau d'une histoire intellectuelle, c'est autour de cette problématique, de l'engagement direct de l'intellectuel − mener les conclusions de ces recherches particuliers vers des points harmonisés avec un discours général dont les racines n'eurent souvent rien à voir avec les domaines 'neutres' (la philologie, l'archéologie ou l'ethnographie) − que pourrait se jouer l'essentiel du jugement porté sur Wikander. Et il est assez clair qu'il ne resta pas du tout indifférent à ce qui se passait à l'époque et que, plus ou moins conscient, il joua la carte d'une idéologie dont il n'eut pas la capacité d'entrevoir à temps les racines et les conséquences. Ce n'est que plus tard qu'il fera l'apologie du savant qui fut Abraham Hyacinthe Anquetil Duperron (1731−1805), le seul ou parmi les seuls «chevaliers de la science», autrement dit non asservi davantage à autre chose qu'à son propre ardeur de connaissance et faire connaître, ou de l'âge premier de l'orientalisme, celui des frères Schlegel, qu'il croyait non encore contaminé d'aucune idéologie. Mais on était déjà dans les années 1960.[49] Ce «chevalier de la science», était-il encore raisonnable à l'imaginer au 19ᵉ siècle?

Qui plus est, il y a eu incontestablement une prédisposition anti-judaïque, avec des développements assez compliqués d'ailleurs, du maintien de l'intérêt européen pour la religion de Zoroastre, et cela

---

[49] Voir M. Timuş, *C'est toujours l'orient*, p. 218−219 et p. 221.

remonte aux 17ᵉ–18ᵉ siècles.⁵⁰ De cela il ne peut être tenu pour responsable. Mais il travailla en dépit de cette conscience. Le coût de cette
indifférence fut d'abord le livre sur le 'Männerbund', tel qu'il peut être
reçu aujourd'hui, comme témoignage remarquable de la capacité de
fantasmer, et avec cela Wikander resta, à l'époque, un esprit beaucoup
moins ouvert du point de vue épistémologique qu'animé d'un étrange
besoin de confirmation – autant répandue que possible – d'une idéologie
poussée en tant que religion d'une prophétie politique.⁵¹ On peut bien
se rendre compte que Zoroastre, dont la religion avait était précédée
par les guerriers de Wikander, est dans les années d'avant la Deuxième
Guerre bien plus proche de Weimar que du Badakhshan. De surcroît,
l'Asie n'arrive pas à alimenter une plus vaste compréhension, mais peut
devenir le terrain souhaité de quelques implants.⁵² En effet, ce n'est pas
tant le zoroastrisme qui attire Wikander que des formes religieuses et
sociales très anciennes qui auraient précédé ou concurrencé l'orthodoxie
zoroastrienne. En s'orientant vers le passé de l'Asie iranienne, le poids

---

⁵⁰ Pour une bonne introduction à cette perspective on peut lire encore avec profit
Jacques-Duchesne Guillemin, *The Western Response to Zoroaster* (Oxford, Ratanbai Katrak
Lectures, 1958), surtout le premier chapitre «The pre-history of Iranian Studies»,
p. 1–19.

⁵¹ Après la très riche enquête, exhaustif dévoilement d'un rêve européen, celui d'un
Zoroastre métaphysique (voir Michael Stausberg, *Faszination Zarathushtra. Zoroaster und die
Europäische Religionsgeschichte der Frühen Neuzeit* (Berlin-New York, Walter de Gruyter, 1998),
on assiste à nos jours à la fin de la fabuleuse carrière du mot 'aryen': «*Arya* est une
désignation ethnique et qui n'a pas de sens que dans le contexte culturel iranien (...).
Il ne faut ni le reproduire tel quel, ni l'adapter dans l'une ou l'autre langue moderne,
mais le traduire, et la traduction est évidente de *airiia: Arya-* est 'iranien'», voir Jean
Kellens, «Le mot 'aryen' ou le fantasme contre l'analyse», *Bulletin de la Classe des Lettres*,
Académie Royale de Belgique, 6ᵉ série, tome 14, 1–6 (2003), p. 99–112.

⁵² L'affaire du 'Männerbund' iranien semble conduire à pas mal d'autres éclaircis-
sements philologiques ou historiques. En revanche l'ami de Wikander, Monchi-Zadeh
se sent poussé à constituer des formations de type SA en Perse: «Monchi-Zadeh war
im Iran politisch tätig gewesen und hatte dort eine Kampftruppe nach dem Vorbild
der SA aufgebaut. Kurze Zeit war er Minister gewesen, danach einige Jahre in Haft.
Gegen Ende des Krieges wurde er in Berlin schwer verwundet, ihm fehlte ein Teil des
Beckens, und er ging an einer Krücke. Seine politischen Ambitionen hatte er schon
lange abgelegt», Bernfried Schlerath, *Das geschenkte Leben*, p. 207. Pour les rapports
entre l'Allemagne et la Perse dans les années 1918–1945, voir Oliver Bast, «German-
Persian Diplomatic Relations», in Ehsan Yarshater, éd., *Encyclopaedia Iranica* 10–5
(New York: Bibliotheca Persica Press, 2001), p. 506–519 (avec une riche et instructive
bibliographie). Le phénomène est assimilable au cas du culte dédié à Hitler en Inde,
voir Nicholas Goodrick-Clarke, *Hitler's Priestess: Savitri Devi, the Hindu-Aryan Myth, and
Neo-Nazism* (New York/London, New York University Press, 1998), et le compte rendu
de Stefan Arvidsson dans *History of Religions* 40–4 (2001), p. 393–396.

de l'intérêt penche plutôt vers le vocable *passé* que sur celui d'*Asie*.
Fut-ce cela parce que le zoroastrisme, à savoir une religion dont les
traces vivantes étaient (et le sont encore) décelables dans l'Iran et l'Inde
contemporains au troisième Reich, ne représentait que des «misérables
restes des anciens Mages ou Ignicoles»,[53] comme pour certains au 18ᵉ
siècle? L'occultation du phénomène religieux zoroastrien ne peut pas
être scientifiquement une chose coupable. Mais on peut entrevoir par
ce fait comment, une fois de plus, inconsciemment peut-être, *Der arische Männerbund* pouvait être souhaité pour une nouvelle édition, chez
l'Ahnenerbe, à être diffusée dans une Allemagne où les discours officiels
incriminaient l'asiatisme.[54]

Immergé dans des analyses philologiques, Wikander procède, du
point de vue historiographique, à une sorte de suspension de critères.
Mises en parenthèse les conditions qui permettent au savant du 20ᵉ
siècle s'interroger sur des *realia* dont la temporalité échappe à peu près
au discernement historique, le savant pratique un plongeon dans le
passé, légitime en principe, mais dépourvu dans ce cas-là de mesures de
sécurité. A une seule exception. L'immense *ambitus* temporel ouverte
par l'orientation vers des communautés indo-iraniennes (donc passé
asiatiques, dont l'histoire à peine la découvrait-on en Europe) décrit
un abîme qui ne donne le vertige que par l'ancrage dans le *présent*.[55]
Un présent où l'exemplaire du rapport entre politique et religion dans
l'ancien monde iranien (c'est-à-dire non chrétien et de la même famille
que les vieux germains), sa *continuité* à travers les empires parthe et
arsacide, pouvaient bien s'accorder avec l'idéal prêché par le troisième
Reich, celui d'une nouvelle foi allemande façonnant ou façonnée par un
appareil politique et idéologique. Dans ce présent se retrouve également

---

[53] L'abbé Fenel, «Premier mémoire sur ce que les Anciens Payens ont pensé de la
résurrection», *Mémoires de littérature tirés des registres de l'Académie Royale des Inscriptions et
Belles-Lettres*, XIXᵉ tome (1753), p. 323.

[54] En admettant qu'une telle affaire n'aurait pas été pour Wikander qu'une simple
solution financière, la promesse de sauvetage d'une difficulté personnelle, le manque
de lucidité face aux conséquences de ses alliances n'est plus une excuse.

[55] C'est vrai, on ne retrouve pas à travers l'œuvre de Wikander aucune expression
précise de la confiance dans le présent; on ne pourrait que la deviner plutôt, en ajoutant
ses lettres ou ses articles dans la presse. Par cela, sa position est différente de celle de
Hermann Güntert, par exemple, qui déclare dans son *Der Ursprung der Germanen*: «my
book might also assist in defining the goal of German culture in the present: it might
clarify and 'awake', and be perceived as a contribution to a 'spiritual reconstruction'»,
voir Bruce Lincoln, «Hermann Güntert in the 1930s: Heidelberg, Politics, and the
study of Germanic/Indogermanic Religion», dans ce volume.

des conséquences d'un processus qui marqua en Allemagne, dans la deuxième moitié du 19ᵉ siècle les débuts de l'institutionnalisation de l'étude comparée des religions, à laquelle un Paul de Lagarde assignait le rôle d'une nouvelle théologie, non-dogmatique, d'une nouvelle religion.[56] Foi ou étude objective? Cette disjonction, si réelle à nos yeux, ne fut pas claire assez longtemps. Et ceux qui annoncèrent une Mecque des études comparées des religions, restèrent le plus souvent à la recherche de la Kaaba.

Dans le sillage de telles étapes la réflexion à l'intérieur des études iraniennes, des études historico-religieuses incluant les religions iraniennes pré-islamiques, dans l'histoire desquelles l'école d'Uppsala, y compris Wikander, joua un rôle important, devrait devenir plus avertie.[57] Historiquement, méthodologiquement. Et pour nous, c'est là que se trouve l'enjeu le plus significatif de cette enquête.

---

[56] Pour de Lagarde: «L'État devra effectuer un autre changement institutionnel: abolir les facultés de théologie protestante et catholique dans les universités allemandes. La théologie cessera d'être une exégèse du dogme chrétien: elle deviendra l'étude comparée de toutes les religions», voir Fritz Stern, *Politique et désespoir. Les ressentiments contre la modernité dans l'Allemagne préhitlérienne,* traduit de l'américain par Catherine Malamoud (Paris, Armand Colin, 1990), p. 71 (le chapitre «La religion germanique», p. 59–75).

[57] Le processus scientifique contre les «scholarly myths» commence peu à peu, voir par exemple la critique de l'étymologie donnée par Widengren et Wikander au mot 'drafsha' chez Albert De Jong, «*Vexillologica sacra*: searching the cultic banner», in Cereti et al., éd., *Religious themes and texts,* p. 191–202.

Bibliographie

1. *Articles de Stig Wikander publiés dans la presse suédoise avant et pendant la guerre**

Wikander, Stig, «Sven Stolpe i Uppsala» [Sven Stolpe à Uppsala]. *Ergo* 8 (1931), p. 30.

———. «Utlänningarna vid svenska universitet» [Les étrangers dans l'université suédoise]. *Ergo* 10 (1933), p. 108.

———. «Nationalistika prolegomena» [Prolégomènes nationalistes]. *Ergo* 10 (1933), p. 112.

———. «Den nordiska folkfrontens melodi» [Le chant du front populaire nordique]. *Fri Opposition* II–3 (1937), le 22 janvier.

———. «Ett revolutionärt val i Franska akademien. Dreyfusmotståndaren Maurras bland Frankrikes odödliga» [Une élection révolutionnaire. Maurras, opposant de Dreyfus, parmi les immortels de la France], n.n., le 18 juin 1938.

———. «En tysk kulturkritiker» [Un critique allemande de la culture], *Sverige-Tyskland* 3 (1939), p. 14–17.

———. «1809 och 1940», *Folkets Dagblad*, le 1ᵉʳ mars 1940.

———. *Der arische Männerbund. Studien zur indo-iranischen Sprach- und Religionsgeschichte.* Lund, Gleerupska univ. bokh., 1938.

———. *Vâyu. Texte und Untersuchungen zur indo-iranischen Religionsgeschichte.* Lund, Lundequistska bokh., 1941.

2. *Documents d'archive***

a. Correspondance Otto Höfler à Stig Wikander (*Uppsala University Library*, archive de Stig Wikander).
   1. Kiel 29.5.1935, 2. Kiel 7.6.1935, 3. Kiel 25.11.1935, 4. Kiel 27.5.1937, 5. Bayreuth 1.3.1937, 6. Kiel 22.11.1937, 7. Kiel 29.1.1938, 8. Kiel 24.5.1938, 9. Kiel 20.6.1938, 10. München-Grünwald 20.9.1939, 11. Wien (Nachlass Höfler) 20.3.1941, 12. Berlin 24.2.1945, 13. 16.05.?? (l'année n'est pas précisée; cette lettre se trouve dans le *Nachlass* Höfler, Wien).

b. Correspondance Stig Wikander à Otto Höfler (*Österreichische National Bibliothek*, Wien, Nachlass Otto Höfler).
   1. non-datée, 2. Köpenhamn 7.5.1936, 3. Uppsala 25.5.1937, 4. Uppsala 27.11.1937, 5. Uppsala 21.12.1937, 6. Uppsala 31.1.1938, 7. Lund 16.5.1938, 8. Uppsala 23.6.1938, 9. Kuokkala 19.7.1938, 10. Kuokkala 4.8.1938, 11. Kuokkala 11.8.1938, 12. Lund 4.10.1938, 13. Lund 18.10.1938, 15. Södertälje 29.10.1938; 16. München 6.3.1939, 17. Uppsala 13.9.1938, 18. Stockholm 22.9.1939, 19. Södertälje 26.9.1939, 20. Lund 28.3.1941.

---

* Je donne ici la liste des articles cités dans cet article. Il est très probable que la liste soit plus longue. Toujours est-il que ce sont les articles dont Wikander lui-même avait gardé des coupures, de sorte qu'ils ont pu être retrouvés dans l'archive donnée par sa famille à la *Carolina Rediviva*. Sans doute, une enquête exhaustive de toutes ses contributions dans la presse suédoise serait souhaitable.

** Je donne ici la liste entière des lettres qui se retrouvent dans les deux archives (Uppsala et Vienne), en revanche elle n'y est pas employée d'une manière exhaustive.

c. Le rapport de soutenance de la thèse de Wikander, Uppsala, 1938 (*Uppsala University Library*, archive de Stig Wikander).

3. *Littérature secondaire*

Arvidsson, Stefan. *Ariska idoler. Den indoeuropeiska mytologin som ideologi och vetenskap.* Stockholm-Stehag, Brutus Östling Bokförlag Symposion, 2000.
——. Compte-rendu de Nicholas Goodrick-Clarke, 'Hitler's Priestess: Savitri Devi, the Hindu-Aryan Myth, and Neo-Nazism'. New York-London, New York University Press, 1998. *History of Religions* 40-4 (2001), p. 393–396.
——. «Stig Wikander och forskningen om ariska mannaförbund». *Chaos* 38 (2002), p. 55–68.
Boyce, Mary. «Priests, cattle and men». *Bulletin of the School of Oriental and African Studies* 50-3 (1987), p. 508–526.
Capps, Walter H. «Geo Widengren on syncretism: On parsing Uppsala methodological tendencies». *Numen* 20-3 (1973), p. 163–185.
Curiel, Raoul. «En souvenir de Jean de Menasce (1902–1973)». *Studia Iranica* 7-2 (1978), p. 289–291.
Dubuisson, Daniel. «Contribution à une épistémologie dumézilienne: l'idéologie». *Revue de l'Histoire des Religions* 208-2 (1991), p. 123–140.
Dumézil, Georges. «Science et politique. Réponse à Carlo Ginzburg». *Annales. Économies. Sociétés. Civilisations*, 40-5, septembre-octobre (1985), p. 985–989.
Dürkop, Martina. «'...er wird sehen, dass das Archiv wirklich ein Geschäft ist, wenn es richtig behandelt wird...'. Wissenschaftlicher und wirtschaftlicher Existenzkampf des ARW 1919–1939». *Archiv für Religionsgeschichte* 1-1 (1999), p. 107–128.
Edsman, Carl-Martin. *Res aut verba? Erinringar med anledning av sakkunnigutlåtandena rörande preceptorsbefattningen i religionshistoria vid Uppsala universitet.* Lund, Lindstedts univ.-bokh., 1949.
——. «Ein halbes Jahrhundert Uppsala-Schule». In Michael Stausberg, éd., *Kontinuität und Brüche in der Religionsgeschichte. Festschrift für Anders Hultgård zu seinem 65. Geburtstag am 23.12.2001* (Ergänzungsbände zum Reallexikon der Germanischen Altertumskunde 31). Walter de Gruyter, 2001, p. 194–209.
Eliade, Mircea. *Naissances mystiques. Essai sur quelques types d'initiation.* Paris, Gallimard, 1959.
——. *De Zalmoxis à Gengis-khan. Études comparatives sur les religions et le folklore de la Dacie et de l'Europe orientale.* Paris, Payot, 1970.
——. *Les religions australiennes*, trad. de l'anglais par L. Jospin. Paris, Payot, 1972.
Engelhard, Isrun. «Tibetan Triangle. German, Tibetan and British Relations in the Context of Ernst Schäfer's Expedition, 1938–1939», *Asiatische Studien/Études Asiatiques* 58-1 (2004), p. 57–113.
Ginzburg, Carlo. «Mythologie germanique et nazisme». *Annales. Économies. Sociétés. Civilisations* 40-4 (1985), p. 695–715.
Gnoli, Gherardo. *Zoroaster's Time and Homeland. A Study on the Origins of Mazdeism and Related Problems.* Naples, Istituto Universitario Orientale, 1980.
Grenet, Frantz. «The Second of Three Encounters between Zoroastriansim and Hinduism: Plastic Influences in Bactria and Sogdiana». In Gilbert Lazard et D.R. Sar-Desai, *James Darmesteter Memorial Lectures.* Bombay, Asiatic Society, 1994, p. 41–57.
Guillemin, Jacques-Duchesne. *The Western Response to Zoroaster.* Oxford, Ratanbai Katrak Lectures, 1958.
Handoca, Mircea. *Mircea Eliade şi corespondenţii săi*, vol. I. Bucarest, Minerva, 1993.
De Jong, Albert. «*Vexillologica sacra*: searching the cultic banner». In Carlo G. Cereti, Mauro Maggi, Elio Provasi, éds., *Religious themes and texts of Pre-islamic and Central Asia. Studies in honour of Professor Gherardo Gnoli on the occasion of his 65th birthday on 6th December 2002.* Wiesbaden, Ludwig Reichert Verlag, 2003, p. 191–202.

Junginger, Horst. *Von der philologischen zur völkischen Religionswissenschaft. Das Fach Religionswissenschaft an der Universität Tübingen von der Mitte des 19 Jahrhunderts bis zum Ende des Dritten Reiches.* Stuttgart, Franz Steiner Verlag, 1999.

Kellens, Jean. «Le mot 'aryen' ou le fantasme contre l'analyse». *Bulletin de la Classe des Lettres*, Académie Royale de Belgique, 6ᵉ série, tome 14, 1–6, 2003, p. 99–112.

——. «Langues et religions indo-iraniennes». *Annuaire du Collège de France* 103 (2002–2003), p. 815–845.

——. «Sur quelques grandes tendances des études avestiques et mazdéennes au XXᵉ siècle». In Carlo G. Cereti, Mauro Maggi, Elio Provasi, éd., *Religious themes and texts of Pre-islamic and Central Asia. Studies in honour of Professor Gherardo Gnoli on the occasion of his 65th birthday on 6th December 2002.* Wiesbaden, Ludwig Reichert Verlag, 2003, p. 213–222.

Lincoln, Bruce. «Rewriting the German War God: Georges Dumézil, Politics and Scholarship in the Late 1930s». *History of Religions* 37–3 (1998), p. 187–208 (repris dans idem, *Theorizing Myth*, p. 121–137).

——. *Theorizing Myth. Narrative, Ideology, and Scholarship.* Chicago/London, Chicago University Press, 1999.

De Menasce, Jean. Compte-rendu de 'Feuerpriester im Kleinasien und Iran'. *Revue de l'Histoire des Religions* 132, juillet-décembre (1946), p. 170–175.

Nyberg, Henrik Samuel. *Die Religionen des alten Iran*, 2ᵉ éd. Osnabrück, Otto Zeller, 1966.

Pettazzoni, Raffaele. «Il neo-paganismo germanico» [1945]. In idem, *Italia religiosa.* Bari, Laterza, 1952, p. 115–131.

Schlerath, Bernfried. *Das geschenkte Leben. Erinnerungen und Briefe.* Dettelbach, J.H. Röll, 2000.

Söderblom, Nathan. *La vie future d'après le mazdéisme.* Paris, Leroux, 1901.

Stausberg, Michael. *Faszination Zarathushtra. Zoroaster und die Europäische Religionsgeschichte der Frühen Neuzeit*, 2 vols. Berlin-New York, Walter de Gruyter, 1998.

Stern, Fritz. *Politique et désespoir. Les ressentiments contre la modernité dans l'Allemagne préhitlérienne*, traduit de l'américain par Catherine Malamoud. Paris, Armand Colin, 1990.

Timuş, Mihaela. «La bibliographie annotée de Stig Wikander (1908–1983)». *Studia Asiatica* 1–1/2 (2000), p. 209–234.

—— et Eugen Ciurtin. «The Unpublished Correspondence between Mircea Eliade and Stig Wikander (1948–1977) – 2nd Part». *Archaeus* 4–4 (2000), p. 179–211.

——. «Le corps eschatologique (*tan ī pasēn*) d'après la théologie zoroastrienne». In Eugen Ciurtin, éd., *Du corps humain, au carrefour de plusieurs savoirs en Inde. Mélanges offerts à Arion Roşu pas ses collègues et ses amis à l'occasion de son 80e anniversaire* (= Studia Asiatica 4.2003–5.2004), sous la direction de O. Botto, C. Caillat, P. Delaveau, P.-S. Filliozat, S. Lienhard, G.J. Meulenbeld et P.V. Sharma. Bucarest, Centre d'histoire des religions – Paris, De Boccard, 2004, p. 779–808.

—— éd. roum. *Întotdeauna Orientul. Corespondenţa Mircea Eliade – Stig Wikander (1948–1977)* [C'est toujours l'Orient. Correspondance Eliade-Wikander]. Préface par Giovanni Casadio, postface par Frantz Grenet. Iasi-Bucarest, Polirom, 2005.

——. «Stig Wikander», Lindsay Jones (ed.), *Encyclopedia of Religion, Second Edition*, Detroit etc., Thomson Gale, 2005, vol. 14, p. 9734a–9736b.

Ţurcanu, Florin. *Mircea Eliade, le prisonnier de l'histoire.* Paris, La Découverte, 2003.

BERNHARD KUMMER (1897–1962)

THE STUDY OF RELIGIONS BETWEEN RELIGIOUS DEVOTION FOR THE ANCIENT GERMANS, POLITICAL AGITATION, AND ACADEMIC HABITUS[1]

Fritz Heinrich

1. *Introduction*

Looking at Bernhard Kummer's writings, one could easily get the impression that the impact of National Socialist ideology could severely damage a thinking subject and its expressions. In other, more moderate words: Ideological tendencies have undermined a reasoning which otherwise could have introduced into contemporary academic discussions some new, fruitful and thought-provoking perspectives with regard to the analysis and description of the old German culture and religion. It seems at least questionable whether Kummer's publications should be a matter for serious academic discussion or not. Too much ideological propaganda or, what Walter Baetke calls "wishful thinking," has slipped into the texts and has rendered them useless outside a specific mental context, which is influenced by National Socialism or a comparable fascist ideology.[2]

But it would be too easy to stop here and put the writings of Bernhard Kummer aside. They are in different ways both dangerous and instructive: Kummer's work gives insights into the persuasive function of ideology, in particular how critical questions are eliminated and how one's thinking is obstructed by implicit convictions which are taken for granted without reflection. The suggestive style of Kummer's writings exerts a convincing sway over the author as well as his readers. The power of persuasion is increased by the authority which Kummer

[1] For their efforts to improve the English of the presented article I would like to sincerely thank Vanessa Cisz and the always patient Chris Collins (his son Luis predominantly had the proper reactions with regard to the presented papers).
[2] Cf. Walter Baetke, *Art und Glaube der Germanen* (Hamburg: Hanseatische Verlagsanstalt, 1934), p. 6f. Baetke's book ran into three editions until 1938.

claimed by emphasizing his affiliation to the academic world.[3] The
short time he spent at the University of Jena as professor of German
and Nordic language and literature gave his publications a lasting
scholarly aura despite his dismissal after the end of the Hitler regime.
Thus in contemporary neo-Nazi circles, Kummer's writings are still
used as academic legitimation for their crude opinions.[4] With the
superficial academic framework of his texts Kummer generates the
appearance of scientifically proven truth and capitalizes on the social
appreciation of scholarship.[5] Applying Pierre Bourdieu's description
of the pre-1968 French university field to the circumstances under
which Kummer's career proceeded, the style of his argumentation
could be characterized as "a rhetoric of scientificity" to impress the
text's scholarly quality upon the readers.[6] Kummer's academic habit
could support the publisher's efforts to sell his books, and the strategy
paid off: Kummer was recommended in promotional articles as one
of the most capable scholars writing about the religion and culture
of the Germans. Kummer was praised in particular for his ability to

---

[3] On the front pages of his books Kummer frequently added the "Dr." to his name,
cf. Dr. Bernhard Kummer, *Mission als Sittenwechsel. Mit einer Antwort an Prof. D Rückert: 'Die
kulturelle und nationale Bedeutung der Missionierung Germaniens für das deutsche Volk'* (Leipzig:
Adolf Klein Verlag, 1933) and idem, *Herd und Altar. Wandlungen altnordischer Sittlichkeit im
Glaubenswechsel*, vol. 1: *Persönlichkeit und Gemeinschaft* (Leipzig: Adolf Klein Verlag, 1934),
and vol. 2: *Der Machtkampf zwischen Volk, König und Kirche im alten Norden* (Leipzig: Adolf
Klein Verlag, 1939). Publishing under addition of the academic title, besides marketing
reasons, was in particular not unusual in the case of authors with strong ideological
tendencies. It seems that these writers were aware of their scholarly deficiencies and
therefore tried to compensate this by pointing out their academic qualification.
[4] The new neo-right radical Jürgen Rieger called, for instance, Kummer's *Midgards
Untergang* a publication without any voelkish bias (www.asatru.de/lp_gewalt.htm), likewise
a Dr. Herbert Lenz in the *Nordische Zeitung* edited by Rieger. Lenz refers to Kummer's
article "Die Wikinger: Räuber oder Helden?," in Bernhard Kummer et al., eds., *Der
nordische Mensch der Wikingerzeit* (Leipzig: Adolf Klein Verlag, 1935), pp. 3–24 in order
to demonstrate the fortitude and ethical perfection of the Old Vikings. See also www.
nordzeit.de/wikzug.htm.
[5] This formulation picks up considerations of Pierre Bourdieu and relates them to
Kummer, cf. Pierre Bourdieu, *Homo Academicus*, trans. Peter Collier (Stanford/California:
Stanford University Press, 1988), p. 16 and p. 28 (German ed. trans. by Bernd Schwibs,
Frankfurt a.M.: Suhrkamp, 1992, p. 52 and p. 71).
[6] Cf. Bourdieu, *Homo Academicus*, p. 28 (German translation, p. 70). Despite some
evident differences between the academic situation in Germany under the impact of
National Socialism and the circumstances at French universities before 1968, it seems
possible and fruitful to use Bourdieu's analysis to explain the conditions in which
Kummer's writing and acting unfolded.

combine objective sobriety and to control his passion while struggling for the mental renewal of the nation.[7]

Yet dealing with Kummer's writings is instructive in another sense. Looking at an extreme mentality makes it easier to grasp the problems and limitations of methodical improper ways of scholarly reasoning compared with more or less moderate cases. And finally, the examination of Kummer's texts could enrich the sustaining discussion among historians and political scientists whether the character of National Socialism should be comprehended as 1) totalitarianism, 2) fascism, or 3) as a singular and incomparable phenomenon unable to be subsumed under usual terms. Kummer's attitude towards National Socialism could exemplify all three approaches. Similar to a totalitarian ideology, his thoughts depended on a set of ideas represented by the NSDAP.[8] Kummer was an ardent party follower supporting its success with his writings and convictions which could at the very least be described as quasi-religious. On the other hand, his views were closer to a fascist ideology, more similar to the Italian prototype than to the state ideology of the Soviet Union.[9] With both the fascist state doctrine and the socialist ideology in the period of Stalinism, Kummer shared the radical attitude against differing opinions targeted in order to destruct the antagonist as was the case during his conflict with the Viennese scholar of German language and literature Otto Höfler.[10] Although racist and

---

[7] Cf. e.g. the publisher's advertisement of Bernhard Kummer, *Nordisches Lebensgefühl. Einführung in das altisländische Schrifttum* (Leipzig: Adolf Klein Verlag, 1935), likewise a quotation of the *Nationalsozialistische Landpost* edited by Richard Walter Darré on the back of the front page of the book.

[8] For totalitarian ideologies, see Karl-Dietrich Bracher, *Die totalitäre Erfahrung* (München-Zürich: Piper, 1987), pp. 23–25, Wolfgang Wippermann, *Totalitarismustheorien. Die Entwicklung der Diskussion von den Anfängen bis heute* (Darmstadt: Primus Verlag, 1997), Klaus-Dietmar Henke, "Achsen des Augenmerks in der historischen Totalitarismusforschung," in Klaus-Dietmar Henke, ed., *Totalitarismus. Sechs Vorträge über Gehalt und Reichweite eines klassischen Konzepts der Diktaturforschung* (Dresden: Hannah-Arendt-Institut für Totalitarismusforschung e.V., 1999), pp. 9–18, Ludolf Herbst, "Das nationalsozialistische Herrschaftssystem als Vergleichsgegenstand und Ansatz der Totalitarismustheorien," ibid., pp. 19–26.

[9] For theories on fascism, see Werner Loh and Wolfgang Wippermann, eds., *Faschismus kontrovers* (Stuttgart: Lucius und Lucius Verlag, 2003), Wolfgang Wippermann, *Faschismustheorien. Zur Entwicklung der Diskussion von den Anfängen bis heute*, 7th ed. (Darmstadt: Primus Verlag, 1997).

[10] For the inherent affinity of totalitarian systems with violence, cf. Philippe Burrin, "Totalitarismus und Gewalt: Die Physiognomie des Nazismus," in K.-D. Henke, ed., *Totalitarismus*, pp. 27–37. See also Philip Morgan, *Fascism in Europe, 1919–1945* (London-New York: Routledge, 2003), p. 17f. and p. 64.

antisemitic aspects are very much visible in Kummer's publications, they are not that pivotal for his reasoning as it might be expected if his ideological convictions were to be classified as fascistic. Though racist ideas played an important role in his argumentation, they were subordinated to his conception of an idealized Nordic society and religion.[11] Kummer used blood and race as central hermeneutical categories of a new historiography. These terms became important in particular in texts published during the procedure of his appointment at the Jena University. Yet his reasoning subordinated these categories to the hypothesis of an advanced Germanic culture ("Hochkultur"), which, as Kummer claimed, had been destroyed through Christian influence.[12] Thus, true Nordic culture and religion could only be recognized indirectly by historic research revealing the truth behind the outward historic events.[13] Finally, some ideas surface in Kummer's publications which can be compared with contemporary ideological movements in Italy, Spain, Romania or other European countries.[14] Such ideas have taken shape in, for example, the challenge of the belief in progress, the refusal of materialistic rationality, and the disdain of urban culture and democracy. It is also important to mention that 'social Darwinism' and a concept of race – a mixture of biological and cultural presumptions – permeated his writings. Yet the framework of Kummer's thoughts remains within the specific German Protestant history of ideas, a romantic 19th century transfiguration of the treasure of fairy tales, myths, legends and sagas. The attempt to comprehend National Socialism as a kind of political religion seems to fail with regard to Kummer.[15] His beliefs

---

[11] Cf. Annett Hamann, "'Männer der kämpfenden Wissenschaft': Die 1945 geschlossenen Institute der Universität Jena," in Uwe Hoßfeld et al., eds., *'Kämpferische Wissenschaft'. Studien zur Universität Jena im Nationalsozialismus* (Köln et al.: Böhlau Verlag, 2003), pp. 202–234, here p. 208.

[12] Cf. Kummer, *Herd und Altar*, vol. 2, pp. 131–154 and pp. 155–181, where the reasoning ends in an annotation about the bankruptcy of the Christian civilization and a call for racial renewal ("Bankerott der christlichen Zivilisation und die Wiederbesinnung auf das Heiligtum der Rasse in letzter Stunde"), ibid., p. 181.

[13] Ibid., pp. 8–29.

[14] Cf. here Morgan, *Fascism*, p. 1. Morgan gives an interesting definition of fascism: "Fascist movements were radical hypernationalist cross-class movements with a distinctive militarist organization and activist political style." Ibid., p. 13. In particular, "radical hypernationalism" and "activist political style" are aspects of this definition which can also be verified in Kummer's interpretations.

[15] The theory of 'secular religion' or 'political religion' was predominantly ushered in by Erich/Eric Voegelin and Jacob L. Talmon. Thereby totalitarian ideologies are understood as compensation for the lost religious paradigms in modern secular societies.

had crossed the border between quasi-religious and religious ideas and were moving towards a kind of neo-German religiosity.

The ideological character of Kummer's reasoning was not always obvious, neither for Kummer nor for his readers. On the contrary, at first sight, his scholarly writings seem to result from a profound and extensive knowledge of ancient Germanic sources and their history.[16] Only a careful and detailed examination will be able to verify the subjective and arbitrary interpretation of the texts and the historical events.

2. Defending Ancient German Culture and Religion against its Supposed Degradation by Christianity

Like other contemporary authors, Kummer drew a picture of the ancient Germans which had more to do with his anti-modern and culture-pessimistic worldview than with the scantily preserved historical sources. Walter Baetke has demonstrated this unremittingly. In Art und Glaube der Germanen, published in 1934, Baetke refuted Herman Wirth's untenable hypothesis regarding the so-called Ura-Linda-Chronik and presented a methodical deconstruction of Bernhard Kummer's book Midgards Untergang.[17] Kummer's doctoral thesis was published six years before the rise of the NS regime in the "Veröffentlichungen des Forschungsinstituts für Vergleichende Religionsgeschichte an der Universität Leipzig," edited by Hans Haas, who also was Kummer's supervisor.[18] In my book Die deutsche Religionswissenschaft und der Nationalsozialismus I have extended Baetke's analysis scrutinizing the way Kummer treated the old Germanic sources from a position critical of modern historical and

---

A qualified summary of these theories and their roots is given by Wippermann, Totalitarismustheorien, pp. 21–24, pp. 107–109, p. 115, and the literature given on p. 122.

[16] Cf. the reviews of the "Thule"-collection of Nordic sources in Kummer, Nordisches Lebensgefühl, pp. 25–64. Another example is chapter 6 of Kummer's Herd und Altar, vol. 2, pp. 98–130: "Das altnordische Schrifttum." Here Kummer offered a superficial critical discussion of the secondary literature and the historic sources, which he profiled with hardly identifiable valuations. But these valuations can be deciphered by the summary at the end of the chapter where he revealed his opinion with regard to the negative influence of Christianity on the Nordic culture.

[17] Cf. W. Baetke, Art und Glaube der Germanen, pp. 11–17 (concerning Wirth) and pp. 27–56 (concerning Kummer).

[18] Bernhard Kummer, Midgards Untergang. Germanischer Kult und Glaube in den letzten heidnischen Jahrhunderten (Veröffentlichungen des Forschungsinstituts für Vergleichende Religionsgeschichte an der Universität Leipzig II-7) (Leipzig: Pfeiffer 1927, 2nd ed. 1935, 3rd enl. ed. 1937).

philological research while projecting the inadequacies of the industrialized society and the inadequacies of contemporary scholarship onto Christianization.[19] Whereas *Midgards Untergang* mainly focused on the hermeneutical question of how the old culture of the Germans could be recognized in the preserved sources, Kummer's interests became more practical in his later publications. In a small book with the meaningful title *Mission als Sittenwechsel* Kummer looked at the consequences he thought to be the result of a collective mental injury Germans sustained with their conversion to Christianity and the loss of their culture. *Der Machtkampf zwischen Volk, König und Kirche im alten Norden*, published in 1939, provides a catalog of what Kummer subsumed under the nuisances of contemporary society. Hardships included usury, homelessness, mass culture, people's indignity, treason against blood and army, cowardice, the disregard of the ancestral heritage, a lacking resistance against the enticements of the day, corruption, disrespect of national interests, a moral of adultery, poverty among children, degeneration of motherly love, and intellectual disbelief.[20]

In the preface to the book series *Reden und Aufsätze zum nordischen Gedanken* Kummer explained the intentions he connected with writing and editing these texts. Though he did nothing else than collecting some interesting texts, he actually wanted to strengthen Nordic and German self-consciousness.[21] The keywords here are "deutsche Selbsterkenntnis" (German self-recognition) and "Befreiung" (liberation). With regard to the further works published in this series, it is no exaggeration to read such concepts as part of a therapeutic program to cure the Germans from the damage caused by the loss of their ancestral values and customs. Combining a 'description' of collective historic experiences with a sort of psychological therapy, Kummer's approach was influenced by Felix Krueger (1874–1948), a psychologist at the University of Leipzig and reviver of the so-called "Leipziger Schule." Krueger focused his

---

[19] Cf. Fritz Heinrich, *Die deutsche Religionswissenschaft und der Nationalsozialismus. Eine ideologiekritische und wissenschaftsgeschichtliche Untersuchung* (Petersberg: Michael Imhof Verlag, 2002), pp. 186–200; for a summary of Baetke's analysis, see p. 59 and p. 279f.

[20] Kummer, *Herd und Altar*, vol. 2, p. 22. The tendentiousness of the German wording is striking and hardly translatable: "also etwa des Bodenwuchers, der Heimatlosigkeit und Vermassung, der Würdelosigkeit des Volkes, des Blutsverrats, des Waffenverrats, der Feigheit, des Ahnenvergessens, der Verführbarkeit, Korruption, Zwietracht, des internationalen Volksvergessens, der Ehebruchsmoral und Kinderarmut, Mütter-Entartung und Elternlieblosigkeit, der Kirchendialektik und intellektuellen Gottlosigkeit."

[21] Cf. Kummer, *Mission als Sittenwechsel*, p. 3.

psychology on the feeling of experience which he declared to be the origin of all psychological phenomena. Krueger gave the "Deutsche Gesellschaft für Psychologie" a stronger ideological profile.[22] Kummer explicitly referred to Krueger's "Ganzheitspsychologie" when pointing to the importance cohesion and inner commitment had among the Nordic population.[23]

The title *Mission als Sittenwechsel* sounds harmless, almost trivial, but in combination with Kummer's hypothesis of an enduring collective mental disease caused by the conversion of the old Germans to Christianity, it acquired a strong ideological meaning. Later, at the end of the 1930s, Kummer explained the term "Sittenwechsel" more widely as embracing all aspects of cultural, religious and mental change which he described in typical tendentious phrases.[24] Originally *Mission als Sittenwechsel* was a lecture given at the "Nordisch-religiöse Arbeitsgemeinschaft Berlin" on November 26, 1932. Already at the beginning of the lecture, the presence of the hypothesis of a collective mental disease in the text is obvious. Kummer deliberately admitted that he was looking back from the misery of the time to the change of customs and beliefs following the Christian mission of the Germans.[25] He continued that the spiritual needs of the Germans had driven them into the arms of false "businessmen of the soul" with which he identified the Catholic church *ultra montes*.[26] A little later Kummer explicitly appealed to all who want to minister to the Germans' ill soul ("an alle, die Ärzte sein wollen an unserer kranken Volksseele") speaking of their responsibility for the national spiritual welfare of the nation ("Auftrag zur völkischen

---

[22] Cf. Werner Traxel, "Zur Geschichte der Deutschen Gesellschaft für Psychologie im so genannten Dritten Reich," *Psychologische Rundschau* 55–7 (2004), pp. 21–32. Krueger was a disciple of Wilhelm Wundt, since 1917 also his successor in Leipzig. Because of his strong national attitude Krueger became a supporter of Hitler's takeover in 1933. See http://www.catalogus-professorum-halensis.de/kruegerfelix.html and Ulfried Geuter, *Die Professionalisierung der deutschen Psychologie im Nationalsozialismus* (Frankfurt a.M.: Suhrkamp, 1988), p. 102f.

[23] Cf. Kummer, *Herd und Altar*, vol. 1, p. 168, n. 19.

[24] Cf. Kummer, *Herd und Altar*, vol. 2, p. 33.

[25] Kummer, *Mission als Sittenwechsel*, p. 5.

[26] "Und je mehr wir uns dieser Bekehrung kritisch annehmen, um so mehr wächst die Sorge aller derer, die ihr Herz den großen Seelengeschäftemachern und Geschichts-fälschern ultra montes in Zahlung gegeben haben. Verteidiger des Bonifatius wachsen wie Pilze aus der Erde, denn man spürt einen wunden Punkt in dem Gefüge unserer christlichen Kulturgeschichte, und man ist selten unbefangen genug, der Wahrheit auch auf Kosten eigener Konfessionssicherheit die Ehre zu geben." Ibid., p. 5.

Seelsorge").[27] In Kummer's eyes, the Germans had lost their history when they converted to Christianity. The "Palestine-psychosis" had then redirected all views from their own history to a foreign one, placing the responsibility for their fate in the hands of a foreign people.[28] Kummer used the history of religions to describe the collective disease of the German soul as a consequence of Christian missionary work. He interpreted the change from a tribal to a universal religion within his ideological framework: The borders of the blood were crossed, the consciousness of the German personality was destroyed, the ancestral heritage was lost and the former gods were turned into devils. Instead, a foreign religion from Palestine entered and brought the Germans alien concepts such as the original sin ("Erbsünde"), a fear of the devil, and the need for salvation.[29] Kummer similarly utilized the history of religions (though with a more racist terminology) to paint the process of Christianization as change from a religion of "related blood" to a world religion illegitimately trespassing voelkish border lines.[30]

3. *The Fanatic Style of Kummer's Reasoning*

The character of Kummer's reasoning can be described as a perlocutionary speech act which is dominated by performative effects to convince the reader, whereas the propositional contents are subordinated. The intended effects were, for the most part, implied and went beyond the issues he was dealing with. These implicit intentions dominated his arguments more intensely than the historic issues he was working on and the scientific methods he was using. Thus the reasoning became an almost irresolvable mixture of matters and interests. At least three intentions can be distinguished: first, being accepted by the scholarly world, second, being recognized as a protagonist of National Socialism in the way Kummer thought it was its real meaning, and third, being perceived as someone who is preaching for the renaissance of ancient pre-Christian German culture and religion. The three aims influenced one another:

---

[27] Ibid., p. 7 and p. 9.
[28] "Die Palästinapsychose richtete alle Blicke von der heimischen Geschichte in die fremde, und gab das Schicksal der Völker fremden Schicksalsmachern in die Hand." Ibid., p. 10.
[29] Ibid., p. 11.
[30] Cf. Kummer, *Herd und Altar*, vol. 2, p. 34.

the struggle for acceptance in the academic world was fought with an ideological and religious impetus, the endeavor to be acknowledged as a leading National Socialist intellectual was undertaken by pointing to his academic and religious seriousness; his religious and cultural intentions were based on scholarly and ideological convictions.

Kummer argued by taking a possible position which inherently was not wrong in general and at least might have been worthy of discussion. He read the medieval sources and their bias in favor of the church critically but interpreted them uncritically on the basis of his positive image of the pre-Christian culture in Northern Europe.[31] Charlemagne, for instance, was portrayed quite negatively as the German emperor under whom Christianity in its Roman-Catholic shape destroyed the Nordic religion and culture. In Kummer's view, Charlemagne's governance was a pivotal step down the wrong path ("Irrweg") of the Franks, pursued by his predecessors and continued by his successors on the throne, a meander which ultimately led to Henry IV's Walk to Canossa.[32] In his mind, Canossa represented the definitive capitulation of mislead German emperors to the Roman Catholic Church.

The issues Kummer was dealing with were framed by a romantic, partially pathetic language, with quotations of German literature like Goethe's Faust,[33] Conrad Ferdinand Meyer, Friedrich Hölderlin, or a "Lübecker Schwerttanzspiel".[34] In his argument, Kummer frequently alluded to voelkish commonplaces such as a general aversion to pure scholarship without reference to life and its needs as well as a strong disrespect of the Roman Catholic Church. Although Kummer demonstrated a distance to the exaggerations of historical interpretation called "Historismus," for instance when he emphasized that not only men made history but also women, he remained within the tradition of historism in focusing on the great persons in history.[35] Kummer repeatedly referred to Leopold von Ranke's world history which he partially elevated into the rank of a historic source.[36] Likewise,

---

[31] Cf. ibid., pp. 64–82.
[32] Ibid., pp. 43–63, for Charlemagne, see pp. 51–56.
[33] See B. Kummer, *Anfang und Ende des faustischen Jahrtausends* (Reden und Aufsätze zum nordischen Gedanken 17) (Leipzig: Adolf Klein Verlag, 1934).
[34] Kummer, *Herd und Altar*, vol. 2, p. 59 and p. 130 (Conrad Ferdinand Meyer), vol. 1, p. 96 (Friedrich Hölderlin), and vol. 2, p. 54 (Lübecker Schwerttanzspiel).
[35] Cf. Kummer, *Herd und Altar*, vol. 1, pp. 6–68 ("Die große Gestalt"), especially p. 6.
[36] Cf. Kummer, *Herd und Altar*, vol. 2, p. 401f.

Kummer's critique of his own perspective remained superficial when he conceded that drawing conclusions from the present into the past has to be made very carefully, and simply noticed that social nuisances named with contemporary catch phrases had existed also in the times of the old Nordic culture.[37]

The character of Kummer's reasoning in which religious, ideological and scientific aspects are mixed together in a propagandistic manner is exemplified by his introduction into the book *Persönlichkeit und Gemeinschaft* where he explained his method. He began by citing Goethe's Faust in order to use its metaphorical wording: Lynkäus, the watchman of a tower, looks from his position from above onto the world below his feet. He greets the world with 'lucky eyes' and says: "Born to see, made to look at." Kummer then summarizes the further action in Goethe's play rather suggestively: Faust becomes a man who had left behind his blind knowledge based only on books ("blinde Bücherweisheit") because he had been blinded by a female personification of worry. Now Faust was able to see life in a new inward light.[38] Kummer used and extended this image as a metaphor to describe the situation of German science since 1933, identifying Lynkäus with research in general. He equated the new scientific method with Faust's path and praised it in religious terms as an act of salvation for future generations ("erlösende Tat für kommende Geschlechter") or as a new piety of looking at the world ("neue Frömmigkeit des Schauens").[39] Literary allusions and tendentious pictorial phrases were aimed at the emotions of the reader and created a mood between darkness and depression on the one side and brightness and optimism on the other, not only in the present case.[40] Kummer avowed himself to a manner of scholarliness, which programmatically used a pictorial style, and was directed to the demands of contemporary life.[41]

---

[37] Ibid., p. 27f.
[38] Kummer, *Herd und Altar*, vol. 1, p. 3: "'Zum Sehen geboren, zum Schauen bestellt', grüßt Lynkäus der Türmer mit 'glücklichen Augen' die Welt zu seinen Füßen." And: "Aber unten im Palast tritt die Sorge ins Gemach zu Faust und blendet ihn. Und jetzt erst sieht der Mann, der seiner blinden Bücherweisheit entflohen und 'durch die Welt gerannt' ist, in einem neuen inneren 'Licht' das Leben."
[39] Ibid., p. 3.
[40] E.g.: "verfluchtes, dumpfes Mauerloch" (damned, musty hole in a wall), ibid., p. 3. Another common tendentious picture against traditional scholarliness used by Kummer was the so called "Bücherstubenweisheit" (bookishness), ibid., p. 4.
[41] "Deswegen bekennen wir uns heute gerade in der Wissenschaft von der altgermanischen Geschichte zu einer Arbeitsweise, die Bilder des Lebens sucht und sehen lehrt, und die über der unbefangenen Suche nach geschichtlicher [sic!] Erkenntnis

With his orientation towards contemporary demands on the sciences and humanities to serve life instead of self-sufficient research, Kummer integrated himself in the mainstream of conventional thought, which was vehemently propagandized by the protagonists of National Socialist policy of education and universities.[42] When he accused traditional scholarliness to produce only cartoons of reality, Kummer conceptualized his own description in a caricature: The old fashioned research he delineated as game with tesserae of a mosaic, which went on behind closed doors, and the scholars are portrayed by their proverbial short-sightedness.[43] As a contrast, Kummer defined the contemporary voelkish conviction ("völkische Gesinnung von heute"), as being far removed from the one St. Paul or the Catholics had in the past ("weit ab schon von der paulinischen oder katholischen von gestern"). The new approach to the life of the Germans ("germanische Leben") was declared different because the contemporary voelkish conviction ("völkische Gesinnung") had its most sacred place neither in Palestine nor in Rome but in the North as the homeland of the nation.[44] Kummer pointed out that the historic trueness in this case would not be affected as in the matter of confessional or nationalistic attitudes.[45] In taking over contemporary political and ideological demands on scholarliness he also distinguished himself as belonging to the academic avant-garde.[46]

---

niemals versäumen möchte, sich an den Notwendigkeiten und Möglichkeiten unseres gegenwärtigen völkischen, germanisch bestimmten Lebens und Wesens auszurichten." Ibid., p. 4.

[42] Cf. e.g. Ernst Krieck, *Wissenschaft, Weltanschauung, Hochschulreform* (Leipzig: Armanen-Verlag, 1934) and idem, *Leben als Prinzip der Weltanschauung und Problem der Wissenschaft.* Mit einem Anhang von Willi Kunz und Karl August Götz (Weltanschauung und Wissenschaft 7) (Leipzig: Armanen-Verlag, 1938), p. 8. Both, Kummer and Krieck, identified Goethe with the new German understanding of "Wissenschaft" against the traditional positivistic and mechanistic conceptions. See Krieck, *Leben als Prinzip,* p. 22f. With regard to Goethe and his reception by NS-theorists, cf. also Willi Kunz, *Das Lebensprinzip bei Goethe,* Anhang 1, in: Krieck, *Leben als Prinzip,* pp. 235–265; Krieck, like Kummer, was affected by aversions against Roman-Catholic thinkers. Cf. Krieck, *Leben als Prinzip,* p. 21.

[43] Kummer, *Herd und Altar,* vol. 1, p. 5.

[44] Die "völkische Gesinnung… hat ihr Heiligstes nicht in Palästina oder Rom, sondern im Norden als der Artheimat unseres Volkes." Ibid., p. 5.

[45] Ibid., p. 5.

[46] "Do not the greatest symbolic profits of science accrue to those kinds of scientific Pharisees who know how to deck themselves with the most visible signs of a scientificity, for example by mimicking the procedures and the languages of the most advanced sciences?" Bourdieu, *Homo Academicus,* p. 30f. (German translation, p. 75).

Not only Kummer's terminology in the outlined rhetoric style was shaped by religious aspects. But religiosity was also an important motive for his approach to the history of religions. Kummer continued the tradition of the "Kulturkampf" against the Roman-Catholic church. Moreover, he extended the controversy adding Protestant dialectical theology and the Jews to his adversaries.[47] He fought with respect towards every true confession in the world,[48] but wanted to defeat the "Prätorianer Roms."[49] In Kummer's eyes, Boniface personified the negative, destructive Roman Catholic Empire.[50] Luther instead embodied the positive German power of the soul.[51] Despite his open apologetic tendencies, Kummer claimed to describe historic events in an objective and incorruptible way. Yet he contradicted himself at the same time by pointing out that his stance had nothing to do with rationalism or enlightenment.[52] Casually Kummer amalgamated his aversion against

---

[47] In regard to the opposition towards dialectical theology cf. Kummer, *Mission als Sittenwechsel*, p. 7, or idem, *Nordisches Lebensgefühl*, p. 18. Antisemitic elements can be found frequently in Kummer's thinking. In addition to the above cited phrase of the "Palästinapsychose," cf. Kummer, *Mission als Sittenwechsel*, p. 10 and Kummer, *Herd und Altar*, vol. 2, p. 23f., p. 139, and p. 159.

[48] Kummer, *Mission als Sittenwechsel*, p. 6: "bei voller Achtung vor jedem ehrlichen Glaubensbekenntnis in der Welt."

[49] Ibid., p. 6. "Prätorianer" usually means the bodyguard of the Roman emperor Augustus and his successors. This group of soldiers had an influence on the Roman politics as well. Kummer used this term to name the followers of the Catholic Church.

[50] Cf. e.g. Kummer, *Herd und Altar*, vol. 1, p. 157: "Die Axt des Bonifatius tut ihre Arbeit, das heilige Land in der Fremde wirkt hinüber hinter die Erobererfront des Nordens, und nimmt dem Wikingergeist das Steuer aus der Hand und den Halt aus dem Herzen. Der wachsende Baum wird zum Strom des Lebens, das nach fremden Ufern drängt. Die Wikingersegel, noch eben der Flügelschlag der nordischen Bauernwelt, verfliegen sich in der Fremde, wie Adler, die den Horst verlassen haben, und wie des Gottes Raben, die sich Mephisto eingefangen hat zu 'seiner Rabentraulichkeit' (Faust 2, 4)." Together with other parts of this first volume, Kummer presented the cited text in the preface of the second volume, cf. Kummer, *Herd und Altar*, vol. 2, p. 4.

[51] Kummer, *Herd und Altar*, vol. 1, p. 20f. gives an example for Kummer's characteristic way of reasoning, when he argues that Martin Luther's great personality was based on his German "Gottesgrund." Quoting and following a speech of Reinhold Seeberg (see idem, *Christentum und Germanentum*, Schriften der Treitschke Stiftung, Leipzig: Dieterich, 1914) Kummer extends the reasoning of this conservative, antidemocratic and culture-pessimistic theologian of German imperialism during the Great War towards his own creeds. Not logically but suggestively connected with what he said before about Luther, Kummer then explains: "Persönlichkeit ist Selbstbewußtsein, das sich nach innen tief und eigenmächtig verbindet mit dem Willen Gottes in Gewissen, Blut und Schicksal und nach außen sich auswirkt in die Tat." Cf. Kummer, *Herd und Altar*, vol. 1, p. 20f. Luther as advocate and defender of Germany against the Roman-Catholic church can be found also in Kummer, *Herd und Altar*, vol. 2, p. 12f.

[52] Kummer, *Mission als Sittenwechsel*, p. 5f.

the Roman-Catholic church with his reservation towards rationalism.[53] The opposition against enlightenment and rationalism was essential for his reasoning in at least two aspects: First, he could eliminate critical questions based on rationality and empirical knowledge, and second, Kummer shared this opinion with the contemporary mainstream of thoughts and was again able to be recognized as part of the scholarly avant-garde.[54]

The style of Kummer's writings published after 1928 was increasingly apologetic, polemic and declamatory. This manner of speech classifies Kummer as a typical representative of National Socialistic rhetoric, according to Victor Klemperer's analysis of the *Lingua Tertii Imperii*.[55] It partially reminds one of sermons spoken by religious fundamentalist preachers which are similarly characterized by a strong dualistic look at the world.[56] Similarly, Kummer's reasoning became acrimonious through simplifying and polemic attacks against opponents, rather than by good arguments. Kummer's accusation that the Christian religion would have caused degenerated sexuality in the German nation gives his reasoning the character of religious fanaticism.[57] And like fundamentalist preachers, Kummer frequently drew upon ungodliness as a reproach against his antagonists.[58] The accusation of ungodliness hit

---

[53] Cf. Kummer, *Herd und Altar*, vol. 2, p. 69f.

[54] Cf. Rainer Flasche, "Der Irrationalismus in der Religionswissenschaft und dessen Begründung in der Zeit zwischen den Weltkriegen," in Hans G. Kippenberg and Brigitte Luchesi, eds., *Religionswissenschaft und Kulturkritik* (Marburg: diagonal Verlag, 1991), pp. 243–257 as well as Heinrich, *Die deutsche Religionswissenschaft*, pp. 71–81. The importance of irrationalism for Hitler and the suggestive style of his propaganda demonstrates Hojer, *Nationalsozialismus und Pädagogik*, pp. 7–15.

[55] Cf. Victor Klemperer, *LTI. Notizbuch eines Philologen* (Leipzig: Verlag Philipp Reclam jun., 1985), pp. 62–67.

[56] Cf. e.g. Kummer, *Mission als Sittenwechsel*, p. 8f. Here Kummer's dealing with the Iro-Scottish Mission is paradigmatically for this manner of 'reasoning': in debate with Otto Wissig Kummer appraises the Iro-Scottish mission as being gradually better than the Roman, but seen from the result there would be no difference. Therefore he argues against a romantic transfiguration of old Ireland: "Das rassisch fremde Alt-Irland kommt so manchmal in ein falsches, nordisches Licht, das das Licht Alt-Islands allzu stark verdunkelt"; as well shaped by a light-dark dualism is, Kummer, *Nordisches Lebensgefühl*, 35.

[57] Cf. Kummer, *Mission als Sittenwechsel*, p. 8f. where mission of the Iro-Scottish monks is made responsible for the "völlige Verdirnung der Frau" in ancient Ireland; see also ibid., pp. 20–23; Kummer, *Herd und Altar*, vol. 1, p. 9 and n. 4 as well as p. 159, where Kummer speaks disrespectfully about the secret sins of the catholic priests.

[58] Cf. e.g. Kummer, *Nordisches Lebensgefühl*, p. 42: "Das heißt, mit dem Religiösen wandelt sich das Ethische, und aus den Heldentaten frommer Heiden werden Schurkenstreiche getaufter Atheisten."

authors like Hans von Schubert or Hanns Rückert[59] who, as church historians, wrote about the Christianization of the Germans: Kummer was convinced that they were godless and only working for the Roman Catholic church which he names as hospice for all ungodliness in need of salvation.[60]

The pivotal question Kummer was dealing with was a religious one: Following Kummer, it was necessary for everybody who wanted to understand the issue that the old Germans had no need of salvation which the Christian missionaries could have satisfied, not to have any need of salvation by himself.[61] Kummer's main problem was that pure historic or philological research is in no way a means to prove this

---

[59] Cf. Kummer, "Die kulturelle und nationale Bedeutung der Missionierung Germaniens für das deutsche Volk. Entgegnung auf die gleichnamige Ausführung von Prof. D. Rückert im Lutherischen Missionsjahrbuch, Jg. 44, 1931," in *Reden und Aufsätze zum nordischen Gedanken* 1 (1933), pp. 25–32.

[60] Kummer, *Mission als Sittenwechsel*, p. 6: "Auch hier arbeiten Gottlose nur für Rom, das große Hospiz aller erlösungsbedürftigen Gottlosigkeit." The "Kulturkämpfer" Kummer gets enraged each time when he believes to have found justifications for the Christian mission of the Germans in theological or church historical literature. Cf. also Kummer, *Nordisches Lebensgefühl*, pp. 47–50. This anti-Catholic polemic brings Kummer very close to the mentality of Alfred Rosenberg, *Protestantische Rompilger: der Verrat an Luther und der 'Mythus des 20. Jahrhunderts'*, 2nd–10th ed. (München: Hoheneichen-Verlag, 1937). Indeed Rosenberg struggled in this scripture against his opponents in the "Kirchenkampf." Germanic references are only accidental, but his polemic aversion against Protestant and Roman-Catholic common grounds and cooperation is comparable to Kummer's reasoning. Especially when Rosenberg speaks about the "Charakterzersetzung der einst aus deutschem Charakter geborenen Reformation" and that "reiner Buchstabenglaube und priesterlicher Größenwahn über germanische Denkart gesiegt haben," he is not far from Kummer's thoughts, cf. ibid., p. 15. Likewise when Rosenberg points to the "germanische Charakterprotest" of Martin Luther, cf. ibid., p. 17. It is Karl Thieme and not Kummer who approves of him in his *Deutsche evangelische Christen auf dem Wege zur katholischen Kirche* (Schlieren-Zürich: Neue Brücke, 1934), cf. Rosenberg, *Protestantische Rompilger*, p. 22f. Rosenberg also speaks about "characterliche Verheerungen" which allegedly had been caused by the dogmatic of the Old Testament and which now would characterize the expressions of contemporary authors of the Christian churches, cf. ibid., 24. Compared to Kummer, Rosenberg does not try to write in a scholarly style. In fact Rosenberg emphasizes his "persönliche religionsphilosophische Überzeugungen", ibid., p. 31, but he does not exert himself in covering ideological stereotypes with academic language or reasoning, cf. especially the antisemitic chapter "Die Judenvergötzung", ibid., pp. 33–39. With regard to the dialectical theology Rosenberg's opinions are also close to the above mentioned convictions of Kummer. Rosenberg calls the "bekennende Kirche" a "Sektenbewegung" and Karl Barth her head, cf. ibid., pp. 43–47.

[61] Kummer, *Mission als Sittenwechsel*, p. 6: "Nur wer selber nicht erlösungsbedürftig ist, kann den großen Irrtum widerlegen, daß die Mission ein Erlösungsbedürfnis befriedigt habe, als sie uns das Erbe aus der Seele nahm und das Bekenntnis zu Rom und Palästina hineintat, als sie das Licht da drin auszublasen suchte, damit uns das messianische Licht der römischen Hierarchie zum Erlöser werden konnte."

intrinsic religious assumption. Historians or philologists may investigate the Germanic sources and look if a need of salvation is recognizable or not. Kummer connected the success of such an investigation with the proper religiosity of the researcher and bound historical description at normative, religious evaluations. As a result, Kummer gave religious answers to historical questions and historical answers to religious issues.[62] With his emotionally charged and fanatic language, Kummer tried to blur this logical flaw which can be named a *metabasis eis allo genos* by enthusiastically pointing out that the last thousand years since Christianization were like one day. Thanks to their racial kinship and a related blood only separated by the Christian mission and its consequences, contemporary Germans are able to understand their pagan ancestors.[63]

Kummer built the bridge into the past following the contemporary religious tradition in the study of religions.[64] Like Rudolf Otto, Nathan Söderblom, Friedrich Heiler or Jakob Wilhelm Hauer, Kummer was searching for inner religious powers underlying the external historical

---

[62] For instance when Kummer tried to demonstrate that the power struggle between the church and the German emperor during the 11th century was caused by the church and its theology and not by the sake of the emperor, he reasons solely with religious-ideological 'arguments', cf. Kummer, *Herd und Altar*, vol. 2, pp. 37–42.

[63] "Nein, diese tausend Jahre seitdem sind 'wie ein Tag'. Die germanischen Heiden von gestern werden von den Deutschen heute und morgen verstanden als ihresgleichen, je mehr sie sich mit ihnen befassen. Nicht Spuren befremdlicher Urmenschheit finden wir in diesem gestrigen Leben verwandten Blutes, sondern unsere unmittelbare Herkunft und damit uns selbst. Und der tiefe Unterschied zwischen uns und jenen Heiden liegt nicht an den kurzen 1000 Jahren des Älterwerdens, sondern an dem einschneidenden Sittenwechsel und Kulturbruch der Mission, an diesem Versuch, unsere ererbte Art, zu lieben und zu glauben, gewaltsam neu zu regeln und einer fremden Art zu unterwerfen." Kummer, *Herd und Altar*, vol. 1, p. 98.

[64] Horst Junginger speaks about a "theologische Religionswissenschaft" with regard to this group of scholars, cf. idem, *Von der philologischen zur völkischen Religionswissenschaft. Das Fach Religionswissenschaft an der Universität Tübingen von der Mitte des 19. Jahrhunderts bis zum Ende des Dritten Reiches* (Contubernium. Tübinger Beiträge zur Universitäts- und Wissenschaftsgeschichte 51) (Stuttgart: Franz Steiner 1999), p. 300f., and idem, "Einführung: Das Überleben der Religionswissenschaft im Nationalsozialismus," *Zeitschrift für Religionswissenschaft* (ZfR) 9 (2001), pp. 155–157. For the differentiation between religious and philological-historical trends in the German study of religion during the first half of the 20th century see also the systematization of Heinrich, *Die deutsche Religionswissenschaft*. The religious background and fundament of Jakob Wilhelm Hauers – who in many ways seems comparable to Kummer – manner of practicing study of religions in the tradition of Rudolf Otto was recently examined and excellently presented by Hiroshi Kubota, *Religionswissenschaftliche Religiosität und Religionsgründung. Jakob Wilhelm Hauer im Kontext des Freien Protestantismus* (Tübinger Beiträge zur Religionswissenschaft 5) (Frankfurt a.M.: Peter Lang 2005).

events.[65] He saw this inner religious power as unmistakably having a racist connotation, since Kummer was frequently pointing to the community of blood, which connected all Germans.[66] Significantly in many cases when he intended to outline his academic method, Kummer used a neo-romantic poetic style with allusions to religious phrases. He identified science, humanities and history with the tree of life and the tree of knowledge alluding to the biblical Garden of Eden, specified as history of the own blood.[67] Alongside the scholars participating in the religious tradition of the study of religions, Kummer also shared the opinion that the own faith is a necessary pre-condition for a successful research in history of religions.[68]

---

[65] Cf. Kummer, *Nordisches Lebensgefühl*, p. 25. In this context Kummer, in following Le Roy and Karl Beth, demands: "Es ist endlich an der Zeit, daß die Forschung vom dichtenden zum betenden Germanen übergeht, von den verworrenen Spielen der Phantasie zu der Frömmigkeit einfacher Menschen." Ibid., p. 26. The nearness of Kummer to Rudolf Otto or Friedrich Heiler in regard to the religious ideals projected into the history of religions is also demonstrated in Walter Baetke's analysis: "Die germanische Religion wäre danach so etwas wie ein mythischer Pantheismus gewesen oder, wie Kummer sagt: eine 'Freiwillige Versenkung in die eigene Tiefe'. Nun ist ja klar, daß diese 'Vergeistigung' germanischer Religion mit wissenschaftlicher Interpretation nichts mehr zu tun hat." Baetke, *Art und Glaube*, p. 44f. A little later Baetke explains how Kummer, following Nathan Söderblom, intended to give the mystical German understanding of god a scholarly reason, cf. ibid., pp. 46–49. It certainly was no coincidence that Jakob Wilhelm Hauer was backing Kummer during his efforts to become a Professor at the University of Jena, cf. Universitätsarchiv Jena, Bestand 4, Abt. IV Nr. 20, Bl. 408: "Brief Prof. Dr. Hauer Tübingen, Langemarkstr. 10 an Herrn Dr. Reimar Schulze, Jena Kahlaische Str. 1 vom 29.06.1938": "Ich habe mich ja für Kummer immer wieder eingesetzt, weil ich ihn sowohl wissenschaftlich wie persönlich sehr schätze... Kummer hat leider, wie ich auch immer wieder betonen musste, ebenfalls eine einseitige Art... ich glaube aber, dass Kummer doch auch in den letzten Jahren sehr viel hinzugelernt hat und ich würde es für einen ganz schweren Schaden sowohl für die Wissenschaft, wie für den weltanschaulichen Kampf halten, wenn Kummer nicht endlich eine feste Professur bekäme, sofern er sie nicht schon hat. Ich bin überzeugt, dass sobald er an diesem Punkte einmal zu Ruhe kommt, er auch noch ganz anders wissenschaftlich produktiv sein wird."

[66] Cf. e.g. Kummer, "Die Wikinger," p. 4.

[67] "...für die Wissenschaft ist der Baum des Lebens der Baum der Erkenntnis; das ganze große Wachsen geschichtlicher Wirklichkeit – das in Menschenwiegen beginnt und nicht in Götterhainen – ist der Baum des Lebens, den die Wissenschaft uns erkennen lehrt am Lebensgang unseres Blutes." Kummer, *Herd und Altar*, vol. 2, p. 15.

[68] Ibid., p. 31.

4. *Supporting the National Socialist Regime as the Institutionalized*
Rebirth of the Pre-Christian Culture and Religion in Germany

The writings of Bernhard Kummer were engaged pleas for the rehabilitation of the old Germans and at the same time political propaganda
for the movement of Adolf Hitler and the NS state. This combination
was not accidental. Kummer belonged to those Germans who supported
Hitler and his regime – the personification of a fanatic follower of
National Socialism. In his eyes it must have been tragic that he had
been unable to find a prominent supporter for his concerns apart
from Alfred Rosenberg although he had been working for the success
of the National Socialist ideology since the late 1920s. Kummer was
a member of the NSDAP from 1928 to 1930. He then left the party
due to financial reasons – the economic situation for Kummer and
his family was strained at that time, and as member of the NSDAP
he could not get a public position of scholarship – but certainly not
because he had changed his mind.[69] The dean of Jena's Philosophy
Department reported in his proposal from July 12, 1939 concerning
the career Kummer had made in various NS organizations: Kummer
was member of the NSDAP in Leipzig since 1928 as well as member
of the SA. He published articles in the NS magazines *NS-Schulungsbrief*
and *NS-Monatshefte* from 1927 on. Despite Kummer's temporary resignation, the dean attested to his inner relationship to the NSDAP. As
proof of Kummer's reliability, he mentioned his activities in various NS
organizations.[70] Beginning with 1933, Kummer made earnest attempts

---

[69] Cf. Hamann, "'Männer der kämpfenden Wissenschaft'," p. 210 and Heinrich,
Religionswissenschaft und Nationalsozialismus, p. 199f. and pp. 365–367.

[70] "Kummer war seit 1928 (Mitgliedsnummer 87 841) Mitglied der NSDAP, Orts-
gruppe Leipzig und im SA.-Sturm 62 aktiv. Seit dem Jahre 1927 brachte der *Völkische
Beobachter*, später der *NS-Schulungsbrief* und die *NS-Monatshefte* Beiträge von ihm. 1930
trat Kummer aus wirtschaftlichen Gründen aus der Partei aus, der er aber innerlich
stets zugehörte. Seit 1933 wurde Kummer ungezählte Male von der Partei und ihren
Gliederungen zu Schulungsvorträgen aufgefordert. 1938 wurde er in den Arbeitskreis
für Weltanschauung und Kultur der SA-Gruppe Thüringen berufen." Universitätsarchiv
Jena, Bestand C, Nr. 876, Vorschlagsbericht betreffend Errichtung eines ordentlichen
Lehrstuhls für altnordische Sprache und Kultur vom 12. Juli 1939, Bl. 2–4, here Bl. 4.
A curriculum vitae of Kummer reads: "Kummer trat wegen wirtschaftlicher Notlage
seiner Familie mit Rücksicht auf die damaligen Verhältnisse äußerlich aus der NSDAP
aus... Kummer gehörte nie einer anderen Organisation politischer Art an und war
Mitglied des Kampfbundes für Deutsche Kultur seit dem 7. März 1932 (Mitgliedsnum-
mer 2 483)." Lebenslauf von Dr. Bernhard Kummer, ibid., Bestand 4, Abt. IV, Nr. 20,
Bl. 165–167, here Bl. 165.

to restart what he had had.[71] Relatively late, supposedly shortly before
the end of the regime, Kummer was re-affiliated to the NSDAP. This
had nothing to do with an opposition against the NS regime, as Kummer pretended after the end of the Third Reich. His problems resulted
from conflicts with other protagonists of the movement, internal quarrels
based on different interpretations of a disparate ideology.[72] Kummer
was backed by the Nationalsozialistische Deutsche Dozentenbund which
did not doubt his political and ideological reliability.[73]

Kummer offered his service to the mental preparation of Germany
for the war since 1933. In his small book *Nordisches Lebensgefühl. Einführung in das altisländische Schrifttum* he already idealized life and death as
a soldier at the front four years before the Second World War began.[74]
Kummer declared that the Nordic experience of life sees – especially
in the dreadfulness of the struggle for survival – the call of god.[75] Four
years later, in the atmosphere of the rising war, Kummer spoke about
the agreement of the parents with the struggle of their children and
confessed that the intention of his book *Wandlungen altnordischer Sittlichkeit
im Glaubenswechsel* was to demonstrate with the terms "Persönlichkeit"
(personage) and "Gemeinschaft" (community) how the life of a Ger-

---

[71] Cf. Willy Schilling, "NS-Dozentenschaft und Nationalsozialistischer Deutscher
Dozentenbund an der Universität Jena," in Hoßfeld, *'Kämpferische Wissenschaft'*, pp.
180–201, especially p. 190.

[72] For the re-affiliation of Kummer to the NSDAP, cf. Uwe Hoßfeld, "'Kämpferische
Wissenschaft': Zum Profilwandel der Jenaer Universität im Nationalsozialismus," in
ibid., pp. 23–117, here p. 80 and p. 119, n. 427 with reference to documents published
by the Institut für Zeitgeschichte: *Akten der Partei-Kanzlei der NSDAP. Rekonstruktion eines
verloren gegangenen Bestandes; Sammlung der in anderen Provenienzen überlieferten Korrespondenzen,
Niederschriften von Besprechungen usw. Mit dem Stellvertreter des Führers und seinem Stab bzw. Der
Partei-Kanzlei, ihren Ämtern, Referaten und Unterabteilungen sowie mit Heß und Bormann persönlich*
(München: Oldenbourg, 1983–1992).

[73] For Kummer's ideological activities in the NSD Dozentenbund in order to be
accepted as member of the NSDAP and to get the professorship, see Schilling, "NS-
Dozentenschaft," p. 189f. and p. 195

[74] Cf. Kummer, *Nordisches Lebensgefühl*, pp. 15–17. Here Kummer alludes in glorifying
manner to the experience at the front during the First World War: "Eine neue Freiheit
und Würde der Seele ist uns zwischen Leben und Tod der Front geboren worden,
ein helles nordisches Lebensgefühl über den fallenden Freunden: kein Wissen um ein
Paradies oder um eine Hölle oder um einen Richter da oben, der diese Toten je nach
Wert auf Himmel und Hölle verteilt, sondern nur ein Gefühl vom Leben, das den Tod
überdauern kann und muß, weil es die Freiheit hat, von der blutenden Erde empor
nach den Sternen zu fassen, und dem, was hinter den Sternen ist, die Tiefe der Seele
beglückend aufzutun." Ibid., p. 16.

[75] "Das nordische Lebensgefühl erlebt gerade in der Furchtbarkeit des Lebenskamp-
fes den Anruf Gottes an sein anderes ich in der Menschenbrust, zu bestehen in der
Welt." Ibid., p. 17.

man farmer and fighter is free as well as bound between the clan and the front.[76] In view of the preparations for the war, Kummer used the history of the old German religion to provide the soldiers and their supporters with a strong morale. He romanticized former times when there was a sacredness of weapons which he described as result of peace within the community. They watched over them above the fire in the hall or at the high stand of the ancestors ("Hochsitz der Ahnen"). The arms were ornamented with divine signs, and behind them recognized Kummer a military ethos of parents who gave the weapons to their sons in order to incite them to deeds and glory.[77]

How Kummer adapted his scholarly work to the demands of National Socialism is demonstrated by the end of his preface to *Der Machtkampf zwischen Volk, König und Kirche im Alten Norden*. Here he explained the political circumstances under which the volume had been compiled relating his writings to the political development. All those events like the annexation of Austria, the return of the Sudeten Germans ("große Heimkehr der Sudetendeutschen"), or, in former times, the beginnings of the conquests of the Vikings, even the contemporary emergence of racial ideas were placed under the Nordic light which was supposed to drive away the superstition from the south.[78] In Kummer's idealized perception of the ancient Icelandic society, the Third Reich was the perfect expression of the Nordic attitude to life.[79] Communism and liberalism were seen as alien to the Nordic nature, whereas Adolf

---

[76] Kummer, *Herd und Altar*, vol. 2, p. 3 (with regard to *Herd und Altar*, vol. 1): "Ja der Eltern zum Kampf der Kinder" and "die Freiheit und die Bindungen des germanischen Bauern- und Kämpferlebens zwischen Sippe und Kampffront."

[77] Kummer, *Herd und Altar*, vol. 2, p. 25: "Tatsächlich gab es schon einmal die Heiligkeit der Waffe und ihre Weihung vom inneren Frieden der Gemeinschaft aus, die sie hütete über dem Feuer in der Halle oder dem Hochsitz der Ahnen, mit göttlichen Zeichen verziert. Tatsächlich gab es hinter dieser Waffe einmal schon eine Wehrgesinnung, die mit Mütter- und Vater-Händen die Waffen zu Tat und Ruhm den Söhnen gab..."

[78] "Das vorliegende Buch wurde im wesentlichen, nach jahrelangen Vorarbeiten, fertiggestellt in dem Sommer, der sich so seltsam ankündigte mit jenem tiefen Nordlicht am Himmel, das in Berlin und Wien gesehen wurde, und der der Vereinigung Österreichs mit dem Reich dann jene andere große Heimkehr der Sudetendeutsche folgen ließ. Auch am Beginn des Wikingersturms und der Umbruchszeit damals standen seltsame Flammenzeichen am Himmel, aber sie deuteten den Abergläubischen Schrecken, Gottlosigkeit und Krieg aus dem Norden, der um des Glaubens willen den Süden bekämpfte. Da nun der Rassengedanke von Norden nach Süden Europa einen soll, möge sich auch der Aberglaube für immer verflüchtigen, der meint, aus Norden komme die Zerstörung und Vernichtung der Religion." Ibid., p. 7.

[79] Kummer, *Nordisches Lebensgefühl*, p. 20.

Hitler's "Führerstaat" was delineated as the only possible form of government for the Germans and legitimated by the history of the old Nordic Religion. Furthermore, Kummer, it should be remembered, belonged to those professors of Jena University, who also taught in the concentration camp Buchenwald.[80]

The propaganda as demonstrated in this case is an extreme example of how scholarly reasoning can be politicized. Returning to Bourdieu and applying his criteria to Kummer, this can be categorized as a compensatory strategy which tends to maintain scholarly credibility and to assert professional advancement against the rules of academic "market."[81] Gaps in the chain of proof were covered and a lack of approval in the academia was compensated.

5. *Struggle for Acceptance and Membership in the Academic World*

If the history of the study of religions under the impact of National Socialist ideology would be analyzed and described with Bourdieu's model of the university field and understood as being involved in the rules of this marketplace, the insight could also be applied to the scholarly world during the NS regime,

> that the university field is, like any other field, the locus of a struggle to determine the conditions and the criteria of legitimate membership and legitimate hierarchy, that is, to determine which properties are pertinent, effective and liable to function as capital so as to generate the specific profits guaranteed by the field.[82]

Such a struggle occurs in every scholarly context and can hardly be criticized. Under normal circumstances these correlations are typical of the academic business and scholars' interaction in scientific and public debates. But under the conditions of a totalitarian dictatorship, normal academic conflicts mutate into severe ideological fights, minefields for academics to denounce their opponents with arguments

---

[80] Cf. Ronald Hirte and Harry Stein, "Die Beziehungen der Universität Jena zum Konzentrationslager Buchenwald," in Uwe Hoßfeld et al., eds., *'Kämpferische Wissenschaft'*, pp. 361–398, here p. 384 and Susanne Zimmermann and Thomas Zimmermann, "Die Medizinische Fakultät der Universität Jena im 'Dritten Reich' – ein Überblick," in: ibid., pp. 401–436, here p. 421.

[81] Bourdieu, *Homo Academicus*, p. 21 (German translation, p. 59).

[82] Ibid., p. 11 (German translation, p. 45).

which would not have the same resounding effect in other contexts. The case of Kummer demonstrates how such a struggle for acceptance in the academic world is formed by external influences and positions scholars receive outside the universities, for instance as members of political or religious organizations. Surely, Kummer is not a singular phenomenon. His behavior is typical of many others in the university field in that time.

The two professors who assisted Kummer in establishing himself at the university were above all Hans Haas in Leipzig and Gustav Neckel in Berlin. Kummer mentioned them in his writings – frequently and with kind commentaries.[83] Haas, who succeeded Nathan Söderblom as historian of religions in Leipzig, was considered as scholar of great integrity with a profound knowledge in the history of religions.[84] From 1920 to 1935, and again from 1937 to 1940, Neckel held the most prominent chair of German language and literature studies in Germany at the University of Berlin.[85] But Neckel's publications and the way he interpreted the sources pertaining to the old German religion and culture raised objections, for instance by Carl Clemen.[86] Together with Eugen Mogk, Haas supervised Kummer's doctoral thesis.[87] Kummer's relationship to Haas could best be described by Bourdieu: A "docile and submissive, even somewhat infantile, attitude which characterizes the good pupil of all eras."[88] Kummer's relationship with Haas probably

---

[83] Cf. e.g. the reference to Gustav Neckel in Kummer, *Liebe und Ehe bei den vorchristlichen Germanen* (Leipzig: Teubner 1932), quoted from Kummer, *Mission als Sittenwechsel*, p. 20f., or Kummer, "Die kulturelle und nationale Bedeutung," p. 26.

[84] Cf. Kurt Rudolph, "Die Bedeutung von Hans Haas für die Religionswissenschaft," *Zeitschrift für Religions- und Geistesgeschichte* 21 (1969), pp. 238–252, re-published in idem, *Geschichte und Probleme der Religionswissenschaft* (Leiden: Brill, 1992), pp. 340–356.

[85] For a survey of Neckel's career see Julia Zernack, "Gustav Karl Paul Christoph Neckel," in *Internationales Germanistenlexikon*, vol. 1 (Berlin-New York: Walter de Gruyter, 2003), p. 1311f.

[86] See Carl Clemen, *Altgermanische Religionsgeschichte* (Bonn: Röhrscheid 1934), p. 14. Neckel kept an open mind on racial issues and partly considered them in the fields of his interests. Cf. Gustav Neckel, *Germanen und Kelten. Historisch-linguistisch-rassenkundliche Forschungen und Gedanken zur Geisteskrisis* (Heidelberg: Winter 1929).

[87] Dietrich Germann underestimates Haas's role in Kummer's career. His portrayal of Kummer's work focused on the influence of Mogk and Kummer's language and literature studies and minimizes the ideological aspects. As a consequence, the picture of Kummer becomes quite positive. Cf. Dietrich Germann, *Geschichte der Germanistik an der Friedrich-Schiller-Universität Jena*, vol. 3 (Diss. Jena 1954), p. 325f. According to the Universitätsarchiv Jena, Bestand 4, Abt. IV, Nr. 20, Lebenslauf von Dr. Bernhard Kummer, Jena, Reinbergstr. 15, Bl. 165–167, here Bl. 165, Kummer became mark 1 for his doctoral thesis.

[88] Bourdieu, *Homo Academicus*, p. 88 (German translation, p. 155).

remained untroubled only because Haas died in 1934 at the beginning of the Third Reich. It can only be speculated if his political and
ideological agitations would have affected the devotion for his teacher
and would have lead to frictions with him. Haas seems to have been
deceived by the philological knowledge Kummer's work shows at the
first sight, and his disinterest in the old German religion had hindered
a thorough reading.

The questionable interpretations Kummer presented in his first book
Midgards Untergang were on the other hand an important reason for
Gustav Neckel to protect him at the beginning of the 1930s. Neckel
supported and justified his reading of the Edda as a testimony of the
religious sensitivity of the old Germans.[89] With the change from Haas
to Neckel, Kummer changed his academic profile. Now the ideological aims became more prominent in his scholarly work. At the end of
1929, Neckel applied for a scholarship in behalf of Kummer to allow
him to pursue further postdoctoral studies. Kummer and his family
lived under miserable financial circumstances in that time. His literary activities, primarily consisting of propaganda in favor of National
Socialism, were insufficient to sustain himself, his wife and his two
children.[90] The two volumes later published in 1934 and 1939 under
the title *Herd und Altar, Wandlung altnordischer Sittlichkeit im Glaubenswechsel*
were originally planned as his habilitation (a post-doctoral lecturing
qualification in Germany),[91] but they were printed without serving as
a formal qualification. Because of their ideological reliability, they did
further his advancement, though with considerable delay. Kummer
often pointed to the fact that his economic situation and his political
activities had hampered his academic career.[92] This was only the half-

---

[89] Cf. the reference to Neckel's interpretation of the Edda, in Kummer, *Nordisches Lebensgefühl*, p. 25.

[90] Cf. Heinrich, *Die deutsche Religionswissenschaft*, p. 199f. and pp. 365–367.

[91] Universitätsarchiv Jena, Bestand C, Nr. 876, Vorschlagsbericht betreffend Errichtung eines ordentlichen Lehrstuhls für altnordische Sprache und Kultur vom 12. Juli
1939, Bl. 2–4, here Bl. 3.

[92] Cf. ibid. This is based on the curriculum vitae of Kummer, Universitätsarchiv Jena,
Bestand 4, Abt. IV, Nr. 20, Bl. 165–167, Bl. 166: "Kummers Habilitation verzögerte
sich durch die Notwendigkeit, Geld zu verdienen (das Stipendium betrug monatlich RM
140,– bis 180,–) und aktiv teilzunehmen am kulturpolitischen Kampf der Gegenwart.
Er übernahm sehr viel Schulungs- und Vortragsarbeit im Kampfbund für Deutsche
Kultur, NS-Lehrerbund, BDM, SS, Hochschule für Politik usw. Seit 1933 hat er ohne
irgend welche eigenen Bemühungen fast 800 Schulungsvorträge vor allen Gliederungen
der Partei gehalten. Er wurde zur Mitarbeit an den NS-Schulungsbriefen, am Schu-

truth. The relationship between Kummer and Neckel was not without complications and Kummer's success suffered due to them.[93] After all, Kummer was jointly responsible for displacing Neckel from Berlin to the Georg-August University of Göttingen in 1935.[94]

Therefore Kummer's career had to proceed without protection of the Berlin specialist in German language and literature studies. Yet the racial features of Kummer's publications produced interest in circles which tended to reform the universities according to the National Socialist ideology. Fritz Sauckel, "NSDAP-Gauleiter" and "Reichsstatthalter" in Thüringen, and Karl Astel, president of the "Thüringisches Landesamt für Rassewesen" since July 1933 and full professor of "Menschliche Züchtungslehre und Vererbungsforschung" since June 1934 at the University of Jena, lobbied for Kummer's potential professorship at the University of Jena.[95] This support for Kummer was part of their efforts to profile Jena as a distinguished university of National Socialism.[96]

Beside his doctoral thesis, his contributions to the *Handwörterbuch des Deutschen Aberglaubens* won Kummer academic merits and reputation.[97] The encyclopedia was an ambitious and prestigious project of German

---

lungshaus des Rassenpolitischen Amtes und des Außenpolitischen Amtes herangezogen und ist bis heute Dozent an der Hochschule für Politik in Berlin."

[93] Cf. Heinrich, *Die deutsche Religionswissenschaft*, p. 365f. and p. 368f.; the reference to Gustav Neckel is 1939 significantly more reserved than 10 years before, cf. Kummer, *Herd und Altar*, vol. 2, p. 89. The disruption between both is highly visible in Kummer's remarks on Neckel in Kummer, *Germanenkunde*, pp. 30–33.

[94] Cf. Julia Zernack, "'Wenn es sein muß, mit Härte' – Die Zwangsversetzung des Nordisten Gustav Neckel 1935 und die 'Germanenkunde im Kulturkampf'," in idem and Klaus von See, eds., *Germanistik und Politik in der Zeit des Nationalsozialismus. Zwei Fallstudien: Hermann Schneider und Gustav Neckel* (Heidelberg: Winter, 2004), pp. 113–208; for Kummer's not executed habilitation see p. 145f. and p. 184; how his ideological reliability was used to compensate for this lack of qualification see pp. 181–184; the conflict with Neckel in which Kummer acted in his characteristic manner, combining his anti-Catholic attitude and suspicions of sex offence on his antagonist with scholarly accusations, is described at great length with regard to Kummer on pp. 145–151, pp. 155–158, p. 161, p. 164, and p. 170; cf. also Fritz Paul, "Zur Geschichte der Skandinavistik an der Georg-August-Universität Göttingen. Eine vorläufige Skizze," http://www.skandinavistik.uni-goettingen.de/semgesch.htm. With regard to Kummer's denunciation, see Kummer, *Germanenkunde*, p. 32f.

[95] Cf. Hamann, "'Männer der kämpfenden Wissenschaft'," p. 202f., and pp. 205–209.

[96] Cf. Uwe Hoßfeld, "Von der Rassenkunde, Rassenhygiene und biologischen Erbstatistik zur Synthetischen Theorie der Evolution: Eine Skizze der Biowissenschaften," in idem, ed., *'Kämpferische Wissenschaft'*, pp. 519–574, especially pp. 531–534.

[97] Regarding the importance of encyclopedias for a scholarly influence, cf. Bourdieu, *Homo academicus*, p. 175f. For the *Handwörterbuch des Deutschen Aberglaubens*, see Nicole Fritz, *Bewohnte Mythen – Joseph Beuys und der Aberglaube* (Diss. Tübingen, 2002), pp. 53–81.

anthropology ("Volkskunde") which tried to collect and evaluate the complete knowledge of German folk beliefs ("Volksglauben"). Articles concerning the study of religions were predominantly written by Karl Beth and Friedrich Pfister. Kummer took part in the encyclopedia from the first volume published in 1927. He wrote articles on family matters: men and women, marriage, sexuality and children.[98] Here Kummer demonstrated a profound knowledge of the historic sources. Nevertheless, his political development until the last volume was published in 1942 becomes also visible. It could be said that, in general, his convictions on the old German culture remained nearly the same. But his arguments became more and more ideological and his style was increasingly propagandistic, as outlined above.

Kummer had a vision of the German university system and his place in it. He aspired to a new type of scholarship as part of the new political university which was frequently postulated by the NS regime. In Kummer's view, an academic should serve the nation with his work and imbue the propaganda an aura of academic seriousness. Moreover, he intended that his writings should deepen the political ideas and explain them correctly, giving them, as he would say, a German fundament in god ("Gottesgrund").[99] With his work, Kummer wanted to provide his contemporaries with a scientific explanation of the ideology of National Socialism.[100] As mentioned above, he compared his way of working with the view Lynkäus had from his tower onto the world. Kummer contrasted this new vision with the old one which only depended on books. His new method would deal with the real life of the German folk and would give new insights in its problems, whereas the old-fashioned scholarship was confined by feeble artificial illumination.[101]

Kummer intended to live this conception of scholarliness. With his appearance he aimed to enhance the profile of Jena University in particular with regard to racial issues. From October 14, 1936 Kummer held a teaching position for Nordic language and culture and history of the old German religion.[102] As of the summer 1941 he can be found

[98] For the complete list of articles, see Bibliography at the end.

[99] Cf. Kummer, *Nordisches Lebensgefühl*, p. 23f.

[100] Cf. Kummer, *Herd und Altar*, vol. 2, p. 21f. Here Kummer presented a catalogue of almost every catch phrase which was used at that time in ideological texts on the history of old German religion and culture, e.g. Volksrecht, Blut und Erblichkeit, Heldenehrung, Führerrecht, Kameradschaft etc.

[101] Cf. Kummer, *Herd und Altar*, vol. 1, p. 5.

[102] Germann, *Geschichte der Germanistik*, p. 326.

in the university calendar as director of the Nordic section in the German seminary. On May 1, 1942 Kummer was appointed professor of old Nordic language and culture as well as of Germanic history of religions ("altnordische Sprache und Kultur sowie germanische Religionsgeschichte") at the University of Jena. On March 2, 1943 he gave his inaugural lecture.[103] He took over the former chair of philosophy hold by Hans Leisegang who was dismissed on June 1, 1937.[104] Yet Hamann is correct in disbelieving whether Kummer's institute took up it's work at all.[105]

Kummer's career and place in the academic field seems contradictory and paradox: On the one hand made him his political agitation an outsider in the academic society despite his doctoral thesis and his cooperation at the renowned encyclopedia. On the other hand he obtained a lectureship at the University of Jena in 1936 and eventually became full professor in 1942 predominantly because of his ideological reliability.[106] Therefore it is accurate to say that Kummer belonged to the National Socialist avant-garde at the university. Yet his academic career was considerably hampered by the fanatic manner in which he defended his creeds.[107] Beside the mentioned break with Gustav Neckel and other

---

[103] Cf. Hamann, "'Männer der kämpfenden Wissenschaft'," p. 209. Kummer was following Hans Leisegang, who has been imprisoned and than discarded because of a denunciation, cf. Hans-Joachim Dahms, "Jenaer Philosophen in der Weimarer Republik, im Nationalsozialismus und der Folgezeit bis 1950", in: 'Kämpferische Wissenschaft', pp. 723–771 and pp. 746–749.

[104] Cf. Germann, Geschichte der Germanistik, p. 327; for the dismissal of Hans Leisegang, see Universitätsarchiv Jena, Bestand BA, Nr. 933, Bl. 195.

[105] Hamann explains: "Nachdem die Errichtung seines Seminars im Frühjahr 1944 endlich offiziell genehmigt wurde, wurde Kummer am 2. September 1944 einberufen. Es erscheint aufgrund der kurzen Zeit bis zur Einberufung als unwahrscheinlich, daß die Errichtung des Seminars praktisch umgesetzt werden konnte. Im September 1945 wurde das Nordische Seminar wieder als Nordische Abteilung in das Deutsche Seminar eingegliedert." Hamann, "'Männer der kämpfenden Wissenschaft'," p. 210. "Das Seminar hat nur ein Semester erlebt, in dem in ihm wirklich gearbeitet wurde: das SS 1944," assesses Germann the situation. Germann, Geschichte der Germanistik, p. 327.

[106] Cf. Hoßfeld, 'Kämpferische Wissenschaft', p. 67f.

[107] How difficult the appointment of Kummer was because of the opposition provoked by his polemic agitation demonstrates a letter from November 1936 which is quoted by Uwe Hoßfeld. There Lothar Stengel von Rutkowski, assistant of Karl Astel, spoke about the energy which was necessary to be successful in this case and that further efforts have to be undertaken to make a full professor out of Kummer. Cf. Uwe Hoßfeld, "Von der Rassenkunde", pp. 519–574, and p. 553f. with reference to the letter in the archive of the Ernst-Haeckel-Haus. Lothar Stengel von Rutkowski is described by Hoßfeld as a "Rassenpolitiker und Pseudo-Philosoph von ganz besonderer politischer Couleur, der zu den charismatischsten Protagonisten einer 'Deutschen Biologie' und 'Deutschen Philosophie' an der Universität Jena gehörte." Ibid., p. 538.

controversies, his career was delayed by the escalation of an academic conflict, in which Kummer acted with unbending fanaticism.

6. *Kummer's Conflict with Otto Höfler*

The conflict with Otto Höfler had been inflamed by a detailed note in Höfler's book *Kultische Geheimbünde der Germanen* where he had discussed Kummer's *Midgards Untergang* quite critically, partially in an ironic manner. For example, Höfler accused Kummer of being rationalistic and unhistorical.[108] Kummer's keen reaction was not only motivated by the somehow arrogant and patronizing style of Höfler but also by Höfler's appointment to a chair at the University of Kiel.[109] In return, Kummer placed Höfler's book in line with Herman Wirth's *Ura-Linda-Chronik* which had been exposed as forgery and therefore had discredited the whole new discipline "Germanenkunde" (Germanic studies). Kummer portrayed himself as someone who had intended to prevent another scandal by questioning Höfler's scholarly abilities and credibility.[110] Kummer struggled with almost every weapon he could get.[111] Therefore he asked rhetorically if Höfler's equation of the Germans with the primitives and his historical construction could be called science.[112] In the following Kummer predominantly criticized Höfler's associative

---

[108] Cf. Otto Höfler, *Kultische Geheimbünde der Germanen* (Frankfurt a.M.: Verlag Moritz Diesterweg, 1934), pp. 335–339. As a result of his examination Höfler says: "Es steht in Kummers Buch vieles Gute und Feinfühlige. Doch bei den Problemen, von denen hier die Rede ist, hat er sich gründlich verrannt. Aber es wäre bei ihm, glaube ich, nicht notwendig, daß das Verständnis für die eine Seite der altgermanischen Kultur zu einer derartigen Unterschätzung der anderen Seite führt. Nur müßte er trachten, die historische Wirklichkeit zu verstehen, statt sie zu schmähen." Ibid., p. 339.

[109] For Kummer's aversion to Höfler's appointment see Universitätsarchiv Jena, Bestand 4, Abt. IV, Nr. 20, Dr. Bernhard Kummer, Jena, Weinbergstrasse 15: Antwort auf das mir durch den Herrn Rektor der Friedrich-Schiller-Universität Jena zugänglich gemachte Schreiben des Herrn Reichsministers für Wissenschaft, Erziehung und Volksbildung vom 20. März 1939, Bl. 538–550, Bl. 549 and Bl. 550 verso.

[110] Cf. B. Kummer, *Germanenkunde im Kulturkampf. Beiträge zum Kampf um Wissenschaft, Theologie und Mythus des 20. Jahrhunderts* (Leipzig: Adolf Klein Verlag, 1935), pp. 17–33; in another context Kummer accused Höfler for having no idea of the "Lebensmitte des germanischen Volkstums," cf. Kummer, "Die Wikinger," p. 8.

[111] The metaphoric terminology which uses martial vocabulary to describe the conflicts and strategies within the university field is applied following Bourdieu, *Homo academicus*, e.g. p. 136 and p. 154.

[112] "Ist das Wissenschaft, wenn Otto Höfler, der die Germanen vielfach mit primitiven Völkern gleichsetzt, folgende Konstruktion vollbringt?" Kummer, *Germanenkunde*, p. 17.

method at length, and then concluded in an extreme polemical manner that the chain of evidence which was presented by Höfler perhaps could lead to the moon or to the primitives but not to a recognition of the Germans.[113]

After summarizing the incidents concerning Herman Wirth, Kummer turned to Höfler and intimated that the author of the *Kultische Geheimbünde der Germanen* had been unknown in the scholarly world before the book had been published. Höfler's theories should be seen as improper and not good enough to get a chair at a German University.[114] At the end of his polemical attack against Höfler, Kummer turned to the NSDAP. The party should deal with this issue which he connected to anti-German and even 'terroristic' activities.[115] And furthermore, Kummer demanded to those in charge of cultural and educational policies that it was high time to take action against such kind of scholarship, if necessary strict measures.[116] Kummer criticized Höfler's methodical approach and rejected the notion that Höfler was competent to understand the character of the German nation ("Volkstum").[117] In Kummer's eyes, Höfler's research was wrong since Höfler interpreted the old Germanic culture from a southern perspective, with all negative implications

---

[113] "Man mag im Einzelnen zu Höflers Buch stehen, wie man will. Man soll sich vergegenwärtigen, welche widerspruchsvollen und heute belachten Germanenbilder uns solch eine bekannte 'Kette des Beweises' schon eingetragen hat. Man kommt, wenn es gut geht, auf den Mond damit, oder zu den Kaffern, aber zu den Germanen eigentlich nur, wenn es der Zufall dieser Beweise will." Kummer, *Germanenkunde*, p. 19.

[114] Kummer, *Germanenkunde*, p. 27.

[115] "Wir rufen die Partei an, der wir im Kampf gegen das Widerdeutsche, u.a. gegen 'terroristische Geheimbünde' seit vielen Jahren dienten, daß sie sich dieser Frage annehme." Kummer, *Germanenkunde*, p. 29.

[116] "Es wird höchste Zeit, daß man kulturpolitisch sich dieser Wissenschaft annimmt, wenn es sein muß, mit Härte, statt mit Vertuschen seltsamer Dinge." Kummer, *Germanenkunde*, p. 33. This remark is directed at Neckel, but Höfler is meant as well. That Kummer's motivation was based on frustration with regard to the stagnation of his own scholarly career, can be seen also in his declaration from the March 30, 1938, Universitätsarchiv Jena, Bestand 4, Abt. IV, Nr. 20, Bl. 246–271, 267: "Zunächst muß ich noch einmal auf das Persönliche hinweisen: Seit 1930 empfehlen mich erstrangige Gelehrte für eine Professur, Seit 1927 bin ich tätig in nationalsozialistischer Geistesarbeit und Presse. Seit 1933 werde ich zu vielen hundert Schulungsvorträgen in der Bewegung eingesetzt. 1935 haben Männer wie Hans F.K. Günther, Alfred Rosenberg, Prof. Meinerth, Ludw. Ferd. Clauß, Hermann Mandel, auch Alfred Bäumler, mich einer Professur für würdig erklärt, und zwar ausdrücklich mit dem Hinweis auf eine mögliche Ausnahme bezüglich Habilitation, die infolge der peinlichen Vorfälle 1934 um Prof. Neckels Professur in Berlin ohne eine Schuld meinerseits abgebrochen werden musste. Seit 1936 bin ich beauftragt für Jena, mit bestimmter Aussicht auf eine Professur, und werde in Presse und Öffentlichkeit mit dem Professorentitel versehen…"

[117] Cf. Kummer, "Die Wikinger," p. 8.

Kummer usually ascribed the Mediterranean culture, instead of the only true northern perspective Kummer had chosen.[118]

Höfler reacted immediately. On November 2, 1935, he complained about Kummer's attacks to the Reich Ministry of Education and Culture, repeating his accusations two years later when Kummer had become a part-time lecturer in Jena.[119] The former petition was unsuccessful because Kummer did not fall within the jurisdiction of the "Disziplinargewalt des Reichserziehungsministeriums," but now, in light of Kummer's new teaching position, Höfler was searching for a second chance. Like Kummer, Höfler questioned the scholarly abilities and the political correctness of his opponent. Höfler pointed out that Kummer's behavior was singular, especially the manner in which Kummer criticized the NS government when he complained about the appointment of Höfler.[120] Once he had compiled Kummer's polemics, Höfler explained the factual and methodical differences between himself and Kummer.[121] Höfler tried to expose Kummer's strategy by demonstrating the superficial scientific basis in his opponent's reasoning. And he countered reproaches for his Viennese provenance by which Kummer tried to question Höfler's political reliability. Höfler in particular refused to be connected with Sigmund Freud and with other issues which could discredit him.[122] Then Höfler launched his counterattack: He questioned Kummer's morale in a fight ("Kampfmoral"),[123] accused him of pacifism,[124] and asked the Minister of Education and Culture

---

[118] Cf. ibid., p. 14.

[119] Universitätsarchiv Jena, Bestand 4, Abt. IV Nr. 20, Bl. 197–204: Abschrift eines Schreibens von Professor Otto Höfler, Kiel, Hindenburgufer 80, vom 26. November 1937.

[120] "Es ist dem Herrn Minister bekannt, dass meine Berufung nach Kiel auf regulären Vorschlag der Fakultät erfolgt ist; auch eine Reihe anderer Universitäten hat mich auf Grund meines Buches gleichzeitig oder kurz darauf auf ihre Vorschlagsliste für Germanistik gesetzt. Es ist m.W. der einzige Fall, dass gegen eine Massnahme der nationalsozialistischen Regierung öffentlich in dieser Weise agitiert worden ist." Ibid., Bl. 198f.

[121] Ibid., Bl. 199f.

[122] "...werde ich geflissentlich als der 'Schüler Wiens' bezeichnet und an kaum versteckter, und ich muss als alter österreichischer Nationalsozialist sagen: niederträchtiger Form sowohl mit dem Wiener Juden Siegfried [sic] Freud als auch mit der eingehend dargestellten römisch-deutschfeindlichen Dollfusspolitik in Zusammenhang gebracht. Ich käme eben 'von Süden'...und nicht von der heldischen Volksgemeinschaft des Nordens." Ibid., Bl. 200.

[123] Ibid., Bl. 202.

[124] Ibid., Bl. 202.

to determine if Kummer's way of fighting was honest and dignified enough for a German scholar.[125] Then he referred to the weak fact in Kummer's political integrity. Alluding to his resignation from the party, Höfler denied Kummer the right to call himself an old fighter for the NSDAP. Moreover, he accused him of having been disloyal during hard times.[126]

The conflict not only delayed Kummer's career but also played a significant role in his academic ambitions. Both Kummer and Höfler acted as exponents of contrary parties within the NS establishment. Kummer sided with the wing of Alfred Rosenberg and his followers against Heinrich Himmler and its SS-Ahnenerbe, the group to which Höfler was bound. Unfortunately, space does not allow an in-depth analysis of the controversy which became a life-and-death struggle. Finally, in 1942 Kummer became a professor at the University of Jena, when the influence of Himmler and his SS-Ahnenerbe on the application policy of the Reich Ministry of Education and Culture diminished.

The conflict between Kummer and Höfler demonstrates how contents depend on the standing one has in the academic world. Kummer started from outside the university and had set his sights on an academic career. Höfler, already a professor of Germanic language and literature, wanted to defend his reputation. Both cases show that that their scientific manner of reasoning depended on their participation in different wings in the NS regime to which they belonged. Whereas Höfler gave the SS-Ahnenerbe a scholarly justification with his books, Kummer's interests can be subsumed under the intentions of Alfred Rosenberg and his religious-ideological mixture of reasoning.[127] Kummer and Höfler accused each other of being unscholarly and ideologically wrong by neglecting their own ideological position. Pierre Bourdieu seems to address both figures in the German translation of his *Homo Academicus* of "interessegeleiteter Hellsicht," which blinds them to their own

---

[125] "...ob Kummers Kampfmethoden der Ehrlichkeit und Würde der deutschen Wissenschaft entsprechen." Ibid., Bl. 203.

[126] "...wer in der entscheidenden Kampfzeit so schreiben... konnte wie Dr. Kummer, [hat] kein Recht, sich als alten nationalsozialistischen Kämpfer zu bezeichnen. Wenn er 1928 bei der SA gewesen war, wie er angibt (Nord. Stimmen 1937, S. 202), dann wiegt sein treueloses Verhalten in der kritischsten Zeit meines Erachtens nur umso schwerer." Ibid., Bl. 203f.

[127] Cf. e.g. Kummer, *Herd und Altar*, vol. 2, p. 18, where he cites Rosenberg as if he were a accepted scholar and his reasoning would meet academic standards.

position. The English version has to make do without such a concise formulation, but illustrates perfectly how to describe such a scholar: "trapped within the lights of his self-interest, he is entirely blind, as blind as those whose blindness he denounces."[128]

---

[128] Cf. Bourdieu, *Homo academicus*, p. 16 (German translation, p. xvi).

Bibliography

Baetke, Walter. *Art und Glaube der Germanen.* Hamburg: Hanseatische Verlagsanstalt, 1934 (2nd ed. 1934, 3rd ed. 1938).

Bourdieu, Pierre. *Homo Academicus,* trans. Peter Collier. Stanford/California: Stanford University Press 1988 (German ed. trans. Bernd Schwibs, Frankfurt a. M.: Suhrkamp, 1992).

Bracher, Karl-Dietrich. *Die totalitäre Erfahrung.* München-Zürich: Piper, 1987.

Burrin, Philippe. "Totalitarismus und Gewalt: die Physiognomie des Nazismus." In Klaus-Dietmar Henke, ed., *Totalitarismus. Sechs Vorträge über Gehalt und Reichweite eines klassischen Konzepts der Diktaturforschung.* Dresden: Hannah-Arendt-Institut für Totalitarismusforschung e.V. 1999, pp. 27–37.

Clemen, Carl. *Altgermanische Religionsgeschichte.* Bonn: Röhrscheid, 1934.

Dahms, Hans-Joachim. "Jenaer Philosophen in der Weimarer Republik, im Nationalsozialismus und der Folgezeit bis 1950." In Uwe Hoßfeld et al., eds., *'Kämpferische Wissenschaft.'* Köln et al.: Böhlau Verlag, 2003, pp. 723–771.

Flasche, Rainer. "Der Irrationalismus in der Religionswissenschaft und dessen Begründung in der Zeit zwischen den Weltkriegen." In Hans G. Kippenberg and Brigitte Luchesi, eds., *Religionswissenschaft und Kulturkritik.* Marburg: diagonal, 1991, pp. 243–257.

Fritz, Nicole. *Bewohnte Mythen – Joseph Beuys und der Aberglaube.* Diss. Tübingen 2002 (online resource 2004: http://www.bsz-bw.de/cgi-bin/xvms.cgi?SWB11244235).

Germann, Dietrich. *Geschichte der Germanistik an der Friedrich-Schiller-Universität Jena,* vol. 3. Diss. Jena 1954.

Geuter, Ulfried. *Die Professionalisierung der deutschen Psychologie im Nationalsozialismus.* Frankfurt a.M.: Suhrkamp, 1988.

Hamann, Annett. "'Männer der kämpfenden Wissenschaft': Die 1945 geschlossenen Institute der Universität Jena." In Uwe Hoßfeld et al., eds., *'Kämpferische Wissenschaft.'* Köln et al.: Böhlau Verlag, 2003, pp. 202–234.

Heinrich, Fritz. *Die deutsche Religionswissenschaft und der Nationalsozialismus. Eine ideologiekritische und wissenschaftsgeschichtliche Untersuchung.* Petersberg: Michael Imhof Verlag, 2002.

Henke, Klaus-Dietmar. "Achsen des Augenmerks in der historischen Totalitarismusforschung." In idem, ed., *Totalitarismus. Sechs Vorträge über Gehalt und Reichweite eines klassischen Konzepts der Diktaturforschung.* Dresden: Hannah-Arendt-Institut für Totalitarismusforschung e.V. 1999, pp. 9–18.

Herbst, Ludolf. "Das nationalsozialistische Herrschaftssystem als Vergleichsgegenstand und Ansatz der Totalitarismustheorien," ibid., pp. 19–26.

Hippler, Fritz. *Wissenschaft und Leben.* Heidelberg: Carl Winter's Universitätsbuchhandlung, 1937.

Hirte, Ronald and Harry Stein. "Die Beziehungen der Universität Jena zum Konzentrationslager Buchenwald." In Uwe Hoßfeld et al., eds. *'Kämpferische Wissenschaft'.* Köln et al.: Böhlau Verlag, 2003, pp. 361–398.

Hitler, Adolf. *Mein Kampf,* 2 vols. München: Eher, 1937.

Höfler, Otto. *Kultische Geheimbünde der Germanen.* Frankfurt a. M.: Verlag Moritz Diesterweg, 1934.

Hojer, Ernst. *Nationalsozialismus und Pädagogik: Umfeld und Entwicklung der Pädagogik Ernst Kriecks.* Würzburg: Königshausen & Neumann, 1996.

Hoßfeld, Uwe, ed. *'Kämpferische Wissenschaft.' Studien zur Universität Jena im Nationalsozialismus.* Köln et al.: Böhlau Verlag, 2003.

——. "Zum Profilwandel der Jenaer Universität im Nationalsozialismus." In ibid., pp. 23–117.

——. "Von der Rassenkunde, Rassenhygiene und biologischen Erbstatistik zur Synthetischen Theorie der Evolution: Eine Skizze der Biowissenschaften." In ibid., pp. 519–574.

Junginger, Horst. *Von der philologischen zur völkischen Religionswissenschaft. Das Fach Religionswissenschaft an der Universität Tübingen von der Mitte des 19. Jahrhunderts bis zum Ende des Dritten Reiches* (Contubernium. Tübinger Beiträge zur Universitäts- und Wissenschaftsgeschichte 51). Stuttgart: Franz Steiner 1999.

——. "Einführung: Das Überleben der Religionswissenschaft im Nationalsozialismus." *Zeitschrift für Religionswissenschaft* 9 (2001), pp. 149–167.

Klemperer, Victor. *LTI. Notizbuch eines Philologen.* Leipzig: Verlag Philipp Reclam jun., 1985.

Krieck, Ernst. *Leben als Prinzip der Weltanschauung und Problem der Wissenschaft,* mit einem Anhang von Willi Kunz und Karl August Götz (Weltanschauung und Wissenschaft 7). Leipzig: Armanen-Verlag, 1938.

——. *Wissenschaft, Weltanschauung, Hochschulreform.* Leipzig: Armanen-Verlag, 1934.

Krüger, Friedrich. *Wissenschaft und Leben: Rede gehalten bei der Feier des 50. Geburtstages des Führers und Reichskanzlers Adolf Hitler am 20. April 1939* (Greifswalder Universitätsreden 52). Greifswald 1939.

Kubota, Hiroshi. *Religionswissenschaftliche Religiosität und Religionsgründung. Jakob Wilhelm Hauer im Kontext des Freien Protestantismus* (Tübinger Beiträge zur Religionswissenschaft 5). Frankfurt a.M.: Peter Lang, 2005.

Kummer, Bernhard. *Midgards Untergang. Germanischer Kult und Glaube in den letzten heidnischen Jahrhunderten* (Veröffentlichungen des Forschungsinstituts für Vergleichende Religionsgeschichte an der Universität Leipzig II-7.). Leipzig: Pfeiffer, 1927 (2nd ed. Leipzig 1935, 3rd ed. Leipzig 1937).

——. "Braut, Bräutigam." In *Handwörterbuch des Deutschen Aberglaubens,* ed. by Hanns Bächtold-Stäubli, vol. 1. Berlin, Leipzig: Walter de Gruyter & Co (1927), col. 1522–1536.

——. "bräutlen, Bräutlingsbaden." Ibid., vol. 1 (1927), col. 1536f.

——. "Ehe," "Empfängnis," "Frau, Weib." Ibid., vol. 2 (1929/30), col. 564–592, col. 806–814, and col. 1732–1774.

——. "Freyja," "Freyr," "Frija-Frigg," "Frô," "Fulla," "Geburt," "Geburtsbaum," "Geburtstag," "Geschlecht," "Geschlechtsverkehr," "Geschlechtswechsel, Geschlechtsverwandlung," "Gevatter, Pate." Ibid., vol. 3 (1930/1931), col. 79–82, col. 82f., col. 103–112, col. 113–115, col. 210f., col. 406–419, col. 419–422, col. 422–424, col. 725–730, col. 735–752, col. 752–755, and col. 789–804.

——. "Hochzeit," "Jungfrau, Jungfräulichkeit, jungfräulich," "Kind," "Kinderherkunft," "Kinderlied," "Kindersegen und Kinderlosigkeit," "Kinderspiel." Ibid., vol. 4 (1931/1932), col. 148–174, col. 841–854, col. 1310–1341, col. 1342–1360, col. 1360f., col. 1374–1385, and col. 1385–1387.

——. "ledig," "Liebe," "Liebeszauber," "Mann, männlich," "Männerkindbett." Ibid., vol. 5 (1932/1933), col. 1003–1012, col. 1273–1276, col. 1279–1297, col. 1569–1573, and col. 1573–1576.

——. *Mission als Sittenwechsel. Mit einer Antwort an Prof. D. Rückert: 'Die kulturelle und nationale Bedeutung der Missionierung Germaniens für das deutsche Volk'* (Reden und Aufsätze zum nordischen Gedanken 1, ed. "in Gemeinschaft mit Mitarbeitern der 'Nordischen Stimmen' von Dr. Bernhard Kummer"). Leipzig: Adolf Klein Verlag, 1933.

——. "Die kulturelle und nationale Bedeutung der Missionierung Germaniens für das deutsche Volk. Entgegnung auf die gleichnamige Ausführung von Prof. D. Rückert im Lutherischen Missionsjahrbuch, Jg. 44, 1931." In: *Reden und Aufsätze zum nordischen Gedanken* 1 (1933), pp. 25–32.

——. *Persönlichkeit und Gemeinschaft* (Herd und Altar. Wandlungen altnordischer Sittlichkeit im Glaubenswechsel 1). Leipzig: Adolf Klein Verlag, 1934.

——. *Anfang und Ende des faustischen Jahrtausends* (Reden und Aufsätze zum nordischen Gedanken 17). Leipzig: Adolf Klein Verlag, 1934.

——. "Nachgeburt." In *Handwörterbuch des Deutschen Aberglaubens*, vol. 6 (1934/1935), col. 760–766.

——. *Germanenkunde im Kulturkampf. Beiträge zum Kampf um Wissenschaft, Theologie und Mythus des 20. Jahrhunderts* (Reden und Aufsätze zum nordischen Gedanken 25). Leipzig: Adolf Klein Verlag, 1935.

——. "Schwangerschaft, Schwangere, schwanger." In *Handwörterbuch des Deutschen Aberglaubens*, vol. 7 (1935/1936), col. 1406–1427.

——. *Nordisches Lebensgefühl. Einführung in das altisländische Schrifttum* (Reden und Aufsätze zum nordischen Gedanken 11). Leipzig: Adolf Klein Verlag, 1935

——. "Die Wikinger: Räuber oder Helden?." In idem et al., eds., *Der nordische Mensch der Wikingerzeit*. Leipzig: Adolf Klein Verlag, 1935, pp. 3–24.

——. *Der Machtkampf zwischen Volk, König und Kirche im alten Norden* (Herd und Altar. Wandlungen altnordischer Sittlichkeit im Glaubenswechsel 2). Leipzig: Adolf Klein Verlag, 1939.

Kunz, Willi. "Das Lebensprinzip bei Goethe, Anhang 1." In Ernst Krieck. *Leben als Prinzip der Weltanschauung und Problem der Wissenschaft* (Mit einem Anhang von Willi Kunz und Karl August Götz; Weltanschauung und Wissenschaft 7), Leipzig: Armanen-Verlag, 1938, pp. 235–265.

Loh, Werner and Wolfgang Wippermann, eds. *Faschismus kontrovers*. Stuttgart: Lucius und Lucius Verlag, 2003.

Morgan, Philip. *Fascism in Europe, 1919–1945*. London-New York: Routledge, 2003.

Müller, Gerhard. *Ernst Krieck und die nationalsozialistische Wissenschaftsreform: Motive und Tendenzen einer Wissenschaftslehre und Hochschulreform im Dritten Reich* (Studien und Dokumentationen zur deutschen Bildungsgeschichte), Weinheim: Beltz, 1978.

Neckel, Gustav. *Germanen und Kelten. Historisch-linguistisch-rassenkundliche Forschungen und Gedanken zur Geisteskrisis*. Heidelberg: Winter, 1929.

——. *Liebe und Ehe bei den vorchristlichen Germanen*. Leipzig: Teubner, 1932 (2nd rev. and enl. ed. 1934, 3rd rev. ed., Schkeuditz-Gartenstadt: Adolf Klein, 1939).

Rosenberg, Alfred. *Protestantische Rompilger. Der Verrat an Luther und der 'Mythus des 20. Jahrhunderts'*, 2nd–10th ed. München: Hoheneichen-Verlag, 1937.

Rudolph, Kurt. "Die Bedeutung von Hans Haas für die Religionswissenschaft." *Zeitschrift für Religions- und Geistesgeschichte* 21 (1969), pp. 238–252, republished in Kurt Rudolph, *Geschichte und Probleme der Religionswissenschaft*, Leiden: Brill, 1992 (Studies in the History of Religions 53), pp. 340–356.

——. *Die Religionsgeschichte an der Leipziger Universität und die Entwicklung der Religionswissenschaft. Ein Beitrag zur Wissenschaftsgeschichte der Religionswissenschaft* (Sitzungsberichte der Sächsischen Akademie der Wissenschaften zu Leipzig, Philologisch-historische Klasse 107–1). Berlin: Akademie-Verlag, 1962.

——. "Walter Hugo Hermann Baetke." In Christoph König, ed., *Internationales Germanistenlexikon 1800–1950*, vol. 1. Berlin-New York: Walter de Gruyter, 2003, pp. 75–77.

Schilling, Willy. "NS-Dozentenschaft und Nationalsozialistischer Deutscher Dozentenbund an der Universität Jena." In Uwe Hoßfeld, ed., *'Kämpferische Wissenschaft'*. Köln et al.: Böhlau Verlag, 2003, pp. 180–201.

Seeberg, Reinhold. *Christentum und Germanentum* (Schriften der Treitschke Stiftung). Leipzig: Dieterich, 1914.

Stöwesand, Rudolf. *Ein Eigener und Besonderer. Meinem Freunde Bernhard Kummer (21.1.1897–1.12.1962) zum Gedächtnis* (offprint of Forschungsfragen unserer Zeit, 10. Jg., 1963, Lfg. 1.2).

Thieme, Karl. *Deutsche evangelische Christen auf dem Wege zur katholischen Kirche*. Schlieren-Zürich: Neue Brücke, 1934.

Traxel, Werner. "Zur Geschichte der Deutschen Gesellschaft für Psychologie im so genannten Dritten Reich," in *Psychologische Rundschau* 55 (2004), pp. 21–32.

Winnkel, Roel Vande: "Nazi Germany's Fritz Hippler (1909–2002)." *Historical Journal of Film, Radio and Television* 23 (2003), pp. 91–99.

Wippermann, Wolfgang. *Faschismustheorien. Zur Entwicklung der Diskussion von den Anfängen bis heute*, 7th rev. ed., Darmstadt: Primus, 1997.

——. *Totalitarismustheorien. Die Entwicklung der Diskussion von den Anfängen bis heute.* Darmstadt: Primus, 1997.

Wüst, Walther. "Von Indogermanischer Religiosität. Sinn und Sendung." *Archiv für Religionswissenschaft* 36 (1939), pp. 64–108.

Zernack, Julia. "Gustav Karl Paul Christoph Neckel." In Christoph König, ed., *Internationales Germanistenlexikon 1800–1950*, vol. 1. Berlin-New York: Walter de Gruyter, 2003, pp. 1311–1312.

——. " 'Wenn es sein muß, mit Härte' – Die Zwangsversetzung des Nordisten Gustav Neckel 1935 und die 'Germanenkunde im Kulturkampf'," in idem and Klaus von See, eds., *Germanistik und Politik in der Zeit des Nationalsozialismus. Zwei Fallstudien: Hermann Schneider und Gustav Neckel.* Heidelberg: Winter, 2004, pp. 113–208.

Zimmermann, Susanne and Thomas Zimmermann. "Die Medizinische Fakultät der Universität Jena im 'Dritten Reich' – ein Überblick." In Uwe Hoßfeld, ed., *'Kämpferische Wissenschaft'*. Köln et al.: Böhlau Verlag, 2003, pp. 401–436.

IRRATIONAL EXPERIENCES, HEROIC DEEDS AND THE EXTRACTION OF SURPLUS

Gustavo Benavides

Entbehren sollst du! sollst entbehren!

Faust I, 4

On April 19, 1944, when the defeat of Nazi Germany was almost certain, Pierre Drieu la Rochelle, the novelist and collaborator, wrote in his diary that he wanted to die in the faith of Nietzsche's *Zarathustra* and the *Bhagavad Gita*.[1] It would be pointless to ask whether Drieu had read Jakob Wilhelm Hauer's analyses of the *Bhagavadgītā*, the ones in which the Tübingen indologist extolls prince Arjuna's decision to fight, a virile decision brought about by Krishna's mix of metaphysical sermon and emotional blackmail; or whether Drieu was familiar with the orientalist Giuseppe Tucci's hymns to the saint and the hero. Death and sacrifice, virility and heroism, prominent already in fin-de-siècle works such as Richard Strauss' *Tod und Verklärung* (1888–89), *Also sprach Zarathustra* (1895–96) and *Ein Heldenleben* (1897–98), and earlier among the romantics,[2] had been very much in the air since the nineteen-twenties, as much among war veterans such as Drieu and Ernst Jünger, as among established orientalists such as Hauer and Tucci. From 1934 to 1958 Hauer had published three almost identical versions of his essay on the yoga of action (*karmayoga*) in the *Bhagavadgītā*. The first appeared in 1934 as *Eine indo-arische Metaphysik des Kampfes und der Tat*, a small volume, dedicated to "Dem kämpfenden Geschlechte," in which Hauer, without betraying the spirit of the Indian text, validated the bellicose aims of

---

[1] Pierre Drieu la Rochelle, *Journal 1939–1945*. Édition établie, présentée et annotée par Julien Hervier (Paris: Gallimard, 1992), p. 380: "Je meurs dans la foi de la 'Bhagavad-Gita' et du 'Zarathoustra': c'est là qu'est ma vérité, mon credo;" cf. p. 355 (September 10, 1943). See also Robert Soucy, *Fascist Intellectual: Drieu La Rochelle* (Berkeley: University of California Press, 1979), p. 93.

[2] See Gerhard Kaiser, *Pietismus und Patriotismus im literarischen Deutschland. Ein Beitrag zum Problem der Säkularisation*, 2nd ed. (Frankfurt am Main: Athenäum, 1973), ch. 9, "Patriotischer Blut- und Wundenkult."

the national socialists in power.[3] This study was reprinted with minor modifications in 1937, as the fifth chapter, "Visnu, der Wirkende und der tragische Heroismus des Gottgeborgenen," of the first and only volume of Hauer's *Glaubensgeschichte der Indogermanen*.[4] It appeared, finally, in 1958, as the third chapter of *Der Yoga. Ein indischer Weg zum Selbst*.[5] What concerns Hauer in this work is the need to forget oneself and to fulfill one's heroic duty violently. For Hauer, as for the authors of the *Bhagavadgītā*, death is ultimately irrelevant, for in killing one does not kill the self, as this self — *Ātman, puruṣa* — relates to the body as bodies relate to clothes: We discard the old and soiled ones and put on new ones (II, 22). As Krishna tells Arjuna, one should fight because the highest form of yoga is *karmayoga*, the yoga of action, for, contrary to what some hypocritical renouncers claim, one cannot not act since the mere act of breathing constitutes an action (III, 5–6). One should act, then, but without becoming attached to the fruits of one's deeds (IV, 18, VI, 1)[6] — as it has been repeated admiringly by countless teachers of introductions to Indian philosophy and religion, without realizing the implications of this position.

At the time Hauer published the first version of his study of the *Bhagavadgītā*, we find the classicist Walter F. Otto writing about the need to have a will for the most difficult tasks and, more ominously, about regarding heroism with awe.[7] Similarly, Tucci, the foremost Italian Buddhologist of the twentieth century, who as a member of the Fascist

[3] J.W. Hauer, *Eine indo-arische Metaphysik des Kampfes und der Tat. Die Bhagavadgītā in neuer Sicht mit Übersetzungen* (Stuttgart: W. Kohlhammer, 1934).

[4] J.W. Hauer, *Glaubensgeschichte der Indogermanen, Erster Teil: Das religiöse Artbild der Indogermanen und die Grundtypen indo-arischen Religion* (Stuttgart: W. Kohlhammer, 1937), pp. 114–173.

[5] J.W. Hauer, *Der Yoga. Ein indischer Weg zum Selbst. Kritisch-positive Darstellung nach den indischen Quellen mit einer Übersetzung der maßgeblichen Texte, 2. umgearbeitete und um den 2. Band erweiterte Auflage des 'Yoga als Heilweg'* (Stuttgart: W. Kohlhammer, 1958).

[6] For more details, see Gustavo Benavides, "Jakob Wilhelm Hauer, or Karmayoga as a Cold War Weapon," in Dalibor Papoušek et al., eds., *The Academic Study of Religion during the Cold War: East and West* (New York: Peter Lang, 2001), pp. 225–238.

[7] W.F. Otto, "Der junge Nietzsche" (1934), *Wissenschaft und Gegenwart* 10, Frankfurt a.M. 1936, repr. in W.F. Otto, *Mythos und Welt* (Stuttgart: Ernst Klett, 1962), pp. 159–178, esp. pp. 175f. On Otto, see Hubert Cancik, "Die Götter Griechenlands 1929. Walter F. Otto als Religionswissenschaftler und Theologe am Ende der Weimarer Republik I," in Heinrich von Stietencron, ed., *Theologen und Theologien in verschiedenen Kulturkreisen* (Düsseldorf: Patmos, 1986), pp. 214–238; idem, "Dionysos 1933. W.F. Otto, ein Religionswissenschaftler am Ende der Weimarer Republik," in Richard Faber and Renate Schlesier, eds., *Die Restauration der Götter. Antike Religion und Neo-Paganismus* (Würzburg: Königshausen & Neumann, 1986), pp. 105–123.

Party published two short books and a number of articles devoted to the glorification of heroism and self-sacrifice, writes that renunciation, the slow burning of passions, is not the only form of sacrifice: Sacrifice can also be accomplished by rendering passions titanic, and by annihilating oneself in the service of a demonic or saintly idea.[8] Later, with the war already under way, Tucci writes that "the Bodhisattva is not only the being who loves and sacrifices himself, but someone who fights. He is an armor-clad warrior"[9] – in a statement which, it must be stressed, contradicts neither traditional Buddhist exegesis nor the way in which Buddhism has been actually lived.[10]

Through a heroic deed one grabs reality and bends it to one's will, paying no consideration to everyday constraints, to ordinary morality or even to the rules of logic. Ultimately, a heroic deed must appear as gratuitous, as grounded upon itself, as similar in this regard to Schmitt's sovereign decision.[11] As I have tried to show elsewhere, there are affinities between Rudolf Otto's conception of the Holy and Schmitt's *Ausnahmezustand*, for one can describe the relation between Otto's Holy (or Eliade's hierophanies) and the world of the profane with the words used by Schmitt to portray the exception: "In der Ausnahme durchbricht die Kraft des wirklichen Lebens die Kruste einer

---

[8] Giuseppe Tucci, "Il cinema indiano," *La lettura* 38 (1938), pp. 350–357, repr. in G. Tucci, *Forme dello spirito asiatico* (Milano-Messina: Casa editrice Giuseppe Principato, 1940–XVIII), pp. 159–169, esp. p. 167: "…sacrificio non è solo nella rinuncia, nel lento bruciare le pasioni umane, ma anche nel renderle potenti e titaniche fino a che nella loro esaltazione travolgano e annientino l'uomo, soggiogato e trascinato da un'idea santa o demoniaca." A discussion of Tucci's career can be found in G. Benavides, "Giuseppe Tucci, or Buddhology in the Age of Fascism," in Donald S. Lopez, Jr., ed., *Curators of the Buddha: The Study of Buddhism under Colonialism* (Chicago: University of Chicago Press, 1995), pp. 161–196.

[9] G. Tucci, "Il Buddhismo e l'uomo," *Forme dello spirito asiatico*, pp. 61–65, esp. p. 62: "Il Bodhisattva non è soltanto colui che ama e si sacrifica, ma anche colui che lotta. È un eroe, un guerriero coperto di corazza."

[10] See Benavides, "Giuseppe Tucci," p. 176, and n. 115.

[11] On decisionism, see Christian Graf von Krockow, *Die Entscheidung. Eine Untersuchung über Ernst Jünger, Carl Schmitt, Martin Heidegger* (Stuttgart: Ferdinand Enke Verlag, 1958, repr. Frankfurt am Main: Campus, 1990). Schmitt's decisionism is of more than historical interest these days, given that it has become the official, if unnamed, doctrine among the lawyers who declared that the decisions of George Bush supersede, among other things, international law forbidding the torture of prisoners. Foremost among those jurists is Alberto Gonzales, the current attorney general of the United States. The key text, now and then, is Carl Schmitt, "Der Führer schützt das Recht. Zur Reichtagsrede Adolf Hitlers am 13. Juli 1934," *Deutsche Juristen-Zeitung* 39. Jahrgang, Heft 15, Berlin, den 1. August 1934, col. 945–950.

in Wiederholung erstarrten Mechanik."[12] Likewise, Tucci's hymn to the annihilation of oneself in the service of a demonic or saintly idea, free as it is from ordinary moral constraints, is an embodiment of the sovereign decision, although in this case the concept that underlies it is not Schmitt's *Entscheidung* but Giovanni Gentile's *atto puro*. This *atto puro*, twin of Schmitt's *Entscheidung*, presents itself as gratuitous, heroic, unconcerned with profit – in short, as the opposite of the economically motivated actions of the Marxists. As Mussolini (or perhaps Gentile) writes in the official article on fascist doctrine, published 1932 in the *Enciclopedia Italiana*, fascism still believes in sanctity and heroism, that is, in acts that have no economic motive, direct or indirect.[13]

Boundless heroism is also to be found in the early works of Ernst Jünger – known to scholars of religion as co-editor of *Antaios*.[14] In *Der Kampf als inneres Erlebnis*, first published in 1922, Jünger celebrates the collapse of the refinement of the spirit and of the tender cult of the brain: "Die Verfeinerung des Geistes, der zärtliche Kultus des Hirns gingen unter in einer klirrenden Wiedergeburt des Barbarentums,"[15] and asks himself, "Denn was ist das Verständnis des Hirns gegen das des Herzens?"[16] Jünger's description of the experience of battle – "In göttlichen Funken spritzt das Blut durch die Adern..."[17] – becomes apophatic theology when he deals with the ecstasy, the frenzy above all frenzies – "Rausch über allen Räuschen" – the madness, the merging into the universe, that takes place in battle. Considering Jünger's pivotal position during the years between the wars, the fact that his book *Der Arbeiter* was required reading for Heidegger's students and, above all,

---

[12] Carl Schmitt, *Politische Theologie. Vier Kapitel zur Lehre von der Souveränität* (Berlin: Duncker und Humblot, 1st ed. 1922, 2nd ed. 1934 = 7th ed. 1996), p. 21. See G. Benavides, "Holiness, State of Exception, Agency," in Brigitte Luchesi and Kocku von Stuckrad, eds., *Religion im kulturellen Diskurs. Festschrift für Hans G. Kippenberg zu seinem 65. Geburtstag* (Berlin-New York: Walter de Gruyter, 2004), pp. 61–73.

[13] Benito Mussolini [Giovanni Gentile?], "Fascismo–Dottrina," *Enciclopedia Italiana di Scienze, Lettere ed Arti* 14 (1932–X), pp. 847–851, esp. p. 849: "Il fascismo crede ancora nella santità e nell'eroismo, cioè in atti nei quali nessun motivo economico – lontano o vicino – agisce."

[14] *Antaios. Zeitschrift für eine freie Welt*, ed. by Mircea Eliade and Ernst Jünger, I,1, Mai 1959 to XII,6, März 1971, Stuttgart, Ernst Klett Verlag. The subtitle, *Zeitschrift für eine freie Welt*, appears only in the first six issues, I,1 to I,6, Mai 1959 to März 1960. The short text introducing the first issue of *Antaios* has been reprinted in Jünger, *Sämtliche Werke* 14 (Stuttgart: Klett, 1982), p. 167f.

[15] Ernst Jünger, *Der Kampf als inneres Erlebnis* (Berlin: Mittler, 1922, repr. in E. Jünger, *Sämtliche Werke* 7, pp. 9–103, here p. 35.

[16] Jünger, *Sämtliche Werke* 7, p. 39.

[17] Ibid., p. 48.

his long friendship with Eliade, the other editor of *Antaios*, it may be worth quoting the passage in full:

> Ein letztes noch: die Ekstase ... das ist ein Rausch über allen Räuschen, eine Entfesselung, die alle Bande sprengt. Es ist eine Raserei ohne Rücksicht und Grenzen, nur den Gewalten der Natur vergleichbar. Da ist der Mensch wie der brausende Sturm, das tosende Meer und der brüllende Donner. Dann ist er verschmolzen ins All, er rast den dunklen Toren des Todes zu wie ein Geschoß dem Ziel.[18]

Among scholars of religion as much as literary figures, the concern with the heroic act goes hand in hand with the concern with irrational experience. Thus, in 1939, equating Zen with mysticism, Tucci writes that mystical systems "are based on an inner experience which, emerging mysteriously within the darkness of our life, transforms night into day, so that as soon as we are touched by its grace we feel reborn in another level where everything is new, luminous and blissful."[19] The heroic act, the violence, seem to require another act of violence, one in which one oneself is seized by a power greater than one's own, a power that, like the heroic deed, violates logic and morality. What we encounter at the other end of the heroic deed is experience, *Erlebnis*. This irrational experience has as its object the numinous, as described by Rudolf Otto in *Das Heilige*. There is no need to elaborate upon Otto's numinous, but it may be useful to point out that experiencing of the kind described by Otto plays a central role in his contemporaries of various political persuasions, including, at one end, National Socialists such as Hauer and, at the other, scholars whose academic position was threatened by the Nazis, such as Friedrich Heiler, or who were forced to leave Germany, such as Joachim Wach.

In *Das Gebet*, a book which, published in 1918, had reached its fifth edition in 1923, Heiler writes:

> Den Ausgangs- und Mittelpunkt der Religionswissenschaft muß stets die *reine, naive* Religion bilden. Die Religion muß vor allem an ihren Quellen und Höhepunkten studiert werden, dort, wo sie spontan und frei mit produktiver Kraft aus starken seelischen Erlebnissen hervorbricht, wo sie

---

[18] Ibid., p. 54.

[19] G. Tucci, "Lo Zen e il carattere del popolo giapponese," *Asiatica* 5 (1939), pp. 1–9, esp. p. 3: "...i sistemi di mistica si vivono: non sono basati su un convincimento logico, ma su un'esperienza interiore la quale misteriosamente sorgendo nelle tenebre della nostra vita, fa della notte giorno così che appena tocchi della sua grazia ci sintiamo renati in altri piani ove tutto è novo, luminoso e beatifico."

noch nicht erstarrt ist in stabilen, konventionellen Kultformen und noch
nicht überwuchert durch das ausdeutende mythologische Denken oder
die klärende philosophisch-theologische Spekulation.[20]

For Heiler, therefore, mysticism has to be considered as the core of
religion: mysticism defined as "jene Form des Gottesumganges, bei der
die Welt und das Ich radikal verneint werden, bei der die menschliche
Personalität sich auflöst, untergeht, versinkt in dem unendlichen Einen
der Gottheit."[21] Mysticism, constituted by extraordinary experiences,[22]
is based on a subjective, inner revelation,[23] and in its pure form is
individualistic, asocial, and knows nothing other than God and the
soul.[24] Forty years later, in *Erscheinungsformen und Wesen der Religion*, his
vast phenomenology of religion, personal religious experience continues
to be demanded from those who wish to study religion.[25]

Similarly, in *Die Religionen, ihr Werden, ihr Sinn, ihre Wahrheit*, whose first
and only part, *Das religiöse Erlebnis auf den unteren Stufen*, was published in
1923, Hauer writes that although many regard with mistrust the term
Erlebnis, he does not shy away from it, because religious experience is
the source from which religion flows,[26] the deepest roots of religion
reaching the inaccessible abyss of the suprarational and resting in the
irrational.[27] A year later, in his *Religionswissenschaft*, Wach, who because
of his Jewish ancestry was eventually forced to leave Germany, echoes

---

[20] Friedrich Heiler, *Das Gebet. Eine religionsgeschichtliche und religionspsychologische Untersuchung* (München: Ernst Reinhardt, 4th ed. 1921 [1st ed. 1918, 2nd ed. 1919, 3rd ed.
1920]), p. 17, cf. also p. 21. Ultimately, "Die Religionswissenschaft wird gekrönt von
einer *Metaphysik der Religion*, welche nach der Realität des von der Phänomenologie
herausgestellten Glaubens an ein Transzendentes und Absolutes und an die Verbindung
des Menschen mit ihn fragt" (p. 25).
[21] F. Heiler, *Das Gebet*, p. 249; the same formulation can be found in his study of
mysticism, *Die Bedeutung der Mystik für die Weltreligionen* (München: Ernst Reinhardt,
1919), p. 6.
[22] F. Heiler, *Das Gebet*, pp. 257f.
[23] Ibid., p. 265.
[24] Ibid., p. 272.
[25] F. Heiler, *Erscheinungsformen und Wesen der Religion* (Stuttgart: W. Kohlhammer, 1961),
p. 17, pp. 19–21, and pp. 541–558: "Die Erlebniswelt der Religion."
[26] J.W. Hauer, *Die Religionen, ihr Werden, ihr Sinn, ihre Wahrheit. Erstes Buch: Das religiöse
Erlebnis auf den unteren Stufen* (Berlin-Stuttgart-Leipzig: Kohlhammer, 1923). See "Vorwort," pp. V–X, esp. p. VI: "Ich scheue mich nicht, das Wort Erlebnis zu gebrauchen,
obwohl ihm heute viele mit Misstrauen begegnen." On Hauer see Margarete Dierks,
Jakob Wilhelm Hauer 1881–1962. Leben. Werk. Wirkung (Heidelberg: Lambert Schneider,
1986).
[27] "Ihre tiefste Wurzeln reichen in den unzugänglichen Abgrund des Übervernünf-
tigen, ruhen im Irrationalen." Hauer, *Die Religionen*, p. 27; see also p. 43: "Die Wurzel
aller Religion ist, wie jede echte Erfahrung zeigt, ein irrationales Erlebnis…"

both Otto and Hauer by claiming, "So gibt es auch eine Voraussetzung, ohne die keiner Religion verstehen kann: das ist *religiöser Sinn*."[28] But even though, according to Wach, every human being may be able to understand what religion is, this member of the George circle[29] warns in a text from 1931 that

> Mit dem Demokratismus des Vernunft-Glaubens wird man im Bereich der Religion nun freilich nicht viel ausrichten; daß die Gaben des Geistes verschiedene sind, daß es so etwas wie Charisma, Stufung usw. gibt, sollte eine elementare Erkenntnis sein. Und was die Alleinherrschaft der ratio anlangt, so sind heute die, die von religiösen Dingen wissen, nicht mehr die einzigen, die ihr skeptisch gegenüberstehen.[30]

This hymn to hierarchy and denunciation of reason, found in a critique of Freud's approach to religion, could have been written by a member of the German nobility during the Weimar years[31] or by an eighteenth or nineteenth-century enemy of the Enlightenment.[32] What could also have been found in one of those texts is Wach's almost caricaturesque contrasting of light and darkness. Wach opposes Freud's use of a couple of verses of Schiller's *Der Taucher*, "Es freue sich, wer da atmet im rosigen Licht," with his own approving reference to the words of Orest in the third act of Goethe's *Iphigenie auf Tauris*, "[Und laß dir raten], habe die Sonne nicht zu lieb und nicht die Sterne, komm, folge

---

[28] Joachim Wach, *Religionswissenschaft. Prolegomena zu ihrer wissenschaftstheoretischen Grundlegung* (Leipzig: J.C. Hinrich'sche Buchhandlung, 1924), p. 36; see also p. 150. On Wach see Rainer Flasche, *Die Religionswissenschaft Joachim Wachs* (Berlin, New York: Walter de Gruyter, 1978).

[29] On the George circle "als geistiger Wegbereiter der nationalsozialistischen Ideologie" and on the Jewish members of the circle, see Karl Löwith, *Mein Leben in Deutschland vor und nach 1933. Ein Bericht* (Stuttgart: J.B. Metzlersche Verlagsbuchhandlung, 1986), pp. 19–24.

[30] J. Wach, "Das religiöse Gefühl," *Das Problem der Kultur und die ärztliche Psychologie* (Vorträge des Instituts für Geschichte der Medizin an der Universität Leipzig 4, ed. by Henry E. Sigerist) (Leipzig: Georg Thieme, 1931), p. 22.

[31] On attitudes towards reason, charisma and hierarchy among the German nobility and its non-aristocratic ideologues, see Stephan Malinowski, *Vom König zum Führer. Deutscher Adel und Nationalsozialismus* (Frankfurt am Main: Fischer, 2004, originally published as *Vom König zum Führer. Sozialer Niedergang und politische Radikalisierung im deutschen Adel zwischen Kaiserreich und NS-Staat*, Berlin: Akademie Verlag, 2003), pp. 87, pp. 104–116, and p. 490.

[32] See Klaus Epstein, *The Genesis of German Conservatism* (Princeton: Princeton University Press, 1966), pp. 67–76; Jacques Droz, *Le romantisme allemand et l'état* (Paris: Payot, 1966), ch. 1, "La destruction des valeurs rationnelles;" Darrin McMahon, *Enemies of the Enlightenment. The French Counter-Enlightenment and the Making of Modernity* (Oxford-New York: Oxford University Press, 2001), esp. p. 68 and p. 131.

mir ins dunkle Reich hinab."³³ Knowing what happened on January 30, 1933, that is, less than two years after the publication of this essay, it is perhaps all too easy for us to deplore Wach's being seduced by Orest's speech, rather than being warned by the verses of *Der Taucher* that follow the ones he quotes: "Da unten aber ist's fürchterlich, und der Mensch versuche die Götter nicht und begehre nimmer und nimmer zu schauen, was sie gnädig bedeckten mit Nacht und Grauen." Poetry aside, Wach's defense of hierarchy seems to have as its *raison d'être* the concerns expressed in a text he published twenty years later; one in which Wach uses ominous military metaphors to describe the advances of materialism: "Materialistic naturalism, relentlessly advancing from the eighteen-fifties to the end of the century, became the philosophical creed of the victoriously advancing natural sciences and of the Marxist social teaching with its mass-appeal."³⁴ Wach was not alone in distrusting reason: Three years after Wach's critique of Freud, Walter F. Otto writes about the severe blows suffered by scientific optimism,³⁵ and with the National Socialists already in power, laments the loss of the capacity for myth.³⁶

Was it because of the relentless advance of materialism, scientism and above all Marxism that an idealistic counteraction of a military-scholarly kind was needed? Was this the reason for the irruption of the irrational *Entscheidung* or for the gratuitousness of an *atto puro* claimed by Mussolini/Gentile to be unsoiled by base economic concerns? Was it necessary, in order to counteract a violence based ultimately on material interests, to transfigure one's violence and to present it as gratuitous, even though its being interest-based was transparent, as even

³³ Wach, "Das religiöse Gefühl," p. 33. Was Wach familiar with Hans Pfitzner's *'Das dunkle Reich'*, *Chorphantasie mit Orchester, Orgel, Sopran- und Bariton-Solo*, op. 38, whose title was taken from Goethe's Iphigenie auf Tauris? Pfitzner's piece, a non-liturgical requiem for his wife, was composed in 1929, two years before the publication of Wach's critique of Freud (a 1993 recording conducted by Rolf Reuter is available: CPO 999 158–2). Pfitzner's polemic against "die neue Ästhetik der musikalischen Impotenz" echoes Wach's attacks against reason.

³⁴ J. Wach, *Types of Religious Experience, Christian and Non-Christian* (Chicago: University of Chicago Press, 1951), ch. 10, "Rudolf Otto and the Idea of the Holy," pp. 209–227, esp. p. 212.

³⁵ W.F. Otto, "Der junge Nietzsche," *Mythos und Welt*, p. 175f.

³⁶ W.F. Otto, "Der Durchbruch zum antiken Mythos im XIX. Jahrhundert," in Wolfgang Frommel, ed., *Vom Schicksal des deutschen Geistes* (Berlin: Die Runde, 1934, p. 35ff.), repr. in W.F. Otto, *Die Gestalt und das Sein. Gesammelte Abhandlungen über den Mythos und seine Bedeutung für die Menschheit* (Düsseldorf-Köln: Wissenschaftliche Buchgesellschaft, 1955), pp. 211–225, esp. p. 221.

the embodiments of the gratuitous act, the members of the nobility, were forced to recognize, sometimes obliquely, sometimes openly?[37] Was this the reason for the two-pronged violence that constitutes the hero: on the one hand, the violence exercised by the hero and, on the other, the violence exercised on the hero by the sacred, the numinous, *das ganz Andere*, the state of *Ergriffenheit?*[38] If the answer to these questions is yes, then we face a case of ideological transfiguration in which both religion and its counterpart, the study of religion, play a central role. But one can go a step further and instead of maintaining that religion and its study merely sanctified claims to the products of someone else's labor, one can hypothesize that in engaging in the transfiguration of fascism, religion and its scholars fulfilled one of religion's central functions, namely, the sacrificial one. For it must be remembered that the violence of the heroic deed is not only directed against others: It also touches the hero and to that extent there is an ascetic, sacrificial, component to violence. It is also necessary to keep in mind in this context the intimate connection between violence and dispossession. What is meant by this is not the obvious fact that dispossession is generally accompanied by violence or at least by the threat of violence against those whose goods or labor one wants to appropriate. What is meant has to do with the fact that in order to dispossess others it is sometimes necessary to engage in a symbolic act of self-dispossession. This may involve nothing more than token self-restraint, such as a degree of circumspection in the manner in which one eats one's food – as if trying to show that one is not really hungry, because one is, in principle, beyond need; or, as in the case of the Prussian nobility, an idealization of penury,[39] along with an exaggerated, sacrificial, sense of duty

---

[37] See the statement by Erwin Freiherr von Aretin, quoted in Malinowski, *Vom König zum Führer*, p. 102; as well as the description of the attempts on the part of the German nobility to acquire land in the newly conquered territories in eastern Europe: ibid., pp. 500–503.

[38] See Steven M. Wasserstrom, *Religion after Religion. Gershom Scholem, Mircea Eliade, and Henry Corbin at Eranos* (Princeton: Princeton University Press, 1999) along with the critique found in G. Benavides, *"Afterreligion* after Religion," *Journal of the American Academy of Religion* 69 (2001), pp. 449–457.

[39] On the practice and ideal of *Kargheit, Entsagung* and similar values, especially among the Prussian lower nobility, see Malinowski, *Vom König zum Führer*, p. 85, and pp. 90–103. English readers can find insights into the economic conditions of the old German nobility in Penelope Fitzgerald's novel about Novalis, *The blue flower* (London: Flamingo 1995).

towards the king who allows one to extract labor from one's serfs;[40] or it may require the creation of orders of full-time ascetics, devoted to the consumption and purification of the gifts bestowed on them by those in power.[41] With this in mind, we can understand the theorists of the heroic death, of the *atto puro*, of the irrational experience, as ideologists and priests of sacrifice: as those who by glorifying deprivation purified the consumption of those in power.

We may note in this context that after a visit to Germany in 1934 – that is, the year that saw the publication of the first version of Hauer's essay about the *Bhagavadgītā* – Drieu la Rochelle claimed to be impressed – positively impressed – by the fact that the German standard of living was lower than before. In an essay he wrote after this visit he asks himself "si la pauvreté ne cache pas une richesse morale," and answers "Eh bien oui, il y a dans l'Allemagne hitlérienne une force morale, comme il y en a une dans l'Italie mussolinienne." For him, as for fascists in general, the foundation of the fascist moral force is "une disposition au sacrifice, une volonté de combat..."[42] Eight years later, in the midst of the war, Tucci claims also that Japan is a force in modern history because of its spiritual riches, shaped by the discipline of poverty.[43] What impressed Drieu and Tucci about Germany and Japan was also found in Italy, where prices rose and wages declined during the 1930s. It would seem, then, that in praising a sacrificial social order that did not appear to them to have as its aim something as base as economic growth, Drieu and his fellow intellectual fascists, fulfilled their function as ideologists of the gratuitous, irrational act, and in so doing purified the process of extraction. Was this also the function of the theories about irrational experience, *sui generis* religion and heroic

---

[40] See Epstein, *The Genesis of German Conservatism*, p. 61; Malinowski, *Vom König zum Führer*, p. 78.

[41] This issue is discussed in an different context in G. Benavides, "Economy," in Donald S. Lopez, Jr., ed., *Critical Terms for the Study of Buddhism* (Chicago: University of Chicago Press, 2005), pp. 77–102, as well as in id., "Buddhism, Manichaeism, Markets and Empires," in Luther H. Martin and Panayotis Pachis, eds., *Hellenisation, Empire and Globalisation: Lessons from Antiquity* (Thessaloniki: Vanias Edition, 2004), pp. 21–40.

[42] Drieu la Rochelle, "Mesure de l'Allemagne" (dated March 1934), in *Socialisme fasciste* (Paris: Gallimard, 1934), pp. 201–216, esp. pp. 201f.; a portion of this passage is quoted in the English translation and discussed in Soucy, *Fascist Intellectual*, p. 139f.

[43] See Benavides, "Giuseppe Tucci, or Buddhology in the Age of Fascism," p. 170, quoting G. Tucci, *Il buscidô* (Firenze: Felice Le Monnier, 1942-XX); see also Tucci, *Forme dello spirito asiatico*, p. 202: "Il Tibet è povero: ma, come succede da per tutto, questa povertà ha provocato la sua ricchezza spirituale," a passage discussed in Benavides, "Giuseppe Tucci," p. 166, n. 33.

deed disseminated by academics? This hypothesis is supported by a letter from Jakob Freiherr von Uexküll to Prince Eulenburg in early 1919,
in which the Freiherr writes about the two ways out of the postwar
crisis: the amputation of the Bolshevik abscess and the great mystical
religious reaction.[44] It is true that the privileges enjoyed by academics
were minimal compared to those of industrialists or large landowners;
nevertheless, compared to the life of workers in the 1920s and 30s,
academics, like military officers, were part, if only metaphorically, of
the *Herrenklub*. In that respect, academics were not different from Drieu,
who more than once confessed in his diary that despite his sympathy
for radical Socialism, he was not able to overcome his visceral dislike
of the lower classes.[45]

There is a running controversy among scholars of fascism concerning
the position of this movement along the traditional left/right spectrum.
For some, the best-known of whom is Sternhell, fascism is a neither-
left-nor-right movement, whereas for others, such as Soucy, when it
came to concrete policies, despite their revolutionary language fascists
constituted no threat to the propertied classes. It would be impossible to
examine here the evidence concerning fascist attitudes towards wages,
working conditions, unions and taxes, on the one hand, and industrial
conglomerates and land tenure, on the other. It may suffice to point
out that a neither-left-nor-right, or even revolutionary understanding of
fascism may be justified if one focuses on the programs of the fascist
factions that sought a radical alteration of the social conditions – such
as the National Socialist faction headed by Otto and Gregor Strasser.
As it is well-known, however, insofar as they threatened the established
social arrangements or the status of the army, such groups were brought
under control and their leaders killed, as it happened to the SA, Ernst
Röhm and Gregor Strasser, or neutralized, as it happened to Achille
Starace, the national secretary of the Fascist Party from 1931 to 1939.
The fact is that Italian fascism was a reactive phenomenon, the proof
of this being that it became strong only in places with a strong Socialist

---

[44] Jakob Frhr. v. Uexküll an Fürst Eulenburg, 13.1.1919, Brandenburgische Lan-
deshauptarchiv (Potsdam), Rep. 37 Liebenberg, Nr. 657, fol. 33f.: "Zweierlei Auswege
sehe ich. Ein fremder Chirurg, der das Bolschewistengeschwür ausschneidet. Dabei
wird der Staat stark amputiert werden. Und zweitens die grosse mystisch-religiöse
Reaktion, wenn das allgemeine Hungern beginnt." Quoted in Malinowski, *Vom König
zum Führer*, p. 223, n. 126.

[45] *Journal*, p. 320 (December 27, 1943), p. 380 (April, 19 1944).

party.[46] In Italy and Germany ownership of the means of production did not change; on the contrary, the Italian and German upper classes supported the new order, a support that involved a sizeable participation of members of the German nobility in the upper ranks of the Nazi party and the SS, as demonstrated beyond any doubt by Stephan Malinowski. Regarding the working classes' rejection of fascism, it may be pointed out, for instance, that during the rituals that commemorated the first anniversary of the March on Rome, the police was instructed to pay attention to the neighborhoods where "popular elements" lived;[47] likewise, the fascists were aware that they could not count on support among the factory workers of Bologna and Milan.[48] This is understandable, given the deterioration of working conditions, the result of the 1926 reduction of salaries and repeal of the eight-hour-day law – a reduction that affected women more than men, as the fascist regimes, with the blessing of the Roman church, sought to relegate women to the reproductive sphere.[49] As this was happening, Mussolini cut business taxes. The same suppression of workers' rights took place in Hitler's Germany, where the working day grew longer just as wages decreased or froze. The same would have occurred in France if the fascist right-wing had attained power. For example, François de La Rocque, leader of the Croix de Feu, advocated in 1937 a sixty or seventy hour workweek, which he justified in part pragmatically, as preparation for war against Germany, and in part spiritually, as a form of Christian asceticism.[50] Similarly concerned with spiritual values, the Solidarité française leader Louis Mouilliseaux criticized the Marxist rejection of "the transcendental, the supra-Human, the Divine,"[51] in a manner that resembles the position of members of the German nobility during the Weimar years.

What we encounter in the discourse of European fascists – some of whom, it must be remembered, were prepared to go to war against

---

[46] See Adrian Lyttelton, *The Seizure of Power. Fascism in Italy 1919–1929*, 2nd ed. (London: Weidenfeld and Nicholson, 1987), p. 188.

[47] See Mabel Berezin, *Making the Fascist Self. The Political Culture of Interwar Italy* (Ithaca: Cornell University Press, 1997), p. 86.

[48] Berezin, *Making the Fascist Self*, p. 93.

[49] Maria-A. Macciocchi, "Les femmes et la traversée du fascisme," in eadem, *Éléments pour une analyse du fascisme*, 1st ed. (Paris: Union générale d'éditions, 1976), pp. 191ff.

[50] The contrast between the revolutionary language and the pro-business attitudes of the French extreme right is examined in Robert Soucy, *French Fascism: The Second Wave 1933–1939* (New Haven: Yale University Press, 1995), p. 188, p. 190, et passim.

[51] Soucy, *French Fascism*, p. 97.

each other – parallels the discourse of the *Religionswissenschaftler* whose words we have cited: in both cases we find that in order to fight off those who sought to improve their living conditions, their material demands were demonized and contrasted to an ascetic lack of concern with base materiality. That in some cases the extolled sacrificial conduct was presented as rooted in the Pagan cult of blood and soil and in some others in heroism for heroism's sake and still in others in the tradition of the selfless Christian knights, embodiments of French identity, is ultimately less relevant than the fact that those who had to sacrifice themselves, either as workers or as soldiers, had little to gain, whereas the choreographers of gratuitousness were defending their own privileges. This does not mean that many of those who uttered the grandiloquent formulas about self-sacrifice or who actually died in battle did not mean what they said.[52] The letters, obituaries and battlefield reports, published by Berezin indicate that some young Italian fascists died in battle believing that they were dying for a glorious cause;[53] indeed, there is no reason to doubt that in some cases the Italian soldiers who died at the Russian or the Greek fronts died as fascist ascetics, invoking *fascismo* or *il Duce*. That this could occur is the result of the confluence of various processes. One of them, as Berezin points out, following Gramsci, is the high value of drama, of the beautiful, operatic, gesture in Italian culture – and, one could add, the accompanying terror of the *bruta figura*. Another, crucial one, is the orchestration of feelings to which Italians were subject since 1922 through parades, demonstrations and speeches.

These political rituals and their intended effects bring us back to the theories of religion we have been examining, for we must consider the extent to which the discourse of scholars of religion, during the 1920s, 30s and beyond, functioned in a manner analogous to that of the political rituals just mentioned. To be sure, it would be a mistake to exaggerate the effects of the writings of Otto, Hauer, Wach, Tucci and others; but while remaining aware of their limited scope, it is still necessary to recognize how invocations of irrational experience, distrust of reason, heroism, sacrifice and search for a master, contributed to the orchestration of feelings and thus to the eliciting of behavior in a

---

[52] See Malinowski, *Vom König zum Führer*, p. 216.
[53] *Making the Fascist Self*, pp. 196–244. This applies *a fortiori* to some of the Men of the Archangel Michael in Romania.

manner that parallels, if only at the textual, academic, level, the massive liturgies of the fascist state. In this regard and, while being fully aware of the difference in scale and medium, we can say that our theorists functioned as Leni Riefenstahl did: While the cinematographer mobilized masses of people, light, angles and movement, our theorists set in motion concepts, words, rhetorical devices. This mobilization does not mean that these theorists misused religion, for the unfortunate truth is that one of the functions of religion is precisely to transfigure violence, to bless weapons, to assist in the process of extraction.[54] It is therefore necessary that, while being aware of the responsibility that the *Nachgeborene* may feel regarding the complicitous deeds of some of their academic ancestors, we recognize that the political, violent, indeed genocidal uses of religion as well as of scholarship on religion that took place during the age of fascism may be extreme, but are not by any means exceptional. This issue has to be approached in the context of attempts to understand religion from evolutionary perspectives, especially those concerned with the role played by religion in leading members of groups to act as if those groups were organisms.[55] In that context, in assuming the reality of a world constituted by organic hierarchies, essences, irrational experiences and heroic deeds, the theorists we have discussed functioned as the theologians of that world.

---

[54] See "The Religiousness of Violence," introduction to *Numen* 52 (2005), pp. 1–4.
[55] See David Sloan Wilson, *Darwin's Cathedral. Evolution, Religion, and the Nature of Society* (Chicago: University of Chicago Press, 2002).

Bibliography

Benavides, Gustavo. "Giuseppe Tucci, or Buddhology in the Age of Fascism." In Donald S. Lopez, Jr., ed., *Curators of the Buddha: The Study of Buddhism under Colonialism.* Chicago: University of Chicago Press, 1995, pp. 161–96.
———. "Jakob Wilhelm Hauer, or Karmayoga as a Cold War Weapon." In Dalibor Papoušek, Luther H. Martin, and Iva Doležalová, eds., *The Academic Study of Religion during the Cold War: East and West.* New York: Peter Lang, 2001, pp. 225–38.
———. "*Afterreligion* after Religion." *Journal of the American Academy of Religion* 69 (2001), pp. 449–57.
———. "Holiness, State of Exception, Agency." In Brigitte Luchesi and Kocku von Stuckrad, eds., *Religion im kulturellen Diskurs. Festschrift für Hans G. Kippenberg zu seinem 65. Geburtstag* (Religionsgeschichtliche Versuche und Vorarbeiten 52). Berlin-New York: Walter de Gruyter, 2004, pp. 61–73.
———. "Buddhism, Manichaeism, Markets and Empires." In Luther H. Martin and Panayotis Pachis, eds., *Hellenisation, Empire and Globalisation: Lessons from Antiquity.* Thessaloniki: Vanias Publications, 2004, pp. 21–40.
———. "Economy." In Donald S. Lopez, Jr., ed., *Critical Terms for the Study of Buddhism.* Chicago: University of Chicago Press, 2005, pp. 77–102.
Berezin, Mabel. *Making the Fascist Self. The Political Culture of Interwar Italy.* Ithaca: Cornell University Press, 1997.
Cancik, Hubert. "Die Götter Griechenlands 1929. Walter F. Otto als Religionswissenschaftler und Theologe am Ende der Weimarer Republik I." In Heinrich von Stietencron, ed., *Theologen und Theologien in verschiedenen Kulturkreisen.* Düsseldorf: Patmos, 1986, pp. 214–38.
———. "Dionysos 1933. W.F. Otto, ein Religionswissenschaftler am Ende der Weimarer Republik." In Richard Faber, Renate Schlesier, eds., *Die Restauration der Götter. Antike Religion und Neo-Paganismus.* Würzburg: Königshausen & Neumann, 1986, pp. 105–23.
Dierks, Margarete. *Jakob Wilhelm Hauer 1881–1962. Leben. Werk. Wirkung.* Heidelberg: Lambert Schneider, 1986.
Drieu la Rochelle, Pierre. *Socialisme fasciste.* Paris: Gallimard, 1934.
———. *Journal 1939–1945.* Édition établie, présentée et annotée par Julien Hervier. Paris: Gallimard, 1992.
Droz, Jacques. *Le romantisme allemand et l'état.* Paris: Payot, 1966.
Eliade, Mircea and Ernst Jünger, eds. *Antaios. Zeitschrift für eine freie Welt,* I,1, Mai 1959 to XII,6, März 1971. Stuttgart: Ernst Klett Verlag.
Epstein, Klaus. *The Genesis of German Conservatism.* Princeton: Princeton University Press, 1966.
Faber, Richard and Renate Schlesier, eds., *Die Restauration der Götter. Antike Religion und Neo-Paganismus.* Würzburg: Königshausen & Neumann, 1986.
Flasche, Rainer. *Die Religionswissenschaft Joachim Wachs.* Berlin-New York: Walter de Gruyter, 1978.
Hauer, Jakob Wilhelm. *Die Religionen, ihr Werden, ihr Sinn, ihre Wahrheit. Erstes Buch: Das religiöse Erlebnis auf den unteren Stufen.* Berlin, Stuttgart, Leipzig: Kohlhammer, 1923.
———. *Eine indo-arische Metaphysik des Kampfes und der Tat. Die Bhagavadgītā in neuer Sicht mit Übersetzungen.* Stuttgart: W. Kohlhammer, 1934.
———. *Glaubensgeschichte der Indogermanen, Erster Teil: Das religiöse Artbild der Indogermanen und die Grundtypen der indo-arischen Religion.* Stuttgart: W. Kohlhammer, 1937.
———. *Der Yoga. Ein indischer Weg zum Selbst. Kritisch-positive Darstellung nach den indischen Quellen mit einer Übersetzung der massgeblichen Texte, 2. umgearbeitete und um den 2. Band erweiterte Auflage des 'Yoga als Heilweg.'* Stuttgart: W. Kohlhammer, 1958.
Heiler, Friedrich. *Die Bedeutung der Mystik für die Weltreligionen,* München: Ernst Reinhardt, 1919.

———. *Das Gebet. Eine religionsgeschichtliche und religionspsychologische Untersuchung.* 4th ed. München: Ernst Reinhardt, 1924.

———. *Erscheinungsformen und Wesen der Religion* (Die Religionen der Menschheit 1). Stuttgart: W. Kohlhammer, 1961.

Jünger, Ernst. *Sämtliche Werke* 7. Stuttgart: Klett, 1982.

———. *Sämtliche Werke* 14. Stuttgart: Klett, 1982.

Kaiser, Gerhard. *Pietismus und Patriotismus im literarischen Deutschland. Ein Beitrag zum Problem der Säkularisation*, 2nd ed. Frankfurt am Main: Athenäum, 1973.

Krockow, Christian Graf von. *Die Entscheidung. Eine Untersuchung über Ernst Jünger, Carl Schmitt, Martin Heidegger.* Stuttgart: Ferdinand Enke Verlag, 1958, repr. Frankfurt am Main: Campus, 1990.

Löwith, Karl. *Mein Leben in Deutschland vor und nach 1933. Ein Bericht.* Stuttgart: J.B. Metzlersche Verlagsbuchhandlung, 1986.

Lopez, Donald S. Jr., ed. *Curators of the Buddha: The Study of Buddhism under Colonialism.* University of Chicago Press, 1995.

———, ed. *Critical Terms for the Study of Buddhism.* Chicago: University of Chicago Press, 2005.

Luchesi, Brigitte and Kocku von Stuckrad, eds. *Religion im kulturellen Diskurs. Festschrift für Hans G. Kippenberg zu seinem 65. Geburtstag* (Religionsgeschichtliche Versuche und Vorarbeiten 52). Berlin-New York: Walter de Gruyter, 2004.

Lyttelton, Adrian. *The Seizure of Power. Fascism in Italy 1919–1929.* 2nd ed. London: Weidenfeld and Nicholson, 1987.

Macciocchi, Maria-A. "Les femmes et la traversée du fascisme." In idem, ed., *Eléments pur une analyse du fascisme.* Paris: Union générale d'éditions, 1976, pp. 191ff.

Malinowski, Stephan, *Vom König zum Führer. Deutscher Adel und Nationalsozialismus.* Frankfurt am Main : Fischer, 2004.

McMahon, Darrin. *Enemies of the Enlightenment. The French Counter-Enlightenment and the Making of Modernity*, Oxford-New York: Oxford University Press, 2001.

Mussolini, Benito [Giovanni Gentile?]. "Fascismo–Dottrina." *Enciclopedia Italiana di Scienze, Lettere ed Arti*, 1932–X, vol. 14, pp. 847–51.

Otto, Walter F. "Der junge Nietzsche." *Wissenschaft und Gegenwart* 10, Frankfurt a.M. 1936. Reprinted in W.F. Otto, *Mythos und Welt.* Stuttgart: Ernst Klett, 1962, pp. 159–78.

———. "Der Durchbruch zum antiken Mythos im XIX. Jahrhundert." In *Vom Schicksal des deutschen Geistes*, Berlin: Die Runde, 1934, pp. 35ff.

———. *Die Gestalt und das Sein. Gesammelte Abhandlungen über den Mythos und seine Bedeutung für die Menschheit.* Düsseldorf-Köln: Wissenschaftliche Buchgesellschaft, 1955.

Papoušek, Dalibor, Luther H. Martin, and Iva Doležalová, eds., *The Academic Study of Religion during the Cold War: East and West.* New York: Peter Lang, 2001.

Schmitt, Carl. *Politische Theologie. Vier Kapitel zur Lehre von der Souveränität.* Berlin: Duncker und Humblot, 1922 (2nd ed. 1934 = 7th ed. 1996).

———. "Der Führer schützt das Recht. Zur Reichtagsrede Adolf Hitlers am 13. Juli 1934." *Deutsche Juristen-Zeitung* 39. Jahrgang, Heft 15, Berlin, den 1. August 1934, col. 945–950.

Soucy, Robert. *Fascist Intellectual: Drieu La Rochelle.* Berkeley: University of California Press, 1979.

———. *French Fascism: The Second Wave 1933–1939.* New Haven, Yale University Press, 1995.

Stietencron, Heinrich von, ed. *Theologen und Theologien in verschiedenen Kulturkreisen.* Düsseldorf: Patmos, 1986.

Tucci, Giuseppe. "Il cinema indiano." *La lettura* 38 (1938), pp. 350–57. Reprinted in G. Tucci, *Forme dello spirito asiatico*, pp. 159–69.

———. *Forme dello spirito asiatico.* Milano-Messina: Casa editrice Giuseppe Principato, 1940–XVIII.

———. "Lo Zen e il carattere del popolo giapponese." *Asiatica* 5 (1939), pp. 1–9.

———. *Il buscidô* (Biblioteca popolare di cultura politica 21). Firenze: Felice Le Monnier, 1942–XX.

Wilson, David Sloan. *Darwin's Cathedral. Evolution, Religion, and the Nature of Society.* Chicago: University of Chicago Press, 2002.

Wach, Joachim. *Religionswissenschaft. Prolegomena zu ihrer wissenschaftstheoretischen Grundlegung* (Veröffentlichungen des Forschungsinstituts für vergleichende Religionsgeschichte an der Universität Leipzig 10). Leipzig: J.C. Hinrich'sche Buchhandlung, 1922.

———. "Das religiöse Gefühl." In Henry E. Sigerist, ed., *Das Problem der Kultur und die ärztliche Psychologie* (Vorträge des Instituts für Geschichte der Medizin an der Universität Leipzig 4). Leipzig: Georg Thieme, 1931.

———. *Types of Religious Experience, Christian and Non-Christian.* Chicago: University of Chicago Press, 1951.

Wasserstrom, Steven M. *Religion after Religion. Gershom Scholem, Mircea Eliade, and Henry Corbin at Eranos.* Princeton: Princeton University Press, 1999.

PART TWO

THE POLITICAL IMPACT IN SOUTH-EASTERN EUROPE

LEONIDAS PHILIPPIDIS AND THE BEGINNINGS OF THE HISTORY OF RELIGIONS AS AN ACADEMIC DISCIPLINE IN GREECE

Vasilios N. Makrides

It will be perhaps of no surprise that the history of religions is a discipline with a relatively recent history in Greek academia. Like many other countries in the European periphery, Greece's progress in this domain remained under the formative influence of the developments that took place in West European countries including Germany. The specific question here is what Greece may have to do with the study of religions under the impact of National Socialist and Fascist ideologies in Europe. To anticipate my conclusions, I will mention two fundamental points.

First, the institutionalization of the history of religions within the Divinity School of the University of Athens, an Orthodox denominational school, owes much to Leonidas Philippidis (1898–1973).[1] Among other things, Philippidis had been studying history of religions at the University of Leipzig since the winter term of 1926/27 and had obtained his doctorate there under the supervision of Hans Haas in 1929. His stay in Germany coincided with a critical period in which National Socialism was gaining strong footholds within German society, including academia, even before coming to power in 1933. This fact poses naturally questions as to what extent Philippidis might have been influenced by the developments of this discipline in Germany and if there was a potential transfer of related ideas to Greece.

---

[1] Biographical and other information on Philippidis are taken from the autobiography of Leonidas I. Philippidis, *Αυτοβιογραφικόν σημείωμα (1898–1963) και πνευματική προσφορά (1913–1963)* (Athens: G.D. Kypraios, 1963), and from the volume *Εις Λεωνίδαν Ιω. Φιλιππίδην τακτικόν καθηγητήν της ιστορίας των θρησκευμάτων εν τη Θεολογική Σχολή του Πανεπιστημίου Αθηνών. Τιμητικόν αφιέρωμα επιτροπής εκ μαθητών του επι τη μετατάξει του εις ομότιμον καθηγητήν. Ομιλούν τα κείμενα* (Athens 1970). See also Anastasios Yannoulatos, "Λεωνίδας Ιω. Φιλιππίδης, ο επιστήμων, ο άνθρωπος," *Επιστημονική Επετηρίς της Θεολογικής Σχολής Πανεπιστημίου Αθηνών* 21 (1974), pp. ια΄ – νε΄; Aristeidis Panotis, "Φιλιππίδης, Λεωνίδας," *Θρησκευτική και Ηθική Εγκυκλοπαιδεία* 11 (1967), pp. 1093–1096.

Second, Philippidis was elected as a fully tenured professor of the history of religions at the above Divinity School in 1939. At that time Greece was under the control of the military regime of Ioannis Metaxas (1936–1941), a dictatorship with strong fascist inclinations. In addition, from 1930 until 1939 Philippidis held various political and ecclesiastical posts, including a leading one in the Ministry of Education and Religious Affairs. In other words, his long service included four years of the Metaxas regime. Philippidis' involvement with politics and its potential interferences with his own academic pursuits and career pose again the question as to whether the institutionalization of the history of religions as an academic discipline in Greece was influenced by the political climate of the period and, if so, to what extent.

Prior to Philippidis, the study of religions from a historical perspective was practiced in the Greek context in a fragmentary way and was almost exclusively situated within the Orthodox theological domain. After all, this remains the main context for the scholarly study of religions until today, although interdisciplinary research on religions is increasingly conducted by many scholars coming from outside the theological domain. This highlights the issue of the separation between Orthodox theology and the scholarly study of religions in Greece, a topic not previously studied. Given this situation, it is not surprising that Philippidis came originally from the Orthodox theological domain. He initially studied Orthodox theology in Athens (1915–1919) where he obtained a doctorate in theology in 1923 with a thesis addressing Greek ecclesiastical history. Considering the extensive and strong intellectual and cultural relations between Greece and Germany at the time, it is not coincidental that until the Second World War most Greek theologians favored almost exclusively Germany as the place for their postgraduate studies. The same is true for Philippidis, who went to Leipzig for further studies and enrolled in the faculty of philosophy. His major subject and area of specialization was the history of religions, while his minor subjects were philosophy and pedagogy. In Leipzig, Philippidis followed other courses as well, such as in Old Testament studies, in which he successfully passed the examinations for the *Hebraicum*. His main mentor in Leipzig was Hans Haas, who had been professor there since 1915. He was an eminent representative of a philologically-oriented history of religions[2] and supervised Philippidis'

---

[2] On Haas in the context of the development of the history of religions in Leipzig, see the exhaustive study by Kurt Rudolph, *Die Religionsgeschichte an der Leipziger Universität*

dissertation on the "golden rule" in the context of the history of religions.[3] In December 1929 Philippidis was awarded the title of *Doctor
philosophiae*. Philippidis also attended the lectures of Joachim Wach,
whose reputation in the scholarly study of religions at the international
level later increased significantly. Supported by Haas, Wach taught in
Leipzig from 1924 onwards as a *Privatdozent* and later as an associate
professor of religious studies until 1935.[4] In addition, Philippidis listened
to the lectures of many other scholars in Leipzig and participated in
their seminars (theologians: Alt, Balla, Achelis, Rendtorff, Fiebig; philologists: Bethe, Körte, Gulkowitsch; philosophers: Driesch, Dittrich,
Wirth; pedagogues: Volkelt, Litt, Klemm, Frenzel, Schneider, Lipsius).
In this way, he profited in many scholarly areas, in addition to his main
specialization in the history of religions.

Upon his return to Greece, Philippidis continued his research and
writing activities and submitted his *Habilitation* in 1934 on the Vedânta-
theory about sorrow and redemption.[5] He taught as a *Privatdozent* at
the Divinity School of the University of Athens from 1934 until 1939
and subsequently as a professor of the history of religions until his
retirement in 1968. He also taught the same subject at the Arsakeios
Teacher's Training College since 1937. Generally, Philippidis' important
contribution to this field is that he supported and developed a historical-philological approach to religions. This departed from the earlier
approaches to religions in Greece, which were mostly favored by theologians with philosophical interests. This was the case with professor
Nikolaos Louvaris of the same department of theology, who initially
began teaching this subject in 1932. Philippidis was a very energetic
person and a prolific author. He touched upon a variety of topics and
left a strong legacy among his numerous students, as well as in his
academic, ecclesiastical and socio-political environment. His scholarly
contributions were acknowledged by the international academic community, especially when he was awarded an honorary doctorate by the
faculty of theology of the University of Marburg in 1960 in the wake of

---

und die Entwicklung der Religionswissenschaft (Sitzungsberichte der Sächsischen Akademie
der Wissenschaften zu Leipzig, Philologisch-historische Klasse, Bd. 107, Heft 1) (Berlin:
Akademie-Verlag, 1962), pp. 123–133.

[3] Leonidas J. Philippidis, *Die 'Goldene Regel' religionsgeschichtlich untersucht*, Inaugural-
Dissertation zur Erlangung der Doktorwürde der Hohen Philosophischen Fakultät der
Universität Leipzig (Leipzig: Adolf Klein, 1929).

[4] See Rudolph, *Die Religionsgeschichte an der Leipziger Universität*, pp. 137–149.

[5] L.I. Philippidis, *Η περί θλίψεως και λυτρώσεως θεωρία της Βεδάντα της δογματικής
του Ινδικού Βραχμανισμού* (Athens: Pyrsos, 1934).

a proposal by professor Friedrich Heiler. This took place in the context of the 10th International Congress for the History of Religions.[6]

Aside from his successful academic career, Philippidis obtained early enough important posts outside academia. Before going to Germany he had served as director of the Metropolitan Office for the Metropolitan of Smyrna Chrysostomos (1919–1921) and later as director of the Patriarchal Office for the Patriarch of Alexandria Photios (1923–1925). In addition, from July 1930 up to December 1939 he served as the Director of the Department of Ecclesiastical/Religious Affairs at the Ministry of Education and Religious Affairs. It is worth mentioning that Philippidis held this office during the ecclesiastical crisis of 1938 regarding the election of the new archbishop of Athens and of all Greece. (The election of Archbishop Damaskinos was annulled by the Council of State, which paved the way for the election of Archbishop Chrysanthos, supported by Metaxas himself.[7]) Philippidis also served as the Royal Commissioner to the Holy Synod of the Church of Greece. At the same time, he was a member of several boards of ecclesiastical and state organizations. This shows his active involvement in church and political affairs of the day under various governments and ministers. During this period, Philippidis dealt with a variety of issues and legislation, ranging from the administration of the church to religious education and inter-Christian relations. It is in this period (September 1938) that the notorious law 1363 originates; it quite specifically regulated the status of the non-Orthodox minorities within Greek territory and is still valid today, despite criticism and reactions.[8] Philippidis was highly honored in 1937 and 1939 by King George II for his long career and services to the Greek state and the Orthodox Church. However, he gave up these various posts when he became professor in 1939. From then on he devoted himself primarily to teaching and scholarly research.

---

[6] For details see Εις Λεωνίδαν Ιω. Φιλιππίδην, pp. 233–265.

[7] On this crisis, see Yiorgos Karayiannis, Εκκλησία και κράτος 1833–1997. Ιστορική επισκόπηση των σχέσεών τους (Athens: To Pontiki, 1997), pp. 51–57. See also Gunnar Hering, "Aspekte der Kulturpolitik des Metaxas-Regimes 1936–1940)," in Reinhard Lauer, Peter Schreiner, eds., Die Kultur Griechenlands in Mittelalter und Neuzeit (Abhandlungen der Akademie der Wissenschaften in Göttingen, Philologisch-historische Klasse, dritte Folge, Nr. 212) (Göttingen: Vandenhoeck und Ruprecht, 1996), pp. 285–321, here pp. 300–302.

[8] See Nicos C. Alivizatos, "The Constitutional Treatment of Religious Minorities in Greece," in René-Jean Dupuy, ed., Mélanges en l'honneur de Nicolas Valticos: droit et justice (Paris: Pedone, 1999), pp. 629–642, here p. 639.

To understand Philippidis' overall career and scholarly output, it is vital to keep in mind that he remained throughout his life a believer and an Orthodox theologian. This did not leave his research in the history of religions unaffected because he always put the study of non-Christian religions in the service of Orthodox theology and Church. In this way, he dissociated himself from the tradition of Leipzig and specifically from his teachers, Hans Haas and Joachim Wach, who clearly attempted in various ways to distance the history of religions from theological studies.[9] In fact, Haas supported the harmonious and complementary relationship between theology and the study of religions, but he did not use the latter in apologetic terms in favor of Christianity. Wach, on the other hand, emphasized the divergence of the two disciplines in a more systematic way, as it is evident in his important study *Religionswissenschaft. Prolegomena zu seiner wissenschaftstheoretischen Grundlegung* (Leipzig 1924).

Philippidis was aware of these ideas and cited, for example, Wach's above-mentioned study, but he followed a different path, more adapted to the Greek Orthodox situation. His main ideas concerning the relationship between the study of religions/comparative religion and Orthodox theology were exposed on various occasions during the 1930s. Given the fact that such a topic was basically absent from the Greek Orthodox milieu until then, his contribution was instrumental in that it offered a first acquaintance with this discipline within Greek academia and an explanation of its relations to Orthodox theology. In his inaugural lecture of 1935 as a *Privatdozent* on the history of religions as a scholarly discipline, Philippidis first offered a historical overview of this area of study from antiquity up to the contemporary period, referring particularly to its institutional establishment since the 19th century in Western Europe.[10] He made also a brief reference to the background of this discipline in Greece.[11] Further, he tried to outline the basic currents within this broad field of research, especially in their relation to Christian theology, and criticized the unprofessional approach and the lack of depth of some scholars.[12] Finally, he attempted to articulate the

---

[9] See Rudolph, *Die Religionsgeschichte an der Leipziger Universität*, pp. 129–130 and pp. 144–148.

[10] L.I. Philippidis, *Η Ιστορία των Θρησκευμάτων ως επιστήμη* (Athens: Pyrsos, 1935), pp. 8–18.

[11] Ibid., pp. 18–20.

[12] Ibid., pp. 20–24.

character of this new discipline, which – in his view – consisted of a combination of history, philosophy and Christian theology. He under-lined the advantages of its teaching in the Greek Orthodox context, and in the end he considered its future development from the perspec-tive of Orthodox theology. In his opinion, the history of religions aims to demonstrate that Christianity is in all respects the superior religion and that it has clear supernatural origins. The new discipline would then certainly contribute to the strengthening of the Christian faith and the verification of the Christian truth. The historical study of religions was thus clearly situated in the service of Orthodox theology and apologetics.[13]

Philippidis expounded his ideas on a "theologically-oriented history of religions" more systematically and at length in a book entitled *The History of Religions in Itself and Within Christian Theology.*[14] His ample use of the relevant foreign literature in this book clearly shows that he was familiar with the situation in this field on an international level. He began with a short account of a Christian theology directed and adjusted to the study of religions, explained the historical develop-ment of the discipline, considered the most recent trends, and – most importantly – dealt with its relationship to Christian theology.[15] In this context he emphasized again the importance of this discipline for demonstrating the uniqueness of Christianity among religions and its concomitant and unquestionable superiority to these others. He also placed particular emphasis on the development of a history of religions *sui generis*, specifically destined for the Orthodox Christian milieu. To this end, he drew on the Church Fathers and other Christian writers, whose dealing with non-Christian religions could offer insights for the future development of this discipline. All in all, the use of the history of religions for clear Christian purposes and priorities repeated itself. This fundamental perspective can be observed in Philippidis' writings during the same period, which dealt with non-Christian religions from a comparative perspective.[16] The same is true of his later writings as well: for example, when he enthusiastically supported the theory of Wilhelm

---

[13] Ibid., pp. 24–35.
[14] L.I. Philippidis, *Η Ιστορία των Θρησκευμάτων καθ᾽ εαυτήν και εν τη Χριστιανική Θεολογία* (Athens: Pyrsos, 1938).
[15] Ibid., pp. 124–180.
[16] See for example L.J. Philippidis, *Das Liebesprinzip im Buddhismus und im Christentum* (Athen: Pyrsos, 1938), esp. pp. 26–29.

Schmidt about primordial monotheism and revelation (*Urmonotheismus/Uroffenbarung*), which had a clear Christian background and concomitant objectives.[17] All these attest to the fact that Philippidis remained primarily and pre-eminently an Orthodox Christian theologian and that he always saw his scholarly research in the context of Orthodox theology and in the service of the Orthodox Church.

As expected, such a position was quite normal within the fairly conservative socio-political and religious milieu of Greece during that period. Its openness towards non-Orthodox others was usually connected with a re-affirmation of its own Orthodox identity and superiority. One remaining question pertains to the potential relations between Philippidis' career and ideas and the ideology of the aforementioned military regime of Ioannis Metaxas (1871–1941). The latter was an army officer and dictator,[18] who between 1936 and 1941 had imposed a regime similar in many ways to other European dictatorships of the period, during which the state became increasingly important. Metaxas had close contacts with Germany and spent four years (1899–1903) studying in the War Academy (*Kriegsakademie*) of Berlin.[19] After an adventurous career as a high army officer, Metaxas gained power as prime minister in 1936 through the support of King George II and rapidly proclaimed a state of emergency on 4 August. He suspended parliament, abolished the freedom of the press and introduced secret police surveillance, censorship and measures against dissidents.[20] Though not fascist, the Metaxas regime soon enough endorsed many of the attributes of the authoritarian regimes of the period. These included order, discipline, indoctrination, propaganda measures, anti-communism, clear hierarchical structures, glorification of youth, theories of

---

[17] See L.I. Philippidis, "† P. Wilhelm Schmidt, S.V.D. (1868–1954). Πρώτη Αποκάλυψις και αφετηριακός μονοθεϊσμός. Εθνολογική και θρησκειολογική επιβεβαίωσις της περί τούτων Βιβλικής αληθείας," *Θεολογία* 26 (1955), pp. 310–327; idem, *Das Unwiderlegliche der Forschungsergebnisse des verewigten Prof. Dr. Rev. P. Wilhelm Schmidt* (Athen 1968).

[18] On his personality, see Gunnar Hering, "Rache am Vaterland? Anmerkungen zur Persönlichkeit des Ioannis Metaxas," in idem, *Nostos. Gesammelte Schriften zur südosteuropäischen Geschichte*, ed. by Maria A. Stassinopoulou (Frankfurt a.M.: Peter Lang, 1995), pp. 131–148.

[19] See Panayiotis J. Vatikiotis, *Popular Autocracy in Greece 1936–41: A Political Biography of General Ioannis Metaxas* (London: Frank Cass, 1998), pp. 39–48; Joachim G. Joachim, *Ioannis Metaxas: The Formative Years 1871–1922* (Peleus 5) (Mannheim – Möhnesee: Bibliopolis, 2000), pp. 28–43.

[20] See Hering, "Aspekte der Kulturpolitik des Metaxas-Regimes," passim.

natural selection and segregation of minorities based on the principle of a pure national identity.[21] Members of his organization, the Εθνική Οργάνωση Νεολαίας (National Youth Organization),[22] modeled after the fascist youth organizations in Italy, Spain and Portugal, had to be true Hellenes, not Jews or members of other minorities. In October 1939 this organization numbered about 750,000 members. Yet the Metaxas regime (usually referred to as the "4th of August Regime") was in some ways less repressive than other dictatorships of the period. This is evident, for example, by its more tolerant policies towards Jews and the fact that it did not proclaim a belligerent ethic.[23] Its ideal was the creation of a "Third Hellenic Civilization," which would incorporate and synthesize elements of the first two civilizations, namely that of ancient Greece and that of Byzantium; particularly, the creativity of the former and the religiosity and the strong state administration of the latter.[24] Metaxas also lessened the linguistic schism in Greece, which had polarized the country in the past. He thus promoted the use of a demotic Greek over the antiquated language.[25] He also encouraged a mythology of the nation-state as the highest and absolute value with an analogous symbolism, while he embarked on a long-term program of public works to improve the country's infrastructure. Among titles given to Metaxas were "First Peasant," "Great Governor," "First Worker," "First Warrior," "National Father," and "Leader." Things changed however in October 1940 when Italy turned to Greece after occupying Albania. Metaxas rebuffed the ultimatum set by Italy, and subsequently the Greek army successfully resisted the invasion of fascist forces. Metaxas did not live to see the further course of warfare, because he died unexpectedly in January 1941.[26] Despite being a dictator, his resistance to Italian fas-

---

[21] On the character of the Metaxas regime, see Susanne-Sophia Spiliotis, "Die Metaxas-Diktatur in Griechenland 1936–1941 – ein faschistoides Regime?," in Erwin Oberländer, ed., *Autoritäre Regime in Ostmittel- und Südosteuropa 1919–1944* (Paderborn: Schöningh, 2001), pp. 403–430.

[22] See Maria Alexopoulou, "Die 'nationale Jugendorganisation' des Metaxas-Regimes (1936–1941): Instrument der 'Umwandlung' Griechenlands," *Bulletin für Faschismus- und Weltkriegsforschung* 17 (2001), pp. 36–65.

[23] See Nikolaos Papanastasiou, *Die Metaxas-Diktatur und das nationalsozialistische Deutschland (1936–1941)* (diss. phil., Augsburg 2000), pp. 54–57.

[24] Hering, "Aspekte der Kulturpolitik des Metaxas-Regimes," p. 290. For details see Chrysanthi Avlami, "Η χρήση της ιστορίας από τους θεωρητικούς της 4ης Αυγούστου," Ίστωρ 2 (1990), pp. 121–149.

[25] See Hering, "Aspekte der Kulturpolitik des Metaxas-Regimes," pp. 296–299.

[26] For various evaluations of the Metaxas period, see Heinz A. Richter, *Griechenland zwischen Revolution und Konterrevolution (1936–1946)* (Frankfurt a.M.: Europäische Verlags-

cism improved his posthumous reputation in a way. It also showed that, despite his pro-fascist inclinations, Metaxas was not ready to sacrifice Greek national interests and priorities.[27] The same is evident from the overall German-Greek political relations at the time. Although close and multifaceted, they never led to an identification of the Metaxas regime with the political ambitions of the Nazis.[28] On the other hand, Metaxas had developed a quite positive relationship with the British and their interests in South Eastern Europe.[29]

It is interesting to note here that, on the ideological level, the "Third Hellenic Civilization" and "The New State"[30] proclaimed by Metaxas were connected not only by a revival of the Hellenic tradition, but also by a new and very positive appreciation of religious phenomena and specifically of Orthodoxy. Although Metaxas himself may have undergone a period of agnosticism and even atheism, he later appeared to be a believer, albeit in his own way.[31] He exhibited in many instances the image of a pious and religious person and supported the view that Orthodoxy was a cornerstone of Greece and specifically of his own politico-ideological system. The latter intended to create a new morality beyond selfish individualism, but never went so far as to create a new

anstalt, 1973), pp. 54–116; Jon V. Kofas, *Authoritarianism in Greece: The Metaxas Regime* (East European Monographs 133) (Boulder/New York: Columbia University Press, 1983), pp. 42–97; Susanne-Sophia Spiliotis, *Transterritorialität und nationale Abgrenzung. Konstitutionsprozesse der griechischen Gesellschaft und Ansätze ihrer faschistoiden Transformation, 1922/24–1941* (München: R. Oldenbourg, 1998), pp. 123–209; Vatikiotis, *Popular Autocracy*, pp. 153–195. See also various articles in Robin Higham and Thanos Veremis, eds., *Aspects of Greece 1936–40: The Metaxas Dictatorship* (Athens: Eliamep – Vryonis Center, 1993); Hagen Fleischer and Nicos Svoronos, eds., *Πρακτικά Α΄ Διεθνούς Συνεδρίου Σύγχρονης Ιστορίας. Η Ελλάδα 1936–1944: Δικτατορία – Κατοχή – Αντίσταση* (Athens: Morfotiko Institouto ATE, 1989, 2nd ed. 1990); Hagen Fleischer, ed., *Η Ελλάδα '36–'49. Από τη Δικτατορία στον Εμφύλιο. Τομές και συνέχειες* (Athens: Kastaniotis, 2003).

[27] See Spyros Linardatos, *Η εξωτερική πολιτική της 4ης Αυγούστου* (Athens: Dialogos, 1975); idem, *Ο Ιωάννης Μεταξάς και οι Μεγάλες Δυνάμεις 1936–40* (Athens: Proskinio, 1993).

[28] See Emmanouil Zacharioudakis, *Die deutsch-griechischen Beziehungen 1933–1941. Interessengegensätze an der Peripherie Europas* (Husum: Matthiesen, 2001); Annivas Velliadis, *Μεταξάς – Χίτλερ. Ελληνογερμανικές σχέσεις στη μεταξική δικτατορία 1936–1941* (Athens: Enalios, 2003); Papanastasiou, *Die Metaxas-Diktatur*, passim.

[29] See John S. Koliopoulos, *Greece and the British Connection 1935–1941* (Oxford: Oxford University Press, 1977); Ilias Iliopoulos, *Metaxas als Realist. Griechische Eindämmungsstrategie und britisches 'Appeasement'* (München: Hieronymus, 2001).

[30] On the homonymous review, see Georgios Kokkinos, *Η φασίζουσα ιδεολογία στην Ελλάδα. Η περίπτωση του περιοδικού 'Νέον Κράτος' (1937–1941)* (Athens: Papazisis, n.d.).

[31] Vatikiotis, *Popular Autocracy*, p. 205.

religion. It is however obvious, that, though highly regarded, religion
was placed on a scale of priorities in which the state and the nation
came first.[32] It was clearly a case of the political instrumentalization
of religion in order to achieve various goals.

Positive references to religion abound in Metaxas' texts. To cite just
one example, on 19 October 1939 he gave a speech to parents and
teachers on the significance of the family. He pointed out that the
majority of Greeks were Orthodox and that the Church emphasized
the sacraments of marriage and baptism, thus presenting the family
as the basic unit of Greek society. He also criticized the separation
between church and state in the West and the social marginalisation of
the church by virtue of its exclusion from the education system. The
Greek situation, however, was for Metaxas quite different.

> Here in Greece, Church and Nation constitute one whole. The Greek
> Nation and the Greek church share the same history since the rise of
> Christianity. Thus the State in Greece never dared seek anti-religious
> aims: even the parliament of 1927, when and where there was such an
> inclination, did not dare undermine the special position of the Ortho-
> dox Church. So that one of the conditions that gave rise to the 4th of
> August Regime was the period of irreligion preceding it. But now Family,
> Nation and Church are the new pillars of the Greek society, nation and
> the state. State and Church work each in its own way towards the same
> national goals.[33]

Given the fact that the state acquired a central role in all aspects of
Greek life during this regime, Orthodoxy had to play a leading role by
supporting the state-directed ideology of national cohesion and solidarity. Educators thus had no right to remain neutral and indifferent
vis-à-vis religion or to claim that religion is of no interest whatsoever.
On the contrary, they were obliged to indoctrinate young people by
instilling in them the sound principles of religiosity.[34] The connection
between Orthodoxy and important events in Greek history was also
especially emphasized. The catalytic role of religion and specifically of
Orthodox Christianity in the new social order is also apparent in many
cases during the Metaxas regime: for example, within the context of

---

[32] See Constantine Sarandis, "The Ideology and Character of the Metaxas Regime,"
in Robin Higham and Thanos Veremis, eds., *Aspects of Greece 1936–40: The Metaxas Dictatorship* (Athens: Eliamep – Vryonis Center, 1993), pp. 147–177, here pp. 159–160.

[33] Cited in Vatikiotis, *Popular Autocracy*, p. 187.

[34] See Kofas, *Authoritarianism in Greece*, p. 86.

the construction and ideological underpinnings[35] of the *National Youth Organization*, which was once referred to by Metaxas as a "Christian organization."[36]

The enhanced role of religion should also be understood in the context of the anti-communist struggle during the interwar period. Greek communism gained at that time significant ground in Greek society. In the elections of January 1936 the Communist Party acquired 15 out of 300 seats in Parliament. This was an alarming signal for the opposing political forces because the impact of communist ideology was becoming stronger among the population.[37] In fact, the Metaxas regime was instituted following a period of social uprising and unrest and appeared to bring order and discipline in a tormented country. In this respect, anticommunism became a cardinal feature of this period and permeated all sectors of Greek society. This explains the numerous repressive measures taken by Metaxas against the communists,[38] in which a leading role was undertaken by his deputy minister for public security, Konstantinos Maniadakis.[39] The same was true with regard to religion and the Orthodox Church. Greek communists and other anti-religious intellectuals criticized religion in general as a serious impediment to the realization of their ideals and to socio-economic progress,[40] and this triggered in turn a religiously-motivated anticommunist critique in various Orthodox circles, which was also supported by the Metaxas regime.

Quite apart from this, it is also known that the Metaxas regime controlled academic life: it helped some of its sympathizers to be elected in professorial chairs, and these scholars later supported the regime

---

[35] For details see Eleni Machaira, *Η νεολαία της 4ης Αυγούστου* (Ιστορικό Αρχείο Ελληνικής Νεολαίας, 13) (Athens: Geniki Grammateia Neas Genias, 1987), pp. 50–65.

[36] Sarandis, "The Ideology and Character of the Metaxas Regime," p. 160.

[37] See Kofas, *Authoritarianism in Greece*, pp. 31–52; Papanastasiou, *Die Metaxas-Diktatur*, pp. 30–31.

[38] See Kofas, *Authoritarianism in Greece*, pp. 129–145 and Haris Vlavianos, "The Metaxas Dictatorship: The Greek Communist Party Under Siege," in Robin Higham and Thanos Veremis, eds., *Aspects of Greece 1936–40: The Metaxas Dictatorship* (Athens: Eliamep – Vryonis Center, 1993), pp. 193–225.

[39] See the book entitled *Ο Κομμουνισμός στην Ελλάδα*, published by the *Εθνική Εταιρία* (Athens 1937) with a congratulatory preface by K. Maniadakis (p. 3f.).

[40] See Zoi Spanakou, "Η κριτική της θρησκείας στο σοσιαλιστικό και μαρξιστικό τύπο του μεσοπολέμου," *Τα Εκπαιδευτικά* 41–42 (1996), pp. 158–176.

ideologically.[41] Philippidis' election as a fully tenured professor of the history of religions in 1939 should be viewed within this general context. The Divinity School of the University of Athens was strengthened with new positions during this period, a development probably not unrelated to the long-term goals of the Metaxas regime. In the same year as Philippidis, another theologian was elected professor in the chair of practical theology, Panayiotis N. Trembelas (1886–1977).[42] He was a founding member of the *Zoi* brotherhood, a semi-monastic religious movement, which had initiated an important revival in Greek religious life and whose power and influence were steadily increasing. Trembelas had already been well known for his apologetic works against various anti-Christian currents including Marxism and communism. Seen from this perspective, his election was certainly not at odds with the general ideological campaign of the Metaxas regime, which was sympathetic to religion and did not support the division between religion, modernity and science (e.g., by eliminating the Darwinian theory of evolution from school curricula).[43] After all, the *Zoi* movement and its affiliated organizations tried to keep good relations with the Metaxas regime and supported the changes it induced.

During the same year, 1939, Alexandros Tsirindanis (1903–1977) was elected professor of mercantile law at the Law School of the University of Athens. Tsirindanis had founded, in 1937, the "Christian Union of Scientists," which had clear apologetic purposes in favor of Christianity and against its various ideological and political enemies. Since October 1937 his organization had published the scholarly and literary review *Ακτίνες* (Sun Rays), which targeted the anti-Christian views of the period and intended to show the compatibility between Christianity, science and the modern world. Tsirindanis later became well known as the initiator of the *Διακήρυξις της Χριστιανικής Ενώσεως Επιστημόνων* (Manifesto of the Christian Union of Scientists), published in 1946.

---

[41] See Spiliotis, *Transterritorialität*, pp. 182–186; Papanastasiou, *Die Metaxas-Diktatur*, p. 45f.

[42] On Trembelas' personality and writings, see Evangelos D. Theodorou, "Παναγιώτης Ν. Τρεμπέλας (Σπουδαί, τίτλοι, δράσις, δημοσιεύματα)," *Επιστημονική Επετηρίς της Θεολογικής Σχολής Πανεπιστημίου Αθηνών* 17 (1971), ζ′ – πδ′.

[43] See Hering, "Aspekte der Kulturpolitik des Metaxas-Regimes", 306–307. See also the book by Dimitrios I. Magkriotis, published by the "National Youth Organization," on the harmonious relations between faith and science (*Πίστις και επιστήμη*, Athens: EON, 1940), in which the author extols in the preface the religious objectives of the Metaxas regime and draws, among other things, on the apologetic material provided by *Zoi* publications including Trembelas' works.

This controversial text intended to reveal the tragic consequences of atheism and the immense potential of Christianity. Tsirindanis' organization had collaborated closely with the *Ζοί* movement since 1937. It is certainly characteristic that most of these actions took place during the Metaxas regime, likely occurring because they fitted its ideological background and goals.[44]

What is perhaps more interesting in the case of Philippidis, is that he was well acquainted with professor Nikolaos I. Louvaris (1887–1961), who, as mentioned above, supported institutionalizing the history of religions at the Divinity School. Louvaris had also been educated at the University of Leipzig (1911–1914) and kept close relations with academic circles in Germany, especially with the pedagogue Eduard Spranger (1882–1963). He was an admirer of the German spirit and of idealism and developed an acute interest in the philosophy and the psychology of religion as well as in relations between art, literature and religion.[45] He was the first to teach related courses at the Divinity School, but his perspective on religions was not purely historical. Therefore, he was in favor of creating an independent chair of the history of religions. Louvaris was a very influential intellectual and left his imprint on his era, and his legacy was kept alive by his numerous admirers and students. Louvaris was also a close friend and collaborator of Metaxas and acted as his advisor in issues of education and religious affairs. During 1935–1936 he had served as General Secretary in the Ministry of Education and Religious Affairs and from 14 March to 4 August 1936 as Minister. Louvaris brought Metaxas into contact with the pedagogical ideas of Eduard Spranger, with whom he had a true and long friendship. He was certainly involved in the honorary doctorate that was awarded to Spranger by the University of Athens at that time.[46] Spranger himself reported on the close relations between Louvaris and the political world of his country and considered Metaxas

---

[44] See Vasilios N. Makrides, "Orthodoxy in the Service of Anticommunism: The Religious Organization Zoë during the Greek Civil War," in: Philip Carabott and Thanasis D. Sfikas, eds., *The Greek Civil War: Essays on a Conflict of Exceptionalism and Silences* (London: Ashgate, 2004), pp. 159–174.

[45] On Louvaris' personality and his writings, see Dimitris Stathopoulos, ed., *N. I. Λούβαρις, ο Αποδημητής, ο Μύστης, ο Επόπτης. Αφιέρωμα τιμής και μνήμης από φίλους, συναδέλφους, μαθητές, στα 20 χρόνια από την εκδημία του (1961–1981)* (Athens: Chatzinikolis, 1981). See also Markos A. Siotis, "Λούβαρις, Νικόλαος," *Θρησκευτική και Ηθική Εγκυκλοπαιδεία* 8 (1966), pp. 352–357; Dimitrios Tsakonas, *Ιδεαλισμός και Μαρξισμός στην Ελλάδα* (Athens: Kaktos, 1988), pp. 169–172.

[46] See Spiliotis, *Transterritorialität*, p. 153, p. 155, and p. 266.

a highly educated individual with a rich library of German books.[47] In
a letter to Louvaris (November 28, 1936) Spranger also mentioned a
card in which he had expressed his thanks to Prime Minister Metaxas.[48]
In general, German-Greek contacts at cultural and scholarly levels
were very close during the Metaxas regime and included a variety of
bilateral initiatives and activities.[49]

Bearing these points in mind, it is not difficult to imagine that this
general climate would suit Philippidis as a young theologian with a
German educational background. Philippidis always maintained close
relations with the German academic world, and his voluminous correspondence attests to this.[50] In addition, he always felt indebted towards
Germany and what it had offered him, as expressed in the obituary he
wrote for his mentor Hans Haas.[51] Given this overall situation, we can
understand Philippidis' role in the Metaxas period in two ways.

First, the formal institutionalization of the history of religions at
the University of Athens through Philippidis' election in 1939 can be
interpreted as an attempt to place emphasis on the historical study of
religions from a comparative perspective in order to show religions'
valuable contributions to mankind. To study religions from a scholarly
point of view could represent them as repositories of faith, tradition,
customs and the idiosyncrasies of a people, resulting in an enormous
cultural impact. In the end, this could show that religions have played
a positive role in human history and that the ideological critique of
them was unfounded and biased. On the other hand, the historical
study of religions did not aim to question the superiority and truth
claimed by Orthodox Christianity, but rather to uphold them. This was
of paramount importance in the Greek case, in which the position of
Orthodoxy remained unchallenged. It is also not coincidental that during the Metaxas period the negative attitude of the regimes in Germany
and in Italy towards Christianity was criticized as potentially leading

---

[47] See Eduard Spranger, "Gedenken an Nikolaos Louvaris," *Universitas* 17 (1962),
pp. 457–468, here p. 459.

[48] Eduard Spranger, *Briefe 1901–1963*, ed. by H.W. Bähr (= E. Spranger, Gesammelte
Schriften, VII) (Tübingen: Max Niemeyer Verlag, 1978), p. 172.

[49] For a good overview, see Papanastasiou, *Die Metaxas-Diktatur*, pp. 89–107. See also
Johannes Irmscher, "Academic Links Between Berlin University and Fascist Greece,"
Journal of the Hellenic Diaspora 13 (1986), pp. 71–90.

[50] See *Εις Λεωνίδαν Ιω. Φιλιππίδην*, passim.

[51] In the *Εκκλησιαστικόν Βήμα* (Athens), 15 October 1934 (and separately: Athens
1934).

to their demise. Thus, the creation of a chair for Philippidis can be understood within the overall climate of the period. It was prompted by the need to fight the anti-religious campaigns of communist and other intellectuals by showing the value of religions from an Orthodox Christian point of view. The positive role ascribed to religions is evident in Philippidis' publications during the Metaxas period, as in his two public speeches at the Literary Society "Parnassos" (in 1935 and 1936 respectively) on the relations between religion, life and death. These were published separately in 1938. Religions were presented as intrinsically related to all forms of individual and social life and as supporting belief in the immortality of the soul, which found its foremost articulation in Christianity in the light of Divine Revelation.[52]

Second, a basic ideological element promoted by the Metaxas regime was the particular connection between Hellenism and Orthodox Christianity and its relevance to the future survival and glorification of the Greek nation. Despite the fact that this regime showed a great predilection for the cult of antiquity, the revival of Greek antiquity did not lead to neo-Pagan movements, as in Germany and Italy, but allowed space for the integration of the Orthodox Christian tradition. The "Third Hellenic Civilization" was not meant to increase Greece's territory (as the irredentist "Great Idea" in earlier periods), but to revive and synthesize the ideals of Ancient Greece and Byzantium, simply because these two previous periods were not considered to be as perfect and as promising as the third one. Considering that Hellenism and Orthodox Christianity had historically experienced various phases of tension and conflict, the ideal of a Helleno-Christian synthesis was a common topic of state ideology, promoted systematically in various forms since the 19th century. In the Metaxas period this was connected with a demonstration of Greece's cultural superiority as well as of its calling and quasi-messianic role in universal history. The "Greek miracle" was thus considered to be the product of both Hellenism and Orthodox Christianity in the context of Divine Providence and its worldwide advancement as a unique privilege of modern Greeks. Seen from this perspective, the scholarly study of religions could contribute significantly to this ideological aim by showing the valuable role that religions (ancient Greek and Orthodox Christian) have always played in Greek

---

[52] See L.I. Philippidis, *Θρησκεία και ζωή* (Athens: Pyrsos, 1938); idem, *Θρησκεία και θάνατος* (Athens: Pyrsos, 1938).

history. Philippidis seems to have shared such views in his publications during the Metaxas period. In his text *Believing Greece* (1937),[53] based on his panegyric at the Literary Society "Parnassos" on the anniversary of the Greek War of Independence (March 25, 1821), he extolled the role of the Orthodox faith and traditional Greek piety in the survival and victories of the Greek nation since antiquity. His statements thus set the agenda for the future success and glorification of the Greeks. Religiosity was viewed as a perennial characteristic of the Greek people and the source of their historical survival. Philippidis also interpreted the "Greek path" as having been predetermined by a special calling and mission for the whole world, which had to be realized some time in the future, not through the use of force, but through the worldwide dissemination of the Greek spirit. It is worth mentioning that Philippidis sent several copies of this speech to Metaxas. The latter responded on 7 May 1937 thanking him and claiming that Philippidis' ideas were in complete congruence with those of his regime.[54] In addition, Philippidis delivered many speeches that portrayed Greek involvement and victories during the Second World War (e.g., on 15 January 1941) as supported by God and the Virgin Mary.[55] Finally, in his inaugural address as a fully tenured professor in 1939, Philippidis talked about divine providence and fate in ancient Greek religion, thus presenting again emphatically the enormous, multi-faceted and valuable role that religion has always played in the history of the Greek people.[56]

In this paper I have tried to present the beginnings of the history of religions as an academic discipline in Greece within the socio-political context of the period by relying on published sources and other related information. Undoubtedly, archival material can shed more light on still unknown aspects of these developments and on the actors involved in them. Yet, based on the above presentation, we can argue that the beginnings of the history of religions in Greece coincided with the emergence of a fascist-like regime, which enabled this discipline to develop within a specific frame *à la grecque*. The ideology and political preferences of the period undoubtedly had an impact on the institutionalization of the history of religions within Greek academia.

---

[53] L.I. Philippidis, *Ελλάς πιστεύουσα* (Athens: Pyrsos, 1937).
[54] See *Εις Λεωνίδαν Ιω. Φιλιππίδην*, p. 134.
[55] Machaira, *Η νεολαία της 4ης Αυγούστου*, p. 52.
[56] L.I. Philippidis, *Θεία Πρόνοια και Μοίρα εν τη θρησκεία των αρχαίων Ελλήνων* (Athens: Pyrsos, 1939).

Furthermore, Philippidis reworked some of the values promoted by the Metaxas regime in a scholarly manner in the context of a Greek history of religions, particularly insofar as they were compatible with Orthodox doctrines and orientations. This is not to say that Philippidis was completely identified with the Metaxas regime or that he adopted its ideological support as his prime objective. It simply means that Philippidis' early academic career and ideas in the history of religions were part of this general intellectual and socio-political context and that the development of this discipline in Greece was accordingly influenced to some extent. This is not surprising, given the fact that the Metaxas regime was viewed positively by many Orthodox prelates as well as by various Orthodox circles at the time. In this respect, the Greek case, despite its idiosyncrasies, presents some analogies to the study of religions in Western Europe under the impact of National Socialist and Fascist regimes.

Bibliography

Alexopoulou, Maria. "Die 'nationale Jugendorganisation' des Metaxas-Regimes (1936–1941): Instrument der 'Umwandlung' Griechenlands." *Bulletin für Faschismus- und Weltkriegsforschung* 17 (2001), pp. 36–65.

Alivizatos, Nicos C. "The Constitutional Treatment of Religious Minorities in Greece." In René-Jean Dupuy, ed., *Mélanges en l'honneur de Nicolas Valticos: droit et justice.* Paris: Pedone, 1999, pp. 629–642.

Avlami, Chrysanthi. "Η χρήση της ιστορίας από τους θεωρητικούς της 4ης Αυγούστου" [The Use of History by the Theoreticians of the 4th August Regime]. *Ίστωρ* 2 (1990), pp. 121–149.

Εις Λεωνίδαν Ιω. Φιλιππίδην τακτικόν καθηγητήν της ιστορίας των θρησκευμάτων εν τη Θεολογική Σχολή του Πανεπιστημίου Αθηνών. Τιμητικόν αφιέρωμα επιτροπής εκ μαθητών του επι τη μετατάξει του εις ομότιμον καθηγητήν. Ομιλούν τα κείμενα [A Honorary Publication Dedicated to Leonidas Io. Philippidis, Ordinary Professor of the History of Religions at the Divinity School of the University of Athens, for Becoming an Emeritus Professor, edited by a Committee of his Students. The Texts Speak for Themselves]. Athens 1970.

Fleischer, Hagen and Svoronos, Nicos, eds. *Πρακτικά Α΄ Διεθνούς Συνεδρίου Σύγχρονης Ιστορίας. Η Ελλάδα 1936–1944: Δικτατορία – Κατοχή – Αντίσταση* [Proceedings of the First International Congress of Modern History. Greece 1936–1944: Dictatorship – Occupation – Resistance]. Athens: Morfotiko Institouto ATE, 1989, 2nd ed., 1990.

Fleischer, Hagen, ed. *Η Ελλάδα '36–'49. Από τη Δικτατορία στον Εμφύλιο. Τομές και συνέχειες* [Greece 1936–1949. From Dictatorship to Civil War. Ruptures and Continuities]. Athens: Kastaniotis, 2003.

Hering, Gunnar. "Rache am Vaterland? Anmerkungen zur Persönlichkeit des Ioannis Metaxas." In idem, *Nostos. Gesammelte Schriften zur südosteuropäischen Geschichte*, ed. by Maria A. Stassinopoulou, Frankfurt a.M.: Peter Lang, 1995, pp. 131–148.

——. "Aspekte der Kulturpolitik des Metaxas-Regimes (1936–1940)." In Reinhard Lauer and Peter Schreiner, eds. *Die Kultur Griechenlands in Mittelalter und Neuzeit* (Abhandlungen der Akademie der Wissenschaften in Göttingen, Philologisch-historische Klasse, Dritte Folge, Nr. 212), Göttingen: Vandenhoeck und Ruprecht, 1996, pp. 285–321.

Higham, Robin and Thanos Veremis, eds. *Aspects of Greece 1936–40: The Metaxas Dictatorship.* Athens: Eliamep – Vryonis Center, 1993.

Iliopoulos, Ilias. *Metaxas als Realist. Griechische Eindämmungsstrategie und britisches 'Appeasement.'* München: Hieronymus, 2001.

Irmscher, Johannes. "Academic Links Between Berlin University and Fascist Greece." *Journal of the Hellenic Diaspora* 13 (1986), pp. 71–90.

Joachim, Joachim G. *Ioannis Metaxas: The Formative Years 1871–1922* (Peleus 5). Mannheim – Möhnesee: Bibliopolis, 2000.

Karayiannis, Yiorgos. *Εκκλησία και κράτος 1833–1997. Ιστορική επισκόπηση των σχέσεών τους* [Church and State 1833–1997. A Historical Review of Their Relations]. Athens: To Pontiki, 1997.

Kofas, Jon V. *Authoritarianism in Greece: The Metaxas Regime* (East European Monographs 133). Boulder/New York: Columbia University Press, 1983.

Kokkinos, Georgios. *Η φασίζουσα ιδεολογία στην Ελλάδα. Η περίπτωση του περιοδικού 'Νέον Κράτος' (1937–1941)* [The Fascistoid Ideology in Greece. The Case of the Journal 'Neon Kratos' (1937–1941)]. Athens: Papazisis, n.d.

Koliopoulos, John S. *Greece and the British Connection 1935–1941.* Oxford: Oxford University Press, 1977.

Linardatos, Spyros. *Η εξωτερική πολιτική της 4ης Αυγούστου* [The Foreign Policy of the 4th August Regime]. Athens: Dialogos, 1975.

——. *Ο Ιωάννης Μεταξάς και οι Μεγάλες Δυνάμεις 1936–40* [Ioannis Metaxas and the Great Powers 1936–1940]. Athens: Proskinio, 1993.

Machaira, Eleni. *Η νεολαία της 4ης Αυγούστου* [The Youth of the 4th August Regime] (Ιστορικό Αρχείο Ελληνικής Νεολαίας, 13). Athens: Geniki Grammateia Neas Genias, 1987.

Magkriotis, Dimitrios I. *Πίστις και επιστήμη* [Faith and Science]. Athens: EON, 1940.

Makrides, Vasilios N. "Orthodoxy in the Service of Anticommunism: The Religious Organization Zoë during the Greek Civil War." In Ph. Carabott and Th. D. Sfikas, eds. *The Greek Civil War: Essays on a Conflict of Exceptionalism and Silences*. London: Ashgate, 2004, pp. 159–174.

Panotis, Aristeidis. "Φιλιππίδης, Λεωνίδας" [Philippidis, Leonidas]. *Θρησκευτική και Ηθική Εγκυκλοπαιδεία* 11 (1967). pp. 1093–1096.

Papanastasiou, Nikolaos, *Die Metaxas-Diktatur und das nationalsozialistische Deutschland 1936–1941*, diss. phil. Augsburg 2000.

Philippidis, Leonidas, J. *Die 'Goldene Regel' religionsgeschichtlich untersucht*, Inaugural-Dissertation zur Erlangung der Doktorwürde der Hohen Philosophischen Fakultät der Universität Leipzig. Leipzig: Adolf Klein, 1929.

——. *Η περί θλίψεως και λυτρώσεως θεωρία της Βεδάντα της δογματικής του Ινδικού Βραχμανισμού* [The Vedânta-Theory of Brahmanism About Sorrow and Redemption]. Athens: Pyrsos, 1934.

——. *Η Ιστορία των Θρησκευμάτων ως επιστήμη* [The History of Religions as a Scholarly Discipline]. Athens: Pyrsos, 1935.

——. *Ελλάς πιστεύουσα* [Believing Greece]. Athens: Pyrsos, 1937.

——. *Η Ιστορία των Θρησκευμάτων καθ' εαυτήν και εν τη Χριστιανική Θεολογία* [The History of Religions in Itself and Within Christian Theology]. Athens: Pyrsos, 1938.

——. *Das Liebesprinzip im Buddhismus und im Christentum*. Athen: Pyrsos, 1938.

——. *Θρησκεία και ζωή* [Religion and Life]. Athens: Pyrsos, 1938;

——. *Θρησκεία και θάνατος* [Religion and Death]. Athens: Pyrsos, 1938.

——. *Θεία Πρόνοια και Μοίρα εν τη θρησκεία των αρχαίων Ελλήνων* [Divine Providence and Fate in the Religion of the Ancient Greeks]. Athen: Pyrsos, 1939.

——. *Αυτοβιογραφικόν σημείωμα (1898–1963) και πνευματική προσφορά (1913–1963)* [Autobiographical Note (1898–1963) and Intellectual Contribution (1913–1963)]. Athens: G.D. Kypraios, 1963.

——. *Das Unwiderlegliche der Forschungsergebnisse des verewigten Prof. Dr. Rev. P. Wilhelm Schmidt*. Athen 1968.

Richter, Heinz A. *Griechenland zwischen Revolution und Konterrevolution (1936–1946)*. Frankfurt a.M.: Europäische Verlagsanstalt, 1973.

Rudolph, Kurt. *Die Religionsgeschichte an der Leipziger Universität und die Entwicklung der Religionswissenschaft* (Sitzungsberichte der Sächsischen Akademie der Wissenschaften zu Leipzig, Philologisch-historische Klasse, Bd. 107, Heft 1). Berlin: Akademie-Verlag, 1962.

Sarandis, Constantine. "The Ideology and Character of the Metaxas Regime." In R. Higham and Th. Veremis, eds., *Aspects of Greece 1936–40: The Metaxas Dictatorship*. Athens: Eliamep – Vryonis Center, 1993, pp. 147–177.

Siotis, Markos A. "Λούβαρις, Νικόλαος" [Louvaris, Nikolaos]. *Θρησκευτική και Ηθική Εγκυκλοπαιδεία* 8 (1966), pp. 352–357.

Spanakou, Zoi. "Η κριτική της θρησκείας στο σοσιαλιστικό και μαρξιστικό τύπο του μεσοπολέμου" [The Critique of Religion in the Socialist and Marxist Press of the Interwar Period]. *Τα Εκπαιδευτικά* 41–42 (1996), pp. 158–176.

Spiliotis, Susanne-Sophia. "Die Metaxas-Diktatur in Griechenland 1936–1941 – ein faschistoides Regime?." In Erwin Oberländer, ed., *Autoritäre Regime in Ostmittel- und Südosteuropa 1919–1944*. Paderborn: Schöningh, 2001, pp. 403–430.

Spranger, Eduard. "Gedenken an Nikolaos Louvaris." *Universitas* 17 (1962), pp. 457–468.

Tsakonas, Dimitrios. *Ιδεαλισμός και Μαρξισμός στην Ελλάδα* [Idealism and Marxism in Greece]. Athens: Kaktos, 1988.

Vatikiotis, Panayiotis J. *Popular Autocracy in Greece 1936–41. A Political Biography of General Ioannis Metaxas*. London: Frank Cass, 1998.

Velliadis, Annivas. *Μεταξάς – Χίτλερ. Ελληνογερμανικές σχέσεις στη μεταξική δικτατορία 1936–1941* [Metaxas – Hitler. Greek-German Relations During the Metaxas Dictatorship 1936–1941]. Athens: Enalios, 2003.

Vlavianos, Haris. "The Metaxas Dictatorship: The Greek Communist Party Under Siege." In R. Higham and Th. Veremis, eds., *Aspects of Greece 1936–40: The Metaxas Dictatorship*. Athens: Eliamep – Vryonis Center, 1993, pp. 193–225.

Yannoulatos, Anastasios. "Λεωνίδας Ιω. Φιλιππίδης, ο επιστήμων, ο άνθρωπος" [Leonidas Io. Philippidis, the Scholar, the Man], *Επιστημονική Επετηρίς της Θεολογικής Σχολής Πανεπιστημίου Αθηνών* 21 (1974), pp. ια' – νε'.

Zacharioudakis, Emmanouil. *Die deutsch-griechischen Beziehungen 1933–1941. Interessengegensätze an der Peripherie Europas*. Husum: Matthiesen, 2001.

WAR-TIME CONNECTIONS: DUMÉZIL AND ELIADE, ELIADE AND SCHMITT, SCHMITT AND EVOLA, DRIEU LA ROCHELLE AND DUMÉZIL

Cristiano Grottanelli

1. *War-time Connections*

To study the subject to which this conference is dedicated, some help may be provided by analyzing the connections between the intellectuals who produced the discourse and committed the deeds we are trying to decipher. Such connections, at once scientific, political, and personal, are especially useful because they provide information on the reciprocal interpretations and attitudes of the persons who met and interacted. More specifically, the study of the relationships between these intellectuals can tell us what some of them meant to some others and how such constructions (Eliade's view of Dumézil, for example, or Dumézil's view of Eliade, or Carl Schmitt's view of Eliade or of Evola) were created, used, and eventually modified. In this paper, I shall provide a glance at some of these relationships, and I shall concentrate especially on the connections that took shape at the very peak of the conflict, while war was actually being waged, and all mediations were made impossible.

2. *Eliade and Dumézil 1943*

As we know from Dumézil's *Entretiens* with Didier Eribon,[1] Mircea Eliade and Georges Dumézil were probably in contact before 1940; they met in November 1943 (as we read in Eliade's wartime journal, now available as *Diario Portugués*),[2] when Eliade, who was then an attaché in the Romanian embassy in Lisbon, managed to spend two weeks in Paris. Finally, when Eliade obtained a visa and arrived in the French capital in September 1945, he contacted Dumézil who became, to say it with

---

[1] Georges Dumézil, *Entretiens avec Didier Eribon* (Paris: Gallimard, 1987), p. 93f.
[2] Mircea Eliade, *Diario portugués* (Barcelona: Editorial Kairós, 2001), p. 112.

Florin Turcanu,[3] his "parrain" in the French academic world. But how important were the respective political positions of the two scholars in creating the friendship that lasted until the end of their lives?

In order to minimize the political import of their friendship and cooperation, Didier Eribon stated in his *Faut-il brûler Dumézil?* that Dumézil disliked the Romanian Iron Guard, as he wrote on December 31, 1933 and on April 1934 in two of his "pro-fascist and anti-Nazi" articles published in the daily newspaper *Le Jour* under the pseudonym Georges Marcenay.[4] But one should consider that respectively ten and nine years elapsed between Marcenay's articles and the first meeting between Eliade and Dumézil, not to speak of the difference in time and circumstance between those articles and the years of their friendship, 1945–1986. And to this one should add that, even in 1943, Eliade's relationship with what remained of the Iron Guard was far from simple, given the fact that he worked for the Antonescu regime after the violent break between Antonescu and that political organization.[5]

The desire to keep Eliade and Dumézil separate in spite of their important relationship is a typical aspect of contemporary French culture, as I wrote in my half of the introduction to the Italian edition of Daniel Dubuisson's *Mythologies du XXe siècle*.[6] In that book, Dumézil is presented as a great master, Eliade is described as a facist, and their friendship is forgotten. I think I detect something of the kind in Alexandra Laignel-Lavastine's important book *Cioran, Eliade, Ionesco. L'oubli du fascisme*, which claims "Eliade noue... de solides amitiés avec plusieurs savants tenus dans l'ignorance de son passé politique, comme Georges Dumézil..."[7] I believe it is impossible to imagine that the *Parisiens* met by Eliade in 1943, when he was probably on leave, but still an attaché of the Romanian embassy in Lisbon, knew nothing of his function, and I believe that his function qualified him politically.

If my way of reasoning is correct, then it is most probable that Dumézil had made a realization by the time he met Eliade in Paris

---

[3] Florin Turcanu, *Mircea Eliade. Le prisonnier de l'histoire* (Paris, Éditions de la Découverte, 2003), p. 344.

[4] Didier Eribon, *Faut-il brûler Dumézil?* (Paris: Flammarion, 1993), pp. 135f.

[5] Turcanu, *Mircea Eliade*, pp. 279–309.

[6] Daniel Dubuisson, *Mitologie del XX secolo* (Bari: Dedalo, 1994), pp. 5–11. The original edition of Dubuisson's book is *Mythologies du XXe siècle. Dumézil, Lévi-Strauss, Eliade* (Lille: Presses Universitaires de Lille, 1993).

[7] Alexandra Laignel-Lavastine, *Cioran, Eliade, Ionesco. L'oubli du fascisme* (Paris: Presses Universitaires de France, 2002), p. 474.

in 1943. Dumézil was aware, or became aware upon meeting him, of Eliade's affiliation, if not to the Iron Guard and to the Antonescu regime whose troops were fighting side by side with those of Nazi Germany. The precise implication of this in the context of their relationship deserves to be discussed: The least one can do is to connect it to the best, and also most cautious, reflection available on the reasons for the friendship between the two scholars, that I find in Florin Turcanu's biography, p. 351f. Turcanu asks why Dumézil constantly helped Eliade between 1945 and 1950, "les années plus sombres de votre vie," as the French scholar wrote to his Romanian friend in a postcard of 1973. After *l'estime intellectuelle*, Turcanu lists a series of political stances that were common to the two scholars.[8]

3. *Mircea Eliade and Carl Schmitt 1942*

To understand the first meeting between Eliade and Dumézil, it is useful to compare it to the first meeting between the Romanian scholar and writer and another intellectual. I refer to Eliade's visit to the Dahlem home of Carl Schmitt during August 1942. In other words: Twelve months and a few days before his trip to Paris and his first sight of Georges Dumézil. Both contacts took place during the war, as Eliade was working for the Romanian embassy in Lisbon, and, as far as we know, during a short leave.[9]

In a recent issue of the *Revue de l'Histoire des Religions*, I published an article on that meeting.[10] All that must be said here is that in 1942 Schmitt was a member of the Nazi party (he had become a member in 1933, after Hitler's rise to power) but had lost practically all the influence he had exerted until his clash with the SS in 1936, and that he was working on his small book *Land und Meer* that was published in Leipzig that same year. That book dealt with empires based upon land and empires based upon sea power, and this subject guided the conversation

---

[8] Turcanu, *Mircea Eliade*, p. 351f.

[9] On the meeting between Eliade and Carl Schmitt, see Eliade, *Diario português*, p. 43. One should note that, according to Alexandra Laignel-Lavastine (*Cioran, Eliade, Ionesco*, p. 313), Eliade's meeting with Carl Schmitt was sponsored by a Romanian institution in Berlin, the *Rumänisches Institut Deutschland*, whose President and Vice-President had both been famous members of the Iron Guard.

[10] Cristiano Grottanelli, "Mircea Eliade, Carl Schmitt, René Guénon, 1942," *Revue de l'Histoire des Religions* 219–3 (2002), pp. 325–356.

to "Portugal, Salazar, and maritime cultures." The Romanian attaché wrote in his diary that his German host reminded him of Nae Ionescu, Eliade's teacher and mentor, who had been influenced by Schmitt's early publication *Romantische Politik*. The *Diario Português* says nothing about his host's opinion of Nae Ionescu, but at the end of the page describing the visit, we find an abrupt quotation of the German professor's interest for René Guénon, who was, Schmitt said to Eliade (p. 43), "the most interesting man today."

In the first volume of Eliade's *Mémoires, Les moissons du solstice*, 1988, the Romanian attaché's visit to Schmitt's Dahlem home is described, but there is no mention of Guénon. But the French traditionalist must have been important, at least in Schmitt's view of his visitor. We know this from two sources. First, in volume 1 of Ernst Jünger's wartime diary, published in 1955 under the title *Strahlungen*, we find an account of Jünger's stay in Dahlem, as a guest of his friend Carl Schmitt, from the 12th to the 17th November, 1942. In that entry, dated November 15, Jünger praises an article by Eliade, *Le symbolisme aquatique*, in the review *Zalmoxis*, that Schmitt had given him to read, and adds that Schmitt had provided detailed information on "Mircea Eliade and on his *Meister* René Guénon." The second source is a letter from Schmitt to Armin Mohler dated December 4, 1948, answering a letter by Mohler, dated October 19 with questions about Schmitt's book *Der Leviathan in der Staatslehre des Thomas Hobbes. Sinn und Fehlschlag eines politischen Symbols*, 1938, and about René Guénon. Mohler was reading *Der Leviathan* where he found, in a footnote, a quotation from *La crise du monde moderne*, 1927, and that quotation seemed puzzling to him, so he asked Schmitt to explain it. In his letter, Schmitt stated that his book *Der Leviathan* was completely esoteric ("voller Esoterik"), and added that he had read many, but alas not all of Guénon's writings, and that he had never met him personally, but that he had met two friends of him. Immediately after these words, Schmitt wrote: "You shall be interested to learn that the Baron Julius Evola was a faithful follower ("ein unbedingter Adept") of Guénon."[11]

In my article, I tried to explain Schmitt's interest in Guénon as the converging of two very different minds upon a guiding principle I called *théorie du complot*, and to envisage the very different "esoteric" atti-

---

[11] All the documents mentioned here are quoted in my article "Mircea Eliade, Carl Schmitt, René Guénon, 1942." Eliade quoted in Jünger's journal: Ernst Jünger, *Strahlungen I* (Stuttgart: Klett-Cotta, 1998), p. 416.

tudes of the two authors as consequences of such theories. I must add
that Schmitt saw the *complot* as a Jewish plot against the State,[12] while
Guénon viewed it differently. Rather than dwell on that interpretation,
I would like to draw attention to what is important in the present context: Schmitt's view of Eliade, and the identity of the two "friends of
Guénon" mentioned by Schmitt in his letter to Mohler, six years after
his first meeting with the Romanian attaché.

4. *Schmitt and Evola*

These "two friends" were, I think, Julius Evola and Mircea Eliade. As
for Eliade, I need not repeat what I have stated so far about the fact
that Carl Schmitt took Guénon to be, to use Ernst Jünger's words, the
Meister of his visitor from Bucharest. As for Evola, who cooperated with
the *Ahnenerbe*, and is actually mentioned by Schmitt in his letter, as a
follower of Guénon,[13] I think it would be interesting to quote a few
documents attesting his relationship with Schmitt before and during
the Second World War.

It is now possible to show that Schmitt met Evola in 1937 and mentioned this meeting in a letter to Jünger dated December 12, and that he
invited him to dinner in his Dahlem home on "Freitag, 17. Juni 1938."[14]
The evidence for this invitation is found in a volume edited by Antonio
Caracciolo and published in 2000.[15] The book contains seven letters
from Evola to Schmitt, written from 1951 to 1963, as well as a few writings of Julius Evola. In the first letter, dated December 15, 1951, Evola
says he had been given Schmitt's address by Armin Mohler, and that he
is taking the initiative of writing to him *après le déluge*.[16] The letter was
extremely friendly: the Italian "philosopher" gave important information about himself, asked Schmitt to send him news of his own situation,

---

[12] See Raphael Gross, *Carl Schmitt und die Juden* (Frankfurt a.M.: Suhrkamp, 2000),
pp. 267–300.

[13] On Evola, see Grottanelli, "Mircea Eliade, Carl Schmitt, René Guénon, 1942,"
esp. pp. 354–356, with some bibliography in footnotes 58–61. See also Sandro Barbera
e Cristiano Grottanelli, "Ammiratori di Evola" *Belfagor* 57-5 (2002), pp. 555–565.

[14] Ernst Jünger-Carl Schmitt, *Briefwechsel*, herausgegeben, kommentiert und mit einem
Nachwort von Helmuth Kiesel (Stuttgart: Klett-Cotta, 1999), p. 72f.

[15] Antonio Caracciolo, ed., *Lettere di Julius Evola a Carl Schmitt* (Quaderni di testi
evoliani 36) (Roma: Europa Liberia Editrice, 2000), p. 82.

[16] Ibid., p. 31f.

enquired after the "hübsche Wohnung" in Dahlem, and asked his German friend to send him a copy of his essay on Donoso Cortés.

In the present context, it is striking that on that same day Julius Evola wrote to Mircea Eliade.[17] In this case, the letter was not the first one *après le déluge*: On the contrary, Evola referred to a previous letter of Eliade, "votre lettre de l'année passée." And the contents of the message differed somewhat from the cordial tone of Evola's letter to Schmitt: The Italian traditionalist accused Eliade of never quoting René Guénon or "other authors" whose ideas were similar ("bien plus voisines") to those that allowed him to find his bearings in the subject he studied. On this letter, and on the following one, dated December 31, much has been written and need not be repeated here. I think it is more important here to note that Evola wrote these two letters on the same day, and to attempt to interpret this fact.

The explanation is found, I think, in Evola's letter to Schmitt, where the Italian traditionalist recounted the salient mishaps of his life *pendant et après le déluge*, beginning with the "Kriegsverletzung" that caused his motor paralysis. In 1948, he wrote, he returned to Italy, and then "geschah etwas komisches: ich war – verhaftet." Here, Evola refers to the legal apprehension, in the spring of 1951, and to the trial, in the month of November of the same year, of about fifty neo-fascists, some of whom were members of a group called *Fasci di Azione Rivoluzionaria* (F.A.R). As Evola himself writes to Schmitt, these neo-fascists "haben sich in Bünden organisiert, die auch Dummheiten (Bombenanschläge) begangen haben." Evola was also arrested in May 1951. According to him, this was because he was considered to be the "geistige Vater" (spiritual father) of these adepts of *Neufaschismus*, but in fact he was accused of *apologia del fascismo*, and suspected of being among the leaders of the F.A.R. group. The trial ended on November 20, 1951: three of the leading neo-fascists were condemned to one year of imprisonment, a few others were sentenced to shorter periods, and others still, among them Julius Evola, were acquitted as not guilty ("per non aver commesso il

---

[17] Mircea Handoca, *Mircea Eliade şi corespondenţii săi*, vol. I (A-E) (Bucureşti: Editura Minerva, 1993), pp. 276–278. On this letter, see Marin Mincu e Roberto Scagno, eds., *Mircea Eliade e l'Italia* (Milano, Jaca Book, 1987), pp. 252–257; Gianfranco De Turris, "L'Iniziato' e il Professore. I rapporti 'sommersi' fra Julius Evola e Mircea Eliade," in the volume by various authors *Delle rovine e oltre. Saggi su Julius Evola* (Roma: Antonio Pellicani Editore, 1995), pp. 219–249; and Paola Pisi, *I 'tradizionalisti' e la formazione del pensiero di Eliade*. In Luciano Arcella et al., eds., *Confronto con Mircea Eliade. Archetipi mitici e identità storica* (Milano: Jaca Book, 1998), pp. 43–133.

fatto") – as Evola puts it in his letter *Freispruch* ("assoluzione con formula piena") – and released from prison after a six-month detainment (*custodia cautelare*).[18]

In all probability, Evola's two letters of December 15, 1951 were the gesture of a man who, having overcome an immediate danger, tried to renew his connections with two friends. As I have already stated, it is important to note the difference in tone and contents of the two letters: to Eliade, a mild reproach for his unfaithfulness to Guénon and to Evola himself; to Schmitt, a warmer greeting and the account of the main events since the contact was broken off, including the latest political news and a mention of his own six-months imprisonment, that must surely have been meaningful to the author of *De captivitate salus*. In any case, these two letters are at least an indication of the credibility of Schmitt's interpretation of the relationship between Eliade, Evola, and Guénon. As for Guénon himself, 1951 marks his death in Cairo, where he had been living for twenty years.

5. *Drieu La Rochelle and Dumézil 1941*

At this point, I can start addressing some of the issues I mentioned at the beginning of my presentation. As for the reciprocal interpretation of the figures discussed in the Eribon interview Dumézil explained that, before 1940, he saw Eliade as a talented and authoritative writer and as the founder of the periodical *Zalmoxis*, dedicated to the history of religions.[19] In 1943, a date he never mentioned, he probably knew of the Romanian's involvement with the Antonescu regime, while Eliade envisaged Dumézil as an interesting scholar, and, when he was a refugee in Paris, saw him as his main friend and sponsor, and, most important, as a respected scholar who defended him against the accusations of the new Romanian State. As for Schmitt and Eliade, the Romanian attaché considered his Dahlem host an important cultural figure of Nazi Germany and compared him to his own beloved teacher Nae

---

[18] Evola's own account of these facts may be found in his autobiography: Julius Evola, *Le Chemin du Cinabre* (Milano-Carmagnola: Arché-Arktos, 1983), pp. 162–165. A slightly more detailed "evolian" account has recently been offered by Gianfranco de Turris, *Elogio e difesa di Julius Evola. Il barone e i terroristi* (Roma: Edizioni Mediterranee, 1997), pp. 45–82.

[19] Dumézil, *Entretiens avec Didier Eribon*, p. 93f. See note 1 above.

Ionescu.[20] They would meet again in Lisbon in 1944, while Eliade was anguished by the news of the American bombing of Bucharest. To Schmitt, Eliade was a follower of Guénon, who in turn was a friend of the Italian Baron Julius Evola he had met in 1937 and invited to dinner in 1938.

This picture is clear, but it is also problematic. Among the many problems it raises, the main one, is, I think, Dumézil's political position during the war and in the immediate aftermath of the conflict, when, in 1947, he defended Eliade against what he called a "political intrigue" that deprived him of a position in the *Centre national de la recherché scientifique*. To shed some light of this specific problem, it would be useful to consider a further case, the connection of Georges Dumézil with the writer Pierre Drieu la Rochelle, anti-Semite, fascist and collaborator, who from 1940 directed the *Nouvelle Revue Française*[21] as a faithful ally of the German Ambassador in Paris, Otto Abetz.[22] This episode has been explored more than once in recent publications: Didier Eribon dealt with it at length, and I examined it in an article that was published in 1998.[23] Here I shall briefly consider a few aspects of that connection.

In his text *France, Angleterre, Allemagne*, published first as an article in the official periodical of the German Cultural Institute in Paris, *Deutschland-Frankreich*, 1943, and again in his book *Les Français d'Europe*, Balzac, 1944, Drieu praised Georges Dumézil for contributing greatly to the knowledge of the ancient harmonies connecting Vedic India, early Rome, Druidic Gaul, Germany and Scandinavia. On such a historical foundation, he explained, a solid and high-spirited future Europe could be built. Of course, Didier Eribon was right in observing that Dumézil was not responsible for Drieu's interpretation of his work; but in the relationship between the two men, in Dumézil's production of 1941, and most specifically in the book most admired by Drieu, *Jupiter, Mars, Quirinus*, there are aspects that show the matter was more complicated than Eribon thought. In my article, I referred in particular to five ideas, expressed in *Jupiter Mars Quirinus*, in a part of that book's introduction,

[20] Eliade, *Diario portuguès*, p. 112.
[21] Lionel Richard, "Drieu la Rochelle et la 'Nouvelle Revue Française' des années noires," *Revue d'histoire de la deuxième guerre mondiale* 25 (1975), pp. 67–84.
[22] Barbara Lambauer, *Otto Abetz et les Français, ou l'envers de la collaboration* (Paris, Fayard, 2001). On Drieu la Rochelle see especially pp. 53–66, pp. 107–113, pp. 233–242.
[23] See Eribon, *Faut-il brûler Dumézil?*, pp. 219–231, and Cristiano Grottanelli, "Dumézil's 'Aryens' in 1941," *Zeitschrift für Religionswissenschaft* 6 (1998), pp. 207–219.

published in Drieu la Rochelle's *La Nouvelle Revue Française*, 1941, as *L'étude comparée des religions indo-européennes*, and in an article, *Le nom des Arya* that also appeared in 1941 in the *Revue de l'Histoire des Religions*.[24]

As for two of these ideas, the name *Aryens* used as a synonym of *Indo-Européens*, and the racial quality of the Indo-European phenomenon, the scholar's decision not to discuss those aspects in the *Nouvelle Revue Française* article has been used by Didier Eribon as evidence of Dumézil's wish to leave the most "dangerous" ideas expressed in *Jupiter Mars Quirinus* out of a text that would be read not by specialists but by all sorts of cultivated readers. Yet one should notice that the French scholar willingly presented to the leaders of the literary periodical perspectives that were just as loaded. These standpoints included not only the description of the Indo-European *triomphes* throughout the planet, but also the interpretation of the Second World War as an internecine conflict between Indo-European nations, and the possible view of that war as the painful birth of a new order (*le dur accouchement d'un ordre stable*). These two ideas were strongly interconnected, but they were expressed in ways that made it difficult to understand what precise political position they implied. Yet both were open to interpretations in line with two ideas dear to Drieu la Rochelle: first, that the Nordic races (the British, the French and the Germans) should have fought together, and not against each other (see Drieu's article *France, Allemagne, Angleterre*, quoted above); second, that the Nazi victory prepared, or should have prepared, a new, united, and powerful Europe, transcending nations (see Drieu's old book of 1931, *L'Europe contre les patries*, or his *Les Français d'Europe*, 1944, also quoted above).

In my article of 1998, I pointed out that, as Eribon had shown, Dumézil was pro-fascist in the 1930s, but was probably anti-German (Eribon writes: "anti-Nazi") in 1939, and that in the texts I have just mentioned he quoted his Jewish colleague Émile Benveniste as an authority on *les Indo-Européens*. Faced with these apparently contradictory attitudes, I tried to suggest a possible explanation of Dumézil's short-lived ideas of 1941. Rather than repeating my hypothesis, I shall turn to Drieu, and to his reading of Dumézil, in order to understand one of the constructions I referred to at the beginning of this paper.

---

[24] Grottanelli, "Dumézil's 'Aryens' in 1941," pp. 207–214, with full bibliography.

Pierre Drieu la Rochelle committed suicide in the summer of 1945. His *Journal* of the years 1939–1945 was published only in 1992.[25] Dumézil is never mentioned in that diary, but many pages help us to understand what he meant to Drieu. As I have stated above, in 1943 he presented that scholar as a specialist who allowed his readers "de prendre une conscience plus large et beaucoup plus precise" of Aryan harmonies. This theme returns often in the *Journal*, and not only did the collaborator envision a better understanding of the wide repercussions of *la pensée aryenne* as a weapon in his ideological battle (January 18, 1944); but at one time he even described what he calls "ma légère intromission dans les affaires politiques" as meant to intensify his preparation for the Netherworld ("pour mieux me rapprocher de la mort, pour intensifier ma préparation à l'au-delà," September 20, 1941). On the other hand, he sometimes saw the study of *l'histoire des religions* as an alternative to his political engagement (July 6, 1940). On January 28, 1944, this connection between a radical change in his life and a religious choice reaches its highest degree. It is striking to see this mystical climax connected with Mircea Eliade's old *Meister* – borrowing a phrase from Ernst Jünger's war diary:

> I would have liked to live a few years without writing in order to become what I am today. And to think that I met Guénon around 1922 in the home of (Daniel) Halévy, and that I did not guess! But I shall never forget his emaciated face. Maybe with a fleeting glance he had touched me forever.[26]

6. *A Few Final Remarks*

The picture I have tried to draw is so complex and variegated that it would be ridiculous even to mention the term "conclusions." Though my research has just begun, the documents I have presented so far allow for a few general remarks. First of all, the intricacy of the interconnections I have hinted at, and the variety of constructions I have been able to mention, are great: A very complex picture presents itself, and the simple tools we have worked with so far are insufficient. Second, in spite of these often unexpected complexities, *a cultural 'front' of the totalitarian*

---

[25] Pierre Drieu la Rochelle, *Journal 1939–1945*, présenté et annoté par Julien Hervier (Paris: Gallimard, 1992).

[26] Drieu la Rochelle, *Journal 1939–1945*, p. 262f., p. 270f., and pp. 361–364.

right existed, and in many different ways many different intellectuals formed, or joined, and fought for, that front. One should beware of the misconception according to which practically no "respectable" member of the cultural elite actually belonged to that front – and of the false impression, encouraged by the retrospective self-presentations offered by many of those members, that most of the *differences* existing among the fighters, and representing different strategies in the same struggle, were better understood as indifferent attitudes, or even as *secret forms of opposition* to the regimes upheld by that front.[27] Third, the "front" was made up not only of German National Socialists or pro-Nazis, or of Italian fascists or pro-fascists, but it was *a vast European front*. Fourth, the members of this cultural and trans-national *Männerbund* kept in contact, or re-contacted each other, after what Evola (and Eliade, in his Portuguese *Journal*, July 24, 1944) called *le déluge*, and in different and new ways continued what they saw as their battle. It is only after a vast general discussion on such observations that the subject to which our conference is dedicated can be properly understood, and a collection of data such as the one I have briefly presented in this paper shall acquire its true meaning.[28]

---

[27] On two intellectuals who skillfully re-constructed their own ideas and behavior during the Second World War, see Cristiano Grottanelli, "Fruitful Death: Mircea Eliade and Ernst Jünger on Human Sacrifice, 1937–1945," *Numen* 52 (2005), pp. 116–145.

[28] I owe some of these last remarks to Bruce Lincoln.

Bibliography

Arcella, Luciano, Paola Pisi, and Roberto Scagno, eds. *Confronto con Mircea Eliade. Archetipi mitici e identità storica.* Milano: Jaca Book, 1998.
Barbera, Sandro and Cristiano Grottanelli. "Ammiratori di Evola." *Belfagor* 57–5 (2002): pp. 555–565.
Antonio Caracciolo, ed. *Lettere di Julius Evola a Carl Schmitt* (Quaderni di testi evoliani 36). Roma: Europa Liberia Editrice, 2000.
Drieu la Rochelle, Pierre. *Journal 1939–1945*, présenté et annoté par Julien Hervier. Paris: Gallimard, 1992.
Dubuisson, Daniel. *Mythologies du XXe siècle. Dumézil, Lévi-Strauss, Eliade.* Lille: Presses Universitaires de Lille, 1993.
——. *Mitologie del XX secolo.* Bari: Dedalo, 1994.
Dumézil, Georges. *Entretiens avec Didier Eribon.* Paris: Gallimard, 1987.
Eliade, Mircea. *Diario portugués*, translated from the original Romanian by Joaquín Garrigós. Barcelona: Editorial Kairós, 2001.
Eribon, Didier. *Faut-il brûler Dumézil?.* Paris: Flammarion, 1993.
Evola, Julius. *Le Chemin du Cinabre.* Milano-Carmagnola: Arché-Arktos, 1983.
——. *Lettere di Julius Evola a Carl Schmitt,* introd. e cura di Antonio Caracciolo (Quaderni di testi evoliani 36). Roma: Europa Liberia Editrice, 2000.
Gross, Raphael. *Carl Schmitt und die Juden.* Frankfurt am M.: Suhrkamp, 2000.
Grottanelli, Cristiano. "Dumézil's 'Aryens' in 1941." *Zeitschrift für Religionswissenschaft* 6 (1998), pp. 207–219.
——. "Mircea Eliade, Carl Schmitt, René Guénon, 1942." *Revue de l'Histoire des Religions* 219 (2002), pp. 325–356.
——. "Fruitful Death: Mircea Eliade and Ernst Jünger on Human Sacrifice, 1937–1945." *Numen* 52 (2005), pp. 116–145.
Handoca, Mircea. *Mircea Eliade şi corespondenţii săi,* vol. I (A–E). Bucureşti: Editura Minerva, 1993.
Jünger, Ernst: *Strahlungen* I. Stuttgart: Klett-Cotta, 1998.
—— und Carl Schmitt. *Briefwechsel,* herausgegeben, kommentiert und mit einem Nachwort von Helmuth Kiesel. Stuttgart: Klett-Cotta, 1999.
Laignel-Lavastine, Alexandra. *Cioran, Eliade, Ionesco. L'oubli du fascisme.* Paris: Presses Universitaires de France, 2002.
Lambauer, Barbara. *Otto Abetz et les Français, ou l'envers de la collaboration.* Paris: Fayard, 2001.
Mincu, Marin and Roberto Scagno, eds. *Mircea Eliade e l'Italia.* Milano: Jaca Book, 1987.
Pisi, Paola. "I 'tradizionalisti' e la formazione del pensiero di Elide." In Luciano Arcella et al., eds. *Confronto con Mircea Eliade. Archetipi mitici e identità storica.* Milano: Jaca Book, 1998, pp. 43–133.
Richard, Lionel. "Drieu la Rochelle et la *Nouvelle Revue Française* des années noires." *Revue d'histoire de la deuxième guerre mondiale* 25 (1975), pp. 67–84.
Turcanu, Florin. *Mircea Eliade. Le prisonnier de l'histoire.* Paris: Éditions de la Découverte, 2003.
Turris, Gianfranco De. "L''Iniziato' e il Professore. I rapporti 'sommersi' fra Julius Evola e Mircea Eliade." In *Delle rovine e oltre. Saggi su Julius Evola.* Roma: Antonio Pellicani Editore, 1995, pp. 219–249.
——. *Elogio e difesa di Julius Evola. Il barone e i terroristi.* Roma: Edizioni Mediterranee, 1997.

ENTRE IDEOLOGIE DE LA CULTURE ET POLITIQUE

MIRCEA ELIADE ET L'ÉTUDE DES RELIGIONS DANS LA ROUMANIE DE L'ENTRE-DEUX-GUERRES

Florin Țurcanu

L'œuvre d'historien des religions de Mircea Eliade abrite une tension entre, d'une part, ses ambitions et sa portée universelles, visibles au plus haut degré dans l'*Histoire des croyances et des idées religieuses* et, d'autre part, son ancrage initial dans une forte tradition culturelle nationale, celle de la Roumanie de l'entre-deux-guerres. L'intensité de cette tension entre l'universel et le particulier, qui est à la fois intellectuelle et biographique, varie dans le temps. Elle ne traverse pas tous ses écrits. Elle a néanmoins conditionné la sensibilité et la quête intellectuelle d'Eliade dans les années 1930 et 1940 et se trouve à l'origine de plusieurs thèmes de sa pensée et de quelques-uns de ses livres.

Que fait l'histoire des religions sinon «introduire l'élément universel dans une recherche 'locale', 'provinciale'» afin de révéler «le vrai sens» des manifestations fragmentaires du phénomène religieux, note Eliade dans son journal en avril 1967.[1] Sa première conception du mythe, dans les années 1930, comme «récit central» et définitoire d'une culture,[2] la valorisation de la préhistoire et de la protohistoire comme âge matriciel de la pensée symbolique et mythique, la question des rapports entre le christianisme et le substrat religieux préchrétien, sa théorie de la «terreur de l'histoire» − tous ces thèmes portent la marque de ses tentatives d'articuler l'identité culturelle roumaine et balkanique sur des phénomènes culturels, et plus spécifiquement religieux, de portée universelle. Les *Commentaires à la légende du Maître Manole* parues en 1943, *Le Mythe de l'éternel retour* publié en 1949 et le recueil d'études intitulé *De Zalmoxis à Gengis Khan* achevé en 1970, sont issues de cette tension intellectuellement féconde.

---

[1] Mircea Eliade, *Fragments d'un journal*, tome I (Paris, Gallimard, 1973), p. 539.
[2] Florin Țurcanu, *Mircea Eliade. Le prisonnier de l'histoire* (Paris, Editions La Découverte, 2003), p. 256 et p. 332.

Il est important de cerner l'enracinement de cette tension ou si l'on veut de cette dialectique de l'universel et du local dans les conditions intellectuelles, institutionnelles et politiques qui ont pesé sur la formation et sur les débuts de carrière de Mircea Eliade. Dans une telle perspective il ne suffit pas de s'en tenir, comme on l'a fait souvent ces derniers temps, à une quête des éléments de sa pensée qui pouvaient s'accorder avec son engagement politique dans les rangs de la Garde de fer. Il faut aller plus loin et prendre en compte le rapport entre cet engagement politique et la position occupée par Eliade, par l'indianisme et par l'histoire des religions dans le champ intellectuel et dans le réseau des institutions culturelles roumaines de l'époque. Il importe donc de reconstituer tout un environnement culturel, la hiérarchie de sa problématique et de ses acteurs ainsi que son fonctionnement afin de mieux comprendre dans quelle mesure et pour quelles raisons Eliade a-t-il essayé d'insérer ses préoccupations d'historien des religions dans les débats identitaires qui dominent le monde intellectuel roumain de l'entre-deux-guerres. Il s'agit en deuxième lieu d'éclairer, à travers le cas particulier de l'engagement fasciste d'Eliade, les rapports ambigus ou franchement conflictuels entre culture et politique, entre légitimité et marginalité intellectuelle dans la Roumanie de l'époque.

Malgré l'existence de quelques timides précurseurs,[3] Mircea Eliade est le premier indianiste et le premier historien des religions roumain digne de ce nom. Son apparition singulière se produit au milieu d'une culture nationale qui, en dépit des traits modernes qu'elle intègre après la première guerre mondiale, demeure encore, notamment dans les années 1920, profondément conservatrice, très dépendante à l'égard de l'Etat et de la monarchie et solidement encadrée par des institutions qui servent à la consolidation culturelle de l'Etat-Nation : l'Académie, les universités, certains instituts de recherche ainsi que les fondations culturelles royales. L'innovation culturelle n'est pas absente, mais, face au canon national elle trouve assez vite ses limites, comme le montre le sort de l'avant-garde littéraire et artistique – Tristan Tzara, Benjamin Fondane, Constantin Brancuși, Victor Brauner – devenus tous parisiens.[4] A cela s'ajoute la primauté traditionnelle de la littérature et de

---

[3] Pour les débuts modestes de l'intérêt pour l'Inde dans la Roumanie du 19e siècle voire Eugen Ciurtin «Imaginea și memoria Asiei în cultura română 1675–1928» [L'image et la mémoire de l'Asie dans la culture roumaine 1675–1928], *Archaeus* 2–2 (1998), p. 213–449.

[4] En 1925, l'Exposition d'art roumain ancien et moderne organisée au Musée du Jeu de Paume à Paris ne comprend aucun œuvre de Constantin Brancuși qui, pour-

l'historiographie dans le champ intellectuel, une réalité qui heurte le jeune Eliade dès l'âge de vingt ans, comme le montre ses articles des années 1926–1928.[5] L'autonomisation du champ intellectuel à l'égard de l'Etat et du canon culturel national s'accélère, certes, après 1918, surtout dans le domaine littéraire, mais la crise économique des années 1929–1933 va ralentir beaucoup cette tendance. Ceci explique pourquoi, après la crise, ce sera la monarchie roumaine qui va intervenir directement avec des moyens financiers et politiques, notamment par l'entremise des Fondations royales, pour revitaliser la vie culturelle en augmentant implicitement la dépendance de nombreux intellectuels vis-à-vis des institutions.

Dans ce monde culturel conservateur, fortement hiérarchisé, institutionnalisé, l'histoire des religions et l'indianisme n'ont pas eu une place réservée d'avance. En 1928, l'année du départ d'Eliade pour l'Inde, la Faculté de théologie de l'Université de Bucarest ne propose aucun cours d'histoire des religions non chrétiennes et limite son enseignement à l'histoire de l'Eglise roumaine et universelle.[6] Cette situation n'avait guerre changée en 1933 lorsque Eliade intègre lui aussi l'université en tant qu'enseignant. Quant aux historiens et aux archéologues, leur intérêt pour l'histoire du christianisme au Bas-Danube dans les derniers siècles de l'Empire Romain s'inscrivait dans la problématique à forte charge identitaire de la christianisation des ancêtres latinophones du peuple roumain.[7] De même, lorsqu'il fait son entrée dans la conscience culturelle nationale grâce aux fouilles archéologiques des années 1920,[8] le problème de la civilisation et de la religion des Daces (les habitants de l'actuelle Roumanie avant la conquête romaine) arrive à temps pour rafraîchir l'imaginaire nationaliste roumain avec un thème nébuleux destiné à faire carrière notamment à l'époque du national-communisme de Nicolae Ceausescu.

---

tant, était déjà connu en Europe et encore plus aux Etats-Unis. Voir Ioana Vlasiu, «L'expérience roumaine», in *La vie des formes. Henri Focillon et les arts* (Gand, Snoeck éditions, 2004), p. 232.

[5] F. Ţurcanu, *Mircea Eliade*, p. 72f. et p. 76.

[6] *Călăuza studentului. Vademecum academicum 1928–1929* [Guide de l'étudiant. Vademecum academicum 1928–1929] (Bucarest, Editura Cartea Românescă, 1928), p. 97–99.

[7] Le fondateur de l'archéologie scientifique en Roumanie, Vasile Pârvan, avait publié en 1911 un ouvrage pionnier intitulé *Contribuţi epigrafice la istoria creştinismului daco-român* [Contributions épigraphiques à l'histoire du christianisme daco-romain].

[8] Qui se trouvent à la base de l'*opus magnum* de Vasile Pârvan, *Getica. O protoistorie a Daciei* [Getica. Une protohistoire de la Dacie] (Cultura Naţionala, Bucarest, 1926).

Pourtant, un des stimulants intellectuels les plus importants du jeune Eliade est venu, de son propre aveu, du sein de l'université sous la forme du cours de philosophie de la religion inauguré en 1924 par le maître de conférences Nae Ionescu dans le cadre de la Faculté de lettres et de philosophie. A cette époque, remarquait Eliade à propos de l'enseignement de Nae Ionescu,

> parler de christianisme et de philosophie chrétienne à l'université était (...) une véritable révolution. Parler de 'rédemption', de 'sainteté', d''orthodoxie', d''hérésie' dans des cours de métaphysique et de logique était une déviation par rapport à une tradition bien établie d'idéalisme et de positivisme.[9]

Véritable réhabilitation intellectuelle du vécu religieux «dans une faculté de philosophie (...) attachée au néo-kantisme officialisé et même au néopositivisme du 'Cercle de Vienne'» comme le dit l'un de ses étudiants,[10] les cours de Nae Ionescu s'opposaient à la fois à l'enseignement traditionnel de la philosophie dans l'université et à la suffisance où campait depuis le 19ᵉ siècle l'enseignement théologique. Ceci ne manquera pas de lui attirer des adversités durables, d'abord au sein de l'Eglise orthodoxe dont il dénonce dès le milieu des années 1920 non seulement les compromis avec l'esprit moderne et avec l'Etat, mais aussi l'indigence intellectuelle. Il croît même que «la véritable doctrine, vivante et actuelle (de l'orthodoxie) naîtra par les efforts de croyants laïques» et non pas dans les rangs des hommes d'Eglise.[11]

Même si, aux yeux de ses admirateurs inconditionnels, Nae Ionescu semblait issu d'une atmosphère intellectuelle européenne où, écrit Eliade, se croisaient « la vogue du néo-thomisme, les débuts de la théologie dialectique, la popularité croissante de Martin Buber, la découverte de Kierkegaard»,[12] sa position officielle dans l'université restera toujours marginale. Il avait acquis au début de sa carrière universitaire le sentiment aigu de sa singularité intellectuelle et se pensait lui-même comme un démolisseur: «Le système n'est pas bon et je suis décidé à

---

[9] Mircea Eliade, «Si un cuvânt al editorului» [Un mot de l'éditeur], in Nae Ionescu, *Roza vânturilor*, [La rose des vents] (Bucarest, Cultura Naționala, 1937), p. 439.

[10] Mihai șora cité in Gabriel Stănescu, *Nae Ionescu în conştiinţa contemporanilor săi* [Nae Ionescu dans la conscience de ses contemporains] (Bucarest, Criterion Publishing, 1998), p. 370.

[11] Nae Ionescu, «Duminica» [Le Dimanche], *Cuvântul* [La Parole], 13 décembre 1926.

[12] M. Eliade, «Profesorul Nae Ionescu. 30 de ani de la moarte» [Le professeur Nae Ionescu. 30 ans depuis sa mort], *Prodromos* 10 (1970).

le changer», écrit-il fin 1925 à son maître et protecteur, le philosophe
Constantin Rădulescu-Motru, au sujet de la sélection des enseignants
dans le département de philosophie.[13] En réalité, Nae Ionescu n'arrivera
pas à «changer le système». «Figure non universitaire par excellence»,[14]
comme le décrit Cioran qui fut lui aussi son élève, partagé entre l'enseignement et le journalisme politique, Ionescu n'accédera jamais au poste
de professeur dans l'université et finira par heurter Rădulescu-Motru
lui-même. Dès le milieu des années 1926 ce dernier – chef de fil des
philosophes roumains et ancien étudiant de Wilhelm Wundt – commence à prendre ses distances par rapport au regain d'intérêt pour le
christianisme qu'affichait une partie du monde intellectuel roumain
et qu'illustrait à sa manière son ancien élève Nae Ionescu.[15] Il finira
par reprocher précisément à Nae Ionescu son parti pris orthodoxe et
«mystique» au sein de l'université, qu'il qualifiera publiquement comme
«une pure farce engendrée par la névrose d'après-guerre».[16]

Dans les années 1929–1931 Rădulescu-Motru avait montré, d'autre
part, un certain intérêt pour les études de philosophie indienne et de
philologie sanscrite que son ancien étudiant Mircea Eliade était en train
d'entreprendre à Calcutta. Surendranath Dasgupta, le maître indien
d'Eliade et professeur à Calcutta avait plaidé auprès de Motru pour la
création en Roumanie d'une chaire de philosophie indienne que son
élève roumain aurait pu occuper dès son retour d'Inde.[17] En 1930 et
1931, Eliade publie par ailleurs trois articles d'indianisme dans la *Revista
de filosofie* patronnée par Rădulescu-Motru tandis que celui-ci caresse à
cette même époque l'idée de placer le jeune indianiste à la tête d'une
chaire de philologie sanscrite ou d'histoire des religions spécialement
créée pour lui à l'université de Bucarest.[18] La rupture entre Motru et
Nae Ionescu n'est pas étrangère à ce projet : «Nous avons grand besoin
d'une chaire et pas seulement d'un cours d'histoire des religions, car

---

[13] Lettre de Nae Ionescu à Constantin Rădulescu-Motru publiée par Marin Diaconu
in *Viaţa Românească* [La Vie Roumaine] 3–4 (1994), p. 78.

[14] Gabriel Liiceanu, *Itinéraires d'une vie: E.M. Cioran* (Paris, Michalon, 1995), p. 102.

[15] Constanin Rădulescu-Motru, «Sufletul mistic» [L'âme mystique], *Gândirea* [La
Pensée] 4/5, 1926.

[16] «O scrisoare a d-lui profesor C. Rădulescu-Motru» [Une lettre de M. le professeur
C. Rădulescu-Motru], *Dreptatea* [La Justice], 20 décembre 1930.

[17] Lettre de S. Dasgupta à Rădulescu-Motru publiée dans *Steaua* [L'Etoile], novem-
bre-décembre 1990.

[18] M. Eliade, *Europa, Asia, America. Corespondenţă*, tome I (Bucarest, Humanitas, 1999),
p. 300, p. 307 et p. 310 ; lettre de Rădulescu-Motru à Mircea Eliade, datée du 21
janvier 1931, *România Literară* [La Roumanie littéraire], 5–11 mai 1999.

chez nous ces choses sont étudiées plutôt *terre à terre* à la manière ortho-
doxiste», écrivait Rădulescu-Motru à Eliade en janvier 1931 dans le
sillage d'une récente polémique avec Nae Ionescu en faisant allusion
à l'enseignement discutable de ce dernier.

L'idée de fonder une chaire d'histoire des religions n'aura cependant
pas de suite. Le fait qu'Eliade retourne d'Inde à Bucarest fin 1931 sans
avoir en poche le titre de docteur de l'Université de Calcutta n'était
pas le seul obstacle à une idée née chez Rădulescu-Motru de sa riva-
lité intellectuelle et personnelle avec Nae Ionescu. A cette époque la
légitimité de l'histoire des religions tout comme celle de la philosophie
indienne ou de la philologie sanscrite ne pouvait être forte à l'intérieur
de l'Université de Bucarest. Aucune de ces disciplines «exotiques»
n'était soutenue ni par une tradition intellectuelle, ni par une idéologie
de l'identité nationale, ni par une vision instrumentale liée à la formation des élites nécessaires au jeune Etat national roumain. Même au
sujet de la philosophie indienne qui avait connu son heure de gloire
dans l'Allemagne de ses études de jeunesse, Rădulescu-Motru avouait
à Eliade en septembre 1929 : « J'ai essayé de lire quelques traductions
d'après les philosophes indiens, mais jamais je n'ai acquis de connais-
sances profitables ».[19]

Tout ceci va influer durablement sur la position d'Eliade dans le
champ intellectuel roumain le long des années 1930, au-delà de ses
succès en tant qu'écrivain ou d'un commencement de reconnaissance
internationale après la publication de son *Yoga* en 1936. Eliade va finalement pénétrer, à l'automne 1933, dans l'université, mais par la petite
porte, en tant que suppléant de Nae Ionescu qui lui verse une partie de
son propre salaire. Il s'agit d'une position précaire et semi-officielle qui
risque facilement d'être mise en cause comme cela se passera d'ailleurs
à deux reprises – à l'automne 1934 et en juin 1937.[20] Le nom d'Eliade
ne figure d'ailleurs pas dans l'annuaire de l'université pour les années
1933–1938 – ce qui trahit l'ambiguïté de sa position et de son enseignement. Néanmoins, c'est de cette position fragile que Mircea Eliade
va introduire l'histoire des religions dans l'Université de Bucarest : « Je
voulais encourager l'étude scientifique de l'histoire des religions en
Roumanie. Dans les milieux académiques, cette discipline n'y existait

---

[19] Lettre de C. Rădulescu-Motru à M. Eliade, datée du 24 septembre 1929, publiée
dans *Romănia Literară*, 5–11 mai 1999.
[20] Mircea Handoca, *Viaţa lui Mircea Eliade* [La vie de Mircea Eliade] (Cluj, Editura
Dacia, 2000), p. 71.

pas encore d'une façon autonome».[21] Ce n'est que grâce à l'appui de
Nae Ionescu qu'Eliade s'engage dans cette voie: «Il m'a cédé le cours
d'histoire de la métaphysique et un séminaire d'histoire de la logique,
en m'invitant à faire précéder l'histoire de la métaphysique par un
cours d'histoire des religions» se souvient-il dans ses entretiens avec
Claude-Henri Rocquet.[22] A l'indianiste roumain Arion Roşu il écrit
dans une lettre de décembre 1966: «Autour de 1934–1935, lorsque
j'étais déjà le suppléant de Nae Ionescu à la chaire de métaphysique
(...) j'enseignais plutôt l'histoire des religions».[23] Il s'agissait, en fait,
d'une véritable substitution d'une matière par une autre. En poussant
son ancien étudiant à inaugurer le premier enseignement d'histoire
des religions dans l'Université de Bucarest, Nae Ionescu l'engageait à
pratiquer la même forme d'innovation potentiellement subversive du
point de vue intellectuel qu'il avait lui-même appliqué en inaugurant
son cours de philosophie de la religion une décennie plus tôt.

Son premier cours qui débute en novembre 1933 concerne «Le
problème du mal et de la rédemption dans la philosophie indienne» et
sera suivi, dans les années 1934–1938 par d'autres cours sur «Le salut
dans les religions orientales», «Le symbolisme religieux» et «L'histoire
du bouddhisme».[24] La matière du cours consacré au «Symbolisme»
se retrouvera dans les «Notes sur le symbolisme aquatique» publiées
en 1939 dans le deuxième numéro de la revue *Zalmoxis*,[25] et c'est
toujours à partir d'exposés, tenus devant les étudiants pendant l'hiver
1936–1937 qu'Eliade rédigera au printemps 1943 les *Commentaires sur
la légende du Maître Manole*.[26] On peut donc dire que ces cours d'histoire
des religions qui s'étendent sur un peu plus de quatre ans ont servi en
partie de laboratoire où Eliade a donné une première forme à certaines
de ses études futures.

On a remarqué les rapports étroits qui liaient Mircea Eliade à Nae
Ionescu ainsi que leurs effets aussi bien intellectuels que politiques
sur l'itinéraire du jeune historien des religions. Eliade «se comportait

---

[21] M. Eliade, *L'Epreuve du labyrinthe. Entretiens avec Claude-Henri Rocquet* (Paris, Belfond,
1978), p. 91.
[22] Ibid., p. 90.
[23] Voire la lettre de Mircea Eliade à Arion Roşu in Eliade, *Europa, Asia, America.
Corespondenţă*, tome III (Bucarest, Humanitas, 2004), p. 103.
[24] M. Handoca, éd., *Mircea Eliade. Biobibliografie*, tome I (Bucarest, Editura Jurnalul
Literar, 1997), p. 16–18.
[25] Handoca, *Viaţa lui Mircea Eliade*, p. 73.
[26] Ţurcanu, *Mircea Eliade*, p. 329.

sans arrêt en disciple», se souvient Cioran.[27] La permission que Nae Ionescu lui avait donné de substituer l'histoire des religions à l'histoire de la métaphysique ne pouvait que renforcer sa dépendance personnelle à l'égard de son ancien professeur. En fait, dans le cas du couple Nae Ionescu-Mircea Eliade il s'agit de l'alliance de deux personnages notoirement marginaux au sein de l'université. Leur grande popularité parmi les étudiants est celle dont jouissent les intellectuels subversifs et non pas celles que l'on témoigne aux autorités établies. Nae Ionescu jouissait de ce genre de popularité depuis une décennie. Mais, de même que sa philosophie des religions n'avait jamais acquis une pleine reconnaissance dans l'université, l'histoire des religions, représentée par Mircea Eliade, entrera et demeurera dans cette même l'université sous le signe du provisorat et du déficit de légitimité institutionnelle. Dans la même lettre adressée à Arion Roşu, Eliade évoquait une tentative qu'il avait entreprise en 1934 ou 1935 pour faire accepter par la Faculté de Lettres un cours de sanskrit doublé par un enseignement de l'histoire des religions dont il aurait été lui-même le titulaire.[28] A cette occasion, sa proposition avait été abruptement rejetée par un de ses anciens professeurs, Petre P. Negulescu au nom d'autres priorités intellectuelles qu'il n'avait même pas daigné spécifier.[29]

Eliade lui-même reconnaîtra deux décennies plus tard, en France, que, dans son pays d'origine, il avait été valorisé en tant qu'écrivain plutôt que comme savant ce qui, même en comptant avec son puissant narcissisme littéraire, a été une source de frustrations permanente. Ses succès en tant qu'indianiste et historien des religions – la publication par les Fondations Royales de son premier ouvrage sur le yoga en 1936 et la sortie de la revue *Zalmoxis* – ne doivent rien à l'université mais sont dus plutôt à ses relations personnelles et familiales qui s'avèrent parfois elles aussi chancelantes. On peut même se demander quelle aurait été la carrière roumaine d'Eliade s'il n'avait pas épousé début 1934, une femme dont l'oncle maternel était le bibliothécaire du roi de Roumanie Carol II. C'est précisément à ce personnage, le général Condeescu ainsi qu'à un autre proche du roi, Alexandru Rosetti, éditeur et philologue, que Mircea Eliade doit la publication en France de son *Yoga* de 1936.[30]

---

[27] Liiceanu, *Itinéraires d'une vie*, p. 102.
[28] Eliade, *Europa, Asia, America*, tome III, p. 103.
[29] Ibid., p. 103.
[30] M. Eliade, *Les promesses de l'équinoxe* (Paris, Gallimard, 1980), p. 417.

D'autre part, quoique cet ouvrage qui inaugurait chez l'éditeur parisien Paul Geuthner une collection intitulée «bibliothèque de philosophie roumaine» n'avait pas de précédent dans l'histoire intellectuelle de la Roumanie, le silence gardé à son sujet par les principales personnalités culturelles roumaines suggère bien l'isolement du savant Eliade dans son pays. Lorsque, par contre, un an plus tard, Eliade est accusé publiquement par le plus important des historiens roumains, Nicolae Iorga, de pornographie littéraire, son expulsion, même temporaire, de l'université, souligne la précarité de sa position.

Le problème qu'affronte Eliade en tant qu'historien des religions dans la Roumanie des années 1930 peut donc se résumer ainsi : ses préoccupations sont trop éloignées par rapport aux repères consacrés de l'université et de la culture nationale, ce qui empiète sur leur reconnaissance intellectuelle et empêche en fin de compte leur institutionnalisation. Ceci explique l'admiration doublée de frustration, qu'Eliade manifeste dans plusieurs articles, pour la reconnaissance dont jouit en Italie fasciste le spécialiste du Tibet Giuseppe Tucci, nommé directeur de l'IsMEO (l'Istituto Italiano per il Medio ed Estremo Oriente) par le régime de Mussolini.[31] Ceci explique aussi les espoirs, vite déçus, qu'il attache à l'éventuelle création, à Bucarest, d'un Institut Oriental. En août 1934 il écourte son premier séjour dans les bibliothèques de Berlin à cause d'une fausse bonne nouvelle : «Il semble que d'ici dix à quinze jours un Institut d'études orientales sera créé sous le patronage des Fondations Royales, avec un budget très limité pour commencer, mais dont les perspectives s'annoncent vastes», écrit Eliade dans une lettre du 5 septembre 1934. «Je serais le secrétaire de cet Institut», précise-t-il, car «il semble que personne n'est disposé à assumer cette tâche. De surcroît, le roi lui-même désire une direction qui soit 'jeune'».[32] Et il prend le soin d'ajouter : «Je rêvais depuis longtemps de quitter l'université où seule une révolution pourrait changer quelque chose, afin de travailler dans mon domaine – l'histoire des religions, l'orientalisme».[33] Le projet d'un Institut Oriental à Bucarest n'allait pas se concrétiser ni cette fois, ni en 1937 lorsque Alexandru Rosetti annonçait Eliade qu'il avait initié

---

[31] M. Eliade, «Tucci», *Vremea* [Le Temps] du 21 janvier 1934 ; «'Dictatura' şi 'personalitatea'» ['Dictature' et 'personnalité'], *Vremea* du 28 mars 1937 ; «Un institut oriental», *Cuvântul* du 14 février 1938.

[32] Eliade, *Europa, Asia, America*, tome I, p. 24.

[33] Ibid.

de nouvelles démarches pour la fondation d'un tel établissement sous le patronage du roi.[34]

Néanmoins, la réaction d'Eliade contre la marginalité à laquelle l'université condamnait ses études ne s'est cristallisée que progressivement après son retour de l'Inde. Elle consiste, d'une part, dans la recherche de l'indispensable reconnaissance intellectuelle à l'étranger non pas seulement par la publication de son premier *Yoga* en 1936 mais aussi par celle de la «revue des études religieuses» *Zalmoxis* dont le premier numéro, prêt dès 1938, sort en avril 1939 avec la collaboration de plusieurs orientalistes et historiens des religions tel Jean Przyluski, Carl Hentze, Ananda K. Coomaraswamy et Raffaele Pettazzoni.[35]

En parallèle, Eliade entreprend, à la même époque, une tentative de «nationaliser» ses préoccupations d'indianiste et d'historien des religions afin de les justifier aux yeux du public intellectuel de son pays en leur donnant une légitimité propre et originale, adaptée aux critères d'évaluation de l'œuvre dans l'environnement roumain. Dans deux préfaces[36] Eliade va même jusqu'à suggérer que son œuvre savante, notamment son étude sur le yoga, a aussi une signification politique liée à l'ascension de la Garde de Fer, mouvement nationaliste et antisémite roumain qu'il ne mentionne pas dans ces textes mais auquel il adhère début 1937. Dans cette entreprise de «nationalisation» de ses préoccupations l'évolution même de sa sensibilité intellectuelle dans la seconde moitié des années 1930 compte beaucoup. Pendant la période qui va de la publication de son premier *Yoga* jusqu'à la sortie, en 1943, des *Commentaires à la légende du Maître Manole*, la pensée d'Eliade se meut sur trois axes majeurs qui se recoupent : 1) une équivalence abrupte entre pensée religieuse d'une part, pensée symbolique et mythique de l'autre, qui favorise la valorisation de la pré- et de la protohistoire comme âge matriciel des représentations mythiques et symboliques; 2) une préoccupation intense pour faire du folklore roumain, et plus généralement balkanique, une voie d'accès nouvelle vers l'histoire des religions en

---

[34] Lettre d'Alexandru Rosetti à Mircea Eliade datée du 27 août 1937, publiée dans *România Literară* du 8–14 septembre 1999.

[35] *Zalmoxis. Revue des études religieuses* I (1938).

[36] M. Eliade (dir.), «Introduction» au recueil de textes de Bogdan Petriceicu Haşdeu, *Scrieri literare, morale şi politice* [Ecrits littéraires, moraux et politiques] (Bucarest, Fundaţia pentru literatură si artă 'Regele Carol II' [Fondation pour la littérature et l'art 'Roi Carol II'], 1937) ; «Préface» à *Cosmologie şi alchimie babiloniană* [Cosmologie et alchimie babylonienne] (Bucarest, Editura Vremea, 1937, traduction française Gallimard, Paris, 1991).

général; 3) une tentative de concevoir l'espace roumain et balkanique comme intégré dans l'espace et l'héritage spirituel oriental considéré à son tour comme opposé à la tradition culturelle occidentale.

La cristallisation de ces trois coordonnés de la réflexion éliadienne ne se produit pas simultanément. Son intérêt affiché pour le folklore roumain, son idée d'un mythe folklorique central de la culture roumaine remonte aux années 1932–1933, cinq à six ans avant sa vision d'un grand espace spirituel oriental qui s'étendrait de l'Indonésie au cœur des Balkans, et de la Chine aux contreforts des Carpates.[37] La valorisation la plus explicite de la préhistoire comme horizon ultime à la fois de la créativité mythique et symbolique des communautés humaines et des recherches de l'orientaliste et de l'historien des religions date des années 1936–1937.[38] Elle procède d'une réinterprétation dans le contexte culturel et politique roumain de l'intérêt déjà ancien d'Eliade pour la préhistoire et la protohistoire de l'Inde.[39] La convergence de ces trois coordonnées apparaît dans les écrits d'Eliade dans les années 1937–1939 et elle exprime clairement une tentative de redéfinir les bases de l'identité nationale roumaine par le biais de nouvelles disciplines intellectuelles.

De par sa formation même Eliade associe encore étroitement à cette époque orientalisme et histoire des religions. Cette association se retrouve en filigrane le long de plusieurs articles qu'il publie dans des hebdomadaires ou des revues culturelles en langue roumaine pendant les années 1938 et 1939.[40] Eliade reprend ici en des termes renouvelés un débat qui avait fait rage dans le monde intellectuel roumain au milieu des années 1920: la culture roumaine moderne doit-elle

---

[37] F. Ţurcanu, «De l'histoire au mythe. La formation de l'image du Sud-Est européen dans l'œuvre de Mircea Eliade», *Studia Politica. Romanian Political Science Review* I–1 (2001), p. 185–194; «Occident, Orient şi fascinaţia originilor la Vasile Pârvan şi Mircea Eliade» [Occident, Orient et la fascination des origines chez Vasile Pârvan et Mircea Eliade], *Studia Politica. Romanian Political Science Review* II–3 (2002), p. 761–770.

[38] Voir en ce sens M. Eliade, «Protohistoire ou Moyen Age», in idem, *Fragmentarium* (Paris, L'Herne, 1989), p. 46–53 ainsi que l'«Introduction» (en roumain) de Mircea Eliade (dir.) au recueil de textes de Bogdan Petriceicu Haşdeu. *Scrieri literare, morale şi politice* [Ecrits littéraire, moraux et politiques], 2 tomes (Bucarest, Editura Fundaţiei Regale pentru Arta şi Literatură, 1937).

[39] Ţurcanu, *Mircea Eliade*, p. 273.

[40] M. Eliade, «Un institut oriental», *Cuvântul* du 14 février 1938; «Când Asia devine asiatica» [Quand l'Asie devient asiatique], *Vremea* du 27 mars 1938; «Orientul viu» [L'Orient vivant], *Cuvântul* du 14 avril 1938; «Echos d'Orient», *Cuvântul* du 16 avril 1938; «Mediterana şi Oceanul Indian» [La Méditerranée et l'Océan Indien], *Revista Fundaţiilor Regale* [Revue des Fondations Royales] 10 (1939), p. 203–208.

se tourner résolument vers l'Occident ou, au contraire, se ressourcer dans la matrice culturelle de l'Orient ? Si pour les tenants du débat des années 1920 l'Orient n'était rien d'autre que Byzance et l'orthodoxie, pour Eliade ce qu'il appelle lui-même «l'Orient vivant» recouvre un espace géographique et culturel à la fois beaucoup plus vaste et plus ancien qui n'avait jamais été pris en compte par les réflexions précédentes sur les sources de l'identité roumaine. Dans ces articles Eliade défend le repositionnement de cette identité sur des bases nouvelles qui renvoient à la fois à une temporalité, à une mémoire et à une géographie alternatives : à la place du Moyen Age cher à l'historiographie nationale romantique et positiviste, la préhistoire et la protohistoire qui relient l'espace balkanique au Levant, à l'Iran, à l'Inde et à la Chine ; à la place de l'Occident avec sa mémoire historique, l'Orient avec sa mémoire mythique et sa préférence pour le langage symbolique.

«On sait que la culture européenne moderne est la création presque exclusive des nations qui ont eu un Moyen Age glorieux», remarque Eliade dans un article d'octobre 1937 intitulé «Protohistoire ou Moyen Age».[41] Il n'est donc pas étonnant que la conscience historique de l'homme moderne et l'historicisme du 19e siècle soient les créations de ces mêmes nations. En choisissant de se doter elles aussi au 19e siècle d'une mémoire historique, les sociétés balkaniques ont dû constater qu'elles avaient vécu, dès le Moyen Age, sur le palier d'une histoire mineure.

> L'individualisme, le positivisme, l'asymbolisme qui découlaient naturellement du siècle de l'historicisme n'avaient pas grand-chose à trouver dans le passé des nations sans Moyen Age glorieux, c'est-à-dire sans grandes personnalités, sans assez de documents écrits, sans transformations sociales et économiques assez importantes pour offrir des fondements brillants à une théorie.[42]

Le phénomène proprement moderne du développement des historiographies nationales balkaniques n'a pas amélioré la place que ces nations occupent dans la conscience historique européenne, remarque Eliade. Autour de 1900, précise-t-il sans ironie aucune, on a montré «une curiosité plus soutenue et plus sincère à l'égard de n'importe quelle tribu africaine et australienne (évidemment pour leur valeur

---

[41] Article repris en traduction française dans Eliade, *Fragmentarium*, p. 46–53.
[42] Ibid.

ethnographique et sociologique) qu'envers l'histoire de la Roumanie, de la Bulgarie ou de la Serbie».[43]

Pourtant, si «la Roumanie n'a pas eu un Moyen Age glorieux (...) elle a eu une préhistoire égale si ce n'est supérieure à celle des grandes nations d'Europe».[44] L'alternative serait de faire valoir en Roumanie et dans tout le Sud-Est européen l'héritage culturel préhistorique et protohistorique conservé dans cette région comme nulle part ailleurs en Europe. Dans une telle perspective le rôle joué par les historiographies nationales devrait revenir dorénavant à d'autres disciplines:

> Notre intérêt inquiétant pour 'l'histoire' doit être corrigé par un déve-loppement urgent des études d'anthropo-géographie, de préhistoire, de protohistoire et de folklore. Les études de balkanologie doivent être portées jusqu'à leur extrême limite – la préhistoire de la péninsule.[45]

On rencontre dans ce texte deux des trois termes-clé à travers lesquels Eliade entend redéfinir à cette époque l'identité roumaine et plus généralement balkanique: «préhistoire» et «folklore» qui à leur tour renvoient au troisième: «Orient». D'ailleurs, à cette même époque, les «Balkans» de l'âge préhistorique ne représentent pour lui que l'extrémité occidentale d'une vaste aire géographique et culturelle orientale organisée selon deux axes. Un d'entre eux reliait l'ancienne Dacie à l'Asie Centrale, voire à la Chine,[46] l'autre, plus important, liait «le Pacifique à la Méditerranée» à travers l'Inde et le Proche Orient.[47] Ce deuxième axe, celui de la néolithisation, a rapproché autrefois les communautés humaines du sud de l'Asie et de l'Europe méridionale. L'histoire a ultérieurement brisé cette unité préhistorique mais, souligne Eliade en octobre 1939, «un nombre considérable de faits ne peut être expliqué de manière satisfaisante si l'on ne prend pas en compte une longue et fertile préhistoire indo-méditerranéenne».[48]

Retrouver l'importance réelle et les racines identitaires de l'espace balkanique suppose la redécouverte du rôle matriciel de la préhistoire pour cette région, la reconnaissance de son caractère essentiellement «oriental» et la prise en compte de son folklore comme voie d'accès aux mythes et aux symboles préchrétiens. Les *Commentaires à la légende*

---

[43] Ibid.
[44] Ibid.
[45] Ibid.
[46] M. Eliade, «Orientul viu» [L'Orient vivant], *Cuvântul* du 14 avril 1938.
[47] Eliade, «Mediterana şi Oceanul Indian», p. 205.
[48] Ibid.

du Maître Manole publiées en 1943 seront, en partie au moins, l'accomplissement de ce projet.

Sur le plan épistémologique le résultat d'une telle redécouverte serait ni plus ni moins qu'un renversement des critères de l'histoire universelle. « Qu'elle est fausse notre vision d'une histoire validée exclusivement par les documents ! » s'exclame Eliade dans son journal en 1942. Pourtant «l'histoire universelle ne peut être rédigée sur la base de documents écrits – mais uniquement sur la base de documents spirituels, c'est-à-dire sur la base de mythes et de croyances. L'Europe, mais spécialement l'Occident, doit être comparée à l'Orient et aux steppes des nomades non pas à travers ses documents écrits mais à travers ses mythes». Et il ajoute : «L'histoire roumaine, par exemple, devrait être comparée à l'histoire occidentale à travers ses mythes : la (ballade) *Miorița* («L'Agnelle voyante»), (la légende du) *Maître Manole*, les ballades héroïques (…)».[49] Même si Eliade ne le dit pas explicitement ce renversement des critères historiographique évacue l'historien, figure intellectuelle dépassée attachée à l'étude du Moyen Age, au profit de l'historien des religions tourné vers la préhistoire et l'Orient.

L'Orient est donc le véritable espace de l'historien des religions, tandis que l'Occident des cités médiévales qui «participent à l'histoire uniquement parce qu'elles avaient une douzaine d'hommes qui sachant écrire ont laissé quelques centaines de documents» tombe dans le lot des historiens tout court.[50] L'espace balkanique, pauvre en documents historiques, mais riche en mythes et symboles préhistoriques, doit se tourner vers l'historien des religions pour retrouver une identité non seulement véritable mais aussi prestigieuse et qui n'aurait rien à envier à l'Europe occidentale.

On comprend ainsi mieux les plaidoyers répétés de Mircea Eliade en 1938 pour la création d'un Institut Oriental ou d'une chaire d'études orientales à Bucarest ainsi que sa critique de l'ignorance autochtone à l'égard des cultures de l'Asie qu'il assimile à une forme condamnable de cécité intellectuelle.

> Quoique nous soyons aux portes de l'Orient et l'ensemble de l'Orient devrait nous intéresser à cause de nos rapports historiques avec sa culture (…) la Roumanie est un des quelques pays européens, peu nombreux, qui

---

[49] Eliade, *Jurnal*, tome I (Bucarest, Humanitas, 1993), p. 19.
[50] Ibid.

ne disposent pas de chaires universitaires d'études orientales, ni même
d'un Institut d'études et de renseignement sur les affaires orientales,

se plaint Eliade en mars 1938.[51]

> Nous oublions que les influences orientales sont encore vivantes dans
> la langue et le folklore roumain. Nous oublions que pour comprendre
> l'authentique existence roumaine il nous est plus utile de connaître
> comment s'habille et construit sa maison un paysan indien plutôt que
> les arcanes de la philosophie kantienne

écrit-il ailleurs à la même époque.[52] Cet «oubli de l'Orient» date en
Roumanie du milieu du 19e siècle car, depuis la révolution de 1848,
«nous sommes aveuglés par tout ce qui nous vient de l'Occident»[53]
et les Roumains sont plutôt «complexés» par l'idée qu'ils pourraient
tout de même appartenir à une aire culturelle orientale.[54] Néanmoins,
souligne Eliade, si ce n'est pas à cause d'une conscience retrouvée de
leurs racines orientales, ce serait à cause du réveil national et de la fin
du colonialisme occidental en Asie que les Roumains devraient se doter
de structures d'enseignement et de recherche consacrées à l'Orient.
Dans une «Asie redevenue asiatique» qui sait quelle pourrait être les
opportunités économiques et politiques d'une Roumanie désireuses elle-
même de s'éloigner du modèle culturel et politique occidentale qu'elle
a adoptée depuis un siècle?[55]

Un Institut Oriental roumain était-il aux yeux d'Eliade une forme
d'institutionnalisation «camouflée» de l'histoire des religions en Roumanie? C'est ce qui nous fait croire sa manière de valoriser simultanément
les études de la préhistoire, du folklore balkanique et de l'Orient comme
autant de voies d'accès à la pensée mythique et aux représentations
symboliques opposées à l'interprétation discursive du monde et la préé-
minence du document écrit chères à l'Europe occidentale.

Quel est le rapport entre, d'une part, cette préférence pour l'Orient
en tant que domaine à la fois de l'histoire des religions et d'une nouvelle
identité culturelle roumaine et, d'autre part, l'engagement politique
fasciste d'Eliade dans les années 1937–1938? Derrière le renouveau

---

[51] Eliade, «Când Asia devine asiatică », *Vremea* du 27 mars 1938.
[52] Eliade, «Un institut oriental», *Cuvântul* du 14 février 1938.
[53] Ibid.
[54] Eliade, *Cuvântul* du 14 avril 1938.
[55] «Orientul viu» et «Când Asia devine asiatica», *Cuvântul* du 14 avril 1938 et
Vremea du 27 mars 1938.

intellectuel qu'appelle la revalorisation de la préhistoire, de la pensée mythique et symbolique, Eliade place, en toile de fond, une dynamique qu'il salue et qui est celle des messianismes politiques modernes.[56] Lorsqu'il remarque au sujet de l'absence d'intérêt des intellectuels et des hommes politiques roumains pour l'Orient que «l'on pourrait dire sans exagération que la culture roumaine est encore dominée par l'esprit de la révolution de 1848»[57] on voit bien à quel point l'option d'Eliade en faveur d'une identité roumaine «orientalisée» est synonyme d'antilibéralisme. Une renaissance culturelle roumaine sous le signe de l'Orient et d'une nouvelle valeur accordée au folklore, au mythe et à la pensée symbolique va de paire avec le rejet des effets culturels et politiques de l'occidentalisation de la société roumaine. On peut donc penser qu'il y avait aux yeux d'Eliade un rapport d'homologie entre la position marginale de sa discipline – l'histoire des religions – et celle du mouvement subversif radical représenté par la Garde de fer roumaine des années 1930. L'ascension de la Garde de fer a pu lui apparaître comme l'occasion unique pour résoudre, dans le contexte d'un bouleversement identitaire général, le problème de la marginalité de l'histoire des religions dans le paysage culturel roumain. Celle-ci aurait pu migrer ainsi vers le centre d'une culture nationale refondée qui se serait débarrassée des «illusions» et des frustrations identitaires issues de l'occidentalisation de la Roumanie. On tient ici à mon avis l'un des ressorts les plus plausibles de son engagement politique.[58]

---

[56] Eliade, «Protohistoire ou Moyen Age», in idem, *Fragmentarium*, p. 49; «Folclor și creație cultă» [Folklore et haute culture], *Sânzana* [nom intraduisible d'une fée du folklore roumain] du 19 décembre 1937.

[57] Eliade, «Un institut oriental».

[58] Pour les rapports entre la quête intellectuelle d'Eliade et son engagement politique voir aussi Țurcanu, *Mircea Eliade*, p. 273–277 et p. 328–333.

Bibliographie

Călăuza studentului. Vademecum academicum 1928–1929 [Guide de l'étudiant. Vademecum academicum 1928–1929]. Bucarest, Editura Cartea Românescă, 1928.

Ciurtin, Eugen «Imaginea şi memoria Asiei în cultura română 1675–1928». *Archaeus* II–2 (1998), p. 213–449.

Diaconu, Marin, «Chipul epistolar al lui Nae Ionescu» [Nae Ionescu à travers ses épîtres]. *Viaţa Românească* [La Vie Roumaine] 3–4, 1994.

Eliade, Mircea. «Tucci». *Vremea* [Le Temps], 21 janvier 1934.

——. «Introducere». In Bogdan Petriceicu Haşdeu, *Scrieri literare, morale şi politice* [Ecrits littéraires, moraux et politiques], 2 vol. Bucarest, Fundaţia pentru literatură si artă 'Regele Carol II', 1937.

——. «şi un cuvânt al editorului» [Un mot de l'éditeur]. In Nae Ionescu, *Roza vânturilor* [La rose des vents]. Bucarest, Cultura Naţionala, 1937.

——. «Folclor şi creaţie cultă» [Folklore et haute culture]. *Sânzana* [nom d'une fée du folklore roumain], 19 décembre 1937.

——. «Un institut oriental». *Cuvântul* [La Parole], 14 février 1938.

——. «Când Asia devine asiatica» [Quand l'Asie devient asiatique]. *Vremea*, 27 mars 1938.

——. «Orientul viu» [L'Orient vivant]. *Cuvântul*, 14 avril 1938.

——. «Echos d'Orient». *Cuvântul*, 16 avril 1938.

——. «Mediterana şi Oceanul Indian» [La Méditerranée et l'Océan Indien]. *Revista Fundaţiilor Regale* [Revue des Fondations Royales] 10 (1939), p. 203–208.

——. «Profesorul Nae Ionescu. 30 de ani de la moarte» [Le professeur Nae Ionescu. 30 ans depuis sa mort]. *Prodromos* 10, 1970.

——. *Fragments d'un journal*, tome I. Paris, Gallimard, 1973.

——. «*L'Epreuve du labyrinthe. Entretiens avec Claude-Henri Rocquet*. Paris, Belfond, 1978.

——. «*Les promesses de l'équinoxe*. Paris, Gallimard, 1980.

——. «Protohistoire ou Moyen Age». In idem, *Fragmentarium*. Paris, L'Herne, 1989, p. 73–79.

——. «Préface» in *Cosmologie et alchimie babylonienne*. Paris, Gallimard, 1991.

——. *Jurnal*, tome I. Bucarest, Humanitas, 1993.

——. «*Europa, Asia, America. Corespondenţă*, tome I–III. Bucarest, Humanitas, 1999 et 2004.

——. «'Dictatura' şi 'personalitatea'» ['Dictature' et 'personnalité']. *Vremea*, 28 mars 1937.

Handoca, Mircea, *Mircea Eliade. Biobibliografie*, tome I. Bucarest, Editura Jurnalul Literar, 1997.

——. «Corespondenţă Alexandru Rosetti – Mircea Eliade». *România Literară*, 8–14 septembre 1999.

——. «Corespondenţă C. Rădulescu-Motru – Mircea Eliade». *România Literară*, 5–11 mai 1999.

——. *Viaţa lui Mircea Eliade* [La vie de Mircea Eliade] . Cluj, Editura Dacia, 2000.

Ionescu, Nae, «Duminica» [Le Dimanche]. *Cuvântul*, 13 décembre 1926.

Liiceanu, Gabriel, *Itinéraires d'une vie: E.M. Cioran*. Paris, Michalon, 1995.

Pârvan, Vasile, *Contribuţi epigrafice la istoria creştinismului daco-roman* [Contributions épigraphiques à l'histoire du christianisme daco-romain]. Bucarest, Editura Socec, 1911.

——. *Getica. O protoistorie a Daciei* [Getica. Une protohistoire de la Dacie]. Bucarest, Cultura Naţionala, 1926.

Rădulescu-Motru, Constantin, «Sufletul mistic» [L'âme mystique]. *Gândirea* [La Pensée] 4/5, 1926.

——. «O scrisoare a d-lui profesor C. Rădulescu-Motru» [Une lettre de M. le professeur C. Rădulescu-Motru]. *Dreptatea* [La Justice], 20 décembre 1930.

Stănescu, Gabriel, *Nae Ionescu în conştiinţa contemporanilor săi* [Nae Ionescu dans la conscience de ses contemporains]. Bucarest, Criterion Publishing, 1998.

Țurcanu, Florin, «De l'histoire au mythe. La formation de l'image du Sud-Est européen dans l'œuvre de Mircea Eliade». *Studia Politica. Romanian Political Science Review* I–1, 2001, p. 185–192.

——. «Occident, Orient şi fascinaţia originilor la Vasile Pârvan şi Mircea Eliade». *Studia Politica. Romanian Political Science Review* II–3, 2002, p. 761–767.

——. «*Mircea Eliade. Le prisonnier de l'histoire*». Paris, Editions La Découverte, 2003.

Vlasiu, Ioana, «L'expérience roumaine». In *La vie des formes. Henri Focillon et les arts.* Gand, Snoeck éditions, 2004, p. 231–239.

Zalmoxis. Revue des études religieuses, I (1938).

RAFFAELE PETTAZZONI ET MIRCEA ELIADE
HISTORIENS DES RELIGIONS GÉNÉRALISTES DEVANT LES FASCISMES (1933–1945)[1]

Eugen Ciurtin

Biographies croisées

Raffaele Pettazzoni[2] (1883–1959) est né, tout comme Mircea Eliade[3] (1907–1986), dans un pays où la forme académique, universitaire et, au sens large, culturelle proprement dite de l'histoire des religions était à peu près absente. Même ailleurs, d'après Franz Cumont (1868–1947), l'histoire des religions était un «enfant encore débile, qui devait devenir un géant».[4] A un quart de siècle d'intervalle, Raffaele Pettazzoni et Mircea Eliade ont joué un rôle essentiel pour fonder, soutenir, illustrer, renouveler ou défendre (d'après leur vocabulaire même) une nouvelle discipline dont la dimension propre et les objectifs distincts étaient en

---

[1] Je voudrais remercier Mmes Tereza Culianu-Petrescu et Gabriela Cursaru, et MM. Giovanni Casadio, Mario Gandini, Horst Junginger, Andrei Oişteanu et Michael Stausberg de leurs observations, avant, après et pendant les journées de Tübingen.
[2] Sur Pettazzoni, y compris sur l'encrage culturel italien et international de son œuvre, voir surtout les enquêtes visant l'exhaustivité d'un concitadin, disciple et biographe, Mario Gandini. Il a publié notamment dans *Strada Maestra. Quaderni della Biblioteca comunale 'G.C. Croce' di San Giovanni in Persiceto* (Bologna) depuis 1989 des *Materiali per una biografia* qui constituent en fait la meilleure biographie à jamais écrite d'un historien des religions, comptant en 2005, pour 1883–1946, 20 parties et 2525 pages (voir la bibliographie; plus loin *Pettazzoni* suivi de l'année; un index sera indispensable). Voir aussi Mario Gandini, «Il Fondo Pettazzoni della Biblioteca comunale 'G.C. Croce' di San Giovanni in Persiceto (Bologna)», *Archaeus* 7–3/4 (2003), p. 293–298, et la contribution de Michael Stausberg dans ce même volume.
[3] Sur les écrits roumains d'Eliade, y compris sur ses rapports politiques, voir, d'une ample littérature en allemand, anglais, espagnol, français, italien et roumain, surtout I.P. Culianu 1978/2004; M.L. Ricketts 1988 et 2003; B. Rennie 1996 et 2001; L. Arcella, P. Pisi, R. Scagno 1998; R.S. Ellwood 1999; B. Lincoln 1999; S. Wasserstrom 1999; M. Călinescu 2001 et 2002; D. Allen 2002; C. Grottanelli 2002 et 2005; F. Ţurcanu 2003/2005; A. Oişteanu 2004, 2004² et 2007.
[4] Franz Cumont, «L'histoire des religions», *Le Flambeau* 18 (1935), p. 291–294, cité par Corinne Bonnet, éd., *La correspondance scientifique de Franz Cumont conservée à l'Academia Belgica de Rome* (Bruxelles-Rome, Institut historique belge de Rome, Diffusion Peeters, 1997), p. 59.

train de s'imposer, voire de se raffiner. Ni l'un, ni l'autre n'avaient de
limites une fois pour toutes fixées à leur appétit scientifique ou à leur
courage intellectuel, qui embrassaient des disciplines entières pour
laquelle il est difficile aujourd'hui de connaître les noms, seulement,
des collègues qui y travaillent. Le fait est palpable dans l'édition de
leur correspondance.[5] Tous les deux ont évolué une bonne période sans
avoir, à Rome et à Bucarest, de vrais collègues dont le dialogue pourrait faire pressentir, au moins, les corporations savantes qui rythment
aujourd'hui la vie académique des sciences religieuses. Leurs œuvres
reflètent abondamment les mérites et les démérites d'une époque, et
surtout sa tension contradictoire face au vertige historique de la guerre.
Mais les louanges les plus sagaces à imaginer ne sauraient éliminer un
problème persistant qui fait l'objet délicat et nécessaire de cette enquête,
au but d'une littérature qui risque de transformer la méditation avertie
en une discipline et l'exercice historique en une découverte pénible,
pourtant indispensable. Tous les deux ont dû admettre que la perspective politique funeste, aux alentours de 1940, a été bien plus généralisée
qu'on ne pourrait être généraliste leur travail d'historiens des religions.
Dans le sillage de cette pression qui éclate ici et là dans leurs écrits
nous nous proposons de gloser dans cette intervention.

Comme on le sait bien, Eliade écrit à Pettazzoni au début de 1926.[6]
D'après la phrase désormais célèbre, et à juste titre, d'Eliade – «de
Pettazzoni j'ai appris non comment, mais *quoi* faire»[7] – leur dialogue
scientifique a été plusieurs fois suivi comme exemple unique de rencontre de deux œuvres majeurs de généralistes en histoire des religions,
préoccupés à palper non seulement les structures mais aussi les contours
de la discipline. Si la géographie de leur savoir les prédisposait à l'uni-

---

[5] Voir Natale Spineto, éd., *Mircea Eliade, Raffaele Pettazzoni. L'histoire des religions a-t-elle
un sens ? Correspondance 1926–1959* (Paris, Éditions du Cerf, 1994). Il est probable que
Pettazzoni et Eliade n'ont pas parlé de ces sujets lors de leurs rencontres, ni même dans
le cercle de l'IAHR ou bien celui d'Eranos ; en tout cas, l'exégèse que nous connaissons
n'en fait guère preuve.

[6] N. Spineto, éd., *Mircea Eliade, Raffaele Pettazzoni*, p. 33 et suiv. et p. 89 et suiv. ;
M. Gandini, «Raffaele Pettazzoni negli anni 1926–1927», *Strada Maestra* 47-2 (1999),
p. 101–104 et p. 216–220.

[7] Voir p. ex. *Journal* (le 1er décembre 1977). En dépit de cette filiation encore à
exploiter, il existe un déséquilibre entre l'exégèse accordée à Eliade et celle pettazzonienne, signalée par Giovanni Casadio, «Per Ugo Bianchi. Introduzione», in idem,
éd., *Ugo Bianchi. Una vita per la storia delle religioni* (Roma, Il Calamo, 2002), p. 22,
n. 12. M. Gandini constat l'absence du nom de Pettazzoni dans nombre de débats
historiographiques postérieurs à 1959 : «Il punto sugli studi pettazzoniani», *Strada
Maestra* 23-2 (1987), p. 151–162.

fier dans un ensemble assez vaste d'où résultaient des entreprises sans
pareille comme *La confessione dei peccati* ou le *Traité d'histoire des religions*,
l'ambitus chronologique susceptible d'être couvert par l'historien généraliste dans leur vision n'a pas été étudié jusqu'à présent, et il nous semble
qu'il peut apporter quelques précisions importantes sur la biographie
de Pettazzoni et d'Eliade, ainsi que sur l'évolution de l'histoire des
religions sous l'impact des idéologies d'extrême droite.

> *«Se è vero – come fu detto – che la seconda guerra mondiale*
> *fu una 'guerra di religione'…»*[8]

Parmi les écrits de Pettazzoni qui méritent ce débat, on dispose des
articles, conférences, comptes rendus et interventions qu'il a publiés pendant une vingtaine d'années. D'ailleurs, sauf les études biographiques
consacrées avec tant de soin par Mario Gandini, on ne dispose pas d'un
examen historiographique complet. Il est un peu étrange de constater
que les opinions d'un redoutable maître de l'histoire des religions sur
l'époque contemporaine ne soient pas assez lisibles dans sa production
majeure ; nous avouons n'avoir pu trouver aucune mention dans les
sommes qui restent *La confessione dei peccati*[9] ou *Miti e leggende*. Une rare
et timide allusion sur le choix des sujets par l'historien des religions
se retrouve dans le texte de l'allocution de 1959.[10] Mais les interventions jugées mineures nous montrent quelques paradoxes directement
politiques.

---

[8] Raffaele Pettazzoni, *Italia religiosa* (Bari, Laterza, 1952), p. 103 (article de juillet
1945).

[9] Outre la synthèse en trois volumes (1929–1936), dont le troisième recensé en tête
de la rubrique par Eliade dans *Zalmoxis* 1 (1938), p. 226–228 (= 2000, p. 230–231),
avec les félicitations de Pettazzoni (voir Spineto, *Mircea Eliade, Raffaele Pettazzoni*, p. 129),
republiée en 1968 et qui devait comporter une refonte dans l'hypothétique édition
allemande (Gandini, «Raffaele Pettazzoni 1941–1943», p. 235–237), Pettazzoni avait
publié plusieurs articles de synthèse comme «Recherches sur la confession des péchés
(résumé)», in Paul-Louis Couchoud, éd., *Congrès d'histoire du christianisme. Jubilé Alfred
Loisy*, tome I (Paris, Rider / Amsterdam, Holkema & Warendorf, 1928) p. 96–98, «La
Confession des péchés dans l'histoire des religions», *Annuaire de l'Institut de Philologie et
d'Histoire Orientales et Slaves. Mélanges Franz Cumont* 4 (1936), p. 893–901 ou «La confession
des péchés : méthodes et résultats», *Scientia*, avril (1937), p. 1–6.

[10] M. Gandini, «Raffaele Pettazzoni (1883–1959) : '…La mia via, la mia verità, la
mia vita…'. Discorso tenuto nell'Università di Roma il 3 febbraio 1959», *Strada Maestra*
38–39 (1995), p. 371–392, ici p. 382 : «la mia risposta sarebbe stata questa, che sì, fra
la vita interiore e l'opera di uno studioso c'è un legame profondo, una sola radice».

Si on parle de nos jours de la nécessité d'une historiographie prenant en compte les implications politiques dans l'histoire des religions, c'est surtout à cause d'un manquement d'esprit critique qui a entraîné une partie des ces études dans le tourbillon de la deuxième guerre mondiale. Arnold van Gennep, lisant la «prolusione» de Pettazzoni, *Svolgimento e carattere della storia delle religioni* (Bari, Laterza, 1924), l'avait vu très tôt dans une clé politique: «M. Pettazzoni juge que, vu la période actuelle, il serait dangereux de parler de l'esprit critique français dans son pays». Pettazzoni lui a répondu en 1925 en excluant la «sua accusa di raffinato machiavellismo».[11] Pourtant, en 1931, juste pour préserver son enseignement romain, Pettazzoni a dû signer à contrecœur le pacte demandé par le gouvernement mussolinien, ne se rangeant pas avec l'intransigeance d'Ernesto Buonaiuti ou de Giorgio Levi della Vida. Dans un compte rendu de 1934 aux Hibbert Lectures de Robert Seymour Conway (*Ancient Italy and Modern Religion*), il ne s'abstient pas de commenter la similitude entre l'histoire du temps présent (Allemagne et Italie) et la crise romaine de l'an 33 av. J.-C.[12] On a signalé un *foglietto* inédit du 17 mars 1936, où Pettazzoni réagit aux frénésies de la romanité païenne adoptées par le fascisme, tout en les immisçant avec un christianisme politiquement obligé par le concordat de 1929. L'historien des religions fait amender l'irrecevable de la propagande avec son propre outil: la grandeur de Rome a été celle républicaine et impériale, et cela est en contradiction avec le christianisme, car «Fu questa Roma persecutrice dei Cristiani che fu grande».[13]

Au premier chef, on a des mentions politiques dans des articles touchant le Japon. Pour ne donner qu'un seul exemple, dans une conférence soutenue le 21 mars 1934 et publiée par l'IsMEO (l'Istituto Italiano per il Medio ed Estremo Oriente) nouvellement fondé par G. Gentile et G. Tucci, Pettazzoni parlait de la religion et de la politique religieuse

---

[11] Pettazzoni, «Intorno ad una prolusione», *Studi e materiali di storia delle religioni* 1 (1925), p. 152–154, ici 154; Gandini, «Raffaele Pettazzoni 1924–1925», p. 166–167 et, autour de la fondation de la chaire de Rome, Valerio Salvatore Severino, «Giovanni Gentile e Raffaele Pettazzoni (1922–1924). Un carteggio sulla storia delle religioni e l'università in Italia», *Storiografia* 6 (2002), p. 107–126 (je remercie Prof. Grottanelli de m'avoir signalé ce titre).
[12] «ideali che oggi effettivamente sono più vivi che mai, sebbene – almeno in parte – in un senso che non è precisamente quello che ha in mente il Conway», *Gnomon* 10–6 (1934), p. 301.
[13] Gandini, «Raffaele Pettazzoni 1935», p. 180–181.

au Japon moderne.[14] De manière très claire, Pettazzoni discutait un changement de situation au Japon contemporain : modernisme au Japon d'après 1868 signifiait, pour beaucoup de commentateurs, adéquation de l'État et de la laïcité. Cependant, observe Pettazzoni :

> Oggi, in Occidente, le cose sono cambiate, e forse sono in via di cambiare ancor più. Noi assistiamo oggi in Europa al formarsi di una nuova coscienza religiosa della nazione e della patria. Lo stato, come espressione della nazione, ne è a sua volta investito. Lo stato, come non vuol più essere agnostico, così non vuole più essere laico. Lo stato, che ha realizzato il suo contenuto etico, non tarderà a realizzare il suo contenuto religioso. (...) La religione della nazione e della patria sta oggi cercando, in Europa, le sue forme. Queste forme, essa le possiede in Giappone da tempo immemorabile, come le possedeva nello scomparso paganesimo occidentale.[15]

Curieusement, parler dans un tel contexte, et abruptement, du néo-paganisme occidental n'était pas chose simple. Le rapport évoqué entre shintoïsme, religion d'état et laïcité au Japon, avait indiqué à Pettazzoni une similitude qui échappait aux lecteurs historiens. L'examen du contexte nous permet de montrer qu'il s'agit d'une référence à l'Allemagne nazie, et non pas directement à l'Italie. Pettazzoni se montre averti mais allusif : des grands problèmes d'histoire des religions étaient présentés d'après une parallèle typologique qui percutait dans la stricte contemporanéité. L'affection japonaise du grand professeur italien pouvait avoir aussi une monture lisible de manière politique. Plus tard, le seul voyage asiatique de Pettazzoni sera japonais (1958). Dans un article du juillet 1945, consacré à Hirohito, il dénonce «quel rigurgito di spirito pagano che affiorò in nome della nazione eletta e della razza dominatrice e dello stato totalitario».[16] Ce qu'il avait recommandé au Japon en 1934 est jugé totalement erroné en 1945, car ce pays n'avait en ce moment qu'à dépasser les emprunts des *formes* occidentales extérieures et vides «en technique et en politique».[17]

---

[14] R. Pettazzoni, «Religione e politica religiosa nel Giappone moderno» (Roma, IsMEO, 1934), p. 5–17. Un article précédent de cette série est en effet «La religione nazionale del Giappone e la politica religiosa dello Stato giapponese», *Nuova Antologia* 1, giugno (1929), p. 3–19. Sur ses relations plus tardives avec Gentile, voir Gandini, *Pettazzoni 1941–1943*, p. 272.

[15] R. Pettazzoni, *Religione e politica religiosa nel Giaponne moderno* (Roma, IsMEO, 1934), p. 17. Plus tard, il donnera une conférence à la radio sur le même sujet (Gandini, «Raffaele Pettazzoni 1935», p. 174–175).

[16] Pettazzoni, *Italia religiosa*, p. 103.

[17] Ibid., p. 109–110; Gandini, «Raffaele Pettazzoni 1934–1935».

Ces hésitations inquiétantes avaient été taxées négativement ou éliminées seulement après qu'il ait connu le résultat de la guerre. Le contexte et la relecture invitent à voir dans la tonalité de ce fragment un soulagement, attendu beaucoup des années de la part d'un savant lié dans sa jeunesse plutôt aux formations socialistes de gauche.[18] S'il manque quelque chose dans la bibliographie de 1945 et après, filtre personnel à étudier soigneusement, c'est justement sa conférence de 1934, curieusement absente de la bibliographie japonaise.

Dans le contexte de la guerre, invité et par ailleurs accompagné de ses collègues académiciens, Pettazzoni collaborera à *Giappone. Volume dedicato all'amicizia italo-giapponese*, paru à Rome en été 1942.[19] Il a voulu quelques années durant contribuer à un volume axé sur *Les racines religieuses de l'héroïsme au Japon, en Allemagne, en Italie*, tripartite quant aux éditeurs (Heinrich Frick, Junyû Kitayama, lui-même) et à la publication (langues et pays), mais unitaire et risquant du point de vue idéologique, projet qui n'a finalement pas abouti.[20]

Le Convegno Volta de Rome, en 1938, consacré aux études africaines, montre un Pettazzoni intéressé au discours du colonialisme italien, très tardivement apparu, par rapport à l'ethnologie, dans ses écrits. En parlant d'une «Africa Italiana», il ajoute «la réaffirmation de la valeur pratique et politique de l'ethnologie».[21] Un an plus tard, dans la nécrologie de son collègue Carlo Alfonso Nallino, il affirme sa vive sensibilité politique, en lui louant aussi la capacité de convaincre «la nostra amministrazione coloniale, lo spirito di una politica coloniale illuminata», car il avait vu, dans la génération de C.A. Nallino «il presagio lungimirante degli islamisti inverato e potenziato nella nuova politica islamica dell'Italia di Mussolini».[22] Ce texte a été gentiment

---

[18] Nombreuses références chez Gandini, Pettazzoni 1928–1929, 1931–1933, 1934–1935, passim.

[19] Discussion chez Gandini, «Raffaele Pettazzoni 1941–1943», p. 163.

[20] Gandini, «Raffaele Pettazzoni 1937–1938», p. 192; ibid., 1939–1940, p. 264–266; ibid., 1941–1943, p. 124–126 et p. 238. Voir aussi la contribution de Hiroshi Kubota dans ce volume.

[21] «Credo che il Convegno Volta 1938 avrà ottenuto un risultato importante se riaffermerà *il valore pratico e politico della etnologia*, in specie della etnologia contemporanea ed applicata; e se varrà a dimostrare, non dico l'utilità delle ricerche etnologiche da parte di studiosi specializzati, ma *la necessità che l'Amministrazione Coloniale disponga di un personale fornito di una adeguata preparazione etnologica*», voir «Orientamenti attuali dell'Africanistica», *Atti dell'VIII Convegno tema: l'Africa, Roma, 4–11 Ottobre 1938–XVI* (Roma, Reale Accademia d'Italia, 1940), p. 11 (c'est moi qui le souligne).

[22] R. Pettazzoni, «'De probitate': Carlo Alfonso Nallino», *Nuova Antologia*, 1 Aprile 1939–XVII, p. 256–257; Gandini, «Raffaele Pettazzoni 1937–1938», p. 195–202.

critiqué par Giorgio Levi della Vida dans une lettre du 19 mai 1939, car Nallino «in politica era un ingenuo».[23]

Pettazzoni a risqué plus d'une fois d'offrir une comparaison entre la situation politique et le programme scientifique en Italie et en Allemagne, comme dans un article de la *Civiltà fascista* de 1938, où il voyait que «la storia delle religioni (…) è particolarmente sensibile alle esigenze dello spirito nazionale» et que

> l'*Archiv für Religionswissenschaft* (…) sentì due anni fa il bisogno, pur mantenendo il suo carattere [sic!], di darsi un nuovo orientamento e un nuovo contenuto conforme al mutato clima spirituale della nuova Germania, e annunziò di avere posto al centro delle sue ricerche questo tema: 'La religione e la religiosità dei popoli germanici e dei loro capi (Führer) religiosi'. Senza essere una nazione pluriconfesionale e senza essere travagliata da una crisi religiosa come quella che agita oggi il popolo tedesco, l'Italia ha pure un suo intimo interesse per una 'storia della religione in Italia'.[24]

Le 14 août 1938, moment où Eliade était emprisonné, Pettazzoni écrit à Cumont pour solliciter l'avis avant d'écrire au président de l'Accademia d'Italia, Luigi Federzoni, pour proposer que le congrès d'histoire des religions soit organisé à Bologne en 1940, et le 12 juin 1939, peut-être sans soupçonner encore l'immédiateté de la guerre, il assure le maître belge établi à Rome que l'Italie ne s'isolera point sur le plan scientifique, la loi sur la fonction des deux académies, qu'il cite, n'excluant pas les membres étrangers comme Cumont.[25]

Son séjour en Allemagne[26] comme conférencier invité à Frankfurt, Marburg et Berlin (5–19 avril 1942) n'a pas eu de dimension politique, Pettazzoni parlant de divinités pluricephales devant un public des professeurs (parmi eux, à Marburg, Bultmann, Heiler et Nobel).[27] Plus tard, en octobre 1942, Pettazzoni doit répondre à une invitation du recteur

---

[23] Publiée par Gandini, «Raffaele Pettazzoni 1939–1940», p. 168.

[24] R. Pettazzoni, «Gli studi storico-religiosi in Italia», *Civiltà fascista* 5–3 (1938), p. 5–6. Sur les transformations subies par la discipline en Allemagne, voir Horst Junginger «Das Überleben der Religionswissenschaft im Nationalsozialismus», *Zeitschrift für Religionswissenschaft* 9 (2001), p. 149–167.

[25] Références résumées fournies par Corinne Bonnet sur le site de l'Academia Belgica, http://cipl.philo.ulg.ac.be.

[26] Gandini, *Pettazzoni 1941–1943*, p. 207–211.

[27] Comme le note Gandini, *Pettazzoni 1934–1935*, p. 156, «il nome e il valore di Pettazzoni sono più noti all'estero che in Italia», ce qui correspond, quant à l'œuvre scientifique, à la situation d'Eliade, tous les deux ayant une attirance vers le système universitaire allemand en général et la Religionswissenschaft en particulier. Aux mois d'été de recherche en Allemagne d'Eliade (1934, 1936 et 1937) correspondent les conférences faites là-bas par Pettazzoni.

de l'Université romaine, de Francisci, pour parler (péniblement) dans ces termes du fascisme:

> Gli studi italiani di storia religiosa debbono al Regime l'istituzione (primo Ministero Mussolini) della prima cattedra di Storia delle Religioni, nella R. Università di Roma, e, più ancora, la formazione di un clima spirituale dal quale è emersa, e dovrà emergere sempre più la loro capitale importanza.[28]

Une seule fois, peut-être, Pettazzoni a été considéré par ses compatriotes sous l'angle d'une culpabilité politique: avec l'acte d'épuration envoyé par un Haut Commissariat à la Commission d'épuration à la fin de 1944, l'historien des religions figurant sur une liste de 54 noms. L'incertitude et l'amertume ne dureront que peu de jours, du 18 décembre 1944 à 9 février 1945 — en effet la décision prise le 13 janvier lui étant le même jour communiqué par un ami et confrère, Luigi Salvatorelli (1886–1974).[29] (La cause était imaginaire et pouvait se résoudre à l'intérieur d'une même culture, mais au camp de Buchenwald, Henri Maspero était inculpé et anéanti pour une cause imaginaire — «Verdacht terroristischer Betätigung».)[30] Après la guerre, d'après Gandini, Pettazzoni «sembra che le sue simpatie vadano alle correnti di sinistra».[31] D'ailleurs, Pettazzoni écrit assez clairement à un ancien ami le 12 août 1946 sur la sympathie qu'il a pour le PSIUP (Parti socialiste italien de l'unité prolétaire): «non mi sono ancora iscritto ufficialmente, non mi sento molto portato a partecipare attivamente alla politica, alla mia età e nella mia posizione di studioso; in seguito vedremo».[32] En fait, il peut regagner de cette manière la distance qu'il avait en 1920–1921 pour la

---

[28] Gandini, «Raffaele Pettazzoni 1941–1943», p. 235.

[29] Eléments chez M. Gandini, «Raffaele Pettazzoni 1943–1946», p. 77–78. En 1959, Pettazzoni évoque Salvatorelli sans reprendre l'épisode pénible (Gandini, «Raffaele Pettazzoni 1883–1959», 1995, p. 378). Aussi «Socialismo e cultura storico-religiosa», in R. Pettazzoni, *Religione e società*, a cura di Mario Gandini (Bologna, Ed. Ponte Nuovo, 1966), p. 173–179.

[30] Arrêté inopinément et attendu en vain à la séance de l'Académie des Inscriptions et Belles-Lettres, vendredi le 28 juillet 1944, qu'il devait présider, Henri Maspero, auquel on a dédié la rencontre de Tübingen, avait été déporté en Allemagne avec le tout dernier train du 15 août; il est mort peu de temps avant l'arrivé des alliés. Voir Paul Demiéville, «Nécrologie. Henri Maspero (1883–1945)», *Journal Asiatique* 234 (1943–1945), p. 245–280, surtout p. 259–263, et Paul Pelliot, ibid., p. 453.

[31] Gandini, «Raffaele Pettazzoni 1943–1946», p. 163.

[32] Cité par Gandini, ibid. p. 59.

politique[33] et il ne renforcera que ses rapprochements socialistes.[34] De ce point de vue, traverser la période de la guerre tout en conservant ses relations professionnelles allemandes n'était pas pour Pettazzoni une affiliation, même si Franz Cumont avait abandonné l'idée de visiter l'Institut allemand de la Via Sardegna déjà en 1939.[35] Pettazzoni, quant à lui, écrit ironiquement à Arnaldo Momigliano en 1945 qu'il lui reste, après le transfert de cette bibliothèque en Allemagne, de s'occuper des peuples incultes (…).[36]

«(…) non mi sento molto portato a partecipare attivamente alla politica» (1946)

Déjà en 1924, Pettazzoni attire l'attention sur la nouvelle religiosité en Allemagne dans son texte et il ne manque pas d'annoter l'entrecroisement entre le néo-paganisme et l'antisémitisme.[37] Attaquant le thème du rapport entre politique et religion, il annote les mouvements nationalistes parmi les *Ersatzreligionen* deux années avant.[38] Pendant la guerre Pettazzoni maintiendra son intérêt pour ce sujet, comme le montre plusieurs épisodes.[39] Il reviendra aussi, et surtout, le 8 avril 1945, avec la conférence «Il neo-paganesimo germanico». C'est le texte que nous connaissons de son livre *Italia religiosa*, et qui n'accepte pas les prétentions du mouvement.[40] En effet, bien qu'étant assez récent, il le

---

[33] Gandini, «Raffaele Pettazzoni 1919–1922», p. 140–142.

[34] En août 1945, Pettazzoni présente un discours devant les socialistes de San Giovanni di Persiceto où il affirme : «L'Italia è a terra. L'Italia è depressa, ma il socialismo è vittorioso. E il socialismo non conosce paesi vincitori né paese vinti. Proletari di tutto il mondo unitevi. L'Italia è a terra, è boccheggiante, è sfinita. Ma il socialismo non la lascerà morire ; sarà salvata, sarà salvata dal socialismo», en ajoutant dans ses notes : «La guerra fascista ha portato al socialismo» (p. 108 ; aussi ibid., «Raffaele Pettazzoni 1941–1943», p. 128), Pettazzoni citant un an après Marx, Engels, Lenin et Trotski (Gandini, «Raffaele Pettazzoni 1943–1946», p. 82).

[35] C. Bonnet, éd., *La Correspondance scientifique de Franz Cumont*, p. 37.

[36] Gandini, «Raffaele Pettazzoni 1943–1946», p. 47.

[37] Gandini, «Raffaele Pettazzoni 1922–1923», p. 219 ; Gandini, «Raffaele Pettazzoni 1934–1935», p. 145–148, avec une liste de livres achetés et lectures.

[38] Gandini, «Raffaele Pettazzoni 1919–1922», p. 175–177.

[39] Gandini, «Raffaele Pettazzoni 1941–1943», p. 254 (liste de livres demandés à Alberto Carlo Blanc le 5 mars 1943, parmi les auteurs étant Hauer et Wüst).

[40] R. Pettazzoni, «Il neo-paganesimo germanico», in idem, *Italia religiosa*, p. 115–131 (repris de *Idea* du mai 1945). Pour la préparation de cette conférence devant l'«Associazione per il progresso degli studi morali e religiosi» et son contexte, voir Gandini, «Raffaele Pettazzoni 1943–1946», p. 90–94 et Giuseppe Trevisi, «Religione dello stato e religione dell'uomo in *Italia religiosa* di Raffaele Pettazzoni», *Strada Maestra* 12 (1979), p. 49–55.

voit dans l'encrage d'une histoire religieuse de l'Europe traumatisée par l'opposition entre un fond indo-européen et un autre sémite. Le 15 mai 1946, il suggèrera toutefois à un éditeur la traduction du livre de Hauer sur le néo-paganisme allemand pour une collection sur la religion dans le monde moderne.[41] Cette attitude n'est pas singulière, et elle a une résonance chez les fervents du fascisme qui voudraient imposer d'ores et déjà l'équation fascisme = nouvelle religiosité. Alberto Gianola, pour nous maintenir dans la compagnie des scientifiques, proposait en 1927 à Pettazzoni de prendre avec lui et de diffuser auprès des participants au Congrès sur l'histoire du christianisme de Paris une liste de « Questions sur le Fascisme » qui s'achevait ainsi : « et qu'en pensez-vous de la force de propagation de cette nouvelle foi, qui, comme toutes les croyances religieuses, a ses ennemis acharnés et ses admirateurs enthousiastes ? ».[42] Pettazzoni n'a évidemment pas répondu à cette sollicitation. Par contre, il a pu écouter et donner l'assentiment à une communication d'Émile Bouvier, professeur à Montpellier, portant sur « Les religions depuis 1914 » – « Nous assistons aujourd'hui (…) à une contre-offensive des religions », affirmait Bouvier –, ou à Alfred Loisy même.[43] Cependant l'insatisfaction de ne pas pouvoir entreprendre une histoire religieuse complète de l'Italie Pettazzoni la confesse lors de la cérémonie en son honneur de 1959.[44]

Relations indirectes

Au-delà des problèmes scientifiques, dans leur pays d'origine, et Pettazzoni et Eliade se sont encrés dans une logique culturelle plus vaste. En effet, le rapport scientifique d'Eliade avec Nae Ionescu (1890–1940) semble répéter celui des orientalistes italiens, une vingtaine d'années avant, vers un promoteur et grand lecteur comme Giovanni Papini, s'inscrivant ainsi dans une logique culturelle du « patron » polymathe.[45]

---

[41] Gandini, « Raffaele Pettazzoni 1943–1946 », p. 169.

[42] Gandini, « Raffaele Pettazzoni 1926–1927 », p. 169.

[43] E. Bouvier, « Les religions depuis 1914 », in P.-L. Couchoud, éd., *Congrès d'histoire du christianisme*, tome III, p. 207–225. Loisy souhaitait aux savants de « mettre fin aux rivalités sanglantes qui n'ont jamais produit que la ruine des civilisations » (ibid., tome I, p. 26).

[44] Gandini, « Raffaele Pettazzoni 1883–1959 », 1995, p. 385–386.

[45] Ajoutons, aux références de Gandini, « Raffaele Pettazzoni 1912 », Ferdinando Belloni-Filippi, qui parle d'un Papini contribuant à la divulgation des philosophies

Même si on ne dispose pas de correspondance après le 18 avril 1939 et avant le 20 février 1946, même si après le retour de l'Inde d'Eliade et la parution de *Yoga* il y a peu de lettres, il y a d'autres signes qu'encourageont plus tard une reprise solide des contacts, tout en expliquant par ailleurs la confiance du professeur italien pour le jeune roumain, illustrée assez tôt, en 1934 déjà, même par des intermédiaires.[46] Ce qui nous semble plus important, chacun d'eux, même indépendamment, s'est intéressé à la culture de l'autre. Ainsi, à l'époque même où Eliade manifeste un intérêt pour le zoroastrisme et son influence,[47] Pettazzoni s'intéresse au motif iranien du Pont Cinvat, connu aussi dans la littérature populaire roumaine déjà à l'époque de Moses Gaster, et même transcrivait, pour une étude ensuite abandonnée, un passage significatif du folkloriste roumain Simion Florea Marian.[48] Eliade célébrait Gaster à Bucarest en roumain et cherchait à le rencontrer à Londres sans succès.[49] Pettazzoni était en revanche présent dans le volume sorti à Londres en 1936,[50] Gaster ayant recensé *I Misteri* un peu avant Eliade,[51]

---

orientales, voir *Due Upanisad. La dottrina arcana del bianco e del nero Yajurveda* (Lanciano, Editore R. Carabba, 1912), p. 19. Nae Ionesco recensait à son tour Paul Masson-Oursel en 1924.

[46] Une lettre de Rome envoyée par Haig Acterian à son frère Arşavir le 18 novembre 1934 (voir Arşavir Acterian, *Cioran, Eliade, Ionesco*, Cluj-Napoca, Eikon, 2003, p. 61–62) lui annonce une rencontre inouïe. En faisant la queue au bureau de la poste pour envoyer un titre de Pettazzoni à Eliade, Haig Acterian lit sur l'enveloppe d'un «petit monsieur» devant lui «expéditeur R. Pettazzoni», se présente et rappel le nom de son ami de Bucarest. Pettazzoni répond sur le vif «Oh mais je connais bien son nom!». «Il s'intéresse beaucoup à lui», glosait l'ami de *Criterion*, invité de suivre l'ouverture du cours de Pettazzoni (Gandini, «Raffaele Pettazzoni 1934–1935», p. 149–150, indique toutefois comme date de reprise le 12 novembre).

[47] Voir Mihaela Timuş, éd., *Întotdeauna Orientul. Corespondenţa Mircea Eliade – Stig Wikander (1948–1977)* [C'est toujours l'Orient. Correspondance Eliade-Wikander] (Iasi-Bucarest, Polirom, 2005), p. 54–57.

[48] Voir Gandini, «Raffaele Pettazzoni 1935», p. 208–209 (d'après *Înmormântarea la români*, Bucarest, 1892).

[49] Eliade, «Doctorul Gaster», *Vremea* [Le temps], 21 juin 1936, p. 9 ; E. Ciurtin, éd., *Zalmoxis. Revistă de studii religioase, sub direcţia lui Mircea Eliade* (Iasi-Bucarest, Polirom, 2000), p. 22 et p. 46. L'article sur «la mort du Dr Gaster» publié en 1939 le met en parallèle avec deux autres géants orientalistes récemment disparus, Berthold Laufer et Sylvain Lévi.

[50] Raffaele Pettazzoni, «Confessions of Sins in Hittite Religion», Bruno Schindler (en collaboration avec A. Marmorstein), éd., *Occident and Orient* (London, Taylor's Foreign Press, 1936), p. 467–471, ou encore Gandini, «Raffaele Pettazzoni 1931–1933», p. 163–165. Pettazzoni a écrit une note sur ce volume dans *Studi e materiali di storia delle religioni* 1937, fasc. 1, p. 125–126; aussi Gandini, «Raffaele Pettazzoni 1931–1933», p. 109 and «Raffaele Pettazzoni 1935», p. 105, p. 110, p. 189, p. 249 et «Raffaele Pettazzoni 1937–1938», p. 77.

[51] M. Gaster, in *Folk-Lore* 36-2 (1925), p. 194–195.

le recevant, ce qui plus est, au *Jubilee Congress of the Folk-Lore Society* (où
il avait été président), en septembre 1929.[52] Plus tard son fils Theodor
H. Gaster cherchera à Londres une maison d'édition pour les œuvres
de Pettazzoni en 1938,[53] mais il sera moins chanceux qu'Eliade à Paris
en 1953.[54] Pettazzoni a eu beaucoup plus de contacts en Roumanie à
l'époque, comme le note soigneusement Gandini : surtout parmi les
archéologues et les classicistes, surtout en liaison avec ses études sur les
Thraces (D.M. Pippidi, collaborateur lui aussi à *Zalmoxis* et cité dans
ses travaux par Pettazzoni ; aussi M. Beza, C. Isopescu, S. Lambrino,
E. Panaitescu etc.) et il devient en 1943 membre de l'«Associazione
Amici della Romania».[55] En outre, il fut, semble-t-il, au courant de
l'ambiant politique roumain même, car il cite sur un brouillon, hélas,
la Légion, voulant discuter l'histoire comme histoire religieuse dans
toutes ses ramifications : «La storia religiosa della Romania dalle origini pre-romane fino al movimento mistico della Legione dell'Arcangelo Gabriele [sic! le patron était l'archange Michel] e della Guardia
di ferro», complétée par une affirmation : «La storia religiosa della
Romania, come la storia religiosa dell'Italia, è ancora da fare».[56] La
source peut bien être, en effet, les lectures de Pettazzoni, car il détenait
la traduction italienne d'un livre de Corneliu Zelea Codreanu : *Guardia
di Ferro (per i legionari)*, publié en 1938 (Rome-Turin).[57] Et l'écriture de
cette histoire amène Pettazzoni au postulat : «La storia d'Italia dovrà
essere anche storia religiosa», qu'il a soutenu plus d'une fois et même,
en 1942, comme jugement sur le fascisme vingt ans après (voir plus
loin)[58] ou bien dans un texte de 1948.[59] A la reprise des contacts, après

---

[52] Gandini, «Raffaele Pettazzoni 1928–1929», p. 125–127 et p. 157–158.
[53] Gandini, «Raffaele Pettazzoni 1937–1938», p. 204. Une fois M. Gandini se trompe
croyant Moses Gaster un «ebreo-ungherese» («Raffaele Pettazzoni 1928–1929», p. 241,
n. 41) : il est l'un des grand juifs expulsés par les lois raciales roumaines en 1885. Sur
cette période on dispose actuellement d'une édition roumaine par Victor Eskenasy de
ses mémoires (Bucarest, Hasefer, 1998).
[54] Gandini, «Raffaele Pettazzoni 1935», p. 105.
[55] Gandini, «Raffaele Pettazzoni 1941–1943», p. 199. Cette association était présidée
par Emilio Bodrero, qui l'invite à faire partie de son conseil directeur (ibid., p. 267).
Pettazzoni ne sympathisait pas trop avec ce sous-secrétaire au Ministère de l'Éducation
Nationale (ibid., p. 127). Il participait aussi à l'inauguration d'une société «Amici del
Giappone», le 11 février 1942 (ibid., p. 193).
[56] Ibid., p. 198.
[57] D'après Gandini («Raffaele Pettazzoni 1937–1938», p. 154) on ne connaît pas
quand et comment il a obtenu ce livre.
[58] Gandini, «Raffaele Pettazzoni 1941–1943», p. 235.
[59] Pettazzoni, «Per la storia religiosa d'Italia», *Ricerche Religiose* 19-1 (1948),
p. 1–12.

quelques six ans d'absence, Pettazzoni lui indique : « Je fréquente assez
souvent l'accademia di Romania ici. J'y ai donné une conférence en
1942 », avec un sujet qui motive une fois de plus le projet de *Zalmoxis* :
« Il culto del sole nella religione dell'antica Tracia »,[60] à une époque où
le symbolisme solaire déclinait.[61]

Les camouflages d'Eliade

Pour analyser la totalité des textes et contextes politiques d'Eliade,
l'éventualité d'un rapprochement à signaler entre ses écrits et son
engagement, fut-il passager, et suivre l'exégèse consacrée pendant plusieurs décennies il faudra peut-être tout un livre.[62] Qu'il nous soit permis,
en revanche, d'attaquer ici seulement quelques étapes anciennes par des
documents nouveaux. L'article « Pourquoi je crois dans la victoire du
mouvement légionnaire » de 1937 a suscité une telle littérature, qu'on
peut comparer la difficulté de lui attribuer la signature (ou la conception) à Eliade avec la querelle autour de *Die Nachtwachen des Bonaventura*
(1804). Le manque de références sur ses implications politiques dans
la correspondance avec Pettazzoni, interrompue justement à cause de
l'arrestation d'Eliade et puis par la guerre, a d'ailleurs empêché de
suivre la complexité de leurs relations.[63]

Parmi les fautes de jeunesse qu'Eliade reconnaîtra plus tard, et qui
sont toutes en rapport avec l'atmosphère idéologique de l'époque,[64] on
rencontre quelques épisodes liés à la rédaction de la thèse sur le yoga.
La réécrire au Musée Guimet presque une vingtaine d'années plus tard,

---

[60] Spineto, p. 131 ; Gandini, « Raffaele Pettazzoni 1941–1943 », p. 197–199 et aussi
Pettazzoni, « Antichi culti solari nella penisola Balcanica », *Rivista d'Albania* 2-2 (1941),
p. 109–114 (tiré à part : p. 3–8) et Gandini, « Raffaele Pettazzoni 1941–1943 », p. 129.

[61] Lettre du février ou mars 1946, dans Spineto, *Mircea Eliade, Raffaele Pettazzoni*,
p. 131.

[62] L'essentiel actuellement disponible se retrouve dans deux chapitres de la monographie de F. Turcanu, *Mircea Eliade*, 2003, p. 251–301 (« L'engagement ») et p. 477–487
(« L'impossible aveu ») (éd. roum. 2005, p. 322–382 et p. 593–618).

[63] Déjà entre la date de sa parution (1994) et celle du compte rendu de Maurice
Olender, *History of Religions* 37-1 (1997), p. 86–90, on a beaucoup publié sur les enga-
gements politiques des historiens des religions. Pour une liste de 35 comptes rendus de
Spineto, voir Gandini, « Raffaele Pettazzoni 1926–1927 », p. 219, n. 3.

[64] La dérive de sa position politique a commencé pour Eliade avec une contradiction avec ses propres opinions antérieures (par exemple : « race, religion et nation (...)
comme vous voyez, seulement des zones dynamitées », « Rasă şi religie », *Vremea*, 21
février 1935).

confesse-t-il à Stig Wikander, signifie corriger les «fautes de jeunesse».[65] La préface de 1936 exprime un courage que nous n'avons pas pu dépister dans un autre ouvrage scientifique sur le même sujet: «nous essayons de prouver que le yoga, loin d'être le patrimoine de quelques sectes ascétiques, est une catégorie spécifique de l'esprit indien, ayant une histoire ininterrompé [sic!] du Chalcolithique jusqu'à nos jours». Une fois, dans un article en roumain de la même année et qui porte notamment le titre «Éléments pré-aryens dans l'hindouisme»,[66] Eliade exprimait sa surprise de constater que ni la civilisation de Mohenjo-Daro n'était pas pure: c'est la perplexité gauche de quelqu'un qui veut trouver, sinon postuler la pureté au début d'une série historique, et c'est la coercition d'un modèle dévolutif qui préjudicie non seulement des œuvres comme celle de Pater Wilhelm Schmidt, mais même celle de son critique Pettazzoni,[67] qui cite justement cette phrase dans un article de 1937, le considérant «a symptom of the actual orientation of studies in this direction».[68] En dépit des plusieurs adhésions des indianistes, Eliade a été critiqué par Jean Filliozat.[69]

Plus d'une fois, l'ambiguïté foncière du discours d'Eliade a égaré même les chercheurs les plus attentifs à ces imbrications, comme c'est le cas de la préface de *Cosmologie et alchimie babylonienne*.[70] Ainsi, un examen plus attentif du climat scientifique roumain de l'époque prouve d'ailleurs qu'Eliade avait ses raisons de poursuivre une critique (après

---

[65] M. Timuş, *Corespondenţa Mircea Eliade – Stig Wikander*, p. 105–106, p. 158 et p. 231–232 (lettres du 2 novembre 1948 et 15 février 1954).

[66] «Elemente preariene în hinduism», *Revista Fundaţiilor Regale* [Revue des Fondations royales] 3–1 (1936), p. 149–173.

[67] Voir Jonathan Z. Smith, «Acknowledgements: Morphology and History in Mircea Eliade's *Patterns in Comparative Religion* (1949–1999) [I–II]», *History of Religions* 39–4 (2000), p. 315–35 and Mac Linscott Ricketts 2000, p. 51–77 et 2002, p. 283–311, ainsi que la poursuite, M.L. Ricketts, «Straightening some 'Tangles' in the Tale of the *Traité*», *Archaeus* 6–1/2 (2002), p. 211–212 et J.Z. Smith, *Relating Religion* (Chicago, Chicago University Press, 2004), p. 79.

[68] R. Pettazzoni, «A Functional View of Religions», *The Review of Religion* 1–3 (1937), p. 236, n. 13. Aussi Gandini, «Raffaele Pettazzoni 1935», p. 225–227.

[69] Par exemple Jean Filliozat, «Les origines d'une techniques mystiques indienne», *Revue philosophique* 1946, p. 208–220.

[70] On ne peut pas voir, comme Ţurcanu, *Mircea Eliade*, 2003, p. 273–274 (2005, p. 348–349) un engagement dissimulé dans la préface qu'Eliade écrit à la *Cosmologie şi alchimie babiloniană* qui date, il est vrai, toujours de 1937. *Pace* Ţurcanu, ce texte se prête aussi à des analyses d'un autre genre, que nous avons commentées dans E. Ciurtin, «Cincizeci de ani în Asia», p. 11–81. Nous avons développé cette analyse dans *Histoire des études indiennes en Europe occidentale et orientale. Quatre conférences à l'École Pratique des Hautes Études* (Paris, à paraître).

l'*Itinéraire spirituel* il avait en chantier un *Itinéraire critique*, non achevé,
et pour cause, vu l'abolissement de l'esprit critique dans l'atmosphère
légionnaire) des appétits scientifiques de la culture officielle, liée à la
fondation de *Zalmoxis*, aux études indiennes qu'il menait et à une
échelle comparative plus large de l'aire balkanique et est-européenne,
tout en gardant les propriétés de l'examen de sources.[71] Au moins en
grand cela permet une parallèle avec la fondation de l'Institut oriental
à Prague.[72]

D'ailleurs, Pettazzoni avait proposé le 15 février 1940 à la *Reale
Accademia d'Italia* (qu'il ne regrettera pas lors de son anéantissement en
1945)[73] l'organisation du Congrès international d'histoire des religions,
qui devait être le septième: il suggère, afin d'obtenir «un unità più sos-
tanziale», le «concept de substrat».[74] Parmi les sujets les plus difficiles en

---

[71] D'ailleurs sur ce plan l'écrit a été élégamment validé par Pietro Mander, «60 anni
da *Cosmologia e alchimia babilonesi*», in L. Arcella et al., éds., *Confronto con Mircea Eliade:
archetipi mitici e identità storica* (Milano, Jaca Book, 1998), p. 219–238.

[72] Alois Musil parlait en 1919, dans un article programmatique sur «Nos devoirs dans
les études orientales et envers l'Orient» (texte tchèque publié, traduit et discuté dans
Archív Orientální, 2002, p. 561–562), d'une tâche de construire les liaisons avec l'Asie, de
renforcer l'intérêt de sa culture pour l'Orient et de l'Orient pour la Tchécoslovaquie,
comme Eliade dans plusieurs articles dont surtout «Un institut oriental», *Cuvântul* du
14 février 1938. Sympathie, réciprocité, généralité et urgence: des invariants dans la
promotion des études indiennes et orientales qui surgissaient encore plus à l'Est. D'après
Hana Navrátilová et Roman Míšek, «Alois Musil and the Rise of Czech Oriental
Studies: A Perspective of a Non-classical Orientalism», *Archív Orientální* 70–4 (2002),
p. 558–564, here p. 561, «this political background deserves attention, as it underscores
the history of Oriental studies in the Middle and Eastern Europe, as condition-specific
and distinct comparison to other Western countries». En Roumanie par exemple, le
prince régnant Charles II avait fait un long voyage à travers l'Asie, en compagnie
d'une suite incluant aussi quelques intellectuels, au moment même où le président de
la nouvelle Tchécoslovaquie, T.G. Masaryk, était attiré par l'Orient et s'était montré
ouvert et efficient en vue de la fondation d'un institut oriental à Prague, ce que Charles
II a hésité plusieurs années d'inaugurer, en dépit des espoirs ardents d'Eliade. Il a écrit
d'ailleurs sur «L'arbitre Masaryk» dans *Vremea* du 1er novembre 1936, p. 2. L'Italie était
aussi le modèle possible, car les subventions de Tucci pour les expéditions au Tibet
étaient admirées à Bucarest (A. Acterian, *Cioran, Eliade, Ionesco*, p. 61).

[73] Gandini, «Raffaele Pettazzoni 1943–1946», p. 53.

[74] R. Pettazzoni, «Criteri per l'ordinamento scientifico del VII congresso internazionale di storia delle religioni», *Atti della Reale Accademia d'Italia. Rendiconti della Classe di
Scienze Morali e Storiche*, serie VII, volume II, fascicolo 1–5, p. 1–3 (ici p. 1–2). Cf. aussi
p. 3: «Si tratta di farvi circolare uno spirito nuovo», phrase qui, même soutenue par
le projet strictement scientifique, risquait d'être commenté en 1940–1941 de manière
politique. L'Europe des savants opposés bel et bien au fascisme comprenait assurément
autre chose par «substrat» et par «esprit nouveau». Ce substrat était en Allemagne
responsable aussi de l'institution d'un *Arische Seminar*, voir H. Junginger, *Von der philologischen zur völkischen Religionswissenschaft* (Stuttgart, Steiner, 1999), p. 216–223 et idem, «Das

histoire des religions, le «substrat» était – Pettazzoni l'avait commenté (parfois avec Cumont),[75] Eliade l'avait prouvé – un problème qui faisait surface aussi dans les débats politiques allemands, italiens, roumains.

Le nom de la revue d'études religieuses *Zalmoxis*, que Pettazzoni trouve «heureusement choisi»,[76] n'était pas sans rapport avec cette même «revalorisation du fond autochtone» qui, Eliade le reconnaissait,[77] a été un chapitre suffisamment délicat dans l'histoire de la culture roumaine moderne. En effet, Jean Przyluski, Georges Dumézil et d'autres encore, de l'Europe centrale et orientale, étaient impliqués, à Paris et à partir de 1936, dans une petite «Société intime d'Études paléo-méditerranéennes (...)», mais, d'après un orientaliste russe exilé en France, Basile Nikitine, «la guerre interrompit brutalement notre activité qui portait sur la couche pré-indo-européenne en Europe».[78] D'après Nikitine, Przyluski «accepta la présidence de la Société, en assurera la tenue scientifique et l'anima de ses théories hardies». Comme sa collaboration pour *Zalmoxis* datait de 1938, on a ici une raison de plus de penser que Dumézil prendra connaissance très tôt de la revue de Bucarest et qu'il existait une communication européenne

'Arische Seminar' der Universität Tübingen 1940–1945», in H. Brückner, K. Butzenberger, A. Malinar, G. Zeller, éds., *Indienforschung im Zeitenwandel. Analyse und Dokumente zur Indologie und Religionswissenschaft in Tübingen* (Tübingen, Attempto Verlag, 2003), p. 177–207. A comparer avec Gandini, «Raffaele Pettazzoni 1937–1938», p. 185–186 et Pettazzoni, «Domenica 17 Aprile. Inaugurazione del congresso», *Atti dell'VIII Congresso Internazionale di Storia delle Religioni* (Firenze, G.-C. Sansoni, [1956]), p. 29–34.

[75] Corinne Bonnet signale 31 lettres envoyées par Pettazzoni à Cumont, de 1922 (l'année de leur rencontre, cf. Gandini, «Raffaele Pettazzoni 1919–1922», p. 154–155) à la fin de 1941 (deux de 1937–1938 étant déjà publiées en 1997, p. 392–394) et dont plusieurs attestent des démarches de Pettazzoni pour le congrès de Rome et le concours des officialités italiennes.

[76] Lettre du 9 mars 1938, in Spineto, *Mircea Eliade, Raffaele Pettazzoni*, p. 117; voir *Zalmoxis* 1938–1942 et E. Ciurtin «La première revue d'histoire des religions en Roumanie : *Zalmoxis* (1938–1942) de Mircea Eliade», *Archaeus* 4–1/2 (2000), p. 327–365 et idem, éd., *Zalmoxis*, p. 7–55. Les publications de l'époque de *Zalmoxis* ont été traduites dans Mircea Eliade, *I riti del costruire. Commenti alla Leggenda di Mastro Manole. La Mandragola e i miti della 'Nascita miracolosa'. Le erbe sotto la Croce* (Milano, Jaca Book, 1990). Aussi Gandini, «Raffaele Pettazzoni 1937–1938», p. 153–154. Toujours en Portugal, il est présumable qu'Eliade ne contrôle plus totalement la parution des volumes de *Zalmoxis*, les deux derniers contenant des études moins brillantes ainsi que des comptes rendus douteux.

[77] M. Eliade, *De Zalmoxis à Gengis Khan* (Paris, Payot, 1970), p. 30–31 (étude sur Zalmoxis datée «1944, 1969»).

[78] Voir Basile Nikitine, «The Society for Palaeo-Mediterranean Studies», *Georgica*, Londres (1937), p. 322–323, souvenir repris dans ses notes autobiographiques «Réminiscences polono-orientales», *Folia Orientalia* 2–1/2 (1960), p. 153–176, ici p. 174.

considérable autour du thème choisi par Pettazzoni.[79] Concept dont
la vogue indéniable concourrait avec celle de l'irrationalisme calqué
sur l'atmosphère de l'époque,[80] le substrat s'opposait génériquement
au « suprastrat » et, en site roumain, évoquait toujours la pureté (pos-
tulée) et la résistance qui offrait le sens de propagande historique aux
mouvements fascisés. En fin de compte, ce qui était conçu comme rôle
de l'histoire des religions à une échelle culturelle plus vaste n'était pas
vraiment protégé contre les mystifications diverses, même si, dans son
article de l'*Enciclopedia Italiana* de 1936, il défend l'histoire des religions
italienne comme une école qui a pu offrir une autonomie croissante
de cette discipline et abandonner clairement les interférences extras-
cientifiques.[81] Pour simplifier tous ce qui peut être simplifié : religion et
politique, mythologie et pouvoir étaient déjà bel et bien des thèmes de
l'histoire des religions ; parmi les meilleurs qui les ont aperçu comme
tel on compte évidemment Pettazzoni et Eliade. En revanche, ni l'un ni
l'autre ne semblent être suffisamment exactes et directes au moment où
ils appliquent l'histoire des religions au rapport, d'une contemporanéité
immédiate, entre religion et politique. Ils n'avaient que des exemples du
passé (et dans d'autres espaces) : ils les transfèrent, puis les appliquent
(ainsi Pettazzoni sur la *Deutsche Glaubensbewegung*) au présent. Comme
ceux qui ont instrumentalisé le discours sur la religion au profit d'une
idéologie politique, les historiens des religions ont cru en leur capacité
d'expliquer ou de critiquer les nouvelles théories nazies. Mais pour
Pettazzoni, plutôt que d'être subrepticement convaincu par l'évolution
politique fasciste et nazi annonçant la guerre, il était stimulé dans ses
détours vers la politique allemande par un souci – difficile à expliquer,
car il ne l'a pas fait assez directement – de grandir les perspectives et
la fonction d'une discipline scientifique. Au même moment, Hauer,
avec un autre timbre, évidemment, raccordait de même manière ses
options historico-religieuses et finalement sa chaire de Tübingen avec

---

[79] Eliade ne connaissait probablement pas toutes ces initiatives, comme il ne cite
pas dans le *Yoga* de 1936 une étude important de Constantin Regamey, « Bibliographie
analytique des travaux relatifs aux éléments anaryens dans la civilisation et les langues
de l'Inde », *Bulletin de l'École française d'Extrême-Orient* 34 (1935), p. 429–566.

[80] Voir Rainer Flasche « Der Irrationalismus in der Religionswissenschaft und
dessen Begründung in der Zeit zwischen den Welkriegen », in Hans G. Kippenberg,
Brigitte Luchesi, éds., *Religionswissenschaft und Kulturkritik* (Marburg, diagonal, 1991),
p. 243–258.

[81] R. Pettazzoni, « La Storia delle Religioni », *Enciclopedia Italiana* 29 (1936), p. 32,
col. 2 : « sempre più autonoma e scevra d'interferenze extrascientifiche ».

le programme de revitalisation néo-païenne devenu nazi. L'explicite de Pettazzoni était en revanche beaucoup plus neutre que celui du professeur allemand, mais non sans rapprochement avec quelques écrits d'Eliade (à partir de ses articles légionnaires,[82] de ses tribulations politiques en Roumanie, à Londres et finalement au Portugal et ensuite, à partir du septembre 1945, à Paris).

Pour comparer les comparatistes Pettazzoni et Eliade, on peut rappeler leurs liaisons avec Jakob Wilhelm Hauer, titulaire de la chaire de l'Université de Tübingen et fondateur de la *Deutsche Glaubensbewegung*, mouvement d'un néo-paganisme qu'indiquait à Pettazzoni, déjà en 1938, aussi en 1945, la crise religieuse de l'Allemagne nazifiée. Avec Hauer, Eliade entre en correspondance d'une manière très confuse, en lui écrivant de l'Inde en 1929.[83] Hauer serait cité après Surendranath Dasgupta sur la première page du *Yoga* de 1936. Ce livre inconnu à vrai dire même en Roumanie ou en France finit avec une phrase qui n'est assurément pas la conclusion de l'indianiste : « on se libère de la mort en mourant ».[84] Un mois avant, on pourrait lire la même opinion dans le livre troglodyte de Moța,[85] légionnaire mort au même moment en Espagne avec son collègue Marin (qu'Eliade connaissait personnellement depuis 1925 !), l'objet du premier article légionnaire publié par Eliade en 1937, qui spécule sur la mort en tant que « belle obsession virile ». Ni belle, ni virile, la mort a toujours restée le fond d'inflation obsessionnel de la Légion, allant jusqu'à interpréter le tremblement de

---

[82] Les articles politiques d'Eliade étaient disposés à entretenir la primauté de la guerre et de l'extase comme Ernst Jünger le faisait dans *Der Kampf als inneres Erlebnis* (Berlin, 1926, p. 53); sur ce point, voir Walther Müller-Seidel 1998, p. 104.

[83] Țurcanu, *Mircea Eliade*, p. 115 et 130 (2005, p. 160 et p. 178). Sur Hauer, aussi Gregory Alles, « The Science of Religion in a Fascist State : Rudolf Otto and Jakob Wilhelm Hauer during the Third Reich », *Religion* 32 (2002), p. 177–204.

[84] En page 311; la fin a été radicalement changée, voire réécrite en 1954.

[85] L'occultiste guénonien Tuliu, personnage à demi caractère autobiographique du roman *Viață nouă* [Vie nouvelle] commencé à Oxford en 1940 et abandonné au Portugal deux ans plus tard, allant revoir Nae Ionescu lors de son cours à l'université en 1935, rencontre dans l'amphithéâtre un Ion Moța auréolé, « surtout ces dernières années où la Légion commençait à être connue à Bucarest aussi ». Le soir, Tuliu raconte l'épisode à son amie clairvoyante Nușa qui lui dit que Moța va mourir sous peu, et d'une mort violente. Il s'agit d'un projet romanesque où, pour Eliade, « évidemment, la tragédie légionnaire jouera le rôle essentiel » (note du journal du roman, le 1er novembre 1940). De Moța, à Oxford, Eliade se rappelle les deux phrases mentionnées dans les articles de 1937–1938 où il mentionnait les deux combattants en Espagne. Voir Mircea Eliade, *Viața nouă* (Bucarest, Jurnalul literar, 1999), p. 115–116, p. 158 et p. 203.

terre dévastateur du 10 novembre 1940 comme un avertissement divin pour n'avoir pas encore vengé la mort de Codreanu.[86]

Eliade n'était pas le seul qui avait cherché en Roumanie et à partir d'une science circonscrite de comprendre l'actualité, de s'impliquer ainsi : la diversité des positions à l'intérieur de cette justification était considérable.[87] Eliade semble avoir ainsi participé de manière synchronique (comme le faisait aussi ailleurs)[88] à une collecte d'opinions politiques somme toute funestes pour son travail. Mais « après la guerre », rappelle Dumézil dans ses entretiens, « il vint à Paris, démuni et calomnié par les Roumains du nouveau régime »[89] : mais ces Roumains avaient plusieurs orientations politiques, comme ses amis et collègues, et la calomnie insistait sur son passé politique, son contact et ses connexions légionnaires notamment. Il n'était pas non plus un simple anti-communiste détesté, à son honneur, par certains citoyens de la République Populaire Roumaine : il était suivi par des accusations d'un autre combat, d'où il est sorti en effet avec beaucoup de chance (ce qu'il répète à plusieurs reprises en commencent avec le *Journal lusitain*).[90] Dans une lettre du 15 octobre 1948 à un bon ami de la période portugaise, Brutus Coste, le

---

[86] D'après l'un de ceux qui ont assassiné Iorga le 29/30 novembre 1940, voir Nicholas Nagy-Talavera, *Nicolae Iorga. A Biography* (Iaşi, The Romanian Cultural Foundation – The Center for Romanian Studies, 1996), p. 424.

[87] A la même époque, Mircea Djuvara (1886–1944), juriste et philosophe du droit, a été invité par Sextil Puşcariu à l'Institut roumain de culture de Berlin en 1942. Il a donné des conférences également aux Université de Berlin, Vienne et Marburg, où « les réalités historiques d'une communauté concrète » étaient subsumées par Djuvara à une sorte de « Volksgemeinschaft », pour expliquer, à partir de ce terme et non sans évoquer le fascisme italien, le fondement du droit positif du people roumain par l'idée de « nation » (*naţiune*). Voir M. Djuvara, *Eseuri de filosofie a dreptului* [Essai de philosophie du droit], éd. N. Culic (Bucarest, Trei, 1997), p. 318–319.

[88] Pour nous maintenir aux exemples non encore discutés, en 1935 et 1937 Eliade écrivait deux librettos sagace sur l'alchimie asiatique, qui ont présagé une incorporation du sujet parmi les objectifs de l'historien des religions. On peut le considérer un pionnier, mais un qui coïncidait avec les besoins de recherche exprimés, quant aux manuscrits alchimiques, par e.g. l'Union Académique Internationale, qui recommandait : « La Commission adresse un pressant appel aux jeunes orientalistes pour qu'ils s'intéressent à ce genre de travaux », cf. *Compte rendu de la dix-septième session annuelle du compte (11–14 mai 1936)*, Bruxelles, secrétariat administratif de l'U.A.I., 1936, p. 21.

[89] Georges Dumézil, *Entretiens avec Didier Eribon* (Paris, Gallimard, 1987), p. 94. Les dénonces et les calomnies à des ingrédients divers se sont succédé plusieurs années, et Eliade les craignait même en Amérique et en 1952, lors de la traduction d'un de ses livres (lettre du 20 décembre 1952 à Brutus Coste, ibid., p. 521). Eliade ajoutait : « Je ne suis pas fait pour la politique, ni même pour celle de vitrine ».

[90] Mircea Eliade, *Diario portugués (1941–1945)*, traducción del rumano de Joaquín Garrigós (Editorial Kairós, Barcelona, 2001), passim.

dédicataire du *Mythe de l'éternel retour*: « Quant à moi, je me suis résigné.
Je sais qu'il n'y a rien qui soit maintenu pur jusqu'à moi. En 1938,
j'ai adhéré à la Garde de Fer pour la mémoire de Moţa, pour voir en
1940 une garde dirigée par de haïdouks, gens de rien (*haimanale*) et semi
doctes, en compromettant même le souvenir de l'idéal de Moţa. C'est
ainsi « l'Histoire » – et ainsi j'opte pour la Métaphysique ».[91]

Le sens de « l'historien des religions généraliste » et les rapprochements fascistes

« La propagande 'néo-païenne' dans l'Allemagne nouvelle est certes
un phénomène intéressant pour l'historien des religions », écrivait
G. Dumézil dans son *Mythes et dieux des Germains*, livre publié en 1939
(p. 153). *La confession des péchés* pettazzonienne restait, en 1937, une synthèse inachevée, sans plonger dans l'analyse de ce morphème religieux
en site chrétien.[92] La confession comme thématique et typologie restait
symboliquement inachevée, et ce qui peut nous intéresser ici est « la
confession négative » (c'est-à-dire: après la mort, grâce à une invocation
des morts et aux procédures stipulées afin de permettre de poursuivre
non seulement la faute, mais aussi son expiation).

Deux correspondances de Ioan Petru Culianu connues depuis peu,
celle avec son maître après la publication de la monographie de 1978,[93]
et celle avec son ami Gianpaolo Romanato, permettrons de mieux saisir

---

[91] Mircea Eliade à Brutus Coste, Paris, le 15 octobre 1948, lettre publiée dans Mircea
Eliade, *Europa, Asia, America... Corespondenţă*, éd. Mircea Handoca, vol. III (Bucarest,
Humanitas, 2004), p. 475 sans mentionner si la source, la *Hoover Institution* de Stanford University, en a approuvé la publication. Eliade ajoutait: « Les légionnaires, eux
non plus ne font pas signes de sagesse politique. (...) J'ai intoxiqué mes jours [mi-am
otrăvit zilele] plaidant une formule de transition, sans résultat. (Mais je ne renonce
pas encore. Au risque d'être considéré « traître », j'essaierai de les convaincre/ouvrir
leur têtes [să le deschid capetele] ». Une semaine avant que la Roumanie devienne une
« république populaire », Eliade écrit toujours à Coste: « L'entrée en clandestinité de
l'entière opposition roumaine transforme tout le pays dans une Garde de Fer quelques
peu plus terroriste et moins bien organisée par rapport à son archétype de 1938–1939.
Comment se venge-t-elle l'histoire! » (ibid., p. 463).
[92] Gandini, « Raffaele Pettazzoni 1935 », p. 205–207 publie toutefois un résumé
d'un possible quatrième volume, jamais paru, traitant de « religions modernes (au
sens typologique ») . C'est ici peut-être une raison pour les historiens du christianisme
occidental comme Jean Delumeau (*L'aveu et le pardon*, Paris, Fayard, 1990) de ne pas
mentionner son travail pionnier, encore à exploiter.
[93] Eliade réponds à Culianu dans plusieurs lettres, notamment celle du 17 janvier
1978, Culianu-Eliade 2004 (108 lettres dont 70 appartenant à Eliade) et Eliade-Culianu
2004, p. 343–346.

la position d'Eliade.[94] Culianu racontait à Romanato, parmi les avatars de la publication de son premier livre, la résistance d'Eliade de ne pas répondre à certaines questions touchant à sa période bucarestoise. Il s'agissait, pour Eliade, d'une impossibilité d'attaquer le sujet de la Légion de Codreanu «après Buchenwald et Auschwitz», l'objectivité (qu'Eliade met par ailleurs en guillemets) étant impossible même pour l'historien honnête, et même dangereuse. On voit comment, d'après le raisonnement même d'Eliade, sa réponse était incomplète et ses raisons étaient ailleurs. Si «après Auschwitz» avait un sens pour Eliade, un sens qui déterminait son propre silence, pourquoi la première phase, qu'il croit pourtant encore «mystique», «entièrement spirituelle» de la Légion, n'aurait-elle pas été, elle aussi, perçue comme un mouvement d'extrême droite au sens stricte du terme?[95]

Le 9 novembre 1978, Culianu confesse à son collègue et ami italien son désespoir d'être entré dans une problématique que lui transfère regrettablement Eliade.[96] Plus tard, il parlera d'une «légende noire» d'Eliade.[97] Avec Matei Călinescu (son ancien professeur à l'Université de

---

[94] Version originale dans Sorin Antohi, éd., *Religion, Fiction, and History. Essays in Memory of Ioan Petru Culianu*, 2 vols. (Bucarest, Nemira, 2001), vol. I, p. 74–152, traduction roumaine (S. Antohi, éd., *Ioan Petru Culianu. Omul si opera*, Iasi-Bucarest, Polirom, 2003), p. 101–161 (34 lettres de 1978–1987).

[95] Parmi les plus délicats moments de ce que țurcanu nomme «l'impossible aveu» on doit noter la perspective historique d'après laquelle Eliade répond aux questionnements épistolaires de Culianu: «Je ne crois pas qu'il est possible d'écrire une histoire objective du mouvement légionnaire, ni un portrait de C.[orneliu] Z.[elea] C.[odreanu]. Les documents à l'appui sont insuffisants. Ce qui plus est, une attitude 'objective' peut être fatale à l'auteur. Aujourd'hui, ne sont acceptées que les apologies (pour un petit nombre de fanatiques, de toutes les nations) ou les exécutions (pour la majorité des lecteurs européens et américains. Après Buchenwald et Auschwitz, même les honnêtes gens ne peuvent pas se permettre d'être 'objectifs'» (*Dialoguri întrerupte. Corespondența Mircea Eliade – Ioan Petru Culianu* [Dialogues interrompus. Correspondance Eliade-Culianu], édition et notes par Tereza Culianu-Petrescu et Dan Petrescu, préface de Matei Călinescu, Iasi-Bucarest, Polirom, 2004, p. 126; aussi Robert S. Ellwood, *The politics of myth: a study of C.G. Jung, Mircea Eliade and Joseph Campbell*, Albany, Suny, 1999, p. 91). Quoi qu'il en soit, cette phrase résonne avec l'article «Meditație asupra arderii catedralelor» [Méditation sur l'incendie des cathédrales], *Vremea* du 7 février 1937, où il compare les pillages communistes et nazis ayant l'opinion que «Lucifer est en totale liberté seulement à l'Est»: «*Sine ira et studio*... Je ne sais si on peut écrire encore, aujourd'hui, et sur des circonstances comme celles-là, *sine ira et studio*».

[96] Lettre à G. Romanato dans Antohi, *Religion, Fiction, and History*, vol. I, p. 116–120 (traduction roumaine, p. 133–136).

[97] Lettre à G. Romanato du 19 septembre 1984, dans Antohi, *Religion, Fiction, and History*, vol. I, p. 141 («la 'leggenda nera'»; traduction roumaine, p. 152), se référant probablement à son article «Mircea Eliade und die blinde Schildkröte» in Hans Peter Duerr, *Die Mitte der Welt* (Frankfurt a.M., Suhrkamp, 1984), p. 216–243.

354   EUGEN CIURTIN

Bucarest) et Wendy Doniger, avait l'intention de publier aux Etats-Unis, en 1988, tous les articles politiques d'Eliade aptes à focaliser et expliquer les dimensions de la question, trop variables et, fautes de sources fiables et d'examen historiographique pertinent et exhaustif, scandant depuis trois décennies une exégèse internationale et/ou roumaine dépourvue d'homogénéité et sans des conclusions nettes pour l'historien qui n'est pas politiquement affilié.[98]

«Corneliu Codreanu a fait de moi un Roumain fanatique» notait Eliade le 1er décembre 1942 dans son journal.[99] Il tiendrait toutefois confesser à Culianu en 1977 qu'il n'étais «jamais antisémite ou filonazi»,[100] caractéristiques de la Légion en débat fervent parmi ses amis légionnaires lors de son dernier passage à Bucarest en juillet 1942.[101] Encore après, invité par l'ambassadeur allemand à Lisbonne au nom de Walther Wüst, dans un contexte nébuleux, à l'inauguration de l'Institut Sven Hedin à Munich en 1943,[102] Eliade montre dans son journal lusitain qu'il gardait des relations parmi les milieux scientifiques nazifiés.

Il est pourtant clair qu'Eliade juge le destin de la Garde de fer avec

---

[98] La réalisation de cette édition n'a jamais été publiée; voir Thérèse Culianu-Petrescu, «Ioan Petru Culianu: A Biography», in Antohi, *Religion, Fiction, and History*, vol. I, p. 46 (traduction roumaine, p. 71); Matei Călinescu, *Despre Ioan P. Culianu și Mircea Eliade. Amintiri, lecturi, reflecții* [Souvenirs, lectures, réflexions], 2e éd. (Iasi-Bucarest, Polirom, 2002), p. 20 et p. 31–32.

[99] «Pero Corneliu Codreanu hizo de mí un fanático rumano», Eliade, *Diario portugués*, p. 62; Țurcanu, *Mircea Eliade*, 2003, p. 242 (2005, p. 312).

[100] Mihail Sebastian, *Journal 1935–1944* (Paris, Stock, 1998, édition incomplète; édition roumaine Bucarest, Humanitas, 1996). Recensant l'édition américaine (Chicago, 2000) de ce *Journal*, B. Rennie écrit: «Still, inaction, opportunism and self-preservation are not rabid, virulent or strident anti-Semitism, even when they unquestionably contribute to the spread of such evil», in *Religion* 33 (2003), p. 175. Voir Radu Ioanid, *The Sword of Archangel* (New York: Columbia University Press, 1990). Seulement en 2004 les autorités roumaines ont établie une journée pour la commémoration du Holocauste et l'enquête historiographique préparée par la *Commission Elie Wiesel* et portant sur l'implication des autorités roumaines et la sorte des Juifs de Roumanie avant et pendant la guerre paraîtra sous peu.

[101] Pendant les discussions du juillet 1942 à Bucarest avec tous ses amis («todos mis amigos») de *Criterion* (sauf Mihail Sebastian), Eliade note une «réplique violente de Mircea [Vulcănescu] accusant la Légion de créer un nouveau dreyfusisme» (*Diario portugués*, p. 42–43).

[102] Eliade, *Diario portugués*, p. 72 (13 janvier 1943); Mihaela Timuș, *Corespondența Mircea Eliade – Stig Wikander*, p. 73–74. Il s'agit du *Sven-Hedin-Reichsinstitut für Zentral-*(ou *Inner-*)*asienforschung* dirigé par le zoologue Ernst Schäfer (1910–1992). L'invitation pour les cérémonies munichoises du 13–20 janvier 1943, où l'ouverture combine Bach et le recteur nazi Walther Wüst, est publiée par Hartmut Walravens, éd., *W.A. Unkrig (1883–1956) Korrespondenz mit Hans Findeisen, der Britischen Bibelgesellschaft und anderen über Sibirien und den Lamaismus* (Wiesbaden, Harrassowitz, 2004), p. 162–164.

ses compétences herméneutiques d'historien des religions,[103] car le 4 octobre 1945, justement arrivé à Paris, il note une analyse personnelle du mouvement légionnaire qu'il avait présenté à Eugène Ionesco. Pour Eliade,

> comme victime de la mort violente, la Garde s'est transformée dans un revenant/vampire [*strigoi*].[104] Il ne peut pas se reposer, soit dans une tombe, soit dans l'histoire. Avec le sang des Légionnaires et des ceux tués par les Légionnaires, le revenant/vampire a continué à 'vivre'. Cela doit finir ; c'est-à-dire, être intégré (…). La psychiatrie cure les asthénies et les troubles neurales en aidant le patient d'intégrer dans sa personnalité certains conflits, traumatismes, obsessions, etc., qui font de sa vie un échec. Il faut que nous procédions de la sorte, par l'intégration des traumatismes, des injuries, des erreurs, des crimes, des frénésies de la Garde – et de les dépasser. Il ne s'agit pas de clore le procès, mais d'un acte créatif de volonté et compréhension.[105]

La médicalisation du passé s'opérait, pour Eliade, à travers le diagnostic de l'historien des religions. Le thème du sacrifice, thème ethnicisé et politisé de la Légion, est aussi un thème de son travail d'historien des religions,[106] comme, on l'a vu, celle de la mort. Mais « la morte violente »

---

[103] Cette perspective a été partiellement pressentie par Culianu dans la refonte française de 1983 de sa monographie : « Est-ce qu'il a jamais eu Eliade de l'admiration pour Codreanu ? (…) Son intérêt devait avoir eu quelque chose de professionnel et de détaché. » Ion Petru Culianu, *Mircea Elide* (Assisi: Cittadella Editrice, 1978 ; édition roumaine avec de textes inédits, Bucarest, Nemira, 1995), p. 235.

[104] Il y a ici évidemment un renversement de perspective par rapport à l'article « Strigoii… » [Les vampires] publié par Eliade dans *Cuvântul* du 21 janvier 1938.

[105] Le passage a été signalé et traduit par Matei Călinescu, « The 1927 Generation in Romania: Friendship and Ideological Choices (Mihail Sebastian, Mircea Eliade, Nae Ionescu, Eugène Ionesco, E.M. Cioran)», *East European Politics and Society* 15-3 (2001), p. 649–677, ici p. 668–669: «Returning to the discussion of the Guard, I tell him that this problem must be laid to rest once for all. After the death of Codreanu and the other leaders, the Guard became a vampire. Indeed, we have witnessed a strange case of vampirism. The attempt has been made to keep alive an organism that had been assassinated. As the victim of a violent death, the Guard turned into a vampire. It cannot rest, either in the grave or in history. With the blood of the Legionaries or of those killed by the Legionaries, the vampire has continued to 'live'. This must be brought to end; that is, integrated. (…) Psychiatry cures asthenias and neuroses by helping the patient to integrate into his personality certain conflicts, traumas, obsessions, etc., which make his life a failure. We must proceed likewise, by integrating the traumas, the injuries, the mistakes, the crimes, the frenzies of the Guard, – and move on. This is not a question of closing the trial but of a creative act of will and understanding».

[106] Plus récemment Cristiano Grottanelli, « Fruitful Death: Mircea Eliade and Ernst Jünger on Human Sacrifice, 1937–1945», *Numen* 52-1 (2005), p. 116–145. La mise à mort de Ana, femme du Maître Manole, interprétée comme sacrifice de fondation, a

est aussi une section d'un article qu'il publie dans le dernier volume de *Zalmoxis*.[107] La «mort violente» devait figurer, comme annoncé, parmi les sujets d'un livre sur la *Mythologie de la mort*, jamais écrit (projet de la fin des années '30).[108] Il ne s'agit pas d'une contamination entre biographie et discours scientifique, mais d'un cheminement de pensée qui a, pour Eliade, ses analogies. Ainsi,

> le *fait* du meurtre par violence, et le plus souvent par ruse, d'un être innocent et supérieur, semble dès lors entraîner la *création* d'une plante. (...) L'on en pourrait tirer certaines conclusions. La mort naturelle n'est pas créatrice; d'un être extraordinaire seulement, dont on tranche brusquement le cours de la vie, quelques chose peut 'naître'. Une vie de cette qualité consommée incomplètement dans la condition humaine du héros veut se prolonger sous une autre forme: de plante, d'arbre, de fleur.

Pour ajouter immédiatement, en signe de différence: «nous n'affirmons certes pas que cette idée, telle du moins que nous venons de la formuler, soit le fondement des légendes et des contes qui nous préoccupent. Il s'agit bien moins d'idées (...) que de mythes».[109] «La mort violente» est à rappeler dans ce contexte politique, car on conserve le pendant

---

ses parallèles dans la mort rituel d'un juif (ou d'un tsigane), ou par l'enterrement de son ombre, attestée par un certain nombre de croyances est-européennes signalées par Andrei Oişteanu, «Ritual and Symbolic Genocide in Central and Eastern Europe», *Archaeus* 5–3/4 (2001), p. 33–43.

[107] «5. La 'mort violente'», dans «La mandragore et les mythes de la 'naissance miraculeuse'», *Zalmoxis* 3 (1942) [1943], p. 30–38 (*Zalmoxis* 2000, p. 396–402). Le passage est un peu différemment repris en 1949 (voir *Traité d'histoire des religions*, § 113), mais cette dernière forme figure déjà dans la rédaction roumaine intermédiaire du *Traité* (Bibliothèque de l'Académie roumaine, Ms 5926, chap. 4, § 20), datant de 1944. Une continuation se retrouve dans *Mythes, rêves et mystères* (Paris, Gallimard, 1957). Un article de *Buna vestire* [«L'Annonciation»] du 14 janvier 1938 répète que «la mort [de Moţa et Marin] a fructifié».

[108] Eliade, *Diario portugués*, p. 27–28 (plan du 12 janvier 1942); M.L. Ricketts «The Tangled Tale of Eliade's Writing of *Traité d'histoire des religions*», *Archaeus* 4–4 (2000), p. 51–77, ici, p. 56; Ciurtin, éd., *Zalmoxis*, p. 9, n. 19. Dans un texte de 1953, Eliade admet une contradiction quant à la date: «rien n'a été publié de *Mythologies de la mort*, commencé en 1938...», mais *La mademoiselle Christina* (1936) dérive de ce livre; voir Mircea Eliade, *Les moissons du solstice. Mémoires II (1937–1960)*, traduit du roumain par Alain Paruit (Paris, Gallimard, 1988), p. 270 et p. 272. Son cours traitait du même problème, comme il l'écrivait à Pettazzoni le 23 juin 1936: «je m'occupe ces derniers temps des représentations de la mort chez les Roumains et leur ancêtres» (Spineto, *Mircea Eliade, Raffaele Pettazzoni*, p. 113).

[109] Eliade, *Diario portugués*, p. 37. Entre 1938 et 1943 Eliade a parlé à plusieurs reprises de son futur livre *La Mandragore. Essai sur la formation des légendes*, jamais paru; pour une discussion, voir Ciurtin, éd., *Zalmoxis*, p. 16–17 et p. 39–40. Il a écrit un premier article en 1933 (il indique dans ses *Mémoires* 1935 comme date du début du livre) et encore en 1951 parlait dans une lettre d'une édition française (chez Payot).

par son journal lusitain : le 12 septembre 1942, après avoir achevé une
refonte de cet article même, il note qu'il a eu «l'intuition d'une nouvelle
interprétation de la mort chez les indo-européens», sans davantage de
précision,[110] et contrastant sur ce point avec la position contemporaine
de Pettazzoni, critique du substrat et se limitant au caractère linguistique
des «indo-européens».[111]

Si Eliade s'oppose aux questions de Scholem, de Culianu et d'autres,
amis, collègues, critiques, Eliade le fait surtout car il ne voit pas dans
l'ouverture du dossier une possibilité raisonnable de le solutionner,
après avoir à lui seul «intégré» la «morte violenta» de la Garde, qu'il
a jugée dans ses *Mémoires* même, avant d'être vampirisé, comme un
mouvement «innocent» (car seulement spirituel), «supérieur» (car
visant la régénération politique) et dont la «morte violenta» entraîne,
quoi qu'il soit – seulement pour lui, un «acte créatif». Au lieu des
plantes comme la mandragore, on a une littérature à clef (*Viaţa nouă*,
fresque inachevée, *La forêt interdite*, plus tard les nouvelles fantastiques), où
«l'intégration» dont il parlait à Ionesco «veut se prolonger», elle aussi,
«sous une autre forme», celle de l'interprétation littéraire camouflée,
solitaire mais «créative», des années de la guerre.

Qui tacet confirmat?

Eliade n'a en tout cas jamais expliqué sa *felix culpa* par les moyens d'Ernst
Jünger, c'est-à-dire comme affinité d'un leader politique funeste pour
son œuvre. Si les journaux jüngeriens remontent au moment où Hitler
était attiré par des écrits de jeunesse comme *Der Arbeiter*,[112] Eliade, moins
précoce, mais décidément plus jeune, a toujours compté ses troubles
parmi ses attractions propres, et non comme une réaction de lecture
provenant, en 1937–1938, des chefs légionnaires. Si ceux-ci possédaient

---

[110] Eliade, *Diario portugués*, p. 45.

[111] Voir la fin de l'article de Pettazzoni, «Per la storia religiosa d'Italia» dans *Ricerche
Religiose* 19–1, 1948, p. 12 : «Come è illusoria l'assegnazione a Barbari e Greci rispetti-
vamente, così conviene guardarsi da una troppo semplicistica ripartizione fra indeuropei
e preindeuropei. Il concetto di 'popol[o] indeuropeo' è un concetto linguistico e non
ci dice, da solo, gran che nel senso storico-culturale».

[112] Voir en outre Ernst Jünger, *Journal de guerre et d'occupation (1939–1948)*, trad. Henri
Plard (Paris, Julliard, 1965), p. 481–483 (note de Kirchhorst, le 2 avril 1946); *Soixante-dix
s'efface. Journal 1971–1980*, trad. Henri Plard, Paris, Gallimard, 1980, vol. 2, p. 285–286
(lettre à Manfred Schwartz sur Hitler, Überlingen, le 29 mai 1977).

des *Strahlungen* tournées en sa direction, ils les avaient épuisées dans les débats avec leurs adversaires démocratiques au moment de campagnes électorales violentes où Eliade figurait comme sympathisant net de la Garde de Fer. Par contre, les données nous obligent à considérer son interprétation immédiate de la Garde comme chapitre d'une nouvelle religiosité dans une histoire culturelle roumaine, européenne et globale, ou au moins de la Garde telle qu'il l'a connue avant la mort de Codreanu.

Ni avant ni après l'acmé de Pettazzoni, en fait, le sens du travail généraliste en histoire des religions n'a eu une plus pleine vigueur, et sur l'échelle des climats religieux, et sur celle chronologique, où il allait jusqu'à la contemporanéité très proche. L'éclosion de ce modèle généraliste de Pettazzoni, qui a avancé aussi ses pièges avant et pendant la guerre, a été héritée par Eliade, mais des nouvelles exigences ont dévié de ce qui semblait pour lui incontournable dans le caractère même de l'histoire des religions et qui, dans la logique de l'accroissement de la discipline, devait rester un moment unique.[113] Les menaces divers de leur modèle sont à l'origine de la véritable critique de leur intérêt pour les religiosités de la société immédiatement et de manière troublante contemporaine. Reconnue comme toujours plus autonome, «insaisissable»[114] ou «en passe de s'émietter»,[115] l'histoire des religions exigera un autre modèle du professionnel qui s'y consacre. Là où il y a compromis chez les deux, pour le maître il s'agissait d'un compromis de maturité, limité et contrôlé, tandis que celui de jeunesse d'Eliade, accusé en conséquence plus tard parmi les «fautes de jeunesse», s'est montré plus nuisible. Au-delà des âges enregistrés par l'histoire des religions, les cultures d'origine fonctionnaient aussi dans la bipolarité maturité-adolescence.

Pourquoi, en fait, cette analyse? Quels sont les résultats d'une telle enquête? On sait très bien, d'une part, qu'aucune démarche scientifique ou humaniste n'a pu traverser l'idéologisation meurtrière de la

---

[113] Pendant des longues décennies, Eliade a voulu interpréter aussi la créativité religieuse du monde moderne et contemporain, sans réaliser le desideratum de l'inclure dans *L'histoire des croyance et des idées religieuses* (pour une interprétation, voir B. S. Rennie, *Reconstructing Eliade. Making Sense of Religion* (Albany, Suny, 1996).

[114] Voir la lettre d'Eliade à Pettazzoni du 2 novembre 1947, dans Spineto, *Mircea Eliade, Raffaele Pettazzoni*, p. 165–166.

[115] Henri-Charles Puech, «Allocution inaugurale», in *Le symbolisme cosmique des monuments religieux. Conférences*, Serie Orientale Roma XIV (Roma, Istituto italiano per il Medio ed Estremo Oriente, 1957), p. 7–16.

seconde guerre mondiale sans enregistrer, de manière assez différente, son immixtion, et aussi qu'il était improbable pour l'histoire des religions de dépasser mieux la fusion explosive des enjeux de l'époque. Pour les généralistes qu'ont été Pettazzoni et Eliade, l'historien des religions a dû rencontrer, s'intéresser à, expliquer – dans ses limites propres et d'après ses méthodes et intuitions – la nouvelle religiosité de leurs pays d'origine, qu'il convient aujourd'hui de verser, dans plus d'un cas, au dossier politique d'une hystérie condamnable. Sans prendre la distance propre à l'historien, tous les deux, à des degrés différents, ont tâché d'interpréter ces religiosités politiques en misant sur la capacité friable de l'histoire des religions, une discipline alors encore très jeune, de rencontrer la plus stricte contemporanéité.[116] Au-delà des faits aujourd'hui connus dans leur grande majorité, notre préoccupation pour cette période doit être vue dans son flux historiographique complet, qui suit le bassin qui se forme de manière capillaire pendant le Grand Siècle[117] et propose un estuaire multiforme dans laquelle naviguent les études encore aujourd'hui. A la sécularisation indispensable à la naissance de l'histoire des religions, on associe le caractère obligatoire de sa maintenance ; le péril des immixtions impropres a ses analogies bien avant et beaucoup après la période trouble des années 1933–1945. Pettazzoni reste ainsi le grand maître, car, comme il l'a bien vu en 1936, « l'autobiographie dérive en grande partie de la confession des péchés ».[118]

---

[116] Son cours de 1935–1936 portait aussi sur l'histoire donc l'historicité de la discipline. Publication de cette cartothèque chez Gandini, *Pettazzoni 1935*, p. 144–145 (« Introduzione. Svolgimento della storia delle religioni » ou bien « Alcune lezioni introduttive sul formarsi di una storia delle religioni »).

[117] Recouvrir une plus ample préhistoire de ces problèmes arrive finalement à considérer le 17e siècle d'un point de vue pour maintes raisons similaires : siècle des guerres de religions qui voit naître une discipline comparative au cœur de l'humanisme européen. Pettazzoni avait utilisé ce terme de « préhistoire » plus tard cher à Eliade (Pettazzoni, « Intorno ad una prolusione », *Studi e materiali di storia delle religioni* 1, 1925, p. 152–154). Pour la dimension de cette préhistoire, voir Pettazzoni, « La Storia delle Religioni », p. 30, col. 2, qui signale « come sintomatica l'opera del teologo anglicano John Spencer » ; voir maintenant Guy G. Stroumsa, « John Spencer and the Roots of Idolatry », *History of Religions* 41-1 (2001), p. 1–23.

[118] Texte de Pettazzoni publié par Gandini (éd.) 1993, p. 67–75 ; Gandini, *Pettazzoni 1935*, p. 170–172, 195.

360 EUGEN CIURTIN

Bibliographie

Alles, Gregory. « The Science of Religion in a Fascist State : Rudolf Otto and Jakob Wilhelm Hauer during the Third Reich ». *Religion* 32 (2002), p. 177–204.

Antohi, Sorin, éd. *Religion, Fiction, and History. Essays in Memory of Ioan Petru Culianu*, 2 vols. Bucarest, Nemira, 2001.

——, éd. *Ioan Petru Culianu. Omul şi opera* [Ion Petru Culianu. L'homme et l'œuvre]. Iasi-Bucarest, Polirom, 2003.

Arcella, Luciano, Paola Pisi, and Roberto Scagno, éds. *Confronto con Mircea Eliade. Archetipi mitici e identità storica*. Milano, Jaca Book, 1998.

Acterian, Arşavir. *Cioran, Eliade, Ionesco*, avant propos de Mihai şora, éd. Fabian Anton. Cluj-Napoca, Eikon, 2003.

Bonnet, Corinne, éd. *La correspondance scientifique de Franz Cumont conservée à l'Academia Belgica de Rome*, Institut historique belge de Rome. Bruxelles-Rome, Diffusion Peeters, 1997.

Călinescu, Matei. « The 1927 Generation in Romania : Friendship and Ideological Choices (Mihail Sebastian, Mircea Eliade, Nae Ionescu, Eugène Ionesco, E.M. Cioran) ». *East European Politics and Society* 15–3 (2001), p. 649–677.

——. *Despre Ioan P. Culianu şi Mircea Eliade. Amintiri, lecturi, reflecţii* [Autour de Culianu et Eliade. Souvenirs, lectures, réflexions], 2e éd. Iasi-Bucarest, Polirom, 2002.

Casadio, Giovanni. « Per Ugo Bianchi. Introduzione ». In idem, éd., *Ugo Bianchi. Una vita per la storia delle religioni*. Roma, Il Calamo, 2002.

Ciurtin, Eugen. « La première revue d'histoire des religions en Roumanie : *Zalmoxis* (1938–1942) de Mircea Eliade ». *Archaeus* 4–1/2 (2000), p. 327–365.

——, éd. *Zalmoxis. Revistă de studii relgioase, sub direcţia lui Mircea Eliade*. Iasi-Bucarest, Polirom, 2000.

——. « Cincizeci de ani în Asia » [Cinquante ans en Asie] et « 'Secretul doctorului Honigberger' : verificarea 'in concreto' » [Le secret du Dr Honigberger : la vérification *in concreto*], dans Johann Martin Honigberger, *Treizeci şi cinci de ani în Orient* [Trente-cinq ans en Orient (1852)], éd. par E. Ciurtin, avant propos de Arion Roşu. Iasi-Bucarest, 2004, p. 11–81 et p. 363–440.

——. *Histoire des études indiennes en Europe occidentale et orientale. Quatre conférences à l'École Pratique des Hautes Études* (à paraître).

Culianu, Ioan Petru. *Mircea Eliade*. Assisi: Cittadella Editrice, 1978. Édition roumaine avec de textes inédits, Bucarest, Nemira, 1995 (2e éd., Iasi-Bucarest, Polirom, 2002).

——. *Dialoguri întrerupte. Corespondenţa Mircea Eliade – Ioan Petru Culianu* [Dialogues interrompus. Correspondance Eliade-Culianu], édition et notes par Tereza Culianu-Petrescu et Dan Petrescu, préface de Matei Călinescu, Iasi-Bucarest, Polirom, 2004.

Demiéville, Paul. « Nécrologie. Henri Maspero (1883–1945) ». *Journal Asiatique* 234 (1943–1945), p. 245–280.

Ellwood, Robert S. *The politics of myth: a study of C.G. Jung, Mircea Eliade and Joseph Campbell*. Albany, Suny, 1999.

Eliade, Mircea. « Elemente preariene în hinduism [Éléments pré-aryens dans l'hindouisme] ». *Revista Fundaţiilor Regale* 3–1 (1936), p. 149–173.

——, éd. *Zalmoxis. Revue des études religieuses*, vol. I–III. Bucarest, Imprimeriile Naţionale – Paris, Librairie Orientaliste Paul Geuthner, 1938–1942.

——. *De Zalmoxis à Gengis Khan*. Paris, Payot, 1970.

——. *Les moissons du solstice. Mémoires II (1937–1960)*, traduit du roumain par Alain Paruit. Paris, Gallimard, 1988.

——. *I riti del costruire. Commenti alla Leggenda di Mastro Manole. La Mandragola e i miti della 'Nascita miracolosa'. Le erbe sotto la Croce*. Milano, Jaca Book, 1990.

——. *Diario portugués (1941–1945)*, traducción del rumano de Joaquín Garrigós. Barcelona, Editorial Kairós, 2001.

——— et Ioan Petru Culianu. «The correspondance between Mircea Eliade and Ioan Petru Culianu», notes by Tereza Culianu-Petrescu and Dan Petrescu, forword by Matei Călinescu. *Archaeus* 8–1/4 (2004), p. 341–364.

Filliozat, Jean. «Les origines d'une techniques mystiques indienne». *Revue philosophique* 1946, p. 208–220.

Flasche, Rainer. «Der Irrationalismus in der Religionswissenschaft und dessen Begründung in der Zeit zwischen den Welkriegen». In Hans G. Kippenberg, Brigitte Luchesi, éds., *Religionswissenschaft und Kulturkritik*. Marburg, diagonal, 1991, p. 243–258.

Gandini, Mario. «Il punto sugli studi pettazzoniani (1987)». *Strada Maestra* 23–2 (1987), p. 151–162.

———, éd. «Raffaele Pettazzoni: Interpretazione religiosa di Pirandello ('Non si sa come')». *Ariel. Quadrimestrale di dramaturgia dell'Istituto di Studi Pirandelliani e sul Teatro Italiano Contemporaneo* 8–1 (1993), p. 67–75.

———. «Raffaele Pettazzoni nell'anno cruciale 1912». *Strada Maestra* 36–37 (1994), p. 177–298.

———, «Raffaele Pettazzoni (1883–1959): '…La mia via, la mia verità, la mia vita…'. Discorso tenuto nell'Università di Roma il 3 febbraio 1959». *Strada Maestra* 38–39 (1995), p. 371–392.

———. «Raffaele Pettazzoni nel primo dopoguerra (1919–1922)». *Strada Maestra* 44–1 (1998), p. 97–214.

———. «Raffaele Pettazzoni dall'incarico bolognese alla cattedra romana (1922–1923)». *Strada Maestra* 45–2 (1998), p. 157–241.

———. «Raffaele Pettazzoni negli anni del noviziato universitario romano (1924–1925)». *Strada Maestra* 46–1 (1999) p. 77–223.

———. «Raffaele Pettazzoni negli anni 1926–1927». *Strada Maestra* 47–2 (1999), p. 95–226.

———. «Raffaele Pettazzoni negli anni 1928–1929». *Strada Maestra* 48–1 (2000), p. 81–249.

———. «Raffaele Pettazzoni nelle spire del fascismo (1931–1933)». *Strada Maestra* 50–1 (2001), p. 19–183.

———. «Raffaele Pettazzoni dal gennaio 1934 all'estate 1935». *Strada Maestra* 51–2 (2001), p. 81–212.

———. «Raffaele Pettazzoni intorno al 1935». *Strada Maestra* 52–1 (2002), p. 99–268.

———. «Raffaele Pettazzoni negli anni 1937–1938». *Strada Maestra* 54–1 (2003), p. 53–232.

———. «Raffaele Pettazzoni negli anni 1939–1940». *Strada Maestra* 55–2 (2003), p. 121–271.

———. «Il Fondo Pettazzoni della Biblioteca comunale 'G.C. Croce' di San Giovanni in Persiceto (Bologna)». *Archaeus. Études d'Histoire des Religions* 7–3/4 (2003), p. 293–298.

———. «Raffaele Pettazzoni nei primi anni Quaranta (1941–1943)». *Strada Maestra* 56–1 (2004), p. 93–279.

———. «Raffaele Pettazzoni dall'estate 1943 alla primavera 1946». *Strada Maestra* 57–2 (2004), p. 21–199.

———. «Raffaele Pettazzoni dall'estate 1946 all'inverno 1947–1948». *Strada Maestra* 58–1 (2005), p. 53–249.

Grottanelli, Cristiano. «Mircea Eliade, Carl Schmitt, René Guénon, 1942». *Revue de l'histoire des religions* 219 (2002), p. 325–356.

———. «Fruitful Death: Mircea Eliade and Ernst Jünger on Human Sacrifice, 1937–1945». *Numen* 52–1 (2005), p. 116–145.

Junginger, Horst. *Von der philologischen zur völkischen Religionswissenschaft. Das Fach Religionswissenschaft an der Universität Tübingen von der Mitte des 19. Jahrhunderts bis zum Ende des Dritten Reiches*. Stuttgart, Franz Steiner, 1999.

——. «Das Überleben der Religionswissenschaft im Nationalsozialismus». *Zeitschrift für Religionswissenschaft* 9 (2001), p. 149–167.

——. «Das 'Arische Seminar' der Universität Tübingen 1940–1945», in Heidrun Brückner, Klaus Butzenberger, Angelika Malinar, Gabriele Zeller, éds., *Indienforschung im Zeitenwandel. Analyse und Dokumente zur Indologie und Religionswissenschaft in Tübingen*. Tübingen, Attempto Verlag, 2003, p. 177–207.

Lincoln, Bruce. *Theorizing Myth. Narrative, Ideology, and Scholarship*. Chicago-London, University of Chicago Press, 1999.

Mander, Pietro. «60 anni da 'Cosmologia e alchimia babilonesi'». In Luciano Arcella, Paolo Pisi et Roberto Scagno, éds., *Confronto con Mircea Eliade : archetipi mitici e identità storica*. Milano, Jaca Book, 1998, p. 219–238.

Navrátilová, Hana, et Roman Míšek. «Alois Musil and the Rise of Czech Oriental Studies: A Perspective of a Non-classical Orientalism». *Archív Orientální* 70–4 (2002), p. 558–564.

Nikitine, Basile. «Réminiscences polono-orientales (Notes autobiographiques)», *Folia Orientalia* 2–1/2 (1960), p. 153–176.

Oişteanu, Andrei. «Ritual and Symbolic Genocide in Central and Eastern Europe». *Archaeus* 5–3/4 (2001), p. 33–43.

——. *Imaginea evreului în cultura română. Studiu de imagologie în context est-central european* [2001], 2e éd. Bucarest, Humanitas, 2004 (éd. anglaise, *The Imaginary Jew in Romanian Culture*, préface de Moshe Idel, Nebraska, University of Nebraska Press, à paraître).

——. «Mircea Eliade between Political Journalism and Scholarly Work». *Archaeus* 8–1/4 (2004), p. 323–340.

——. *Religie, politică şi mit. Texte despre Mircea Eliade şi Ioan Petru Culianu* [Religion, politique et mythe. Textes sur M. E. et I. P. C.], 'Biblioteca Ioan Petru Culianu', Iasi, Polirom, 2007.

Pettazzoni, Raffaele. «Intorno ad una prolusione». *Studi e materiali di storia delle religioni* 1 (1925), p. 152–154.

——. «Recherches sur la confession des péchés (résumé)». In Paul-Louis Couchoud, éd., *Congrès d'histoire du christianisme. Jubilé Alfred Loisy*, tome I. Paris, Rider/Amsterdam, Holkema & Warendorf, 1928, p. 96–98.

——. «La religione nazionale del Giappone e la politica religiosa dello Stato giapponese». *Nuova Antologia*, 1 Giugno 1929, p. 3–19.

——. «Religione e politica religiosa nel Giappone moderno», Roma, IsMEO, 1934, p. 5–17.

——. «La Storia delle Religioni». *Enciclopedia Italiana* 29 (1936), p. 29–33.

——. «Confessions of Sins in Hittite Religion». In Bruno Schindler [et A. Marmorestein], éd., *Occident and Orient being Studied in Semitic Philology and Literature, Jewish History and Philosophy and Folklore in the widest sense. In Honour of Haham Dr. M. Gaster 80th Birthday (Gaster Anniversary Volume)*. London, Taylor's Foreign Press, 1936, p. 467–471.

——. «La Confession des péchés dans l'histoire des religions». *Annuaire de l'Institut de Philologie et d'Histoire Orientales et Slaves. Mélanges Franz Cumont* 4 (1936), p. 893–901.

——. «La confession des péchés: méthodes et résultats». *Scientia*, avril 1937, p. 1–6.

——. «A Functional View of Religions». *The Review of Religion* 1–3 (1937), p. 225–237.

——. «Gli studi storico-religiosi in Italia». *Civiltà fascista* 5–3 (1938), p. 3–6.

——. «De probitate: Carlo Alfonso Nallino». *Nuova Antologia*, 1 Aprile 1939, p. 253–258.

——. «Criteri per l'ordinamento scientifico del VII congresso internazionale di storia delle religioni». *Atti della Reale Accademia d'Italia. Rendiconti della Classe di Scienze Morali e Storiche* 7, vol. 2, 1–5 (1940), p. 1–3.

——. «Orientamenti attuali dell'Africanistica». *Atti dell'VIII Convegno tema: l'Africa, Roma, 4–11 Ottobre 1938–XVI*, Roma, Reale Accademia d'Italia, 1940, p. 5–11.

——. «Antichi culti solari nella penisola Balcanica». *Rivista d'Albania* 2–2 (1941), p. 109–114 (tiré à part p. 3–8).

——. «Per la storia religiosa d'Italia» *Ricerche Religiose* 19–1 (1948), p. 1–12.

——. *Italia religiosa*, Bari, Laterza, 1952.

——. «Socialismo e cultura storico-religiosa». In idem, *Religione e società*, a cura di Mario Gandini. Bologna, Ed. Ponte Nuovo, 1966, p. 173–179.

Puech, Henri-Charles. «Allocution inaugurale». *Le symbolisme cosmique des monuments religieux. Conférences*, Serie Orientale Roma XIV, Roma, Istituto italiano per il Medio ed Estremo Oriente, 1957, p. 7–16.

Rennie, Bryan S. *Reconstructing Eliade. Making Sense of Religion*. Albany, Suny, 1996.

——, éd. *Changing Religious Worlds. The Meaning and End of Mircea Eliade*. Albany, Suny, 2001.

Ricketts, Mac Linscott. *Mircea Eliade : The Romanian Roots (1907–1945)*. East European Monographs vol. 248, 2 vols. Boulder, Colorado, East European Monographs, 1988.

——. «The Tangled Tale of Eliade's Writing of *Traité d'histoire des religions*». *Archaeus* 4–4 (2000), p. 51–77.

——. «Eliade and Goethe». *Archaeus* 6–3/4 (2002), p. 283–311.

——. *Former Friends and Forgotten Facts*. Norcross, GA, Criterion Publishing, 2003.

Sebastian, Mihail. *Journal 1935–1944*. Paris, Stock, 1998 (éd. roumaine complète Bucarest, Humanitas, 1996; trad. anglaise New York, 2001).

Severino, Valerio Salvatore. «Giovanni Gentile e Raffaele Pettazzoni (1922–1924). Un carteggio sulla storia delle religioni e l'università in Italia». *Storiografia* 6 (2002), p. 107–126.

Smith, Jonathan Z. «Acknowledgements: Morphology and History in Mircea Eliade's *Patterns in Comparative Religion* (1949–1999) [I–II]». *History of Religions* 39–4 (2000), p. 315–351.

Spineto, Natale, éd. *Mircea Eliade, Raffaele Pettazzoni. L'histoire des religions a-t-elle un sens ? Correspondance 1926–1959*, édition originale par Natale Spineto, préface de Michel Meslin. Paris, Éditions du Cerf, 1994.

Timuş, Mihaela, éd. *Întotdeauna Orientul. Corespondenţa Mircea Eliade – Stig Wikander (1948–1977)* [C'est toujours l'Orient. Correspondance Eliade-Wikander]. Iasi-Bucarest, Polirom, 2005.

Trevisi, Giuseppe. «Religione dello stato e religione dell'uomo in *Italia religiosa* di Raffaele Pettazzoni». *Strada Maestra* 12 (1979), p. 49–55.

Ţurcanu, Florin. *Mircea Eliade: Le prisonnier de l'histoire*, préface de Jacques Julliard. Paris, La Découverte, 2003 (éd. roumaine légèrement revue: *Mircea Eliade. Prizonierul istoriei*, avec une préface de Zoe Petre. Bucarest, Humanitas, 2005).

Walravens, Hartmut, éd. *W.A. Unkrig (1883–1956) Korrespondenz mit Hans Findeisen, der Britischen Bibelgesellschaft und anderen über Sibirien und den Lamaismus*. Wiesbaden, Harrassowitz, 2003.

Wasserstrom, Steven. *Religion after Religion. Gershom Scholem, Mircea Eliade and Henry Corbin at Ascona*. Princeton, Princeton University Press, 1999.

RAFFAELE PETTAZZONI AND THE HISTORY OF RELIGIONS IN FASCIST ITALY (1928–1938)

Michael Stausberg[1]

Raffaele Pettazzoni (1883–1959), who had lost his Catholic faith during his studies in Bologna but who would never lose his interest in religious matters, clearly stands out as one of the towering figures of the history of the history of religions in the 20th century.[2] Through his numerous scholarly works[3] Pettazzoni contributed to shaping the scientific identity of the discipline.[4] Moreover, Pettazzoni was instrumental to establishing lasting elements of the discipline's scholarly infrastructure both on an international and a national scale. For example, from 1950 to his death Pettazzoni served as the second president (after Gerardus van der Leeuw) of the International Association for the Study of the History of Religions (later International Association for the History of Religions)[5] and he was among the founders of the review *Numen* and

[1] I wish to express my sincere gratitude to Giovanni Casadio (Faenza, Roma, Salerno) for a good number of corrections, comments, and references.
[2] Sadly, Pettazzoni is not listed as one of the classics of the discipline in the otherwise useful anthology edited by Axel Michaels, *Klassiker der Religionswissenschaft. Von Friedrich Schleiermacher bis Mircea Eliade* (München: C.H. Beck, 1997).
[3] For Pettazzoni's scholarly bibliography see Mario Gandini, "Nota bibliografica degli scritti di Raffaele Pettazzoni," *Studi e Materiali di Storia delle Religioni* 31 (1960), pp. 3–21; idem, "Il contributo di Raffaele Pettazzoni agli studi storico religiosi," *Strada maestra* 2 (1969), pp. 1–48; idem, "Presenza di Pettazzoni," *Strada maestra* 3 (1970), pp. 1–69.
[4] For some of the more recent assessments of his scholarly work see Mario Gandini, "Pettazzoni, Raffaele," *Encyclopedia of Religion*, 2nd ed., vol. 10 (2005), pp. 7072–7077; Giuseppe Mihelcic, *Una religione di libertà. Raffaele Pettazzoni e la Scuola Romana di Storia delle Religioni*. Premessa di Piero Coda, prefazione di Carlo Prandi (Roma: Città Nuova, 2003); Riccardo Nanini, "Raffaele Pettazzoni e la fenomenologia delle religione," *Studia Patavina* 50 (2003), pp. 377–413; Natale Spineto, "Raffaele Pettazzoni e la comparazione, fra storicismo e fenomenologia," *Storiografia* 6 (2002), pp. 27–48; Natale Spineto, "Raffaele Pettazzoni e la verità del mito," *Rivista di storia della storiografia moderna* 17 (1996), pp. 59–65; Michael Stausberg, "Pettazzoni, Raffaele," *Theologische Realenzyklopädie* 26 (1996), pp. 319–324; Paola Pisi, "Storicismo e fenomenologia nel pensiero di Raffaele Pettazzoni," *Studi e Materiali di Storia delle Religioni* 56 (1990), pp. 245–277; Ugo Casalegno, *Dio, esseri supremi, monoteismo nell'itinerario scientifico di Raffaele Pettazzoni* (Torino: Lit. Coggiola, 1979).
[5] See also Ugo Bianchi, "Raffaele Pettazzoni e la I.A.H.R.," *Strada maestra* 12 (1979), pp. 11–18 [= *Studi e Materiali di Storia delle Religioni* 49 (1983), pp. 21–28].

the corresponding book-series *Studies in the History of Religions* (in which
this volume is published!). In Italy, Pettazzoni had already founded
several book series (*Storia delle religioni* 1920ff.; *Testi e documenti per la storia
delle religioni* 1929ff.) and a journal (*Studi e Materiali di Storia delle Religioni*
1925ff.).[6] It is probably no exaggeration to claim that the coming into
existence of the history of religions (*storia delle religioni*) as a non-con-
fessional academic discipline in Italy would probably be unimaginable
without the passionate and enthusiastic efforts of Pettazzoni,[7] whose life
was equally devoted to the development of the discipline as that of his
long-time correspondent and admirer Mircea Eliade.[8]

Compared to Eliade, however, Pettazzoni's fame is not overshad-
owed by political accusations. Quite on the contrary, Pettazzoni even
enjoys the reputation of having been an 'anti-fascist' (see below). If it
is agreed that the successful establishment of the history of religions in
Italy is in great part due to Pettazzoni's efforts, the question may also
be permitted whether the fascist government did not in the first place
provide the fertile ground that would allow Pettazzoni's efforts to bear
fruit. As a matter of fact, the lasting institutional establishment of the
history of religions in Italy occurred soon after the fascist government
was established in October 1922.[9]

---

[6] See Pier Angelo Carozzi, "Prima della fondazione di SMSR," *Strada maestra* 12
(1979), pp. 19–28; Giulia Piccaluga, "SMSR. Una rivista, un metodo, una scuola,"
Strada maestra 12 (1979), pp. 29–37.

[7] For the history of the discipline in Italy see also Georg Dörr and Hubert Mohr,
"Religionswissenschaft und Kulturwissenschaft. Die 'Schule von Rom' und die deutsche
Religionswissenschaft des zwanzigsten Jahrhunderts." In Christoph Auffarth and Jörg
Rüpke, eds., *Epitome tes oikumenes. Studien zur römischen Religion in Antike und Neuzeit für Hubert
Cancik und Hildegard Cancik-Lindemaier* (Stuttgart: Franz Steiner, 2002), pp. 263–284.

[8] The correspondence between the two stretched over more than three decades.
See Natale Spineto, *Mircea Eliade/Raffaele Pettazzoni: L'histoire des religions a-t-elle un sens?
Correspondence 1926–1959* (Paris: Les Éditions du Cerf, 1994). On Eliade see also the
papers of István Keul and Eugen Ciurtin in this volume.

[9] Valerio Salvatore Severino, "Giovanni Gentile e Raffaele Pettazzoni (1922–1924).
Un carteggio sulla storia delle religioni e l'università in Italia," *Storiografia* 6 (2002),
pp. 107–126 has thrown light on the circumstances of Pettazzoni's appointment. I
owe a reference and a Xerox of Severino's paper to Cristiano Grottanelli. For earlier
attempts at establishing the discipline (since the late 1880s) see Paolo Siniscalco, "Gli
insegnamenti storico-religiosi nell'Univsersità di Roma. Origini e primi sviluppi." In
G. Sfameni Gasparro ed., *Agathe elpis. Studi storico-religiosi in onore di Ugo Bianchi* (Roma:
L'Erma di Bretschneider, 1994), pp. 149–170; Pier Angelo Carozzi, "L'introduzione
della storia delle religioni nell'insegnamento universitario italiano. Il contributo di
Umberto Pestalozza e di Tomaso Gallarti Scotti," *Studi e Materiali di Storia delle Religioni*
49 [= NS 7] (1983), pp. 389–415.

The Establishment of the Roman Chair

Since 1914, Pettazzoni had been teaching the history of religions at the University of Bologna. The academic year 1919–20 was the first and only time his teaching assignment was reimbursed. Apparently for lack of funds, in 1920, the Italian minister of education (who happened to be Benedetto Croce at the time!) decided that Pettazzoni had to teach for free again.[10]

In the same year, an application by his faculty in Bologna for an opening in the history of religions was approved by the "Consiglio Superiore della Publica Istruzione," but the ministry did not take any action to implement that decision.[11] In autumn 1922 – when the matter was still pending –, upon initiative of the influential philosopher Giovanni Gentile, who at that time was professor of philosophy at the University of Rome,[12] the decision was made to create the chair at 'his' university instead of Bologna.[13]

Pettazzoni had recently got in touch with Gentile by sending him a review copy of his recent book on the development of monotheism in the history of religions.[14] Soon afterwards, on September 20, 1922, Gentile published a critical review of Pettazzoni's book in *La critica* (vol. 20, pp. 298–301), but interestingly his academic critique of Pettazzoni's approach by stressing the need for a concept of religion as a starting-point of the endeavour did not prevent him from personally supporting Pettazzoni.[15] Already in his first letter to Pettazzoni, Gentile expresses his hopes that Pettazzoni would soon get the position that

---

[10] See Severino, "Giovanni Gentile e Raffaele Pettazzoni," p. 113 (nn. 5 and 6).

[11] Ibid., p. 113.

[12] For a survey of recent research on Gentile see Gabriele Turi, "Giovanni Gentile: Oblivion, Remembrance, and Criticism," *Journal of Modern History* 70 (1998), pp. 913–933. See also A. James Gregor, *Giovanni Gentile. Philosopher of Fascism* (New Brunswick: Transaction Publishers, 2001).

[13] At least Gentile claims that this was due to his own initiative (in a letter to Pettazzoni, dated October 19, 1922), published by Severino, "Giovanni Gentile e Raffaele Pettazzoni," p. 121. In this letter, Gentile argues that Rome was more suitable because of the many belated studies available at the university.

[14] Raffaele Pettazzoni, *Dio. Formazione e sviluppo del monoteismo nella storia delle religioni. Vol. 1: L'essere celeste nelle credenze dei popoli primitivi* (Roma: Atheneum, 1922).

[15] In a way, then, the topic of the 1990 congress of the IAHR ("The Notion of 'Religion' in Comparative Research") that was arranged by Pettazzoni's student Ugo Bianchi brought that heritage full circle.

he deserved.[16] Subsequently, Gentile assumed the role of Pettazzoni's benefactor, and Pettazzoni would several times in his letters appeal to him in that capacity. Gentile became a particular powerful patron when, on October 31, 1922, Mussolini appointed him to serve as minister of education ("Pubblica Istruzione", later changed to "Educazione Nazionale") for his first government.[17] In this new capacity, Gentile was in a position to push Pettazzoni most efficiently. Already in late December 1922, the post in the history of religions at the University of Rome was advertised – Gentile informed Pettazzoni already two days in advance –, and hardly a year later, on December 2, 1923, Pettazzoni was appointed as extraordinary professor on the newly created Roman chair.[18] In a letter to Gentile, Pettazzoni ascribed the (for him) happy outcome of the proceedings to Gentile's intervention on his behalf.[19] That this was more than mere private flattery is evidenced by the fact that Pettazzoni publicly devoted the printed version of his programmatic inaugural lecture that he held on January 17th, 1924,[20] to Gentile as "the minister who would create the first Italian chair in the History of Religions in Rome."[21] Of course, it ultimately remains a matter of speculation whether the chair would eventually have been instituted (either in Bologna or Rome) and whether Pettazzoni would have been appointed to that chair if Mussolini had not come into power; the fact remains that things happened because of Pettazzoni's rapports with Gentile and Gentile's position in Mussolini's government.

---

[16] Gentile to Pettazzoni on July 21, 1922 (Severino, "Giovanni Gentile e Raffaele Pettazzoni," p. 112).

[17] Gentile joined Mussolini's National Fascist Party PNF (Partito Nazionale Fascista) half a year later, in May 1923.

[18] See Severino, "Giovanni Gentile e Raffaele Pettazzoni," p. 125, n. 39.

[19] Pettazzoni to Gentile on December 20, 1923: "...sento di doverLe esprimere, ora che la battaglia è vinta, tutta la mia gratitudine, perché a Lei debbo se ho potuto combatterla, e, nonostante gli intrighi degli avversari, riportare piena vittoria", Severino, "Giovanni Gentile e Raffaele Pettazzoni," p. 124 ("I feel the duty to express my sincerest gratitude to you, now that the battle has been won, because I owe it to you that I was in a position to fight it [the battle] in the first place, and to report victory despite the intrigues of the adversaries." Trans. mine).

[20] Raffaele Pettazzoni, *Svolgimento e carrattere della storia delle religioni* (Bari: Laterza, 1924), reprinted (with some typos) in Sonia Giusti, *Storia e mitologia. Con antologia di testi di Raffaele Pettazzoni* (Roma: Bulzoni, 1988), pp. 352–376. This lecture is in part a reaction to Gentile's criticism.

[21] "A Giovanni Gentile ministro che volle istituita in Roma la prima cattedra italiana di Storia delle Religioni", see Severino, "Giovanni Gentile e Raffaele Pettazzoni", p. 125f. (also with reference to an interview in the journal *L'Impero* where Pettazzoni once again publicly praised Gentile).

The story, however, does not finish with the establishment of Pettazzoni's chair. For subsequent to Pettazzoni's appointment, the discipline witnessed an astonishing blossoming at Italian universities. Nobody expressed the positive effects that the fascist government would have on the development of the history of religions in Italy with greater clarity than Pettazzoni himself. In a paper contributed to the review *Civiltà fascista* and published in 1938 (see also below), Pettazzoni states:

> La Storia delle Religioni è entrata nel nostro insegnamento universitario, ufficiale e definitivamente, dopo l'avvento del Fascismo, con la istituzione della cattedra di Roma nel 1923. Oggi è professata, a titolo ufficiale, nelle Facoltà di lettere delle Università di Roma, Milano, Cagliari, Firenze, Pisa, Padova; ed è compresa fra gli insegnamenti delle Facoltà di Genova, Napoli, Palermo e Catania.[22]

Looking back in 1938, Pettazzoni can thus – and be it only for reasons of rhetoric, flattery, or propaganda – trace a truly remarkable development: In a country where the discipline had previously been virtually absent (ignored or suppressed),[23] within 15 years after the takeover of fascism it was officially established at six universities and taught at ten.[24] For a historian, this situation raises many questions. In what follows, however, I shall focus on the person Raffaele Pettazzoni and try to analyze his way of maneuvering under the political circumstances.

This task is facilitated by the fact that we have at our disposal what is probably the most extensive biography of a historian of religions ever written. Since 1989, the local historian Mario Gandini, in his capacity as the former (now retired) director of the public library "G.C. Croce"

---

[22] Raffaele Pettazzoni, "Gli studi storico-religiosi in Italia," *Civiltà fascista* 5 (1938), pp. 194–197, p. 194 ("The History of Religions has officially and definitely entered our university teaching after the advent of fascism, with the establishment, in 1923, of the chair in Rome. Nowadays, it is officially taught at the faculties of arts at the universities of Rome, Milan, Cagliari, Florence, Pisa, and Padova. Moreover, it is included in the syllabus of the universities of Genoa, Naples, Palermo, and Catania." Trans. mine.).

[23] But see n. 9 above.

[24] The passage quoted above obscures the fact that the history of religions was established as an ordinary chair at three universities. At the remaining universities, the discipline was not taught on a permanent basis. Hence, Aldo Natale Terrin, "The Study of Religions in Italy. Some Data and Reflections." In Johannes G. Platvoet and Gerald A. Wiegers, eds., *Modern Societies & the Science of Religions. Studies in Honour of Lammert Leertouwer* (Leiden: Brill, 2002), pp. 373–387, p. 374 may be right when he states that "the history of religions as a discipline fully entered into the academic study of Italian Universities in the 1960s." As a matter of fact, it is at that time when the students of Pettazzoni would occupy the major chairs. Terrin, "The Study of Religions in Italy," p. 375 regards Pettazzoni as "the true inspirator of the history of religions in Italy."

and director of its review *Strada maestra* in Pettazzoni's place of birth, San Giovanni in Persiceto (situated roughly between Modena and Bologna), has published a series of extremely rich and long articles providing "materials for a biography of Raffaele Pettazzoni" (as the subtitle reads). The articles are provided with extensive, carefully compiled, and very useful bibliographical references. In these articles, Gandini follows Pettazzoni's life on a year to year – and sometimes on a day to day – basis. In this truly remarkable and unique work, Gandini reconstructs almost every aspect of Pettazzoni's life that has left traces in the available sources. The articles document Pettazzoni's readings (professional and leisure) and other research work, his leisure and professional travels, his lectures, courses, his correspondence, his involvement in publication projects, each and every of his scholarly publications (including their genesis and their reception in form of reviews and letters), his institutional work (including meetings), his financial situation, his acquaintances with colleagues (belonging to almost all intellectual and political camps), his relationships with his family and his girlfriend (whom he, much to her despair, married only many years after she had already dedicated her life to him), and opinions that other people uttered about Pettazzoni (including statements about Pettazzoni in works of reference). In this article, I shall gratefully exploit that mine of information. The reason why this article focuses on the decade stretching from 1928 to 1938 is that professor Gandini has generously put at my disposal copies of the relevant issues of *Strada maestra* (published between 2000 and 2003) that contain his articles covering those years of Pettazzoni's life.[25] The period covered here is thus framed by two events that are relevant in our context: the Lateran Treaty in 1929 and the Racial Legislation in 1938.

---

[25] See Mario Gandini, "Raffaele Pettazzoni negli anni 1928–1929. Materiali per una biografia," *Strada maestra* 48 (2000), pp. 81–249; idem, "Raffaele Pettazzoni intorno al 1930. Materiali per una biografia," *Strada maestra* 49 (2000), pp. 141–254; idem, "Raffaele Pettazzoni nelle spire del fascismo (1931–1933). Materiali per una biografia," *Strada maestra* 50 (2001), pp. 19–183; idem, "Raffaele Pettazzoni dal gennaio 1934 all'estate 1935. Materiali per una biografia," *Strada maestra* 51 (2001), pp. 81–212; idem, "Raffaele Pettazzoni intorno al 1935. Materiali per una biografia," *Strada maestra* 52 (2002), pp. 99–268; idem, "Raffaele Pettazzoni negli anni 1937–1938. Materiali per una biografia," *Strada maestra* 54 (2003), pp. 53–232.

An Anti-Fascist Servant of the Fascist State?

As mentioned earlier, Pettazzoni enjoys the reputation of having been an 'anti-fascist'. Indeed, from his earlier biography it seems that nothing points to any fascist leanings of Pettazzoni and that he remained committed to the socialist ideas of his student years. Is that, however, enough to claim that he actually was an 'anti-fascist'?

Found in the articles covering the years 1928 to 1938, the documentation provided by Gandini contains several explicit statements pointing in that direction.[26] To begin with, in a late paper Arnaldo Momigliano in passing categorically refers to "Pettazzoni who was an anti-fascist".[27] Obviously, for Momigliano Pettazzoni's 'anti-fascism' was a fact that did not require any further elaboration. It goes without saying Momigliano's is an important testimony.[28]

Gandini's articles contain two other written testimonies, both however of a private nature. For one, there is a letter by Pettazzoni's brother who referred to Pettazzoni's ideas as being "contrary to fascism."[29] Secondly, Tullia Romagnoli, who studied under Pettazzoni in the later 1930s, wrote to Gandini in 1996 saying:

---

[26] Apart from the sources mentioned in what follows, Gandini himself sometimes comes up with some statements about Pettazzoni's non-fascism; see, e.g., "Raffaele Pettazzoni intorno al 1935," p. 147: "Pettazzoni, quanto a gradi di temperatura fascista, è sotto lo zero...".

[27] Arnaldo Momigliano, "Per la storia delle religioni nell'Italia contemporanea: Antonio Banfi ed Ernesto De Martino tra persona e apocalissi," *Rivista storica italiana* 99 (1987), pp. 435–456, p. 441: "Pettazzoni, che era antifascista". In the same paper, Momigliano creates a causal link between Pettazzoni's laicism and his commitment to the historical study of religion: "Laico nel profondo, e storico della religione [sic: Momigliano uses the singular here] appunto perché laico..." (p. 440).

[28] The reliability of Momigliano's statement, however, needs to be qualified as he himself was sympathetic to fascism until he was expelled from the country. Pettazzoni had a high esteem of his younger colleague's scholarly capacities and several times he tried to advance Momigliano's scholarly career. By way of example, in 1934/35 he tried to obtain a prize for Momigliano, see Giorgio Fabre, "Arnaldo Momigliano: autobiografia scientifica (1936)," *Quaderni di storia* 41 (1995), pp. 85–94, p. 86. Momigliano, "Per la storia delle religioni nell'Italia contemporanea," p. 441 recalls Pettazzoni's generosity ("la generosità che gli era caratteristica"). Giovanni Casadio who knew Momigliano personally comments that Momigliano later always proudly referred to his friendship with Pettazzoni.

[29] Gandini, "Raffaele Pettazzoni nelle spire del fascismo (1931–1933)," Giuseppe writes to Raffaele: "...tu essendo contrario colle tue idée al fascismo..." In this letter, his brother (who was living in London) was worried that he could harm his anti-fascist brother by adopting British citizenship.

> Ma da Pettazzoni io non imparai solo la storia delle religioni. Esso fu per noi giovani, nel fascismo, un maestro di democrazia e libertà. Lo ricordo insistere sul tema della libertà e poi via che qualcuno di noi maturava e si orientava farsi più esplicito. Molti di noi – ed io fra questi – se divenimmo antifascisti lo dobbiamo anche a Pettazzoni.[30]

The question arises whether these statements *about* Pettazzoni are corroborated by any direct statements *by* Pettazzoni or by any actions of distancing from, if not resistance to, any of the political actions undertaken by the fascist government.[31] To be brief, I did not find any evidence for that in the exhaustive body of materials provided by Gandini, at least for the decade under scrutiny. If he did take a distance from the regime at all, than this must have happened silently.

Moreover, even if we have every reason to assume that he did so against his own convictions, as almost everybody else Pettazzoni performed all the acts of confession of public loyalty to the fascist government that were expected of him as an employee of the Italian state. As required by a law passed in August 1931, on November 20 of the same year, Pettazzoni publicly professed his loyalty to the King and his successors and to the fascist Government and his commitment to educate citizens in the spirit of devotion to the fatherland and the fascist regime.[32] There are no signs of resistance on Pettazzoni's side. Clearly, any such public heroic proclamation of his anti-fascist ethos would have cost him his job and although he could probably have quite easily found a position abroad he would have had to renounce everything that he had built up in terms of institutional achievements over

---

[30] Gandini, "Raffaele Pettazzoni nelle spire del fascismo (1931–1933)," p. 132 ("But from Pettazzoni I did not just learn the history of religions. During fascism, for us youngsters he was a teacher of democracy and freedom. I remember him insisting on the topic of freedom and that he got more explicit when some of us little by little found their way. Many of us, and I among them, if we happened to turn into anti-fascists, then this happened also thanks to him." Trans. mine.).

[31] It seems that the postwar political authorities were not immediately convinced that Pettazzoni was an anti-fascist, for on December 18, 1944, Pettazzoni was informed that he, together with 54 colleagues, was deferred to the commission for the "cleansing" of the employees at the university. Fortunately for him, his friend, the (church) historian Luigi Salvatorelli, a pronounced anti-fascist, happened to be appointed as "Commissario Aggiunto della Commissione." Salvatorelli revoked any measures against Pettazzoni, see Mario Gandini, "Raffaele Pettazzoni dall'estate 1943 alla primavera 1946. Materiali per una biografia," *Strada maestra* 57 (2004), pp. 21–200 (non vidi; references kindly provided by Giovanni Casadio).

[32] For the circumstances see Gandini, "Raffaele Pettazzoni nelle spire del fascismo (1931–1933)," pp. 38–40.

the past years. His anti-fascism did not stretch as far as to commit that sacrifice (for him and 'his' discipline). As a matter of fact, in the whole of Italy only twelve professors refused to take the oath of fidelity to the fascist regime.[33] Remarkably, three of them were eminent colleagues of Pettazzoni at the Roman faculty of arts: Ernesto Buonaiuti (history of Christianity), Gaetano De Sanctis (ancient history), and Giorgio Levi Della Vida (oriental studies). Pettazzoni decided not to follow suit.

But that wasn't all. Two years later, Pettazzoni had to, or decided to (depending on the moral perspective), perform a further act of obedience. In 1933, each and every civil servant, including the university professors, was required to apply for membership in the National Fascist Party (PNF). Gandini speculates that Pettazzoni may have experienced some pressure and that some 'friend' may have suggested to him that he owed the establishment of his chair to a fascist Minister.[34] However that may have been, on July 31, 1933, our anti-fascist took the decisive step and became a member of the party.[35] Nevertheless, it seems that he did not participate in any party activities, nor did he wear the black shirt.[36] In a private note from June 1945 Pettazzoni articulates some excuses for that fateful decision: He felt that antifascism had been practically disbanded and was inexistent at the time, and the only way to get rid of the fascist regime would have been by means of a foreign power.[37] Amongst his old, like-minded friends Pettazzoni's decision was controversial: While it was resented by one if not several, another one (Giuseppe Calzati) found that Pettazzoni had never been attracted by fascism and that Pettazzoni even was a victim of the regime's attempt to benefit from his international fame.[38] Judging from the materials compiled by Gandini, however, it seems that Pettazzoni never made any, not even modest, attempts to exploit this symbolic capital in order to influence political decisions in the non-academic sphere.

---

[33] See Helmut Goetz, *Der freie Geist und seine Widersacher. Die Eidverweigerer an den italienischen Universitäten im Jahre 1931* (Frankfurt am Main: Haag und Herchen, 1993); Giorgio Boatti, *Preferirei di no. Le storie dei dodici professori che si opposero a Mussolini* (Torino: Einaudi, 2001).

[34] See Gandini, "Raffaele Pettazzoni nelle spire del fascismo (1931–1933)," p. 132.

[35] Ibid., p. 132.

[36] Ibid., p. 132.

[37] Quoted by Gandini, "Raffaele Pettazzoni nelle spire del fascismo (1931–1933)," p. 132 ("nel '33 l'antifasc.o era sbandato, inesistente. / Il fasc.o poteva essere abbatutto solo dall'esterno, cioè con una guerra perduta").

[38] See Gandini, "Raffaele Pettazzoni nelle spire del fascismo (1931–1933)," p. 132.

In 1938, a racist campaign was started by the fascist regime and racial legislation was passed and enforced.[39] As a consequence, it was impossible for people of Jewish descent to work at Italian universities. First, all the institutions had to perform a 'racial census' of their own organisations that would pave the way for the expulsion of the Jewish intellectuals. Recent research has shown "that, among the members of Italy's roughly 150 cultural institutes, only two individuals – Benedetto Croce and Gaetano De Sanctis – refused to co-operate."[40] In November 1938, around a hundred professors were dismissed. Among them we find several scholars with whom Pettazzoni was on good terms and with some of whom he even entertained amicable relations.[41] That included the Rabbi and Hebraist Umberto Cassuto, the archaeologist Alessandro Della Seta, Arnaldo Momigliano, and Alberto Pincherle, a student of Buonaiuti who taught history of Christianity in Rome and (since 1937) history of religions at Cagliari.[42]

Gandini points out that it would have been simply impossible to voice any public protest – in fact, only Croce publicly protested – or to perform any public act of solidarity with the people concerned.[43] As justified as these observations are, they are of course meant as an excuse that there is no evidence for any such act on the side of Pettazzoni. It should be added that Gandini does not produce any private or unpublished materials in which Pettazzoni condemned the racial politics of the regime.

Not only professors but also assistants and assistant lecturers were subject to the legislations and were 'removed' from the universities. This directly affected Pettazzoni's chair: His extraordinary assistant Paola Franchetti who had taken her doctorate with Pettazzoni in 1936 and who, after a brief period in the United States, had been hired in 1937, was suspended in October 1938 as she 'belonged to the Jewish

---

[39] For recent scholarship on the issue of Italian antisemitism and the response by Italians to Mussolini's anti-Jewish campaign see Stefano Luconi, "Recent Trends in the Study of Italian Antisemitism under the Fascist Regime," *Patterns of Prejudice* 38 (2004), pp. 1–17. See also Roberto Finzi, *L'università italiana e le leggi antiebraiche. Seconda edizione* (Roma: Editori riuniti, 2003, 1st ed. 1997).

[40] Luconi, "Recent Trends in the Study of Italian Antisemitism under the Fascist Regime," p. 6 with a reference to Annalisa Capristo, *L'espulsione degli ebrei dalle accademie italiane* (Torino: Zamorani, 2002).

[41] See Gandini, "Raffaele Pettazzoni negli anni 1937–1938," p. 189 where some further names are listed.

[42] On Pincherle's rapports with Pettazzoni see Gandini, "Raffaele Pettazzoni dal gennaio 1934 all'estate 1935," p. 87.

[43] Gandini, "Raffaele Pettazzoni negli anni 1937–1938," p. 189.

race' (*appartenente alla razza ebraica*).[44] Pettazzoni tried to interest his colleague Arthur D. Nock in her, but nothing seems to have resulted from this initiative. One year later, he tried to get Franchetti admitted to the reading rooms of the library and in 1944/45 he assigned her the task to translate texts from English into Italian for a publication he was preparing.[45] Franchetti's dismissal paved the way for the Italian career of the young Hungarian scholar Angelo Brelich, who became Pettazzoni's assistant in 1939 and who would later on become Pettazzoni's successor on the chair.[46]

A Fruitful Working Relationship

As mentioned above, Pettazzoni's chair was established by the fascist government shortly after it had come to power. Giovanni Gentile, Pettazzoni's benefactor, eventually was dismissed as minister of education in 1924. In February 1925, the "Istituto Giovanni Treccani" was founded in Rome. It was named after the industrialist who sponsored its work. The institute was to publish a national encyclopedia, the *Enciclopedia Italiana* (modelled on the Britannica and other 'national' encyclopedias). The task of acting as the 'scientific director' of the encyclopedia was assigned to Gentile who in his turn appointed a 'technical committee' consisting of around 50 scholars covering what Gentile

---

[44] Ibid., p. 209.
[45] Ibid., p. 133.
[46] The 'irony' of his appointment was not lost on Brelich, see Angelo Brelich, *Storia delle religioni: perché?* (Napoli: Liguori, 1979), p. 31. In order to obtain his position as an assistant, Brelich had to produce his membership card of the National Fascist Party, see Gandini, "Raffaele Pettazzoni negli anni 1937–1938," p. 209. Brelich does not comment on this in his autobiography. Maybe he was not overtly concerned with that step because it seems that he was close to right-wing ideas in that period of his life anyhow. At least there is evidence that Brelich, who later became an outspoken leftist, was under the influence of Julius Evola at that time. In that connection, Giovanni Casadio draws my attention to Brelich's papers "Antica spiritualità eroica," *Regime fascista* (*Diorama filosofico quindicinale*, diretto da Julius Evola), February 25, 1937 and "Giove e l'idea romana dello Stato," *Regime fascista*, January 18, 1940 (non vidi). Interestingly, even Dario Sabbatucci (1923–2003), a later exponent of the scuola di Roma (founded by Pettazzoni), had right-wing sympathies, see Gianni Scipione Rossi, *La destra e gli ebrei. Una storia italiana* (Soveria Mannelli: Rubbettino, 2003), pp. 175–179. His colleague Enrico Montanari, who now holds a chair in the history of religions, contributed to the journal *Occidentale* that was published by Sabbatucci's 'Circolo dei Selvatici', see Rossi, *La destra e gli ebrei*, p. 176, n. 43. Giovanni Casadio drew my attention to Rossi's book when it was first published.

perceived to be the relevant academic disciplines. Interestingly, this also included the history of religions for which Pettazzoni was assigned responsibility. In that capacity he did editorial work including the revision of incoming contributions, and he recruited contributors and wrote a good number of articles himself.[47] Neither all of the members of the 'technical committee' were fascists, nor all of the authors, nor were all articles colored by fascist ideology.[48] That, however, is not necessarily a sign of 'tolerance',[49] nor must it obscure the fact that the project of the *Enciclopedia Italiana* was part of the overall scheme of " 'fascism of culture' – a culture that was not intended to remain within the party but that was supposed to bring all of Italy's cultural expressions within the embrace of fascist principles."[50] Pettazzoni faithfully played his role in that scheme.[51]

While the political direction that the government would take was not clear when Mussolini came to power in late 1922, by 1925 the political stance taken by the fascist government was pretty clear, and Gentile had clearly emerged as Italy's "leading fascist ideologue."[52] In 1925, Gentile's former companion, Benedetto Croce, "arguably the world's best known anti-fascist,"[53] who, like many intellectuals, had first "adopted a wait-and-see attitude...committed himself unequivocally to opposition."[54] Maybe out of a sense of gratitude and loyalty towards the man whom

---

[47] In his biographical essays, Gandini provides an extensive coverage of Pettazzoni's time-consuming work for the *EI*. The *EI* also contained an entry on Pettazzoni (vol. 25, 1935, p. 65f.).

[48] Classical antiquity, for instance, was confided to Gaetano De Sanctis. Some intellectuals, such as Croce and Luigi Einaudi, however, refused to write for the *Enciclopedia Italiana*, see Turi, "Giovanni Gentile," p. 931.

[49] See Turi, "Giovanni Gentile," p. 931.

[50] Ibid., p. 930. On the *Enciclopedia Italiana* see also Gabriella Nisticò, "Scienze sociali nell'EI." In Giuliana Gemelli, *Enciclopedie e scienze sociali nel XX secolo* (Milano: Angeli, 1999), pp. 220–252; Gabriele Turi, *Il mecenate, il filosofo e il gesuita. L'Enciclopedia italiana specchio della nazione* (Bologna: Il mulino, 2002).

[51] According to Turi, "Giovanni Gentile," p. 931, "the only group within the *Enciclopedia* that managed to stand up against the fascist ideology was the Catholics, under the leadership of Pietro Tacchi Venturi, a Jesuit." Tacchi Venturi was responsible for 'ecclesiastical matters'. Certainly one needs to recall that the Jesuits were not necessarily antithetical to the regime which after all had achieved 'conciliation' with the Catholic Church.

[52] David D. Roberts, "How Not to Think about Fascism and Ideology, Intellectual Antecedents and Historical Meaning," *Journal of Contemporary History* 35 (2000), pp. 185–211, p. 201.

[53] Roberts, "How Not to Think," p. 209.

[54] Ibid., p. 209.

he felt he owed his chair, and maybe because he did not see anything wrong in it – for wasn't the encyclopedia after all primarily a useful project? –, Pettazzoni did not take any visible steps into that direction. He would remain faithful to Gentile and the regime and establish a working relationship that would benefit both parts.[55]

While it must be an unpleasant experience (to say the least) to live under any totalitarian government for anybody apart from the passionate supporters of the system, Pettazzoni himself, it seems, did not personally suffer from the politics of the fascist regime. While Gandini claims that Pettazzoni was forced into some sort of isolation,[56] as a matter of fact, by appointing him as member of the Accademia d'Italia (in 1933), Pettazzoni was promoted to the rank of one of the most illustrious public intellectuals and figureheads of public life in the fascist state.

The Accademia d'Italia had been instituted in 1926 and was officially inaugurated in 1929. Mussolini was present at the opening ceremony, and the founding of the Accademia d'Italia was part of the above-mentioned political scheme to foster the spirit of fascism – in contradistinction from the existing academies, in particular from the ancient Accademia dei Lincei that would maintain its independence from fascism until it was eventually 'fused' in the Accademia d'Italia in 1939.[57] However, in order to legitimate the new institution and to commit eminent personalities to the regime, not only fascists and open sympathizers were nominated as members. Apart from the prestige of being a member of the Academy, the members also obtained some direct and indirect financial benefits.[58] As a member of the Academy, Pettazzoni repeatedly received subsidiaries that allowed him to continue with the publication of 'his' journal, the *Studi e materiali di Storia delle religioni*. In that way, Pettazzoni's membership in the Academy was instrumental to advance the history of religions in Italy.

While Momigliano held that Mussolini nominated Pettazzoni as a non-Catholic counterpart to cardinal Gasparri who was nominated

---

[55] In one way (at least), Gentile's political action was antithetical to Pettazzoni's project, for in the reform of the school system that Gentile had effectuated as minister of education in 1923, he had introduced compulsory religious education – and the religion in question was Catholicism.

[56] Gandini, "Raffaele Pettazzoni intorno al 1930," p. 190. The statement refers to summer 1930.

[57] Pettazzoni became a member of the Accademia dei Lincei in september 1946.

[58] See Gandini, "Raffaele Pettazzoni nelle spire del fascismo (1931–1933)," p. 105f.

at the same time,[59] more recent research has evidenced that Pettazzoni had been ranked second by the scientific evaluation committee,
behind the archaeologist Alessandro Della Seta. Della Seta had already
been ranked first (and not been nominated) in the year before (1932).
In 1932, before ignoring Della Seta's candidacy, Mussolini had even
pointed to Della Seta's imminent nomination (which then did not occur!)
as a proof for the inexistence of antisemitism in Italy![60] As a matter
of fact, no Jew was ever nominated into the Accademia d'Italia, and
hence the way was paved for Pettazzoni who unhesitatingly accepted
the nomination.[61]

As a member of the Accademia d'Italia, the time was soon ripe for
another oath of loyalty. Within the scope of spreading fascist ideology throughout the cultural life of the country, the fascist government
decided in 1933 that the members of all the academies – and that
included the Accademia dei Lincei – had to profess an oath to remain
faithful (*fedele*) to the king, and his successors, and to the fascist regime.
Again, only very few people abstained from, or rejected, the oath.[62]
And, again, Pettazzoni did not belong to that group.

The Project of an International Congress in Italy

As one of Italy's most prestigious intellectuals, even before he was
nominated for the Accademia d'Italia, Pettazzoni regularly attended
the international congresses of the history of religions where he
'represented' his country. His membership in the Accademia d'Italy
facilitated these travels, because it was easier for him to obtain travel
subsidiaries in his capacity as an 'academician'. As a matter of fact,
Pettazzoni had personally paid the expenses for his travels to attend
previous congresses in Paris (Congrès d'histoire du Christianisme: Jubilé
Alfred Loisy, 1927) and London (Jubilee Congress of the Folk-Lore

[59] See Momigliano, "Per la storia delle religioni nell'Italia contemporanea," p. 441.
[60] See Luconi, "Recent Trends in the Study of Italian Antisemitism under the
Fascist Regime," p. 10.
[61] See Gandini, "Raffaele Pettazzoni intorno al 1935," p. 109. There are no traces
in the materials gathered by Gandini that Pettazzoni was ever concerned about the
political implications in his acceptance of the nomination.
[62] See Gandini, "Raffaele Pettazzoni dal gennaio 1934 all'estate 1935," p. 103; see
also Goetz, *Der freie Geist und seine Widersacher.*

Society, 1928), and it took him considerable efforts to procure travel subsidiaries from the government and his university that would enable him to attend the fifth international congress of the history of religions in Lund (1929).[63] In Lund, the international committee decided to have the subsequent congress, scheduled for 1933, in Berlin.[64] Because of Hitler's takeover, however, on rather short notice it was decided to postpone the congress and to have it take place elsewhere.[65] The Norwegian indologist Sten Konow and the holder of the chair in Berlin, Alfred Bertholet, suggested to shift the congress to Rome where it could be held coincidently with the international orientalist congress scheduled for 1935, but the colleague in charge of that congress, Carlo Alfonso Nallino, whom Pettazzoni contacted immediately, was not in favor of such an arrangement. As a result, the idea to move the congress to Rome was eventually dropped.[66]

Instead, the congress was held in Brussels (in September 1935). Pettazzoni got his travel to Brussels sponsored by the government, and in his application he had flatteringly argued that the history of religions had started much later in Italy than in most other countries and that it had been established only thanks to the ascent of fascism. He also obtained the authorization of the government to propose that the subsequent congress (scheduled for 1939) could be held in Italy.[67] At the Brussels congress this proposal was accepted by the international committee.[68] The political circumstances reigning in Italy, it seems, did not irritate the committee – neither in 1935 nor in the following years. Rather, what seems to have caused some concern for some members of the committee – in particular its head, Franz Cumont – was the question whether the Vatican would allow Catholic scholars to attend

---

[63] See Gandini, "Raffaele Pettazzoni negli anni 1928–1929," p. 152f.

[64] Ibid., p. 201.

[65] A letter by the "Deutsche Kongreß-Zentrale" to the Reichsminister für Wissenschaft, Erziehung und Volksbildung dated February 13, 1942, gives the membership of some Jews ("die Mitgliedschaft einiger Juden") as the reason why the conference could not be held in Germany (Barch Berlin R 49.01, 3164, fol. 44; Horst Junginger generously shared a copy of that letter). Neither Horst Junginger nor I could identify the name of the author of that letter.

[66] See Gandini, "Raffaele Pettazzoni dal gennaio 1934 all'estate 1935," p. 103f. From Gandini's materials, it seems that, strangely, political considerations did not make any impact on that decision.

[67] See Gandini, "Raffaele Pettazzoni dal gennaio 1934 all'estate 1935," p. 190.

[68] See Gandini, "Raffaele Pettazzoni negli anni 1937–1938," p. 149.

the congress.[69] In order to avoid problems on that front, it seems, the idea was born to hold the congress not in Rome, but in Bologna.

In spring 1938, Pettazzoni worked on the issue and got in contact with the relevant people. For that matter, he could draw on his network of contacts that he had established in his capacity of one of the most prestigious intellectuals of the fascist state. In March and April he met the national minister of education and the president of the Senate (who happened to be the president of the Accademia d'Italia as well) in order to discuss organizational and financial matters.[70] In July 1938, Pettazzoni received an official letter confirming that the Duce had personally agreed to make £50,000 available for the purpose of the congress[71] – which was around half the amount that Pettazzoni had hoped for.[72] At the same time, the letter invited Pettazzoni to consider the option to postpone the congress to the year 1942, when the 20th anniversary of fascist reign was supposed to be celebrated in great style (in the "E 42", also known as the 'Olympic games of Civilisations').[73] If not postponing the congress, the letter suggested making sure that another international congress of the history of religions would take place in Rome in 1942.[74] Pettazzoni declined both suggestions – viz., to postpone the event and to have another congress in 1942 – for organizational reasons, but at the same time he jumped on the occasion by suggesting that the third international congress of the anthropological and ethnological sciences might be held in Rome in connection with the E 42 in Rome. At the same time, for organizational reasons he suggested postponing the 1939 conference to 1940 (while leaving the question whether to hold it at Rome or Bologna, still undecided).[75] Eventually, the war came in between and put an end to the project.[76]

---

[69] Ibid., p. 149.

[70] Ibid., p. 150.

[71] Ibid., p. 177.

[72] Ibid., p. 150.

[73] Ibid., p. 177. On the E 42 (EUR) see also Tullio Gregory, *E 42, utopia e scenario del regime* (Venezia: Cataloghi Marsilio, 1987).

[74] See Gandini, "Raffaele Pettazzoni negli anni 1937–1938," p. 177.

[75] Ibid., p. 185.

[76] In 1955 Pettazzoni eventually saw his dream of having an international congress taking place at Rome fulfilled. However, there were some obstacles against holding the congress in Rome, see Giusti, *Storia e mitologia*, p. 139f.; Dörr and Mohr, "Religionswissenschaft und Kulturwissenschaft," p. 271; see also Spineto, *Mircea Eliade/Raffaele Pettazzoni*, p. 255.

The way in which Pettazzoni handled the congress project illustrates the economy of prestige that Pettazzoni and the regime involved each other in, where each part could offer what the other lacked. Pettazzoni provided scholarly prestige and the links to an international scholarly community, and having such a conference take place in Rome would have been a propagandistic victory for the regime. Pettazzoni obviously was happy to be part of this political scheme as long as he was not required to compromise on his professional academic standards, and as long as he would obtain the logistical and financial benefits that would help him to go ahead with his mission of fostering the history of religions as an academic discipline (first of all in Italy, but also internationally).

A Fascist Design of the History of Religions and the Myth of Rome

In January 1936, Pettazzoni published the third and final volume of his opus magnum on the confession of sins.[77] Drawing on his extensive network of national and international contacts, he tried to get his work circulated and reviewed as widely as possible. Moreover, he wished to address a wider audience, and in February, he got an extract of the book published by the *Giornale d'Italia*, formerly a liberal newspaper that had been brought in line with fascist ideology since 1926.[78]

Less than a year later, the editor of the *Giornale d'Italia* approached Pettazzoni asking him to contribute to the paper – and Pettazzoni did. On February 28, 1937, on its third page, the newspaper carried an article by Pettazzoni titled "Roma è il centro della storia religiosa" ("Rome is at the center of religious history").[79] Pettazzoni's article has two parts. First, he recounts the rise of the history of religions in fascist Italy, with due homage to Mussolini. Moreover, Pettazzoni states that the further growth of the discipline was only limited by the

---

[77] Raffaele Pettazzoni, *La confessione dei peccati. Parte seconda. Volume terzo. Siria-Hittiti-Asia Minore-Grecia. Indice dei volumi I–III* (Bologna: Zanichelli, 1936).

[78] See Gandini, "Raffaele Pettazzoni intorno al 1935," p. 164; Gandini, "Raffaele Pettazzoni negli anni 1937–1938," pp. 77f.

[79] The draft had a different title ("Storia delle religioni" [history of religions]), see Gandini, "Raffaele Pettazzoni negli anni 1937–1938," p. 78.

scarce availability of qualified scholars to fill prospective positions.[80] In the second part, Pettazzoni suggests Rome to be the central point of reference for the entire history of religions, since Rome offered a perspective that would allow regarding the religious history of mankind from a unified point of view. According to Pettazzoni it was in Rome that the religious history of the ancient world ended and the religious history of the modern world began. Finally, Pettazzoni argues that there is a deep continuity connecting what seems to be antithetic: Paganism and Christianity fascism.[81]

This exaltation of the historical significance of Rome reminds the reader of the myth of Rome that, together with the cult of the Duce, was one of the pillars of the symbolical universe of Italian fascism.[82] Mussolini had referred to Rome as the 'point of reference' of fascism[83] – and Pettazzoni proclaimed it to the 'point of reference' for global religious history. Moreover, the 'mystery of the continuity of Rome' (Mussolini)[84] was another pivotal point for the fascist myth of Rome. Pettazzoni seems to tie up to that motive in his speech with the – possibly significant – omission of the third step in the account of continuity as devised by Gentile, who linked Romanness (*Romanità*), Catholicism, and fascism.[85]

---

[80] In 1935, Pettazzoni was heading the commission evaluating the candidates who had applied for the chair of history of religions at the University of Milan. For the report prepared by the commission see Gandini, "Raffaele Pettazzoni intorno al 1935," pp. 132–138. Interestingly, Pettazzoni himself did not produce any students who would make a lasting impression on the discipline in the 1920s and 1930s. His well-known later students Ugo Bianchi and Vittorio Lanternari studied with him in the 1940s. On Bianchi see the volume edited by Giovanni Casadio, *Ugo Bianchi. Una vita per la storia delle religioni* (Roma: Il Calamo, 2002) which also contains a brief essay comparing Pettazzoni and Bianchi (Sonia Giusti, "Analogia metodologica e contrasti teorici fra Raffaele Pettazzoni e Ugo Bianchi," pp. 393–400). Ernesto de Martino was something like an 'adopted' student of Pettazzoni. It is only since the early 1940s that something like the 'scuola romana' emerged, see also Dörr and Hubert Mohr, "Religionswissenschaft und Kulturwissenschaft," p. 272. For reflections on the achievements (and flaws) of some later exponents of the 'Roman school', see Giovanni Casadio, "Historiography: Western Studies [Further Considerations]," *Encyclopedia of Religion*, 2nd ed., vol. 6 (2005), pp. 4042–4052, p. 4050.

[81] See Gandini, "Raffaele Pettazzoni negli anni 1937–1938," p. 78f.

[82] See Emilio Gentile, *Il culto del littorio. La sacralizzazione della politica nell'Italia fascista* (Bari: Editori Laterza, 2003 (1993)), p. 130.

[83] In an article published on the occasion of the "Natale di Roma" on April 21, 1922, quoted by Gentile, *Il culto del littorio*, pp. 130f.

[84] "...mistero della continuità di Roma," words used in a speech on April 21, 1924, quoted by Gentile, *Il culto del littorio*, p. 134.

[85] See Gentile, *Il culto del littorio*, p. 129.

Pettazzoni's main scholarly projects such as his work on the confession of sins remained unaffected by the fascist environment. In the case of Pettazzoni, at least to my eyes, hunting for a hidden political subtext underneath the academic discourse does not seem to be a very promising task.[86] Nor does his scholarly work, as I read it, "reinforce...the ideological machinery of the [fascist] state",[87] as was the case with the writings of Pettazzoni's Roman colleague Giuseppe Tucci, an ardent wearer of the black shirt. However, one cannot fail to notice that Pettazzoni developed a modest interest in matters of ancient Roman religion[88] – and it is not difficult to imagine that this new interest may have been stimulated by the fascist agenda of the myth of Rome.[89] At a national conference on Roman studies organized by the "Istituto di studi romani" (founded in 1925/26 with the project of studying 'latinità' under the ideological auspices of fascism) – Pettazzoni would not participate in the regular activities of the Istituto, however[90] – in April 1928, he suggested applying the comparative method when approaching Roman religion.[91]

As in most areas of global religious history, Pettazzoni attempted to be up to date with recent research on Roman religion, for instance by regularly reading the *Archiv für Religionswissenschaft*. Eventually, Pettazzoni invited Franz Altheim to contribute to his journal (*SMSR*). Altheim published some pieces in *SMSR* and he dedicated his book *Epochen der römischen Geschichte* [1934] to Pettazzoni and Kerényi. Pettazzoni

---

[86] But see the paper of Eugen Ciurtin in this volume.

[87] Gustavo Benavides, "Giuseppe Tucci, or Buddhology in the Age of Fascism." In D.S. Lopez, Jr., ed., *Curators of the Buddha. The Study of Buddhism under Colonialism* (Chicago-London: University of Chicago Press, 1995), pp. 161–196, p. 182.

[88] Syncretism and conversion (and their mutual relations) are further topics that captivated his attention since around 1932.

[89] On which see (apart from Gentile, *Il culto del littorio*), Romke Vesser, "Fascist Doctrine and the Cult of the Romanità," *Journal of Contemporary History* 1 (1992), pp. 5–21; Andrea Giardina and André Vauchez, *Il mito di Roma. Da Carlo Magno a Mussolini* (Roma: Laterza, 2000); and several papers in Beat Näf and Tim Kammasch, eds., *Antike und Altertumswissenschaft in der Zeit von Faschismus und Nationalsozialismus. Kolloquium Universität Zürich 14.–17. Oktober 1998* (Mandelbachtal: edition cicero, 2001). On architecture and planning see Leonardo Benevolo, *Roma. Dal 1870 al 1990* (Roma, Bari: Laterza, 1992); John Agnew, "The Impossible Capital. Monumental Rome under Liberal and Fascist Regimes, 1870–1943," *Geografiska Annaler* 80B (1998), pp. 229–240.

[90] See Gandini, "Raffaele Pettazzoni negli anni 1928–1929," p. 97.

[91] Ibid., p. 98. Interestingly, Pettazzoni did not read the last part of his paper, in which he argued that the church had posed a new sort of religious problem, viz., the relationship between the church and society and nation respectively. Probably Pettazzoni did not find it suitable to address that issue in public.

corresponded with Altheim until 1937 and later on again in 1942.[92] As Altheim's active engagement with Himmler's "Ahnenerbe" (founded in 1935) can be traced to around 1937,[93] one may wonder if that may be the reason why the contact seems to have been discontinued. But I am not aware of any evidence that Pettazzoni was concerned about Altheim's political commitments, and the two eventually resumed contact.

Pettazzoni was also in contact with Altheim's teacher Walter F. Otto,[94] for whom he would even write an expertise attesting the academic value of *Paideuma* in 1941.[95] As late as March 1942, Pettazzoni was supposed to give a talk about "Mehrköpfige Gestalten in den Religionen der alteuropäischen Völker" in a lecture series arranged by the Deutsche Gesellschaft für Volkskunde in Frankfort.[96] According to Gandini, at least since 1935 Pettazzoni had been aware of the persecution of the Jews in Germany.[97] This, however, apparently did not have any impact on his academic collaboration with German colleagues including visits to Germany.

In 1934, Pettazzoni's interest in the early religious history of Lazio and Rome obtained some publicity through an interview with a journalist which was published several times (in modified versions), in the papers *L'Illustrazione italiana* (July 1, 1934) and *Il Giornale d'Italia* (April 14, 1935).[98] In 1935, among many other things, he occupied himself with the scandal of the Bacchanalia and their repression,[99] a subject on

---

[92] See Gandini, "Raffaele Pettazzoni nelle spire del fascismo (1931–1933)," p. 70.

[93] See Volker Losemann, *Nationalsozialismus und Antike. Studien zur Entwicklung des Faches Alte Geschichte 1933–1945* (Hamburg: Hoffmann und Campe, 1977), p. 125. On Altheim and the "Ahnenerbe" in general see Losemann, *Nationalsozialismus und Antike*, pp. 123–132 and some stray remarks in Michael H. Kater, *Das 'Ahnenerbe' der SS 1935–1945. Ein Beitrag zur Kulturpolitik des Dritten Reiches. 2., um ein ausführliches Nachwort ergänzte Auflage* (München: Oldenbourg, 1997), e.g., pp. 78, 99, 106, 108, 286, 389.

[94] According to Losemann, *Nationalsozialismus und Antike*, p. 124, Altheim's presumed attachments to the 'third humanism' of his teacher raised the suspicions of the fascist authorities, and around 1935 Altheim was still far from being 'politically correct' (in NS-terms). In 1942, however, assessors who were close to Rosenberg positively commented on the fact that Atheim had broken ties with W.F. Otto's humanism, see Losemann, *Nationalsozialismus und Antike*, p. 124.

[95] Otto had asked Pettazzoni that favor; see the litteral remains of Pettazzoni. I owe a copy of those documents to Horst Junginger.

[96] Literal remains, Pettazzoni. I owe a copy of the program to Horst Junginger.

[97] See Gandini, "Raffaele Pettazzoni intorno al 1935," p. 240.

[98] See Gandini, "Raffaele Pettazzoni dal gennaio 1934 all'estate 1935," p. 95f., p. 109f.

[99] Ibid., p. 180f.

which he gave three lectures at the University of Padova in February/ March 1936.[100] In the final lecture, he already touches upon a topic that he would return to repeatedly throughout his remaining career: The idea of a 'religious history of Italy' as the only way of obtaining a unified perspective (*una visione unitaria*), in contrast to pure political history (*pura storica politica*).[101]

In September 1937, the great exhibition commemorating the second millennium of Augustus was opened in Rome. The "Mostra Augustea della Romanità" was one of the big events of national propaganda during the fascist period and a public celebration of the myth of Rome.[102] The intelligentsia was expected to play their part in the propagandistic spectacle. The presidency of the Accademia nazionale dei Lincei decided to honor the occasion with an anthology devoted to the imperator and the different aspects of his reign. Pettazzoni was assigned the task to take care of the section on religion, and he prepared a paper on religion in Augustan times for the "Festschrift" resulting from the endeavor of the Accademia.[103] Pettazzoni also devoted his course in the academic year 1937–38 to that topic and gave a number of speeches on that topic which would result in some journalistic publications.[104] As I have not seen those works, I cannot address the questions whether there is a political subtext (be it subversive or affirmative) to be detected. However that may be, it is to be noted that Pettazzoni in his capacity as a scholar actively participated in this discursive and symbolic universe.

Late in 1937 (the year when his articles for the *Giornale d'Italia* were published), Pietro de Francisci, the president of the National Institute of fascist Culture (Istituto nazionale di cultura fascista) and one of the main promoters of the fascist myth of Rome,[105] asked Pettazzoni

---

[100] On the notes and manuscripts of these lectures and the traces they left in his later publications, see Gandini, "Raffaele Pettazzoni intorno al 1935," pp. 175–180.

[101] Quoted from the manuscript by Gandini, "Raffaele Pettazzoni intorno al 1935," p. 179.

[102] See Friedemann Scriba, "Il mito di Roma. L'estetica e gli intellettuali negli anni del consenso: la Mostra Augustea della Romanità," *Quaderni di storia* 41 (1995), pp. 67–84; idem, *Augustus im Schwarzhemd? Die Mostra Augustea della Romanità in Rom, 1937/38* (Frankfurt am Main-New York: Peter Lang, 1995).

[103] Raffaele Pettazzoni, "La religione." In *Augustus. Studi in occasione del Bimillenario augusteo.* Roma: 1938, pp. 217–249 (non vidi).

[104] See Gandini, "Raffaele Pettazzoni negli anni 1937–1938," p. 119, and pp. 158–160.

[105] See Gentile, *Il culto del littorio*, p. 130.

to contribute an article to their official monthly national paper, *Civiltà fascista*.[106] De Francisci requested an article on the study of religion and on the history of religions in Italy, its past and recent developments and new tendencies.[107] Pettazzoni granted the request and contributed the article on "Gli studi storico-religiosi in Italia" (The Study of the history of religions in Italy) that was already quoted above (p. 369). When preparing this article, Pettazzoni made inquiries with the ministry of education in order to get up-to-date information on the teaching of the history of religions at all the Italian universities.[108]

In this article, Pettazzoni reviews the delay of the establishment of the history of religions as an academic discipline compared to the countries with a Protestant or a mixed Protestant and Catholic population, starting with the debates leading to the abolishment of the faculties of theology in Italy in 1873.[109] He finds that it was only when the agnostic spirit of secularism or laicism (*laicismo*) was superseded by the fascist government that the history of religions found itself in a position to blossom.[110] Pettazzoni holds that one should 'emulate' the example of more successful countries when it comes to foster the future development of the discipline. In those countries, Pettazzoni writes, religious studies have a wider resonance in the national life of the people.[111]

In the later part of his article Pettazzoni states that the totalitarian state promotes the history of religions according to the necessities of national culture. The history of religions, he goes on, in its turn was sensitive to the requirements of the national spirit.[112] In that connection – and probably meant as an example to 'emulate' – Pettazzoni refers to the recent changes in the *Archiv für Religionswissenschaft*. According to Pettazzoni's account, while the journal maintained its scholarly

---

[106] On this paper see Gandini, "Raffaele Pettazzoni negli anni 1937–1938," p. 140 (as usual) with further references.

[107] See Gandini, "Raffaele Pettazzoni negli anni 1937–1938," p. 139.

[108] The document is quoted by Gandini, "Raffaele Pettazzoni negli anni 1937–1938," p. 140. Gandini adds some further pieces of information.

[109] See Pettazzoni, "Gli studi storico-religiosi in Italia," p. 195.

[110] Ibid., p. 196.

[111] Ibid., p. 194: "...altri paesi dove gli studi religiosi hanno una più larga risonanza nelle vita nazionale."

[112] Ibid., p. 196: "Disperso lo spirito agnostico del laicismo, lo stato totalitario provvede all'incremento degli studi religiosi secondo la necessità della cultura nazionale. Dal canto suo la storia delle religioni, per la congenita consapevolezza del valore della religione nella vita dei popoli, è particolarmente sensibile alle esigenze dello spirito nazionale."

character, it had two years ago felt the need to change its previously 'purely technical, strictly philological' outlook to accommodate the 'changed political climate of the new Germany' by focusing on the religion of the ancient Germanic people and their leaders.[113] As I read the text, there is not the slightest move of critical distance towards the dramatic "völkisch" change of course in the direction taken by the new editors of the *Archiv*.[114] As a matter of fact, he even suggests following suit: While Italy was not a multi-confessional nation and did not undergo a 'religious crisis' similar to what was going on in Germany,[115] Pettazzoni nevertheless claims that Italy had a genuine interest in a religious history of Italy, and he regards that project – with the basic assumption of a continuity from the Roman Empire to the Roman Church as one of the great axes on which to build a universal religious history – as the "opera massima" to be undertaken.[116] This idea was not only uttered in an official publication of the fascist regime, but it was also clearly inspired both by the focus on Rome placed by fascist ideology and by the fascist tendencies in German Religionswissenschaft that Pettazzoni unhesitatingly suggested to emulate and thus implicitly subscribed to.

The idea of a religious history of Italy remained with Pettazzoni even after the fall of fascism. He published two programmatic essays in the years after the war.[117] Eventually, his research resulted in his

---

[113] This is a paraphrase of the programmatic paper by Friedrich Pfister, "Die Religion und der Glaube der germanischen Völker und ihrer religiösen Führer," *Archiv für Religionswissenschaft* 33 (1936), pp. 1–14. For the history of journal see Horst Junginger, "Archiv für Religionswissenschaft" (unpublished) and Martina Dürkop, "'…er wird sehen, daß das Archiv wirklich ein Geschäft ist, wenn es richtig behandelt wird…'. Wissenschaftlicher und wirtschaftlicher Existenzkampf des ARW 1919–1939," *Archiv für Religionsgeschichte* 1 (1999), pp. 107–128.

[114] As a matter of fact, despite its new programmatic bias, many, if not most contributions followed the established standard of the journal (until 1939). See Junginger, "Archiv," p. 3: "Noch immer kennzeichnete der Geist einer vergangenen Epoche viele Artikel im ARW. Eine eindeutige Rücksichtnahme auf Inhalt und Terminologie der nationalsozialistischen Weltanschauung blieb die Ausnahme."

[115] Pettazzoni had already around 1934/35 shown an interest in recent German neo-Paganism and the Deutsche Glaubensbewegung, see Gandini, "Raffaele Pettazzoni dal gennaio 1934 all'estate 1935," pp. 145–148. Ten years later, after the fall of fascism, he eventually published a paper on 'germanic neo-Paganism', see Pettazzoni 1945.

[116] Pettazzoni, "Gli studi storico-religiosi in Italia," p. 196f.

[117] Raffaele Pettazzoni, "Idea di una storia religiosa d'Italia," *Rassegna d'Italia* 2 (1947), pp. 69–76; idem, "Per la storia religiosa d'Italia," *Richerche religiose* 19 (1948), pp. 29–41.

book *Italia religiosa* (1952).[118] At the outset of the book, once more he emphasizes the fundamental idea of a continuity of the development of Italy's religious history that would go beyond the opposition of Christianity and Paganism, but instead revolve around two 'heterogeneous religious forms' (*due forme religiose eterogenee*) which he calls 'the religion of the state' and the 'religion of Man' (*la religione dell'Uomo*).[119] In the second chapter, Pettazzoni traces some main stages of the religious history of Italy, starting with the most ancient period in evidence, through Rome, Paganism and Christianity, the Medieval "Comuni," the Renaissance, "Il Risorgimento," all the way to "La Resistenza." In that last chapter, he comments on a collection of letters written by members of the resistance who happened to be on the death row.[120] Pettazzoni presents a religious reading of the documents in which he finds an intense religious belief (*una fede religiosamente professata*) and a continuation of the 'religious spirit of the Risorgimento'.[121] In this way, seven years after Mussolini's execution, Pettazzoni constructs a line of historical development that is characterized by substantial continuity and culminates in the resistance to fascism.[122]

Colonialism and the Establishment of Ethnology in Italy

Roman imperialism and its domination of the Mediterranean and North Africa was the political model that Mussolini hoped to emulate. The Augustus exhibition of 1937 fell in a period when the political climate underwent severe changes in fascist Italy: Since 1935 (when Italy

---

[118] This book is rather a collection of essays than a monograph in the stricter sense. Among other essays, it comprises a reprint of his paper on Germanic paganism [= Raffaele Pettazzoni, "Il neo-paganesimo germanico," *Idea* 1 (1945), pp. 15–20], see Raffaele Pettazzoni, *Italia religiosa* (Bari: Laterza, 1952), pp. 115–132.

[119] Pettazzoni, *Italia religiosa*, pp. 7f. On this conceptual scheme see Enrico Montanari, "Religione dello stato e religione dell'uomo nel pensiero di Raffaele Pettazzoni," *Studi e Materiali di Storia delle Religioni* 56 (1990), pp. 7–23 [= idem, *Categorie e forme nella storia delle religioni* (Milano: Jaca Book, 2001), pp. 15–32].

[120] Pietro Malvezzi and Giovanni Pirelli, *Lettere di condannati a morte della Resistenza italiana, 8 settembre 1943–25 aprile 1945* (Torino: Einaudi, 1952).

[121] Pettazzoni, *Italia religiosa*, p. 73.

[122] Gentile, *Il culto del littorio*, p. 276 comments on the fact that Pettazzoni fades out the religious dimension of Fascism "che pure è stato nell'Italia unita...l'unica religione istituzionalizzata dallo Stato."

invaded Ethiopia[123]) the country had entered its imperialist-colonialist phase.[124] The territorial expansion went along with the internal exclusion of the Jews (see above) and the colonial subjects – other groups such as Slavs, communists, socialists, democrats, and Freemasons had already been excluded previously.[125]

Pettazzoni was a member of the honorary committee for the second conferences of colonial studies that had been arranged by the Istituto coloniale Fascista in 1934.[126] However, he did not attend the third conference that was held in 1937,[127] but it is unclear if this to be interpreted as a sign of political distancing or due to other circumstances.

Pettazzoni had always paid close attention to ongoing ethnographic research and had made ample use of its results in his scholarly work, e.g. in his studies on the developments of conceptions of the divine.[128] However, at that time ethnology (or anthropology) was not an established academic subject at Italian universities.[129] At least on paper, in

---

[123] The Accademia d'Italia was convened on March 14, 1936, in order to celebrate the Italian victory. The King and the Duce were praised. Pettazzoni did attend the meeting, see Gandini, "Raffaele Pettazzoni intorno al 1935," 210. On the picture he is shown seated in the last row.

[124] See Alexander De Grand, "Mussolini's Follies. Fascism in Its Imperial and Racist Phase, 1935–1940," *Contemporary European History* 13 (2004), pp. 127–147. Ever since the seminal volumes by Angelo Del Boca (1976ff.) a lot has been published on the issue in Italian. The debate has recently intensified; see Nicola Labanca, *Oltremare. Storia dell'espansione coloniale italiana* (Bologna: Il mulino, 2002) and Jacqueline Andall, Charles Burdett and Derek Duncan, "Italian Colonialism: Historical Perspectives. Introduction," *Journal of Modern Italian Studies* 8 (2003), pp. 370–374.

[125] See Grand, "Mussolini's Follies", p. 143.

[126] See Gandini, "Raffaele Pettazzoni nelle spire del fascismo (1931–1933)," p. 158. At the first conference of the Istituto Pettazzoni was asked to give a paper; he had accepted the invitation, but did not attend the conference, see Gandini, "Raffaele Pettazzoni intorno al 1930," pp. 219f.

[127] See Gandini, "Raffaele Pettazzoni intorno al 1935," p. 257.

[128] The Catholic priest and leading anthropologist Father Wilhelm Schmidt – according to Thomas Hauschild, "Christians, Jews, and the Other in German Anthropology," *American Anthropologist* 99 (1997), pp. 746–753, p. 749 "a radical anti-Semite in theory and practice" who would also write "outspokenly in favor of Italian fascism" in antisemitic journals – was Pettazzoni's archenemy (scholarly, but also culturally and politically, one should guess); their feuds are amply documented by Gandini. On Pater Schmidt see now also Joseph Henninger and Alessandra Ciattini, "Schmidt, Wilhelm," *Encyclopedia of Religion*, 2nd ed., vol. 12 (2005), pp. 8167–8171, and the article by Udo Mischek in this volume.

[129] For the development of ethnology/anthropology in Italy see Vinigi Grottanelli, "Ethnology and/or Cultural Anthropology in Italy: Traditions and Developments," *Current Anthropology* 18 (1977), pp. 593–514. There is a brief passage on Pettazzoni

the academic year 1932–33 for the first time there was a course in ethnology at the University of Rome.[130] However, it would take several years until the subject was eventually taught regularly. That happened after the renewed colonial expansion, and the teaching was at first, starting with the academic year 1936/37, assigned to Pettazzoni who successfully campaigned to achieve a regular status for that discipline. In a private letter written in 1947 Pettazzoni claims to have introduced ethnology at the Italian universities.[131]

As a matter of fact, on January 20, 1937, Pettazzoni gave the inaugural lecture in ethnology at the University of Rome (13 years after his inaugural lecture in the history of religions). As a title he chose "Ethnology as a Historical Science" (*L'Etnologia come scienza storica*).[132] At the outset he mentions the fact that the *tabula gratulatoria* of the Frazer-Festschrift published in 1934 contained the name of two Italians: his own and that of Mussolini. Even if meant as an amusing episode, a rhetoric *captatio benevolentiae*, Pettazzoni does not hesitate to publicly link himself to the Duce. Despite the title of the lecture, towards the end of the lecture, Pettazzoni addresses the actuality of the discipline in the sense of an 'applied ethnology': The 'practical-political value' of the discipline when it, based on a 'morphology and typology of cultural encounters', results in a 'technique' ensuring to discipline these encounters and a 'formative didactics' of the colonial administrators.[133] Pettazzoni's vision of 'applied ethnology' puts the discipline into the service of colonial politics. He is well aware of the fact that the origin of the discipline is intimately linked to the colonial expansion of the European powers,[134] but he does not seem to regard that heritage as inherently problematic[135] – instead, a sympathetic reading of the text

---

(p. 596f.), but the paper is more interested in the history of ideas than in the institutional side.

[130] See Gandini, "Raffaele Pettazzoni nelle spire del fascismo (1931–1933)," p. 88.

[131] The letter (to Griselda Cosentini) from December 31st, 1947, reads: "Qualche cosa sono riuscito a fare: sono riuscito a far introdurre l'Etnologia nelle Facoltà di Lettere delle nostre Università," quoted by Gandini, "Raffaele Pettazzoni intorno al 1935," p. 256.

[132] The text is published by Gandini, "Raffaele Pettazzoni negli anni 1937–1938," pp. 70–73.

[133] Ibid., p. 73.

[134] Ibid., p. 73.

[135] In a speech held at a conference in October 1938, however, Pettazzoni cautions against a too hasty destruction of the primitive civilisations that would lead to a complete destruction of their 'system of life' in a period when they were not yet mature to completely share the European lifestyle, see Gandini, "Raffaele Pettazzoni

might suggest that he was (naively?) optimistic about the benevolent impact that an adequate ethnological training might have on future colonial functionaries.

In summer 1937 Pettazzoni took the initiative in suggesting to the vice chancellor of his University to establish an "Istituto di Etnologia e Scienze Coloniali." This institute was to serve the purpose of a 'scientific preparation' of the higher functionaries of the colonial administration.[136] He mentioned that project also in a paper given at a conference.[137]

In October 1938 he drafted a letter to the national minister of education in which he requested the minister to include ethnology among the complementary courses of the Faculty of Arts at his university. The letter was written for a number of reasons, among them the importance of ethnological researches for colonial administration and politics. In order to support his suggestion he argues:

> In linea contingente, e cioè in rapporto con l'importanza oggi assunta dai problemi della razza, sembra opportuno che gli Studenti di Lettere, oltre a giovarsi di insegnamenti in altre Facoltà per il perfezionamento della loro cultura razzistica, trovino nella loro Facoltà stessa, nel clima omogeneo della loro formazione culturale e scientifica, un insegnamento che, per l'organica complementarità degli studi su la civiltà e degli studi sulla razza, li ponga direttamente a contatto con i problemi razziali.[138]

For a moment Pettazzoni was prepared to play on the official politics of the fascist government in order to achieve his goal. However, it seems that he himself felt that he had gone too far, because a note on the draft says that he had stopped short of sending it to the minister ("Non fu inoltrata").[139] This episode illustrates the ideological limits that Pettazzoni was not prepared to cross (at least after he had thought things

---

negli anni 1937–1938," p. 199. Pettazzoni's concern here is not so much the fact that the civilisations of the indigenous people were destroyed, but rather that this happened too fast; he does not seem to doubt the evolutionary vision leading them to give up their lifestyles in order to participate in that of the Europeans.

[136] From minutes published by Gandini, "Raffaele Pettazzoni negli anni 1937–1938," p. 99.

[137] Published by Gandini, "Raffaele Pettazzoni negli anni 1937–1938," p. 171f.

[138] Quoted by Gandini, "Raffaele Pettazzoni negli anni 1937–1938," p. 203 ("...with regard to the importance that problems of race have currently gained, it seems opportune that the students in the Faculty of Arts, apart from availing themselves of the other Faculties in order to improve their racist culture, should find in their own Faculty...a discipline...that puts them directly in touch with the racial problems." Trans. mine.).

[139] See Gandini, "Raffaele Pettazzoni negli anni 1937–1938," p. 203.

over) and his struggle to maintain his scholarly integrity while at the same time attempting to foster his academic projects.

In a sense, then, this episode may exemplify Pettazzoni's maneuvering throughout the entire period studied in this essay. Pettazzoni was certainly not an enthusiastic supporter of the regime, but on the other hand he never clearly distanced himself in any discernible manner explicitly from the political frameworks set by the fascist regime. It seems that the circumstances leading to his appointment on the newly created Roman chair caused the take-off of his career to coincide with the establishment of fascist rule, tied Pettazzoni into a web of loyalty to Gentile and the regime in general. Instead of questioning the regime and its politics, he advanced his own academic projects – and letting himself be promoted by the authorities, Pettazzoni hoped to, and also did, promote his academic interests. It was only the war that came into the way of his apotheosis at the planned international congress. Pettazzoni engaged in several give-and-take relationships with the regime and to some extent he acted as an opportunist.[140] However, he was always careful never to let his institutional compromises have any impact on the rigorous academic standards that he had set for his scholarly work.

---

[140] Opportunism is here understood as "the art, policy, or practice of taking advantage of opportunities or circumstances often with little regard for principles or consequences" ("opportunism," *Merriam-Webster Online Dictionary*, 2005. http://www. merriam-webster.com, April 23rd, 2005) In the case of Pettazzoni, the question was not that of consequences but rather that of principles.

Bibliography

Agnew, John. "The Impossible Capital. Monumental Rome under Liberal and Fascist Regimes, 1870–1943." *Geografiska Annaler* 80B (1998), pp. 229–240.

Andall, Jacqueline, Charles Burdett and Derek Duncan. "Italian Colonialism: Historical Perspectives. Introduction." *Journal of Modern Italian Studies* 8 (2003), pp. 370–374.

Benavides, Gustavo. "Giuseppe Tucci, or Buddhology in the Age of Fascism." In D.S. Lopez, Jr., *Curators of the Buddha. The Study of Buddhism under Colonialism.* Chicago-London: University of Chicago Press, 1995, pp. 161–196.

Benevolo, Leonardo. *Roma. Dal 1870 al 1990.* Rom, Bari: Laterza, 1992.

Bianchi, Ugo. "Raffaele Pettazzoni e la I.A.H.R." *Strada maestra* 12 (1979), pp. 11–18 [= *Studi e Materiali di Storia delle Religioni* 49, NS 7 (1983), pp. 21–28].

Boatti, Giorgio. *Preferirei di no. Le storie dei dodici professori che si opposero a Mussolini.* Torino: Einaudi, 2001.

Brelich, Angelo. *Storia delle religioni: perché?.* Napoli: Liguori, 1979.

Capristo, Annalisa. *L'espulsione degli ebrei dalle accademie italiane.* Torino: Zamorani, 2002.

Carozzi, Pier Angelo. "L'introduzione della storia delle religioni nell'insegnamento universitario italiano. Il contributo di Umberto Pestalozza e di Tomaso Gallarati Scotti." *Studi e Materiali di Storia delle Religioni* 49 [= NS 7 (1983), pp. 389–415].

Carozzi, Pier Angelo. "Prima della fondazione di SMSR." *Strada maestra* 12 (1979), pp. 19–28.

Casadio, Giovanni. "Historiography: Western Studies [Further Considerations]." *Encyclopedia of Religion,* 2nd ed., vol. 6 (2005), pp. 4042–4052.

———, ed. *Ugo Bianchi. Una vita per la storia delle religioni.* Roma: il Calamo, 2002.

Casalegno, Ugo. *Dio, esseri supremi, monoteismo nell'itinerario scientifico di Raffaele Pettazzoni.* Torino: Lit. Coggiola, 1979.

De Grand, Alexander, "Mussolini's Follies. Fascism in Its Imperial and Racist Phase, 1935–1940." *Contemporary European History* 13 (2004), pp. 127–147.

Dörr, Georg and Hubert Mohr. "Religionswissenschaft und Kulturwissenschaft. Die 'Schule von Rom' und die deutsche Religionswissenschaft des zwanzigsten Jahrhunderts." In Christoph Auffarth and Jörg Rüpke, *Epitome tes oikumenes. Studien zur römischen Religion in Antike und Neuzeit für Hubert Cancik und Hildegard Cancik-Lindemaier.* Stuttgart: Franz Steiner, 2002, pp. 263–284.

Dürkop, Martina, "'...er wird sehen, daß das Archiv wirklich ein Geschäft ist, wenn es richtig behandelt wird...'. Wissenschaftlicher und wirtschaftlicher Existenzkampf des ARW 1919–1939." *Archiv für Religionsgeschichte* 1 (1999), pp. 107–128.

Fabre, Giorgio. "Arnaldo Momigliano: autobiografia scientifica (1936)." *Quaderni di storia* 41 (1995), pp. 85–94.

Finzi, Roberto. *L'università italiana e le leggi antiebraiche.* 2nd ed., Roma: Editori riuniti, 2003 (1st ed., 1997).

Gandini, Mario. "Il contributo di Raffaele Pettazzoni agli studi storico religiosi." *Strada maestra* 2 (1969), pp. 1–48.

———. "Nota bibliografica degli scritti di Raffaele Pettazzoni." *Studi e Materiali di Storia delle Religioni* 31 (1960), pp. 3–21.

———. "Pettazzoni, Raffaele." *Encyclopedia of Religion.* 2nd ed., vol. 10 (2005), pp. 7072–7077.

———. "Presenza di Pettazzoni." *Strada maestra* 3 (1970), pp. 1–69.

———. "Raffaele Pettazzoni negli anni 1928–1929. Materiali per una biografia." *Strada maestra* 48 (2000), pp. 81–249.

———. "Raffaele Pettazzoni intorno al 1930. Materiali per una biografia." *Strada maestra* 49 (2000), pp. 141–154.

———. "Raffaele Pettazzoni dal gennaio 1934 all'estate 1935. Materiali per una biografia." *Strada maestra* 51 (2001), pp. 88–212.

——. "Raffaele Pettazzoni nelle spire del fascismo (1931–1933). Materiali per una biografia." *Strada maestra* 50 (2001), pp. 19–183.
——. "Raffaele Pettazzoni intorno al 1935. Materiali per una biografia." *Strada maestra* 52 (2002), pp. 99–268.
——. "Raffaele Pettazzoni negli anni 1937–1938. Materiali per una biografia." *Strada maestra* 54 (2003), pp. 53–232.
——. "Raffaele Pettazzoni dall'estate 1943 alla primavera 1946. Materiali per una biografia." *Strada maestra* 57 (2004), pp. 21–200.
Gentile, Emilio. *Il culto del littorio. La sacralizzazione della politica nell'Italia fascista.* Bari: Editori Laterza, 2003 (1st ed., 1993).
——. *The Sacralization of Politics in Fascist Italy.* Cambridge, Mass.: Harvard University Press, 1996 (English trans. of Gentile 2003, 1st ed., 1993).
Giardina, Andrea and André Vauchez. *Il mito di Roma. Da Carlo Magno a Mussolini.* Roma: Laterza, 2000.
Giusti, Sonia. "Analogia metodologica e contrasti teorici fra Raffaele Pettazzoni e Ugo Bianchi." In Giovanni Casadio, ed., *Ugo Bianchi. Una vita per la storia delle religioni.* Roma: il Calamo, 2002, pp. 393–400.
——. *Storia e mitologia. Con antologia di testi di Raffaele Pettazzoni.* Roma: Bulzoni, 1988.
Goetz, Helmut. *Der freie Geist und seine Widersacher. Die Eidverweigerer an den italienischen Universitäten im Jahre 1931.* Frankfurt am Main: Haag und Herchen, 1993.
Gregor, A. James. *Giovanni Gentile. Philosopher of Fascism.* New Brunswick: Transaction Publishers, 2001.
Gregory, Tullio. *E 42, utopia e scenario del regime.* Venezia: Cataloghi Marsilio, 1987.
Grottanelli, Cristiano. "Ethnology and/or Cultural Anthropology in Italy: Traditions and Developments." *Current Anthropology* 18 (1977), pp. 593–614.
Hauschild, Thomas. "Christians, Jews, and the Other in German Anthropology." *American Anthropologist* 99 (1997), pp. 746–753.
Henninger, Joseph and Alessandra Ciattini. "Schmidt, Wilhelm." *Encyclopedia of Religion*, 2nd ed., vol. 12 (2005), pp. 8167–8171.
Junginger, Horst. "Archiv für Religionswissenschaft" (unpublished manuscript).
Kater, Michael H. *Das 'Ahnenerbe' der SS 1935–1945. Ein Beitrag zur Kulturpolitik des Dritten Reiches. 2., um ein ausführliches Nachwort ergänzte Auflage.* München: Oldenbourg, 1997.
Labanca, Nicola. *Oltremare. Storia dell'espansione coloniale italiana.* Bologna: Il mulino, 2002.
Malvezzi, Pietro and Giovanni Pirelli, eds. *Lettere di condannati a morte della Resistenza italiana, 8 settembre 1943–25 aprile 1945.* Torino: Einaudi, 1952.
Losemann, Volker. *Nationalsozialismus und Antike. Studien zur Entwicklung des Faches Alte Geschichte 1933–1945.* Hamburg: Hoffmann und Campe, 1977.
Luconi, Stefano. "Recent Trends in the Study of Italian Antisemitism under the Fascist Regime." *Patterns of Prejudice* 38 (2004), pp. 1–17.
Michaels, Axel, ed. *Klassiker der Religionswissenschaft. Von Friedrich Schleiermacher bis Mircea Eliade.* München: C.H. Beck, 1997.
Mihelcic, Giuseppe. *Una religione di libertà. Raffaele Pettazzoni e la Scuola Romana di Storia delle Religioni. Premessa di Piero Coda, prefazione di Carlo Prandi.* Roma: Città Nuova, 2003.
Momigliano, Arnaldo. "Per la storia delle religioni nell'Italia contemporanea: Antonio Banfi ed Ernesto De Martino tra persona e apocalissi." *Rivista storica italiana* 99 (1987), pp. 435–456.
Montanari, Enrico. *Categorie e forme nella storia delle religioni.* Milano: Jaca Book, 2001.
——. "Religione dello stato e religione dell'uomo nel pensiero di Raffaele Pettazzoni." *Studi e Materiali di Storia delle Religioni* 56 (1990), pp. 7–23.
Nanini, Riccardo. "Raffaele Pettazzoni e la fenomenologia delle religione." *Studia Patavina* 50 (2003), pp. 377–413.

Nisticò, Gabriella. "Scienze sociali nell'EI." In Giulina Gemelli, *Enciclopedie e scienze sociali nel XX secolo.* Milano: Angeli, 1999, pp. 220–252.

Pettazzoni, Raffaele. *Italia religiosa.* Bari: Laterza, 1952.

——. "Per la storia religiosa d'Italia." *Richerche religiose* 19 (1948), pp. 29–41.

——. "Idea di una storia religiosa d'Italia." *Rassegna d'Italia* 2 (1947), pp. 69–76.

——. "Il neo-paganesimo germanico." *Idea* 1 (1945), pp. 15–20.

——. "La religione." In *Augustus. Studi in occasione del Bimillenario augusteo.* Roma: 1938, pp. 217–249.

——. "Gli studi storico-religiosi in Italia." *Civiltà fascista* 5 (1938), pp. 194–197.

——. *La confessione dei peccati. Parte seconda. Volume terzo. Siria-Hittiti-Asia Minore-Grecia. Indice dei volumi I–III.* Bologna: Zanichelli, 1936.

——. *Svolgimento e carrattere della storia delle religioni.* Bari: Laterza, 1924.

——. *Dio. Formazione e sviluppo del monoteismo nella storia delle religioni. Vol. 1: L'essere celeste nelle credenze dei popoli primitivi.* Roma: Atheneum, 1922.

Pfister, Friedrich. "Die Religion und der Glaube der germanischen Völker und ihrer religiösen Führer." *Archiv für Religionswissenschaft* 33 (1936), pp. 1–14.

Piccaluga, Giulia. "SMSR. Una rivista, un metodo, una scuola." *Strada maestra* 12 (1979), pp. 29–37.

Pisi, Paola. "Storicismo e fenomenologia nel pensiero di Raffaele Pettazzoni." *Studi e Materiali di Storia delle Religioni* 56 (1990), pp. 245–277.

Roberts, David D. "How Not to Think about Fascism and Ideology, Intellectual Antecedents and Historical Meaning." *Journal of Contemporary History* 35 (2000), pp. 185–211.

Rossi, Gianni Scipione. *La destra e gli ebrei. Una storia italiana.* Soveria Mannelli: Rubbettino, 2003.

Scriba, Friedemann. *Augustus im Schwarzhemd? Die Mostra Augustea della Romanità in Rom, 1937/38.* Frankfurt am Main, New York: Peter Lang, 1995.

——. "Il mito di Roma. L'estetica e gli intellectuali negli anni del consenso: la Mostra Augustea della Romanità." *Quaderni di storia* 41 (1995), pp. 67–84.

Severino, Valerio Salvatore. "Giovanni Gentile e Raffaele Pettazzoni (1922–1924). Un carteggio sulla storia delle religioni e l'università in Italia." *Storiografia* 6 (2002), pp. 107–126.

Siniscalco, Paolo. "Gli insegnamenti storico-religiosi nell'Univsersità di Roma. Origini e primi sviluppi." In G. Sfameni Gasparro, ed. *Agathe elpis. Studi storico-religiosi in onore di Ugo Bianchi.* Roma: L'Erma di Bretschneider, 1994, pp. 149–170.

Spineto, Natale. "Raffaele Pettazzoni e la verità del mito." *Rivista di storia della storiografia moderna* 17 (1996), pp. 59–65.

——. "Raffaele Pettazzoni e la comparazione, fra storicismo e fenomenologia." *Storiografia* 6 (2002), pp. 27–48.

Stausberg, Michael. "Pettazzoni, Raffaele." *Theologische Realenzyklopädie* 26 (1996), pp. 319–324.

Terrin, Aldo Natale. "The Study of Religions in Italy. Some Data and Reflections." In Johannes G. Platvoet and Gerarld A. Wiegers, eds. *Modern Societies & the Science of Religions. Studies in Honour of Lammert Leertouwer.* Leiden: Brill, 2002, pp. 373–387.

Turi, Gabriele. "Giovanni Gentile: Oblivion, Remembrance, and Criticism." *Journal of Modern History* 70 (1998), pp. 913–933.

——. *Il mecenate, il filosofo e il gesuita. L'Enciclopedia italiana specchio della nazione.* Bologna: Il mulino, 2002.

Vesser, Romke. "Fascist Doctrine and the Cult of the Romanità." *Journal of Contemporary History* 1 (1992), pp. 5–21.

POLITISCHE MYOPIE, MYSTISCHE REVOLUTION, GLÜCKLICHE (UN)SCHULD?

MIRCEA ELIADE UND DIE LEGIONÄRE BEWEGUNG: REZENTERE RUMÄNISCHE PERSPEKTIVEN

István Keul

1. *Einleitung*

Im Vorfeld der rumänischen Parlamentswahlen im Winter 1937 beglei-
tete Mircea Eliade eine Gruppe von legionären Aktivisten (darunter
seine langjährigen Freunde Mihai Polihroniade und Haig Acterian) zu
einer Wahlkampfveranstaltung der rechtsextremen Eisernen Garde.
„Ich weiß nicht, ob auch Mircea Reden gehalten hat", notierte der
Schriftsteller Mihail Sebastian, ebenfalls ein naher Freund Eliades, am
7. Dezember 1937 in sein Tagebuch.[1] Die Aufzeichnungen Sebastians,
der 1944 bei einem Verkehrsunfall ums Leben kam, wurden in Rumänien 1996 veröffentlicht und boten einem breiten Publikum nicht nur
die Gelegenheit, ein turbulentes Jahrzehnt des rumänischen – genauer,
des Bukarester – politischen und kulturellen Lebens aus der Sicht eines
jüdischen Intellektuellen nachzuempfinden, sondern ermöglichten auch
eine Begegnung mit einem Eliade, dessen sukzessive Annäherung an die
nationalistische, antisemitische Eiserne Garde aus den Zeilen Sebastians

---

[1] Mihail Sebastian, *Jurnal* [Tagebuch] *1935–1944* (Bucureşti: Humanitas, 1996),
S. 132. Die Zersplitterung des politischen Spektrums Großrumäniens erreicht 1937
ihren Höhepunkt: An der Wahl am 20. Dezember nehmen 13 größere politische Parteien und 53 kleinere Gruppierungen teil. Die politische Organisation der Legionäre,
die Partei „Alles für das Land" erreicht die dritthöchste Stimmenzahl (15,58%), hinter
der bis dahin regierenden Liberalen Partei (35,92%) und der Nationalen Bauernpartei
(20,40%), und vor der Christlich-Nationalen Partei (9,15%). Nach versuchten Block-
bildungen und einer missglückten Regierungsbildung unter dem designierten Pre-
mierminister Octavian Goga (Christlich-Nationale Partei) kommt König Carol II. von
Hohenzollern einem geplanten Staatsstreich zuvor, löst das Parlament auf und regiert
ab Februar 1938 allein. Vgl. Vlad Georgescu, *Istoria românilor. De la origini pînă în zilele
noastre* [Geschichte der Rumänen. Von den Anfängen bis heute], 4. Aufl. (Bucureşti:
Humanitas, 1995), S. 214f.

deutlich hervorscheint.[2] Eine interessierte rumänische Öffentlichkeit
nahm um die Mitte der 1990er Jahre neben diesen sehr persönlichen,
stellenweise verbittert klingenden Einsichten eines Eliade nahestehenden
Zeitgenossen auch zwei aufsehenerregende politik- und kulturhistori-
sche Arbeiten von Leon Volovici bzw. Zigu Ornea zur Kenntnis, die
die nationalistischen Bewegungen der rumänischen Zwischenkriegszeit
umfassend und kenntnisreich analysierten und dabei – neben zahllosen anderen – auch die Position und Rolle Eliades in der politischen
Landschaft jener Zeit kritisch beleuchteten.[3]

Die Reihe der Versuche, im postkommunistischen Rumänien Eliades
legionäre Vergangenheit zu diskutieren,[4] hatte einige Jahre zuvor (1992)
bereits Norman Manea eröffnet, der in einem ausführlichen Beitrag
Eliade vorwarf, sich von seinen politischen Ansichten der dreißiger
Jahre nicht losgesagt zu haben. Manea weitete darin den Ausdruck *felix
culpa*, den Eliade im Zusammenhang mit der Verehrung seines Lehrers
Nae Ionescu gebraucht hatte, auf die Nähe/Zugehörigkeit Eliades zum
Legionarismus im Allgemeinen aus.[5]

Alle erwähnten Veröffentlichungen zogen in Rumänien vielstimmige
Reaktionen nach sich: Während Maneas Artikel überwiegend Proteste

---

[2] Zur Eisernen Garde siehe Armin Heinen, *Die Legion ‚Erzengel Michael' in Rumä-
nien. Soziale Bewegung und politische Organisation. Ein Beitrag zum Problem des internationalen
Faschismus* (München: R. Oldenbourg Verlag, 1986, (rumänische Ausgabe: Bucureşti:
Humanitas, 1999), Nicholas Nagy-Talavera, *The Green Shirts and the Others. A History of
Fascism in Hungary and Romania* (Stanford: Hoover Institution Press, 1970), Francisco
Veiga, *La mística del ultranacionalismo (Historia de la Guardia de Hierro). Rumania 1919–1941*
(Bellaterra: Publicacions de la Universitat Autònoma de Barcelona, 1989, rumänische
Ausgabe: Bucureşti: Humanitas, 1991 und 1995).

[3] Leon Volovici, *Ideologia naţionalistă şi ‚problema evreiească' în România anilor' 30* [Die
nationalistische Ideologie und das ‚jüdische Problem' im Rumänien der dreißiger Jahre]
(Bucureşti: Humanitas, 1995). Eine englische Ausgabe liegt bereits seit 1991 vor: Leon
Volovici, *Nationalist Ideology and Antisemitism. The Case of Romanian Intellectuals in the 30s*
(Oxford: Pergamon Press, 1991), Zigu Ornea, *Anii treizeci. Extrema dreaptă românească*
[Die dreißiger Jahre. Die rumänische äußere Rechte] (Bucureşti: Editura Fundaţiei
Culturale Române, 1995).

[4] Als Zäsur dient hier der Dezember 1989, als das Regime Nicolae Ceauşescus
beseitigt wurde.

[5] Norman Manea, „Culpa fericită. Mircea Eliade, fascismul şi soarta nefericită a
României [Glückliche Schuld. Mircea Eliade, der Faschismus und das unglückliche
Schicksal Rumäniens]", in *22* (1992), S. 6–8. Maneas Beitrag erschien zwischen 1991
und 1995 in mehreren Periodika, u.a. in *The New Republic* (1991), *Les temps modernes*
(April 1992) und *Lettre International* (Frühjahr 1995, unter dem Titel „Felix Culpa.
Erinnerung und Schweigen – Mysterien bei Mircea Eliade") sowie in Maneas Band,
Despre clovni. Dictatorul şi artistul [Über Clowns. Der Diktator und der Künstler] (Cluj:
Apostrof, 1997), S. 97–132.

hervorrief, fiel das Echo auf die späteren Publikationen differenzierter aus. Eingefleischte Apologeten setzten ihrerseits – scheinbar unbeeindruckt – ihre Gegenangriffe auf Eliades „Verleumder" fort.[6] Doch es gab auch eine Reihe nachdenklicher Kommentatoren, die in ihren Arbeiten versuchten, auf die komplexen politischen, historischen und sozialen Zusammenhänge zu verweisen, auf deren Hintergrund zahlreiche Vertreter des kulturellen Lebens im Rumänien der 1930er Jahre zunehmend radikale, rechtsextreme Positionen einnahmen.

Nach einem Abriss der rumänischen Eliaderezeption bis 1989, in dem der Fokus auf Aussagen zum politischen Engagement Eliades in den 1930er Jahren liegt, sollen in den folgenden Abschnitten einige der eindringlicheren, in rumänischer Sprache erfolgten Wortmeldungen der letzten Jahre vorgestellt werden. Beabsichtigt wird insgesamt ein schneller Blick in ausgewählte neuere rumänische Veröffentlichungen mit vorrangiger Berücksichtigung jener Stimmen, die Eliades Involvierung in die rechtsextremen politischen Bewegungen seiner Zeit im Licht der soziohistorischen Rahmenbedingungen und der daraus resultierenden Konditionierungen eher wohlwollend (aber keineswegs verharmlosend) interpretieren, als Ergebnis situativer Konstellationen, die aus dem politischen, historischen, kulturellen Kontext der späten rumänischen Zwischenkriegszeit entstehen sowie gleichzeitig als unvermeidliche Konsequenz einer gewollt selektiven, individuell eingefärbten Wahrnehmungsweise dieser Konstellationen durch Eliade.

---

[6] In diese Kategorie gehört vor allem Mircea Handoca, ein äußerst beflissener Archivar und Herausgeber von Eliades Schriften in Rumänien, dessen wenig überzeugenden, apodiktisch vorgetragenen Verteidigungsversuche (z.B. im Vorwort des Bandes Mircea Eliade, *Textele ‚legionare' şi despre ‚românism'* [Die ‚legionären' Texte und die Texte zum ‚Rumänismus'] (Cluj-Napoca: Dacia, 2001), S. 7–35, oder in den Einleitungen zu seinem mehrbändig angelegten *„Dosarul" Eliade* [Das Eliade-„Dossier"] (Bucureşti: Curtea Veche Publishing, 1998f.) in meinem Tagungsvortrag mit dem Titel „Just another Futile Attempt? Eliade, Handoca, and the Case for the Defence" umrissen wurden. Das im Rahmen der Tagung vorgestellte (und kontrovers diskutierte) Material erwies sich für eine ausführlichere schriftliche Fassung als nur begrenzt ausbaufähig und fand für den vorliegenden Beitrag daher keine Berücksichtigung. Es wird aber in eine geplante spätere Arbeit einfließen. Für wertvolle Anregungen am Rande der Tagung bedanke ich mich besonders bei Florin Ţurcanu.

2. Der Prophet in seinem Vaterland: Eliaderezeption in Rumänien bis 1989[7]

Als Mircea Eliade im Frühling des Jahres 1940 Rumänien in Richtung London verließ, war er ein im Land vielgelesener Schriftsteller und Essayist. Seine zahlreichen Zeitungs- und Zeitschriftenbeiträge trugen neben der intensiven Vortragstätigkeit (sei es im Rahmen seiner Universitätsvorlesungen, im Rundfunk[8] oder in den Veranstaltungen der Gruppe „Criterion") zu seiner Bekanntheit erheblich bei. Bis 1944 sind mehrere Neuauflagen seiner literarischen Werke zu verzeichnen, aber auch Erstveröffentlichungen von Essaysammlungen und anderen Schriften.[9] Die Auseinandersetzung mit Eliades Arbeiten blieb in diesen Jahren lebhaft, und es erschienen zahlreiche Aufsätze und Besprechungen, die seine Werke zum Gegenstand hatten.[10]

Nach der kommunistischen Machtübernahme, eingeleitet durch den Frontwechsel Rumäniens im August 1944, wurde der Druck und der Verkauf von Eliades Büchern schrittweise eingedämmt. 1946 erschien zwar noch die 6. Auflage seines Bestsellers *Maitreyi*, die politische Zugehörigkeit Eliades vor dem Krieg prägte jedoch zunehmend die auf ihn bezogenen Stellungnahmen. Oscar Lemnarus 1947 im linksorientierten Blatt *Dreptatea nouă* [Die neue Gerechtigkeit] erschienenen Zeilen sind diesbezüglich bezeichnend:

---

[7] Teile dieses Abschnitts stützen sich auf den Text eines im Frühjahr des Jahres 2000 an der Abteilung für Religionswissenschaft der Universität Tübingen gehaltenen Vortrags (I. Keul, „Der Prophet in seinem Vaterland. Neuere Veröffentlichungen zu Mircea Eliade in Rumänien", unveröffentlichtes Manuskript.).

[8] Ein Großteil der Beiträge ist mittlerweile veröffentlicht worden, zuletzt in Mircea Eliade, *50 de conferinţe radiofonice* [50 Rundfunkvorträge] *1932–1938* (Bucureşti: Humanitas, 2001).

[9] Neuauflagen bereits erschienener literarischer Werke (Auswahl): *Domnişoara Christina* [Fräulein Christina], (2. Aufl. 1943), *Întoarcerea din rai* [Die Rückkehr aus dem Paradies] (2. Aufl. 1943), *Huliganii* [Die Hooligans] (3. Aufl. 1943), *Maitreyi* (5. Aufl. 1943), *Şarpele* [Die Schlange] (2. Aufl. 1944). Einige der hier aufgeführten Werke sind später auch ins Deutsche übersetzt worden und erhielten zum Teil leicht abgewandelte Titel, z.B. *Der Versucher und die Schlange* oder *Das Mädchen Maitreyi*. Zu den Neuveröffentlichungen aus dieser Zeit zählen u.a. *Mitul reintegrării* [Der Mythos der Reintegration] (1942), *Insula lui Euthanasius* [Die Insel des Euthanasius] (1942), *Salazar şi revoluţia din Portugalia* [Salazar und die Revolution in Portugal] (1942). Zu Eliade als Erfolgsautor der vierziger Jahre siehe auch Cornel Ungureanu, *Mircea Eliade şi literatura exilului* [Mircea Eliade und die Exilliteratur] (Bucureşti: Editura Viitorul Românesc, 1995), S. 45.

[10] Eine Aufstellung dieser Beiträge ist zu finden in Mircea Handoca, *Mircea Eliade: Biobibliografie*, Bd. 2: *Receptarea critică* [Mircea Eliade: Biobibliographie, Bd. 2: Die kritische Rezeption] *1925–1986* (Bucureşti: Editura ‚Jurnalul Literar', 1998), S. 170–178.

Gestern sah ich am Elisabeta-Boulevard Bände von Mircea Eliade und Emil Cioran. Die kulturellen Aktivitäten dieser Leute sind wohlbekannt. Sie schürten den Haß der Menschen und waren, was ihre politische Ideologie anbelangt, notorische Hitleristen, Legionäre, Faschisten. Es ist nicht gut, daß ihre Anschauungen weiter verbreitet werden, auch wenn ihre Bücher nicht mehr in den Buchhandlungen vorhanden sind, sondern nur in den Auslagen von Antiquariaten. Es sollten in dieser Hinsicht strenge Maßnahmen ergriffen werden. Man müsste es den Antiquaren verbieten, Werke solch infamer Autoren zu verbreiten. Selbst wenn diese Bücher literarische Themen behandeln, bleiben sie dennoch gefährlich, sind sie doch getränkt mit einem nebulösen, finsteren Mystizismus, der den Geist verwirrt, das Gewissen trübt, die Seelen zersetzt.[11]

Ein Jahr später wurden mehrere Bücher Eliades auf den Index gesetzt, darunter u.a. das Buch über Salazar, außerdem *Die Hooligans* sowie auch ein Band mit Indienberichten (*In einem Kloster im Himalaya*). Ab dem gleichen Jahr 1948 erreichten seine aus Frankreich und später aus den USA nach Rumänien gesandten Briefe ihren Empfänger in der Regel nicht mehr.[12] Die Brisanz, die Eliades Bücher in den 1950er Jahren in Rumänien hatten, lässt sich an dem Schauprozess illustrieren, den das damalige Regime gegen eine Gruppe von 23 Intellektuellen inszenierte, und in dem das Lesen und Verbreiten des Romans *Der verbotene Wald*

---

[11] Oscar Lemnaru, „Anticarii şi cărţile interzise" [Die Antiquare und die verbotenen Bücher], *Dreptatea nouă*, 4. November 1947, S. 2. Lemnaru veröffentlichte in den Jahren 1944–1946 mehrere gegen Eliade gerichtete Beiträge in *Dreptatea* und *Dreptatea nouă*: „Er fischte im trüben Gewässer eines peinlichen Mystizismus solange er nur konnte, und als seine Angel stumpf wurde und ihm sein Köder ausging, wurde er plötzlich Diplomat." „Mircea Eliade", *Dreptatea*, 28. September 1944, S. 2. „Von den Schuldigen, die diese große, auch von ihnen gewollte Schlacht überlebt haben, halte ich Mircea Eliade für verantwortlich, die Jugend, deren Mentor er war, angesteckt zu haben. Wie alle erfolgreichen Betrüger genoß dieser Mann ein hohes Ansehen in den verwunderten Augen all jener, die Ehrlichkeit und Farce, Lüge und Wahrheit, Gerechtigkeit und Infamie nicht unterscheiden können. Man müsste ihn zur Rechenschaft ziehen für die vielen Ideen, die er in die Welt setzte, für die vielen Irrtümer, die er pries, für die vielen Proselyten, deren trüben Geist er, der als unumstrittene ‚Leitfigur seiner Generation' galt, beflügelte." „Mircea Eliade", *Dreptatea nouă*, 3. Februar 1946, S. 2; vgl. M. Handoca, *Mircea Eliade: Biobibliografie*, Bd. 2, S. 178–180. Alle Übersetzungen von rumänischen Textpassagen im vorliegenden Beitrag stammen von mir; auf eine Wiedergabe der rumänischen Originalzitate wurde aus Gründen der Übersichtlichkeit verzichtet.

[12] Der letzte unter eigenem Namen versandte und auch zugestellte Brief ist auf den 9. März 1948 datiert und an die Eltern adressiert. Bezogen auf seinen wissenschaftlichen Ruhm leicht antizipierend, drückt Eliade darin vor allem seiner Mutter seine Dankbarkeit aus und zieht eine Zwischenbilanz: „Ich habe 25 Bücher veröffentlicht (...), halte Vorlesungen an der Sorbonne, bin auf der ganzen Welt bekannt, meine Studien und Artikel werden auf drei Kontinenten gedruckt, ich werde in unzählige Sprachen übersetzt (...)." Mircea Eliade, *Europa, Asia, America...*, Bd. 1: A-H, hg. von Mircea Handoca (Bucureşti: Humanitas, 1999), S. 342–344, hier S. 343.

mit einen der Hauptanklagepunkte darstellte.[13] Noch in den Jahren
1961–1963, als bereits deutliche Anzeichen für eine innenpolitische
Entspannung in Rumänien zu vernehmen waren, verfassten eine Reihe
von Mitarbeitern der im Auftrag des kommunistischen Regimes in
Ostberlin erscheinenden Zeitschrift *Glasul patriei* [Die Stimme des Vater-
landes] gegen Eliade gerichtete Texte, in denen auch Eliades legionäre
Vergangenheit wiederholt heraufbeschworen wurde.[14]

1965 wurde Nicolae Ceauşescu Generalsekretär der kommunistischen
Partei Rumäniens RKP. Er setzte den bereits unter seinem Vorgänger
Gheorge Gheorghiu-Dej begonnenen nationalkommunistischen Kurs
fort. Eine kontrollierte ‚Liberalisierung' des politischen und kulturellen Lebens kennzeichnete die unmittelbar nachfolgenden Jahre. Im
konzertierten und groß angelegten Versuch, genuin rumänische (und
nicht sowjetische) kulturelle Werte in den Vordergrund zu stellen, aufrechtzuerhalten oder wiederzubeleben, geriet auch Eliade, mittlerweile
ein renommierter Auslandsrumäne, schnell ins Blickfeld der verantwortlichen Kulturfunktionäre. Eliades innerrumänische Repräsentation
wandelte sich innerhalb nur weniger Jahre in spektakulärer Weise von
einem „zynischen legionären Intellektuellen" (1961) und „manischen
Pornographen" (1963) zu einem Autor, über den es in der Zeitschrift
des Rumänischen Schriftstellerverbandes 1967 heißt:

---

[13] Der Prozess endete im Februar 1960 mit der Verhängung langjähriger Haft-
und Zwangsarbeitsstrafen. Aufschlussreich zu diesem Thema ist der Band *Prigoana*
[Die Verfolgung]. *Documente ale procesului C. Noica, C. Pillat, N. Steinhardt, Al. Paleologu,
A. Acterian, S. Al-George, Al. O. Teodoreanu, etc.* [Bucureşti: Editura Vremea, 1996]. Vgl.
hierzu auch Florin Ţurcanu, *Mircea Eliade. Le prisonnier de l'histoire* (Paris: Éditions La
Découverte, 2003), S. 465f.

[14] „Herr Mircea Eliade ist – wie jedermann weiß – einer jener legionären ‚Intellektuellen', die zusammen mit ihren Kameraden für die schreckliche Ermordung Nicolae
Iorgas verantwortlich sind." Aus: „Legionarii şi Nicolae Iorga" [Die Legionäre und
N. Iorga], *Glasul patriei*, 1. Mai 1961, der Verfasser bleibt anonym. Und zwei Jahre davor
heißt es im gleichen Publikationsorgan: „Als ich ihn einen manischen Sexologen nannte,
war das noch ein Euphemismus. In Wirklichkeit ist M(ircea) E(liade) ein manischer
Pornograph, der seine Obsessionen in der irreführenden Gestalt gelehrter Abhandlun-
gen verbreitet. Wissenschaftlich-pornographische Schriften gibt es nun massenhaft im
Westen. Mircea Eliade sticht allerdings hervor durch den Versuch, der Pornographie
einen mystischen, heiligen Sinn zu verleihen, und aus dem Inzest und dem orgiastischen
Akt ein kosmisches Prinzip zu machen", schreibt Nichifor Crainic in einem Kommentar
zu Eliades Roman *Isabel şi apele diavolului* [Isabel und die Wasser des Teufels], in
N. Crainic, „M. Eliade, un sexolog maniac" [M. Eliade, ein manischer Sexologe], *Glasul
patriei*, 10. September 1963, veröffentlicht u.a. auch in Mircea Handoca, *Viaţa lui Mircea
Eliade* [Mircea Eliades Leben] (Cluj-Napoca: Dacia, 2000), S. 134f.

Mircea Eliades Arbeiten fehlt das oberflächliche Schillern: Er arbeitet gründlich und ernst, ja sogar mit der feierlichen Würde eines Gelehrten, der im heiligen Innenraum grundlegender Dinge ein Amt versieht.[15]

Im gleichen Jahr druckte eine ostrumänische Zeitschrift eine Erzählung Eliades, und 1969 erschien die siebte Auflage von *Maitreyi* sowie ein umfangreicher Prosaband: *La ţigănci şi alte povestiri* [Bei den Zigeunerinnen und weitere Erzählungen], beide in Bukarest veröffentlicht.[16] Bei allem scheinbaren Wohlwollen am Ende der 1960er, Anfang der 1970er Jahre Eliade gegenüber: Die Zensur passierten nur ausgewählte Schriften von und über Eliade, die mit dem kulturpolitischen Programm des Regimes kompatibel waren. Äußerst selektiv rezipiert und kommentiert wurden vor allem Eliades wissenschaftliche Arbeiten, wobei jene bevorzugt wurden, die im Einklang mit der zunehmend tendenziösen Beschäftigung und Glorifizierung der rumänischen Geschichte zu sein schienen. Der raschen Besprechung von Eliades 1970 in Paris erschienenem Sammelband *De Zalmoxis à Gengis Khan* folgte erst zehn Jahre später (1980!) die Veröffentlichung einer rumänischen Übersetzung.[17] Außer diesem Band erschien vor 1990 in Rumänien von den umfangreichen Arbeiten Eliades zur Religionsgeschichte nur noch seine *Geschichte der religiösen Ideen.*[18]

---

[15] Zoe Dumitrescu-Buşulenga, „Un filosof al miturilor" [Ein Philosoph der Mythen], *Secolul XX*, 9, 1967, S. 4f. Zitiert nach M. Handoca, *Mircea Eliade: Biobibliografie*, Bd. 2, S. 216. Vom September 1967 und bis zum Februar 1968 erscheinen in mehreren Zeitschriften insgesamt mehr als ein Dutzend wohlwollende Beiträge vor allem zu den literarischen Arbeiten Eliades, der auf diesem Weg sukzessive und selektiv in eine Positivliste eingegliedert, teilweise rehabilitiert, und für die rumänische Kultur somit „zurückgewonnen" wird. Siehe auch F. Ţurcanu, *Mircea Eliade*, S. 468–469.

[16] Die Erzählung *Un om mare* [Der Makranthropus] erschien in Iaşi in *Cronica* 49, 1967, S. 6f. Zum ersten Mal hatte Eliade die 1945 geschriebene Erzählung in Frankreich in der ersten Ausgabe der von ihm gegründeten Zeitschrift *Luceafărul* [Der Abendstern] im Jahr 1949 abgedruckt.

[17] Der Band behandelte die Religion und Folklore Dakiens und Südosteuropas. „Zum ersten Mal wird die archaische Spiritualität unseres Volkes, werden die Mythen und die sie verkörpernden Meisterwerke der Kunst im Rahmen einer ausführlichen Synthese dargestellt und in den Kontext der Weltkultur gestellt." Dumitru Micu, „O carte despre arhaicul românesc [Ein Buch über die rumänische Vorgeschichte] De Zalmoxis à Gengis Khan de Mircea Eliade", *România literară* 27 (1970), S. 11, zitiert nach M. Handoca, *Mircea Eliade: Biobibliografie*, Bd. 2, S. 223.

[18] *Istoria credinţelor şi ideilor religioase*, 3. Bde. (Bucureşti: Editura ştiinţifică şi enciclopedică, 1981, 1986 und 1988, die französische Originalausgabe: Paris: Payot, 1976, 1978 und 1983).

Die 1972 in Israel aufkommende und kurz darauf international aufgegriffene Diskussion um Eliades legionäre Vergangenheit wurde in Rumänien stillschweigend übergangen.[19] In den folgenden Jahren erschienen – mit wenigen Ausnahmen – in rumänischen Periodika überwiegend solche Beiträge, die sich in der Regel in einem positiven Ton mit Eliades Belletristik oder mit hermeneutischen und mythos-theoretischen Aspekten seiner Werke befassten.[20] Das Gleiche gilt für die wenigen umfassenderen Studien und Monographien zu Eliade, die bis 1989 gedruckt werden konnten; unter ihnen befand sich auch ein indologischer sowie ein äußerst kritischer soziologischer Beitrag.[21]

Erst in den 1990er Jahren wurden die meisten Werke Eliades zum ersten Mal auch in Rumänien veröffentlicht. Mittlerweile ist ein Großteil seiner wissenschaftlichen, literarischen, autobiographischen und publi-zistischen Arbeiten erschienen und findet in vielen Fällen reißenden Absatz. Zur Faszinationskraft des facettenreichen Werkes gesellte sich spätestens seit 1992 die intensiv und leidenschaftlich geführte Diskussion um die in den 1930er Jahren von Eliade eingenommene ideologische Position. Teil der späteren Phase dieser Diskussion, engagiert und moderat in Ton und Urteil, sind die Stellungnahmen von Sorin Alex-andrescu und Matei Călinescu.

---

[19] Siehe dazu: „Dosarul Mircea Eliade", *Toladot*, Januar-März 1972.

[20] Literarische Werke Eliades wurden auch in den 1980er Jahren in Rumänien gedruckt, z.B. der mehr als 600 Seiten umfassende Sammelband, der den Titel einer seiner Erzählungen trägt: *În curte la Dionis* [Im Hof bei Dionysos] (Bucureşti: Editura Cartea Românească, 1981). Siehe außerdem die Einträge in M. Handoca, *Mircea Eliade: Biobibliografie*, Bd. 2, 226–306. Auf Handocas Beitrag „Mircea Eliade gazetarul" [Mircea Eliade als Journalist], *Vatra* 5, Mai 1984, S. 8, antwortete Marius Godeanu mit dem Artikel „Spălarea statuilor" [Das Reinwaschen von Statuen] in der rumänischsprachigen Zeitschrift aus Israel *Revista mea* vom 31. August 1984, S. 6f.: „Es ist bekannt, daß in den dreißiger Jahren M. Eliade eine breite publizistische Tätigkeit entfaltete, besonders mit Beiträgen in *Vremea*, *Cuvîntul* und *Credinţa*. Genausogut bekannt ist die Tatsache, daß der große Philosoph und Schriftsteller in einem Großteil seiner damaligen Artikel eine deutlich legionäre und antisemitische Haltung an den Tag legte. Und jetzt kommt *Vatra* und reinigt den Genannten mit nur wenigen Federstrichen."

[21] Ion Lotreanu, *Întroducere în opera lui Mircea Eliade* [Einführung in das Werk Mircea Eliades] (Bucureşti: Editura Minerva, 1980), Adrian Marino, *Hermeneutica lui Mircea Eliade* [Die Hermeneutik Mircea Eliades] (Cluj-Napoca: Dacia, 1980), Sergiu Al-George, *Arhaic şi universal* [Das Archaische und das Universale] (Bucureşti: Editura Eminescu, 1981), Henri H. Stahl, *Eseuri critice despre cultura românească* [Kritische Essays zur rumänischen Kultur] (Bucureşti: Editura Minerva, 1983).

3. *Eliade und das ‚legionäre Phänomen'*

Weite Teile des 1998 erschienenen Bandes *Paradoxul român* [Das rumänische Paradoxon] aus der Feder des Literaturwissenschaftlers und
Historikers Sorin Alexandrescu sind unterschiedlichen Aspekten der
rumänischen Zwischenkriegszeit gewidmet, darunter auch dem ‚legionären Phänomen'.[22] Einige der einführenden methodologischen und
theoretischen Überlegungen Alexandrescus sind wesentlich für das
Verständnis seines Eliadebildes: Von Bedeutung erscheint für unseren
Zusammenhang die von ihm geübte Kritik an der von einer Reihe von
Autoren – unter ihnen werden auch Ornea und Volovici genannt –
vorgenommenen, zu starren, zuweilen dichotomisierenden Einteilung
der politischen und kulturellen Strömungen der behandelten Epoche in
Traditionalisten vs. Modernisten, oder Demokraten vs. Rechtsextreme,
eine Einteilung, die – so Alexandrescu – der inhaltlichen Vielschichtig-
keit der Äußerungen im Bereich des Politischen (Texte wie Handlungen)
jener Zeit nicht gerecht werden könne. Der Verfasser bezieht sich dabei
auf Aussagen und Agieren maßgeblicher Gestalten der Epoche wie
Iuliu Maniu, Carol II., Nae Ionescu, Zelea-Codreanu und Antonescu,
aus deren Aktivitäten er deutlich unterschiedliche Normen und Standpunkte hervorscheinen sieht, die einen gemeinsamen historischen Bezug
vermissen lassen, auch wenn alle aufgezählten politischen (Wort)Führer
erklärtermaßen das „Wohl des Landes" im Auge haben. Die Verschie-
denheit des von ihnen jeweils imaginierten, sie zugleich antreibenden
Bildes von „ihrem" (gegenwärtigen sowie zukünftigen) Land habe die
Möglichkeit eines Kompromisses oder eines Dialogs ausgeschlossen,

---

[22] Unter der Überschrift *Fenomenul legionar* [Das legionäre Phänomen] erschienen
1940 und 1993 Aufzeichnungen von vier Vorträgen, die Nae Ionescu im Mai 1938
vor seinen Mitgefangenen (Legionären und Sympathisanten) im Gefangenenlager von
Miercurea Ciuc gehalten hatte. Alexandrescu differenziert in seinen Ausführungen
zwischen dem historischen bzw. sozialen Phänomen der legionären Bewegung und dem
Bild, das (sich) die Ideologen und intellektuellen Sympathisanten des Legionarismus
von diesem schufen. „Es ist meine Überzeugung, daß Nae Ionescu, Mircea Eliade
und andere Intellektuelle, die über die Legionäre geschrieben haben, ihrerseits in das
Netz fielen, in dem auch die Legionäre gefangen waren, nämlich in die Illusion, daß
die ‚Taten' nicht an die ‚Worte' gebunden waren, und daß nur die letzteren für die
Beurteilung der Bewegung ausschlaggebend waren." Sorin Alexandrescu, *Paradoxul român*
[Das rumänische Paradoxon] (București: Editura Univers, 1998), S. 223.

was folgerichtig nur zu exzessiven, multidirektionalen Gewalttaten in jenen Jahren führen konnte.[23]

Gegen die in historischen Arbeiten häufig anzutreffende teleologische Ausrichtung der dargestellten Ereignisse plädiert Alexandrescu nicht zuletzt in Anbetracht der vorhin erwähnten zahlreichen unterschiedlichen Standpunkte für eine konsequente, wenn auch etwas eingeschränkte, Kontingenzpräsumtion: Die persönliche Entscheidung der Handelnden bleibt – unabhängig davon, ob sie sich der Implikationen einer Zugehörigkeit zum System, in dem sie sich bewegen, bewusst sind – bis zu einem gewissen Punkt unvorhersehbar und kann nicht direkt aus dem System abgeleitet werden. Die sich hieraus ergebende Herangehensweise für eine Analyse der Äußerungen jener Intellektuellen, die der legionären Bewegung nahestanden, sieht so aus:

> Ich habe zum Beispiel versucht, die legionäre Mentalität zu verstehen, und auch jene von legionsnahen Intellektuellen wie Nae Ionescu und Mircea Eliade, indem ich danach fragte, in welcher Weise und bis zu welchem Punkt die Annäherung erfolgt war, eine Annäherung, die ich nicht als schuldhaft ansah, sondern nur als verfehlt, auch wenn der Fehler sich als tragisch erweisen sollte. Die Annahme politischer Unschuld bei den Personen führt zur Annahme einer nichtrichterlichen Haltung beim Historiker: Dieser ist kein politisches oder moralisches Tribunal für die geschichtlichen Abläufe, die er untersucht, und er hat es auch nicht zu sein.[24]

Und nun zur versuchten Reevaluation von Eliades Verhalten in unterschiedlichen Zusammenhängen: Auffallend für Alexandrescu ist z.B. das offensichtliche Desinteresse, mit dem Eliade den Lageralltag während seiner Inhaftierung in Miercurea Ciuc (August-Oktober 1938) verfolgte. In seinem Band *Erinnerungen* widmete Eliade diesem Thema nur wenige Zeilen, während er sich in den restlichen zehn Seiten dieses Fragments mit Ausführungen Nae Ionescus zum Apostel Paulus sowie mit seinen eigenen Arbeiten aus jener Periode befasste.[25] Für Eliades politische Haltung und gleichermaßen für ein Verständnis des legionären Phänomens insgesamt erscheint die Frage nach der „Realität des Desinteresses für die Realität" wichtig. Die Analyse einer Reihe von (zeitgenössischen und retrospektiven) Aussagen Eliades, in denen dieser die religiöse, nichtpolitische Motivation der Legion und seinen

---

[23] S. Alexandrescu, *Paradoxul român*, S. 16f.
[24] Ebd., S. 18.
[25] M. Eliade, *Memorii*, Bd. 2 (Bucureşti: Humanitas, 1991), S. 28–37.

Glauben an ihren Sieg betont,[26] lassen in den Augen Alexandrescus keinen Zweifel an den Annäherungsmotiven Eliades an die Garde in den Jahren 1936–1937 zu: Eliade glaubte, wie viele andere, an die „Worte" der Legionäre, ohne die Übereinstimmung von „Wort" und „Tat" zu überprüfen. Und dass er 1938 dem Legionarismus nicht – wie viele andere Gefangene – abschwor, sieht Alexandrescu nicht vorrangig als Beweis für die fortdauernde prolegionäre Haltung Eliades, sondern plädiert für Nuancierungen: Die Zustimmung Eliades erstreckte sich – wenn überhaupt – nur auf die von ihm als religiös interpretierten Aspekte der Bewegung, und nicht auf die von ihr verübten Morde, die Eliade später ausdrücklich verurteilte. Nicht aus einem engen politischen Partisanentum, sondern aus seiner besonderen Sichtweise auf die Ereignisse lässt sich Eliades Interesse für die Garde am Besten erklären, so Alexandrescu, und dieses Interesse flaut in dem Moment ab, in dem er – nach den Morden an Iorga und Madgearu – zu erkennen meint, dass aus der „mystischen Sekte" eine politische Bewegung wurde. Nicht der an Eliade gerichtete Vorwurf der politischen Naivität sei demnach zutreffend, sondern jener der „politischen Myopie": die Morde nicht zu sehen, oder sie nicht als „wirklich" zu erachten, wobei Alexandrescu hier den Bezug zu Eliades späteren Theorien über das „mythische Denken" herstellt. Nur jene Handlungen und Dinge seien von Bedeutung und somit „wirklich", die auf Ereignisse im *illud tempus* verweisen, oder sie wiederholen.

> Wie soll Eliade von den Morden nichts gewusst haben? (...) Er ‚wusste' davon, und genauso ‚wusste' er auch, was im Lager in Miercurea Ciuc vorging, so wie er (und jeder Gefangene) ‚wusste', daß er dort auch umgebracht werden konnte. Etwas ‚zu wissen' bedeutete aber für ihn (...) nicht, seine Haltung grundlegend zu ändern, zum Beispiel sich von der Legion

---

[26] „Die Bedeutung der Revolution, deren Verwirklichung Herr Corneliu Codreanu [der politische Führer der Legion, I. K.] verfolgt, ist so tiefgehend mystisch, daß ihr Erfolg den Sieg des christlichen Geistes in Europa bedeuten würde." (M. Eliade in *Vremea*, 21. Februar 1937); „Ich glaube an diesen Sieg, weil ich vor allem an den Sieg des christlichen Geistes glaube. Eine Bewegung, die dem christlichen Geist entspringt und von diesem genährt wird, eine spirituelle Revolution, die in erster Linie gegen die Sündhaftigkeit und der Unwürdigkeit kämpft, ist keine politische Bewegung. Sie ist eine christliche Revolution (...). Ich glaube an die Bestimmung des rumänischen Volkes, und deshalb glaube ich an den Sieg der legionären Bewegung." (Aus dem mit „M. Eliade" unterschriebenen Beitrag in *Buna Vestire*, 17. Dezember 1937.) Alexandrescu neigt nach einer lexikalischen und syntaktischen Analyse des Textes dazu, ihn nicht Eliade zuzuschreiben, die inhaltliche Übereinstimmung mit Eliades Haltung aus jenen Monaten ist für ihn jedoch offensichtlich. Vgl. S. Alexandrescu, *Paradoxul român*, S. 226f.

zu ,desolidarisieren'. (Die These einer ,politischen Myopie' macht auch
deswegen so betroffen, weil der Autor des Werkes *Roman eines kurzsichtigen
Jungen* sein ganzes Leben lang tatsächlich kurzsichtig war!)[27]

Während Eliades Lehrer und Mentor Nae Ionescu sich bereits 1933
offen zum Legionarismus bekannte, wird Eliades „gardistische Konversion" erst in den Jahren 1936/37 deutlich. Alexandrescu rückt die
unterschiedlichen Zugänge und Entscheidungsgründe der beiden in den
Vordergrund. Nae Ionescus offene Parteinahme erfolgte aus politischen
Erwägungen, als Carol II. erneut die Liberalen mit der Regierungsbildung
betraute. Eliades Annäherung verfolgt Alexandrescu anhand einer
Reihe von Veröffentlichungen aus den Jahren 1935/36, deren zentrale
Themen die ,spirituelle Revolution' der Intellektuellen sowie die Überwindung des Politischen/der Politik sind.[28] Ist Nae Ionescus Publizistik
in der besagten Periode eher von politischer Taktiererei geprägt, gelangt
Eliade auf einer vordergründig wenig realpolitischen Ebene schrittweise
zur Einsicht, dass die legionäre Ideologie seine seit mehreren Jahren
vertretenen Ansichten am besten verkörpert. Die letzten Impulse, die
zu Eliades offenem Eintreten für die Garde führte, sieht Alexandrescu
schließlich in zwei Vorgängen vom Anfang des Jahres 1937: in der
zunehmenden Distanzierung der Garde von den politischen Strate-
giespielen Carols II. (wodurch der Eindruck einer gewissen politischen
Aufrichtigkeit Codreanus entstehen konnte), und im „Opfertod" zweier
rumänischer Legionäre im spanischen Bürgerkrieg (samt den aufwen-
digen und aufsehenerregenden Bestattungsfeierlichkeiten).[29]

---

[27] S. Alexandrescu, *Paradoxul român*, S. 230. Zum nächsten Abschnitt vgl. ebd.
[28] Erschienen in *Vremea* in den Ausgaben vom 21 April, 27. Oktober, 1. Dezember
1935 und vom 26. April und 4. Oktober 1936.
[29] Auszüge aus dem Nachruf, den Eliade in der Zeitung *Vremea* vom 24. Januar 1937
(S. 3) veröffentlichte: „Selten begegnet man in der Geschichte eines Volkes einem so
bedeutungsvollen Tod wie dem dieser beiden legionären Führer, die ihr Leben an der
spanischen Front ließen. (...) Diese letzte und verhängnisvolle Probe – die Reise nach
Spanien – hatten sie sich selber ausgesucht, als den höchsten Beweis ihres Glaubens
und ihres christlichen Heldentums. (...) Der freiwillige Tod von Ion Moța und Vasile
Marin hat einen mystischen Sinn: den eines Opfers für das Christentum. Es ist dies
ein Opfer, das den Heroismus und den Glauben einer ganzen Generation bestätigt.
Ein Opfer, das dafür bestimmt ist, eine Erfüllung, eine Bestärkung im christlichen
Glauben zu sein und eine junge Generation zu dynamisieren." *Mircea Eliade. Textele
,legionare'și despre ,românism'* [Die ,legionären' Texte und die Texte zum ,Rumänismus'],
hg. v. M. Handoca (Cluj-Napoca: Dacia 2001), S. 36–38. Der tiefe Eindruck, den der
Tod von Moța und Marin auch in Eliade hinterließ, geht aus dem Tagebuch Sebastians hervor: „Es fällt mir schwer, mit Mircea darüber zu sprechen. Ich fühle, daß er
trauert." Sebastians unmittelbar darauffolgenden Einträge stellen eine zeitgeschichtliche

Dass Eliade in den Jahren 1935–1937 wahrscheinlich weniger den politischen Kontext, sondern vielmehr die religiöse Verwertbarkeit der Ideologien zeitgenössischer sozialer Bewegungen vor Augen hatte, wird noch einmal aus einem Brief ersichtlich, den Cioran im Sommer 1936 von seinem Freund Eliade aus Berlin erhielt. Im Auftrag des Königs war Eliade zuvor nach England gereist, um sich ein Bild von der *Oxford Group Movement* zu machen:

> Ich bin dann nach England gereist, ziemlich unerwartet. Du weißt, dass ich geplant hatte, Anfang Juni nach Berlin zu kommen, um saubere Luft zu atmen (es ist halt so), und um in der Bibliothek vernünftig zu arbeiten. (…) Jedenfalls schickt mich der König – über Gusti – nach Oxford, damit ich schaue, was mit der Oxford Group Movement ist. Ich war da und hab es mir angesehen; die großartigste Sache in Europa. Übertrifft auch den Hitler. Schade nur, dass es so schwer ist: dich von Gott führen zu lassen, wie sie sagen, und dennoch in der Welt zu verbleiben, in der Familie, Politik zu treiben, Literatur zu schreiben, und sogar zu lehren – all dies scheint mir engelhaft einfach, also unmöglich.[30]

Wie Alexandrescu betont, scheint es also für Eliade unerheblich zu sein, dass die eine Bewegung, eine religiöse Erneuerungsbewegung, in eine Demokratie wie Großbritannien eingebettet ist, und die andere Bewegung, der Nationalsozialismus, von einem diktatorischen Regime vorangetrieben wird. Aus einem völlig entkontextualisierten und (auf den ersten Blick) enthusiastisch-„kurzsichtigen" Vergleich von (imaginierten) „religiösen Qualitäten", in dem Hitler den kürzeren zieht, wird eine Selektivität in Eliades Wahrnehmung deutlich, unter dem Gesichtspunkt der alles bestimmenden „Obsession einer ‚religiösen Renaissance' ".[31]

Momentaufnahme dar, die in wenigen Worten die in den Reihen seiner Generationskollegen und (ehemaligen) Freunde vorherrschende politische Euphorie treffend und ohne jeden Weichzeichnereffekt erfasst: „Was mich angeht, so macht mich diese Begebenheit traurig. In ihrem Lager ist viel mehr Verblendung denn Verstellung, und wohl mehr Aufrichtigkeit als Betrug. Wie kann es denn überhaupt möglich sein, daß sie ihren furchtbaren, fürchterlichen Fehler nicht erkennen?" M. Sebastian, *Jurnal*, S. 108.

[30] M. Eliade, *Europa, Asia, America…*, S. 153. Der Brief ist auf den 24. Juli 1936 datiert.

[31] S. Alexandrescu, *Paradoxul român*, S. 235. Zumindest eine Schattierung, im äußersten Fall eine andere interpretatorische Richtung erhält der etwas sorglos hingeschrieben und vielleicht nicht ganz ernstgemeint anmutende Vergleich mit Hitler, wenn die politischen Sympathien des Adressaten (Cioran) in jenen Jahren mit berücksichtigt werden. Und auch Frank Buchman, Gründer und Leiter der Oxford Group Movement, war alles andere als ein Kritiker des Nationalsozialismus, wenn man bedenkt, dass er Hitler als Gegenspieler des kommunistischen Antichrists sah und dem Himmel für seine Existenz

4. *Eliade, Culianu und die ‚mystische Sekte'*

Persönlicher im Ton, konziliant und nachdenklich zugleich, doch für ein rumänisches Publikum im Subtext nicht minder kritisch mutet ein fragmentierter Essay des Literaturwissenschaftlers Matei Călinescu an.[32] Der Text ist, wie der Autor in seiner Einführung hervorhebt, ein (seinerseits verästeltes) Nebenprodukt eines Beitrags für die Ion Petru Culianu gewidmete, im Jahr 2001 in Rumänien erschienene posthume Festschrift,[33] und stellt ein Geflecht aus persönlichen Reminiszenzen und Textanalyse, von Anekdotischem und hermeneutischen Hypothesen dar. Unter den zahlreichen Strängen des dichten Essays befinden sich unter anderem verstreute, dann wieder dicht aneinandergereihte Momentaufnahmen der schrittweise – epistemologisch wie auch affektiv begründeten – Distanzierung Culianus von seinem Lehrer, aus denen ein zunehmend diffiziler Umgang Culianus mit der politischen Vergangenheit Eliades hervorgeht. Daneben finden sich Reflexionen am Rande der Lektüre literarischer Texte Eliades, Texte, die, auf den Hintergrund historischer Ereignisse projiziert, Möglichkeiten für neue, überraschende und – auch in politischer Hinsicht – aufschlussreiche Lesarten generieren; eindringliche, resümierende Verweise auf zahlreiche ausführliche Analysen der ideologischen Position und der Werke (nicht nur) rumänischer Intellektueller der Zwischenkriegszeit.

Die politische Einstellung Eliades in den 1930er Jahren war das Thema zahlreicher Gespräche, die der damals in Chicago lehrende Culianu 1989 mit Călinescu führte, als dieser für ein geplantes Buch im

---

dankte. Siehe Anders Jarlert, *The Oxford Group, Group Revivalism, and the Churches in Northern Europe 1930–1945* (Lund: Lund University Press, 1995), S. 404 und F. Țurcanu, *Mircea Eliade*, S. 253. Über seine Erkenntnisse, die er in Oxford und in Birmingham über die Oxford Group Movement gewonnen hatte, lieferte Eliade in einem Rundfunkvortrag am 13. September 1936 einen ausführlichen Bericht, in dessen abschließenden Teil er auch Überlegungen zu Rumänien einschloss: „Unser Land kann von dieser Revolution [der christlichen, I. K.] nur profitieren. Rumänien, ein christliches Land, kann sich nur freuen über jeden Erfolg des christlichen Geistes in diesem luziferischen Europa. (…) In einem christlichen Europa wird Rumänien ruhiger atmen. Nur, wir können nicht mit verschränkten Armen auf den Sieg der christlichen Revolution warten. Die Vertreter der Kirche und die revolutionären Laien haben das entscheidende Wort." „O revoluție creștină la Oxford" [Eine christliche Revolution in Oxford], 13. September 1936, in M. Eliade, *50 de conferințe radiofonice*, S. 213–220, hier S. 219f.

[32] Matei Călinescu, Despre *Ioan P. Culianu și Mircea Eliade. Amintiri, lecturi, reflecții* [Über I.P. Culianu und M. Eliade. Erinnerungen, Lesarten, Reflexionen], 2. Aufl. (Iași: Polirom, 2002, 1. Aufl. 2001), S. 9–107.

[33] Sorin Antohi, Hg., *Religion, Fiction and History: Essays in Memory of Ioan Petru Culianu*, 2 Bde. (București: Nemira, 2001).

neu eingerichteten Eliade-Archiv der Chicagoer Regenstein-Bibliothek forschte. Călinescu berichtet über den von ihm gefühlten inneren Zwiespalt bei Culianu, der seine Verehrung Eliades und die Unmöglichkeit, die politischen Ansichten seines Meisters zu rechtfertigen, betraf. Der Plan der beiden, die legionären publizistischen Beiträge Eliades mit einer Einleitung und Kommentaren in einem Band herauszugeben, scheiterte am Widerstand von Eliades Frau Christinel. Culianus Position in den Jahren 1987/88 in Bezug zu Eliades legionärer Vergangenheit wird aus einem Brief an Adrian Marino ersichtlich, in welchem er den Inhalt von Eliades prolegionären Artikeln anspricht:

> Ich glaube, wir müssen hermeneutische Anstrengungen unternehmen und eine kaum abstreitbare Kontiguität (aber *keine* völlige Identifizierung!) eingestehen. Freilich sind einige chauvinistisch eingefärbte Aussagen ärgerlich. Aber sie scheinen nicht verhängnisvoll [im Original: *dezastruoase*, I.K.] zu sein.[34]

Verglichen mit früheren Wortmeldungen[35] stellten diese Aussagen – trotz der abschwächenden Nachbemerkung – eine merkliche Veränderung der Haltung Culianus dar. In Gesprächen mit Călinescu drückte er sein Bedauern darüber aus, keine frühere Kenntnis einiger Schriften Eliades gehabt zu haben, die ihm schließlich die Einsicht brachten, Eliade habe sich in den 1930er Jahren in der Politik falsch orientiert und sich von dem „‚salvationistisch'-nationalistischen" Glauben seiner Generation anstecken lassen.[36] Andererseits, und hier scheint Călinescu mit ihm

---

[34] M. Călinescu, *Despre Ioan P. Culianu și Mircea Eliade*, S. 33. Der Brief wurde am 11. Oktober 1987 verfasst. Ein Jahr später, so Călinescu, war Culianu noch der gleichen Meinung.

[35] Etwa seine zuerst in Italien veröffentlichte Studie *Mircea Eliade* (Assisi: Cittadella Editrice, 1978), oder die lange Zeit unpubliziert gebliebene, 1982–1983 verfasste Arbeit *Mircea Eliade necunoscutul* [Der unbekannte M. E.], die beide (neben weiteren Texten) in den in Rumänien erschienenen Band von Ioan Petru Culianu, *Mircea Eliade* (București: Nemira, 1995) Aufnahme fanden. In den letzten Jahren wurden darüber hinaus zahlreiche Editionen und Übersetzungen von Culianus wissenschaftlichen Werken aufgelegt, unter anderem: *Călătorii în lumea de dincolo* [Reisen ins Jenseits], 3. Aufl. (Iași: Polirom 2002, 1. und 2. Aufl.: 1994, 1996, engl.: *Out of this World. Otherworldly Journeys from Gilgamesh to Albert Einstein*, Boston u.a.: Shambhala Publications, 1991], *Jocurile minții. Istoria ideilor, teoria culturii, epistemiologie* [Denkspiele. Ideengeschichte, Kulturtheorie, Epistemiologie] (Iași: Polirom, 2002), *Studii românești* [Rumänische Studien], Bd. 1 (București: Nemira, 2000), *Păcatul împotriva spiritului* [Die Sünde wider den Geist] (București: Nemira 1999). Zur vielstimmigen Culianurezeption in Rumänien siehe neben zahlreichen Zeitschriftenbeiträgen z.B. die einführende Studie von Sorin Antohi, *Laboratorul lui Culianu* [Culianus Laboratorium], in I.P. Culianu, *Jocurile minții*, S. 9–81.

[36] M. Călinescu, *Despre Ioan P. Culianu și Mircea Eliade*, S. 91.

konform zu gehen, stand Culianu den ungenauen und übertriebenen
Interpretationen von Eliades politischer Involvierung unversöhnlich
gegenüber. Insgesamt entfernte sich Culianu in den Jahren 1988/89
zunehmend von Eliade, besonders auch in wissenschaftlicher Hinsicht.
Die methodologischen Alterserscheinungen seines Werkes seien kaum
noch zu übersehen, das mittlerweile fragile Interesse der Fachwelt für
seine Hypothesen würde nach und nach schwinden, führte Culianu
in seinen Gesprächen mit Călinescu aus. Seine moderate Haltung
gegenüber dem legionären Engagement Eliades änderte Culianu jedoch
auch in den folgenden Jahren nicht. Von der sich über Rumänien
ergießenden nationalistischen Strömung mitgerissen, sei Eliade zu
keinem Zeitpunkt ein Antisemit gewesen. Auch Călinescu neigt dazu,
Eliades vieldiskutiertem Abstreiten der Verfasserschaft eines glühenden
prolegionären Bekenntnisses aus dem Dezember des Jahres 1937 Glauben zu schenken:

> Meine Meinung ist – gestützt auf die direkte Kenntnis von Gepflogenheiten
> der rumänischen Presse aus der kommunistischen Zeit, Gepflogenheiten,
> die die Kommunisten aber nicht selber erfunden haben – daß Eliades
> Erklärung plausibel ist, auch wenn sie ihn nicht der Schuld enthebt, und
> daß er (…) nach dem Krieg die genuin humanistische Ader, einen gewissen
> Ökumenismus seines frühen Denkens wiedergefunden hat.[37]

Culianu war es auch, dessen Interpretation der Eliade'schen Erzählung
Un om mare [Der Makranthropus] Călinescu dazu anregte, in einem
weiteren Schritt nach einer verborgenen politischen Botschaft in diesem
Text zu suchen.[38] In der Konzeption der – pathologisch und mythologisch – unaufhaltsam wachsenden Hauptfigur der in den ersten Wochen
des Jahres 1945 in Portugal verfassten Erzählung sah Culianu deutliche
Parallelen zu Corneliu Codreanu, dem Führer der Eisernen Garde.[39]
Călinescu schlägt eine alternative Interpretation vor: Die zentrale Gestalt
Cucoaneş wird darin zu einem Beispiel prophetischer Erwählung, zu
einem „Berufenen wider Willen" (beides treffend ausgedrückt durch
die Metapher „Makranthropie"). Bis zum Zeitpunkt der Erkrankung

---

[37] Ebd., S. 93.

[38] Eine deutsche Übersetzung liegt vor in Mircea Eliade, *Magische Geschichten* (Frankfurt
a.M. u.a.: Insel Verlag, 1997), S. 133–164.

[39] Diese Interpretation der Erzählung ist nachzulesen bei I.P. Culianu, *Mircea Eliade*,
S. 234f. „Der Makranthropus" war der erste Text Eliades, der 1967 die kommunistische
Zensur passierte (siehe Anm. 16). Zum folgenden Abschnitt vgl. M. Călinescu, *Despre
Ioan P. Culianu şi Mircea Eliade*, S. 77f.

ein unauffälliger junger Mann, wird Cucoaneş plötzlich berühmt und muss in die Berge fliehen, wo er, mittlerweile zu einem Riesen mutiert, zu einer sagenumwobenen Märchenfigur wird. Doch die Culianu'sche Allegorie Codreanu-Cucoaneş bietet, einmal entschlüsselt, keine politische Handlungsanweisung, liefert keinen deutlichen Ausdruck wie auch immer gearteter ideologischer Standpunkte. Es sind nicht zuletzt Eliades Aufzeichnungen, die Călinescu Anhaltspunkte für seine „egoistische Hypothese" bieten, Cucoaneş als symbolisches Selbstbildnis Eliades aufzufassen: Das Wachsen, Folge einer durch „mystische Konversion oder einer machtvollen Epiphanie" hervorgerufenen Wandlung, hindert den Helden an der Forstsetzung des Dialogs mit der profanen Wirklichkeit und zwingt ihn, in den „Bergen der Seele" Zuflucht zu suchen.[40] Călinescu argumentiert in einem weiteren Kapitel seines Buches auch gegen den vereinfachenden „Vulgärbiographismus", den etwa Claudio Mutti auf Eliades Erzählung *Nouăsprezece trandafiri* [Neunzehn Rosen] anwendet. Bei C. Mutti wird die Hauptfigur *dieser* Erzählung mit Codreanu gleichgesetzt, die Zahl 19 auf die neunzehn Mitglieder der legionären Führungsriege, die 1938 verurteilt wurden, gemünzt.[41] Călinescu verweist auf die von Eliade intendierte, „kalkulierte literarische Ambiguität", welche exklusivistische, rein politisch gelagerte Lesarten von vornherein unmöglich mache.

Aufschlussreich erscheinen die Überlegungen Călinescus zu Personenkonstellationen (einschließlich der inhaltlichen Verknüpfung ihrer Werke) um Eliade vor und nach dem Krieg.[42] Berücksichtigung finden u.a. Mihail Sebastian, Nae Ionescu, Eugen Ionescu (Eugène Ionesco), Carl Gustav Jung, Gershom Scholem, Henry Corbin. Die Beziehung Eliades zu seinem jüdischen Freund Sebastian gestaltete sich zunehmend komplizierter in den Jahren 1936/37, als sich Eliade immer offener zur Legion bekannte und sich Antisemitismusvorwürfen ausgesetzt sah. Zu einem völligen Abbruch der Verbindung kam es bis zur Abreise Eliades nach London (1940) dennoch nicht: Man besuchte sich gegenseitig, selbst in Zeiten ideologischer Differenzen. Călinescu

---

[40] Ebd., S. 78f.
[41] Claudio Mutti, *Mircea Eliade şi Garda de Fier* (Sibiu: Editura Puncte Cardinale, 1995), hier S. 61–66. Vom gleichen Autor liegt in einer rumänischen Übersetzung vor: *Penele arhangelului. Intelectualii români şi Garda de Fier* [Die Federn des Erzengels. Die rumänischen Intellektuellen und die Eiserne Garde] (Bucureşti: Anastasia, 1997).
[42] Vgl. zu den folgenden Abschnitten besonders M. Călinescu, *Despre Ioan P. Culianu şi Mircea Eliade*, S. 42–52 (Eliade und Sebastian, Eliade und der Eranos-Kreis) und S. 82–89 (Eliade und Ionesco).

spricht von einer „reziproken Faszination, genährt durch verstörende Ambivalenzen, aber auch durch subtile intellektuelle und gefühlsmäßige Übereinstimmungen",[43] die er auch in einer bislang unveröffentlichten Tagebucheintragung Eliades bestätigt fand: „Selbst in meiner legionären Klimax fühlte ich ihn mir nahe".[44] Von der gleichen Faszination geprägt war das Verhältnis der beiden Freunde zu ihrem Lehrer Nae Ionescu. Sebastian hegte noch lange Zeit nach Ionescus Verwandlung in einen Ideologen des Legionarismus und sogar noch nach dessen antisemitischen Vorwort zu Sebastians Roman *De două mii de ani* [Seit zweitausend Jahren] (1934) Bewunderung und Sympathie für Ionescu.[45] In diesem Licht besehen ist freilich auch ein aufsehenerregendes spätes Bekenntnis Eliades zu Nae Ionescu keineswegs zwingend als ideologische Reminiszenz zu werten, sondern kann durchaus „nur" ein Ausdruck persönlicher Verbundenheit sein.[46] Eugène Ionescos Mitte der 1940er Jahre in Paris wieder aufgenommener Dialog mit Eliade weist vielleicht in eine ähnliche Richtung. Ein scheinbar irreparables, ideologisch begründetes Zerwürfnis erweist sich in jenem Augenblick als illusorisch, als der spätere Dramatiker von Weltruhm nach Dialogpartnern sucht, deren kulturelle Sensibilitäten und Matrizen mit den seinen übereinstimmen. Auf dem Hintergrund einer gemeinsamen kultur- und „generationsspezifischen *forma mentis*" (inklusive einer geteilten diffusen Religiosität) finden die beiden Exilrumänen zueinander.[47] In Bezug

---

[43] Ebd., S. 42.

[44] Auf die Nachricht von Sebastians Tod schrieb Eliade in Portugal am 29. Mai 1945 in sein Tagebuch: „Ich erinnere mich an unsere Freundschaft. In meinen Träumen war er einer von 2–3 Menschen, die Bukarest für mich erträglich gemacht hätten. Selbst in meiner legionären Klimax fühlte ich ihn mir nahe. Ich hatte auf diese Freundschaft gezählt, um ins rumänische Leben, in die rumänische Kultur zurückzukehren." Unveröffentlichtes Manuskript, Regenstein Library, University of Chicago; zitiert nach Călinescu, *Despre Ioan P. Culianu și Mircea Eliade*, S. 67, Anm. 23.

[45] Mihail Sebastian, *De două mii de ani. Cum am devenit huligan* [Seit zweitausend Jahren. Wie ich zu einem Hooligan wurde] (București: Humanitas 1992).

[46] Im Zusammenhang mit seiner Kandidatur für den Literaturnobelpreis schreibt Eliade an Culianu am 24. März 1978: „Ich habe stets erklärt: Sollte ich diese Auszeichnung bekommen, fahre ich sofort nach Rumänien, um meine Identität als ,rumänischer Schriftsteller' zum Ausdruck zu bringen. Ich habe aber niemandem gesagt, was ich in Bukarest tun werde. Ich sage es Dir: Ich werde auf den Friedhof Bellu gehen und die Gräber meines Vaters, meiner Mutter, meines Bruders und Nae Ionescus mit ihren Lieblingsblumen bedecken." Ted Anton, *Eros, magie și asasinarea profesorului Culianu* [Eros, Magie und die Ermordung des Professors Culianu] (București: Nemira, 1997), S. 171.

[47] „Wir kommen aus dem gleichen Land. Wir haben eine gemeinsame Herkunft, auch wenn ich das nur ungern zugebe und Rumänien ablehne, das Land, in dem ich Furchtbares erleben musste (…) in der Nazifizierungsatmosphäre um 1935. Dessen

auf die Mitglieder des Eranos-Kreises hebt Călinescu (ausgehend von Wasserstrom[48]) den überaus wichtigen Stellenwert des Geheimen, des Verborgenen als Kategorie des „Heiligen" bei Scholem, Corbin und Eliade gleichermaßen hervor und bezeichnet aus dieser Perspektive Eliades Überzeugung, die Legion sei eine „mystische Sekte" gewesen, die ihre Berufung durch die Morde aus dem November 1940 verfehlt habe, als einen „zwar seltsamen, doch durchaus erklärbaren Fall von Selbsttäuschung".[49] Aus eben diesem Grund ist Eliade in den Augen Călinescus kein Ideologe, kein politischer Doktrinär der Legion, sondern vielmehr ein „rechter ,Revolutionär', wenn auch nur in der existentialistisch-vitalistischen und frivol-mystischen, für das Bukarest der dreißiger Jahre typischen Spielart".[50] Gegen Ende seines Essays liefert Călinescu

---

ungeachtet gibt es einen gemeinsamen Hintergrund, der mich mit den Auffassungen der Rumänen, in anderen Bereichen als der Politik, verbindet, und dies war der Grund dafür, daß ich, ohne es zu wissen, ohne mir dessen bewusst zu sein, Eliade und seiner Auffassung über das Heilige nahestand." Auszug aus einem Interview mit Ionescu, veröffentlicht in Marie-Claude Hubert, *Eugène Ionesco* (Paris: Seuil, 1990), S. 235, zitiert nach M. Călinescu, *Despre Ioan P. Culianu și Mircea Eliade*, S. 86. In einem in Paris geschriebenen Brief vom 19. September 1945 umreißt Ionescu sowohl sein ,Dialog-Dilemma' als auch die politische Haltung seiner Generationskollegen: „(Ohne) meine Feinde fühle ich mich einsam. Ich war dazu verdammt, sie zu hassen und mit ihnen verbunden zu sein: Mit wem soll ich reden? Ich bin mit dem gleichen Mal gezeichnet. (...) Was mich anbelangt, kann ich mir nicht vorwerfen, Faschist gewesen zu sein. Doch man kann dies fast allen anderen vorwerfen (...). In diesen Tagen wird Eliade eintreffen, vielleicht ist er auch schon da. Für ihn ist alles verloren, da ,der Kommunismus gesiegt hat'. Er ist einer der großen Schuldigen. Doch auch er, und Cioran (...) sind Opfer des hassenswerten Toten Nae Ionescu. Wenn Nae Ionescu nicht gewesen wäre (oder wenn er sich mit dem König nicht gestritten hätte), hätten wir heute eine wertvolle Führungsgeneration gehabt, zwischen 35 und 40 Jahre alt. Wegen ihm sind alle zu Faschisten geworden. Er schuf ein stupides, erschreckendes, reaktionäres Rumänien. Der zweite Schuldige ist Eliade (...). Auch Eliade beeinflusste einen Teil seiner ,Generationskollegen' sowie den gesamten intellektuellen Nachwuchs." *Scrisori către Tudor Vianu II (1936–1949)* [Briefe an Tudor Vianu] (București: Editura Minerva, 1994), S. 274.

[48] Steven Wasserstrom, *Religion after Religion: Gershom Scholem, Mircea Eliade, and Henry Corbin at Eranos* (Princeton: Princeton University Press, 1999).

[49] „Die legionäre Bewegung hatte die Struktur und die Berufung [*vocație*] einer mystischen Sekte und nicht einer politischen Bewegung. (...) Die einzige massive Widerlegung des bekannten Refrains, das rumänische Volk sei nicht religiös (...) waren die Handlungen einiger Tausend Rumänen in den Jahren 1938–1939, in Gefängnissen oder Lagern, verfolgt oder frei." M. Călinescu, *Despre Ioan P. Culianu și Mircea Eliade*, S. 49, aus M. Eliade, *Memorii* (București: Humanitas, 1991), S. 352f.

[50] M. Călinescu, *Despre Ioan P. Culianu și Mircea Eliade*, S. 68. Alexandru George beschreibt in seinem Essay *Bolșevismul alb* [Der weiße Bolschevismus] den Weg der „Jungen Generation" der Zwischenkriegszeit, der auch Eliade angehörte, wie folgt: Die Ideologen „der Jungen Generation, (...) gelangen direkt in den aristokratischen Anarchismus, in die revolutionäre Pose, in die Amoralität, die frei ist von jeder Verantwortung, das

eine Einschätzung der Bedeutung Eliades für die rumänische Kultur, der den Schlusspunkt des vorliegenden Beitrags setzen soll:

> Was die rumänische Kultur anbelangt, (...) wird Eliade – trotz seiner ideologischen Entgleisung – weiterhin eine Ikone der Vervollkommnung bleiben, ein Genie in einer letztendlich transpolitischen Konstellation von Rumänen (...); eine Zielscheibe für die seltenen Ikonoklasten, eine Inspiration für die noch selteneren Gelehrten auf dem Gebiet der Religionsgeschichte, der Folklore oder der Anthropologie; ein Modell oder ein Antimodell – auch Antimodelle können manchmal genauso wichtig sein, wie die positiven Vorbilder (...).[51]

‚Abenteuer' suchend, stets auf den eigenen Vorteil bedacht." *În istorie, în politică, în literatură* [In Geschichte, Politik, Literatur] (Bucureşti: Albatros, 1997), S. 138. Auch Eliade betonte den Abenteuercharakter (*aventură spirituală*), der den Entscheidungen für gewisse politische Richtungen inhärent sei (z.B. in einem Tagebucheintrag vom 2. Oktober 1946, Unveröffentlichtes Manuskript, Special Collections, Regenstein Library, University of Chicago; vgl. M. Călinescu, ebd.).

[51] Ebd., S. 92.

Bibliographie

Alexandrescu, Sorin. *Paradoxul român* [Das rumänische Paradoxon]. Bucureşti: Editura Univers, 1998.

Antohi, Sorin, Hg. *Religion, Fiction and History: Essays in Memory of Ioan Petru Culianu*, 2 Bde. Bucureşti: Nemira, 2001.

Anton, Ted. *Eros, Magic, and the Murder of Professor Culianu*. Illinois 1996 (rumänische Ausgabe Bucureşti: Nemira, 1997).

Călinescu, Matei. *Despre Ioan P. Culianu şi Mircea Eliade. Amintiri, lecturi, reflecţii.* [Über Ioan P. Culianu und Mircea Eliade. Erinnerungen, Lesarten, Reflexionen], 2. Aufl. Iaşi: Polirom, 2002 (1. Aufl. 2001).

Culianu, Ioan Petru. *Mircea Eliade*. Bucureşti: Nemira, 1995.

Dubuisson, Daniel. *Mythologies du XXe siècle. Dumézil, Lévi-Strauss, Eliade*. Lille: Presse Universitaires de Lille, 1993.

Eliade, Mircea. *Memorii* [Erinnerungen], Bd. 2. Bucureşti: Humanitas, 1991.

———. *Coloana nesfârşită. Teatru* [Die endlose Säule. Theaterstücke], hg. von Mircea Handoca. Bucureşti: Minerva, 1996 (darin die 1939 verfasste, 1941 in Bukarest uraufgeführte Tragödie in drei Akten ‚Iphigenie‘).

———. *Europa, Asia, America...*, Bd. 1: A-H, hg. von Mircea Handoca. Bucureşti: Humanitas, 1999.

———. *Textele ‚legionare‘ şi despre ‚românism‘* [Die ‚legionären‘ Texte und die Texte zum ‚Rumänismus‘], hg. von Mircea Handoca. Cluj-Napoca: Dacia, 2001.

———. *50 de conferinţe radiofonice* [50 Rundfunkvorträge] *1932–1938*. Bucureşti: Humanitas, 2001.

Georgescu, Vlad. *Istoria românilor. De la origini pînă în zilele noastre* [Geschichte der Rumänen. Von den Anfängen bis heute], 4. Aufl. Bucureşti: Humanitas, 1995.

Handoca, Mircea. *‚Dosarul‘ Eliade* [Das Eliade-‚Dossier‘]. Bucureşti: Curtea Veche Publishing, 1998f.

———. *Mircea Eliade: Biobibliografie* [Mircea Eliade: Biobibliographie], 3 Bde. Bucureşti: Editura ‚Jurnalul Literar‘, 1997, 1998, 1999.

———. *Viaţa lui Mircea Eliade* [Mircea Eliades Leben]. Cluj-Napoca: Dacia, 2000.

Heinen, Armin. *Die Legion ‚Erzengel Michael‘ in Rumänien. Soziale Bewegung und politische Organisation. Ein Beitrag zum Problem des internationalen Faschismus*. München: R. Oldenbourg Verlag, 1986 (rumänische Ausgabe Bucureşti: Humanitas, 1999).

Ionescu, Nae. *Între ziaristică şi filosofie. Texte publicate în ziarul ‚Cuvântul‘ (15 august 1926–26 martie 1938)* [Zwischen Journalismus und Philosophie. In der Zeitung ‚Cuvântul‘ veröffentlichte Texte (15. August 1926–26. März 1938)]. Iaşi: Editura Timpul, 1996.

Laignel-Lavastine, Alexandra. *Cioran, Eliade, Ionesco: L'oubli du fascisme*. Presses Universitaires de France: Paris 2002.

Lotreanu, Ion. *Introducere în opera lui Mircea Eliade* [Einführung in das Werk Mircea Eliades]. Bucureşti: Editura Minerva, 1980.

Manea, Norman, „Culpa fericită. Mircea Eliade, fascismul şi soarta nefericită a României" [Glückliche Schuld. Mircea Eliade, der Faschismus und das unglückliche Schicksal Rumäniens]. 22 (1992), Nr. 6–8.

Marino, Adrian. *Hermeneutica lui Mircea Eliade* [Die Hermeneutik Mircea Eliades]. Cluj-Napoca: Dacia, 1980.

Mutti, Claudio. *Le penne dell‘ Arcangelo. Intellettuali e Guardia di Ferro*, Società Editrice Barbarossa: Milano, 1994 (rumänische Ausgabe: *Penele arhangelului. Intelectualii români şi Garda de Fier* [Die Federn des Erzengels. Die rumänischen Intellektuellen und die Eiserne Garde]. Bucureşti: Anastasia, 1997).

———. *Mircea Eliade, Legiunea şi Noua Inchiziţie* [Mircea Eliade, die Legion und die neue Inquisition]. Bucureşti: Editura Vremea.

Nagy-Talavera, Nicholas. *The Green Shirts and the Others. A History of Fascism in Hungary and Romania*. Stanford: Hoover Institution Press, 1970.

Oişteanu, Andrei. „"Eclipsa raţiunii' în cazul Antonescu şi ,miopia politica' în cazul Eliade" [Die ,Verfinsterung der Vernunft' im Fall Antonescu und die ,politische Myopie ' im Fall Eliade]. *22*, 1 (1999), S. X–Y.

——. „Mircea Eliade between political journalism and scholarly work". *Archaeus* 8–1/4 (2004), S. 323–340.

Ornea, Zigu, *Anii treizeci. Extrema dreaptă românească* [Die dreißiger Jahre. Die rumänische äußere Rechte]. Bucureşti: Editura Fundaţiei Culturale Române, 1995.

Sebastian, Mihail. *De două mii de ani. Cum am devenit huligan* [Seit zweitausend Jahren. Wie ich zu einem Hooligan wurde]. Bucureşti: Humanitas, 1992.

——. *Jurnal* [Tagebuch] *1935–1944*. Bucureşti: Humanitas, 1996 (deutsche Ausgabe Berlin: Claassen, 2005).

Stahl, Henri. *Eseuri critice despre cultura românească* [Kritische Essays zur rumänischen Kultur]. Bucureşti: Editura Minerva, 1983.

Totok, William. „Die Generation von Mircea Eliade im Bann des rumänischen Faschismus". *Halbjahresschrift für südosteuropäische Geschichte, Literatur und Politik* 1 (1995), S. 42–55.

Ţurcanu, Florin. *Mircea Eliade. Le prisonnier de l'histoire*. Paris: Éditions La Découverte, 2003.

Ungureanu, Cornel. *Mircea Eliade şi literatura exilului* [Mircea Eliade und die Exilliteratur]. Bucureşti: Editura Viitorul Românesc, 1995.

Veiga, Francisco. *La mística del ultranacionalismo (Historia de la Guardia de Hierro). Rumania 1919–1941*. Bellaterra: Publicacions de la Universitat Autònoma de Barcelona, 1989 (rumänische Ausgaben: Bucureşti: Humanitas, 1991 und 1995).

Volovici, Leon. *Nationalist Ideology and Antisemitism. The Case of Romanian Intellectuals in the 30s*. Oxford: Pergamon Press, 1991 (rumänische Ausgabe: *Ideologia naţionalistă şi ,problema evreiească' în România anilor '30* [Die nationalistische Ideologie und das , jüdische Problem' im Rumänien der dreißiger Jahre]. Bucureşti: Humanitas, 1995.

Vulcănescu, Mircea. *Nae Ionescu. Aşa cum l-am cunoscut* [Nae Ionescu. So wie ich ihn kannte]. Bucureşti: Humanitas, 1992.

PART THREE

THE CATHOLIC PERSPECTIVE

MARIA LAACHS „LITURGISCHE BEWEGUNG" IM ALLGEMEINEN UND ODO CASELS „MYSTERIENTHEOLOGIE" IM BESONDEREN

EIN DOPPELTER RÜCKBLICK AUF KATHOLISCHE RELIGIONSGESCHICHTE, MIT SEITENBLICKEN AUF MIRCEA ELIADE UND STEFAN GEORGE

Richard Faber

> Im kirchlichen Ritual, in Liturgie, Messe, Prozession
> überlebt heute noch repräsentative Öffentlichkeit (...):
> sie basiert auf einem Arkanum.
> (Jürgen Habermas)

> Kirche ist Eucharistie.
> (Josef Ratzinger)

> Religionsgeschichtliche Untersuchungen laufen, zumal
> in labilen Situationen, Gefahr, religiöse Regressionen zu
> befördern.
> (Hubert Cancik)

1. *Mysterientheologie*

Der früher sehr kritische, in seiner Habilitationsschrift über *Katholizismus und Moderne in der Weimarer Republik* weithin politologisch vorgehende Systematische Theologe Thomas Ruster hat der Maria Laacher Mysterientheologie – Odo Casels speziell – 1994 eine „*reductio in mysterium*" nachgesagt: in mysterium *cultus*, und sich dabei vor allem auf folgende Mysteriums-Definition in Casels Buch über *Das christliche Kultmysterium* von 1932 gestützt:

> Das Mysterium ist eine heilige *kultische* Handlung, in der eine Heilstatsache unter dem Ritus *Gegenwart* wird; indem die Kultgemeinde diesen Ritus vollzieht, *nimmt* sie an der Heilstatsache *teil* und erwirbt sich *dadurch* das Heil.[1]

---

[1] Thomas Ruster, *Die verlorene Nützlichkeit der Religion. Katholizismus und Moderne in der Weimarer Republik* (Paderborn u.a.: Schöningh, 1994), S. 257.

Ruster, der einen „gleichsam selbstreferentiellen Vollzug des Kult-
mysteriums" bei den Laachern konstatiert,[2] interpretiert dennoch religions*geschichtlich*: „Mysterium im engeren Sinn meint bei Casel einen
Vollzug, eine dramatisch-liturgische Handlung, die die Feiernden mit
dem *Kultheros* vereint".[3] Ruster, der festhält, dass für Casel die religiösen
Formen des ‚Heidentums‘ generell die Natur sind, auf der nach dem
scholastischen Axiom die Gnade aufbaut, pointiert mit seiner Rede vom
Kult*heros* die ‚pagane‘ Dimension der Mysterientheologie auf besonders
archaisierende Weise.[4]

Über den spezifisch soziopolitischen Charakter der Kult*gemeinde* urteilt
Ruster als Zeithistoriker, obwohl gleichfalls *Un*gleichzeitigkeit, wenn
nicht schlechte Romantik diagnostizierend:

> Der standesbewußte Katholizismus des 19. Jahrhunderts zog sich bei ihm
> [Odo Casel, R.F.] in die Liturgie zurück. Dort ergänzten und bestärkten
> sich die Theologie und das Wissen um die natürlichen Gliederungen unter
> den Menschen (...) gegenseitig in dem Bemühen, das zu leisten, was der
> traditionelle Katholizismus für die ganze römisch-katholische Gesellschaft
> geleistet hatte: ‚Einweisung in die soziale Rolle‘, ‚Disziplinierung‘ und
> ‚Verklärung‘.[5]

Auf diesen gesellschafts- bzw. gemeinschafts-sakralisierenden und deshalb extrem affirmativen Charakter der Mysterien-Theologie ist nicht
weniger einzugehen als auf ihren extrem *irrationalen*, dem eine hoch
selektive Rezeption des Hellenismus entsprach (sei es als Voraussetzung
oder als Folge solchen Irrationalismus). Besonders fatal war dabei – nicht
nur des aufziehenden „Dritten Reiches" wegen – die Eliminierung alles
irgend Jüdischen, sogar „Alttestamentlichen":

---

[2] Ebd., S. 262.
[3] Ebd., S. 257.
[4] Ebd., S. 262. Wie richtig Ruster damit zugleich die (prä-)faschistische Dimension
Laachs akzentuiert, belegen besonders gut Reden, die der Laacher Abt Ildefons Herwegen im Jahre 1933 gehalten hat. Vgl. Marcel Albert, *Die Benediktinerabtei Maria Laach
und der Nationalsozialismus* (Paderborn u.a.: Schöningh, 2003), S. 60 und S. 62f. sowie
die letzten Absätze meines vorliegenden Beitrages. Was das ‚Archaisieren‘ angeht,
vgl. Richard Faber, „Archaisch/Archaismus", in Hubert Cancik u.a., Hg., *Handbuch
religionswissenschaftlicher Grundbegriffe*, Bd. 2 (Stuttgart: Kohlhammer, 1990), S. 51–56
und ders., „‚Pagan‘ und Neo-Paganismus", in ders. und Renate Schlesier, Hg., *Die
Restauration der Götter. Antike Religion und Neo-Paganismus* (Würzburg: Königshausen &
Neumann, 1986), S. 10–25.
[5] Ruster, Die verlorene *Nützlichkeit der Religion*, S. 267.

Die Schriften des Alten Bundes finden in der mysterien-theologischen Literatur so viel wie gar keine Verwendung. Der Grund liegt nach der Behauptung Casels darin, daß dem Alten Testament der Begriff des kultischen Mysteriums fremd gewesen sei.[6]

So hat Theodor Filthaut bereits 1947 konstatiert und Hubert Cancik 1974 – wie in logischer Fortführung des Laach-kritischen Theologen: „Casel unterdrückt die *synagogale* Tradition, den jüdischen Wortgottesdienst: die demokratischste und rationalste Tradition innerhalb des christlichen Kultus."[7] Diese Unterdrückung bzw. Verdrängung ist aber, wie ich hinzusetze, nur konsequent; denn „ je mehr die Religion zu einer Religion des verkündeten Wortes wird und im Sagbaren ihr Schwergewicht erhält, desto mehr schwindet" – mit Worten des mythomanen Heidegger-Schülers Eugen Fink von noch 1960 – „die magische Substanz, das *mythische* Schauspiel."[8]

Casel, der 1938 dem Judentum – von ihm mit den „Semiten" überhaupt identifizierbar – generell nur „eine ,Episode' in der Heilsveranstaltung Gottes" konzedierte,[9] verdrängte es sogar zugunsten der griechisch-römischen Antike – was das für ihn entscheidende, sein Christentum geradezu ausmachende Kultmysterium anging. Dass dieses mehr als das entsprechende und ihm vorangehende Gedächtnis des jüdischen Volkes am Pessachfest Gedächtnisfeier des „Pascha-Mysteriums" sein soll,[10] ist gleichsam normal christlich. Casel deklariert aber darüber hinaus die *griechisch-römischen* Mysterienkulte zur entscheidenden „Vorschule Christi", indem er die Meinung vertritt, daß das Pascha-Mysterium dem „einseitig jüdischen Geiste ein *Greuel*" gewesen sei.[11] Auf

---

[6] Theodor Filthaut, *Die Kontroverse über die Mysterienlehre* (Warendorf: Schnell, 1947), S. 75.

[7] H. Cancik, Brief an den Verfasser vom Juli 1974.

[8] Eugen Fink, *Spiel als Weltsymbol* (Stuttgart: Kohlhammer, 1960), S. 186.

[9] Vgl. Ruster, *Die verlorene Nützlichkeit der Religion*, S. 263f.; zum Laacher Antijudaismus bis Antisemitismus siehe jetzt auch Marcel Albert, *Die Benediktinerabtei Maria Laach und der Nationalsozialismus* (Paderborn u.a.: Schöningh, 2003), S. 163f. und, was Stefan George und nicht wenige der Seinen angeht, Gert Mattenklott u.a. Hg., *Verkannte Brüder? Stefan George und das deutsch-jüdische Bürgertum zwischen Jahrhundertwende und Emigration* (Hildesheim: Olms, 2001), bes. die Beiträge von J. Egyptien, M. Philipp und R. Kolk (ebd., S. 15ff.).

[10] Ruster, *Die verlorene Nützlichkeit der Religion*, S. 258. „Zu dem bloß vergegenwärtigenden Erinnern kommt [nach Casel, R.F.] im christlichen Kult die reale, mystische Vereinigung der Gläubigen mit Christus hinzu, die das Erinnerte zur wirksamen, heilschaffenden Gegenwart werden läßt." (Ebd.).

[11] Vgl. Ruster, *Die verlorene Nützlichkeit der Religion*, S. 260.

der für das Christentum vorbildlichen religiösen Formgebung durch die vor- und nichtjüdische Antike beruhe dagegen „der *absolute* Wert, den wir (…) dem hellenistisch-römischen Zeitalter zugesprochen haben."[12]

Casel fand die Grundelemente seines Verständnisses vom Kultmysterium in den ‚paganen' Mysterienkulten vor und übernahm sie von dort, wobei nicht genügend betont werden kann, dass religionsgeschichtliche und heilsgeschichtlich-theologische Betrachtungsweise bei Casel *unentwirrbar* miteinander verbunden sind. Nach ihm wollten bereits die griechisch-römischen Mysterienkulte ihre Kultgenossen zur Einheit mit der Gottheit führen. Sie waren Gedächtnisfeiern, und sie vollzogen die mystische Einheit mit der Gottheit in einem dramatischen Ablauf, in den die Mitfeiernden eingeweiht und hineingenommen wurden. „Allzu klar stehen die Analogien jedem vor Augen", wie Casel überzeugt ist. „Auf beiden Seiten haben wir einen Kult, der auf dem Weg liturgischer Mystik die Menschen zur innigsten Gottesgemeinschaft führen soll."[13]

Bis in die Einzelheiten hinein glaubt Casel zeigen zu können, dass alle Elemente der ‚paganen' Mysterien in den christlichen Sakramenten ihre Entsprechung finden: der Glaube an die „Wiedergeburt", die Vereinigung mit der Gottheit im Opfer, die Übungen der Einweihung. Und auch darin sieht er eine Analogie, dass die Eingeweihten der Mysterien bereits hier auf Erden aus der Menge der Sterblichen hinausgenommen sind und unter sich eine „heilige Gemeinschaft unter der Führung einer auserwählten auctoritativen Priesterschaft" bilden. Casel empfindet es generell als glückliche Fügung, ja als „Vorsehung", dass dem jungen Christentum in den griechisch-römischen Kulten die religiösen Formen zur Verfügung standen, die seinem eigenen Wesen zutiefst entsprachen und in denen es das Christusmysterium ausdrücken konnte[14] – besser jedenfalls als in den Formen des synagogalen Gottesdienstes.

Ich selbst habe bereits 1981 darauf aufmerksam gemacht, dass Casel zitiert, was „Paulus von den Kultriten des Alten Bundes" sagt: „Das Gesetz enthielt nur einen Schattenriß der zukünftigen Güter, nicht das Bild der Dinge selbst", und dass Casel diese Passage *kommentiert* mit den Worten: „Wieviel mehr gilt das von den Riten der Antike!" Nur wenige Sätze zuvor *spezifiziert* er jedoch:

---

[12] Vgl. ebd., S. 251.
[13] Vgl. ebd., S. 259.
[14] Vgl. ebd., S. 259f.

(...) die Welt, die [‚pagane‘, R.F.] Gemeinde braucht immer neues Leben. Deshalb vollzieht sich im Kult *immer von Neuem* jene Epiphanie, jene rettende, heilbringende Tat des Gottes. Der Kult ist das Mittel, sie *wieder* zur Wirklichkeit und dadurch zur Heilsquelle werden zu lassen.

Eben dies ist er für die christliche Kirche auch noch; Casel läßt keinen Zweifel daran: „In jedem Kirchenjahr begehen wir *wieder* die Urheilstat und werden dadurch heil." „Das Kirchenjahr ist [also, R.F.] nicht Linie, sondern *Kreis*. Im Kirchenjahr gibt es nichts Neues, sondern immer *Dasselbe*." Mit jedem „ersten Adventssonntag" beginnt der „Kreislauf (...) von Neuem", wie Casel veranschaulicht.[15]

Mir kommt es im Folgenden – wie schon 1981 – ganz entscheidend auf die Differenz zur, vor allem aber auf die Identität der der Mysterientheologie zugrundeliegenden Zeit-Metaphysik mit der antik-‚heidnischen' an:

> Die Natur ist das ewig Fließende. (...) Aber Christus und die Kirche stehen über der Natur im Reiche des ewigen Geistes. (...) Wenn also die Kirche von einem ‚Kirchenjahr‘ oder besser *mit den Alten* von einem ‚Jahreskreis‘ (anni circulus) spricht, so verbindet sie damit andere Gedanken. Der Kreis ist *für die Alten* gerade das Gegenteil aller Entwicklung; er ist als das an sich vollkommen Abgerundete das Symbol des Ewigen und Göttlichen. (...) Der heilige Kreislauf der Liturgie soll also [wie *bei den Alten*, R.F.] vom Ewigen künden, nicht von dem Leben der Natur, das heute keimt, morgen blüht (...) und übermorgen hinwelkt.

Dennoch ist und bleibt auch die Liturgie „Kreislauf ".[16]

Die mythische Form der identischen Wiederholung bietet sich – kritisch gesehen – als die naheliegendste und machtvollste Gestalt für das Bewusstsein historischer Kontinuität an. Diese wird allerdings nicht mehr als historische gewusst, sondern gegen den Fortgang der Geschichte aufrechterhalten, im Sprung über die historische Differenz hinweg, die die Gegenwart immer weiter vom maßgeblichen Ursprung

---

[15] Vgl. R. Faber, *Roma aeterna. Zur Kritik der ‚Konservativen Revolution‘* (Würzburg: Königshausen & Neumann, 1981), S. 111–113; mein vorliegender Text stützt sich insgesamt auf die Kapitel I, 5/6 dieses Buches bzw. deren verselbständigte Version mit dem Titel „Politischer Katholizismus. Die Bewegung von Maria Laach", in H. Cancik, Hg., *Religions- und Geistesgeschichte der Weimarer Republik* (Düsseldorf: Patmos, 1982), S. 136–158.

[16] Odo Casel, *Das christliche Kultmysterium* (Regensburg: Pustet, 4. Aufl. 1960, 1. Aufl. 1932), S. 91.

trennt.[17] Und *der* Sprung-Stab dazu ist der Kult; vor allem in ihm gewinnen Überlieferungen, die von ihrem Inhalt her noch keineswegs als mythische identifizierbar sind, diesen ‚Sinn': „Ein Christ nimmt", um den affirmativen Mircea Eliade zu zitieren,

> nicht an einer Gedenkfeier eines geschichtlichen Ereignisses, z.B. des 14. Juli oder des 11. November, teil. Er gedenkt nicht eines Ereignisses, er vergegenwärtigt ein *Mysterium*. Für einen Christen stirbt und aufersteht Jesus vor ihm, ‚hic et nunc'. Durch das Mysterium der Passion und der Auferstehung überwindet der Christ die profane Zeit, wird er in die heilige Urzeit eingeführt.[18]

Zwei Seiten vorher heißt es bei dem − Casel vielfach kongenialen − von Haus aus rumänisch-orthodoxen Eliade,

> daß das Christentum (…) zumindest *einen* mythischen Zug hat bewahren müssen: die *liturgische* Zeit, das heißt die Ablehnung der profanen Zeit und die periodische Wiedergewinnung der Großen Zeit, des ‚illud tempus' des ‚Anbeginns'.[19]

Und − Pointe der Pointe − Casel wusste solche ‚Religionswissenschaft' von vornherein zu schätzen, schon 1938 − Eliade sympathisierte in dieser Zeit mit Rumäniens „Eiserner Garde"[20] − schrieb Casel:

> Erst ganz allmählich kehren wir heute unter dem erschütternden Eindruck des Bankerotts des Humanismus zur älteren, vorwissenschaftlichen Auffassung der Religion zurück. Hier liegt vielleicht der tiefste Wert der religionsgeschichtlichen Forschung für unsere Zeit und auch der Grund ihres Wiederauflebens in unserer Zeit: die geheime Sehnsucht nach den

---

[17] Vgl. Wolfhart Pannenberg, „Späthorizonte des Mythos in biblischer und christlicher Überlieferung", in Manfred Fuhrmann, Hg., *Terror und Spiel. Probleme der Mythenrezeption* (München: Fink, 1971), S. 473–525, hier S. 500.

[18] Mircea Eliade, *Mythen, Träume und Mysterien* (Salzburg: Müller, 1961), S. 30.

[19] Eliade, Mythen, Träume und Mysterien, S. 28. Carsten Colpe hat im Gespräch mit mir immer wieder auf die seines Erachtens fundamentale Wichtigkeit der liturgischen Sozialisiation des jungen Eliade für den späteren Religionswissenschaftler hingewiesen.

[20] Vgl. Mac Lincsot Ricketts, *Mircea Eliade. The Romanian Roots, 1907–1945*, 2 Bde. (Boulder, Col.: East European Monographs, 1988); zum bis zuletzt anhaltenden Antijudaismus der Eliadeschen Religionsideologie vgl. in aller Kürze R. Faber, „‚Der Zersetzer'", in Julius H. Schoeps und Joachim Schlör, Hg., *Antisemitismus. Vorurteile und Mythen* (München: Piper, 1995), S. 260–264. In unserem Zusammenhang besonders bemerkenswert ist die Eloge des späteren rumänischen Pressereferenten in Lissabon auf Oliveira Salazar *Salazar si revulotia din Portugalia* [Salazar und die Revolution in Portugal], Bukarest 1942. Was die deutsch-katholische Begeisterung für Salazar angeht, über 1945 hinaus, vgl. R. Faber, *Lateinischer Faschismus. Über Carl Schmitt den Römer und Katholiken* (Berlin-Wien: Philo, 2001), Kap. III, 2.

ursprünglichen und den ganzen Menschen umwandelnden Formen der Religion, wie sie dem Altertum eigen waren und im alten Christentum, durch göttliche Offenbarung unterstützt, zu ihrem Gipfel gelangten.[21]

Casels Programm einer Religionsgeschichte zugunsten *vorwissenschaftlicher* Religionsauffassung benennt im voraus den Entstehungsgrund auch der Eliadeschen Religionsphilosophie, wenn nicht *-ideologie*. Schon Casel sah sich mit seinem Werk an einer „Weltenwende" stehen,

> wie sie in solchem Ausmaß vielleicht noch nie über diese Erde hingegangen ist. Nie hatte allerdings auch die Menschheit die Wende, die conversio, die Bekehrung, die Neubelebung mehr notwendig als heute. Denn nie war sie so weit vom göttlichen Mysterium abgeirrt, nie hatte sie sich so sehr dem Tode hingegeben.

Die epochale Wende, die Casel damals – man schrieb das Jahr 1932 – „zuerst in kleinen Kreisen" sich vollziehen sah, sollte die Überwindung des rationalistischen und subjektivistischen Geistes bringen;

> in den Niederungen der Masse ist (dieser) zwar heute lebendiger als je, aber auf den Höhen rötet sich ein neuer Tag, der über den Rationalismus und Materialismus hinweg zu einem neuen symbolischen Denken, zu einer Mystik, zurückstrebt.

Und Casel *sah* sich in seinen Bestrebungen mit „den Besten unserer Zeit" vereint, die

> aus all der Äußerlichkeit einer durch Industrialismus, Mammonismus, Demokratismus entgotteten Welt sich in die Tiefen der Seele zurückziehen und dort den geheimnisvollen Stimmen lauschen, die aus einer besseren Welt herübertönen.[22]

Es war also wohl richtig, Casels Werk in den Zusammenhang der nach dem Ersten Weltkrieg verbreiteten Suche nach dem „Objektiven", dem „Irrationalen", dem „Ganzheitlichen" und der „wahren Volksgemeinschaft" zu rücken,[23] wie ich es mit als erster getan habe. Casel glaubte aber auch, dieser Suche durch die von ihm betriebene Wiederentdeckung des „Mysteriums" die entscheidende Richtung weisen zu können. Bereits die ‚paganen' Mysterienreligionen hätten

---

[21] O. Casel, *Das christliche Opfermysterium. Zur Morphologie und Theologie des eucharistischen Hochgebetes* (Graz: Styria, 1968), S. 198; was den auch von Casel und Eliade geteilten Antihumanismus angeht, vgl. R. Faber, Hg., *Streit um den Humanismus* (Würzburg: Königshausen & Neumann, 2003), bes. Kap III.

[22] Vgl. Ruster, *Die verlorene Nützlichkeit der Religion*, S. 252f.

[23] Ebd., S. 253.

„die unbedingte Gottesherrschaft und den Gemeinschaftsgedanken in ihrer alles überragenden Stellung" in Geltung gesetzt. Indem nun die römisch-katholische Liturgie das Erbe der Mysterienkulte bewahrt, ja sie in ihrem eigentlichen Sinne „erfüllt" habe,[24] seien von ihr die Kräfte für die Überwindung der entgotteten Welt zu beziehen,[25] und eben auch in socio-politicis.

2. *Hierarchische Gemeinschaftslehre*

Casel führt ausdrücklich die Verwandtschaft zwischen liturgischem und kirchlich-*politischem* Handeln auf und nennt dabei zuerst die „Idee der *Gemeinschaft*":

> Die katholische Aktion will den Grundsatz verwirklichen: Alle für einen und einer für alle. Sie will jene Erkenntnis durchsetzen, (…) daß nämlich der einzelne durch seine Tüchtigkeit dem Ganzen nicht wesentlich nützen kann, daß aber, wenn das Ganze blüht, auch der einzelne sich wohlbefindet. Wo ist dieser Grundsatz (…) besser und großartiger durchgeführt als in der katholischen Liturgie?[26]

Ferner kann sich die Kirchenpolitik die Liturgie auch darin zum Vorbild nehmen, dass sie die Mitarbeit der Laien unbedingt will, aber nur unter Führung der kirchlichen Autorität. In der Liturgie ist dieses Verhältnis von Laien und Führern vorgebildet: Einerseits ist die Anteilnahme aller Feiernden Bedingung für die Feier des Mysteriums, andererseits ist die Liturgie „wesentlich an das Priestertum der Kirche gebunden", die Kirche erlebt sich dort als „sichtbare, *monarchische* Gemeinschaft". Dazu kommt, dass nur der Mann diese führende Rolle in der Liturgie einnehmen kann, während die Frau dort nicht herrschen kann und soll, „sondern in Liebe dienen und dadurch mit dem Herrn einswerden". An solchen Hinweisen sollte die von der Hierarchie gesteuerte „Katholische Aktion" nicht achtlos vorbeigehen. Casel fasst zusammen:

---

[24] Wörtlich heißt es in O. Casels *Christlichem Opfermysterium* (Graz: Styria, 1968), S. 439: „Wer Christus hat, besitzt das wahre und höchste Mysterium, in dem alle anderen Mysterien erfüllt sind." Vgl. auch Casel, „Das Weihnachtsmysterium", *Hochland* 27–1 (1929/30), S. 193–201, hier S. 201.

[25] Vgl. Ruster, *Die verlorene Nützlichkeit der Religion*, S. 253, aber auch Albert, *Die Benediktinerabtei Maria Laach und der Nationalsozialismus*, S. 76 und S. 229.

[26] Ruster, *Die verlorene Nützlichkeit der Religion*, S. 254f. und Albert, *Die Benediktinerabtei Maria Laach und der Nationalsozialismus*, S 136.

> Die Autorität der Hierarchie tritt nirgends in so klarer und liebenswerter Weise hervor wie in der Liturgie, wo der Priester als der Vater im Pneuma, als der Erzeuger des übernatürlichen Lebens und damit als größter Wohltäter erscheint.[27]

Ich lasse Casels so patriarchale wie mystifizierende Sprache auf sich beruhen und gebe sofort dem Maria Laach und seiner „Liturgischen Bewegung" gleichfalls eng verbundenen Romano Guardini das Wort, der zugleich dem auch staatlichen, ja gesamtgesellschaftlichen, sprich *volksgemeinschaftlichen* Anspruch dieser Bewegung Ausdruck verleiht – schon im Ersten Weltkrieg:[28]

> Das Ich, welches die liturgische Gebetshandlung trägt, ist nicht die einfache Zusammenzählung aller gleichgläubigen Einzelnen. Es ist deren Gesamtheit, aber sofern die Einheit als solche etwas ist, abgesehen von der Menge derer, die sie bilden: *die Kirche*. Hier liegt etwas Ähnliches vor wie im Staatsleben. Der Staat ist mehr als die Gesamtzahl der Bürger, Behörden, Gesetze und Einrichtungen usw. Die Glieder des Staates fühlen sich nicht nur als Teile einer größeren Zahl, sondern irgendwie als Glieder eines übergreifenden, lebenden Einheitswesens. Etwas Entsprechendes, freilich in einer wesentlich anders gearteten Ordnung, der übernatürlichen, stellt die Kirche dar.[29]

Guardini bestätigt – per Selbstaussage – was der Carl Schmitt- und Othmar Spann-Schüler Christoph Steding 1932, eine entwickelte „katholische" Soziologie vor Augen, gleichsam von außen feststellen wird: Zum Wesen des katholischen Ethos gehört, „daß das Ganze, der gesellschaftliche Organismus, die Gemeinschaft, die *Institution* (...) grundsätzlich dem Individuum ‚vorhergeht'."[30] Guardini selbst lässt keinen Zweifel, dass die Liturgie *total* ist, wie ihre Kirche und der dieser entsprechende Staat:

> Das Einzelwesen muß darauf verzichten, seine eigenen Gedanken zu denken, seine eigenen Wege zu gehen. Es hat den Absichten und Wegen der Liturgie zu folgen. Es muß seine Selbstverfügung an sie abgeben; mitbeten, statt selbständig vorzugehen; gehorchen, statt frei über sich

---

[27] Ruster, *Die verlorene Nützlichkeit der Religion*, S. 255.

[28] Auf keinen Fall weniger einschlägig als Guardinis eigene Ausführungen ist das schon 1918 den Christlichen Ständestaat propagierende Vorwort, das der Laacher Abt Ildefons Herwegen zu Guardinis Buch beigesteuert hat. Siehe Romano Guardini, *Vom Geist der Liturgie* (Freiburg: Herder, 6. Aufl. 1962), S. 7–14.

[29] Ebd., S. 45f.; heute liegt Guardinis Buch in 20. Auflage (Mainz 1997) vor.

[30] Christoph Steding, *Politik und Wissenschaft bei Max Weber* (Breslau: Korn, 1932), S. 90.

zu verfügen; in der Ordnung stehen, statt sich nach eigenem Willen zu bewegen.[31]

Offensichtlich ist von der Liturgie *jemandes* die Rede, *dessen* „Absichten und Wegen" das „Einzelwesen" folgen, *dem* es „gehorchen" muss: Die „Ordnung" hat ihre Ordner; mythisch-affirmativ, in der hauptsächlich von Dionysius Areopagitas „Hierarchie der Engel" inspirierten Sprache Erik Petersons: die Engel. *Ihre* himmlische Liturgie bildet die irdische vor; diese ist nur ihr Abbild – ein hierarchisches: „Den Gesängen der Kirche korrespondieren himmlische Gesänge, und *je* nach der Art der Teilnahme am himmlischen Gesang gliedert sich auch das innere Leben der Kirche." – „Die Engel mit ihrem Gesange (...) gliedern (...) die Kirche in ‚Engelähnliche' und in ‚Volk'".[32]

Um zu entmythologisieren: Die „Engel-Ähnlichen" tun das: die Mönche und Priester. Und *mythologisch* wird das dadurch möglich, dass die „untersten (Engel-)Chöre die oberste Stufe der Kirche berühren". Infolgedessen „schließt sich das ganze Gefüge der übereinander getürmten Ränge zu *einer* (...) Einheit, und *eine* geistige Leiter entsteht, die vom *Mönch* bis zum Herzen der Gottheit führt"[33] – unter Ausschluss des Volkes.

Als Antwort auf die Frage: „Cui bono?" läßt sich mit Hugo Balls – freilich affirmativen – Worten sagen: Der „himmlischen Hierarchie (...) obliegt die Vergottung des *Priester*reichs".[34] Und nicht nur das der Priester, wie es bei Peterson mit seiner Ablehnung *jeder* „Politischen Theologie" den Anschein hat[35] – auch und gerade im Mittelalter nicht: „*Seit* dem Pseudo-Dionysos wiederholt sich immer wieder der Vergleich zwischen der Hierarchie der himmlischen Chöre und der irdischen

---

[31] Guardini, *Vom Geist der Liturgie*, S. 48; vgl. auch Albert, *Die Benediktinerabtei Maria Laach*, S. 55f.

[32] Erik Peterson, *Das Buch von den Engeln. Stellung und Bedeutung der heiligen Engel im Kultus* (Leipzig: Hegner, 1935), S. 98f.; vgl. auch Jürgen Habermas, *Strukturwandel der Öffentlichkeit. Untersuchungen zu einer Kategorie der bürgerlichen Gesellschaft* (Neuwied und Berlin: Luchterhand, 4. Aufl. 1969), S. 18f.

[33] Hugo Ball, *Byzantinisches Christentum. Drei Heiligenleben* (München/Leipzig: Duncker & Humblot, 1923), S. 202.

[34] Ebd., S 232

[35] Vgl. Peterson „Kaiser Augustus im Urteil des antiken Christentums", in Jacob Taubes, Hg., *Der Fürst dieser Welt. Carl Schmitt und die Folgen* (München: Fink, 1983), S. 174–180 und ders., *Der Monotheismus als politisches Problem* (Leipzig: Hegner, 1935) sowie Schmitt, *Politische Theologie II. Zur Legende von der Erledigung jeder Politischen Theologie* (Berlin: Duncker & Humblot, 1970) und Faber, *Die Verkündigung Vergils: Reich – Kirche – Staat. Zur Kritik der ‚Politischen Theologie'* (Hildesheim/New York: Olms, 1975), bes. „Einleitung".

Hierarchie der Kirche *und* der Herrschaftsverbände",[36] wobei – direkt – jene diese rechtfertigt.

Der spätere Kardinal-Erzbischof Joseph Höffner weist 1939 in aktualisierender Absicht darauf hin:

> Der herrschaftsständische Gesellschaftsaufbau kam dem (...) [mittelalterlichen, R.F.] Menschen umso natürlicher vor, als man ja auch in der kirchlichen Hierarchie dasselbe Prinzip verwirklicht sah. Man zählte deshalb (...) ohne Bedenken die weltlichen und geistlichen Stände in derselben Reihe auf. Die katholische Kirche war ja auch, in ihrer inneren Organisation einem deutschen Herrschaftsverband' (O. v. Gierke) sehr ähnlich.[37]

Dies ist der „sakral *politische*" Kern des „hierarchischen Prinzips" (Georg Weippert), aber es ist ein universal-metaphysisches: „*Jedes* Ding der Welt muß sein officium erfüllen, und jedes Ding hat seinen Stand, ordo, status in der Weltordnung. Die *Welt* ist ‚ständisch' gegliedert" und „das himmelriche" nur ihre „höchste politische Gemeinschaft". Die Frage nach dessen Ständen ist

> darum ein so brennendes, jedermann interessierendes, vitales Problem, weil sie auf das Engste zusammenhängt mit der Frage der endgültigen sozialen Stellung jedes einzelnen Menschen, mit seiner Rangordnung im Himmelreich. Nicht nur der Mönch und Asket streben nach einem hohen Rang im Jenseits, sondern dies ist das natürliche Verlangen *jedes* Menschen.

Wer aber „einen hohen Stand" haben will, muss sich auf *Erden* darum bemühen.

> Der Mensch ist bestimmt, in die englischen Stände aufgenommen zu werden; jeder wird in den Engelstand aufgenommen, den er auf Erden nachgeahmt hat: (...) 'Got wil *dort* iechelicheme geben den kor den hie gedienet sin leben mit tugentlicher arbeit.'[38]

Um den hierarchiekritischen Friedrich Heer weiter zu zitieren:

> Der himmlische (...) Stand (...) entspricht dem realen irdischen Stand jedes Menschen; dieser ist, wenn auch nur ein schwaches, so doch ein wirkliches Abbild der himmlischen Ordnung. Daher werden oft die

---

[36] Friedrich August von der Heydte, *Die Geburtsstunde des souveränen Staates* (Regensburg: Habbel, 1952), S. 13.

[37] Joseph Höffner, *Kirche und Bauer im deutschen Mittelalter* (Paderborn: Schöningh, 1939), S. 80.

[38] Friedrich Heer, *Die Tragödie des Heiligen Reiches* (Stuttgart: Kohlhammer, 1952), S. 137f.

irdischen Stände mit den himmlischen in Beziehung gesetzt. (…) Gott
sendet zum Beispiel die himmlischen Fürsten, das heißt den Engelstand
der Fürstentümer, um die irdischen Fürsten – die er nach dem Bilde der
himmlischen Fürsten geformt hat –, zu lenken und zu leiten; die irdischen
Fürsten erhalten dann auch einen ihrer irdischen Stellung entsprechenden
Rang im Himmel. Welt und Überwelt erscheinen gleichmäßig gestuft und
ineinander verzahnt; die irdische Rangordnung gleicht der himmlischen,
ja, sie soll sich geradezu nach dem Muster der überweltlichen Hierarchie
aufbauen und ausordnen. Auf der Höhe der Scholastik entwirft der
Bischof von Paris, Wilhelm von Auvergne, eine himmlische Staats- und
Ständelehre, die dem irdischen Staat als Vorbild dienen soll.[39]

Im Laufe der geschichtlichen Entwicklung (so sieht es Hugo von St. Victor) gleicht sich der soziale Aufbau der irdischen Familie Christi immer
mehr der himmlischen an. Aufgabe jeder irdischen Politik, sei sie nun
‚weltlich‘ oder ‚geistlich‘, ist daher die Organisierung und Ausformung
des Diesseits nach der Ordnung des Jenseits. Vorbild jedes irdischen
Gemeinwesens, sei es nun des Staats oder der Kirche, ist der Staat Gottes,
das himmlische Jerusalem, dessen glanzvolle Mauern geschichtet sind
aus den verschiedenen ordines – eine untrennbare Einheit, in der kein
ordo fehlen darf.[40]

Damit es insgesamt *ein* ordo ist: „ordo *universi*". Und an seiner Stelle muss
jeder einzelne der Ordines sein, verharrend auf der ihm zugeordneten
Stufe: „In der Sache der Ordnungen (…) sind wir Hierarchisten."[41]

3. *Literarisches „Interregnum" der ersten deutschen und österreichischen Republik*

Apodiktisch heißt es beim zuletzt zitierten Theodor Haecker:

Ordnung ist nichts anderes, als daß jedes Ding, das ist, zunächst einmal
in sich selber ganz sei, nicht mehr und nicht weniger, und also auch
nicht mehr beanspruche, als was ihm gemäß seinem Sein zukommt,
hinwiederum aber auch nicht mit weniger sich zufrieden gebe, als was
ihm seinem Sein gemäß gebührt. Ordnung ist das äußere und innere
rechte Verhalten zu sich selber und zu allem anderen.[42]

---

[39] Ebd., S. 138f.
[40] Ebd.
[41] Theodor Haecker, *Werke*, Bd. 5 (München: Kösel, 1967), S. 219.
[42] Haecker, *Werke*, Bd. 3, S. 495f.

Diese Definition vorausgesetzt, ist *jetzt* Unordnung, was gerade Haecker mit seiner Rede vom „Chaos" auch behauptet.[43]

Gleichsam transzendental war die Unordnung immer schon möglich; die Bewahrung vor ihr verlangt eine irdische Macht, die *als solche* erschütterbar ist; dass sie Gottes Stelle vertritt und *seine* Ordnung bewahren soll, hindert das nicht: sie *soll* dies nur tun. Deswegen liegt kein Anachronismus vor, wenn ein „konservativer Revolutionär" wie Hugo von Hofmannsthal die „Weisheit" seines „Salzburger Großen Welttheaters" den König mahnen lässt: „Gedenk: das Hohe hoch, das Niedrige niedrig *halten*."[44] Doch freilich, der Carl Schmitt verbundene Hofmannsthal[45] spricht ausdrücklich aus einer Situation heraus, wo es *keinen* „katechon" – von Schmitt auch als „Niedrighalter" übersetzt[46] – mehr gibt, jedenfalls keinen institutionell abgesicherten, und Hofmannsthal deswegen sich genötigt sieht, selbst aktiv zu werden, ersatzweise *literarisch*.[47] (Dass sein neobarockes Mysterienspiel 1922 in der Salzburger Kollegienkirche uraufgeführt wurde, doch eben im Rahmen der Salzburger *Festspiele*, dementiert diese Charakteristik keineswegs.[48])

„Dichtung ist der Ort der Gegenwart der *Götter*", schreibt der Heidegger-Schüler Walter Bröcker in seiner Interpretation der Hölderlin'schen

---

[43] Vgl. Haecker, *Werke*, Bd. 5, S. 46f.; kritisch: Joachim Schumacher, *Die Angst vor dem Chaos. Über die falsche Apokalypse des Bürgertums* (Frankfurt/M.: Makol-Verlag, 2. Aufl. 1972), S. 139 und Max Horkheimer, „Der Wolkenkratzer", in ders., *Notizen 1950 bis 1956 und Dämmerung. Notizen in Deutschland*, hg. von Werner Brede (Frankfurt a.M.: S. Fischer Verlag, 1977, nach der Erstauflage unter dem Pseudonym Heinrich Regius, *Dämmerung. Notizen in Deutschland*, Zürich: Precht & Helbing, 1934), S. 287f. sowie ders. „Zu Theodor Haeckers ‚Der Christ und die Geschichte'" (1936), in: ders., *Kritische Theorie. Eine Dokumentation*, hg. von A. Schmidt, Bd. I und II Studienausgabe (Frankfurt/M.: Fischer, 1977, S. 361–373.

[44] Hugo von Hofmannsthal, *Das Schrifttum als geistiger Raum der Nation* (München: Verlag der Bremer Presse, 1927) und ders., *Das Salzburger Große Welttheater* (Frankfurt/M.: Fischer, 1957), S. 33.

[45] Vgl. neuerdings Marcus Twellman, *Das Drama der Souveränität. Hugo von Hofmannsthal und Carl Schmitt* (München: Wilhelm Fink, 2004).

[46] Carl Schmitt, „Drei Stufen historischer Sinngebung", *Universitas* 5 (1960), S. 927–931, hier S. 929.

[47] Ausführlicher Faber, *Roma aeterna*, S. 175f.

[48] Vgl. zur Ideologie der Salzburger Festspiele generell Michael P. Steinberg, *Ursprung und Ideologie der Salzburger Festspiele 1890–1938* (Salzburg: Pustet, 2000); was Laachs Salzburg-Connections angeht, verweise ich auf Dagmar Pöpping, *Abendland. Christliche Akademiker und die Utopie der Antimoderne 1900–1945* (Berlin: Metropol 2002), S. 133–137.

„Friedensfeier" noch 1960.[49] Hofmannsthal hat an Hölderlin selbst –
bereits in den 1920er Jahren – als „Vorläufer" eines *politischen* „Führers"
erinnert; er berichtete (einem US-amerikanischen Publikum), dass in
„kleinen Konventikeln" jungkonservativer Literaten „der Führer oder
Vorläufer des Führers (...) in der Gestalt eines Toten", Hölderlins
eben, „heraufbeschworen" würde.[50] Hofmannsthal dürfte vor allem
an den Stefan George-Kreis gedacht haben. Jedenfalls heißt es 1930 beim
„Jünger" Friedrich Wolters – auch im Blick auf George selbst –, was
der „Urdichter" singe, sei „Gesang des Gottes durch seinen Mund".[51]
Wie die „beiden brüderlichen Vates" Vergil und Hölderlin[52] verkünde
„Meister" George die „*Wiederkunft* der Götter" und wie Hölderlin (in der
„Friedensfeier"), indem er Christus (im „Gespräch des Herrn mit dem
römischen Hauptmann") zu ihrem archaisch-paganen „Reigenführer"
macht. Der Georgeaner F.W. L'Ormeau, alias Wolfgang Frommel,[53]
schreibt darüber noch 1953: „Das von der vorchristlichen Esoterik
angerufene Sonnenkind" – Vergils „puer" –

> ist durch Christus in den historischen Raum eingetreten. Im Lichte seiner
> Inkarnation erlöschen die Mysterien, eine götterlose Zeit hebt an. Die
> geschichtliche Präsenz des Herrn saugt durch ihre gewaltige Strahlung
> gleichsam alle anderen, bis dahin die Welt beseelenden Götterwesen in sich
> ein. Da Christus im jüdischen Raum erscheint, wird er dem Weltbild der
> Propheten eingefügt: der zielgerichtete Messianismus des frühen Christen-
> tums zersprengt die runde Einighelligkeit des (...) griechischen Kosmos.
> Wenn nun George – wie vor ihm Hölderlin – Christus als ‚Reigenführer'
> im Sinne der großen Mysterientradition versteht, so verbindet er ihn damit
> dem in sich selbst kreisenden Kosmos, dem tanzenden Ring aionischen
> Lebens. In diese Schau mündet eine im Christentum lang schon sich
> vorbereitende und immer wieder hervorbrechende Tendenz, die escha-
> tologischen, transzendenten Messiaserwartungen in den Raum des ganz-

---

[49] Walter Bröcker, „Hölderlins Friedensfeier entstehungsgeschichtlich erklärt", *Wissen-schaft und Gegenwart* 2 (1960), S. 32. Dass man Hölderlin(s „Friedensfeier") ganz anders interpretieren kann bzw. muss, zeigt neuerdings Jürgen Link, „,Lauter Besinnung aber oben lebt der Äther'. Ein Versuch, Hölderlins Griechenland-Entwürfe in der Episteme von 1800 zu lesen", in Christoph Jamme u.a., Hg., *Es bleibet aber eine Spur, doch eines Wortes'. Zur späten Hymnik und Tragödientheorie Friedrich Hölderlins* (München: Fink, 2004), S. 77–103.

[50] Von Hofmannsthal, *Aufzeichnungen* (Frankfurt/M.: Fischer, 1959), S. 312.

[51] Friedrich Wolters, *Stefan George und die Blätter für die Kunst. Deutsche Geistesgeschichte seit 1890* (Berlin: Bondi, 1930), S. 400.

[52] Vgl. Karl Kerényi, „Vergil und Hölderlin", in Hans Oppermann, Hg., *Wege zu Vergil* (Darmstadt: Wissenschaftliche Buchgesellschaft, 1966), S. 320–337, hier S. 337.

[53] Vgl. Günter Baumann, *Dichtung als Lebensform. Wolfgang Frommel zwischen George-Kreis und Castrum Peregrini* (Würzburg: Königshausen & Neumann, 1995).

heitlichen Lebens zurückzubiegen und von der geschichtstheologischen, linearen Zeitbetrachtung einer extensiven Ewigkeit abzukommen.[54]

Ohne Zweifel: Eliade wie Casel lassen bei Frommel grüßen. Im Blick auf Casel und Laachs „Liturgische Bewegung" generell zitiere ich auch George persönlich: „Die antiken Mysterien sind der ewige Typus des höheren Wissens. Der Katholizismus hat etwas davon bewahrt und könnte sich von da aus erneuern."[55] Es ist, als ob der Carl Schmitt-Schüler Rüdiger Altmann dieses von Ernst Robert Curtius überlieferte George-Diktum gekannt hätte,[56] als er noch 1970 − in einem SPIEGEL-Essay − formulierte: „Die Zukunft der Kirchen liegt wahrscheinlich allein in der Wiederherstellung des Kultus." Freilich fügte Altmann schon damals hinzu, dass das „reaktionär" sei und vor allem *zu spät*. In absehbarer Zeit werde die „kritische", ja „negative Theologie" den Kult zerstört haben − auch den katholischen; der „Charakter der Mysterienfeier" werde der Messe nicht erhalten bleiben können. Altmann glaubte mit Recht nicht, dass es möglich sei, „die Auferstehung Jesu und seine Himmelfahrt, die Unbefleckte Empfängnis und vieles andere gegen die theologische Kritik, gewissermaßen als sakrale Folklore, zu erhalten." Wird aber der Kult zerstört, so prognostizierte Altmann weiter, ist auch „die Struktur des (...) Kirchentums" betroffen, „zu dessen Schwerpunkten der Kultus und seine Öffentlichkeit gehört."[57]

---

[54] L'Ormeau alias Wolfgang Frommel, *Die Christologie Stefan Georges* (Castrum Peregrini 15) (Amsterdam: Castrum-Peregrini-Press, 1953), S. 88f.

[55] Stefan George, nach Ernst Robert Curtius, „Stefan George im Gespräch", in ders., *Kritische Essays zur europäischen Literatur* (Bern: Francke, 3. Aufl. 1963), S. 100–116, hier S. 114; kritisch gegenüber George und den Seinen u.a. R. Faber, *Männerrunde mit Gräfin* (Frankfurt/M.: Lang, 1994), Kap. IV, vor allem aber Wolfgang Braungart, *Ästhetischer Katholizismus. Stefan Georges Rituale der Literatur* (Tübingen: Niemeyer, 1997).

[56] Curtius, besonders aber Schmitt standen in engerem Kontakt mit Laach; was Schmitt angeht vgl. vor allem Andreas Koenen, *Der Fall Carl Schmitt. Sein Aufstieg zum ‚Kronjuristen des Dritten Reiches'* (Darmstadt: Wissenschaftliche Buchgesellschaft, 1995). (Koenen ist ebenso meinen Vorarbeiten verpflichtet wie W. Braungart, Th. Ruster und D. Pöpping.)

[57] Rüdiger Altmann, „Abschied von den Kirchen", *Der Spiegel* 28 (1970), S. 121. Josef Ratzinger setzt heute noch auf die Mysterientheologie, nicht zuletzt in seinem − Guardini schon im Titel verpflichteten − Buch *Der Geist der Liturgie* aus dem Jahr 2000. Kirche sei emphatisch „Eucharistie". Vgl. Ratzinger, *Der Geist der Liturgie. Eine Einführung* (Freiburg: Herder, 2000) sowie ders., *Aus meinem Leben. Erinnerungen (1927–1977)* (Stuttgart: Deutsche Verlags-Anstalt 1998), *Zur Gemeinschaft gerufen: Kirche heute verstehen* (Freiburg: Herder, 1991), *Das Fest des Glaubens. Versuche zur Theologie des Gottesdienstes* (Einsiedeln: Johannes-Verlag, 1981) und grundlegend *Die sakramentale Begründung der christlichen Existenz* (Meitingen: Kyrios-Verlag, 1966). Kritisch gegenüber Ratzinger (und der Laacher Tradition insgesamt) Arnold Angenendt, *Liturgik und Historik. Gibt es eine organische Liturgie-Entwicklung?* (Freiburg u.a.: Herder, 2001) sowie Hermann Häring,

4. *Intimes Wechselverhältnis von ‚esoterisch' und ‚exoterisch'*

Öffentlichkeit steht zunächst einmal im strikten Gegensatz zu Geheimnis, der wörtlichen Bedeutung von „mysterium". Und Casel *verstand* die ‚paganen' Kultgemeinden als „Geheimbünde": „Solche Kultgemeinden scharen sich durch Einzelberufung aus religiös besonders hochstehenden Menschen zusammen; sie bilden einen *Geheimbund*, der sich von den Profanen abschließt".[58] Auch der lange ‚führende' Patristiker Hugo Rahner vertrat die Meinung – noch nach dem Zweiten Weltkrieg:

> (...) so sehr die christliche Verkündigung öffentlich ist, ‚von den Dächern gepredigtes Mysterium', das sich an alle Menschen wendet, so muß es sich doch vom dritten Jahrhundert an gegen den Einbruch der Masse wehren: jetzt, und erst jetzt, entsteht die sogenannte Arkandisziplin, ja ihre eigentliche Ausgestaltung ist erst im vierten Jahrhundert erfolgt. Da ist es nur zu verständlich, daß die vom Neuplatonismus kommenden Väter der Kirche dafür eine Sprache prägen, die zweifellos (...) aus der religiösen Welt des absterbenden *Mysterienwesens* gebildet ist. Die Mysterien der Taufe und des Opferaltars werden mit verhüllenden Riten ehrfürchtiger Scheu umgeben, und bald verbirgt die Ikonostase den Uneingeweihten jeden Blick ins Allerheiligste: sie werden zu den (...) ‚schauervollen Mysterien, die frieren machen'.[59]

Rahner läßt – im Unterschied zu Casel – erst das etablierte (ja vom Staat sanktionierte) Christentum Geheimreligion werden. Und (der mit Rahner durch den „Eranos"-Kreis bekannte) Eliade verficht die (in diesem Punkt) *völlig* abweichende These,

> daß das Christentum gerade deshalb den Sieg davontrug und eine universale Religion wurde, weil es sich von den griechisch-orientalischen Mysterien *losgelöst* hatte und eine Religion des *jedermann* zugänglichen Heils verkündigte.[60]

„Haus Gottes – Hüterin des Abendlandes? Josef Ratzingers Katholizismus als europäisches Kulturprojekt", in Richard Faber, Hg., *Katholizismus in Geschichte und Gegenwart* (Würzburg: Königshausen & Neumann, 2005), S. 159–187.

[58] Casel, *Das christliche Kultmysterium*, S. 79.

[59] „‚Es wissen das die Eingeweihten' klingt es durch alle griechischen Predigten, und noch der Pseudo-Areopagite warnt den eingeweihten Christen, der die göttliche Mystagogie durchgemacht hat, vor dem Ausplaudern: ‚Schau, daß du das Allerheiligste nicht ausschwätzest, wahre die Mysterien des verborgenen Gottes so, daß Uneingeweihte nicht daran teilnehmen können, indem du nur Heiligen vom Heiligen in heiliger Erleuchtung mitteilst.'" Hugo Rahner, *Griechische Mythen in christlicher Deutung* (Zürich: Rhein-Verlag, 2. Aufl. 1957), S. 65f.

[60] M. Eliade, *Das Mysterium der Wiedergeburt. Initiationsriten, ihre kulturelle und religiöse Bedeutung* (Zürich: Rascher, 1961), S. 9.

Ich kann hier nicht entscheiden, wer mehr Recht hat: Casel oder Eliade. Wahrscheinlich schließen sich ihre Sätze gar nicht aus; synchron richtig ist jedenfalls diese Feststellung *Rahners* (unbeschadet des ihrerseits theologischen Charakters):

> Das christliche Mysterium ist immer eine ‚geheime Offenbarung': geheim, weil hienieden immer nur an den Glauben sich wendend und innerhalb des gläubigen Annehmens nur langsame Aufstiege in das Verstehen, in die heilige Gnosis eröffnend; offenbar, weil ‚von den Dächern gepredigt' und sich an die Gesamtmenschheit wendend, mit Ausschluß jeglichen Esoterismus und jeglicher Geheimlehre.[61]

Mehr als synchron, nämlich *zeitgenössisch*, erklärt Rahner damit auch, dass die katholische Kirche kein − wie immer gearteter − George-Kreis ist (davon abgesehen, dass selbst dieser eines Tages aufhörte, strikt esoterisch zu sein[62]). Im Blick auf die katholischen *Akademiker* hatte Peter Wust in den 1920er Jahren allerdings eine „heilige Schar" gefordert, die „selbst darüber wachen" müsste,

> daß ein jedes ihrer Mitglieder seine Kräfte, statt sie zu verzetteln, ganz auf die eine große Aufgabe konzentriert, die eben ihm aus der Gesamtaufgabe des Kreises erwächst. Daß so etwas möglich ist,

bewies Wust „die wunderbare Einheitlichkeit des *Georgekreises*, mag man auch im Übrigen über diesen Kreis denken, wie man will."[63] Pointe der Pointe: Wust dachte daran,

> einen solchen Kreis gleichsam in die Liturgische Bewegung von Abt Ildefons Herwegen einzugliedern und ihm in gewissem Sinne die Abtei Maria Laach als eine ganz besondere Basis anzuweisen.

Denn: „Was in der Georgeschule jene merkwürdige Idealgestalt des Jünglings Maximin ist, hier müßte es die reale Idealgestalt Christi sein."[64] George ist zeitlebens bei „Maximin" geblieben, doch auch er war einmal genügend katholisch *gewesen*, um wie Casel und die Seinen zu wissen, dass der Katholizismus etwas von den antiken Mysterien bewahrt hat, dem „ewigen Typus des höheren Wissens", wie George sie

---

[61] Rahner, *Griechische Mythen in christlicher Deutung*, S. 52f.

[62] Vgl. Günter Baumann, „Der George-Kreis", in R. Faber und C. Holste, Hg., *Kreise − Gruppen − Bünde* (Würzburg: Königshausen & Neumann, 2000), S. 65−84.

[63] Peter Wust, *Aufsätze und Briefe. Gesammelte Werke*, Bd. 7 (Münster: Regensburg, 1966), S. 185.

[64] Ebd., S. 186.

nennt, *und* dass sich der Katholizismus „von da aus erneuern" könnte (wie wir bereits gehört haben).

Kein anderer als Hugo Rahner schreibt noch nach 1945 und katholischerseits in der Einleitung seines Buches „Griechische Mythen in christlicher Deutung":

> Friedrich Wolters hat einmal von Augustinus gesagt: ‚Ein Jahrhundert vor der Schließung der Platonischen Akademie durch Justinian hat er den ganzen Schatz des griechischen Geistes in die Civitas Dei gerettet und so bewahrt bis zur schöneren Geburt: so daß wir heute wieder den Weg zurück über die Brücken des Kreisstroms finden, auf unseren Fahnen das flammende Wort: ‚Hellas ewig unsere Liebe.' Und Stefan George, sein Meister [persönlich, R.F.], leihe uns das abschließende Wort zum Ausdruck dessen, was der beste Sinn auch dieses Buches sein soll: ‚Aus diesen Trümmern hob die Kirche dann ihr Haupt, / die freien nackten Leiber hat sie streng gestaupt, / doch erbte sie die Prächte, die nur starrend schliefen / und übergab das Maß der Höhen und der Tiefen / dem Sinn, der beim Hosiannah über Wolken blieb / und dann zerknirscht sich an den Gräberplatten rieb.'[65]

Was George und die Seinen mit „Gräberplatten" vorhatten, speziell *kaiserlichen*, daran lassen geradezu magische Verse aus dem Gedicht „Die Gräber in Speyer" keinen Zweifel – unmittelbar anschließend an das Gedicht „Leo XIII", in dem George dem Papst diese – deutlich Vergils IV. Ekloge nachempfundene – Verse in den Mund legt: „Komm heiliger knabe! Hilf der welt die birst / Dass sie nicht elend falle! einziger retter!"[66] Wie spätestens die – von Anfang an und immer wieder – exoterische Rezeption der IV. Ekloge beweist,[67] provoziert gerade Esoterisches Popularisierung und Politisierung. Georges und der Seinen (Gedanken-)Lyrik ist ein prominent moderner Beleg dafür und Laachs Mysterientheologie ein nicht weniger prominenter. Auf der dritten „Soziologie"-Tagung des „Katholischen Akademikerverbandes" vom 21. bis 23. Juli 1933 in der Laacher Abtei erklärte deren Abt Herwegen

---

[65] Rahner, *Griechische Mythen in christlicher Deutung*, S. 16f.

[66] Stefan George, *Werke. Ausgabe in vier Bänden*. Bd. 2 (München: dtv, 1983), S. 17.

[67] Vgl. neben meinen bereits erwähnten Büchern *Roma aeterna* und *Die Verkündigung Vergils* auch R. Faber, *Politische Idyllik* (Stuttgart: Klett, 1977), ders., *Abendland. Ein politischer Kampfbegriff*, 2. Aufl. (Berlin-Wien: Philo-Verlag) und ders., „ ,Présence de Virgil': Seine (pro-)faschistische Rezeption", *Quaderni di storia* 18 (1983), S. 233–271 sowie ders., „Faschistische Vergil-Philologie", *Hephaistos* 10 (1991), S. 111–133. Zu Casel selbst: O. Casel, „Das Weihnachtsmysterium", S. 201.

persönlich und unumwunden: „Was auf religiösem Gebiet die Liturgische Bewegung ist, ist auf dem politischen Gebiet der Faschismus."[68]
Schon 1924 behauptete Herwegen:

> Zwei unvergleichliche Werte haben wir Katholiken unseren Volksgenossen [!] zu bieten: Objektivität gegenüber dem auflösenden Subjektivismus, und Gemeinschaft gegenüber dem atomisierenden Sozialismus. Eine unübertreffliche Schule, in der wir diese Lebensgüter ausbilden, ist die *Liturgie*.[69]

Wie allgemein-katholisch im ersten dieser beiden Sätze heißt es dann auch Juli 1933: „Sagen wir ein rückhaltloses Ja zu dem neuen soziologischen Gebilde des totalen Staates, das durchaus analog gedacht ist zu dem Aufbau der Kirche."[70] (Zwar haben nicht „wir Katholiken unseren Volksgenossen" die „zwei unvergleichlichen Werte" geboten, dennoch sieht sie Herwegen offensichtlich im „Dritten Reich" verwirklicht – „das durchaus analog gedacht ist zu dem Aufbau der Kirche".)
Was speziell Laachs Mysterientheologie angeht, sei abschließend aus einem Brief von Casels zeitweise engstem Mitarbeiter, dem Münsteraner Theologie-Professor Anton Baumstark an Herwegen vom 1. Januar 1934 zitiert:

> Insbesondere beschäftigt mich (...) immer wieder die starke Wesensverwandtschaft, die gerade nach der Seite der liturgischen Bewegung hin mit deren Betonung des Mysteriums und der religiösen Subjektivismus überwindenden Gemeinschaftsidee besteht. Ich gedenke, im nächsten Semester in einem einstündigen Publicum über ‚Nationalsozialismus als geistesgeschichtliche Zeitenwende' den Versuch zu machen, den Dingen, so wie ich sie sehe, bis in die letzten Gründe nachzugehen, wobei sich etwa herausstellen würde, daß wir dort heute geistig wieder anzuknüpfen hätten, wo der Einfluß nicht der großen und heldischen Antike Homers und der griechischen Tragiker, sondern der selbst innerlich müde und morsch gewordenen Spätantike, deren erste Vorfrucht bereits das rationalistische Zeitalter der Sophistik darstellte, altchristliche und germanische Geistesart aus ihren Bahnen geworfen und beide verhindert hat, diejenige Art eines Bundes miteinander einzugehen, die möglich gewesen wäre und ein durchaus anderes Gesicht gezeigt haben würde, als es die geistige Entwicklung von der Hochscholastik über Cartesius und französische Aufklärung bis zum modernsten Positivismus und Technizismus aufweist.[71]

---

[68] Zit. nach H. Rink, „Reformer aus der Kraft der Tradition. Zum 25. Todestag: Ildefons Herwegen und die kirchliche Erneuerung in Deutschland", *Publik* 36 (1971), S. 25.

[69] Ildefons Herwegen, *Lumen Christi. Gesammelte Aufsätze* (München: Theatiner-Verlag, 1924), S. 91.

[70] Zit. nach *Kölnische Volkszeitung*, 30.7.1933.

[71] Zit. nach Albert, *Die Benediktinerabtei Maria Laach und der Nationalsozialismus*, S. 22.

Bibliographie

Albert, Marcel. *Die Benediktinerabtei Maria Laach und der Nationalsozialismus.* Paderborn u.a.: Schöningh, 2003.

Altmann, Rüdiger. „Abschied von den Kirchen". *Der Spiegel* 28 (1970), S. 120f.

Angenendt, Arnold. *Liturgik und Historik. Gibt es eine organische Liturgie-Entwicklung?.* Freiburg u.a.: Herder, 2001.

Ball, Hugo. *Byzantinisches Christentum. Drei Heiligenleben.* München: Duncker & Humblot, 1923.

Baumann, Günter. *Dichtung als Lebensform. Wolfgang Frommel zwischen George-Kreis und Castrum Peregrini.* Würzburg: Königshausen & Neumann, 1995.

——. „Der George-Kreis". In Richard Faber und Christine Holste, Hg., *Kreise – Gruppen – Bünde. Zur Soziologie moderner Intellektuellenassoziation.* Würzburg: Königshausen & Neumann, 2000, S. 65–84.

Braungart, Wolfgang. *Ästhetischer Katholizismus. Stefan Georges Rituale der Literatur.* Tübingen: Niemeyer, 1997.

Bröcker, Walter. „Hölderlins Friedensfeier entstehungsgeschichtlich erklärt". *Wissenschaft und Gegenwart* 2 (1960), S. 32.

Cancik, Hubert, Hg., *Religions- und Geistesgeschichte der Weimarer Republik.* Düsseldorf: Patmos, 1982.

——, u.a., Hg. *Handbuch religionswissenschaftlicher Grundbegriffe*, Bd. 1–5. Stuttgart: Kohlhammer, 1988–2001.

Casel, Odo. „Das Weihnachtsmysterium". *Hochland* 27–1 (1929/30), S. 193–201.

——. „Religionsgeschichte und Liturgiewissenschaft". *Jahrbuch für Liturgiewissenschaft* 14 (1938), S. 197–224.

——. *Das christliche Kultmysterium.* Regensburg: Pustet, 4. Aufl. 1960 (1. Aufl. 1932).

——. *Das christliche Opfermysterium. Zur Morphologie und Theologie des eucharistischen Hochgebetes.* Graz: Styria, 1968.

Curtius, Ernst Robert. „Stefan George im Gespräch". In ders. *Kritische Essays zur europäischen Literatur.* Bern: Francke, 3. Aufl. 1963, S. 100–116.

Eliade, Mircea. *Mythen, Träume und Mysterien.* Salzburg: Müller, 1961.

——. *Das Mysterium der Wiedergeburt. Initiationsriten, ihre kulturelle und religiöse Bedeutung.* Zürich: Rascher, 1961.

Faber, Richard. *Die Verkündigung Vergils: Reich – Kirche – Staat. Zur Kritik der ‚Politischen Theologie'.* Hildesheim: Olms, 1975.

——. *Politische Idyllik. Zur sozialen Mythologie Arkadiens.* Stuttgart: Klett, 1977.

——. *Roma aeterna. Zur Kritik der ‚Konservativen Revolution'.* Würzburg: Königshausen & Neumann, 1981.

——. „Politischer Katholizismus. Die Bewegung von Maria Laach". In Hubert Cancik, Hg., *Religions- und Geistesgeschichte der Weimarer Republik.* Düsseldorf: Patmos, 1982, S. 136–158.

——. „‚Présence de Virgil': Seine (pro-)faschistische Rezeption". *Quaderni di storia* 18 (1983), S. 233–271.

—— und Renate Schlesier, Hg. *Die Restauration der Götter. Antike Religion und Neo-Paganismus.* Würzburg: Königshausen & Neumann, 1986.

——. „‚Pagan' und Neo-Paganismus. Versuch einer Begriffsklärung". In ebd., S. 10–25.

——. „Archaisch/Archaismus". In Hubert Cancik u.a., Hg., *Handbuch religionswissenschaftlicher Grundbegriffe*, Bd. 1. Stuttgart: Kohlhammer, 1988, S. 51–56.

——. „Faschistische Vergil-Philologie. Zum Beispiel Hans Oppermann". *Hephaistos* 10 (1991), S. 111–133.

——. *Männerrunde mit Gräfin. Die ‚Kosmiker' Derleth, George, Klages, Schuler, Wolfskehl und Franziska zu Reventlow.* Frankfurt/M.: Lang, 1994.

——. „„Der Zersetzer'". In Julius H. Schoeps und Joachim Schlör, Hg., *Antisemitismus. Vorurteile und Mythen*. München: Piper, 1995, S. 260–264.

—— und Christine Holste, Hg. *Kreise – Gruppen – Bünde. Zur Soziologie moderner Intellektuellenassoziation*. Würzburg: Königshausen & Neumann, 2000.

——. *Lateinischer Faschismus. Über Carl Schmitt den Römer und Katholiken*. Berlin-Wien: Philo, 2001.

——. *Abendland. Ein politischer Kampfbegriff*. Berlin-Wien: Philo, 2. Aufl. 2002.

—— Hg. *Streit um den Humanismus*. Würzburg: Königshausen & Neumann, 2003.

—— Hg. *Katholizismus in Geschichte und Gegenwart*. Würzburg: Königshausen & Neumann, 2005.

Filthaut, Theodor. *Die Kontroverse über die Mysterienlehre*. Warendorf: Schnell, 1947.

Fink, Eugen. *Spiel als Weltsymbol*. Stuttgart: Kohlhammer, 1960.

Frommel, Wolfgang [F.W. L'Ormeau]. *Die Christologie Stefan Georges* (Castrum Peregrini 15). Amsterdam: Castrum-Peregrini-Press, 1953.

Fuhrmann, Manfred, Hg. *Terror und Spiel. Probleme der Mythenrezeption*. München: Fink, 1971.

George, Stefan. *Werke. Ausgabe in vier Bänden*. Bd. 2, München: dtv, 1983.

Guardini, Romano. *Vom Geist der Liturgie*. Freiburg: Herder, 6. Aufl. 1962.

Habermas, Jürgen. *Strukturwandel der Öffentlichkeit. Untersuchungen zu einer Kategorie der bürgerlichen Gesellschaft*. Neuwied und Berlin: Luchterhand, 4. Aufl. 1969.

Haecker, Theodor. *Werke*, Bd. 3. München: Kösel, 1961.

——. *Werke*, Bd. 4. München: Kösel, 1965.

——. *Werke*, Bd. 5. München: Kösel, 1967.

Häring, Hermann. „Haus Gottes – Hüterin des Abendlandes? Josef Ratzingers Katholizismus als europäisches Kulturprojekt". In: Richard Faber, Hg., *Katholizismus in Geschichte und Gegenwart*. Würzburg: Königshausen & Neumann, 2005, S. 159–187.

Heer, Friedrich. *Die Tragödie des Heiligen Reiches*. Stuttgart: Kohlhammer, 1952.

Herwegen, Ildefons. *Lumen Christi. Gesammelte Aufsätze*. München: Theatiner-Verlag, 1924.

Heydte, Friedrich August von der. *Die Geburtsstunde des souveränen Staates*. Regensburg: Habbel, 1952.

Höffner, Joseph. *Kirche und Bauer im deutschen Mittelalter*. Paderborn: Schöningh, 1939.

Hofmannsthal, Hugo von. *Das Schrifttum als geistiger Raum der Nation*. München: Verlag der Bremer Presse, 1927.

——. *Das Salzburger Große Welttheater*. Frankfurt/M.: Fischer, 1957.

——. *Aufzeichnungen*. Frankfurt/M.: Fischer, 1959.

Horkheimer, Max. „Der Wolkenkratzer". In ders., *Notizen 1950 bis 1956 und Dämmerung. Notizen in Deutschland*, hg. von Werner Brede. Frankfurt a.M.: S. Fischer Verlag, 1977 (nach der Erstauflage unter dem Pseudonym Heinrich Regius, *Dämmerung. Notizen in Deutschland*, Zürich: Precht & Helbing, 1934), S. 287f.

——. „Zu Theodor Haeckers ‚Der Christ und die Geschichte'" (1936). In ders., *Kritische Theorie. Eine Dokumentation*, hg. von A. Schmidt, Bd. I und II, Studienausgabe. Frankfurt/M.: Fischer, 1977, S. 361–373.

Kerényi, Karl. „Vergil und Hölderlin". In Hans Oppermann, Hg., *Wege zu Vergil*. Darmstadt: Wissenschaftliche Buchgesellschaft, 1966, S. 320–337 (auch als Sonderdruck zum 60. Geburtstag des Altertumsforschers am 19.1.1957. Zürich: Rhein-Verlag, 1957).

Koenen, Andreas. *Der Fall Carl Schmitt. Sein Aufstieg zum ‚Kronjuristen des Dritten Reiches'*. Darmstadt: Wissenschaftliche Buchgesellschaft, 1995.

Jamme, Christoph u.a. Hg. *‚Es bleibet aber eine Spur, doch eines Wortes'. Zur späten Hymnik und Tragödientheorie Friedrich Hölderlins*. München: Fink, 2004.

Link, Jürgen. „‚Lauter Besinnung aber oben lebt der Äther'. Ein Versuch, Hölderlins Griechenland-Entwürfe in der Episteme von 1800 zu lesen". In ebd., S. 77–103.

Mattenklott, Gert u.a. Hg. ‚Verkannte Brüder?' Stefan George und das deutsch-jüdische Bürgertum zwischen Jahrhundertwende und Emigration. Hildesheim: Olms, 2001.

Oppermann, Hans, Hg. Wege zu Vergil. Darmstadt: Wissenschaftliche Buchgesellschaft, 1966.

Pannenberg, Wolfhart. „Späthorizonte des Mythos in biblischer und christlicher Überlieferung". In: Manfred Fuhrmann, Hg., Terror und Spiel. Probleme der Mythenrezeption. München: Fink, 1971, S. 473–525.

Peterson, Erik. Das Buch von den Engeln. Stellung und Bedeutung der heiligen Engel im Kultus. Leipzig: Hegner, 1935.

——. Der Monotheismus als politisches Problem. Ein Beitrag zur Geschichte der Politischen Theologie im Imperium Romanum. Leipzig: Hegner, 1935.

——. „Kaiser Augustus im Urteil des antiken Christentums". In Jacob Taubes, Hg., Der Fürst dieser Welt. Carl Schmitt und die Folgen. München: Fink, 1983, S. 174–180.

Pöpping, Dagmar. Abendland. Christliche Akademiker und die Utopie der Antimoderne 1900–1945. Berlin: Metropol 2002.

Rahner, Hugo. Griechische Mythen in christlicher Deutung. Zürich: Rhein-Verlag, 2. Aufl. 1957.

Ratzinger, Joseph. Die sakramentale Begründung der christlichen Existenz. Meitingen: Kyrios-Verlag, 1966.

——. Das Fest des Glaubens. Versuche zur Theologie des Gottesdienstes. Einsiedeln: Johannes-Verlag, 1981.

——. Zur Gemeinschaft gerufen: Kirche heute verstehen. Freiburg: Herder, 1991.

——. Aus meinem Leben. Erinnerungen (1927–1977). Stuttgart: Deutsche Verlags-Anstalt, 1998.

——. Der Geist der Liturgie. Eine Einführung. Freiburg: Herder, 2000.

Ricketts, Mac Lincsot. Mircea Eliade. The Romanian Roots, 1907–1945, 2 Bde. Boulder, Col.: East European Monographs, 1988.

Rink, H. „Reformer aus der Kraft der Tradition. Zum 25. Todestag: Ildefons Herwegen und die kirchliche Erneuerung in Deutschland". Publik 36 (1971), S. 25.

Ruster, Thomas. Die verlorene Nützlichkeit der Religion. Katholizismus und Moderne in der Weimarer Republik. Paderborn u.a.: Schöningh, 1994.

Schmitt, Carl. „Drei Stufen historischer Sinngebung". Universitas 5 (1960), S. 927–931.

——. Politische Theologie II. Die Legende von der Erledigung jeder Politischen Theologie. Berlin: Duncker & Humblot, 1970.

Schoeps, Julius H. und Joachim Schlör, Hg. Antisemitismus. Vorurteile und Mythen. München: Piper, 1995.

Schumacher, Joachim. Die Angst vor dem Chaos. Über die falsche Apokalypse des Bürgertums. Frankfurt/M.: Makol-Verlag, 2. Aufl. 1972.

Steding, Christoph. Politik und Wissenschaft bei Max Weber. Breslau: Korn, 1932.

Steinberg, Michael. P. Ursprung und Ideologie der Salzburger Festspiele 1890–1938. Salzburg: Pustet, 2000.

Taubes, Jacob, Hg. Der Fürst dieser Welt. Carl Schmitt und die Folgen. München: Fink, 1983.

Twellmann, Marcus. Das Drama der Souveränität. Hugo von Hofmannsthal und Carl Schmitt. München: Wilhelm Fink, 2004.

Wolters, Friedrich. Stefan George und die Blätter für die Kunst. Deutsche Geistesgeschichte seit 1890. Berlin: Bondi, 1930.

Wust, Peter. Aufsätze und Briefe. Gesammelte Werke, Bd. 7. Münster: Regensburg, 1966.

Für wichtige Hinweise danke ich Horst Junginger, István Keul und Bernd Wacker.

FRIEDRICH ANDRES (1882–1947)

EIN THEOLOGISCHER RELIGIONSWISSENSCHAFTLER AN DER UNIVERSITÄT BONN

Ulrich Vollmer

Über das Verhalten von Friedrich Andres im Dritten Reich gehen die Meinungen, wie es den ersten Anschein hat, auseinander. Während er bei Ulrich von Hehl als „Priester unter Hitlers Terror" aufgelistet ist,[1] ist für Martin Persch der Entzug seines Lehrauftrages an der Universität Frankfurt „wahrscheinlich aus weltanschaulichen Gründen" erfolgt.[2] Hans-Paul Höpfner wiederum paraphrasiert ohne Kommentar einen Abschnitt aus einem Brief des damaligen Bonner Leiters der Dozentenschaft Karl Franz Chudoba vom 9. März 1938 an den Rektor der Universität Bonn, in dem es im Original heißt:

> Prof. A[ndres] ist mir seit Jahren als Dozent bekannt und hat vor der Machtübernahme dem politischen Katholizismus absolut fern gestanden und nach der Machtübernahme Verständnis und große loyale Einstellung gegenüber der neuen Zeit und dem neuen Staat an den Tag gelegt. Er gehört zu den wenigen katholischen Dozenten unserer Universität, die den deutschen Gruß mit ‚Heil Hitler' offen und uneingeschränkt anwenden.[3]

Ziel des folgenden Aufsatzes ist es, diese ganz offensichtlich unterschiedlichen Beurteilungen, die das Verhalten von Friedrich Andres erfahren hat, vor dem Hintergrund seiner Biographie, seines wissenschaftlichen Werks und Wirkens, seiner Selbstdarstellungen und der Einschätzungen von Zeitgenossen, wie sie sich in verschiedenen Archiven finden, sowie schließlich durch Analyse einiger Dokumente aus der Zeit des 2. Weltkriegs zu evaluieren.

---

[1] Ulrich von Hehl, *Priester unter Hitlers Terror*, 4. Aufl. (Paderborn: Schöningh, 1998), S. 816.

[2] Martin Persch, „Andres, Friedrich", in *Biographisch-Bibliographisches Kirchenlexikon* 15 (1999), Sp. 21f.

[3] Universitätsarchiv Bonn, Personalakte Andres. Die Paraphrase dieses Abschnitts aus dem Gutachten Chudobas findet sich bei Hans-Paul Höpfner, *Die Universität Bonn im Dritten Reich* (Bonn: Bouvier, 1999), S. 201.

I

Die biographischen Daten von Friedrich Andres, der bisher in der Forschung noch keine umfassende Würdigung gefunden hat, sind bis zum Beginn des Dritten Reichs relativ schnell vorgestellt.[4] Friedrich Andres wurde am 28. März 1882 im lothringischen Neunkirchen bei Saargemünd geboren. Nach seinem Abitur im Jahre 1901 studierte er zunächst an der Universität Straßburg Klassische Philologie, dann im Bischöflichen Priesterseminar in Trier Philosophie und katholische Theologie. Nach seiner Priesterweihe im Jahre 1906 war er zunächst drei Jahre lang in der Seelsorge tätig. Von 1909 bis 1911 studierte er in Berlin, von 1911 bis 1914 in Breslau vor allem griechische Philologie sowie Dogmen- und Religionsgeschichte. 1913 wurde er in Breslau zum Doktor der Theologie promoviert. In seiner Dissertation behandelte er *Die Engellehre der griechischen Apologeten des 2. Jahrhunderts und ihr Verhältnis zur griechisch-römischen Dämonologie*, die im folgenden Jahr im Druck erschien. Der Plan einer Habilitation fand die Unterstützung seiner akademischen Lehrer. Bezeichnend für das geistige Klima jener Zeit ist die Einschätzung durch den Breslauer Theologen Joseph Pohle, der am 9. Dezember 1913 über Andres an den Trierer Bischof schrieb:

> Seine Tüchtigkeit namentlich auf dem so wichtigen, fast nur vom Unglauben bebauten und gegen die christliche Religion gerichteten Gebiet der vergleichenden Religionsgeschichte steht absolut außer Zweifel.[5]

Im gleichen Jahr 1913 nahm Friedrich Andres an der 2. *Semaine d'ethnologie religieuse* teil und knüpfte so Verbindungen zu Wilhelm Schmidt und dessen Schülern.[6] Nach dem Oberlehrer-Examen wechselte er 1915 in den Schuldienst über und arbeitete daneben an seiner Habilitation, die am 16. Juli 1920 an der Universität Bonn für das Fachgebiet „Allgemeine Religionswissenschaft, vergleichende Religionsgeschichte und Religionspsychologie" erfolgte. Die unveröffentlichte

---

[4] Neben den Lebensläufen in den Personalakten im Bistumsarchiv Trier, im Universitätsarchiv Bonn und in der Entnazifizierungsakte im Hauptstaatsarchiv Düsseldorf vgl. vor allem Otto Wenig, Hg., *Verzeichnis der Professoren und Dozenten der Rheinischen Friedrich-Wilhelms-Universität zu Bonn 1818–1968* (Bonn: Bouvier/L. Röhrscheid, 1968), S. 4 und M. Persch, a.a.O., Sp. 21f. sowie ders., „Andres, Friedrich", in Heinz Monz, Hg., *Trierer biographisches Lexikon* (Trier: Wissenschaftlicher Verlag Trier, 2000), S. 5.

[5] Bistumsarchiv Trier, Personalakte Andres, Blatt 8 verso.

[6] Vgl. Friedrich Andres, „Löwener religionsgeschichtlich-ethnologische Kurse", *Pastor bonus* 26 (1913/14), S. 215–222.

Habilitationsschrift trug den Titel *Das mystische Schauen bei Plotin und Richard von St. Viktor. Ein religionsgeschichtlicher und religionspsychologischer Versuch zur Geschichte der Mystik.* Seine Antrittsvorlesung hielt er über das Thema „Die Psychologie der Ekstase". Von 1920 an lehrte er an der Universität Bonn, zunächst als Privatdozent, dann als Lehrbeauftragter, von 1927 an als nichtbeamteter außerordentlicher Professor. Neben seiner Lehrtätigkeit in Bonn war er seit 1926 mit der Durchführung von Lehrveranstaltungen zur katholischen Weltanschauung an der Universität Frankfurt beauftragt.

In die frühen 1920er Jahre fällt die Bekanntschaft mit dem niederländischen Theologen Thomas Goossens, die offensichtlich von der gemeinsamen Teilnahme an der 3. *Semaine d'ethnologie religieuse* in Tilburg herrührt. Wie der Briefwechsel zeigt, war Andres von 1922 an als Gastdozent mit den von Goossens an der Handelshochschule in Tilburg organisierten „Roomsch-katholieke leergangen" verbunden, in deren Rahmen er Vorlesungen zu ethnologischen und religionsgeschichtlichen Themen hielt.[7] Der Briefwechsel zeigt zudem, dass sich Andres 1927 durch die Vermittlung von Goossens Hoffnung darauf machte, den durch den Wechsel von Johann Peter Steffes nach Münster freigewordenen Lehrstuhl für Religionsgeschichte in Nijmegen zu erhalten.[8] Berufen wurde allerdings nicht er, sondern Karel Leopold Bellon.

Dass Friedrich Andres in dieser Zeit auch weiterhin Kontakt mit Wilhelm Schmidt hatte, erhellt aus der Tatsache, dass er zusammen mit Schmidt, Martin Gusinde und Wilhelm Koppers 1924 an den beiden Sessionen des 21. Amerikanistenkongresses in Den Haag und Göteborg teilnahm.[9] Daneben stehen weitere Studien im Bereich der Völkerkunde, die er, obwohl schon habilitiert, zusammen mit dem damals noch jungen

---

[7] Vgl. zu diesen „leergangen" allgemein Thomas Goossens, „Leergangen, Roomsch-Katholieke", in *De katholieke encyclopaedie* 16 (1936), S. 226f. Die Lehrtätigkeit von Friedrich Andres lässt sich allerdings nur schwer dokumentieren; eine kurze Erwähnung findet sich bei Johannes A. Bornewasser, *Vijftig jaar katholieke leergangen. 1912–1962* (Tilburg: Katholieke Leergangen, 1962), S. 129; in der hier zusammengestellten Liste der Dozenten (ebd., S. 244–259) fehlt sein Name ebenso wie bereits in der entsprechenden Liste im *Gedenkboek bij gelegenheid van het vijf-en-twintig jarig bestaan van de R.K. leergangen. 1912–1937* (Tilburg: R.K. Leergangen, 1937), S. 83–88.

[8] Bistumsarchiv s'-Hertogenbosch, Nachlass Goossens, Briefe von Andres vom 6. und 10. Oktober 1927. Für eine Übersendung der Kopien des Briefwechsels bin ich Dr. Jan Peijnenburg, s'-Hertogenbosch, sehr verbunden.

[9] Vgl. dazu Fritz Bornemann, *P. Martin Gusinde (1886–1969). Mitglied des Anthropos-Institutes* (Rom: Collegium Verbi Divini, 1971), S. 83.

Hermann Trimborn bei Fritz Graebner durchführte.[10] Nach Graebners Wechsel nach Köln blieben die Verbindungen erhalten; auch mit dessen Nachfolger in der Leitung des Rautenstrauch-Joest-Museums, dem Ethnologen Julius Lips, hatte er offensichtlich Kontakt.[11]

II

In dem – zugegeben – sehr schmalen wissenschaftlichen Werk von Friedrich Andres lässt sich vom Jahr 1933 an kein Wandel feststellen. In einer offenkundigen Kontinuität mit den Jahren zuvor behandelt er in einer Reihe von Aufsätzen und in zahlreichen Rezensionen im Wesentlichen zunächst drei Themenkomplexe. Da ist zum einen der Bereich der Religionsethnologie, der ja zunehmend in den Mittelpunkt seines Interesses gerückt war. Seine Beiträge liegen hier ganz auf der von Wilhelm Schmidt und dessen Schülern vertretenen Linie, wenngleich im Detail doch eine andere Grundstimmung spürbar ist. So stellt Andres in engem Anschluss an Martin Gusinde die Yamana äußerst positiv und von Sympathie getragen dar;[12] er unterscheidet sich bei der Darstellung schriftloser Völker von Gusinde, der sich – allerdings in anderem Zusammenhang – durchaus darüber Gedanken gemacht hat, „ob die unsteten Pygmäen (...) kolonial brauchbar gemacht [sic!] werden könnten".[13] Ähnliches gilt auch für den Artikel von Andres über die „Epische Dichtung der Naturvölker" aus dem Jahr 1939, der nach der Aufforderung zu weiterer Feldforschung mit den Worten schließt:

> Dann wird man erkennen, dass auch bei diesen Stämmen mit ihrer primitiven materiellen Kultur die Gabe epischer Dichtung nicht selten ist. Auch diese Völker haben ihren Beitrag zur Menschheitsdichtung gegeben.[14]

---

[10] Vgl. dazu Paul Leser, „Fritz Graebner – Eine Würdigung", *Anthropos* 72 (1977), S. 45 und Josef-Thomas Gröll, *Zur Geschichte der Völkerkunde an der Universität Bonn* (Bonn: Seminar für Völkerkunde, 1986), S. 52.

[11] Gusinde berichtet in seinem leider nur sporadisch erhaltenen Tagebuch unter dem 12. September 1927 von einem Treffen mit Andres und Trimborn anlässlich eines Vortrags von ihm in Köln (Anthropos-Institut, St. Augustin, Nachlass Gusinde). Für den 9. März 1930 weist das Programm des Vereins zur Förderung des Rautenstrauch-Joest-Museum für Völkerkunde Köln einen Vortrag von Friedrich Andres zum Thema „Geheimkulte bei primitiven Völkern" aus. Es findet sich dazu aber der handschriftliche Vermerk „ausgefallen" (Historisches Archiv der Stadt Köln, 614/125).

[12] Vgl. Andres, „Yamana – ein aussterbender Urstamm Südamerikas", *Kölnische Volkszeitung*, 24.7./21.8.1938.

[13] Das Zitat nach Hans Fischer, *Völkerkunde im Nationalsozialismus* (Hamburg: D. Reimer, 1990), S. 116.

[14] Andres, „Epische Dichtung der Naturvölker", *Kölnische Volkszeitung*, 19.2.1939.

Ein weiterer Themenkomplex sind die Megalithe in Europa, zunächst im Rheinland, dann vor allem in Frankreich, denen er insgesamt vier Aufsätze widmet und dabei in immer neuen Wendungen – um es mit Eliade zu sagen – „die ‚Undurchsichtigkeit' vorgeschichtlicher Dokumente" artikuliert.[15]

Einen dritten Schwerpunkt bildet seine Mitarbeit an dem niederländischen Nachschlagewerk *De katholieke encyclopaedie*, das von 1933 bis 1939 in insgesamt 25 Bänden erschien. In der Liste der Redakteure bzw. Mitherausgeber ist Friedrich Andres der einzige Deutsche. Aus den Themen, die er in seinen insgesamt 27 Beiträgen bearbeitet hat, darf man wohl mit Recht schließen, dass er das Fachgebiet Ethnologie betreute oder zumindest einen Teilbereich unter seiner Verantwortung hatte. In der Liste der Mitarbeiter tauchen kaum ausländische Wissenschaftler auf. In Band 2 werden Hermann Trimborn aus Bonn und Ferdinand Hestermann aus Münster genannt; bei der langjährigen Bekanntschaft mit beiden ist es ganz offensichtlich, dass Friedrich Andres sie wie später auch Martin Gusinde als Mitarbeiter gewonnen hatte. Die Verbindung mit Hermann Trimborn und Ferdinand Hestermann ist für die Einschätzung von Friedrich Andres sicher nicht unwichtig. Während die Meinungen über Trimborn geteilt sind[16] und die Entnazifizierungsakte Trimborns Opposition gegen den Nationalsozialismus von Anfang an dokumentieren soll,[17] lassen sich bei Hestermann, den Andres bei der 2. *Semaine d'ethnologie religieuse* kennen gelernt hatte, eine Reihe von Verbindungen zum Widerstand gegen das Dritte Reich aufzeigen. Dazu gehört seine Hilfe bei der Flucht des katholischen Jugendführers Franz Ballhorn und dessen späterer Frau in die Niederlande 1934 bzw. 1935[18] und sein geradezu konspirativer Einsatz für die Rettung der Bibliothek des Anthropos-Instituts nach dem Einmarsch der Deutschen in

---

[15] Vgl. Andres, „Uralte Denkmalsteine im westdeutschen Gebiet", *Umschau* 41 (1937), S. 800–803, „Carnac und seine megalithischen Monumente", *Kölnische Volkszeitung*, 7.7.1940, „Loqmariaquer und seine megalithischen Monumente", in ebd., 21.7.1940 und „Carnac und seine Steindenkmäler", *Umschau* 46 (1942), S. 185–189. Das Eliade-Zitat in Mircea Eliade, *Geschichte der religiösen Ideen*, Bd. 1: *Von der Steinzeit bis zu den Mysterien von Eleusis* (Freiburg u.a.: Herder, 1978), S. 17.

[16] Man vergleiche nur Eva Lips, *What Hitler Did to Us. A Personal Record to the Third Reich* (London: M. Joseph, 1938), S. 115–117 mit Lothar Pützstück, *'Symphonie in Moll'. Julius Lips und die Kölner Völkerkunde* (Pfaffenweiler: Centaurus, 1995), S. 252, bes. Anm. 209, der an der Darstellung von Eva Lips erhebliche Zweifel hat.

[17] Hauptstaatsarchiv Düsseldorf, Entnazifizierungsakte Trimborn. Vgl. dazu Höpfner, *Die Universität Bonn im Dritten Reich*, S. 438–440.

[18] Hauptstaatsarchiv Düsseldorf, Entnazifizierungsakte Hestermann. Zu Ballhorn vgl. Paul Jakobi, „Franz Ballhorn", in Joël Pottier, Hg., *Christen im Widerstand gegen das Dritte Reich* (Stuttgart/Bonn: Burg-Verlag, 1988), S. 519–526.

Österreich.[19] Wie kompromisslos das niederländische Nachschlagewerk Rassismus und Nationalsozialismus gegenüber eingestellt ist, erhellt aus den einschlägigen Stichwörtern, etwa dem Eintrag „Arische bewegingen", der die entsprechenden Strömungen in Deutschland und in den Niederlanden mit sarkastischem Spott schlichtweg lächerlich macht.[20]

Bei aller Aufgeschlossenheit für die geistigen Werte der ethnischen Kulturen, die Andres in seinen Artikeln und Rezensionen dokumentiert, darf man freilich nicht übersehen, dass sich bei ihm kein kritisches Wort gegenüber den Rassetheorien des von ihm verehrten Wilhelm Schmidt findet.[21] Auch muss man erwähnen, dass er Jahre zuvor, 1929, in der in den Niederlanden erscheinenden und von Thomas Goossens mit herausgegebenen *Historisch Tijdschrift* eine umfangreiche und sehr positive Rezension des Buches von Benedikt Momme Nissen über den *Rembrandtdeutsche[n] Julius Langbehn* veröffentlicht hat. Julius Langbehn wird „viel Gütiges, Edles" attestiert, freilich werden auch „gewisse Unvollkommenheiten seines Charakters, Züge herrenmenschlichen Selbstbewusstseins" festgestellt – eine doch erschreckend zurückhaltende Formulierung angesichts des von Langbehn propagierten Rassismus und Antisemitismus.[22]

Das Wirken von Friedrich Andres im akademischen Raum stellt sich zunächst in seinen Vorlesungen an der Universität Bonn dar. Auch hier treten bereits im Verlauf der 1920er Jahre zunehmend vier Themenkomplexe in den Mittelpunkt: 1. Fragen der Religionspsychologie – von 1940 bis zum Kriegsende ist dies der fast ausschließliche Schwerpunkt, 2. das Verhältnis des Christentums zu den nichtchristlichen Religionen, 3. Zeugnisse der vorchristlichen Religion im Rheinland und schließlich

---

[19] Vgl. Ferdinand Hestermann, *Eine Rede, die nicht gehalten werden konnte* (Berlin: Kongress-Verlag, 1948), S. 1. Auch Hestermanns Münsteraner Schülerin Gertrud Pätsch schildert ihren Lehrer in späteren Jahren und unter anderen politischen Vorzeichen als einen Menschen, der, „wo immer eine Gelegenheit sich bot, gegen den menschenunwürdigen Rassebegriff auftrat", so Gertrud Pätsch, „In memoriam Ferdinand Hestermann", in *Beiträge zur Ethnolinguistik. Gedenkschrift zum 100. Geburtstag von Ferdinand Hestermann* (Jena: Friedrich-Schiller-Universität, 1980), S. 7.

[20] Criton [i.e. Hubert Cuypers], „Arische bewegingen", in *De katholieke encyclopaedie* 2 (1933), S. 827–829.

[21] Zu Schmidts Ansichten vgl. Ernest Brandewie, *When Giants Walked the Earth. The Life and Times of Wilhelm Schmidt, SVD* (Fribourg: University Press, 1990), S. 200–242, ferner Fischer, *Völkerkunde im Nationalsozialismus*, S. 54–63 und den Beitrag von Udo Mischek in diesem Band.

[22] Die beiden Zitate: Andres, Rezension von „Der Rembrandtdeutsche Julius Langbehn. Von seinem Freunde Benedikt Momme Nissen, Freiburg i.Br. 1926", *Historisch Tijdschrift* 8 (1929), S. 72.

4. der Bereich der Religionsethnologie, wobei sich Friedrich Andres offenbar in der Wortwahl – und ich glaube: nur in der Wortwahl – dem Geist der Zeit anpasst. Er kündigt regelmäßig eine einstündige Vorlesung für Hörer aller Fakultäten an. Im Wintersemester 1928/29 und im Wintersemester 1929/30 „Der Ursprung der Gottesidee und die Religion der Naturvölker", im Sommersemester 1932 „Die Religion der Primitiven (Einführung in die völkerkundlichen Grundlagen der Religionsgeschichte)", im Wintersemester 1934/35 hingegen „Die Religionen der Eingeborenen der deutschen Kolonien", schließlich im Wintersemester 1936/37 und im Wintersemester 1939/40 „Religion der Naturvölker (mit besonderer Berücksichtigung der Eingeborenen der deutschen Kolonien)".

Anders als die Vorlesungen an der Universität Bonn sind die Vorlesungen an der Universität Frankfurt nahezu ganz theologischen und religionsphilosophischen Themen vom Standpunkt der katholischen Kirche aus gewidmet. Sie sind daher für die hier gegebene Fragestellung nicht relevant. Die behandelten Themen lassen, mit einer Ausnahme, die gleich im Zusammenhang mit der Selbstdarstellung von Friedrich Andres kurz betrachtet werden soll, keinen aktuellen Zeitbezug erkennen. Dass ihm mit Schreiben des Reichsministeriums vom 8. Februar 1937 der Lehrauftrag ohne Begründung entzogen wurde, liegt nicht in seiner Person begründet, sondern hängt mit dem nationalsozialistischen Programm der „Entkonfessionalisierung des öffentlichen Lebens" zusammen.[23]

Neben seiner Lehrtätigkeit hat sich Friedrich Andres auch in verschiedenen wissenschaftlichen Vereinigungen engagiert. Dazu gehörte die Frankfurter Gesellschaft für Ethnologie und Anthropologie und vor allem die Bonner Gesellschaft für Erd- und Völkerkunde, in der er neben dem 1940 verstorbenen Carl Clemen sogar zum Vorstand gehörte.[24]

---

[23] Vgl. allgemein zu den Ereignissen des Jahres 1937 Ulrich von Hehl, *Katholische Kirche und Nationalsozialismus im Erzbistum Köln 1933–1945* (Mainz: M. Grünewald, 1977), S. 136–173. In der ausführlichen Darstellung der Geschichte der Frankfurter Universität bis zum Jahr 1950 bei Notker Hammerstein, *Die Johann Wolfgang Goethe-Universität Frankfurt am Main*, Bd. 1: *Von der Stiftungsuniversität zur staatlichen Hochschule, 1914–1950* (Neuwied/Frankfurt: A. Metzner, 1989) kommt Friedrich Andres nicht vor.

[24] Bei Karlheinz Pfaffen, Hg., *50 Jahre Gesellschaft für Erd- und Völkerkunde zu Bonn* (Bonn: Dümmler, 1960), S. 22 wird zwar ein Vortrag von Andres, nicht aber dessen Zugehörigkeit zum Vorstand der Gesellschaft erwähnt. In dieser Eigenschaft hatte Andres in Briefen vom 6. Februar und 2. März 1938 an den Geographen Carl Troll diesem zur Berufung nach Bonn gratuliert und ihn gebeten, den 1. Vorsitz der Gesellschaft zu übernehmen (Geographisches Institut der Universität Bonn, Nachlass Troll). Zu Carl

Sein Engagement für die Vortragsveranstaltungen dieser Gesellschaft erhellt aus dem umfangreichen Briefwechsel mit Andreas Scheller, der ohne vorherigen Studienabschluss und nur aufgrund seiner politischen Konformität seinem von den Nazis abgesetzten Lehrer Julius Lips in der Leitung des Kölner Rautenstrauch-Joest-Museums gefolgt war. Der erhaltene Briefwechsel beginnt mit dem Durchschlag eines Briefes von Scheller an Andres vom 6. Juli 1934 und endet mit einem Brief von Andres an Schellers Nachfolger Martin Heydrich vom 14. November 1940. In dem Briefwechsel mit Scheller geht es nahezu ausschließlich um die gemeinsame Organisation von Vorträgen in Bonn und Köln, zum Teil auch in Frankfurt. Unter dem Datum vom 9. Oktober 1936 bietet Scheller Andres an, einen Bericht von Andres über die Tagung der „Gesellschaft für Völkerkunde" in Leipzig, der im *Westdeutschen Beobachter* erscheinen soll und „unter Umständen auch ausführlicher sein kann", an die Zeitung zu vermitteln.[25] Andres, der Scheller zuvor eine detaillierte Darstellung über den Kongress hatte zukommen lassen, antwortet am 10. Oktober, die Offerte missverstehend und lapidar: „Falls Sie einen Artikel für den WB verfassen wollen, so müssen Sie das unter Ihrem Namen tun."[26] Warum es nach dem Brief an Heydrich, in dem Andres um ein persönliches Gespräch bittet, keine weiteren Briefe gibt, lässt sich nicht feststellen. Auch ist nicht mehr zu eruieren, ob es Kontakte von Andres zu Julius Lips gab, die über die Vereinbarung eines Vortrags hinausgingen.[27]

Clemen siehe Ulrich Vollmer, „Carl Clemen (1865–1940) als Emeritus", *Zeitschrift für Religionswissenschaft* 9 (2001), S. 185–203.

[25] Der *Westdeutsche Beobachter* hatte den Untertitel *Amtliches Organ der NSDAP und sämtlicher Behörden*.

[26] Der Briefwechsel befindet sich im Historischen Archiv der Stadt Köln, 614/595. Vgl. dazu Pützstück, ‚*Symphonie in Moll*‘, S. 304.

[27] Eva Lips berichtet (*What Hitler Did to Us*, S. 288) von insgesamt sechs Anrufen, die sie und ihr Mann Julius Lips am 21. März 1934 unter dramatischen Umständen während einer im Rundfunk übertragenen Rede Hitlers erhielten, weil die Anrufer allesamt glaubten, die Mitarbeiter der Telefonüberwachung würden sich die Rede anhören. Unter ihnen war „[a] friendly catholic priest", über dessen Identität sie nichts weiter mitteilt.

III

In den verschiedenen konsultierten Archiven finden sich Materialien, die zum einen zeigen, wie sich Friedrich Andres in dieser Zeit selber darstellte. Es geht in der Regel um Anträge, die er aus unterschiedlichen Anlässen gestellt und in denen er bei der Begründung auch etwas von sich preisgeben hat, sei es durch die Art und Weise der Formulierung, sei es aber auch dadurch, dass er etwas verschwiegen hat. Auf der anderen Seite steht die Einschätzung dieser seiner Anträge und damit auch seiner Person in Form von Stellungnahmen offiziöser oder offizieller zeitgenössischer Stellen.

Das erste Dokument in diesem Zusammenhang betrifft den VI. Internationalen Kongress für Religionsgeschichte, der im September 1935 in Brüssel stattfand. In Bonn hat sich lediglich die Ablehnung seines Antrags durch das Berliner Ministerium erhalten, die auf den 17. Juli 1935 datiert ist. Die Erlaubnis zur Teilnahme erhielten – in der Reihenfolge des Schreibens des Ministeriums vom 10. Juli – Alfred Bertholet, Johannes Witte, Karl Bornhausen, Friedrich Heiler, Otto Weinreich und Wilhelm Gundel.[28] Am 17. Juni des folgenden Jahres beantragte Andres, bei den schon erwähnten Fortbildungskursen der Handelshochschule in Tilburg

> an einigen Samstagen des bevorstehenden Wintersemesters in der erd- und völkerkundlichen Abteilung (...) Vorträge über die heidnischen Religionen zu halten, die für die deutschen und niederländischen Kolonien in Betracht kommen.

Von dem Organisator der Kurse, dem schon genannten niederländischen Theologen Thomas Goossens, sagt Andres, er sei ihm „seit vielen Jahren als Deutschfreund [sic!] bekannt". Gegen Ende heißt es:

> Wenn es mir gestattet würde, die Einladung zu diesen Vorträgen anzunehmen, so hätte ich die von mir sehr begrüßte Möglichkeit, für das Deutschtum und im Interesse der deutschen Wissenschaft zu wirken.[29]

---

[28] Universitätsarchiv Bonn, Personalakte Clemen.

[29] Universitätsarchiv Bonn, Personalakte Andres. Zu Thomas Goossens vgl. Johannes A. Bornewasser, „Thomas Johannes Adrianus Josephus Goossens", in *Jaarboek van de Maatschappij der Nederlandse Letterkunde te Leiden 1971–1972* (Leiden: E.J. Brill, 1973), S. 136–142. Die Charakterisierung des niederländischen Theologen, die Andres hier vornimmt, muss vor dem Hintergrund gesehen werden, dass Goossens 1942 von der deutschen Besatzungsmacht einige Zeit in Haft genommen wurde. Der Briefwechsel zwischen ihm und Andres wurde bis in die Nachkriegszeit fortgeführt.

452   ULRICH VOLLMER

Im Gegensatz zu seinem Antrag im Vorjahr genehmigte das Berliner
Ministerium mit Schreiben vom 7. Juli 1936 die Reisen nach Tilburg.
1938 wurde Andres eine Studienreise nach Frankreich gestattet. Vom 1.
bis zum 6. August fand in Kopenhagen der 2. Internationale Kongress
für Anthropologie und Ethnologie statt. Andres beantragte offensichtlich
die Erlaubnis zur Teilnahme. Erhalten hat sich in Bonn lediglich die
Antwort des Ministeriums, das ihn unter dem Datum vom 2. März
1938 an Eugen Fischer, den Direktor des Kaiser-Wilhelm-Instituts für
Anthropologie, menschliche Erblehre und Eugenik in Berlin-Dahlem
verweist. Von einem entsprechenden Briefwechsel mit Eugen Fischer
findet sich in den Bonner Akten keine Spur. Die Reise kam jedenfalls
nicht zustande.[30]

Im gleichen Jahr 1938 beantragte Friedrich Andres eine Erhöhung
seiner Vergütung für den Bonner Lehrauftrag, da sich seine Bezüge
durch den Fortfall des Frankfurter Lehrauftrags erheblich verkürzt
hatten. Interessant sind die Anlagen, die diesem Antrag beigefügt sind.
Da gibt es einmal ein Verzeichnis seiner in Frankfurt gehaltenen Vorlesungen. Im Unterschied zu einem analogen Verzeichnis, das Andres im
Jahr zuvor selber angefertigt und einem Schreiben an den Limburger
Bischof beigefügt hatte,[31] fehlen in dem neuen Verzeichnis die Angaben
der jeweiligen Semester; außerdem ist es nach den verschiedenen theologischen Disziplinen gegliedert, denen Andres die Vorlesungen inhalt-
lich zuordnete – mit der Folge, dass die im Wintersemester 1932/33
gehaltene Vorlesung „Die religiöse und geistige Krisis der Gegenwart"
sozusagen im Kleingedruckten verschwindet. Beigefügt ist ferner ein
Verzeichnis seiner Publikationen. Hier fällt auf, dass es keinerlei Hinweis
auf seine doch maßgebliche Beteiligung an *De katholieke encyclopaedie* gibt.
Schließlich folgt eine Liste der geplanten Publikationen:

– Die Mystik des Richard von St. Viktor
– Kritische Neuausgabe der wichtigsten mystischen Traktate des
  Richard von St. Viktor
– Wesen und Erscheinungsformen des Opfers in den nichtchristlichen
  Religionen
– Theologische und psychologische Grundlagen der Mystik

---

[30] Vgl. die Angaben über Auslandsreisen im Fragebogen zur Entnazifizierung,
Hauptstaatsarchiv Düsseldorf, Entnazifizierungsakte Andres.
[31] Diözesanarchiv Limburg, DAL 57/C1, Blatt 310.

– Religionsgeschichtliche Grundlagen der Religionsphilosophie
– Religionspsychologische Ergebnisse der Forschungen über die Medizinmännerschule süd-amerikanischer Indianer

In einem Gutachten vom 9. März 1938 befürwortet der Leiter der Dozentenschaft, der spätere Rektor Karl Franz Chudoba, den Antrag. Der erste Teil dieses Gutachtens wurde bereits eingangs zitiert. Weiter heißt es in diesem Gutachten:

> Gleichzeitig sei auch vermerkt, dass die Wohlmeinung über Prof. A[ndres] auch der Rektor der Frankfurter Universität, Prof. Platzhoff, in einem Gutachten an mich zum Ausdruck gebracht hat. A[ndres] wird von ihm als der Typus eines etwas weltfremden Gelehrten, der ganz seiner Wissenschaft lebt, geschildert, dessen innere Stellung zum Nationalsozialismus natürlich nicht beurteilt werden kann.[32]

Nach der Wiedergabe einer Beurteilung durch den Kurator der Frankfurter Universität („Prof. A[ndres] ist ein stiller Gelehrter, guter Wissenschaftler, aber völlig unpolitischer Mensch") schreibt Chudoba weiter:

> Hervorzuheben bleibt, dass sich Prof. A[ndres] neben seinem Fachgebiet aus besonderer Neigung mit vor- und kulturgeschichtlichen Dingen befasst, die sich besonders auf die deutsche und Frühgeschichte beziehen. Nach Urteilen von Fachleuten hat sich A[ndres] jeweils mit einer erfreulichen Objektivität der Erforschung germanischer Kultur gewidmet, wobei er durch den Hinweis auf die ursprünglichen Inschriften, Runen und Zeichen jeweils darzulegen bemüht ist, dass unsere Vorfahren keine kulturlosen Nomaden, sondern sesshafte Bauern mit ernsten, kulturgeschichtlichen [sic!] Gebräuchen gewesen seien.[33]

---

[32] Der von Chudoba paraphrasierte Abschnitt im Gutachten des Frankfurter Rektors vom 18. November 1937 lautet (Universitätsarchiv Frankfurt a.M., Personalakte Andres): „Er [Andres, U.V.] gehört nach meiner Meinung nicht zu jenen katholischen Theologen, die ihre politischen Anschauungen hinter einem sicheren und gewandten Auftreten verbergen, sehr glatt und deshalb gefährlich sind. Wie Professor Andres innerlich zum National-Sozialismus [sic!] steht, kann ich nicht beurteilen. Aber da nun einmal die katholisch-theologischen Fakultäten bestehen und Dozenten benötigen, so halte ich ihn, der mir auch stets einen irenischen Eindruck gemacht hat, für geeigneter als manchen anderen."

[33] Universitätsarchiv Bonn, Personalakte Andres. Was Chudoba hier über die „Erforschung germanischer Kultur" durch Andres schreibt, ist an dessen Veröffentlichungen nicht auszumachen (bis zu diesem Zeitpunkt lag nur der kurze Aufsatz über „Uralte Denkmalsteine im westdeutschen Gebiet" [1937] vor); es entspricht auch nicht seinen damaligen Arbeitsschwerpunkten, wie er sie zumindest in der Anlage seines Antrags auflistet.

Trotz dieses positiven Gutachtens fiel in der Sache zunächst ganz offensichtlich keine Entscheidung. Stattdessen beantragte Andres im folgenden Jahr die Ernennung zum „beamteten außerplanmäßigen Professor
mit Diäten", die dann auch – u.a. nach einem weiteren Gutachten des
neuen Dozentenführers auf der Grundlage des Gutachtens von Chudoba – am 18. Oktober 1939 erfolgte. Zwar hatte diese Ernennung für
Andres kaum finanzielle Vorteile – sein Gehalt war nur wenig höher als
vor 1937 in seiner Zeit als Lehrbeauftragter –, aber sie stellte zu diesem
Zeitpunkt doch eine bevorzugte Behandlung dar, die möglicherweise
auch vor dem Hintergrund der besonderen Binnenstruktur der Bonner
katholisch-theologischen Fakultät zu sehen ist.[34]

Am 16. September 1941 beantragte Andres im Zusammenhang
mit seinen Forschungen an Megalithen die Erlaubnis für eine Reise in
das von den Deutschen besetzte Frankreich. In der Zwischenzeit war
der luxemburgische Theologe und Jurist Nikolaus Majerus, seit 1934
Honorarprofessor für „Deutsch-französische Rechtsvergleichung",[35]
am 16. Juli 1941 „wegen seiner francophilen Einstellung", wie es in
einem Schreiben der SD-Hauptaußenstelle Köln vom 18. September
1941 heißt, in das unbesetzte Frankreich abgeschoben worden. Das
Schreiben schließt mit dem Hinweis:

> Bei der Sichtung des sichergestellten Schrifttums bei Majerus wurden u.a.
> auch Schreiben des Prof. Dr. Andres, Bonn, Beethovenstr. 19, erfasst.[36]

Aus den erhaltenen Unterlagen geht nicht hervor, welcher Art die
sichergestellten Schreiben waren. Unter bloßer Berufung darauf, dass
Andres „nach hier eingegangenen Mitteilungen in Briefwechsel mit
Prof. Majerus" steht, machte der Dozentenführer in einem Schreiben
an den Rektor unter dem Datum des 2. Oktober „Bedenken gegen die
Ausreise von Prof. Andres geltend". Am 15. Dezember schreibt das
Ministerium an den Rektor:

---

[34] So war Friedrich Andres nicht an der Vorbereitung und Abfassung der *Studien
zum Mythus des 20. Jahrhunderts* (1934) beteiligt; vgl. die Auflistung der Beteiligten bei
Wilhelm Neuss, *Kampf gegen den Mythus des 20. Jahrhunderts* (Köln: Bachem, 1947), S. 14f.,
ferner Raimund Baumgärtner, *Weltanschauungskampf im Dritten Reich. Die Auseinandersetzung
der Kirchen mit Alfred Rosenberg* (Mainz: M. Grünewald, 1977), S. 154–168 sowie Hehl,
Katholische Kirche und Nationalsozialismus, S. 88–90.
[35] Zu Majerus vgl. Wenig, *Verzeichnis der Professoren und Dozenten*, S. 186, ferner René
Fisch, „Dr. Nicolas Majerus", in *Die Luxemburger Kirche im 2. Weltkrieg* (Luxemburg:
Éditions Saint-Paul, 1991), S. 284f.
[36] Universitätsarchiv Bonn, Personalakte Majerus.

Im Einvernehmen mit dem Auswärtigen Amt und mit dem Herrn Militärbefehlshaber konnte dem Antrage von Professor Andrees [sic!] auf Durchführung einer Studienreise nach Frankreich nicht entsprochen werden. Der Reisepass ist in der Anlage beigefügt.[37]

IV

Mit dem „Fall Majerus" ist die Zeit des 2. Weltkriegs erreicht, die auch in Leben und Werk von Friedrich Andres ihren Niederschlag gefunden hat. In seinen Vorlesungen konzentrierte er sich nahezu ganz auf theologische und religionspsychologische Fragen. Dies hängt wohl auch damit zusammen, dass im Zuge einer von den Nationalsozialisten angestrebten Zurückdrängung der Kirchen mit Schreiben des Ministeriums vom 26. Juni 1942 seine Lehrbefugnis auf das theologische Kernfach „Fundamentaltheologie" abgeändert wurde.

Obwohl er, wie oben aufgezeigt, mit der Bonner Gesellschaft für Erd- und Völkerkunde eng verbunden war, ist er 1942 aus dieser renommierten und für das kulturelle Leben der damals noch kleinen Universitätsstadt Bonn sicherlich maßgebenden Gesellschaft ausgetreten. Der Grund für diesen Austritt lässt sich nicht mehr eruieren. Als Dokumente liegen heute nur vor: 1. die damaligen Kassenbücher (Andres hat letztmalig 1941 seinen Beitrag gezahlt) und 2. ein Zettel mit Notizen, die sich Carl Troll, damals 1. Vorsitzender der Gesellschaft, bei der Vorstandssitzung am 21. Dezember 1942 gemacht hat.[38] Auf diesem Zettel finden sich unter dem Tagesordnungspunkt „Verschiedenes" lediglich zwei Zeilen: In der ersten Zeile steht „Austritt von Andres" und in der zweiten Zeile „Konkurrenz des Volksbildungswerkes", das zu der Nazi-Organisation „Kraft durch Freude" gehörte und dessen Leitung zuvor Gustav Mensching übernommen hatte. Beide Einträge stehen aber sicherlich nicht in einem ursächlichen Zusammenhang. Mensching hat im Rahmen seines Entnazifizierungsverfahrens u.a. eine Auflistung der von ihm organisierten Vorträge und der aus dem Universitätsbereich herangezogenen Referenten erstellt; in dieser Liste taucht Friedrich Andres nicht auf.[39] Was immer die Motive für sei-

---

[37] Universitätsarchiv Bonn, Personalakte Andres.

[38] Die Dokumente befinden sich im Geographischen Institut der Universität Bonn, Nachlass Troll.

[39] Hauptstaatsarchiv Düsseldorf, Entnazifizierungsakte Mensching.

nen Austritt gewesen sein mögen, sie lassen sich nicht mehr erhellen; vielleicht hatte sich das geistige Klima verändert.[40] Der letzte Vortrag, den die Gesellschaft veranstaltete, fand am 9. Juni 1944 statt. Herman Lommel sprach über „Die Jünglingsweihe bei den Indern und Iraniern". Der Bericht über diesen Vortrag im *Westdeutschen Beobachter* schließt mit den Worten: „Mit zahlreichen Einzelheiten (...) gab Prof. Lommel ein anschauliches Bild dieser eigenartigen, aus urarischer Zeit entstammenden Riten."[41]

Als Mitglied der Katholisch-theologischen Fakultät der Universität Bonn hat Friedrich Andres auch an den von der Fakultät herausgegebenen *Feldunterrichtsbriefen* mitgearbeitet.[42] Die Abhandlungen *Die Absolutheit des Christentums und die vergleichende Religionsgeschichte* und *Das religiöse Leben und seine psychologische Erforschung* sind stark von theologischen Zielsetzungen her geprägt.[43] Sie sollen daher hier im Detail nicht berücksichtigt werden.

Anders ist es mit dem *Feldunterrichtsbrief* vom Oktober 1944, der zugleich die letzte bibliographisch nachweisbare Veröffentlichung von Friedrich Andres darstellt und den Titel *Nationalreligion und Weltreligion in Japan* trägt. In einem Brief an den Trierer Generalvikar Heinrich von Meurers schreibt Andres am 6. Oktober 1944:

> Aufrichtig freue ich mich, dass dieser mein neuer Feldunterrichtsbrief noch gedruckt werden konnte, so dass ich Dir ihn senden kann. Das Thema ist gewählt worden, weil aus dem Felde so viele Anfragen darüber kamen und weil im letzten Semester so manche Vorträge in der Universität von in Deutschland lebenden japanischen Gelehrten zur Propaganda des Shintoismus gehalten worden sind, in denen er idealisiert wurde.[44]

---

[40] Im Rahmen des Entnazifizierungsverfahrens gab Andres an, dass er von 1935 bis 1944 [sic!] Mitglied der Nationalsozialistischen Volkswohlfahrt war, ohne ein Amt zu bekleiden. Falls es sich bei der Zahl 1944 nicht um einen Schreibfehler handelt, muss er noch während des Dritten Reichs aus dieser Organisation ausgetreten sein. Hauptstaatsarchiv Düsseldorf, Entnazifizierungsakte Andres.

[41] Gustav Mensching, „Jünglingsweihen", *Westdeutscher Beobachter*, 12.6.1944.

[42] Zu den Hintergründen vgl. Heiner Faulenbach, *Theologisches Fernstudium im II. Weltkrieg. Die Lehrbriefe und Feldunterrichtsbriefe der Bonner theologischen Fakultäten* (Bonn: Bouvier, 1987), S. 43f. und S. 55f.

[43] F. Andres, *Die Absolutheit des Christentums und die vergleichende Religionsgeschichte*. Hektographiertes Manuskript. Katholisch-theologische Fakultät der Rheinischen Friedrich-Wilhelms-Universität Bonn, Feldunterrichtsbrief Oktober 1942 [= *Pastor bonus* 53 (1942), S. 165–181] und ders., *Das religiöse Leben und seine psychologische Erforschung* (Bonn: J.F. Carthaus, 1943).

[44] Bistumsarchiv Trier, Personalakte Andres, Blatt 42. Zu Heinrich von Meurers vgl. allgemein Martin Persch, „Meurers, Heinrich von", in *Biographisch-Bibliographisches*

Bei den hier genannten japanischen Gelehrten handelt es sich einmal um Toyofumi Murata, damals Leiter des Instituts für Japankunde der Universität Wien. Er hielt am 21. Juni 1944 einen Vortrag über „Shinto, Staatsmythos und Weltanschauung der Japaner". Der Bericht über diesen Vortrag im *Westdeutschen Beobachter* schließt mit den Worten:

> Sie [die Japaner, U.V.] kennen nicht das Gebet für das Wohl des Einzelnen, sondern ewigen Dienst und Dank und das Gelöbnis, den Ahnen keine Schande zu machen. ‚Sieg unseren Waffen, Sieg unserem Glauben, das ist das heilige Gebot der Stunde!' schloss der japanische Gast seine fesselnden Ausführungen.[45]

Der zweite Gelehrte war Kenju Moriya, seinerzeit Lektor an der Universität Leipzig. Er sprach am 12. Juli 1944 über das Thema „Die japanische Malerei". Im *Westdeutschen Beobachter* heißt es dazu unter anderem: „Die überaus zahlreiche Hörerschaft spendete dem Redner lebhaften Beifall."[46]

Ganz im Gegensatz zu den beiden Referenten sieht Friedrich Andres im Shintoismus ein Gemenge aus verschiedenen Komponenten, wobei sich der Eindruck aufdrängt, dass er zwar „Shintoismus" sagt, aber in der negativen Charakterisierung dieser Form nationalreligiöser Frömmigkeit „auch" die germanische Religion, näherhin die aktuellen Versuche zu ihrer Revitalisierung meint. Ihm begegnet hier „in erster Linie ein primitiver polytheistischer Naturkult (...) und dann ein Seelen- und Ahnenkult".[47] Das Ganze sieht er „von einer bestimmten dynastisch-politischen Tendenz beherrscht". Zur shintoistischen Religion bemerkt er lakonisch:

> Der shintoistischen Religion fehlen die individuell persönlichen Züge. Ihr religiöser Gehalt ist gering. Die Äußerungen der Frömmigkeit sind schlicht, ja dürftig. Die Gebete, die man an die Götter richtet, sind kurz;

Kirchenlexikon 5 (1993), Sp. 1401f., zu seinen Konflikten mit den Nationalsozialisten Alois Thomas, *Kirche unter dem Hakenkreuz. Erinnerungen und Dokumente* (Trier: Paulinus-Verlag, 1992), S. 61–79.

[45] Gustav Mensching, „Ein Japaner sprach über Japan. Shinto, Staatsmythos und Weltanschauung der Japaner", *Westdeutscher Beobachter*, 23.6.1944. Wesentlich distanzierter ist die Darstellung im Bonner *General-Anzeiger*: N.N., „Staatsmythos und Weltanschauung der Japaner. Professor Dr. Murata sprach als Gast der Universität", ebd., 22.7.1944.

[46] Johannes Peters, „Die japanische Malerei. Gastvorlesung des Professors Kenju Moriya", *Westdeutscher Beobachter*, 15./16.7.1944.

[47] Dies und die beiden folgenden Zitate nach Andres, *Nationalreligion und Weltreligion in Japan* (Bonn: J.F. Carthaus, 1944), S. 3f.

sie sind ebenso wie die Opfergaben, die man vor den Götterschreinen darbringt, auf das Motiv ‚do, ut des' eingestellt. Der Shintoismus kennt keine Ethik im eigentlichen Sinne des Wortes.

Weiten Raum nimmt sodann die Darstellung des Buddhismus und seiner verschiedenen Gruppierungen ein. Der „Armut der Nationalreligion des Shintoismus" stellt er „die Weltreligion des Buddhismus mit ihrem Reichtum an religiösen und ethischen Inhalten" gegenüber.[48] In der Schlussbetrachtung skizziert er einen religiösen Entscheidungskampf, dessen Ausgang letztlich offen, wenngleich in der grundlegenden Tendenz bereits entschieden ist:

> Ob sich der shintoistische Staatsmythos von der Abstammung von der Sonnengöttin usw. auf die Dauer gegenüber der weiter fortschreitenden Aufklärung und dem wachsenden Unglauben wird halten können? (...) Alle Anzeichen deuten darauf hin, dass eine Nationalreligion auch [sic!] im fernen Osten gegenüber einer Weltreligion nicht standhalten wird. Der religiöse Entscheidungskampf im fernen Osten wird unter der Parole stehen: Christus oder Buddha.[49]

Die Auseinandersetzung wird zwischen den Weltreligionen – zwischen Buddhismus und Christentum – stattfinden. Die Nationalreligionen sind durch die religionsgeschichtliche Entwicklung überholt, im Falle der Germanen und eben „auch" im Falle des Shintoismus.[50]

Am Ende dieser Darstellung von Friedrich Andres ist nun noch ein Dokument zu analysieren, das auf den ersten Blick der ganzen Tendenz seiner Haltung, wie sie sich zumindest uns darstellt, zu widersprechen scheint. Es handelt sich um den einzigen Brief von Andres an den Bonner Philosophen und Psychologen Erich Rothacker, der sich im Nachlass Rothacker erhalten hat und der das Datum des 22. September 1944 trägt:

---

[48] Ebd., S. 5.

[49] Ebd., S. 19.

[50] Andres, *Die Absolutheit des Christentums und die vergleichende Religionsgeschichte* nach der Fassung in *Pastor bonus* 53 (1942), S. 174, wo es ganz in diesem Sinne und unter ausdrücklicher Berufung auf Menschings Monographie *Volksreligion und Weltreligion* aus dem Jahr 1938 heißt: „In diesen Vergleich [des Christentums mit den anderen Religionen, U.V.] brauchen nur die sogenannten Weltreligionen einbezogen zu werden. Die Volksreligionen sind ja zeitlich und örtlich bedingt, relativ (...). So gehen primitive [sic!] Religionen unter, wenn sie mit höheren zusammenstoßen." Zu dem Problem Volksreligion und Weltreligion im Kontext der damaligen Zeit vgl. Ulrich Vollmer, „Volksreligion und Weltreligion in der Deutung von Gustav Mensching", in Wolfgang Gantke u.a., Hg., *Religionswissenschaft im historischen Kontext. Beiträge zum 100. Geburtstag von Gustav Mensching* (Marburg: Diagonal-Verlag, 2003), S. 61–85, bes. S. 82–85.

Für Ihre freundliche Zusendung Ihres Vortrags über die Kriegswichtigkeit der Philosophie, den ich mit Interesse und Zustimmung gelesen habe, danke ich Ihnen bestens. Darf ich Ihnen übersenden sowohl meinen kleinen Artikel zu Dölgers 60. Geburtstag (aus der damals noch erscheinenden Kölnischen Volkszeitung) als auch meinen Aufsatz über die experimentelle Religionspsychologie, über den ich gerne gelegentlich einmal mit Ihnen reden würde?[51]

Den Vortrag mit dem bombastischen Titel hatte Erich Rothacker am 31. Mai 1944 an der Universität Bonn im Rahmen der Vortragsreihe *Wissenschaft im Kampf für Deutschland* gehalten. Der Vortrag war anschließend in der vom Rektor Karl Franz Chudoba herausgegebenen Reihe der *Kriegsvorträge der Rheinischen Friedrich-Wilhelms-Universität* im Druck erschienen. Wie an der Person Erich Rothacker, so scheiden sich auch an diesem Vortrag die Geister. Volker Böhnigk sieht vor dem Hintergrund seiner Deutung des Bonner Philosophen und Psychologen hier einen Vortrag, „der klar [sic!] den nationalsozialistischen Vernichtungskrieg unterstützt",[52] ohne sich allerdings näher mit dem Inhalt dieses Vortrags zu beschäftigen, mit dem immerhin Friedrich Andres d'accord geht. Während in den Augen von Böhnigk Rothacker das ganze Dritte Reich hindurch und auch noch darüber hinaus an seinen nationalsozialistischen Ideen festgehalten habe, glaubt Heinrich Lützeler,[53] dass sich Rothacker, bedingt durch eine ganze Reihe von Faktoren, u.a. den

---

[51] Universitätsbibliothek Bonn, Handschriftenabteilung, Nachlass Rothacker. Bei den beiden Schriften von Andres handelt es sich zum einen um den Artikel von Andres zu „Franz Joseph Dölgers 60. Geburtstag" in der *Kölnischen Volkszeitung* vom 18.10.1939; in einer Postkarte vom 19. September 1940 teilt Andres Thomas Goossens mit, dass zwei Tage zuvor „der mit mir eng befreundete Bonner Prof. Dölger gestorben" sei (Bistumsarchiv s'-Hertogenbosch, Nachlass Goossens). Bei der anderen Schrift handelt es sich um Andres' Aufsatz über „Das religiöse Leben und seine psychologische Erforschung" von 1943. Eine Antwort von Rothacker ist nicht erhalten.

[52] Volker Böhnigk, *Kulturanthropologie als Rassenlehre. Nationalsozialistische Kulturphilosophie aus der Sicht des Philosophen Erich Rothacker* (Würzburg: Königshausen & Neumann, 2002), S. 21.

[53] Vgl. Heinrich Lützeler, *Persönlichkeiten. Konrad Adenauer, Paul Clemen, Kardinal Frings, Johannes XXIII., Erich Rothacker, Max Scheler* (Freiburg i.Br.: Herder, 1978), S. 33–60, bes. S. 52–56 („Gegnerschaft [gegen den Nationalsozialismus, U.V.]"); ferner ders., *Bonn, so wie es war*, Bd. 2 (Düsseldorf: Droste, 1980), S. 15–17, bes. S. 16: „Er wandte sich nun [1941, U.V.] von der Partei aus einem unbedingt wissenschaftlichen Ethos ab. Bald war er wegen seiner lebensgefährlichen Äußerungen im Studenten- und Kollegenkreis bekannt." Vgl. ferner Hans-Joachim Dahms, „Philosophie", in Frank-Rutger Hausmann, Hg., *Die Rolle der Geisteswissenschaften im Dritten Reich 1933–1945* (München: R. Oldenbourg, 2002), S. 193–217, bes. S. 217.

Kriegstod seines einzigen Sohnes im Jahr 1941, von seinen Vorstellungen zu Beginn des Dritten Reichs deutlich distanziert habe.[54]

Sieht man sich den Vortrag nun genauer an, so begegnet der Begriff „Kriegswichtigkeit" bzw. das Adjektiv „kriegswichtig" im Zusammenhang mit Philosophie tatsächlich mehrmals,[55] aber immer in einer Argumentation, die in ihrer logischen Durchsichtigkeit eigentlich aufgesetzt und banal erscheint. Im Grunde geht es Erich Rothacker darum, die grundlegende Notwendigkeit philosophischer Reflexion vor jeder fachwissenschaftlichen und für jede fachwissenschaftliche Arbeit aufzuweisen. An drei Stellen wird die Linie dann als Syllogismus durchgezogen: Wissenschaften sind für den Krieg wichtig; Voraussetzung für jede Wissenschaft ist die Philosophie; also ist Philosophie für den Krieg wichtig. Wenn man diese drei Stellen aus dem Kontext löst, ändert dies nichts an der grundlegenden Position des Autors, was die wissenschaftskonstituierende Funktion der Philosophie angeht; und es ändert nichts am Ergebnis seiner umfangreichen philosophiegeschichtlichen Betrachtung, dass in der Vergangenheit häufig Fachwissenschaft und Philosophie in einer Person vereinigt waren.

Man mag trotz allem über die Position des Autors streiten. Aus der Perspektive des Historikers ist ein Blick auf die zeitgenössische Reaktion aufschlussreich. Im *Westdeutschen Beobachter* erschien ein vergleichsweise kurzer Bericht über diesen Vortrag, in dem die Argumentation des Vortragenden in ihren Grundzügen korrekt skizziert wird. Es ist bezeichnend, dass selbst in einem so exponierten Organ wie dem *Westdeutschen Beobachter* im Text selber der Begriff „Kriegswichtigkeit" nicht begegnet;[56] dem Berichterstatter war wohl die eigentliche Intention des Referenten nicht entgangen, und diese Intention war es offensichtlich, mit der Friedrich Andres übereinstimmte.[57]

---

[54] Unter dem Datum des 28. März 1941 schrieb der zu diesem Zeitpunkt bereits emeritierte Bonner Kunsthistoriker Paul Clemen, der jüngere Bruder von Carl Clemen, aus seinem Altersdomizil in Endorf an Erich Rothacker; gegen Ende des Briefes findet sich der folgende Passus, der zeigt, dass sich Clemen der Einstellung seines Briefpartners ganz offensichtlich sicher sein konnte (Universitätsbibliothek Bonn, Handschriftenabteilung, Nachlass Rothacker): „(...) Radio hören − aber keine Landkarte ansehen. Ich sitze wohl am Schreibtisch − aber ich schreibe nur zu meinem Plaisir. Je m'amuse. Für das Übrige habe ich auch nur ein französisches Wort: Merde."

[55] Erich Rothacker, *Die Kriegswichtigkeit der Philosophie* (Bonn: Scheur, 1944), S. 5, S. 16 und S. 22.

[56] A. D., „Die Kriegswichtigkeit der Philosophie. Ein Vortrag von Professor Dr. Rothacker", *Westdeutscher Beobachter*, 2.6.1944.

[57] Erich Rothacker hat mit einem Vortrag, den er knapp acht Tage später bei der Feier zum 9. Gründungstag des von Gustav Mensching geleiteten Volksbildungswerks

V

Auch für Friedrich Andres ging nach der Zäsur des Kriegsendes 1945 die Geschichte weiter. Am 3. November 1945 wendet er sich in einem Brief an den Rektor der Universität Bonn:

> Darf ich Ew. Magnifizenz die beiden Anliegen, die ich mündlich mit Ihnen zu besprechen heute Gelegenheit hatte, empfehlen:
>
> 1.) Seit 1920 bin ich in der Kath.-theol. Fakultät habilitiert für ‚Allgemeine Religionswissenschaft, vergleichende Religionsgeschichte und Religionspsychologie'. Für diese Fächer erhielt ich einen Lehrauftrag zu Beginn 1922. Während der Kriegsjahre – 1941 oder 1942 – wurde (nicht von der Fakultät) dieser Lehrauftrag umschrieben die ‚Fundamentaltheologie' [sic!]. Ich bitte, genehmigen zu wollen, dass mein Lehrauftrag nunmehr umschrieben wird: ‚Fundamentaltheologie mit besonderer Berücksichtigung der Allgemeinen Religionswissenschaft, der vergleichenden Religionsgeschichte und der Religionspsychologie'.
> 2.) Seit 1920 doziere ich in Bonn. 1927 war ich zum nichtbeamteten außerord. Professor ernannt worden, 1939 zum beamteten außerpl. Professor mit Diäten. Ich bitte, erwägen zu wollen, ob ich nicht, damit meine Pension gesichert würde, ein beamtetes Extraordinariat bekommen könnte.
> 3.) Wäre es möglich, dass ich meine Übungen über Religionsgeschichte und Religionswissenschaft in dem Seminar für Religionswissenschaft, das allerdings der Philos. Fakultät angegliedert ist, abhalten könnte, da diese Abteilung in dem Kath.-theol. Seminar vernichtet ist und das gesamte Seminar der Philos. Fakultät in einem sehr schönen Raum des Universitätshauptgebäudes bereits eingerichtet ist und die Bücher aufgestellt sind.[58]

Die Antworten auf diese insgesamt drei Anfragen fallen unterschiedlich aus: Die Umwandlung der Venia wird – da mit keinerlei Kosten verbunden – durch Schreiben des Oberpräsidenten der Nord-Rheinprovinz vom 6. März 1946 gewährt; was die Umwandlung seiner Stelle in eine

---

zum Thema „Was ist Bildung?" hielt, erhebliche Schwierigkeiten bekommen. Während der *Westdeutsche Beobachter* in seiner Berichterstattung entgegen seiner sonst üblichen Praxis den Inhalt von Rothackers Vortrag schlichtweg verschweigt, bietet der Bericht im Bonner *General-Anzeiger* als Resümee der Position Rothackers den abschließenden Satz (dr. th. 1944): „Der gebildete Mensch ist also im Sinne dieses Vortrags der zum geistigen Leben und Erleben erweckte Mensch." Inge Andersson, Menschings Sekretärin beim Volksbildungswerk, erklärte unter dem Datum vom 2. Januar 1946 (Hauptstaatsarchiv Düsseldorf, Entnazifizierungsakte Mensching): „Zu einem offenen Konflikt mit der Gestapo kam es (…) nach einem Vortrag von Prof. Rothacker über ‚Was ist Bildung?' Dieser Vortrag war so offen antinationalsozialistisch, dass die Gestapo sofort eingriff und auch die Arbeitsfront aufs neue gegen Prof. Menschings Amtsführung protestierte."

[58] Universitätsarchiv Bonn, Personalakte Andres.

pensionsberechtigte Professur angeht, so wird auf die zuvor nötige Feststellung einer freien Planstelle verwiesen. Über diesem Verfahren ist Friedrich Andres am 1. Dezember 1947 verstorben. Was den dritten Punkt betrifft: Zu einem „Streit der Fakultäten" ist es nicht gekommen. Die Anfrage ist ganz offensichtlich im Sande verlaufen.

Bibliographie

1. *Archivquellen*

Anthropos-Institut, St. Augustin, Nachlass P. Martin Gusinde S.V.D.
Bistumsarchiv s'-Hertogenbosch, Nachlass Thomas J.A.J. Goossens.
Bistumsarchiv Trier, Abt. 85 / Nr. 23, Personalakte Friedrich Andres.
Diözesanarchiv Limburg, DAL 57 C/1, Errichtung einer theologischen Fakultät in Frankfurt am Main.
Geographisches Institut der Universität Bonn, Nachlass Carl Troll.
Hauptstaatsarchiv Düsseldorf, NW 1049–50884, Entnazifizierungsakte Friedrich Andres.
Hauptstaatsarchiv Düsseldorf, NW 1039–H-4234, Entnazifizierungsakte Ferdinand Hestermann.
Hauptstaatsarchiv Düsseldorf, NW 1049–53429, Entnazifizierungsakte Gustav Mensching.
Hauptstaatsarchiv Düsseldorf, NW 1049–2372, Entnazifizierungsakte Hermann Trimborn.
Historisches Archiv der Stadt Köln, 614/125 und 127, Vorträge des Vereins zur Förderung des Rautenstrauch-Joest-Museums für Völkerkunde Köln.
Historisches Archiv der Stadt Köln, 614/595, Briefwechsel Andreas Scheller / Friedrich Andres.
Universitätsarchiv Bonn, Personalakte Friedrich Andres.
Universitätsarchiv Bonn, Personalakte Carl Clemen.
Universitätsarchiv Bonn, Personalakte Nikolaus Majerus.
Universitätsarchiv Frankfurt a. M., Personalakte Friedrich Andres.
Universitäts- und Landesbibliothek Bonn, Handschriftenabteilung, Nachlass Erich Rothacker.

2. *Gedruckte Quellen*

Andres, Friedrich. „Löwener religionsgeschichtlich-ethnologische Kurse". *Pastor bonus* 26 (1913/14), S. 215–222.
――. Rezension von „Der Rembrandtdeutsche Julius Langbehn. Von seinem Freunde Benedikt Momme Nissen. Freiburg i.Br. 1926". *Historisch Tijdschrift* 8 (1929), S. 71–73.
――. „Uralte Denkmalsteine im westdeutschen Gebiet". *Umschau* 41 (1937), S. 800–803.
――. „Yamana – ein aussterbender Urstamm Südamerikas". *Kölnische Volkszeitung*, 24.7./21.8.1938.
――. „Franz Joseph Dölgers 60. Geburtstag". *Kölnische Volkszeitung*, 18.10.1939.
――. „Carnac und seine megalithischen Monumente". *Kölnische Volkszeitung*, 7.7.1940.
――. „Loqmariaquer und seine megalithischen Monumente". *Kölnische Volkszeitung*, 21.7.1940.
――. *Die Absolutheit des Christentums und die vergleichende Religionsgeschichte*. Hektographiertes Manuskript. Katholisch-theologische Fakultät der Rheinischen Friedrich-Wilhelms-Universität Bonn, Feldunterrichtsbrief Oktober 1942 [= *Pastor bonus* 53 (1942), S. 165–181].
――. *Das religiöse Leben und seine psychologische Erforschung* (Katholisch-theologische Fakultät der Rheinischen Friedrich-Wilhelms-Universität Bonn. Feldunterrichtsbrief Oktober 1943). Bonn: J.F. Carthaus 1943 [= *Zeitschrift für Askese und Mystik* 19 (1944), S. 39–52].
――. *Nationalreligion und Weltreligion in Japan* (Katholisch-theologische Fakultät der Rheinischen Friedrich-Wilhelms-Universität Bonn, Feldunterrichtsbrief Oktober 1944). Bonn: J.F. Carthaus, 1944.

Baumgärtner, Raimund. *Weltanschauungskampf im Dritten Reich. Die Auseinandersetzung der Kirchen mit Alfred Rosenberg* (VKZG.F 22). Mainz: M. Grünewald, 1977.

Böhnigk, Volker. *Kulturanthropologie als Rassenlehre. Nationalsozialistische Kulturphilosophie aus der Sicht des Philosophen Erich Rothacker.* Würzburg: Königshausen & Neumann, 2002.

Bornemann, Fritz. *P. Martin Gusinde (1886–1969). Mitglied des Anthropos-Institutes* (Divini Verbum Supplementum 15). Rom: Collegium Verbi Divini, 1971.

Bornewasser, Johannes A. *Vijftig jaar katholieke leergangen. 1912–1962.* Tilburg: Katholieke Leergangen, 1962.

———. „Thomas Johannes Adrianus Josephus Goossens". In *Jaarboek van de Maatschappij der Nederlandse Letterkunde te Leiden 1971–1972.* Leiden: E.J. Brill 1973, S. 136–142.

Brandewie, Ernest. *When Giants Walked the Earth. The Life and Times of Wilhelm Schmidt, SVD* (SIA 44). Fribourg: University Press, 1990.

Criton [i.e. Hubert Cuypers]. „Arische bewegingen". In *De katholieke encyclopaedie* 2 (1933), S. 827–829.

Dahms, Hans-Joachim. „Philosophie". In Frank-Rutger Hausmann, Hg., *Die Rolle der Geisteswissenschaften im Dritten Reich 1933–1945* (Schriften des Historischen Kollegs 53). München: R. Oldenbourg, 2002, S. 193–227.

Eliade, Mircea. *Geschichte der religiösen Ideen. Bd. 1: Von der Steinzeit bis zu den Mysterien von Eleusis.* Freiburg u.a.: Herder, 1978.

Faulenbach, Heiner. *Theologisches Fernstudium im II. Weltkrieg. Die Lehrbriefe und Feldunterrichtsbriefe der Bonner theologischen Fakultäten* (Bonner Akademische Reden 65). Bonn: Bouvier, 1987.

Fisch, René. „Dr. Nicolas Majerus". In *Die Luxemburger Kirche im 2. Weltkrieg. Dokumente, Zeugnisse, Lebensbilder.* Luxembourg: Éditions Saint-Paul, 1991, S. 284f.

Fischer, Hans. *Völkerkunde im Nationalsozialismus. Aspekte der Anpassung, Affinität und Behauptung einer wissenschaftlichen Disziplin* (Hamburger Beiträge zur Wissenschaftsgeschichte 7). Berlin/Hamburg: D. Reimer, 1990.

Gedenkboek bij gelegenheid van het vijf-en-twintig jarig bestaan van de R. K. leergangen. 1912–1937. Tilburg: R. K. Leergangen, 1937.

Goossens, Thomas. „Leergangen, Roomsch-Katholieke". In *De katholieke encyclopaedie* 16 (1936), S. 226f.

Gröll, Josef-Thomas. *Zur Geschichte der Völkerkunde an der Universität Bonn* (Bonner Amerikanistische Studien. Sondernummer). Bonn: Seminar für Völkerkunde, 1986.

Hammerstein, Notker. *Die Johann Wolfgang Goethe-Universität Frankfurt am Main. Von der Stiftungsuniversität zur staatlichen Hochschule. Bd. 1: 1914 bis 1950.* Neuwied/Frankfurt: A. Metzner, 1989.

Hehl, Ulrich von. *Katholische Kirche und Nationalsozialismus im Erzbistum Köln 1933–1945* (VKZG.F 23). Mainz: M. Grünewald, 1977.

———. *Priester unter Hitlers Terror. Eine biographische und statistische Erhebung.* 4. Aufl. Paderborn: Schöningh, 1998.

Hestermann, Ferdinand. *Eine Rede, die nicht gehalten werden konnte* (Schriftenreihe für Einheit und gerechten Frieden). Berlin: Kongress-Verlag, 1948.

Höpfner, Hans-Paul. *Die Universität Bonn im Dritten Reich. Akademische Biographien unter nationalsozialistischer Herrschaft* (Academica Bonnensia 12). Bonn: Bouvier, 1999.

Jakobi, Paul. „Franz Ballhorn". In Joël Pottier, Hg., *Christen im Widerstand gegen das Dritte Reich.* Stuttgart/Bonn: Burg-Verlag, 1988, S. 519–526.

Leser, Paul. „Fritz Graebner – Eine Würdigung". *Anthropos* 72 (1977), S. 1–55.

Lips, Eva. *What Hitler Did to Us. A Personal Record to the Third Reich.* London: M. Joseph, 1938.

Lützeler, Heinrich. *Persönlichkeiten. Konrad Adenauer, Paul Clemen, Kardinal Frings, Johannes XXIII., Erich Rothacker, Max Scheler* (HerBü 668). Freiburg i.Br.: Herder, 1978.

———. *Bonn, so wie es war.* Bd. 2. Düsseldorf: Droste, 1980.

Mensching, Gustav. „Jünglingsweihen". *Westdeutscher Beobachter*, 12.6.1944.

——. „Ein Japaner sprach über Japan. Shinto, Staatsmythos und Weltanschauung der Japaner". *Westdeutscher Beobachter*, 23.6.1944.

Neuss, Wilhelm. *Kampf gegen den Mythus des 20. Jahrhunderts. Ein Gedenkblatt an Clemens August Kardinal Graf Galen*. Köln: Bachem, 1947.

N.N. „Staatsmythos und Weltanschauung der Japaner. Professor Dr. Murata sprach als Gast der Universität". *General-Anzeiger*, 22.7.1944.

—— [A. D.]. „Die Kriegswichtigkeit der Philosophie. Ein Vortrag von Professor Dr. Rothacker". *Westdeutscher Beobachter*, 2.6.1944.

—— [dr. th.]. „Vortrag von Professor Dr. Rothacker ‚Was ist Bildung?'". *General-Anzeiger*, 7.6.1944.

Pätsch, Gertrud. „In memoriam Ferdinand Hestermann". In *Beiträge zur Ethnolinguistik. Gedenkschrift zum 100. Geburtstag von Ferdinand Hestermann*. Jena: Friedrich-Schiller-Universität, 1980, S. 7–9.

Persch, Martin. „Meurers, Heinrich von". In *Biographisch-Bibliographisches Kirchenlexikon* 5 (1993), Sp. 1401f.

——. „Andres, Friedrich". In *Biographisch-Bibliographisches Kirchenlexikon* 15 (1999), Sp. 21f.

——. „Andres, Friedrich". In Heinz Monz, Hg., *Trierer biographisches Lexikon*. Trier: Wissenschaftlicher Verlag Trier, 2000, S. 5.

Peters, Johannes. „Die japanische Malerei. Gastvorlesung des Professors Kenju Moriya". *Westdeutscher Beobachter*, 15./16.7.1944.

Pfaffen, Karlheinz, Hg. *50 Jahre Gesellschaft für Erd- und Völkerkunde zu Bonn*. Bonn: Dümmler, 1960.

Pützstück, Lothar. *‚Symphonie in Moll'. Julius Lips und die Kölner Völkerkunde* (Kulturen im Wandel 4). Pfaffenweiler: Centaurus, 1995.

Rothacker, Erich. *Die Kriegswichtigkeit der Philosophie* (KRFWU 37). Bonn: Scheur, 1944.

Thomas, Alois. *Kirche unter dem Hakenkreuz. Erinnerungen und Dokumente* (VBAT 27). Trier: Paulinus-Verlag, 1992.

Vollmer, Ulrich. „Carl Clemen (1865–1940) als Emeritus". *Zeitschrift für Religionswissenschaft* 9 (2001), S. 185–203.

——. „Volksreligion und Weltreligion in der Deutung von Gustav Mensching". In Wolfgang Gantke u.a., Hg., *Religionswissenschaft im historischen Kontext. Beiträge zum 100. Geburtstag von Gustav Mensching* (RWR 21). Marburg: Diagonal-Verlag, 2003, S. 61–85.

Wenig, Otto, Hg. *Verzeichnis der Professoren und Dozenten der Rheinischen Friedrich-Wilhelms-Universität zu Bonn 1818–1968*. Bonn: Bouvier/L. Röhrscheid, 1968.

ANTISEMITISMUS UND ANTIJUDAISMUS IN DEN WERKEN UND ARBEITEN PATER WILHELM SCHMIDTS S.V.D. (1868–1954)

Udo Mischek

1. *Einleitung*

Bis zur Mitte des 20. Jahrhunderts war Pater Wilhelm Schmidt eine schillernde Figur der deutschsprachigen Ethnologie und Religionswissenschaft. Er prägte nicht nur eine Schule – die historische Ethnologie Wiener Provenienz –, sondern hinterließ auch ein kaum zu überschauendes wissenschaftliches und publizistisches Oeuvre. Dabei erreichten nicht nur seine wissenschaftlichen Werke zahlreiche Leser, auch seine religiöse Erbauungsliteratur zur Aufmunterung der deutschen und österreichischen Katholiken, oft verquickt mit zeitkritischen Betrachtungen, erlebte mehrere Auflagen.[1] Neben diesen theologischen Handreichungen verfasste er noch Artikel in der katholischen Wochenpresse Österreichs. Hierin beschäftigte er sich vornehmlich mit tagespolitischen Themen, freilich in dezidiert konservativ-katholischer Perspektive. Insbesondere seine politischen Analysen sind themenabhängig stark antijüdisch. Ein antijüdischer Zug lässt sich jedoch auch in seinen theologischen Schriften finden und noch weiter abgeschwächt auch in einzelnen Passagen seiner wissenschaftlichen Arbeiten.

Ausführlicher werden hier Schmidts populäre Werke und Zeitungsbeiträge der 1920er und 1930er Jahre vorgestellt, da sie eine sehr viel breitere Öffentlichkeit ansprachen. Seine wissenschaftlichen Publikationen wurden zwar in der Wissenschaftsgemeinde wahrgenommen, ihre Außenwirkung ist aber geringer zu veranschlagen als etwa sein öffentliches Auftreten auf Kirchenveranstaltungen. Die Artikel und Gegendarstellungen in den Zeitungen lösten teilweise heftige Kontroversen

---

[1] Siehe etwa Wilhelm Schmidt, *Ein Jesus-Leben* (Wien: Mayer, 1948) bzw. ders., *Die Völker in der Heilsgeschichte der Menschheit* (Kaldenkirchen: Steyler Verlagsbuchhandlung, 1953).

innerhalb der katholischen Presse aus.[2] Seine theologischen Erbauungs-
schriften dürften über den Kreis der Katholiken nicht hinausgelangt
sein. Damit soll keineswegs in Abrede gestellt werden, dass es zwischen
den einzelnen Domänen keine Verbindungen gegeben hätte. Im Gegenteil: seine gesamte Arbeit bestand aus einzelnen Themenblöcken, die er
je nach Bedarf und Kontext verschieden gewichtete, die aber in allen
Tätigkeitsfeldern nachweisbar sind.

2. *Biographische Skizze und wissenschaftlicher Standpunkt*

Pater Wilhelm Schmidt wurde 1868 in Hörde – heute ein Teil Dort-
munds – in Westfalen geboren. Im Jahr 1883 trat er in den katholischen
Missionsorden Societas Verbi Divini (Gesellschaft des Göttlichen Wortes)
ein, der während des Kulturkampfes seine Zentrale in das holländische
Steyl verlegt hatte. Im Alter von 20 Jahren machte Wilhelm Schmidt
sein Abitur, durchlief dann das Noviziat und absolvierte ein theologisches Studium. 1892 wurde er zum Priester geweiht. Von 1893–1895
studierte er orientalische Sprachen und islamische Theologie bei Martin
Hartmann in Berlin. Danach wurde Schmidt in das österreichische
Haus des Ordens St. Gabriel versetzt. Hier in Mödling bei Wien nahm
Schmidt Kontakt zur Wiener Universität auf. Neben seiner Lehrver-
pflichtung für die Ordensschüler übernahm er bald Lehrveranstaltungen an der Wiener Hochschule. Sein Engagement für den Orden und
seine Interessen für die universitäre Ethnologie, Religionswissenschaft
und Sprachforschung ließen sich auch deshalb gut miteinander vereinbaren, weil der Orden ab 1879 missionarisch tätig wurde, zunächst
in China, 1888 in Argentinien, 1892 in Togo und schließlich 1896 in

---

[2] So hatte *Das Neue Reich*, die Vorläuferzeitung der *Schöneren Zukunft*, für die Schmidt
über zwei Jahrzehnte Artikel verfasste, eine Wochenauflage von 20.000 Exemplaren,
wie das Titelblatt der Nr. 39 vom 30. Juni 1923 vermerkt. Einen Überblick und eine
Einschätzung der katholischen Presselandschaft in Österreich im fraglichen Zeitraum
gibt Rudolf Ebneth, *Die Österreichische Wochenschrift 'Der Christliche Ständestaat'* (Mainz:
Matthias Grünewald, 1976). Ebneth beurteilt die *Schönere Zukunft* als pronazistisch (ebd.,
S. 23 und S. 103), was aber keineswegs auf alle Artikel zutrifft, wie Schmidts Beispiel
belegt. Weinzierl-Fischer verweist auf die wechselhafte Beurteilung des Nationalsozialis-
mus im *Neuen Reich* und der *Schöneren Zukunft*, die ab 1932 auf Wunsch der österreichi-
schen Bischöfe auf einen einheitlich nationalsozialismuskritischen Kurs einschwenkte.
Schmidts unten wiedergegebene Artikel belegen diese Aussagen beispielhaft. Vgl. Erika
Weinzierl-Fischer „Österreichs Katholiken und der Nationalsozialismus", in: *Wort und
Wahrheit* 18 (1963), S. 417–439 und S. 493–526, hier bes. S. 431–436.

Papua Neuguinea. 1902 nahm Schmidt die österreichische Staatsbürgerschaft an. In das Jahr 1906 fiel die Gründung der Zeitschrift *Anthropos*. Seit dieser Zeit beschäftigte ihn „Der Entwicklungsgedanke in der Religionswissenschaft", so ein Titel eines Vortrages, der schließlich in die 12 Bände *Der Ursprung der Gottesidee*, die zwischen 1912 und 1955 erschienen, einmündete. Schmidt war unermüdlich tätig, um seine Auffassung über die Ethnologie und Religionswissenschaft auch außerhalb der Universitäten bekannt zu machen. Die Gründung des päpstlichen Missionsmuseums im Lateranpalast in Rom – zunächst als missionsethnologische Ausstellung im Dezember 1924 eröffnet – gehört ebenso hierher wie der Aufbau des Anthropos-Instituts in Mödling bei Wien im Jahr 1931. Das Institut und sein Direktor mussten nach der Annektierung Österreichs durch das Deutsche Reich Wien 1938 verlassen und siedelten in die Schweiz über. Hier in Froideville bei Fribourg, wirkte Schmidt bis zu seinem Tod 1954 sowohl als Ordinarius für Ethnologie an der Université de Fribourg als auch am Anthropos-Institut.[3]

Neben seiner wissenschaftlichen Arbeit war Schmidt politisch tätig, um seine katholische Weltsicht auch praktisch umzusetzen. Seine Zusammenarbeit mit dem habsburgischen Thronfolger und letzten Kaiser Karl, der ihn im 1. Weltkrieg als Militärkaplan an die österreichische Galizienfront berief, gehört hierher, ebenso seine Arbeit für katholische Verbände.[4] Da Schmidt sich immer darum bemühte, die Ergebnisse seiner Forschungen einem breiteren Publikum vorzustellen, kam diesen außerwissenschaftlichen Aktivitäten für die Popularisierung seiner Ideen eine erhebliche Rolle zu. So war er auf vielen Veranstaltungen und Kongressen, die vor allem vom politischen Katholizismus organisiert

---

[3] Siehe zu Schmidts Leben Joseph Henninger, „P. Wilhelm Schmidt S.V.D. 1868–1954. Eine biographische Skizze", *Anthropos* 51 (1956), S. 19–60, Fritz Bornemann, *P. Wilhelm Schmidt S.V.D. 1868–1954* (Rom: Apud Collegium Verbi Divini, 1982), Ernest Brandewie, *When Giants walked the Earth. The Life and Times of Wilhelm Schmidt* (Fribourg: University Press, 1990) und Hans Waldenfels, „Wilhelm Schmidt (1868–1954)", in Axel Michaels, Hg., *Klassiker der Religionswissenschaft* (München, Beck, 1997), S. 185–197. Über Schmidts Haltung nach der Annexion Österreichs gibt Maximilian Liebmann, *Theodor Innitzer und der Anschluß. Österreichs Kirche 1938* (Graz u.a.: Styra, 1988), S. 129–139 Hinweise. Friedrich Heer, *Gottes Erste Liebe* (München-Esslingen: Bechtle, 1967), S. 361 und S. 375, macht Schmidt als Steigbügelhalter der nationalsozialistischen Judenverfolgung aus.

[4] Brandewie, *When Giants walked the Earth*, S. 143 erwähnt die Arbeit als Militärkaplan. Schmidt war mit der Einrichtung von Frontheimen für Soldaten beschäftigt, in denen diese sich erholen konnten. Seine diesbezüglichen Bemühungen führten zu Spannungen mit der Armeeführung und seiner endgültigen Entlassung als Militärkaplan noch vor Ende des 1. Weltkrieges.

und getragen wurden, mit Reden und Vorträgen präsent. Zu diesen Aktivitäten zählten auch seine Auftritte auf katholischen Kirchentagen der 1920er und 1930er Jahre, seine Bemühungen um die Gründung einer katholischen Universität in Salzburg Mitte der 1930er Jahre und die von ihm betreute ethnologische Ausstellung im Vatikan.

Neben all diesen Tätigkeiten unterrichtete Schmidt im Missionsseminar seines Ordens und an der Wiener Universität.[5] Viele seiner wissenschaftlichen Arbeiten, gingen auf Anstöße von Außen zurück, so etwa seine Beschäftigung mit dem Thema „Rasse", dem er sich erstmals 1926 zuwandte.[6] Schmidt verfasste darüber hinaus zahlreiche Artikel in Fachzeitschriften, etwa in dem von ihm gegründeten und bis heute wichtigen ethnologischen Organ *Anthropos*, oder schrieb Beiträge für die Zeitschrift *Hochland*, die sich vor allem an die katholischen Intellektuellen richteten.[7] Daneben stehen seine voluminösen Monographien. Insbesondere die 12 Bände *Der Ursprung der Gottesidee* oder Bücher zu anderen Themen der Zeit, etwa seine Betrachtungen *Rasse und Volk*, sind hier zu nennen.[8]

Unverkennbar war jedoch auch die wissenschaftliche Arbeit von Schmidts katholischem Glauben motiviert. So veranstaltete er zwischen 1911 und 1929 so genannte „Religions-ethnologische Wochen" in verschiedenen katholischen Hochschulorten, um die katholische Religionswissenschaft zu stärken, die ein Gegengewicht zu der von ihm als antiklerikal empfundenen akademischen Religionsforschung bilden sollte.[9] Schmidts Hauptanliegen in seinen wissenschaftlichen wie

---

[5] Zu seinen zahllosen Aktivitäten siehe die genannten Arbeiten von Brandewie, Bornemann, Henninger und Waldenfels sowie Karl Josef Rivinius, „Schmidt, Wilhelm SVD", in *Biographisch-Bibliographisches Kirchenlexikon* 17 (2000), Sp. 1231–1246 (bzw. www.bautz.de/bbkl, s.v. Schmidt).

[6] W. Schmidt, *Rasse und Volk. Eine Untersuchung zur Bestimmung ihrer Grenzen und zur Erfassung ihrer Beziehungen* (München: Kösel & Pustet, 1927). Auf Einladung des „Landesvereins katholischer Edelleute Südwestdeutschlands" hatte sich Schmidt mit dem Thema „Rasse und Volk" beschäftigt und diesen Vortrag zunächst in der katholischen Zeitschrift *Hochland* abgedruckt, bevor er eine erweiterte Fassung dem Verlag vorlegte. Eine nochmals um fast 200 Seiten erweiterte Ausgabe erschien 1935 in Österreich im Verlag Pustet, Salzburg.

[7] Siehe beispielsweise W. Schmidt, „Die Pygmäenvölker als älteste derzeit uns erreichbare Menschheitsschicht", *Hochland* 1 (1925/26), S. 574–592.

[8] Siehe W. Schmidt, *Der Ursprung der Gottesidee: eine historisch-kritische und positive Studie*, 12 Bde. (Münster: Aschendorffsche Verlagsbuchhandlung, 1912–1955) und ders. *Rasse und Volk. Ihre allgemeine Bedeutung. Ihre Geltung im deutschen Raum* (Salzburg/Leipzig: Pustet, 1935).

[9] Vgl. zu dieser Tätigkeit von Schmidt auch den Beitrag von Ulrich Vollmer in diesem Band.

populären Veröffentlichungen war es, dem schwindenden Einfluss der katholischen Lehre entgegenzuwirken. Seine katholische Sozialisation hatte großen Einfluss auf seine wissenschaftlichen und politischen Auffassungen. Da das geistige Prinzip für ihn entscheidend war, lehnte er die materialistischen Strömungen in der Politik und in der Wissenschaft ab. Sein Glaube lieferte ihm dafür das Interpretationsschema: jede Seele, von Gott neu geschaffen, manifestiert sich in jedem Menschen. Alle Menschen sind daher „Kinder eines Vaters", eines Schöpfergottes.[10] Geisteswissenschaften wie Ethnologie und Religionswissenschaft fiel die Aufgabe zu, die aus diesem Schöpfungsprozess hervorgegangenen Religions- und Gesellschaftsformen dingfest zu machen. In seinen ethnologischen und religionswissenschaftlichen Arbeiten setzte er dies um, indem er einen eigenen katholischen Ansatz entwickelte, der mit seiner Urmonotheismusidee in Verbindung stand. Schmidt projizierte in dieses Konzept die Vorstellung eines goldenen Zeitalters der Uroffenbarung hinein, das durch den rechten Glauben und intakte Familienstrukturen geprägt war: der Vatergott bringt soziale Sicherheit, er fungiert als Gesetzgeber und Überwacher, begründet die monogame Familienstruktur und „schenkt dem Menschen die Kraft zum Leben und Lieben".[11] Dieser ideale Urzustand war Anfechtungen ausgesetzt, so dass die Menschen in der Folge den rechten Weg verließen. Wie noch gezeigt wird, ist diese Idee das Einfallstor für Schmidts antijüdische und antikapitalistische Tiraden, die sich gehäuft in seinen Gegenwartsanalysen finden.

Schmidt stellte nun fest, dass Kulturen vom Hochgottglauben der Urzeit signifikant abwichen und konstruierte daraufhin eine Gliederung der Kulturen, die diesem Glaubensabfall Rechnung trug. Die Urkulturkreise – Schmidt trennte zwischen unterschiedlichen Urkulturen, etwa der pygmäischen Urkultur und der arktischen Urkultur –, die er dann von seinen Schülern und Mitarbeitern auch ethnologisch dokumentieren ließ, hatten den ursprünglichen Glauben noch bewahrt. Ethnien wie die Selknam auf Feuerland oder die zentralafrikanischen Bambuti (Pygmäen) waren für Schmidt Beispiele, mit deren Hilfe er

---

[10] W. Schmidt, *Die Stellung der Religion zu Rasse und Volk* (Augsburg: Haas & Grabherr, 1932), S. 17.
[11] W. Schmidt, *Ursprung und Werden der Religion. Theorien und Tatsachen* (Münster: Aschendorffsche Verlagsbuchhandlung, 1930), S. 274.

seine Theorien untermauerte.[12] Neben den Urkulturkreisen entstanden die primären Kulturkreise: der agrarische, der jägerisch-totemistische und der hirtennomadische Kulturkreis. Aus diesen ergaben sich durch Überlagerungsvorgänge seitens der „Herrscherhirten" die ersten Hochkulturen in Ägypten oder im Zweistromland. Am weitesten vom ursprünglichen Zustand hatte sich die „mutterrechtlich-agrarische Kultur", mit den ihr von Schmidt zugeschriebenen blutigen Opferriten, entfernt.[13] Der „patriarchalische Kulturkreis der Nomadenhirten" hatte neben den noch existierenden Urkulturvölkern den Hochgottglauben jedoch am reinsten bewahrt. Diese Nomadenhirten, von Schmidt auch als „Herrschervölker" bezeichnet, gab es in zwei Varianten: die „(Ural-)Altaier und die „Semitohamiten".[14]

Auch die jüdische Religion war dem Kulturkreis der Nomadenhirten zugeordnet und nahm von daher im Vergleich zu anderen Kulturkreisen und deren Religionen eine privilegierte Stellung ein.[15] Allerdings war die Lage der jüdischen „Semitohamiten" durchaus ambivalent, denn nun waren die Juden nicht mehr die ersten Monotheisten. Dieser Rang wurde ihnen von den Urkulturvölkern und dem anderen Zweig der Hirtenvölker, den Altaiern, streitig gemacht, die nach Schmidts Meinung die älteren Anrechte auf den Eingottglauben hatten. Schmidts katholische Sozialisation ließ eine völlige Missachtung der Juden und des Alten Testaments aber nicht zu.[16] Die Relativierung der jüdischen Position als erste Monotheisten eröffnete ihm eine Möglichkeit der Kritik, ergänzt durch die negative Rolle, die er ihnen in seiner Auslegung des Neuen Testaments zuwies. Auf der anderen Seite stand der im Vergleich mit anderen Völkern reine Monotheismus des Alten Testaments. Zwischen diesen beiden Polen oszillierte denn auch

---

[12] Wilhelm Koppers (1886–1961), Martin Gusinde (1886–1969) und Paul Schebesta (1878–1967) alle Mitglieder der Gesellschaft des göttlichen Wortes, konnten mit Hilfe der von Schmidt beim Vatikan losgeeisten Gelder Feldforschungen insbesondere in Feuerland (Koppers und Gusinde) und Zentralafrika (Schebesta), betreiben. Einen Überblick über die Wiener Schule gibt Werner Petermann, *Die Geschichte der Ethnologie* (Wuppertal: Peter Hammer, 2004), S. 605–610.
[13] Schmidt, *Ursprung und Werden der Religion*, S. 278.
[14] Eine Zusammenfassung des Gedankens findet sich bei Sylvester Pajak, *Urreligion und Uroffenbarung bei P.W. Schmidt* (St. Augustin: Steyler, 1978), S. 207ff.
[15] Schmidt, *Die Stellung der Religion zu Rasse und Volk*, S. 18.
[16] Zu diesem Punkt schon Edouard Conte, *Völkerkunde und Faschismus* (Manuskript, o.O., o.J.: Bibliothek des Ludwig-Uhland-Instituts für empirische Kulturwissenschaften der Universität Tübingen), S. 12.

das Bild, das Schmidt von der jüdischen Religion und ihren Anhängern zeichnete.

3. Antijüdische und antisemitische Passagen in Schmidts Werken

Das Idyll der Vergangenheit bildete auch Schmidts Maß für die Gegenwart. Er konnte in der Geschichte Deutschlands, insbesondere seit der Reformation, einen beschleunigten Verfall auf religiösem Gebiet erkennen. Im protestantischen Teil Deutschlands sah er den Totengräber des Heiligen Römischen Reiches, dem Pater Schmidt nachtrauerte. Der Höhepunkt dieser Verfallsentwicklung war die Zeit nach dem verlorenen 1. Weltkrieg, gekennzeichnet durch die versuchte Machtübernahme seitens der vom Materialismus verseuchten Bolschewisten. Weil nach Schmidts Lesart die meisten der sozialistischen und sozialdemokratischen Politiker Juden waren, finden sich gerade in der Auseinandersetzung mit diesem Teil des politischen Spektrums die meisten seiner antisemitischen und antijüdischen Äußerungen.[17] Es bedurfte aber des protestantischen Hohenzollernkaisers, um der Revolution den Weg zu bereiten. Weil nach dem desaströsen Ausgang des Krieges der deutsche Protestantismus mit seiner engen Anbindung an das Haus Hohenzollern – bis 1918 war der deutsche Kaiser auch Oberhaupt der Protestanten in Preußen – geschwächt war, konnte eine Heilung der geschundenen Seelen eigentlich nur vom Katholizismus her geleistet werden. Um sich aber von anderen Heilsversprechen abzugrenzen, kam es darauf an, diese falschen Prophetien zu demaskieren. Aus diesem Grund suchte Schmidt die Auseinandersetzung mit dem linken Lager, wobei er hier besonders häufig solche antisemitischen Stereotypen verwendete, die sich nicht allein aus seinen religiösen Vorurteilen speisten. In ähnlicher Weise polemisierte er aber auch gegen die sich etablierende völkische Szene,

---

[17] Schon Bornemann, *P. Wilhelm Schmidt*, 279f. hat in seiner materialreichen Arbeit auf Passagen mit antijudaistischem Inhalt in Schmidts Werken aufmerksam gemacht. Ihm folgten Artikel von Edouard Conte, „Wilhelm Schmidt: Des Kaiers letzter Beichtvater und das ‚neudeutsche Heidentum'", in Helge Gerndt, Hg., *Volkskunde und Nationalsozialismus* (München: Münchener Vereinigung für Volkskunde, 1987), S. 261–278 sowie ein Abschnitt bei Michael Spöttel, *Hamiten: Völkerkunde und Antisemitismus* (Frankfurt u.a.: Lang, 1996), S. 66f.; Brandewie, *When Giants walked the Earth*, widmet in seiner Schmidt-Biographie dem „Antisemitismus" ein Kapitel (ebd., S. 233).

insbesondere die Nationalsozialisten, auch wenn er hier verständlicherweise keine antisemitische Rhetorik benutzte.[18]

Erste Belege für einen handfesten Antijudaismus finden sich in seiner politisch-religiösen Zeitdiagnose *Der deutschen Seele Not und Heil,* die 1920 im katholischen Schöningh Verlag in Paderborn erschien. Hier zog Schmidt ein Resümee aus dem verlorenen Weltkrieg, dessen Folgeerscheinungen er vor allem dem in weiten Bevölkerungskreisen angeblich virulenten Materialismus anlastete. Als Verbreiter des Materialismus machte er vor allem die Juden aus, sowohl in der Unterschicht als Funktionäre der Sozialisten, als auch in der Oberschicht. Selbst der Kaiser war vor ihnen nicht gefeit, da er die Gesellschaft des antisemitischen Hofpredigers Stoecker verschmähte und sich stattdessen „den Juden Ballin, Bleichröder, Dernburg u.a." zuwandte. Diese Freundschaft verhinderte es nach Schmidts Dafürhalten, „einen unzerstörbaren Damm gegen Sozialdemokratie und Judentum" aufzurichten.[19]

Folgerichtig musste die ganze Entwicklung im Zusammenbruch des deutschen Reiches enden. Doch das kaiserliche Deutschland war zum Teil auch an seinen inneren Widersprüchen zerbrochen: Auf der einen Seite standen die verarmten Massen, die ihr Heil in der Sozialdemokratie suchten, auf der anderen das Bildungsbürgertum, das, von Schmidt als „Bildungsphilistertum" karikiert, „dank der jüdischen Presse, üppig ins Kraut schoß."[20] Hinzu kam das Wirtschaftsbürgertum, das nur noch den wirtschaftlichen Erfolg im Auge hatte und die „Niederkonkurrierung des Gegners" betrieb. Auch hier war es vor allem „das jüdische Element, das sich immer rücksichtsloser vordrängte".[21] So ließ sich der moralische Verfall nicht mehr aufhalten und als letzte Konsequenz kam es dazu,

> daß ein paar land- und stammfremde, förmlich dahergelaufenen Menschen von teilweise abenteuerlichster Vergangenheit und zweifelhaften moralischen und intellektuellen Qualitäten in mehreren Staaten und

---

[18] Antisozialistisch war Schmidts Schrift, *Der Ödipus-Komplex der Freudschen Psychoanalyse und die Ehegestaltung des Bolschewismus* (Berlin/Wien: Erneuerungs-Verlag, 1933), antinationalsozialistisch „Zur Aussprache über den Nationalsozialismus", *Schönere Zukunft* 37 (1932), S. 861f. sowie „Das Rasseprinzip des Nationalsozialismus, ebd., Nr. 43, S. 999f.

[19] W. Schmidt, *Der Deutschen Seele Not und Heil. Eine Zeitbetrachtung* (Paderborn: Schöningh, 1920), S. 29.

[20] Ebd., S. 15.

[21] Ebd., S. 17.

Städten die Herrschaft an sich reißen und sie Wochen und Monate lang diktatorisch, selbst tyrannisch ausüben konnten (...).[22]

Auch wenn er in diesem Absatz die Juden nicht namentlich erwähnte, ist unschwer zu dechiffrieren, wem Schmidt die Schuld an der Revolution anlastete. So schrieb er einige Seiten später:

denn seitdem der Jude auf die Stimmen seiner alten Propheten nicht mehr gehört hat, ist er dazu verurteilt, selbst das Zerrbild eines Propheten zu sein, der mit hastiger Vordringlichkeit und lautem Geschrei überall die Aufmerksamkeit der Menge an sich zu reißen sich bemüht. Seitdem er den wahren Messias verleugnet und ans Kreuz geschlagen hat, ist es sein Fluch, aller Welt ein Messias sein zu wollen.[23]

Das in dieser frühen Schrift deutlich zu Tage tretende Muster einer Verquickung von genuin religiösen Antijudaismen und anderen stereotypen Judenbildern, etwa als blutsaugende Kapitalisten, geifernde Pressemagnaten oder die Ordnung zersetzende Revolutionäre, bildete in den folgenden Jahren die Vorlage, nach der Schmidt seine Artikel webte. Ausfälle gegen Juden häuften sich vor allem in den Arbeiten zu Beginn der 1920er Jahre. Das Thema verblieb aber in seinem Ideenfundus und Schmidt benutzte antisemitische Stereotypen auch weiterhin als Versatzstücke in seinen Artikeln.

Diese „Patchworktechnik" zeigt sich auch in seiner Auseinandersetzung mit der Freudschen Psychoanalyse, der Schmidt am Ende der 1920er Jahre entgegentrat. Hier waren aber, das verdient hervorgehoben zu werden, keine direkten antisemitischen Angriffe auf Freud und seine Schule zu finden. Allenfalls verweist die Wortwahl die Schmidt benutzte, um Freuds Stellung in der Wissenschaft zu beschreiben, auf eine kritische Haltung. So war von „starken organisatorischen Kräften" und einer „Rührigkeit der Bewegung" die Rede. Insbesondere Freuds kritische Analyse des Neuen Testaments wurde von Schmidt als „Gipfelpunkt der Atrocität" verworfen.[24]

Der eigentliche Vorwurf, den Schmidt der Theorie des Ödipus-Komplexes machte, war ein anderer. Wenn Religion, Verwandtschaft und Familienbeziehungen auf einem Verbrechen, dem Mord an dem Vater fußten, dann konnte die logische Folgerung nur darin liegen, konsequent mit dieser Vergangenheit und der Familie zu brechen. Schmidt verwies

---

[22] Ebd., S. 42.
[23] Ebd., S. 162f.
[24] Schmidt, *Der Ödipus-Komplex der Freudschen Psychoanalyse*, S. 3 und S. 11.

darauf, dass die Sowjetunion eine Liberalisierung des Familien- und Eherechts eingeleitet habe, um eben dies in die Tat umzusetzen. Insbesondere die Lockerung der monogamen Ehe empfand Schmidt als „radikalste Vergewaltigung" und fuhr fort:

> Mit entschlossener Hand wird hier Dynamit gelegt an den innersten Kern der sozialen und sittlichen Ordnung der Menschheit und an die tiefsten Grundlagen selbst ihrer materiellen, physischen Existenz.[25]

Für Schmidt war die psychoanalytische Theorie ein Werkzeug, das half, die „Familienautorität zu vernichten", und dafür waren die Bolschewisten verantwortlich. Nach seiner Auffassung bestand in dieser Sache zwischen Freud und den sowjetrussischen Kommunisten „eine nicht wegzudisputierende entente cordiale".[26] Das hier verwendete Interpretationsmuster Schmidts, die Verbindung von Kommunismus und Juden, tauchte bei ihm in unterschiedliche Gewänder gekleidet immer wieder auf, nur die Wertigkeiten werden leicht verschoben. Waren in einem Fall die kommunistischen und sozialistischen Funktionäre Juden, so benutzen im Fall der Psychoanalyse die „Bolschewisten" jüdisches Handwerkszeug: das Resultat blieb das gleiche.

Zur Jahreswende 1933/34 rückten die Juden erneut in das Zentrum seiner Überlegungen. Der Nationalsozialismus war in Deutschland an die Macht gelangt und in Österreich hatte das autoritäre Dollfuß-Regime im März 1933 die Regierung übernommen. Auf einer Tagung der „Katholischen Aktion" – einer vom Vatikan geförderten Laienbewegung zur Eindämmung von liberalen, sozialistischen und nationalsozialistischen Einflüssen[27] – hatte Schmidt sich erneut mit den Juden, insbesondere mit jüdischstämmigen Konvertiten, befasst. Er brachte an dieser Stelle sehr deutlich zum Ausdruck, dass er den von den deutschen Nationalsozialisten geführten Rassendiskurs ablehnte. Dabei verwies er auf die sich widersprechenden Aussagen der Anthropologen, auf denen sich schwerlich eine „Weltanschauung" aufbauen lasse.[28] Andererseits betonte er aber, dass eine Lösung der Judenfrage auch in Österreich nötig wäre, denn, so Schmidt, „wenn man jetzt daran vorbeiginge", bestünde die Gefahr, „daß sie später in gewaltsamer Weise gelöst würde,

---

[25] Ebd., S. 19.
[26] Ebd., S. 21.
[27] Siehe hierzu bes. Luigi Civardi, *Das Handbuch der katholischen Aktion* (Innsbruck/Wien: Tyrolia, 1938).
[28] W. Schmidt, „Zur Judenfrage", *Schönere Zukunft* 17 (1934), S. 408.

die weder dem österreichischen deutschen, noch dem jüdischen Volke günstig wäre."[29] Die Frage war nach Schmidt deshalb so akut geworden, weil die „Vormacht der Juden in den kulturellen Institutionen nicht länger" ertragen werden konnte. Zur Begründung führte er die verhältnismäßig hohe Zahl von Juden in den akademischen Berufen, in der Filmbranche, der Presse und dem Theater an.

Das eigentliche Problem der Juden war für Schmidt aber nicht ihre Rasse, wie von anderer Seite suggeriert wurde, sondern beruhe auf „geistigen Faktoren":

> Das jüdische Volk hatte als nationalen Beruf den höchsten erhalten, der einem Volk übertragen werden kann: dem Heiland der Welt die menschliche Natur vorzubereiten, die er aus ihm annehmen sollte, und ihm als Wegbereiter in die Menschheit zu dienen. Den ersten Teil dieser Aufgabe hat es erfüllt, den zweiten nicht (...). Deshalb hat diese Volk als solches seinen nationalen Beruf verfehlt. Ein solches Verfehlen aber verzerrt ganz allgemein das Wesen eines jeden Volkes; bei der Verfehlung eines so hohen Berufes aber wie beim jüdischen Volk geht diese Verzerrung weiter und tiefer; corruptio optimi pessima. Zur Strafe dieser Verfehlung wurde dieses Volk, wie Christus selber es vorhersagte, von seinem Heimatboden vertrieben und irrt seitdem umher, seines heimatlichen Wurzelbodens beraubt, als entwurzeltes Volk.[30]

Die einzige Möglichkeit für die Juden, diesem Schicksal zu entrinnen, bestehe darin, sich taufen zu lassen. Nur der Übertritt eines Juden zur katholischen Kirche räume die „eigentlichste und tiefste Ursache seines Andersseins" beiseite. Allerdings nicht vollständig, denn an dieser Stelle führte Schmidt erstmals eine rassistisch geprägte Argumentationslinie in die Diskussion ein, die sich bis dato in keinem seiner Werke nachweisen lässt. Er gewährte der Rassenideologie sozusagen durch das Hintertürchen Einlass, wenn er schreibt:

> Aber die rassischen Auswirkungen dieser Ursache, die im Laufe dieser zwei Jahrtausende sich eingestellt haben, werden nicht mit einem Male, auch nicht durch die Taufe, aufgehoben; dazu braucht es viel Zeit und innere Arbeit, so daß er wohl zu uns gehört, aber nicht so wie unsere deutschen Volksgenossen.[31]

Mit dieser Aussage hebelte Schmidt seine gesamte bisherige Argumentation aus, denn sie bedeutet in letzter Konsequenz, dass das Sakrament

---

[29] Ebd., S. 408.
[30] Ebd., S. 408f.
[31] Ebd., S. 409.

der Taufe und der heilige Geist doch schwächer als die Natur und die
Rasse sind.

Schmidt muss diesen Widerspruch erkannt haben, denn er verfasste
für die katholische Wochenzeitung *Schönere Zukunft* eine Richtigstellung
seiner Aussagen, die er auf der Tagung der „Katholischen Aktion"
gemacht hatte. Auch hier ist seine Argumentationsführung beeindruk-
kend, gelingt es ihm doch, seine zuvor gemachten Aussagen abzu-
schwächen und sogar ins Gegenteil zu verkehren. Nun bewertete er
nämlich den rassischen Unterschied zwischen Juden und Nichtjuden
als etwas Positives. Es handele sich um „Rasseverschiedenheiten", die
das jüdische Volk aus jener Zeit mitbekommen habe, als es „von Gott
noch nicht verworfen war," um hinzuzufügen, dass es unsinnig sei, diese
Eigenschaften aufgeben zu wollen, die „seinerzeit eine berechtigte und
wertvolle Eigenart darstellten und die nach ihrer Reinigung nichts von
ihrer Berechtigung und ihrem Wert verloren haben."[32]

Deutlich wird durch diese zitierten Stellen der Versuch Schmidts
belegt, den rassischen Antisemitismus mit dem christlichen Antijudaismus zu vermengen. Dieser Ansatz scheiterte und Schmidt verzichtete
in den folgenden Jahren darauf. Seinem christlich geprägten Judenhass
hat er aber nicht abgeschworen.

Das gespannte Verhältnis einer rassisch argumentierenden Judenfeindschaft und einer katholischer Sichtweise wird auch in Schmidts
Arbeiten zum Verhältnis von Rasse und Volk sichtbar. In der ersten
Ausgabe von *Rasse und Volk* aus dem Jahr 1927 äußerte er sich in einigen
Absätzen stark antijüdisch. Dieses Werk, zunächst als Vortrag für den
„Landesverein katholischer Edelleute Südwestdeutschlands" in Stuttgart
verfasst, stellte eine Zusammenfassung des damaligen Rassendiskurses
dar. Schmidt zitierte die neuesten Arbeiten aus der Anthropologie,
kritisierte aber Rassenkundler, die am Rand des wissenschaftlichen
Spektrums standen und von denen einige im Nationalsozialismus später
mit Lob und Ehren überschüttet werden sollten.[33] Für ihn stand außer
Zweifel, dass es zwar Rassen gab, diese aber unter dem Primat der Seele
und des Geistes standen. Eine Verbindung von Rasse und Seele lehnte

---

[32] Ebd., S. 409.
[33] So polemisierte Schmidt (*Rasse und Volk*, S. 22f.) gegen Hans F.K. Günther, den
er als „Hellseher" bezeichnete, der eher das „Gebiet des Komischen" beackerte, als
Wissenschaft zu treiben. Zu Günthers Karriere im Nationalsozialismus siehe Katja
Geisenhainer, *Rasse ist Schicksal. Otto Reche (1879–1966) – ein Leben als Anthropologe und
Völkerkundler* (Leipzig: Evangelische Verlagsanstalt, 2002), bes. S. 260f., dort auch wei-
terführende Literaturangaben.

er ab, da „jede Seele in ihrem eigensten Wesen neu geschaffen wird"
und daher gelte: "Die Seele hat als solche keine Rasse."[34]

In sein eigenes Gedankengebäude baute Schmidt die Rasse insofern ein, als er von einer relativen Isolierung seiner Urkultur- und
Primärkulturkreise ausging, die daher auch unterschiedliche Rassen
ausgebildet hätten. Hochkulturen aber entstanden, so Schmidt, durch
Rassenmischung, die erst die unterschiedlichen Talente voll zur Geltung
bringen könne.[35] Mit dieser Ansicht brachte er sich in Opposition zur
sich entwickelnden nationalsozialistischen Rassenideologie, die ihr Heil
allein in der nordischen Rasse zu finden glaubte. Nach der Machter-
greifung sollte daher konsequenterweise auch die zweite Auflage von
Rasse und Volk auf dem nationalsozialistischen Index landen.[36]

Etwas unverbunden finden sich antijüdische Äußerungen am Ende
der ersten Auflage dieser Schrift, die Schmidt ohne jegliche Bezüge zu
seiner vorhergehenden Darstellung unter der Überschrift „Die Bedeutung der Aristokratie im Kulturganzen" vortrug. Seinem Publikum, dem
„Landesverein katholischer Edelleute Südwestdeutschlands", huldigend
führte er aus, dass der bodenständige Adel besser geeignet sei, größeren
Landbesitz zu bewirtschaften und für das Allgemeinwohl nutzbar zu
machen, als „Mitglieder des rassisch und national zumeist fremden und
deshalb mehr international orientierten Finanz- und Bankkapitals."[37]
Gleichzeitig seien die „entwurzelten jüdischen Führer" der städtischen
Arbeiterschaft nicht in der Lage, eine „wirkliche Kultur" aufzubauen,
da sie „feindselig aller tieferen Einwurzelung widerstreben".[38]

In den folgenden Jahren thematisierte Schmidt die rassische Anders-
artigkeit der Juden nicht mehr, auch nicht in der zweiten Auflage
von *Rasse und Volk*, die 1935 erschien. Gleichwohl blieb er seiner religiös begründeten antijüdischen Einstellung treu. Zu Tage tritt diese
religiös motivierte Geringschätzung der Juden besonders in seiner
Leben-Jesu-Darstellung, die erstmals in den Jahren 1940–1944 und als
zweite Auflage 1948 erschien. Zur Stärkung der katholischen Seelen

---

[34] Schmidt, *Rasse und Volk*, S. 16.
[35] Ebd., S. 37.
[36] Nach dem Krieg meinte Schmidt (*Rassen und Völker*, Bd. 1, Luzern: Stocker, 1946,
S. IX) dies sei Wilhelm Emil Mühlmann zu verdanken gewesen, der 1937 in der NS-
Zeitschrift *Volk und Rasse* einen Verriss veröffentlichte. Mühlmann, „Politisch-katholische
Rassenforschung" (ebd., 1937, S. 35) wollte eine zuvor in der gleichen Zeitschrift
erschienene positive Darstellung des Schmidtschen Buches richtig stellen.
[37] Schmidt, *Rasse und Volk*, S. 61.
[38] Ebd. S. 63.

in Deutschland gedacht, wollte das Buch eine „positive und konkrete Darstellung der Person Jesu" entwerfen und ein Gegenbild zu dem nationalsozialistischen „Haß gegen die Person Jesu" sein.[39] Schmidt gelingt dies, wenn auch auf Kosten der Juden, die in seiner Darstellungen zu Gegenspielern Jesu werden. Auch nach der Ermordung des europäischen Judentums durch die Nationalsozialisten blieben die Juden das Volk der Gottesmörder. Eine Verurteilung dieses Verbrechens sucht man bei Schmidt vergebens. Im Gegenteil, Schmidt beschreibt die Juden als Feinde Jesu, als „hitzige Stürmer und Fanatiker" und als „materialistische Genussmenschen", denen sich bereits Jesus widersetzt habe.[40] Seine antijüdische Darstellung kulminiert in den Kapiteln, die sich mit Jesu Verurteilung und Kreuzigung befassen. Hier wird Pilatus Opfer einer Verschwörung, die das Volk gegen Jesu aufhetzt. Es waren die „hohen jüdischen Hintermänner, die das Volk missbrauchen, um ihre dunklen Ziele zu erreichen" und die letztlich auch für Jesu Tod verantwortlich waren.[41]

Obwohl Schmidt sehr viel abwertender über die Juden spricht, so ist doch auch Pilatus nicht ganz unschuldig:

> Der gigantische Haß dieses Volkes und ihrer Aufwiegler für sich allein ist nicht stark genug, den Kreuzestod über Jesus zu verhängen, wenn dein Mund nicht das Todesurteil spricht, und deine Hand es nicht unterzeichnet. Freilich dieses Volk in seiner Wut gebärdet sich wie vom Teufel besessen, es erklärt sich bereit, den vollen Anteil der Blutschuld auf sich und seine Kinder zu übernehmen, und so gellt der unheimliche Ruf vieltausendstimmig über den Platz, durch den das jüdische Volk selbst sein Strafurteil über sich spricht, noch ehe Pilatus das seinige über Jesus ausgesprochen hat: ‚Sein Blut komme über uns und unsere Kinder!'[42]

Noch kurz vor seinem Tod schrieb er 1953 in einer anderen religiösen Erbauungsschrift über die Juden, dass sie sich der „göttlichen Berufung versagten", „Jesus verwarfen und an das Kreuz lieferten".[43] Auch in seinem nachgelassenen wissenschaftlichen Werk *Das Mutterrecht* finden sich religiös motivierte antijüdische Ausfälle. Hier verweist er darauf, dass es lediglich dem Christentum gelungen sei, der Frau ihre wahre

---

[39] W. Schmidt, *Ein Jesus-Leben*, 2 Bde. (Wien: Mayer, 1948), S. X.
[40] Ebd. Bd. 2, S. 44.
[41] Ebd., Bd. 2, S. 192.
[42] Ebd., Bd. 2, S. 194. Ein Wort über die Blutschuld der nazistischen Häscher findet sich in keiner einzigen Passage.
[43] W. Schmidt, *Die Völker in der Heilsgeschichte der Menschheit* (Kaldenkirchen: Steyler Verlagsbuchhandlung, 1953), S. 15.

Aufgabe, die Mutterschaft, zurückzugeben. Die Unauflöslichkeit von Ehe und Familie zu garantieren, war für die Erfüllung dieser Pflicht Voraussetzung. Genau dies aber sei von den Juden missachtet worden. Christus musste eingreifen, so Schmidt, um die „Frau vor der Übermacht des Mannes" zu schützen, „die beim jüdischen Volk eingerissen war in grenzenloser Willkür des Mannes bei der Ehescheidung".[44] Erst das Christentum schafft es, das „weibliche Ideal, das Eva die erste Menschenmutter nicht zu verwirklichen vermocht hatte", in Maria zu vervollkommnen.[45] Die jungfräuliche Gottesmutter war im Gegensatz zu ihrer Vorläuferin auf keinen jüdischen Adam angewiesen, um Jesus zu empfangen.

Kennzeichnend für Schmidts Judengegnerschaft war die religiöse Begründung, die er immer wieder anführte, ohne allerdings eine Auseinandersetzung mit den betreffenden Bibelstellen zu suchen. Juden waren in seiner Lesart verstockte Jesusmörder, deren „Verworfenheit" aber eben nicht in ihrer körperlich rassischen Eigenart sondern in ihrer geistigen Einstellung lag. Deutlich wurde das Primat der Seele nach dem verunglückten Versuch hervorgehoben, den Rassendiskurs in seine antijüdische Argumentation einzubauen. Nach seiner Kehrtwende verzichtete er auf dieses Stereotyp, ohne jedoch seinem religiös begründeten Antijudaismus ganz abzuschwören. Ungeklärt bleiben letztlich Schmidts Motive. Ob seine Abneigung gegen die Juden in erster Linie während seiner Ausbildung vermittelt wurde, oder ob die Familie oder die Umgebung entscheidende Impulse gaben, sind Fragen, für deren Beantwortung andere Quellen erschlossen werden müssen.[46]

4. Antinazistische Stellen in Schmidts Arbeiten

Schmidts antijüdische Ausfälle sollen nicht dazu verleiten, in ihm einen Parteigänger oder Sympathisanten der Nationalsozialisten zu vermuten. Das Gegenteil war der Fall. Den deutschen und österreichischen Nationalsozialismus lehnte er entschieden ab. In nicht zu überbieten-

---

[44] W. Schmidt, *Das Mutterrecht* (Wien-Mödling, Missionsdruckerei St. Gabriel), S. 185.
[45] Schmidt, *Das Mutterrecht*, S. 186.
[46] Arye Maimon u.a. Hg., *Germanica Judaica* 3 (Tübingen: Mohr, 1987), S. 245 und S. 566. Der Eintrag des Lexikons weist für den Ort Hörde eine sehr kleine jüdische Bevölkerung nach. 1511 ist erstmals das Aufenthaltsrecht für einen Juden bezeugt und die Zahl der jüdischen Familien stieg auch im 19. Jahrhundert nicht stark an. Im Gegensatz dazu ist für das benachbarte Dortmund eine größere Judengemeinde belegt.

der Schärfe und in aller Deutlichkeit wies er das Heilsversprechen des
Nationalsozialismus zurück.

Für ihn fußte die nationalsozialistische Ideologie letztlich auf den
gleichen falschen Grundlagen, wie er sie auch bei Sozialisten erkannt
zu haben glaubte: dem Materialismus. Insbesondere in der Diskussion
um die Bedeutung der Rasse zeigt sich der grundlegende Unterschied
zwischen Schmidts Interpretation und der nazistischen Lesart. Für
ihn bestand das deutsche Volk aus unterschiedlichen gleichwertigen
Rassen. In der NS-Ideologie herrschte dagegen eine Rassenhierarchie
vor, außerdem huldigte das NS-Regime einem

> neuen Materialismus eben in der Maßlosigkeit seiner Rassentheorien, die
> das Höchste und Beste im Menschen von dem Blute ableiten und damit
> die Geistigkeit und Eigenständigkeit der Seele und die Freiheit sittlichen
> Wollens entweder einfach leugnen oder sie in geschwollenen Redensarten
> verschwinden lassen.[47]

Das Rassenprinzip des Nationalsozialismus und die damit verbundene
Bevorzugung des Körperlichen vor dem Geistigen war es, die es einem
„wirklich denkenden und lebendigen Katholiken" unmöglich machte,
zu einem Gefolgsmann der Nazis zu werden. Für Schmidt bestand der
fundamentale Unterschied zwischen den Juden und den christlichen
Völkern in ihrer „seelischen Struktur". Er wurde nicht müde seinen
Hauptvorwurf zu wiederholen, dass die Juden ihrer „Geschichte und
Berufung" zuwidergehandelt hätten, woraus ihre Verdorbenheit und
ihre „schlechten und gefährlichen Eigenschaften" hervorgegangen
seien.[48] Seine Warnungen vor den völkischen Ideologen richteten sich
vor allen Dingen an die katholische Jugend Österreichs, die sich nicht
vor einen „fremden Heerhaufen" spannen lassen solle, schon gar nicht
vor einen, der das christliche Kreuz entweiht und es als Hakenkreuz
über das christliche Symbol gestellt hatte. Um die alte Weltordnung
wieder aufzurichten bleibe nichts anderes übrig als

> zu jedem Haken an allen vier Enden des Hakenkreuzes noch zwei andere
> hinzuzusetzen, um auch an den vier Enden ein Kreuz entstehen zu lassen,
> um dadurch zum Ausdruck zu bringen, daß das Kreuz nach allen vier
> Weltgegenden hin und in allen seinen Folgerungen angenommen und
> anerkannt werden muß. Das ist dann das fünffache Kreuz: das Kreuz in
> der Mitte und die Kreuze an den vier Enden, das sich auch gegen den

---

[47] Schmidt, *Das Rasseprinzip*, S. 999.
[48] Ebd., S. 999.

fünfzackigen Sowjetstern richtet und das allen Völkern von der Mitte der Erde wie von ihren vier Enden zuruft: In hoc signo vinces![49]

5. *Schmidts Position und die aktuelle Diskussion um den „Katholischen Antisemitismus"*

In Schmidts dualistischer Weltsicht stehen dem Glaubensabfall und der Abkehr vom rechten Weg die Wiederbesinnung auf die katholischen Werte gegenüber. Kennzeichnet die von ihm beschriebene „älteste Zeit" mit ihrem Glauben an den einen Gott und ihrer nahezu vollkommenen Verfassung den Idealzustand, kam es in den folgenden Epochen zu einer geistigen Erosion. Nahezu alle Gebiete waren davon betroffen. Der Monotheismus wurde zugunsten eines „zersplitterten Polytheismus" aufgegeben und im Rechtsleben wurde der Eigentumsbegriff von seinen sozialen Bindungen gelöst und zu einer „heidnisch-römischen", den „Rechtsindividualismus auf die äußerste Spitze" treibenden Institution, der dadurch sämtliche Regelmechanismen abhanden kamen.[50]

Zu den positiven Zäsuren der deutschen Geschichte zählte Schmidt das Reich Karls des Großen, der die Heiden besiegte und die Einheit der Kirche beförderte. In negativer Hinsicht war es vor allem die Reformation, mit der das eigentliche Übel seinen Anfang nahm. Von nun an war das Heilige Römische Reich geschwächt und der Protestantismus gewann langsam die Überhand. Dies zeige sich am deutlichsten bei der Gründung des neuen deutschen Reiches 1871, das nun mehrheitlich von Protestanten bewohnt wurde, weil man das katholische Österreich ausgeschlossen hatte. Die Folgen ließen nicht auf sich warten: Liberalismus und Materialismus blühten auf und führten ins Chaos, hatten sie sich doch von den christlich-katholischen Grundlagen immer weiter entfernt. Folgerichtig kam es vor allem nach dem verlorenen 1. Weltkrieg zur bisher schlimmsten Katastrophe, die selbst die französische Revolution in den Schatten stellte: die kommunistische Machtübernahme in Russland. Schmidts Antijudaismus ist in diese Weltsicht eingepasst. Juden sind nicht nur durch die Emanzipationsbewegung, die von Seiten liberaler Parteien und Abgeordneter vorangetrieben wurden, mit der liberalen Bewegung des 19. Jahrhunderts verbunden, sondern wurden

---

[49] Schmidt, „Zur Aussprache über den Nationalsozialismus", S. 832.
[50] Schmidt, „Der Eigentumsgedanke hinter der Enzyklika ‚Rerum novarum'", *Schönere Zukunft* 36 (1931), S. 851f.

über die „Judenpresse" integraler Bestandteil dieser politischen Richtung. Aber nicht nur im Liberalismus, auch im Bolschewismus und in
der Sozialdemokratie sind die Juden eine tragende Säule. Eine solche
Gemengelage war freilich nicht nur für die Sichtweise Pater W. Schmidts
typisch, vielmehr wurde diese Einstellung von vielen Katholiken geteilt,
die im unkontrollierten kapitalistischen Wachstum mit seinen Folgen für
das gesamte soziale Klima die Juden am Werke sahen, die die Arbeiter-
massen ausbeuteten und für ihre umstürzlerischen Ziele einspannten. In
dieser selektiven Wahrnehmungsweise finden nichtjüdische Industrielle
keine Beachtung, wie Schmidts Biograph Brandewie feststellte.[51] Ähnliches galt für die Säkularisierungstendenzen im Staat, der die Zivilehe
einführte und das Bildungsmonopol beanspruchte, das zuvor von der
Kirche verwaltet wurde.

In Schmidts Werken lässt sich neben deutlich antijüdischen Passagen
auch immer eine gewisse Hochachtung erkennen, die er dem mosa-
ischen Monotheismus entgegenbringt. In seiner 1932 veröffentlichten
Broschüre zum Thema *Religion und Rasse* findet sich kein einziger
negativer Abschnitt über die jüdische Religion. Im Gegensatz zu seinen
sonstigen Gepflogenheiten führt er hier aus, dass nur ein Volk beim
gemeinsamen Vater geblieben sei, „auserwählt, geleitet und geschützt
von Gott selbst".[52] Auch in dem 1935 erschienenen Band *Rasse und
Volk* finden sich keinerlei Hinweise auf seine Einstellung zur jüdischen
Religion und ihrer Anhänger. Dafür hatte er 1934 in seiner rassenan-
tisemitisch angehauchten Rede zur „Judenfrage" kein Blatt vor den
Mund genommen. Wie Schmidts gegensätzliche Positionen zu erklären
sind, kann nur eine weitere Untersuchung des Kontextes, in denen
die Schriften entstanden bzw. des Leserkreises, für den sie geschrieben
wurden, ergeben.

Die Analyse der Äußerungen von Pater Wilhelm Schmidt über
das Judentum bietet instruktives Material für die in der Geschichtswissenschaft geführte Debatte um den katholischen Antisemitismus.
Insbesondere von Olaf Blaschke und Aram Mattioli wurde die Dop-
pelgründigkeit des katholischen Antisemitismus hervorgehoben, der
einerseits dem alten christlichen Antijudaismus verpflichtet war, sich auf
der anderen Seite aber auch solcher Stereotypen bediente, die keine
religiösen Wurzeln aufwiesen. Wie Blaschke feststellte, existierte für

---

[51] Brandewie, *When Giants walked the Earth*, S. 236.
[52] Schmidt, *Die Stellung der Religion zu Rasse und Volk*, S. 16.

die Katholiken ein „doppelter Antisemitismus", der „zwischen einem guten, katholischen, gerechten Antisemitismus und einem schlechten, unchristlichen, blindwütigen Judenhass" unterschied.[53]

Ein solches Konglomerat von Stereotypen, aus dem sich die Judenfeindschaft zusammensetzt, lässt sich auch bei P.W. Schmidt erkennen. Daher kann man die religiösen Motive nicht aus der Betrachtung ausblenden.[54] Vorurteile gegen Juden, die sich vor allem gegen die ihnen im Modernisierungsprozess zugeschriebene Rolle (jüdische Pressemagnaten, Industrielle oder Arbeiterführer) richten, werden mit antijüdischen Ausfällen (entwurzeltes und verworfenes Volk der Gottesmörder) kombiniert, die auf einer religiösen Grundlage fußen.

Die strikte Trennung von Antijudaismus und Antisemitismus aufzuheben, wie es Blaschke fordert, findet ihre richtige Begründung in der Tatsache, dass beide Spielarten der Judenfeindschaft – insbesondere im 19. Jahrhundert – gleichen Einflussfaktoren ausgesetzt waren und eine „Modernisierung und Transformation erlebten".[55] Die Gefahr eines solchen Ansatzes besteht darin, dass die Analyse der Beweggründe und der jeweiligen Dynamik zu kurz kommt. War das Judesein nach christlichem Verständnis eine geistige Eigenschaft, die durch die Taufe aufgehoben werden konnte, war sie in der rassischen Lesart ein körperliches Merkmal, das sich nicht mehr verändern ließ.[56]

Die Verwobenheit beider Begründungsebenen lässt sich auch in Schmidts Werken erkennen. Ganz offensichtlich ist dies in seinen zeitkritischen Artikeln, aber auch in seiner religiösen Apologetik und in seinen wissenschaftlichen Arbeiten, obwohl er hier sehr vorsichtig und eher indirekt dem Judentum seinen Platz in der Weltgeschichte

---

[53] Olaf Blaschke und Aram Mattioli, Hg., *Katholischer Antisemitismus im 19. Jahrhundert. Ursachen und Traditionen im internationalen Vergleich* (Zürich: Orell Füssli, 2000), S. 9.

[54] Brandewie (*When Giants walked the Earth*, S. 242) nennt Schmidt einen politischen Antisemiten. Der religiöse Gehalt seines Antisemitismus wird dadurch aber nicht analysiert.

[55] Blaschke und Mattioli, Hg., *Katholischer Antisemitismus*, S. 6. Freilich wird nirgends deutlich gemacht, wo sich am religiösen Fundament der Judenfeindschaft etwas geändert hätte.

[56] Blaschke und Mattioli tun sich in dem genannten Werk schwer, in ihrer Analyse die spezifisch christlichen Anteile des Antisemitismus und seine Verankerung in der Bibel zu benennen. Ähnlich auch Olaf Blaschke, „Antijudaismus und Antisemitismus im deutschen Katholizismus", in Richard Faber, Hg., *Katholizismus in Geschichte und Gegenwart* (Würzburg: Königshausen & Neumann, 2005), S. 143–156. Auch bei Daniel Jonah Goldhagen, *Die katholische Kirche und der Holocaust. Eine Untersuchung über Schuld und Sühne* (Berlin: Siedler, 2002), S. 37f. verwischt die von ihm eingeführte Kategorie des „eliminatorischen Antisemitismus" die Unterschiede.

streitig macht, weil die Juden in seiner Theorie der Uroffenbarung ihre Position als ursprüngliche Träger des wahren Gottesglaubens verlieren. Zum Schluss bleibt darauf hinzuweisen, dass Schmidt und sein Werk auch in aktuellen Zusammenhängen noch immer relevant ist. So hat Katharina Lange in ihrer Untersuchung über Indigenisierungsansätze in den arabischen Sozialwissenschaften darauf verwiesen, dass Schmidt hier von islamistischen Intellektuellen als Kronzeuge des Monotheismus angeführt wird. Insbesondere der Exponent des islamischen Ansatzes in der arabischsprachigen Ethnologie, der emeritierte Hochschullehrer Zaki Muhammad Ismail (geb.1928), führt Schmidt als Gegenspieler des Durkheimschen Religionsverständnisses an. Das koranische Monotheismusverständnis bildet hier den Anknüpfungspunkt, sich auf P. Wilhelm Schmidt zu berufen.[57]

---

[57] Katharina Lange, „Zurückholen, was uns gehört". Indigenisierungstendenzen in der arabischen Ethnologie. Bielefeld: Transcript, 2005), S. 127 und S. 217.

Bibliographie

Blaschke, Olaf. *Katholizismus und Antisemitismus im Deutschen Kaiserreich.* Göttingen: Vandenhoeck & Ruprecht, 1997.

——. „Antijudaismus und Antisemitismus im deutschen Katholizismus". In Richard Faber, Hg., *Katholizismus in Geschichte und Gegenwart.* Würzburg: Königshausen & Neumann, 2005, S. 143–156.

Blaschke, Olaf und Aram Mattioli, Hg. *Katholischer Antisemitismus im 19. Jahrhundert. Ursachen und Traditionen im internationalen Vergleich.* Zürich: Orell Füssli, 2000.

Bornemann, Fritz. *P. Wilhelm Schmidt S. V.D. 1868–1954* (Analecta SVD 59). Rom: Apud Collegium Verbi Divini, 1982.

Brandewie, Ernest. *When Giants walked the Earth. The Life and Times of Wilhelm Schmidt, S.V.D.* (SIA 44). Fribourg: University Press, 1990.

Civardi, Msgr. Luigi. *Das Handbuch der katholischen Aktion.* Innsbruck/Wien: Tyrolia, 1938.

Conte, Edouard. „Wilhelm Schmidt: Des letzten Kaisers Beichtvater und das ‚neudeutsche Heidentum' ". In Helge Gerndt, Hg., *Volkskunde und Nationalsozialismus.* München: Münchener Vereinigung für Volkskunde, 1987, S. 261–278.

——. *Völkerkunde und Faschismus,* Manuskript (o.O., o.J.). Bibliothek des Ludwig-Uhland Instituts, Eberhard-Karls-Universität Tübingen.

Ebneth, Rudolf. *Die Österreichische Wochenschrift ‚Der Christliche Ständestaat'.* Mainz: Matthias-Grünewald, 1976.

Geisenhainer, Katja. *Rasse ist Schicksal. Otto Reche (1879–1966) – ein Leben als Anthropologe und Völkerkundler.* Leipzig: Evangelische Verlagsanstalt, 2002.

Goldhagen, Daniel Jonah. *Die katholische Kirche und der Holocaust. Eine Untersuchung über Schuld und Sühne.* Berlin: Siedler, 2002.

Heer, Friedrich. *Gottes Erste Liebe.* München-Esslingen: Bechtle, 1967.

Henninger, Joseph. „P.W. Schmidt S.V.D. 1868–1954. Eine biographische Skizze." *Anthropos* 51 (1956), S. 19–60.

Lange, Katharina. *‚Zurückholen, was uns gehört'. Indigenisierungstendenzen in der arabischen Ethnologie.* Bielefeld: Transcript, 2005.

Liebmann, Maximilian. *Theodor Innitzer und der Anschluß. Österreichs Kirche 1938.* Graz/Wien/Köln: Styra, 1988.

Maimon, Arye, u.a. Hg. *Germanica Judaica* 3. Tübingen: Mohr, 1987.

Mühlmann, Wilhelm Emil. „Politisch-katholische Rassenforschung?". *Rasse und Volk* 1 (1937), S. 35–38.

Pajak, Sylvester. *Urreligion und Uroffenbarung bei P.W. Schmidt.* St. Augustin: Steyler, 1978.

Petermann, Werner. *Die Geschichte der Ethnologie.* Wuppertal: Peter Hammer, 2004.

Rivinius, Karl Josef. „Schmidt, Wilhelm SVD", in *Biographisch-Bibliographisches Kirchenlexikon* 17 (2000), Sp. 1231–1246 (bzw. www.bautz.de/bbkl, s.v. Schmidt, Wilhelm).

Schmidt, P. Wilhelm. *Der Ursprung der Gottesidee: eine historisch-kritische und positive Studie,* 12 Bde. Münster: Aschendorffsche Verlagsbuchhandlung, 1912–1955.

——. *Der Deutschen Seele Not und Heil. Eine Zeitbetrachtung.* Paderborn, Schöningh, 1920.

——. „Die Pygmäenvölker als älteste derzeit uns erreichbare Menschheitsschicht". *Hochland* 1 (1925/26), S. 574–592.

——. *Rasse und Volk. Eine Untersuchung zur Bestimmung ihrer Grenzen und zur Erfassung ihrer Beziehungen.* München: Kösel & Pustet, 1927.

——. *Ursprung und Werden der Religion. Theorien und Tatsachen.* Münster: Aschendorffsche Verlagsbuchhandlung, 1930.

——. „Der Eigentumsgedanke hinter der Enzyklika ‚Rerum novarum' ". *Schönere Zukunft* 36 (1931), S. 851–852.

——. „Zur Aussprache über den Nationalsozialismus". *Schönere Zukunft* 37 (1932) S. 861–862.

——. „Das Rassenprinzip des Nationalsozialismus". *Schönere Zukunft* 43 (1932), S. 999–1000.

——. *Die Stellung der Religion zu Rasse und Volk.* Augsburg: Haas & Grabherr, 1932.

——. *Der Ödipus-Komplex der Freudschen Psychoanalyse und die Ehegestaltung des Bolschewismus.* Berlin-Wien: Erneuerungs-Verlag, 1933.

——. „Zur Judenfrage". *Schönere Zukunft* 17 (1934), S. 408–409.

——. *Rasse und Volk. Ihre allgemeine Bedeutung. Ihre Geltung im deutschen Raum.* Salzburg/Leipzig: Pustet, 1935.

——. *Rassen und Völker*, Bd. 1. Luzern: Stocker, 1946.

——. *Ein Jesus-Leben*, 2 Bde., 2. Aufl. Wien: Mayer, 1948 (1. Aufl. unter dem Pseudonym Arnoldus Fabricius, Paderborn: Schöningh, 1944).

——. *Die Völker in der Heilsgeschichte der Menschheit.* Kaldenkirchen: Steyler Verlagsbuchhandlung, 1953.

——. *Das Mutterrecht.* Wien-Mödling: Missionsdruckerei St. Gabriel, 1955.

Spöttel, Michael. *Hamiten: Völkerkunde und Antisemitismus.* Frankfurt u.a.: Lang, 1996.

Waldenfels, Hans. „Wilhelm Schmidt (1868–1954)". In Axel Michaels, Hg., *Klassiker der Religionswissenschaft.* München: Beck, 1997, S. 185–197.

Weinzierl-Fischer, Erika. „Österreichs Katholiken und der Nationalsozialismus". *Wort und Wahrheit* 18 (1963), S. 417–439 und S. 493–525.

PART FOUR

THE PROTESTANT PARADIGM

RELIGIONSWISSENSCHAFT ZWISCHEN RATIONALISMUS UND IRRATIONALISMUS

EIN NORWEGISCHES BEISPIEL: DER FALL KRISTIAN SCHJELDERUPS

Sigurd Hjelde

1. *Zur Einleitung: Die norwegische Religionswissenschaft
zwischen den Weltkriegen*

Zwischen den beiden Weltkriegen war die norwegische Religionswissenschaft streng genommen auf einen einzigen Professor, Wilhelm
Schencke (1869–1946),[1] und – in den 1930er Jahren – dessen einzigen
Stipendiaten, Albert Brock-Utne (1906 bis ca. 1990),[2] beschränkt.
Schenckes wissenschaftliche Interessen galten dem Nahen Osten,
zunächst der altägyptischen Religion und dem frühen Judentum,
später vorwiegend dem Islam; Brock-Utnes Hauptinteresse waren die
primitiven Religionen. Sowohl Schencke als auch Brock-Utne hatten
ihr Studium mit dem theologischen Staatsexamen abgeschlossen, beide
standen sie aber dennoch aller akademischen Theologie recht kritisch
gegenüber; ein paarmal war Schencke sogar in der Öffentlichkeit mit
der Forderung hervorgetreten, dass man die theologische Fakultät – „ein
entzündeter Blinddarm" – aus der Universität herausnehmen müsse.[3]

Als Religionswissenschaftler in einem weiteren Sinne lassen sich
aber im selben Zeitraum auch einige Theologen einordnen, deren
Interessen – zumindest in der ersten Phase ihrer akademischen Lauf-
bahn – zu einem großen Teil in religionswissenschaftlicher Richtung
gingen. Drei prominente Namen sollen hier genannt werden: Eivind
Berggrav (1884–1959), Sigmund Mowinckel (1884–1965) und Kristian Schjelderup (1894–1980). Berggrav wurde auf dem Feld der

---

[1] Stipendiat 1901–1914, Professor 1914–1939.
[2] Stipendiat 1934–1940; während des 2. Weltkriegs musste Brock-Utne Norwegen
verlassen, danach blieb er in den USA.
[3] So in der Tageszeitung *Tidens Tegn* vom 28.1.1913; vgl. auch Schenckes Aufsatz
„Hører et teologisk fakultet hjemme ved et universitet?", *Samtiden* (1917), S. 293–313.

Religionspsychologie,[4] Schjelderup auf dem der Religionsphilosophie promoviert,[5] während sich der Alttestamentler Mowinckel, der als Stipendiat auch noch Assyriologie studiert hatte,[6] gelegentlich mit Fragen der altmesopotamischen Religionsgeschichte beschäftigte. Allen drei fiel es aus persönlichen Gründen lange schwer, wenn nicht unmöglich, in das Pfarramt einzutreten; mit der Zeit fanden sie jedoch alle zu ihrer ursprünglichen Zugehörigkeit innerhalb der norwegischen Staatskirche zurück. Berggrav und Schjelderup wurden beide markante Bischöfe, aber auch Mowinckel, der zeitlebens Professor der alttestamentlichen Theologie blieb, ließ sich schließlich 1940 ordinieren, um Gottesdienste halten zu können.

Wie fast alle anderen Theologiestudenten ihrer Zeit lernten Schencke, Berggrav, Mowinckel und Schjelderup vor allem deutsche theologische Traditionen kennen, und deutsche Universitäten waren auch das erste Ziel ihrer Studienreisen. Sie waren also mit deutscher Sprache, Wissenschaft und Kultur wohl vertraut und wurden allmählich auch mit deutschen Freunden und Kollegen persönlich verbunden. Vor diesem Hintergrund wäre es an sich verständlich, wenn sie im ersten Weltkrieg zu denjenigen Mitbürgern zählten, die im neutralen Norwegen mit Deutschland sympathisierten; zumindest zwei von ihnen – Mowinckel und Schjelderup – haben das auch offen und eindeutig getan.[7] Ganz anders war die Situation im zweiten Weltkrieg; da hat

---

[4] Eivind Berggrav, *Religionens terskel. Et bidrag til granskningen av religionens sjelelige frembrudd* (Kristiania: Aschehoug, 1924), deutsch *Der Durchbruch der Religion im menschlichen Seelenleben* (Göttingen: Vandenhoeck & Ruprecht, 1929).

[5] Kristian Schjelderup, *Religionens sandhet i lys av den relativitetsteoretiske virkelighetserkjennelse* [Die Wahrheit der Religion im Lichte der relativitätstheoretischen Erkenntnis der Wirklichkeit] (Kristiania: Aschehoug, 1921); die Disputation fand allerdings erst 1923 statt.

[6] Bei Peter Jensen in Marburg (1911–1913); wichtiger noch waren für die wissenschaftliche Entwicklung Mowinckels die Einflüsse von Hermann Gunkel und Vilhelm Grønbech, die er in seinen bahnbrechenden *Psalmenstudien* I–VI (1921–1924) und überhaupt durch seine „kultgeschichtliche Methode" weiter entwickelte.

[7] In einem Brief an Hermann Gunkel vom 14.12.1914 gibt Mowinckel zwar zu, dass die Mehrheit seiner Landesleute „aus alter Gewohnheit englischfreundlich" sei, kann aber seinem verehrten Lehrer (aus dem Sommersemester 1912 in Gießen) dennoch versichern, dass es genug Norweger gebe, die sich „sowohl aus Herzen als auch aus politischer Überzeugung" auf die Seite Deutschlands stellten: „Besonders unter den Akademikern; fast die ganze Universität, und ich glaube, ein recht großer Teil der Hauptstadt, ist deutschfreundlich." – Schjelderup unternahm im Frühjahr 1915 eine Studienreise nach Deutschland und vermittelte seine vielen positiven Eindrücke in Zeitungsartikeln weiter.

sich in der norwegischen Religionswissenschaft – der institutionalisierten wie der theologischen – niemand auf die Seite Deutschands gestellt. Als Bischof von Oslo leitete Berggrav den Kampf der norwegischen Christenheit gegen die nationalsozialistische Regierung, und sowohl er als auch Schjelderup wurden über längere Zeit in Hausarrest oder Gefangenschaft gehalten. Weniger dramatisch war in den Kriegsjahren das Schicksal Mowinckels, aber durch illegale Privatgottesdienste nahm er ebenfalls am Widerstand gegen die Okkupationsmacht teil. Brock-Utne hat schon früh das Land verlassen – oder verlassen müssen,[8] und der alte Schencke fristete in seinem Ruhestand ein eher einsames und resigniertes Rentnerdasein.

Der norwegische Widerstand gegen die deutsche Politik im zweiten Weltkrieg hängt natürlich teilweise direkt mit dem deutschen Überfall im April 1940 zusammen; auch vor dem Krieg aber gab es nur wenige Norweger, die wirklich mit dem Nationalsozialismus sympathisierten. In den ersten Jahren nach Hitlers Machtübernahme scheint auf der politisch konservativen Seite die Auffassung relativ verbreitet gewesen zu sein, dass ein starkes Deutschland als Bollwerk gegen den kommunistischen Osten wertvoll sei, und diejenigen, die die moderne Auflösung traditioneller Normen und Werte beklagten, mögen sich aus der nationalen und moralischen Aufrüstung des Dritten Reichs zunächst glaubwürdige Ansätze zu einer positiveren Gesellschaftsentwicklung erhofft haben. Einen besonders fruchtbaren Nährboden hatten aber faschistische Ideen in der Bevölkerung nicht, und je mehr die nationalsozialistischen Machtansprüche und -missbräuche offenbar wurden, desto skeptischer wurde die allgemeine Haltung.

Vor diesem Hintergrund könnte es nahe liegen, einen Bericht über das Verhältnis der norwegischen Religionswissenschaft zu faschistischen und nationalsozialistischen Ideologien ganz einfach mit diesem negativen Ergebnis abzuschließen: dass kaum etwas zu sagen ist – wenn nicht der Fall Schjelderups wäre. Kristian Schjelderup, der in der damaligen norwegischen Öffentlichkeit als liberaler, weltoffener, humanistisch

---

[8] Zwei andere jüngere Religionswissenschaftler theologischer Herkunft hielten sich in den Kriegsjahren ebenfalls im Ausland auf: Herman Ludin Jansen (1905–1981), von 1953 bis 1975 Professor der Religionsgeschichte, flüchtete 1940 über Schweden nach England und dann weiter in die USA; der Mowinckel-Schüler Harris Birkeland (1904–1961), von 1946 bis 1961 Dozent bzw. Professor für Semitische Philologie, zog 1943 nach Schweden (Uppsala).

orientierter Theologe und Religionswissenschaftler allgemein bekannt
war, zeigte in den 1930er Jahren ein solches Interesse für die Deutsche Glaubensbewegung Jakob Wilhelm Hauers, ja eine solche Aufgeschlossenheit ihr gegenüber, dass er auf antifaschistischer Seite als
„ein unfreiwilliger Apostel des Faschismus" verdächtigt wurde.[9] Wem
heute der Name Kristian Schjelderup ein Begriff und sein Lebenswerk
bekannt ist, den muss diese Tatsache überraschen. Aus diesem Fall,
scheint mir, könnte darum für ein Studium der Geschichte der europäischen Religionswissenschaft zwischen den zwei Weltkriegen einiges
zu lernen sein. Als Vorbereitung zu einer näheren Untersuchung dieses
Beispiels wird es aber notwendig sein, die Lebensgeschichte Schjelderups
ganz kurz zu skizzieren.[10]

2. *Kristian Schjelderup: ein Blick auf seine Lebensgeschichte*

Als Kristian Vilhelm Koren Schjelderup, Sohn eines Bischofs mit dem
gleichen Namen, 1912 im Alter von 18 Jahren sein Theologiestudium
begann, hatte er immer noch eine tiefe, gefühlsmäßige Verankerung in
jener gemäßigt konservativen Frömmigkeit, in der er in seinem Elternhaus aufgewachsen war. Während des Studiums trafen ihn aber mit
voller Wucht die vielen Fragen der modernen Religionskritik, und nach
abgeschlossenem Studium vertrat er – sechs Jahre später – eine recht
radikale theologische Position. Auf der Suche nach einer Religion, die
neben den Erkenntnissen der modernen Wissenschaft würde bestehen
können, schien es ihm unmöglich, an den überlieferten Glaubensvor-
stellungen der Kirche festzuhalten.

Trotz seiner kritischen Einstellung zu Theologie und Kirche ist Schjelderup 1921 theologischer Stipendiat geworden, eine Stelle, die er bis
1927 innehatte. Seine Doktorarbeit über die religionsphilosophischen
Konsequenzen von Einsteins Relativitätstheorie, die er schon 1921
lieferte,[11] war zum großen Teil der Ertrag eines Studienaufenthalts in
Marburg im Wintersemester 1920/21. Hier hatte Schjelderup sowohl
bei Rudolf Otto als auch bei Friedrich Heiler studiert, und insbesondere

---

[9] Vgl. Anm. 27 unten.
[10] Vgl. Pål Repstad, *Mannen som ville åpne kirken. Kristian Schjelderups liv* [Der Mann,
der die Kirche öffnen wollte. Das Leben Kristian Schjelderups] (Oslo: Universitetsforlaget, 1989).
[11] Vgl. Anm. 5 oben.

zu Otto trat er in eine freundschaftliche Beziehung.[12] Durch Otto inspiriert, unternahm er 1922 eine längere Studienreise in den Fernen Osten, um den Hinduismus und den Buddhismus aus der Nähe kennen zu lernen;[13] außerdem hatte ihn Otto dazu aufgefordert, Kontakte für seinen „Religiösen Menschheitsbund" zu knüpfen.

Als Stipendiat beschäftigte sich Schjelderup in Vorträgen, Aufsätzen und Büchern weiter mit der Frage, wie sich in der modernen Welt Glaube und Wissen in tragfähiger Weise verbinden ließen. Eine aufsehenerregende Artikelserie im Herbst 1924 über „Die Entstehung des Christentums in religionshistorischem Lichte" verwickelte ihn in einen bitteren Streit mit den verantwortlichen Vertretern der theologischen Fakultät, weil er die liberale Theologie wegen ihrer Halbheit und Zweideutigkeit kritisierte.[14] Seine geistige Offenheit führte ihn dazu, auf den unterschiedlichsten Wegen die Wahrheit zu suchen: in den fernöstlichen Religionen, in der Parapsychologie und in der Anthroposophie. Seit Mitte der 1920er Jahre wandte er sich auch der Religionspsychologie zu. 1926 suchte er in Zürich Oskar Pfister auf, um bei ihm die Theorie und die Praxis der Psychoanalyse zu lernen;[15] er übersetzte Werke von Freud ins Norwegische, und dreimal (1927, 1930, 1935) besuchte er die Stigmatikerin Therese Neumann in Konnersreuth.

Als die Stipendienjahre vorüber waren, hat sich Schjelderup, dieses *enfant terrible* der liberalen Theologie, 1928 letztlich doch um eine Pfarrstelle beworben, sogar um einen denkbar wenig attraktiven Posten an der äußersten Nordlandküste. Er war der einzige Bewerber – und hat

---

[12] In einem Artikel in der Hauptstadtzeitung *Aftenposten* mit dem Titel „En religionernes liga som verdens samvittighed" (datiert Marburg, den 26.1.1921), in dem Schjelderup über „deutsche und englische Pläne eines religiösen Menschheitsbundes" berichtet, rechnet er Otto zu den „Enthusiasten, die die Idee des Guten so stark ergriffen hat, dass sie im Kampf für den Sieg des Guten sich selbst opfern", und stellt ihn weiter als „einen der bedeutendsten Religionsforscher der Gegenwart, einen selten feinen und originellen Denker" vor. Im Nachlass Schjelderups (im Staatsarchiv in Kristiansand) finden sich aus den 1920er Jahren etliche Briefe Ottos, die von einer relativ engen Beziehung zwischen den beiden zeugen.

[13] Über diese Reise berichtete Schjelderup in mehreren Reisebriefen an norwegische Zeitungen, in Vorträgen sowie im Buch *Der mennesker blir guder* [Wo Menschen Götter werden] (Kristiania: Aschehoug, 1923).

[14] Als Buch erschienen diese Artikel unter dem Titel *Hvem Jesus var og hvad kirken har gjort ham til* [Wer Jesus war, und was die Kirche aus ihm gemacht hat] (Kristiania: Aschehoug, 1924).

[15] Eine Frucht seiner psychoanalytischen Orientierung war das größere Werk *Die Askese* (Berlin: de Gruyter, 1928).

die Stelle dennoch nicht bekommen. Ein paar Jahre später fand er aber
eine Anstellung an einem kulturwissenschaftlichen Forschungsinstitut
in Bergen, wo er seine Studien auf dem Feld der Religionspsychologie
zielbewusst weitertreiben konnte.[16] Zusammen mit seinem Bruder, dem
Psychologen Harald Schjelderup (1895–1974), gab er 1932 die Arbeit
*Über drei Haupttypen der religiösen Erlebnisformen und ihre psychologische Grund-
lage* heraus.[17] Allmählich wurde ihm aber klar, dass sein Interesse nicht
so sehr den rein theoretischen Fragestellungen galt als vielmehr den
aktuellen Problemen der Gegenwart. Parallel zum Heranwachsen des
Faschismus richtete sich seine Aufmerksamkeit darum in zunehmendem
Maße auf die Themen der Humanität, der Freiheit und der Toleranz,
und zusammen mit einem guten Freund, Anders Wyller, nahm er die
Initiative zu einer humanistischen Akademie, die 1939 unter dem
Namen „Nansenskolen" (Nansen-Schule) in Lillehammer eröffnet, aber
schon im Jahr danach durch die Nazis geschlossen wurde.[18]

   In den ersten Kriegsjahren fand Schjelderup endlich zur norwegischen Kirche zurück. In Gefangenschaft ist er seinen Mitgefangenen
gegenüber sowohl als Verkündiger als auch als Seelsorger tätig gewesen. Kurz nach Kriegsende wurde er in den Pfarrdienst aufgenommen
und 1947 zum Bischof des ostnorwegischen Bistums Hamar ernannt.
Seiner liberalen Grundeinstellung blieb er aber auch in diesem hohen
Amt treu: 1953 wurde er in einen langjährigen Streit um die ewigen
Höllenstrafen verwickelt, und 1961 war er als einziger Bischof dazu
bereit, die erste Pastorin der norwegischen Kirche zu ordinieren.

3. *Schjelderup und die Deutsche Glaubensbewegung*

Nach diesem biographischen Ausblick kehren wir jetzt zu der Zeit
zwischen den beiden Weltkriegen zurück, zu jener Zeit also, als Schjelderup immer noch unterwegs war, ständig auf der Suche nach einer
Religion für den modernen Menschen. In dieser Situation wurde in
den frühen 1930er Jahren sein Interesse für die nationalreligiöse Neu-
orientierung in Deutschland geweckt. Durch die Zeitschrift *Fritt ord*

---

[16] Es handelte sich dabei um das Chr. Michelsens Institutt for Videnskap og Åndsfrihet.
[17] Harald Schjelderup und Kristian Schjelderup, *Über drei Haupttypen der religiösen
Erlebnisformen und ihre psychologische Grundlage* (Berlin: de Gruyter, 1932).
[18] Nach dem Krieg wurde der Betrieb wieder aufgenommen, und die Schule besteht
heute noch als eine „humanistische Akademie".

(Freies Wort), die er 1931 als Organ für einen 1927 von ihm selbst ins Leben gerufenen „Verein für freisinniges Christentum" gegründet hatte, kam er in Kontakt mit Herbert Grabert, einem Schüler des deutschen Religionswissenschaftlers Jakob Wilhelm Hauer. Grabert hatte die erste Nummer von Schjelderups Zeitschrift gelesen und meinte, in diesem Organ eine Parallele zu der von Hauer herausgegebenen *Kommende Gemeinde* zu sehen.[19] In den folgenden Jahren war Schjelderup mehrmals in Deutschland, um die politische und religiöse Entwicklung im Lande zu studieren, und lernte auf diesen Reisen auch Grabert und Hauer persönlich kennen. Insbesondere Hauer hat offensichtlich einen starken Eindruck auf ihn gemacht; in ihm sei er, so bekannte Schjelderup in einem Zeitungsinterview, einem der „hervorragendsten" Religions-historiker Europas, einer „außerordentlich tiefen, genuin religiösen Persönlichkeit" begegnet.[20]

Die Eindrücke von diesen Studienreisen hat Schjelderup durch sein vielseitiges publizistisches Wirken an die norwegische Öffentlichkeit weitervermittelt.[21] In seiner eigenen Zeitschrift ließ er sowohl Grabert (1931 und 1932) als auch Hauer (1935) zu Wort kommen, und als im Herbst 1935 von verschiedenen Seiten der Versuch gemacht wurde, einen Besuch Hauers in Norwegen (und Schweden) zu organisieren, nahm er aktiv an der Planung teil. Hauer wollte gerne kommen, letztlich scheiterten aber die Pläne daran, dass ihm von den Behörden in Berlin die Ausreiseerlaubnis verweigert wurde.[22] Im gleichen Herbst erschien aber ein Buch, in dem Schjelderup unter dem Titel *På vei mot hedenskapet* (Auf dem Weg zum Heidentum) eine zusammenfassende Darstellung und Analyse der von Hauer geleiteten „Deutschen Glaubensbewegung" bot. Kritisch reagiert Schjelderup hier auf die nationalistischen und militaristischen Töne innerhalb der zeitgenössischen deutschen Politik

---

[19] Vgl. Pål Repstad, *Teologisk profilering i sosial kontekst: Kristian Schjelderups liv, tid og teologi* [Theologische Profilierung in sozialem Kontext: Das Leben Kristian Schjelde-rups, seine Zeit und seine Theologie], Diss. Oslo (Kristiansand: Agder distriktshøgskole 1994), S. 408.

[20] *Aftenposten* vom 17.10.1934; vgl. Terje Emberland, *Religion og rase. Nyhedenskap og nazisme i Norge 1933–1945* [Religion und Rasse. Neuheidentum und Nazismus in Nor-wegen 1933–1945] (Oslo: Humanist forlag, 2003), S. 75.

[21] Vgl. insbesondere K. Schjelderup, *Den tyske religionskamp og nutidens religiøse krise* [Der deutsche Religionskampf und die religiöse Krise der Gegenwart] (Bergen: Chr. Michelsens institutt, 1935, mit einer deutschen Zusammenfassung, S. 27–34) und ders., *På vei mot hedenskapet. Trekk av den tyske religionskamp* [Auf dem Weg zum Heidentum. Züge des deutschen Religionskampfs] (Oslo: Aschehoug, 1935).

[22] Vgl. Emberland, *Religion og rase*, S. 77f.

und Kultur, nicht zuletzt auf alle Tendenzen zu Rassismus, Judenhass und aggressiver Christentumsfeindlichkeit. Vor diesem Hintergrund ist auch seine Einstellung zur Deutschen Glaubensbewegung von einer grundlegenden Zweideutigkeit geprägt. Auf der einen Seite erkennt Schjelderup hier Züge, die von „tiefem religiösem Ernst" zeugten und für die Zukunft Verheißungsvolles versprächen; auf der anderen Seite scheint ihm aber die Form, die das Neuheidentum so weit angenommen habe, in der Hauptsache zeitbedingt zu sein. Sein letztes Wort bleibt darum die folgende Warnung: „Politisch kann die Bewegung dadurch gefährlich werden, dass sie die chauvinistischen Tendenzen im national-sozialistischen Deutschland verstärkt. Und religiös ist sie mit Elementen verbunden, die leicht dazu führen, dass man in altheidnischen Formen erstarrt."[23]

Im Frühjahr 1936, als es innerhalb der Deutschen Glaubensbewegung zum Bruch kam und Hauer die Kontrolle verlor, reiste Schjelderup sofort wieder nach Deutschland, um sich vor Ort über die letzte Ent-wicklung und die aktuelle Situation zu informieren. In einem Zeitungs-artikel über die „Krise im deutschen Heidentum" fasste er nach seiner Heimkehr den neuen Stand der Dinge dahingehend zusammen, dass der politische Flügel nunmehr die Oberhand gewonnen habe und die Deutsche Glaubensbewegung folglich aufgehört habe, eine religiöse Bewegung zu sein.[24] Damit war aber auch Schjelderups Interesse für sie am Ende. Von nun an galt seine volle Sympathie jenen evangeli-schen und katholischen Geistlichen, deren konsequenten Widerstand gegen die nationalsozialistische Gleichschaltungspolitik er schon 1935 respektvoll gelobt hatte. Auf diese religiösen Kräfte setzte er jetzt seine ganze Hoffnung für die Zukunft.[25]

4. *Ein unfreiwilliger Apostel des Faschismus?*

Dass Kristian Schjelderup schon früh ein entschlossener Kritiker des Faschismus und des Nationalsozialismus war, steht außer Zweifel. Dem

---

[23] Schjelderup, *På vei mot hedenskapet*, S. 137 (eigene Übersetzung).

[24] *Tidens Tegn* vom 2.5.1936; vgl. Emberland, *Religion og rase*, S. 79ff.

[25] So in zwei Zeitungsartikeln aus dem Jahre 1937: „Vor einer neuen Phase im deutschen Religionskampf?" (*Tidens Tegn* vom 20.4. und *Bergens Arbeiderblad* vom 23.4), wo es in einer Überschrift heißt: „Die deutschen Pfarrer sind heute die einzige geistige Opposition im Lande."

Verleger seiner Zeitschrift missfiel deren redaktionelles Profil denn auch
so sehr, dass er nur dann gewillt war, die Zusammenarbeit fortzusetzen,
wenn Schjelderup durch ein antikommunistisches Bekenntnis für ein
gewisses Gleichgewicht zur antifaschistischen Programmerklärung sor-
gen würde. Obwohl sich Schjelderup bereit erklärte, dieser Forderung
ein Stück weit entgegenzukommen, kamen Redakteur und Verleger
doch nicht überein, so dass sich Schjelderup im Spätwinter 1934 letzten
Endes nach einem neuen Verlag umsehen musste.[26]

Vor diesem Hintergrund kann man sich schon fragen, wieso ausge-
rechnet Schjelderup, dessen ganzes Leben und Denken den freiheitlichen
Idealen des liberalen Humanismus verpflichtet war, der bedeutendste
Vermittler deutschen Neuheidentums auf norwegischem Boden werden
konnte? Wie ist es zu erklären, dass er der heranwachsenden Deutschen
Glaubensbewegung nicht nur mit kritischem Interesse begegnete, sondern ihr auch so viel Offenheit und Sympathie entgegenbrachte, dass
er von einem zeitgenössischen Kritiker als „ein unfreiwilliger Apostel
des Faschismus in Norwegen" charakterisiert worden ist?[27]

Mit dieser Frage haben sich in den letzten Jahren zwei norwegische
Religionsforscher beschäftigt. Der Religionssoziologe Pål Repstad, der
1989 eine solide Biographie Schjelderups veröffentlichte, die er 1994 in
erweiterter und umgearbeiteter Form als Doktorarbeit vorlegte, weist
als mögliche Erklärung auf Schjelderups persönliche Sympathie für
Hauer hin sowie auf sein Misstrauen allem dogmatischen Christentum gegenüber.[28] Über diese Erklärung hinaus hat Terje Emberland,
Redakteur der Zeitschrift des norwegischen Humanistenverbandes, eine
tieferliegende geistige und religiöse Verwandtschaft zwischen Hauer
und Schjelderup in Betracht gezogen. In einer Abhandlung über
„Neuheidentum und Nationalsozialismus in Norwegen 1933–1945"
vergleicht er beide Männer sowohl unter biographischem als auch
unter religionsphilosophischem Blickwinkel und kommt auf dieser
doppelten Grundlage zu dem Schluss, dass es sich hier um zwei „verwandte Seelen" gehandelt habe, die dieselbe Entwicklung durchliefen:
Beide hätten einen konventionell christlichen Familienhintergrund, an

---

[26] Als Schjelderups „Verein für freisinniges Christentum" 1933 aufgelöst worden war,
wollte Schjelderup die Zeitschrift auf selbständiger Basis weiterführen. In diesen Zusammenhang gehört der Streit um die redaktionelle Programmerklärung, die den Jahrgang
1934 einleiten sollte. Vgl. Repstad, *Teologisk profilering i sosial kontekst*, S. 391ff.

[27] Der Pfarrer Karl Møll 1935 in einem Artikel in *Arbeiderbladet*, vgl. Emberland,
Religion og Rase, S. 104.

[28] Repstad, *Mannen som ville åpne kirken*, S. 261.

dem sie nach der Begegnung mit moderner Wissenschaft und fremden
Religionen nicht länger festzuhalten vermochten; beide hätten sich dann
zunächst auf dem ökumenischen bzw. interreligiösen Felde eingesetzt,
bis ihre Glaubensschwierigkeiten sie schließlich über das Christentum
hinaus führten.[29]

Auch im Hinblick auf ihr religionsphilosophisches Denken deckt
Emberland eine ganze Reihe von Parallelen zwischen Schjelderup und
Hauer auf – hier seien nur einige besonders wichtige angeführt:[30] Sie
standen beide in der von Schleiermacher ausgehenden liberaltheologischen Traditionslinie Ritschls und Ottos; sie betrachteten beide
die individuelle religiöse Erfahrung des Numinosen als das religiöse
Urphänomen und die Mystik demzufolge als die eigentliche Form
wahrer Religiosität; sie gingen beide von einem essentialistischen
Religionsbegriff aus, der ihnen eine kategorische Unterscheidung zwischen dem universalen Wesens- und Wahrheitskern der Religion und
den kulturspezifischen Erscheinungsformen der einzelnen Religionen
ermöglichte; ein elitistischer Zug sei ebenfalls beiden gemeinsam, indem
sie nicht nur die entscheidende Rolle der religiösen Meister hervor-
hoben, sondern auch darauf bestanden, dass nur derjenige wirklich
Religionswissenschaft betreiben könne, der aus eigener Erfahrung wisse,
was Religion sei. Der einzige Punkt von Gewicht, wo Schjelderup dem
verehrten Deutschen nicht restlos folgen konnte, sei die Frage nach dem
Verhältnis von Rasse und Religion. Wenn nämlich auch Schjelderup die
Bedeutung rassemäßiger Faktoren für die religiöse Entwicklung nicht
gänzlich abweisen wollte, sei ihm Hauers Behandlung dieser Frage doch
zu einseitig, schematisch und vereinfacht erschienen.[31]

5. Rationalismus oder Irrationalismus?

Im Rahmen dieses Referats muss ich mich darauf beschränken, die
wichtigsten Gesichtspunkte Emberlands kurz wiederzugeben, ohne sie
im Einzelnen prüfen zu können; in der Hauptsache scheinen sie mir
denn auch durchaus treffend und plausibel. Größere Schwierigkeiten
habe ich mit den beiden mit einander verbundenen Fragen, in die

---

[29] Emberland, *Religion og rase*, S. 72f.
[30] Ebd., S. 84ff.
[31] Ebd., S. 102.

Emberland seine Schjelderup-Analyse einmünden lässt. Zunächst: inwiefern war die nationalsozialistische Ideologie, der die Deutsche Glaubensbewegung huldigte, eine Folge ihrer Religionsauffassung? Und zweitens – grundsätzlicher betrachtet: besteht ein Zusammenhang zwischen einer irrationalistischen Religionsauffassung und totalitärem Denken?[32]

Was die erste Frage betrifft, gibt Emberland Schjelderup gegen seine Kritiker Recht: es bestehe kein *notwendiger* Zusammenhang zwischen jener Religionsauffassung, die Hauer und Schjelderup gemeinsam teilten, und einer totalitären Ideologie.[33] Auf dem relativistischen Standpunkt, wo die Wahrheit der Religion an die persönliche und subjektive Erfahrung geknüpft wird, verliere die Religion „ihre Möglichkeit, moralische Grenzen zu ziehen", und könne sich folglich „mit jedweder politischen Bewegung" verbünden. Auf Grund dieser Erkenntnis fragt aber Emberland – im Anschluss an Karl Poppers Überlegungen in *The Open Society and its Enemies*[34] – weiter, ob das Verhältnis von Irrationalismus und totalitärem Denken nicht doch zumindest durch eine *Affinität* geprägt sei?[35]

Hier ist der Punkt, wo ich Emberland nicht weiter zu folgen vermag. Seine Interpretation von Poppers Analyse und sein Gebrauch von dessen Argumentation scheinen mir an sich einwandfrei zu sein, nur stellt sich die Frage: was hat denn das alles mit *Schjelderup* zu tun? Ein erstes Anzeichen dafür, dass hier irgend etwas nicht stimmt, ist die grundlegende Unklarheit, die Emberlands Problemformulierung anhaftet: Dort, wo er sie das erste Mal präsentiert, ist von einer „irrationalistischen *Religionsauffassung*"[36] die Rede; ehe er aber diese Frage aufgreift, um sie gründlicher zu erörtern, hat unmerklich ein nicht unwesentlicher Perspektivenwechsel stattgefunden. Im Vordergrund seines Interesses steht jetzt der Irrationalismus *ganz allgemein*, dessen „Hauptproblem" seine erkenntnistheoretische Position sei:

> Weil die tiefste Wahrheit über den Menschen nicht von der Vernunft ergriffen werden kann, verwirft man den rationalen Dialog und die

---

[32] Ebd., S. 105.
[33] Ebd., S. 106.
[34] Vgl. Karl R. Popper, *The Open Society and its Enemies* (London: George Routledge, 1949/50, Nachdruck 1956); Emberland bezieht sich hier insbesondere auf das Kapitel 24: „Oracular Philosophy and the Revolt Against Reason" (ebd., S. 410–442).
[35] Emberland, *Religion og rase*, S. 107.
[36] Ebd., S. 105 (vgl. Anm. 32 oben); meine Unterstreichung.

kritische Überprüfung als äußerste Appellinstanz für den Wahrheitsgehalt von Behauptungen. (…) Man steht so vor der Notwendigkeit, Wahrheitspostulate ohne Debatte und kritische Prüfung zu akzeptieren, was dazu führt, dass der Irrationalismus zu unkritischem Autoritätsglauben tendiert.[37]

Als ein weiteres Kennzeichen des Irrationalismus führt Emberland – immer noch im Anschluss an Popper – dessen Tendenz zu einer dualistischen Auffassung der Menschheit und zum Elitismus an. Eine Folge davon sei, dass der Fokus nicht auf die Qualität der Meinungen als solcher ausgerichtet werde, sondern auf die Person, die sie äußert:

> Das führt leicht zu einer Einteilung von Menschen in solche, die an der tieferen und unaussprechlichen Wahrheit Anteil haben, und solche, die es nicht haben. Die Wahrheit ist also einer auserwählten Gruppe von Menschen vorbehalten, die von geistig hellsichtigen Propheten angeführt werden.[38]

Bei Hauer, meint Emberland nun, sei „das autoritäre Potential des Irrationalismus in voller Blüte" aufgegangen, bei Schjelderup dagegen sei es nur als „eine untergründige Tendenz" da, die durch seinen ethischen „Gesinnungshumanismus" in Schach gehalten werde. Was mir hier an der Analyse Emberlands problematisch vorkommt, sind weder sein Begriff des Irrationalismus noch seine Charakterisierung Hauers, nur sein Umgang mit Schjelderup. An diesem Punkt nämlich scheint mir seine konsequente Parallelisierung dieser beiden Religionsforscher nicht länger haltbar zu sein. Gewiss hat Schjelderup – wie beispielsweise Otto und Hauer – das numinose Urphänomen im irrationalen Bereich der Seele lokalisiert, wo es der kritischen Vernunft letztlich unzugänglich bleibt, und gewiss hat er – wiederum in Übereinstimmung mit den beiden Deutschen – vom Religionsforscher gefordert, dass dieser aus eigener Erfahrung das religiöse Grunderlebnis kenne.[39] Lassen aber religionstheoretische bzw. methodische Ansätze wie diese gleich den Schluss zu, dass Schjelderup selbst damit ohne weiteres auch als „Irrationalist" zu gelten habe?

Nun sind Rationalismus und Irrationalismus in der Tat ebenso komplexe wie flexible Begriffe, die in verschiedenen Sinnzusammenhängen recht unterschiedliche Bedeutungen annehmen können, und deren

---

[37] Ebd., S. 107.
[38] Ebd., S. 107f.
[39] Vgl. K. Schjelderup, *Religion og religioner* (Oslo: Gyldendal Norsk Forlag, 1926).

Gebrauch darum mit erheblichen Unsicherheitsfaktoren verbunden ist. Auf den Versuch einer sauberen Begriffsklärung kann ich mich hier nicht einlassen; wenn aber bei Schjelderup von einer „untergründigen Tendenz" die Rede sein sollte, fragt sich in der Tat, ob diese nicht eher der „rationalistischen" als der „irrationalistischen" Position zuzurechnen wäre? Zumindest scheint er den beiden zentralen Kriterien Poppers – und Emberlands – ziemlich genau zu entsprechen: zum einen der Bereitschaft dazu, „sich kritische Argumente anzuhören und aus der Erfahrung zu lernen" und zum anderen dem festen Glauben an die Einheit der Menschheit.[40] Wenn man bedenkt, wie Schjelderup eben den offenen Dialog – mit den fremden Religionen ebenso wie mit der modernen Welt – als den angemessenen Weg zu wahrer Erkenntnis betrachtet und praktiziert hat, wird man, wenn ich recht sehe, seinen Humanismus mit größerem Recht auf den Nenner des Rationalismus als auf den des Irrationalismus bringen müssen.

6. *Religionswissenschaft zwischen Rationalismus und Irrationalismus*

Den Fall Schjelderups habe ich nicht in erster Linie deswegen thematisiert, um norwegische Fachgeschichte zu betreiben oder eine innernorwegische Diskussion zu führen. Zum Schluss bleibt uns darum noch die Frage, ob aus diesem Beispiel etwas zu lernen sei, was in einer breiteren wissenschaftshistorischen Perspektive von Interesse und Bedeutung sein könnte? Zu diesem Zweck möchte ich zwei Fragen formulieren, die ich freilich nicht selber zu beantworten vermag, die mir aber zumindest überlegenswert vorkommen. Die eine, die in diesem Abschnitt im Zentrum der Aufmerksamkeit steht, betrifft die europäische Religionswissenschaft der Zwischenkriegszeit; die andere, in der es um die Identität der Religionswissenschaft überhaupt als einer akademischen Disziplin geht, möchte ich abschließend nur ganz kurz andeuten.

---

[40] Vgl. Popper, *The Open Society and its Enemies*, wo Rationalismus „in terms of practical attitudes or behavior" erklärt und wie folgt definiert wird:. „an attitude of readiness to listen to critical arguments and to learn from experience" (ebd., S. 410f); ähnlich hebt Popper den Glauben an die Einheit der Menschheit („unity of mankind") als ein Merkmal des Rationalismus hervor, wie er überhaupt bei dem Verhältnis von „(critical) rationalism" und „irrationalism" nicht nur eine erkenntnistheoretische, sondern auch – ja, in erster Linie – eine *ethische* Alternative im Blick hat: „The choice before us is not simply an intellectual affair, or a matter of taste. It is a moral decision" (ebd., S. 417).

Wo heute von der europäischen Religionswissenschaft der Zwischenkriegszeit die Rede ist, scheint es üblich zu sein, den „Irrationalismus"
bzw. die „Irrationalität" derselben hervorzuheben und sie damit unter
ein disqualifizierendes Urteil zu stellen. Nicht zuletzt trifft ein solches
Verdikt die führenden Vertreter der religionsphänomenologischen
Richtung, wie etwa Nathan Söderblom, Rudolf Otto, Friedrich Heiler, Joachim Wach und Gerardus van der Leeuw. Bei Rainer Flasche,
einem profunden Kenner dieser Wissenschaftsepoche, taucht dieser
Gesichtspunkt öfters auf,[41] und in einem Standardwerk wie dem *Handbuch religionswissenschaftlicher Grundbegriffe* dominiert ebenfalls die religionswissenschaftliche Aktualisierung des Irrationalismusbegriffs.[42] Die
Argumente, die für eine derartige Sichtweise sprechen, liegen auf der
Hand: sowohl in der Religionstheorie als auch in der religionswissenschaftlichen Methodologie erhält die subjektive Erfahrung des Forschers
hier die Funktion eines leitenden Prinzips, wodurch der Charakter des
Studiums als eines rationalen, allgemeingültigen Diskurses aufs Spiel
gesetzt wird. Mir kann es darum nicht daran gelegen sein, die Kritik
an diesen Religionsmodellen und Erkenntnisprinzipien grundsätzlich
in Frage zu stellen, wohl aber frage ich mich, ob es nicht recht und
billig wäre, allzu vereinfachende Pauschalurteile über jene „irrationalistischen" Religionswissenchaftler durch nuanciertere Charakteristiken
zu ersetzen?[43]

Abgesehen davon, dass die Religionswissenschaft der 1920er und
1930er Jahre – und zwar die „irrationalistische" wie die „rationalistische" – in der Praxis natürlich eine ganze Menge guter Arbeit geleistet

---

[41] Siehe etwa Rainer Flasche, „Religionsmodelle und Erkenntnisprinzipien der
Religionswissenschaft in der Weimarer Zeit", in Hubert Cancik, Hg., *Religions- und
Geistesgeschichte der Weimarer Republik* (Düsseldorf: Patmos Verlag, 1982), S. 261–276 sowie
ders., „Der Irrationalismus in der Religionswissenschaft und dessen Begründung in der
Zeit zwischen den zwei Weltkriegen", in Hans G. Kippenberg und Brigitte Luchesi,
Hg., *Religionswissenschaft und Kulturkritik* (Marburg: diagonal-Verlag, 1991), S. 223–257
und im Anschluss an Flasche Fritz Heinrich, *Die deutsche Religionswissenschaft und der
Nationalsozialismus. Eine ideologiekritische und wissenschaftsgeschichtliche Untersuchung* (Petersberg:
Michael Imhof Verlag, 2002), S. 71–75.

[42] Vgl. Hanna Gekle, „Irrationalismus/das Irrationale", in Hubert Cancik u.a., Hg.,
Handbuch religionswissenschaftlicher Grundbegriffe, Band 3 (Stuttgart: Kohlhammer, 1993),
S. 302–317, insbesondere S. 314–317.

[43] Was Otto betrifft, weisen sowohl Jack Stewart Boozer in der „Einleitung" der von
ihm herausgegebenen *Aufsätze zur Ethik* Rudolf Ottos (München: Verlag C.H. Beck,
1981), S. 18 als auch Todd A. Gooch, *The Numinous and Modernity. An Interpretation of
Rudolf Otto's Philosophy of Religion* (Berlin-New York: Walter de Gruyter, 2000), S. 134 und
S. 178ff. den Vorwurf des Irrationalismus als vereinfacht und irreführend zurück.

hat, die durchaus den Ansprüchen einer strengen kritischen Methode genügt,[44] ist meine Frage auf dem Hintergrund von dem Fall Schjelderups, ob es nicht auch in diesem weiteren Zusammenhang sinnvoll wäre, etwas deutlicher zwischen einer irrationalistischen *Religionsauffassung* und einer irrationalistischen *Grundhaltung* zu unterscheiden? Zweifellos waren in der Religionswissenschaft der Zwischenkriegszeit − und zwar insbesondere in der theologischen − irrationalistische Ansätze theoretischer und methodischer Art weit verbreitet, Ansätze, die sich historisch zu romantischen Einflüssen in Beziehung setzen lassen. In dem Maße aber, wie diese Einflüsse durch die protestantische liberale Theologie vermittelt wurden, machen sich hier ebenfalls Motive geltend, die eher mit einer rationalistischen, aufklärerischen Grundhaltung verwandt sind. Denn so viel wenigstens stand in der liberaltheologischen Religionsphilosophie fest, dass Religion nur dann „ursprünglich", „wahr" und „echt" sei, wenn sie der Gläubige persönlich und selbständig verantworten könne. Echte, wahre, ursprüngliche Religiosität war darum auf dem Standpunkt der liberalen Theologie eben der diametrale Gegensatz zu allerlei Formen des Dogmatismus und des Autoritätsglaubens. Das heißt aber wiederum, dass die von der liberalen Theologie herkommende Religionswissenschaft der 1920er und 1930er Jahre in Wirklichkeit keine besondere „Affinität" zu einer irrationalistischen Grundhaltung kennzeichnet; trotz der irrationalistischen Züge ihrer Religionstheorie und Methodologie war sie zugleich einem ethischen Rationalismus im Sinne Poppers verpflichtet, und es dürfte von daher fraglich sein, ob sie schon durch ihre religionswissenschaftliche Irrationalität „in gefährliche Nähe" zu faschistischen oder nationalsozialistischen Ideen gebracht worden wäre.[45]

Eine Art „Seelenverwandschaft" mag Kristian Schjelderup sowohl

---

[44] Das bestätigt auch Flasche im Hinblick auf die deutsche Religionswissenschaft der Jahre 1933–1945. Siehe ders., „Gab es Versuche der Ideologisierung der Religionswissenschaft während des Dritten Reiches", in Holger Preißler und Hubert Seiwert, Hg., *Gnosisforschung und Religionsgeschichte. Festschrift für Kurt Rudolph zum 65. Geburtstag* (Marburg: diagonal-Verlag, 1994), S. 420.

[45] So in Flasche, „Religionsmodelle und Erkenntnisprinzipien", S. 276: „(...) gerät die Religionswissenschaft mit ihren Religionsmodellen und Erkenntnisprinzipien in gefährliche Nähe zu anderen irrationalen Denkansätzen und -möglichkeiten", und S. 261: „Diese irrationalen Strömungen [der Weimarer Zeit, S.H.] haben letztlich den Boden bereitet für die geistigen Tonlagen, die sich in der nachfolgenden historischen Periode verheerend durchzusetzen und auszuwirken vermochten", sowie in „Der Irrationalismus in der Religionswissenschaft", S. 257: „Was sich aus solchen an ‚Stimmungen' festgemachten Erkenntnissen erheben kann, hat Europa damals ‚erfahren' (...)".

mit Rudolf Otto als auch mit Jakob Wilhelm Hauer verbunden haben; zugleich sind aber, was die Haltung zum Nationalsozialismus betrifft, schwerwiegende Unterschiede festzustellen – zumindest im Verhältnis zwischen Schjelderup und Hauer,[46] obwohl es Schjelderup selbst offenbar nicht leicht gewesen ist, sich über diesen Abstand zwischen Hauer und ihm klar zu werden.[47] Die Erklärung aber, warum der eine sein Denken und Handeln von nationalistischen und rassistischen Motiven bestimmen ließ, der andere dagegen nicht, kann man kaum in der gemeinsam geteilten Religionsauffassung oder religionswissenschaftlichen Grundposition suchen. Hier müssen andere Faktoren in Betracht gezogen werden. Welches diese Faktoren sind, ist eine Frage, auf die ich hier keine Antwort geben kann, es sei denn die naheliegende Vermutung, dass sich Hauer eben als Deutscher faktisch in einer größeren „Nähe" zum Nationalsozialismus – und insofern in einer größeren „Gefahr" – befand als Schjelderup. Jedoch ist das auf keinen Fall eine Antwort, die die diametral unterschiedlichen Entscheidungen der rationalistischen und der irrationalistischen Grundhaltung erklären kann – oder gar erklären darf.

7. Zum Schluss: Die Frage nach Ort und Identität der Religionswissenschaft

Als Religionswissenschaftler standen Kristian Schjelderup, Rudolf Otto und Jakob Wilhelm Hauer irgendwo im Spannungsfeld von Rationalismus und Irrationalismus. Auf je ihre Weise taten das wohl auch alle anderen Religionswissenschaftler der 1920er und 1930er Jahre. Es stellt sich deshalb zum Schluss die Frage, ob das nicht auch der Ort der

---

[46] Gregory D. Alles, „Rudolf Otto (1869–1937)", in Axel Michaels, Hg., *Klassiker der Religionswissenschaft* (München: Verlag C. H. Beck, 1997), S. 208 zufolge ist das Verhältnis Ottos zur NS-Ideologie „schwierig zu beurteilen"; darum halte ich ihn hier aus dem Vergleich mit Schjelderup heraus.

[47] Ohne Schjelderups Hauer-Begeisterung zu teilen, hat mein Vater, Oddmund Hjelde, in einer kritischen Analyse der nationalsozialistischen Eckhart-Interpretation Hauer immerhin das Attest ausgestellt, dass man bei ihm [d.h. in Hauers Buch *Deutsche Gottschau*, S.H.] „mehr echter Religiosität und größerer wissenschaftlicher Redlichkeit" begegne als etwa bei Alfred Rosenberg: „Hauer besitzt selber etwas vom Geist der Mystik, und mit seinem religionshistorischen Wissen vermeidet er die oberflächlichen Missdeutungen. Aber auch er sieht den Meister im Lichte seiner eigenen neuheidnischen Religion." Oddmund Hjelde, „Mester Eckhart og den nazistiske tolkning av ham" [Meister Eckhart in der Interpretation des Nationalsozialismus], *Norsk Teologisk Tidsskrift* 47 (1946), S. 1–44, hier S. 2. Die Abhandlung wurde 1939/40 als Staatsarbeit im Fach Germanistik geschrieben, konnte aber erst nach dem Krieg gedruckt werden.

Religionswissenschaft überhaupt als einer akademischen Disziplin sein muss? Als Wissenschaft muss sie sich natürlich prinzipiell zur kritischen Rationalität bekennen und in ihrer Arbeit diese Grundsatzerklärung so weit möglich in die Praxis umsetzen; andererseits sind aber weder Religion noch Wissenschaft ohne irrationale Elemente, und folglich kommt auch die Religionswissenschaft letztlich nie aus der Dualität von Rationalität und Irrationalität heraus.

In einer gewissen Parallele zu diesem prinzipiellen Gegensatz von Rationalismus und Irrationalismus scheint die historische Alternative von Aufklärung und Romantik zu stehen, und auch in diesem Spannungsfeld muss die Religionswissenschaft den Ort suchen, der ihr rechtmäßig zukommt. In diesen Prozess ihrer Selbstfindung gehört zweifellos auch die kritische Auseinandersetzung mit essentialistischen Religionstheorien und subjektivistischen Erkenntnisprinzipien, aber ist damit schon gesagt, dass wir klug daran tun, all unser romantisches Traditionsgut gleich in den Mülleimer zu werfen? Stünden wir dann nicht in Gefahr, das Kind mit dem Bad auszuschütten? Wenn nämlich auch das rationalistische Erbe der Aufklärung das grundlegende Element aller modernen Religionswissenschaft ist, ohne das sie ganz einfach undenkbar wäre, sollten wir vielleicht bedenken, dass sie ihre faktische Existenz als eine eigenständige akademische Disziplin in erster Linie eben der Romantik zu verdanken hat. Wäre es ohne deren enthusiastischen Sinn für „Religion" als ein zentrales Grunddatum allen Menschenlebens überhaupt zu einer Institutionalisierung der Religionswissenschaft gekommen? Vielleicht hätten wir dann aus den verschiedensten Ecken des akademischen Hauses – aus den vielen Abteilungen der Philologie und der Geschichte, aus der Soziologie, Psychologie und Kultur- oder Sozialanthropologie – erst zueinander finden müssen?

Bibliographie

Alles, Gregory D. „Rudolf Otto (1869–1937)“. In Axel Michaels, Hg., *Klassiker der Religionswissenschaft*. München: Verlag C.H. Beck, 1997, S. 198–210.

Berggrav, Eivind. *Religionens terskel. Et bidrag til granskningen av religionens sjelelige frembrudd* (Kristiania: Aschehoug, 1924), deutsch *Der Durchbruch der Religion im menschlichen Seelenleben* (Göttingen: Vandenhoeck & Ruprecht, 1929).

Boozer, Jack Stewart. „Einleitung“. In ders., Hg., Rudolf Otto, *Aufsätze zur Ethik*. München: Verlag C.H. Beck, 1981, S. 7–52.

Emberland, Terje og Arnfinn Pedersen. „Religion for en ny tid. Kristian Schjelderup og den alternative åndelighet“. In Bodil Stenseth, Hg., *På tampen av det 20. århundre. Om ideologier, eksperter og amatører*. Oslo: Universitetsforlaget, 1999, S. 63–95.

Emberland, Terje. *Religion og rase. Nyhedenskap og nazisme i Norge 1933–1945* [Religion und Rasse. Neuheidentum und Nazismus in Norwegen 1933–1945]. Oslo: Humanist forlag, 2003.

Flasche, Rainer. „Religionsmodelle und Erkenntnisprinzipien der Religionswissenschaft in der Weimarer Zeit“. In Hubert Cancik, Hg., *Religions- und Geistesgeschichte der Weimarer Republik*. Düsseldorf: Patmos Verlag, 1982, S. 261–276.

———. „Der Irrationalismus in der Religionswissenschaft und dessen Begründung in der Zeit zwischen den zwei Weltkriegen“. In Hans G. Kippenberg und Brigitte Luchesi, Hg., *Religionswissenschaft und Kulturkritik*. Marburg: diagonal-Verlag, 1991, S. 223–257.

———. „Gab es Versuche der Ideologisierung der Religionswissenschaft während des dritten Reiches“. In Holger Preißler und Hubert Seiwert, Hg., *Gnosisforschung und Religionsgeschichte. Festschrift für Kurt Rudolph zum 65. Geburtstag*. Marburg: diagonal-Verlag, 1994, S. 413–420.

Gekle, Hanna. „Irrationalismus/das Irrationale“. In Hubert Cancik u.a., Hg., *Handbuch religionswissenschaftlicher Grundbegriffe*, Band 3. Stuttgart: Kohlhammer, 1993, S. 302–317.

Gooch, Todd A. *The Numinous and Modernity. An Interpretation of Rudolf Otto's Philosophy of Religion* (Beihefte zur Zeitschrift für die alttestamentliche Wissenschaft 293). Berlin-New York: Walter de Gruyter, 2000.

Grabert, Herbert. „Viljen til religiøs fornyelse hos Tysklands ungdom“ [Der Wille zur Erneuerung in der Jugend Deutschlands]. *Fritt ord* [Freies Wort] 1 (1931), S. 264–268.

———. „Frem for forståelse mellem religionene“ [Für Verständigung zwischen den Religionen]. *Fritt ord* 2 (1932), S. 121–130.

Graf, Friedrich Willhelm, Hg. *Liberale Theologie. Eine Ortsbestimmung*. Gütersloh: Gütersloher Verlagshaus, 1993.

Hauer, Wilhelm. „Det tyske hedenskaps forutsetninger“ [Die Voraussetzungen des deutschen Heidentums]. *Fritt ord* 5 (1935), S. 76–86.

Heinrich, Fritz. *Die deutsche Religionswissenschaft und der Nationalsozialismus. Eine ideologiekritische und wissenschaftsgeschichtliche Untersuchung*. Petersberg: Michael Imhof Verlag, 2002.

Hjelde, Oddmund. „Mester Eckhart og den nazistiske tolkning av ham“ [Meister Eckhart in der Interpretation des Nationalsozialismus]. *Norsk Teologisk Tidsskrift* 47 (1946), S. 1–44.

Hjelde, Sigurd. *Die Religionswissenschaft und das Christentum. Eine historische Untersuchung über das Verhältnis von Religionswissenschaft und Theologie* (Studies in the history of religions 61). Leiden u.a.: Brill, 1994.

———. „Sigmund Mowinckels Lehrjahre in Deutschland“. *Zeitschrift für die Alttestamentliche Wissenschaft* (1997), S. 589–611.

———. „The Science of Religion and Theology: The Question of their Interrelationship“. In Arie L. Molendijk und Peter Pels, Hg., *Religion in the Making. The Emergence of the Sciences of Religion*. Leiden u.a.: Brill, 1998, S. 99–128.

——— Hg. *Man, Meaning, and Mystery. 100 Years of History of Religions in Norway. The Heritage of W. Brede Kristensen.* Leiden u.a.: Brill, 2000.

———. „From Kristiansand to Leiden: The Norwegian Career of W. Brede Kristensen". In ebd., S. 207–222.

———. „Das Christentum als Gegenstand der Religionswissenschaft". In Gebhard Löhr, Hg., *Die Identität der Religionswissenschaft. Beiträge zum Verständnis einer unbekannten Disziplin.* Frankfurt a.M.: Peter Lang, 2000, S. 171–189.

———. *Sigmund Mowinckel und seine Zeit. Leben und Werk eines norwegischen Alttestamentlers.* Mohr Siebeck, 2006.

Junginger, Horst. *Von der philologischen zur völkischen Religionswissenschaft. Das Fach Religionswissenschaft an der Universität Tübingen von der Mitte des 19. Jahrhunderts bis zum Ende des Dritten Reiches.* Stuttgart: Franz Steiner Verlag, 1999.

Krech, Volkhard. *Wissenschaft und Religion. Studien zur Geschichte der Religionsforschung in Deutschland 1871–1933.* Tübingen: Mohr Siebeck, 2002.

Nanko, Ulrich. *Die Deutsche Glaubensbewegung. Eine historische und soziologische Untersuchung.* Marburg: diagonal Verlag, 1993.

Popper, Karl R. *The Open Society and its Enemies.* London: George Routledge, 1945/1950 (Nachdruck 1956).

Repstad, Håkon. *En mystikk for det moderne menneske. Kristian Schjelderups mystikk i idéhistorisk kontekst.* Hovedoppgave i idéhistorie [Eine Mystik für den modernen Menschen. Die Mystik Kristian Schjelderups in ideengeschichtlichem Kontext. Staatsarbeit in Europäischer Geistesgeschichte]. Universität Oslo, 2001.

Repstad, Pål. *Mannen som ville åpne kirken. Kristian Schjelderups liv* [Der Mann, der die Kirche öffnen wollte. Das Leben Kristian Schjelderups]. Oslo: Universitetsforlaget, 1989.

———. *Teologisk profilering i sosial kontekst: Kristian Schjelderups liv, tid og teologi* [Theologische Profilierung in sozialem Kontext: Das Leben Kristian Schjelderups, seine Zeit und seine Theologie]. Diss. Oslo. Kristiansand: Agder distriktshøgskole 1994.

Schjelderup, Kristian. *Religionens sandhet i lys av den relativitetsteoretiske virkelighetserkjennelse* [Die Wahrheit der Religion im Lichte der relativitätstheoretischen Erkenntnis der Wirklichkeit]. Kristiania: Aschehoug, 1921.

———. *Der mennesker blir guder* [Wo Menschen Götter werden]. Kristiania: Aschehoug, 1923.

———. *Hvem Jesus var og hvad kirken har gjort ham til* [Wer Jesus war, und was die Kirche aus ihm gemacht hat]. Kristiania: Aschehoug, 1924.

———. *Religion og religioner* [Religion und Religionen]. Oslo: Gyldendal Norsk Forlag, 1926.

———. „Hvad vi vil" [Was wir wollen]. *Fritt ord* 1 (1931), S. 3–6.

———. „Fritt ord". *Fritt ord* 4 (1934), S. 1–3.

———. *Den tyske religionskamp og nutidens religiøse krise* [Der deutsche Religionskampf und die religiöse Krise der Gegenwart]. Bergen: Chr. Michelsens institutt, 1935 (mit einer deutschen Zusammenfassung, ebd., S. 27–34).

———. *På vei mot hedenskapet. Trekk av den tyske religionskamp* [Auf dem Weg zum Heidentum. Züge des deutschen Religionskampfs]. Oslo: Aschehoug, 1935.

———. *Oppgjør med nazismens ideologi* [Auseinandersetzung mit der Ideologie des Nationalsozialismus]. Oslo: Aschehoug, 1945.

———. *Veien jeg måtte gå* [Der Weg, den ich gehen musste]. Oslo: Aschehoug, 1962.

———. *Under åpen himmel* [Unter offenem Himmel]. Oslo: Aschehoug, 1969.

Thomassen, Einar. „Wilhelm Schencke – Norway's First Professor in History of Religions". In Sigurd Hjelde, Hg., *Man, Meaning, and Mystery. 100 Years of History of Religions in Norway.* Leiden u.a.: Brill, 2000, S. 223–236.

HARALDS BIEZAIS (1909–1995)
EIN RELIGIONSHISTORIKER ZWISCHEN THEOLOGIE UND RELIGIONSWISSENSCHAFT

Iveta Leitāne

1. *Einleitung*

Der lettische Theologe und Religionswissenschaftler Haralds Biezais ist als bedeutender Religionshistoriker bekannt. Er verfasste Standardwerke zur lettischen Religion und entwickelte wichtige Fragestellungen zur Systematik der Religionswissenschaft. Außerdem wirkte er als Herausgeber bedeutsamer religionswissenschaftlicher Werke.[1] Während seines ganzen Lebens blieb er ordinierter Pfarrer der evangelischen Kirche. Biezais' frühe Werke, die noch in Lettland geschrieben wurden und in die Zeit des Nationalsozialismus fallen, sind einem breiten akademischen Publikum zumeist unbekannt. Man spricht deshalb öfters von zwei verschiedenen Biezais: dem frühen theologischen und späten religionswissenschaftlichen. Dazu hat nicht zuletzt Biezais selbst beigetragen, da er beide Wissensbereiche sorgfältig trennte. Im Gegensatz zu seinen späteren Kollegen an der Theologischen Fakultät der Universität in Riga – hier wäre unter anderem Eduards Zicāns, Ludvigs Adamovičs, Eduards Rumba und Alberts Freijs zu nennen – führte Biezais in seinen frühen Jahren fast keine religionswissenschaftlichen Studien durch. Der späte Biezais hat sich allem Anschein nach nicht auf sein frühes Werk bezogen. Erst im Zuge der Erforschung der „Neuen Religionen" kam Biezais wieder auf die weltanschaulichen Grundlagen seiner systematischen Arbeit zurück. Was verbindet die

---

[1] Siehe etwa Haralds Biezais, „Transformation und Identifikation der Götter im Synkretismus", *Temenos* 11 (1976), S. 5–25, ders., „Vom Sinn der religionswissenschaftlichen Forschung", *Theologia practica* 13 (1978), S. 159–163, ders., „Typology of Religion and the Phenomenological Method", in Lauri Honko, ed., *Science of religion, studies in methodology. Proceedings of the study conference of the international association for the history of religions, held in Turku, Finland August 27–31, 1973* (The Hague: Mouton, 1979), S. 143–161, ders. Hg., *New Religions. Based on Papers read at the Symposium on New Religions held at Åbo on the 1st–3rd of September 1974* (Stockholm: Almqvist & Wiksell, 1975) heraus. Biezais war einer der ersten, die sich im akademischen Bereich dem Thema „Neue Religionen" zuwandten.

Theologie der Zwischenkriegszeit mit der Religionswissenschaft in den
Jahren danach? Gibt es in Biezais' Religionsforschung Grundannahmen, die von seinem Theologieverständnis vorgeprägt sind? Inwieweit
wurde seine Religionswissenschaft in der Nachkriegszeit durch diese
Grundannahmen beeinflusst? Gibt es eine Diskrepanz zwischen den
theologischen Erwartungen der Zwischenkriegszeit und den Ergebnissen
der religionshistorischen Forschungen von Biezais nach dem Krieg?
Die folgenden Ausführungen versuchen, auf diese Fragen Antworten
zu geben, wobei davon auszugehen ist, dass die Auswirkungen solcher
Ideen, die eine immanente Nähe oder zumindest eine Kompatibilität
mit nationalsozialistischem Gedankengut aufweisen, weit über das Jahr
1945 hinausreichen.

2. *Biographischer Hintergrund*

Haralds (Fritz Theodor) Biezais wurde am 10. Juli 1909 in Lestene in
einer armen evangelischen Bauernfamilie geboren. Die Familie besuchte
nur unregelmäßig den Gottesdienst und stand der ‚deutschen' Kirche
mit ihren ‚deutschen' Pfarrern kritisch gegenüber. Die ältere Generation achtete noch in traditioneller Weise die Autorität des Pfarrers.
Doch am Anfang der 1920er Jahre vollzog sich ein Nationalitäten- und
Gesinnungswechsel bei der lettischen Pfarrerschaft. An die Stelle der
deutschen und deutschorientierten Pfarrer traten lettische und national
gesinnte Geistliche. Das lässt sich besonders im Jahr 1924 feststellen,
als der erste Lehrgang die Theologische Fakultät der Universität
Lettlands in Riga absolvierte. Davor studierte man Theologie an der
Landesuniversität Dorpat (Estland). Von 1802 bis 1919 haben dort etwa
150 lettische Studenten Theologie studiert. Zur ersten Generation, die
ein Theologiestudium in Riga absolvierten, gehörte unter anderem
Roberts Slokenbergs, der Gemeindepfarrer in der Heimatgemeinde
von Biezais. Wie Biezais später schrieb, hätte er nach Abschluss der
Schulzeit in Džūkste bereits im Konfirmandenunterricht bei Pfarrer
Slokenbergs „furchtlos über verschiedene christliche Dogmen und
ethische Fragen von religiösen und sozialethischen Gesichtspunkten
aus gestritten" und sich nicht zuletzt deswegen zum Theologiestudium
entschlossen.[2] Die Suche nach einem authentischen Christentum heftete

---

[2] H. Biezais, *Saki tā, kā tas ir* [Sag' mal, wie es ist] (Rīga: Svētdienas Rīts, 1995),
S. 72f. In den Diskussionen mit Slokenbergs habe er gelernt, dass „es eine Sache ist, was

sich an das persönliche Charisma von Pfarrern lettischer Herkunft, von Biezais später als Problem der Persönlichkeit thematisiert.[3] Während seiner Jugendzeit war Biezais in die traditionelle Lebensweise Lettlands integriert, was sowohl seine existentiellen Identifikationsmuster als auch seine Kritik an einer romantisierend-idealistischen Sicht der lettischen Kultur beeinflusste. Die Tradition wiederzubeleben, war keineswegs Biezais' Absicht.

Nach Abschluss des Gymnasiums in Tukums immatrikulierte sich Biezais 1929 in der Theologischen Fakultät der Universität Lettland für ein Studium der evangelischen Theologie, das er in drei Jahren absolvierte. 1934/35 und 1936/37 betrieb er in Zürich und in Straßburg auf eigene Kosten ein Aufbaustudium. Bereits in seinem letzten Rigaer Studienjahr trat er in Gramzda, einem Dorf an der lettisch-litauischen Grenze mit einer großen Anzahl von Baptisten und Herrnhutern, ein Pfarramt an, das er bis zur deutschen Besatzungszeit innehatte. Es gelang ihm durch verschiedene Aktivitäten, etwa über individuelle Gespräche mit Konfirmanden und ihren Eltern, vor allem aber mit dem Versuch einer Verbindung von christlichen und altlettischen Ritualen, die Zahl der Gemeindemitglieder beträchtlich zu vergrößern. Zusammen mit seinen Konfirmanden und deren Eltern unternahm er Wallfahrten zum Brüderfriedhof in Riga, wo die im 1. Weltkrieg gefallenen lettischen Soldaten bestattet waren. Die Kirchenführung sah dieses neue Brauchtum zwar als heidnisch an, tolerierte es jedoch zunächst.[4] Als weitere Neuerung führte Biezais in der Gramzder Gemeinde das Feiern von Friedhofsfesten ein. Dies sei, wie Biezais später schrieb, Zeugnis seiner liberalen Einstellung gewesen.[5]

---

die Kirche und die Pfarrer tun, und eine andere, was den tieferen Sinn des Christentums ausmacht." Ebd., S. 74. Biezais widmete Slokenbergs einen Erinnerungsband, in dem er insbesondere die Konflikte zwischen Kirche und Staatsmacht, vorrangig im lettischen Exil nach dem 2. Weltkrieg, nachzeichnete: *Ne ikkatrs, kas uz mani saka... Mācītāja Roberta Slokenberga piemiņas rakstu krājums* [Nicht jeder, der zu mir sagt... Erinnerungsband zu Ehren von Pfarrer Roberts Slokenbergs] (Vasteras: Andersson & Kagardt Tryckeri AB, 1975). Siehe dabei v.a. den Aufsatz „Roberta Slokenberga dzīves meti" [Umrisse des Lebens von Roberts Slokenbergs], ebd., S. 9–61. Alle Übersetzungen aus dem Lettischen stammen von der Autorin.

[3] „Der tiefere Sinn des Christentums ist von den politischen und ideologischen Überzeugung der deutschen oder lettischen Pfarrer unabhängig. (...) Christentum ist mehr als eine Kirche. (...) Die Idee einer politisierten Kirche ist für mich nicht akzeptabel. Gott wollte mich in den Zeiten des Exils in die widerlichste, durch und durch politisierte Kirche Schwedens hineinversetzen." H. Biezais, *Saki tā, kā tas ir*, S. 77.

[4] H. Biezais, *Saki tā, kā tas ir*, S. 128.

[5] Ebd., S. 128

Liberalismus bedeutete für Biezais aber nicht die Verweltlichung der
Kirche sondern die Aufnahme traditioneller Elemente, d.h. in diesem
Fall ein Art Ahnenkult in der Form von Friedhofsfesten, die auf eine
breite öffentliche Akzeptanz stießen. Nach seiner Auffassung stand der
Gemeinde und nicht der Kirchenleitung das Recht zu, die Form der
christlichen Rituale und des Gemeindelebens zu bestimmen. Das führte
zu mehreren Konflikten mit der Kirche. Im Zusammenhang einer
Auseinandersetzung mit Erzbischof Theodors Grīnbergs drohte Biezais
sogar die Absetzung als Pfarrer. Er hatte sich geweigert, staatlichen
Feiern mit seinen Gottesdiensten eine sakrale Weihe zu verleihen. Statt
dessen trat er für die Unabhängigkeit der Kirche von den staatlichen
Behörden ein. Nach der Machtübernahme durch Kārlis Ulmanis im
Jahr 1936 setzte eine genau entgegengesetzte Entwicklung ein, die eine
erhebliche Stärkung der Macht der Bischöfe mit sich brachte.

Die Kirche in Gramzda wurde kurz nach dem Einmarsch der Nazis
Ende Juni 1941 niedergebrannt. Biezais bewirkte aber, dass sie – mit
dem von der Besatzungsmacht bewilligten Einsatz von Juden – in nur
wenigen Monaten wieder aufgebaut wurde. Seit Anfang Juni 1941
Privatdozent an der lettischen Staatsuniversität Riga, arbeitete Biezais
ab dem 1. September 1941 im Kirchlichen Zentralarchiv in Riga, dessen Direktor er 1942 wurde. Seine Tätigkeit bestand vor allem darin,
Ariernachweise für Deutschbalten aus der Wehrmacht anzufertigen.
Auch während der Zeit der deutschen Besatzung hörte Biezais nicht
auf zu publizieren. Zwischen 1941 und 1942 schrieb er zahlreiche
kleine Artikel wie zum Beispiel „Finden des Menschen",[6] „Wächter der
Volksehre",[7] „Zum Andenken an Prof. Maldonis",[8] „Die Vision vom
künftigen Menschen",[9] „Einsicht in die Heiligkeit des Lebens",[10] „Gott
in Schicksalskämpfen".[11] 1943 veröffentlichte er nicht nur das Buch *Christentum im Zeitenwandel* sondern auch die Aufsätze „Der vitale Mensch",[12]
„Wunde im Lebensbaum",[13] „Die positive Rolle der Leidenschaften",[14]

---

[6] H. Biezais, „Cilvēka atrašana", *Tēvija* [Vaterland], 7.10.1941.
[7] Ders., „Tautas goda sargātāji", ebd., 12.11.1941.
[8] Ders., „Profesoru V. Maldoni pieminot", ebd., 21.2.1942.
[9] Ders., „Nākamā cilvēka vīzija", *Daugavas vēstnesis* [Daugavas Bote], 10.5.1942.
[10] Ders., „Dzīvības svētuma ieskatījums", ebd., 26.7.1942.
[11] Ders., „Dievs likteņa cīņās", *Baznīcas ziņas* [Kirchennachrichten], 30.8.1942.
[12] Ders., „Vitālais cilvēks", *Mana māja* [Mein Zuhause] 22, 1943.
[13] Ders., „Brūce dzīvības kokā", *Daugavas vēstnesis*, 13.6.1943.
[14] Ders., „Kaislību pozitīvā jēga", ebd., 12.9.1943.

„Instinkt und Intelligenz".[15] Außer der erweiterten zweiten Auflage von *Christentum im Zeitenwandel* erschienen 1944 die Aufsätze „Auferweckte Menschen",[16] „Traditionen und Neuschöpfung",[17] „Das organische und mechanische Lebensmodell",[18] „An den Quellen des Lebens",[19] „Aufruf an die Pfarrer".[20] 1945 schrieb er für ein lettisches Kalenderbuch „Die ethischen Werte und ihre Träger",[21] „Dem Morgen entgegen",[22] „Das lebendige Volk"[23] sowie einige Berichte auf schwedisch über die lettische Kirche während der deutschen Besatzungszeit.

Im Studienjahr 1943/44 hielt Biezais einen zweisemestrigen Vorlesungskurs über „Geschichte der Philosophie und Ethik" und im Sommersemester 1944 führte er zusammen mit Prof. Kārlis Kundziņš und Dekan Eduards Zicāns die Prüfungen der Studenten durch. Das war der Anfang seiner Lehrtätigkeit an der Universität Riga, da 1941 nach dem Einmarsch der Nazis die Fakultät geschlossen wurde. Biezais erlebte auch die sowjetische Besatzung: 1941 wurden Bewohner seines Hauses von eindringenden Sowjets verhaftet. Noch dreizehn Jahre nach diesem Erlebnis habe er unter Albträumen seiner eigenen Verhaftung, Verfolgung und Flucht gelitten.[24] Dieses Ereignis ließ in Biezais die Überzeugung reifen, dass Widerstand gegen Terror unmöglich sei.[25] Außerdem habe es seine völlige Desillusionierung hinsichtlich linker Ideologien bewirkt. Bei der Einberufung der ersten lettischen Legionäre zur Wehrmacht predigte Biezais 1943 in der Domkirche zu Riga. Nach dem erneuten Einmarsch der Roten Armee flüchtete Biezais am 13. Oktober 1944 von Lettland nach Schweden. Er war einer der elf emigrierten lettischen Pfarrer in Schweden, wo er sich bei der Einrichtung

---

[15] Ders., „Instinkts un inteliģence", *Tēvija*, 27.11.1943.

[16] Ders., „Augšāmceltie cilvēki", *Mana māja* 6, 1944.

[17] Ders., „Tradīcijas un jaunradīšana", *Daugavas Vanagu Mēnešraksts* [Monatsschrift der Daugavas Falken], 1944.

[18] Ders., „Organiskais un mehāniskais dzīves modelis (T. Celma lekcija)", *Līdums* [Neuland] 9, 1944.

[19] Ders., „Pie dzīvības avotiem", *Laika balss* [Die Stimme der Zeit], 10.5.1944.

[20] Ders., „Aicinājums mācītājiem", ebd., 14.12.1944.

[21] Ders., „Ētiskās vērtības un to nesēji", *Latviešu kalendārs* 1946, Stokholmā 1945, S. 74–84.

[22] Ders., „Rītdienai pretī", *Upsalas raksti* [Upsalas' Schriften] 2, Stokholmā 1945, S. 2–4.

[23] Ders., „Dzīvā tauta", ebd. 5, 1945, S. 11–13.

[24] H. Biezais, *Saki tā, kā tas ir*, S. 147f.

[25] „Unter dem Lebensdruck ist der Mensch kein Held. Wenn er zu ihm wird, ist er ein Heiliger. Und das sind in der Geschichte der Menschheit nur wenige." Ebd., S. 148.

einer vorläufigen Verwaltung der lettischen Kirche beteiligte. In einem Lager lettischer Flüchtlinge in Stockholm leistete er seelsorgerliche Arbeit. Die lettischen Insassen des Flüchtlingslagers waren gespalten, einem liberalen und linken Flügel standen die Konservativen und Nationalgesinnten gegenüber.[26]

An der Universität Uppsala wurde Biezais zunächst Assistent am Lehrstuhl für Systematische Theologie, doch studierte er dann auch noch Philosophie und Geschichte. 1952 legte er sein Geschichtsexamen ab, um drei Jahre später mit einer Dissertation über *Die Hauptgöttinnen der alten Letten* den philosophischen Doktorgrad zu erwerben. 1971 wurde er auf eine Professur für Religionsgeschichte an der Theologischen Fakultät der Universität Åbo/Turku in Finnland berufen. Biezais nahm rege an internationalen Konferenzen zu religionswissenschaftlichen Themen teil. Nach Lettland ist er niemals mehr zurückgekehrt, obwohl er nach 1991 die Gelegenheit dazu gehabt hätte. Unter dem Titel *Saki tā, kā tas ir* erschienen 1983 seine auf lettisch geschriebenen Memoiren. Sie waren vor allem an das lettische Exil gerichtet und entsprachen dessen Erwartungen. Gleichwohl bilden sie eine wichtige Quelle für die biographische Forschung.

Biezais distanzierte sich mit Nachdruck von der Politik. Sein einziges politisches Ziel habe darin bestanden, für die Unabhängigkeit der lettischen Kirche einzutreten, was in den 1930er Jahren zu Auseinandersetzung mit der kirchlichen Obrigkeit führte. Allerdings stellte Biezais weder den Nationalsozialismus noch den lettischen Nationalismus und Autoritarismus je in Frage. Den lettischen Nationalismus hat er sogar vollkommen akzeptiert. Zu Juden und zum Judentum hatte Biezais ein zwiespältiges Verhältnis, das zuerst durch einen wirtschaftlichen Antisemitismus geprägt war. Später fühlte er sich durch den christlichen Antisemitismus in seinen Ansichten bestätigt. Als 1940/41 die unsichere Zukunft des lettischen Volkes und der eigenen Situation zu belastend wurde, spielte er fast jeden Tag Schach und führte ein künstlerisch-philosophisches Leben. Er besuchte literarische Salons, verkehrte mit Theaterstars und studierte Philosophie. In dieser Zeit beschäftigte er sich sehr stark mit philosophischen Fragen, besonders mit den Positionen des Phänomenologen Theodor Celms. Wenn er es für richtig hielt, scheute sich Biezais nicht, Bitten oder Forderungen an die deutsche Besatzungsmacht zu richten, wodurch er ein gewisses Risiko einging. Anlässe dafür

---

[26] H. Biezais, *Ne ikkatrs, kas uz mani saka*, S. 26.

waren z.B. der Wiederaufbau seiner zerstörten Kirche im Herbst und Winter 1941 oder die Wiedereröffnung der Theologischen Fakultät Ende 1942. Dem Nazi-Terror im Lande widmete Biezais im ersten Teil seiner Autobiographie kein Wort. Der zweite Teil, der sein Leben in Exil zum Thema haben sollte, ist noch nicht erschienen. Man kann Biezais aber sicherlich nicht zu den Freunden und Bundesgenossen des Nationalsozialismus rechnen. Im Hinblick auf die Rolle der lettischen Legionäre, die im 2. Weltkrieg in die Wehrmacht einberufen worden waren und an deren Seite kämpften, nahm er eine Zwischenposition ein.[27] Er wollte sie weder zu Freiheitskämpfern des lettischen Volkes hochstilisieren noch als reine Parteigänger der Nazis diffamieren. Seine Einschätzung beruhte auf der grundsätzlichen Annahme, dass unter dem Druck der Besatzungsmacht die Absichten und Ziele der davon Betroffenen unerheblich waren.

Biezais' Hiwendung zur religionshistorischen Forschung erfolgte Anfang der 1950er Jahre. Innerhalb von etwa zwei Jahrzehnten entstanden seine vier religionswissenschaftlichen Hauptwerke: *Die Hauptgöttinnen der alten Letten* (1955), *Die Gottesgestalt der lettischen Volksreligion* (1961), *Die himmlische Götterfamilie der alten Letten* (1972) und *Lichtgott der alten Letten* (1976). Alle Bücher erschienen im Verlag Almqvist & Wiksells Boktryckeri AB in Uppsala. In diesen Büchern bezog sich Biezais nicht ausdrücklich auf seine früheren Arbeiten. Es wäre jedoch falsch, hierin eine Distanzierung von seinen theologischen und ethischen Positionen zu sehen. 1974 wirkte Biezais an der Organisation einiger internationaler Konferenzen zum Thema der „Neuen Religionen" mit. Er sah sich als Pionier auf diesem Gebiet der religionsgeschichtlichen Forschung, wobei er sich der deutschen Religionswissenschaft sehr verbunden fühlte. Auch seine Tätigkeit als Pfarrer wollte er keineswegs herunterspielen. Er führte sie auf „meine hervorragende Pfarrerberufung" zurück und brachte sie mit seinem zweiten Namen Theodor in Verbindung.[28] In seiner Autobiographie schwebte Biezais zwischen einer christlich religiösen Umdeutung seiner Lebensgeschichte und einer Mythisierung derselben, ein Schweben, das jenes Konditionalgefüge verrät, deren Nebensätze mit metasprachlicher Distanz und ‚protestantischer' Bescheidenheit den jeweiligen dogmatischen Gehalt anspricht, wobei der Hauptsatz

---

[27] Siehe H. Biezais, *Kurelieši. Nacionālās pretestības liecinieki* [Die Kurelisleute. Zeugen des nationalen Widerstands] (Ithaka: Mežābele, 1991).
[28] Biezais, *Saki tā, kā tas ir*, S. 9.

Biezais' distanzlose Folgerung aufnimmt und fortführt. So bekennt sich der spätere Religionswissenschaftler: „Wenn ich abergläubischer [sic!] wäre, könnte ich sagen: das silberne oder goldene Kreuz, das ich in meinem späteren Leben auf der Brust trug, hat das Kreuz meines eigenen Lebens so leicht gemacht."[29] Und noch deutlicher: „Wenn ich theologischer eingestellt und heuchlerisch genug wäre, hätte ich gesagt, dass ich früh die Süße des ‚stellvertretenden Leidens‘ kennen gelernt habe."[30]

3. Beziehung zum lettischen Nationalismus und zur lettischen evangelischen Kirche

Biezais' Beziehung zur nationalen Idee wird besonders an seinem Verhältnis zu evangelisch-lutherischen Kirche Lettlands und deren Lettisierungsbestrebungen sowie später an seiner Beteiligung an lettischen Exilorganisationen ersichtlich. Das Ausgangsdilemma für die Kirche schilderte er folgendermaßen:

> Wir waren Fremde auch in der geistigen Welt, in dem Milieu, in das wir eingetreten waren. Die ältere Pfarrergeneration, obwohl lettischer Herkunft, lebte größtenteils weiter im erstarrten traditionellen Erbe. Sie war vom deutschen Geist der äußerlichen Traditionen durchdrungen, vor allem von den Korporationen, und vom Geist der deutschen Theologie geprägt.[31]

Nach dem 1. Weltkrieg wurde die Notwendigkeit einer Neugestaltung der lettischen Kirche auf einer neuen national-ethischen und religiösen Grundlage als drängendes Bedürfnis empfunden. Nach Biezais' Einschätzung waren 1919 90 Prozent aller Pfarrer, auch in den lettischen Gemeinden, Deutsche.[32] Als allgemein verbindlich galten die Gegensatzpaare deutsch (deutschorientiert) und lettisch; konservativ, dogmatisch und modern liberal; nüchtern, rhetorisch und stürmisch, offen, z.T. sogar avantgardistisch. Der auf den staatlichen Institutionen gegründeten öffentlichen Autorität wurde die errungene und erkämpfte Autorität

---

[29] Ebd., S. 18.
[30] Ebd., S. 31.
[31] Ebd., S. 94.
[32] Ebd., S. 94.

der jungen Generation gegenüberstellt.[33] Als Gemeindepfarrer wirkte
Biezais ausgesprochen integrierend. Indem er nationale Elemente in
das Gemeindeleben einbezog, entschärfte er die Kritik an der Kirche,
wie sie etwa von den Baptisten und Herrnhutern vorgebracht wurde.
Seine Erfahrungen im Umgang und in der Auseinandersetzung mit
ihnen hat ihm bei der Ausformulierung seiner späteren Theorie der
„Neuen Religionen" geholfen, da sie seine Sensibilität für religiöse
Meinungsunterschiede verfeinerte.

Die Theologische Fakultät der Universität Riga galt insgesamt als
liberal. Ihren liberalen und eher apolitischen Flügel repräsentierten
insbesondere der Theologe Kārlis Kundziņš und der Religionsphilosoph
Valdemārs Maldonis. Es gab aber auch eine Strömung, die eng mit
den Korporationen und später mit der autoritären nationalistischen
Regierung in Verbindung stand.[34] Biezais lehnte sich an die Liberalen
an, wobei sein Verhältnis zum autoritären lettischen Staat nach der
Machtübernahme durch Kārlis Ulmanis ambivalent blieb. Seine frühe
Auseinandersetzung mit dem Nationalismus ist von seiner Haltung
der lettischen Kirche gegenüber nicht zu trennen. 1936 schrieb er
einen Aufsatz, in dem er sich unter anderem für die Lettisierung der
evangelischen Kirche und des Gottesdienstes einsetzte, aber auch auf
ungeklärte Fragen im Hinblick auf die Kirchenverfassung nach der
Machtübernahme durch Ulmanis im Jahre 1934 hinwies.[35] Biezais
vermied es allerdings, diesen direkt zu kritisieren. Nachdem Ulmanis
zur Macht gekommen war, wurde die demokratische Verfassung der
evangelisch-lutherischen Kirche von 1928 außer Kraft gesetzt.[36]

---

[33] Vgl. Biezais, *Ne ikkatrs, kas uz mani saka*, S. 16. Die jungen lettischen Pfarrer sollten
vor allem folgende Eigenschaften haben: ein guter Rednergabe, eine laute, musikali-
sche Stimme, die die Zuhörer ergreift, sie sollten herzlich und geradezu distanzlos im
Umgang sein und aus den eigenen Reihen stammen (ebd., S. 16f., S. 64 und S. 71).
Biezais' Parallelisierung künstlerischer Berufe war offensichtlich. Während der Nazi-Zeit
verkehrte er mit bekannten Theater- und Opernstars. Lilita Bērziņa, die erfolgreichste
Schauspielerin der 1930er Jahre, äußerte sogar den Wunsch, in die Gemeinde von
Biezais einzutreten.

[34] Die Konservativen gründeten 1923 ein eigenes theologisches Institut in Riga, das
der Ausbildung der Pfarrer und der Gemeindemitarbeiter diente. Es ist bezeichnend,
dass die Exilletten nach dem 2. Weltkrieg K. Kundziņš in die Richtung des Autoritarismus drängten.

[35] H. Biezais, „Vienas lietas vajag" [Man braucht eines], *Brīvā zeme* [Das freie Land],
30.11.1936.

[36] Nach 1945 übernahm die Exilkirche die uneingeschränkte Macht der Bischöfe
vom autoritären Regime, wobei es nur wenige freie Gemeinden gab, die sich auf eine
Wahl der Kirchenleitung stützen konnten. Den Sonderdruck seines Aufsatzes „Der
Gegengott als Grundelement religiöser Strukturen" (*Saeculum* 34–3/4, 1983, S. 280–291)

Die Folgen dieser ungeklärten kirchenpolitischen Probleme hatte
Biezais während seiner Tätigkeit als Pfarrer praktisch zu spüren
bekommen. In dem genannten Aufsatz „Man braucht eines" stellte er
den Pfarrer als Träger des Pfarramts auf der einen Seite dem Pfarrer
als ethische und religiöse Persönlichkeit auf der anderen Seite gegenüber. Im Anschluss an die Theologie Richard Rothes, die das Ethos
der Kirche in das des Staates auflöste, folgerte Biezais, dass sich ein
geistiges Amt biblisch nicht begründen lasse.[37] Biezais betrachtete das
Pfarramt als eine rein administrative Angelegenheit und wandte sich
daher gegen die Versuche der dialektischen Theologie, das geistliche
Amt als „eine Sache der guten und zweckmässigen Ordnung" in den
Vordergrund zu stellen.[38] Unter einer religiösen Persönlichkeit verstand
er jemanden, der seine Aufgabe direkt von Gott empfängt, unter einer
ethischen Persönlichkeit jemanden, der ehrlich und wahrhaftig ist.[39]
Der Pfarrer müsse eine ethische Entscheidung treffen, wenn seine
subjektiven Erlebnisse mit den objektiven Normen der Tradition in
Konflikt geraten. Biezais übernahm die Sichtweise Martin Schians,
der gegenüber der Objektivität der Norm das Gewissen des Pfarrers
hervorhob.[40] Die religiöse und ethische Persönlichkeit stand für Biezais
eindeutig über dem Pfarramt.[41]

Biezais schilderte Kārlis Ulmanis mit den gleichen Worten, mit denen
er die ethische und religiöse Persönlichkeit des Pfarrers charakterisierte.
Der autoritäre lettische Präsident wurde von ihm in diesem eben
zitierten Aufsatz nach dem Vorbild eines Seelsorgers gestaltet. Ulmanis
verkörperte dieses Vorbild und wurde so zur großen und tragischen
Persönlichkeit, ja zum Märtyrer, der mit seinem Leben die Treue zum
freien Lettland bezeugt habe. Ihm gegenüber empfand Biezais eine „tiefe
Ehrfurcht und Bewunderung".[42] Ulmanis habe es zwar nicht vermocht,

---

widmete Biezais dem Erzbischof der Lettischen Ausländischen Kirche Arnolds Lūsis
mit den Worten: „Der Autor, der ins Amt des Erzbischofs nicht eingesetzte alte Stu-
dienkamerad – Haralds".

[37] Biezais, „Domu izmaiņai. Mācītāja reliģiskā un ētiskā personība" [Zum Gedan-
kenaustausch. Die religiöse und ethische Persönlichkeit des Pfarrers], Ceļš [Der Weg]
6 (1936), S. 374–383, hier S. 376.

[38] Ebd., S. 377f.

[39] Ebd., S. 380.

[40] Ebd., S. 381.

[41] Ebd., S. 383 sowie ders., Kristiānisms laikmetu maiņā [Christentum im Wandel der
Zeit] (Rīgā: Grāmatu apgādniecība A. Gulbis, 1943), S. 132.

[42] H. Biezais, Šķautnes. Meditācija par dieviem, cilvēkiem un tautu [Facetten. Meditation von
Göttern, Menschen und Volk] (Istlansinga: Gaujas apgāds, 1983), S. 120.

das Schicksal seines Volkes zu wenden, er konnte aber „in der Tragödie an seinem Platz bleiben".[43] Biezais rückte Ulmanis hier in die Nähe eines Heiligen, wobei es sich offensichtlich erneut um eine Widerspiegelung der Figur einer ethisch-religiösen Persönlichkeit handelte, die er ansonsten für Widerstandskämpfer gegen den Terror reserviert wissen wollte. Widerstand und passive Zurückhaltung wurden von ihm dabei aporetisch zu einem Konzept zusammengefügt, das Passivität in eine Form des Widerstandes verwandelte.

1938 hatte Biezais einen Aufsatz über „Das Problem des christlichen und des staatlichen Bewusstseins" veröffentlicht, in dem er von der Grundannahme ausging, dass jede Wahrheit historisch bedingt sei.[44] Auch die Beziehung zwischen Staat und Kirche ordnete er diesem Paradigma unter. Was das konkret für ihn bedeutete, zeigt sich an seinem Hinweis darauf, dass das aktuelle Zeitalter das „Zeitalter des wachsenden Nationalbewusstseins" sei. Da ein „christliches Bewusstsein auch außerhalb der Kirche" existiere, sei der Anspruch der Kirche, Trägerin des christlichen Bewusstseins zu sein, höchst zweifelhaft geworden.[45] Auf der Suche nach dem Träger des christlichen Bewusstseins besann sich Biezais auf die Kategorie des Volkes. Das Volk war nach seiner Auffassung eine natürliche Größe, seine Wurzeln biologischer Natur.[46] Es gründe sich auf einen angeborenen Egoismus und würde dem Einfluss der christlichen Ethik zunächst ablehnend gegenüber stehen. Diese im Gefolge Schopenhauers vertretene Ansicht lässt Biezais als Fürsprecher des Voluntarismus erkennen, bei dem das Volk als Träger des irrationalen Willens auftritt. Auch das Individuum treffe ethische Entscheidungen aufgrund tief verwurzelter Impulse, da die moralischen Prinzipien als solche urtümlich und irrational seien.[47] Biezais' Gebrauch des Begriffs des Irrationalen zeigt eine zeitgemäße Vermengung des rational nicht Begründbaren mit dem Transzendenten (dem göttlichen Willen), dem Willkürlichen, Zufälligen und Schicksalhaften, wobei das Biologische und das Transzendente eine Verbindung eingehen. Dass

---

[43] „Jede Tragödie zeichnet sich durch den Kampf zwischen äußeren unüberwindbaren Umständen und der siegreichen moralischen Kraft des Menschen aus. (...) Ulmanis hatte diese Kraft zur Genüge. Das hebt ihn aus der tragischen realen Welt in die mythische Welt der Symbole heraus." Ebd., S. 130f.

[44] H. Biezais, „Kristīgās un valstiskās apziņas problēma" [Das Problem des christlichen und staatlichen Bewusstseins], Sējējs [Der Sämann] 6 (1938), S. 573–579.

[45] Ebd., S. 573.

[46] Ebd., S. 575.

[47] Ebd., S. 575.

gerade das Volk zum Träger der genannten Eigenschaften werden kann, lag nach Biezais darin begründet, dass das Volk schon von vornherein im Schöpfungsplan Gottes enthalten sei.[48]

Um den Staat sozialpsychologisch begründen zu können, bezog Biezais die beiden staatstragenden Faktoren Ehrfurcht und Angst in seine Überlegungen mit ein. Die Würde einer Nation bestehe darin, neue Werte zu schaffen und diese dem Volke zu übereignen.[49] In der Frontstellung gegen die dialektische Theologie behauptete Biezais, dass der Staat die Erfüllung der Existenz des Volkes sei. Ohne dass die kulturprotestantische Komponente bestimmend wurde, wollte Biezais hier zum Ausdruck bringen, dass die Existenz und Entwicklung eines Volkes ohne einen eigenen Staat nicht normal verlaufen könne.[50] Da er sich aber der Gefahr des Immanentismus dieser Erklärung selbst bewusst war, fügte er hinzu, dass die Begründung des Staates zwar nicht mehr christlich aber im Grunde doch religiös sei.[51] Die Betonung des Staates verlangte nach der Ausweitung des Religionsbegriffs zu einem Wertbegriff. Das Christentum sollte deshalb auf seinen Absolutheitsanspruch verzichten und das Nebeneinanderbestehen gleichrangiger Werte dulden. Solche parallelen Werte waren für Biezais etwa die christliche und die weltliche Macht, deren Dualismus sich nicht ohne weiteres versöhnen lasse. Gut kantianisch erklärte Biezais, dass die echte christliche Persönlichkeit heilig sei, weil sie die Kluft zwischen Macht und Liebe überwunden habe. Im gleichen Atemzug beschrieb er das Ideal der christlichen Persönlichkeit als eine Bürgerpflicht.[52] Der Begriff der Liebe hatte demnach die Funktion, den fehlenden Bezug auf externe Bestimmungskriterien des Volkes auszugleichen. Zugleich diente er dazu, sich der Notwendigkeit der Suche nach solchen Kriterien dezisionistisch

---

[48] „Den Völkern und ihren Organisationen wohnt eine eigenartige Kraft inne, die vor dem christlichen Universalitätsprinzip und internationalen Forderungen nicht zurückweicht und nie versiegt. Das lässt uns den Willen und die Vernunft Gottes in der Existenz des Volkes erkennen. Alle Reden von der Brüderlichkeit der Menschheit ohne Völkerunterschiede sind als unrealistische romantische Träume zu sehen." Ebd., S. 576.

[49] Ebd., S. 576.

[50] Ebd., S. 576.

[51] Ebd., S. 578. Der deutsche Idealismus stehe mit seiner Idee der Humanität und der Immanenz Gottes in gewisser Spannung zum Christentum. Der Idealismus bringe einerseits die Diesseitigkeit der Welt, die „Sehnsucht nach der profanen Welt", andererseits die eng mit dem Humanismus verbundene Idee der Freiheit zum Ausdruck. Siehe H. Biezais, *Kristiānisms laikmetu maiņā*, S. 71.

[52] Biezais, „Kristīgās un valstiskās apziņas problēma", S. 578.

zu entheben.[53] Biezais' eigenes Verhalten war gerade auf das Einhalten der nächstliegenden Pflichten im Rahmen des Nationalen beschränkt. Dieses Thema hat er viel später noch einmal aufgegriffen und ist dabei wiederum gut kantianisch vorgegangen.

Eine Erzählung von Ēvalds Vilks, der Biezais einen Aufsatz widmete, stellt einen lettischen Bauern während der deutschen Besatzungszeit dar, dem der Dorfälteste einen jüdischen Jungen als Hirten überlässt gegen das Versprechen, ihn im Herbst der Polizei in einer benachbarten Stadt zur Erschießung zu bringen.[54] Über die Analyse dieses Beispiels wollte Biezais die evolutionistische Ethik und die Frage des Verhältnisses von Egoismus und Altruismus thematisieren. Biezais meinte, die Voraussetzung der Anwendung der Normen untersucht zu haben, wie sie aus dem lebensweltlichen Hintergrund hervortreten. Der Bauer wird als Normadressat aufgefasst, dem gegenüber die „moral community" als Empfänger der Normbefolgung auftritt. Der jüdische Junge gehört nicht zu den moralisch zu berücksichtigenden Wesen, er wird als das vom Dorfältesten und der Polizei Verfügbare konzipiert. Das Problem der Unzumutbarkeit, das hier den Hintergrund bildet, ist letztlich eine Frage der Perspektive, aus der heraus sich das Können beurteilen lässt.

Den Wahrheitsbegriff, der seinem Geschichts- und Religionsverständnis zugrunde liegt, begründete Biezais unter anderem mit Erkenntnissen aus verschiedenen theologischen Teildisziplinen. Im Jahre 1940 schrieb er einen konzeptionell wichtigen Aufsatz über den „Dynamischen Charakter historischer Wahrheiten".[55] Darin betonte er, dass es der Forschung nicht möglich sei, der Prägung durch das Zeitalter zu entkommen. Auch das Christentum als historische Erscheinung stehe unter diesem Gesetz.[56] Biezais begründete diese Behauptung mit der Leben-

---

[53] Soweit ich sehe hat sich Biezais aber nicht auf Carl Schmitt bezogen. Vgl. dazu Emil Brunner, *Das Gebot und die Ordnungen* (Tübingen: Mohr, 1932), S. 118: „Die Liebe ist okkasionalistisch und gerade darin ist sie erst wirklich an Gott-selbst und an den Nächsten-selbst gebunden. Die Entscheidung ist nicht vorweggenommen; sie kann nicht im ethischen Gesetzbuch ‚nachgeschlagen' werden. Die ganze Verantwortung liegt auf dem Einzelnen selbst; diese Liebe allein ist frei von Heteronomie, wie von der Selbstherrlichkeit der Autonomie. Sie ist darum in ihrer Entscheidung ‚opportunistisch', ‚prinzipienlos', während doch sie allein frei ist von aller Willkür."
[54] Siehe Ēvalds Vilks, „Pusnakts stundā" [In der Mitternacht], *Kopoti raksti 5 sējumos* [Gesammelte Werke in 5 Bänden], Werkausgabe, Bd. 2 (Rīga: Liesma, 1982), S. 339–362 sowie H. Biezais, „Meditācija par noskrandušo vēsturi" [Meditation über die Geschichte in Fetzen], in *Reliģiski-filozofiski raksti* [Religionsphilosophische Schriften], Bd. 7 (Rīga: FSI [Institut für Philosophie und Soziologie], 2001), S. 223–237.
[55] Biezais, „Vēsturisko patiesību dinamiskais raksturs", *Ceļš* 4 (1940), S. 249–259.
[56] Ebd., S. 249.

Jesu-Forschung: auch Jesus, obwohl über allen Zeiten stehend, sei ein Kind seines Zeitalters geblieben.[57] Anhand der Fallbeispiele von Wertungen Jesu (Gustav Pfannmüller) zeigte er, dass auch wissenschaftliche Methoden und Werturteile zeitbedingt und antizipatorisch ausgerichtet sein können. Neben dem Erkannten im Erbe der Vergangenheit spricht aber immer auch ein letztes Unerkanntes mit. Was nun den Wahrheitsanspruch vieler Wahrheiten anbetrifft, werden alle Wahrheiten einer Epoche in einer anderen zweifelhaft oder sogar falsch.[58] Den Begriff der Wahrheit, der die profane und die theologische Erkenntnis gleichzeitig betrifft, bettete Biezais in einen Gesamtzusammenhang ein, den er als funktionellen dynamischen Organismus begreift.[59] „Die höchste historische Wahrheit besteht darin, die eigene Zeit zu enträtseln. Man darf nie die eigene Epoche missverstehen, sonst fällt die Geschichte ihr strenges Gerichtsurteil." Als Beispiele für Verfehlungen dieser Art nannte Biezais die Versuche deutschbaltischer Autoren, das ganze lettische Leben durch deutschen Einfluss zu erklären, so als ob die Letten keine eigene Kultur gehabt hätten oder haben könnten.[60] Die Deutschbalten „leben das Leben ihres Zeitalters nicht und sind mit ihm nicht organisch verbunden." „Wenn jemand unsere Erfolge durch äußere Zwänge oder durch die Umstände hervorgerufen sehen wollte, fiele diese Erklärung aus seinem Zeitalter, d.h. aus dem Dynamismus des Lebens hinaus und hätte als Folge den Verlust jedes Wahrheitswertes."[61]

Dem Vorwurf des Subjektivismus und Relativismus meinte Biezais dadurch entgehen zu können, dass er das Gewicht auf den Verantwortungsbegriff verlegte: Die Erkenntnis des dynamischen Charakters historischer Wahrheiten verpflichte den Wissenschaftler (Theologen) darauf, sich seine eigene Epoche anzueignen. Es sei nicht möglich, in der Welt theologischer Denkformen zu leben, die vor einigen hundert oder tausend Jahren geprägt worden sind. Das von Biezais gezogene Fazit lautete: „Das höchste Ziel und die Aufgabe der historischen Wahrheit ist es, sich in den sinnvollen Zusammenhang ihrer Epoche einzufügen."[62]

---

[57] Ebd., S. 252.
[58] Ebd., S. 252.
[59] Ebd., S. 256.
[60] Ebd., S. 257.
[61] Ebd., S. 257.
[62] Ebd., S. 259.

Wesentliche Aspekte von Biezais' Positionen beleuchtet auch sein 1953 in Kopenhagen erschienenes Buch *Christentum. Nationalismus. Humanismus*, das die Diskussionen resümiert, die lettische Intellektuelle der Nachkriegszeit in Uppsala über das Wesen des Christentums, des Volkes und der Nation geführt haben.[63] Dies war das letzte große Werk von Biezais, in dem er die Themen Religion und Nationalismus behandelte. Biezais spielte hier den Begriff des Humanismus gegen den damals politisch verdächtig gewordenen Biologismus und Vitalismus aus.[64] Der Gedanke des Humanismus bzw. der Humanität war bereits durch seine Dissertation vorbereitet worden. Auch noch 1953 vertrat er die Auffassung, dass das unreduzierbar Individuelle an der Weltanschauung des Einzelnen auf die biologische Bestimmtheit des Menschen und seinen irrationalen, mit der Vernunft nicht vereinbaren Glauben zurückgehe.[65] Das Christentum fasste Biezais jetzt aber nicht mehr als einen paradoxen Gegenwert zu anderen gleichrangigen Werten auf. Vielmehr griff er nun auf das alte Konzept des Kulturprotestantismus zurück, wonach das Christentum notwendigerweise mit anderen Weltanschauungen eine Verbindung eingehe. In einer noch späteren Arbeit versuchte Biezais, an Richard Rothe geschult, am Beispiel des lettischen Traditionalisten Edvarts Virza den Kulturprotestantismus auf lettischem Boden zu exemplifizieren.[66] Dies war nun aber eine Position, die sich in Lettland kaum durchsetzen konnte, da man dort das Christentum nicht als Voraussetzung und Legitimierung der modernen lettischen Kultur, sondern als deren Alternative sehen wollte. Als am Ende der 1980er Jahre das nationale Erwachen Lettlands anbrach, standen sich zwei konkurrierende Auffassungen des Volkes gegenüber. Die eine behauptete die rettende Kraft des Christentums und fasste das Volk als christliche Gemeinde auf, die andere beschwörte eine nationale lettische Mentalität und deren Aufrechterhaltung. Biezais' weiter Begriff des Christentums aus den 1930er bis zu den 1950er Jahren hat dieses

---

[63] H. Biezais, *Kristiānisms. Nacionālisms. Humānisms* [Christentum, Nationalismus, Humanismus] (Kopenhavn: Imanta, 1953), siehe außerdem ders., *Kristiānisma vēsturiskā vide. Ieskatītais un atzītais, veltīts Prof. Teodoram Celmam* [Die historische Umwelt des Christentums. Das Eingesehene und das Erkannte, gewidmet Prof. Teodors Celms] (Stockholm: Daugava, 1963).

[64] H. Biezais, *Kristiānisms. Nacionālisms. Humānisms*, S. 9.

[65] Ebd., S. 14.

[66] H. Biezais, „Edvarta Virzas reliģiskā dzīve" [Das religiöse Leben von Edvarts Virza], *Ceļa zīmes* [Wegzeichen] 3–7 (1950), S. 289–298.

Dilemma nicht gekannt. Christentum und Nationalismus verlangten hier gerade nacheinander und bedingten sich gegenseitig.

Für die Verarbeitung der jüngsten Vergangenheit griff Biezais noch 1953 auf eine vermeintlich falsche Gegenüberstellung der von ihm als jüdisch bezeichneten Lehre vom Menschen als Sünder einerseits und der Einzigartigkeit des Menschen als Ebenbild Gottes und Mitarbeiters an seinem Reich andererseits zurück.[67] In Übereinstimmung mit der Mehrheit der lettischen Bevölkerung betonte Biezais, dass der Lette die Arbeit mit dem Leben gleichsetze. Im Gegensatz dazu stellte Biezais bei den Juden eine angebliche Abneigung gegenüber der Arbeit fest: „Beim jüdischen Volk ist eine Moral entstanden, die sich gravierend von den Einstellungen unterscheidet, die in der Arbeit einen positiven Sinn sehen."[68] Auf der anderen Seite lehnte Biezais aber eine Bestimmung des Volkes durch ein biologistisches Rassenkonzept ab, da dies dem Leben nicht entspreche und da außerdem der Rassebegriff „noch sehr unklar sei".[69] Die von ihm ebenfalls kritisierte Identifikation von Volk und Staat entsprach einem Denken, das im lettischen Exil weit verbreitet war. An Stelle eines rassischen Biologismus findet sich bei Biezais aber weiterhin eine völkische und sozialdarwinistische Tendenz, die besagt, dass sich „jedes Volk mit anderen Völkern in ständigem Kampf befindet, da es von anderen in seiner Existenz bedroht wird."[70] Die Geschichte und Wirklichkeit des Lebens zeige, dass der Fortbestand eines Volkes sehr eng mit seinem geographischem Raum verbunden sei: „Das Volk, das seinen geographischen Raum verliert, ist dem Untergang freigegeben," es wird der Assimilation ausgeliefert.[71] Als abschreckendes Beispiel nannte Biezais wiederum die Juden, die „riesige Verluste lebendiger Kraft durch Assimilation" aufweisen würden.[72]

Die These von der biologischen Einheit des Volkes wollte Biezais weiterhin gelten lassen, auch wenn sie „in den letzten Jahrzehnten in unnötige Extreme getrieben wurde." Zum ersten Mal sprach Biezais nun aber davon, dass gerade den nationalen Religionen (der christlichen

---

[67] H. Biezais, *Kristiānisms. Nacionālisms. Humānisms*, S. 44.
[68] Ebd., S. 109.
[69] Ebd., S. 79.
[70] Ebd., S. 83.
[71] Ebd., S. 84.
[72] Ebd., S. 85. Diese Ansicht gibt die Argumentationsweise sowohl der Zionisten, als auch Autonomisten der Zwischenkriegszeit in Lettland wieder. In Riga lebten und veröffentlichten ihre Werke beispielsweise Simon Dubnow, Max Schatz-Anin, Michael Yoffe.

wie vorchristlichen) bei der Herstellung der Volkseinheit eine besondere
Rolle zukäme, wobei er auch den Katholizismus mit einschloss.[73] Ungeachtet seiner biologischen Bestimmung sei das Wesen des Volkes in erster
Linie als eine geistige Größe aufzufassen, die sich durch Unabhängigkeit,
Geist und Charakter ihrer Werke kennzeichne.[74] Die genannten Prädi-
kate entnahm Biezais seiner Charakterisierung von Kirche, Staat und
Persönlichkeit (Elite) und verschmolz sie zu einer neuen Einheit. Da er
den Moralbegriff in seiner Definition des Volkes unbedingt beibehalten
wollte, verortete er das Volk zwischen der „Masse", die keine Moral
und individuelle Verantwortung kennt, und der „Armee", die eine sehr
starke Verantwortung gegenüber überindividuellen Werte hat.[75] Die
Tradierung dieser Werte werde durch einen Prozess des „organischen
Wachstums" gesichert. „Das Vererben des Volksgeistes von einer Generation zur anderen" sorge dafür, dass sich die Völker nur sehr langsam
verändern.[76] Dasselbe Gesetz des organischen Wachstums bedinge auch
das Hervortreten eines Führers. Die Person des Volksführers sei weder
durch Wahl noch durch Gewalt zu bestimmen, da jede Führerperson
seinem Milieu nach organischen Gesetzen entwachse. Die Führer des
Volkes seien „typische Erscheinungen des Volksgeistes", um das Volk
zusammenzuhalten.[77]

Vom biologisch verankerten Lebenswillen des Volkes setzte Biezais
einen geistigen Volksbegriff ab. Dessen Funktion sei „die Erfüllung seines
höchsten Bewusstseins, das seine Impulse von den Weisheitsschätzen
des Volkes und seinen Gefühlserlebnissen empfängt."[78] Die in seinem
Volksbegriff enthaltene Heterogenität des Biologischen und Geistigen
wurde von Biezais nicht wirklich reflektiert, doch er griff immer wieder
darauf zurück und versuchte, beide Teile konzeptionell zusammenzu-
fügen. Die Volksverbundenheit nannte Biezais eine mythisch-mystische
Verbindung, von der man sich nicht einfach aufgrund einer freien Wil-
lensentscheidung losreißen könne.[79] Die Ethik eines Volkes entwachse

---

[73] Ebd. „Ob das der primitive Mensch im afrikanischen Urwald mit seiner heiligen
Magie oder der gegenwärtige Katholik ist, sie alle fühlen sich in ihrem religiösen Verhalten eng mit Ihresgleichen verbunden, mit ihrem Stamm oder Volk." Ebd., S. 85f.
[74] Ebd., S. 88.
[75] Ebd., S. 90f.
[76] Ebd., S. 93.
[77] Ebd., S. 95f.
[78] Ebd., S. 99.
[79] Ebd., S. 123.

seinem Selbstbewusstsein und seiner Überlebenskraft.[80] „Der gesunde
Volksegoismus" bedeute, dass „Völker ihre Lebensinteressen keinen
Prinzipien universaler Ethik unterwerfen", selbst wenn diese christlich
sind. Für alle Menschen gültige ethische Prinzipien würden sich nicht
verwirklichen lassen. Für die genannte Heterogenität prägt Biezais den
Begriff des Kompromisses: alle großen Religionen würden Kompro-
misse mit den Lebensinteressen der unterworfenen Völker und deren
ethischen Anschauungen schließen.[81]

Das traditionalistische lettische Geschichtsverständnis der Zwischenkriegszeit tritt bei Biezais deutlich zum Vorschein und wurde in
seiner Konzeption durch eine theologische Komponente ergänzt. Es
ist daher verständlich, dass weder pagane Rekonstruktionen, die sich
einem dynamistischen Geschichtsverständnis widersetzten, noch die
radikale Abweisung vorchristlicher Schichten, die das Erbe und die
Tradition in ihrer biologisch-religiöser und geistigen Einheit verkennt,
für Biezais eine Lösung darstellten. In dem vier Jahre vor seinem Tod
veröffentlichten Werk *Lächelnde Götter und eine Menschenträne* kritisierte er
sowohl die antichristlich argumentierenden Befürworter der lettischen
Religion (die Bewegung „Dievturi") als auch jene Christen, die die
Bedeutung der altlettischen Religion oder die Notwendigkeit einer Dif-
ferenzierung zwischen den Konfessionen des Christentums verkennen.
Biezais endete Anfang der 1990er Jahre pathetisch und ganz im Geiste
seiner Jugendansichten:

> All die Streitereien und Kämpfe zwischen den Kirchen um die Frage,
> welche denn nun die echte Wegweiserin zu Gott sei, stellen tatsächlich
> eine Verleumdung Gottes dar, so als ob Gott selbst nicht vermochte hätte,
> sich an dem Ort, den Menschen und zu der Zeit zu zeigen, wenn er es
> will. Diesen Kampf mit den religiösen Gegnern teilen auch die Prediger
> der nationalen Religion, indem sie den wichtigsten Gehalt ihrer Predigt,
> die Güte nämlich, vergessen.[82]

---

[80] Ebd., S. 111.
[81] Ebd., S. 119f.
[82] H. Biezais, *Smaidošie dievi un cilvēka asara* [Die lächelnde Götter und eine Men-
schenträne] (Plön: Senatne, 1991), S. 6.

4. Wissenschaftlicher Werdegang

Der gemeinsame Nenner der beiden Bereiche Theologie und Religions-wissenschaft war für Biezais zweifelsohne die Religionsphänomenologie Rudolf Ottos, die an der Theologischen Fakultät der Universität Riga fest verankert war. Die Religionsphänomenologie, deren Rezeption dadurch erleichtert wurde, dass sie zwar christlich, jedoch akonfes-sionell war, prägte schon das Religionsverständnis des jungen Biezais. Bereits sein Gemeindepfarrer Roberts Slokenbergs verbrachte auf Anregung von Prof. Maldonis im Sommersemester 1931 einige Zeit in Marburg.[83] Seine theologische Diplomarbeit schrieb Biezais 1932 über den *Religionsbegriff bei R. Otto*. Der von Biezais als einer seiner Lehrer bezeichnete Valdemārs Maldonis hatte in Marburg unter anderem bei Rudolf Otto studiert und 1921/22 an der Universität Marburg den Doktor der Philosophie erworben. Von Maldonis, der auch als Schüler des Marburger Neukantianers Paul Natorp galt, übernahm Biezais die zentrale Ausrichtung auf das Heilige als Teil der Religionspsychologie. Maldonis lehrte in Riga außer Religionspsychologie auch Religionsphi-losophie, Ethik und Dogmatik. Den Otto-Schüler Gustav Mensching nannte Biezais dagegen seinen ersten „Lehrer der Religionsgeschichte", den er 1978 mit einem Nekrolog würdigte.[84] Gustav Mensching, der an der Theologischen Fakultät der Universität Riga von 1927 bis 1935 die Religionsgeschichte vertrat, war von Otto persönlich der Fakultät empfohlen worden. Im Vergleich zu Menschings späterer Zeit in Bonn beurteilte Biezais dessen Rigaer Lehrtätigkeit weniger günstig. Men-schings Dissertation nannte er „schwach" und seine Aufsätze lediglich „populär".[85] Im Gegensatz zu seinen lettischen Kollegen wollte Biezais ihm aber den wissenschaftlichen Charakter seiner Arbeiten nicht grund-sätzlich absprechen. Der Einfluss Rudolf Ottos war hingegen an der Rigaer Universität fächerübergreifend. Außer den bereits Genannten beeinflusste Ottos Denken auch die Theologen A. Freijs, E. Rumba, K. Kundziņš sowie die Vertreter religiöser Bewegungen wie z.B. die Röricheaner (R. Rudzītis).

Zu einem weiteren prägenden Faktor, insbesondere in der Argumen-tation gegen die dialektische Theologie, wurde für Biezais der Persona-

---

[83] Siehe H. Biezais, *Ne ikkatrs, kas uz mani saka*, S. 17.

[84] Siehe Biezais, *Die Hauptgöttinnen der alten Letten*, S. VI und „Profesoram Menšingam aizejot" [Zum Abschied von Prof. Mensching], *Latvija* [Lettland], 4.11.1978.

[85] Biezais, *Saki tā, kā tas ir*, S. 188.

lismus in einem weit gefassten Sinn.[86] Der Lehrer seiner Studienzeit *par excellence* war der in Dorpat bei dem Personalisten und Nachfolger von Gustav Teichmüller Jēkabs Osis (Oze) ausgebildete Kārlis Kundziņš.[87] Dem Personalismus ist auch Biezais' Züricher Lehrer Emil Brunner zuzurechnen. Biezais belegte alle Seminare und Vorlesungen Brunners, die sich durch eine scharfe Kritik an Karl Barth auszeichneten. Eine personalistische Komponente (Liebesbegriff) hat Biezais auch bei Brunners Gegner Albert Schweitzer empfunden, den er während seines ersten ausländischen Studienjahres in Zürich 1934/35 persönlich kennen lernte.[88]

Nach Abschluss seines Studiums an der Theologischen Fakultät der Universität Riga wurde Biezais zunächst am Lehrstuhl für Systematische Theologie tätig. Damit begann seine akademische Karriere. Bei der Wahl seines Forschungsschwerpunktes verzichtete Biezais ganz auf Dogmatik und unterrichtete in erster Linie Ethik und Religionspsychologie. Weil Systematische Theologie und Ethik für Biezais eines höheren Ranges waren, wollte er unbedingt auf diesen Gebieten tätig sein, da er fürchten musste, als Liberaler und nicht zum politischen und kirchlichen Establishment Gehöriger in die von ihm weniger gewünschte Religionsgeschichte oder das Alte Testament abgedrängt zu werden. Im Februar 1940 reichte Biezais seine Habilitationsschrift über *Die anthropologischen Anschauungen E. Brunners* ein. Das im Mai 1940 von der Fakultät vorgegebene Thema seiner Probevorlesung, die zweite Bedingung für die Habilitation, lautete: „Sind die Dogmen ewig?"[89] Doch erst der Universitätsrat war berechtigt, seine Ernennung zum

[86] Der Personalismus bezeichnet solche philosophische Lehren, die die ‚Person' dem ‚Individuum' gegenüber stellen. Gegenüber der überspannten Forderung individueller Freiheit und Verantwortung tritt der Personalismus für den Wert des konkreten menschlichen Lebens ein. Zu seinen Vertretern gehören etwa Max Scheler, Emmanuel Mounier, Nikolaj Berdjajev, Gerhard Teichmüller, Jēkabs Osis (Oze) und Emil Brunner. Der Begriff hat sich insbesondere im russischen und französischen philosophiegeschichtlichen Diskurs eingebürgert, im Deutschen spricht man eher von einem ethischen oder kritischen Personalismus.
[87] Siehe K. Kundsin, *Das Urchristentum im Lichte der Evangelienforschung* (Giessen: Verlag Alfred Töpelmann, 1929).
[88] Emil Brunner schreibt über Albert Schweitzer: „‚Ehrfurcht vor dem Leben' (...) ein merkwürdiger Bastard der pantheistischen Lebensmystik der Guyau und Fourier auf der einen und des kantianischen humanistischen Personalismus auf der anderen Seite. Wenig eignet sich für die Begründung der Ethik." Ders., *Das Gebot und die Ordnungen*, S. 582. Auf Jean-Marie Guyau nahm Biezais in seiner Dissertation Bezug.
[89] Als Biezais bei Maldonis nachfragte, was es mit diesem Thema auf sich habe, bekam er die ermutigende Antwort seines Lehrers „Sag' mal, wie es ist!" (*Saki tā, kā tas ir*), die er als Titel für seinen Erinnerungsband wählte.

Privatdozenten auszusprechen. Ehe dies erfolgen konnte, wurde Biezais am ersten Jahrestag des Deutsch-Sowjetischen Nichtangriffspaktes am 23.8.1940 entlassen, nachdem Lettland am 5.8.1940 von sowjetischen Truppen besetzt worden war. Auch nach dem Einmarsch der deutschen Truppen am 22. Juni 1941 änderte sich nichts daran. Die Universität blieb bis Ende 1942 geschlossen. Der Bitte von Biezais, einen Abschluss für diejenigen Theologie-Studenten zu ermöglichen, die vor der deutschen Okkupation immatrikuliert waren, wurde von der national-sozialistisch dominierten Verwaltung entsprochen. Daraus ergab sich aber kein legaler Status für die theologische Fakultät. Biezais schrieb sich dann für ein philosophisches und psychologisches Studium an der Philosophischen Fakultät Universität Lettland ein, das er bis September 1944 betrieb. Bis zum Zeitpunkt seiner Flucht legte er etwa die Hälfte aller Prüfungen am Psychologischen Seminar ab.[90] Eine besondere Attraktivität hatte für Biezais der bei Edmund Husserl und Paul Natorp ausgebildete lettische Phänomenologe Theodor Celms. Celms sah es als seine Aufgabe an, die phänomenologische Methode seines Lehrers Husserl vom Idealismus zu entkoppeln.[91] Seine Lehrtätigkeit an der Theologischen Fakultät trat Biezais im Herbstsemester 1943 mit einer Vorlesung über „Religionsphilosophie und Ethik" an. Das Thema der gut besuchten und von Celms herzlich begrüßten Antrittsvorlesung des jungen Privatdozenten lautete „Wissenschaftlichkeit der Theologie".[92] Von Celms übernahm Biezais die Sicht auf die Philosophie als Welt-anschauung der Gebildeten, die eine kritische Erkenntnis einbezieht und jeden Mythos bzw. jede Religion überwindet.[93] Diesen Gedanken versuchte er in seine Vorstellung eines undogmatischen Christentums zu integrieren. Eine philosophische Religion oder natürliche Theologie hat ihn dagegen nie ernstlich beschäftigt.

1939 veröffentlichte Biezais seine im Jahr davor eingereichte theo-logische Dissertation zum Thema *Synthesis von Leben und Liebe in der christlichen Humanität. Eine christliche Bewertung der ethischen Grundprinzipien*

---

[90] Ebd., S. 212.

[91] Siehe dazu das von Celms auf Deutsch verfasste Werk *Der phänomenologische Idea-lismus Husserls*, das 1928 in den *Acta Universitatis Latviensis* erschien und 1979 in den USA neu aufgelegt wurde.

[92] H. Biezais, *Saki tā, kā tas ir*, S. 209f.

[93] T. Celms, *Tagadnes problēmas* [Probleme der Gegenwart] (Rīga: Valters un Rapa, 1934), S. 201

von biozentrisch orientierten Denkern.[94] Das Werk ist der Begegnung der
Lebensphilosophie mit der christlichen Theologie unter besonderer
Berücksichtigung ethischer Fragestellungen gewidmet. Unter Lebensphilosophie verstand Biezais eine organische Ganzheit, die sich auch
methodisch am Zusammenhang der Erscheinungen orientierte.[95] Um
zu veranschaulichen, dass er einen Ausgleich zwischen Theologie und
Lebensphilosophie anstrebte, nannte er seine Methode historisch-orga-
nisch. Die Brücke zwischen beiden Auffassungen sah er darin, dass
auch der Lebensbegriff letztlich in Gott begründet sei. Biezais bezog
dabei auch das Unbewusste, das seiner Meinung nach für ethische
Entscheidungen eine zentrale Bedeutung hatte, in seine Überlegungen
mit ein.[96] Nach der Widerlegung bisheriger Syntheseversuche erörterte
er im Anschluss an den praktischen Theologen Alfred Dedo Müller eine
neue Synthese, die er unter den Oberbegriff eines „dritten Humanismus" subsumierte. Der „zweite", an der Antike ausgerichtete Humanismus der Renaissance hätte zu einer „Absolutsetzung des Menschen
geführt" und sei an seiner „religiösen Unentschiedenheit" zugrunde
gegangen.[97] Im Gegensatz zum „dritten Humanismus" Werner Jaegers
orientierte sich Biezais nicht am Vorbild der Griechen. Die Vollendung
des Christentums sah er in dessen Hinwendung zur Welt und in einer
Profanität, die ebenfalls von Gott her komme.[98] Dadurch meinte Biezais, gewichtige Argumente gegen die Orthodoxie der dialektischen
Theologie geliefert zu haben.

In seinen religionshistorischen Studien zur altlettischen Religion
äußerte sich Biezais ausgesprochen vorsichtig und zurückhaltend. Wegen
der unsicheren Quellenlage hielt er eine genaue Rekonstruktion für

---

[94] H. Biezais, *Dzīvības un mīlestības sintēze kristīgajā humanitātē. Disertācija* (Riga: Autora
izdevums, 1939). Siehe dazu die wichtige Rezension von V. Maldonis in der Zeitschrift
Ceļš 1 (1940), S. 49–51.

[95] H. Biezais, *Dzīvības un mīlestības sintēze kristīgajā humanitātē*, S. 6f.

[96] Ebd., S. 130.

[97] Ebd., S. 202.

[98] „Das Christentum muss wissen, dass es der humanitären Gestaltwerdung bedarf,
um nicht mit seinem eigenen Verwirklichungsauftrag in Widerspruch zu geraten. Der
Humanismus muss wissen, dass er der christlichen Universalität und Nüchternheit
bedarf, um den Zusammenhang mit der tiefsten Realität der Dinge nicht zu verlieren.
Das Christentum muss seine starre Abgrenzung gegen die Welt verlieren: es bedarf der
Profanität zu seiner Selbstvollendung. Der Humanismus muss seine starre Weltlichkeit
aufgeben: der Mensch bedarf Gottes, um zu sich selbst zu kommen." So Alfred Dedo
Müller, *Ethik: der evangelische Weg der Verwirklichung des Guten* (Berlin: Töpelmann, 1937),
S. 201f.

ausgeschlossen, und um jede Spekulation zu vermeiden, beschränkte er sich auf rein wissenschaftliche Aussagen. Dabei stellte er viele Thesen in Frage, die von Forschern in- und außerhalb Lettlands zur lettischen Religionsgeschichte vorgetragen wurden. Im Gegensatz etwa zu Leopold von Schröder und Wilhelm Mannhardt betonte Biezais die nur relative Gültigkeit von Aussagen über die lettische Religionsgeschichte. Den Lichtgott wollte er z.B. nicht voreilig mit der Sonne oder dem Sonnenkult identifizieren, wie das Leopold von Schröder und August Bielenstein getan hatten. Auch eine Sonnenmythologie lehnte Biezais ab, da sie seiner Meinung nach zu viel zu erklären beanspruchte.[99] Dennoch anerkannte er: „Saule steht als Göttin im Mittelpunkt der Religion der alten Letten."[100] Skeptisch äußerte sich Biezais auch zu Behauptungen über den Lichtgott Ūsiņš, der für ihn typologisch zu den Himmelsgöttern gehörte: „Inhalt und Art der Quellen lassen in seinem Wesen phänomenologisch nur solche Züge erkennen, die es erlauben, ihn mit den Erscheinungen des Lichtes zu verbinden." Eine direkte Aussage darüber sei in den Quellen nicht zu finden.[101] Biezais beschäftigte die Frage, ob man tatsächlich einen irreduziblen Wesenskern der Religion herausfinden könne, auch wenn sich diese nicht oder nicht im gewünschten Umfang rekonstruieren lasse. Im Grunde genommen sei dieser Wesensgehalt auf das Eintauchen der Religionen in das „Mysterium des Lebens und des Todes" zurückzuführen.[102] Das Lebensmysterium der lettischen Religion finde sich beispielhaft im Johannisfest abgebildet.[103]

Die Totenrituale, die das Mysterium des Todes zum Ausdruck bringen sollen, wurden von Biezais dagegen viel weniger behandelt. Sicherlich kann man sagen, dass die „Himmelsgötter" und der „himmlische Seite" der Religion in der wissenschaftlichen Arbeit von Biezais eine

---

[99] Leopold von Schröder meinte, dass „Saule" [Sonne] die Tochter Gottes sei. Siehe ders., *Arische Religion, Bd. 1: Einleitung – Der altarische Himmelsgott – Das höchste Wesen* (Leipzig: H. Hassel, 1914, Nachdruck 1923), S. 527. Die Kenntnis der lettischen Mythologie und Religion hatte Schröder Mannhardts Werken entnommen, die sich jedoch vornehmlich auf das litauische Material beziehen. In der Tat gibt es in der lettischen Überlieferung die Jungfrau Sonne und die Mutter Sonne, doch der Gottvater „Dievs" hat keine Töchter. Siehe H. Biezais. *Die himmlische Götterfamilie der alten Letten* (Uppsala: Almqvist & Wiksells Boktryckeri AB, 1972), S. 483–493.

[100] H. Biezais, *Lichtgott der alten Letten* (Uppsala: Almqvist & Wiksells Boktryckeri AB, 1976), S. 186.

[101] Ebd., S. 187.

[102] H. Biezais, *Saki tā, kā tas ir*, S. 18.

[103] H. Biezais, *Die himmlische Götterfamilie der alten Letten*, S. 303–414.

weitaus größere Rolle spielten. Dies scheint durch die „Einbürgerung"
des lettischen Polytheismus in die herrschaftslegitimierende indoeuro-
päische Pantheonbildung bedingt, die eine politische oder wenigstens
psychologische Komponente des Lettentums im Exil zum Ausdruck
bringt. Eine gewisse Meidung des Todes und der chthonischen Seite
des Lebens könnte man auch als Ausdruck einer Strategie der Distanzierung sehen. Zur Zeit der Herrschaft des Nationalsozialismus bediente
sich Biezais einer „vitalistischen" Terminologie, die man sogar den
Titeln seiner Essays und Artikel entnehmen kann. Andererseits sollte
die nationale Religion ebenso wie der Nationalismus über den Topos
des „Generationenfluss" ohne das Problem des Todes auskommen Die
Todesproblematik berücksichtigte Biezais lediglich in einem biographischen Essay über Kai Munk, in dem die Distanz von der „Strategie
des de Sade" (bewusstes Ausleben und Akzeptanz des ganzen Leidens
auf der Seite des Opfers) fast verschwindet.[104]

Biezais hat um die Mitte der 1950er Jahre einige biographische
Essays geschrieben. Die Auswahl der dargestellten Personen ist mit zwei
ausländische Literaten – Kai Munk und Nikos Kazantzakis[105] – auffal-
lend. Jede Biographie kann man als eine Art projektive Biographie oder
Auto-Biographie sehen, wobei die Biographie einerseits die Elemente
zum Ausdruck bringt, die man sich nicht traut, als autobiographische
zu bezeichnen, andererseits, über-schreibt und korrigiert man das eigene
Leben, indem man einen virtuellen Zwilling, hier die beiden Autoren
Munk und Kazantzakis, herstellt. Beide kritisierten den traditionellen
Gottesbegriff der christlichen Kirche, folgerten aber unterschiedliche
Konsequenzen, die sich daraus für das ethische Verhalten des Menschen
ergeben würden.

Der Begriff des Heiligen in der Prägung Rudolf Ottos, Friedrich
Heilers, Nathan Söderbloms und später Mircea Eliades war die tragende

---

[104] H. Biezais, „Kajs Munks, ziemeļzemju dzejnieks, pravietis un moceklis" [Kai
Munk, Dichter, Prophet und Märtyrer der Nordländer], *Ceļa zīmes* [Wegzeichen]
16 (1953/54), S. 27–32, später (1983) veröffentlicht in H. Biezais, *Šķautnes*, S. 39–69.
Nach dem Vorbild und den Erzählungen Kai Munks, der durch seinen Widerstand
gegen die Nazis bekannt wurde, thematisierte Biezais die Stellungnahme eines Pfarrers,
der sein ganzes Leben den Menschen diente, dann aber von der Kirche abgesetzt
wurde, weil die kirchliche Obrigkeit feststellte, dass er nicht mehr an Gott glaubt.
Aus Überzeugung bietet er den gläubigen Gemeindemitgliedern aber weiterhin seine
kirchlichen Dienste an.
[105] H. Biezais, „Niks Kazantzakis – dieva cīnītājs" [Nikos Kazantzakis – Gottesbe-
kämpfer], veröffentlicht in ders., *Šķautnes*, S. 108.

Säule des Religionsverständnisses von Biezais.[106] Bei der Rekonstruktion der lettischen Religion griff Biezais in starkem Maße auf die Psychologie zurück. Das Heilige unterschied er in späteren Werken nicht mehr vom Sakralen und wurde von ihm nicht mehr nur phänomenologisch gedacht sondern bezog auch die Soziologie und Sozialpsychologie mit ein, worunter Biezais die gemeinsamen Normen, die in einem bestimmten kulturellen Milieu gepflegt werden und dort verbindlich sind, verstand.[107] Eine seiner letzten Publikationen aus dem Jahre 1991 griff das Thema seiner Diplomarbeit über *Die sozialanthropologische Begründung der Kategorie des 'Heiligen'* wieder auf.[108] Biezais erörterte hier theoretische Probleme, die auf die Anwendung der Kategorie des Heiligen zurückgehen. Wenn das Heilige nur in Relation zum Profanem zu begreifen ist, werde die Dichotomie unvermeidlich, dass der Mensch in zwei Welten, einer sakralen und einer profanen, beheimatet ist. Er sei dann gleichzeitig ein biologisches und transempirisches Wesen. Sowohl Rudolf Otto als auch Mircea Eliade konnten dieser Konsequenz nicht ausweichen. Nach Biezais Auffassung ist das Heilige kein Phänomen sui generis. Er lehnte es ab, das Heilige über das Supranaturale zu begründen. Aber das Heilige Otto'scher Prägung ist gerade dem supranaturalem Gehalt entnommen worden, ist seine Vergegenständlichung. Biezais' Betonung der Psychologie, die von ihm aber nur unscharf von der Sozialpsychologie getrennt wird, bedeutete eine Vorentscheidung für eine a-theologische Religionsforschung. Biezais führte den Begriff des Heiligen auf

---

[106] Zum Lichtgott Ūsiņš äußert Biezais seine Überzeugung, dass er vorchristlichen Ursprungs sei. Das ließe sich zwar nicht mit völliger Sicherheit entscheiden, aber man könne generell festhalten, dass es seine Haupfunktion sei, „die Fruchtbarkeit der Felder zu sichern und sich vor bösen und schädlichen Kräften zu schützen." Biezais, *Lichtgott der alten Letten*, S. 181. Diese Hauptfunktion werde letztlich von der Grunderfahrung des religiösen Erlebens gesteuert. Über die tiefere Bedeutung von ūsiņš, die in seinem Ritt über den Berg zum Ausdruck kommt, wobei er den Bäumen die Blätter und den Feldern das grüne Gras bringt, sagte er, dass dies ein anschaulicher Beweis dafür sei, „daß das Leben wiederkehrt". Ebd., S. 184. Biezais leitete die ūsiņš zugesprochenen Funktion der völligen „Abhängigkeit des Bauern vom Erwachen der Natur" zu und erinnerte daran, dass von den Bauern das Frühjahr als eine Hungerzeit bezeichnet wird. Auf Seite 185 warnte er: „Nur der Drang des Wissenschaftlers nach Systematisierung, der einen Gott einzig an seine besonderen Funktionen binden will, schafft Probleme, wo solche im Bewusstsein des Bauern im wirklichen Leben gar nicht bestehen."

[107] Siehe hierzu etwa den 1981 in Uppsala vor Exilletten gehaltenen Vortrag „Lette – Stiefkind der Demokratie, Kultur und Subkultur", veröffentlicht in H. Biezais, *Skautnes*, S. 181–197.

[108] H. Biezais, „Svētā kategorijas sociālantropoloģiskais pamatojums" [Die sozialanthropologische Begründung der Kategorie des Heiligen], in *Filozofija un teoloģija. Rakstu krājums* [Philosophie und Theologie. Aufsätze] (Rīga: FSI, 1991), S. 32–37.

Söderblom zurück, ohne allerdings auf dessen Genese einzugehen. Die Bemerkung von Biezais, dass Söderblom seinen Begriff des Heiligen an der iranischen Religion entwickelt habe, entspricht auch nicht ganz dem Forschungsstand. Wenn Biezais zwei Begriffe des Heiligen postuliert (einen weiten und einen engen) und die supranaturalen Kategorien als zu eng abweist, übersieht er, dass dies bereits von Otto getan wurde. Bereits Rudolf Otto hatte auf supranaturale Kategorien als nur eine mögliche Manifestationsform des Heiligen verwiesen und alle Formen letztendlich anthropologisch verankert gesehen.

Für Biezais konnte jeder Gegenstand oder jedes Ereignis heilig sein oder auch entheiligt werden. Dafür prägte er den Ausdruck „die heilige Entheiligung des Heiligen",[109] die den möglichen Schwund des Heiligen auffängt (das Heilige wird immer nur ersetzt, nur durch anderes Heiliges beseitigt), und gibt dem Heiligen eine soziale Verankerung.[110] Die religiösen Bewegungen der Seele, die empirisch zu beobachten Biezais den Religionswissenschaftler auffordert, um sich gegen eine Theologisierung zu wappnen, sind zunächst als solche zu erkennen. Das Ergebnis ist letztendlich eine Ontologisierung des Heiligen auf Kosten einer instabilen Balance zwischen psychologischen und sozial-psychologischen Zugangsweisen aufrechtzuerhalten.

In einem breiteren Diskurs von Historikern und Schriftstellern wurde die lettische Geschichte als ein „Schicksalsweg" aufgefasst, der zum Teil auch über die Schicksalsgötting in der lettischen Religionsgeschichte verortet wurde.[111] Der „Schicksalsbegriff"[112] in der lettischen Religion brachte das Sich-nicht-entscheiden-Können und die (göttliche)

---

[109] H. Biezais, „Reliģiju zinātne atver brīvības vārtiņus. Nikandra Gilla intervija ar Prof. H. Biezo" [Die Religionswissenschaft öffnet die Türe zur Freiheit. Interview von Nikandrs Gills mit Prof. H. Biezais], ebd., 2001, S. 248–265, bes. S. 251ff.

[110] H. Biezais, „Svētā kategorijas sociālantropoloģiskais pamatojums", S. 33.

[111] Die Schicksalsgöttin Laima ist neben Dievs „Bestimmerin des menschlichen Lebens", „Bestimmerin des Lebenslaufes" (Biezais, *Die Hauptgöttinen der alten Letten*, S. 123f.). Ihre Setzung ist unabänderlich und für sie „sind schon am Anfang alle künftigen Lebensereignisse bekannt" (ebd., S. 126). Laima wird auch „paralell mit Gott erwähnt, als Bestimmerin über diejenigen, die leben oder sterben müssen. (...) Sie allein bestimmt über die Länge des Lebenslaufes" (ebd., S. 129).

[112] Den Begriff des Schicksals thematisierte in der zeitgenössischen Philosophie in Lettland Teodor Celms, doch es ist hier nicht möglich, darauf näher einzugehen. Es sei nur darauf hingewiesen, dass Celms damit der „Faktizität des Lebens" nachgehen und sie als eine irrationale Gegebenheit sehen wollte. Celms bewertete Husserls Phänomenologie als einen einseitigen Rationalismus: „Alles weist wie wier schon zur Genüge wissen auf die Faktizität des Lebens zurück, und diese als solche ist, trotz aller absoluten apriorischen Regelung, ewig irrational." T. Celms, *Der phänomenologische Idealismus Husserls*, S. 423.

Bejahung dessen zum Ausdruck, was Biezais mit dem Begriff der „weinenden Laima" meinte. Bereits zu Beginn der 1950er Jahre schrieb er, dass anscheinend sogar „Laima selbst ihren Beschluss nicht mehr ändern" kann, so dass „die Bestimmerin des Lebenslaufes selbst über ihre Bestimmung weint".[113] Die Ursache dafür sah Biezais darin, dass diese selbst die „Mängel und Schwächen" ihrer Beschlüsse erkenne.[114] Später gab er in seinem Aufsatz „Die weinende Laima" diese Sicht der „weinenden Reflexion" der Göttin wieder auf.[115] Es ist nun nicht mehr die mangelnde Selbstkorrektur, die an Laima festgemacht wird, sondern die unfreiwillige Bejahung des Schicksals: „Man konnte das Leben nicht ändern, nur darüber weinen." Das stand nicht einmal in der Macht der angebeteten Göttin Laima. Der lettische Bauer musste sich damit abfinden, „dass seine Göttin zusammen mit ihm weint."[116] Ein solches Schicksalsverhängnis konterkarierte Biezais 1953 mit seinem Verweis auf den Begriff der Menschenwürde bei dem italienischen Humanisten Pico della Mirandola als ein sich frei entscheiden können und auch müssen.[117] Der Dezisionismus eines Mirandola ist die Kehrseite des Schicksalsbegriffs der an der Gestalt der Laima exemplifiziert wird.

Den fehlenden Einfluss auf die Geschichte kann man entweder göttlich rechtfertigen (die Weinende ist ja die Göttin und selbst ihr Weinen ist daher eine Art Bejahung) oder durch eine entschieden dezisionistische Theorie verdecken, die nicht nach dem Grund des konkreten Entscheidens fragt, das Entscheiden selbst aber auch nicht in Frage stellt. Die Aporie ist dann die, dass man sich der Entscheidung oder zumindest ihrer Begründung entzieht, die Realität aber akzeptiert und im Nachhinein mangels einer rationalen Begründung fast als heilig ansieht.[118] Ähnliche strukturelle Aporien finden wir bei Biezais öfters: Ulmanis war autoritär, durch Aktivität ausgezeichnet,[119] gleichzeitig soll

---

[113] H. Biezais, *Die Hauptgöttinnen der alten Letten*, S. 134.

[114] Ebd., S. 136.

[115] H. Biezais, „Raudošā Laima" [Die weinende Laima], in ders., *Latviešu kultūra laikmetu maiņās* [Die lettische Kultur im Wandel der Zeiten] (Stockholm: Ronzo Boktryckeri, 1966), S. 45–64.

[116] H. Biezais, *Die Hauptgöttinnen der alten Letten*, S. 58.

[117] Siehe H. Biezais, „Pico della Mirandolas anthropologische Anschauungen", *Spiritus et Veritas* (1953), S. 13–41.

[118] Die Holocaust-Debatte wird heute in Lettland auf ähnliche Weise geführt. Man hat nichts gemacht und dennoch alles richtig gemacht, was sich gegenseitig ausschließt.

[119] Seinen Widerpart in der lettischen Exil Kirche Teodors Grīnbergs nannte Biezais sogar „Träger der absoluten Macht". H. Biezais, *Ne ikkatrs, kas uz mani saka*, S. 56.

er als tragische Persönlichkeit (besonnene Passivität) fast „heilig" gewesen sein. Das neutestamentliche Gebot der Liebe, das sich reibungslos zu „anderen Werten" nur in der Heiligkeit verwirklichen lässt – eine Sicht die Biezais bereits in seiner Dissertation vertreten hat –, wird von ihm als eine schlichte Bürgerpflicht der Christen gesehen, um die Reflexionslücke im Entscheidungsprozess zu füllen. Da das Verhältnis von Liebe und Macht letztendlich paradox ist (E. Brunner), verhalten sich Liebe und Bürgerpflicht aporetisch zueinander.

Die strukturellen Aporien haben Biezais auch methodisch interessiert.[120] Ein solches Gegensatzpaar ist auch die versöhnende Gewalt: „Der dynamische Entwicklungsprozess selbst zwingt unaufhaltsam zu Gewalt, zur Zerstörung des ursprünglichen, historisch gebundenen, des Ganzen, da das der einzige Weg ist, zum Sinn der historischen Erscheinung zu gelingen".[121] Das Thema der Gewalt thematisierte Biezais auch am Beispiel des von Kai Munk 1936 geschriebenen Dramas „Sieger". Herodes, der Sadist fällt in Inkonsequenz und identifiziert sich mit der Gewalt Gottes.[122] Die religionsgeschichtlichen Studien zur lettischen Religion fungieren bei Biezais dagegen als ein Rückzugsort für seine wissenschaftliche Skepsis, stützen die Idee der Zugehörigkeit der lettischen zur indogermanischen (europäischen) Gemeinschaft. Zu einer Zeit, als sich Lettland unter sowjetischer Besatzung befand, soll die Berufung auf die hohe Kultur (das himmlische Pantheon, den Lichtgott) dazu beitragen, die strukturellen Aporien der Nachkriegszeit unter einem anderen „Schicksal" zum Ausdruck zu bringen.

Zusammenfassung

Haralds Biezais ist – wenn man sich der heuristischen Einteilung der Religionswissenschaft zur Zeit des Nationalsozialismus von Horst

---

[120] „Die Qualität des Göttlichen ist nicht abhängig von Funktionen und Ausdrucksformen, durch welche sie demonstriert wird. (...) Bei der Einordnung ist nur die jeweilige Situation entscheidend. (...) Dann ist der erlebte Teufel immer da." H. Biezais, „Der Gegengott als Grundelement religiöser Strukturen", S. 291.
[121] H. Biezais, *Kristiānisms laikmetu maiņā*, S. 116.
[122] „Sonst wäre er ja kein teuflischer Mensch, sondern Teufel." Biezais, *Šķautnes*, S. 58. Die Identifizierung Gottes mit der Gewalt sieht Biezais auch in der Darstellung von Batsebas Liebe zu David in dem Munk'schen Drama „Auserwählte": „Wer ist stärker in mir als ich selbst, wer ist der stärkste in der Welt? Also, Jahve treibt mich. (...) Also, meine Liebe zu dir ist ebenso heilig wie das Leben." Ebd., S. 65.

Junginger bedient – einer theologischen oder religiösen Religionswissenschaft zuzurechnen. Von Hause aus Theologe, wurde er während seiner Studienzeit an der Theologischen Fakultät in Riga religionsphänomenologisch ausgebildet. Die Religionsphänomenologie Rudolf Ottos war dort stark vertreten. Biezais relativierte das orthodox christliche Glaubensverständnis und lehnte deren religiöse Dogmatik weitgehend ab. Bis zu seinen letzten Werken hat er die Ansicht vertreten, dass Religion eine „eigenartige universelle Erscheinung des menschlichen Lebens" sei.[123] Bei Biezais trifft die „Relativierung des christlichen Absolutheitsanspruches" und die Beschwörung einer „Vielfalt religiöser Verhaltensweisen" vollkommen zu.[124] Mehr noch, diese Vielfalt entsprach für ihn als Anhänger eines freien Christentums seinem eigentlichen Religionsverständnis. In seiner frühen theologischen Periode fungierten jedoch nicht die historischen Religionen als Beleg für eine kirchlich nicht mehr gebundene Religionsauffassung sondern die Kulturwerte des lettischen Volkes bzw. die religiöse Persönlichkeit schlechthin. Auch darin erwies sich Biezais als guter Schüler Emil Brunners, dem die ekklesiologische Komponente zugunsten einer im Geist zusammengeführten Christusgemeinschaft zu kurz kam. Biezais' phänomenologischer Religionsauffassung und sein dynamischer Wahrheitsbegriff bildeten die formalen Voraussetzungen dafür, dass verschiedene religiöse Gehalte austauschbar wurden, ohne dass man den christlichen Bezugsrahmen verlassen musste. Das machte es überflüssig, bei der Rekonstruktion der lettischen Religion die christlichen Einflüsse auszublenden. Biezais wurde nie von der Intention getragen – und darin unterschied er sich von anderen Religionshistorikern und Volkskundlern in Lettland –, mit Hilfe einer Rekonstruktion des lettischen Heidentums das Christentum überwinden zu wollen. Er hatte nie die Idee, dass andere Religionen die Erwartungen, die an das Christentum gestellt werden, besser erfüllten könnten als dieses selbst. Geschult an der Dialogphilosophie Brunners und mit dem Vorbild Albert Schweitzers vor Augen, bildeten die Nüchternheit des Wissenschaftlers und das Ethos eines freien Christen bei ihm das erwünschte Selbstideal.

---

[123] H. Biezais, „Jauno reliģiju krāšņajā pasaulē", in *Reliģiski-filozofiski raksti* (Rīga: FSI, 1997), S. 178.

[124] Horst Junginger, „Einführung. Das Überleben der Religionswissenschaft im Nationalsozialismus", *Zeitschrift für Religionswissenschaft* 2 (2001), S. S. 149–167, hier S. 156.

540   IVETA LEITĀNE

Bibliographie

Biezais, Haralds. „Vienas lietas vajag" [Man braucht eines]. *Brīvā zeme* [Das freie Land], 30.11.1936.

——. „Domu izmaiņai. Mācītāja reliģiskā un ētiskā personība" [Die religiöse und ethische Persönlichkeit des Pfarrers]. *Ceļš* [Weg] 6, (1936), S. 374–383.

——. „Kristīgās un valstiskās apziņas problēma" [Das Problem des christlichen und staatlichen Bewusstseins]. *Sējējs* [Sämann] 6 (1938), S. 573–579.

——. *Bergsona reliģiskās atziņas* [Die religiösen Erkenntnisse Bergsons]. *Izglītības Ministrijas Mēnešraksts* [Monatschrift des Bildungsministeriums] 12 (1938), S. 681–686.

——. *Dzīvības un mīlestības sintēze kristīgajā humanitātē. Disertācija* [Synthese des Lebens und der Liebe in der christlichen Humanität]. Rīga: Autora izdevums, 1939.

——. *A. Šveicers, Lielais zinātnieks un ārsts āfrikas mūža mežos* [A. Schweitzer, Der große Wissenschaftler und Arzt in Urwäldern Afrikas]. Rīga: Ev.lut. Baznīcas Virsvalde, 1940.

——. „Vēsturisko patiesību dinamiskais raksturs" [Der dynamische Charakter der historischen Wahrheiten]. *Ceļš* 4 (1940), S. 249–259.

——. „Cilvēka atrašana" [Finden des Menschen]. *Tēvija* [Vaterland], 7.10.1941.

——. „Tautas goda sargātāji" [Wächter der Volksehre]. Ebd., 12.11.1941.

——. „Profesoru V. Maldoni pieminot" [Zum Andenken an Prof. Maldonis]. Ebd., 21.2.1942.

——. „Nākamā cilvēka vīzija" [Die Vision vom künftigen Menschen]. *Daugavas vēstnesis* [Daugavaser Bote], 10.5.1942.

——. „Dzīvības svētuma ieskatījums" [Einsicht in die Heiligkeit des Lebens]. *Daugavas vēstnesis*, 26.7.1942.

——. „Dievs likteņa cīņās" [Gott in Schicksalskämpfen]. *Baznīcas ziņas* [Kirchennachrichten], 30.8.1942.

——. „Vitālais cilvēks" [Der vitale Mensch]. *Mana māja* [Mein Zuhause] 22, 1943.

——. „Brūce dzīvības kokā" [Wunde im Lebensbaum]. *Daugavas vēstnesis*, 13.6.1943.

——. „Kaislību pozitīvā jēga" [Die positive Rolle der Leidenschaften]. *Daugavas vēstnesis*, 12.9.1943.

——. „Instinkts un inteliģence" [Instinkt und Intelligenz]. *Tēvija*, 27.11.1943.

——. *Kristiānisms laikmetu maiņā* [Christentum im Wandel der Zeit]. Rīga: Grāmatu apgādniecība A. Gulbis, 1943.

——. „Augšāmceltie cilvēki" [Auferweckte Menschen]. *Mana māja* 6, 1944.

——. „Organiskais un mehāniskais dzīves modelis (T. Celma lekcija)" [Das organiche und mechanische Lebensmodell]. *Līdums* [Neuland] 9, 1944.

——. „Tradīcijas un jaunradīšana" [Tradition und Neuschöpfung]. *Daugavas Vanagu Mēnešraksts* [Monatsschrift der Daugavas Falken], 1944.

——. „Pie dzīvības avotiem" [An den Quellen des Lebens]. *Laika balss* [Die Stimme der Zeit], 10.5.1944.

——. „Aicinājums mācītājiem" [Aufruf der Pfarrer]. *Latvju ziņas*, 14.12.1944.

——. „Ētiskās vērtības un to nesēji" [Die ethischen Werte und ihre Träger]. *Latviešu kalendārs*, Stokholmā 1946, S. 74–84.

——. „Rītdienai pretī" [Dem Morgen entgegen]. *Upsalas raksti* [Upsalas Schriften] 2, Stokholmā 1945, S. 2–4.

——. „Pico della Mirandolas anthropologische Anschauungen". *Spiritus et Veritas* (1953), S. 13–41.

——. „Reliģiskie motīvi Andreja Eglīša jaunajā dzeju krājumā" [Die religiösen Motive im jüngsten Band von Andrejs Eglītis]. *Latvija Amerikā* [Lettland in USA], 15.8.1953.

——. *Die Hauptgöttinnen der alten Letten*. Uppsala: Almqvist & Wiksells Boktryckeri AB, 1955

——. *Die Gottesgestalt der lettischen Volksreligion.* Uppsala: Almqvist & Wiksells Boktryckeri AB, 1961.

——. *Kristiānisms. Nacionālisms. Humānisms* [Christentum. Nationalismus. Humanismus]. Kopenhavn: Imanta, 1953.

——. „Kristiānisma vēsturiskā vide" [Die historische Umwelt des Christentums]. In ders., Hg., *Ieskatītais un atzītais, veltījums Prof. Teodoram Celmam* [Das Eingesehene und das Erkannte. Prof. Theodor Celms gewidmet]. Stokholma: Daugava, 1963, S. 55–78.

——. „Raudošā Laima" [Die weinende Laima]. In ders., *Latviešu kultūra laikmetu maiņās* [Die lettische Kultur im Wandel der Zeiten]. Stockholm: Ronzo Boktryckeri, 1966, S. 45–64.

——. *Die himmlische Götterfamilie der alten Letten.* Uppsala: Almqvist & Wiksells Boktryckeri AB, 1972.

—— Hg. *New Religions. Based on Papers read at the Symposium on New Religions held at Abo on the 1st–3rd of September 1974.* Stockholm: Almqvist & Wiksell, 1975.

—— Hg. *Ne ikkatrs, kas uz mani saka... Mācītāja Roberta Slokenberga piemiņas rakstu krājums* [Nicht jeder, der zu mir sagt... Erinnerungsband zu Ehren von Roberts Slokenbergs]. Vasteras: Andersson & Kagardt Tryckeri AB, 1975.

——. *Lichtgott der alten Letten.* Uppsala: Almqvist & Wiksells Boktryckeri AB, 1976.

——. „Transformation und Identifikation der Götter im Synkretismus". *Temenos* 11 (1976), S. 5–25.

——. „Vom Sinn der religionswissenschaftlichen Forschung". *Theologia practica* 13 (1978), S. 159–163.

——. „Typology of Religion and the Phenomenological Method. In Lauri Honko, ed., *Science of religion, studies in methodology. Proceedings of the study conference of the international association for the history of religions, held in Turku, Finland August 27–31, 1973.* The Hague: Mouton, 1979, S. 143–161.

——. *Šķautnes, Meditācija par dieviem, cilvēkiem un tautu* [Facetten. Meditation von Göttern, Menschen und Volk]. Istlansinga: Gaujas apgāds, 1983.

——. „Kajs Munks, ziemeļzemju dzejnieks, praviets un moceklis" [Kai Munk, Dichter, Prophet und Märtyrer der nordischen Länder]. Ebd., S. 39–69.

——. „Niks Kazantzakis – dieva cīnītājs" [Nikos Kazantzakis – Gottesbekämpfer]. Ebd., S. 70–81.

——. „Der Gegengott als Grundelement religiöser Strukturen". *Saeculum* 34–3/4 (1983), S. 280–291.

——. *Smaidošie dievi un cilvēka asara* [Die lächelnden Götter und eine Menschenträne]. Plön: Senatne, 1991.

——. *Kurelieši. Nacionālās pretestības liecinieki* [Kurelisleute. Zeugen des nationalen Widerstands]. Ithaka: Mežābele, 1991.

——. „Svētā kategorijas sociālantropoloģiskais pamatojums" [Die sozialanthropologische Begründung der Kategorie des Heiligen]. In Maija Kūle, Hg., *Filozofija un teoloģija. Rakstu krājums* [Philosophie und Theologie. Aufsätze]. Rīga, FSI, 1991, S. 32–37.

——. *Saki tā, kā tas ir* [Sag' mal, wie es ist]. Rīga: Svētdienas Rīts, 1995 (1. Aufl. Īstlansinga: Gauja, 1986).

——. *Latvija kāškrusta varā* [Lettland unter der Macht des Hakenkreuzes]. Īstlansinga: Gauja, 1992

—— Hg. *Reliģiski-filozofiski raksti,* Bd. 6. Rīga: FSI, 1997.

——. „Reliģiju zinātne atver brīvības vārtiņus. Nikandra Gilla intervija ar Prof. H. Biezo" [Die Religionswissenschaft öffnet die Türe zur Freiheit. Interview von Nikandrs Gills mit Prof. H. Biezais]. Ebd., 2001, S. 248–265.

——. „Meditācijas par noskrandušo vēsturi" [Meditationen von der Geschichte in Fetzen]. In *Reliģiski-filozofiski raksti,* Bd. VII. Rīga: FSI, 2001, S. 223–237.

——. „Jauno reliģiju krāšņajā pasaulē" [In der schillernden Welt der neuen Religionen]. Ebd., 2003, S. 266–276.

Brunner, Emil. *Das Gebot und die Ordnungen. Entwurf einer protestantisch-theologischen Ethik.* Tübingen: Mohr, 1932.

Celms, Theodor. *Tagadnes problēmas* [Probleme der Gegenwart]. Rīga: Valters un Rapa, 1934.

——. *Der phänomenologische Idealismus Husserls.* Riga: Acta Universitatis Latviensis 19, 1928 (Nachdruck, New York: Garland, 1979).

Junginger, Horst. Einführung: Das Überleben der Religionswissenschaft im Nationalsozialismus. *Zeitschrift für Religionswissenschaft* 2 (2001), S. 149–167.

Leese, Kurt. *Die Religion des protestantischen Menschen.* München, J. & S. Federmann Verlag, 1938.

Luven, Yvonne. *Der Kult der Hausschlange. Eine Studie zur Religionsgeschichte der Letten und Litauer.* Böhlau Verlag Köln, Weimar, Wien. 2001.

Müller, Alfred Dedo. *Ethik: der evangelische Weg der Verwirklichung des Guten.* Berlin: Toepelmann, 1937.

Schweitzer, Albert. *Kultur und Ethik. Kulturphilosophie*, Bd. 2., 3. Aufl. München, Becksche Verlagsbuchhandlung, 1923.

THE ESSENCE OF CONCRETE INDIVIDUALITY
GERARDUS VAN DER LEEUW, JAN DE VRIES, AND NATIONAL SOCIALISM

Willem Hofstee

> The existence of a vital tradition of scientific analysis of cultural and social issues, such as religion and its relation to politics, is one of the most effective guarantees against ideological extremism
> — Clifford Geertz[1]

In the early morning on May 10th, 1940, German troops invaded the Netherlands and occupied the whole country after a heavy five days battle with the Dutch army. The country was ripped of a home-made neutrality, nourished since the beginning of the First World War, within the blink of an eye.

That same day an article appeared in the widely read Dutch magazine *General Weekly for Christianity and Culture*, in which the reader is told to trust the political neutrality of the Dutch government because it will be respected by everyone, and not to hope for a victory of the allied forces because "such a victory would only differ gradually from a victory of the totalitarians." The article continues by saying that

> victories, including the one in 1918, are always a disaster for all parties involved; the best thing to do is staying neutral...It is certain that only a small part of the German population is in favor of National Socialist ideas, and that only a small part of that particular group supports the German leadership with devotion.

The author of the article was Gerardus van der Leeuw, professor at the University of Groningen, and at the time a leading scholar of religion in the Netherlands and Europe.[2]

A few months after the invasion, a small booklet was published in which the Dutch population is called upon to act in favor of nationalism

---

[1] Clifford Geertz, *The Interpretation of Cultures* (New York: Harper & Row, 1973), p. 232.
[2] Gerardus van der Leeuw, "De positieve waarde van onze neutraliteit," *Algemeen Weekblad voor Christendom en Cultuur* 16, May 10, 1940.

and socialism, being two important aspects of the 'new order'.[3] In the book it is stated that "atrocities never can be a reason to criticize or condemn a certain ideology, because the only way to change things is the radical one."[4] The book advocates the acceptance of German leadership in Europe, the promotion of a nationalist and colonialist policy, and the elimination of democracy as the political structure of the state. The author of the booklet was Jan de Vries, professor at the University of Leiden, and a well known expert on the comparative study of Indo-European languages, and the religion and mythology of the ancient Germans.

In my short contribution to this conference I will look both at Van der Leeuw's and De Vries' struggle in coping with the political events in Europe between 1933 and 1945. And I must confess that I have more questions than answers when it comes to this issue. Looking at the socio-political writings of both scholars during the inter-war years, there is not so much difference between them regarding the analysis of the general cultural crisis. But in the case of Van der Leeuw the outcome has been different from De Vries. Van der Leeuw was arrested by the Germans in 1943, De Vries joined the SS in the same year; Van der Leeuw was appointed to the government just after the war, De Vries was convicted to twelve months imprisonment for 'intellectual collaboration' with the German Nazis, and lost his professorship and his political rights. Despite the differences in outcome, there is at the same time a similarity between the two which I consider as being crucial: Both scholars were not satisfied with the actual political system of parliamentary democracy, and both were convinced that the community (*Gemeinschaft*) should be placed above the individual. It seems to me that precisely this could be a key to understand both Van der Leeuw and De Vries in their dealings with National Socialism. Both scholars were also very concerned with big issues like 'the future of western civilization', 'the loss of values and moral', 'the decadence in art and music', and so on. Their cultural critique is in fact only critical to a certain extent: Most of it seems to be more a cultural pessimism, and a moral disagreement with ideas and practices which they both

---

[3] Jan de Vries, *Naar een betere Toekomst* (Amsterdam: Elsevier, 1940).
[4] Ibid., p. 45.

considered harmful to the *Gemeinschaft.* First I will look at Van der Leeuw's ideas, then I will turn to De Vries.[5]

Van der Leeuw (1890–1950) considered German National Socialism and Russian communism as equally great threats to western civilization because of their nihilistic character. A few years before the Nazis came to power in Germany, Van der Leeuw expressed his concern about the loss of values in modern society, and about the cultural crisis in Europe. For him the three main shortcomings of modern times were the lack of community, authority, and belief. These three inseparable 'basics' he saw as antidotes to modern man falling victim to nihilism and despair. In both 'primitive society' and the ancient world, these notions were present because there collective representation was a central element. Lucien Lévy-Bruhl's notion of the *mentalité primitive* has had a great influence on Van der Leeuw's ideas about the structure of the human mind. Not only in his phenomenological method and in his idea of science in general, but also in his critique of culture Van der Leeuw recalls Karl Jaspers' existential analysis of modern society.[6] Because of his many contacts in Germany, Van der Leeuw was well aware of the difficult situation which many German intellectuals, Jews in particular, were facing. Already in 1933 he urged, together with a few colleagues in Groningen, to help Jews who were in need, but the Dutch Protestant Church did not respond. At first Van der Leeuw is mainly concerned with theological and ecclesiastical issues, but after 1933 his critique of culture becomes more sermonizing, more concerned with social institutions, cultural forms, and ways of life. In 1935 Van der Leeuw considered the thoughts of Hitler's ideologist Alfred Rosenberg as an illustration of the decline of values and morals.

Despite all this, he did not join one of the most important protest groups of Dutch intellectuals against National Socialism and antisemitism,

---

[5] On Van der Leeuw see Willem Hofstee, *Goden en Mensen. De Godsdienstwetenschap van Gerardus van der Leeuw 1890–1950* (Kampen: Agora, 1997). A revised English edition is in preparation. See also W. Hofstee, "Religion and Ideology: Dutch Science of Religion during the Cold War," in Iva Doležalová et al., eds., *The Academic Study of Religion During the Cold War* (New York: Peter Lang, 2001), pp. 239–252. There is still no intellectual biography on Jan de Vries. Biographical information in this article is based on Pieter J. Meertens, "Jan de Vries," *Volkskunde* 65 (1964), pp. 97–113 and on Andries Dierk. Kylstra, *Het naoorlogse beeld van de oudgermanist Jan de Vries* (Groningen: no publisher, 1999).

[6] About Jaspers' influence on Van der Leeuw see also Jürgen Kehnscherper, *Theologisch-philosophische Aspekte der religionsphänomenologischen Methode des Gerardus van der Leeuw* (Frankfurt a.M.: Peter Lang, 1998).

the "Committee of Vigilance." This group was founded in 1936, following the French *Comité de vigilance des intellectuels antifascistes*. The group also protested against the Dutch government, dominated by a coalition of conservative Christian democrats, because it banned meetings, theater plays, exhibitions, and radio broadcasts, which could be interpreted as being 'anti-German'. The Dutch government wanted to stay neutral at any price: In 1936 one could end up in jail for insulting Hitler, and in 1937 in The Hague a theater play was forbidden because it criticized the Nazis. The Dutch government even recognized the invasion of Ethiopia by Mussolini's fascist army. But none of this convinced Van der Leeuw to join the group of protesting intellectuals. For two reasons. First, he wanted to be neutral himself, to be above any political party or group. For him it could not be possible that Germany, the country of philosophers, musicians, writers, and scientists, had turned into a terrorist state. Secondly, the "Committee of Vigilance" also consisted of communists. At the time Van der Leeuw was asked to join the group, his irritated answer was: "I prefer Franco!"[7] This reaction has to be seen as an illustration of the strong anti-communist atmosphere in The Netherlands in those days, which was much more widespread than for instance in France. Communism was seen as anti-religious, and Franco and Mussolini at least were defending the church against the pagan Bolsheviks.

In 1939 Gustav Mensching had asked Van der Leeuw to consider leaving out the names of Jewish authors, in this case Lévy-Bruhl and Cassirer, in a planned German translation of one of his major works.[8] Van der Leeuw only agreed with the omission of the address to Lévy-Bruhl at the beginning of the book. Because of difficulties with the translation, the German edition of this book never appeared.[9] Van der Leeuw's anti-communism was stronger than his fear of National Socialism and fascism, which does not mean that he was in favor of these last two ideologies, given the fact that on many places he has written against National Socialism and fascism. Not only for Van der

---

[7] Letter of H.J. Pos to H. Plessner on October 2, 1936 (Personal Archives of Helmuth Plessner, University Library Groningen); see also Menno ter Braak & Edgar du Perron, *Briefwisseling. Een Bloemlezing* (Amsterdam: Van Oorschot, 1952), p. 486.

[8] I am referring to G. v.d. Leeuw, *De Primitieve Mensch en de Religie* (Groningen: J.B. Wolters, 1937), not to be confused with his *Der Mensch und die Religion* (Basel: Haus zum Falken, 1941). The letter with Mensching's request to Van der Leeuw is dated June 16, 1939 (Van der Leeuw Archives, University Library Groningen).

[9] See for more details Hofstee, *Goden en mensen*, pp. 78–81.

Leeuw, but for many people in the Netherlands communism was 'the big fear', because of its economic state monopolism, and its anti religious doctrine. At first Hitler was given the benefit of the doubt, because everyone felt it necessary to end "the nude gymnastics and left wing policy of the Weimar Republic." Besides, all the wild stories about the Germans planning to capture all of Europe were told by communists, and who would believe them? Many were the silent admirers of what had been achieved in Italy and Germany concerning the organization of *Volkseinheit*. Many were the politicians who favored powerful political leadership, who criticized parliamentary democracy as it existed, and who suggested political reorganizations along corporative lines.[10] The 'crisis of democracy' was a favorite theme of discussion, and precisely this is one of the reasons for the rise of fascist ideologies.

So, looking at the general picture, Van der Leeuw has not been much of an exception when it comes to his critique of culture. Neither was he an exception when he joined the political movement which proposed a 'critical collaboration' with the German oppressors in 1940, since many intellectuals and politicians did the same. The movement collapsed after a year, because 'critical' collaboration turned out to be impossible. In the meantime the Nazis had taken over the universities, and especially in Groningen their influence was strong. All Jewish scholars were already fired in 1940, and in 1943 all the students were forced to sign a document of loyalty to the Nazis. Many refused, among them Van der Leeuw's two sons. They both had joined the student resistance, and presumably because of their activities Van der Leeuw was arrested and interrogated by the *Sicherheitsdienst* in Groningen. They could not find anything against him, so he was released. During the rest of the war Van der Leeuw kept a low profile. He published a few articles on ancient Egypt and a book about the poetry of Novalis, and succeeded in surviving without much personal damage.

Jan de Vries (1890–1964) had already been active in an anti-democratic, nationalist right-wing group in 1919. His interest in Germanic studies arose earlier during his years as a student in Amsterdam. In 1926 he was appointed professor at the University of Leiden. He developed himself into a well-known expert, especially in ancient Germanic mythology and religion. Between 1926 and 1940 De Vries published many articles and books not only on the religion and myths

---

[10] Ernst H. Kossmann, *De Lage Landen 1780–1940* (Amsterdam: Elsevier, 1976), p. 440.

of ancient Germans (in which we find ideas similar to those of scholars like Stig Wikander and Georges Dumézil), but also on the nature of Dutch culture and its *voelkish* national identity. Before the Second World War Jan de Vries was a well-respected academic. His conservative anti-democratic ideas, his anti-British sentiment as a result from his favoring of the South African Boers, and his pro-German sentiment during the First World War did not cause much criticism because it fitted rather well into the general atmosphere in The Netherlands during the inter-war years.

However, things rapidly changed after May 10, 1940. After their take-over the Germans looked for co-operators, also among university professors. De Vries was important for the Germans in their attempt to convert the Dutch nation to their National Socialist ideology, although he had criticized the anti-Christian racist ideology of the Nazis. Nevertheless De Vries turned out to be a co-operative National Socialist who was useful for the Germans. He published in NS magazines, participated in conferences organized by the Nazis, made trips to Germany and the occupied territories in Eastern Europe, and even joined the *Allgemeine SS* in 1943. Earlier De Vries had also joined *Das Ahnenerbe*, the continuation of the *Studiengesellschaft für Geistesurgeschichte Deutsches Ahnenerbe*, founded by Heinrich Himmler and others in 1935. Although De Vries never participated in any military action, nor was given any assignment as a member of *Das Ahnenerbe*, his association with both organizations and his active collaboration with the German oppressor has been the major ground for his arrest after the war. After the invasion of the allied troops in Normandy in 1944, De Vries decided to leave the city of Leiden. He fled to Leipzig, where he was welcomed by members of the *Ahnenerbe*. He got a job, paid by the *Deutsche Forschungsgemeinschaft*, and started working on a 13th century Nordic text. But again his scientific work was interrupted, this time by the invasion of the Russian troops and the capitulation of Germany. He managed to escape to the western area, and settled down in the neighborhood of Göttingen. But he was arrested in October 1946. After a year of imprisonment in Fallingbostel and Recklinghausen, he was transported to the Dutch prison of Vught. His trial took place in May 1948, and he was convicted of 'serious intellectual collaboration'. After his release he earned his money with teaching at a high school in Zeeland, and managed to continue his scientific work. In 1957 he moved to the city of Utrecht. Until his death in 1964 he published many articles and books on the religion and culture of the Celts and Germans, and on northern mythology and etymology.

As I have said before: I have more questions than answers. Did the spirit of the inter-war years shape both Van der Leeuw's and De Vries' study of religion, and if so, how did this process of shaping took place? What then would be the prime movers in this process? The intellectual field is a social composition of human relations in which competition, authority and prestige play a role. The reconstruction of these kinds of relations seems relevant for the understanding of the genesis of intellectual products. At the same time the socio-cultural and political situation in which both scholars operated seem crucial when it comes to the shaping of ideas. The question is: How do both factors relate to each other? During the inter-war years European cultural history is marked by a decline of the belief in progress, and the predictions of the Enlightenment were met by skepticism. Many were the diagnoses of the crisis in western culture. In The Netherlands the dominant conservative sentiment succeeded in creating a period of political stability after the First World War, despite the ideological and religious contradictions, and the existence of a poignant social inequality. This political stability was mainly due to the pillarized structure of Dutch society, where the people were brought together in separate social organizations based on different religious denominations. Due to the relative safety of these organizations, the people became more and more dependent on them, and, as a result of that, became more politically apathetic at the same time.

In this situation parliamentary democracy was threatened in two ways. First, the system was dependent on the passivity of the subjects, and, secondly, it gave room for politicians to question the consistency of the democratic parliamentary system. The American historian Robert Paxton has stated that the role of intellectuals lies precisely there where they question both the values of the Enlightenment, and the consistency of the parliamentary system.[11] The affirmation or rejection of the legitimacy of authority is a major preoccupation of every form of intellectual life. It could not be otherwise, since intellectual life could not exist without the authority of tradition: An inherited corpus of works/texts and standards for the production of works of high quality,

---

[11] Robert Paxton, *The Anatomy of Fascism* (New York: Knopf, 2004).

or without the creativity which challenges the authority of tradition. Authority, furthermore, engages the minds of intellectuals, especially those active in primary intellectual production, for instance philologists like De Vries. The American sociologist Edward Shils has described the involvement in primary intellectual production as a pursuit of 'the essential' and the sacred, and political authority claims a similar involvement on behalf of its legitimacy. Intellectual action, arisen out of religious preoccupations, continues to share with genuine religious experience the fascination with the sacred, or the ultimate ground of thought and experience, and the aspiration to enter into intimate contact with it. In secular intellectual work this concern involves the search for the truth, for the principles embedded in events and actions and for the establishment of a relationship between the empirical self and the 'essential,' whether the relationship be cognitive, appreciative, or expressive. It is therefore no stretching of the term 'religion' to say that science and philosophy, and even politics, even though they are not religious in a conventional sense, are as concerned with the sacred as religion itself.[12] In this respect it is important again to investigate the religious aspect of today's American political leadership, and the way it uses religious phrases and symbols.

Here we are discussing men of science (it is a gender problem also, since there are no women involved so far!), in this case scholars of religion who have been wrong or partly wrong in the past, but do we know where we stand right now? How critical are we at this very moment towards ourselves as scholars of religion when it comes to the hidden agendas of today's politics? This question is even more relevant since both Van der Leeuw and De Vries share their heritage in the romantic tradition, which starts with the appreciation of the spontaneous manifestations of the essence of concrete individuality, a theme which is still popular today. Institutions with rules prescribing the conduct of the individual in the public sphere, are viewed as destroying life. The bourgeois family, mercantile activity, civil society in general, with its curb on enthusiasm and its sober acceptance of obligation, are repugnant to the romantic tradition. All are regarded as the enemies of spontaneity and genuineness, since they impose a role on the individual and do not permit him to be himself. They also

---

[12] Edward Shils, "Intellectuals," *International Encyclopedia of the Social Sciences* 7 (New York: Macmillan, 1970), pp. 399–414.

kill what is really living in the general population, that is the spontaneous and undeliberate. Civil society is thought to have no place for the intellectual who thus becomes afflicted with a sense of his moral solitude within it. Moral solitude is viewed as the natural condition of the spontaneous individuality in a society of philistines living a routine existence. Again according to Shils, the romantic tradition is one of the most explosively anti-authoritarian and even anti-civil powers of modern intellectual life.

Together with one of its offsprings, populism, the belief in the creativity and superior moral power of the ordinary people, romanticism can be found in several New Religious Movements and New Age groups today. It is high time to study these movements not only for their interesting religious contents, but also for the political implications these contents might have.[13] Only then it is possible to develop a critical attitude towards oneself, and to be able to understand others.

---

[13] Pioneering work in this field has been done by Nicolas Goodrick-Clark, *Black Sun. Aryan Cults, Esoteric Nazism and the Politics of Identity* (New York-London: New York University Press, 2002).

Bibliography

Braak, Menno ter and Edgar Du Perron. *Briefwisseling. Een Bloemlezing*. Amsterdam: Van Oorschot, 1952.

Geertz, Clifford. *The Interpretation of Cultures*. New York: Harper & Row, 1973.

Kippenberg, Hans G. and Brigitte Luchesi, eds. *Religionswissenschaft und Kulturkritik*. Marburg: Diagonal Verlag, 1991.

Hofstee, Willem. *Goden en Mensen. De Godsdienstwetenschap van Gerardus van der Leeuw 1890–1950*. Kampen: Agora, 1997.

——. "Religion and Ideology: Dutch Science of Religion during the Cold War." In Iva Dolezalová et al., eds., *The Academic Study of Religion During the Cold War*. New York: Peter Lang, 2001, pp. 239–252.

Doležalová, Iva et al., eds. *The Academic Study of Religion During the Cold War*. New York: Peter Lang, 2001.

Cancik, Hubert, ed. *Religions- und Geistesgeschichte der Weimarer Republik*. Düsseldorf: Patmos, 1982.

Schuller, Wolfgang, ed. *Antike in der Moderne*. Konstanz: Universitätsverlag, 1985.

Faber, Richard and Renate Schlesier, eds. *Die Restauration der Götter. Antike Religion und Neo-Paganismus*. Würzburg: Königshausen & Neumann, 1986.

Geertz, Clifford. *The Interpretation of Cultures*. New York: Harper & Row, 1973.

Goodrick-Clarke, Nicholas. *Black Sun. Aryan Cults, Esoteric Nazism and the Politics of Identity*. New York-London: New York University Press, 2002.

Gugenberger, Eduard et al., eds. *Weltverschwörungstheorien: Die neue Gefahr von Rechts*. Wien: F. Deuticke, 1998.

Kehnscherper, Jürgen. *Theologisch-philosophische Aspekte der religionsphänomenologischen Methode des Gerardus van der Leeuw*. Frankfurt a.M.: Peter Lang, 1998.

Kossmann, Ernst H. *De Lage Landen 1780–1940*. Amsterdam: Elsevier, 1976.

Kylstra, Andries Dierk. *Het naoorlogse beeld van de oudgermanist Jan de Vries*. Groningen: no publisher, 1999.

Leeuw, Gerardus van der. *La Structure de la Mentalité Primitive*. Paris: Alcan, 1928.

——. *De Primitieve Mensch en de Religie*. Groningen: Wolters, 1937.

——. *Phänomenologie der Religion*. Tübingen: J.C.B. Mohr, 1933.

——. *Gemeenschap, Gezag, Geloof*. Groningen: Wolters, 1937.

——. "De positieve waarde van onze neutraliteit." *Algemeen Weekblad voor Christendom en Cultur* 16, May 10, 1940.

——. *Der Mensch und die Religion*. Basel: Haus zum Falken, 1941.

Lijphart, Arend. *The Politics of Accomodation: Pluralism and Democracy in The Netherlands*. Berkeley: University of California Press, 1968.

Meertens, Pieter J. "Jan de Vries." *Volkskunde* 65 (1964), pp. 97–113.

Paxton, Robert. *The Anatomy of Fascism*. New York: Alfred Knopf, 2004.

Shils, Edward. "Intellectuals." *International Encyclopedia of the Social Sciences* 7 (New York: Macmillan, 1970), pp. 399–414.

Vries, Jan de. *Naar een betere Toekomst*. Amsterdam: Elsevier, 1940.

——. *Perspectives in the History of Religions*. Berkeley: University of California Press, 1977 (1st ed. 1961).

ÅKE OHLMARKS IN THE THIRD REICH

A SCIENTIFIC CAREER BETWEEN ADAPTATION, COOPERATION AND IGNORANCE

Andreas Åkerlund

1. *Preface*

In November 1944 an institute of science of religions was founded at the Ernst Moritz Arndt University of Greifswald. The institute was short-lived and only existed until the end of the war. Its director and co-founder was the Swedish philologist and historian of religions Åke Ohlmarks who had been a lecturer in Swedish at the university since 1941. This post as director was to be the peak of his scientific career in the Third Reich.

Although not a very central person in the history of the academic study of religions, there are reasons to take a closer look at the biography of Ohlmarks. At a time when many scientists had been forced to leave Germany he had chosen to go in the opposite direction, leaving the neutral country of Sweden for the National Socialist state. The first bundle of questions which I will try to answer in this article therefore considers Ohlmarks' motives: Why did an academic career in the Third Reich seem more attractive to Ohlmarks than staying in Sweden? Was he a right-wing *voelkish* scholar, moving to Germany out of sympathy for the National Socialist movement or did he have other reasons than ideological ones?

Another set of questions concerns Ohlmarks' position in the academic field. His rise to director of the institute of science of religions in Greifswald would have been impossible without support from groups and persons supporting the National Socialist state. Fritz Heinrich has investigated the founding of this institute, suggesting in his article that Ohlmarks took advantage of the chances existing in the Third Reich for Scandinavian scholars.[1] Which were these chances for Ohlmarks in

---

[1] Fritz Heinrich, "Das religionswissenschaftliche Institut der Ernst Moritz Arndt-Universität Greifswald 1944–1945," *Zeitschrift für Religionswissenschaft* 5 (1997), pp. 215f.

particular? Or, to formulate the question more precisely: Which were his contacts in the scientific field of the study of religions in the Third Reich and why did he profit from them? Another question addresses Ohlmarks' position within the context of a *voelkish* science. How did he position himself towards *voelkish* scholars of religion such as Jakob Wilhelm Hauer or Otto Höfler? In contrasting Ohlmarks' writings with the academic and political context in which they were written, I will try to show that a cooperation with National Socialist groups did not necessarily lead to an embracement of *voelkish* positions.

2. Åke Ohlmarks' Scientific Advancement in Sweden

Åke Ohlmarks was born in 1911 near Kristianstad in the south of Sweden. He studied philosophy, history of religions and Nordic philology at the University of Lund between 1929 and 1932 where he also acted as editor in chief of the student magazine *Lundagård*.

Like most of his fellow students Ohlmarks had a conservative worldview. The majority of the Swedish students came from the upper and middle classes, disliking the workers' movement and the coalition government between social democrats and liberals who ruled Sweden in the 1930s. In the political discussion leftist groups were accused of receiving financial aid from the Soviet Union. In 1809 Russia, the old enemy of Sweden, had conquered Finland and destroyed the Swedish empire. Ohlmarks was no exception to the rule, often taking a strong anti-communist stance in his articles for *Lundagård* as well as in his autobiography.[2]

The attitude of Swedish conservative groups towards Nazi Germany and National Socialism, the German NSDAP and its Swedish counterparts, was ambivalent.[3] On one hand they distanced themselves from

---

[2] See Åke Ohlmarks, *I Paradiset. Levnadsminnen I* [In paradise. Memories of my life I] (Uddevalla: Zindermans, 1965), p. 271 and idem, *Efter mig Syndafloden. Greifswald-Berlin-Hamburg 1941–1945* [After me the flood] (Köping: Lindfors, 1980), p. 154.

[3] For an overview of the research on Swedish fascism and National Socialism, see Bernt Hagtvet, "On the Fringe: Swedish Fascism 1920–1945," in Stein Ugelvik Larsen et al., eds., *Who were the Fascists? Social Roots of European Fascism* (Bergen: Universitetsforlaget, 1980), pp. 715–742 and Lena Berggren, "Swedish Fascism – Why Bother?," *Journal of Contemporary History* 37-3 (2002), pp. 395–417. The Swedish political parties on the extreme right are treated by Helene Lööw in *Hakkorset och Wasakärven. En studie av nationalsocialismen i Sverige 1924–1950* [Swastika and Wasa-sheaf. A study of National Socialism in Sweden 1924–1950] (Göteborg: Göteborgs Universitet, 1990) and idem

the small Swedish parties of the extreme right. But on the other hand they saw parts of NS politics such as a strong army and harder laws against 'communists' as a possibility for Sweden as well. Last but not least the Swedish conservatives had been great admirers of culture and science of the old German empire and many hoped that Nazi Germany in one way or the other would develop into a resurrection of the old imperial Germany as it had existed before 1914.[4]

Ohlmarks shared the same ambivalence. He had learned German at school and admired the German cultural and scientific tradition. To some extent he seems to have been an admirer of National Socialism as well, at least in his student years. In 1933 Ohlmarks published an article in *Lundagård*, in which he attacked liberals and leftists at the university, accusing them of being elitists, lame and over-intellectualizing. As a counterexample Ohlmarks pointed to the German Nazi movement and called it a youth organization possessing a goal to fight for.[5] In this article, the 22-year old student is clearly showing sympathy for the new Germany although it remains unclear how big these sympathies were. But Ohlmarks was politically inactive and not a member of a political group or party.

After finishing his studies, Ohlmarks worked as a lecturer in the Swedish language at the universities of Tübingen (1933–1934) and Reykjavik (1935). In 1937 he presented his doctoral thesis *Heimdalls*

Nazismen i Sverige 1924–1979: pionjärerna, partierna, propagandan [Nazism in Sweden: the pioneers, the parties the propaganda] (Stockholm: Ordfront, 2004). Contemporary publications on antisemitism and *voelkish* ideology include Mattias Tydén, *Svensk antisemitism 1880–1930* [Swedish antisemitism 1880–1930] (Uppsala: Centre for Multiethnic Research, 1986), Lars Trädgårdh, "Varieties of Volkish Ideologies: Sweden and Germany 1848–1933," in Bo Stråth, ed., *Language and the Construction of Class Identities. The Struggle for Discursive Power in Social Organisation: Scandinavia and Germany after 1800* (Göteborg: Göteborgs Universitet, 1990), pp. 25–54, Lena Berggren, *Nationell upplysning. Drag i den svenska antisemitismens idéhistoria* [National enlightenment: Traits in the history of Swedish antisemitism] (Stockholm: Carlsson, 1999), and Lars M. Andersson, *En jude är en jude är en jude: Representationer av 'juden' i svensk skämtpress omkring 1900–1930* [A Jew is a Jew is a Jew: Representations of the Jew in Swedish comic press 1900–1930s] (Lund: Nordic Academic Press, 2000).

[4] Cf. Jonas Hansson, "Sweden and Nazism," in Stig Ekman and Klas Åmark, eds., *Sweden's relations with Nazism, Nazi Germany and the Holocaust* (Stockholm: Almqvist & Wiksell International, 2003), pp. 137–196.

[5] Å. Ohlmarks, "De negativistiska kulturessayisterna" [The negative culture essayists], *Lundagård* 6 (1933), p. 118. See also Sverker Oredsson, *Lunds universitet under andra världskriget. Motsättningar, debatter och hjälpinsatser* [The University of Lund during the second world war. Antagonisms, debates and aid-actions] (Lund: Lunds universitetshistoriska sällskap, 1996), pp. 23–25.

Horn und Odins Auge (Heimdall's horn and Odin's eye) which deals with
the Old Norse god Heimdall.[6] His main thesis is that Heimdall has to
be considered one of the oldest Norse gods, originally being the god of
the sun. As a philologist, Ohlmarks read all written sources on Heimdall
in the original. In fact, the philological discussion makes up a large
part of the book. As the written sources are very rare, Ohlmarks used
ethnographic material on beliefs in so-called primitive cultures, basically
from Polynesia, to prove his theory. The theoretical framework is made
up by the paradigm of natural mythology represented by scholars such
as Friedrich Max Müller. Wilhelm Schmidt's theory of cultural circles
(Kulturkreise) had a great impact on the work of Ohlmarks.[7]

Important for Ohlmarks is Schmidt's typology of cultures in matriarchal and patriarchal cultures. The Indo-Germanic culture, to which the
Norse culture belongs, is a patriarchal one, originally being a nomadic
culture of hunters. According to Ohlmarks it is a result of their way
of living that the sun becomes the most important astronomical phenomena. In the matriarchal cultures on the other hand, the moon is
the most important celestial body because of its greater importance to
agriculture.[8] The role this typology played in *Heimdalls Horn and Odins
Auge* cannot be fully grasped without knowing that Ohlmarks planned to
write a second book in which he wanted to show how Heimdall ceases
to be the highest god, leaving place for Odin. Ohlmarks' theory is that
traces of this process are to be found in the poem of *Völuspá*, in which
the "eye of Odin" and the "horn of Heimdall" are used alternately
to describe the same phenomenon.[9] According to Ohlmarks this phenomenon has to be the moon and the difference lies therein that the
horn is a thing whereas the eye is a part of the god, indicating that
Odin originally had to be a moon god. The fact that the importance
of Heimdall ceases and that the 'Shaman' moon god Odin becomes
the highest god is therefore for Ohlmarks an indication of the impact
of a 'matriarchal culture' on the 'patriarchal' Indo-Germanic one.

Ohlmarks' work stands in the philological tradition of religious studies
as represented by Friedrich Max Müller as well as in the ethnographi-

---

[6] Å. Ohlmarks, *Heimdalls Horn und Odins Auge. Studien zur nordischen und vergleichenden
Religionsgeschichte. Erstes Buch (I–II) Heimdallr und das Horn* (Lund: C.W.K. Gleerup,
1937).

[7] See ibid., p. 25.

[8] Ibid., pp. 29–33.

[9] Å. Ohlmarks, *Doktor i Lund. En bok om akademiska intriger* [Doctor in Lund. A book
about academic intrigues] (Stockholm: Sjöstrands, 1980), p. 68.

cal tradition of Leo Frobenius and Fritz Graebner. He shared Müller's view of the first gods as personifications of natural phenomena such as the sun and the rain, but Ohlmarks also stressed the important role of the human imagination and "artistic freedom" for the origin and evolution of religious ideas. It is therefore not surprising that he almost completely ignored the phenomenological tradition of religious studies. The only person somehow representing this tradition to figure in *Heimdalls Horn* is Nathan Söderblom, whose work Ohlmarks calls "superficial" and much too "schematic."[10] But Rudolf Otto's concept of "das ganz Andere" or Gerardus van der Leeuw's encounter of the religious man with the "force," seeing the core of religion as an irrational moment only to be understood by people sharing the same experience, were not treated by Ohlmarks. For him religion was not wholly separated from other spheres of life and did not possess an unchangeable essence since religions were differently shaped depending on the life-situation of the people. In the center of Ohlmarks' interest stood the evolution and changes of religious ideas, especially when originating in the contact between cultures.

Ohlmarks' doctoral promotion was a disaster. The defense lasted over seven hours and, according to Ohlmarks, his opponent, Dag Strömbäck, had done nothing more than attack him personally and at the same time avoided criticizing the book. In the end Ohlmarks received the grade 1.5–2 which gave him the right to bear the doctoral title, but he would have needed at least a 2–2 to become a lecturer at the university, which was what he wanted. Responsible for the bad grade was the historian Lauritz Weibull who wanted to disallow the promotion.[11] In his autobiography, a bitter Ohlmarks claims that Weibull did this out of personal reasons. This may actually be a part of the truth: In 1932 Ohlmarks had ridiculed Weibull in a play set up by the students. Important is that Ohlmarks had no chance of starting an academic career in Sweden without lecturer status.

Heimdalls Horn and Odins Auge was widely criticized in Sweden. His colleagues in Lund, Dag Strömbäck and Birger Pering, accused Ohlmarks of bad philological work, of not taking the specifics of the Old Norse culture into account and of using a speculative and deductive

---

[10] Ohlmarks, *Heimdalls Horn und Odins Auge*, p. 8.
[11] Ohlmarks, *Doktor i Lund*, p. 132.

method.[12] Some scholars were also offended by the harsh sarcastic tone in which Ohlmarks had criticized previous works on Heimdall.[13] This critique is also brought forward by Geo Widengren in a post-war article on the study of religion in Sweden, where he basically tells the reader to ignore everything Ohlmarks has ever written.[14] It is a harsh judgment which may – to some extent – have been rooted in the different scientific approaches of Ohlmarks and the scholars of religion in Uppsala. Widengren represented the old phenomenological tradition whereas others like Stig Wikander worked along the lines being drawn up by Otto Höfler and Georges Dumézil.[15] Both Wikander and Höfler had been lecturers at the University of Uppsala.[16] In his autobiography Ohlmarks polemically calls the academic work of Dumézil "out of touch with reality" regretting that scholars in Uppsala nevertheless tended to see him as a "god and authority."[17] Clear is that Ohlmarks' position in the Swedish scientific community was, as we have seen, very weak, especially considering the fact that Lund and Uppsala were the only existing universities in Sweden at this time. As if this was not enough, Ohlmarks' protector and friend, the professor of Nordic philology Emil Olson, died in 1937, and with him died Ohlmarks' academic chances to become established in the field of philology. In the following years Ohlmarks therefore studied Sanskrit and Hebrew and wrote a second book, which, as he hoped, would give him the possibility to become a

---

[12] Dag Strömbäck, "Philologisch-Kritische Methode und altnordische Religionsgeschichte," *Acta Philologica Scandinavica* 12 (1937–1938): pp. 1–24; Birger Pering, "Anmälan av 'Åke Ohlmarks, Heimdalls Horn und Odins Auge. Erstes Buch. Heimdallr und das Horn'," *Arkiv för nordisk filologi* 54 (1939), pp. 342–353.

[13] Best illustrated by a comment in the review Jan de Vries wrote for *Museum*: "Unpleasant is the art in which he [Ohlmarks] reprimands scholars such as [Hugo] Pipping und [Vilhelm] Grønbech as if they were schoolboys." ("Onaangenaam doet daarbij aan, dat hij aan geleerden als Pipping en Grønbech terechtwijzingen uitdeelt, alsof zij schoolknapen waren."). See Jan de Vries, Review of 'Heimdalls Horn und Odins Auge,' *Museum. Maandblad voor Philologie en Geschiedenis* 7 (1939), p. 190f.

[14] Geo Widengren, "Die religionswissenschaftliche Forschung in Skandinavien in den letzten 20 Jahren," *Zeitschrift für Religions- und Geistesgeschichte* 5 (1953), pp. 193–222 and pp. 320–334, here p. 219.

[15] On the phenomenological tradition in Uppsala see Geo Widengren, "Die religionswissenschaftliche Tradition in Uppsala," *Archiv für Religionspsychologie* 13 (1978), pp. 21–32.

[16] For Wikander see Stefan Arvidsson, "Stig Wikander och forskningen om ariska mannaförbund" [Stig Wikander and the research on Aryan men-societies], *Chaos. Dansk-norsk tidsskrift for religionshistoriske studier* 38 (2002), pp. 55–68 and especially the article of Mihaela Timus in this book.

[17] Ohlmarks, *I Paradiset*, p. 162.

lecturer. In 1939 he published his most famous work *Studien zum Problem des Schamanismus*.

In this book Ohlmarks treated a question which arose from *Heimdalls Horn and Odins Auge*. The title is slightly misleading since it does not bring up the problem of shamanism as such but the issue of shamanistic rituals, as the seiðr, in the context of old Norse religion.[18] In his book *Sejd*, published in 1935, Dag Strömbäck claimed that seiðr was a result of an impact from the Saami or Lapps. In his *Studien zum Problem des Schamanismus*, Ohlmarks instead tried to prove that seiðr, just as Odin, was a takeover from an arctic people which, however, could not have been the Saamis. According to Ohlmarks, arctic Shamanism can be divided into two forms, the "true arctic" and the "sub-arctic." The shamanism of the Saamis is a true arctic form which Ohlmarks considered being a pathological phenomenon determined by the "arctic hysteria." The seiðr on the other hand shows all signs of being of sub-arctic origin as the ecstasy involved is artificially produced through drugs, drumming, singing and dancing. Another difference is that the Saami Shaman is a man whereas the seiðr is carried out by women. Moreover it would be impossible that a primitive culture such as the Saami culture could have had an impact on the higher Norse one as this would be against the "rules of cultural impact."[19] The impact must therefore be of an older date and must originate in an older, more developed "sub-arctic" culture. These theoretical similarities in *Heimdalls Horn und Odins Auge* and *Studien zum Problem des Schamanismus* are not to ignore, especially considering the fact that Ohlmarks counted the "arctic culture" to the 'matriarchal' and the Nordic to the 'patriarchal' cultural circle. For Ohlmarks the seiðr and Odin are just two sides of this old "matriarchal impact" on the Norse culture and religion.[20]

But Ohlmarks was not able to secure his lectureship this time either. His referee, the German ethnologist Friedrich Rudolf Lehmann, sent a long critical review to the University of Lund, resulting in the refusal of Ohlmarks' application.[21] In 1939, Ohlmarks' possibilities to find

---

[18] For an overview of the academic discussion on this topic, see Stefanie von Schnurbein, "Shamanism in the Old Norse Tradition: A Theory between Ideological Camps," *History of Religions* 43–2 (2003), pp. 116–138.

[19] Å. Ohlmarks, *Studien zum Problem des Schamanismus* (Lund & Kopenhagen: C.W.K. Gleerup/Ejnar Munksgaard, 1939), p. 349f. See also Ohlmarks' "Arktischer Schamanismus und altnordischer Seiðr," *Archiv für Religionswissenschaft* 36 (1939), pp. 171–180.

[20] See especially Ohlmarks, *Heimdalls Horn und Odins Auge*, pp. 235–245. For an extensive analysis of Ohlmarks' approach, see Andreas Åkerlund, "Åke Ohlmarks and the 'Problem' of Shamanism," *Archaeus* 10–1/2 (2006), pp. 201–220.

[21] Ohlmarks, *Doktor i Lund*, pp. 179–181.

work at a Swedish university were basically non-existent. After this second failure, Ohlmarks joined the pro-German academic society "Riksföreningen Sverige-Tyskland." The "Swedish-German society" had been founded in 1937 by academics who wanted to support the new Germany. Chairman was the professor of theology in Lund, Hugo Odeberg, an expert on Jewish mysticism and, according to himself, a "competent antisemite."[22] Odeberg was a person with many contacts in Germany, especially to German Christian theologians. Ohlmarks also belonged to a research group on Old Norse religion called "Odal" founded by Odeberg.

Odeberg pushed Ohlmarks' scientific career forward. In 1940 Ohlmarks participated in a conference of the "Lutherakademie Sondershausen" where Odeberg was an important member lecturing on the travels of the dead in the worldview of the Germanic peoples.[23] The "Lutherakademie" was a corporation between the different Lutheran churches in Europe and was at this time receiving financial aid from the German ministry of propaganda.[24] Odeberg was also an active member of the "Institut zur Erforschung und Beseitigung des jüdischen Einflusses auf das deutsche kirchliche Leben" (Institute for the Study and Eradication of Jewish Influence on German Church Life) in Eisenach. Another member of this institute, the professor of theology in Jena, Wolf Meyer-Erlach, had held lectures at the University of Lund in 1941, invited by Odeberg. As in the same year a position as a lecturer in Swedish at the University of Greifswald opened up, Odeberg and Meyer-Erlach supported Ohlmarks' application. In his letter of

---

[22] See Joakim Berglund, *Quislingcentralen. Nazismen i Skåne på 30- och 40-talet* [The Quisling center. Nazism in Scania in the 1930's and 1940's] (Malmö: [n.p.], 1994), p. 115. The relationship between the Swedish church and National Socialism is still not very well investigated. But some publications deserve being mentioned, for instance Lars Gunnarssons book *Kyrkan nazismen och demokratin. Åsiktsbildning kring svensk kyrklighet 1919–1945* [Church, Nazism and democracy. Opinions about the Swedish Church 1919–1945] (Stockholm: Almqvist & Wiksell International 1995) and Anders Jarlert's article on the application of the Nuremberg laws in the Swedish Church: "Die Anwendung der Nürnberger Gesetze in der Schwedischen Kirche 1935–1945," *Kirchliche Zeitgeschichte* 1 (2001), pp. 159–174.

[23] See Dorothea Ott and Martin Seils, *Die Luther-Akademie Sondershausen. Eine Dokumentation* (Münster: Lit, 2003), p. 34. Ohlmarks' lecture was published as "Das Grabschiff. Studien zur vorgeschichtlichen nordischen Religionsgeschichte," *Zeitschrift für systematische Theologie* 18 (1941), pp. 150–158.

[24] J. Hansson, "Sweden and Nazism," p. 184. See also Gunnar Appelquist, *Luthersk samverkan i nazismens skugga. Sverige och Lutherakademien i Sondershausen 1932–1945* [Lutheran Cooperation in the Shadow of Nazism. Sweden and the Luther-Academy in Sondershausen 1932–1945] (Uppsala: Svenska Kyrkohistoriska föreningen, 1993).

recommendation, Meyer-Erlach certified that Ohlmarks was a part of the "National Front in Sweden" and that he "actively worked for the cooperation between the two Germanic nations as a member of the 'Swedish-German Society'."[25] The Swedish Foreign Ministry in Berlin recommended Ohlmarks to the University of Greifswald and the university accepted. In November 1941, Ohlmarks moved to Germany.[26]

The fact that Ohlmarks openly sided with antisemitic theologians calls for an explanation. Ohlmarks was not an active Christian and had refused to try to get a lectureship at a theological faculty, a move which professor Efraim Briem had suggested in 1937.[27] There are also no traces whatsoever of antisemitic prejudices in his written work, neither in his academic texts nor in his articles in *Lundagård*. Ohlmarks was a very productive writer,[28] but did not publish one single article in the journal of the "Swedish-German Society." It can therefore be questioned how actively he actually worked for a Swedish-German cooperation. It is true that Ohlmarks had written an article in 1933, in which he took a stance for the NSDAP, but there are no sources proving that he was of the same opinion in 1941; this, however, cannot be excluded.

It seems that the primary reason for Ohlmarks to side with Odeberg and the German Christians was the fact that they could help him to get an academic position. For Ohlmarks Germany was an attractive country with a strong tradition in the study of religions. He could speak the language and had written books in German drawing primarily on German theoreticians. Contrary to the situation in Sweden, *Heimdalls Horn and Odins Auge* had also received good reviews in German journals.[29] Ohlmarks obviously did not care if he had to cooperate with antisemites and pro-Nazi Christians as long as this cooperation furthered his scientific career.

---

[25] Anders Marell, "Åke Ohlmarks – schwedischer Lektor, Nazimitläufer und/oder Geheimagent?," *Germanisten. Zeitschrift schwedischer Germanisten* 3–1/3 (1998), pp. 93–100, here p. 96.

[26] Ohlmarks, *Doktor i Lund*, pp. 15–17.

[27] Ibid., p. 166.

[28] See the long list of publications in Gunnar Jarring, "Ohlmarks, Åke Joel," *Svenskt Biografiskt Lexikon* 28 (Stockholm: Bonnier, 1992–1994,) pp. 111–117.

[29] See for instance the reviews of Carl Clemen and Gustav Neckel in the *Theologische Literaturzeitung* 26 (1937), p. 467 and the *Zeitschrift für Volkskunde*, Neue Folge 9 (1938), pp. 87–89.

3. *A Scientific Career in the Third Reich: Cooperation and Distance*

Ohlmarks' contacts with the "Institute for the Study and Eradication of Jewish Influence on German Church Life" were to last also after his arrival in Germany. But why did German theologians aiming to free Christianity from the 'Jewish impact' support a scholar specialized in Old Norse religion?

Founded in 1932, the German Christians did not see Christianity and National Socialism as opposing forces. They propagated the model of a "Volkskirche," a people's church to be built on the principles of blood and race.[30] The central moments in the worldview of the German Christians, namely its antisemitism and the idea of an Aryan religiosity shaped by one's racial soul places them in close relationship with non-Christian *voelkish* organizations such as the German Faith Movement of Jakob Wilhelm Hauer. The difference between the two groups was not the idea of a racial and biological fundament of religion, but if Christianity was a true expression of the Germanic race or not. In the religious conflicts that took place in the Third Reich, the German Christians therefore held a kind of middle position between the Confessing Church and anti-Christian *voelkish* groups, forced to battle them both.

German Christian theologians used the term "Religionswissenschaft" for their own work out of two reasons. As Fritz Heinrich has shown, the renaming of theology in science of religion has to be seen as a strategy to protect the theological faculties at the university.[31] On the other hand, the renaming also justified an expansion of the theological work field to include pre-Christian, Indo-Aryan, or Germanic religions as well. The academic program of such a *voelkish* and Christian science of religion was to free Aryan Christianity from all oriental-Jewish influences. In 1938 German Christians were discussing the set-up of an academic institute to carry out this work. The debate led to the "Institute for the Study and Eradication of Jewish Influence on German Church Life" in Eisenach, which was opened on May 6, 1939. Around fourty theolo-

---

[30] See Doris L. Bergen, "Die 'Deutschen Christen' 1933–1945. Ganz normale Gläubige oder eifrige Komplizen?," *Geschichte und Gesellschaft* 29 (2003), pp. 542–574, here p. 546, and idem, *Twisted Cross. The German Christian Movement in the Third Reich* (Chapel Hill and London: University of North Carolina Press, 1996).

[31] Fritz Heinrich, *Die deutsche Religionswissenschaft und der Nationalsozialismus. Eine ideologiekritische und wissenschaftsgeschichtliche Untersuchung* (Petersberg: Imhof, 2002), pp. 213–219.

gians as well as some high church leaders counted among the founding members. Its director was Walther Grundmann, professor of *voelkish* theology at the University of Jena and a colleague of Wolf Meyer-Erlach. First, Grundmann wanted to join the institute to the University of Jena, but his plans were stopped by the rector Karl Astel who had close affinities with the SS. The institute was therefore placed at the old preacher seminar in Eisenach and was financed by a consortium of regional Protestant churches as well as by the church headquarters in Berlin.[32] Some of the institute's projects entailed an "aryanized" version of the New Testament, the so-called "Volkstestament" (people's gospel) and a songbook in which the references to Judaism had been removed from old church hymns such as "silent night."[33]

Susannah Heschel draws attention to the fact that the academic group possessing expertise in Judaism was the theologians as they were able to read texts written in old Hebrew and old Greek.[34] But what they lacked was the knowledge of the old Germanic religion and the ability to utilize Old Norse sources. This was a crucial knowledge for a group wanting to "Germanize" Christianity, especially considering the fact that the anti-Christian German Faith Movement had a professor of indology and science of religion as its "Führer." This shortage clarifies the interest in the person Åke Ohlmarks and his academic work. The fact that Ohlmarks came from Sweden was not unimportant as well, in light of the enthusiasm for everything "Nordic" in the Third Reich. Grundmann used the notion "Religionswissenschaft" for the work being carried out at the institute in order to avoid the accusation of being a confession-bound institute.[35]

The members of the "Institute for the Study and Eradication of Jewish Influence on German Church Life" formed working groups concentrating on different subject matters. The working group "Germanentum und Christentum" formed by Walther Grundmann and

---

[32] See Susannah Heschel, "Theologen für Hitler," in Leonore Siegele-Wenschkewitz, ed., *Christlicher Antijudaismus und Antisemitismus* (Frankfurt am Main: Haag und Herchen, 1994), pp. 125–170 and idem "Deutsche Theologen für Hitler," in Peter von der Osten-Sacken, ed. *Das mißbrauchte Evangelium. Studien zur Theologie und Praxis der Thüringer Deutschen Christen* (Berlin: Institut Kirche und Judentum, 2002), pp. 70–90.

[33] Bergen, "Die 'Deutschen Christen'," p. 169.

[34] Heschel, "Deutsche Theologen für Hitler," p. 72.

[35] See for instance Grundmann's letter to a Mr. Gielen at the ministry of propaganda where he wrote that the work at the institute was carried out by "Religionswissenschaftler" regardless of their confession, in: Léon Poliakov and Joseph Wulf, *Das Dritte Reich und seine Denker* (Wiesbaden: Fourier, 1989, 1st ed. 1959), p. 232.

Wolf Meyer-Erlach was of special interest to Ohlmarks. Together with the working group "Odal" from Lund this group organized two working conferences in Weißenfels an der Saale. 24 of the 62 participants came from Sweden, including the Stockholm priest Nils Hannerz, a leading personality of the upper-class pro-Nazi "Manhem society," and of course Odeberg and Ohlmarks. The conference took place between November 4–8, 1941 near Halle. The choice of Weißenfels and the date were both symbolic. During the 30 Years' War, Weißenfels had been the headquarters of the Swedish king Gustav II Adolf before the battle of Lützen on November 6, 1632. In the foreword to the conference book *Die völkische Gestalt des Glaubens*, Grundmann declared the Swedish king as the savior of Protestantism in Germany representing the Germanic character of Protestantism with a mix of nationalism, Protestantism and *voelkish* thoughts characteristic of the German Christians.[36] The same can be said about the books' articles with titles such as "Luther und Gustav Adolf" by Wolf Meyer-Erlach or "Das germanische Erbe in der schwedischen Frömmigkeit" by Erik Douglas Edenholm. Ohlmarks presented a paper on "Die klassischen Isländersagas und ihr Ehrbegriff."[37] In an anonymous conference report, written for the German Ministry of Education, Ohlmarks is not just described as a scholar of profound scientific knowledge, but also as a person fighting for the pan-Germanic idea and working for a close cooperation between Sweden and Germany.[38]

This was not the only lecture Ohlmarks gave for the "Institute for the Study and Eradication of Jewish Influence on German Church Life". According to the work report recorded for 1941–1942, he had held his lecture on the Icelandic sagas 18 times and a lecture on the Old Norse God Ullr and the origin of the sacral kingdom of the Germanic peoples no less than 36 times.[39] At the next Swedish-German encounter in Weißenfels in 1942, Ohlmarks presented a paper on the construction of the Old Germanic temple and in the same year he held a lecture during a working conference of the Eisenach institute on the sources of the Völuspá in the context of literature and history

[36] Walther Grundmann, ed. *Die völkische Gestalt des Glaubens* (Leipzig: Georg Wigand, 1943).
[37] Printed under the same title in ibid., pp. 157–220.
[38] Bundesarchiv Berlin, R 49.01–2966, fol. 183–185.
[39] Landeskirchenarchiv Eisenach, A 921, fol. 70.

of religions.[40] All of Ohlmarks' lectures were collected and printed as *Studien zur altgermanischen Religionsgeschichte*.[41]

One would expect that Ohlmarks had to adapt his lectures to the *voelkish* Christian context in which they were held but this is only partially the case. As a matter of fact, the continuity of his academic work is remarkable. In the articles presented in *Studien zur altgermanischen Religionsgeschichte*, Ohlmarks more or less treats the subject of Old Norse religion in the same way prior to the migration to Germany. The most substantial changes are to be found on the terminological level as Ohlmarks consequently uses the word Germanic instead of Old Norse. In the article on the Old Icelandic sagas he also uses the word "blood" where he normally would have said "family" or "people." Compared to *Heimdalls Horn and Odins Auge*, his methodology remains unchanged; Ohlmarks still used the paradigm of the cultural circles, comparing the Old Norse writings with myths from other cultures. Totally absent is the *voelkish* concept that religion is something emanating from the racial soul. Ohlmarks also distanced himself from German scholars supporting the Third Reich, drawing on pre-1933 German literature or Scandinavian authors and thereby ignoring the writings of Pagan scholars such as Jakob Wilhelm Hauer.[42] The only German researcher still active during the Third Reich quoted by Ohlmarks is Walter Baetke, an opponent of National Socialism.

Although he cooperated with the "Institute for the Study and Eradication of Jewish Influence on German Church Life," Ohlmarks obviously tried to hold on to the methods and scientific standards of his pre-war academic work, not letting a racial biology or *voelkish* ideology affect his texts. In his practical cooperation with Nazi organizations he made some concessions. But at the same time he kept the academic norms and refrained from totally adapting his scientific work to the demands

---

[40] See Bundesarchiv Berlin, 49.01–2966, fol. 214–227 and Staatsarchiv Marburg, 307a, acc. 1962/12, Nr. 44.

[41] Å. Ohlmarks, *Studien zur altgermanischen Religionsgeschichte. 4 Aufsätze* (Leipzig: Georg Wigand, 1943).

[42] This is interesting considering the fact that Ohlmarks and Hauer knew each other personally. They had met when Ohlmarks worked as a lecturer in Tübingen in 1933 where Ohlmarks had participated in seminars led by Hauer (Ohlmarks, *Doktor i Lund*, p. 33f.). In 1935, Hauer wrote a letter of recommendation for Ohlmarks when he applied for the position as lecturer in Reykjavik (Bundesarchiv Koblenz, Nachlass Hauer, vol. 141, fol. 373f.). Hauer also helped Ohlmarks to publish an article on the connection between shamanism and seiðr in the *Archiv für Religionswissenschaft* 36 (1939), pp. 171–180.

of National Socialism. The German historian Dieter Langewiesche described such a behavior as a very common and widespread position in the academic field under National Socialism.[43] It was not necessary for Ohlmarks to embrace a *voelkish* position in order to comply with the purposes of German Christian theologians. He was merely there to provide them with facts considering the Old Norse religion and, on the other hand, to function as a "token scientist" from Sweden for propaganda reasons. Ohlmarks seems not to have sympathized with the idea of an Aryan Christianity to a greater extent. Cooperating with the German Christians was for him merely a way to get established in Germany.

4. *The Founding of the Institute of Science of Religion in Greifswald in 1944 and the Further Work of Ohlmarks*

During his time as a lecturer in Swedish at the University of Greifswald, Ohlmarks succeeded in extending his work to encompass lectures on Old Norse religion. As Fritz Heinrich has shown, this resulted from the situation of the theological faculty at the university. In the Third Reich the Ministry of Education planed to remove theological departments from the universities completely. As a step in that direction, Martin Bormann suggested to move Greifwald's theological faculty to Kiel.[44] The professor of systematic theology at the University of Greifswald Wilhelm Koepp wanted to avoid this measure and tried to widen the theological program by involving comparative religion. Koepp was also a member of the "Institute for the Study and Eradication of Jewish Influence on German Chruch Life" and had participated in the Weißenfels conferences. It can therefore be assumed that he and Ohlmarks had met each other in 1941.

Ohlmarks and Koepp obviously saw mutual benefits in broadening the work of the theological faculty. For Ohlmarks it was a possibility to get established within the scientific world, whereas for Koepp the inclusion of Ohlmarks, being a non-theologian and covering the ideo-

---

[43] Dieter Langewiesche, "Die Universität Tübingen in der Zeit des Nationalsozialismus. Formen der Selbstgleichschaltung und Selbstbehauptung," *Geschichte und Gesellschaft* 23 (1999), pp. 618–646, here p. 620f.

[44] Heinrich, "Das religionswissenschaftliche Institut der Ernst Moritz Arndt-Universität," pp. 225–228.

logical important field of Old Norse religion, would help him in his plans to keep theology in Greifswald. In spring 1944 Koepp therefore helped Ohlmarks becoming a lecturer in general history of religions with a special reference to the religion of the primitives at the theological faculty.[45] Since the lectureship was only temporary, Ohlmarks and Koepp both worked towards the founding of an institute.

Their work turned out to be successful and Ohlmarks was made director of the new institute, which was opened on November 22, 1944. Lars Åkerberg, a member of the Swedish legation in Berlin and a personal friend of Ohlmarks, had donated 15,000 Reichsmark to the institute and was therefore made honorary senator of the University of Greifswald. Surely, the money and the fact that it was donated by a Swedish diplomat were strong reasons to found such an institute. At the opening celebration Ohlmarks presented the first – and last – publication of the institute: *Thomas Thorild als Vorläufer der neuzeitlichen Religionswissenschaft*, a kind of homage to the Swedish poet and philosopher Thomas Thorild, professor and librarian in Greifswald between 1795 and 1808.[46] Åkerberg figured as a co-author of the book, but this is more due to the fact that he had donated money to the institute. There existed plans to confer the title of an extraordinary professor on Ohlmarks. But they failed because the philosophy department expressed reservations about Ohlmarks and recommended the Minister of Education Bernhard Rust to wait with the appointment.[47]

During his time as a lecturer in Swedish at the University of Greifswald, Ohlmarks balanced between actively participating in the scientific field in Nazi Germany – e.g. through his work for the German Christians and in founding an institute of science of religion together with Koepp – and dissociating himself from other institutions of the Third Reich. He insisted on the remark "nicht Reichsbeamter" after his name in the university calendars and refused to do any work for the so-called

---

[45] Heinrich, *Die deutsche Religionswissenschaft und der Nationalsozialismus*, p. 227f.

[46] Åke Ohlmarks and Lars Åkerberg, *Thomas Thorild als Vorläufer der neuzeitlichen Religionswissenschaft* (Veröffentlichungen des religionswissenschaftlichen Instituts der Universität Greifswald 1) (Greifswald: [n.p.], 1944).

[47] Heinrich, *Die deutsche Religionswissenschaft und der Nationalsozialismus*, p. 233. According to Ohlmarks' autobiography it was the other way round. The idea to make him a professor was an initiative from the rector of the university Carl Engel. Ohlmarks claimed to have turned down this offer because it would have meant to become a German citizen. See Ohlmarks, *Efter mig Syndafloden*, p. 128.

"Nordische Auslandsinstitute" (Nordic Foreign Institutes).[48] Ohlmarks'
will to distance himself from working for the Nordic Foreign Institutes
can be seen as a desire not to become too involved with the official
structures of the NS state, considering the fact that the director of the
Swedish institute, Johannes Paul, participated in radio propaganda
in Königsberg[49] and that the Nordic Foreign Institutes were partially
supported by the pro-Nazi "Volksdeutsche Forschungsgemeinschaften."[50]
Another reason for Ohlmarks to keep distance was his wish not to loose
the possibility of continuing his career outside of Germany. In a letter
to the Minister of Education Bernhard Rust, professor Leopold Magon
from the Nordic Foreign Institutes wrote that Ohlmarks' application for
the succession of Vilhelm Grønbech as regular professor in Copenhagen
had been turned down due to his pro-German attitude.[51]

Ohlmarks' work took an interesting turn during his time in Nazi Germany because he recognizably avoided further references to Schmitt's
'Catholic' theory of cultural circles. In *Heimdalls Horn and Odins Auge* as
well as in *Studien zum Problem des Schamanismus* he had drawn heavily on
this theory, trying to explain major changes in the Norse religion as a
result of cultural contacts with a 'matriarchal', 'arctic' people. In the
1940s Ohlmarks concentrated on other questions, abandoning the use
of 'myths' and written sources and turning to archaeological remains.
In a series of lectures he dealt with the function of Norse temples
arguing that the construction of special houses for rites resulted from a
Christian impact on the Old Norse cult. To support his argumentation
he compared the remains of the temple in Uppsala with the temple
in Arkona on Rügen and with old Norwegian churches.[52] This did not

---

[48] Between 1933 and 1945 "Nordische Auslandsinstitute" was the designation for
the Danish, Swedish, Norwegian, Finnish and Icelandic institutes at the University of
Greifswald. See Wilhelm Friese, "75 Jahre Nordisches Institut der Universität Greifswald," *Skandinavistik* 23 (1993), pp. 110–127, here p. 115f.

[49] Heinrich, "Das religionswissenschaftliche Institut der Ernst Moritz Arndt-Universität," p. 215.

[50] Michael Fahlbusch, *Wissenschaft im Dienst der nationalsozialistischen Politik? Die 'Volksdeutschen Forschungsgemeinschaften' von 1931–1945* (Baden-Baden: Nomos, 1999), p. 227
and p. 589.

[51] Marell, "Åke Ohlmarks – schwedischer Lektor, Nazimitläufer und/oder Geheimagent?," p. 96f.

[52] See Åke Ohlmarks, "Alt-Uppsala und Arkona," in *Vetenskapssocieteten i Lund, Årsbok
1943* (Lund: C.W.K. Gleerup, 1944), pp. 79–120 and idem, *Alt-Uppsala und Urnes. Untersuchung zur Entstehung der Dreischiffstabkirche und des ältesten germanisch-heidnischen Kulthauses*
(Meddelande från Lunds astronomiska observatorium II–115) (Lund: Håkan Ohlssons
Boktryckeri, 1944).

mean that Ohlmarks discarded the theory of cultural circles. In his first post-war book *Gravskeppet* he made extensive use of it.[53] He simply did not use it in his works published in and during the Third Reich.

To understand the turn in Ohlmarks' work, it is important to stress the differences between his early books and the predominating *voelkish* study of religions in the Third Reich. Ohlmarks' concept of religion in general and of Old Norse or Germanic religion in particular is in some crucial points contrary to the *voelkish* view. For Ohlmarks religion does not originate in a racial soul and has no irrational core which cannot be understood in a rational way. This places him in opposition to the approach of Jakob Wilhelm Hauer. In claiming that Odin was not even an original Germanic god, Ohlmarks' ideas opposed the teachings of scholars like Otto Höfler for whom Odin was the most important god in the Germanic pantheon.[54] Instead of criticizing the work of Hauer and Höfler, Ohlmarks changed his scientific interest, avoiding discussions on Old Norse religion carried out by various *voelkish* scholars in the Third Reich. This demonstrates very well the ambivalence of Ohlmarks towards the National Socialist ideology. He was prepared to work with the German Christians as long as he was allowed to do the research he wanted, but he was not prepared to change his scientific position or theoretical viewpoint to fit better with a *voelkish* science of religions. The fact that Ohlmarks avoided confrontations with scholars like Hauer or Höfler clearly shows his opportunistic stance and his eagerness not to get into a position that would make him *persona non grata* in the scientific field in the Third Reich.

In March 1945 as the end of the war drew nearer, Ohlmarks left Greifswald and Germany. The return to Sweden meant the end of his scientific career. He never held a position at a Swedish university. Between 1950 and 1959, Ohlmarks worked as a scriptwriter and head of the script department at "Europafilm." Later he worked as a translator

---

[53] Åke Ohlmarks, *Gravskeppet. Studier i förhistorisk nordisk religionshistoria* [The grave-ship. Studies in pre-historic Nordic history of religions] (Stockholm: Gebers, 1946). Although finished in 1941 or 1942, this book on bronze age ship-graves was not published until 1946.

[54] For Höfler, see Esther Gajek, "Germanenkunde und Nationalsozialismus. Zur Verflechtung von Wissenschaft und Politik am Beispiel Otto Höflers," in Richard Faber, ed., *Politische Religion – Religiöse Politik* (Würzburg: Königshausen und Neumann, 1997), pp. 173–204 and for an overview of Höflers theory of "Männerbünde" in a broader context, Stefan Arvidsson, *Ariska Idoler. Den indoeuropeiska mytologin som ideologi och vetenskap* [Aryan idols. The Indo-European mythology 'as' ideology and science] (Stockholm/Stehag: Symposion, 2000), pp. 217–236.

and freelance author, writing everything from travelers' guides and dictionaries for solving crossword puzzles to historical novels. Åke Ohlmarks died on June 6, 1984 in Crist di Niardo, Brescia, Italy.

5. *Conclusion*

Åke Ohlmarks' main reason for migrating to Nazi Germany was not his political or ideological point of view, but his weak position within the Swedish science of religion. He did not work together with Hugo Odeberg or Wolf Meyer-Erlach out of political conviction – although all of them shared an anti-Bolshevistic point of view – but merely because they could help him with his scientific career. One could honestly say that the main impact of National Socialism on Ohlmarks' life was that the rise of the German Christians opened a completely new field of work for him. Ohlmarks' philological skills in Old Icelandic and his work on Old Norse religion made him interesting for groups who wanted to "aryanize" Christianity such as theologians working for the "Institute for the Study and Eradication of Jewish Influence on German Church Life."

Wilhelm Koepp supported Ohlmarks' appointment to director of the institute of science of religions in Greifswald out of similar considerations. Founded with Swedish money and with a Swedish scholar as director, the institute would help to prevent the closing of the theological faculty and to give the theology in Greifswald a new Nordic profile.

This is interesting insofar the cooperation with the German Christians had little impact on Ohlmarks' theoretical positions. During his time in the Third Reich, he never cast aside his philological approach or the paradigm of the cultural circles. This corresponds with the conclusions Fritz Heinrich draws in his study on the German science of religions during the National Socialist era. According to him, scholars with a philological-historical approach did not "ideologize" their work during the Third Reich to the same extent as did scholars standing in the phenomenological tradition.[55] This is a valid conclusion concerning the writings of Ohlmarks as well.

Ohlmarks' lectures held before the "Institute for the Study and Eradication of Jewish Influence on German Church Life" clearly illustrate

---

[55] Heinrich, *Die deutsche Religionswissenschaft und der Nationalsozialismus*, p. 391f.

that a scholar was not forced to adopt a *voelkish* and antisemitic paradigm to be of interest for organizations supporting National Socialism. Hence, it is very important to contextualize academic scholarship in order to determine the actual "use of science" (Pierre Bourdieu) within a social setting. It is only when Ohlmarks' lectures on Old Norse religion are seen in the antisemitic German Christian context in which they were held that one can understand the role he choose to play within the work of the institute in Eisenach. The career of Åke Ohlmarks in the Third Reich more than adequately exemplifies a scholar who chose to adapt to the demands of National Socialism and to cooperate with an antisemitic group without fully sharing its conviction.

Bibliography

Åkerlund, Andreas. "Åke Ohlmarks and the 'Problem' of Shamanism." *Archaeus* 10–1/2 (2006), pp. 201–220.

Andersson, Lars M. *En jude är en jude är en jude: Representationer av 'juden' i svensk skämtpress omkring 1900–1930* [A Jew is a Jew is a Jew: Representations of the Jew in Swedish Comic Press 1900–1930s]. Lund: Nordic Academic Press, 2000.

Appelquist, Gunnar. *Luthersk samverkan i nazismens skugga. Sverige och Lutherakademien i Sondershausen 1932–1945* [Lutheran cooperation in the shadow of Nazism. Sweden and the Luther-Academy in Sondershausen 1932–1945] (Skrifter utgivna av Svenska Kyrkohistoriska föreningen II, 47). Uppsala: Svenska Kyrkohistoriska föreningen, 1993.

Arvidsson, Stefan. *Ariska idoler. Den indoeuropeiska mytologin som ideologi och vetenskap* [Aryan idols. The Indo-European mythology 'as' ideology and science]. Stockholm/Stehag: Symposion, 2000.

———. "Stig Wikander och forskningen om ariska mannaförbund" [Stig Wikander and the research on Aryan men-societies]. *Chaos. Dansk-norsk tidsskrift for religionshistoriske studier* 38 (2002), pp. 55–68.

Bergen, Doris L. *Twisted Cross. The German Christian Movement in the Third Reich.* Chapel Hill and London: University of North Carolina Press, 1996.

———. "Die 'Deutschen Christen' 1933–1945. Ganz normale Gläubige oder eifrige Komplizen?." *Geschichte und Gesellschaft* 29 (2003), pp. 542–574.

Berggren, Lena. *Nationell upplysning. Drag i den svenska antisemitismens idéhistoria* [National enlightment: Traits in the history if Swedish antisemitism]. Stockholm: Carlsson, 1999.

———. "Swedish Fascism – Why Bother?" *Journal of Contemporary History* 37–3 (2002), pp. 395–417.

Berglund, Joakim. *Quislingcentralen. Nazismen i Skåne på 30- och 40-talet* [The Quisling center. Nazism in Scania in the 1930's and 1940's]. Malmö: [n.p.], 1994.

Clemen, Carl. Review of 'Heimdalls Horn und Odins Auge.' *Theologische Literaturzeitung* 26 (1937), p. 467.

Ekman, Stig and Klas Åkmark, eds. *Sweden's relation with Nazism, Nazi Germany and the Holocaust.* Stockholm: Almqvist & Wiksell, 2003.

Fahlbusch, Michael. *Wissenschaft im Dienst der nationalsozialistischen Politik? Die 'Volksdeutschen Forschungsgemeinschaften' von 1931–1945.* Baden-Baden: Nomos, 1999.

Friese, Wilhelm. "75 Jahre Nordisches Institut der Universität Greifswald." *Skandinavistik* 23 (1993): pp. 110–127.

Gajek, Esther. "Germanenkunde und Nationalsozialismus. Zur Verflechtung von Wissenschaft und Politik am Beispiel Otto Höflers." In Richard Faber, ed., *Politische Religion – Religiöse Politik.* Würzburg: Königshausen und Neumann, 1997, pp. 173–204.

Grundmann, Walther, ed. *Die völkische Gestalt des Glaubens.* Leipzig: Georg Wigand, 1943.

Gunnarsson, Lars. *Kyrkan nazismen och demokratin. Åsiktsbildning kring svensk kyrklighet 1919–1945* [Church, Nazism and democracy. Opinions about the Swedish church 1919–1945]. Stockholm: Almqvist & Wiksell International 1995.

Hagtvet, Bernt. "On the Fringe: Swedish Fascism 1920–1945." In Stein Ugelvik Larsen et al., eds. *Who were the Fascists? Social Roots of European Fascism.* Bergen: Universitetsforlaget, 1980, pp. 715–742

Hansson, Jonas. "Sweden and Nazism." In Stig Ekman and Klas Åmark, eds., *Sweden's relations with Nazism, Nazi Germany and the Holocaust.* Stockholm: Almqvist & Wiksell International, 2003, pp. 137–196.

Heinrich, Fritz. "Das religionswissenschaftliche Institut der Ernst Moritz Arndt-Universität Greifswald 1944–1945." *Zeitschrift für Religionswissenschaft* 5 (1997), pp. 203–230.

———. *Die deutsche Religionswissenschaft und der Nationalsozialismus. Eine ideologiekritische und wissenschaftsgeschichtliche Untersuchung.* Petersberg: Imhof, 2002.

Heschel, Susannah. "Theologen für Hitler." In Leonore Siegele-Wenschkewitz, ed., *Christlicher Antijudaismus und Antisemitismus.* Frankfurt am Main: Haag und Herchen, 1994, pp. 125–170.
———. "Deutsche Theologen für Hitler." In Peter von der Osten-Sacken, ed., *Das mißbrauchte Evangelium. Studien zur Theologie und Praxis der Thüringer Deutschen Christen.* Berlin: Institut Kirche und Judentum, 2002, pp. 70–90.
Jarlert, Anders. "Die Anwendung der Nürnberger Gesetze in der Schwedischen Kirche 1935–1945." *Kirchliche Zeitgeschichte* 1 (2001), pp. 159–174.
Jarring, Gunnar. "Ohlmarks, Åke Joel." In *Svenskt Biografiskt Lexikon* 28. Stockholm: Bonnier, 1992–1994, pp. 111–117.
Junginger, Horst. *Von der philologischen zur völkischen Religionswissenschaft. Das Fach Religionswissenschaft an der Universität Tübingen von der Mitte des 19. Jahrhunderts bis zum Ende des Dritten Reiches.* Stuttgart: Franz Steiner, 1999.
———. "Einführung. Das Überleben der Religionswissenschaft im Nationalsozialismus." *Zeitschrift für Religionswissenschaft* 9 (2001), pp. 149–167.
Langewiesche, Dieter. "Die Universität Tübingen in der Zeit des Nationalsozialismus. Formen der Selbstgleichschaltung und Selbstbehauptung." *Geschichte und Gesellschaft* 23 (1999), pp. 618–646.
Lööw, Helene. *Hakkorset och Wasakärven. En studie av nationalsocialismen i Sverige 1924–1950* [Swastika and Wasa-sheaf. A study of National Socialism in Sweden 1924–1950]. Göteborg: Göteborgs Universitet, 1990.
———. *Nazismen i Sverige 1924–1979: pionjärerna, partierna, propagandan* [Nazism in Sweden: the pioneers, the parties, the propaganda]. Stockholm: Ordfront, 2004.
Marell, Anders. "Åke Ohlmarks – schwedischer Lektor, Nazimitläufer und/oder Geheimagent?," in *Germanisten. Zeitschrift schwedischer Germanisten* 3–1/3 (1998), pp. 93–100.
Neckel, Gustav. Review of 'Heimdalls Horn und Odins Auge.' *Zeitschrift für Volkskunde,* Neue Folge 9 (1938), pp. 87–89.
Ohlmarks, Åke. "De negativistiska kulturessayisterna" [The negativistic culture essayists]. *Lundagård* 6 (1933), p. 118.
———. *Heimdalls Horn und Odins Auge. Studien zur nordischen und vergleichenden Religionsgeschichte. Erstes Buch (I–II) Heimdallr und das Horn.* Lund: C.W.K. Gleerup, 1937.
———. *Studien zum Problem des Schamanismus.* Lund & Kopenhagen: C.W.K. Gleerup/Ejnar Munksgaard, 1939.
———. "Arktischer Schamanismus und altnordischer Seiðr." *Archiv für Religionswissenschaft* 36 (1939), pp. 171–180.
———. "Das Grabschiff. Studien zur vorgeschichtlichen nordischen Religionsgeschichte." *Zeitschrift für systematische Theologie* 18 (1941), pp. 150–158.
———. "Die klassischen Isländersagas und ihr Ehrbegriff." In Walther Grundmann, ed., *Die völkische Gestalt des Glaubens.* Leipzig: Georg Wigand, 1943, pp. 157–220.
———. *Studien zur altgermanischen Religionsgeschichte. 4 Aufsätze.* Leipzig: Georg Wigand, 1943.
——— and Lars Åkerberg. *Thomas Thorild als Vorläufer der neuzeitlichen Religionswissenschaft* (Veröffentlichungen des religionswissenschaftlichen Instituts der Universität Greifswald 1). Greifswald: [n.p.], 1944.
———. "Alt-Uppsala und Arkona." In *Vetenskapssocieteten i Lund, Årsbok 1943.* Lund: C.W.K. Gleerup, 1944, pp. 79–120.
———. *Alt-Uppsala und Urnes. Untersuchung zur Entstehung der Dreischiffstabkirche und des ältesten germanisch-heidnischen Kulthauses* (Meddelande från Lunds astronomiska observatorium II–115). Lund: Håkan Ohlssons Boktryckeri, 1944.
———. *Gravskeppet. Studier i förhistorisk nordisk religionshistoria* [The graveship. Studies in pre-historic Nordic history of religions]. Stockholm: Gebers, 1946.
———. *I Paradiset. Levnadsminnen I* [In paradise. Memories of my life I]. Uddevalla: Zindermans, 1965.
———. *Doktor i Lund. En bok om akademiska intriger* [Doctor in Lund. A book about academic intrigues]. Stockholm: Sjöstrands, 1980.

———. *Efter mig Syndafloden. Greifswald-Berlin-Hamburg 1941–1945* [After me the flood]. Köping: Lindfors, 1980.

Oredsson, Sverker. *Lunds universitet under andra världskriget. Motsättningar, debatter och hjälpinsatser* [The University of Lund during the Second World War. Antagonisms, debates and aid-actions]. Lund: Lunds universitetshistoriska sällskap, 1996.

Ott, Dorothea and Martin Seils. *Die Luther-Akademie Sondershausen. Eine Dokumentation.* Münster: Lit, 2003.

Pering, Birger. "Anmälan av 'Åke Ohlmarks, Heimdalls Horn und Odins Auge. Erstes Buch. Heimdallr und das Horn'," in *Arkiv för nordisk filologi* 54 (1939), pp. 342–353.

Poliakov, Léon and Joseph Wulf. *Das Dritte Reich und seine Denker.* Wiesbaden: Fourier, 1989, 1st ed. 1959.

Schnurbein, Stefanie von. "Shamanism in the Old Norse Tradition: A Theory between Ideological Camps." *History of Religions* 43-2 (2003), pp. 116–138.

Strömbäck, Dag. "Philologisch-Kritische Methode und altnordische Religionsgeschichte." *Acta Philologica Scandinavica* 12 (1937–1938), pp. 1–24.

Trädgårdh, Lars. "Varieties of Volkish Ideologies: Sweden and Germany 1848–1933," In Bo Stråth, ed. *Language and the Construction of Class Identities. The Struggle for Discursive Power in Social Organisation: Scandinavia and Germany after 1800.* Göteborg: Göteborgs Universitet, 1990.

Tydén, Mattias. *Svensk antisemitism 1880–1930* [Swedish antisemitism 1880–1930]. Uppsala: Centre for Multiethnic Research, 1986.

Vonderau, Patrick. *Schweden und das nationalsozialistische Deutschland. Eine annotierte Bibliographie der deutschsprachigen Forschungsliteratur.* Stockholm: Almqvist & Wiksell, 2003.

Vries, Jan de. Review of 'Heimdalls Horn und Odins Auge.' *Museum. Maandblad voor Philologie en Geschiedenis* 7 (1939), p. 190f.

Widengren, Geo. "Die religionswissenschaftliche Forschung in Skandinavien in den letzten 20 Jahren." *Zeitschrift für Religions- und Geistesgeschichte* 5 (1953), pp. 193–222 and pp. 320–334.

———. "Die religionswissenschaftliche Tradition in Uppsala." *Archiv für Religionspsychologie* 13 (1978), pp. 21–32.

PART FIVE

THE QUEST FOR THEORIES

THE 'FAITH OF THE ENLIGHTENED' BY WŁADYSŁAW WITWICKI

AN EXAMPLE OF THE CONFLICT BETWEEN ACADEMIC RESEARCH AND POLITICAL CORRECTNESS

Halina Grzymała-Moszczyńska

1. *Methodological Remarks*

Academics are always under multiple pressures to adhere to the constraints of the methodologies accepted by their particular disciplines. Psychology labors under the general constraints of statistical evaluations and the hope of finding universals that are dependent upon a central processing mechanism and for which all other differences between individuals are irrelevant. Psychology uses terminology that implies universal categories of relevance irrespective of the era and the social context of the researched individuals or groups in question. Nevertheless, it is very important to take steps to ensure the usefulness of psychology for interdisciplinary research. The application of a variety of disciplines, competent in different methodologies and differing levels of analysis, can describe social reality more precisely than psychology alone. This requirement calls for a more wide ranging formulation of the goal of psychology.

In the special case of psychology when it is incorporated into the scientific study of religion, such an adjustment is particularly important. Scientific investigations of religion call for coordinated efforts in pluralistic groups of researchers from diverse disciplines. That does not mean that individual researchers should claim a competence in other disciplines with which they cooperate, but it is important for them to work with theoretical paradigms that are accessible to other members of the interdisciplinary group.

Such a situation occurs when we try to examine some issues concerning the relationship between a scholar's scientific output and the political context in which his research takes place. For this purpose I have chosen to analyze Władysław Witwicki's book *Faith of the Enlightened*.

There have been many publications on Witwicki's research.[1] But very rarely has there been any analysis of the broader social climate in which he conducted his investigations. An invitation to present such an analysis helped me to fill this gap. In order to accumulate a more detailed knowledge about both Witwicki's work and its context, I re-analyzed the most important of his publications. I was also fortunate enough to be able to exchange letters with Witwicki's former student, professor emeritus of the Marie-Curie University in Lublin, Andrzej Nowicki, who has himself witnessed developments relating to the book *Faith of the Enlightened.*

An opportunity arose to reflect on the political milieu in which very important work in Polish psychology of religion was carried out. It appeared in the framework of an academic exchange on the content and methodology of studies of religion under the ideological impact of National Socialism and fascism. To attempt an analysis of Witwicki's studies from within this particular context calls for a perspective which is broader than the traditionally conceived psychology of religion (although Witwicki's work explicitly belongs to that domain) and requires a reflection based on a meta-theoretical approach. In psychology such a standpoint is available in cultural psychology, particularly where it enters into a reflection on *emic* and *etic* perspectives in conducting research on human activities. A clarification of these two approaches is provided by the Dutch psychologist Geert Hofstede:

> An *emic* point of view is taken from within a culture, usually the author's own. An *etic* point of view is a 'view from the bridge', comparing different cultures according to criteria supposed to apply to all of them.[2]

---

[1] See Halina Grzymała-Moszczyńska, "Eksperyment psychologiczny Władysława Witwickiego w badaniach nad wiarą religijną" [Psychological experiment on religious faith by Władysław Witwicki], *Studia Religiologica* [Religious Studies] 5 (1980), pp. 127–132; idem, *Psychologia religii – wybrane zagadnienia* [Psychology of religion – selected problems] (Kraków: Zakład Wydawniczy Nomos, 1991); *Religia a kultura – wybrane zagadnienia z kulturowej psychologii religii* [Religion and culture – selected problems from cultural psychology of religion] (Kraków: Wydawnictwo Uniwersytetu Jagiellońskiego, 2004); Andrzej Nowicki, "Inedita Władysława Witwickiego, 1878–1948. Ankieta w sprawie utraty wiary religijnej (rękopis)" [Unpublished manuscripts by Władysław Witwicki, 1878–1948. Questionnaire about loosing religious faith, manuscript], *Euhemer* 117 (1980), pp. 103–113; idem, *Witwicki* (Warszawa: Wiedza Powszechna, 1982); Teresa Rzepa, "Problemy religii w kontekście uwag na temat wychowania w listach Władysława Witwickiego do syna Tadeusza z lat 1918–1945" [Religious issues in the context of remarks pertaining to education – Władysław Witwicki's letters from 1918–1945 to his son Tadeusz], *Euhemer* 151 (1989), pp. 45–58.
[2] Geert Hofstede, "Foreword," in U. Kim et al., eds. *Individualism and Collectivism* (Thousand Oaks, California: Sage, 1994), p. 12

I personally believe that these approaches do not need to be taken separately. On the contrary, in order to fully understand the reaction to Witwicki's research by the Polish political and academic authorities (and later on placing these reactions in the broader European context of the inter-war period), both approaches should be treated consecutively because they are in fact complementary.

The *emic* approach to the analysis of Witwicki's work requires one to take a close look at his biography and his immediate environment. Both created a context for the content and reception of his work. This procedure allows us to get away from general but vague and ambiguous statements typical of the *etic* approach, concerning the *social climate in Poland* in general or *attitudes of Polish scholars* as a group. The *etic* approach will be used at a later stage of my analysis of Witwicki's work to put it in the context of the political climate in both Poland and Europe.

2. *Biographical Sketch*

Władysław Witwicki (1878–1948) was born into a family of Polish nobility strongly connected to the Roman Catholic Church. His mother's uncle Łukasz Baraniecki was Archbishop of Lvow and his mother's sister became the superior of a convent in Lvow. Witwicki's childhood was filled with multiple daily religious practices, which he perceived mostly as boring, sometimes funny and often tiresome.[3] His family expected him to enter the priesthood, start his theological education and eventually to replace his great-uncle in the position of archbishop. His life, however, took another path. He became a student at the University of Lvow under the famous Polish philosopher Kazimierz Twardowski. Later on in 1919 Witwicki was given a professorship in psychology at Warsaw University.

Witwicki's interests in religion from a psychological point of view had been consistently present in his academic writings since 1904. He started off by composing numerous reviews of publications pertaining to the subject of religious life and later on he initiated his own research. He went on to publish a two-volume handbook of psychology (*Psychologia. Dla użytku słuchaczów wyższych zakładów naukowych*).[4] The

---

[3] See A. Nowicki, "Inedita Władysława Witwickiego," pp. 103–113
[4] Władysław Witwicki, *Psychologia. Dla użytku słuchaczów wyższych zakładów naukowych* [Psychology. For pupils of academic establishments], 2 vols. (Lwów: Lwówska Biblioteczka Pedagogiczna, 1925 and 1927).

first volume drew largely on German publications written by Frobes, Ebbinghaus and Hofler, while the second volume was based on his own analysis. He was well-read in German psychology due to his first hand experience in encountering German colleagues during multiple journeys to Austria and Germany. During the fall semester of 1902 he was awarded a scholarship to study in Vienna where he attended Alois Hofler's lectures. These lectures awakened his interest in methodological issues in psychology and he continued to visit Vienna on several subsequent occasions. He also participated there in the First International Congress of the Psychology of Religion, held between May 26–31 in 1931. His impressions after the congress were highly negative because of its distinctly apologetic, confessional, and non-academic character.[5] The theme of the congress pertained to the sources of unbelief and the papers provided analyses of the phenomena exclusively from the point of view of the presenters who were strongly convinced of their own beliefs.

In April 1902 Witwicki arrived in Leipzig and attended the lectures of Wilhelm Wirth and Wilhelm Wundt. Almost from the beginning of his stay in Leipzig he was invited to join them in their psychological experiments, conducted in Wundt's famous laboratory.

3. The 'Faith of the Enlightened'

The book *Faith of the Enlightened* was completed in 1935 and presented the results of his research on the psychological status of religious beliefs among educated people.[6] Witwicki was always interested in the various products either material (artefacts) or intellectual (thoughts and reflections) of human beings. His methodological approach to the analysis of the human psyche was experimental, probably due to Wundt's influence, although he did not particularly value the content of Wundt's psycho-physical experiments. He found them simplistic and missing the broader reaches of the expression of the human psyche.

---

[5] See Władysław Witwicki "I Międzynarodowy Kongres poświęcony psychologii religii w Uniwersytecie Wiedeńskim w tygodniu Zielonych Świąt 1931" [First International Congress of Psychology of Religion at Vienna University in the week of Pentecost, 1931], *Kwartalnik Psychologiczny* [Psychological Quarterly] 4 (1931), p. 397.
[6] W. Witwicki, *La foi des éclairés* (Paris: Alcan, 1939).

The experimental approach of Witwicki was very new in the Polish academic context. He did not limit his research to the analysis of data collected via introspection or questionnaire, but instead actively explored the psychological mechanisms reconciling opposite or mutually exclusive information. His approach predated what was to become the famous psychological theory of cognitive dissonance introduced by Leon Festinger in the 1950s and extensively used in both social psychology and cognitive psychology up until the present day.[7]

Witwicki's research sample for his study of human religiosity consisted of people who had completed at least secondary school (Gymnasium) and passed the university entrance exam (Abitur). By the standards of the inter-war period the participants were qualified to an educational level equivalent to today's students with an MA degree. The educational level of his subjects suggested to him the term *enlightened* (simply standing for 'well educated'). He had chosen as research subjects people able to understand a text and to present their reasoning in resolving the moral dilemmas included there. The text used by Witwicki for evaluation by the participants in the experiment contained secular versions of Old and New Testament motifs such as Original Sin, the Mission of Jesus Christ, and his death which re-established the bond between God and his people. These motifs were adapted in a rather naive (by today's standards) story about an Indian Rajah, at first benevolent and later viciously angry and vengeful against the inhabitants of his realm who had read a prohibited book from his library. He accepted them back into his kingdom only after his grandson had been martyred.

The members of the research group were asked to answer blocks of questions pertaining to the ethical evaluation of the Rajah's behavior toward his people. The collected material helped Witwicki to find answers to questions concerning the contradictions between one's acquired knowledge and one's religious convictions. Witwicki believed that moving the story away from its religious context would allow his subjects greater freedom of judgment. He found that people used several tactics to reconcile their ethical and religious judgments concerning the behavior of the main character in the story. In contemporary psychological terminology we might say that they used different strategies in order to resolve the cognitive dissonance created by their negative

[7] See Leon Festinger, Henry Riecken, and Stanley Schachter, *When Prophecy Fails* (Minneapolis: University of Minnesota Press, 1956).

evaluation of the Rajah's behavior who as the main character of the story stands in for the God of the Old Testament.

The most common strategy adopted by the participants in the experiment was based on keeping their ethical judgments and their faith at two separate levels which never came into contact or interfered with each other. These results did not contribute to a particularly positive image of popular Polish religiosity. They showed how much the religious convictions and practices of his research subjects were habitual and lacking any deeper reflection. The outcome of the experiment was in agreement with Witwicki's personal view of organized religion, about which he had expressed vehement criticism on many occasions. Most telling in this respect is a collection of 321 unpublished letters to his son in which he denies not only any value to the religious education of children but also the meaningfulness of religious practices.[8]

4. *The Political Context*

The manuscript intended for formally publishing the results of Witwicki's research was completed in October 1935. However, already in 1932 the main part of his analysis had been presented at the monthly meetings of the psychological section of the Warsaw Philosophical Society. The result was that the text he submitted to the editor of *Kwartalnik Psychologiczny* (Psychological Quarterly) in Warsaw was denied publication, mainly because of worries by the editorial board about the reaction of the Bishop of Warsaw and other Church authorities. By presenting his research he strengthened his reputation as a godless person, presumably a Jew. Groups of fiercely nationalistic youths demonstrated in front of his office at Warsaw University, demanding from him to resign his professorship. They also tried on one occasion to invade his classroom during a seminar, intending to assault both him and his students, who obviously (according to the attackers) shared their professor's godless attitude. On this occasion Witwicki was able to block the doors and defend himself and his students against the intruders.

The different political attitudes amongst academic youth in Poland during the inter-war period have been described by Ramet:

---

[8] See the already mentioned article of Teresa Rzepa, "Problemy religii w kontekście uwag na temat wychowania w listach Władysława Witwickiego do syna Tadeusza z lat 1918–1945."

The major part of the Polish student body found itself under the political influence of national democracy and its student organization Młodzież Wszechpolska (*All-Polish Union*), as well as the radical-nationalist organization that arose in the final years before the Second World War. These influences led large numbers of young people to a position of radical nationalism, often a chauvinism that called into question the rights of national minorities, linked with anti-Semitism and racism, and with distinct sympathies for fascism. Moreover, those nationalist tendencies were quite commonly associated with a rather strange religious formation; that was a superficial, sentimental Catholicism – a religion that did not form a worldview and had a rather limited influence on social *mores*. Odrodzenie (*the Catholic Academic Organization*), although it was an apolitical organization and jealously guarded its apolitical character, stood in sharp conflict with the circles of the 'national youth', combating the latter's nationalism and anti-Semitism. For Odrodzenie, nationalism could not be conjoined with Catholicism properly understood, because nationalism was at the same time anti-personal...and anti-universal...[9]

It is an interesting question as to why Witwicki's research on religious reasoning and motivation stirred such strong negative emotions and placed its author in the hateful category of the 'Other'. In order to answer this question it is necessary to take a closer look at the situation of Poland between the wars and even earlier, during the long period of partition (1772–1918). Eva Hoffman offers a helpful examination of this context. She analyzes the phenomenon from an historical and anthropological perspective:

> ...during the long period of the partitions, the visions of the reborn Poland became more abstract and more purist. To some extent this can be understood as a reflex of self-preservation. If 'Polishness' was to survive, it would have to be defined as a strong, distinct entity or quality... In the absence of territory, or sovereignty...'Polishness'...began to be associated with a kind of homogeneity. To qualify as Polish, members of the future nation had to declare unequivocal loyalty to the state and to a 'Polish' system of values. Herein the source of true intolerance – of hostility toward the very existence and presence of Otherness – could be discerned.[10]

Any research on religion, especially any investigations aimed at understanding the very essence of religious convictions and potentially questioning religion's validity was perceived in that context as an immediate

---

[9] See Petra Ramet, *Cross and Commissar: The Politics and Religion in Eastern Europe and USSR* (Bloomington, Indianapolis: Indiana University Press, 1987), p. 63.

[10] Eva Hoffmann, *Shtetl: The Life and Death of a Small Town and the World of Polish Jews* (Boston, New York: Houghton Mifflin Company, 1997), p. 144.

584   HALINA GRZYMAŁA-MOSZCZYŃSKA

threat to Polishness, a construct which had a very uncertain and far from generally-agreed definition. One thing was certain: Adherence to the Roman Catholic religion was in every sense part of the core values that all true Poles should cherish.

'Core value' as a concept in scientific discourse was introduced by Smolicz only in the late 1970s and developed further in the late 1990s.[11] He describes those aspects of a society that are particularly important for the continued existence of a community as a distinct cultural entity. Different groups consider different sets of ideals as their 'core values', being of the utmost importance for a group's cultural survival. According to his theoretical analysis, religion represents a particularly potent factor in that respect. Any threat to religion is easily interpreted as a threat to the very existence of the group. This function of religion in the context of Polish society must certainly have contributed to the hostile reaction to Witwicki's research. He demonstrated that an important *core value* constituting a major part of Polish identity religion had a rather questionable status. The findings from his work on Polish religion showed it to be superficial, traditional, sentimental and lacking deeper reflection and understanding.

During the inter-war period one of the dominating issues in Polish politics was the question of identity. How should 'Polishness' be defined: by citizenship? or by inherited ethnicity? The main political groups present at the creation of the new Poland were asking these questions. The most radical way of responding originated from the "Narodowa Demokracja" (National Democracy Party or "Endencja"). Its radically rightist offshoots were the very people who demonstrated in front of Witwicki's office. The role of "Narodowa Demokracja" can be described as follows:

> This Party strongly rejected tolerance for minorities and favoured instead anti-Semitism and racism. At the same time, however, the Party represented strong resistance towards the spread of Soviet-type of communism and atheism in the country.[12]

---

[11] See Jerzy Smolicz, *Culture and Education in a Plural Society* (Canberra: Curriculum Development Center, 1979); idem, "Tradition, Core Values and Intercultural Development in Plural Societes," in Mark Secombe and John Zajda, eds., *J.J. Smolicz on Education and Culture* (Albert Park: James Nicholas Publishers, 1999), pp. 257–281

[12] H. Grzymała-Moszczyńska, "The Polish Church in the Reconciliation Process," in Lucia Ann McSpadden, ed., *Reaching Reconciliation: Churches in the transitions to democracy in Eastern and Central Europe* (Uppsala: Life and Peace Institute 2000), p. 197.

This characteristic of "Narodowa Demokracja" gives us an insight into why each voice undermining the Roman Catholic religion was treated as extremely threatening to the very essence of 'Polishness' and equivalent to the much hated communist ideology of Russia. One needs to remember that Russia was the object of strong hatred not only for being one of the super-powers that divided Poland during the time of partition, but also as a country actively promoting an atheistic worldview.

Such an extreme ideology also explains why Witwicki was labeled a Jew, the term representing the equivalent of a vicious anti-religious scholar. Again Eva Hoffman's analysis proves very helpful:

> ...in the inter-war period Polish politics became increasingly obsessed with the 'Jewish question'...Jews were still the main Other, the Polish alter ego, but this Otherness was no longer primarily religious or caste-based or even cultural. Instead, it had become political and ideological. In the new Polish nation, the Jews began to be seen as another nation, one whose character was utterly distinct from Polish identity. Jews were becoming, then, not so much a part – no matter how loved or denigrated – of the symbolic and social entity that was Poland, but an entity unto themselves, which was experienced as somehow foreign, and which could be mentally detached or expelled from the symbolic universe of self-contained Polish state.[13]

Interestingly, Jews did not represent a particularly significant social group in terms of numbers. According to the 1921 census, ethnic Poles comprised 69.3 percent of the population, Ukrainians 14.3 percent and Jews constituted only 8 percent of the population. The threat posed by the Jews for Poland's cohesion was based on their distinctiveness and to a large extent on anti-assimilationist attitudes. Such fears were not even decreased by the presence of large numbers of educated, liberal Jews, mostly city dwellers who had completely assimilated into the Polish majority.

Relegating Witwicki to the category of a 'Jew' was a reaction to the perception that his analysis undermined the Roman Catholic religion, while membership of the Church was equated with membership of an important social institution contributing to the cohesion of the nation. After four years of waiting for publication in Poland, Witwicki's book

---

[13] E. Hoffman, *Shtetl*, p. 169.

was translated into French. Several months after submission to the French publisher Alcan, it was published in Paris.

One more interesting point can be made concerning the fate of Witwicki's research. In contemporary terms his findings did not meet the requirements of political correctness for his time. The concept of political correctness entered current social discourse with a somewhat ambivalent overtone. Some scholars consider it as quite new, an American invention referring to the social pressure to give expression to certain issues in a specific way, or to keep silent about them. Looking back into history we can easily demonstrate that the practice of (but not the term) political correctness had already existed for a long time in the academy. The inter-war period in Poland was not an exception in that respect. A large sector of the Roman Catholic authorities insisted on pious religious adherence and the exemption of religion as a research subject for academic scrutiny. Religion was too important a part of the whole package of the correct, dominant ideology.

5. *Final Remarks*

The fate of Witwicki's research was not typical for investigations conducted by Polish scholars in the scientific study of religion. Exhaustive analysis of multiple research projects conducted by Polish scholars in this field during the inter-war period points towards the development of many investigations describing folk religiosity within the territory of Poland, as well as studies of the religious traditions of nations that are geographically and historically far away.[14] This opinion can be supported by examples of research taken from what we can call, broadly speaking, the social sciences of religion. One might mention ethnographic, anthropological and sociological research devoted to the place, role and function of religion inside various cultures. A strict division between these disciplines did not exist during inter-war period, therefore I have listed representative researchers together in one group.[15]

---

[14] See Halina Grzymała-Moszczyńska and Henryk Hoffmann, "The Science of Religion in Poland: Past and Present," *Method and Theory in the Study of Religion* 10 (1998), pp. 352–372 and Eva Hoffmann, *Dzieje polskich badań religioznawczych 1873–1939* [History of Polish research on religion in 1873–1939] (Kraków: Wydawnictwo Uniwersytetu Jagiellońskiego, 2004).

[15] See the publications of Czaplicka (1918), Malinowski (1922), Dobrowolski (1923), Moszyński (1929), Udziela (1931), Czarnowski (1937), and Bystroń (1939).

A detailed analysis of the developments in Polish psychology of religion in the inter-war period also demonstrates the variety and richness of the field.[16] Psychological research was devoted to the investigation of distinct religious phenomena such as magic thinking, occultism, hypnosis as important factor in mystical experiences, and the phenomenon of prayer.[17]

These researchers did not challenge the essence of individual religious conviction because their work remained at the descriptive level of analysis. Investigations of religious thinking and prayer were conducted very much according to a positivistic approach, with a clear separation between the expression of faith and faith in itself. On the other hand, Witwicki's research paradigm was seen as a violation of this division and as a direct attack on faith. Therefore, according to the Polish academic establishment, he deserved punishment by blocking publication of these research results.

The last years of Witwicki's life were marked by Germany's attack on Poland on September 1, 1939 and a rapid deterioration of his health. Until June 1943 he lived in Warsaw, than he moved to Konstancin, a small town 20 kilometers from Warsaw. He stayed there until his death in 1948. His house in Warsaw was burned during the Warsaw Uprising of 1944. In spite of his illness (he eventually lost most of his vision), he remained extremely busy as translator of classic Greek and Roman writings. He also translated Gospels according to St. Mark and St. Matthew. Witwicki also nurtured his interests in arts by preparing a theoretical manual and practical exercise book for teaching drawing and perspective. After the war, he never resumed his lectures at the Warsaw University, although a group of students attended seminars at his home in Konstancin. Witwicki passed away on December 21, 1948.

---

[16] Cf. H. Grzymała-Moszczyńska, *Religia a kultura − wybrane zagadnienia z kulturowej psychologii religii*.

[17] Cf. here Ochorowicz (1916–1917), Abramowski (1923), Lutosławski (1924) and Błachowski (1937).

588   HALINA GRZYMAŁA-MOSZCZYŃSKA

Bibliography

Abramowski, Edward. "Psychologia modlitwy" [Psychology of prayer]. *Myśl Wolna* [Free Thought], vol. 4 (1923), pp. 1–5 and vol. 5 (1923), pp. 1–4.

Błachowski, Stefan. "The Magical Behavior of Children in Relation to School." *American Journal of Psychology* 50 (1937), pp. 347–361.

Bystroń, Jan Stanisław. "Czynniki magiczno-religijne w osadnictwie" [Magic and religion in settlement]. *Przegląd Socjologiczny* [Sociological Review] 7 (1939), pp. 25–46.

Czaplicka, Marie A. *The Turks of Central Asia in History and at Present Day*. Oxford: Clarendon Press, 1918 (repr. Amsterdam: Philo, 1973).

Czarnowski, Stefan. "Kultura religijna wiejskiego ludu polskiego" [Religious culture of Polish farmers]. *Wiedza i Życie* [Knowledge and Life] 4–5 (1937), pp. 271–282.

Dobrowolski, Kazimierz. *Dzieje kultu Świętego Floriana w Polsce do połowy XVI wieku* [Cult of St. Florian's in Poland until the 1st half of the XVI century]. Warszawa: Towarzystwo Naukowe, 1923.

Festinger, Leon, Henry Riecken, and Stanley Schachter. *When Prophecy Fails*. Minneapolis: University of Minnesota Press, 1956.

Grzymała-Moszczyńska, Halina. "Eksperyment psychologiczny Władysława Witwickiego w badaniach nad wiarą religijną" [Psychological experiment on religious faith by Władysław Witwicki]. *Studia Religiologica* [Religious Studies] 5 (1980), pp. 127–132.

———. *Psychologia religii – wybrane zagadnienia* [Psychology of religion – selected problems]. Kraków: Zakład Wydawniczy Nomos, 1991.

——— with Henryk Hoffmann. "The Science of Religion in Poland: Past and Present." *Method and Theory in the Study of Religion* 10 (1998), pp. 352–372.

———. "The Polish Church in the Reconciliation Process." In Lucia Ann McSpadden, ed. *Reaching Reconciliation: Churches in the transitions to democracy in Eastern and Central Europe*. Uppsala: Life and Peace Institute 2000, pp. 191–231.

———. *Religia a kultura – wybrane zagadnienia z kulturowej psychologii religii* [Religion and culture – selected problems from cultural psychology of religion]. Kraków: Wydawnictwo Uniwersytetu Jagiellońskiego, 2004.

Hoffman, Eva. *Shtetl: The Life and Death of a Small Town and The World of Polish Jews*. Boston, New York: Houghton Mifflin Company, 1997.

———. *Dzieje polskich badań religioznawczych* 1873–1939 [History of Polish research on religion in 1873–1939]. Kraków: Wydawnictwo Uniwersytetu Jagiellońskiego, 2004.

Hofstede, Geert. "Foreword." In Uichol Kim et al., eds., *Individualism and Collectivism*. Thousand Oaks, California: Sage, 1994, pp. 10–22.

Kim, Uichol et al., eds. *Individualism and Collectivism*. Thousand Oaks, California: Sage, 1994.

Lutosławski, Wincenty. "Spirytualizm jako pogląd na świat" [Spiritualism as a worldview]. *Przegląd Warszawski* [Warsaw Review] 39 (1924), pp. 310–324.

Malinowski, Bronislaw. *Argonauts of the Western Pacific*. London, New York: Macmillan, 1922.

McSpadden, Lucia Ann, ed. *Reaching Reconciliation: Churches in the transitions to democracy in Eastern and Central Europe*. Uppsala: Life and Peace Institute, 2000.

Moszyński, Kazimierz. *Kultura ludowa Słowian* [Slavic folk-culture]. Kraków: Polska Akademia Umiejetnosci, 1929.

Nowicki, Andrzej. "Inedita Władysława Witwickiego (1878–1948). Ankieta w sprawie utraty wiary religijnej (rękopis)" [Unpublished manuscripts by Władysław Witwicki, 1878–1948. Questionnaire about loosing religious faith, manuscript]. *Euhemer – Przegląd Religioznawczy* [Euhemer – Review for the Science of Religion] 117 (1980), pp. 103–113.

———. *Witwicki*. Warszawa: Wiedza Powszechna, 1982.

Ochorowicz, Julian. *Psychologia i medycyna* [Psychology and medicine]. Warszawa: Alfa, 1916–1917.

Ramet, Petra. *Cross and Commissar: The Politics and Religion in Eastern Europe and USSR.* Bloomington, Indianapolis: Indiana University Press, 1987.

Rzepa, Teresa. "Problemy religii w kontekście uwag na temat wychowania w listach Władysława Witwickiego do syna Tadeusza z lat 1918–1945" [Religious issues in the context of remarks pertaining to education – Władysław Witwicki's letters from 1918–1945 to his son Tadeusz]. *Euhemer* 151 (1989), pp. 45–58.

Secombe, Mark and John Zajda, eds. *J.J. Smolicz on Education and Culture.* Albert Park: James Nicholas Publishers, 1999.

Smolicz, Jerzy. *Culture and Education in a Plural Society.* Canberra: Curriculum Development Center, 1979.

——. "Tradition, Core Values and Intercultural Development in Plural Societes." In Mark Secombe and John Zajda, eds., *J.J. Smolicz on Education and Culture.* Albert Park: James Nicholas Publishers, 1999, pp. 257–281.

Udziela, Seweryn. "Rośliny w wierzeniach ludu krakowskiego" [Plants in beliefs of Cracow's district peasants]. *Lud* [Folk] 30 (1931), pp. 36–75.

Witwicki, Władysław. *Psychologia. Dla użytku słuchaczów wyższych zakładów naukowych* [Psychology. For pupils of academic establishments], 2 vols. Lwów: Lwówska Biblioteczka Pedagigiczna, 1925 and 1927.

——. "I Międzynarodowy Kongres poświęcony psychologii religii w Uniwersytecie Wiedeńskim w tygodniu Zielonych Świąt 1931" [First International Congress of Psychology of Religion at Vienna University in the week of Pentecost of 1931]. *Kwartalnik Psychologiczny* [Psychological Quarterly] 4 (1931), p. 397.

——. *La foi des éclairés.* Paris: Alcan, 1939.

FUTURE'S PAST

C.G. JUNG'S PSYCHOUTOPIA AND THE 'GERMAN REVOLUTION' OF 1933

Petteri Pietikäinen

Historian Sonu Shamdasani has noted that the Swiss depth psychologist Carl Gustav Jung (1875–1961) has been called

> Occultist, Scientist, Prophet, Charlatan, Philosopher, Racist, Guru, Anti-Semite, Liberator of Women, Misogynist, Freudian Apostate, Gnostic, Post-Modernist, Polygamist, Healer, Poet, Con-Artist, Psychiatrist and Anti-Psychiatrist – what has Jung not been called?[1]

To Shamdasani's list, I would like to add that Jung has also been called a völkisch scholar (Noll), pseudo-mythologist (Marcuse), crypto-fascist (Bloch), National Socialist (Reich), sympathizer of Hitler, and 'necrophilous character' – that is, a lover of death (Fromm)!

More recently, the German sociologist Heinz Gess connected Jungian psychology with neo-fascist and New Age movements. Grounding his ideological critique on the Critical Theory of the Frankfort School, Gess discounted Jung's archetypal theory as representing a legitimization of the capitalist society with its emphasis on the mythical, unchanging and eternal. In Jung's pursuit of organic, psychic Wholeness, Gess detected distinct resemblances with Hitler's ambitions and, at the same time, a continuation of a fascist personality type.[2]

From the point of view of historical truth, how serious are these accusations hurled at Jung? Do they correspond to what we know about Jung's beliefs and intentions? In order to answer these questions, I will leave Jung aside for a while and turn my attention to the question of method. (Those who do not care about such questions can proceed straight to the next section).

---

[1] Sonu Shamdasani, *Jung and the making of modern psychology* (Cambridge: Cambridge University Press, 2003), p. 1.
[2] Heinz Gess, *Vom Faschismus zum Neuen Denken – C.G. Jungs Theorie im Wandeln der Zeit* (Lüneburg: Klampen, 1994).

Some Preliminary Remarks on the Historical Method

How to make a 'good' historical interpretation of the ideas, utterances and acts of past peoples and individuals? After musing on this simple but thorny question for twenty years, I think I can make some tentative comments on 'method', using Quentin Skinner's ideas as my guiding light. Skinner is a historian of political ideas who has provided valuable methodological tools for exploring the thinking of historical agents. In my view, Skinner's ideas are relevant to all scholars who are doing historical research on the ideas and practices of German *Bildungsbürgertum*, including scholars of religion, between the years 1933 and 1945.

To put it as succinctly as possible, Skinner's methodological argument goes something like this. In order to determine or clarify what the authors meant in what they wrote or said, we have to find out what were the conventional *illocutive* tones or acts that were typical in the time and place ('culture') in which the authors lived. Skinner has derived the idea of 'illocutive tones' from the linguistic philosopher John L. Austin's theory; Austin argued that all sentences have an illocutive meaning that is determined by the *intention* of the speaker, and that one cannot understand the illocutive meaning merely by analyzing the sentence itself. To understand an utterance such as 'it is cold outside' we have to grasp the speaker's intentions: does 'it is cold outside' mean that we should go skiing? Or should we stay indoors? Should I close the window? Is it a warning, a request, or a suggestion? For Skinner, to understand an expression as an illocutive act is equivalent to understanding the intentions of the historical agent, and this understanding makes it possible to understand the *meaning* of the text, or the meaning the author wanted to express or convey in the text. But the question of the relationship between intentions and meanings is more complicated than that, because texts may have meanings that the author did not intend to convey. Thus Skinner urges historians to "focus not merely on the particular text in which we are interested but on the prevailing conventions governing the treatment of the issues or themes with which the text is concerned."[3]

An interpretation of a particular text requires not only the identification of intentions, but also of beliefs, and these beliefs are something

---

[3] Quentin Skinner, *Visions of politics. Volume I: Regarding method* (Cambridge: Cambridge University Press, 2002), p. 101f.

that the author typically takes for granted and does not articulate – he or she may not be aware of all of his or her beliefs. An intellectual historian who tries to identify and describe particular beliefs places these beliefs in a wider 'network of beliefs' or mentality, which refers to beliefs that were commonplace and typical at a time. Thus historians cannot determine the meaning of texts without recovering beliefs and intentions of the author, and in seeking for *connections* between intentions and (often) unarticulated beliefs, historians are contextualizing their subjects. The search for connections between beliefs and intentions – 'contextualization' – requires first that historians try to recapture the prevailing beliefs or presuppositions that governed the approach to a particular issue in a particular time and place; second, that historians ask questions about what the writers were *doing* as well as what they were saying in a given text, and third, that so far as possible, historians try to see things the way peoples of the past saw them.

The foremost task of an intellectual historian is to identify and describe beliefs, and the starting point of this inquiry is to determine what the historical agents *themselves* have possibly said about their beliefs. This requires a particular, context-bound approach, which in turn requires that we do not evaluate the ideas of past thinkers from the point of view of our own standards of epistemic and moral truth. As Skinner points out, "we are prone to fall under the spell of our own intellectual heritage."[4] For those of us who study past thinkers, to fall under this spell can be intellectually fatal: if we assume that our own cherished values and visions of justice and freedom somehow stand above the battle of conflicting values and visions, we are inclined to evaluate the past intellectual traditions with our own normative concepts. This inevitably leads to distortions and false statements concerning the beliefs and intentions of past thinkers. "What the historical record strongly suggests," writes Skinner, "is that no one is above the battle, because the battle is all there is."[5] To understand different styles of reasoning is not necessarily equal to "being able to translate those styles into more familiar ones"[6] – that is to say, into styles of reasoning that provide frameworks for our own beliefs or presuppositions.

Like Skinner, I believe that in social explanation, human agency

---

[4] Ibid., p. 6.
[5] Ibid., p. 7.
[6] Ibid., p. 47.

is to be privileged over structure. A study of individual thinkers and
scholars should not be seen merely as a preliminary stage to a more
'scientific' or otherwise important study of 'structures' or 'institutions'.
Through a proper study of historical agents, we can understand the
beliefs that in a specific context "governed the treatment of the issues
or themes with which the text is concerned" (Skinner). In other words,
we can understand the intellectual contexts out of which particular
beliefs, ideas and arguments arose. And, for me, this is the ultimate
goal of historical scholarship. While we cannot discover the true reality of the past, we can find out not only the reasons why individual
thinkers held certain beliefs, but also why it was rationally or morally
acceptable or uncontroversial to hold these beliefs in a particular time
and place. To accuse late nineteenth-century thinkers of racism, for
example, may be an edifying exercise of moral reading, but it does not
help us understand why these thinkers (Darwin or Marx, for instance)
thought it rational to hold beliefs that we now consider to be utterly
racist or prejudiced, or what they may have intended or meant in their
texts or utterances.

A study of history can demonstrate why it was rational for thinkers
of the past to hold certain beliefs, but it does not qualify us to draw
moral conclusions about these beliefs. What historians can do is to
insist of a given belief that "it was less than rational for a given agent
to uphold it".[7] In a way, compared to, for example, scholars of völkisch
beliefs, it is easier for Skinner to uphold the idea that historians should
not approach their materials with preconceived paradigms, and that
they should employ the concept of rational acceptability when they
try to recover the points of view of past thinkers. Skinner himself is
a specialist in early modern political thought, and the thinkers he has
studied certainly thought rationally (Machiavelli, Hobbes, etc.) and
developed ideas and theories that were not devoid of consistency and
logic. By contrast, historians who are engaged in the study of the
ideas, beliefs and intentions of völkisch or National Socialist scholars
enter into a conceptual territory where the standards of rationality are
often stretched to the limit, and where sinister political purposes and
disagreeable intentions seem to abound.

How can a historian coolly stick to Skinner's methodological framework when he or she knows that the subject of his or her study was a

---

[7] Ibid., p. 38.

scheming Nazi (such as Walther Wüst)? I believe that if Skinner was a scholar of fascist or National Socialist ideas, his statements about method would differ from the ones he has made as a historian of early modern political thinking. The obscure, simplistic, racialist (etc.) styles of reasoning that völkisch authors represented are difficult to characterize as 'rational', especially if one espouses the paradigmatic Kantian view on the rationality of moral principles. Thus it is exceedingly difficult for a historian of völkisch beliefs to see it as his or her task to study the contexts of beliefs and presuppositions in a way that, as Skinner puts it, "serves to exhibit the utterance in which we are interested as one that it was rational for that particular agent, in those particular circumstances, to have held to be true."[8] It seems to me that the problem lies not in Skinner's sound principle that historians should make the agents who endorsed particular beliefs to appear as rational as possible; the problem is rather that the rationality of historical agents is sometimes extremely difficult to disentangle from morality, or from the 'preconceived' moral standards of historians themselves. The alleged rationality of an executioner is less of an issue than the moral justification (or, as usually is the case, the lack of moral justification) of his executions.

Still, a historical study of fascist or National Socialist thinkers and scholars is not a mission impossible. Beliefs and intentions of even the most fanatical Nazi scholars can be contextualized, elucidated and explained, and a precise contextualization enables historians to recover the ways in which historical agents fell short of some standard of epistemic rationality that was commonly accepted in a particular society. Of course, in the case of Nazi Germany, historians need to confront the issue of the lowering of the standard of epistemic rationality when the Weimar republic was buried in 1933. The true challenge, as I see it, is to try to explain historically why particular agents espoused particular beliefs, and to illustrate the connections between their beliefs and intentions – a German scholar may have presented himself as a dedicated National Socialist for a variety of reasons, and it is the task of historians to examine the interplay of ideological commitments, often unarticulated beliefs (which did not necessarily harmonize with one's ideological commitments) and intentions (e.g. with regard to career opportunities, scholarly reputation, the accumulation of 'symbolic capital' and so forth).

---

[8] Ibid., p. 42.

In what follows, I will try to practice what I preach and uncover some of Jung's beliefs and intentions concerning Nazi Germany. Following Skinner and Wittgenstein, I endorse the statement (made by Wittgenstein in his *Philosophical Investigations*) that "words are also deeds" – we are always doing something as well as saying something. With regard to thinkers like Jung, who made sweeping statements about Hitler's Germany and the Jews, this argument about the performativity of texts is, I believe, incontestable.

"The German revolution has positive and negative aspects."
On Jung's Early Interpretation of National Socialism

In 1933, Jung became president of the reorganized "Überstaatliche allgemeine ärztliche Gesellschaft für Psychotherapie," and the editor of its journal *Zentralblatt*. German psychotherapists, now under the sway of National Socialism, were by far the largest national group in the International Society, and held the main executive positions. Although Jung inserted a circular letter in the December 1934 issue of the *Zentralblatt*, in which he declared that the International Society was neutral in its politics and creed,[9] the official journal of the society published papers and reviews which praised Hitler and extolled National Socialism. It seems that Jung was exploited by the scheming German psychotherapists, who tried to take full advantage of Jung's fame and neutral citizenship in order to legitimize National Socialist ideology and policy.[10] These manipulations and organizational arrangements, together with Jung's questionable 'psychological profiles' of the Jews, written in the late 1920s and early 1930s, provoked legitimate criticism both during his life and after his death.[11]

---

[9] C.G. Jung, "Circular Letter," in idem, *Collected Works* 10 (London: Routledge & Kegan Paul, 1981, 1st ed. 1934), p. 545f.

[10] Deirdre Bair, *Jung A biography* (Boston: Little, Brown and Company, 2003), pp. 444–448.

[11] On Jung's relationship to the Third Reich and its racial psychology, see Bair, *Jung*; Petteri Pietikäinen, "The 'Volk' and its Unconscious. Jung, Hauer, and the 'German revolution'," *Journal of Contemporary History* 35 (2000), pp. 523–539; Stanley Grossman, "C.G. Jung and National Socialism," in Paul Bishop, ed., *Jung in Contexts* (London: Routledge, 1999), pp. 92–121; Geoffrey Cocks, *Psychotherapy in the Third Reich: The Göring Institute*, 2nd rev. and exp. ed. (New Brunswick, NJ: Transaction Publishers, 1997); Andrew Samuels, *Politics and psyche* (London: Routledge, 1993); Aryeh G. Maidenbaum and Stephen A. Martin, eds., *Lingering shadows: Jungians, Freudians, and Anti-Semitism* (Boston: Shambala, 1991).

However, I will not discuss Jung's involvement in the German psychotherapeutic scene here. Instead, I will argue that Jung originally interpreted National Socialism as a social equivalent to what he called 'individuation'. Jung's individuation refers to an archetypal psychic process in which individuals become what they 'truly are' – authentic, Whole, true to themselves, and so forth. My thesis is that, in the 1930s, Jung expanded his psycho-utopian idea of individual authenticity and wholeness to apply not only to individuals but also to nations. During this decade, Jung formulated ideas that had their ultimate source in his belief that what he called the 'German revolution' of 1933 might very well signify individuation writ large, or *national* individuation, a process whereby a whole nation attains a new spiritual and cultural level. It seems to me that it was this promise of a psycho-spiritual regeneration of Germany that attracted Jung to National Socialism in the early years of the Third Reich. What is more, it was this prospect for a national individuation that encouraged Jung to co-operate with the National Socialist indologist Jakob Wilhelm Hauer, whom he first met in the late 1920s at Count Keyserling's School of Wisdom in Darmstadt. Jung and Hauer stayed in contact after National Socialism rose to power.

What makes the relationship between Hauer and Jung so fascinating a subject for historical analysis is that, a few years after Hauer had established the neo-Pagan *Deutsche Glaubensbewegung* in 1933, Jung declared that Hauer and the other members of his movement were possessed by the ancient German Pagan god, Wotan, which had reappeared in Germany as an archetype of the Collective Unconscious (Hauer himself denied that his movement had anything to do with Wotan).[12] In 1936, Jung devoted an (infamous) essay to the depth-psychological analysis of the Wotan archetype, stating that Wotan reveals more about National Socialism than political, economical or psychological (sic) explanations. This is what he said of the *Deutsche Glaubensbewegung* in his essay:

> [T]here are people in the German Faith Movement who are intelligent enough not only to *believe* but to *know* that the god of the *Germans* is Wotan and not the Christian God. This is a tragic experience and no disgrace...We who stand outside judge the Germans far too much as if they were responsible agents, but perhaps it would be nearer the truth to regard them also as *victims*.[13]

---

[12] For the history of the German Faith Movement, see Ulrich Nanko, *Die Deutsche Glaubensbewegung* (Marburg: Diagonal Verlag, 1993).

[13] C.G. Jung, "Wotan," in idem, *Collected Works* 10 (London: Routledge & Kegan Paul, 1981, 1st ed. 1936), pp. 191f.

By 'victims', Jung did not refer to the idea that the Germans were victims of National Socialist tyranny; what he meant rather was that they were victims of the archetypal forces of the Collective Unconscious. Thus, Hauer and the members of his movement were 'possessed' by the archetype of Wotan.

In his seminar on Nietzsche's *Zarathustra* in February 1936, Jung told his audience that "I must say that I am very *grateful* to the Germans for their paganistic movement, at the head of which is my friend Professor Hauer who taught us the Tantric Yoga, and who has now become a savior of the fools" [italics mine].[14] Why was Jung 'grateful' to the Germans? And what sort of archetype was the archetype of Wotan that Jung saw as responsible for the emerging psycho-spiritual revolution in Germany? To answer the latter question first, Jung's Wotan appeared to be a very formidable archetype indeed – an archetype which (or, who?) would first bring about chaos and tumult, and then – after the storm – introduce a new and potentially regenerated or 'individuated' German nation.

Was this promise of a better future for Germany the reason why Jung was 'grateful' to the Germans for Hauer and his *Glaubensbewegung*? "Definitely maybe" is what I would like to answer to this question at this point. But let us move on and return to Jung's gratitude later.

In 1935, a member of his seminar on *Zarathustra* provided Jung with the French phrase to which he would refer a year later when he wrote *Wotan*: *il faut reculer pour mieux sauter* ("to jump farther, one must fall back").[15] Jung concludes his essay on *Wotan* by referring to Wotan's reawakening in the form of National Socialism as a *reculer pour mieux sauter*; it is a stepping back into the past, but such a regression is required before "the water will overleap the obstacle. Then at last we shall know what Wotan is saying when he 'murmurs with Mimir's head'."[16] Historian Stanley Grossman has noted in his analysis of Jung and National Socialism that, in the original 1936 edition, Jung ended his essay with this positive note, but added the supplementary, more sinister quotation from Voluspa (Poetic Edda) after World War II. This

---

[14] *Nietzsche's Zarathustra. Notes of the seminar given in 1934–1939 by C.G. Jung*, vols. I–II, ed. by James L. Jarrett (Princeton: Princeton University Press), p. 813 (February 5, 1936).

[15] Ibid., p. 378 (February 13, 1935). The individual in question was Mrs. Martha Sigg, who used the saying as a comment on Jung's idea that it is difficult to judge Germany, because "[F]rom one aspect things are positive, and from another, quite negative." Ibid.

[16] Jung, *Wotan*, p. 192.

is a detail which, as Grossman suggests, implies that dark future rather than cultural renewal is to be expected in Germany.[17] This minor gesture – which is not noted in the Collected Works edition – indicates a major change in Jung's attitude towards National Socialism between 1936 and 1945, a change that made him revise his essay on Wotan after the war in order to strike a more pessimistic note. It is easy to be wise after the event.

A year before *Wotan* appeared, Jung had interpreted the 'German revolution' in an even more symbolistic fashion. In his seminar on *Zarathustra* in February 1935, he deliberated upon the psychic background of color symbolism, zodiacal signs and national symbolism. He observed, first, how the Soviet-Russians had chosen as their national symbol the five-rayed star, which is the pentagram, the sign of evil magic: "[T]he Soviet star is not only five-rayed, it is also red, the color of blood, so it is an intensely evil sign."[18] Second, he made a social statement based on astrology: "[O]ne can really say there is a tremendous transformation going on throughout the world, and it is coincident with the approach of Aquarius."[19] Third, he paid attention to the 'curious' fact that the swastika is turning the wrong way, to the way of 'evil':

> Now, in choosing the black swastika turning to the left, the Germans have surely expressed the backward movement in many ways. First of all, the swastika is a pagan sun symbol in spite of the fact that it is found in early Christianity, in the catacombs for instance... Then secondly, its backward movement, and thirdly, the black color, the color of evil. Those are regressions into archaism, into the path of the left hand which is the dark unconscious side. So one could say the sun is now transformed into a counter-sun, a sun which is not above but below, which is not bright but dark, which does not go clockwise but counterclockwise. It is a revolution against the old trend of things, and therefore progress is arrested: there is a regression.[20]

This looks like a rather negative interpretation of National Socialism, unless one is aware that Jungian individuation begins with the acknowledgement of the darker and inferior side of one's personality, an encounter with the archetype of the Shadow. This encounter with the Shadow is truly an act of *reculer pour mieux sauter*: you regress and take a

---

[17] Grossman, "C.G. Jung and National Socialism," p. 113f.
[18] Jung, *Nietzsche's Zarathustra*, p. 374 (February 13, 1935).
[19] Ibid., p. 376 (February 13, 1935).
[20] Ibid., p. 377 (February 13, 1935).

step back in order to jump further. But, as was often the case with Jung, his way of expressing his ideas was not exactly crystal-clear. Indeed, his fluency in the art of mystical exegesis is finely exemplified here. Instead of reality-oriented analysis of the developments in Germany, he offered hard-to-decipher interpretations that followed the tradition of esoteric hermeneutics of the likes of Böhme and Swedenborg. Quite effortlessly, he lifted the social and political phenomena from the mundane reality to the transhistorical level of archetypal symbolism, and interpreted National Socialism as an essentially religious phenomenon.

In his Visions seminar on May 10, 1933, Jung referred to the persecution of the German Jews and the recent burning of Jewish literature by students, and went on to say:

> It is a regression and injustice, there is no doubt about that; but they [the Germans] cannot get together as a nation, they cannot celebrate their love feast, if strangers are in between. Of course you can say that Jews are scapegoats; of course they are scapegoats, but other people, individuals, do the same thing: in the process of individuation, for instance, they exclude many things, they may desert their relations, which is unjust, cruel, or foolish perhaps, but it serves that one purpose of individuation, of coming together.[21]

Here Jung explicitly compares the 'German revolution' with individuation process, whereby an individual becomes that which he or she truly is, attaining authenticity and Wholeness. National individuation signifies an attainment of a new condition of collective consciousness, and during the process, the Germans would have to 'exclude many things', Jews among them. While he saw the 'German revolution' as an individuation process writ large, Jung was also worried that 'the suppression of free speech' and expulsion of people who are

> enormously valuable to a nation...may have a very bad influence on the further development of the German mind, because they are isolating themselves from the world...Such things may mean the ultimate defeat of this movement, we don't know, but at all events for the time being we must suspend our judgment. The German revolution has positive and negative aspects.[22]

---

[21] *Visions. Notes of the seminar given in 1930–1934* by C.G. Jung, vols. I–II, ed. by C. Douglas (London: Routledge, 1998), p. 976 (May 10, 1933).
[22] Ibid., p. 976f. (May 10, 1933).

The Significance of Wotan

Central to the argument I am developing here is that although Jung admitted that Wotan's reawakening amounted to cultural regression, he also believed that, after the Germans had overcome the first tumultuous effects of Wotan's resurgence, something more valuable and long-lasting would appear in Germany. For Jung, the reappearance of the archetype of Wotan signaled the beginning of a national individuation in Germany. Inspired by the Heraclitean principle of *enantiodromia* (running towards the opposite), Jung appeared to hold that through the inherently dialectical development of culture, Germany would perhaps enter into a new Golden Age after the initial spiritual regression. What Jung failed to make clear in this context was whether he saw the new Golden Age emerging as a later phase of the National Socialist 'revolution' or as a totally new, post-Nazi, era, although it can be inferred that a political turnover was *not* a prerequisite for a better future for Germany.

I would suggest that this is the main reason he became so interested in Wotan and German neo-Paganism in the early 1930s: It appeared to him that National Socialism had awakened the collective, primordial archetypal forces in the unconscious of the Germans, and that it was the archetype of Wotan that corresponded to the confused and regressed, but extremely vital state of the German unconscious psyche. In fact, he did not confine Wotan's sphere of activity to Germany: After expressing his gratitude to Germans for their 'paganistic movement' (Hauer's *Glaubensbewegung*) in his seminar on Zarathustra in February 1936, he proclaimed that

> Now Old Wotan is in the center of Europe; you can see all the psychological symptoms which he personifies, including his romantic character of the sorcerer, the god of mysteries – all that is living again. As far as the German mentality reaches in Europe – and it reaches, as you know, from the Urals to Spain – we see religion upset; in the most Catholic of all countries, Spain, the Church is completely overthrown. And that is old Wotan, you could not name it better, the wind came and blew the thing into bits. Fascism in Italy is old Wotan again; it is all Germanic blood down there, with no trace of the Romans; they are Langobards, and they all have that Germanic spirit. Of course Switzerland is still a little exception, you know! Oh, we have joined in but we were not so foolish as to say so.[23]

---

[23] Ibid., p. 813f. (February 5, 1936).

I believe it is no coincidence that Jung focused on the ancient German Pagan god when he tried to make sense of the 'German revolution', and of the developments in Spain and Italy. In Jung's utopian vision of national regeneration, religion played an essential role as the symbolic outlet for the cataclysm caused by the social and political turmoil in these countries that in his view were affected by the 'German mentality'.

What I believe is incontestable, it is that Jung was initially enthusiastic over the religious and depth-psychological aspects of the changes taking place in National Socialist Germany. His statements between the years 1933–1937/38 indicate that his fundamental belief during this period was that while the deepest level of the psyche was the matrix of collective psychic epidemics (such as communism or National Socialism), it was *also* the matrix of psycho-utopian renewal (the attainment of a new level of consciousness). This is what Jung suggested in his seminars in the 1930s (Visions, Zarathustra), as well as in his essay on Wotan.

In the end, however, the brutal reality of the Third Reich refused to conform to Jung's psychology, throwing archetypes overboard, as it were. After 1936 and his essay on Wotan, where Hauer and his movement are analyzed as a positive symptom of German *Ergriffenheit*, Jung's attitude towards Hauer and National Socialism became increasingly reserved and disillusioned. By 1938, Jung, whose popularity in the English-speaking world was steadily growing, had probably come to the conclusion that völkisch ideas offered nothing to him, and that National Socialism was not, after all, an invigorating religious movement that would lead the German nation to the path of national individuation.

I will now return to the question whether Jung was 'grateful to the Germans' because they seemed to be on the road to national individuation. My central argument is that, between 1933 and 1937/38, Jung believed that National Socialism was potentially a movement that would help bring about a spiritual and cultural regeneration of the German nation, and that such a national regeneration or individuation would exemplify, and give evidence for, his theory of individuation at the collective, national level. Although confused and misguided about the political goals of National Socialism, for a few years Jung held the assumption that, in an era of western civilization characterized by a deep cultural crisis, one great nation would experience psycho-spiritual and socio-cultural renewal through a process that was violently initiated by National Socialism – or, rather, by the archetype of Wotan.

In my view, Jung's reasoning concerning National Socialism should be seen in the context of his professional life, which inevitably molded his 'mental habits'. Jung was a psychiatrist by training and education, and he worked for nine years as a clinical psychiatrist at the Burghölzli mental hospital in Zurich in the early twentieth century. He resigned in 1909 and for the rest of his long life he made his living as a psychotherapist in private practice. His burning ambition was not only to become a renowned psychotherapist, but, above all, to be a creator of a new psychology and, even beyond that, to develop a new understanding of human nature. I would suggest that it was this ambition that made him evaluate political movements and phenomena in psychological and psychomedical terms. As a psychologically-oriented therapist who was trained to see individuals in terms of sickness, symptoms and suffering, he was prone to apply these terms and categories when he mulled over political and socio-cultural events and phenomena.

That Jung interpreted National Socialism in terms of his own theory, is not that different from the way in which Freud interpreted cultural evolution as a massive neuroticizing process in *Das Unbehagen in der Kultur* (1930). Granted, Freud's pessimistic view of the neurosis-prone western civilization can be placed in the critical Enlightenment tradition, while Jung's more esoteric and obscure references to national individuation are more difficult to contextualize. As Sonu Shamdasani's remark at the beginning of this paper shows, the question of the proper context of Jung's ideas elicits widely diverging answers. In the remaining two sections, I will briefly discuss a mentality and a worldview which, I believe, clarifies the connection between Jung's beliefs (concerning the psychic functioning of people) and intentions (with regard to politics and culture).

Jung in Context I: Antitemporalism

Notwithstanding Jung's increasing aversion to National Socialism at the end of the 1930s, there is one essential point of contact between Jung, a republican Swiss psychologist, and Hauer, a National Socialist German scholar of religion: their common preoccupation with mythical, constant and transhistorical. Hauer examined the religious *Urphänomen*, the commonly-shared basic elements of religious experience (such as the eternal essence of Man and how his ultimate destiny is determined by God), whereas Jung studied the psychic *Urphänomen* called archetypes, with which he approached purely historical phenomena and gave transhistorical interpretations of them. They both searched for some rational justification for their preoccupation with organic totality and wholeness, which could be attained through examining forms, structures and forces that were somehow beyond historical time and were often called with the prefix 'ur' (*Urphänomen, Urkraft, Urform, Urtyp, Urgeschichte, Urgrund*, etc.).

An inclination to give far-reaching mythical *ur*-accounts of history was apparent, for example, in Thomas Mann's 'Jungian' tetralogy *Joseph und seine Brüder*, in the work of the German *Volkskundler* Adolf Spamer, who searched for the *geistig-seelische Urkräfte* in his studies of *Volksseele*, and in the whole scholarly work of Mircea Eliade. Eliade even operated with the term 'archetype', although for him it referred to the existence of Platonic-universal forms in the religious sphere rather than to psychic structures. In the 1930s, many scholars who studied the 'elementary forces' in culture and human nature had either theoretical or overtly political connections to right-wing ideologies, which tended to glorify the mythical and the timeless and downplay the profane time of historical contingencies (the worship of History and its 'laws' was a specialty of Marxists).

It seems to me that Jung's preference for phenomena that he claimed were not subject to contingencies of historical time characterized his utopian yearning for a deeper and more meaningful world than the one in which he and his patients had to live. In Jung's vision of *Ganzheit*, an individual encounters fascinating archetypes, which as mental invariables are essentially beyond time and place. As in all utopias, there is no history nor diachrony in his psychological utopianism – everything is privatized into individual-yet-universal intrapsychic domain. The 'law of motion' that Jung discovered was not that of history and society, as in Marxist and other historically-determined utopias, but that of archetypal processes.

As Jung saw it, historical time with its contingencies lacked sacred aura, mystery and imagination. The more modern individuals were cut off from the world of archetypal symbols, the more intense was their experience of cultural and psychological disenchantment (*Entzauberung*). One could say that Jung reacted against what he saw as the oppression of historical contingency and the seemingly limitless devaluation of timeless truths by devising psycho-utopian ideas about the supratemporal structures of the Collective Unconscious which would function as a cure for the mythic-symbolic impoverishment of western culture. He wanted to create a sense of experiencing Sacred Time by connecting his patients and readers with the inner universe, where the primordial era of myth continues its ur-existence in the form of transhistorical archetypal symbolism. Instituting the absolutism of archetypal images against the oppression of historical time, he represented this transportation to higher time as a healing and a regeneration of the psyche. His psychological antitemporalism signified a therapeutic move from the alleged pathogenicity of historical time to the timeless symbolic universe of (potentially) healing archetypes.[24]

Jung in Context II: German Holism

If antitemporalism was a 'mentality' that governed the way Jung approached issues he was interested in, German anti-positivist holism was a worldview that shaped the way in which many scientists, physicians and scholars, Jung among them, looked at reality. In the interwar years, the holistic attempt to overcome cultural and scientific fragmentation found favor with many Germans, who sought *Ganzheit* in life as well as in culture. As Mitchell G. Ash and Anne Harrington have demonstrated in their respective studies, organic, holistic ideas are in themselves neither fascist nor 'reactionary'.[25] The fact that Jung elaborated on the idea of psychic Wholeness does not transmogrify him, any more than it does the liberal gestalt psychologist Kurt Goldstein, into a fascist. Quite the contrary, a number of respected German scientists and scholars (and not only muddle-headed völkisch obscurantists) were concerned with achieving Wholeness in culture and society. Harrington argues that

> before 1933, various liberal, democratic, and Jewish scientists were attracted to both the intellectual and cultural promises of holism and managed to share concerns about the 'mechanization' of both science and society with their more reactionary, and, in some cases, anti-Semitic colleagues.[26]

---

[24] For a more detailed discussion of Jung's antitemporalism, see Petteri Pietikäinen, *C.G. Jung and the psychology of symbolic forms* (Helsinki: The Finnish Academy of Science and Letters, 1999).

[25] Mitchell G. Ash, *Gestalt psychology in German culture, 1890–1967: Holism and the quest for objectivity* (Cambridge: Cambridge University Press, 1995); Anne Harrington. *Reenchanted science: Holism in German culture from Wilhelm to Hitler* (Princeton: Princeton University Press, 1996).

[26] Harrington, *Reenchanted science*, p. xxi.

Like Jung, these scientists and scholars tended to see modern techno-
logical culture as a mechanical 'Gorilla-Machine', devoid of life and
meaning. What is more, some of them conceived ideas and theories
that had striking resemblances with Jung's psychology.

Here I content myself with short references to two such representatives of holistic thinking, Constantin von Monakow and Felix Krueger.
The renowned Swiss neurologist von Monakow was engaged in a
research on the way past and present experiences were coded in the
brain, coining the term 'horme' in 1918 to designate the 'primal mother
of instinct'. In Harrington's words, Monakow's horme had its origins
"not in the world of visible, material biology, but in a domain that
transcended biology and was inaccessible to direct empirical investigation."[27] Just like Jung with his theory of archetypes, Monakow drew
inspiration from German *Naturphilosophie* and evolutionary vitalism, and,
again like Jung, Monakow was motivated to pursue his psychobiological
vision by his existential observation that the "meaninglessness of life
tortures us. That is today the disease of our age."[28] Yet, Monakow was
hardly a fascist or even a völkisch scholar just because he envisioned
organic unity and Wholeness, and fused the categories of biology and
spirit to create an essentially moral tale of how to heal humanity and
attain wisdom.

Another scholar who was searching for a unifying worldview was
Felix Krueger, head of the Leipzig school of *Ganzheitspsychologie*, a more
conservative holistic psychology which in the Weimar era rivalled the
liberal, Berlin-based *Gestaltpsychologie*. Krueger, who endorsed völkisch
metaphors and the ultraconservative ideology behind them, introduced
the term 'Structure', which resembles Jung's archetype. 'Structure' is a
mental operating system, an 'unconscious force' that is profoundly teleological and purposive as it is designed to meet a need for meaning and
Wholeness. Similarly, Jung's archetypes are 'structures' or 'categories' of
imagination and fantasy, attaching immense importance to our 'inherent
tendency' to realize our psychic potentialities and achieve Wholeness.
Like Jung, most holistic theorists were conservative intellectuals and
academics, who "often employed holistic vocabulary in their efforts to
counter the perceived threats of urbanization, industrialization, and

---

[27] Ibid., p. 90.
[28] Quoted in Harrington, *Reenchanted science*, p. 87.

democratization."[29] In his later theory of synchronicity ('an a-causal connecting principle'), Jung offered a distinctly holistic account of the interdependence of mind and matter, but it would be quite foolish to claim that this sort of holistic thinking, also exemplified in psychosomatic medicine, necessarily has reactionary political implications.

Holism represents a mode of thought that cannot be easily categorized through its political ramifications. In their search for the unifying *Weltanschauung*, Jung and German holistic thinkers manifested thought patterns that seem to testify to the continuity of the questions nineteenth-century representatives of German Romanticism and *Naturphilosophie* had been preoccupied with. This is not to say that holism is an 'intellectual tradition' going back to the early nineteenth century (or even beyond); rather, it is a question of twentieth-century holistic thinkers tracing the lineage of their ideas to such paradigmatic authors as Goethe, who represented the *Urvater* of holism to such authors as Jung.

Conclusion

In their everyday work, historians have to face the fact that their knowledge base is (sometimes frustratingly) uncertain. In fact, the ability to tolerate epistemic uncertainty and the lack of general laws or even historical 'tendencies' is an essential requirement for historians. This being the case, there is nothing very extraordinary in my observation that it is difficult to make final judgments on the degree of Jung's commitment to the belief that the 'German revolution' of 1933 would usher in a new Golden Age for Germans. So much of Jung's correspondence, for example, is still unpublished that we need to know more about his beliefs in order to be more assertive in our statements about the proper historical context of his thinking. What is clear is that, in his elaborated attempt to mythologize man's 'inner nature', Jung derived ideas from a multitude of sources, modifying, abandoning or developing them further. Therefore, Jung's beliefs and intentions in the 1930s cannot be wholly explained by something as vague and diffuse as völkisch ideology, antitemporalism or holism.

What is also clear is that Jung represented a relatively large group of physicians and academics who were (a) fascinated by National Socialism

---

[29] Ash, *Gestalt psychology in German culture*, p. 12.

during the first years of Hitler's regime, (b) formulated ideas tallying with ideas propounded by people who were openly National Socialist or fascist; and (c) became over time disillusioned with National Socialism, which developed into a violent system of terror rather than into a popular movement that would pave the way for the better future for Germany. The political sentiments and opinions about Germany that Jung expressed in the 1930s were in most part shared by, for example, Swedish conservative physicians, who felt great affinity with German culture and initially believed that National Socialism would function as a valuable counterforce against communism, materialism and what they regarded as the moral degeneration of the west.[30] Like Jung, the majority of Swedish doctors were not, however, active supporters of National Socialism, and during the latter half of the 1930s their attitude towards the 'new' Germany cooled down considerably.

Still, I believe it would be wrong to simply assert that Jung was politically naive or that his disregard of 'external reality' made him (partially) blind to the terror that was National Socialism. Like his German contemporary, Martin Heidegger, Jung appeared to be unable to confront the issue of his thought system's relation to politics. Heidegger, who, remarkably enough, later considered *himself* to be a victim of National Socialism, explained away his utterances and maneuvers in the 1930s by referring to his misjudgment about the true nature of National Socialism. As the political scientist Mark Lilla puts it in his account of Heidegger's involvement in politics,

> He [Heidegger] simply had been fooled into thinking that the Nazis' resolve to found a new nation was compatible with his private and loftier resolution to refound the entire tradition of Western thought, and thereby Western existence.[31]

It stretches the historians' imagination to try to see things the way Jung and Heidegger saw them. That they both initially thought that the phenomenon of National Socialism would somehow be compatible with or a testimony to their own assumptions concerning the 'refounding of Western existence' (Heidegger) or 'national individuation' (Jung) suggests that their styles of reasoning were separated from reality. In

---

[30] See Mats Eklöf, *Läkarens ethos. Studier i den svenska läkarkårens identiteter, intressen och ideal 1890–1960* (Linköping: Linköpings universitet, 2000).
[31] Mark Lilla, *The reckless mind: Intellectuals in politics* (New York: New York Review Books, 2001), p. 29.

the case of Jung, such separation was intrinsic to his psychology of archetypes, Jung interpreting contemporary problems through the prism of myths and symbols only dimly connected to them, and transforming politics into 'psychopolitics' that placed the locus of political ideas and acts in the Unconscious.

My conclusion is that, with his archetypal interpretations of the alleged psycho-spiritual forces that were at play in Hitler's Germany, Jung made a serious error in substituting historical contingencies by the absolutism of archetypal images. This error was both epistemic and moral: Jung's theory of archetypes obfuscated rather than clarified the phenomenon of National Socialism, and in his lifting of historical reality to the supratemporal sphere of archetypal symbols, Jung belittled the concrete fact that the storm troopers, no matter which archetype was stirring in their Collective Unconscious, were killing and abusing German citizens. For Jung, the suffering and humiliation of the victims of Hitler's tyranny seemed to pale to insignificance compared with the spectacular unleashing of archetypal forces in the German unconscious. From the moral point of view, I find it disturbing that Jung either did not recognize or did not care about the fact that human dignity and the principles of justice were trampled underfoot in Germany.

The Swiss author Axel von Muralt, who among Jung's contemporaries was perhaps the most trenchant critic of his *Wotan*, argued immediately after the war that Jung's greatest failure was "his unwillingness to warn the world of Hitler's evil, and he [Muralt] damned the entire essay as little more than 'a stab in the back from Switzerland' for those Germans who did try to resist."[32] To me, von Muralt's criticism of Jung's political passivity if not acquiescence vis-à-vis Hitler's Germany is right on target, and an important reminder that all those who are prone to interpret social, political and religious phenomena with the help of archetypes or other 'timeless' categories run the risk of using many words to say nothing of cognitive value, but much that is morally questionable.

In this article, I have not related Jung's ideas concerning the religious aspects of National Socialism to ideas that German scholars of religions developed in the 1930s. Obviously, the beliefs and intentions of German academics differed from those of Jung, who was a Swiss psychologist and therapist, and head of a depth-psychological 'school'. Still, I believe that Jung and the German scholars shared some core

---

[32] Bair, *Jung*, p. 455.

beliefs concerning the significance of National Socialism to the cultural renewal of Germany, and that their pronouncements were very much in accord with the prevailing mentality of the German *Bildungsbürgertum*. Although history teaches us no lessons, it may be instructive to reflect on the suggestion that people like Jung and German scholars of religion created stories and developed theories about the world consonant with their *Weltanschauung*, and that in doing so they may have been inclined to mitigate the destructive implications of ideologies and belief systems that appealed to their imagination, or that seemed to validate their theoretical constructions of psychological or religious phenomena.

Like Robert Musil, I believe that the lack of proportion is a particularly dangerous form of stupidity, because it distorts one's perception of reality and may in some cases (I am thinking of Jung and Heidegger here) prompt respected thinkers and renowned doctors to replace reality with the Second Reality, a reality in which the criteria for truth and morality are grounded on illusory beliefs.[33] In the 1930s, Jung made statements about National Socialism that were grounded on beliefs I would characterize as illusory.

---

[33] See Robert Musil, "Über die Dummheit," in idem, *Gesammelte Werke 8: Essays und Reden* (Reinbek: Rowohlt, 1981, 1st ed. 1937).

Bibliography

Ash, Mitchell G. *Gestalt psychology in German culture, 1890–1967: Holism and the quest for objectivity*. Cambridge: Cambridge University Press, 1995.

Bair, Deirdre. *Jung. A biography*. Boston: Little, Brown and Company, 2003.

Cocks, Geoffrey. *Psychotherapy in the Third Reich: The Göring Institute*, 2nd rev. and exp. ed. New Brunswick, NJ: Transaction Publishers, 1997.

Eklöf, Mats. *Läkarens ethos. Studier i den svenska läkarkårens identiteter, intressen och ideal 1890–1960*. Linköping: Linköpings universitet, 2000.

Gess, Heinz. *Vom Faschismus zum Neuen Denken – C.G. Jungs Theorie im Wandel der Zeit*. Lüneburg: Klampen, 1994.

Grossman, Stanley. "C.G. Jung and National Socialism." In Paul Bishop, ed. *Jung in Contexts*. London: Routledge, 1999, pp. 92–121.

Harrington, Anne. *Reenchanted science: Holism in German culture from Wilhelm to Hitler*. Princeton: Princeton University Press, 1996.

Jung, Carl Gustav. "Circular letter." *Collected Works* 10. London: Routledge & Kegan Paul, 1981, 1st ed. 1934, p. 545f.

———. "Wotan." *Collected Works* 10. London: Routledge & Kegan Paul, 1981, 1st ed. 1936, pp. 173–193.

———. *Nietzsche's Zarathustra. Notes of the seminar given in 1934–1939 by C.G. Jung*, volumes I–II. James L. Jarrett, ed. Princeton: Princeton University Press, 1988.

———. *Visions. Notes of the seminar given in 1930–1934* by C.G. Jung, volumes I–II. Douglas, C., ed. London: Routledge, 1998.

Lilla, Mark. *The reckless mind: Intellectuals in politics*. New York: New York Review Books, 2001.

Maidenbaum, Aryeh, G. and Stephen A. Martin, eds. *Lingering shadows: Jungians, Freudians, and Anti-Semitism*. Boston: Shambala, 1991.

Musil, Robert. "Über die Dummheit." *Gesammelte Werke 8: Essays und Reden*. Reinbek: Rowohlt, 1981, 1st ed. 1937.

Nanko, Ulrich. *Die Deutsche Glaubensbewegung. Eine historische und soziologische Untersuchung*. Marburg: Diagonal Verlag, 1993.

Pietikäinen, Petteri. *C.G. Jung and the Psychology of Symbolic Forms*. Helsinki: The Finnish Academy of Science and Letters, 1999.

———. "The 'Volk' and its Unconscious. Jung, Hauer, and the 'German revolution'." *Journal of Contemporary History* 35 (2000), pp. 523–39.

Samuels, Andrew. *Politics and psyche*. London: Routledge, 1993.

Shamdasani, Sonu. *Jung and the making of modern psychology*. Cambridge: Cambridge University Press, 2003.

Skinner, Quentin. *Visions of politics. Volume I: Regarding method*. Cambridge: Cambridge University Press, 2002.

STRATEGIES IN REPRESENTING 'JAPANESE RELIGION' DURING THE NATIONAL SOCIALIST PERIOD

THE CASES OF KITAYAMA JUNYÛ AND WILHELM GUNDERT

Hiroshi Kubota

Prologue

On November 28, 1940, Heinrich Frick from the University of Marburg wrote a letter to Raffaele Pettazzoni in Rome concerning his plan to publish a booklet entitled *Religiöse Wurzeln des Heroismus in Japan, Italien und Deutschland* (Religious Roots of Heroism in Japan, Italy and Germany).[1] Frick's aim was to elucidate the various religious motives that were historically influential on heroism in these nations. He thereby proposed that he himself would write the part on Germany, Pettazzoni on Italy, and Kitayama Junyû on Japan. At the same time, he stressed that the discipline "Allgemeine Religionswissenschaft" (general study of religion) could demonstrate its value by showing how the characteristics of heroism emerged from great religious traditions and thus contribute significantly to the comparative study of religion.[2]

Frick declared in his letter that the planned booklet had to be built on a scholarly and non-political basis. However, its political reference is more than apparent: Just before this letter was written, the so-called Triple Alliance had been formed in September 1940. This political context together with Frick's proposal urged Kitayama to write a separate book entitled *Heroisches Ethos. Das Heldische in Japan* (Heroic Ethos. The Heroic in Japan),[3] while the German and Italian parts of Frick's plan did not materialize on time.[4]

---

[1] All English translations of German texts originate from H. Kubota.

[2] Frick's letter to Pettazzoni of November 28, 1940, literary remains of R. Pettazoni, Biblioteca Communale 'G.C. Croce' di San Giovanni in Persicieto.

[3] Kitayama, Junyû, *Heroisches Ethos. Das Heldische in Japan* (Berlin: de Gruyter, 1944).

[4] Although Pettazzoni began writing his part on Italy, and finished the most part of his work in 1941, it was only in 1952 when it was published in the complete form. It

1. *Introduction*

Scholarly disciplines normally called and subordinated to area studies have been inevitably involved in foreign policies employed by the
state. Especially in colonial times, area studies stood at the forefront
of academic life, enjoying great support from the authorities thanks to
the subjects' geopolitical connotations. However, the academic study of
religions inside regional studies did not ordinarily show their 'social utility' to be directly applicable to certain aspects of socio-political life and
diplomatic orientation of the state. The study of religions historically
emerged within the humanities, which were not requested to demonstrate their political relevance bluntly, partly because humanistic knowledge was regarded as a self-sufficient educational aim ("Bildung") or a
self-evident precondition for higher promotion in the state bureaucracy.
Humanistic disciplines were accordingly allowed to immerse themselves
in philological quests for the alleged wellspring of either one's own or
others' cultural and intellectual achievements – a quest chiefly inspired
by enlightenment and romanticism. These philological disciplines
were understood as completely independent of concrete sociopolitical
demands. However, the historical and philological preoccupation with
ancient or historical religions all over the world meant groping for an
alleged origin in the chronological sense, or an essence postulated to be
the a-historical and invariable core of "religion" in singular form. In
the context of modernity, such a search for the origin or the essence of
religion acquired the ability to compensate for the 'loss' that modernization and industrialization had caused in society.[5] As a consequence of
that, the alleged scientific quests themselves incorporated an intellectual
attempt to create a new religiosity – at least a new understanding of
religion – corresponding with the concrete given cultural and mental
constellations of society. This academic stance functioned, on one hand,
as a critical moment against the religious status quo, by romantically
idealizing religion. Such a critique did not necessarily mean to be critical against religion itself (e.g. the trend of so-called phenomenology
of religion). On the other hand, it functioned also as a moment of
scientifically strengthening one's own religious tradition. But this was

---

was included in the following publication as a section entitled "Momenti della storia
religiosa d'Italia": Raffaele Pettazzoni, *Italia religiosa* (Bari: Laterza, 1952).
  [5] See Hans G. Kippenberg, *Die Entdeckung der Religionsgeschichte. Religionswissenschaft
und Moderne* (München: C.H. Beck, 1997).

occasionally accompanied by its unexpected self-destructive potential (such as biblical criticism in liberal Protestant theology).

Geopolitical changes in the 1930s coerced the humanities in Germany, including the study of religions, to leave their 'independent' domain and to serve newly emerging political realities. The time of National Socialism was a period in which university disciplines had to demonstrate their social utility. They found themselves forced to legitimize their raison d'être, but in a peculiar way: The demands of the regime consisted not only of political, economic and geopolitical issues, but also – and more emphatically – of issues of *Weltanschauung*, which particularly concerned traditional humanistic fields. Evidently, the ideological pressure led to their discursive self-adjustment. Whether such a discursive adjustment was, despite their declared conviction of conformity between the National Socialist *Weltanschauung* and their 'academic' stance, a mere opportunistic disguise for institutional survival, or was deeply rooted in their pre-reflexive and pre-theoretical presuppositions, is naturally a question to be answered only after examining each case individually. Here I would like to emphasize solely that such a discursive self-adjustment to a current sociopolitical discourse could take place, and also at present can take place and is taking place, in our very 'academic' discourse, if unreflectively or not, and even if with impartiality ('objectivity', or 'neutrality') conviction based on allegedly sufficient self-reflection, particularly with regard to the discipline's applicability in society.[6]

In the context of National Socialism the scholarly occupation with religion(s) in Japan consequently found itself confronted by the following two eminent tasks. On one hand, it had to adapt to the new sociopolitical and diplomatic context of the 1930s. Until 1936, when the Anti-Comintern-Pact between Germany and Japan was concluded, it had seemed quite questionable whether the scholarly occupation with a foreign state that belonged to the victorious nations of World War I – particularly with no direct reference to Germany – could be sufficiently warranted. But new geopolitical developments gradually

---

[6] In regard to religious studies in the times before and after 1933 in Germany see Fritz Heinrich, *Die Deutsche Religionswissenschaft und der Nationalsozialismus* (Petersberg: Michael Imhof, 2002); Horst Junginger, *Von der philologischen zur völkischen Religionswissenschaft* (Stuttgart: Franz Steiner, 1999); Volkhard Krech, *Wissenschaft und Religion* (Tübingen, Mohr Siebeck, 2002); Hiroshi Kubota, *Religionswissenschaftliche Religiosität und Religionsgründung* (Frankfurt a. M.: Peter Lang, 2005).

changed the atmosphere for it to demonstrate its academic utility positively in the new Germany. Followed by the Triple Alliance in 1940,
the Anti-Comintern-Pact brought forth a sort of "Japan boom" in and
outside the academe. For example, from 1939 until 1944 the magazine
*Berlin. Rom. Tokio. Monatsschrift für die Vertiefung der kulturellen Beziehungen
der Völker des weltpolitischen Dreiecks* was published under the patronage of
the Foreign Minister Joachim von Ribbentrop. A number of scholars
of Japanese studies contributed to this magazine. Furthermore, the first
comprehensive dictionary of Japanese studies in German language was
published in 1941, in which both Kitayama and Gundert belonged to
the 35 contributors.[7] In the new diplomatic constellation, the importance of *Japanologie* (Japanese studies) rapidly increased – and parallel
to that scholars became convinced of their growing importance. Its
urgent task was seen to elucidate the spiritual roots of the Japanese
newcomer who had appeared on the stage of world politics only a
half century earlier.

On the other hand, it seemed more precarious to justify the academic
treatment of religions in this region, especially because the traditional
occupation with Japanese religion(s) had, as mentioned above, largely
concentrated on historical-philological inquiries of pre-modern texts.
Now, the historical-philological approach, lacking direct reference to
political, economic and diplomatic requirements, was responsible for
legitimizing itself. The framework of reference within which one tried to
prevail against reproaches of academic irrelevance was partly provided
through adducing the contemporary scholarly tendency to investigate
Germany's pre-Christian religious heritage, which was assumed to be
reconstructed as a homogeneous entity called "Germanic" or "Teu-
tonic" religion. Following this interpretative scheme, Japanese studies
scholars endeavored to give reasons for the relevance and significance
of historical and philological studies on religions in Japan by postulating
a Japanese religion in singular form similar to the alleged pre-Chris-

[7] Martin Ramming, ed., *Japan-Handbuch. Nachschlagewerk der Japankunde, im Auftrag
des Japaninstituts Berlin* (Berlin: Steiniger-Verlag 1941). See also the remark of Worm
concerning the popularity of Japanese studies and the friendship between the axes
("Achsenfreundschaft") in Herbert Worm, "Japanologie im Nationalsozialismus. Ein
Zwischenbericht," in Gerhard Krebs and Bernd Martin, eds., *Formierung und Fall der
Achse Berlin-Tôkyô* (München: Iudicium, 1994), pp. 153–186, here p. 161.

tian religious substance in Germany.[8] Therefore it was no wonder that parallelism between Buddhism and Christianity was given a decisive significance. Both of these two so-called world religions were described to be foreign influences inimical to the declared core of each nation and its *Volkscharakter*.[9] As a result, the scholarly discourse on the history of religions in Japan – much like other academic occupations with religions in several regions, Germany among them – became a very important feature in the midst of Germany's religious constellations mirroring certain aspects of the religious conflicts of that time. Just at the time when the scholarly treatment of the history of religions in Germany could gain its argumentative validity, and became the religious, particularly religio-political conceptual apparatus in the given religious constellations in the Third Reich, the academic occupation with the supposedly indigenous religiosity in Japan was also instrumentalized in the German academe in order to in reverse support and legitimize the authenticity of the Germanic religiosity, and in most cases in order to discredit the hegemonic status of traditional Christianity.[10]

2. *KITAYAMA Junyû and Wilhelm GUNDERT – a Biographical Sketch*

The following sketch examines two scholars within the context outlined above. Both were actively engaged in propagating a singular Japanese religion in the German academic context: Kitayama Junyû (1902–1962) and Wilhelm Gundert (1880–1971).[11]

---

[8] Concerning conceptual problems of constructing a singular Japanese religion, see the papers of the panel "The Consequences of Constituting 'Japanese Religion' as an Object of Concern" at the Annual Meeting of the Association for Asian Studies (March 4–7, 2004, San Diego, CA), especially Gary L. Ebersole's paper on "Ato (Traces): Absence And Presence in the Discourse of 'Japanese Religion'."

[9] Concerning problems of the term 'world religion(s)', see Tomoko Masuzawa, *The Invention of World Religions. Or, How European Universalism Was Preserved in the Language of Pluralism* (Chicago: University of Chicago Press, 2005).

[10] In this point, it is also of great importance to see that the academic representation of Japanese religion was exclusively addressed to a German public and played on the stage of the German academe. Whether or not the academics relied on the discourse of religious homogeneity that had been nursed in Japan is not relevant to this paper. Incidentally, the Japanese government officially claimed so-called Shintô might not be regarded as 'religion'. See also footnote 48.

[11] To understand Kitayama's and Gundert's political involvement in the 1930s and 1940s, the following essays of Eberhard Friese, "Das Japaninstitut in Berlin (1926–1945). Bemerkungen zu seiner Struktur und Tätigkeit," in Hartmut Walravens, ed., *Du verstehst*

Kitayama, son of a Buddhist monk of the Pure-Land-School in Japan, studied first at a Buddhist university in Tokyo.[12] After being ordained, he came to Germany by order of the Pure-Land-School (1924–1929) studying philosophy under Edmund Husserl and Buddhism under Ernst Leumann at the University of Freiburg. He continued his studies at the University of Heidelberg where he studied philosophy under Karl Jaspers and Heinrich Rickert and Buddhism under Heinrich Zimmer. Having written his doctoral thesis under Karl Jaspers on the metaphysics of Mahâyâna Buddhism in 1931,[13] he took an active part in the fields of both Japanese and religious studies. Among other positions, he worked as an assistant of the "Religionskundliche Sammlung" at Marburg – where he closely cooperated with Rudolf Otto and Heinrich Frick – and as director of the Japanese Department at the "Forschungs-institut für Kulturmorphologie," founded by Leo Frobenius. Parallel to that Kitayama was engaged in the field of intercultural exchange acting as deputy of the Japanese director of the Berlin "Japan-Institut" which had been established to foster both cultural and academic mutual understanding and cooperation between Germany and Japan in 1926. In 1944 Kitayama, who had been characterized as a warm and upright friend of National Socialism, was offered an appointment as director of the Department of Japanese Studies at the German "Karls-Universität" in Prague.[14] After the end of World War II, Kitayama was interned as a pro-German collaborator. When he was released, he became a teacher

---

unsere Herzen gut: Fritz Rumpf (1888–1949) im Spannungsfeld der deutsch-japanischen Kultur-beziehungen (Weinheim: VCH, Acta Humaniora, 1989), pp. 73–88 and Annette Hack, "Das Japanisch-Deutsche Kulturinstitut in Tôkyô zur Zeit des Nationalsozialismus. Von Wilhelm Gundert zu Walter Donat," Nachrichten der Gesellschaft für Natur- und Völkerkunde Ostasiens. Zeitschrift für Kultur und Geschichte Ost- und Südostasiens 157/158 (1995), pp. 77–100 are very usefull.

[12] He studied Buddhism, Japanese literature, and German philosophy at the Shûkyô Daigaku (currently Taishô University). My essay on Kitayama, "Ideologiesierbarkeit und Ideologieanfälligkeit der Religionsforschung. Das Beispiel Kitayama Junyû als 'völkischer Religionswissenschaftler' im Dritten Reich," will be published soon.

[13] J. Kitayama, Metaphysik des Buddhismus. Versuch einer philosophischen Interpretation der Lehre Vasubandhus und seiner Schule (Stuttgart: W. Kohlhammer, 1934). Kitayama's doctoral thesis was published as no. 7 of the series Veröffentlichungen des Orientalischen Seminars der Universität Tübingen. Abhandlungen zur orientalischen Philologie und zur allgemeinen Religions-geschichte, edited by Enno Littmann and Jakob Wilhelm Hauer. For its publication Heinrich Frick had advised Kitayama to contact Hauer in Tübingen. See the letter of Kitayama to Hauer on April 18, 1932, Federal Archive Koblenz, literary remains of Hauer, vol. 170, fol. 436.

[14] Note of November 2, 1943 to Ministerialrat Frey, Federal Archive Berlin, BDC-REM, K. 22: Kitayama Junyu, fol. 1084.

of Japanese and judo until his death in 1962. Since his repatriation to Japan was not approved by the Czechoslovakian government, he was obliged to stay in Prague until his death.

Wilhelm Gundert, the cousin of Hermann Hesse and grandson of Hermann Gundert (a missionary, linguist, and founder of the "Calwer Verlagshaus," a Protestant publishing company in the southern Germany), was born in 1880 in Stuttgart. Having studied Protestant theology and philosophy at the universities of Tübingen, Halle, and Heidelberg, he served in Württemberg's Protestant State Church and later acted as a free missionary in Japan until 1936. During his stay in Japan he cooperated with the liberal Protestant *East Asia Mission Society* ("Ostasien-Mission")[15] and worked as a teacher of German. After his return to Germany he was nominated professor of Japanese studies at the University of Hamburg as Karl Florenz's successor in 1936. This was the first appointment of a Japanese studies' professor under National Socialism. Gundert had been a party member since April 1934 and also acted as "Obmann" (representative) of the "Nationalsozialistischer Lehrerbund" (NSLB), the National Socialist teachers' union. In 1937 he was the dean of Hamburg's philosophy department, and from 1938 until 1941 the university's rector. Forced to retire in 1945, Gundert remained active as an independent scholar concentrating on philological works of Buddhist texts until his death in 1971.

3. *Shintō as 'National Religion'*

The beginning of Kitayama's academic career in Germany incidentally corresponded with the outset of the National Socialist regime. In the course of his scholarly activities, he seems to have eagerly attempted to acquire a fashionable academic discourse which was strongly conditioned by the political constellation of the 1930s and 1940s. As a Japanese intellectual living in the German society, he saw his task thus: generalize the religious and intellectual history of Japan by presenting them as a crucial and indispensable key to a better understanding of actual Japanese political events. To make his message attractive, he

---

[15] The organ of this mission society was one of the few scholarly magazines of religious studies at that time: *Zeitschrift für Missionskunde und Religionswissenschaft.*

used a rhetoric inclined to the National Socialist ideology resulting in a rather pompous and artificial diction.

First of all, he pointed to the Japanese *Volk* as an unchangeable essence, moving in the discursive scheme of the popular ideology of the German *Volkstum*. According to Kitayama, the present Japanese polity was "the vital vein" of the Japanese *Volk*. Consequently, the state appeared as the realization of the organic "character of *Volk* and culture."[16] This organic and biological concept was easily connected with current racial ideas of the day. Without touching on antisemitic issues – though Kitayama defined Japan as "free from any Semitic racial character"[17] – he made his thesis known that the Japanese were partly of Aryan origin. Kitayama understood the Japanese *Volk* to be made up of a unitary race, however resulting from the creative mixture of various races:

> This unique mixture of races and their mentalities with different cultures, leading to a unit, was possible by the isolated island location. In this way it created a completely new race and culture...The activity of the nomadic peoples in the north, being united with the cheerful liveliness of the sea peoples in the south, formed the Japanese will toward progress and the Japanese character as fighters. The Chinese immigration, being mixed with the Malay and Indian fantasy talent, shaped the mental ability of the island nation...The Japanese people inherited from these preconditions both the Aryan and Mongolian people's nomadic instinct for conquest as well as the contemplative and aesthetic characteristics of the Indian and Chinese.[18]

---

[16] J. Kitayama, "Tradition und Neuordnung. Das Gesicht der japanischen Kultur," *Berlin. Rom. Tokio. Monatsschrift für die Vertiefung der kulturellen Beziehungen der Völker des weltpolitischen Dreiecks* 2–3 (1940), p. 11f.

[17] Questionnaire of April 10, 1933, Federal Archives Berlin, BDC-REM, J. Kitayama, fol. 0983.

[18] "Diese einzigartige Mischung der Rassen und ihrer Mentalitäten mit verschiedenartigen Kulturen zu einer Einheit war durch die Einsamkeit der Insellage möglich und schuf so eine völlig neue Rasse und Kultur...Die Aktivität der Nomadenvölker des Nordens, vereint mit der heiteren Lebendigkeit der Meervölker des Südens, formte den japanischen Fortschrittswillen und die japanische Kämpfernatur. Die chinesische Einwanderung, gemischt mit der malaiischen und indischen Phantasiebegabung, gestaltete die geistige Fähigkeit des Inselvolkes...Aus diesen Vorbedingungen erbte das japanische Volk sowohl den nomadenhaften Eroberungsinstinkt der arischen und mongolischen Völker als auch die kontemplativ-ästhetischen Eigenschaften der Inder und Chinesen." J. Kitayama, "Japanisches Wachstum. Von Rasse und Kultur," *Schule der Freiheit. Unabhängige Zeitschrift für organische Gestaltung von Kultur, Gesellschaft und Wirtschaft* 9–7/8 (1941), p. 150.

Such an indication of the racial affinity between Aryans and Japanese was not a singular phenomenon, but a commonly accepted thesis in the circle around the German-Japanese Association ("Deutsch-Japanische Gesellschaft") where the declared anti-Semite and anti-Christian Johann von Leers played a role as spokesperson:

> The Japanese *Volk* is a mixed *Volk* that became in the insularity a clearly recognizable *Volkstum*, starting from very different racial components. In it elements of the intrinsic inner-Asian race are to be found, being mixed with elements of the racially also non-uniform Malayanness of the South Pacific. What is not well-known is however the fact of the Japanese *Volk*'s close connections with eastern Turkic people (Tungus and Koreans) in terms of the physical existence, just as well as its language shows with regard to grammar and construction the close similarity to the Turkic languages...Japan's original cultural connection with the early culture of the Nordic race cannot be denied any more today...Thus we have to see the present form of the Japanese *Volk* as a *Volk* that goes back in terms of its roots and origins, despite its multiple mixture in later times, to the same racial forces as ours; while, however, all the state formations of the Nordic race in the pre-Indo-Germanic, or Neolithic period sank, this ancient state form has survived in its insularity, and it still bears today in crucial manners features of the oldest Nordic immigration, in spite of all of its different and special developments.[19]

---

[19] "Das japanische Volk ist ein Mischvolk, das aus sehr verschiedenen Rassenbestand-teilen in insularer Abgeschlossenheit zu einem deutlich erkennbaren Volkstum geworden ist. In ihm finden sich Elemente der eigentlich innerasiatischen Rasse, vermischt mit Elementen aus dem rassisch auch nicht einheitlichen Malaientum der Südsee. Viel zu wenig bekannt ist, daß aber, genauso wie die Sprache in Grammatik und Konstruktion den Türksprachen nahesteht, auch im körperlichen Bestand ein naher Zusammenhang mit den östlichen Türkvölkern (Tungusen und Koreaner) besteht...Kulturgeschichtlich ist der Zusammenhang der japanischen Kultur in ihrer Wurzel mit der Frühkultur der nordischen Rasse heute nicht mehr zu bestreiten...Wir haben also im heutigen japanischen Volke ein Volk zu sehen, das in seinen Wurzeln und Ursprüngen trotz vielfacher späterer Untermischungen auf die gleichen Rassenkräfte zurückgeht, wie wir; während aber alle Staatengründungen nordischer Rasse aus der vorindogermanischen, also jungsteinzeitlichen Periode, versunken sind, hat in der Inselabgeschlossenheit diese sich erhalten und trägt in entscheidenden Formen noch heute unter aller fremdartigen Sonderentwicklung Züge der ältesten nordischen Einwanderung." Johann von Leers, "Denkschrift der Deutsch-Japanischen Gesellschaft zur Frage der Anwendung der Rassen-Gesetzgebung auf die Abkömmlinge aus deutsch-japanischen Mischehen, 25. Oktober 1934," reprinted in Eberhard Friese, *Japaninstitut Berlin und Deutsch-Japanische Gesellschaft Berlin. Quellenlage und ausgewählte Aspekte ihrer Politik 1926–1945* (Berlin: Osta-siatisches Seminar der FU-Berlin, 1980), pp. 39–46, here pp. 43–45. By arguing in this way, von Leers himself depended on Hans F.K. Günther. See also Harald Kleinschmidt, *Württemberg und Japan. Landesgeschichtliche Aspekte der deutsch-japanischen Beziehungen* (Stuttgart: Helfant edition, 1991), pp. 42ff. and p. 54.

Considering Kitayama's racial thinking, it is not surprising that he tried to explain Japan's peculiar cultural quality by using the term "arteigene Kultur."[20] By indicating these racially determined cultural features, he postulated a historically unchangeable substance of an indigenous Japanese culture which he identified with the so-called Shintô.[21]

It is of great importance to understand not only Kitayama's *Volkstum* ideology but also his rhetorical strategy of internalizing the geopolitical concept of Karl Haushofer, precisely speaking, of Heinrich Frick's 'georeligious' version of the concept.[22] According to Frick, the two world religions Christianity and Buddhism could rid themselves of their original "chaotic" characteristics, which were said to stem from the climatic conditions in their birthplaces in Palestine and India. Moreover, Frick believed that these two religions had become completely purified and refined in other climatically milder regions like Germany and Japan taking shape as German Protestantism and Mahâyâna-Buddhism respectively.[23] Certainly, Frick was confronted with an increasing criticism against Christianity from anti-Christian and *völkisch* religious groups. So his primary concern was to present German Protestantism, especially in its theologically liberal version, as a religion purified from its climatically determined "chaos," and therefore racially suitable to Nazi Germany. Accordingly, Frick's 'georeligious' theory was located in a discursive strategy to legitimize and proclaim the racial suitability of Christianity, particularly under the slogan of the "Artgemäßheit" of Christianity.

Arguing in the same way, Kitayama declared that Japanese Mahâyâna-Buddhism was the ideal expression of Buddhism, identifying it with the "East Asian view of the world and the being" as such.[24] He characterized

---

[20] Kitayama, "Japanisches Wachstum," p. 151.

[21] See Kitayama, "Die japanische Urkultur und ihre Auseinandersetzung mit dem Buddhismus," *Ostasiatische Rundschau. Die Zeitschrift für den Fernen Osten* 15–18 (1934), pp. 421–428.

[22] Concerning the "georeligious" concepts of H. Frick, see his book *Deutschland innerhalb der religiösen Weltlage* (Berlin: Alfred Töpelmann, 1936) and his articles "Die religiöse Weltkrise der Gegenwart," in *Die Welt im Fortschritt* (Berlin: F.A. Herbig, 1937), pp. 17–116 and "Regionale Religionskunde. Georeligiöse Erwägungen zum Zusammenhang zwischen Boden und Religion," *Zeitschrift für Geopolitik* 20–8 (1943), pp. 281–291. Cf. also H. Kubota's paper "Political Discourse and Religious Studies in the National Socialist Period: The Case of Heinrich Frick," International Workshop: Neo-Paganism, 'Völkische Religion' and Antisemitism II (October 27–29, 1997, Tübingen).

[23] Frick, "Regionale Religionskunde," pp. 286–288 and idem, "Die religiöse Weltkrise der Gegenwart," pp. 33–38.

[24] "Welt- und Daseinsanschauung Ostasiens." Kitayama, *Heiligung des Staates und Verklärung des Menschen. Buddhismus und Japan* (Berlin: Wilhelm Limpert, 1943), p. 3.

the history of Japanese Buddhism as a "purification process of the Buddhist spirit," concluding: "Thus the intrinsic task of Buddhism was completed, and only in this way did Buddhism become a world religion."[25] Japanese Mahâyâna-Buddhism constituted for him "the final stage and fulfillment of Buddhist religiosity."[26] His understanding of the term "purification" meant nothing else than 'Japanizing', corresponding with Frick's "purified" Protestantism in Germany, that is with a 'Germanized' Christianity. Frick himself intended to synthesize Christianity and "Deutschtum" (Germandom) considering the Reformation of Martin Luther as the religious purification "auf deutschem Boden" (on German soil).[27] Contrary to Frick, who paid no attention to Shintô, Kitayama went even further by affirming that the history of 'Japanized' Buddhism illustrated the Japanese belief in the divine character of the Emperor. According to Kitayamy, this 'Japanized' form of Buddhism, for example in the seventh and eighth century, clearly expressed "the ancient mythological belief in the Emperor as envoy of god – by order of the sun goddess Amaterasu – and the feeling of the relationship between the ruler and his divine ancestral goddess as head of the nation family."[28] Here it is apparent that Kitayama's analysis of Japan's religious history finally led him to propagate one singular religious tradition, which was supposed to have remained constant over time. This indigenous religious tradition that Kitayama identified with a culturally formative power was able to protect the Japanese essence from negative foreign influences:

> Despite the manifold effects of foreign religions from China and India on Japanese religiosity, the impact was not indiscriminate and arbitrary. The substance of the Shintoist core remained untouched. Only such elements of a foreign mentality were accepted which had already been present in the Shintoist ideas latently.[29]

---

[25] J. Kitayama, *Genjo Koan. Aus dem Zen-Text 'Shôbo Ganzô' von Patriarch Dôgen*, translated and commented by Junyû Kitayama (Berlin: Alfred Töpelmann, 1940), p. 8.

[26] Ibid., p. 8.

[27] Frick, *Deutschland innerhalb der religiösen Weltlage*, p. 137 and p. 161.

[28] "Die alte mythologische Überzeugung vom Gottgesandtentum des Kaisers im Auftrag der Sonnengöttin Amaterasu und das Verwandtschaftsgefühl des Herrschers mit seiner göttlichen Ahnherrin als dem Oberhaupt der Volksfamilie kommt in dieser Form wieder zu äußerst lebendigem Ausdruck." Kitayama, "Die japanische Urkultur und ihre Auseinandersetzung mit dem Buddhismus," p. 428.

[29] "Trotz dieser mannigfaltigen Einwirkungen fremder Religionen aus China und Indien auf die japanische Religiosität waren die Einflüsse nicht wahllos und willkürlich. Die Substanz des shintoistischen Kerns blieb unerschüttert. Nur solche Güter fremder Geistigkeit wurden aufgenommen, die bereits keimhaft im shintoistischen Gedankengut

Kitayama endeavored to construct Shintô as national religion completely in line with the *Volkscharakter* which he identified with Japanese culture itself.[30] According to Kitayama, the modality of this national religion is utterly determined through and profoundly rooted in the "Volksgefühl" or "arteigene Kultur", which functions as a mental determinant:

> Each *Volk*, ranging from the most primitive nation in a state of nature to the cultural nation with the highest developed civilization, lives somehow in relation with the divine... The elementary religious thinking that is common to all human beings gains in each nation the appropriate and specific form to be derived from the *Volkscharakter*.[31]

---

vorhanden waren." Kitayama, *Der Shintoismus. Die Nationalreligion Japans* (Berin: Wilhelm Limpert, 1943), p. 8. With regard to Japanese Christians he argued in the same way: "These Christians in Japan found the way back to their own roots in making a detour to Christianity, as any foreign spiritual inclination was for the Japanese people a detour leading to their own mentality." ("Diese Christen in Japan fanden auf dem Umwege des Christentums zu ihrem Ursprung zurück, wie jede fremde Geisteshaltung für das japanische Volk der Umweg zur eigenen Geistigkeit war"). Kitayama, *West-östliche Begegnung. Japans Kultur und Tradition* (Berlin: de Gruyter, 1944), p. 244.

[30] Kitayama, *Der Shintoismus*, p. 3. Concerning Shintô as Japan's "national religion," see Genchi Katô, *A Study of Shinto. The Religion of the Japanese Nation*, 2nd ed. (London and Dublin: Curzon Press, 1971, 1st ed. 1926) and idem, *What is Shintô?* (Tokyo: Mazuzen Company, 1935). KATÔ Genchi (1873–1965) was one of the leading scholars in the field of the history of Shintô before 1945. Like Kitayama he explicated Shintô for Westerners stressing – in contrast to the Japanese government's official standpoint: Shintô is not a religion – that Shintô should be regarded as quite a unique type of religion. According to him, "Shintô is indeed a religion peculiar to and inherent in the Japanese mind, so that it cannot be displaced or eradicated by any conflicting religious power from without." *What is Shintô*, p. 11. Contrasting Shintô with the Greek and Roman religion as "national faiths of Greece and Rome" that had been replaced by Christianity, he emphatically put forward that Shintô "from the beginning down to the present time, through each and every stage of its gradual evolution, has existed unmistakably as the national religion of the Japanese people" (ibid., p. 60f.), because Shintô had been "a religion *a priori* of the heart and life of every Japanese subject, male and female, high and low, old and young, educated or illiterate." He continues: "This is the reason why a Japanese never ceases to be a Shintoist, i.e., an inborn steadfast holder of the national faith, or one who embraces the national faith or the Way of the Gods as a group or folk religion, as distinguished from a personal or individual religion, even though he may accept the tenets of Buddhism or Confucianism – probably Christianity here in Japan not being excepted – as his personal or individual religion." Ibid., p. 64f. Here, one can easily discern the same tenor in Katô's and Kitayama's explication of Shintô. Although it is not clear to what extent Kitayama relied on Katô's publications, he at least knew them, and wrote a short article on him in the *Japan-Handbuch*, p. 288.

[31] "Jedes Volk, das primitivste Naturvolk und das zivilisatorisch höchste entwickelte Kulturvolk, lebt in irgendeiner Beziehung zum Göttlichen... Das eine religiöse Denken, das allen Menschen gemeinsam ist, findet im einzelnen Volk die entsprechende spezifische Gestaltung, die aus dem Volkscharakter herzuleiten ist." Kitayama, *Der Shintoismus*, p. 3.

This quote demonstrates how Kitayama shares a certain understanding of religion that prevailed among scholars of religious studies at that time, especially among the so-called phenomenologists of religion espousing the premise that religion in singular form is, if conscious or not, aprioristically immanent and present in all human beings. Although such a singular religion was understood to be independent of racial and cultural differences, its appearances and phenomenological expressions were thought to vary depending on cultural preconditions. Between the 1920s and the 1940s, some scholars under the influence of the phenomenology of religion shared this premise, on one hand using theological and metaphysical categories (for example, Rudolf Otto), and on the other hand relying on a racial substance ontologically understood in the framework of "Rassenseelenkunde" (for example, J.W. Hauer). Kitayama's understanding has, insofar as he deterministically argues, a certain similarity to that of Hauer.

Kitayama argued that one could understand the mental constitution of a *Volk* only by exploring its religion and explicating the racially determined relation between the *Volk* and the divine. Here Kitayama's message to the Germans, although not explicitly formulated, could be understood as an appeal: go back to your religiosity and discover the authentic quintessence of your own *Volk*.[32] Thus both Shintô and Germanic Religion were according to Kitayama "*völkisch*-orientated."[33]

Such an interpretation of Shintô as invariable and homogeneous cultural core was of course not limited to Kitayama. His intention primarily consisted in deepening the German public's understanding of the Japanese mentality from the perspective of a Japanese scholar of religious studies living in Germany. It was above all Wilhelm Gundert who depicted Shintô as the counterpart of *Germanentum* for the sake of his own *Volk*.

---

[32] This point is obvious in Kityama's critique of European Christianity. But one should not underestimate Kitayama's emphasis in explicating the history of Japanese religion. He implicitly suggested that Japan, in contrast to Germany, had succeeded in unifying religion and politics. It is little wonder that Kitayama's glorification of Japan's success was criticized by some National Socialist officials. See for example Kleinschmidt, *Württemberg und Japan*, p. 608.

[33] Kitayama, *Der Shintoismus*, p. 6.

4. The History of Japanese Religion as Model for an Ideal 'Volk' Formation

As a leading professor of Japanese studies, the chief aims of Wilhelm Gundert lay first of all in justifying a special relevance of the academic study of the religious history of Japan in National Socialist Germany. He wanted to establish *Japanologie* as a " 'German' science for our own 'Volk'."[34] In his inauguration speech at the University of Hamburg, he accentuated this point, reproaching the traditional current of the discipline for lacking self-consciousness. He also criticized the morbid idea of the times ("Zeitkrankheit"), because of which the academe believed that it existed only for itself:

> Japanology in its educational form did nothing else than accumulating a large amount of scientific stuff which undoubtedly possessed great value. But unfortunately it did not ask itself the question how and for whom this material would be useful. Moreover, it has lost itself in leisure pursuits only accessible to a very small circle of initiated being the objective of passionate enjoyment. Some of us have already felt since long that something must be wrong and unhealthy with this situation. But only the experience we owe to the National Socialist movement has opened our eyes what was really lacking: a clear orientation of the japanologist towards his own *Volkstum*.[35]

This quotation clearly shows that the concept of *Volk* played a vital role for Gundert as well. He expressed the *völkisch* idea that the discipline should become strongly aware of its obligation and responsibility to its *Volk*.[36] In this context he emphasized – more than anything – that the research objective of his discipline should be the Japanese *Volk* per se:

> There is for japanology no more fruitful, no more appropriate and there-
> fore no luckier objective than such an understanding of the *Volk* which

---

[34] Gundert, "Die Bedeutung Japans und die Aufgabe der deutschen japanologischen Arbeit," *Zeitschrift der Deutschen Morgenländischen Gesellschaft* 90 (1936), p. 248.

[35] "[D]ie Japanologie diente in ihrer schulmäßigen Form der Anhäufung einer großen Menge von Wissensstoff, der ohne Frage hohen Wert besaß, nur daß sie selbst nicht danach fragte, wie und für wen er zu verwerten wäre, und sie verlor sich darüber hinaus in Liebhabereien, die nur einem ganz engen Kreis von Eingeweihten zugänglich, für ihn aber um so mehr Gegenstand eines oft schwärmerischen Genießens war. Daß an diesem Zustand irgend etwas nicht richtig, nicht gesund sein müsse, das hat wohl mancher von uns schon lange empfunden. Aber erst das Erlebnis, das wir der nationalsozialistischen Bewegung verdanken, hat uns die Augen dafür geöffnet, woran es in Wirklichkeit gefehlt hat: nämlich ganz einfach an der klaren Bezogenheit des Japanforschers auf sein eigenes Volkstum." Ibid., p. 249f.

[36] Ibid., pp. 248–250, and p. 258.

we owe to the fight for the National Socialist alignment of the academe. Nowhere else in the world a human community could be found to be called a *Volk* in this perfect sense than in Japan. The island's secluded location, her geographical dimensions – neither too small nor too large – have, together with the graces of the climate, altogether contributed so that here a *Volk* could develop autonomously, a *Volk* in a shape barely comparable on earth.[37]

For Gundert, the Japanese *Volk* consequently meant "a totality that has been representing a self-sustaining unity from the earliest beginning until the present."[38] Gundert's logic saw inquiries into this historical origin as essential task for Japanese studies which transformed the foundation of the *Volk* into an ideal, making it substantial. Furthermore, the argument legitimized the traditional historical-philological approach.

Simultaneously he tried to shed light on the *völkisch* character of *Japanologie* by distinguishing the cultural and spiritual essence of the Japanese *Volk* from foreign influences in order to uncover a valuable inner force behind the practical behavior of the German *Volk*. For example, Gundert attempted to elucidate how Japan had behaved against foreign cultural influences.[39] For this purpose he listed a series of comparable religious, cultural, and political phenomena both in the German and Japanese history, calling this parallelism a "strange similarity and synchronizing simultaneousness."[40] He compared the Roman and Christian culture with Chinese and Buddhist culture and conceived an explanatory scheme in which the historical religio-cultural course of Germany and Japan could be comparatively described. As a result, Japanese studies could contribute, according to Gundert, to a stronger German self-consciousness. What antiquity and humanism were to

---

[37] "Es gibt für die Japanologie keinen fruchtbareren, keinen ihrem Gegenstand gemäßeren und darum keinen glücklicheren Mittelpunkt als diesen Gedanken des Volkes, den wir dem Kampf um die nationalsozialistische Ausrichtung der Wissenschaft verdanken. Denn kaum irgendwo in der Welt findet sich eine menschliche Gemeinschaft, die in so vollendetem Sinn als Volk zu bezeichnen ist, wie in Japan. Die abgeschlossene Insellage des Landes, seine Ausmaße – weder zu klein noch zu groß, die Gunst des Klimas – alles hat dazu beigetragen, daß sich hier ein Volk sozusagen in Reinkultur entwickeln konnte, ein Volk, das in Form ist wie schwerlich ein anderes auf Erden." Ibid., p. 258.

[38] "[E]in Ganzes, das von den frühesten Anfängen an bis heute eine in sich geschlossene Einheit." Ibid., p. 259.

[39] Ibid., p. 261, and p. 264.

[40] "[D]ie merkwürdige Ähnlichkeit und annähernde Gleichzeitigkeit." Gundert, "Nationale und übernationale Religion in Japan," in *Die religiösen Kräfte Asiens* (Hamburg: Hanseatische Verlagsanstalt, 1937), p. 5.

Germany, was what Confucian moral philosophy was to Japan; what romanized Christianity was to Germany, was what Chinese Buddhism was to Japan. Moreover, Gundert writes:

> This conformity in many fields becomes much more remarkable if we particularly observe the mental development of Japan...What forms the basis both here and there is blood and soil, its racial spirit, as it has grown together with its surrounding nature in mutual effect. The original Japanese disposition there corresponds with our inborn German essence, while the ancient indigenous cult of the national gods or kami, which one has designated with the term Shintô ever since the penetration of foreign beliefs in order to distinguish Shintô from them, corresponds with our Germanic religion.[41]

Religion, according to Gundert, comes therefore in two forms: as a *völkish* and national religion rooted in *Blut und Boden*, and as a supernational (world-)religion. In his explanatory framework of the "conflict between national and supernational religion", he set the *völkisch* faith against supernational religion, equating the latter with foreign religious influences.[42] In doing so, Gundert identified the *völkisch* faith of Japan with Shintô, namely with the veneration of the Emperor.

Gundert's description of the relation between Buddhism and Shintô in Japan provides a great deal of insight on our understanding of his interpretative scheme concerning the religious history of Japan. Since the adoption of Buddhism, particularly on the political level, Shintô had been "annexed to Buddhism, permeated with Buddhist spirit, wrapped in Buddhist rituals, but has continued to exist in the form of a long-standing national cult of native state gods."[43] Similar to Frick's purification theory, Gundert went so far as to mention that the Bud-

---

[41] "Diese Übereinstimmung in den großen Zügen wird noch auffallender, wenn wir im besonderen die geistige Entwicklung Japans beobachten...Die Grundlage bildet hier wie dort Blut und Boden, die Rassenseele, so wie sie mit der sie umgebenden Natur in wechselseitiger Wirkung verwachsen ist. Unserem angeborenen deutschen Wesen entspricht dort die urjapanische Art, unserer germanischen Religion der alteingesessene Kult der nationalen Götter oder Kami, den man seit dem Eindringen fremder Glaubensanschauungen zur Unterscheidung von diesen mit dem Ausdruck Shintô bezeichnet." Ibid., p. 6.

[42] Ibid., p. 7 and p. 9. In this context he regarded indigenous religions as an entity organically grown up. For example, Gundert featured Shintô – he used various termini in order to name it "Schintoreligion," "Schintoismus" etc. – by describing it as "a religious reflex of the whole life of the Japanese *Volk*" ("ein religiöser Reflex des gesamten Lebens des japanischen Volkes"). See ibid., p. 11.

[43] "So wurde im Laufe der Zeit fast das ganze Gebiet des Kamikultes...dem Buddhismus einverleibt, wurde mit buddhistischem Geist durchtränkt, mit buddhistischen

dhist reform movement in the thirteenth century in Japan corresponded with the Protestant Reformation.[44] But contrary to Kitayama's stress on the revival of Shintô in the history of Buddhism, he indefatigably emphasized the danger of this foreign to the indigenous religion. He emphatically appreciated the Meiji Restoration in 1868 through which the *völkisch* faith could be equipped with a certain polity that guaranteed its protection against foreign and supernational influences not only from the Buddhist side but also against Christianity since the last decades of the 19th century.[45] Here Gundert underscored the close relation between the national religion of Japan and the political power firmly grounded in the Imperial Household. However, as Gundert said, the indissoluble union between the indigenous religion and the polity in Japan stood in contrast to the insufficient ties between the Nazi regime and the Germanic or Indo-Germanic religiosity.[46] Therefore the study of Japanese religious history had the task of utilizing this observation of the situation in Japan – which was crystallized even up to a so-called "State Shintô" – in order to deliberate on Germany's own political and religious constellations. His conclusion ended in acknowledging the *Volk* concept popular in the National Socialist society, but still ascertaining the regrettable lack of a close relation between religion and politics in Germany.

Gundert self-confidently declared that the scholarly occupation with Japan in the National Socialist state could only be valuable if it was able to decipher Germany's own essence and to provide the German *Volk* with a new self-assurance and courage to affirm itself.[47] The investigation into a religion politically embodied in the ideal *Volk*, he argued, served just this purpose.

5. *Summary and Conclusion*

Certainly one can discern different motives in the interpretation of "Japanese religion" by Gundert and Kitayama partly resulting from

---

Kultformen überdeckt, und blieb doch als alter nationaler Kult der angestammten Landesgötter bestehen." Ibid., p. 15.

[44] Ibid., pp. 15ff.
[45] Ibid., p. 11f., and p. 18f.
[46] Ibid., p. 12.
[47] Ibid., p. 9.

their biography. On one hand, Kitayama was a Japanese national, a former monk of the Mahâyâna-Buddhist Pure-Land-School and a philosopher specializing in the Indian Mahâyâna philosophy. In National Socialist Germany, he functioned as an intercultural spokesperson of the *Japan-Institut* and as a lecturer at some German universities propagating an authentic Japanese religion. On the other, Gundert was a German scholar who had worked in Japan as a liberal Protestant missionary returning to Germany only after the establishment of the National Socialist regime. Nominated as Professor of Japanese studies at the University of Hamburg, he became a scholarly authority on Japanese history of religions.

Despite these dissimilarities, it is easy to detect common pre-theoretical premises which allowed both scholars to adjust to the popular discourse indicated above. First, both started from the premise that the historically conditioned phenomenon called Shintô was Japan's authentic national religion that, as they thought, was beyond comparison with other religions. According to them, Shintô remained a uniform and homogeneous phenomenon during the whole history of Japan, being the decisive binding factor in the whole spectrum of the Japanese *Volk*. In other words, they assumed that it was possible for a *Volk* – in this case the Japanese *Volk* – to possess a certain singular religiosity independent of various concrete religious affiliations of the members of the *Volk*.[48] This view enabled them to compare the situation in Japan with a singular and authentic German religiosity, which they supposed to determine exclusively the character of the Germans.

Second, by identifying a *Volk* religiosity with the culture of its society in this manner, Kitayama und Gundert reduced the whole range of mental and spiritual aspects of peoples and societies to their religion, which was regarded as the sole determinant of the *Volk* life. Within this framework Japanese culture was constructed as the embodiment of Shintô and praised as a model case of *Volk* formation. It goes without saying that their identification of religion and culture resulted from a view exclusively based on the religious apriority of human beings.[49]

---

[48] Here it is quite interesting to see that the Japanese government officially declared that Shintô was not a religion, and denied its religious features. Instead it was declared that Shintô constituted the "national moral" to make the fundamental basis of Japan. Although knowing this stance of the Japanese government, both scholars presented Shintô as the only Japanese indigenous 'religion.'

[49] This postulation directly originated from Ernst Troeltsch's famous thesis of a "religious apriority" which descended to Rudolf Otto and most other phenomenologists of

Third, man's religious dimension structured in this manner went beyond any critical examination. It constituted an unquestionable fact that observers solely could affirm. This was the necessary consequence of the logic that presupposed the universality of religion as the authentic determinant prescriptive for thinking and behavioral patterns of a *Volk*. Kitayama and Gundert believed not only to be able to explore this hidden dimension of religion but also to have exposed it. This tautology of both scholars was made possible by unquestionably affirming the politically and ideologically constructed religiosity, which coincided with the political status quo.

The religious and political premises witnessed by both scholars led them to adjust their arguments to the popularized ideological discourse. However, one cannot maintain that this kind of reasoning completely vanished after the end of the National Socialist regime. Even now, these types of premises occasionally emerge in some discursive strategies for the purpose of demonstrating religious studies' social utility. A critical treatment of this discipline in the era of National Socialism just might give us a chance to critically dissect our own discursive strategies in representing religion.

---

religion. However, it is necessary to keep in mind that Troeltsch still attributed religion with a potential power in order to criticize culture. He saw the relationship between religion and culture as a tense one and therefore intended to reconcile both. Yet when this tension eased a new interpretative scheme emerged among phenomenologists of religion. Inquiries of ancient and foreign 'religions' became thus synonyms of those of ancient and foreign 'cultures' per se.

Bibliography

Antoni, Klaus and Hiroshi Kubota et al. eds. *Religion and National Identity in the Japanese Context*. Münster, Hamburg, London: LIT, 2002.

Ebersole, Gary L. "Ato (Traces): Absence And Presence in the Discourse of 'Japanese Religion'" (paper of the panel "The Consequences of Constituting 'Japanese Religion' as an Object of Concern," Annual Meeting of the Association for Asian Studies, March 4–7, 2004, San Diego, CA.

Frick, Heinrich. *Deutschland innerhalb der religiösen Weltlage*. Berlin: Alfred Töpelmann, 1936.

———. "Die religiöse Weltkrise der Gegenwart." In *Die Welt im Fortschritt*. Berlin: F.A. Herbig, 1937, pp. 17–116.

———. "Regionale Religionskunde. Georeligiöse Erwägungen zum Zusammenhang zwischen Boden und Religion." *Zeitschrift für Geopolitik* 20–8 (1943), pp. 281–291.

Friese, Eberhard. *Japaninstitut Berlin und Deutsch-Japanische Gesellschaft Berlin. Quellenlage und ausgewählte Aspekte ihrer Politik 1926–1945*. Berlin: Ostasiatisches Seminar der FU-Berlin, 1980.

———. *Philipp Franz von Siebold als früher Exponent der Ostasienwissenschaften. Ein Beitrag zur Orientalismusdiskussion und zur Geschichte der europäisch-japanischen Begegnung*. Bochum: Studienverlag Brockmeyer, 1983.

———. "Das Japaninstitut in Berlin (1926–1945). Bemerkungen zu seiner Struktur und Tätigkeit." In Hartmut Walravens, ed. *Du verstehst unsere Herzen gut: Fritz Rumpf (1888–1949) im Spannungsfeld der deutsch-japanischen Kulturbeziehungen*. Weinheim: VCH, Acta Humaniora, 1989, pp. 73–88.

Gundert, Wilhelm. *Japanische Religionsgeschichte*. Stuttgart: D. Gundert, 1935.

———. *Der japanische Nationalcharakter*. 2nd ed. Leipzig: Otto Harrassowitz, 1935.

———. "Die Bedeutung Japans und die Aufgabe der deutschen japanologischen Arbeit." *Zeitschrift der Deutschen Morgenländischen Gesellschaft* 90 (1936), pp. 247–264.

———. "Nationale und übernationale Religion in Japan." In *Die religiösen Kräfte Asiens*. Hamburg: Hanseatische Verlagsanstalt, 1937, pp. 5–20.

———. "Fremdvölkisches Kulturgut und Eigenleistung in Deutschland und Japan." In Walter Donat, ed., *Das Reich und Japan*. Berlin: Junker und Dünnhaupt, 1943.

———. "Die Entwicklung und Bedeutung des Tenno-Gedankens in Japan." In Hans Heinrich Schaeder, ed., *Der Orient in deutscher Forschung. Vorträge der Berliner Orientalistentagung, Herbst 1942*. Leipzig: Harrassowitz, 1944, pp. 137–157.

Hack, Annette. "Das Japanisch-Deutsche Kulturinstitut in Tôkyô zur Zeit des Nationalsozialismus. Von Wilhelm Gundert zu Walter Donat." *Nachrichten der Gesellschaft für Natur- und Völkerkunde Ostasiens. Zeitschrift für Kultur und Geschichte Ost- und Südostasiens* 157/158 (1995), pp. 77–100.

Heinrich, Fritz. *Die Deutsche Religionswissenschaft und der Nationalsozialismus. Eine ideologiekritische und wissenschaftsgeschichtliche Untersuchung*. Petersberg: Michael Imhof, 2002.

Junginger, Horst. *Von der philologischen zur völkischen Religionswissenschaft. Das Fach Religionswissenschaft an der Universität Tübingen von der Mitte des 19. Jahrhunderts bis zum Ende des Dritten Reiches*. Stuttgart: Franz Steiner, 1999.

Katô, Genchi. *A Study of Shinto. The Religion of the Japanese Nation*, 2nd ed. London and Dublin: Curzon Press, 1971 (1st ed. 1926).

———. *What is Shintô?*. Tokyo: Maruzen Company, 1935.

Kippenberg, Hans G. *Die Entdeckung der Religionsgeschichte. Religionswissenschaft und Moderne*. München: C.H. Beck, 1997.

Kitayama, Junyû. "Die japanische Urkultur und ihre Auseinandersetzung mit dem Buddhismus." *Ostasiatische Rundschau. Die Zeitschrift für den Fernen Osten* 15–18 (1934), pp. 421–428.

———. *Metaphysik des Buddhismus. Versuch einer philosophischen Interpretation der Lehre Vasuband-*

hus und seiner Schule. (Veröffentlichungen des Orientalischen Seminars der Universität Tübingen. Abhandlungen zur orientalischen Philologie und zur allgemeinen Religionsgeschichte, edited by Enno Littmann and Jakob Wilhelm Hauer, no. 7). Stuttgart: W. Kohlhammer, 1934.

———. *Genjo Koan. Aus dem Zen-Text 'Shôbo Ganzô' von Patriarch Dôgen*, translated and commented by Junyû Kitayama. Berlin: Alfred Töpelmann, 1940.

———. "Tradition und Neuordnung. Das Gesicht der japanischen Kultur." *Berlin. Rom. Tôkio. Monatsschrift für die Vertiefung der kulturellen Beziehungen der Völker des weltpolitischen Dreiecks*, vol. 2, no. 3 (1940), pp. 10–15.

———. "Japanisches Wachstum. Von Rasse und Kultur." *Schule der Freiheit. Unabhängige Zeitschrift für organische Gestaltung von Kultur, Gesellschaft und Wirtschaft*, vol. 9, no. 7/8 (1941), pp. 150–152.

———. *West-östliche Begegnung Japans Kultur und Tradition*. Berlin: de Gruyter, 1941.

———. *Der Shintoismus. Die Nationalreligion Japans*. Berlin: Wilhelm Limpert, 1943.

———. *Heiligung des Staates und Verklärung des Menschen. Buddhismus und Japan*. Berlin: Wilhelm Limpert, 1943.

———. *Heroisches Ethos. Das Heldische in Japan*. Berlin: de Gruyter, 1944.

Kleinschmidt, Harald. *Württemberg und Japan. Landesgeschichtliche Aspekte der deutsch-japanischen Beziehungen*. Stuttgart: Helfant edition, 1991.

Krebs, Gerhard, Martin, Bernd eds. *Formierung und Fall der Achse Berlin-Tôkyô*. München: Iudicium, 1994.

Krech, Volkhard. *Wissenschaft und Religion. Studien zur Geschichte der Religionsforschung in Deutschland 1871 bis 1933*. Tübingen: Mohr Siebeck, 2002.

Kubota, Hiroshi. "Political Discourse and Religious Studies in the National Socialist Period: The Case of Heinrich Frick" (paper at the International Workshop: Neo-Paganism, 'Völkische Religion' and Antisemitism II, October 27–29, 1997, Tübingen).

———. *Religionswissenschaftliche Religiosität und Religionsgründung. Jakob Wilhelm Hauer im Kontext des Freien Protestantismus*. Frankfurt a.M.: Peter Lang, 2005.

———. "Ideologiesierbarkeit und Ideologieanfälligkeit der Religionsforschung. Das Beispiel Kitayama Junyû als 'völkischer Religionswissenschaftler' im Dritten Reich" (in print).

Masuzawa, Tomoko. *The Invention of World Religions. Or, How European Universalism Was Preserved in the Language of Pluralism*. Chicago: University of Chicago Press, 2005.

N.N. "Quelle: Bericht des Reichsministeriums über die Lage der Sinologie und Japanologie in Deutschland 1942." *Newsletter Frauen und China* 7 (1994), pp. 1–17.

Pettazzoni, Raffaele. *Italia religiosa*. Bari: Laterza, 1952.

Ramming, Martin ed. *Japan-Handbuch. Nachschlagewerk der Japankunde, im Auftrag des Japaninstituts Berlin*. Berlin: Steiniger-Verlag, 1941.

Walravens, Hartmut ed. *Du verstehst unsere Herzen gut: Fritz Rumpf (1888–1949) im Spannungsfeld der deutsch-japanischen Kulturbeziehungen*. Weinheim: VCH, Acta Humaniora, 1989.

Worm, Herbert. "Japanologie im Nationalsozialismus. Ein Zwischenbericht." In Gerhard Krebs and Bernd Martin, eds., *Formierung und Fall der Achse Berlin-Tôkyô*. München: Iudicium, 1994, pp. 153–186.

JOACHIM WACHS GRUNDLEGUNG DER RELIGIONSWISSENSCHAFT

EIN BEITRAG ZU IHRER IDENTITÄT UND SELBSTÄNDIGKEIT

Kurt Rudolph

Am 29. April 1935 wurde dem Leipziger außerordentlichen Professor für Religionswissenschaft Joachim Wach vom Sächsischen Ministerium für Volksbildung (SMVB) die Lehrbefugnis und Prüfungserlaubnis entzogen; ab 1. Mai erhielt er bereits keine Bezüge mehr.[1] Der Anlass dafür war das bekannte nazistische Gesetz zur Wiederherstellung des Berufsbeamtentums vom 7. April 1933, das unter anderem Juden und „jüdisch Versippten" eine Beamtenstellung untersagte. In einer Sitzung der Philosophischen Fakultät, der Wach angehörte, kam es am 8. Mai darüber zu einer kontroversen Aussprache, da auch einige andere Professoren wie etwa der Assyriologe Benno Landsberger betroffen waren. Einige Mitglieder der Fakultät legten Prostest ein, darunter Werner Heisenberg, Friedrich Hund und Bernhard Schweitzer, aber eine Protestentschließung der Fakultät kam nicht zustande und wurde von dem damaligen Dekan der Philosophischen Fakultät, dem Althistoriker Helmut Berve, auch nicht gewünscht. Da das Ministerium von diesen Vorgängen erfuhr, verlangte es einen Bericht darüber, der am 23. Mai über den Rektor der Universität erfolgte. Auch der Versuch, wenigstens die Studenten bzw. Doktoranden ihre Prüfungen bei Wach ablegen zu lassen, wurde untersagt. Von Wach selbst liegt keine eigene Stellungnahme dazu vor, hatte er doch Anfang April 1935 bereits eine Einladung an die Brown University in Rhode Island für das Wintersemester

---

[1] Für die folgenden Vorgänge verweise ich auf meine Arbeit *Die Religionsgeschichte an der Leipziger Universität und die Entwicklung der Religionswissenschaft* (Berlin: Akademie-Verlag, 1962), S. 137ff., die erstmalig die relevanten Materialien aus dem Leipziger Universitätsarchiv (bes. der Philosophischen Fakultät) benutzte. Außerdem verwende ich eine Leipziger Hauptseminararbeit von Johannes Graul zum Thema „Joachim Wach als Hochschullehrer in Leipzig (1924–1935)" vom Wintersemester 2003/04, die er mir freundlicher Weise zur Verfügung stellte und die die Leipziger Unterlagen noch einmal ausführlich heranzog.

1935/36 erhalten und dafür Urlaub erbeten, der ihm am 11. April erteilt wurde. Wie bekannt, verließ Wach im September 1935 Deutschland und kehrte nicht mehr zurück. Ob ihm dies bei seiner Ausreise tatsächlich bewusst war, bleibt unsicher. Jedenfalls hatte er mit dieser Gastprofessur in den USA letztlich doch noch einen Ausweg aus der für ihn schmerzlichen Situation in seiner Heimat gefunden. In Rhode Island blieb er bis 1945, dann wechselte er an die Divinity School der University of Chicago, der er bis zu seinem Tode 1955 treu blieb. Kurz vor seinem Tod erreichte ihn eine Berufung auf den früheren Lehrstuhl Rudolf Ottos für Systematische Theologie der Philipps-Universität Marburg, die er aber ablehnte.[2]

Man muss bei diesen Vorgängen berücksichtigen, dass, abgesehen von der mageren Quellenlage – Wachs Nachlass in Chicago ist diesbezüglich noch nicht ausgewertet worden –, die Haltung von Wach selbst eindeutig war, wie aus der bereits im Oktober 1933 abverlangten Stellungnahme zu seiner Auffassung vom Hochschullehrerberuf hervorgeht, die keine Anpassung an die zur Herrschaft gelangte Ideologie zeigen, sondern dem von ihm bereits in seiner Habilitationsvorlesung 1924 über „Meister und Jünger" geäußerten Zügen einer idealisierten Beziehung von Lehrer und Schüler im Sinne Stefan Georges folgte. Ein erster Teil der bekannten Druckfassung von 1924 erschien schon 1922 in einer Publikation der „Freideutschen Jugend".[3] Es muss auch bemerkt werden, dass Wach sich in keiner Weise als Jude oder „jüdisch" fühlte. Er war in einem christlichen Elternhaus lutherischer Prägung aufgewachsen und trat noch in einem im April 1934 an die Philosophische Fakultät der Universität Leipzig gerichteten Schreiben Gerüchten entgegen, dass sein berühmter Großvater, der Jurist Adolf Wach, nichtarischer

---

[2] Vgl. dazu die Bemerkungen von Joseph M. Kitagawa, im 1. Band der *Joachim Wach-Vorlesungen der Theologischen Fakultät der Philipps-Universität Marburg/Lahn*, hg. von Ernst Benz, (Leiden: Brill, 1963) (Beihefte der ZRGG VI), S. 4f. und in der Einleitung zu den von ihm und Gregory D. Alles herausgegebenen Wach'schen *Essays in the History of Religions* (New York: Macmillan, 1988), S. XIIff.

[3] J. Wach, „Meister und Jünger/Lehrer und Schüler", *Freideutsche Jugend. Eine Monatsschrift aus dem Geiste der Jugend*, Heft 8/9 (1922), S. 233–239; ders., *Meister und Jünger. Zwei religionssoziologische Betrachtungen* (Abdruck einer Rede vom 3. Mai 1924, Leipzig: Pfeiffer, o.J. [1924], Tübingen: Mohr, 1925). Englische Übersetzung: „Master and Disciple. Two Religio-Sociological Studies", *Journal of Religion* 42 (1972), S. 1–32, wiederabgedruckt in J. Wach, *Essays in the History of Religions*, S. 1–21. Vgl. dazu Rainer Flasche, *Die Religionswissenschaft Joachim Wachs* (Berlin: De Gruyter, 1978), S. 76ff.

Herkunft gewesen sei.[4] Dass sich Wach schon bald nach 1933 dem Vorwurf ausgesetzt sah, ein so genannter „Nichtarier" zu sein, geht aus verschiedenen Äußerungen hervor, etwa von Hans Haas.[5] Sie beruhten darauf, dass seine Eltern in verwandtschaftlicher Beziehung zu der Familie Mendelssohn-Bartholdy standen, eine Familie, die bereits seit zwei Generationen christlich war. Wachs Mutter war eine Tochter des Bruders von Felix Mendelssohn Bartholdy, seine Großmutter die jüngste Tochter des berühmten Komponisten, verheiratet eben mit Adolf Wach. Wach war, so könnte man sagen, durchaus „deutschnational" eingestellt, wie die Mehrheit der Deutschen zu dieser Zeit. Er hatte sich 1916 kriegsfreiwillig gemeldet und nach Ablegung des Notabiturs in Dresden am 1. Weltkrieg teilgenommen, dabei den Offiziersrang (Leutnant im Sächsischen Garderegiment) und das Eiserne Kreuz erhalten. Diese Tatbestände spielten übrigens eine Rolle bei den Protesten gegen seine Entlassung, natürlich vergebens, da es um rassistische Gründe ging. Ein Nachspiel dieser Art erfolgte noch mitten im 2. Weltkrieg, als man 1943 allen promovierten Juden den Doktorgrad aberkannte, diesmal nicht nur Wach, sondern auch seinem Schüler Hans-Joachim Schoeps. Damit sollte diese traurige Seite von Wachs Leben in seiner Heimat zunächst beendet sein. Er war der einzige deutsche Religionswissenschaftler, den das NS-Regime aus dem Land gejagt hat.

Ich möchte mich nunmehr einer seiner Arbeiten zuwenden, die ich nach wie vor für eine der wichtigsten halte, und die zeigt, welchen Verlust die deutsche Religionswissenschaft durch den Weggang von Wach erlitten hat, aber auch welche Impulse von Wach heute noch ausgehen, ohne dass man sich dessen bewusst ist. Wach hatte bis zu seiner Vertreibung schon eine erhebliche Anzahl Arbeiten publiziert, darunter seine Habilitationsschrift *Religionswissenschaft* (1924), eine *Einführung in die Religionssoziologie* (1931), übrigens die erste dieser Art, und die dreibändige Ausgabe *Das Verstehen. Grundzüge einer Geschichte der hermeneutischen Theorie im 19. Jahrhundert* (1926, 1929, 1933; ein 4. Band kam dann nicht mehr zustande). Alle diese Werke, die von zahlreichen kleineren Studien − vornehmlich in der von ihm mitherausgegebenen *Zeitschrift für Missionskunde und Religionswissenschaft* (ZMR) − begleitet wurden, zeichnen sich durch eine enorme Fülle von Material zur Theorie

---

[4] Siehe dazu auch Horst Junginger, „Das Überleben der Religionswissenschaft im Nationalsozialismus", *Zeitschrift für Religionswissenschaft* 9 (2001), S. 149–167, hier S. 158.

[5] Rudolph, *Die Religionsgeschichte*, S. 130.

der Religionswissenschaft aus, und zwar vor allem aus dem Bereich der Geschichtswissenschaft und ihrer Methodologie. Wach hat mit gutem Gespür eben gerade nicht den von der herkömmlichen Religionswissenschaft oder Religionsgeschichte, wie sie damals noch häufig hieß, betretenen Pfad zur Religionsphilosophie und Theologie als Impulsgeber für ihre grundsätzlichen Probleme der Selbstfindung beschritten, sondern sich der historischen Theorie, der Hermeneutik, wie sie sich seit dem frühen 19. Jahrhundert ausgebildet hatte, zugewandt, um von daher Anregungen für die Probleme der Religionswissenschaft zu erhalten. Natürlich hat er in keiner Weise das Gespräch mit der Religionsphilosophie, die ja damals noch oft mit der Religionsgeschichte bzw. Religionswissenschaft verwechselt wurde, oder auch mit der Theologie vernachlässigt, wie seine Arbeiten auf Schritt und Tritt zeigen. Sicherlich war seine Hinwendung zur Geschichtswissenschaft damit verbunden, dass er seit 1924 eine Stellung am Institut für Kultur- und Universalgeschichte der Leipziger Universität innehatte, eine Institution, die 1909 von Karl Lamprecht geschaffen worden war. Die Wendung zu dieser Seite der Geistes- bzw. Kulturwissenschaften halte ich für einen bis heute nachwirkenden wichtigen Einfluss Wachs, auch wenn uns das nicht mehr so deutlich ist. Nur wenn man seine Schriften wieder liest, wird einem dieser Zusammenhang klar. Keiner der zeitgenössischen Religionswissenschaftler hat die Beschäftigung mit methodologischen Fragestellungen so energisch und mit Leidenschaft betrieben wie Wach. Daher war sein erzwungener Weggang ein enormer Schaden für die deutsche Religionswissenschaft. Ob sie nach 1933 einen anderen Weg genommen hätte, glaube ich zwar nicht, aber die Auseinandersetzung mit Wach war zunächst zu Ende und setzte erst nach 1945 mit einiger Verzögerung wieder ein. Wach war in Deutschland ein Fremder geworden, dessen Anfänge nicht mehr aktuell waren.

Damit will ich zu der bereits genannten Arbeit von Wach kommen, seiner *Religionswissenschaft*, die er im Untertitel als eine *Prolegomena zu ihrer wissenschaftstheoretischen Grundlegung* bezeichnet hat. Von ihr erschien erst 1989 eine englische Übersetzung, die von Joseph M. Kitagawa, Wachs Schüler und Nachfolger in Chicago, und dessen Schüler Gregory D. Alles betreut wurde.[6] Wach hat im Vorwort ausdrücklich auf seine

---

[6] Joachim Wach, *Introduction to the history of religions*, ed. by Joseph M. Kitagawa and Gregory D. Alles, with the collaboration of Karl W. Luckert (New York: Macmillan 1988), S. 1–150: *Part one: The History of Religions. Theoretical prolegomena to its foundation as a scholarly discipline*, 1924. Der 2. Teil (S. 151–225: *Essays from Die RGG 1928–1931*)

Vorläufer F.M. Müller und C.P. Tiele verwiesen, die sich im Abstand von 25 Jahren (1874 und 1899) in grundsätzlicher Weise zur Disziplin der Religionswissenschaft geäußert hatten. Da diese aber einer anderen Zeit zugehörten, müssen, wie Wach schrieb, eine Reihe von „Fragen, die die Voraussetzungen der religionswissenschaftlichen Arbeit betreffen", neu aufgeworfen und geklärt werden. „Die Verwirrung in unserer Wissenschaft ist, was ihre methodische Grundfragen angeht, anerkanntermaßen groß". Ein Satz, der zum Teil auch noch heute gilt. Bei dieser Klärung hat Wach ausdrücklich die Hilfe der Nachbarwissenschaften, d.h. der Kulturwissenschaften im Auge, vor allem die in ihnen besonders von Wilhelm Dilthey entwickelte neue Hermeneutik.[7] Wie er schon im Vorwort erklärt, wollte Wach den „empirischen Charakter" der Religionswissenschaft hervorheben, die Trennung von religionsphilosophischen und religionswissenschaftlichen Aufgaben durchsetzen, eine Gleichberechtigung mit den anderen empirischen Geisteswissenschaften erreichen, außerdem die Scheidung zwischen Religionsgeschichte und „systematischer Religionswissenschaft" durchführen und die Grundlinien der letzteren zeichnen.[8] Damit soll keine neue Disziplin eruiert werden, sondern eine „klare Herausarbeitung der Tendenzen, die die Religionswissenschaft bestimmen", erfolgen. Es geht Wach primär um eine Hebung und Klärung des methodischen Bewusstseins, an dem es in der Religionswissenschaft mangelte. Kritik hat er erwartet, vor allem wegen seiner Abgrenzung zur Theologie. Aber er sieht seine Studie auch als einen notwendigen Beitrag zur deutschen Geistesgeschichte seiner Zeit, in der die Klärung von empirischer Forschungsarbeit und philosophischer Spekulation im Bereich der Religionswissenschaft notwendig geworden ist.

Das Programm wird von Wach in fünf Kapiteln durchgeführt, auf die hier kurz eingegangen werden kann, wobei ich mir erlaube, einige

---

enthält Übersetzungen von Artikeln Wachs aus der 2. Auflage der RGG (1928–1931). Das Buch ist von Kitagawa mit einer längeren Einleitung über „Verstehen und Erlösung" versehen worden (S. IX–XXXIV; vgl. bereits *History of Religions* 11, 1971/72, S. 31–35). Ich verweise in den folgenden Bezügen auf das deutsche Original von 1924 (Leipzig: J.C. Hinrichs'sche Buchhandlung; Veröffentlichungen des Forschungsinstituts für vergleichende Religionsgeschichte an der Universität Leipzig, hg. von Prof. Dr. Hans Haas, Nr. 10) und auch auf die englische Übersetzung. Ein Nachdruck der deutschen Ausgabe erschien wenig beachtet 2001 im Verlag Spenner, Waltrop, mit einer Einleitung von Christopher H. Grundmann.

[7] Vgl. bereits Wachs Studie „Methodologie der allgemeinen Religionswissenschaft", *Zeitschrift für Missionskunde und Religionswissenschaft* 38 (1923), S. 33–55.

[8] *Religionswissenschaft*, S. VI.

Aussagen zu zitieren, um deutlich zu machen, wie klar Wach bestimmte
Sachverhalte beschreibt, die für uns nichts Neues sind, damals aber
offensichtlich noch nicht. Hier zeigt sich wieder seine bahnbrechende
Betrachtung und Analyse, die wir in anderen zeitgenössischen Arbeiten
(und teilweise auch heute noch) vermissen.

Im ersten Kapitel geht es Wach um die Emanzipation der Religionswissenschaft von der Theologie und Religionsphilosophie (S. 1–20).
Wach plädiert für eine Verankerung der Religionswissenschaft in der
Philosophischen Fakultät, parallel zu den anderen Geisteswissenschaften,
aber mit deutlicher Distanz zur Religionsphilosophie.[9] Eine Verwendung
der Religionswissenschaft für antireligiöse Polemik lehnt er ab, genauso
wie er später ebenso ausdrücklich der „praktischen Inanspruchnahme
von Religion" in der Religionswissenschaft bzw. deren „religiöse
Abzweckung" eine Absage erteilt.[10] Die Aufgaben der Religionswissenschaft beschreibt Wach im zweiten Kapitel (S. 21–71), wobei er bereits
deutlich die historische von der systematischen Arbeit unterscheidet;
beides gehört aber zur Religionswissenschaft, da sie nicht bloß mit der
Religionsgeschichte identisch ist, sondern auch systematische Fragestellungen aus ihrer Arbeit hervorgehen. Dabei hat die so genannte
Wahrheitsfrage auszusetzen. Wach bemüht hier den Begriff der „Ein-
klammerung", der seitdem in der Religionswissenschaft üblich geworden
ist, so z.B. bei Gerardus van der Leeuw. „Erst durch diese Klammer
entsteht recht eigentlich das Objekt der Religionswissenschaft".[11] Sehr
deutlich sieht Wach, dass damit diesbezügliche Werturteile wegfallen,
und zwar bis in die Terminologie hinein (Häresie, Ketzerei).[12] Den
Vorwurf des Rationalismus hält er in diesem Kontext für unberechtigt
und verweist mit Bezugnahme auf Rudolf Otto darauf, dass auch das
„Irrationale" von der Religionswissenschaft zur Kenntnis genommen
werden muss. Sehr klar spricht sich Wach gegen die Wesensfrage aus:
die Religionswissenschaft hat es nicht mit dem „Wesen von Religion"
zu tun und hat deshalb diese Frage nicht zu erörtern.[13] Es geht ihr
um den „Geist" oder die „Idee" im Sinne des „Lebensmittelpunktes",
des „Zentrums" oder des „Grundgedankens" einer Religion, wobei

---

[9] Ebd., S. 13ff. (englische Übersetzung, S. 4f.).
[10] Ebd., S. 124 (englische Übersetzung, S. 89f.).
[11] Ebd., S. 29 (englische Übersetzung, S. 24).
[12] Ebd., S. 32, S. 53, Anm. 1 und S. 70 (englische Übersetzung, S. 26, S. 208,
Fußnote 21 und S. 51).
[13] Ebd., S. 37ff. und S. 59f. (englische Übersetzung, S. 25ff. und S. 36f.).

allein der empirische Nachweis derselben eine Rolle spielen darf.[14] Diese Betonung der historischen Detailforschung als Ausgangspunkt auch systematischer oder synthetischer Arbeit wird wiederholt von Wach hervorgehoben.[15] Zum Schluss führt Wach eine klare Trennung von der Theologie bzw. den Theologien durch, und zwar mit dem Argument, dass es sich bei der Theologie wie auch bei der Religionsphilosophie um eine normative Wissenschaft handelt.[16] „Es gibt keine normative Religionswissenschaft, es gibt nur Religionsphilosophie und Theologie".[17] Das schließt ein Beschäftigung der Religionswissenschaft mit der Geschichte des Christentums ein, ebenso die Zusammenarbeit mit der exegetisch-biblischen Theologie, obwohl es hier, wie in der Kirchengeschichte, zu unterschiedlichen Ausgangspunkten und Arbeitsweisen kommt.[18] Einige Zitate aus der Zusammenfassung: „die Aufgabe der Religionswissenschaft ist die Erforschung und Darstellung der empirischen Religionen. Sie ist also eine beschreibend-verstehende, keine normative Wissenschaft. Mit der historischen und systematischen Bearbeitung der konkreten Religionsbildungen ist ihre Aufgabe erfüllt".[19] „Als Wissenschaft hat sie voraussetzungslos zu arbeiten. Über die persönliche Stellungnahme des Forschers ist damit nichts präjudiziert (...)."[20] „Aber man muss trennen können zwischen Arbeit und Predigt, zwischen Wissenschaft und Prophetie, zwischen Wissenschaft und Philosophie".[21] Erforderlich ist die „strengste Sachlichkeit" und „das höchstmögliche Maß von Objektivität".[22] Was Wach hier sagt, klingt schon fast wie Positivismus, von dem er sich aber ausdrücklich distanziert.[23] Wach fordert in diesem Kontext sogar eine „Kunde der religiösen Sprache", ja eine Art „religiöse Grammatik", offensichtlich in Anlehnung an die Literatur- und Sprachwissenschaft.[24]

---

[14] Ebd., S. 49f. (englische Übersetzung, S. 38f.).
[15] Ebd., S. 57 (englische Übersetzung, S. 43).
[16] Ebd., S. 60ff. (englische Übersetzung, S. 44ff.).
[17] Ebd., S. 61 (englische Übersetzung, S. 46).
[18] Ebd., S. 65ff. (englische Übersetzung, S. 48ff.).
[19] Ebd., S. 68 (englische Übersetzung, S. 49f.).
[20] Ebd. (englische Übersetzung, S. 50).
[21] Ebd., S. 69 (englische Übersetzung, S. 51).
[22] Ebd. (englische Übersetzung, S. 51).
[23] Ebd., S. 137 (englische Übersetzung, S. 100). Da ich Wachs diesbezüglicher Auffassung oft gefolgt bin, habe ich mir den Vorwurf des „Neopositivismus" von Seiten dogmatischer Marxisten während meiner Leipziger Zeit eingehandelt, der bis in meine Stasi-Akten reichte.
[24] Ebd., S. 70f. (englische Übersetzung, S. 51f.).

In den folgenden zwei Kapiteln geht es Wach zunächst um die Einteilung der Religionswissenschaft (S. 72–112), dann um ihre Methode
(S. 113–164). Für ihn ist die Aufteilung der Religionswissenschaft in
historische und systematische Aufgaben ein wichtiges Grundanliegen,
da er darin einen Fortschritt in der Konzeption der Disziplin als einer
empirischen Geisteswissenschaft sieht, die sich von Religionsphilosophie
und Theologie unterscheidet. Konstruktionen, wie eine allgemeine
Religionsgeschichte oder die Entwicklung der Religion, womöglich
begleitet von einem Fortschrittsgedanken, sind für ihn kein Thema der
Religionswissenschaft.[25] Die systematischen Fragestellungen ergeben sich
oft von selbst aus der empirischen Forschung. Sie bedürfen einer eigenen
Bearbeitung durch die Religionswissenschaft unter Berücksichtigung der
Nachbardisziplinen.[26] Dazu zählen für ihn die Religionspsychologie,
aber nur in kritisch-begrenzter Weise,[27] dann die Religionssoziologie,
für die besonders Max Weber, Ernst Troeltsch und Werner Sombart
angeführt werden,[28] außerdem die von ihm mit Skepsis betrachtete
Religionsgeographie.[29] In dem umfangreichen Methodenkapitel (S. 113–
164) geht es Wach noch einmal um die Auseinandersetzung mit der
Philosophie und deren Betrachtung von Religion. Deren spekulative
Sicht hält er jedoch für unvereinbar mit der Religionswissenschaft, wie
er an den Entwürfen von Ernst Troeltsch, Heinrich Scholz und Max
Scheler kritisch aufzeigt.[30] Die Religionswissenschaft nimmt ihren Ausgang von den geschichtlich gegebenen Religionen und nicht von einer
abstrakten Wesensbestimmung von Religion.[31] „Die Religionen können
aus der Idee der Religion nicht deduziert werden," heißt es.[32] Daher
gehört die Religionsphilosophie nicht zur Religionswissenschaft, was
nicht ausschließt, dass sie bei einigen Fragen zu Rate gezogen werden
kann, so bei der „Durchdenkung und Bereitstellung von Methoden",
der „wesensmäßigen Durchforschung und philosophischen Bestimmung

---

[25] Ebd., S. 79ff. (englische Übersetzung, S. 56ff.).
[26] Ebd., S. 89ff. (englische Übersetzung, S. 63ff.).
[27] Ebd., S. 98ff., ausführlich im Anhang: „Über den Psychologismus in der Religionswissenschaft" (S. 193–205). (englische Übersetzung, S. 76ff. und im Appendix
„Psychologism and the Study of Religion", ebd., S. 143–150).
[28] Ebd., S. 105ff. (englische Übersetzung, S. 75ff.).
[29] Ebd., S. 107ff. (englische Übersetzung, S. 76ff.).
[30] Ebd., S. 120ff. (englische Übersetzung, S. 86ff.).
[31] Ebd., S. 129f. (englische Übersetzung, S. 94f.).
[32] Ebd., S. 131 (englische Übersetzung, S. 95).

ihres Gegenstands" und bei der „philosophischen Einordnung des Phänomens in das Ganze der Erkenntnis".[33]

Ein besonders Anliegen von Wach ist es hier, die Methode des historischen Verstehens im Anschluss an Wilhelm Dilthey als Ziel des religionswissenschaftlichen Erkennens zu beschreiben.[34] Die Voraussetzung dafür sieht er im Interesse am Gegenstand, nicht aber im „bloßen Nachfühlen oder Nacherleben".[35] Daher beschreibt er die Gefahren eines psychologisierenden Verstehens[36] und tritt für eine methodisch streng gelenkte Kommunikation mit dem Objekt ein, ohne jedoch die völlige Distanz zu ihm zu verlieren, was ein persönliches Verhältnis, eine gewisse Affinität und eine Teilhabe nicht ausschließt.[37] Der Charakter des Menschen spielt dabei ebenso eine Rolle wie die Phantasie.[38] Beachtenswert ist, dass Wach bereits die subjektiven Voraussetzungen der Forschung thematisiert, das Wissen um ihre zeitgenössische Einbindung und Abhängigkeit, wobei er ausdrücklich an das europäische Denken und Empfinden erinnert, das von christlichen Auffassungen bestimmt wird.[39] Daher ist die Selbstbesinnung und Selbstprüfung eine wichtige Voraussetzung religionswissenschaftlicher Forschung. Der Wandel der Auffassungen im Laufe der Geschichte, die Affinität zum jeweiligen Zeitgeist,[40] der „Wandel der Bilder",[41] sind gerade für die Religionsgeschichte wichtig und sollen uns an die Vergänglichkeit auch der Forschung erinnern. Hier hat Wach aktuelle Diskussionen vorweggenommen, auch wenn er die jeweiligen Themen nur kurz streift. Zum Schluss werden von Wach noch die „Formen" der Religionen angesprochen, über die das Verstehen ihres Sinnes läuft.[42] Natürlich

---

[33] Ebd., S. 136f. (englische Übersetzung, S. 99f.).

[34] Ebd., S. 132 und S. 139ff. (englische Übersetzung, S. 95 und S. 101ff.). Vgl. dazu auch J. Wach, *Das Verstehen*, Bd. 2 (Tübingen: Mohr, 1929, Nachdruck: Hildesheim 1966), S. 64–71 und seinen Artikel „Verstehen" in der 2. Auflage der *RGG*, Bd. 5, 1931, Sp. 1570–1573 (englische Übersetzung, S. 153–157: „Understanding"); ferner „On understanding", in *Essays in the History of Religions*, S. 171–184 (ursprünglich in *The Albert Schweitzer Jubilee Book*, ed. by A.A. Robach, Cambridge, MA 1946, S. 131–146, erschienen).

[35] Ebd., S. 154 (englische Übersetzung, S. 111).

[36] Ebd., S. 148ff. und S. 158ff. (englische Übersetzung, S. 107ff. und S. 115ff.).

[37] Ebd., S. 150f. und S. 158 (englische Übersetzung, S. 109f. und S. 114).

[38] Ebd., S. 152 (englische Übersetzung, S. 112f.).

[39] Ebd., S. 143f. (englische Übersetzung, S. 104f.).

[40] Ebd., S. 145 (englische Übersetzung, S. 105).

[41] Ebd., S. 146 (englische Übersetzung, S. 106).

[42] Ebd., S. 160f. (englische Übersetzung, S. 120f.).

fehlt bei Wach die Reflexion über die Rolle des Erklärens als Teil des
Verstehens und ihre kritische Wirkung auf die Arbeit des Forschers und
seinen Gegenstand, d.h. die ideologiekritische Komponente historischer
Forschung. Dazu war die Zeit offenbar noch nicht reif genug, obwohl
gerade der Nationalsozialismus auf dem Gebiet der Religionsforschung
ein lohnendes Ziel dafür abgegeben hätte.[43]

Die „systematische Religionswissenschaft" ist das Thema des letzten
Kapitels (S. 164–192).[44] In ihr sah Wach den eigentlich neuen Teil
der Religionswissenschaft und verglich ihn mit dem in der Rechts-
und Sprachwissenschaft ebenfalls bereits vorhandenen Zweig einer
Systematik, der vor allem der vergleichenden Methode verpflichtet ist.
Es geht in der systematischen Religionswissenschaft um die Herausarbeitung von Gleichförmigkeiten und Verläufen, die empirisch, nicht
dogmatisch oder normativ gewonnen werden müssen.[45] Die Betonung
der historischen Basis ist für Wach immer wieder charakteristisch und
wird oft übersehen. Als einzelne Aufgaben führt Wach hier auf: die
Klärung von Grundbegriffen, die Formtypen religiöser Ausdrücke,
die Gewinnung von Strukturen mit Hilfe von Querschnitten durch
die religiöse Formenwelt. Auch die Gefahren, zu denen Wach die
Parallelomanie[46] und die Vernachlässigung individueller Züge rechnet,
werden angesprochen, wogegen er den aus der Soziologie stammenden
„Bündigkeitscharakter" anführt.[47] Schließlich gehört auch die Bildung
von „idealtypischen Begriffen",[48] die Feststellung von Regel- oder Gesetz-

---

[43] Vgl. dazu Charles M. Wood, *Theory and Understanding. A Critique of the Hermeneutics
of Joachim Wach* (Missoula, Mo: Distributed by Scholars Press, 1975), bes. S. 166ff.,
Flasche, *Die Religionswissenschaft Joachim Wachs*, S. 130ff. bzw. zur „ideologiekritischen"
Funktion der Religionswissenschaft meinen so betitelten Beitrag in *Numen* 25 (1978/9),
S. 17–33, ergänzter Abdruck in ders., *Geschichte und Probleme der Religionswissenschaft*
(Leiden: Brill, 1992), S. 81–103. Vgl. auch Fritz Heinrich, *Die deutsche Religionswissenschaft
und der Nationalsozialismus. Eine ideologiekritische und wissenschaftsgeschichtliche Untersuchung*
(Petersberg: Imhof, 2002, diss. theol. Marburg 2001), bes. S. 26ff.

[44] Englische Übersetzung, S. 121–142. Vgl. bereits Wachs „Bemerkungen zum
Problem der ‚externen' Würdigung der Religion", *Zeitschrift für Missionskunde und Religionswissenschaft* 38 (1923), S. 161–183, bes. S. 174ff.

[45] Ebd., S. 167ff. (englische Übersetzung, S. 122ff.).

[46] Ebd., S. 181f. (englische Übersetzung, S. 134f.).

[47] Ebd., S. 185f. mit Verweisen auf W. Dilthey, H. Freyer und G. Simmel (Englische
Übersetzung, S. 136ff.).

[48] Vgl. ebd., S. 189 mit Anm. 1 (englische Übersetzung, S. 139 ohne Anm.), wo
darauf angespielt wird. Wach hat dies dann in seiner Religionssoziologie umzusetzen
versucht: *Einführung in die Religionssoziologie* (Tübingen 1931), *Sociology of Religion* (Chicago
1944, deutsche Fassung nach der 4. Auflage, Tübingen 1951), „Sociology of Religion",
in *Essays in the History of Religions*, S. 81–113 (ursprünglich in *Twentieth Century Sociology*,
ed. by Gregorij D. Gurvitch and Wilbert E. Moore, New York: Philos. Lib., 1945,

mäßigkeiten in den historischen Verläufen, Typologie und Morphologie sowie letztlich der Versuch einer „materialen Systematik" als Ordnung und Zusammenschau des Vielen zu den Aufgaben der Systematischen Religionswissenschaft, deren historische Basis damit nicht verlassen wird, aber der Bildung einer Gesamtschau der religiösen Welt dient, wie sie der wissenschaftliche Zugriff der Religionswissenschaft ermöglicht.

Damit habe ich versucht, einen Einblick in die Bemühungen Wachs für eine systematische Bestimmung der Religionswissenschaft zu geben, von denen ich nach wie vor der Meinung bin, dass sie zu den grundlegenden Versuchen gehört, unsere Disziplin auf einen richtigen und anerkannten Weg zu bringen. Ich habe bewusst die kritischen Fragen an manche Äußerungen und den nicht immer gut gegliederten Argumentationen unterlassen, da ich den positiven, weiterführenden Charakter des Inhalts seiner Prolegomena hervorheben wollte, der oft unterschlagen wird. Schließlich handelt es sich um eine Habilitationsarbeit. Ich weiß um den Wandel von Wach, für den nicht zuletzt sein Schicksal in Deutschland verantwortlich ist, war er doch in den USA in einer Theologischen Fakultät (Divinity School) tätig und von einer anderen Umgebung bestimmt.[49] Es wäre an der Zeit diesen Wandel, wie überhaupt das Leben von Wach an Hand der noch nicht verwendeten Quellen zu studieren und eine Monographie über diesen Religionswissenschaftler, der das Opfer einer unsinnigen und verbrecherischen Politik geworden ist, zu schreiben.[50]

S. 406–437). Vgl. dazu Flasche, *Die Religionswissenschaft Joachim Wachs*, S. 219ff. (Exkurs über Wachs Typenbildung in seiner „Religionssoziologie").

[49] Über Wachs weiteren Weg und Wandel siehe Rudolph, *Die Religionsgeschichte*, S. 145ff.; ders., *Geschichte und Probleme der Religionswissenschaft*, S. 357–367 (bes. S. 365ff.); Kitagawa, *Gibt es ein Verstehen fremder Religionen?*, S. 18ff., S. 26ff. und S. 39ff.; Flasche, *Die Religionswissenschaft Joachim Wachs*, bes. S. 229ff. und S. 253ff. sowie ders., „Joachim Wach", in Axel Michaels, Hg., *Klassiker der Religionswissenschaft* (München: Beck, 1997), S. 291–302, bes. S. 298ff.); Robert A. Segal, „Joachim Wach and the History of Religions", *Religious Studies Review* 20/3 (July 1994), S. 197–201; Heinrich, *Die deutsche Religionswissenschaft und der Nationalsozialismus*, S. 292ff., Anm. 43).

[50] Zu den Wach Papers der University of Chicago, Department of Special Collections, gibt es einen Guide der Joseph-Regenstein-Library von 1980, der mir vorliegt. Danach handelt es sich in der Mehrzahl um Material zu den wissenschaftlichen Arbeiten (Manuskripte, Exzerpte), Vorlesungen und Vorträgen, Universitätsangelegenheiten, Prüfungen, Rezensionen etc. Leider ist nur ein kleiner Bestand an Korrespondenzen aus den 1940er und 1950er Jahren überliefert. Es scheint, dass gerade die Briefliteratur aus der älteren, bes. der Leipziger Zeit, bisher nicht aufgetaucht ist bzw. überhaupt nicht aufbewahrt worden ist, soweit sie nicht unmittelbar beruflichen Charakter hatte und in die Archive gelangt sind. Manches ist vermutlich im Nachlass der Schwester Wachs, Frau Susi Heigl-Wach, die in der Schweiz (Locarno) lebte, vorhanden gewesen. Darüber ist aber nichts weiter bekannt.

646   KURT RUDOLPH

Bibliographie

Flasche, Rainer. *Die Religionswissenschaft Joachim Wachs*. Berlin, New York: De Gruyter, 1978.

——. „Joachim Wach". In Axel Michaels, Hg. *Klassiker der Religionswissenschaft*. München: Beck, 1997, S. 290–302.

Heinrich, Fritz. *Die deutsche Religionswissenschaft und der Nationalsozialismus. Eine ideologiekritische und wissenschaftsgeschichtliche Untersuchung*. Petersberg: Imhof Verlag, 2002.

—— und Kurt Rudolph. „Walter Baetke (1884–1978)". *Zeitschrift für Religionswissenschaft* 9 (2001), S. 169–184.

Junginger, Horst, *Von der philologischen zur völkischen Religionswissenschaft. Das Fach Religionswissenschaft an der Universität Tübingen von der Mitte des 19. bis zum Ende des Dritten Reiches*. Stuttgart: Steiner, 1999.

——. „Das Überleben der Religionswissenschaft im Nationalsozialismus". *Zeitschrift für Religionswissenschaft* 9 (2001), S. 149–167.

Kitagawa, Joseph M. et al., eds. *The history of religions. Essays on the problem of understanding by Joachim Wach*. Chicago: Chicago University Press, 1967.

—— and Gregory Alles, eds. Joachim Wach, *Essays in the history of religions*. New York: Macmillan, 1988.

—— and Gregory Alles, eds. Joachim Wach, *Introduction to the history of religions*. New York: Macmillan, 1988.

——. *Gibt es ein Verstehen fremder Religionen? Mit einer Biographie Joachim Wachs und einer vollständigen Bibliographie seiner Werke* (Joachim Wach-Vorlesungen der Theologischen Fakultät der Philipps-Universität Marburg/Lahn 1, zugl. Beiheft der Zeitschrift für Religions- und Geistesgeschichte 6). Leiden: Brill, 1963.

Rudolph, Kurt. *Die Religionsgeschichte an der Leipziger Universität und die Entwicklung der Religionswissenschaft. Ein Beitrag zur Wissenschaftsgeschichte und zum Problem der Religionswissenschaft* (Sitzungsberichte der Sächsischen Akademie der Wissenschaften zu Leipzig, Philologisch-Historische Klasse 107,1). Berlin: Akademie-Verlag, 1962.

——. „Die ‚ideologiekritische‘ Funktion der Religionswissenschaft". *Numen* 25 (1978), S. 17–39, Nachdruck in ders., *Geschichte und Probleme der Religionswissenschaft* (Studies in the history of religions 53). Leiden: Brill, 1992, S. 81–103.

——. „Joachim Wach (1898–1955)". In Max Steinmetz, Hg., *Bedeutende Gelehrte in Leipzig*, Bd. 1, Leipzig: Karl Marx Universität, 1965, S. 229–237, Nachdruck in ders., *Geschichte und Probleme der Religionswissenschaft*, S. 357–367.

Segal, Robert A. „Joachim Wach and the History of Religions". *Religious Studies Review* 20/3 (July 1994), S. 197–201.

Wach, Joachim. „Meister und Jünger/Lehrer und Schüler". *Freideutsche Jugend. Eine Monatsschrift aus dem Geiste der Jugend*, Heft 8/9 (1922), S. 233–239.

——. „Zur Methodologie der allgemeinen Religionswissenschaft". *Zeitschrift für Missionskunde und Religionswissenschaft* 38 (1923), S. 33–55.

——. „‚Nur‘. Gedanken über den Psychologismus". *Zeitschrift für Missionskunde und Religionswissenschaft* 39 (1924), S. 209–215.

——. *Religionswissenschaft. Prolegomena zu ihrer wissenschaftstheoretischen Grundlegung* (Veröffentlichungen des Forschungsinstituts für Vergleichende Religionsgeschichte an der Universität Leipzig 1, 10). Leipzig: Hinrichs, 1924, Nachdruck Waltrop: Verlag Spenner, 2001.

——. „Wilhelm Dilthey über ‚Das Problem der Religion‘". *Zeitschrift für Missionskunde und Religionswissenschaft* 40 (1925), S. 66–81.

——. *Meister und Jünger. Zwei religionssoziologische Betrachtungen*. Leipzig: Pfeiffer, o.J. [1924] (Abdruck einer Rede vom 3. Mai 1924). Tübingen: Mohr, 1925.

——. *Die Typenlehre Trendelenburgs und ihr Einfluss auf Dilthey. Eine philosophie- und geistesgeschichtliche Studie*. Tübingen: Mohr, 1926.

——. „Max Weber als Religionssoziologe". In *Kultur- und Universalgeschichte. Walter Goetz zu seinem 60. Geburtstag dargebracht von Fachgenossen, Freunden und Schülern*. Berlin: Teubner, 1927, S. 376–394.

——. Die Geschichtsphilosophie des 19. Jahrhunderts und die Theologie der Geschichte. *Historische Zeitschrift* 142 (1929), S. 1–15.

——. „Religionsphilosophie". In *Die Religionen in Geschichte und Gegenwart*, 2. Aufl., Bd. 5, 1931, Sp. 1914–1921.

——. „Religionssoziologie". In *Die Religionen in Geschichte und Gegenwart*, 2. Aufl., Bd. 5, 1931, Sp. 1929–1934.

——. „Religionswissenschaft". In *Die Religionen in Geschichte und Gegenwart*, 2. Aufl., Bd. 5, 1931, Sp. 1954–1959

——. „Verstehen". In *Die Religionen in Geschichte und Gegenwart*, 2. Aufl., Bd. 5, 1931, Sp. 1570–1573.

——. „Und die Religionsgeschichte?" *Zeitschrift für systematische Theologie* 6 (1929), S. 484–497.

——. „Religionssoziologie". In Alfred Vierkandt, Hg. *Handwörterbuch der Soziologie*, Bd. 1. Stuttgart: Enke, 1931, S. 479–494.

——. *Typen religiöser Anthropologie. Ein Vergleich der Lehre vom Menschen im religionsphilosophischen Denken von Orient und Okzident*. Tübingen: Mohr, 1932.

——. *Das Verstehen. Grundzüge einer Geschichte der hermeneutischen Theorie im 19. Jahrhundert*, 3 Bde. Tübingen: Mohr, 1926–1933, Nachdruck, Hildesheim: Olms, 1984.

——. *Einführung in die Religionssoziologie*. Tübingen: Mohr, 1931.

——. *The comparative study of religions*. New York, NY: Columbia University Press, 1958.

——. *Sociology of religion*. Chicago: University of Chicago Press, 1946.

——. *Vergleichende Religionsforschung*. Stuttgart: Kohlhammer, 1962.

Wood, Charles M. *Theory and Understanding. A Critique of the Hermeneutics of Joachim Wach* (AAR Diss. Ser. 12). Missoula, Mo: Distributed by Scholars Press, 1975.

LIST OF CONTRIBUTORS

ANDREAS ÅKERLUND, M.A. in the study of religion, contemporary history and sociology at the Freie Universität Berlin, is a graduate student at the Department of History at the University of Uppsala. His master's thesis deals with the Swedish scholar Åke Ohlmarks. Currently he is writing a dissertation on Swedish lecturers at German universities between 1933 and 1945.

GUSTAVO BENAVIDES teaches history of religions in the Department of Theology and Religious Studies, Villanova University, Pennsylvania, USA. His research and publications focus on the theory, comparison and historiography of religion. He is the co-editor of *Numen* and of the series *Religion and Society*.

EUGEN CIURTIN, PhD, is postdoctoral fellow of New Europe College, of the Institute for Advanced Study, Bucharest, and of the Maison des Sciences de l'Homme, Paris, as well as secretary of the Romanian Association for the History of Religions. Being a co-editor of *Archaeus* and *Studia Asiatica*, his publications and scholarly interests focus on Indian religions, on Romanian cultural history and on the historiography of Asian and religious studies.

RICHARD FABER is professor of sociology at the Freie Universität Berlin. His teaching and publishing areas encompass the sociology of culture, literature, and religion as well as the history of political ideas. He is the editor of a great number of anthologies, among them *Abendland. Ein politischer Kampfbegriff* (2nd ed. 2002), *'Wir sind Eines'. Über politisch-religiöse Ganzheitsvorstellungen europäischer Faschismen* (2005), and *Politische Dämonologie. Über modernen Marcionismus* (2007).

HALINA GRZYMAŁA-MOSZCZYŃSKA is professor of psychology at the Jagiellonian University Cracow and at the School of Social Psychology, Warsaw. Her teachings include the psychology of religion, clinical aspects of religiosity, cultural psychology, as well as multiculturalism and religion. Her research focuses on religious experience in various religious contexts and on the role of religion in the process of cultural adaptation of migrants.

CRISTIANO GROTTANELLI is professor of history of religions at the University of Florence and a Faculty member in the *Dottorato* "Antropologia, Storia e Teoria della Cultura" (ASTEC) at the University of Siena, Italy. He is co-editor of *History of Religions* and *Archiv für Religionsgeschichte*. His recent publications include *Il sacrificio* (1999), *Kings and Prophets* (1999), *Profeti biblici* (2003), and (with Riccardo Contini) *Il saggio Ahiqar* (2005).

FRITZ HEINRICH, Dr. phil. in the study of religion at the University of Marburg. He has worked for a number of museums and is now teaching Religionswissenschaft at the Department of New Testament Studies at the University of Göttingen. His publications include a dissertation on *Die deutsche Religionswissenschaft und der Nationalsozialismus* (2002).

SIGURD HJELDE is professor of history of religions at the University of Oslo in the Department of Culture Studies and Oriental Languages. Among his major works were *Das Eschaton und die Eschata* (1987), *Die Religionsgeschichte und das Christentum* (1994), and *Sigmund Mowinckel und seine Zeit* (2006).

WILLEM HOFSTEE is assistant professor in anthropology of religion at the Faculty of Religious Studies, Leiden University. His research and publications concern the history of the academic study of religion in the 20th century, new religious movements and New Age groups. He is particularly interested in the relation between religious ideas and political actions.

ISTVÁN KEUL, Dr. phil., teaches history of religions at the Freie Universität, Berlin. His fields of research include Hinduism, religion in East Central Europe, and linguistic theories in the study of religion. He is the author of monographs on the Hindu deity Hanuman and on the religious history of Transylvania in the early modern period.

HORST JUNGINGER, Dr. phil. in the study of religion at the University of Tübingen. He has published extensively on antisemitism and on the history of the academic study of religion including *Von der philologischen zur völkischen Religionswissenschaft* (1999) and "Das Überleben

der Religionswissenschaft im Nationalsozialismus," special issue of the
Zeitschrift für Religionswissenschaft (2001).

HIROSHI KUBOTA has received his Dr. phil. in the study of religion from
the University of Tübingen. Now he is teaching as associate professor
in the Department of Christian Studies at Rikkyo University, Tokyo.
He is co-editor of *Religion and National Identity in the Japanese Context* (2002)
and the author of *Religionswissenschaftliche Religiosität und Religionsgründung:
Jakob Wilhelm Hauer im Kontext des freien Protestantismus* (2005).

IVETA LEITĀNE is professor of Religionswissenschaft and Jewish thought
and philosophy in the Department of Theology at the University of
Latvia. Her recent articles deal with the antisemitism in Latvia after
1991, Jewish Cemeteries in Courland (Latvia), Jewish neo-Kantianism,
and with the function of religion in the Latvian society after 1991.

VASILIOS N. MAKRIDES studied theology in Athens, history of religions
and sociology of religion at Harvard and in Tübingen, from where
he obtained his doctorate in 1991. Having taught at the University of
Thessaly (Greece) he is professor of religious studies (specializing in
Orthodox Christianity) at the Faculty of Philosophy, University of Erfurt
since 1999. His main research interest include comparative religious
and cultural history as well as sociology of Orthodox Christianity.

UDO MISCHEK, Dr. phil. in anthropology at the University of Leipzig, has
undertaken extensive fieldwork on the migration of gypsies in Germany
and Turkey. His research into the history of German ethnology has
resulted in a biographical study on the German anthropologist Günter
Wagner (2002).

BRUCE LINCOLN is the Caroline E. Haskell Professor of History of
Religions at the University of Chicago. Among his recent works are
Religion, Empire, and Torture: The Case of Achaemenian Persia (2007), *Holy
Terrors: Thinking about Religion after September 11* (2003), and *Theorizing
Myth: Narrative, Ideology, and Scholarship* (1999).

PIETTERI PIETIKÄINEN, Ph.D. in history at the University of Helsinki,
has published extensively on modern intellectual and medical history,
including *C.G. Jung and the Psychology of Symbolic Forms* (1999), *Neurosis and
Modernity* (2007), and *Alchemists of Human Nature* (2007). He is adjunct

professor (Docent) in the Department of History at the University of Helsinki.

KURT RUDOLPH, Dr. theol. (Leipzig 1956) and Dr. phil. (Leipzig 1958), was professor of history of religions at the University of Leipzig (1963–1984), at the University of California, Santa Barbara (1984–1986), and, after that, at the University of Marburg until his retirement in 1995. Publications include *Die Mandäer* (1965), *Die Gnosis* (4th ed. 2005), *Geschichte und Probleme der Religionswissenschaft* (1992), and *Gnosis und spätantike Religionsgeschichte* (1996).

MICHAEL STAUSBERG is professor of history of religions at the University of Bergen. Apart from the history of the discipline, his research interests include early modern European religious history, Zoroastrianism, modern religions and theories of ritual and religion.

MIHAELA TIMUŞ, PhD candidate in ancient Iranian studies at the École Pratique des Hautes Études, Paris, and Alumna at the New Europe College, Bucharest, is treasurer of the Romanian Association for the History of Religions and co-editor of *Archaeus* and *Studia Asiatica*. She published *The Correspondence Eliade-Wikander (1948–1977)* (2005, in Romanian) and co-edited *New Perspectives on Iranian Religions* (forthcoming).

FLORIN ŢURCANU is a historian specialized in modern intellectual history. He is senior lecturer at the Department of Political Science at the University of Bucharest and a researcher at the Institute of South-East European Studies in Bucharest. He is the author of *Mircea Eliade – le prisonnier de l'histoire* (2003).

ULRICH VOLLMER, M.A., is working at the Institut für Orient- und Ostasienwissenschaften at the University of Bonn. His recent publications focus on the history of the history of religions including articles on Friedrich Andres and Hans-Joachim Klimkeit.

INDEX

Abetz, Otto, 310
Académie Française, 207
Accademia dei Lincei (Accademia d'Italia), 62, 339, 347, 377–378, 380, 385, 389
Achelis, Hans, 285
Achterberg, Eberhard, 165
Acterian, Arşavir, 343
Acterian, Haig, 343, 397
Adamovičs, Ludvigs, 511
Ahnenerbe, 46–48, 50–51, 71, 73–76, 107–108, 117, 120–123, 127–129, 131–133, 140–147, 154–156, 160–170, 198–199, 212–213, 257, 384, 548
Åkerberg, Lars, 567
Alexandrescu, Sorin, 404–409
Alles, Gregory D., 638
Alt, Albrecht, 285
Altheim, Franz, 23, 35, 142, 146, 163, 169, 212, 383–384
Altmann, Rüdiger, 435
Andersson, Inge, 461
Andrae, Tor, 164
Andres, Friedrich, 27, 66–67, 443–462
Anquetil-Duperron, Abraham Hyacinthe, 222
Antaios, 138, 168, 266–267
Anthropos, 67, 469–470
Anthropos-Institut, 67–68, 446–447, 469
Anti-Comintern Pact, 85, 615–616
Anton, Ted, 34
Antonescu, Ion, 57, 304–305, 405
Antonescu, Mihai, 57
Arbman, Ernst, 220
Archiv für Religionswissenschaft (ARW), 46–47, 155–157, 199, 206, 312, 339, 383, 386–387
Aretin, Erwin Freiherr von, 271
Arsakeios Teacher's Training College, 285
Aryan Institute (at the University of Tübingen), ix, 153
Aryan Myth, 44, 109, 148, 152, 170
Ash, Mitchell G., 605
Astel, Karl, 52, 251, 253, 263, 563
Aufhauser, Johannes Baptist, 79

Augustin, Alarich, 75–76
Augustin, Günther, 76
Augustinus, 438
Augustus, 240, 385, 388
Auschwitz (concentration camp), 93, 143, 145–146, 153, 353
Austin, John L., 592
Auvergne, Wilhelm von, 432

Baetke, Walter, 229, 233–234, 244, 565
Baeumler, Alfred, 118, 255
Baillet, Philippe, 35, 167–168
Ball, Hugo, 430
Balla, Emil, 285
Ballhorn, Franz, 447
Ballin, Albert, 474
Baraniecki, Łukasz, 579
Barth, Karl, 4, 242, 530
Bartholomae, Christian, 181
Basler Missionsgesellschaft, 113
Bauer, Fritz, 108
Baumstark, Anton, 439
Beger, Bruno, 153, 167
Bellon, Karel Leopold, 445
Belloni-Filippi, Ferdinando, 342
Benavides, Gustavo, 53–54
Benveniste, Émile, 311
Benz, Ernst, 33
Berdjajev, Nikolaj, 530
Berezin, Mabel, 275
Berg, Alexander, 142
Berger, Adriana, 32
Berger, Gottlob, 75
Berggrav, Eivind, 491–493
Bertholet, Alfred, 27, 379, 451
Berve, Helmut, 635
Bērziņa, Lilita, 519
Best, Werner, 133
Beth, Karl, 112, 122, 244, 252
Bethe, Erich, 285
Beza, M., 344
Bianchi, Ugo, 367, 382
Bielenstein, August, 533
Biezais, Haralds, 69–70, 165, 509–540
Birkeland, Harris, 220, 493
Birkenau (concentration camp), 146
Bittremieux, L., 218

Blaschke, Olaf, 484–485
Blavatsky, Helena, 143
Bleichröder, Gerson, 474
Bloch, Ernst, 591
Boas, Franz, 186
Böhme, Jakob, 600
Bohmers, Assien, 142
Böhnigk, Volker, 459
Boll, Franz, 179, 181
Bopp, Franz, 190
Bormann, Martin, 566
Bornhausen, Karl, 27–28, 112, 114, 117, 451
Bornkamm, Heinrich, 81
Bourdieu, Pierre, 51, 230, 248–249, 257
Bouvier, Emile, 342
Boyce, Marie, 220
Brachmann, Wilhelm, 112–113
Brancuşi, Constantin, 316
Brand, Hans, 142
Brandewie, Ernest, 484
Brandt, Rudolf, 133
Braune, Wilhelm, 181
Brauner, Victor, 316
Braungart, Wolfgang, 435
Brelich, Angelo, 62, 169, 375
Breloer, Bernhard, 151
Briem, Efraim, 561
Bröcker, Walter, 433
Brock-Utne, Albert, 491, 493
Bruckmann, Hugo, 117
Brugmann, Karl, 190
Brunner, Emil, 69, 530, 538–539
Buber, Martin, 64, 66, 72, 318
Buchenwald (concentration camp), x, 71, 248, 340, 353
Buchman, Frank, 409
Bultmann, Rudolf, 339
Bund für deutsche Kirche, 218
Bund deutscher Unitarier, 76
Buonaiuti, Ernesto, 336, 373–374
Burgstaller, Ernst, 165
Burnouf, Eugène, 221
Bush, George, 265

Călinescu, Matei, 353, 404, 410–415
Calzati, Giuseppe, 373
Cancik, Hubert, 421, 423
Cantacuzino, Ion, 36
Căntacuzino-Granicerul, Gheorge, 36, 40
Caracciolo, Antonio, 307
Carol II of Romania, 322, 324, 347, 397, 405, 408

Casadio, Giovanni, 333, 365, 371–372, 375
Casel, Odo, 65–66, 421–428, 435–437
Cassata, Francesco, 137
Cassuto, Umberto, 374
Ceauşescu, Nicolae, 63–64, 317, 398, 402
Celms, Theodor, 516, 531, 536
Chamberlain, Houston Stewart, 127, 140, 190
Charlemagne, 237, 483
Charles II, see Carol II of Romania
Christensen, Arthur, 207
Christian, Viktor, 142
Christodulo, E., 36, 38
Chrysanthos, Filippides, 286
Chrysostomos of Smyrna, 286
Chudoba, Karl Franz, 443, 453–454, 459
Cioran, Emil, 319, 322, 401, 409, 415
Civiltà fascista, 62, 339, 369, 386
Cisz, Vanessa, x
Ciurtin, Eugen, 59–61, 333
Clemen, Carl, 27, 112, 170, 249, 449, 360
Clemen, Paul, 460
Codreanu, Corneliu Zelea, 37, 40–41, 56, 137–138, 344, 351, 353–355, 358, 405, 407, 412–413
Coman, Ioan, 216
Committee of Vigilance, 546
Comité de vigilance des intellectuels antifascistes, 546
Condeescu, Nicolae, 322
Conway, Robert Seymour, 336
Coomaraswamy, Ananda K., 324
Corbin, Henry, 413, 415
Cornelius, Friedrich, 165
Cortés, Juan Donoso, 308
Coste, Brutus, 351–352
Croce, Benedetto, 367, 369, 374, 376
Culianu, Ioan Petru, 34, 40–42, 352–355, 357, 410–413
Culianu-Petrescu, Tereza, 333
Cumont, Franz, 333, 339, 341, 348, 379
Cursaru, Gabriela, 333
Curtius, Ernst Robert, 435

Dachau (concentration camp), 142, 145
Dam, Jan van, 77–78
Damaskinos, Papandreou, 286
Darré, Richard Walther, 120, 184
Dasgupta, Surendranath, 319, 350

Degrelle, Léon, 75
Dernburg, Friedrich, 474
Descartes, René, 439
Deutschbund, 218
Deutsche Forschungsgemeinschaft
    (DFG), x, 74, 121, 140, 548
Deutsche Glaubensbewegung (German
    Faith Movement), 10, 72, 147–149,
    152, 154, 161, 168, 349–350,
    494–496, 501, 562–563, 597–598,
    601
Deutsche Karls-Universität Prag, 87, 618
Deutsche Unitarier
    Religionsgemeinschaft (DUR), 76
Deutsche Vereinigung für
    Religionsgeschichte (DVRG), ix–x, 5,
    68, 79
Deutsche Vereinigung für
    Religionswissenschaft (DVRW), ix
Deutscher Christenbund, 218
Deutscher Glaube, 147
dialectical theology, 4, 240, 242, 522,
    529, 532
Diderichs, Eugen, 115
Diederichs, Niels, 114
Dierks, Margarete, 84
Dieterich, Albert, 45–46, 179, 181,
    186–188, 190
Dietrich, Ernst Ludwig, 81
Dievturi (Latvian new religion), 528
Dilthey, Wilhelm, 639, 643
Dionysius the Areopagite, 430
Dirlmeier, Franz, 142
Dittrich, Ottmar, 285
Divinity School of the University of
    Athens, 54, 283–285, 294
Divinity School of the University of
    Chicago, 42, 636
Djuvara, Mircea, 351
Dölger, Franz Josef, 459
Doniger, Wendy, 354
Dornseiff, Franz, 27
Dreyfus, Alfred, 207
Driesch, Hans, 285
Drieu la Rochelle, Pierre, 56, 263, 272,
    303, 309–312
Dubnow, Simon, 526
Dubuisson, Daniel, 304
Duca, Ion, 36
Dumézil, Georges, 48–49, 179,
    209–210, 216–217, 303–305,
    309–312, 351–352, 548, 558
Durkheim, Émile, 128, 217–218, 486

East Asia Mission, see Ostasien Mission
Ebbinghaus, Julius, 580
Ebel, Wolfgang, 142
Eckhardt, Karl August, 81, 149–150
École Pratique des Hautes Études
    (EPHE), x
Edenholm, Erik Douglas, 564
Edsman, Carl-Martin, 220
Ehrlinger, Erich, 69, 71
Eickstedt, Egon Freiherr von, 185
Eiserne Garde, see Iron Guard
Einaudi, Luigi, 376
Eißfeldt, Otto, 112
Eliade, Christinel, 32, 411
Eliade, Mircea, 30–43, 56–65, 137–143,
    167–170, 218, 303–313, 315–330,
    333–359, 366, 397–416, 426–427,
    435–437, 604
Emberland, Terje, 72, 499–503
Enciclopedia Italiana, 62, 266, 349,
    375–376
Encyclopedia of Religion, 168–169
Endres, Hans, 153
Engel, Carl, 567
Engel, Wilhelm, 81
Engels, Friedrich, 341
Enlightenment, 89, 136, 269, 507, 549,
    603
epoché, 9
Epting, Karl, 81
Eranos movement, 84, 168, 334, 413,
    415, 436
Eribon, Didier, 303–304, 309–311
Erixson, Sigurd, 192
Eulenburg, Philip Prince of, 273
Euler, Friedrich Karl, 81
Europäische Sammlung für
    Urgemeinschaftskunde (ESU), 164
European Association for the Study of
    Religions (EASR), ix
Evola, Julius, 35, 40, 61–62, 127–140,
    166–170, 307–310, 313
Externsteine, 121

Faber, Richard, 65
Fascher, Erich, 79
Fasci di Azione Rivoluzionaria (F.A.R.),
    308
Federzoni, Luigi, 339
Fehrle, Eugen, 117, 184, 188–190, 192,
    201
Feist, Sigmund, 182–183, 185
Ferraresi, Francesco, 166

Festinger, Leon, 581
Fiebig, Kurt, 285
Filliozat, Jean, 346
Filthaut, Theodor, 423
Fink, Eugen, 423
Fischer, Eugen, 452
Flasche, Rainer, 33, 504–505
Florenz, Karl, 619
Fondane, Benjamin, 316
Fourth of August Regime, 55–56, 290, 292
Franchetti, Paola, 374–375
Francisci, Pietro de, 340, 385–386
Franco, Bahamonde, 77, 166, 546
Frank, Walter, 214
Frankfort School, 89, 591
Franz, Günther, 81
Freemasons, 114, 128, 134, 389
Freijs, Alberts, 511, 529
Frenzel, N.N., 285
Freud, Sigmund, 256, 269–270,
    475–476, 495, 603
Fri opposition, 213
Frick, Heinrich, 79, 87–88, 116,
    164–165, 338, 613, 618, 622–623
Fritt ord, 72, 496–497, 499
Frobenius, Leo, 218, 557, 618
Frobes, N.N., 580
Fromm, Erich, 591
Frommel, Wolfgang, 434–435

Galke, Bruno, 122–123
Gandini, Mario, 60, 333–335, 340, 344,
    369–374, 377–378, 384
Garde de Fer, see Iron Guard
Gasparri, Pietro Cardinal, 377
Gaster, Moses, 343–344
Gaster, Theodor H., 344
Găvănescul, Ion, 36, 38
Geertz, Clifford, 543
Geiger, Wilhelm, 148, 151
General Weekly for Christianity and Culture,
    543
Gennep, Arnold van, 336
Gentile, Giovanni, 62, 266, 270, 336,
    367–368, 375–377, 382, 392
George II of Greece, 286, 289
George, Stefan, 421, 423, 434, 438, 636
George-Kreis, 269, 434, 437
German Christians, 17–18, 23, 114,
    561–562, 564, 566–567, 569–570
German Faith Movement, see Deutsche
    Glaubensbewegung
Germanische Glaubensgemeinschaft,
    218

Germanischer Wissenschaftseinsatz
    (GWE), 25, 75–76
Germann, Dietrich, 249
Gess, Heinz, 591
Gestapo, 70, 88, 134, 154, 160, 461
Getreuer-Kargl, Ingrid, 86
Geuthner, Paul, 216, 323
Gheorgieu-Dej, Gheorge, 402
Gianola, Alberto, 342
Gielen, Jos, 78
Gielen, N.N., 563
Gieselbusch, Hermann, 155
Giornale d'Italia, 63, 381, 384–385
Glasenapp, Helmuth von, 148
Glasul patrie, 402
Gleißner, Stephanie, x
Gobineau, Arthur de, 109–110, 140,
    190
Godeanu, Marius, 404
Goegginger, Wolf H., 199
Göring, Hermann, 116, 152
Goethe, Johann Wolfgang von, 237–239,
    269–270, 607
Goga, Octavian, 397
Goldstein, Kurt, 605
Gonzales, Alberto, 265
Goossens, Thomas, 445, 448, 451, 459
Grabert, Herbert, 51, 156, 168, 170,
    497
Grabert, Wigbert, 168
Grabert-Verlag, 168
Graebner, Fritz, 446, 557
Gramsci, Antonio, 275
Graul, Johannes, 635
Grenet, Frantz, 205
Grimm, Jacob, 187, 190
Grīnbergs, Theodors, 514
Grønbech, Vilhelm Peter, 210, 492, 558,
    568
Grönhagen, Yrjö von, 142
Grossman, Stanley, 598–599
Grottanelli, Cristiano, 56, 58, 336, 366
Grundmann, Walther, 17, 563–564
Grzymała-Moszczyńska, Halina, 82
Guardia di ferro, see Iron Guard
Guardini, Romano, 429, 435
Guénon, René, 35, 306–310, 312
Gulkowitsch, Lazar, 285
Gundel, Wilhelm, 451
Gundert, Wilhelm, 85–88, 613–631
Gunkel, Hermann, 70, 492
Güntert, Gisela, 189
Güntert, Hermann, 27, 45–46, 80, 111,
    147, 179–201, 224

Günther, Hans F.K., 185–188, 190, 255, 478, 621
Gusinde, Martin, 445–447, 472
Gustav II Adolf, 564
Gustav IV Adolf of Sweden, 215

Haarnagel, N.N., 142
Haas, Hans, 54, 112, 233, 249–250, 283–285, 287, 296, 637
Haecker, Theodor, 432–433
Hakl, Hans Thomas, 168–169
Hale, Christopher, 167
Halévy, Daniel, 312
Hamann, Annett, 253
Hancke, Kurt, 131, 133–134, 166
Handoca, Mircea, 33, 399, 404
Hannerz, Nils, 564
Hansen, H.T., see Hakl, Hans Thomas
Harmjanz, Heinrich, 74, 142, 153, 156, 199
Harrington, Anne, 605
Hartmann, Martin, 468
Hartog, Hans, 166
Harva, Uno, 220
Hauer, Jakob Wilhelm, 12, 25, 49, 72, 84–85, 111, 113, 147–161, 243–244, 263–269, 275, 342, 349–350, 494, 497–502, 506, 562, 565, 569, 597–598, 602–603, 625
Haushofer, Karl, 88, 622
Haverbeck, Werner, 148
Heberer, Gerhard, 81
Heckel, Johannes, 81
Hedin, Sven, 142, 354
Heer, Friedrich, 431
Hegel, Georg Friedrich Wilhelm, 123
Hehl, Ulrich von, 443
Heidegger, Martin, 266, 423, 433, 608, 610
Heigl-Wach, Susi, 645
Heiler, Christian, 164
Heiler, Friedrich, 4–5, 61–62, 78–79, 163–166, 267–268, 286
Heinen, Armin, 38
Heinrich, Fritz, 50–51, 553, 562, 566, 570
Heisenberg, Werner, 635
Hellenism, 22, 297, 422
Hempel, Johannes, 81
Hentze, Carl, 324
Herder, Johann Gottfried, 187, 190
Hermlink, Heinrich, 116
Herwegen, Ildefons, 422, 429, 437–439
Heschel, Susannah, 563

Hesse, Hermann, 87, 619
Hestermann, Ferdinand, 447–448
Heydrich, Martin, 450
Heydrich, Reinhard, 87, 153
Heymann, Betty, 150–151
Hibbert Lectures, 336
Hielscher, Friedrich, 142
Hildebrand, L., 218
Himmler, Heinrich, 3, 50–51, 119–123, 126–127, 132–134, 141–146, 153, 198, 211–212, 257
Hirohito, Emperor of Japan, 337
Hirt, August, 144, 153
Hirt, Hermann, 185
Historische Tijdschrift, 448
Hitler, Adolf, 10–12, 62, 67, 123–125, 189, 191, 409
Hjelde, Oddemund, 506
Hjelde, Sigurd, 71
Hobbes, Thomas, 306, 594
Hochland, 470
Höfler, Otto, 47–52, 76, 196, 205, 208, 211–212, 254–257, 569
Höffner, Joseph, 431
Hölderlin, Friedrich, 237, 433–434
Höpfner, Hans-Paul, 443
Hörbiger, Hans, 142
Höß, Rudolf, 146
Hoffmann, Eva, 583, 585
Hoffmann, Karl, 214
Hofler, Alois, 580
Hofmannsthal, Hugo von, 433–434
Hofstede, Geert, 578
Hofstee, Willem, 74, 76–77
holocaust, 2, 24, 31, 69, 168, 354, 537
Homer, 439
Hübner, Arthur, 118
Hugo von St. Viktor, 432
Hund, Friedrich, 635
Hunke, Sigrid, 76
Hunke, Waltraud, 76
Hupp, Otto, 142
Husserl, Edmund, 531, 536, 618
Huth, Otto, 25, 51, 71, 76, 108, 118, 141–144, 170

Iliescu, Ion, 31
Institut zur Erforschung und Beseitigung des jüdischen Einflusses auf das deutsche kirchliche Leben, 17, 82, 560, 562–566, 570
International Association for the History of Religions (IAHR), ix, 25–27, 55, 67, 78, 365

International Association for the Study of the History of Religions (IASHR), 5, 78–80, 365
International Congress for the History of Religions, 26, 55, 63, 78, 93, 113–114, 163, 165, 286, 378–380, 392, 451
International Institute for Documentation (Palais Mondial), 26
Ioanid, Radu, 31, 39
Ionesco, Eugène, 355, 357, 413–414
Ionescu, Nae, 39, 59, 306, 318–322, 342, 350, 398, 405–406, 408, 413–415
Iorga, Nicolae, 323, 351, 402, 407
Iron Guard, 31, 34–42, 59, 61, 137–139, 304–305, 316, 324, 330, 344, 350–355, 355, 358, 397–398, 406–408, 412–415
Ismail, Zaki Muhammad, 486
Isopescu, C., 344
Istituto coloniale Fascista, 389
Istituto di Etnologia e Scienze Coloniali, 391
Istituto di studi romani, 383
Istituto Giovanni Treccani, 375
Istituto Italiano per il Medio ed Estremo Oriente (IsMEO), 323, 336
Istituto nazionale di cultura fascista, 385

Jacobsohn, Hermann, 115–116, 149
Jacobsohn, Margarete, 116
Jaeger, Werner, 532
Jankuhn, Herbert, 81, 144, 212
Jansen, Herman Ludin, 493
Japan-Institut, 630
Jaspers, Karl, 87, 545, 618
Jones, Sir William, 190,
Jünger, Ernst, 138, 263, 266, 306–307, 350, 357
Jung, Carl Gustav, 61, 83–85, 413, 591, 596–610
Junginger, Horst, 44–45, 56, 61, 205, 213, 243, 333, 379, 384, 538–539
Justinian, 438

Karl I., last emperor of Austria, 469
Kater, Michael H., 2, 107, 108, 121
katholieke encyclopaedie, De, 452
Katô, Genchi, 624
Kazantzakis, Nikos, 534
Kellens, Jean, 221
Kerényi, Grazia, 146
Kerényi, Karl, 146–147, 169, 383

Keul, István, 63–64
Kienle, Richard von, 142, 198, 201
Kierkegaard, Søren Aaby, 318
Kitagawa, Joseph M., 638–639
Kitayama, Junyu, 85–88, 338, 613–631
Kittel, Gerhard, 17, 23
Klemm, N.N., 285
Klemperer, Victor, 241
Klumberg, Wilhelm, 192
Koenen, Andreas, 435
Koepp, Wilhelm, 82, 566–567, 570
Körte, N.N., 285
Kommende Gemeinde, 497
Konow, Sten, 379
Koppers, Wilhelm, 445, 472
Kossinna, Gustaf, 185
Krause, Wolfgang, 142
Krieck, Ernst, 239
Kriegseinsatz der Geisteswissenschaften, 24–25, 159
Krogman, Willy, 194
Krueger, Felix, 234–235, 606
Kubota, Hiroshi, 85
Kuen, Heinrich, 198
Kuhn, Karl Georg, 81
Kummer, Bernhard, 25, 50–52, 54, 119, 163–165, 229–258
Kuṇdzinš, Kārlis, 515, 519, 529–530
Kwartalnik Psychologizny, 83, 582
Kylstra, Andries Dirk, 80

La Rocque, François de, 274
Lagarde, Paul de, 225
Laignel-Lavastine, Alexandra, 304
Lambrino, S., 344
Lamprecht, Karl, 638
Landsberger, Benno, 635
Langbehn, Julius, 448
Lange, Katharina, 486
Langenhove, G. v., 27
Langewiesche, Dieter, 566
Langsdorff, Alexander, 129, 133
Lanternari, Vittorio, 382
Lateran Treaty, 370
Laufer, Berthold, 343
Leers, Johann von, 119, 621
Leeuw, Gerardus van der, 5, 76–79, 365, 504, 543–550, 640
Lehmann, Friedrich Rudolf, 559
Lehmann, Julius Friedrich, 184
Lehmann, Paul, 142
Leisegang, Hans, 253
Leitane, Iveta, 69–70
Lemnarus, Oscar, 400

Lenin, Vladimir, 341
Lenz, Herbert, 230
LeRoy, N.N., 244
Leumann, Ernst, 618
Levi della Vida, Giorgio, 336, 339, 373
Lévi, Sylvain, 207
Lévy-Bruhl, Lucien, 546
Liljedahl, Ragnar, 213
Lilla, Mark, 608
Lincoln, Bruce, 45–46, 205, 210, 213
Lips, Eva, 447, 450
Lips, Julius, 446–447, 450
Lipsius, N.N., 285
Litt, Theodor, 285
Loisy, Alfred, 342, 378
Lombard, Alf, 210, 216
Lommel, Herman, 151, 163, 179, 214, 456
L'Ormeau, F.W., see Frommel, Wolfgang
Losemann, Volker, 146
Louvaris, Nikolaos, 285, 295–296
Lovinescu, Vasile, 137, 140
Ludendorff, Mathilde, 119
Lüders, Heinrich, 120, 151
Lundagård, 554–555, 561
Lūsis, Arnolds, 520
Luther, Martin, 206, 240, 564, 623
Lützelburg, Philipp Freiherr von, 142
Lützeler, Heinrich, 459

Machiavelli, Niccolò, 594
Mackensen, Lutz, 194
Madgearu, N.N., 407
Männerbund, 48–49, 58, 131, 196, 208–209, 217–224, 569
Magon, Leopold, 568
Mai, Friedrich Wilhelm, 142
Maier, Hans, 194
Majerus, Nicolas, 454–455
Makrides, Vasilios N., 54–55
Maldonis, Valdemārs, 514, 519, 529–530, 532
Malinowski, Stephan, 274
Mandel, Hermann, 25, 51, 255
Manea, Norman, 398
Manhem society, 564
Maniadakis, Konstantinos, 293
Maniu, Iuliu, 405
Mann, Thomas, 604
Mannhardt, Wilhelm, 533
Marcenay, Georges (pseudonym of Georges Dumézil), 304
March on Rome, 274
Marcuse, Herbert, 591

Maria Laach, 65, 422–423, 429, 435, 437–439
Marian, Simion Florea, 343
Marin, Vasile, 138, 350, 408
Marino, Adrian, 411
Martino, Ernesto de, 371, 382
Martire, Egilberto, 135
Marx, Karl, 341, 594
Masaryk, Thomáš Garrigue, 347
Maspero, Henri, x, 340
Masson-Oursel, Paul, 343
Mattiat, Eugen, 114
Mattioli, Aram, 484
Maurras, Charles, 207, 214
Mauss, Marcel, 217
Mausser, Otto, 121
May, Eduard, 142
Meid, Wolfgang, 199
Meiji Restoration, 629
Menasce, Jean de, 220
Mendelssohn Bartholdy, Felix, 89, 637
Mendelssohn, Moses, 89
Mensching, Gustav, 5, 69, 79, 113, 163, 455, 458, 460–461, 529, 546
Merck, Mathilde, 117
Merhart, Gero von, 115
Meringer, Rudolf, 182
Merkel, Rudolf Franz, 27, 165
Metaxas regime, 55, 284, 289–299
Metaxas, Ioannis, 284, 289
Meurers, Heinrich von, 456
Meyer, Conrad Ferdinand, 237
Meyer, Herbert, 144, 212
Meyer-Erlach, Wolf, 560–561, 563–564, 570
Meyer-Lübke, Wilhelm, 182
Mikkola, Joosepi Julius, 182
Mirandola, Pico della, 537
Mişcarea pentru România, 34
Mischek, Udo, 67–68
Mitläufer, 1
Młodzież Wszechpolska (All-Polish Union), 583
Mogk, Eugen, 249
Mohler, Armin, 306–307
Momigliano, Arnaldo, 341, 371, 374, 377–378, 393
Monakow, Constantin von, 606
Monchi-Zadeh, Davoud, 223
Montanari, Enrico, 375
Moriya, Kenju, 457
Mossé, Fernand, 194
Mostra Augustea della Romanità, 385
Moța, Ion, 138, 350, 408

Mouilliseaux, Louis, 274
Mounier, Emmanuel, 530
Mowinckel, Sigmund, 70, 491–492
Much, Rudolf, 182, 194, 196
Mühlhausen, Ludwig, 75, 144
Mühlmann, Wilhelm Emil, 5, 67–68, 163, 479
Müller, Alfred Dedo, 532
Müller, Friedrich Max, 44, 109–110, 556, 639
Müller, Hannelore, 34–36
Müller, Werner, 144, 170, 179
Munk, Kai, 534, 538
Munteanu, Marian, 34
Muralt, Axel von, 609
Murata, Toyofumi, 457
Murko, Matthias, 182
Museo Missionario Etnologico, 67
Musil, Alois, 347
Musil, Robert, 610
Mussert, Anton, 75
Mussolini, Benito, 62, 133, 266, 270, 274, 232, 338, 340, 368, 376–377, 381–382, 388, 390, 546
Mutti, Claudio, 34–35, 167–168, 401, 413

Nallino, Carlo Alfonso, 338–339, 379
Narodowa Demokracja (Polish National Democratic Party), 584–585
National Youth Organization (of the Metaxas regime in Greece), 290, 293
National-Socialistische Beweging (NSB, the Netherlands), 73, 75
Nationalsozialistische Deutsche Arbeiterpartei (NSDAP), 37, 47, 69, 81, 119, 149, 231, 245–246, 251, 255, 257, 554, 561
Nationalsozialistischer Lehrerbund (NSLB), 150, 619
Natorp, Paul, 529, 531
Neckel, Gustav, 118, 249, 250–251, 253
Nederlandsche Kulturraad, 75
Negulescu, Petre P., 322
Neue Reich, Das, 468
Neumann, Therese, 495
Niemczyk, Wiktor, 28
Nietzsche, Friedrich, 76, 124, 263
Nikitine, Basile, 348
Nilsson, Martin P., 156, 206
Nissen, Benedikt Momme, 448
Nobel, Johannes, 339
Nock, Arthur D., 375
Noll, Richard, 591

Nordische Auslandsinstitute, 568
Noua Dreapta (Romanian New Right), 34
Nouvelle Revue Française, 310
Nowicki, Andrzej, 578
Numen, 366
Nuremberg Laws, 89, 560
Nuşa, N.N., 350
Nyberg, Henrik Samuel, 47, 206–208, 210, 213, 217, 219, 221–222

Odeberg, Hugo, 82, 560–561, 564, 570
Oertel, Hanns, 111, 120, 148–149, 151, 199
Ohlmarks, Åke, 81–82, 553–571
Olson, Emil, 558
Ornea, Zigu, 398, 405
Osis, Jēkabs, 530
Ostasien-Mission, 112–113, 619
Otto, Rudolf, 9, 49, 67–69, 116, 165–166, 243–244, 267, 529, 534–536
Otto, Walter F., 264, 270, 384
Oxford Group Movement, 409

Pätsch, Gertrud, 448
Panaitescu, E., 344
Pantazi, N.N., 36
Panzer, Friedrich, 184
Papini, Giovanni, 342
Partito Nazionale Fascista (PNF), 62, 273, 368, 373
Partito Socialista Italiano di Unità Proletaria (PSIUP), 340
Pârvan, Vasile, 317
Paul, Johannes, 568
Paul, Otto, 47, 148
Paxton, Robert, 549
Pering, Birger, 557
Persch, Martin, 443
Peterson, Erik, 430
Pettazzoni, Raffaele, 21, 26, 59–63, 68, 169, 324, 333–359, 365–392, 613
Pfannmüller, Gustav, 524
Pfister, Friedrich, 46, 156, 252
Pfister, Oskar, 495
Pfitzner, Hans, 270
Philippidis, Leonidas, 54–56, 283–299
Photios (Patriarch of Alexandria), 286
Pietikäinen, Petteri, 83
Pincherle, Alberto, 374
Piperescu, N.N., 36
Pippidi, Dionisie M., 344
Pipping, Hugo, 558
Piquet, Félix, 193

Pisi, Paola, 168
Plaßmann, Joseph Otto, 128–129, 131–132, 142, 167
Platzhoff, Walter, 453
Pöpping, Dagmar, 435
Pohle, Joseph, 444
Poliakov, Léon, 44, 109, 183
Polihroniade, Mihai, 37, 40, 397
Popper, Karl, 501–503, 505
Porzig, Walter, 198
Preuss, Konrad Theodor, 117
Preziosi, Giovanni, 136, 138
Protocols of the Elders of Zion, 128–129, 136, 169
Przyluski, Jean, 324, 348
Puhvel, Jaan, 181
Pure-Land-School, 87, 618, 630
Puşcariu, Sextil, 36, 38, 57

Quellmalz, Anton, 142

Rade, Martin, 116
Rădulsescu-Motru, Constantin, 319–320, 331
Rahner, Hugo, 436–438
Ramet, Petra, 582
Ranke, Leopold von, 237, 533
Rascher, Sigmund, 142, 145
Ratzinger, Josef, 421, 435
Rauter, Hanns Albin, 73
Ravensbrück (concentration camp), 146
Reche, Otto, 185
Redeker, Martin, 81
Reformation, 52, 242, 473, 483, 623, 629
Reichsinstitut für Geschichte des neuen Deutschland, 17, 214
Reichsuniversität Posen, x
Reichsuniversität Straßburg, 25, 143, 170
Religiöser Menschheitsbund, 9, 495
Religion in Geschichte und Gegenwart, Die (RGG), 80–81
Religionsgeschichtliche Schule, 17
Religionskundliche Sammlung, 67, 87, 164, 618
Remy, Steven, 199
Rendtorff, Heinrich, 285
Rendtorff, Trutz, 113
Rennie, Bryan S., 31
Repstad, Pål, 499
Révue Germanique, 193
Rhema (PHMA), 163
Ribbentrop, Joachim von, 616

Rickert, Heinrich, 618
Ricketts, Mac Linscott, 39, 58
Riefenstahl, Leni, 276
Rieger, Jürgen, 230
Riksföreningen Sverige-Tyskland, 81, 560
Ritschl, Albrecht, 500
Rocque, François de la, 274
Rocquet, Claude-Henri, 321
Rohde, Erwin, 187
Röhm, Ernst, 273
Romagnoli, Tullia, 371
Romanato, Gianpaolo, 352–353
Römer, Ruth, 199
Rönnow, Kasten Anders, 221
Rosenberg, Alfred, 3, 10, 48, 50, 67, 107, 113, 119–121, 140, 165, 242, 245, 255, 257, 384, 506, 545
Rosetti, Alexandru, 216, 322–324
Rößler, Otto, 142
Rössner, Hans, 75
Roşu, Arion, 321–322
Roşu, Niculae, 36
Rothacker, Erich, 458–461
Rothe, Richard, 520, 525
Ruben, Walter, 150
Rudolph, Kurt, 1–2, 89, 144
Rudolph, Martin, 142
Rudzītis, R., 529
Rumänien Institut, 57–58, 305
Rumba, Eduards, 511, 529
Ruppel, Karl Konrad, 142
Russell, Bertrand, 206
Rust, Bernhard, 47, 114, 568
Rust, Hans, 27
Ruster, Thomas, 421–422
Rutowski, Lothar Stengel von, 253

SA (Sturmabteilung, Stormtroopers), 36, 47, 196, 223, 245, 273
Sabbatucci, Dario, 375
Salazar, António de Oliveira, 57, 306, 401, 426
Salvatorelli, Luigi, 340, 372
Sanctis, Gaetano De, 373–374, 376
Sandberger, Martin, 69
Sangue e Sprito, 133, 137–138
Sauckel, Fritz, 251
Schaeder, Hans Heinrich 25, 47, 162
Schäfer, Ernst, 142
Schatz-Anin, Max, 526
Schebesta, Paul, 472
Scheftelowitz, Isidor, 113
Scheler, Max, 530, 642

Scheller, Andreas, 450
Schemann, Ludwig, 109, 110
Schencke, Wilhelm, 71, 491–493
Scherman, Lucian, 111
Schian, Martin, 520
Schiller, Friedrich, 269
Schjelderup, Harald, 72, 496
Schjelderup, Kristian, 72, 491–506
Schlegel, Friedrich, 206, 222
Schleiermacher, Friedrich, 500
Schmidt, Richard, 151
Schmidt, Wilhelm, 67–68, 81, 289, 346, 389, 444–446, 448, 467–486, 556
Schmitt, Carl, 56–58, 65, 68, 265–266, 303, 305–310, 429, 433, 435, 523, 568
Schneider, Hans-Ernst (alias Hans Schwerte), 25, 73, 75–76, 142
Schneider, N.N., 285
Schönere Zukunft, 468
Schoeps, Hans-Joachim, 637
Scholem, Gershom, 38–39, 42, 357
Scholl, Hans, 160
Scholl, Sophie, 160
Scholz, Heinrich, 642
Schomerus, Hilko Wiardo, 113
Schopenhauer, Arthur, 521
Schrader, Otto, 185
Schröder, Christel Matthias, 166
Schröder, Leopold von, 533
Schubert, Hans von, 242
Schultz, Wolfgang, 48
Schurtz, Heinrich, 218
Schütrumpf, N.N., 142
Schwalm, Hans, 75
Schweitzer, Albert, 530, 539
Schweitzer, Bernhard, 635
Schweizer, Bruno, 73, 142
Schwerte, Hans, see Schneider, Hans-Ernst
Scultetus, Hans Robert, 142
SD (Sicherheitsdienst, Security Service), 52, 71, 73, 75–76, 81, 131, 454, 547
Sebastian, Mihail, 37, 39, 64, 354, 413–414
See, Klaus von, 48
Seta, Alessandro Della, 374, 378
Seyß-Inquart, Arthur, 78
Shamdasani, Sonu, 591, 603
Shils, Edward, 550–551
Sievers, Wolfram, 48, 73, 108, 122–145, 213
Sigg, Martha, 598
Simmel, Georg, 644

Simon, Gerd, 108
Simon, Marcel, 25, 27
Six, Alfred, 134
Skinner, Quentin, 592–596
Slokenbergs, Roberts, 512–513, 529
Smolicz, Jerzy, 584
Snijder, Geerto, 75, 192
Societas Verbi Divini (SVD), 468
Société Asiatique, 207
Söderblom, Nathan, 206–207, 243, 249, 504, 534, 536, 557
Sombart, Werner, 642
Soucy, Robert, 273
Spamer, Adolf, 604
Spann, Othmar, 132, 429
Spengler, Oswald, 127, 140
Spindler, Robert, 151
Spineto, Natale, 59
Spranger, Eduard, 295–296
Srbik, Heinrich Ritter von, 192
SS (Schutzstaffel, Protection Squadron), 25, 52, 73–75, 81, 127, 130–131, 139, 196, 305, 544, 548
Stahlecker, Franz Walter, 69, 71
Stahlmann, Hans, 183
Starace, Achille, 273
Stausberg, Michael, 60–61, 63, 333
Stauß, N.N., 142
Steding, Christoph, 214, 429
Steffes, Johann Peter, 445
Stegmann von Pritzwald, Kurt, 198
Stelescu, Mihael, 139
Stengel von Rutkowski, Lothar von, 370
Sternhell, Zeev, 273
Stoecker, Adolf, 474
Strada maestra, 370
Strasser, Gregor, 273
Strauß, Otto, 113, 149–150
Strauss, Richard, 263
Streitberg, Gerhart, 193
Strömbäck, Dag, 557, 559
Studi e Materiali di Storia delle Religioni (SMSR), 62, 366, 377, 383
Swedenborg, Emanuel, 600
Sven-Hedin-Institut, 142, 354
swastika, 80, 159, 599

Taeschner, Franz, 81
Teichmüller, Gustav, 530
Thorild, Thomas, 567
Tiele, Cornelis Petrus, 639
Till, Rudolf, 142
Tillich, Paul, 28, 114
Timuş, Mihaela, 45, 49

Totul pentru Țara (TPȚ, Romanian All
  for the Country party), 36–37, 39
Tratz, Eduard Paul, 142
Trembelas, Panayiotios N., 294
Trimborn, Hermann, 446–447
Triple Axis-Pact, 85
Troeltsch, Ernst, 630, 642
Troll, Carl, 449, 455
Trotsky, Leon, 341
Tsirindanis, Alexandros, 294–295
Tucci, Giuseppe, 35, 169, 263–267, 272,
  275, 323, 336, 347, 383
Tuliu, N.N., 350
Țurcanu, Florin, 58–59, 304–305, 346,
  399
Twardowski, Kazimierz, 579
Tzara, Tristan, 316

Uexküll, Jakob Freiherr von, 273
Ulmanis, Kārlis, 514, 519–521, 537
Ura-Linda-Chronik, 118–119, 121,
  147–148, 170, 233, 254

Vatican, 67, 379, 470, 472, 476
Venturi, Pietro Tacchi, 376
Vergil, 434, 438
Verein für freisinniges Christentum, 499
Versaille treatise, 109
Vida, Giorgio Levi Della, 336, 339, 373
Vienna Circle, 318
Vikings, 230, 247
Vilks, Ēvalds, 523
Virza, Edvarts, 525
Voegelin, Eric, 232
Volkelt, N.N., 285
Vollmer, Ulrich, 66
Volovici, Leon, 38, 137, 398, 405
Vries, Jan de, 72–77, 80, 543–551

Wach, Adolf, 636
Wach, Joachim, 8, 89–90, 93, 267–270,
  285, 287, 635–645
Waffen-SS, 71, 75, 145, 166
Wahle, Ernst, 185
Watkins, Calvert, 180
Weber, Max, 160
Weber, Roland, 142
Webster, H., 218
Wegner, Max, 119
Weibull, Lauritz, 577

Weinreich, Otto, 27, 156, 451
Weippert, Georg, 431
Weiser, Lilly, 49, 189, 196
Weiße Rose, 160
Westermann, Diedrich, 27
Widengren, Geo, 207, 210, 213, 221,
  558
Wieser, Max, 117
Wikander, Åke Magnus, 207
Wikander, Stig, 46–50, 205–225, 346,
  548, 558
Wiligut, Karl Maria, 154–155, 167
Winkler, Hans Alexander, 27, 88
Winter, Carl, 189
Wippermann, Wolfgang, 232
Wirth, Herman, 5, 109, 114–122,
  163–166, 169–170, 233, 254–255
Wissig, Otto, 241
Witte, Johannes, 112–113, 150, 451
Wittgenstein, Ludwig, 596
Wittram, Reinhard, 81
Witwicki, Władysław, 82–83, 577–587
Wörter und Sachen, 45–46, 182, 198
Wolfram, Richard, 142, 196
Wolters, Friedrich, 434, 438
Würth, Stefanie, 74
Wundt, Max, 81
Wundt, Wilhelm, 235, 319, 580
Wust, Peter, 437
Wüst, Walther, 6–7, 20, 44–52, 56–57,
  71, 73–74, 93, 107–171, 198–199,
  211, 213–215, 354
Wyller, Anders, 496

Yoffe, Michael, 526

Zalmoxis, 57, 61, 216, 306, 309,
  321–324, 344–348
*Zeitschrift für Missionskunde- und
  Religionswissenschaft* (ZMR), 63, 112,
  114, 116, 619, 637
*Zeitschrift für Missionswissenschaft und
  Religionswissenschaft*, 114
Zentralblatt für Psychotherapie, 596
Zeterstéen, K.V., 207
Zicāns, Eduards, 511, 515
Ziegler, Matthes, 165
Zimmer, Heinrich, 618
Zoi movement, 294–295